11TH EDITION

CRIMINAL INVESTIGATION

CHARLES R. SWANSON
University of Georgia (Emeritus)
President, Swanson and Bracken

NEIL C. CHAMELIN
Assistant State Attorney, Leon County,
Florida (Retired) and Attorney at Law

LEONARD TERRITO
Saint Leo University

ROBERT W. TAYLOR
The University of Texas at Dallas

McGraw Hill

Connect
Learn
Succeed™

CRIMINAL INVESTIGATION

Published by McGraw-Hill, a business unit of The McGraw-Hill Companies, Inc., 1221 Avenue of the Americas, New York, NY 10020. Copyright © 2012 by The McGraw-Hill Companies, Inc.

Some ancillaries, including electronic and print components, may not be available to customers outside the United States.

2 3 4 5 6 7 8 9 0 DOW/DOW 0 9 8 7 6 5 4 3 2

ISBN: 978-0-07-811152-5
MHID: 0-07-811152-8

Sponsoring Editor: *William Minick*
Marketing Manager: *Leslie Oberhuber*
Development Editor: *Craig Leonard*
Senior Production Editor: *Mel Valentín*
Text and Cover Designer: *Preston Thomas*
Design Manager: *Leslie Racanelli*
Art Editor: *Ayelet Arbel*
Photo Research Manager: *Brian Pecko*
Buyer II: *Tandra Jorgensen*
Media Project Manager: *Jennifer Barrick*
Composition: *9.5/12 Palatino by Aptara®, Inc.*
Printing: *Acid-free 45# New Era Matte Plus by R. R. Donnelley & Sons*

Vice President Editorial: *Michael Ryan*
Publisher: *Katie Stevens*
Editorial Coordinator: *Amy Mittelman*
Director of Development: *Dawn Groundwater*

Cover image: © William Whitehurst/Corbis.

Credits: The credits section for this book appear on page and are considered an extension of the copyright page.

Library of Congress Cataloging-in-Publication Data

Swanson, Charles R., 1942–
   Criminal investigation / Charles Swanson, Neil Chamelin, Leonard Territo. — 11th ed.
      p. cm.
   Includes bibliographical references and index.
   ISBN-13: 978-0-07-811152-5
   ISBN-10: 0-07-811152-8
   1. Criminal investigation. 2. Criminal investigation—United States.
   I. Chamelin, Neil C., 1942– II. Territo, Leonard. III. Title.
      HV8073.S84 2011
      363.25—dc23
                                                                    2011020729

From Charles R. Swanson: For our daughter Maggie Mercer, who crossed over the Jordan River too soon, always in our prayers and hearts.

From Neil C. Chamelin: For my wife, Vicki, and our children, Chris and Todd; my daughter-in-law Heidi; my granddaughters, Tally and her little sister Casey; and a soon-to-be-born granddaughter whose name is held secret by her parents until she is born.

From Leonard Territo: For my wife, Elena, the kindest and sweetest woman I have ever known, and our children, Lorraine, Kseniya, and Ilia, and my grandchildren, Matthew and Branden.

From Robert W. Taylor: For my beautiful wife Mary and our new grandchildren: Olivia, Auggie, and Brody.

ABOUT THE AUTHORS

Charles R. "Mike" Swanson is the managing partner of Swanson and Bracken, a firm specializing in police promotional testing. He has extensive experience in designing promotional systems and tests for state, county, and municipal public safety agencies, including the Kentucky State Police, the Georgia Bureau of Investigation, the Alabama State Troopers, and the Georgia State Patrol. He has conducted over 60 job-analysis studies and written more than 125 promotional tests. He has designed and implemented at least 75 assessment centers, as well as written their exercises. Mike has trained assessors from 18 different states and has testified in federal court as an expert witness on police promotional matters.

Mike enlisted in the Marine Corps when he was 17 years old and then joined the Tampa Police Department, working as a uniformed officer in the highest crime areas of the city before being promoted to detective. Subsequently, he worked as the senior police planner and later as the acting deputy director of the Council on Law Enforcement in the Office of the Florida Governor. While working in Florida, Mike earned his bachelor's and master's degrees in criminology from Florida State University. After a teaching stint at East Carolina University, Mike accepted a faculty position at the University of Georgia's Institute of Government, where he received a Ph.D. with an emphasis on public administration and rose through the administrative ranks, retiring as the interim director in late 2001. While at the Institute Mike trained over 10,000 law-enforcement officers from 42 states in advanced courses such as homicide investigation and police agency leadership. He remains active as a consultant to law-enforcement agencies and has written more than 200 technical reports for them.

In addition to this book, Mike has coauthored four others, including *Police Administration: Structures, Processes, and Behavior,* and has authored or coauthored a number of monographs, articles, and conference papers pertaining to policing. In 2003 he received the O. W. Wilson Award for Outstanding Police Scholarship. He has received multiple awards from the governors of three states and from the Georgia Association of Chiefs of Police, who recognized his contributions to their association by making him the first Honorary Chief of Police. The University of Georgia twice recognized Mike for "extraordinary work with law-enforcement agencies." He is currently working on a novel, tentatively titled *The Night Man.*

Neil C. Chamelin was an assistant state attorney in Leon County, Florida, and presently is an attorney at law. He previously served as a hearing officer in the Florida Division of Motor Vehicles; director of Criminal Justice Programs for Troy State University—European Region; director of the Florida Police Standards and Training Commission; division director, Standards and Training Division, Florida Department of Law Enforcement; administrator of the Police Science Division, Institute of

Government, at the University of Georgia; and director of the Florida Institute for Law Enforcement. He has also served as a police officer in Sarasota, Florida. Neil is author of *Criminal Law for Police Officers* and coauthor of *Introduction to Criminal Justice* and *Police Personnel Selection Process*.

Leonard Territo is presently a Visiting Distinguished Professor in the Department of Criminal Justice at Saint Leo University, Saint Leo, Florida, and Professor Emeritus in the Department of Criminology at the University of South Florida, Tampa, Florida. He was previously the Chief Deputy (Undersheriff) of the Leon County Sheriff's Office in Tallahassee, Florida. He also served for nine years with the Tampa Police Department as patrol officer, motorcycle officer, and homicide detective. He is a former chairperson of the Department of Police Administration and director of the Florida Institute for Law Enforcement at St. Petersburg Junior College (Now St. Petersburg College), St. Petersburg, Florida.

In addition to writing nearly 50 articles, book chapters, and technical reports, he has authored or coauthored 12 books, including *Police Administration*, which is in its eighth edition; *Crime and Justice in America*, which is in its sixth edition; *Police Civil Liability; College Crime Prevention and Personal Safety Awareness; Stress and Police Personnel; Stress Management in Law Enforcement*, which is in its second edition; *The Police Personnel Selection Process; Hospital and College Security Liability*, and a mystery crime novel based on a true story, *Ivory Tower Cop*. His books have been used in more than a thousand colleges and universities in all 50 states, and his writings have been used and referenced by both academic and police departments in 16 countries, including Australia, Barbados, Belarus Canada, China, Chile, Czechoslovakia, England, France, Germany, Israel, the Netherlands, Poland, Saudi Arabia, South Korea, and Spain.

His teaching awards include being selected from among 200 criminal justice educators from the state of Florida as the Outstanding Criminal Justice Educator of the Year and the Outstanding Teacher of the Year by the College of Social and Behavioral Sciences at the University of South Florida. He has been given awards by both the Florida Police Chiefs Association and the Tampa Police Academy for his years of teaching and meritorious service and has been selected for inclusion in *Who's Who in American Law Enforcement*. He's also been given an award for Distinguished Scholarly Publications at Saint Leo University, Saint Leo, Florida. He is also a qualified police procedures expert in Alaska, Arizona, District of Columbia, Florida, Georgia, Illinois, Iowa, Kansas, Kentucky, Louisiana, Michigan, New Jersey, Ohio, Oregon, Pennsylvania, Tennessee, Virginia, Washington, and Wisconsin.

Robert W. Taylor is currently professor and Program Head for the Public Affairs Program at The University of Texas at Dallas. Before that he was the founding Executive Director of the W. W. Caruth, Jr., Police Institute, an executive training and police research center funded through a $9.5 million grant embedded in the Dallas Police Department. For the past 30 years, Bob has studied police responses to crime and terrorism. He has traveled extensively throughout the Middle East, Europe, and Far East Asia. He currently serves as a consultant to numerous federal, state, and local agencies on policing issues and practices, intelligence analysis, human trafficking, and terrorism. Since September 11, 2001, Bob has been a consultant to the U.S. Department of Justice working with the Institute for Intergovernmental Research. He acts as a lead instructor in the State and Local Anti-Terrorism Training (SLATT) program, which is responsible for training law-enforcement and other related criminal justice professionals (specifically the FBI Joint Terrorism Task Forces—JTTF, the Organized Crime Drug Enforcement Task Forces—OCDETF, and the DEA High Intensity Drug-Trafficking Area Strike Forces—HIDTA) on Middle Eastern groups and other terrorism issues. Bob focuses on the nexus between human trafficking, drug trafficking, and the financing of terrorist incidents internationally and domestically. In 2008 the Academy of Criminal Justice Sciences presented him with the O. W. Wilson Award "in recognition for his outstanding contribution to police education, research and practice," and in 2003 the University of North Texas presented him with the Regent's Lecture Award for his outstanding work on terrorism in the Middle East.

Bob also has written extensively in the area of law-enforcement management and administration, community policing, and public policy. He served as a sworn police officer in Portland, Oregon, for six years, three of which were as a major crimes detective. Aside from this work, Bob has coauthored four additional books: *Juvenile Justice: Policies, Programs, and Practices; Police Administration: Structures, Processes, and Behavior; Police Patrol Allocation and Deployment;* and *Digital Crime and Digital Terrorism*.

BRIEF CONTENTS

CONTENTS

6
FIELD NOTES AND REPORTING   153

7
THE FOLLOW-UP INVESTIGATION AND
INVESTIGATIVE RESOURCES   170

12
HUMAN TRAFFICKING 341

13
ROBBERY 356

As with the previous editions, the first purpose of this book is to provide a useful tool for those on law-enforcement's front lines. Thus, *Criminal Investigation* is once again filled with practical "how to" information, case studies, and color photographs that illustrate important points and checklists that can be adapted to the needs of local agencies.

We have scrutinized all aspects of the book, downsizing and deleting some content while elsewhere adding new cutting-edge topics. The computer crime chapter was dropped; an entirely new chapter, "Cybercrime," takes its place. Another new chapter, "Human Trafficking," examines the crimes associated with it in the United States. Many portions of chapters have been substantially or totally rewritten, including the guidelines for conducting photo lineups, live lineups, and field show-ups; crime scene reconstruction; and forensic odontology. These and other changes are more fully identified shortly.

Criminal Investigation continues to differ from other texts, and the differences are again reflected throughout this edition. First, criminal investigation generally has been conceived of, and touted as, an art. This approach depreciates the precision required to conduct inquiries; it denies the existence of, and adherence to, rigorous methods; and it associates criminal investigation with unneeded mysticism. Criminal investigation is in large part a science. The fact that criminals are not always apprehended does not make it less so. The rational scientific method is, of necessity, supplemented by initiative and occasional fortuitous circumstances, but it is the application of the method rather than shrewd hunches that most frequently produces results. The most successful investigators are those who know how to apply the rational scientific method; therefore, it is this method that we consistently use in *Criminal Investigation*.

A second major difference between this text and others arises from our belief that writing about techniques takes on more substance if one understands something of the nature of the event being investigated. Thus we have discussed typologies—including offenses, offenders, and victims—in depth, so that our readers not only take away a more comprehensive understanding of criminal investigation than they would from another textbook but also have substantial information to use later as a reference.

Third, because crime-prevention technology has been a significant milestone for both the police and the public, we have inserted short sections on prevention in chapters where appropriate. The complexity of crime prevention dictates that it is a specialization within police departments. Yet at the scene of a crime, the investigator may be in a unique position to make a few helpful, if rudi-

mentary, suggestions to a victim on how to avoid further loss. *Criminal Investigation*'s crime-prevention sections give investigators the tools to accomplish this task.

Finally, most investigative books tend to blur the distinction between the roles of uniformed officers and detectives; we draw this line distinctly. Although everyone may not agree with our dichotomizing, the uniformed officer's role must be recognized for the contribution it makes to the ultimate success of an investigation.

THE ELEVENTH EDITION

Criminal investigation is always evolving owing to scientific, legal, and social developments, as well as to changes in the behavior of criminals. Although many investigative techniques are fundamental and remain basically the same over time, significant changes also occur on a continuing basis. In addition to having updated photographs, tables, figures, and citations, this edition reflects both the ongoing and the changing dimensions of criminal investigation by including the following text updates and revisions:

- **Chapter 1, "The Evolution of Criminal Investigation and Forensic Science,"** a historically oriented chapter, has a revised introduction that provides a definition of the investigator and the investigation, as well as an emphasis on the fundamental purpose of investigation and forensic science and its role in discovering the truth. A new section on jurisdiction has been added that discusses the geographic area and the legal/enforcement responsibility. The section on personal identification now includes a focus on biometrics.

- **Chapter 2, "Legal Aspects of Investigation,"** addresses legal topics that uniformed officers and investigators encounter on a daily basis and that are essential for the successful resolution of every criminal case. The chapter includes updated information on case law, including the scope of search of an automobile (*Arizona* v. *Gant*), legality of a search based on erroneous information officers received from another jurisdiction (*Herring* v. *United States*), legality of an arrest and search of a motorist even though state law required only the issuance of a summons (*Virginia* v. *Moore*), and legality of a search based on exigent circumstances (*Michigan* v. *Fisher*).

- **Chapter 3, "Investigators, the Investigative Process, and the Crime Scene,"** includes crime scene sketching and forensic mapping. There are revised and expanded discussions of infection diseases, digital video and photography, Digital Image Management Systems (DIMS), and Automated Digital Imaging of Crime Scenes using panoramic and laser scanning. A number of new photographs have been added, including those pertaining to crime scene control and coordination, detection using sense of smell, latent fingerprint kits, and the use of a privacy screen to shield bodies. The chapter continues to emphasize its strong crime scene and preliminary investigation focus.

- **Chapter 4, "Physical Evidence,"** has been thoroughly revised and streamlined and includes new material on forensic odontology, questioned documents, and new photographs pertaining to electrostatic dust print lifter (EDPL) and Hexagon OBTI.

- **Chapter 5, "Interviewing and Interrogation,"** includes new sections on witness intimidation, the use of electronic recordings for interrogation, why people confess, the detection of deception, and recent Supreme Court rulings relating to the rights of defendants to remain silent under the provisions of the Miranda ruling.

- **Chapter 6, "Field Notes and Reporting,"** has been completely reorganized so that it moves through the process of collecting information, recording notes, understanding and completion of incident reports, supervisory review and alternative dispositions, follow-up investigations, and finally, the preparation of supplementary reports.

- **Chapter 7, "The Follow-Up Investigation and Investigative Resources,"** has been thoroughly updated and includes revised sections on reinterviewing victims and witnesses and the use of facial recognition software. The section on conducting photo and live lineups has been updated to include new standards as well as forms to be used with each of the three types of lineups. The section on crime scene reconstruction now includes a step-by-step guide to using each of the CSR models as well as examples of each. This chapter also includes a number of new visuals pertaining to geoprofiling maps, the use of trained dogs to detect odors of cadavers, and a link/association diagram.

- **Chapter 8, "The Crime Lab,"** includes an updated and expanded section on the measures of crime lab effectiveness and includes recent BAS findings and recommendations regarding the nation's forensic science system. A new section on the Next Generation Identification (NGI) program has been added.

- **Chapter 9, "Injury and Death Investigations,"** includes a new section on the law regarding criminal homicides and felony assaults, a new "dead body checklist," and an updated section on serial murders that includes a discussion of the myths and misconceptions about, and the possible causes of, serial murder.

- **Chapter 10, "Sex-Related Offenses,"** includes new sections on elder sexual abuse and the early recognition and detection of sexual assault of the elderly.

- **Chapter 11, "Crimes against Children,"** contains expanded coverage of assaults against children, including the signs that indicate abuse, shaken baby syndrome, sex tourism, and Internet crimes against children. New sections cover unexplained child fatalities, traumatic brain injuries, and child pornography.

- **Chapter 12, "Human Trafficking,"** is new to this edition and discusses U.S. and state laws concerning human trafficking, the National Anti-Trafficking Task Force, forced labor, involuntary servitude, peonage, debt bondage, the delivery and marketing of women, conducting victim interviews, the psychological effects of sex trafficking on the victims, and information on identifying brothels.

- **Chapter 13, "Robbery,"** includes expanded discussions of taxi cab robberies, various crime prevention strategies, and convenience store robberies. A new section on police robbery prevention recommendations for convenience stores has been added.

- **Chapter 14, "Burglary,"** The references and data in this chapter have been updated. Portions of this chapter were rewritten for clarity.

- **Chapter 15, "Larceny/Theft and White-Collar Crime"** includes new sections on mortgage frauds, Internet frauds and scams, and senior citizens as fraud victims. The section on organized retail crime (ORC) includes a new case box on Target that explains their approach to dealing with ORC. The section on how identity theft occurs includes information on FBI scam letters as well as examples of these letters, debit card skimming, and social security number theft. The section on health care fraud has been expanded to include coverage of Medicare fraud. The section on security and investment frauds includes updates on the Bernie Madoff scandal.

- **Chapter 16, "Vehicle Thefts and Related Offenses,"** All statistics have been updated and show a continued decrease in the number of reported auto thefts in this country but the problem is still of national importance. Cloning of vehicles and obtaining titles using fraudulant paperwork continues to increase. A paragraph on Automated License Plate Recognition Systems has been added to the materials on Major Investigative Resources along with materials on the major involvement of The National Insurance Crime Bureau regarding the theft of heavy equipment.

- **Chapter 17, "Cybercrime,"** has been completely reorganized and rewritten with the objective of preparing first responders with the information needed to perform until a specialist arrives and what to do if one is not available. The chapter distinguishes between cyber- and computer crime; chronicles cybercrime tools and services related to thefts and frauds; and covers computer intrusions, malware, blended threats, drive-bys, herders and botnets, viruses and worms, time, logic, and email bombs, denial of services attacks (DoSs), ransomware, dead drops, keyloggers, rootkits, and scareware.

- **Chapter 19, "Arson and Explosives,"** includes a new section called "Know Your Explosives" which includes a detailed description of the characteristics of various types of explosives as well as the ways in which they can be scientifically analyzed and detected. An entirely new module has been added on "Improvised Explosive Devices" in which we discuss the components of IEDs and provide a series of new photographs that illustrate the various types of commonly used IEDs. A detailed discussion and photos of two of the more infamous cases involving IEDs occurring in the United States in the last couple of years have been added.

- **Chapter 20, "Recognition, Control, and Investigation of Drug Abuse,"** includes expanded coverage of "cheese" heroine, codeine, opiate overdoses, crystallized methamphetamine, synthetic marijuana (K2), drug trafficking and violence in Mexico, and new methods for producing meth. There is a new section discussing the paradigm shift in how our nation is addressing the war on drugs.

- **Chapter 21, "Terrorism,"** has received many updates to reflect recent events regarding Al-Qaeda in Iraq, Afghanistan, Yemen, and Somalia, as well as here in the United States The section on Hizbollah includes updates on the current presidential administration's efforts to normalize relations with it, as well as its involvement in Mexico, Canada, and the United States. The section on HAMAS has also been updated to reflect recent events and activities, including recruiting and fundraising. There are new sections addressing the threat of the Mexican drug trade, homegrown terrorism, and domestic right-wing terrorism. The section on investigation of terrorist activities now has an expanded discussion of investigative tools and techniques, including reference cards developed by New York state and the use of technology to coordinate and disseminate intelligence.

- **Chapter 22, "The Trial Process and the Investigator as a Witness,"** has an expanded section on evaluating the case to include information the prosecutor needs to evaluate the same case.

LEARNING AIDS

Working together, the authors and the editors have developed a format for the text that supports the goal of a readable, practical, user-friendly book. In addition to the changes already mentioned, we have added a host of new photographs, figures, and tables to reinforce and expand the text coverage. A visual presentation of the book's many lists—which are so critical in a text that teaches professionals and future professionals "how to" investigate crime—makes this material easy to digest. The learning aids in the edition go beyond these visual elements, however:

- **Chapter-opening photographs, outlines, and learning objectives** draw readers in and serve as a road map to the chapter.

- **Chapter-opening overviews** provide readers with a snapshot of the entire chapter and are excellent review tools for readers who are preparing for exams.

- **Detailed captions accompany photographs,** clarifying precisely what readers should be looking for and learning when examining each piece of art.

- **End-of-chapter review sections featuring key-term lists, review questions, and Internet activities** make preparing for exams easier than ever.

As mentioned, we have retained our plentiful, widely acclaimed "cases" within every chapter, ensuring that the eleventh edition is not only the most current, definitive text on criminal investigation but also the most practical and relevant. And with the enhancements we have made to the learning aids, *Criminal Investigation* is, simply put, the most mastery-oriented text available for the course.

SUPPLEMENTS

As a full-service publisher of quality educational products, McGraw-Hill does much more than just sell textbooks. The company creates and publishes an extensive array of print, video, and digital supplements for students and instructors. This edition of *Criminal Investigation* is accompanied by a comprehensive supplements package.

FOR THE STUDENT

Online Learning Center Website: This unique, book-specific website features interactive cases that not only are fun to explore but also are terrific learning tools. The website also includes self-grading quizzes and other exercises to assist students in mastering the concepts in the book. Visit it at *www.mhhe.com/swanson11e.*

FOR THE INSTRUCTOR

- *Instructor's Manual and Testbank:* Includes detailed chapter outlines, key terms, overviews, lecture notes, transparency masters, and a complete testbank.

- *Computerized Testbank:* This easy-to-use computerized testing program is for both Windows and Macintosh computers.

- *PowerPoint Slides:* Complete chapter-by-chapter slide shows feature text, art, and tables.

- *Online Learning Center Website:* Password-protected access is provided for important instructor support materials and additional resources.

- *Course Management Systems:* Whether you use WebCT, Blackboard, e-College, or another course management system, McGraw-Hill will provide you with a cartridge that enables you either to conduct your course entirely online or to supplement your lectures with online material. And if your school does not yet have one of these course management systems, we can provide you with PageOut, an easy-to-use tool that allows you to create your own course web page and access all material on the Online Learning Center.

- *Primis Online:* A unique database publishing system that allows instructors to create a customized text from material in this text or elsewhere and deliver that text to students electronically as an e-book or in print format via the bookstore.

- *Videotapes:* A wide variety of videotapes from the *Films for the Humanities and Social Sciences* series is available to adopters of the text.

All the preceding supplements are provided *free of charge* to students and instructors. Orders of new (versus used) textbooks help us defray the cost of developing such supplements, which is substantial. Please contact your local McGraw-Hill representative for more information on any of the preceding supplements.

ACKNOWLEDGMENTS

Without the kindness of many people throughout the country—literally from Alaska to Maine—this book could not have been written. We are grateful for the support of our colleagues around the country who have contributed case histories, reviewed portions of the manuscript within their areas of expertise, written sections for inclusion in the book, contributed photographs, forms, and other illustrations, or otherwise gone out of their way to be helpful. Our continuing concern in writing these acknowledgments is that, inadvertently, we may have omitted someone. If this is so, let us know so that we may correct this oversight, and also please accept our apologies. Our acknowledgments include persons who have contributed to this edition and those who helped with earlier editions. Some of the people identified have retired or taken on new responsibilities since assisting us, but, unless otherwise requested, we include their organizational affiliation and status at the time of the original contribution, since we feel that the agencies then employing them are also deserving of continued recognition.

Colleagues who have contributed photographs, forms, and other illustrations are identified beginning on page xxiii; thank you one and all. We would also like to thank another group of individuals who helped out in a variety of ways: Ross Gardner reviewed the new section of forensic mapping and made helpful suggestions, as did Captain John P. Slater (retired), Training Director, National Institute for Truth Verification with respect to the CVSA II System. Special Agent, Joe Navarro, FBI (retired) was kind enough to provide us with most of the information discussing the detection of deception. Chief Jack Lumpkin and Sgt. David Leedahl, Athens Clarke County (Georgia) Police Department; Chief Dwayne Orrick, Cordele (Georgia) Police Department; Chief Rick Boren, Lt. Ronnie Griffin, and Sgt. Doug Shafer, Columbus (Georgia) Police Department; Major Tolbert and Lt. Zapal, Savannah Police Department; Bob Hopkins, Hillsborough County, Florida, Sheriff's Office gave us information to strengthen the section on follow-up investigations; Commander Michael Frazier, Phoenix, Arizona, Police Department, was helpful with information on arson and explosives, as were Chief Richard Pennington and Officer R. Bonelli from the New Orleans Police Department; Chief Lee Donahue and Major William Gulledge, Honolulu, Hawaii, Police Department; Kenneth V. Lanning, Supervising Special Agent of the Federal Bureau of Investigation and the National Center for Missing and Exploited Children allowed us to reprint in Chapter 11 ("Crimes against Children") from his previously published material on the topics of child molestation and child pornography. Major Andy Garrison and Frank Broadrick, Northeast Georgia Police Academy, reviewed the chapter on report writing and made good suggestions for its revision. Steven Gottlieb, executive director of the Alpha Group Center for Crime and Intelligence Analyst Training, allowed us to adopt portions of his textbook to explain the critical role of crime analysis in law-enforcement investigations. Ron French of the Ecorse, Michigan, Fire Department provided updated commentary on where and how fires start, as well as on fire setting and related mechanisms. Leigh Herbst from the University of Nebraska helped with the new chapter-opening and closing material.

Chief Robert Davis, Lt. Rick Martinez, and Police Artist Gil Zamora, San Jose California Police Department, provided photographs for the robbery chapter. Lt. Anthony Traina, Paterson (NJ) Police Department, provided information and a photograph on using street surveillance cameras to prevent street robberies.

Gene Lazarus, Florida State Fire College, Ocala, and Steve Mraz, formerly with the Pinellas County, Florida, Fire Academy, reviewed and contributed to the arson chapter. Bob Quinn, Tom Costigan, Mike Rendina, Jim Wilder, and Richard Frank, presently or formerly with the Drug Enforcement Administration. Richard Souviron, Chief Forensic Odontologist, Dade County Florida, Medical Examiners Office, was an early major contributor of material dealing with bite marks and dental evidence.

Dr. Wally Graves, Medical Examiner for Lee, Henry, and Glades Counties, Florida, provided information on dental evidence. John Valor, forensic artist and photographer, provided illustrations for the dental section. Dick Williams of the FBI Crime Laboratory read the questioned-documents section and made a number of suggestions to clarify and strengthen it. Don Hampton of the Springfield, Missouri, Police Department did the same for parts of the crime scene chapter. We benefited also from the reviews and research materials provided by Jim Halligan, formerly with the Florida Department of Law Enforcement and then a professor at Florida State University's School of Criminology. He was a superb teacher and a real friend.

Special thanks to Lt. Greg Terp, commander of the Miami-Dade Auto Theft Task Force, and to some special people with the National Insurance Crime Bureau—Special Agent Lawrence "Dave" Dempsey; Regional Manager Ron Poindexter; Vice-President and General Counsel Robert H. "Bob" Mason; and Member Relations Manager Ed Sparkman.

Thanks to professor Gail Anderson of Simon Frazer University in Burnaby, B.C., Canada, for providing us with updated information on forensic entomology. Robert Aristarco, Assistant Vice President for Corporate Communications, American Re-Insurance Company in Princeton, New Jersey, allowed us to reprint material on arson investigation published by his company. Linda Brown and Robyn Royall of Help A Child, Inc. and SAVE (Sexual Assault Victim Examination Program) in Pinellas Park, Florida, provided us with all the material they use to collect the physical evidence of sexual assault cases. Dave Crosbie of the Burnsville Minnesota Fire Department provided us with photos for the "Arson and Explosives" chapter. Michael Dorn of Dorn's, Inc. provided us with current information on crimes in schools. Dr. Thomas B. Kelley of Florida State University in Panama City (Department of Criminology and Criminal Justice) provided us with both narrative information on underwater crime scene investigation and photographs. Debbie Lewis, Records Custodian, William A. Pellan, Director of Forensic Investigations in Pasco and Pinellas Counties, Largo, Florida, and John R. Thogmartin, M.D. provided numerous photographs for Chapter 9 ("Injury and Death Investigations") and Chapter 10 ("Sex-Related Offenses"). Sergeant Jim Markey of the Sex Crimes Unit of the Phoenix, Arizona, Police Department supplied us with information on how to reopen cold case sex crimes; he also provided us with a photograph. Robert Parker, Director, and Major Raul M. Ubieta, Miami-Dade (Florida) Police Department, supplied us with their agency's Robbery Standard Operating Procedure along with model form letters sent to robbery victims. Greg C. Pauley of the Temple Terrace, Florida, Police Department provided us with a computer-generated composite image as well as a police mug shot of a robbery suspect at the time he was arrested. Lieutenant Ted Snodgrass of the Las Vegas, Nevada, Metropolitan Police Department Robbery Sec-

tion supplied us with considerable information about his agency's "Team Approach" in dealing with robbery cases. Detective David Spraggs of the Boulder, Colorado, Police Department provided us with material used in the discussion of opening a cold case homicide investigation, along with several photographs. Laurie A. Ward, Crime Scene Administrator, Laura Sheffield, Forensic Artist, and Sheriff Grady C. Judd, Jr., all of the Polk County Sheriff's Department Office in Barstow, Florida, provided us with information on the use of forensic artists to re-create images of a robbery suspect along with a picture of the suspect at the time he was arrested. Sergeant Scott Whittington of the Colorado Springs, Colorado, Police Department supplied us with a video photo of a robbery in progress. Maryellin Territo and Sal Territo devoted long hours to researching sources for the most current information relating to all facets of criminal investigation.

A special thank you is extended to Mr. Ed Hueske for his invaluable help and assistance on the Physical Evidence and Crime Laboratory chapters. His forensics expertise was instrumental in helping acquire photographs and addressing new techniques in the area. Also, a very special thanks to Ms. Jennifer Davis for her hard work, research, and assistance in developing the book. She was an important coauthor on the "Crimes against Children" chapter. Chief Jimmy Perdue, North Richland Hills, Texas Police Department; Chief Richard Wiles, Deputy Chief Dianna Kirk, and Mr. Stuart Ed, El Paso, Texas Police Department; Chief Robert Lehner and Deputy Chief Chuck Tilby, Eugene, Oregon Police Department; and Chief David Kunkle, Dallas Police Department, provided opportunities within their departments for acquiring photographs and learning new techniques in the investigative process. Dr. Kall Loper has coauthored the "Computer Crime" chapter in previous editions, and some of his work was continued in this edition. Dr. David Carter, Dr. Richard Holden, Dr. Jonathon White, and Mr. Doug Bodrero, Institute for Intergovernmental Relations (Tallahassee, Florida), offered important information on terrorism and intelligence gathering analysis that highlighted the "Terrorism" chapter.

We would also like to thank Professor Barry Glover and Ashlee Castle of the Department of Criminal Justice, Saint Leo University, Saint Leo, Florida for providing us with the material in Chapter 9, Injury and Death Investigation, on the discussion of the Utilization of Criminal Justice College Students to Evaluate Cold Cases. "We also would like to thank Sharon Ostermann for graciously and cheerfully typing up major portions of this edition. Her constructive criticism, research skills, and editing greatly improved the final product."

This eleventh edition of the book benefited from a counsel of reviewers. Thanks to:

Preston Baity, *Milwaukee Area Technical College*
Geriann Brandt, *Maryville University*

Tyler Brewer, *Southwestern College*
John Brooks, *University of Arkansas*
Michael Brown, *Southeast Missouri State University*
Ruben Burgos, *Milwaukee Area Technical College*
Steven Chavez, *Western New Mexico University*
Stephen D'Arcy, *California State University, Sacramento*
Gene Evans, *Camden County Community College*
Anita Bledsoe Gardner, *Cleveland Community College*
Barry Glover, *Saint Leo University*
Don Haley, *Tidewater Community College*
Daniel Hebert, *Springfield Technical Community College*
Edward Jackson, *Baltimore City Community College*
William Kemper, *University of South Florida, Sarasota*
Dwayne Marshall, *Lock Haven University of PA*
Glenn McKiel, *Middlesex Community College*
Joe Morris, *Northwestern State University*
James Parlow, *Winona State University*
Dave Pauly, *Methodist University*
Scott Pray, *Muskingum College*

William Vizzard, *California State University, Sacramento*
Charlene Weitzeil, *Olympic College*
Donna Gaughan Wilson, *Prince George's Community College*

Finally, a few words about the hard-working people at McGraw-Hill who helped make this a better book: We would like to thank our editors Katie Stevens and Craig Leonard; project manager Mel Valentín, who kept this project moving forward and on time; designer Cassandra Chu; photo research manager Brian Pecko, who found us photos and obtained permission to use them in a timely manner; marketing manager Joyce Chiu; copyeditor Stacey C. Sawyer; and everyone else from the McGraw-Hill production staff in San Francisco who worked on this edition of the text.

Charles R. "Mike" Swanson
Neil C. Chamelin
Leonard Territo
Robert W. Taylor

We are grateful to our colleagues from around the country who have been kind enough to contribute photographs, forms, and other figures to the text. The inclusion of such material helps ensure the relevancy and usefulness of the text for all readers in all states. For this, we are indebted to the following individuals, departments, and agencies:

Alaska

State of Alaska Scientific Crime Detection Laboratory

Arizona

Phoenix, Arizona, Police Department

California

California Bureau of Livestock Identification
Kern County, California, Sheriff's Department
Los Angeles County Sheriff's Department
Riverside County, California, Sheriff's Department
San Bernardino County, California, Sheriff's Department
San Diego County Sheriff's Department
San Jose Police Department
Santa Ana, California, Police Department
Santa Barbara County, California, Sheriff's Department

Colorado

Westminster, Colorado, Police Department

Delaware

Delaware State Police

Florida

Big Bend Bomb Disposal Team, Tallahassee, Florida
Dade County Medical Examiner Department, Miami, Florida
Florida Department of Law Enforcement
Leon County Sheriff's Department, Tallahassee, Florida
Miami-Dade Police Department
Pinellas County, Florida, Public Health Unit, Sexual Assault Victim Examination Program
Pinellas County, Florida, Sheriff's Office
Polk County Sheriff's Office
Port Orange, Florida, Police Department
St. Petersburg, Florida, Police Department
Tallahassee Regional Crime Laboratory, Florida Department of Law Enforcement
Tampa, Florida Fire Department
Tampa, Florida Police Department

Georgia

Athens-Clarke County, Georgia, Police Department
Atlanta Police Department
Cordele, Georgia, Police Department
Columbus, Georgia, Police Department
Georgia Bureau of Investigation
Savannah Police Department

Idaho

Idaho Bureau of Investigation

Illinois

Chicago Crime Laboratory
Chicago Police Department
Cook County, Illinois, Sheriff's Department
Illinois Environmental Protection Agency
Illinois State Police

Indiana

Indiana State Police

Iowa

Iowa Criminalistic Laboratory, Department of Public Safety
State Historical Society of Iowa

Kansas

Wichita, Kansas, Police Department

Kentucky

Kentucky State Police

Maine

Lewiston, Maine, Police Department

Maryland

The SANS Institute

Massachusetts

Massachusetts Environmental Police
National Fire Protection Association

Michigan

Ecorse, Michigan, Fire Department
Sterling Heights, Michigan, Police Department

Minnesota

Minneapolis, Minnesota, Police Department
Minnesota Department of Health

Missouri

Regional Criminalistics Laboratory, Metropolitan Kansas City, Missouri
Springfield, Missouri, Police Department
St. Louis County, Missouri, Police Department
St. Louis Police Department

New Jersey

New Jersey State Police
Paterson Police Department

New York

Nassau County, New York, Police Department
New York City Police Department

North Carolina

North Carolina Bureau of Investigation
SIRCHIE Fingerprint Laboratories, Inc.

Ohio

Geauga County, Ohio, Sheriff's Department

Pennsylvania

Pennsylvania State Police
Philadelphia Police Department

South Carolina

Georgetown, South Carolina, Police Department

Tennessee

Nashville Police Department
Tennessee Bureau of Investigation

Texas

Austin, Texas, Police Department
Dallas Police Department
Forensic Training and Consulting, LLC
Texas Department of Public Safety (Garland
   Crime Lab)
Texas Parks & Wildlife

Utah

Utah Department of Public Safety, Bureau of
   Forensic Sciences

Virginia

Alexandria, Virginia, Police Department
Fairfax County, Virginia, Police Department

Washington

Clark County Sheriff's Office, Vancouver, Washington

Washington, D.C.

Police Executive Research Forum
Virginia Department of Forensic Services

Wisconsin

Madison Police Department
Milwaukee County Department of Social Service

Wisconsin Crime Laboratory
Wisconsin State Police

Wyoming

Lincoln County, Wyoming, Sheriff's Office
Wyoming State Crime Laboratory
Wyoming Game and Fish Department
Wyoming State Archives and Historical Department

National & Federal Agencies

Bureau of Justice Statistics, U.S. Department of Justice
Centers for Disease Control
Chester A. Higgins, Jr., and the U.S. Department of
   Justice, Office of Justice Programs
Drug Enforcement Administration
Environmental Protection Agency
Federal Bureau of Investigation
Federal Emergency Management Agency
Immigration and Naturalization Service, Forensic
   Document Laboratory
National Automobile Theft Bureau
National Center for Missing and Exploited Children
National Drug Intelligence Center
National Institute of Justice
National Insurance Crime Bureau
National Park Service
Office of Justice Programs, National Institute
   of Justice
Pinkerton's Archives
U.S. Customs Service
U.S. Department of Justice
U.S. Department of the Treasury, Bureau of Alcohol,
   Tobacco, and Firearms
U.S. Forest Service
U.S. Public Health Service
U.S. Secret Service

International Agencies

London Metropolitan Police
Royal Canadian Mounted Police
Turkish National Police

◄ Sir Robert Peel (1788–1850), whose efforts led to the establishment of the London Metropolitan Police in 1829. English police officers are still referred to as "Bobbies," a play on Peel's first name.

(© The Granger Collection, New York)

1

THE EVOLUTION OF CRIMINAL INVESTIGATION AND FORENSIC SCIENCE

CHAPTER OBJECTIVES

1. Define "investigator."
2. Define the most fundamental purpose of investigation.
3. State four additional objectives of the investigative process.
4. Explain the importance of the Bow Street Runners.
5. Discuss the contribution of Sir Robert Peel's reform to early policing in the United States.
6. Explain the history and contributions of the Pinkerton National Detective Agency.
7. Identify the first major federal investigative agencies and their responsibilities.
8. Explain the Supreme Court's "due process revolution" and its impact on policing.
9. Discuss Bertillon's method of anthropometry.
10. Summarize the historical development of fingerprint identification.
11. Explain the concept and practice of DNA typing.
12. Outline the milestones in the development of firearms identification.

An investigator is someone who gathers, documents, and evaluates evidence and information. This is accomplished through the process of investigation. The most fundamental purpose of criminal investigation and forensic science is to discover the truth. By making this purpose the cornerstone of their behavior, investigators can remain faithful to their oath of office and the accompanying ethical standards. Four additional objectives of the investigative process are to (1) establish that a crime was actually committed; (2) identify and apprehend the suspect(s); (3) recover stolen property; and (4) assist in the prosecution of the person(s) charged with the crime.

JURISDICTION

The authority of law-enforcement officers is limited by such factors as the Constitution, court decisions, federal and state laws, departmental policies, and jurisdiction, which can be thought of as both a *geographical area* and the laws for which an agency has *enforcement responsibility.*

The general rule is that the *geographic jurisdiction* of police officers is limited to the area governed by their employer. Law-enforcement officers employed by state agencies and county, as well as metropolitan and city police departments, follow this general pattern. Depending on the state, Sheriffs' deputies and county police departments usually patrol the unincorporated portions of a county, although by contract they may provide law-enforcement services to municipalities. Sheriff's deputies may or may not have jurisdiction outside their home counties. Investigations beyond the governing authority's geographical boundaries usually are conducted with the assistance of the appropriate law-enforcement agency. Some states have statutorily extended the jurisdiction of peace officers—for example, allowing investigation beyond their normal jurisdiction for offenses committed within the investigating officers' regular jurisdiction, when viewing serious misdemeanors or felonies, or assisting another law-enforcement officer.

The FBI provides a good illustration of *enforcement responsibility.* It has primary enforcement responsibility for all federal criminal laws, except cases for which responsibility is by statute or otherwise assigned specifically to another agency. As a practical matter the enforcement responsibility of the FBI is limited to roughly 200 laws.

CRIMINAL INVESTIGATION AND FORENSIC SCIENCE

For present purposes, the roots of criminal investigation can be traced back to England in the eighteenth century, a period marked by significant social, political, and economic changes. These changes were important to the development of the first modern detective force, the **Bow Street Runners.** In addition, London was the home of the first police reformer, Robert Peel. Both of these factors contributed to the subsequent development of police organizations and criminal investigation in the United States.

Forensic science draws from diverse disciplines, such as geology, physics, chemistry, biology, and mathematics, to study physical evidence related to crime. If it is suspected that a person has died from poisoning, for example, a toxicologist, who specializes in identifying poisons and their physiological effects on humans and animals, can assist in the investigation. Experts in other areas, such as botany, forensic pathology, entomology, and archaeology, may also provide helpful information to criminal investigators.

Over hundreds of years many people have made contributions to the fields of criminal investigation and forensic science. To recognize all of them is beyond the scope of this chapter and requires setting some limits. This chapter presents a brief history of criminal investigation and forensic science. Many volumes have been written about these entwined topics, but the space that can be devoted to them here is limited. Sufficient broad perspectives and supporting details, however, are included in this chapter to enable readers intrigued by these subjects to independently pursue their interest armed with a working knowledge of the basics.

THE EVOLUTION OF CRIMINAL INVESTIGATION

THE IMPACT OF THE AGRICULTURAL AND INDUSTRIAL REVOLUTIONS

During the eighteenth century, two events—an agricultural revolution and an industrial revolution—began a process of change that profoundly affected how police services were delivered and investigations conducted. Improved agricultural methods, such as the introduction in 1730 of Charles Townshend's crop rotation system and Jethro Tull's four-bladed plow, gave England increased agricultural productivity in the first half of the eighteenth century.[1] Improvements in agriculture were essential preconditions to the Industrial Revolution in the second half of the eighteenth century, because they freed people from farm work for city jobs. As the population of England's cities grew, slums also expanded, crime increased, and disorders became more frequent. Consequently, public demands for government to control crime grew louder.

THE FIELDINGS: CRIME INFORMATION AND THE BOW STREET RUNNERS

In 1748, **Henry Fielding** became chief magistrate of Bow Street and set out to improve the administration of justice. In 1750, he established a small group of volunteer, non-uniformed home owners to "take thieves." Known as the **"Bow Street Runners,"** these Londoners hurried to the scenes of reported crimes and began investigations, thus becoming the first modern detective force. By 1752, Fielding began publishing *The Covent Garden Journal* as a means of circulating the descriptions of wanted persons. On his death in 1754, Henry Fielding was succeeded by his blind half-brother, **John Fielding,** who carried on Henry's ideas for another 25 years.[2] Under John Fielding, Bow Street became a clearinghouse for information on crime,

and by 1785 at least four of the Bow Street Runners were no longer volunteers but paid government detectives.[3]

THE METROPOLITAN POLICE ACT OF 1829

In 1816, 1818, and again in 1822, England's Parliament rejected proposals for a centralized professional police force for London as different political philosophies clashed. One group argued that such a force was a direct threat to personal liberty. The other group—composed of reformers such as Jeremy Bentham and Patrick Colquhoun—argued that the absence, rather than the presence, of social control was the greater danger to personal liberty. Finally, in 1829, owing in large measure to the efforts of **Sir Robert Peel,** Parliament passed the **Metropolitan Police Act,** which created a metropolitan police force for London. Police headquarters became known as "Scotland Yard," because the building formerly had housed Scottish royalty. Police constables were referred to as **"Bobbies,"** a play on Peel's first name.[4]

Because French citizens had experienced oppression under centralized police, the British public was suspicious of, and at times even hostile to, the new force. In response to the high standards set for the police force, there were 5,000 dismissals and 6,000 forced resignations from the force during the first three years of operations.[5] This record was a clear indication to the public that police administrators were requiring officers to maintain high standards of conduct. Within a few years, the London Metropolitan Police had won a reputation for fairness, and it became the international model of professional policing. Despite the growing popularity of the uniformed Bobbies, however, there was fear that the use of **"police spies"**—detectives in plain clothes—would reduce civil liberties.

In the years immediately following 1829, some Metropolitan Police constables were temporarily relieved from patrolling in uniform to investigate crimes on their beats.[6] As the distinction between the use of uniformed constables to prevent crime and the use of plainclothes detectives for investigation and surveillance became clear, the public became uneasy. Illustratively, in 1833, a **Sergeant Popay** was dismissed following a parliamentary investigation that revealed that he had infiltrated a radical group, acquired a leadership position, and argued for the use of violence. In 1842, a regular detective branch was opened at **Scotland Yard** (Figure 1-1), superseding the Bow Street force.[7] Initially, the detective force was limited to no more than 16 investigators, and its operations were restricted because of a distrust of "clandestine methods."[8]

AMERICAN INITIATIVES

The success of Peel's reform in England did not go unnoticed in the United States. **Stephen Girard** bequeathed $33,190 to Philadelphia to develop a competent police force. In 1833 Philadelphia passed an ordinance creating

▲ FIGURE 1-1   New Scotland Yard
In 1890 the Metropolitan Police left their original quarters and were housed in New Scotland Yard, pictured above. Subsequently, in 1967 the Metropolitan Police moved again, to their present facilities, which are also referred to as New Scotland Yard.

America's first paid, daylight police force. Although the ordinance was repealed just three years later, the concept of a paid police force would reappear as American cities staggered under the burdens of tremendous population growth, poverty, and massive crime. In 1836 New York City rejected the notion of a police force organized along the lines advocated by Peel. The committee studying the idea concluded it was better in emergencies to rely on citizens than "despotic governments."[9]

Thus, before mid-century, few American cities had police service, and those that existed were inadequate. Many cities had paid police departments only at night or treated day and night police services as entirely separate organizations. Finally, in 1844 the New York state legislature created the first unified police force in the country, although New York City did not actually implement the measure until a year later. Other cities rapidly followed

New York's lead: Chicago in 1851, New Orleans and Cincinnati in 1852, and Baltimore and Newark in 1857. By 1880 virtually every major American city had a police force based on England's Peelian reforms of 1829 and pioneered in this country by New York City.

If one of the problems of the London Metropolitan Police had been getting the public to accept some constables' working out of uniform as detectives, in the United States the problem was getting the police to wear uniforms in the first place. American officers believed that a uniform made them easy targets for public harassment and made them look like servants. Only after the Civil War did the wearing of a uniform—invariably Union blue—become widely accepted by American police officers.

PINKERTON'S NATIONAL DETECTIVE AGENCY

America needed reliable detectives for several reasons: (1) graft and corruption were common among America's big-city police officers; (2) the jurisdiction of sheriffs' offices and municipal officers was limited; and (3) there was little information sharing by law-enforcement agencies. Thus, offenders often fled from one jurisdiction to another with impunity. Information sharing has vastly improved in the last 150 years but is an area that still requires further development.

In 1846 seeing the need for reliable investigators, two former St. Louis police officers formed the first recorded private detective agency.[10] However, the major private detective agency of the nineteenth century was formed by **Allan Pinkerton** (1819–1884, Figure 1-2.). In 1850, after working as a Chicago detective and a U.S. mail agent,[11] Pinkerton formed a private detective agency with attorney Edward Rucker.[12] Pinkerton's trademark was an open eye above the slogan "We never sleep."[13] The trademark gave rise to the use of the term "private eye" in reference to any private investigator.[14] The Pinkertons enjoyed such enormous success in the United States and throughout the world that some people thought "Pinkerton" was a nickname for any American government detective.[15]

The list of achievements by Pinkerton is impressive. Pinkerton reportedly discovered and foiled an assassination attempt on President-elect Lincoln in Baltimore.[16] At the outbreak of the Civil War in 1861, Pinkerton organized a Secret Service Division within the army (not to be confused with the U.S. Secret Service) and worked closely with General McClellan.[17] He infiltrated Confederate lines in disguise on several occasions and usually functioned as a military analyst.[18]

Following the Civil War, the Pinkertons were primarily engaged in two broad areas: (1) controlling a discontented working class, which was pushing for better wages and working conditions, and (2) pursuing bank and railroad robbers.[19] Unrestricted by jurisdictional limits, Pinkerton agents roamed far and wide pursuing lawbreakers. In a

▲ **FIGURE 1-2   Pinkerton at work**
Allan Pinkerton, President Lincoln, and General McClellan at
Antietam, Maryland, about October 3, 1862. Born in Scotland,
Allan Pinkerton was the son of a police sergeant. He found
employment as a barrel maker and advanced to supervisor.
At the same time, this red-headed, strong-willed man
advocated more voice in government for ordinary people,
a position that resulted in him becoming a wanted man.
Narrowly avoiding arrest on his wedding day, Pinkerton
and his wife fled to America, surviving a shipwreck while
en route. He started a successful barrel-making company.
While owner of that business, his initiative led to the arrest
of counterfeiters. This gave him an appetite for police work,
his father's profession, and changed his life and American
policing forever. **(Courtesy Pinkerton's Archives)**

▲ **FIGURE 1-3   Butch Cassidy's Pinkerton record**
Note the "P.N.D.A." initials on the first line, which stand for
Pinkerton National Detective Agency. Pinkerton agents were
highly successful in combating the bank and train robbers of
the Old West, such as the Hole in the Wall gang, so named
because of the small opening through rocky walls that led
to the valley in Johnson County, Wyoming, used as their
hideout. As many as 40 bandits may have lived there in
six cabins. Butch Cassidy and the Sun Dance Kid were both
members of the Hole in the Wall gang at various times.
(Courtesy Wyoming State Archives and Historical Department)

violent time, they sometimes used harsh and unwise
methods. For instance, suspecting that they had found
the hideout of Jesse James's gang, Pinkerton agents
lobbed in a 32-pound bomb, killing a boy and injuring a
woman.[20]

Pinkerton understood the importance of information,
records, and publicity and made good use of all of them.
For example, in 1868, Pinkerton agent Dick Winscott took
on the Reno gang. Winscott located Fred and John Reno
and, after a drinking bout, persuaded them to let him
photograph them.[21] He sent the photographs to Pinkerton
files, and within a year the Reno gang was smashed.[22]
Pinkerton also collected photographs of jewel thieves and
other types of criminals and photographed horses to prevent illegal substitutions before races.[23] The Pinkertons
also pushed Butch Cassidy (Robert Parker) and the Sun
Dance Kid (Harry Longabaugh) into leaving the United
States for South America, where they were reportedly
killed by Bolivian soldiers at San Vincente in 1909 (Figure 1-3.) Because of their better-known antilabor activities, the Pinkertons' other work often is overlooked. But
they were the only consistently competent detectives
available in this country for over 50 years[24] and provided
a good model for government detectives.

THE EMERGENCE OF MUNICIPAL DETECTIVES

As early as 1845 New York City had 800 plainclothes officers,[25] although not until 1857 were the police authorized to designate 20 patrol officers as detectives.[26] In November 1857 the New York City Police Department set up a **rogues' gallery** (Figure 1-4)—photographs of known offenders arranged by criminal specialty and height—and by June 1858, it had over 700 photographs for detectives to study so that they might recognize criminals on the street.[27]

Photographs from rogues' galleries of that era reveal that some offenders grimaced, puffed their cheeks, rolled their eyes, and otherwise tried to distort their appearance to lessen the chance of later recognition.

To assist detectives, in 1884 Chicago established this country's first municipal Criminal Identification Bureau.[28] The Atlanta Police Department's Detective Bureau was organized in 1885 with a staff of one captain, one sergeant, and eight detectives.[29] In 1886 Thomas Byrnes, the dynamic chief detective of New York City, published *Professional Criminals in America*, which included pictures, descriptions, and the methods of all criminals known to him.[30] Byrnes thereby contributed to information sharing among police departments. To supplement the rogues' gallery, Byrnes instituted the **Mulberry Street Morning Parade.** At 9 o'clock every morning, all criminals arrested in the past 24 hours were marched before his detectives, who were expected to make notes and to recognize the criminals later.[31]

FEDERAL AND STATE DEVELOPMENTS

From its earliest days, the federal government employed investigators to detect revenue violations, but their responsibilities were narrow and their numbers few.[32] In 1865 Congress created the U.S. Secret Service to combat counterfeiting. In 1903—two years after President McKinley was assassinated by Leon Czolgosz in Buffalo—the previously informal arrangement of guarding the president was made a permanent Secret Service responsibility.[33]

In 1905 the California Bureau of Criminal Identification was set up to share information about criminal activity, and Pennsylvania governor Samuel Pennypacker signed legislation creating a state police force. Widely regarded then by labor as "strikebusters on management's side," the Pennsylvania State Police nevertheless was the prototype for modern state police organizations (Figure 1-5). New York and Michigan in 1917 and Delaware in 1919 adopted the state police concept. Since then, state police forces have assumed the function of providing local police with help in investigations.

Although Virginia, Kentucky, and Arkansas have a State Police, there are none in the deep South. To a large degree, their use in that area has been foiled by politically potent sheriffs seeking to maintain autonomy.

Where State Police agencies do not exist, a common arrangement is to have a department that focuses primarily on traffic enforcement and another for criminal investigation—for example, in North Carolina there is a

▲ FIGURE 1-5   The Pennsylvania State Police

Troop D, Pennsylvania State Police, Punxsutawney, Pennsylvania, 1906. Note that both plainclothes and uniformed personnel are represented. (Courtesy Pennsylvania State Police)

State Highway Patrol and the State Bureau of Investigation (SBI). In such arrangements the crime laboratory may be a separate department or part of the state investigative agency. Similarly, casino gaming enforcement may be a function of a state police agency or a state gaming commission.

After Prohibition was adopted nationally in 1920, the Bureau of Internal Revenue was responsible for its enforcement. Eventually the ranks of the bureau's agents swelled to a massive 4,000.[34] Because the Bureau of Internal Revenue was lodged in the Department of the Treasury, these federal agents were referred to as T-men.

In 1908 U.S. Attorney General Charles Bonaparte created the embryo of what was later to become the Federal Bureau of Investigation (FBI) when he ordered that investigations were to be handled by a special group. In 1924 J. Edgar Hoover (1895–1972) assumed leadership of the Bureau of Investigation; 11 years later Congress passed a measure giving the FBI its present designation.

When Prohibition was repealed by the Eighteenth Amendment to the U.S. Constitution in 1933, many former bootleggers and other criminals turned to bank robbery and kidnapping.[35] During the Depression, some people saw John Dillinger, "Pretty Boy" Floyd, and Bonnie and Clyde (Figures 1-6 and 1-7) "as plain folks" and did not grieve over a bank robbery or the kidnapping of a

► FIGURE 1-6   Bonnie Parker

Texas-born Bonnie Parker (1910–1934) was part of the murderous Barrow gang, which robbed and murdered its way across Oklahoma, Missouri, Texas, and New Mexico. In 1930, she smuggled a gun into the Waco (Texas) County Jail, helping Clyde Barrow and a companion to escape. From 1932 until 1934, Bonnie and Clyde left a deadly trail before they were stopped. (Courtesy FBI)

▲ **FIGURE 1-7 Clyde Barrow**

Clyde Barrow (1909–1934) was captured after his escape from the Waco County Jail and served two years in prison. Upon his release, he and Bonnie began their rampage. Outside of Black Lake, Louisiana, they were killed by law-enforcement officers who had pursued them tirelessly.

(Courtesy FBI)

millionaire.[36] Given the restricted roles of other federal investigative agencies, it became the FBI's role to deal with these criminals.

Under Hoover, who understood the importance and uses of information, records, and publicity as well as Allan Pinkerton had, the FBI became known for investigative efficiency. In 1932, the FBI established a crime laboratory and made its services available free to state and local police (Figure 1-8). In 1935 it started the **National Academy,** a training course for state and local police. In 1967 the **National Crime Information Center (NCIC)** was made

operational by the FBI, providing data on wanted persons and property stolen from all 50 states. Altogether, these developments gave the FBI considerable influence over law enforcement throughout the country. Although some people argue that such federal influence is undesirable, others point out that Hoover and the FBI strengthened police practices in this country, from keeping crime statistics to improving investigation.

The Harrison Act (1914) made the distribution of non-medical drugs a federal crime. Enforcement responsibility was initially given to the Internal Revenue Service, although by 1930 a separate Federal Bureau of Narcotics (FBN) was established in the Treasury Department. In 1949 a federal commission noted that federal narcotics enforcement was fragmented among several agencies, including the Border Patrol and Customs, resulting in duplication of effort and other ills. In 1968 some consolidation of effort was achieved with the creation of the Bureau of Narcotics and Dangerous Drugs (BNDD) in the Department of Justice, and in 1973, with the creation of its successor, the **Drug Enforcement Administration (DEA).**

Today the DEA devotes many of its resources to fighting international drug traffic. Like the FBI, the DEA trains state and local police in investigative work. The training focuses on recognition of illegal drugs, control of drug purchases, surveillance methods, and handling of informants.

In 2002 several federal agencies were consolidated to form Immigration and Customs Enforcement (ICE) in the Department of Homeland Security (DHS).

THE POLICE AND THE U.S. SUPREME COURT

As the highest court in this country, the Supreme Court is obligated to review cases and to make decisions that often have considerable impact. From 1961 to 1966, a period known as the "due process revolution," the

◀ **FIGURE 1-8**

FBI crime laboratory

In 2003 the FBI occupied its 463,000 square foot state-of-the-art crime laboratory, which cost $130 million.

(© AP Photo/Charles Dharapak)

Supreme Court became unusually active in hearing cases involving the rights of criminal suspects and defendants. Its decisions focused on two vital areas: (1) search and seizure and (2) the right to legal representation. Among those cases was *Miranda* v. *Arizona* (1966), which established the well-known "Miranda rights." *Miranda* and other decisions infuriated the police, who felt that the Supreme Court had "tied their hands."

So what did the due process revolution and subsequent Supreme Court decisions really change? Questionable and improper police procedures and tactics were greatly reduced. In turn, this created the need to develop new procedures and tactics and to make sure that officers were well trained in their uses. To no small extent, this cycle has hastened the continuing professionalization of the police while also asserting the principle that the action of police officers anywhere may be subject to close scrutiny by the Supreme Court.

HISTORICAL MILESTONES OF FORENSIC SCIENCE

The origins of criminalistics or forensic science are largely European. Forensic science draws from diverse disciplines, such as geology, physics, chemistry, biology, and mathematics, to study physical evidence related to crime. The first major book describing the application of scientific disciplines to criminal investigation was written in 1893 by **Hans Gross,** a public prosecutor and later a judge from Graz, Austria.[37] Translated into English in 1906 under the title *Criminal Investigation,* it remains highly respected today as the seminal work in the field.

The Frenchman **Edmond Locard** established the first forensic laboratory in Lyon in 1910. All crime scenes are searched on the basis of Locard's exchange principle, which asserts that when perpetrators come into contact with the scene, they will leave something of themselves and take away something from the scene, for example, hairs and fibers. Expressed somewhat differently, Locard's exchange principle states that there is something to be found. He is also recognized as the father of poreoscopy, the study of pores and for advocating that if there were 12 points of agreement between two compared fingerprints the identity was certain.

Forensic science enjoys periods of stability, but on the whole it is dynamic and in constant progress. To illustrate this principle of dynamic change, the histories of two commonly used services—biometric-based personal identification and firearms identification—are traced in this section.

BIOMETRIC BASED PERSONAL IDENTIFICATION

Biometrics is from the Greek meaning life measurement. The most important goal of biometric measurements is to uniquely identity, or verify the identity of, an individual through characteristics of the human body. Biometrics is superior to eye witness identification because it has a scientific foundation.

Historically, there have been three major scientific systems of biometric-based personal identification of criminals in wide use: anthropometry, dactylography, and deoxyribonucleic acid (DNA) typing. The first was relatively short lived. The second, dactylography, or fingerprint identification, remains in use today throughout the world. The third, DNA, is a relatively contemporary development.

Anthropometry

Anthropometry was developed by **Alphonse Bertillon** (1853–1914), who is rightly regarded as the father of criminal identification (Figure 1-9). The first method of criminal identification that was thought to be reliable, **anthropometry** "was based on the fact that every human being differs from every other one in the exact measurements of their body, and that the sum of these measurements yields a characteristic formula for each individual."[38] Figure 1-10 depicts a New York City police detective taking one type of measurement used in the "Bertillon system."

▲ **FIGURE 1-9 Bertillon**
Alphonse Bertillon (1853–1914), the father of personal identification. In 1882, he began using his system on those incarcerated in Paris's Palais de Justice. (Courtesy Jacques Genthial)

▲ FIGURE 1-10   **Taking a Bertillon measurement**
A New York City Police detective taking a Bertillon measurement of the right ear, one of the 11 measurements that made up anthropometry. This photograph was taken around 1896. Note in this photo and the one that immediately follows that the right ear is consistently part of the measurements made. **(Library of Congress)**

▲ FIGURE 1-11   **Early identification card**
A Bertillon-style identification card, combining both personal measurements and photographs, prepared on February 28, 1917, by the Chicago Police Department. **(Courtesy Chicago Police Department)**

There was little in Alphonse Bertillon's early life to suggest that he would later make significant contributions. He was the grandson of a well-known naturalist and mathematician and the son of a distinguished French physician and statistician, who was also the vice president of the Anthropological Society of Paris.[39] Despite the advantages Bertillon had, he failed in a number of jobs. He was, therefore, able to obtain only a minor position in 1879, filing cards on criminals for the Paris police, because of his father's good connections.[40] The cards described criminals so vaguely that they might have fit almost anyone: "stature: average . . . face: ordinary."[41]

Bertillon wondered why so many resources were wasted on a useless system of identifying criminals.[42] He began comparing photographs of criminals and taking measurements of those who had been arrested.[43] Bertillon concluded that if 11 physical measurements of a person were taken, the chances of finding another person with the same 11 measurements were 4,191,304 to 1.[44] His report outlining his criminal identification system was not warmly received. After reading it, the chief said "your report sounds like a joke."[45]

Yet in 1883 the "joke" received worldwide attention, because within 90 days of its implementation on an experimental basis, Bertillon correctly made his first criminal identification. Soon, almost all European countries adopted Bertillon's system of anthropometry. In 1888 Bertillon's fertile mind produced yet another innovation, the *portrait parlé* or "speaking picture," which combines full-face and profile photographs of each criminal with his or her exact body measurements and other descriptive data onto a single card (Figure 1-11).

After the turn of the century, many countries abandoned anthropometry and adopted the simpler and more reliable system of fingerprints instead. Bertillon himself was not insensitive to the potential of fingerprints. In 1902, he solved the murder of Joseph Riebel when he discovered the prints of Henri Scheffer on the pane of a glass cupboard.[46] Yet Bertillon's rigid personality would not allow him to acknowledge the clear superiority of dactylography to anthropometry. Even so, Bertillon's place in history is secure as the father of criminal identification.

Dactylography

Dactylography is the study of fingerprints. Fingerprints were used on contracts during China's T'ang Dynasty in the eighth century as well as on official papers in fourteenth-century Persia and seventeenth-century England.[47] In the first century, the Roman lawyer Quintilianus introduced a bloody fingerprint in a murder trial, successfully defending a child against the charge of murdering his father.[48]

In a scientific context, in 1684 in England, Dr. Nehemiah Grew first called attention to the system of pores and ridges in the hands and feet.[49] Just two years later, Marcello Malpighi made similar observations.[50] In 1823, John Perkinje, a professor at the University of Breslau, named nine standard types of fingerprint patterns and outlined a broad method of classification.[51] Despite these early stirrings, it was not until 1900 that a country, England, used dactylography as a system of criminal identification.

The Herschel-Faulds Controversy.
Beginning in 1858 William Herschel, a British official in India, requested the palm prints and fingerprints of those with whom he did business, thinking that it might awe people into keeping agreements.[52] Over the next 20 years, Herschel noted from his records that the patterns of the lines on the fingerprints never changed for an individual. Excited by the prospects of applying this knowledge to the identification of criminals, Herschel wrote in 1877 to the inspector general of the prisons of Bengal. The reply made it clear that the inspector general was not interested. Discouraged, Herschel made no further efforts to pursue his discovery. Henry Faulds, a Scottish physician at the Tsukiji Hospital in Tokyo, had been interested in fingerprints for several years before 1880. When a thief left a sooty print on a whitewashed wall, Faulds was able to tell that the person in police custody was not the thief[53] and to match another suspect's fingerprints with those on the wall.[54] Faulds reported his findings in the journal *Nature* in 1880. Herschel read the account and published a reply, claiming credit for the discovery over 20 years before. A controversy broke out that was never resolved to anyone's satisfaction. Because there was also no official interest in using fingerprints, both Herschel and Faulds were even further frustrated.

Galton's and Vucetich's Systems.
In 1888 **Sir Francis Galton** (1822–1911) turned his attention to criminal identification.[55] When Galton contacted the editor of *Nature* for both Herschel's and Faulds's addresses, he was by chance sent only Herschel's. Contacted by Galton, Herschel unselfishly turned over all his files in the hopes that this revived interest would lead to practical uses of fingerprints.[56] In 1892 Galton published the first definitive book on dactylography, *Finger Prints*. It presented statistical proof of the uniqueness of fingerprints and outlined many principles of identification by fingerprints.[57] In Argentina, in 1894, **Juan Vucetich** (1858–1925) published *Dactiloscopia Comparada*, outlining his method of fingerprint classification. In 1892 a disciple of Vucetich's,

Inspector Alvarez, obtained South America's first criminal conviction based on fingerprints by using Vucetich's system to convict a woman of beating her two children to death.[58]

The Henry System.
The final breakthrough for the fingerprint method of personal identification was made by **Edward Henry.** At the age of 23 he went to India and by 1891 had become the inspector general of police of Nepal, the same province in which Herschel had worked some 15 years earlier.[59] Subject to many of the same influences as Herschel, but apparently working independently, Henry developed an interest in fingerprints[60] and instituted Bertillon's system with the addition of fingerprints to the cards. In 1893, Henry obtained a copy of Galton's book and began working on a simple, reliable method of classification. The governor general of India received a report from Henry in 1897 recommending that anthropometry be dropped in favor of Henry's fingerprint classification system. It was adopted throughout British India just six months later.[61] In 1900 Henry's system was adopted in England. The next year, Henry enjoyed two personal triumphs, the publication of his *Classification and Use of Finger Prints* and his appointment as assistant police commissioner of London,[62] rising to the post of commissioner two years later.

Faurot and "James Jones."
In 1904 New York City Detective Sergeant Joseph Faurot was sent to England to study fingerprints, becoming the first foreigner trained in the use of the Henry classification system. Upon Faurot's return, the new police commissioner told him to forget about such "scientific notions" and transferred him to walking a beat.[63] In 1906 Faurot arrested a man dressed in formal evening wear but not wearing shoes, as the man crept out of a suite in the Waldorf-Astoria Hotel.[64] Claiming to be a respectable citizen named "James Jones," the man demanded to see the British consul and threatened Faurot with nasty consequences.[65] Faurot sent the man's fingerprints to Scotland Yard[66] and got back a reply that "James Jones" was actually Daniel Nolan, who had 12 prior convictions of hotel thefts and who was wanted for burglarizing a home in England. Confronted with this evidence, Nolan confessed to several thefts in the Waldorf-Astoria and received a sentence of seven years.[67] Newspaper stories about the case advanced the use of fingerprints in this country.

The West Case.
Despite the fame achieved by Faurot, the most important incident to advance the use of fingerprints in this country was the **West case** (Figure 1-12). In 1903, Will West arrived at the U.S. penitentiary at Leavenworth, Kansas. While West was being processed in through identification, a staff member said that there was already a photograph and Bertillon measurements for him on file. But a comparison of fingerprints showed that despite identical appearances and nearly identical Bertillon

	William West	Will West
Bertillon: Measurements (in centimeters)		
Height	177.5	178.5
Outstretched arms	188.0	187.0
Trunk	91.3	91.2
Head length	19.8	19.7
Head width	15.9	15.8
Cheek width	14.8	14.8
Right ear	6.5	6.6
Left foot	27.5	28.2
Left middle finger	12.2	12.3
Left little finger	9.6	9.7
Left forearm	50.3	50.2

▲ **FIGURE 1-12** **The Two Wests**
William West had been in Leavenworth Prison since 1901; Will West arrived two years later. Given their similar appearances and nearly identical anthropometry measurements, one can understand the confusion created upon Will West's arrival. (Courtesy FBI)

measurements, the identification card on file belonged to a William West, who had been in Leavenworth since 1901. The incident accelerated the recognition that fingerprints were superior to anthropometry as a system of identification.

Rivalry of Vucetich's and Henry's Systems

Vucetich's book on fingerprint classification was published in 1894, seven years before Henry's, but Henry's system has become much more widely used. However, some experts think that Vucetich's system was superior.[68] The rivalry between partisans of the two classification systems deserves attention.

In 1911 the provincial government of Buenos Aires passed a law requiring fingerprint registration for all adults subject to military service and eligible to vote.[69] By 1913 Vucetich had completed the task and decided to travel. In his travels, he was showered with decorations for his classification system. But when he visited Bertillon to pay his respects to the father of criminal identification,[70] Bertillon kept Vucetich waiting and finally opened the door just long enough to yell, "Sir, you have done me great harm," before slamming it shut again.[71] They were never to meet again. On his return to Argentina, Vucetich was to face further humiliation. When Buenos Aires planned an expansion of fingerprint registration, there were strong protests. In 1917 the Argentine government canceled registrations, seized Vucetich's records, and forbade him to continue his work.[72] In 1925 much as Bertillon

had in 1914, Vucetich died a disappointed man. Although Vucetich's system is in use in South America today, Vucetich did not live long enough to see the vindication of his life's work.

In contrast, Henry became the head of what was then the world's most prestigious police organization and enjoyed the support of his government. These advantages, coupled with Vucetich's loss of support in his own country, meant that the Henry classification would become adopted virtually throughout the world.

DNA

DNA as "Blueprint"

Although **deoxyribonucleic acid (DNA)** was discovered in 1868, scientists were slow to understand its role in heredity.[73] During the early 1950s, James Watson and Francis Crick deduced the structure of DNA, ushering in a new era in the study of genetics.[74] Such developments were seemingly of peripheral interest to forensic scientists until 1985, when research into the structure of the human gene by Alec Jeffreys and his colleagues at Leicester University, England, led to the discovery that portions of the DNA structure of certain genes can be as unique to individuals as are fingerprints.[75] According to Jeffreys, the chance of two persons having identical DNA patterns is between 30 billion and 100 billion to 1.[76]

In all life forms—with the exception of a few viruses—the basis for variation lies in genetic material called

Cell

Nucleus

Chromosome

DNA

Gene

◀**FIGURE 1-13**
DNA Structure
The long, stringy DNA that makes up genes is "spooled" or coiled within chromosomes. If unspooled and connected, the DNA is a person's body would stretch approximately 67 billion miles. (Courtesy National Institute of General Medical Sciences, 2010)

DNA.[77] This DNA is a chemical "blueprint" that determines everything from hair color to susceptibility to diseases[78] (Figure 1-13). In every cell of the same human that contains DNA, this blueprint is identical, whether the material is blood, tissue, spermatozoa, bone marrow, tooth pulp, saliva, or a hair root cell.[79] Thus, with the exception of identical twins, every person has distinctive DNA.

The Enderby Cases

The first use of DNA in a criminal case was in 1987 in England.[80] In 1983 Lynda Mann, age 15, was raped and murdered near the village of **Enderby.** This case was unsolved. Three years later, another 15-year-old, Dawn Ashworth, was a victim in a similar offense. Comparing the DNA "fingerprints" derived from semen recovered from both victims' bodies, investigators realized that the same man had raped and killed both women. A 17-year-old man was initially arrested and a sample of his blood was subjected to DNA analysis. This man's innocence, however, was clearly established by the lack of a DNA match, and he was released. Subsequently, all males in the Enderby area between 13 and 30 years of age were asked by the police to voluntarily provide blood samples for DNA typing. Of 5,500 men living in the area, all but two complied with the request. A man then came forward and told the police that he had used false identification to supply a blood sample in the name of a friend. This friend, Colin Pitchfork, was subsequently arrested and convicted of Ashworth's murder, with DNA evidence playing a crucial role in the prosecution's case.

The Orlando Cases

During 1986 a series of rapes and assaults occurred in Orlando, Florida, that resulted in the first use of DNA in criminal investigation cases in this country.[81] The crimes shared a common pattern: the attacks occurred after midnight, in the victims' homes, by a knife-wielding perpetrator. The perpetrator was quick to cover the eyes of the victims with a sheet or blanket, so none of them could give detailed descriptions of their assailant. During early 1987, investigators staking out a neighborhood in which it was believed the rapist might strike saw a blue 1979 Ford speeding out of the area. They followed the car for a short distance before it crashed into a utility pole while making a turn.

The suspect, Tommie Lee Andrews, lived just 3 miles from the home of the first victim, who identified him at a photographic lineup the next morning. The prosecutor's case was certainly not ironclad. The identification rested on the victim's having seen the defendant for 6 seconds in a well-lit bathroom nearly a year before the photo lineup. Standard forensic tests comparing characteristics of the suspect's blood with characteristics derived from the semen found on the victim suggested that only Andrews could have committed the offense; but 30% of the male population of the United States shared these same characteristics. In short, there was enough evidence to prosecute, but a conviction was by no means a certainty.

However, on learning about the Enderby cases, the prosecutor secured DNA processing of the evidence and Andrews was convicted.

DNA Analysis

In 1988 the FBI became the first public-sector crime laboratory in the United States to accept cases for DNA analysis.[82] Private firms also offer DNA testing, including Orchid Cellmark, with forensic labs in Nashville, Tennessee and Dayton, Ohio

Although DNA analysis of blood and other evidence from humans in criminal investigation cases is widely understood and used, there was no application of "genetic fingerprinting" to plant evidence in criminal cases until the 1992 **palo verde seedpod case** in Phoenix, Arizona.[83] Joggers found the body of a female who had been strangled. At the scene, investigators found a beeper, which led them to a suspect. The suspect admitted that (1) he had been with the victim the evening she disappeared, (2) the victim had been in his vehicle, (3) he and the victim had had sex, and (4) he and the victim had struggled. However, the suspect also maintained that the victim had run off with his beeper when he refused to help her to get drugs and that he had not been anywhere near the place the body was found in 15 years. Investigators had found two seedpods from a palo verde tree in the bed of the suspect's truck. A University of Arizona plant geneticist was asked to determine if the seedpods came from a palo verde tree at the scene. The Maricopa County Sheriff's Office collected a total of 41 samples of palo verde seedpods from the crime scene and the surrounding region. The geneticist was able to exactly match the seedpods from the bed of the suspect's truck with those seized from the crime scene as part of the sample of 41 seedpods. Additionally, none of the 41 seedpods exactly matched another. This evidence was admitted at the trial. The defense attacked the evidence, properly arguing that the findings from a study based on 41 trees had substantial limitations and did not establish conclusively that the suspect could have gotten the seedpods only at the crime scene. However, along with other evidence, the testimony given by the geneticist had sufficient weight for the jury to convict the suspect.

FIREARMS IDENTIFICATION

Biometric based personal identification grew as several rival systems. Anthropomorphy lost credibility; Henry's system of fingerprint identification substantially eclipsed Vucetich's, and DNA remains widely used. In contrast, firearms identification moved forward in a series of successive steps.

In the United States, the frequency of shootings has made firearms identification extremely important.[84] As a specialty within forensic science, firearms identification extends far beyond the comparison of two fired bullets. It includes identification of types of ammunition, knowledge of the design and functioning of firearms, restoration of obliterated serial numbers on weapons, and estimation of the distance between a gun's muzzle and a victim[85] when the weapon was fired.

In 1835 **Henry Goddard,** one of the last of the Bow Street Runners, made the first successful attempt to identify a murderer from a bullet recovered from the body of a victim.[86] Goddard noticed that the bullet had a distinctive blemish on it, a slight gouge. At the home of one suspect, Goddard seized a bullet mold with a defect whose location corresponded exactly to the gouge on the bullet. When confronted with this evidence, the owner of the mold confessed to the crime.[87]

Professor Lacassagne removed a bullet in 1889 from a corpse in France. On examining it closely, he found seven grooves made as the bullet passed through the barrel of a gun.[88] Shown the guns of a number of suspects, Lacassagne identified the one that could have left seven grooves. On the basis of this evidence, a man was convicted of the murder.[89] However, any number of guns manufactured at that time could have produced seven grooves. There is no way of knowing whether the right person was found guilty.[90]

In 1898 a German chemist named Paul Jeserich was given a bullet taken from the body of a man murdered near Berlin. After firing a test bullet from the defendant's revolver, Jeserich took microphotographs of the fatal and test bullets and, on the basis of the agreement between both their respective normalities and abnormalities, testified that the defendant's revolver fired the fatal bullet, contributing materially to the conviction obtained.[91] Unknowingly at the doorstep of scientific greatness, Jeserich did not pursue this discovery any further, choosing instead to return to his other interests.

Gradually, attention began to shift from just bullets to other aspects of firearms. In 1913 Professor Balthazard published perhaps the single most important article on firearms identification. In it, he noted that the firing pin, breechblock, extractor, and ejector all leave marks on cartridges and that these vary among different types of weapons. With World War I looming, Balthazard's article was not widely read for some years.

Calvin Goddard (1858–1946, Figure 1-14), a U.S. physician who had served in the army during World War I, is the person considered most responsible for raising firearms identification to a science and for perfecting the bullet-comparison microscope. To no small degree, Goddard's accomplishments were contributed to heavily by three other Americans—Charles Waite, John Fisher, and Phillip Gravelle—working as a team on firearms identification. In 1925, Goddard joined Waite's team and upon Waite's death a year later, Goddard became its undisputed driving force and leader.[92] Like those of many pioneers, Waite's contributions are often overlooked. He had been interested in firearms since 1917, and from 1920 on he visited firearms manufacturers to get data on those manufactured since 1850. Because of Waite, the first significant

▲ FIGURE 1-14   Calvin Goddard, an American pioneer in the study of ballistics

▲ FIGURE 1-15   Atomic Force Microscope (AFM) image of fingerprint on cartridge case. (Courtesy of University of Leicester, Forensic Research Centre, England)

cataloged firearms collection in this country was assembled. Nonetheless, ultimately it was Goddard who raised firearms identification to the status of a science.

OTHER CONTRIBUTORS

There are many other contributors to the evolution of investigation and forensic science. For example, in 1910 **Albert Osborn** (1858–1946) wrote *Questioned Documents,* which is still regarded as a definitive work. **Leone Lattes** (1887–1954) developed a procedure in 1915 that permits blood typing from a dried bloodstain, a key event in forensic serology. Although more an administrator and innovator than a criminalist, **August Vollmer** (1876–1955), through his support, helped **John Larson** produce the first workable polygraph in 1921. Vollmer established America's first full forensic laboratory in Los Angeles in 1923.

In 1935 **Harry Soderman** and **John O'Connell** coauthored *Modern Criminal Investigation,* the standard work for the field for decades until the publication of *Crime Investigation* by **Paul Kirk** in 1953. A biochemist, educator, and criminalist, Kirk helped develop the careers of many criminalists.

RECENT DEVELOPMENTS

The knowledge base, facilities, and capabilities for both criminal investigation and forensic science are constantly advancing. A few illustrations are provided here and other developments are discussed in the appropriate chapters.

If fingerprints are left on cartridge cases which are then fired, attempts to recover fingerprints are successful only 1% of the time using conventional methods. However, in 2009, a new capability, using Atomic Force Microscope (AFM) imaging, was announced by researchers at the University of Leicester, England. When fingerprints come into contact with a polished metal surface, such as a cartridge case, a residue is left behind. This initiates a reaction that continues even if the print is wiped away, and the heat from discharge of a bullet actually enhances the interaction.[93] AFM examinations of fingerprints on polished surfaces produce extremely high-resolution 3-D images of them (Figure 1-15). AFMs also have applicability to the examination of documents.

Research using functional magnetic resonance imaging (fMRI), electroencephalography (EEG), and near infrared light (NIL) on the brain's electromagnetic signals has produced some tantalizing results.[94] Analysis of brain activity suggests that there are different patterns when people are lying, and it appears that brain activity can also reveal whether people are familiar with unpublicized details of crimes.[95] In *United States* v. *Semrau* (2010), a federal district court excluded fMRI evidence at trial because it lacked sufficient scientific support.

There continues to be strong interest in biometrics. Among the biometric-based methods of identifying individuals that are in use or on the horizon are hand geometry, iris scans, ear matching, facial and voice recognition, vein patterns, human body odor, and brain activity. The use of iris scanning presents some challenges, because the iris is affected by alcohol, drug use, pregnancy, and aging. Veins in subcutaneous tissue, the loose flesh immediately under the skin, are unique to each person. Several systems for imaging them are available, such as Vein Viewer and Palm Secure. Vascular pattern recognition (VPR) is focused on palm and finger subcutaneous veins. Electronic noses (E-Noses) have many applications, including food quality control and air pollution measurement. There is some evidence that E-Noses are effective in detecting and classifying human body odor. In 2006, in Nanjing, China, the Chinese government began gathering an odor database, reporting success in using it to solve cases.

"Biometric signatures" also receive research attention. Although handwriting analysis has long been used,

examples of applications in development include identifying computer users by the pattern, speed, and rhythm of their keystrokes and gait or walking analysis, which presents analytical problems, because gait can be disguised or difficult to discern if long, loose-fitting clothing is worn.

KEY TERMS

anthropometry
Bertillon, Alphonse
biometrics
Bobbies
Bow Street Runners
dactylography
deoxyribonucleic acid (DNA)
Drug Enforcement Administration (DEA)
Enderby cases
Fielding, Henry
Fielding, John
forensic science
Galton, Francis
Girard, Stephen

Goddard, Calvin
Goddard, Henry
Gross, Hans
Henry, Edward
investigator
Kirk, Paul
Larson, John
Lattes, Leone
Locard, Edmond
Metropolitan Police Act (1829)
Mulberry Street Morning Parade
National Academy
National Crime Information Center (NCIC)

O'Connell, John
Osborn, Albert
palo verde seedpod case
Peel, Robert
Pinkerton, Allan
"police spies"
Popay, Sergeant
rogues' gallery
Scotland Yard
Soderman, Harry
Vollmer, August
Vucetich, Juan
West case

REVIEW QUESTIONS

1. What is the most fundamental purpose of investigation?
2. What are four other objectives of investigation?
3. Who were the Bow Street Runners, and of what historical importance are they?
4. Why did the British public object to the use of detectives after enactment of the Metropolitan Police Act of 1829?
5. Why did the profession of detective in this country basically evolve in the private sector?
6. Of what significance is the work of Pinkerton and his National Detective Agency?
7. What is a rogues' gallery?

8. Allan Pinkerton and J. Edgar Hoover have what similarities?
9. What is anthropometry, and why was it abandoned in favor of dactylography?
10. What are the milestones in the development of dactylography?
11. Why does the Henry classification system enjoy greater use than Vucetich's system?
12. What are the different human sources of DNA material identified in this chapter?
13. Of what significance is the palo verde case?
14. What are the milestones in the development of firearms identification?

INTERNET ACTIVITIES

1. Research your local, county, and state police agencies. Do these agencies have a criminal investigation unit? Do "general investigators" investigate all types of crimes? Or, in contrast, is there investigative specialization—for example, a homicide unit? How many investigators are assigned to such

units? Do officers have to meet a certain criteria to be assigned to these units? How are officers selected? Is there any history on the creation of these units?
2. Find out more about the FBI's Biometric Center of Excellence (BCOE) by visiting *www.biometriccoe.gov.*

2

LEGAL ASPECTS OF INVESTIGATION

CHAPTER OBJECTIVES

1. Explain the historical evolution of the laws of arrest and search and seizure from the Bill of Rights through the Fourteenth Amendment.

2. Describe and diagram the flow of constitutional rights to a defendant in a federal criminal trial and a defendant in a state criminal trial.

3. Outline the requirements of a valid arrest warrant.

4. Describe whether a "John Doe" arrest warrant is ever valid, and if so, under what circumstances.

5. Define probable cause.

6. Describe the evolution of the Exclusionary Rule.

7. Explain the "Silver Platter" doctrine.

8. Describe the reasons for a search incident to a lawful arrest.

9. Explain the limitations on the search of a motor vehicle incident to an arrest.

10. Describe at least five circumstances that justify a search under exigent circumstances.

11. Define the law-enforcement policy issue that determines whether an inventory search is lawful.

12. Identify the primary requirement that makes a plain view seizure lawful.

13. Describe the limitations of a stop and frisk encounter.

14. Explain the circumstances that would cause application of the "Fruits of the Poisonous Tree" doctrine.

All law-enforcement officers, uniformed and plainclothes, conduct investigations. That is a statement of fact. There are, of course, differing concentrations of the investigative process and varying responsibilities among different units and different people.

Every law-enforcement officer must have a working knowledge of the criminal laws that he or she is charged with enforcing. The greater the knowledge, the better overall job one can do as an investigator. This will become apparent throughout the remainder of this text. It will be reinforced over and over because the criminal law is the foundation on which every investigation is built.

Criminal law is divided into two major components that are interrelated yet serve different functions. The **substantive criminal law** deals with those elements that describe and define a crime. When an investigator has the needed proof to satisfy the particular elements of an offense, it can then be said that the crime did occur.

The other component of criminal law is **procedural criminal law.** It is not enough to know whether a crime has been committed. The investigator must understand what and how things need to be done with the people involved in an investigation, be it a victim, a witness, an informant, or a suspect. Thus, the procedural part of criminal law defines what can and cannot be done with, or to, people. The procedural law changes much more rapidly than does the substantive criminal law. Procedural law deals with processes of arrest, search and seizure, interrogations, confessions, admissibility of evidence, and testifying in court. Some of these topics will be discussed in other portions of this book because they are relevant to specific subject matter covered. Legal matters dealing with interrogations and confessions are dealt with in the chapter on interviews and interrogation. Rules regarding admissibility of evidence and testifying in court round out the book, because they come into play when an investigation is completed and the case is submitted for prosecution. This chapter concerns the concepts of arrest and search and seizure. But knowing the current case law on these topics is not enough. The student must also understand the historical constitutional principles that got us to where we were, where we are, and, perhaps, where we are going tomorrow.

THE BILL OF RIGHTS AND THE STATES

An examination of constitutional history reveals that the powers yielded by the states were specifically granted for the purpose of establishing a national government. However, final ratification of the new constitution was delayed because some states wanted guarantees that individual liberties would be safeguarded from potential oppression by the newly formed government. This desire was based on the experiences of the colonists who supported the Declaration of Independence and fought the revolutionary war that won independence and created the United States of America, all of which occurred because the King of England was oppressing the colonies. The guarantees came in the form of the first ten amendments to the Constitution known as the Bill of Rights (Figure 2-1).

The Bill of Rights, however, restricts actions only by the federal government. It does not apply to, nor guarantee, the same protections from state governments. In addition, the Bill of Rights does not protect people from abuses by others who are not government officials or working on behalf of government officials. Thus, a private citizen could conduct an unreasonable search and seizure, then turn the results over to a government agency for use in court. Despite the fact that the seizing person may be criminally or civilly liable, the evidence seized could be used in court.[1]

The liberties protected by the specific clauses of the Bill of Rights are not exhaustive. One clause of the Fifth Amendment has been interpreted to leave the door open for additional protections. The **due process clause** provides: ". . . nor [shall any person] be deprived of life, liberty or property without due process of law." **Due process** is one of those concepts that has long been the subject of judicial controversy and has no universally accepted definition. The American concept of "fairness" is probably the closest one could get to an acceptable definition, in layman terms, without burdening the effort with reams of judicial history and philosophy. Thus the Supreme Court has the latitude to interpret the Constitution in any manner it

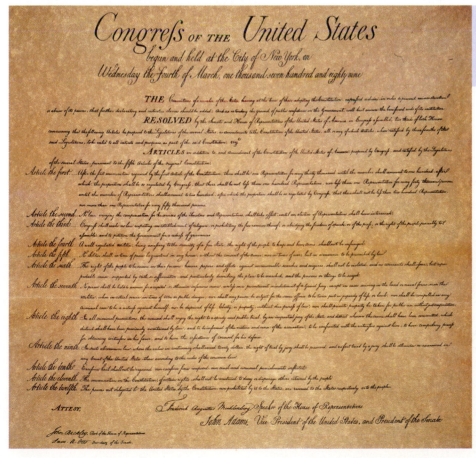

◄ **FIGURE 2-1** **The Bill of Rights**
The Bill of Rights restricts actions only by the federal government.
(© The Granger Collection, New York)

deems to be fair and just under the American judicial system.[2]

During this time period and until the last part of the nineteenth century, the federal courts could insure fairness only in federal criminal proceedings.

EVOLUTION OF THE FOURTEENTH AMENDMENT

The Civil War was over. Slavery had been abolished. The Thirteenth, Fourteenth, and Fifteenth Amendments were all designed to guarantee the freedoms and equal protection of the laws for all citizens, especially the former slaves.

Interpretations given portions of the Fourteenth Amendment provide the foundation for much of modern criminal procedure in the United States today. The relevant portions of the Fourteenth Amendment read:

> No state shall make or enforce any law which shall abridge the privileges and immunities of citizens of the United States; nor shall any state deprive any person of life, liberty, or property, without due process of law; nor deny any person within its jurisdiction the equal protection of the laws.

The first three words of this quote provide the cornerstone to the foundation. Until this amendment was ratified in 1868, the people of the United States had never before granted the federal government the power to tell the states what they could or could not do. This section contains the Fourteenth Amendment's due process clause. This shift in power and authority was enhanced by another part of the Fourteenth Amendment. The first clause of Section 1 of the amendment reads:

> All persons born or naturalized in the United States, and subject to the jurisdiction thereof, are citizens of the United States and the state wherein they reside.

This wording creates what is commonly referred to as "dual citizenship" and gives the federal government the power to tell the states they cannot abuse the freedoms of those people—us; all of us.[3]

A few years after ratification of the Fourteenth Amendment, the United States Supreme Court was asked to determine the meaning of that amendment's due process clause. In the 1884 case of *Hurtado* v. *California*,[4] the defendant urged the Supreme Court to declare that the due process clause of the Fourteenth Amendment incorporated all the guarantees of the first eight amendments to the Bill of Rights. Hurtado was charged with a capital offense in the state court upon an Information filed by the District Attorney. He was convicted and sentenced to hang. The Fifth Amendment expressly requires that capital cases must be based on an indictment or presentment by a grand jury, but because Hurtado was being tried in

a state court on a state charge, the Fifth Amendment was not applicable, as it would have been if he were being tried for a federal offense in federal court. He urged the high court to provide him the same guarantees in state court. This attempt to require carte blanche application of the first eight amendments to the states through the due process clause of the Fourteenth Amendment was rejected by a majority of the Court in this case and in many cases that followed. This attempted process became known as the "shorthand doctrine." The Supreme Court in rejecting the "shorthand doctrine" said that if the people and the states had intended for the Fourteenth Amendment to encompass the rights protected in the Bill of Rights and make them mandatorily applicable to the states, this would have been specified in the wording of the Fourteenth Amendment.[5]

Instead of adopting the "shorthand doctrine," the Supreme Court has reviewed cases on a case-by-case basis, determining whether the particular issue of the case calling into question a clause of the Bill of Rights should be made mandatorily applicable to the states through the due process clause of the Fourteenth Amendment. Although the Supreme Court rejected the quick way, the truth is, today, it doesn't matter anymore, because virtually everything in the first eight amendments has been ruled to apply to the states through the due process clause of the Fourteenth Amendment. It is still important to understand the relationship between the federal government and the states with respect to the Fifth and Fourteenth Amendments to the Constitution of the United States of America.[6] This relationship is diagrammed in Figure 2-2.

Let's now look at some of these processes as they have evolved.

THE FOURTH AMENDMENT

In part, the Fourth Amendment reads:

> The Right of the people to be secure in their persons, houses, papers, and effects, against unreasonable searches and seizures, shall not be violated, and no warrants shall issue, but upon probable cause, supported by oath or affirmation, and particularly describing the place to be searched, and the persons or things to be seized.

It is a common misconception that search and seizure is the sole topic covered by the Fourth Amendment. However, the authority for the laws of arrest is also derived from this amendment, as is seen in the last clause that provides: *"and the persons . . . to be seized."*[7]

By strict construction of the Fourth Amendment, the only time an arrest can be made or a search and seizure be conducted is under the authority of a warrant. However, the courts have not been that stringent in their interpretation of this amendment.

▲ FIGURE 2-2

Federal and State constitutional relationships in criminal cases

This chart represents the legal procedure a defendant would follow to claim a violation of constitutional rights in a criminal case. Line 1 represents a defendant claiming his rights in federal court directly from the Bill of Rights. Lines 2a and 2b are the correct procedure followed by an accused in a state court. Line 3 would be an incorrect attempt by a defendant to claim violation of constitutional rights directly from the protections guaranteed in the Bill of Rights.

(Source: Neil C. Chamelin, Vernon B. Fox, and Paul M. Whisenand, *Introduction to Criminal Justice,* 2nd Edition, Copyright 1979, reprinted with permission of Pearson Education, Inc., Upper Saddle River, NJ)

ARREST

There are a number of definitions of the term **arrest.** They range from "any interference with a person which, if not privileged, would constitute false imprisonment," to "interfering with the freedom of a person who is suspected of criminal conduct to the extent of taking him to the police station for some purpose," to "the taking of custody upon sufficient and proper evidence for the purpose of prosecution."[8] Each of these definitions is valid and depends on context. For example, what may appear to be a simple street stop or field interrogation may, in fact, constitute an arrest according to the first definition. Taking a person to the police station or sheriff's department for interrogation may fit the second definition. When an investigator intends to incarcerate and charge a person with a crime, the third definition applies.

INGREDIENTS OF ARREST

There are three essential ingredients of an arrest:

1. Intention
2. Authority
3. Custody

The officer must have the intention of taking the suspect into custody. This factor distinguishes an arrest from a lesser form of detention, but actual or expressed intention is not always the controlling factor. The intention may be inferred by a court if its estimate of all the conduct and circumstances indicates that an arrest occurred, despite any contrary intent on the part of the law-enforcement officer.

The officer must have real or assumed legal authority for taking the person into custody. The officer must have the actual authority to make a legal arrest or at least believe this to be the case. For example, an investigator may make an arrest under a defective warrant but not know about the defect. The third ingredient is that the person arrested must come within the custody and control of the law. This element can be satisfied either by physical restraint or by the arrestee's voluntary submission to the custody and control of the arresting officer.

ARREST DISTINGUISHED FROM DETENTION

Detention is a temporary and limited interference with the freedom of a person for investigative purposes. Sometimes called investigative detention, it is also commonly referred to by law enforcement as a "street stop" or "field interrogation." In this instance, police are justified in employing **"stop and frisk"** measures—patting down the outer clothing—if they suspect that the person being questioned may be armed and their safety is in jeopardy.[9] This issue of "stop and frisk" is covered later near the end of the search and seizure section of this chapter.

There is a fine line between detention and arrest. Because an officer does interfere with the freedom of the individual stopped, even for only a few minutes, some theorists view any such action as constituting arrest. Most people and most courts recognize the validity of street stops and uphold them as not being arrests if conducted properly.

A valid detention must be brief and made for good reason. The officer must limit questioning and investigation and must then either release the subject or decide to arrest. Detention for an undue length of time could be construed as an arrest if later challenged in court.

ARREST DISTINGUISHED FROM CHARGING

As noted earlier, one definition of arrest is to interfere with the freedom of a person suspected of involvement in a crime to the extent that the person is taken to the police station. But investigators do not always intend to prosecute or have the ability to prosecute at that time. Formally **charging** a suspect with a crime does not automatically flow from an arrest. Charging follows a decision to prosecute. This decision may be made by the police, by the prosecutor, or by both. But they may also decide not to bring charges. For example, the evidence that justified the arrest may not be sufficient to warrant formal charges, because the prosecutor believes he or she cannot prove the case beyond, and to the exclusion of, every reasonable doubt. Perhaps additional information may come to light after the arrest that points to the accused's innocence. Maybe an arrest was unlawful or evidence was obtained in violation of constitutional standards.

ARREST PROCEDURES

The laws of most jurisdictions permit an arrest in at least three and sometimes four types of situations:

1. When a warrant has been issued.
2. When a crime is committed in the presence of an arresting officer.
3. When an officer has probable cause to believe that the suspect being arrested has committed a felony.
4. In statutorily created instances.

THE ARREST WARRANT

The preferred method of effecting an arrest is under the authority of a warrant. In fact, if one were to read the constitutional requirements in their strictest sense, arrests can be justified only if made with a warrant. Of course, the courts have chosen to be more liberal in their interpretation so that warrantless arrests can be made in certain situations. But there are sound reasons for both the warrant requirements and the exceptions created by judicial case law, and, in some instances, by legislation. In the U.S. constitutional system, the functions of government—executive, legislative, and judicial—are each the responsibility of a separate branch. The police function is an executive one, whereas the judicial responsibility obviously belongs to the courts. Although the mechanism of arrest is an executive function, it is subject to judicial scrutiny and review. This position is supported by the very wording of the Fourth Amendment to the U.S. Constitution:

> . . . and no warrant shall issue, but upon probable cause, supported by oath or affirmation, and particularly describing the . . . person . . . to be seized.

The two major benefits derived from securing prior judicial approval for arrests through the warrant process are that the approval relieves law enforcement of the burden of proving the legality of the arrest—so that officers need not fear charges of false arrest, malicious prosecution, or other civil suits—and getting a warrant provides for an independent evaluation of the evidence.

Even the most objective, well-trained, and well-intentioned investigators sometimes become so involved in a case that their involvement may affect their ability to evaluate the case's merits objectively. Presenting the case before a qualified judge has the benefits of allowing an independent third party, with no emotional involvement in the investigation and with the knowledge of legal standards that must be met, to assist the investigator in determining whether those standards have been achieved. It is also logical to assume that the validity of an arrest made after this review and the issuance of a warrant is more likely to be upheld if later challenged in court than an arrest based solely on an officer's own determination of the sufficiency of the evidence. The wise law-enforcement officer recognizes the value of obtaining a warrant whenever practical. The word "practical" has significance with regard to the propriety of securing an arrest warrant. The law recognizes that the innumerable situations encountered by law-enforcement officers in daily activities and the variety of conditions inherent in the nature of the law-enforcement function make it impossible and unrealistic to expect an officer to obtain a warrant in every situation before effecting an arrest—hence, the exceptions to the warrant requirement.

The procedure required for obtaining a warrant is often time-consuming and inconvenient. Frequently, the process in major felony cases requires that the investigator seek out the prosecutor; present the facts, which will be reduced to paper in affidavit form for a probable cause determination; find a judge who is authorized to issue warrants; present the case again for a determination of the sufficiency of the grounds for arrest; and then wait for the warrant to be typed up and signed. In many cases, the procedure can take several hours, even during the normal workday. On weekends and late at night, it may take even longer, as the prosecutor, judge, or both are located or roused from bed. As a consequence, officers sometimes tend to take the easy way out by making a warrantless arrest, hoping they are right and believing they have sufficient grounds to act. By conducting themselves in this manner, they neglect the basic rule of thumb—get a warrant—and its underlying rationale. But the warrantless arrest is not always a shortcut. As clear as the law may appear to be on the need for warrants, each case must rest on its own facts. There are relatively few cases in which it is obvious that an arrest can be made without a warrant. Similarly, the clear-cut instances for which a warrant is absolutely needed are relatively few. The majority of cases fall within that vast plane requiring evaluation of the merits of each case. An arrest without a warrant, however, does not save time. In reality, the time an officer spends on justifying this decision in motion hearings demanded by the defense attorney will equal or exceed the time it would have taken to get a warrant in the first place. The potential consequence is that the case may be dismissed for want of a valid arrest or that important evidence, seized as a result of the arrest, may be suppressed.

The investigator is not relieved of all responsibility for the legality of the arrest simply because a warrant was obtained. The investigator must be aware of what constitutes a valid warrant to ensure that the one he or she possesses permits a legal arrest.

An **arrest warrant** is a judicial order commanding the person to whom it is issued or some other person to

▲ **FIGURE 2-3   Review of affidavit for arrest warrant**
Investigator and judge review the paperwork prepared by
the investigator in support of seeking the arrest warrant.
(© Mike Karlsson/Arresting Images)

▲ **FIGURE 2-4**
**Swearing or affirming to contents of affidavit for arrest
warrant**
When the judge is satisfied that the arrest warrant affidavit is
in order, and probable cause to arrest exists, he places the
investigator under oath and the affidavit becomes a sworn
document. (© Mike Karlsson/Arresting Images)

arrest a particular individual and to bring that person
promptly before a court to answer a criminal charge. The
arrest warrant generally must be written. By legislation,
some jurisdictions allow for verbal authorization supported by written authorization in warrant form that is
issued later (Figures 2-3 and 2-4).

In most cases, particularly major felonies, the warrant
must be issued by a judge who personally reviews the
facts to determine the existence of reasonable grounds as
required by the Constitution. The warrant must be supported by an **affidavit**—a written statement of the information known to the officer that serves as the basis for
the issuance of the warrant. In major cases, the requirements vary on whether the warrant must be issued in the
county in which the offense occurred, but once issued,
major case warrants can be served anywhere in the state.

The form and contents of an arrest warrant usually
include:

1. The authority under which the warrant is issued
   (the name of the state).
2. The person who is to execute the warrant (generally addressed to any peace officer of the state).
3. The identity of the person to be arrested.
4. The designation of the offense.
5. The date, time, and place of the occurrence.
6. The name of the victim.
7. A description of the offense and how it occurred.

Blank warrants are not constitutionally valid. Before a
warrant can be issued, the identity of the perpetrator
must be known. The mere fact that a crime has been committed by someone unknown will not support a warrant's issuance. The Constitution requires that the warrant
contain a particular description of the suspect. This
description must be specific enough to permit an officer
not acquainted with the case to identify the person to be
arrested with reasonable certainty. Aliases may be used.
If the suspect's name is not known, "John Doe" may be
used provided there are other methods of describing the
person to be arrested, such as place of residence, occupation, and a physical description.

A reprint of an Associated Press story appeared on the
web on August 8, 2004, reporting that in Boston, prosecutors found a way to prevent the 15-year statute of limitations from destroying the possibility of bringing rapists

▶ **FIGURE 2-5**
Placing felon under arrest
A San Antonio, Texas, police officer arrests a person he has probable cause to believe just committed a felony battery. (© Bob Daemmrich/ PhotoEdit)

to trial. In cases that have DNA evidence, prosecutors are obtaining indictments against "John Does" based on their DNA profiles. Massachusetts followed the lead of Wisconsin that started doing this in 1999. New York has also begun using the process. In a Wisconsin appellate case challenging the constitutionality of the statute claiming that the indictment does not specifically name the defendant, the court said that DNA evidence was the best method of identification available.

Herring v. *United States*[10] involved a warrant issued on erroneous information that the police did not know was in error. Officers in one Alabama county arrested Herring based on a warrant that was listed in a neighboring county's database. Search incident to arrest yielded drugs and a gun. It was then learned that the warrant had been recalled months earlier but someone forgot to remove the warrant from the neighboring county's database. Herring was tried on federal gun and drug possession charges. The federal district court refused to suppress the evidence and Herring was convicted. The U.S. Supreme Court held: When police mistakes leading to an unlawful search are the result of isolated negligence leading up to the search, rather than systematic error or disregard of constitutional requirements, the exclusionary rule does not apply.

Crime Committed in Presence

Any offense committed in the presence of an officer, whether felony or misdemeanor, can be the basis of an arrest without a warrant. The in-presence requirement is usually thought of in the narrow context of sight. However, to satisfy the legal requirements, perception of some or all of the elements of an offense as they occur, through the use of any or all of the five senses—sight, hearing, taste, touch, or smell—can justify a warrantless arrest.

PROBABLE CAUSE

The third major category in which a lawful arrest is generally permitted involves offenses not committed in the officer's presence and for which a warrant has not been issued. The law allows an officer to make warrantless arrests in felony cases provided reasonable grounds or probable cause exists to make the arrest (Figure 2-5). (As previously noted, probable cause also must be shown in an affidavit to support the issuance of a warrant.)

Probable cause is a difficult term to define, because in no two instances are circumstances identical. One acceptable definition of **probable cause** is that it is more than suspicion but less than actual knowledge. It is suspicion plus facts and circumstances that would lead a reasonable person exercising ordinary caution to believe that a crime has been, is being, or is about to be committed (see Figure 2-6).

Probable cause may be based on a number of sources of information, not all of which have to be the kind of evidence admissible at trial. However, if prosecution is an aim of the arrest, there must also be sufficient evidence to take the case to court. In addition, the probable cause must exist at the time the arrest is made and may not be developed by subsequently acquired evidence.

Mere suspicion is not enough to justify an arrest; there must be supporting facts and circumstances. Certain factors may help to decide the existence of probable cause. The most common is the personal knowledge of the officer/ investigator. Information obtained from informants also may be of value, although that information may not be admissible at a subsequent hearing or trial. The investigator must be able to establish the reliability of the information and the informant by indicating the length of time the investigator has known or dealt with the informant, the general character and reputation of the informant, the

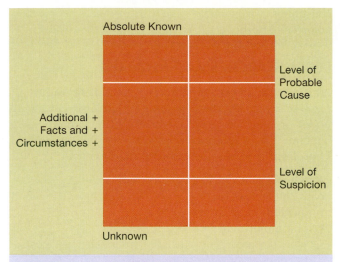

▲ FIGURE 2-6   Probable cause

(Source: Neil C. Chamelin, Vernon B. Fox, and Paul M. Whisenand, *Introduction to Criminal Justice*, 2nd ed. Copyright 1979, reprinted with permission of Pearson Education, Inc. Upper Saddle River, NJ)

number of tips received from the informant in the past, the accuracy of previous information, whether the informant is paid for the information, and the informant's motives for volunteering the information. One of the current common instances is the use of confidential informants to make drug buys.

Other sources of probable cause include information from a police department or from other law-enforcement agencies, such as notice of outstanding warrants, the past criminal record of the suspect, physical evidence found at the scene of the crime, other evidence detected in the follow-up investigation, crime laboratory analyses, and reports of victims and eyewitnesses.

There is a third exception to the warrant requirement for a valid arrest. By legislation, states allow officers to make arrests in nonfelony cases even though the offense is not committed in the officer's presence. Examples include domestic violence situations, violations of injunctions against domestic violence, and cases of battery.[11]

SEARCH AND SEIZURE

The evolution of the law of **search and seizure** illustrates the relationship described earlier between federal and state court systems and between the Bill of Rights and its application to the states through the due process clause of the Fourteenth Amendment.[12]

Under early English common law, an illegal search and seizure that produced incriminating evidence was allowed, and the evidence obtained was admissible in court. Surprisingly, federal law-enforcement officers in the United States were permitted to follow the same rule until 1914. Up to that time, the search and seizure practices

of federal officials had not been scrutinized in light of the wording of the Fourth Amendment. In 1914 the case of *Weeks* v. *United States*[13] was decided by the United States Supreme Court. Weeks was charged by federal agents with using the mails for transporting materials that represented chances in a lottery. After his arrest for this federal offense, Weeks's room was searched twice without the authority of a valid search warrant. But Weeks had been arrested at his place of employment, not his home. During the **search,** the agents found and seized various incriminating papers and articles. This evidence was admitted at his trial for the federal violation, and Weeks was convicted. On appeal to the United States Supreme Court, the Court established what became known as the "Federal Exclusionary Rule." The Court ruled that any evidence unreasonably obtained by federal law-enforcement officers could no longer be admissible in federal prosecutions. The Court made it quite clear that, because this was a federal case, the decision was applicable only to federal law-enforcement officers and federal courts and was in no way applicable to the states. But this decision, as do many Supreme Court decisions, left a number of unanswered questions. Out of one question arose the "Silver Platter Doctrine." The *Weeks* decision prohibited federal officers from illegally seizing evidence but it did not prevent law-enforcement officers of the states from illegally seizing the evidence and handing it over to federal agents on a "silver platter" for use in federal courts. This method of circumventing the Federal Exclusionary Rule remained unchallenged until 1960. In that year, the Supreme Court prohibited the introduction in federal courts of all illegally seized evidence obtained by state officers in violation of the Fourth Amendment.[14]

After the *Weeks* decision, very few states adopted their own exclusionary rule applicable within their own state. It was not until 1949 that a serious attempt was made to seek mandatory application of the exclusionary rule to the states through the due process clause of the Fourteenth Amendment. In *Wolf* v. *Colorado,*[15] the defendant was charged with abortion. Based on suspicion of similar prior offenses, officers searched Wolf's office, arrested him, and seized certain documents that were later admitted into trial. Wolf appealed his conviction contending that the unreasonable search and seizure was a denial of due process under the Fourteenth Amendment, as it would be under the Fourth Amendment had he been in federal court. The Supreme Court held that unreasonable searches and seizures by state officials in state cases did not constitute a denial of Fourteenth Amendment due process but added that the Court did have the authority to rule otherwise if the Justices so desired. The interesting point in this case seemed to be that the Court was giving the states fair warning that they disapproved of unreasonable searches and seizures by state authorities and that sooner or later they would rule in favor of incorporating the Fourth Amendment protection in the due process clause of the Fourteenth Amendment. Many states took the hint.

By 1961 only 18 states had not adopted an exclusionary rule. In that year, the warning that the Supreme Court had given 12 years earlier in the *Wolf* case came to pass. In May 1957 three Cleveland police officers arrived at Dolree Mapp's residence in that city with information that a person who was wanted for questioning in a recent bombing was hiding out in her home and that there was a large amount of gambling paraphernalia being hidden in the home. The officers knocked on the door and demanded entrance, but Ms. Mapp, after telephoning her attorney, refused to admit them without a search warrant. The officers advised their headquarters of the situation and undertook a surveillance of the house. Some three hours later, the officers, with reinforcements, again sought entrance. When Ms. Mapp did not come to the door immediately, one of the doors was forcibly opened and the officers gained entry. Ms. Mapp demanded to see the search warrant. One of the officers held up a paper that he claimed was the search warrant. She grabbed the paper and stuffed it down the front of her dress. A struggle ensued in which the officers recovered the piece of paper and handcuffed Ms. Mapp for her "belligerency" in resisting the attempt to recover the "warrant." A subsequent widespread search of the entire premises disclosed obscene materials. Ms. Mapps was convicted for possession of these materials. No search warrant was ever produced at the trial.

Following Ms. Mapp's conviction and the denial of her appeals in the state courts, her case was appealed to the United States Supreme Court. *Mapp* v. *Ohio*,[16] decided in 1961, established the rule that any evidence unreasonably searched and seized would no longer be admissible in any court—state or federal. The Exclusionary Rule was now applicable in all courts at all levels.

Among the many unanswered questions created by the *Mapp* decision, the crucial question revolved around the definition of the word **unreasonable.** It did not take the state courts long to find the loophole. In order to avoid applying the decision in the *Mapp* case to instances arising in state courts, state officials merely called previously unreasonable searches and seizures reasonable searches. Because no standards had been set for determining what constitutes a reasonable or unreasonable search, many of the state courts felt free to make their own determination on this issue. In effect, *Mapp* had little impact on these states. However, within two years of the *Mapp* decision, the Supreme Court had the opportunity to rule on this matter. The Court held in *Ker* v. *California*[17] that the state court judges were still free to determine the reasonableness of searches but that in making those determinations they would now be guided by the same standards as had been followed in the federal courts, which were established in the line of cases decided since the *Weeks* case in 1914. In essence, the Court said that states would be held to federal standards in search and seizure matters.

The long line of cases evolving since *Mapp* and *Ker* have essentially revolved around the single issue of what constitutes a reasonable search in instances where law-enforcement officers act with or without a warrant.

LEGAL SEARCHES AND SEIZURES

As is true for arrests, the Fourth Amendment also recognizes searches and seizures only by government agents under the authority of a warrant. The United States Supreme Court recognizes judicially created exceptions. Thus, legal searches and seizures can be made:

1. when a warrant has been issued;
2. with consent;
3. incident to an arrest;
4. of a motor vehicle;
5. when an emergency (exigent circumstances) exists;
6. to conduct an inventory.

There are two additional areas that are closely related but can't truly be called searches and seizures—plain view seizures and stop and frisk encounters. These will also be covered.

SEARCH WITH A WARRANT

A **search warrant** is a written order, in the name of the state, signed by a judicial officer, exercising proper authority, and directing a law-enforcement officer to search for certain specific property and bring it before the court. To be valid, the warrant must be signed by one who is authorized to sign. Normally, this is a judicial officer. In rare instances, state law may allow a prosecutor or law-enforcement officer to sign the warrant to expedite the process but only after the facts and circumstances have been reviewed over the telephone by a judicial officer, being later subject to that judicial officer's signature. In no case is a prosecutor or law-enforcement officer permitted to sign a warrant without that judicial review. The independent impartial review is what provides the warrant with validity.

A warrant to search must be based upon probable cause. In this instance, probable cause can best be defined as facts and circumstances that would lead a reasonable person to believe that the place to be searched and the things to be seized are to be found. The probable cause is established by a written affidavit prepared by the law-enforcement officer/investigator, stating all those known facts and circumstances. As is true for an arrest warrant, probable cause may be established by any number of sources, including information supplied by informants. In drug cases, probable cause is often established by confidential informants who make repeated drug buys from a specific house or store. The affidavit is then presented to the judicial officer, who independently evaluates it and, if she or he finds it sufficient, issues the warrant. As is pretty evident from the process described so far, probable cause must be established before the warrant is issued. Anything found as a result of the service of the warrant cannot be used to establish the probable cause.

The search warrant must particularly describe the place to be searched. Although the Constitution does not define "particularly," the description must be sufficient to distinguish the place from all others. Normally, one might think of a building on a piece of property as a place to be searched. Using the legal description is not necessary; however, a street address may not be sufficient. There are many appellate cases involving invalid warrants because the address failed to distinguish between two identical numbers on houses on "Main Street" because one was on "North Main" and the other on "South Main." In addition, numbers may be missing from the house or mailbox causing problems. What happens when a warrant is issued for "999 Main Street" but the numbers have come loose and flipped over at "666 Main Street" and now read "999"? Have investigators ever served a warrant at the wrong location? The appellate cases are full of examples. The warrant should contain information such as the color of the house, the type of floor plan (for example, ranch style home); apartment on the third floor, east side of a brownstone tenement; cream colored, vinyl siding, one story house with green trim, green shutters, an American flag on a pole in the front yard, and so forth.

The phrase "particularly describe" also applies to the things to be seized. This governs the extent of the search. For example, if the affidavit and warrant are for the search and seizure of drugs in a house, the search can be pretty extensive. Thus, it would be permitted to search closets, under beds, in dresser drawers, in medicine cabinets, and in kitchen cupboards—and anything found, even evidence of other crimes, may be properly seized and considered admissible. For example, the search turns up a firearm; but the occupant of the house, being a previously convicted felon, is not allowed to possess firearms. The discovery of the weapon could be the legal basis for adding a charge of illegal possession of a firearm. But if the warrant is based on the belief that the house contains stolen tires, the places that can legally be searched in that same house are significantly reduced. A search of dresser drawers, kitchen cupboards, and medicine cabinets would be improper, and, if the firearm in the previous example is found under the pillow on the bed occupied by the suspect, its seizure would be improper unless the investigator could convince the court, during a hearing on a motion to suppress the seizure of the firearm, that the investigator reasonably believed there might have been a stolen tire under the pillow.

In another example, a law-enforcement officer went outside the scope of his authority to search when, with consent, while searching for a stolen boat motor and a shotgun, picked up and opened a tackle box that contained drugs and drug paraphernalia. This served as the basis for charging. The court stated there was no reasonable belief the boat motor or shotgun was in the tackle box.[18]

Normally, investigators should include in their affidavits in support of a search warrant the justification for

▲ **FIGURE 2-7   Preparing to serve a search warrant**
An investigator and a uniformed officer, each positioned to react if trouble should occur, are the advance party for the service of a search warrant. Other investigators wait to see if anyone inside opens the door. (© Tony Savino/The Image Works)

searching persons found at the place where the warrant is to be executed and the search conducted. In the absence of such authority in the warrant, persons found on the scene may not be searched unless they are first lawfully arrested.

Once issued, a warrant must be executed within whatever time limits the law of the state requires; time of day/night limits are applicable. In some instances, the warrant may specify that it may be served at nighttime if the probable cause supporting the warrant can justify that the specific criminal activity only occurs at night. Until recently, state laws required officers/investigators executing warrants to knock, announce their purpose and the fact that they were in possession of a warrant, and giving the occupants a reasonable time to answer and open the door (Figure 2-7). In 2006 the Supreme Court ruled in *Hudson* v. *Michigan*[19] that violation of the knock and announce requirement for the service of a search warrant will no longer result in the suppression of evidence found during execution of the search warrant. The Court said the social cost of applying the exclusionary rule to knock and announce violations was considerable.

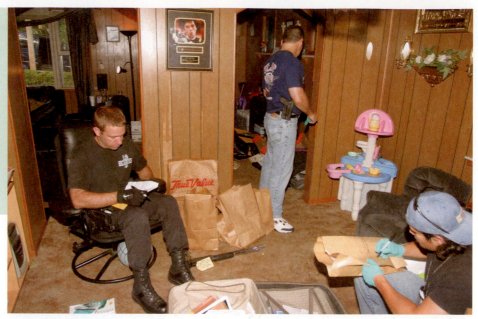

▶**FIGURE 2-8**
Investigators conducting a search
Investigators conduct a home search. Note that while one of the investigators searches, another records the location where each piece of evidence was found, and a third officer packages and marks each piece of evidence. All these steps are important in maintaining and protecting the chain of custody.
(© Mike Karlsson/Arresting Images)

During the search, particularly if several investigators are involved, one investigator should be designated the property custodian. A detailed record must be kept of each piece of evidence, with a specific description, where it was found, and by whom. This list then becomes part of the return on the warrant that must be brought back and presented to the judge for review. It, of course, also becomes part of the case file (Figure 2-8).

In 2005, in *Muehler* v. *Mena*,[20] the Supreme Court held that officers executing a search warrant of a house seeking weapons and evidence of gang membership in the wake of a drive-by shooting acted reasonably by detaining the occupants of the house in handcuffs during the search, especially since there were only two officers to watch over four people.

SEARCH WITH CONSENT

One of the most common situations arising today is when a uniformed officer, in encountering a citizen during a traffic stop or other routine activity, asks the person if he/she has any weapons or drugs on his/her person or in the vehicle. Sometimes the person says yes, and that might lead to an immediate arrest. Often the person says no, and the officer may then ask if he/she can search the person and/or the vehicle. If the person gives affirmative consent, the search may be conducted. If the person denies consent, which he/she has the right to do, no search may be made unless there is probable cause to conduct a search under one of the other exceptions to the warrant requirement. A refusal to allow a search, standing alone, does not constitute probable cause to justify any further action.

The crux of a consent search is that the consent must be voluntarily given. It can't be based on intimidation or threats of any kind.

A person may give consent to the search of his/her home, but in the case where there are roommates living in the same house or apartment and each has his/her own bedroom, an occupant may give consent to the search only of his/her private room and any area shared in common by the roommates, such as the kitchen or living room.

Once consent is given for search of a home, car, office, or any other place, it may be withdrawn at any time by the person who had the authority and gave the consent. When consent is withdrawn, the search must stop. Any incriminating evidence found after consent is withdrawn is illegally seized and is not admissible.

It is always wise to get documentation of the consent to search. Figure 2-9 is a generic form that may be used.

SEARCH INCIDENT TO ARREST

The courts have regularly recognized the right of law-enforcement officers to search people who have been arrested without a warrant. Such searches are justified for officer safety and to preserve evidence.[21] In 1969 the United States Supreme Court limited the scope of a search when it ruled in *Chimel* v. *California*[22] that a warrantless search of the defendant's entire house, following his lawful arrest in the house on a burglary charge, was unreasonable. This case set the benchmark for searches incident to a valid arrest by holding that such searches may be made of the person arrested and the area under his/her immediate control from which he or she might obtain a weapon or destroy evidence. Initially, searches were reasonable only if conducted in conformity with *Chimel.* Over the years, case law has expanded the allowable area of search following a legal arrest, particularly as applied to automobile searches, but as to searches of an arrestee's home, *Chimel* is still followed closely. In

◄ **FIGURE 2-9**
Consent to search form—generic

PERMISSION TO SEARCH AND SEIZE

I, _____, agree to permit members/officers

of the _____ to search my

(agency name)

vehicle(s)/apartment/house/other structure(s) or other areas as described below, which

are in my control.

Area to be Searched: Located At:

_____

And I further agree to permit members/officers of the _____

(agency name)

_____ to remove from the above listed areas any item(s) of

property they deem relevant to their investigation. It is further understood that I will

receive a receipt for any and all items removed by the _____

(agency name)

_____.

I am giving this written permission to the _____

(agency name)

freely and voluntarily, without any threats or promises having been made to me, and

after having been informed that I have a right to refuse to permit this search and

seizure. I further understand that any item(s) seized, may be used in a court of law

during a criminal procedure/prosecution.

Signed: _____

Address: _____

Date: _____ Time: _____

Witness: _____

Witness: _____

◄ **FIGURE 2-9**
Consent to search form—generic

Maryland v. *Buie*,[23] a 1990 case, the Supreme Court reported that:

> Two men committed an armed robbery. The police obtained warrants for their arrest. Buie was one of the people to be arrested. The officers went to Buie's home to arrest him. When they entered, they found Buie coming from the basement. That is where he was arrested. One of the officers went into the basement, allegedly on a protective sweep, to make sure no one else was down there. While in the basement he saw "in plain view" a red running suit that matched the description of clothing that witnesses said one of the robbers was wearing. The officer seized the suit and it was used in evidence to help convict Buie.

The Supreme Court said that:

> . . . as an incident to the arrest of the accused, the officers could, as a precautionary measure and without a search warrant, probable cause, or reasonable suspicion, look in closets and other spaces immediately adjoining the place of arrest from which an attack could be immediately launched . . .[24]

As to conducting protective sweeps, the Supreme Court went on to say:

> . . . beyond that, the Fourth Amendment permits a warrantless protective sweep in conjunction with an in-home arrest—extending only to a cursory inspection of those spaces where a person may be found, lasting no longer than is necessary to dispel the reasonable suspicion of danger, and in any event no longer than it takes to complete the arrest and depart the premises—when the searching officer possesses a reasonable belief based on specific and articulable facts which, taken with the rational inferences from those facts, would warrant a reasonably prudent officer in believing that the area to be swept harbors an individual posing a danger to those on the arrest scene.[25]

The Court made it clear that the officers had the right, pursuant to the arrest warrant, to search anywhere in the house, even the basement, until they found Buie.[26]

SEARCH OF A MOTOR VEHICLE

The search of a motor vehicle, sometimes referred to as the automobile exception to the requirement that a search be conducted with a warrant, really involves two distinct legal issues under modern law. The first can be traced back to a 1925 Supreme Court case. In *Carroll* v. *United States*,[27] the Court created the "moveable vehicle" rule. The Court held that if there was sufficient probable cause to get a warrant, but, because the vehicle was moveable, it might be gone if time were taken to get a warrant, a warrantless search was justified. In this case, the vehicle was moving and contained bootleg whiskey during Prohibition. The search of the entire vehicle, including the trunk was justified in this case.

In *Chambers* v. *Maroney*[28] a service station was robbed by two armed men. About the time of the robbery, two teenagers saw a blue station wagon circling the block around the service station and later sped off with four men. The service station attendant described one of the robbers as wearing a green sweater and the other wearing a trench coat. Sometime after, a vehicle fitting the description, carrying four men, one of whom was wearing a green sweater, was stopped. A trench coat was seen in the car. The occupants were arrested, and the car was searched without a warrant. The money, guns, and other evidence of the robbery were found. The Supreme Court approved of the search under the motor vehicle exception. The motor vehicle exception is still very viable.

In *Maryland* v. *Dyson*,[29] the Supreme Court continued to follow the ruling in *Carroll.* But it is not necessary that the vehicle actually be moving to justify such a warrantless search. Early on, the Supreme Court held that where a car was legally parked, agents did not have to speculate as to when the owner would return and whether there was time to obtain a search warrant.[30]

The second issue involves the search of a vehicle incident to a lawful arrest. Keeping in mind the foundation principle of the *Chimel* case, that a search may be made of the area under the arrestee's immediate control, the Supreme Court ruled in the 1981 case of *New York* v. *Belton*[31] that when a police officer makes a lawful custodial arrest of the occupant of an automobile, the officer may search the vehicle's passenger compartment as a contemporaneous incident of arrest. The right to search includes any open or closed containers found in the passenger compartment. It does not include the trunk.

On May 24, 2004, the Supreme Court decided *Thornton* v. *United States*.[32] In 2001 Officer Nichols was driving behind Thornton's Lincoln town car. He ran the town car's license plate. The response from the Department of Motor vehicles (DMV) reported that the tag belonged on a 1982 Chevrolet. Before Nichols had a chance to pull the car over, Thornton drove into a parking lot, parked, and got out of his car. Officer Nichols saw Thornton leave his vehicle as he pulled in behind him. The officer parked, got out of his car, and accosted Thornton. He asked Thornton for his driver's license and told Thornton that the license plate did not match the vehicle to which it was properly attached. Nichols then asked Thornton if he could pat him down. Thornton agreed. Nichols felt a bulge In Thornton's left front pocket and again asked him if he had any illegal narcotics on him. This time Thornton said that he did and pulled out two bags, one containing marijuana and the other crack cocaine. The officer handcuffed Thornton, informed him that he was under arrest, and put him in the back seat of the patrol car. Officer Nichols then searched the vehicle and found a 9-mm handgun under the driver's seat. Thornton was charged with federal firearms and drug offenses. He was convicted. His case was affirmed on appeal by the district court of appeals and then was appealed to the Supreme Court.

In brief, the Supreme Court said that the right to search the passenger compartment of a car still exists even if the officer does not make contact until the person arrested has left the vehicle (Figure 2-10). The issue in this case asked the question on the reasonableness of the search whether the defendant was inside or outside the vehicle when first contacted and subsequently arrested. The opinion points out that the length of time the person had been out of the car and how far away from the vehicle the person was may all come into play in determining reasonableness of a search. Interestingly, in this case, the defendant had already been secured and was in the back seat of the patrol car when this search took place. This, of course, was pointed out by the dissenting Justices, who said there was no longer any chance to obtain a weapon or destroy evidence and the officer should have obtained a warrant before searching.

Five years after *Thornton* and 28 years after *Belton*, the Court seemed to revert to the *Chimel* foundation. In *Arizona* v. *Gant*,[33] the Supreme Court said that *Belton* had been expanded beyond what the Court intended. Although the majority opinion doesn't specifically overrule *Belton* and *Thornton*, the holding severely limits the situations in which law enforcement may search incident to a lawful arrest. Gant was arrested for driving with a suspended license. He was handcuffed and locked in the back seat of a patrol car. Two other individuals were with Gant. They were also secured in patrol vehicles. Then the passenger compartment of his vehicle was searched and officers found cocaine in the pocked of a jacket in the back seat. Gant was charged and convicted of possession of cocaine and a related charge. The Supreme Court held that once the scene was secured, that is, the driver was handcuffed and locked in the back of a patrol car, he

◄ FIGURE 2-10
Officer and investigator searching the passenger compartment of a motor vehicle
Uniformed officers search a vehicle in a warehouse district after making a major bust of cocaine traffickers.
(© James Shaffer/PhotoEdit)

could no longer reach a weapon to harm an officer or reach to destroy any potential evidence. Consequently, a search and seizure, without a warrant, under these circumstances would be reasonable. However, the Court waivered slightly by concluding "that circumstances unique to the automobile context justify a search incident to arrest when it is reasonable to believe that evidence of the offense of arrest might be found in the vehicle." Thus, when a person is arrested on a traffic charge and secured, there would be no evidence in the vehicle related to the charge. But if the vehicle driver is arrested on a drug charge, there may be evidence in the vehicle related to that charge and a search may be reasonable even though the driver is secured in the back of a patrol car. In *Belton*, there were four people in the vehicle. They were separated and were away from the vehicle at the time of the search but were not secured and not under arrest. That was the narrow context in which the Court intended *Belton* to be applicable. The Court pointed out that at least eight states followed the narrow interpretation based on state constitutional provisions. The states were Vermont, New Jersey, New Mexico, Nevada, Pennsylvania, New York, Oregon and Wyoming. In *Thornton*, the driver was away from the vehicle when arrested on a drug charge after a consent pat down. Thornton was secured and placed in a patrol car but, because this was a drug case, search of the vehicle incident to arrest was reasonable and evidence found was admissible.

A vehicle search is not reasonable if conducted pursuant to stopping a vehicle for a traffic violation and writing a citation. A citation is not an arrest and no right to search arises. Does the same rule hold true if an officer issues a summons (sometime called a Notice to Appear)? Generally, the answer is yes; but consider the case of *Virginia* v. *Moore*,[34] decided by the Supreme Court in 2008. Moore was arrested for driving on a suspended license. He was searched and cocaine was found on his person. He

was charged with the possession of cocaine and convicted. The kink in this story is that Virginia law specified that when officers stopped the vehicle Moore was driving, he should have been given a summons. Had that been done, there would not have been a search. But when they arrested him instead, they searched incident to the arrest. The Supreme Court held that police did not violate the Fourth Amendment by arresting Moore instead of following state law requiring the issuance of a summons, thereby making the search and seizure reasonable.

EMERGENCY (EXIGENT CIRCUMSTANCES)

The **exigent circumstances** exception recognizes that a warrantless entry by law-enforcement officials may be legal when there is a compelling need for official action and no time to get a warrant. The exception covers several common situations including: danger of flight or escape, loss or destruction of evidence, risk of harm to the public or police, mobility of a vehicle (discussed earlier), and hot pursuit.[35] In *Warden* v. *Hayden*,[36] two taxi drivers reported seeing an armed robber run into a residence. Police arrived within minutes, entered the house without a warrant, found the defendant in an upstairs bedroom where he was arrested, and then conducted a search. They found and seized a shotgun and a pistol in the adjoining bathroom flush tank. They also seized a jacket and pants that were of the type witnesses said the robber was wearing. Hayden was convicted, and when the case reached the Supreme Court, it held the search and seizure was legal. The Court said that speed was essential to find out if other people were in the house who might be in danger and to protect the officers themselves by insuring they had possession of all weapons that could be used against them or to effect an escape. In all cases of exigent circumstances, there must be an emergency that justifies the warrantless search.

Officers responded to a residence after receiving two 911 calls saying that there was loud arguing and numerous shots had been fired. On arrival, a husband and wife were on the porch of their mobile home. Officers, while behind their vehicle doors and with weapons drawn, ordered the people off the porch and told them to lie down with their palms facing up. After finally getting compliance and securing the pair along with a neighbor who appeared from the side of the house, officers entered the house to see if anyone was inside and hurt. In the process, when stepping on the porch, they found a shotgun leaning against the side of the mobile home about 3 feet from where the defendant had been standing and a number of expended shells on the porch and ground nearby. These were seized. The defendant was convicted of possession of a firearm by a convicted felon. He challenged the officers' actions of stepping on the porch as an illegal search.

When the case finally reached the Supreme Court, the search and seizure was upheld under exigent circumstances. The Court reasoned that there certainly was a reasonable belief by the officers that there might be injured people inside the home based on the multiple calls that shots had been fired. This emergency justified the warrantless entry and the seizure of the weapon that formed the basis of the charge.[37]

In *Brigham City* v. *Stuart*,[38] the Supreme Court held that law-enforcement officers may enter a home without a warrant when there is an objectively reasonable basis to believe that an occupant is seriously injured or imminently threatened with serious injury.

In *Michigan* v. *Fisher*[39] officers arrived at Fisher's home in response to a call for service by a couple who reported that Fisher was "going crazy." The officers found the homestead trashed and a pickup truck in the driveway was smashed. There was blood on the hood and on clothes inside the truck. Fence posts along the side of the property were damaged, and three windows to the house were smashed. Through the window, officers could see Fisher smashing things in the house. The back door was locked and Fisher had pushed a couch against the front door. The officers knocked but Fisher would not answer the door. The officers saw a cut on Fisher's hand and asked him if he needed medical attention. Fisher told officers to get a search warrant. One officer forced his way in but he retreated when Fisher pointed a rifle at him. Officers entered the house and finally subdued Fisher. He was charged with assault with a deadly weapon and possession of a firearm in the commission of a felony. Fisher argued that the entry of the police was an unreasonable search and seizure and anything he said to a police officer should not be admitted. The trial court agreed, and the State appealed. After several remands and reversals, the case ended in the U.S. Supreme Court. The Court cited the *Brigham City* case for the proposition that an "emergency aid" exception exists justifying an entry into a residence without warrant. The State courts in this case found that an "emergency" did not exist. The Supreme Court, however, said that officers did not need iron-clad proof that a serious injury had occurred. There was ongoing violence and an objective basis for believing that medical attention was needed. Therefore, the officers were justified in entering without a warrant. The case was remanded, and the trial court was required to deny the defendant's motion to suppress the statements made by the defendant to officers who entered his home.

Conducting an Inventory

Law-enforcement agencies have not only the right but also the obligation to inventory property taken from a person arrested. This includes property taken from the person and from their presence, such as a motor vehicle. The inventory is done for the purpose of protecting the property of the person arrested and documenting what was found with a receipt given to the person arrested. In this manner, law enforcement can prevent accusations of stealing an offender's money or property. Similarly, law enforcement should inventory a vehicle that was impounded pursuant to an arrest. This includes the contents of the trunk (Figure 2-11). If contraband or evidence of a crime are found by virtue of a valid inventory search, the results are admissible. To justify admissibility of the fruits of an inventory search, the agency must have a standing policy that specifies the inventory in all cases. If such a policy does not exist, but this particular vehicle was inventoried, it will be ruled a pretext for a warrantless search and will be deemed unreasonable.

PLAIN VIEW SEIZURES

If an investigator/officer is lawfully in a place and sees contraband or evidence in plain view, the investigator may seize the evidence, and it will be admissible. For example, investigators were called to a hotel room door, because the occupant wanted to turn himself in on an outstanding warrant. When the defendant opened the door, officers could see crack cocaine lying on the counter inside the room. Their entry and seizure was lawful. Investigators are not required to turn their backs on a crime being committed in their presence. It is critical that the officer has a lawful right to be where she/he can see the evidence in plain view. An investigator on the street outside a house who looks in a window and sees contraband can legally seize it, but if that same investigator is standing on a box, peering inside a window overlooking the backyard, he/she cannot expect any subsequent seizure to be upheld.

Consider this example: The men's restroom in a local club, frequented by young adults, is known for drug use. Users go in the stalls, lock the doors, and ingest cocaine. Off-duty, uniformed officers check out the whole club, including the men's room. Underneath the stall door they see an individual's feet turned sideways to the toilet. It's pretty obvious that the person is not using the toilet for

◀ **FIGURE 2-11**

Officer and K-9 partner inventorying trunk of impounded vehicle
A police officer and his K-9 partner conduct an inventory search of an impounded vehicle's trunk. The driver of the vehicle had been arrested for selling large quantities of MDMA, better known as Ecstasy. Pursuant to departmental policy, all vehicles impounded are inventoried to protect the possessions of the arrested person. In drug-related arrests, dogs are used. (© Bob Daemmrich/PhotoEdit)

its intended purpose. The officer looks through a crack between the stall door and the frame and sees the individual snorting cocaine. The officer tells the man to open the door, then arrests him for possession of cocaine. Whether this is a plain view seizure depends on two things. First, is a person in a public bathroom stall entitled to an expectation of privacy? Second, was the officer in a place where he had a lawful right to be when he viewed the offense? The answer to the first question is yes. A person does have a right to expect privacy in a bathroom stall. That's why there are stalls with doors on them. It doesn't matter that it was a restroom used by the public. The answer to the second question is a little trickier. If the opening between the door and the frame was small and, in order for the officer to see what was going on, he had to get right up to the door and peek in through the small space, this will likely be found to be an unwarranted invasion of privacy and in violation of the Fourth Amendment. However, if the space was large enough that anyone walking by might see what the accused was doing from a couple of feet away from the stall, there is no reasonable expectation of privacy, and a subsequent seizure would be reasonable.

STOP AND FRISK

Earlier in this chapter, the stop and frisk topic was mentioned to distinguish arrest from detention. There is, of course, a search and seizure aspect to this concept. In *Terry* v. *Ohio*[40] (Figure 2-12), Cleveland Police Officer

◀ **FIGURE 2-12**

Officer frisking a suspicious person
An officer conducts a "stop and frisk" of the outer clothing of a man to determine if he is armed, as authorized by *Terry* v. *Ohio*. This individual was driving on a back road near the Mexican border, acting very nervous, continually looking out the side window toward a distant point, and frequently checking his rearview mirror. (© Bob Daemmrich/The Image Works)

► **FIGURE 2-13**
Investigator checking identification
An investigator checks the identification of a young person in an abandoned house. Originally thought to be burglary suspects, these youths, it was discovered, were looking for a place to smoke marijuana. (© Kwame Zikomo/SuperStock)

McFadden observed three men walking back and forth in front of a jewelry store. Believing the men were casing the store for commission of a crime, he approached them. The defendant, one of the three, was acting strangely and the officer, concerned for his own safety, patted down the defendant's outer clothing for weapons. The officer removed a pistol from the defendant's overcoat pocket. Over the defendant's objection, the weapon was introduced in evidence. The appellate process took the case to the Supreme Court. The defendant's challenge was that the officer conducted an unreasonable search because he did not first arrest Terry and there was no probable cause or exigent circumstances justifying a search. The Court ruled that under circumstances where a person is acting suspiciously and the officer is concerned about his own safety when approaching such an individual, the officer may pat down the outer clothing to determine if the person has a weapon even though there was no arrest. If a weapon is found, it may be seized, and, if its possession is a violation of the law, it is admissible in a subsequent proceeding. The Court said that officer safety in a detention situation justifies the frisk. The Court held that an officer cannot frisk for illegal drugs but only for weapons. If, however, the officer feels something that she/he believes might be a weapon but turns out to be contraband, it is admissible. However, if it is readily apparent that the item is not a weapon, its seizure is unreasonable. To illustrate, in the case of *Minnesota* v. *Dickerson*,[41] officers stopped the defendant whose actions were evasive when approached by police just after he left a building known for cocaine traffic. One officer conducted a pat down and found no weapon, but he did feel a lump in the defendant's jacket pocket. After feeling it and examining it with his fingers, the officer believed it to be crack cocaine. He reached into the pocket and withdrew a bag containing cocaine. The Supreme Court held that even though the detention and frisk were lawful under the *Terry* doctrine, it was obvious to the officer that the lump in the pocket was not a weapon. Therefore, the seizure of the cocaine was based on an unlawful search and should not have been admitted into evidence.

In an interesting collateral issue to a *Terry* stop, the Supreme Court, in 2004, upheld a conviction under a Nevada statute that requires a person to identify himself, when so requested, during a *Terry* stop. When the defendant refused to identify himself after 11 requests by the officer, he was arrested and charged with violating the statute.[42] In addition to Nevada, the following states have **stop and identify** statutes: Alabama, Arkansas, Colorado, Delaware, Florida, Georgia, Illinois, Kansas, Louisiana, Missouri, Nebraska, New Hampshire, New Mexico, New York, North Dakota, Rhode Island, Utah, Vermont, and Wisconsin[43] (Figure 2-13).

FRUITS OF THE POISONOUS TREE

A final point is necessary to fully comprehend the consequences of an unreasonable search and seizure. The **fruits of the poisonous tree doctrine** provides that evidence obtained from an unreasonable search and seizure cannot be used as the basis for learning about or collecting new admissible evidence not known about before. Not only is the evidence obtained from the unreasonable search and seizure inadmissible; any evidence resulting from the unreasonably seized evidence is also tainted and is not admissible as fruits of the poisonous tree. This doctrine resulted from a 1963 decision of the high court in which a confession was obtained from the defendant after evidence was produced that had been obtained unreasonably.[44]

KEY TERMS

affidavit	due process clause	search and seizure
arrest	exigent circumstances	search warrant
arrest warrant	fruits of the poisonous tree doctrine	stop and frisk
charging	procedural criminal law	stop and identify
detention	probable cause	substantive criminal law
due process	search	unreasonable

REVIEW QUESTIONS

1. Define *arrest*.
2. Distinguish arrest from detention.
3. Distinguish arrest from charging.
4. What are the benefits to a police officer and the case if an arrest is made under the authority of a warrant?
5. Is a "John Doe" arrest warrant valid under any circumstances? Explain.
6. Define and describe *probable cause*.
7. During an ongoing criminal investigation, what factors must the criminal investigator consider in deciding whether to make an arrest and when to make it?
8. Explain how the laws of arrest and search and seizure flow from the Bill of Rights.
9. Distinguish the effects of the Fifth and Fourteenth Amendments on defendants in criminal cases.
10. List the requirements of a valid arrest warrant.
11. What is the Exclusionary Rule, and how did it evolve?
12. Describe the "Silver Platter" Doctrine. Is it still followed? Why or why not?
13. Under what circumstances may a search be conducted without a search warrant?
14. For what reasons do the courts allow searches incident to a lawful arrest?
15. What limitations have judicial cases placed on the search of a motor vehicle incident to a lawful arrest?
16. Give five examples justifying a search under exigent circumstances.
17. How does a law-enforcement agency's policy affect the lawfulness of an inventory search of a motor vehicle?
18. What is meant by a plain view seizure, and what are the requirements for conducting such a seizure by a law-enforcement officer?
19. What are the limitations on a law-enforcement officer conducting a stop and frisk?
20. Explain the "fruits of the poisonous tree" doctrine.

INTERNET ACTIVITIES

1. Locate the requirements in two states for the legal issuance of a search warrant. These requirements can be found as a list or on a blank search warrant form. How alike or unalike are the two? What explanation do you have for your conclusion?
2. In this country and abroad, newspaper stories about defendants alleging unlawful arrest by police are not uncommon. Take three such stories from this country and three from foreign countries and compare the fact situations for the arrest. Are there common denominators? For example, in some countries people are arrested because their speaking or writings are critical of a totalitarian government or "strong man" regime or they advocate for greater civil rights for citizens.

► Crime scene personnel documenting the scene of a murder. The number of yellow "tents" indicates numerous evidence items were found. The use of "Police Line" tape creates a buffer zone to keep bystanders from interfering with the investigation. (© Gary Listort/New York Daily News)

3

INVESTIGATORS, THE INVESTIGATIVE PROCESS, AND THE CRIME SCENE

CHAPTER OBJECTIVES

1. Understand the skills and qualities needed by investigators.
2. Identify the objectives of crime scene investigation.
3. Distinguish between the preliminary and follow-up investigations.
4. Explain the importance of crime scene coordination.
5. Explain the factors that may affect crime scene processing plans.
6. Discuss three broad categories of evidence.
7. Explain the "rules" for crime scene investigators.
8. Identify crime scene health issues.
9. Summarize the four major considerations that dominate the crime scene search.
10. Identify different methods of visually documenting the crime scene.

Although crime is a national problem, its control is primarily the responsibility of local government. When officials cannot prevent or deal effectively with crime, other problems are created. First, if individuals commit crime and escape prosecution, future illegal acts are encouraged. Second, unchecked crime requires that resources, which could be devoted to other social problems, be diverted to crime control, resulting in further entrenchment of such ills as poverty and substandard housing. Third, as crime increases, our system of government faces the real possibility of a crisis of confidence in its ability to maintain public welfare. Finally, crime tears the fabric of social relations and living patterns. People become fearful of strangers and of being on the streets after dark, homes become fortresses, and families move to new locations in search of a secure life. A terrible reality is that until significant inroads are made in controlling crime, the overall quality of life is lower than it could be.

Certain qualities are common to successful investigators, such as good communication skills, strong ethics, initiative, and resourcefulness. All crimes assigned to investigators must be investigated effectively and thoroughly. This responsibility includes not only complete preliminary and follow-up investigations but also understanding the importance of physical evidence in a criminal investigation. The contributions of physical evidence to an investigation are diminished primarily by the inability, unwillingness, or failure to locate, properly collect, mark, and preserve the evidence, and by the drawing of improper conclusions from its analysis.

TYPES OF OFFENSES

A **crime** is the commission (doing) of any act that is prohibited or the omission (failing to do) of any act that is required by the penal code of an organized political state. There can be no crime unless there is advance notice that the conduct is prohibited or required.

Legislatures enact criminal laws that distinguish between felonies and misdemeanors. In most states, a **felony** is an act punishable by imprisonment for a term of one or more years, or by death. Generally, violations of the criminal code that are not felonies are designated as **misdemeanors,** lesser offenses that may be punishable by a fine, ordinarily not to exceed $500, and/or imprisonment for no more than a year. Some states have a third crime category called **violation** (for example, criminal littering), which is punishable only by a fine, usually no more than $250.

THE INVESTIGATOR AND THE IMPORTANCE OF INVESTIGATION

In the search for truth, the most important skill of an investigator is the ability to converse equally well with a wide range of people, from corporate executives to the homeless. This is essential because much of what we learn during an investigation comes from people. The competent investigator is aware of the difference between knowing things and doing things. Such an investigator will therefore consistently translate his or her special knowledge into actual investigative behaviors.

The investigation of any crime places significant responsibilities on the investigator. These responsibilities are particularly heavy during an arrest for a violent felony, since the investigator may have to use deadly force: investigators cannot legally use such force prematurely, but from a tactical standpoint they cannot be even a split second too late in responding to deadly force directed at them. When a person is arrested, whether for a felony or a misdemeanor, the arrest is often publicized, and the person, even if not convicted, incurs economic and/or social costs. The more heinous the charge, the greater these costs will be. If a criminal charge is sustained, the person may suffer any of the penalties authorized for conviction of a felony, misdemeanor, or violation, which run from a fine to execution. This means that investigators must evaluate information accurately and use sound judgment in making investigative decisions.

ESSENTIAL QUALITIES OF THE INVESTIGATOR

Some investigators have a reputation of being lucky, and good fortune sometimes does play a role in solving a case. Most often, however, the "lucky" investigator is someone with strong professional training and solid experience who, by carefully completing every appropriate step in an investigation, leaves nothing to chance. By doing so, he or she forfeits no opportunity to develop evidence. In addition, successful investigators:

1. Invariably have a strong degree of self-discipline. It is not the presence or absence of a supervisor that causes them to get things done.
2. Use legally approved methods and are highly ethical.
3. Have the ability to win the confidence of people with whom they interact.
4. Do not act out of malice or bias.
5. Include in their case documentation all evidence that may point to the innocence of the suspect, no matter how unsavory his or her character.
6. Know that investigation is a systematic method of inquiry that is more science than art.
7. Realize that successful investigations are not always produced by rote application of the appropriate steps and therefore supplement the investigative procedures with their own initiative and resourcefulness.
8. Have wide-ranging contacts across many occupations.
9. Are not reluctant to contact experts from many different fields to help move the investigation forward.
10. Use both **inductive** and **deductive reasoning.** Inductive reasoning moves from the specific details to a general view. It uses the factual situation of a case to form a unifying and logically consistent explanation of the crime. In contrast, deductive reasoning creates a hypothesis about the crime. The explanation is tested against the factual situation. If the fit is not good, the hypothesis is reformulated and tested again. The process is repeated until everything "fits together."
11. Know that inductive and deductive reasoning can be distorted—by untenable inferences, logical fallacies, the failure to consider all alternatives, and bias—and self-monitor themselves to ensure effective use of these reasoning processes.
12. Learn something from every person with whom they come into contact, knowing that the wider their understanding of different lifestyles, occupations, vocabularies, views, and other factors, the more effective they will be.
13. Have the empathy, sensitivity, and compassion to do their job without causing unnecessary anguish (for example, when interviewing a rape victim).
14. Avoid becoming calloused and cynical from their constant contact with criminals, keeping in mind that the criminal element does not represent everyone. The failure to keep this distinction in mind can be the precursor of unethical behavior.

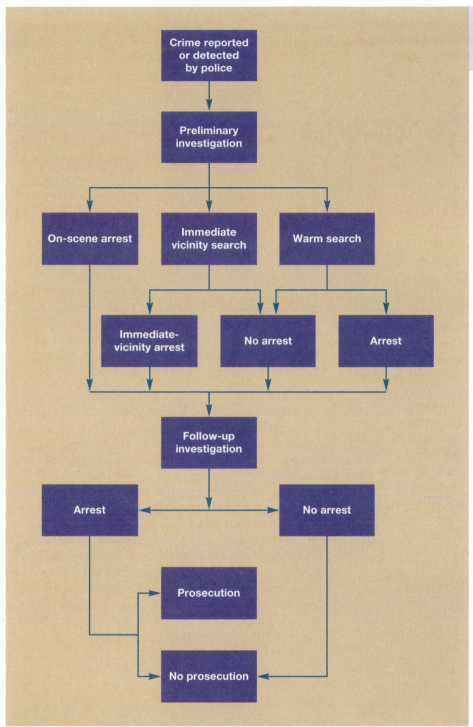

◄ FIGURE 3-1
Major events in the investigation of a crime

ORGANIZATION OF THE INVESTIGATIVE PROCESS

The major events in the investigation of crime are depicted in Figure 3-1. These elements provide an overview of the investigative process and introduce concepts covered in greater detail in subsequent chapters.

Once a criminal offense has been committed, three immediate outcomes are possible; it may: (1) go undetected, as in the case of a carefully planned and conducted murder by organized-crime figures, in which the body is disposed of in such a way that it will remain undiscovered; (2) be detected, but not reported, for example, because the loss is minor or the victim wants to avoid contact with the police, or (3) come to the attention of the police through their observation, a complaint by the victim or witnesses, or a tip.

Regardless of the outcome, a crime has occurred in each of the three preceding instances. However, only in the last case, when it is both detected and reported, is the offense of concern to the investigator, because only at that time does it become subject to formal processing.

THE PRELIMINARY INVESTIGATION

The actions taken by the first officer to arrive at the scene of a crime after its detection and reporting are collectively termed the **preliminary investigation**. The **follow-up investigation** is the police effort expended after the initial incident report is completed until the case is ready for prosecution. Normally the preliminary investigation is conducted by a uniformed officer from the Patrol Division and consists of the following steps:

1. RECEIPT OF INFORMATION, INITIAL RESPONSE, AND OFFICER SAFETY PROCEDURES

a. *Note all dispatch information:* time, date, type of call, location, names of parties involved, their descriptions, past history of incidents at the location, and, if known, whether any weapons are involved in this call.[1] Rough **field notes** must be made intermittently throughout the preliminary investigation. In those notes, the condition and placement of people and things at the scene are recorded, for example, where was the victim, assailant, and witnesses, what were they doing, what types of weapons were where, and what was said as you arrived. Often the type of call to which you are dispatched is actually what happened at the scene. However, people who call 911 may be excited, confused, misinformed, or have only partial information. In turn, dispatchers may have a hard time hearing or understanding callers or fail to get sufficient information. Finally, what is going on at the scene at the time of the call may have violently escalated by the time officers arrive:

A solo unit was dispatched to a domestic disturbance in progress. The caller reported that it involved a man and a woman arguing on the small porch of a home. A backup was also dispatched. When the first unit arrived, the officer saw the man stab the woman. When the second unit arrived, less than 20 seconds later, the man had already stabbed the first officer and was attempting to stab him again.

b. *Be alert for people and cars leaving the crime scene or its immediate proximity and note their numbers and descriptions.* Information about the factors needed for full descriptions are identified later on in Section 4, in the context of issuing an APB (All Points Bulletin) or BOLO (Be-On-The-Lookout) for persons and vehicles identified by victim or witness interviews as being involved in a crime to which a patrol officer is the first responder. Do not deviate from going to the call to which you are assigned, except for the most compelling reasons, for example, being fired on or discovering a violent crime in progress.

c. *Approach the scene cautiously,* scan the entire area thoroughly, assess the scene, and be aware of people and vehicles in the vicinity that may be related to the call. Consider suspect may have hidden near the scene or be within the building in which the crime occurred. Prioritize what needs to be done. Wait for or request backup as needed.

d. *In assessing the scene, use all your senses:* look, listen, smell (Figure 3-2). Be alert for:

- *The possibility that violence is still ongoing.*
- *Dangers from "ordinary" people,* for example, a backup gunman for bank robbery was dressed as a nun and shot a policeman in the back as he ran past the "nun" toward the scene.
- *Dangers from special hazards,* for instance, natural gas leaks, and the possibility of one or more other bombs yet to explode). The first arriving officer must inform other responders about dangers and request specialized help and equipment, for example, hazmat and canine teams, the bomb squad, fire department, and EMTs, as the situation dictates. Maintain a safe distance from special hazards. Do not just rush in; you cannot warn other responders if you are incapacitated or dead.

e. *Determine whether a tactical situation exists,* such as a barricaded subject with a gun or a robber who took a hostage because police arrived before he/she could flee the scene. Get help from other officers or specialized units as needed.

f. *Remain alert and attentive.* Assume that the crime is in progress until you can safely conclude—not assume—that it is over and the suspects are no longer on the scene.

g. *Make sure that you follow departmental contact protocols* for notifying supervisors or others immediately in special situations, for example, requesting approval for crime scene processing or the notification of the medical examiner.

h. *Treat the location as a crime scene until you conclude otherwise.* Sometimes this is not an easy determination, as demonstrated by the following case histories:

A badly wounded man called the police and reported an assailant had tried to rob him and his pregnant wife and that she had been shot in the head. With two victims, no gun at the scene, and no witnesses, the husband's version of events initially held up. However, there were lingering questions about what the two victims were doing in that area late at night. The wife died in the hospital as the investigation continued. Ultimately, the investigation established that the husband had been the shooter. His brother reportedly took the gun from the scene. When the husband's story unraveled, he committed suicide.

◀ **FIGURE 3-2   Crime scene odor**
A quiet neighborhood was plagued with strong stench. Ray's Sausage Shop, next to this house, was first thought to be the source of the odor. The drainpipe was flushed and a sewer line replaced. Still, the smell persisted. Investigators searching the house, where a convicted sex offender lived, discovered the bodies of 11 murdered women. Note the investigator at the left covering his nose and mouth. (© AP Photo/The Plain Dealer, John Kuntz)

◀ **FIGURE 3-3**
Conducting a search of a suspect
The investigator in the right foreground is handing a weapon discovered on the subject he is searching to the investigator at his immediate left. Note that he carefully keeps his finger outside the trigger guard. However, the proper action to take is to have the partially visible covering investigator at the left side of the picture approach the investigator who found the weapon, who would hand it directly back to him. The action depicted distracts both investigators and keeps an unsecured weapon near the suspects, making the situation more dangerous. (© Mike Karlsson/Arresting Images)

For over a year, a woman was tormented by a person dubbed the "Poet" because he sent threatening mail in verse form to her, as well as committing other acts. Among the acts reported to the police were having her telephone line cut, chunks of concrete thrown at her home, and being abducted and stabbed. When the woman was discovered mailing a "Poet" letter to herself at the post office, along with her normal bills, the truth came out. A psychologist speculated that the "Poet" incidents were motivated by the prior victimization of the woman, at that time age 16, when she was drugged, assaulted, and branded on both thighs by an assailant.[2]

i. *If suspect is still at the scene, arrest him/her,* conduct a search of his/her person, seize weapons, drugs, fruits of the crime, and other evidence (Figure 3-3). Legal rules apply as to just how far you may search a person beyond his or her actual person (for example, the immediate area, other rooms, and any vehicle involved). Make sure you know and follow such rules. If you intend to interrogate suspects, make sure they are given their Miranda warnings and document this action. In some situations (for example, a growing hostile crowd), you may need to have suspects removed immediately from the scene.

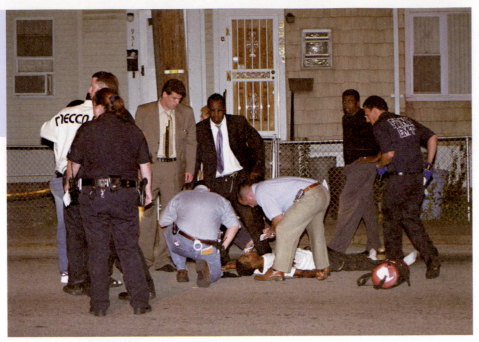

▶ **FIGURE 3-4**
Crime scene interview
Detectives question a shooting victim as EMTs prepare to transport him. Note the yellow crime-scene barrier tape in the left rear of the photo.
(© Seth Gottfried)

j. *An officer's field notes should also include information about a variety of scene conditions* initially observed that may prove to be significant later. Illustrations include what doors or windows were open or unlocked, what light switches were on, the condition of appliances (on-off, warm-cold, open-shut), and the general condition of the scene (for example, clothes and items thrown about and temperature). If the victim has a motor vehicle, is the engine cold, warm, or hot?

2. EMERGENCY CARE

a. If there are no satisfactory options to causing or allowing the contamination or destruction of evidence, remember that *saving the victim's life has a higher value than preserving physical evidence.*

b. *Assess level of injuries to the victim and request any needed medical assistance,* which is usually provided by emergency medical technicians (EMTs). You may need to provide first aid, taking appropriate precautions, to the victim until EMTs arrive.

c. *Point out potential evidence to medical personnel,* and ask them to have no contact with it or to have minimum contact with it. Instruct emergency personnel to preserve all clothing and personal effects; do not allow them to cut clothing through or along bullet holes or knife openings. Document all movement of people and items (for example, furniture and blankets, weapons) by medical personnel. Also make note of things EMTs may have added to or left at the scene, such as hypodermic needles and bandage wrappings, as well as personal items, such as jackets. Restrict the movement of the EMTs to areas at the scene where they are actually needed.

d. *Obtain as much information as possible from the victim before he/she is moved to the hospital by EMTs* (Figure 3-4).

e. *Do not allow EMTs to clean the scene,* because they may eradicate trace or larger types of evidence.

f. *Get the names of attending medical personnel, as well as their locator information,* including their employer, telephone numbers, and email addresses. Find out to which hospital the victim will be taken and send an officer, whenever possible, in the ambulance with the victim to get additional information. If that is not possible have an officer check with the transporting EMTs regarding any statements made by the victim or suspect. If this is not done on a timely basis, it may be 24 hours or more before the EMTs are available to be interviewed and valuable information could be lost.

g. *If there is a chance that the victim may die, attempt to get a dying declaration.* Also document other statements, comments, and spontaneous exclamations by victims, suspects, EMTs, and witnesses.

3. SECURE SCENE AND CONTROL PERSONS AND EVIDENCE

a. *As rapidly as possible, identify the boundaries of the crime scene and secure it* (Figure 3-5). Establishing the boundaries could entail checking an open field for additional bodies and physical evidence or all the rooms in a structure to determine if there are multiple scenes. A classic example of multiple scenes occurred in 1966 in a Chicago townhouse, where Richard Speck killed eight student nurses in different rooms. Checking for multiple scenes may also identify other victims who are still alive and require medical attention. On rare occasions, such victims or witnesses

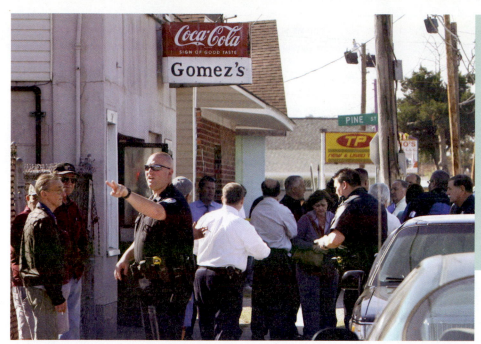

may have hidden themselves in closets or elsewhere, fearing the return of their assailant, as did a ninth nurse who eluded Speck. Crime scene control is also covered in different contexts, for example, dealing with the news media, in subsequent portions of this chapter.

b. *In defining the scene, officers must make sure that they also identify possible or actual lines of approach to, and flight from, the scene and protect them also.* These lines may contain shoe or tire impressions or residues, weapons, discarded fruits of the crime on which fingerprints may have been left, or other things which may provide investigative leads.

c. *Maintaining* **crime scene control** *is a crucial element in the preliminary investigation.* To the extent possible while meeting emergency care and other responsibilities, prevent individuals at the scene from committing any acts of theft, altering/destroying evidence, or attacking others. Identify all individuals at the scene, such as suspects, victims, bystanders, family, and friends.

Do not delay medical treatment for victims to identify them or accomplish other investigative tasks. Occasionally, situations will dictate seizing evidence before it is photographed for safety reasons:

An officer arrived at a bar where a shooting had just occurred. The victim was lying on the cement floor and had been shot several times in his upper thighs and lower groin area by a small caliber pistol, which was lying on the bar. Two seats down the bar, his girlfriend was having a drink. When she saw the officer she spontaneously said, "Yea, that's right, I shot the son-of-a-bitch, caught him with another woman and me

working and paying all the bills." Friends of the victim and the shooter were shouting back and forth and emotions in the crowd were running high. The officer immediately seized the weapon.

d. *Separate any potential combatants* to avoid violence; *separate persons arrested* so they cannot "get their story together"; and *separate witnesses* so they don't contaminate each other's recollection.

e. *Set up a physical barrier to protect the scene, prevent the contamination or theft of evidence and for your own safety.* Use yellow crime scene tape or employ natural barriers such as doors, walls, gated areas, request additional personnel as needed. Cover fragile evidence with a box or other container that will not disturb or contaminate the evidence.

f. *Maintain a crime scene entry log of persons coming to and leaving the scene* (Figure 3-6). Brief those entering on the situation and any special conditions or hazards.

4. ISSUE A BE-ON-THE-LOOKOUT

a. If the suspect is not arrested at the scene, conduct interviews and issue an **APB/BOLO (All Points Bulletin/Be-on-the-Lookout),** which is broadcast to other officers. The APB/BOLO is crucially important, because without its information other officers could be caught in the situation of approaching someone whom they think is a minor traffic violator when they have actually stumbled on a violent criminal fleeing the scene.

b. *Whenever possible, an APB/ BOLO should include* the following points: number of suspects, age, race, sex, height, weight, build, coloration, birthmarks, hair color

▶ **FIGURE 3-6**
Crime scene entry log sheet

CRIME SCENE ENTRY LOG SHEET

ALL PERSONS ENTERING THE CRIME SCENE MUST SIGN THIS SHEET

AGENCY: _____ INCIDENT #: _____

SCENE LOCATION: _____

NOTE: Officers assigned to maintain scene security must also log in and out on this sheet and should state their reason as "Log Officers."

NAME & TITLE	INITIALS	AGENCY	IN DATE / TIME	OUT DATE / TIME	REASON FOR ENTERING
			/	/	
			/	/	
			/	/	
			/	/	
			/	/	
			/	/	
			/	/	
			/	/	
			/	/	
			/	/	
			/	/	
			/	/	
			/	/	
			/	/	
			/	/	
			/	/	

Copyright 2000, Imprimus Forensic Services, LLC - This form may be reproduced for law enforcement purposes only.   Page_____of _____

and length, mustaches and beards, names and/or nicknames, clothing, hats, scars, marks, tattoos, jewelry worn, deformities (for example, missing finger), any prosthesis, and accent, as well as whether the suspects were unarmed or armed, numbers and descriptions of weapons, the method and direction of flight, and a full description of their vehicle, including year, make, model, color, stickers, damage, things hanging from the mirror, and loud mufflers. The importance of details in APB/BOLOs is demonstrated by the following case:

A convenience store was hit by an armed robber. The first responding officer determined that a toy gun may have been used and that the suspect's vehicle had a white "hard hat" on the rear shelf. This information was included, along with a description of the suspect and his vehicle on the BOLO. Another officer found a vehicle matching the suspect's behind a tavern. A toy gun box was found on the rear floorboard, and a white hard hat was on the rear shelf. The bartender said a man matching the suspect's description had entered the tavern, called a taxi, had a quick drink, and left in the taxi when it arrived. The cab company reported that the fare was taken to the airport. There it was learned that he had boarded a flight to another city, where he was arrested when he got off of the plane.

5. CONDUCT NEIGHBORHOOD AND VEHICLE CANVASS

A **neighborhood canvass** is an attempt to locate witnesses who may have heard, seen, or smelled something of investigative importance. The "neighborhood" may be other tenants in an apartment building, business owners and their employees in a commercial district, or some similar grouping. The neighborhood canvass may be conducted by uniformed officers, investigators, or some combination thereof. It may occur while the crime scene is still being processed. If not conducted at the time of the preliminary investigation, the investigator assigned to do the follow-up will determine whether the fact situation warrants one. All results of the canvass, both positive and negative, should be carefully recorded because information that seems unimportant to the canvasser may have significance to someone else (Figure 3-7):

BUILDING / NEIGHBORHOOD CANVASS

AGENCY: _____

INCIDENT#: _____

INSTRUCTIONS: Document whether or not all occupants of the residence were interviewed. Document locations where no persons were contacted. If available, list pager and / or cellphone numbers in the remarks column. Use the back side of this sheet for notes.

MULTIPLE UNIT OCCUPANCY: Address _____   Number of Units _____

(List only unit numbers below)

ADDRESS (indicate residence, business, etc.)		PERSON CONTACTED	DOB	HOME TX#	WORK TX#	REMARKS (pager / cell phone)
	# OF OCC.					☐ FOLLOW-UP RQ'D ☐ NOTES ON BACK
	# OF OCC.					☐ FOLLOW-UP RQ'D ☐ NOTES ON BACK
	# OF OCC.					☐ FOLLOW-UP RQ'D ☐ NOTES ON BACK
	# OF OCC.					☐ FOLLOW-UP RQ'D ☐ NOTES ON BACK
	# OF OCC.					☐ FOLLOW-UP RQ'D ☐ NOTES ON BACK
	# OF OCC.					☐ FOLLOW-UP RQ'D ☐ NOTES ON BACK
	# OF OCC.					☐ FOLLOW-UP RQ'D ☐ NOTES ON BACK
	# OF OCC.					☐ FOLLOW-UP RQ'D ☐ NOTES ON BACK
	# OF OCC.					☐ FOLLOW-UP RQ'D ☐ NOTES ON BACK
	# OF OCC.					☐ FOLLOW-UP RQ'D ☐ NOTES ON BACK
	# OF OCC.					☐ FOLLOW-UP RQ'D ☐ NOTES ON BACK
	# OF OCC.					☐ FOLLOW-UP RQ'D ☐ NOTES ON BACK
	# OF OCC.					☐ FOLLOW-UP RQ'D ☐ NOTES ON BACK
	# OF OCC.					☐ FOLLOW-UP RQ'D ☐ NOTES ON BACK
	# OF OCC.					☐ FOLLOW-UP RQ'D ☐ NOTES ON BACK
	# OF OCC.					☐ FOLLOW-UP RQ'D ☐ NOTES ON BACK
	# OF OCC.					☐ FOLLOW-UP RQ'D ☐ NOTES ON BACK

CANVASSING OFFICER (Print): _____

INITIALS: _____   DATE: _____   START TIME _____   TIME END: _____

▲ **FIGURE 3-7 Building/neighborhood canvass**
(Courtesy of Imprimus Forensic Services, LLC)

On a Sunday morning, a residential burglary resulted in the theft of $3,800 in rare coins. The uniformed officer making the original investigation received permission to conduct the neighborhood canvass. Usually the follow-up investigator did the canvass, but the uniformed officer was allowed to do it. The victim's home was situated on a cul-de-sac along with four other homes with some view of the victimized premises. There were no homes to the rear of the victim's residence. After interviewing residents of the four neighboring homes, including a teenage boy, the uniformed officer recorded the identities and statements of those with whom he had talked in his report. All indicated they had seen nothing. Because of the value of the property taken, the case was referred for follow-up investigation.

The investigator assigned to the case recently had been transferred from the Youth Services Bureau to the Burglary Section and recognized the name of the youth identified in the interview section of the uniformed officer's report as an individual with an extensive juvenile record for breaking and entering. Investigation revealed that the youth had committed the offense, and all coins taken were recovered.

Interviews should be conducted first at businesses or dwellings with a clear view of the crime scene and at the suspect's avenues of approach and flight. When there are substantial numbers of locations involved, several teams of officers canvassing simultaneously are helpful.

If the crime was committed near a public transit system, visit the system at the same time and on the same day of the week as the time and day of the crime. If victims and witnesses have been intimidated or otherwise dissuaded from testifying investigators should notify their supervisors and protective services considered.

It is estimated that a systematic neighborhood canvass soon after the commission of an offense results in information of investigative value in approximately 20% of all cases. The extent of the canvass depends on variables such as the type of offense, time of day, and characteristics of the crime scene. The timing of a neighborhood canvass is an important consideration. People not only move randomly through areas but also ebb and flow on a variety of schedules. To mistime a neighborhood canvass by 30 minutes, for example, may mean eliminating the possibility of locating persons who regularly catch a bus at a particular time and who, on the day of an offense, might have seen something of considerable investigative value.

Offenders may have driven near to the scene to commit their crimes, but not have sufficient time to get back to their car afterwards. Alternatively, the co-conspirator who was to drive the suspect from the scene may have panicked as he/she saw or heard police cars approaching

and walked away from the "get-away" car. The **vehicle canvass** makes a record of all vehicles in the area to provide another investigative avenue (Figure 3-8). The address or location of each vehicle must be recorded, as well as its description and plate/tag number. Anything unusual about a vehicle should be noted, such as bullet holes; blood; odd appearance of the interior; recent damage; noteworthy stickers; unusual articles; items hanging from the rearview mirror, and whether the car is hot, warm, cold, muddy, or clean.

6. ADMINISTRATIVE PROCEDURES FOR PROCESSING CRIME SCENES

Procedures for handling specific types of evidence are discussed in Chapter 4, "Physical Evidence." This section discusses the administrative procedures for crime scene processing.

a. In smaller departments that do not have specialists, roughly those with 20 or fewer sworn personnel, the responding officer must recognize and identify physical evidence, document its location through sketching and photographs, collect it and mark it, package it (Figure 3-9), and take it to the station for storage in the evidence room, where a written receipt for it will be given to the officer. This receipt is then attached to the incident/offense report, which the officer subsequently writes. When serious crimes are committed in smaller jurisdictions, assistance with the crime scene may be available through mutual aid agreements with larger agencies or from the state investigative agency.

b. At all stages of handling the evidence, the chain of custody or control of it must be established. The **chain of custody** is the witnessed, unbroken, written chronological history of who had the evidence when. It also accounts for any changes in the evidence, noting, for example, if any portion was used for laboratory analysis.

c. In larger agencies that have sworn and/or civilian crime scene technicians, these specialists will process the crime scene. More detailed information about this subject is presented later in this chapter.

d. One or more plainclothes investigators may also come to the scene, depending on the severity of the crime. If they do, the first responding officer has the following crime scene turnover responsibilities: (1) briefing the personnel taking charge, (2) assisting in controlling the scene, (3) turning over responsibility for starting another crime scene entry log, and (4) remaining at the scene until relieved.

7. THE INCIDENT/OFFENSE REPORT

The officer assigned to the call must prepare an **incident/offense report** on his or her part in the investigation. (Additional information on this subject is presented in Chapter 6, "Field Notes and Reporting.") A supervisor reviews and approves the incident report; the case may be

VEHICLE INFORMATION CANVASS

AGENCY: _____   INCIDENT#: _____

INSTRUCTIONS: Document all vehicles in the area you have been assigned. Include vehicles parked in the streets, driveways, alleyways and yards. Under "Remarks" list anything unusual noted about the vehicle (manner of parking, warm engine, fresh damage, etc.)

For vehicles without license plates, enter the VIN in the "Remarks" column.

ADDRESS (indicate alley, driveway, street, etc.)	MAKE	MODEL	COLOR	PLATE	REMARKS (VIN)

CANVASSING OFFICER (Print): _____   INITIALS: _____   DATE: _____   START TIME _____   TIME END: _____

▲ **FIGURE 3-8   Vehicle information canvass**
(Courtesy of Imprimus Forensic Services, LLC)

▶**FIGURE 3-9**
Crime scene investigators handling physical evidence
A crime scene investigator examines blood-stained clothes before placing them in an evidence bag. Note that the investigators are going to place the clothes in a paper evidence bag, which is the appropriate action when seizing blood soaked clothing; each article should be placed in a separate bag to avoid cross-contamination. (Chapter 4, "Physical Evidence" has additional information on identifying and collecting such evidence.)
(© Seth Gottfried)

retained in the patrol division for further investigation, referral to the investigative division for follow-up, or inactivated and receive no further investigative effort unless new information is received.

TYPES OF CRIME SCENES

From Chapter 1, we recall that the fundamental assumption on which crime scene searches are carried out is **Locard's principle:** there is something to be found. We usually think of a crime scene as one particular place. Although this is often true, consider the 1988 terrorist bombing of Pan Am Flight 103 over Lockerbie, Scotland. Among the dead were 259 people on the plane and 11 people on the ground. Evidence from the explosion rained down over 800 square miles. In one of the greatest investigations ever, evidence was collected that led to the identification, arrest, and conviction of the bomber, who was a former Libyan intelligence officer.

Crime scenes vary in regard to the amount of physical evidence that is ordinarily expected to be recovered, for instance, a murder scene will yield more than a yard from which a lawn mower was stolen. At the most basic level, a **crime scene** is the location where the offense was committed. As discussed earlier, the search of the crime scene for physical evidence must include a wider area, such as the perpetrator's lines of approach to, and flight from, the scene.

The basic definition of a crime scene works well for many crimes, such as a burglary or a robbery at a liquor store. But where was the crime scene for Pan Am Flight 103? On a much smaller geographic scale, consider the example of a victim who is abducted from a mall parking lot and raped by one accomplice while the other one drives the van from one county to another. Later, the vic-

tim is taken to a secluded area, removed from the van, further abused, and executed, and her body is dumped into a ravine in yet another jurisdiction. Clearly, we need additional ways to think about what a crime scene is.

1. Criminal incidents may have more than one crime scene. The **primary scene** is the location where the initial offense was committed; the locations of all subsequent connected events are **secondary scenes.**[3] Illustrating this statement is a Utah case in which a husband shot his wife while she was sleeping. He disposed of the body in a trash bin that ended up in a landfill. After 33 days of picking through 4,600 tons of compacted garbage up to 20 feet deep, investigators located the body (Figure 3-10).

2. On the basis of size, there are macroscopic and microscopic scenes.[4] A **macroscopic scene** is the "large view." It includes such things as the relevant location(s), the victim's and the suspect's bodies, cars, and buildings. The **microscopic scene** consists of the specific objects and pieces of evidence that are associated with the commission of the crime, including knives, bite marks, hairs and fibers, shoe and tire impressions, cigar butts, blood, and so on.[5]

3. Other useful ways of thinking about crime scenes are based on the type of crime (larceny versus aggravated assault), the location (indoors or outdoors), the condition of the scene (organized or disorganized), and the type of criminal action (active or passive). Some further breakdown of these types may also be useful, such as if outside, whether the body is on the surface, buried, or underwater.[6]

The usefulness of having several frames of reference for crime scenes is that they can help organize your thinking about how to approach and process a crime scene. If there are multiple crime scene locations, the primary and secondary scenes may be located in different legal jurisdictions, a situation requiring a high level of cooperation

◄ **FIGURE 3-10**
Crime scene investigation
Officers from the Salt Lake City Police Department search for the body of murder victim Lori Hacking. Her body was eventually found three months after her death. Her husband subsequently pleaded guilty in the case. (© George Frey/Getty Images)

and informational exchange between agencies. In cases where a serial offender is active and working across several jurisdictions, the case may be assigned to a standing interagency investigative task force, or a special one may be created. In such situations, it is important that departmental jealousies, the issue of who is going to get credit for solving the case, and other factors do not impede the success of the operation.

ORGANIZATION OF THE CRIME SCENE INVESTIGATION

Crime scene investigation is purposeful behavior and is intended to accomplish specific objectives:

1. Establish what happened; for example, was the purpose of the murder to kill the home owner or did she surprise a burglar when she came home unexpectedly? Or, more difficult, to often impossible, to determine, was it a murder-suicide versus an accidental discharge followed by a remorseful suicide?
2. Determine the sequence of events.
3. Find out what the suspect did or didn't do at the scene.
4. Establish the modus operandi, the method of operation, used by the suspect.
5. Determine what property was stolen and what articles were left by the suspect.
6. Note inconsistencies. For example, if the crime appears to be a home invasion that resulted in a murder, why wasn't the victim's cash and jewelry taken? Did the perpetrator panic and flee the scene before taking them, or is something else at work, such as a love triangle?

7. Locate and interview witnesses.
8. Document and recover physical evidence.[7]
9. Provide investigative leads.

Some of these objectives may not be attainable during the crime scene investigation phase and will require the services of specialists. At a complex scene with multiple victims and considerable evidence, determining the sequence of events, for example, in what order were the victims killed, may only be possible when autopsy and lab reports are available. Even then, the subsequent services of a crime scene reconstructionist may be needed. Lurking behind Point 6 in the preceding list is the determination of the motive for the crime, ordinarily the work of a specialist in criminal profiling. (Crime scene reconstruction and criminal profiling are discussed in Chapter 7, "The Follow-up Investigation and Investigative Resources.")

To achieve the objectives of crime scene investigation, the work at the scene is divided into three major functions: (1) overall coordination of the scene, (2) forensic services, and (3) investigative services.

OVERALL COORDINATION

The senior criminal investigator assigned to a case usually has overall responsibility for what happens at a crime scene. In order to fulfill this responsibility he/she must conduct a visual inspection, the "walk through," of the scene and develop a preliminary plan for its investigation. Members of the investigate team typically know their jobs and little direct "standing over their shoulder" supervision is required or desired, although the senior investigator may direct that additional processing be done or otherwise provide investigative direction.

A crucially important task for the senior investigator is coordination (Figure 3-11). It is usually accomplished by the senior investigator as he/she moves from one point to another. Some scenes may be so large or victims

▶ FIGURE 3-11
The need for scene coordination
Maine State Police searching multiple sites for human remains in a forest. Without coordination, the investigative effort can lose focus and fail to capitalize on opportunities for locating physical evidence. (© Bangor Daily News/Bill Trotter)

so numerous that layers of coordination may be needed, which may require using a mobile incident command van or a temporary "headquarters" such as a tent or a building (Figure 3-12).

The senior investigator at the scene is also responsible for requesting whatever types of additional resources are needed—for example: (1) obtain a search warrant; (2) if there is a dead body, the medical examiner or the coroner must be called to the scene. Generally, this official has jurisdiction over a dead body, which should not be searched or removed from the scene without his/her prior consent;[8] (3) fire truck ladders may be needed to search rooftops for evidence; (4) transportation of vehicles to impound lots; (5) aerial photography of scene; and (6) personnel with specialized knowledge and experience, such as being able to interpret gang graffiti/tattoos/markings.

The senior investigator must ensure that all the members of the crime scene team are briefed simultaneously

so that everyone hears and knows the same thing. The senior investigator is also responsible for ensuring that there is a continuous flow of information between members of the team as evidence is recovered. Other duties include making his/her own evaluation of potential

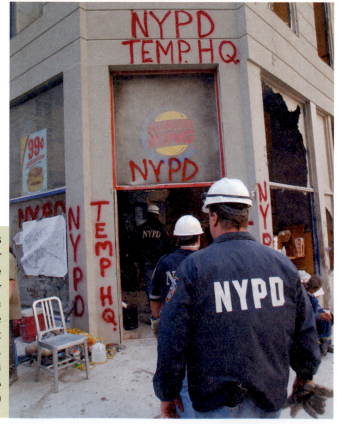

▶ FIGURE 3-12   **NYPD Temp Headquarters**
When there is an unusual event, such as a barricaded criminal or a hostage situation, an incident commander comes to the scene to take control. In fast-moving situations, the incident commander may have to operate out of his/her assigned vehicle until a mobile command van arrives. In other situations, the police use an existing building, with the permission of the owner, as a point from which to operate. Following the attack of September 11, 2001, members of the New York City Police Department established a temporary headquarters near ground zero. (© Andrea Booher/FEMA News Photo)

◀ **FIGURE 3-13**
Latent fingerprint kit
A latent fingerprint kit, which includes different color powders, several types of brushes, scales, clear lifting tape, and cards to which the lifted prints are affixed. (Courtesy of Mike Grimm Jr./Evident, Inc.)

◀ **FIGURE 3-14**
Police department mobile crime scene unit
The inside of a crime scene van; note the portable Kawasaki generator on the left and the light on the right. The balance of the van is filled with various types of equipment needed at crime scenes, such as gunshot residue, blood, fingerprint, and other collection kits. Many departments buy prepared evidence kits; others assemble kits to better meet their specific needs and capabilities. (Courtesy Chief Jack Lumpkin, Athens Clarke County (Georgia) Police Department)

safety issues, reviewing the actions of the person who conducted the preliminary investigation, allocating resources among the primary and any secondary scenes, establishing a secure area for the temporary storage of evidence, and establishing a command post and media function if the situation warrants them. The senior investigator also does a walk through of the scene with those responsible for forensic services to make sure there is a common understanding of how the scene will be approached and processed.[9]

FORENSIC SERVICES

Forensic services is the responsibility of the senior representative of the department's central crime laboratory or a crime scene processing unit. He/she may arrive to process the scene carrying one or more crime scene investigation kits (Figure 3-13) or have the more substantial resources carried in a crime scene van (Figure 3-14). Some jurisdictions also have a mobile crime laboratory in which technicians can carry out limited scientific tests.

Figure 3-15 is a list of supplies and equipment that are available for crime scene processing. Although law-enforcement agencies are varied, the core tasks that need to be completed at scenes dictate that they will use many of the supplies and equipment listed, but there will also be some variation in what is actually used. Because at least 92% of all law-enforcement agencies in this country use **digital cameras** their use is specified in Figure 3-15.[10]

Advanced methods of crime scene documentation, laser scanning, and panoramic cameras are discussed later in this chapter.

▶ **FIGURE 3-15**
Crime scene supplies and equipment

Crime Scene Security

- Barrier tape—for example, "Police Line Do Not Cross," in locally spoken languages, such as Spanish, "La Linea de la Policia No Cruza"
- Scene flags—such as "Sheriff's Line Do Not Cross" and "BioHazard Line Do Not Cross"
- Waterproof tarps and tents
- Sawhorses
- Chalks—standard/reflective/fluorescent spray/assorted colors
- Spray paint/standard/fluorescent/assorted colors
- Marked police vehicles
- Cord, rope
- Flares, chem-lites
- Preprinted signs—such as "Command Center" and "Media Relations" and poles
- Traffic cones

Safety/Personal Protection Equipment (PPE)

- Reflective vests and gloves
- Neoprene, Latex, nitrile (synthetic latex), polyvinyl, and cut/puncture resistant gloves, such as TurtleSkin®
- Disposable air-filtering masks/respirators
- Safety glasses/chin length face shield/coveralls/shoe covers
- First responder spray—such as MyClyns™ for potential pathogenic exposures
- EPA registered wipes/spray (for example, Sporicidin) and bleach (for instance, Ultra Clorox Germicidal Bleach)
- Chemical/Biological/Radiological/Nuclear (CBRN) threat environments require specialized PPE
- First aid kit/insect repellant

Washington County (Maine) Sheriff's Deputy searching underwater for stolen guns using a metal detector. (© Bangor Daily News/Diana Grattinger)

An investigator in Rothbury, England examines the scene where a fugitive shot himself, dying later in a hospital. The tent shields public observation of the process. Note the high-intensity lights, the carefully lined path, and the coveralls, hair net, gloves, and air-filtering mask being worn. Gun ownership rates are low in England, and suicide by them there is therefore rare. (© Dan Kitwood/Getty Images)

Telecommunications

- Cell/smart phones
- Fax machine
- Tablet/netbook/laptop/computers
- Copier/printer
- Teleconferencing capability
- Departmental handheld radios
- Key telephone numbers/telephone directories

Miscellaneous Equipment

- Audio recorder
- Consent search forms
- Large magnet
- Handheld Global Positioning System (GPS)
- Magnetic compass
- Portable generator
- High-intensity lights—for example, two 750-watt halogens/telescoping arm/adjustable legs
- Evidence refrigeration capability
- Flashlights/spare batteries
- Numbered evidence location marking cones/tents/flags
- Metal detectors
- Thermometers
- Logbooks
- Tents/tarps to protect evidence/personnel/equipment from inclement weather
- Extension cords/adapters
- Ladders
- Privacy/body screen
- Area map
- Pruning shears/wood saws/axes to clear vegetation from core search area
- Rakes/shovels/trowels/paintbrushes
- Soil probe
- Business cards

Equipment for Basic Crime Scene Photography

- Digital single-lens reflex (DSLR) camera for still photography
- Memory cards/extras
- Gray card/other color checker
- External flashes and cords
- Remote shutter release

▶ **FIGURE 3-15**
Crime scene supplies and equipment (*continued*)

- Various lens, macro/normal/wide-angle/telephoto
- Lens filters
- Supplemental light meter
- Digital video recorder
- Lens cleaning material
- Tripods
- External rechargeable battery packs/extra batteries
- Auxiliary lighting
- Scales/adhesive scales/rulers
- Owner's manuals for cameras
- Stepladder
- Numbered evidence location marking cones/tents/flags

Equipment for Basic Crime Scene Sketching/Diagramming

- Sketching/drafting board
- "T" square, assorted transparent triangles: 45/90 and 30/60 degrees
- Drafting compass/dividers/protractor/straight-edge rulers
- Paper/tape/pencils/pens
- Several retractable tape measures, 6- to 100-feet lengths, steel, and fiberglass
- Distance measuring wheel with visible reader for longer distances up to 1,000 feet
- Laser/ultrasonic measuring device
- Magnetic compass
- Laptop computer/crime scene diagramming software, for example, The Crime Zone
- Sketching templates

▶ **Sketching templates**
Two types of templates used in sketching crime scenes: the Human Figure Template (*left*) and the Crime Scene Template (*right*).
(Courtesy Lynn Peavey Company)

General Evidence Collection Equipment

- Stainless steel/disposable tweezers/forceps/hemostats/metal probes/scalpel
- Hard-metal scribes
- Tongue depressors
- Nets for flying insects
- Framed sifting screens and tubes
- Utility knife/scissors
- Assorted tools, wire and bolt cutters/hacksaw, extra blades/hammers/screwdrivers/wood and metal chisels/pliers/wrenches/pry bar/vise grips/drills, bits
- Mirror with telescoping arm
- Magnifying glasses

Specialized Evidence Collection Kits and Material

- Sexual assault
- Gunshot residue (GSR)
- DNA/biological evidence
- Laser trajectory
- Entomology/insect
- Latent fingerprint
- Trace evidence vacuum
- Latent fingerprint
- Blood spatter
- Presumptive field tests, for example, blood and drugs
- Body excavation
- Electrostatic lifting for dust and residue prints

- Forensic light source(s)/goggles
- Adjustable casting frames for foot/shoe/tire impressions
- Casting preparation materials/dust, sand, and dirt hardeners/wax hardener for snow impressions/snow print powder (red) to contrast impression to be photographed with surrounding snow
- Casting materials, for instance, Durocast, silicone, dental stone, low-density impression foam such as BioFoam, and Mikrosil. AccuTrans, a silicone product, which won an innovation award in 2006, is finding favor as a casting medium. The silicone is dispensed from a chalk-gun-like gun, dries in four minutes, is highly flexible after drying, and captures fine details. Self-contained kits for casting tire and shoe impressions, such as Shake-N-Cast, are also gaining in popularity. The Shake-N-Cast kits contain dental stone and a water vial in the same pouch; the vial is broken while inside of the pouch and the kit massaged, producing the same correct consistency to pour into an impression each time.

Evidence Packaging Materials

- Evidence tags/general identification labels
- Evidence control/chain of custody labels
- Sharpie permanent markers, assorted colors
- Assorted sizes of Kraft paper evidence envelopes/bags
- Rolls of Kraft/butcher paper
- Assorted adhesive/"sticky" labels—for example, "Biohazard" and "Latent Print Evidence"
- Weapons and other sized boxes
- Clear plastic tubes for syringes and knives
- Clear plastic jars, assorted sizes
- Antistatic bags for computer and other digital evidence
- Nylon bags and metal cans for arson evidence
- Evidence sealing tape, sensitive to tampering efforts, ½" to 3" wide
- Document sleeves
- Polyethylene evidence tubing
- Assorted sizes of Ziploc bags
- Heat sealer for polyethylene/nylon bags
- Sterile swabs/swab boxes
- Blood tubes, with, and without, preservative coating
- "Peel and Seal" evidence bags, which cannot be opened without destroying the bag

Source: Content drawn from Henry C. Lee, Timothy M. Palmbach, and Marilyn T. Miller, *Crime Scene Handbook* (San Diego: Academic Press, 2001), pp. 321–324; Technical Working Group on Crime Scene Investigation, *Crime Scene Investigation* (Washington, D.C.: U.S. Department of Justice, 2001), pp. 33–36; National Institute of Justice, *Crime Scene Investigation: A Reference for Law Enforcement* (Washington, D.C.: NIJ, June 2004), pp. 55–57 and additional content from the authors.

Evidence located in areas that are "open-view" to the public are ordinarily processed first and then the out-of-view areas. Similarly, fragile evidence should be documented and collected before more durable physical evidence. The open-view "rule" is especially important when bodies are in plain sight because common talk and potential news media photography will cause family members and friends great pain (Figure 3-16).

The forensic services function includes (1) establishing a central point to collect trash generated by processing the scene, including biohazard bags for the collection of disposable evidence equipment and personal protection equipment (PPE); (2) establishing a decontamination point as needed; and (3) carrying out the identification, documentation, collection, marking, packaging, and transmission of physical evidence to the evidence room or the crime laboratory.

A variety of factors shape the initial plan for processing crime scenes, which may need revisions in light of new information/developments. Among these factors are these:[11]

1. Remote or difficult terrain—for example, steep ravines, swamp areas, and forested areas with thick underbrush. In 2002 a man walking his dog found the remains of murder victim Chandra Levy in a remote part of Washington D.C.'s 2,000-acre Rock Creek Park. The Federal Bureau of Prisons intern had disappeared a year earlier. Based on information in the victim's computer, police thought she may have disappeared in the park. Although the police had twice searched much of it, they did not search the park's most remote area, judging it unlikely to yield results.

▶ **FIGURE 3-16**
Use of privacy screen to shield body
St. Tammany Parish, Louisiana, Sheriff's Office investigators use a privacy screen to shield the body of a homicide victim from morning rush hour traffic. A second victim was found on the same highway, two miles away. Gunshots killed both victims and investigators proceeded on the theory of a double homicide. (© David Grunfeld/Times-Picayune)

▶ **FIGURE 3-17**
Maine State Police, Department of Inland Fish and Wildlife wardens, and officers from several municipalities reach a small island on which a light plane had just crashed, unsure if their mission is rescue or body recovery. Aluminum canoes were the safest choice to cross the water because of increasing ice in it. In extreme cold, hypothermia is a risk factor for investigators. (© Bangor Daily News/ Kevin Bennett)

2. Physical hazards that imperil crime scene technicians—for instance, downed power lines, unsafe structures, and booby traps.
3. A hostile crowd.
4. Human remains that are widely scattered because of animal predation.
5. Weather, including rain/sleet/snow, extreme heat/ cold temperatures (Figure 3-17), blowing sand/ dust, and nearby lightning strikes.
6. Potential presence of chemical/biological/ radiological/nuclear (CBRN) weapons agents—for example, following the attacks on September 11, 2001, a biological agent, anthrax, was mailed to several dozen recipients, including two members of Congress.
7. Presence of dangerous chemicals and vapors—for example, at meth labs or from fields recently sprayed with agrichemicals.

8. Limited personnel or the availability of additional personnel—such as cadets from a police academy.
9. Infectious disease risks, which have led some law-enforcement agencies to require crime scene investigators to undergo health screening twice each year as a precaution. (Infectious disease risks and the precautions investigators should take regarding them are discussed in detail later in this chapter.)

INVESTIGATIVE SERVICES

Investigative services include: (1) interviewing witnesses; (2) conducting and documenting the neighborhood canvass; (3) a field interrogation of the suspect if he or she is in custody; and (4) carrying out and recording the results of a vehicle canvass.

TYPES OF EVIDENCE

There are three broad categories of evidence in which investigators have a particular interest: (1) corpus delicti, (2) associative, and (3) tracing. The task of developing such evidence is spread across the three main crime scene functions, but the data from the different types of evidence are combined to create a larger and more unified picture of the crime. This picture helps determine, to a large extent, how the follow-up investigation will be conducted.

CORPUS DELICTI EVIDENCE

Each criminal offense contains a distinct set of elements whose commission or omission must be demonstrated to have occurred in order to prove a case; **corpus delicti evidence** substantiates these elements. Thus, at each crime scene the investigator must keep in mind the unique requirements of proof for the case and attempt to locate related evidence.

ASSOCIATIVE EVIDENCE

Associative evidence is bidirectional in that it connects the perpetrator to the scene or victim, or connects the scene or victim to the suspect. A case history illustrates this:

A silent burglar alarm was triggered at a bar in a high-crime area. Officers responding to the scene found a point of forced entry at a rear window of the building. An individual was detected hiding in a small shed attached to the building. His statement was that when walking up the alley, he suddenly saw police cars, panicked, and hid in the shed. The search of this person following his arrest revealed the presence of valuables and materials taken from the burglarized premises, connecting the suspect with the scene.

TRACING EVIDENCE

The identification and location of the suspect are the goals of **tracing evidence;** corpus delicti and associative evidence may also serve these purposes:

A 20-year-old female was at a laundromat washing her clothes. A male loitered nearby, observing her. When the woman was alone, he walked rapidly to the laundromat and entered the men's room. A few minutes later, with his pants and underwear around his ankles, he approached the woman, shook his genitals at her, pulled up his clothing, and ran off. The officer who responded to the call found a man's wallet on the floor of the men's rest room. A records check on the identification contained in it revealed that the owner of the wallet had a history of sex offenses and lived in the neighborhood of the laundromat. When the victim identified the suspect from a series of photographs, a warrant for the suspect's arrest was obtained.

TYPICAL CRIME SCENE PROBLEMS

Although the procedures to be followed at a crime scene investigation may be neatly delineated in theory, any number of conditions may render their accomplishment a good bit less orderly than the ideal. In a perfect world, every crime scene would be fastidiously processed. In reality, the scenes of misdemeanor offenses receive a cursory examination and even the thoroughness with which felony crime scenes are processed is frequently affected by the severity of the offense. A crime scene processing unit cannot be called out to process every crime scene. To victims, the crime committed against them is important regardless of the severity. To investigators, that crime may be important or "just another report to fill out." Regardless of the situation, officers must convey a genuine interest in the complainant's situation.

At the scenes of violent crimes, especially those that are interracial, emotions may run high. Even a small crowd may add considerable confusion to the process of ascertaining what has happened and along what lines the investigation should proceed. In such situations, it is not unusual for witnesses to be lost, for their versions and perceptions of what occurred to be altered by contamination through contact with the crowd, or even for so-called witnesses to be added. In this last circumstance, a bystander may hear actual witnesses talking and suddenly believe they personally know something they should tell the police.

Police officers and supervisors occasionally make investigations more difficult when they drop by to see if they "can be of help," when in reality they are simply curious. Too many people at the scene can lead to confusion of assignments or the accidental alteration or destruction of evidence.

RULES FOR THE CRIME SCENE INVESTIGATOR

Regardless of the type of crime involved, five fundamental rules must be observed.

MAINTAIN CONTROL

Although mentioned previously in this chapter, the issue of control is so important that it warrants further elaboration. Without control, a life might be lost, evidence destroyed, assignments overlooked, or the investigation conducted in a generally haphazard manner. At the scene of sensational crimes, such as bank robberies, criminal homicides, or those involving well-known victims, members of the news media typically arrive shortly after the investigation begins and immediately attempt to quickly obtain information and/or videotape investigators, witnesses, or bystanders in order to meet their deadlines. Unless properly handled, this situation has the potential to create both confusion and complicate the investigative process.

The person in charge of the crime scene should cooperate with the press, but the scope of cooperation is limited by the need to avoid interference with the investigation, to protect the legal rights of a suspect, avoid placing a witness in danger, and other factors. All investigators should have a thorough knowledge of their agency's media relations policy.

Although some states have enacted "shield laws" so that news media personnel are not required to divulge their sources, as a general matter reporters have no legal rights beyond those granted each citizen. Although news officials may be permitted to enter a crime scene, they do so at their own risk; if their presence in any way jeopardizes police operations, it should not be allowed. The arrest of a news media worker at a crime scene should be made only on the most serious provocation and with full awareness of the adverse publicity that is certain to follow.

News media personnel may photograph or report anything that they observe while legally at a crime scene or covering any other incident involving the police. If in this process they obtain information that could endanger people or adversely affect the investigative process, both they and their supervisors should be notified of the possible consequences.

When suspects have been interviewed but not arrested, their identities should not be disclosed. It is appropriate for the crime scene coordinator to *generally* describe to reporters the physical evidence found at the scene, proceeds of the crime, weapons involved, and the issuance of warrants. However, detailed descriptions of evidence, proceeds, or weapons should not be disclosed, nor should information pertaining to how physical evidence, proceeds of the crime, or weapons were located.

It is also appropriate to withhold certain details about the crime scene, such as how a victim was mutilated, messages left at the scene by the perpetrator, particular types of evidence seized, or the exact words spoken to a rape victim. Such information could be vital in solving the case, evaluating informants' tips, or determining the authenticity of statements or confessions made by subse-

▲**FIGURE 3-18** **Investigations and the media**
Washington, D.C. Police Chief Cathy Lanier speaks at a press conference following the 2009 shooting attack at the Holocaust Museum, which resulted in the death of a security guard. A persistent question is whether news media coverage helps or hinders investigations. The answer is that it all depends on the fact situation, but that excessive details revealed in the news media can hamper investigations.
(© Alex Wong/Getty Images)

quently identified suspects. If a suspect has been identified and an identity established or a likeness generated by an artist's sketch or by facial composite software (see Chapter 12, "Robbery"), it may be advantageous to widely publicize this information if it is not likely to hinder apprehension of the suspect.

Relevant information can be supplied in **media statements** if it cannot be characterized as being prejudicial to a fair trial for the defendant (Figure 3-18). Among the actions and statements that are permissible and impermissible under the policies of many departments are these:

1. If a suspect is not in custody, investigators may:
   a. Release the type of call received and the time of dispatch.
   b. Disclose known facts and circumstances related to the commission of the crime to the extent it will not hinder or prejudice investigation and prosecution.
   c. Give a general description of the suspect(s).
   d. State the age, race, sex, and occupation of the suspect(s).
   e. Provide the name(s) of the suspect(s).

f. Release the number, sex, and age of the victim(s) unless a juvenile is involved.

g. Give general information about injuries.

h. Release the identities of deceased victims if the families have been previously notified.

i. Provide the identities of the investigators assigned if this does not place them at risk or hinder the investigation.

j. If a victim has been transported to a hospital, refuse to release the name of that facility to the news media.[12]

k. At this or any other stage, refuse to release information or reports that reveal information about confidential informants, or other information, such as medical conditions, which is privileged.

2. If a suspect is in custody, investigators should not do the following for the media:

a. Require the suspect to pose for photographers.

b. Give detailed descriptions of suspects or evidence that may jeopardize the successful conclusion of an investigation or prosecution.

c. Reenact the crime.

d. Provide the suspect's prior criminal record of arrests or other criminal charges that did not result in a final conviction.

e. Disclose that the suspect told where weapons, proceeds of the crime, or other materials were located.

f. Use derogatory terms to refer to the suspect, such as "depraved character," "real no-good," "sexual monster," and other terms.

g. Reveal that the suspect declined to take certain types of tests or that the suspect did take certain tests (for example, a blood alcohol test to determine the degree, if any, to which the suspect was under the influence of drugs or alcohol).

h. Tell the results of any tests to which the suspect submitted.

i. Make statements as to the guilt or innocence of a suspect.

j. Release the identities of prospective witnesses or comment on the nature of their anticipated testimony or credibility.

k. Release information about the existence or content of any confession, admission, or statement given by suspects in custody.

l. Make statements of a purely speculative nature about any aspect of the case.

3. If a suspect is arrested, it is permissible in most states to release the following types of information about him/her:

a. The defendant's name, age, sex, residence, employment, marital status, and similar background information, unless the defendant is a juvenile.

b. The nature of the crime for which the arrest was made and the identity of the complainant (as long as disclosing this information does not create a danger for the complainant and is not seriously embarrassing to him or her—as can be the case for victims of sexual offenses—or does not run counter to other reasons of good judgment or applicable laws).

c. The identities of any other agencies participating in the investigation, and/or making the arrest, as well as those of the individual officers involved.

d. The circumstances surrounding the arrest, such as the time and place, the extent of any pursuit, amount of resistance, possession and use of weapons, injuries to an officer (notification of the family should precede disclosing an individual officer's identity), and a general description of items seized at the time of arrest.

CONCEPTUALIZE EVENTS

Outside the Bar Code nightclub, a 24-year-old man was shot five times and killed. Other shots were also fired. By conceptualizing how the crime was committed, Washington State Police officers believed that the face of the club might contain places where bullet evidence could be recovered, but which they could not see. They called in for a bucket truck and were successful in locating important evidence (Figure 3-19).

Even experienced investigators may not take the time to conceptualize how a crime was committed. Or they develop a premature concept of how the crime was committed. This often results in available evidence not being recovered, as happened in the Chandra Levy murder. During the course of an investigation facts known to investigators and inferences they have made must be periodically reviewed. This facilitates the reconstruction of the offense and identification of the perpetrator's method of operation, suggests the possible existence of certain types of physical evidence, and assists in establishing appropriate lines of inquiry:

Multiple female murder victims were found strangled and stabbed in an apartment. The lead investigator studied the crime scene very carefully. One of the victims was lying near the doorway to one of the bedrooms with a pillow under her head. The investigator concluded that the perpetrator may have touched the very lowest portion of the door to steady himself as he stood up after killing that victim. The crime scene technician processed that portion of the door and located the only fingerprint of the suspect found at the crime scene. The suspect was identified by this print and subsequently convicted of the murders.

▶ **FIGURE 3-19**
Investigators searching for bullet holes
Investigators from the Washington State Police Crime Laboratory search for bullet holes in the front of the Bar Code, a local club. Note WSP officers in the "bucket," which can be moved to search higher spots. (Courtesy The Olympian.com. Photo by Ron Soliman)

Without the investigator's thoughtful examination of the crime and reconstruction of how the perpetrator may have acted, that lower portion of the door would not have been dusted for fingerprints because it would have been illogical to expect to find a fingerprint there. Consequently, the most important piece of evidence would never have been located.

Assumptions that are made must be checked for accuracy as quickly as possible. The failure to do so may result in an offender's escaping prosecution and in embarrassment for the investigator and the department. It may also produce confusion in, or misdirect, the investigation:

> A woman was murdered in her apartment. The investigators assumed that the woman's husband had thoroughly searched the apartment for their missing infant child when he first arrived and found his wife's body. Thus, they further assumed that the baby had been kidnapped. Some four days later the baby's body was found by the grandmother in the apartment under a sofa cushion.[13]

Human behavior is rich in its variety; in reconstructing the crime, investigators must be alert to the danger of imparting their own probable motives or actions to the perpetrator unless there are solid grounds for so doing. Alternatively stated, this proposition dictates that simply because, under the same or a similar set of circumstances, we would not have acted in a particular fashion does not preclude the possibility that the perpetrator may have acted in that way. Two cases illustrate the importance of this point:

> In Woodbridge, New Jersey, a series of burglaries was solved when it was established that two inmates had been breaking out of a correctional facility to commit the offenses, and then returning nightly to the facility.[14]

> In Palm Beach, Florida, a guard at a bank was surprised one night by an intruder who took $50,000 in gold coins. Unable to find a point of entry, investigators were puzzled until they received an anonymous tip that the intruder had shipped himself into the bank in a crate and broken out of it after the regular employees had gone home.[15]

Large physical evidence, such as a handgun used in a criminal homicide, is often easily found at the crime scene and requires little in the way of conceptualization. However, there is the possibility that much smaller types of evidence are also present; these will be located only if the investigator is able to conceptualize events:

> A university student claimed that several hours previously her date had raped her at his apartment. This had been their second date. In addition to being able to identify her assailant, the victim showed the investigator a digital photograph taken on her phone earlier in the evening of her and her assailant. In examining the photograph, the investigator noticed that the victim was wearing a sorority pin in the photograph, but

the victim's pin was now missing. Believing that the pin could have been lost at the crime scene, the investigator went to the suspect's apartment. The suspect's version of events was that he told the victim he no longer wanted to date her and she swore to get even for "being dumped." The suspect also said that the woman had never been in his apartment and consented to a search. The investigator found the missing sorority pin in the perpetrator's bedroom, and the suspect subsequently gave her a confession.

It does not take a great deal of conceptualization to recognize larger items of evidence at a crime scene. Where this ability pays substantial dividends is in locating **trace evidence,** which is present in extremely small or limited amounts. Such evidence may be, but is not exclusively, microscopic in size.

Often this trace evidence is located using **alternative light systems (ALSs)** (Figure 3-20). Illustrations include the Polilight, BlueMaxx, and Luma-Lite. As illumination from ALSs sweep over a crime scene, the various lights cause many types of evidence to fluoresce. Trace evidence that reacts to such illumination includes fingerprints, bodily fluids, hairs, fibers, drugs, glass and metal fragments, bite marks, bruises, human bone fragments, and gunshot residues. The following case illustrates the value of ALSs:

A small leaf was found on the windowsill where a burglar entered the building. The burglar had worked barefoot, and investigators located a portion of his footprint on the leaf using a Luma-Lite. Confronted with this and other evidence, the suspect pled guilty.[16]

Portable **trace-evidence vacuums** are also quite useful in locating very small items of evidence. To prevent the accidental contamination of the evidence, the nozzle and the evidence filter unit (which sits on top of the vacuum's nozzle) is packaged and sealed at the factory's "clean room." At the crime scene, as each different area is vacuumed, the nozzle and the filter are detached and sealed as evidence. These systems are particularly effective in gathering hairs, fibers, and certain types of drug evidence, such as cocaine. Thus, trace-evidence vacuum systems can often be effectively used in assault, rape, and some drug cases. If clothing is seized as evidence and fiber, hair, or other evidence from the suspect or victim may be on it, crime laboratories generally prefer that the clothing not be vacuumed at the scene but instead be sent to the laboratory for processing to prevent the possibility that other valuable evidence may be lost during the vacuuming.

PROCEED WITH CAUTION

Many crime scenes provide an immediate focus; in criminal homicide, for example, there is a tendency to move directly to the body. Such action, when the person is obviously deceased, has a number of disadvantages. In approaching the point of focus, small but extremely important evidence may be altered or destroyed, the area to be searched may be too rapidly defined, and other areas that might be fruitfully explored are overlooked or given only a cursory examination.

APPLY INCLUSIVENESS

The rule of inclusiveness dictates that every available piece of evidence be obtained and, where there is a question as to whether a particular item constitutes evidence, be defined as such. The rationale is that mistakes made

◄FIGURE 3-20 Forensic light
Forensic light illuminating latent finger fingerprints. Chapter 4, "Physical Evidence," contains a major section on fingerprint evidence. Such illumination helps to find fingerprints that might otherwise be overlooked. (Courtesy Chief Jack Lumpkin, Athens Clarke County (Georgia) Police Department)

in excluding potential evidence often cannot be rectified. One cannot always return to the crime scene and recover evidence. Sound judgment is required in applying the rule of inclusiveness. If you pick up everything that remotely could have some evidentiary value, scarce laboratory resources are going to be wasted.

The rule of inclusiveness also requires that standard samples and elimination prints always be obtained when appropriate. If, for example, a burglary has been committed and a safe inside the building successfully attacked, exposing the insulation of the safe, then standard samples of the insulation should be obtained. This will ensure that if at some future time a suspect is identified, comparisons can be made between the standard sample of safe insulation and any traces of safe insulation that might be recovered from the soles of the suspect's shoes or his or her car floor mat.

Elimination prints are useful in determining whether a latent fingerprint found at a crime scene belongs to the suspect. In the case of a residential burglary, for example, if a latent print was discovered inside the house on the window ledge where the perpetrator entered, the residents of the household should be fingerprinted and a comparison made between the latent fingerprint and those of the residents. If the latent fingerprint does not belong to any of the residents, it may belong to the perpetrator. In some instances, the fingerprint might belong to someone having authorized access to the dwelling. In cases where this is found to be true, however, the possibility cannot be overlooked that the person with authorized access may be the perpetrator. An example of this is the case of a licensed real estate dealer operating in the Washington, D.C., area who may have entered more than 100 homes that were being offered for sale, stealing furs, tape recorders, silverware, and other valuables worth between $200,000 and $300,000.[17]

MAINTAIN DOCUMENTATION

Documentation of the crime scene is a constant activity, starting with the rough, shorthand record created by field notes. Other types of documentation that need to be maintained include:

1. The **crime scene entry log,** which was shown in Figure 3-6.
2. The **administrative log,** which is the responsibility of the crime scene coordinator and details such things as who is assigned to what function at the crime scene and the sequence of events at the scene, including its release.
3. **Assignment sheets,** which are completed by each individual who is given specific work to do and which document the results—both positive and negative.
4. The incidence/offense report, which is the responsibility of the first officer on the scene.
5. **Photographic logs,** detailing who took which shots, from where, when, and under what circumstances, for example, type of lighting (Figures 3-21a and 21b). Separate logs are kept for each camera used.
6. The rough sketch of the crime scene; the data used to prepare the finished or final diagram, which may be drawn by hand or by computer.
7. The **evidence recovery log,** which lists each item of evidence; the names of the collector and witness; the location, date, and time of the collection; and documentation such as photos or diagrams (Figure 3-22).

▶ **FIGURE 3-21a**
Photo Log Sheet
(Courtesy Imprimus Forensic Services, © 2000, by permission)

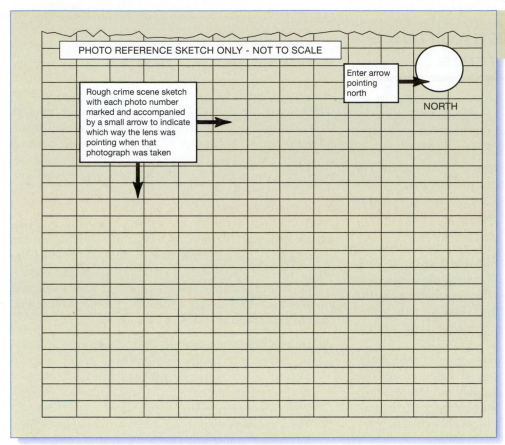

◄FIGURE 3-21b
Photo Log Sheet (*continued*)

PHOTO REFERENCE SKETCH ONLY - NOT TO SCALE

Rough crime scene sketch with each photo number marked and accompanied by a small arrow to indicate which way the lens was pointing when that photograph was taken

Enter arrow pointing north

NORTH

◄FIGURE 3-22
Evidence recovery log
(Courtesy Imprimus Forensic Services, © 2000, by permission)

| Incident # | | Offense: | | Victim: | | Location: | | | | | |

Item No.	Description	Collector	Witness	Location	Time/Date Collected	Photos		Diagramed	
						Y	N	Y	N
1									
2									
3									
4									
5									
6									
15									

Recorded by:
Name: _____
ID No.: _____
Unit: _____

Date: _____
Start Time: _____
End Time: _____

Recorded by:
Name: _____
ID No.: _____
Unit: _____

Page____of____Pages

8. Emergency medical personnel documents.
9. The **lifted-prints log,** which contains the same type of basic information as the evidence recovery log.
10. If applicable, the consent search form or search warrant.

In lesser offenses, a single officer may be the only representative of the police department at the scene. Thus, everything that is learned will be a result of his/her investigation. In such cases, the only documentation that may exist is the officer's field notes and the incident/offense report.

INFECTIOUS DISEASE RISKS AND PRECAUTIONS FOR INVESTIGATORS

On a daily basis, investigators are at risk of exposure to infectious pathogens (disease-causing agents), such as HIV, hepatitis B, hepatitis C, and tuberculosis. These diseases and the precautions that can be taken are discussed in the sections that follow.

HIV/AIDS

The **human immunodeficiency virus (HIV)** is a blood-borne pathogen that is also present in some body fluids—that is, blood, semen, vaginal secretions, and breast milk. In the United States it is most commonly transmitted by vaginal and anal intercourse. Less commonly, some HIV mothers may pass the pathogen to their baby at birth. The exposure risk from blood transfusions and organ transplants is extremely remote given the rigid testing associated with those procedures.[18]

If HIV progresses into acquired immunodeficiency syndrome (AIDS), the body's natural defenses against many types of diseases are substantially reduced, leaving victims vulnerable to "opportunistic infections," such as pneumonia, from which they ultimately die. There is no HIV/AIDS vaccine.

HIV is not spread from casual contact. You cannot get it from toilet seats, telephones, swimming pools, door knobs, a drinking fountain, or air.[19] There is no present evidence that HIV is spread through sweat, tears, saliva, or urine.[20] However, the co-presence of blood is not always obvious in such materials, nor may blood be immediately apparent on clothing, guns, knives, cars, drugs, and hypodermic needles; therefore, consistent caution is always warranted. It should be noted that HIV (and hepatitis B and C) can also be spread through shared razors, toothbrushes, and other personal care items. Biting insects, such as mosquitoes, do not transmit HIV.[21]

HIV/AIDS and Investigator Precautions. In general, the risk of HIV infection after an accidental needle stick is extremely low.[22] However, given the frequency with which investigators deal with special populations, such as intravenous drug users (IDUs), homosexuals, and prostitutes, the risk for them may be somewhat greater because of repeated exposure. The greatest danger to officers arises when they are making arrests, seizing drug-related evidence, and processing crime scenes and accidents where blood and other bodily fluids are exposed.

At all crime, accident, and other scenes with a potential or known HIV risks, investigators should use the appropriate personal protective equipment provided by their departments. If they have a suspected exposure it should be immediately reported to their supervisor and all treatment and decontamination protocols followed (Figure 3-23). Additionally:

1. Be cautious when conducting all types of searches; never put your hands anyplace you cannot see. Instead, use a mirror, or probe with a flashlight, pen, wooden dowel, or metal rod. Disinfect these items immediately after using them.
2. The most important protective barrier against HIV infection is intact skin. Even the slightest opening in the skin can be a portal through which HIV enters the body. Protect skin wounds, abrasions, and openings with 360-degree fluid-proof bandages.
3. About 20% of AIDS patients develop raised, purplish-colored lesions (Kaposi's sarcoma), which may be present anywhere on the body (Figure 3-24). Most commonly these are seen on the head, neck, and oral cavity. Some of these are "weeping lesions" that let out an HIV-carrying fluid. You should be particularly careful around such lesions.

▶ **FIGURE 3-23**
HIV post-exposure–prevention (PEP)

The risks of HIV exposures are well understood by law-enforcement agencies. The responsibilities of the officer at risk and the obligations of the employing department are detailed in policy manuals. Such policies usually require that exposures be reported immediately and medical treatment obtained where there has been a significant blood or other body fluid exposure to a known high-risk individual.

However, such policies typically stop short of identifying potential medical interventions. An HIV post-exposure-prophylaxis (PEP) treatment, a combination of several antiretroviral drugs, may be appropriate in some fact situations. PEP has been available since 1996 and changed as newer drugs became available. Although study results vary, its efficacy is about 75%. The treatment lasts four weeks and its side effects include headaches, vomiting, diarrhea, and fatigue. Some people cannot tolerate the full course of treatment.

The Chandler (Arizona) Police Department has a model policy that emphasizes rapid screening for PEP treatment. Its "Hazardous Body Fluid Exposure Control Plan" requires officers to report high risk exposures *within 15 minutes* to the agency's designated health provider. Although the Centers for Disease Control (CDC) advise that treatment started as late as 72 hours after an exposure may have benefit, needed treatment started within hours is more promising.

FIGURE 3-24   AIDS purple-colored lesion
(© SPL/Photo Researchers, Inc.)

Another condition, pseudo–Kaposi's sarcoma, or acroangiodermatitus, has a similar appearance but is not HIV related.

4. If you are bitten by a suspect, have a medical assessment made. Do not place your mouth to the bite area. There are only a few, rare reports of transmission of the HIV virus by biting, although other types of infections may result.[23]

5. Bites, needle sticks, cuts, or similar incidents involving broken or punctured skin, however slight, should be washed immediately with soap in warm water for at least 30 seconds and treated medically.[24]

Use soap from a dispenser, not a shared bar. Some agencies recommend the use of germicidal wipes approved by the Environmental Protection Agency (EPA). There is no evidence that squeezing or "milking" wounds reduces the risk of HIV.

6. If splashed in the eyes or on mucous membranes (for example, inside the nose), flush the area for 15 minutes using water, sterile water, or a saline solution.

7. Do not attempt to recap hypodermic needles seized as evidence, and use care when seizing any other sharp items (for instance, knives, razor blades, broken glass, scissors, and metal pieces) at crime scenes. When handling sharp objects, use disposable tongs or forceps and place the objects in appropriate rigid, puncture-resistant containers.

8. The use of latex or nitrile gloves significantly reduces exposure from body fluids and may reduce the amount of blood transferred by an accidental needle stick by 50%.[25] To prevent the possibility of piercing your gloves, remove any rings before placing them on your hands. When wearing gloves, check them frequently for wear and tear; replace them often. When you remove gloves, wash your hands and use an approved germicidal wipe on them. High risk/cut-resistant gloves further reduce chance of accidental needle sticks and other wounds.

9. In addition to gloves, other **personal protection equipment (PPE)** may be necessary at high-risk scenes with exposed body fluids. Examples of such equipment are listed in Figure 3-25.

10. All disposable worn PPE should be placed in a biohazard waste bag when you have completed your work at a crime scene. When removing PPE, do so in a manner that does not contaminate your clothing. Clean your hands in the appropriate manner immediately afterward.

- Gloves—cotton, latex (natural rubber), nitrile, polyvinyl chloride (PVC), and neoprene. Each of these has different characteristics and limitations; more detailed information on this can be obtained by referring to the FBI's Forensic Science Handbook, which is available on the Internet.
- Cut-resistant glove liners.
- Protective or impermeable "booties" or shoe covers, disposable gowns, coveralls or jumpsuits, aprons, hoods, chin-length face shields, eyewear with side shields.
- Masks—infiltration masks for protection from highly contagious people and situations; nuisance odor masks for reduction of unpleasant odors; and half-mask particulate respirators for protection from fumes, particulate/dust, and airborne pathogens. Self-contained breathing apparatus (SCBA).
- EPA-registered bleach, germicidal disinfectants, and wipes.
- First-aid kit.
- Biohazard bags.
- Insect repellant.

Source: Content drawn from Henry C. Lee, Timothy M. Palmbach, and Marilyn T. Miller, *Crime Scene Handbook* (San Diego: Academic Press, 2001), pp. 321–324, and Technical Working Group on Crime Scene Investigation, *Crime Scene Investigation* (Washington, DC: U.S. Department of Justice, 2000), pp. 33–36; additional content supplied by the authors.

◀FIGURE 3-25
Crime scene personal protection equipment (PPE)

11. Maintain a high sense of personal awareness at potential HIV scenes. When you are wearing gloves, do not handle personal items (such as your pen or clipboard), and do not put your hands in your pockets, touch your face, or scratch your head.

    If you do touch personal items or body areas, they should be immediately disinfected.

12. Always carry a flashlight, even during daylight hours, so that you can search dark areas more safely.

13. Do not eat, drink, smoke, handle contacts, or apply lip balm or cosmetics at HIV-risk crime scenes.

14. Contaminated evidence should be collected, marked, and packaged as appropriate for the particular type of evidence. If the evidence might be contaminated, mark it prominently as such or apply a "Biological Hazard" sticker.

15. Carefully follow department policy regarding decontamination of your uniform, equipment, and vehicle.

16. Make sure you understand federal and state confidentiality laws that pertain to disclosing information about HIV to others, including the news media.

Hepatitis B and C. **Hepatitis B (HBV)** is the most common serious disease in the world and is the leading cause of liver cancer; about 500,000 people die annually from liver cancer and another 5,000 from chronic HBV and associated complications.[26] It also results in cirrhosis (scarring) of the liver and liver failure. Symptoms include appetite loss, fatigue, nausea, vomiting, pain over the location of the liver, stools that are pale gray or clay colored, and dark urine with a tea or cola color. Since 1982 there has been a safe and effective HBV vaccine.

HBV is a major health concern. It is spread by contact with the blood or body fluids of an infected person, for example, blood to blood contact; unprotected sex; sharing earrings; nail-clippers; toothbrushes; razors, and unsterile needles. Well regulated acupuncture, tattooing, and body piercing services are not viewed as a serious risk. In the absence of precautions, officers are 100 times more likely to contract HBV than HIV.[27]

Hepatitis C (HCV) may be transmitted from an infected woman to her newborn during delivery. Also at risk are persons with an HIV infection, accidental needle sticks, recipients of blood transfusions and organ transplants before 1992, and chronic hemodialysis patients. There is no vaccine for HCV.

Unless effective new therapies are developed, deaths due to HCV will double or even triple over the next 15 to 20 years simply because 80% of those infected have no signs or symptoms and therefore may have been infected for a long time without knowing it.[28] The symptoms are similar to those of HBV: jaundice—the yellowish coloring of the skin and whites of the eyes, dark urine, fatigue, abdominal pain, nausea, and loss of appetite.[29] There is no vaccine for HCV. Neither HBV nor HCV is spread by casual contact.

Tuberculosis. **Tuberculosis (TB)** is a chronic bacterial infection that is spread by air. Accountable for more deaths worldwide than any other infectious disease, it usually infects the lungs, although other organs may be involved.[30] One third of the world's population is infected with TB, although most will never develop active TB. The mortality rate for treated cases is about 10%.[31] The existence of some drug-resistant strains of TB is of concern to public health officials.[32]

When a person with active TB coughs into the air, infectious droplets are released; repeated exposure to them can cause the disease. People who eat healthy diets and lead healthy lifestyles are less at risk than others when such exposure occurs. Conversely, the homeless, alcoholics, drug addicts, and people in poor health are at greater risk.

A vaccine (BCG) is given to infants in some parts of the world where the disease is common; the effectiveness of BCG in adults varies widely, and in the United States its general use is not recommended.[33] Several drug therapies are available for people who have a high risk of developing active TB, that is, those who are in close contact with persons who are infected with TB or have active TB.[34]

The Americans with Disabilities Act. Investigators who contract the infectious diseases discussed previously may be covered by the federal **Americans with Disabilities Act (ADA).** Under this act, it is illegal to discriminate against an otherwise qualified employee in regard to employment actions—such as assignments and promotions—solely because the employee is thought to have, or actually has, a covered disability. Employers may be required to make "reasonable accommodations" for such employees. Reasonable accommodations include redesigning jobs, offering part-time hours, and modifying equipment and facilities. The legal provisions of ADA are broad and cover more than just infectious diseases; additional information is readily obtainable in personnel offices, from police unions, and on the Internet.

As a final note, some police agencies have taken the view that if an officer cannot fully perform all the functions required of a certified peace officer, she or he may be separated from the service or placed on involuntary medical retirement, depending on the situation. Other police departments have chosen to inventory their positions each year in order to determine how many of them could, with reasonable accommodations, be staffed by persons covered by ADA.

THE CRIME SCENE SEARCH

The purpose of the crime scene search is to obtain physical evidence useful in establishing the fact that an offense has been committed, identify the method of operation employed by the perpetrator, reduce the number of suspects, and identify the perpetrator. Four major considerations dominate the crime scene search.

1. BOUNDARY DETERMINATION

In terms of the boundary of the crime scene, it is useful to think of an inner perimeter and an outer perimeter. The inner perimeter delineates the area where the specific items of evidence are known to be, along with the lines of entry into, and exit from, the scene. The outer perimeter is set farther back than the inner perimeter and helps establish control of, and entry into, the scene.

The crime scene coordinator is responsible for deciding the positions of the inner and outer perimeters, which are determined by the locations of the primary and any secondary crime scenes—such as the perpetrator's lines of approach to and from the scene. Along these lines, the perpetrator may have accidentally left or dropped valuable evidence, such as items taken from the scene, the perpetrator's wallet or distinctive jewelry, matches from an establishment he or she works at or frequents, a water bottle the perpetrator drank from while waiting for the victim, and the butt from a cigarette he or she smoked. Saliva traces from the bottle and the butt could yield DNA evidence.

For an indoor crime scene, the physical limitations of the building can help determine where the inner and outer boundaries should be. More problematic is determining the boundaries for an outdoor crime scene. As a general rule, in such situations, it is better to establish the perimeters more broadly. Although doing so may result in some "wasted" search effort, items of evidence are occasionally found.

2. CHOICE OF SEARCH PATTERN

There are five basic **crime scene search patterns** from which the crime scene coordinator may choose:

1. The spiral, depicted in Figure 3-26(a) is usually employed in outdoor scenes and is normally executed by a single person. The searcher walks in slightly decreasing, less-than-concentric circles from the outermost boundary determination toward a central point. This pattern should not be operated in the reverse—beginning at some central point and working toward the perimeter of the crime scene in increasing, less-than-concentric circles—as there is a real danger that some evidence may be inadvertently destroyed while walking to the central point to initiate the search.

2. The strip/line search, diagrammed in Figure 3-26(b), involves the demarcation of a series of lanes down which one or more persons proceed. On reaching the starting point, the searchers proceed down their respective lanes, reverse their direction, and

▲ FIGURE 3-26   Crime scene search patterns

continue in this fashion until the area has been thoroughly examined. If multiple searchers are being used, then whenever physical evidence is encountered, all searchers should stop until it is properly handled and they have received information with respect to its nature. The search is then resumed in the fashion described previously.

3. The grid search is a variation of the strip/line pattern and is depicted in Figure 3-26(c). After completing the strip pattern, the searchers double back perpendicularly across the area being examined. Although more time-consuming than the strip search, the grid offers the advantage of being more methodical and thorough; examined from two different viewpoints, an area is more likely to yield evidence that might otherwise have been overlooked.

4. Figure 3-26(d) shows the zone/quadrant search pattern, which requires that an area be divided into four large quadrants, each of which is then examined using any of the methods already described. If the area to be searched is particularly large, each of the quadrants can be subdivided into four smaller quadrants.

5. The pie/wheel search, shown in Figure 3-26(e), entails dividing the area into a number of pie-shaped sections, usually six. These are then searched, usually through a variation of the strip method.

   In practice, both the spiral and the pie search patterns are rarely employed. When the area to be searched is not excessively large, the strip or grid pattern is normally used. When the crime scene is of significant size, the zone search pattern is normally employed.

3. INSTRUCTION OF PERSONNEL

Although instruction of personnel was mentioned earlier in the chapter, its importance requires some further elaboration. Even when the same type of criminal offense has been committed, the variation among crime scenes may be enormous, for example, the murder weapon may be recovered at the scene or in a distant body of water (Figure 3-27.) These variations are due to such factors as the physical settings, the manner and means that the perpetrators used to execute the offenses, and the lengths to which they may have gone to eliminate or destroy evidence. Thus, it is of paramount importance that the crime scene coordinator call together all the individuals who will be, in various capacities, processing the scene and share with them all the available information concerning the case. Doing so serves to minimize the possibility of excluding any available evidence. On receipt of this information, the members of the crime scene processing team may then begin their work.

4. COORDINATION

As discussed earlier, one of the most important responsibilities of the person in charge of the crime scene is integrating the efforts of those assigned to the technical and investigative service functions, along with ensuring the timely flow of pertinent information. For example, if a suspect is in custody and the interrogation yields information concerning the weapon or tool that may have been used, or where it may be located, then the crime scene coordinator should rapidly relay this information to those involved in crime scene processing so that they will be alert to specific possibilities for the recovery of

►**FIGURE 3-27**
Police diver finds evidence
Police scuba diver with pistol used in murder case that was recovered from a lake. It is kept in the same type of water in which it was found until it arrives at the crime laboratory to be properly processed, preventing the accidental destruction or contamination of the evidence. (© AP Photo/Paul Kuehnel)

physical evidence. Conversely, as significant physical evidence is recovered, the information should be conveyed to the crime scene coordinator, who can then transmit it to other investigators so they can move toward apprehending a suspect or use the information during the interrogation of a possible perpetrator already in custody.

SUSPENDED SEARCHES, DEBRIEFING, AND RELEASE OF THE SCENE

Occasionally, it may be necessary to suspend an operation temporarily. In one of the most common situations, a priority crime with evidence subject to decay requires the temporary diversion of personnel from another scene where delayed processing will not result in any loss of physical evidence. If it becomes necessary to stop the examination of a scene for a time, that scene should be secured in such a fashion that there is no possibility of contamination, alteration, or accidental destruction of any evidence that may exist.

Immediately before the **crime scene release,** the coordinator calls all team members together. In addition to ensuring that assignments were properly executed, the coordinator checks to make sure that all equipment brought to the scene has been retrieved and that all trash generated in processing the scene has been removed. Because each participant shares information during the debriefing, additional opportunities to develop evidence may be identified allowing all parties to leave the scene with a common understanding of the crime and of what the next steps are going to be. When the scene is finally released, the name of the party to whom it is released and his/her locator information should be noted in the administrative log.

Once a scene is released, the person to whom it is released will usually clean it up. Additionally, if the person is living there, the countless small things he/she does each day will alter and contaminate the scene, so that returning to it for further processing is not a viable option. Therefore, the decision to release a scene must be well thought out. An absolute must is to photograph the scene again just before it is turned over to the responsible party. These photos will counter claims that the police "tore my sister's house apart when they were there."

COLLECTION AND CARE OF EVIDENCE

The location of physical evidence during the crime scene search merely marks the first step in its long journey toward presentation in court. To satisfy legal requirements related to its introduction in a judicial proceeding, investigators must be able to:

1. identify each item of evidence they collected or handled;
2. describe the location and condition of the evidence at the time it was collected;
3. state who had contact with or handled the evidence;
4. state when, or during what time periods, the evidence was handled;
5. declare under what circumstances, and why, the evidence was handled;
6. explain what changes, if any, were made to the evidence.[35]

The essence of packaging any evidence is to do it in a way that will make any tampering with it clearly evident. For example, if evidence is placed in a plain Kraft envelope, the envelope should be sealed with tamper-evident evidence tape. As a further measure, when the officer signs her or his initials or signature, the writing can start on the envelope, cross the tape, and go back onto the envelope. Using a preprinted label or otherwise just writing on the envelope, the following information should be provided: type of offense and agency case number; the item number, the date recovered/received; and the investigator's name and badge number/departmental identifier. The entries made on evidence, and strong evidence room procedures, such as the use of bar codes to track evidence handling, can eliminate many barriers to introducing evidence in a courtroom.

VISUAL DOCUMENTATION OF THE CRIME SCENE

Occasionally, the value of an otherwise excellent investigation is reduced by improper or inadequate visual documentation of the scene. People process information differently, so the more ways a crime scene is properly documented, the greater the likelihood that other people will accurately understand the scene and what happened there.

This section examines three basic methods of documenting crime scenes: (1) digital video recording, (2) digital still photography, and (3) sketching. In general, the methods should be used in that order with documentation progressing from the general to the more specific. More advanced crime scene digital imaging techniques are discussed later in the chapter.

DIGITAL VIDEO RECORDING

Using **digital video recording** to document the crime scene offers several advantages. Such cameras are relatively inexpensive, they incorporate audio, their use can be quickly learned, the motion of videotapes holds the attention of viewers, and the images collected can be

▶ FIGURE 3-28

Police officer photographing the body of a 29-year-old mother of six who was found murdered in a parking lot. The words on the yellow crime scene tape are hard to read because they are printed on the opposite side, but they can be plainly seen by people approaching the crime scene. (Courtesy Lexington Hearld-Leader. Photo by Pablo Alcala)

played back immediately. On the downside, neither the resolutions nor the color accuracy can compete with those of digital still photography. Video recorded images are not an acceptable alternative to high-resolution digital photographs. Several protocols should be followed when video recording a crime scene:

1. Keep the camera's lens clean to produce sharper images.
2. To avoid dragging electrical cords through the scene, battery packs should be used for the camera and portable lights. Use the camera's title generator and make sure that the time/date indicators are correct before recording begins.
3. The recording should begin with an identification of the location, case number, type of offense, and other pertinent information. It should progress to what viewers will be seeing. Some agencies display a simple overhead view of the scene during the narration to help orient viewers.
4. After the narration ends a dummy microphone plug should be inserted in the camera to avoid recording unwanted and potentially embarrassing extraneous comments being recorded.
5. Once recording begins, the camera should be kept running; gaps may be hard to satisfactorily explain to jurors.
6. Most crime scenes can be documented within 30 minutes. Pan each area in 360 degrees.
7. The use of a rolling tripod or shoulder brace with the camera will produce smoother, less jerky images.
8. The most common mistake in video recording is going too fast; the speed you think is right may be as much as 50% too fast. Take your time and use the camera's capabilities for wide-area pans, close-ups, and very tight shots of the evidence.

DIGITAL STILL PHOTOGRAPHY

Digital (DSLR) still photography is the primary means of documenting major crime scenes. Although digital video recordings capture images, they are supplemental to the four classes of photographs that must be taken with digital still cameras; they are often taken in this progression:

1. *Orientation*—long/longer range shots, general views of the entire scene.
2. *Relationship*—medium range, photos of evidence and their positional relationship to each other (see Figure 3-28).
3. *Identification*—close-ups that show specific features, such as the serial number on a firearm.
4. *Comparison*—close-ups that document characteristics for future laboratory examination, for example, 1:1 shots of developed fingerprints.[36]

These general guidelines are appropriate for still photography of almost any scene; some previously mentioned points in this chapter are reiterated to consolidated them:[37]

- Photograph the crime scene as soon as possible.
- Prepare the photographic log.
- Photograph from eye level to represent the normal view.
- Photograph the most fragile areas of the crime scene first.
- Photograph all stages of the crime scene investigation, including discoveries.
- Photograph the condition of evidence before recovery.
- Take all photographs intended for examination purposes without a scale, and then with one.
- Photograph the interior crime scene in an overlapping series using a normal lens, if possible. Overall photographs may be taken using a wide-angle lens.

- Photograph the exterior crime scene, establishing the location of the scene by a series of overall photographs including a landmark. Photographs should have 360 degrees of coverage. Consider using aerial photography, when appropriate.
- Photograph entrances and exits from the inside and the outside.
- Photograph important evidence twice: (1) a medium-distance shot that shows the evidence and its position to other evidence and (2) a close-up shot that includes a scale and fills the frame.

Some law-enforcement agencies have concluded that although many crimes committed do not warrant full crime scene processing, there is a need to supplement some reports with photographs—for instance, a misdemeanor assault that produces visible injuries. In those departments low-end "point and shoot" digital cameras are issued to officers or to their Sergeants.

DIGITAL IMAGE MANAGEMENT SYSTEMS

Whether digital video recordings or still digital photographs, digital images from different crime scenes should not be comingled on the same storage media. These images are evidence and should be handled as such. Many agencies use **Digital Image Management System (DIMS)** software to help accomplish this. DIMS have a digital authentication capability that verifies that the images from the storage media and those uploaded are exactly the same. The initial storage media can then be wiped clean and reused at another scene, although many agencies also treat the original storage media as evidence. Other DIMS capabilities include setting levels of user access and image searching across the entire database.

One DIMS uploaded copy is kept as the "electronic negative" and others can be processed for analytical/investigative purposes, for example, alterations of the color contrast to make visible what otherwise could not be seen; image enhancement/sharpening, and resizing. Each processing or transformation of an image must be logged; some software, such as Adobe Photoshop, automatically compiles this data. Although the original image is never altered, the ability to "manipulate" digital images has resulted in some legal changes to them. Departments must have standard operating procedures (SOPs) regarding their digital image capturing and processing practices, as well as specifying how the images are managed and their integrity maintained.

The existence of a DIMS SOP does not guarantee compliance with its provisions. One department lost over 600 digital crime scene photographs because they were not backed up. The responsibility for ensuring compliance must be fixed; that person is usually the head of the crime laboratory, or in smaller agencies, whoever supervises the person capturing the images.

CRIME SCENE SKETCHING AND FORENSIC MAPPING

A **crime scene sketch** is a basic diagram of the scene showing important points, such as the locations where various pieces of physical evidence were located. Often, the sketch is not drawn to scale. Sketches made by hand in the field are called **"rough sketches"** as opposed to the more polished **"smooth or finished" sketches** typically drawn in the office. Finished sketches may also be drawn by hand, although it is often done using specialized computer software. Although there is a learning curve with any software, once the package is mastered computer generated sketches produce substantial reductions in the time required to make them—perhaps 75%–versus traditional sketching methods.

Forensic mapping is the process of taking and recording the precise measurements of items of evidence to be drawn or "fixed" on the sketch.[38] In theory, a crime scene sketch and associated mapping data should allow someone to return to the crime scene and place an item of evidence in exactly the same place as it was recovered. As a practical matter, the sketch allows the positioning of the evidence back into its original location with a reasonable degree of accuracy because there is some variation in the precision of sketching methods. The process of mapping the scene inherently intrudes into the scene, because the investigator must move through and around the scene taking and recording measurements.[39] This process requires a degree of caution in order to prevent the accidental moving, alteration, or destruction of physical evidence, all of which have the potential to confuse or misdirect the investigation.

It is critical that the entries on the sketch be as accurate as possible. Errors noted call into question not only the accuracy of the sketch but also the investigation as a whole. For example, distances should not be paced off and then recorded as so many feet and inches. Distances may be measured using rulers or tape measures, as well as by using more sophisticated methods, such as laser devices. Sketching and mapping methods are covered in the sections that follow.

Sketching Views

Regardless of the method, sketches typically employ one of three different views: (1) **overhead** or **bird's-eye view** (Figure 3-29), which is the most common; (2) the **elevation view** (Figure 3-30), which shows heights; and (3) the **cross-projection view** (Figure 3-31), which "lays" the walls to a room down so objects of interest in the wall can be mapped.[40]

Forensic Mapping Methods

The choice of mapping methods can be influenced by a variety of factors, including the nature and the amount of evidence, the overall size of the crime scene, the number of personnel available, the number, size and types of

▶ **FIGURE 3-29**
Overhead or bird's-eye view of a crime scene
No measurements are included in this sketch because it is intended merely to portray the overhead or bird's-eye view. Occasionally it is also called a floor-plan sketch. As a convention, North is usually oriented toward the top of the sketch.

▶ **FIGURE 3-30**
North wall elevation view of the crime scene
In common language, *elevation* refers to the height of something above a reference point. In this view, the reference point is the floor. An elevation view represents the front, sides, or rear of a building. It is an excellent tool to record evidence on vertical surfaces. This view shows the North interior wall using the following legend: A: Apparent bullet hole in glass window. B: Apparent bullet hole in glass window.

line-of-sight-obstructions, and weather conditions.[41] It is not necessary to map everything that you can see; it is important to show the location of the items of physical evidence and any decedent(s). Typically, each crime scene sketch employs only one of these mapping methods; the choice begins with the seriousness of the crime. More severe crimes dictate the use of more precise mapping methods.[42]

This section summarizes major mapping methods, including: (1) rectangular coordinates, (2) triangulation, (3) baseline coordinates, (4) polar coordinates, and (5) the grid system.

1. Rectangular Coordinates. This method is the best to use with scenes having clear and specific boundaries, such as interior walls, because **rectangular coordinates** can

be measured fast and accurately, especially if one is using a laser measuring device.[43] The crime scene investigator (CSI) usually takes two measurements at right angles from the center mass of the evidence to the two nearest walls. It has one deficiency: Although evidence can be fixed at a particular location, the orientation of the evidence can be changed simply by rotating it on the axis where the two measurements intersect. In the case of Figure 3-32, this means the knife's tip could point in 360 different degrees.[44] This deficiency can be overcome by taking and recording additional measurements or, as is the more usual case, by using a different sketching technique, such as triangulation.

2. Triangulation. The **triangulation** method is useful both for interior scenes in buildings, as well as for outdoor

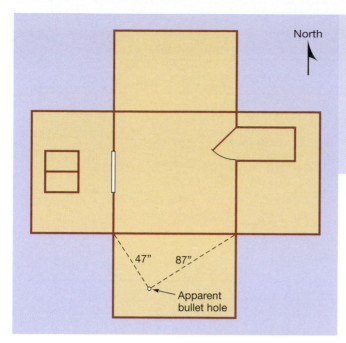

◄**FIGURE 3-31   Cross-projection view of a crime scene**
The cross-projection, or "exploded," view "lays" the walls down flat, as though the room had been unfolded like a box. The purpose of doing this is to be able to show points of interest in the wall, which can also be done with an elevation sketch. The advantage of using the cross-projection method is that when there are multiple points of interest in several different walls, they can be displayed simultaneously in one sketch, as opposed to having to make and refer to multiple elevation sketches.

(1) top of the foremost portion of the gun barrel and (2) nearest portion of the grip, fixing the location of the handgun with precision.[46]

In the aftermath of the 1992 Ruby Ridge shootout, the FBI was criticized for not using triangulation to memorialize the location of physical evidence, a remark that failed to take into account the limitations of using it when the terrain is very uneven.

3. Baseline Coordinates. "The baseline method of fixing evidence is very similar to the rectangular coordinates process."[47] **Baseline coordinates** can be used both inside and outside. Figure 3-34 depicts its use in an interior location. Establishing a straight baseline in a room is straightforward; once it exists, the distance on a right angle (90 degrees) between the center mass of the evidence and where it intersects with the baseline is recorded. The distance from this intersection along the baseline to a fixed

scenes, where measurements must spring from distinct, "permanent" features or landmarks, such as the corner of a home, telephone, mailbox and lighting poles, fences, stop sign posts, the intersections of paved driveways and roads, and other similar features (Figure 3-33). Each pair of measurements is anchored by a reference point (RP), forming two sides of the triangle.[45] In Figure 3-33, two measurements from separate points were made to the

◄**FIGURE 3-32**
Rectangular coordinates
In this example the legend block is blank, because the two items of evidence were drawn in the sketch. If numbers or letters had been used to indicate the locations of the evidence, then the legend would read: 1, pool of blood, and 2, knife with blood on blade. Some investigators prefer to use letters rather than numbers to indicate the location of evidence, because letters are more easily differentiated from the measurements that appear in the sketch.

▶**FIGURE 3-33** **Triangulation**

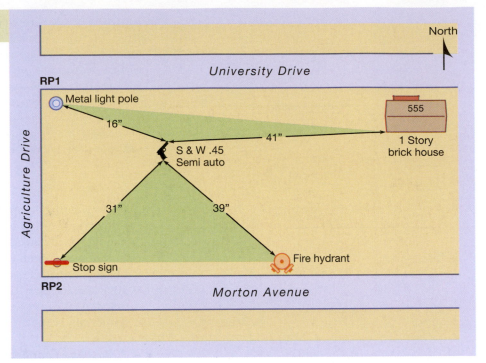

point is also recorded. If greater precision in fixing the location of the Glock 40 in Figure 3-34 was desired, several 90-degree measurements from distinct parts of the Glock back to the baseline and then, respectively, along the baseline to the West wall could be made. Without those additional measurements, the orientation of the Glock could be rotated in the same manner described earlier regarding the use of the rectangular coordinates method.

When this method is used outside, the baseline may be established by running a string or non-stretching tape measure between distinct features or landmarks. Some agencies do not use baseline coordinates when the distance from the physical evidence back to the baseline is more than 30 feet, because as the distance to be measured increases, so does the potential for error.[48] However, this error potential may be greater with handheld tape measures than with lasers and other very accurate measuring devices. Therefore, it should be considered a rule of thumb rather than an iron-clad requirement.

4. Polar Coordinates. When you are mapping outdoor scenes at which evidence is scattered over a fairly large open area, the **polar coordinate** method is an effective tool; it is not useful at scenes where the line of sight is limited.[49] For example, when human remains in an open field are dispersed because of animal predation, polar-coordinates are useful in fixing them. At its simplest, the polar-coordinates method requires measuring the straight line distance from a known reference point along a direction (angle) to the physical evidence to be fixed, as shown in Figure 3-35.[50]

The starting or **datum point** for polar coordinates may be established using a number of methods, including the baseline or triangulation, or in the absence of other possibilities, a global positioning system (GPS) can establish the datum point at which a metal rod may be driven into the ground as it can subsequently be located using a metal detector.[51] The distance from the datum point to the physical evidence may be measured using steel or fiberglass tapes, which are not subject to stretching or shrinkage, while the angle may be set by a handheld

▲**FIGURE 3-34** **Baseline coordinates**

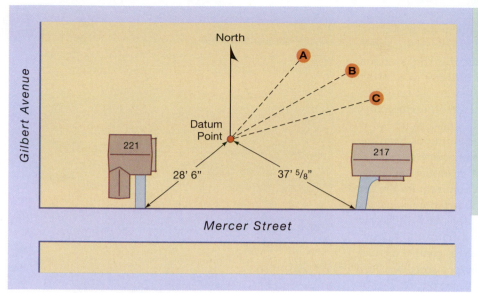

◄ FIGURE 3-35
Polar coordinates
The datum, or starting point, is established by triangulation using the points at which two paved driveways intersect with Mercer Street to form the base of the triangle. In this example, no elevation measurements were taken. Elevation is measured as the difference between the elevation of the datum point and each item of evidence.

compass or protractor. Because of its greater accuracy, a surveyor's transit or similar device, which can also establish the elevation of evidence if this is important, is preferred to a handheld compass. In Figure 3-33, triangulation is used to establish the datum point from which the angles and distances to the evidence is determined.

5. Grid Systems. A **grid system** (See Figure 3-36) is an excellent tool to use when there is a large outdoor scene with no significant features or landmarks.[52] For many years archaeologists have used grid systems to record where artifacts are found at a site; during the mid-1980s, there was a noticeable transfer of this technology as archaeologists instructed investigators on using the grid system and other techniques to process buried body scenes.[53] Both archaeologists and crime scene investigators typically lay out grids with sides of 3 meters or 10 feet, although they may be of any dimensions so long as they are of uniform size; grids as large as 30 feet to a side have been used. When dealing with buried bodies or human remains scattered in a relatively compact area, a grid system of smaller dimensions may be useful.[54]

The boundary of each grid is fixed by a metal or wooden stakes; smaller sized grids may be connected using twine, although this may be impractical with large grids. If several search teams are working, each should be responsible for certain grids and as they find physical evidence, information about it should be immediately communicated to all other search teams. Laying out the grids and marking the boundaries of each is time consuming, but essential;[55] evidence may be fixed within the grids by employing whatever method is most useful; this is an exception to the earlier guideline that typically each crime scene sketch uses only one mapping method; another exception is the use of triangulation to establish the datum point for the polar coordinates method.

Automated Digital Imaging of Crime Scene

Although digital video recording, digital still photography, and sketching are the predominant methods of crime scene documentation, there appears to be some potential for a slow and quiet convergence of them, fueled by advances in two methods of digital imaging: (1) laser

▲ **FIGURE 3-36   Grid system**

scanning and (2) panoramic (360-degree-view) cameras. Originally conceived of as a supplement to traditional sketching and photography, some departments are experimenting with them as an alternative. The systems, depending on their capabilities, cost $40,000 to $250,000 and are often purchased with forfeited assets seized by law-enforcement agencies and federal government grants. They are automated in the sense that once set up by an operator, the systems do not require continuous handling as with video recordings and still photography.

Although the capabilities of laser scanning and panoramic camera imaging systems vary and require the use of specialized software, their *combined* advantages include these: (1) The systems can easily be deployed; (2) scenes can be documented very rapidly and more thoroughly; (3) the 3-D models and panoramic images created are easily stored and can be referred to days after a scene has been released up to years later; (4) the results can be accessed by investigators working similar cases at a distant precinct or across the country; (5) questions that were not fully explored or contemplated at the scene can be carefully studied later; (6) investigators can view the crime scenes, panning left and right and zooming in and out; in 3-D models they can "walk" through the virtual crime scenes to any location for any viewpoint; (7) bullet and blood spatter trajectories can be inserted; (8) victims can be captured and displayed in the precise location they were found; (9) animation of the actions of the assailant and victim can be created; (10) with a DSLR, hundreds of still photographs could be taken and still not produce the complete coverage of these newer techniques; (11) if one points at and clicks on any two different points, their precise distance apart is calculated and shown as if the scene still existed; and (12) in addition to being powerful tools for courtroom presentations and training, they are being used by some agencies as part of the interrogation process. Whichever technology is used, place the imaging unit in several locations at the scene to completely capture the scene. Specific equipment for laser scanning and panoramic imaging of crime scenes is discussed in the sections that follow as examples of what is available in the market place.

Although a number of *combined* advantages for these two methods were discussed, the specific advantages actually acquired by an agency will depend on the type of imaging system selected.

Laser Scanning

The DeltaSphere-3000 is a 25-pound easily portable **laser scanning** system that can be set up in 10 minutes and complete a 360-degree scan in 3 to 15 minutes. Through a data-fusion process, the DeltaSphere "marries" data from its two major components: (1) high-resolution panoramic photos and (2) millions of data points ("point clouds") measured by a laser scanner to produce photorealistic 3-D computer graphics models accurate to 0.25 inch (Figure 3-37).

▲ FIGURE 3-37
A DeltaSphere 3-D laser scan model of a mock crime scene with mannequins as two victims. The white lines above the woman's head show the major axes of the blood spatters on the wall. The blue line is perpendicular through their point of intersection. The red lines are the blood spatter trajectory. Where the red and blue lines intersect appears to be the woman's position when she was shot. In a working model, a click on the "Officer A" annotation at the left of the image would produce the same field of view the first arriving responder had. **(Courtesy of Dough Schiff, 3rdTech, Durham, North Carolina)**

Training for use of the DeltaSphere is conducted over a three-day period. The first half-day is devoted to setting up and using the equipment, that is, capturing the data, and the remaining time is spent using the associated SceneVision 3-D software building the 3-D computer graphics model, annotating the model and images with measurements and notes, making diagrams, linking close-up photographs, and preparing viewpoints, and the "walk through." The final step is creating the finished presentation.

Panoramic Cameras

A **panoramic camera** provides an unbroken, continuous view of the area that encircles it. The PanoScan rotates a full 360 degrees as it takes high-resolution photographs of the crime scene, a process of about 11 minutes. Individual photographs can be studied or they can be viewed as a seamless image of the entire the scene. Investigators can scene, pan left and right, and zoom in on features (Figure 3-38). Return to Scene (R2S) software bundles the ultra-high resolution images with full measurement capabilities. Users can insert "hotspots" into the images to indicate the position of relevant features, for example, fingerprints and other forensic evidence, and links to associated files, such as laboratory reports.

SUBMISSION OF EVIDENCE TO THE CRIME LABORATORY

As a preamble to discussing the submission of evidence to the crime laboratory, we note that there is some potential for our country's laboratory system to be significantly restructured within the near-term future. In 2009 the National Research Council issued a report highly critical of this country's forensic laboratory system. The report called for forensic laboratories to be separated from law enforcement and placed under a new federal body—the National Institute of Forensic Science (NIFS)—that would oversee their operation. At least one Congressional hearing has been held to review the report's recommendations. They are further discussed in Chapter 8, "The Crime Laboratory".

Faced with exploding demands for service, the FBI made a policy decision several decades ago to accept only those state and local law-enforcement requests for evidence examinations that involved violent crimes and to virtually cease accepting their property crimes evidence. For example, the FBI no longer accepts evidence from state and local law-enforcement agencies for burglaries, thefts and frauds involving losses of less than $100,000, arson and explosive incidents involving unoccupied premises, auto thefts not involving a ring, and hit-and-run automobile accidents not involving personal injury.[56] However, if a property crime involves personal injuries or the intent to cause them, the FBI may examine the associated evidence.

When a heart artery becomes clogged and narrowed, new blood vessels, collateral arteries, develop to help circulate the blood. Much like collateral arteries, when the FBI reduced the scope of its services state and local units of government developed new capacities for the analysis of forensic evidence, creating stronger central laboratories at the state level and smaller regional ones, reducing their dependence on the FBI. In the longer view, the FBI's policy shift was a positive development.

The result is that procedures for submitting evidence for examination are similar, but varied, across the country. Evidence submitted to a crime laboratory is most often transmitted by courier, air express, or registered mail. In the ideal situation, the investigator most knowledgeable about the case takes it to the laboratory so he/she can discuss the case with appropriate examiners. Given the caseloads all crime laboratories have, this situation is the exception. In general, the method of transmitting evidence is determined by the nature of the evidence and the urgency of getting an analyst's conclusions.

Rules established by federal and state agencies regulate how some special classes of evidence must be sent. Examples of these classes are chemicals, blasting caps, flammable materials, and biological and chemical agents. Check with laboratories before submitting these types of evidence.

Unsurprisingly, many state and local laboratories leverage resources through the use of Laboratory Information Management Systems (LIMS) software for various tasks, including the automated tracking of physical evidence and reporting examination results. Laboratory internet sites provide information useful to investigators, such as an *Evidence Handbook* on acceptable procedures for collecting, marking, and packaging evidence and guidance on submitting it.

Laboratories may have one "universal form" or separate forms for different types of evidence on their Internet site and/or require a letter on agency letterhead stationary formatted in a specific way. Either way, an investigator submitting evidence will need to provide the following information:

- The investigator's name, agency, address, telephone number, and email address.
- Copies of any previous correspondence about the case, including any pertaining to other evidence that was examined earlier.
- The type of criminal act and the basic case facts related to each item of evidence.
- The name(s) and descriptive data about the individual(s) involved (subject, suspect, victim, or a combination of those categories) and the agency-assigned case number.
- A list of the evidence being submitted.
- What type(s) of examination is requested.
- Where the evidence should be returned and where the laboratory report should be sent.
- A statement if the evidence was examined by another expert in the same field, if there is local controversy, or if other law-enforcement agencies have an interest in the case.
- Any reason(s) justifying an expeditious examination request.
- The name and locator information for the assigned prosecutor, if designated already.

Some law-enforcement agencies maintain a list of crimes that the Patrol Division may retain for follow-up investigation. This list adds variety to patrol duties, creates skills that will be useful if the officers become detectives, and preserves the resources of the Investigative Division. If cases are retained for further investigation by the Patrol Division, the submission of evidence to the lab usually requires the approval of a supervisor. For cases referred for follow-up investigation, the assigned investigator often makes that decision. If submission to a private lab for analysis is contemplated a supervisor's approval is typically required because of the cost involved.

INVESTIGATIVE SUCCESS

The public thinks an investigation is a success when the perpetrator is arrested, property recovered, and the perpetrator convicted. However, law enforcement considers a case successful if it can be administratively classified in one of two different ways:

1. **"Cleared by exceptional means,"** meaning that the police can demonstrate who committed the crime but for any of several reasons cannot pursue the case further. Examples of this are when the suspect is dead, witnesses refuse to testify, and another jurisdiction refuses to extradite. Two common reasons for one state declining to extradite a suspect to a second state are he/she will be tried on more serious charges in state one or is already incarcerated there on serious charges.

2. **"Cleared by arrest,"** meaning that the perpetrator has been arrested and there is sufficient evidence to file criminal charges against him/her. Note that this definition of success does not require a conviction.

Table 3-1 shows that many types of crimes committed do not result in arrest and conviction. This is frustrating to investigators who want to take violent, predatory, and other offenders off the street. In these situations, police have to accept the fact that some crimes are simply not going to be solved because of insufficient evidence or legal restrictions. In such situations, investigators have to draw comfort from knowing they did their best, pursued all lines of inquiry, and then go on to the next case. Ultimately, time is on the side of law enforcement and eventually many suspected offenders will commit acts for which they can be arrested. The tragedy, of course, is the harm they do between when they first come to the attention of investigators and when they are ultimately arrested.

If investigators allow case disappointments to get the best of them, they run the risk of slipping into cynicism, an unattractive trait, and over a period of years will become vulnerable to engaging in unethical behavior, such as planting evidence or committing perjury.

TABLE 3-1	Crimes Cleared by Arrest or Exceptional Means	
OFFENSE		**PERCENTAGE CLEARED**
Murder/Non-negligent Manslaughter		66.6%
Aggravated assault		56.8
Forcible rape		41.2
Robbery		28.2
Larceny-theft		21.5
Motor vehicle theft		12.4
Burglary		12.5
Arson		18.5

Source: Federal Bureau of Investigation, Crime in the United States—2009 (September 2010), Table 25, no page number, www.FBI.gov/about-us/cjis/ucr/crime-in-the-u.s./2009.

KEY TERMS

administrative log
All Points Bulletin (APB)
alternative light systems (ALSs)
Americans with Disabilities
   Act (ADA)
assignment sheet
associative evidence
baseline coordinates
be-on-the-lookout (BOLO)
chain of custody
cleared by arrest
cleared by exceptional means
corpus delicti evidence
crime
crime scene
crime scene control
crime scene entry log
crime scene release
crime scene search patterns
crime scene sketch
cross-projection view
datum point
deductive reasoning

digital camera
Digital Information Management
   System (DIMS)
digital video recording
elevation view
elimination prints
evidence recovery log
felony
field notes
follow-up investigation
forensic mapping
grid system
hepatitis B (HBV)
hepatitis C (HCV)
human immunodeficiency
   virus (HIV)
incident/offense report
inductive reasoning
laser scanning
lifted-prints log
Locard's principle
macroscopic scene
media statements

microscopic scene
misdemeanor
neighborhood canvass
overhead or bird's eye view
panoramic cameras
personal protection
   equipment (PPE)
photographic log
polar coordinates
preliminary investigation
primary scene
rectangular coordinates
rough sketch
secondary scenes
smooth or finished sketch
trace evidence
trace-evidence vacuums
tracing evidence
triangulation
tuberculosis (TB)
vehicle canvass
violation

REVIEW QUESTIONS

1. What skills and qualities are needed by investigators?
2. What are the objectives of crime scene investigation?
3. How would you describe the "lucky" investigator?
4. What are preliminary and follow-up investigations?
5. How are inductive and deductive reasoning used in investigation?
6. Why is crime scene coordination so important?
7. What factors can shape or impact a plan to process a crime scene?
8. What are the three broad categories of evidence?
9. How is a crime scene entry log properly used?
10. What is a neighborhood canvass?
11. What are the "rules" for crime scene investigators?
12. What four considerations dominate the crime scene search?
13. Define *primary scene* and *secondary scene(s)*.
14. What are macroscopic and microscopic scenes?
15. What infectious disease risks are faced by crime scene investigators?
16. What methods are available to visually document the crime scene?
17. Draw a rough crime scene sketch of your bedroom, assuming that there are two shell casings on the floor and one bullet hole in the west wall.

INTERNET ACTIVITIES

1. Visit the Crime Scene Investigator Network website at *www.crime-scene-investigator.net*. Read the section on "Crime Scene Response."
2. Learn more about laser and panoramic camera imaging of crime scenes at *www.3rdTech.com* and *www.panoscan.com*.

▶ Weapons are often found at the scene of a crime. Here, a large "bolo" type knife is found at the exit of the front door leading to the living room where a young woman was murdered in a domestic quarrel. This is the eighth piece of physical evidence found at the scene. A rigid ruler is included to give an indication of size and proportionality.

(Courtesy Dallas Texas Police Department)

4

PHYSICAL EVIDENCE

If physical evidence is to be useful in exonerating the innocent and pursuing suspects it must be treated in accordance with its importance. The evidence must be located, its position documented, be collected, be identified by marks/writing on it and/or on the package in which it is placed, and be transmitted to the evidence room or the crime laboratory while the collector maintains the chain of custody.[1] This chapter describes the proper protocols of dealing with various types of physical evidence. Adherence to approved procedures maintains the potential that the evidence can be a powerful part of the investigative process and avoids the embarrassment that careless handling is sure to bring. Even more serious is the possibility that but for the careless handling of evidence the prosecutor would have filed charges against a suspect.

CLASS VERSUS INDIVIDUAL CHARACTERISTICS

To fully appreciate the potential value of physical evidence, the investigator must understand the difference between class and individual characteristics. Characteristics of physical evidence that are common to a group of objects or persons are termed **class characteristics.** Regardless of how thoroughly examined, such evidence can be placed only into a broad category; an individual identification cannot be made because there is a possibility of more than one source for the evidence.[2] Examples of this type of evidence include all unworn Nike athletic shoes of a particular model, the new, unmarked face of a manufacturer's specific type of hammer, and soil. In contrast, evidence with **individual characteristics** can be identified, with a high degree of probability, as originating with a particular person or source (Figure 4-1).[3] The ability to establish individuality distinguishes this type of physical evidence from that possessing only class characteristics. Some examples of evidence with individual characteristics are fingerprints, palm prints, and footprints.

Conceptually, the distinction between class and individual characteristics is clear. But as a practical matter, the crime scene technician or investigator often may not be able to make this differentiation and must rely on the results

▲ **FIGURE 4-1   Individual class evidence**
(*Top left*) Shoeprint left on face of murder victim; (*top right*) shoeprint left on hood of car at scene; (*bottom left*) duplicating the bottom of a shoe seized from suspect; (*bottom right*) wear patterns and slight nicks in the shoe's tread made it individual characteristic evidence. Additionally, DNA from blood caught in the shoe tread and the victim tied the shoe to contact with the victim. (Courtesy Detroit Michigan State Police)

yielded by crime laboratory examination (Figure 4-1). Thus, although the investigator must recognize that physical evidence that allows for individualization is of more value, he or she should not dismiss evidence that appears to offer only class characteristics, because it may show individual characteristics through laboratory examination. Furthermore, a preponderance of class-characteristic evidence tying a suspect (or other items in the suspect's possession) to the scene strengthens the case for prosecution. Note also that occasionally class-characteristic evidence may be of such an unusual nature that it has much greater value than that ordinarily associated with evidence of this type. In an Alaska case, a suspect was apprehended in the general area where a burglary had been committed; the pry bar found in his possession contained white stucco, which was of considerable importance, since the building burglarized was the only white stucco building in that town.[4] Finally, class-characteristic evidence can be useful in excluding suspects in a crime, resulting in a more effective use of investigative effort.

COMPARISON SAMPLES

Much of the work of forensic science involves comparing various types of samples. Special terms are used to refer to these samples, and you must know what they mean to communicate with the laboratory and understand its reports. At the most general level, comparison samples may be from **unknown or questioned sources** or from **known sources;** each of these two main categories has three subcategories.

Unknown or Questioned Samples

1. *Recovered crime scene sample whose source is in question:* This evidence may have been left, for example, by either victims or suspects. A typical question is "Whose fingerprints are on the window used as the point of entry?"

2. *Questioned evidence that may have been transferred to an offender during the commission of a crime and been*

taken away by him or her: When compared with the evidence from a known source, this evidence can be used to link the suspect to a person, vehicle, tool, or weapon. For example, the question might be "Do any of the hairs combed from the suspect's hair match those of the victim?"

3. *Evidence from an unknown or questioned source that can be used to link multiple offenses:* This material might link crimes that were committed by the same person, tool, or weapon. Assuming that a suspect is arrested at a murder scene with a pistol in his overcoat, the question raised could be "Did this gun fire the bullets recovered from the victims of a double homicide a week ago?"[5]

Known Samples

1. *Standard or reference sample:* This is material from a known or verifiable source. It is compared to similar material from an unknown source to determine whether an association or linkage exists between a crime scene, a victim, and the offender. For example, a sample of blood is taken under medical conditions from the suspect so that it can be compared with blood on the victim's shirt.

2. *Control or blank sample:* This is material from a known source that was uncontaminated by the crime (for example, carpet fibers taken from the far corner of a room in which a body was found). It is used to make sure that the material on which evidence was deposited—for instance, carpet fibers, under the body, on which there is blood, does not interfere with laboratory testing.

3. *Elimination sample:* This type of sample is taken from a source known to have had lawful access to the crime scene, such as a police officer, medical technician, or the occupant. It is compared with unknown samples of the same type from the scene so that matches can be eliminated, thereby highlighting non-matches. An example is elimination prints. If latent fingerprints recovered at a crime scene do not match the fingerprints of those who have lawful access to the area, they immediately become of investigative interest in terms of determining whose prints they are.[6]

SOIL AND POLLEN

Soil can be the natural accumulation of earth materials, such as weathering rocks, minerals, and decomposing plants, pollen, bacteria and fungus.[7] It may also contain human-made materials, including pieces of brick, glass, and paint. By comparing color, texture, and composition in soil examinations, one can determine whether soils share a common origin.[8] Although soil is class-characteristic evidence, its analysis can help focus investigations and discredit alibis:

A man was arrested and charged with the beating of a young girl. The scene of the crime was a construction site adjacent to a newly poured concrete wall. The soil was sand, which had been transported to the scene for construction purposes. As such, it had received additional mixing during the moving and construction process and was quite distinctive. The glove of the suspect contained sand that was similar to that found at the scene and significantly different in composition and particle size from that in the area of the suspect's home. This was important because the suspect claimed that the soil on the gloves came from his garden.[9]

An elderly woman was robbed and murdered in a Washington, D.C., park, and her body was found under a park bench. Within a short time, a suspect was apprehended as a result of a description given by a witness who had seen the person leaving the park on the night of the murder. It was obvious that the suspect had been involved in a struggle and had soil adhering to his clothing and inside his trouser cuffs. He claimed to have been in a fight in another part of the city and gave the location of the fight. Study of the soil near the park bench and of that collected from the scene of the alleged fight revealed that the soil from the suspect's clothing was similar to soil near the park bench but did not compare favorably with samples from the area of the described fight. These comparisons strongly suggested that the suspect had been in contact with the ground in that area and cast strong doubt on his statement that he had not been in the park for years. Furthermore, the lack of similarity between the clothing soil samples and those from the area in which he claimed to have been fighting questioned the validity of his alibi.[10]

The pollen in soil or on plants and grass can also be very significant in determining whether or not a suspect was at the scene:

In a case of alleged sexual assault, the pollen content of samples from a grassy crime scene were compared to pollen recovered from the suspect's clothes and shoes. A very strong correlation with the variety of pollens present on the suspect's clothing and the sample collected at the scene strongly supported the conclusion that the suspect was at the scene.[11]

Although soil and pollen are class-characteristic evidence, their specificity can approach the level of individual characterization:

> In a rape case, the knees of the suspect's trousers contained encrusted soil samples; the sample from the right knee was different from that collected from the left. In examining the crime scene, investigators found two impressions in the soil corresponding to a right and a left knee; samples taken from these two impressions were different. The soil sample from the left-knee impression compared with that removed from the left trouser knee of the suspect, as did the right-knee impression and the right trouser knee soils. The significant difference in soil type between the two knee impressions and their consistency with samples obtained from the suspect's trousers strongly indicated his presence at the scene.[12]

LOCATING AND HANDLING SOIL EVIDENCE

Soil residues and smears on such surfaces as clothing, people, and vehicles may not be of sufficient quantity for analysis. Unless the suspects were apprehended at the scene or in very close proximity to it, the soil on their feet/shoe soles and the tires of their cars may have been contaminated, and therefore may not be of evidentiary value.[13]

Soil evidence may be important when the suspect drives or walks on unpaved areas, since it is picked up by tire treads or the bottom of shoes and the cuffs of pants. It may also be recovered in a number of other places, such as on the floorboard of the subject's car or on articles in the trunk of the vehicle, including shovels and blankets. In hit-and-run accidents, soil samples may be encountered, for example, in one unusual case, a solid soil sample in the rough shape of a triangle with 3-inch sides was found and later substantially matched to a space on the underside of the suspect's vehicle. The guidelines shown next should be followed in handling soil evidence:

1. Soil conditions at the scene can change, so gather the soil as quickly as sound action permits.
2. Collect soil not only from the crime scene but also from the logical points of access to, and escape from, the scene. Place the samples in clean plastic vials and labeled with the date, time, name of the crime scene technician, and the case number, if known.
3. Collect soil samples where there are noticeable changes in color, texture, and composition.
4. Collect soil samples from a depth that is consistent with the depth at which the questioned soil may

have originated. In most cases, samples will be a tablespoon of material taken no more than ½ inch from the surface.
5. When possible, collect soil samples from alibi areas, such as the worksite, yard, or garden of the suspect.
6. Make a detailed drawing or map documenting where and at what depth you collected each soil sample.
7. Do not remove soil adhering to shoes, clothing, and tools. Do not process tools for latent prints at this time. Air dry the soiled garments and package them separately in paper bags. Avoid jostling and transport to the crime lab for analysis and further processing.
8. Submit unknown or questioned soil and known samples in separate leak-proof containers such as film canisters or plastic pill bottles. Avoid the use of paper envelopes or glass containers. If there are lumps in the soil, pack it in a way that keeps the lumps intact.[14]
9. In packaging soil or other types of evidence, take care to avoid **cross contamination** of the samples.
10. Soil impressions made by footwear should be photographed to scale and cast before any soil samples are taken.
11. At indoor crime scenes, special vacuums may be used to collect soil samples from carpets and floors that may have been introduced by the suspect(s). Collect and document each procedure before transporting the contents to the crime lab.[15]

The guidelines for collecting pollen evidence are consistent with those for soil evidence. It may be necessary to take grass or other clippings from different heights.

FOOTWEAR, FOOT, AND TIRES: PRINTS AND IMPRESSIONS

Prints may be made from (1) footwear, including shoes, boots, and sandals; (2) the soles of feet; and (3) tires, and all are common types of evidence.[16] These prints are formed when the soles of footwear, soles of feet, and tires are contaminated with foreign matter such as blood or dust and leave a print on a firm base, such as a floor, the seat of a chair, paper, or cloth (Figure 4-2).[17] Such prints are called **residue prints.** In contrast, **impressions** result from footwear, feet, and tires treading in some moldable material, such as earth, clay, and snow.[18] For residue prints and impressions the sequence is always photograph and then collect the evidence.

Residue and impression evidence can provide investigative leads, such as the number of suspects at the scene, where they walked in the scene, some indication of the

▲ **FIGURE 4-2**

Tire print left on pedestrian victim's shirt by hit-and-run vehicle

Police located a potentially involved vehicle. Tire print and other physical evidence established it struck the pedestrian. However, the car's owner still needed to be put behind the wheel. Confronted with the evidence, he confessed. (Courtesy Seattle Washington State Police)

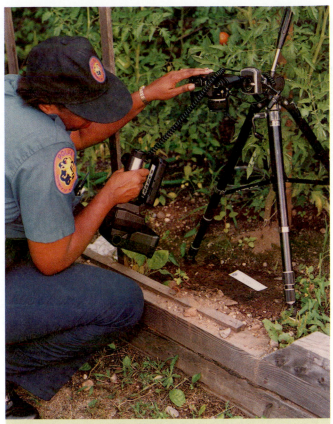

▲ **FIGURE 4-3   Footwear impression photography**

A crime scene technician documenting a footwear impression. The impression runs left to right, roughly between the front legs of the tripod. The white slip of paper "North" of the impression has the case number and other information on it. (Courtesy Nassau County, New York Police Department)

sequence of events, the direction taken by the suspects as they left the scene, the type and brand of shoe or tire, and the type of vehicle involved.[19] Although European agencies report collecting footwear evidence in over 70% of their cases, its use in this country is much less, possibly due to a lack of awareness and proper training by crime scene technicians.[20]

A number of software programs, such as SICAR, can compare footwear and tire evidence. **SoleMate** contains the records of 24,000 sports, work, and casual footwear. Its purpose is to identify footwear prints recovered at a crime scene. It is updated continuously and distributed on CD to users quarterly. **CrimeShoe** has a collection of 23,000 shoe and sole images representing 950 brands. Using the Internet, investigators can upload their prints. If CrimeShoe cannot make an identification or provide other relevant information there is no charge. **TreadMate** is a reference collection of 8,500 tires, available for a fee on CD issued annually.

PRESERVING RESIDUE PRINTS

Residue prints are two dimensional; they have a length and a width and no appreciable height. They may be from a dry origin, such as dust, or a wet one, for example, stepped in oil.[21] Residue prints may or may not be readily visible. If they are not immediately apparent, turn off the lights and search for prints using a flashlight held close to, but obliquely from, the surface you are examining or use a forensic light source. When you find prints:

1. Take general crime scene photos showing the location of the prints.
2. Take photos from directly overhead using lighting and a tripod. A photo with a label near the print should be taken to correlate photos with the photo log (Figure 4-3). Subsequent shots should include a scale near the print. Ideally, "L"-shaped footwear/tire photographic scale should be used to capture

width and length dimensions. Alternatively, two regular scales can be crossed and used for the same purpose. These directions also apply to photographing impressions.

There are several methods by which residue prints can be recovered. The best approach is to send the original evidence to the lab. It should be taped in a rigid container so that there is no opportunity for accidental erasure of the footwear print; do not wrap it in plastic, because this can cause a partial erasure of the image.

Residue prints may be collected by using a large transparent adhesive lifter and then mounting the lifter on an appropriately colored card. Similarly, an appropriately colored and sized rubber-gelatin lifter can be employed. Coated with a thin film of very sensitive gelatin, the lifter is carefully placed over the print and then removed. Transparent, black, and white lifters are available. Transparent and white lifters can be used for dark prints; a black lifter should be used for light prints.[22] Residue prints can also be lifted through the use of an electrostatic dust print lifter (EDPL) (Figure 4-4). The resulting image must be photographed as soon as possible, since it is in dust and therefore not permanent.

PRESERVING IMPRESSIONS

Impressions are three-dimensional; they have a length, width, and height (see Figure 4-5). Impressions are physically preserved by casting. Plaster of Paris is no longer recommended for use in casting impressions. **Dental stone** or die stone—for example, Traxtone—is the most used casting medium because of greater strength, quicker setting time, and ease of use; also, cleaning casts made doesn't result in any loss of detail, and provides more detailed impressions. Because of the strength of dental stone and die stone, the cast does not need to be reinforced.

The first step in casting is the preparation of the impression. The rule is that the impression should not be disturbed. Thus, if twigs, leaves, or other materials are stuck *in* the impression, they should remain there. Only loose material lying *on* the impression, such as leaves, should be moved. If the impression to be cast is in sandy soil, hair spray may be used to "fix" the details, taking care not to disturb them as it is applied. The use of a casting frame may not be necessary if the ground is fairly level.

In Chapter 3, "Investigators, the Investigative Process, and the Crime Scene," impression casting materials were identified—for instance, Shake-N-Cast, which has all the mixing materials preassembled in one bag. This section covers preparing and using dental stone "from scratch" to cast a shoe impression. About 2 pounds of dental stone and 12 ounces of water are needed.

Place the dental stone in a 1-gallon Ziplock bag and add the water.[23] Massage the Ziplock bag; you want to reach a consistency of thick paint or pancake batter. The

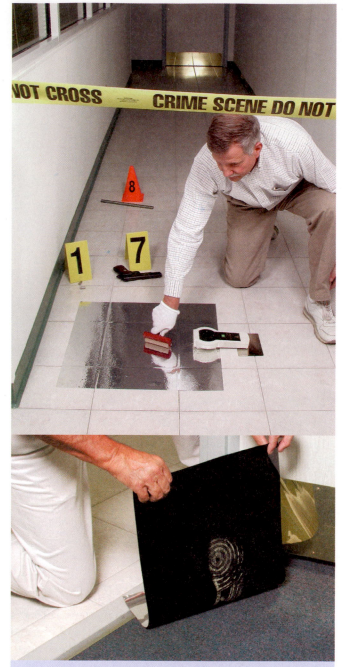

▲ **FIGURE 4-4**
Use of electrostatic dust print lifter (EDPL)
(*top*) A lifting mat is laid over a shoe dust print and electrically charged using the high voltage power supply unit on the right side of the mat. An insulated roller systematically is moved across the silver side of lifting mat. (*bottom*) The dust print is transferred to the dark-colored underside of the lift mat. (**Courtesy SIRCHIE Fingerprint Laboratories, Inc.**)

dental stone is then poured alongside the impression and allowed to flow into it as opposed to pouring it directly on the impression. Make sure you pour it so that the contents of a single Ziplock bag cover the entire impression.

Otherwise, there will be a lap mark in the cast that is likely to cause a loss of detail.

Dental stone sets fairly rapidly. Die stone sets up quicker, in 12 to 15 minutes. Soil evidence should be collected from the bottom of the impression after the cast is removed.

If there is standing water in the impression, the following steps should be taken: (1) place a casting frame around the impression so that a cast 2 inches deep can be made; (2) gently sift dental stone that has not been mixed with water directly into the impression to a depth of about 1 inch; (3) add enough mixed dental stone to form a second 1-inch layer; and (4) allow the cast to set in place for at least 1 hour.[24]

The crime scene technician or other person casting the footwear impression should enter her or his initials, the date, and other relevant details on the bottom of the cast before it dries.[25] For submission to the laboratory, wrap the cast in tissue, clean paper, packing peanuts, or multiple paper bags. The laboratory examiner will clean the cast and examine it after it has dried for 24–48 hours.

PRESERVING SHOE IMPRESSIONS IN SNOW

Dental stone is also the preferred material for casting impressions in snow, replacing the more difficult and time-consuming process of using sulfur, which had to be heated. Impressions in snow should first be photographed in the manner previously described; however, impressions in snow are difficult to photograph because of a lack of contrast.[26] To overcome this, lightly spray several layers of red-colored Snow Print Wax (SPW) or spray paint over the impression at a 45-degree angle from the surface (Figure 4-6). Pause briefly between layers to let the SPW dry; in addition to coloring the impression, SPW

leaves a waxy surface on it that prevents the small amount of heat generated by the drying dental stone from erasing the fine details of the impression. To combat heat formation when casting in snow, use snow or cold-water mix in the dental stone.

The spray nozzle should be held 24 inches to 36 inches from the impression so the force of the aerosol doesn't alter it. An impression highlighted in this manner will absorb heat from the sun and should be shielded until ready to photograph and cast. Because some heat is generated when dental stone is mixed, a box should be placed over the cast for at least 1 hour as it dries.

PAINT

Paint evidence may be encountered in many types of investigation, but perhaps most commonly it is transferred from one source to another in burglaries and hit-and-run accidents. Paint is transferred as fresh smears, dried chips, or "chalking" from old, dry paint. Many burglaries involve a tool that was used to pry a door or window open, transferring paint from the building to the suspect's tools or clothing. In hit-and-run accidents, paint from the fleeing vehicle may be found on a pedestrian or another car.

In hit-and-run cases, the make and model of the involved vehicle might be identified by comparing paint evidence to the records in the FBI's National Automotive Paint File on original-manufacturer finishes. **Paint Data Query (PDQ),** another database, is a global information system on the paint used by the original manufacturer. Each of the roughly 22 countries participating in this system maintains a central point of information; in

▲ **FIGURE 4-6   Snow print wax use**
Having already photographed the shoe impression in the snow, the officer sprays red-colored Snow Print Wax on the impression (*top*); the impression is rephotographed (*middle*); and the dental-stone mix is poured from a plastic pouch onto the impression (*bottom*). (Courtesy Lewiston, Maine Police Department)

A 53-year man was hit by an unidentified vehicle and dragged more than 200 feet, dying from his injuries. No witnesses were present, and the police did not have any other leads regarding the suspect vehicle. A gold metallic painted plastic fragment recovered from the scene was sent to the lab, along with the victim's clothing containing gold metallic paint particles.

The PDQ system found one color, Aztec Gold, which closely matched the paint particles recovered from the victim's clothing. It was used on 11,000 Ford Mustangs made in 1997. Only two of these vehicles were registered in the jurisdiction of the offense. An officer located a 1997 Aztec Gold Ford Mustang with scratches on its hood and a piece of painted plastic missing from the flair molding on the left side. The flair molding and paint samples were collected from the vehicle and submitted for comparison to the materials recovered from the scene and victim's clothing. The painted plastic piece was physically fitted together with the flair molding and the recovered gold metallic paint particles were consistent with paint samples taken from the suspect vehicle.

Although these results provided some closure to the victim's family, the suspect had been deported for other reasons several days before the vehicle was located.[27]

Usually, paint is class-characteristic evidence, although in some cases it reaches the level of individual evidence. If the chips are large enough, it may be possible to make a fracture match between a questioned and a known source (Figure 4-7). A **fracture match** occurs when it is established that two physical items were once co-joined. For example, a paint chip recovered from a tool in a burglary suspect's possession exactly fits an area on a paint sample recovered from the point of forced entry in a burglary. If a building or car has been painted multiple times, the layer structure of a questioned sample can be compared to a known source as to the number of layers, the sequence of colors, the thickness of each layer, and the chemical composition of each layer (Figure 4-8).[28] Thus, when one is recovering paint chips, one must go all the way to the base surface.

If paint evidence is collected from a burglary's point of entry, the samples should be collected from an area immediately adjacent to the area damaged by the suspect while forcing entry.[29] This principle also applies to taking paint samples from automobiles that have been involved in a hit-and-run. Each chip sample taken should be packaged separately. One rule of thumb is to collect four

the United States and Canada it is the FBI and the Royal Canadian Mounted Police (RCMP).

The value of paint evidence is seen in the case study that follows.

◀ FIGURE 4-7
Paint chip fracture match
(Courtesy Texas Department of Public Safety)

▲ **FIGURE 4-8   Side view of a multilayered paint chip**
(Courtesy Wisconsin Dept of Justice - State Crime Laboratory)

they are often fragile. A clear solid plastic container is ideal for packaging a paint chip, because it can be seen. Paper envelopes are acceptable if they are properly sealed and protected from being bent or compressed.

The sheets placed under and over hit-and-run victims in the ambulance while they are being transported may also be a good source of paint evidence; the clothing and sheets may have fresh blood on them. These items should be allowed to air dry naturally in properly ventilated lockers. Before hanging these items in the lockers or other secure place, place fresh paper under the items so any evidence that falls as the drying occurs can be recovered. When dried, place the items separately in their own paper bag and submit them to the laboratory.

samples around each separate area that is involved with the incident.

A new razor blade or evidence scalpel should be used for each paint chip recovered to avoid contamination. Burglary tools that may contain paint evidence should be carefully wrapped and submitted to the lab without disturbing the evidence. Similarly, the clothes of a burglary suspect arrested at the scene or in its vicinity and the clothes of a pedestrian hit-and-run victim should be submitted to the lab without attempting to collect paint evidence. Paint smears may also be useful, and it is desirable to submit the item on which the smear is found—for example, a car's bumper, to the laboratory.

Do not collect paint chips or particles with transparent tape or use it to fix the evidence to a card. Paint chips and particles should not be placed in plastic bags, because they will develop a static electrical charge that makes them hard to handle. Placing paint chips in cotton is not good practice, because separating them is difficult and

GLASS

Generally, glass is class-characteristic evidence, although in some fact situations it may be individual class. Glass is important as physical evidence because it is so common. Suspects may take it from the scene in their clothing or hair. Laboratory examination of glass evidence may be able to determine:

1. the type of glass, such as tempered or container;
2. the direction of force used to break the glass (Figure 4-9);
3. the direction and sequence of shots fired through a closed glass window;
4. similarity between evidence glass and standards;
5. a fracture physical match, establishing that the pieces were formerly joined (Figure 4-10).[30]

▲ **FIGURE 4-9**

Determining the direction of a bullet's penetration of glass

Police were called to a home where the occupant alleged that while standing in the living room someone standing outside of the house fired a shot at him. The complainant dropped to the floor, crawled to a nearby desk, and retrieved his revolver. After a short time he stood up and the person outside fired a sec-ond and third time. At that point the complainant fired a single shot at the outsider, whom he recognized as a man who lived nearby. The alleged shooter had a different version of events. He was walking past the complainant's house and was shot at three times before he shot once in self-defense at the man in the house. All shots passed through the glass of a single window. Both man said there was "bad blood" between them.

Figure 4-11 illustrates the four bullet holes found in the window by the police. When a glass window is broken by a shot, both **radial fracture** and **concentric fracture** lines may develop. Radial fractures move away from the point of impact; concentric fracture lines more or less circle the same point. From Figure 4-9 we know that shot B came before shot A, because the radial and concentric fracture lines of shot B stop those of shot A. From 4-11, we know nothing of the relationship of holes C and D. However, as shown in Figure 4-9, we can determine the direction from which a bullet penetrated glass: on the side opposite the surface of initial impact, there will be a characteristic cone-shaped area. In the case being illustrated, shots A, B, and D all contained a cone-shaped characteristic on the inside of the window, indicating that these three shots had been fired from the outside. Shot C had the cone-shaped area on the outside, revealing that it had been fired from inside the house. Thus the physical evidence substantiated the complainant's statement.

► **FIGURE 4-10**

Glass fracture match of a rear tail light and assembly

Pieces of red tail light were found at the scene of a hit-and-run and matched with pieces still intact in the tail light assembly when the suspect vehicle was located. (Courtesy Mr. Ed Hueske and Ms. Sherry Bethune, Forensic Training and Consulting, LLC, 2007)

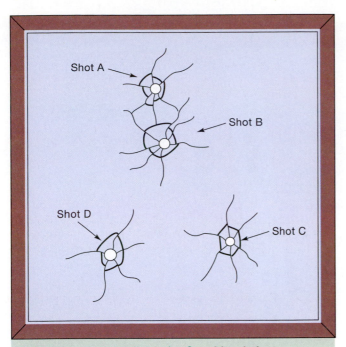

▲ **FIGURE 4-11   Bullet holes found in window**

Walking a beat in a downtown business section in the late evening hours, a uniformed officer heard an alarm go off and saw an individual round the corner and run toward him at full speed. On seeing the officer, the individual started to double back the other way and then stopped. As the office approached, the man started to flee, but he stopped when commanded to do so. The man then told the officer that he had observed two people standing in front of a jewelry store window take a brick from a shopping bag and throw it through the window. The person said that, on seeing this, he became frightened and ran. Subsequent investigation revealed that the person who had rounded the corner was in fact the perpetrator of the offense and that he had fled before obtaining any material from the display window, because a lookout had seen a police car responding to a call in an adjacent block and had given warning. Processing of the perpetrator's clothing revealed pieces of glass in the cuff of his pants sufficiently large to make fracture matches with glass at the scene.

It is essential that the crime scene technician and investigator understand the ways in which glass reacts to force. Often this knowledge is critical in determining whether a crime has been committed, establishing the sequence of action, and evaluating the credibility of statements given by parties at the scene. Before any glass or window pane is moved at all, it should be photographed

in detail to reflect the exact features of the existent glass fractures. Moving the evidence may cause fracture extensions that could change the conclusions of the investigator and laboratory analyst. At crime scenes involving automobiles, the utility of glass evidence may be compromised by rescue personnel working to free occupants and wreckers pulling involved vehicles to the side of the road.

This example underscore the importance of the investigator's paying particular attention to determining what occurred between the time of the crime and the time he/she arrived at the scene. A key question that the investigator must attempt to answer with glass and other types of evidence is whether the position and characteristic of evidence could have been altered by the suspect, a witness, the victim, emergency medical personnel, or another officer. Stated differently, do not assume that the position of evidence you locate is in its original position.

HANDLING GLASS EVIDENCE

Ordinarily, if glass evidence is to be processed for fingerprints, it will be done in the laboratory.[31] Tape should not be used to collect glass evidence in the field because it interferes with laboratory processing. As with other types of evidence, photography precedes the collection of glass evidence.

The physical properties used for comparison of known and questioned glass specimens are color, fluorescence, thickness, surface features, and curvature.[32] If glass is being submitted for comparison purposes, that is, to determine whether the particles may have originated from a common source, they are ordinarily small, and the following precautions should be taken: (1) glass evidence from combing hair should be done over clean paper; (2) clothing and shoes should be packaged separately, and in no case should the victim's and suspect's items be comingled in any way; (3) if clothing items are wet, air dry them in the manner previously described; (4) glass may be embedded in the skin and open wounds of victims and suspects, and recovery by qualified medical personnel may be required; (5) submit weapons and tools without disturbing glass evidence; (6) samples of laminated glass—for example, windshields, should be labeled "inside" and "outside" and separately packaged in leak proof containers; (7) if a vehicle is involved, use a vacuum to collect the glass from each area of the vehicle; evidence collected from different areas should be packaged separately, and a new vacuum bag should be used for each new area processed; and (8) known and questioned glass samples, and evidence from victims and suspects, should be shipped separately to avoid contamination. These types of evidence should be wrapped in clean paper and sealed in a rigid container, such as a box, or if sufficiently small, a plastic container. Do not submit the evidence in a glass container.

If door, window, or other framed glass is to be submitted for possible fracture matches, submit the entire frame

▲ FIGURE 4-12   Comparison of cotton fibers
The victim, who was wearing a red shirt, was stabbed by a man. Fibers from the victim's shirt (*above*) were compared to fibers collected from the assailant's pants (*right*). The two sets of fibers were consistent in all respects, although this finding does not exclude other sources for the fibers on the assailant's pants. (**Courtesy Chicago Police Department**)

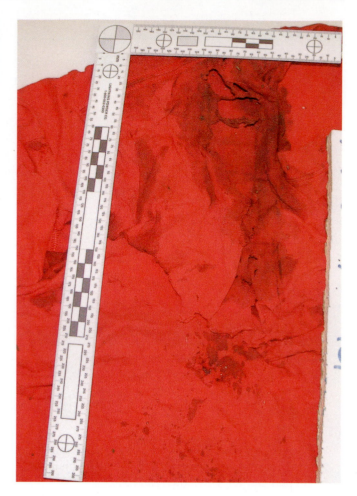

in which all glass originally existed, marking the sides of the frame to show which way is inside and outside, along with marking it "top," "bottom," "left," and "right." Broken pieces should be carefully packaged in separate containers to avoid breakage in transit. Depending on the sizes involved, it may be necessary to place the glass between sturdy pieces of cardboard or plywood.[33]

FIBERS, CLOTH FRAGMENTS, AND IMPRESSIONS

Fibers are of value as evidence because they incorporate such variables as material type, number of fibers per strand, number of strands, thickness of fibers and strands, amount and direction of twists, dye content, type of weave, and the possible presence of foreign matter embedded in them. When something composed of fibers, such as clothing, comes into contact with other clothing or objects, there is the opportunity for the exchange or transfer of fibers. Fibers may also be located on the body of the victim or the suspect, serving to connect one to the other (Figure 4-12).

Cloth fragments may be found at the scene of violent crimes or along the perpetrator's point of approach to, or exit from, a crime scene (Figure 4-13). They may be found on such diverse points as a chain fence, the splintered edge of a wooden building, or protruding nails. In hit-and-run offenses, cloth fragments may be found in the grille or undercarriage of the striking vehicle. Cloth impressions are found infrequently in investigations, usually on wet paint or some surface of a vehicle involved in striking a pedestrian.

Both fibers and cloth fragments should be packaged in a pillbox or in folded paper that is taped shut. Only on rare occasions will it be possible to obtain a cast of a cloth impression. This effort, however, should invariably be preceded by the taking of several photographs; at least one of these photos should show a scale to allow for comparisons at some future date.

STRING, CORD, ROPE, AND TAPE

String, cord, rope, and tape evidence is usually found in robbery, murder, rape, and kidnapping cases. It is also associated with accidental hangings by children and accidental

◀ **FIGURE 4-13   Fabric match**
Physical matching (sometimes called *physical* fit or *jigsaw* fit) is powerful and incontrovertible evidence. Shown here is a fragment from a victim's clothing found in the grille of the suspect's vehicle involved in a hit-and-run case. The fabric fragment fitted the victim's raincoat and conclusively established the contact between the suspect's vehicle and the victim. (© The McGraw-Hill Companies, photographer Keith Eng)

◀ **FIGURE 4-14   Tape match**
In a particularly violent rape, the suspect used gray duct tape to tie the victim's hands and cover her mouth. The victim was left for dead, but she managed to crawl out an open window and seek help. The top portion of the photograph is the filament tape recovered from the victim's face covering her mouth. The bottom part of the photograph is the end of the tape roll found in the suspect's pocket. By showing that these two ends of the duct tape match, a physical match is established. (Courtesy Portland, Oregon Police Bureau)

sexual asphyxiations. String, cord and rope have essentially the same characteristics and share some characteristics of fibers. Known samples of these types of evidence can be compared to crime scene evidence on the basis of composition, diameter, color, and construction; if a tracer is present, it is possible to identify the manufacturer. There is some preliminary evidence if string, cord, and rope is made from plant material, and contains cells from the plant of origin, then DNA analysis techniques can exclude or include as a source remnants found in a suspect's possession as compared to a length used to bind a victim.[34]

In instances where the victim was tied, it may be possible to match the ends of the string, cord, rope, and tape with the rest of the roll in the suspect's possession (Figure 4-14). When rope evidence is removed from a victim or from anyplace, knots should never be severed. Instead, a place away from the knot should be cut and a piece of twine used to loop the two ends together. A tag should be attached to indicate that the investigator has cut the rope. Evidence about knot tier handedness and use of habitual knots has been scarce and conflicting. A 2010 study of 562 subjects did reveal differences in patterns of knot tying between left and right handers.[35] Ordinarily, because of its resilient nature, the packaging of this type of evidence poses no particular problem when standard procedures are followed.

FINGERPRINTS

Several different parts of the body—such as palms, fingers, toes, and the soles of the feet—have friction ridges that can form a "fingerprint." All such prints are collected, preserved, and identified using similar methods. But it may not be immediately apparent which part of a body made the print; as used here, "fingerprint" includes all prints made by friction ridges. Basically, a **fingerprint** is a replica of the friction ridges that touched the surface on which the print was found. These ridge characteristics are also called **minutiae.**

▶ FIGURE 4-15
Fingerprint patterns
Fingerprints are initially classified into one of the major classifications shown here.

Plain Arch   Tented Arch   Ulnar Loop   Radial Loop

Plain Whorl   Central Pocket Loop   Double Loop Whorl   Accidental Whorl

With just a few exceptions—persons with birth defects or amputations—everyone has fingerprints. This universal characteristic is a prime factor in establishing a standard of identification. Since a print of one finger has never been known to duplicate exactly another fingerprint—even of the same person or an identical twin[36]—it is possible to identify an individual with just one impression. The relative ease with which a set of inked fingerprints can be taken as a means of identification is a further reason for using this standard. Despite such factors as aging and environmental influences, a person's fingerprints do not change. This unaltering pattern is a permanent record of the individual throughout life.

BASIS FOR FINGERPRINT IDENTIFICATION

The ridge detail of fingerprints—including ends of ridges, their separations, and their relationship to one another—constitutes the basis for identification of fingerprints. There are as many as 150 ridge characteristics in an averaged-sized fingerprint.[37] The major **fingerprint patterns** are shown in Figure 4-15. About 65% of the population have loops, roughly 30% have whorls, and the remaining 5% have arches.[38] Points are identical characteristics that are found in fingerprints from known and questioned sources. Positive identification cannot be made when an unexplained difference appears, regardless of the points of similarity.

There is no reliable method for judging the age of latent fingerprints, although the context in which they are found may provide some information. However, both here and in England over the past decade, research has been conducted on how the chemical composition of latent fingerprints varies from the time they are deposited; there is also interesting work suggesting that the chemical composition of latent fingerprints may at some point allow us to make some statements about the

approximate age of the donor.[39] The more immediate application of the research on the chemical composition of latent fingerprints will be improvements in the methods of developing them.

There is no standard requirement of print size for positive identification. It is necessary only that the partial print be large enough to contain the necessary points of individuality. This number may be found in an area as small as the flat end of a pencil. Thus, the rule whenever an investigator develops a partial latent print that appears to have only a few ridges is that it should be submitted to the laboratory.

Some persons erroneously believe that the points used for identification of the fingerprint occur only in the pattern area of the finger. In fact, all the different types occur outside the pattern area on the finger as well as on the first and second joints of the finger and the entire palm of the hand. They are also present on the toes and the entire sole of the foot; they may be found in any area where friction ridges occur.

LATENT FINGERPRINTS

Latent prints can be used in two different ways: (1) to refer to all three categories of prints identified below, in the sense that they have been found at the scene of the crime or on items of investigative interest—for example, a murder weapon recovered from a lake far from the primary crime scene—and (2) to refer specifically to latent/invisible prints. Ordinarily, the context in which the term is used helps in understanding which meaning is intended.

1. **Plastic prints** are three-dimensional; they are molded, indented, or impressed into some pliable surface (Figure 4-16). They are created when fingers touch material such as a painted surface that is still "tacky," oil films, explosives, edible fats, putty, dust, caulking, and similar surfaces.

◄ **Figure 4-16 Plastic print**
A suspect left this print in a child's "silly putty" while keeping his victims at bay during a home invasion robbery. (© The McGraw-Hill Companies, Inc./Jill Braaten)

2. **Patent/contaminated/visible prints** result after fingers, contaminated with foreign matter such as soot, oils, face powder, ink, and some types of safe insulation, touch a clean surface. The most common type of contaminated print results when a finger is pressed into a thin layer of dust before touching a smooth surface. Fingerprints that result from blood contamination are sometimes less distinct than those that result from other types of contamination. Patent prints are readily visible to the eye.

3. **Latent/invisible prints** are unseen or hidden. When a crime scene is processed for latent fingerprints, they are made visible by "developing" them, a process described later in this chapter. Latent prints are associated with the small amounts of body perspiration and oil that are normally found on the friction ridges. A latent fingerprint is created when the friction ridges deposit these materials on a surface.

CONDITIONS AFFECTING THE QUALITY OF LATENT FINGERPRINTS

The quality of latent fingerprints is affected by a number of conditions, including these:

1. *The surface on which the print is deposited:* The type of surface on which latent prints are left affects their durability and the type of process used to develop them. There are three broad categories of surfaces:[40]
   a. nonporous surfaces, which are not absorbent. These surfaces often appear polished and repel moisture. Examples include mirrors, glass, smooth ceramics, plastic, and painted wood. Prints on these types of surfaces are more susceptible to damage, because they are on the outermost surface. Undisturbed, they might last for years.
   b. porous surfaces, which are absorbent, such as documents and cardboard. Prints on documents, for example, may be durable and fairly stable over a period of years or they can quickly fade or deteriorate beyond the point of being useful it they are subject to high humidity or if they become wet.
   c. semiporous surfaces, which don't fit easily into the previous two categories, because they both resist and absorb fingerprints, which may or may not soak into the surface. Semiporous examples include glossy cardboard, magazine covers, and some types of cellophane. The durability of prints on these surfaces is variable.

   Textured surfaces, such as the "pebbled" effect of some computer monitors are both nonporous and porous, because the pebbled effect creates an inconsistent contact between the friction ridge skin and the surface, producing a discontinuous appearance when developed and a lack of fine detail.

2. *The nature of the material contaminating the fingerprint:* patent fingerprints resulting from contamination by soot, safe insulation, and face powder are quickly destroyed; those made with blood, ink, or oil can last longer periods of time under favorable conditions.[41]

3. *Any physical or occupational defects of the person making the print.*

4. *How the object on which the prints appear was handled:* The distance between friction ridges is very small, and if the finger moves even slightly, that ridge detail can be lost.

5. *The amount of the contamination:* When the finger leaving the print is very contaminated, both the ridge surfaces and their "valleys" get filled up, resulting in a smeared appearance with little value as evidence.

LOCATING LATENT FINGERPRINTS

Proper latent print processing begins with wearing latex, nitrile, or other suitable gloves.[42] Latent prints are such valuable evidence that extraordinary efforts should be made to recover them. The investigator must adopt a positive attitude about this, regardless of apparent problems or past failures.

It is imperative that the investigator thoroughly search all surface areas in and around the crime scene that might retain prints. Shining a flashlight at an oblique angle to the surface being examined is often helpful in this search. The fact that an individual may have worn gloves in no way lessens the need for a complete search. On occasion, gloves themselves leave impressions as individualized as fingerprints. Moreover, although unusual, it may be possible to develop a latent fingerprint on the inside of a glove recovered at a crime scene.[43] Particular attention should be paid to less obvious places, such as the undersides of toilet seats, toilet handles, tabletops, and dresser drawers; the surfaces of dinner plates and filing cabinets; the backs of rearview mirrors; and the trunk lids of automobiles. Frequently handled objects, such as doorknobs and telephones, ordinarily do not yield good prints. But because they are likely to have been touched, they should always be processed.

Never assume that the offender took precautions against leaving prints or destroyed those left. The commission of a criminal offense involves stress, and the offender may have made a mistake. If gloves were worn, for example, the suspect may have removed them for some operation.

It helps to attempt to view the scene as the criminal did. Such conditions as time of day, weather, and physical layout may suggest that certain surfaces should be more closely examined. In conducting the examination for latent prints in a burglary case, for example, the investigators should begin at the point of entry. For other crimes, such as the issuance of worthless checks, the point of entry often takes on less importance. Ordinarily, however, whatever the crime and its attending circumstances, reconstruction by the investigator gives direction to the search.

A person who is familiar with the environment, such as the owner of the building or the occupant of an apartment, may give valuable aid in obtaining latent prints. The person should be allowed to observe the scene so that he or she can indicate any items out of place or brought to the scene by the suspect.

When neither the ambient lighting nor the use of a bright flashlight reveals latent prints, other methods of searching for them—a forensic light or laser unit—may provide results. A **forensic light source (FLS)** is a powerful light source that has one or more specialized light capabilities, such as infrared (IR) or ultraviolet (UV) light capabilities. UV lights, in addition to causing naturally fluorescent/glowing prints to be visible, are useful in locating small amounts of body fluids, hairs, fibers, and other evidence too small to be visible to the naked eye. Historically, lasers had superior illumination capabilities, but their size and cost precluded their use in most law-enforcement agencies. With the recent arrival of less costly, handheld third-generation laser systems, which are green-light-based, laser systems are becoming more widely used in the field. Appropriate safety precautions prescribed by FLS and laser system manufacturers, for example, wearing approved goggles, should be followed.

METHODS OF DEVELOPING LATENT FINGERPRINTS

Plastic and contaminated prints require little or no development. However, there are numerous ways to develop latent prints. Four methods that investigators should be familiar with are (1) use of traditional powders, (2) use of fluorescent powders, (3) application of chemicals, and (4) cyanoacrylate or superglue fuming. The most common method of developing latent/invisible prints is through the use of traditional powders (Figure 4-17). Because it may be possible to obtain a DNA sample from a print, the method selected for development should not eliminate this possibility.

Traditional Powders

Commercially prepared **traditional powders** come in a number of colors, including black, white, silver, red, and gray. To provide a good contrast between the print and the background on which it has been made, darker powders are used to locate latent/invisible prints on lighter-colored surfaces, and lighter ones are used on darker backgrounds (Figure 4-17). There are also dual-use powders, which appear black when dusted on a light-colored surface and silver when applied to a dark one. The tip of the brush is gently placed into the wide-mouthed powder container and then lightly tapped to allow excess powder to drop away. Caution must be used when applying the powder to a latent print. Too much powder creates a print in which the details are difficult to identify. This is why powder is never sprinkled directly on the surface to be dusted. The entire area to be dusted should be covered with smooth, light brush strokes until the ridge detail begins to show. Then, the brush strokes should follow the contours of the ridges until the latent/invisible print is fully visible. Even if the first attempt to develop a print is not successful, a second one may be. The choices of brushes include tips made of fiberglass, feathers, and camel hair. Most latent print development is done with traditional powders.

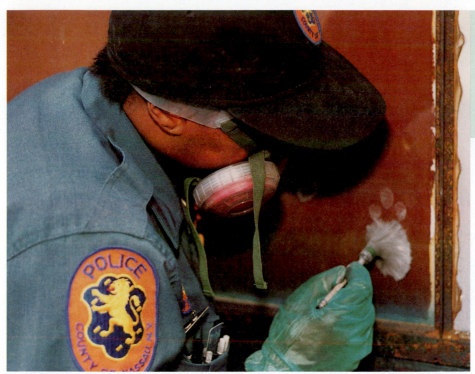

◀ **FIGURE 4-17 Locating prints**
A crime scene technician uses protective equipment while dusting for fingerprints. Several developed prints can be seen in the area the technician is dusting. (Courtesy Nassau County, New York Police Department)

Magnetic applicators may be used in lieu of a brush. A magnetic applicator has a magnet in its head and when placed close to a magnetic powder container, it attracts the powder, forming a virtual brush. Magnetic powders commonly come in black, gray, and white. There are also dual-use magnetic powders. Magnetic powders are only used on nonmetallic surfaces.

Fluorescent Powders

As mentioned earlier, low concentrations of some naturally occurring substances will cause a latent print to fluoresce, or glow, under FLS or laser illumination. To compensate for the typically low level of naturally occurring fluorescence, investigators can dust the area to be examined with a special **fluorescent powder,** which chemically enhances the print when viewed under FLS or laser illumination (Figure 4-18). Fluorescent powders are also available in several colors for use with a magnetic applicator.

CHEMICALS

A variety of chemicals are used to develop and enhance latent prints. These chemicals are applied by spraying or brushing the surface being examined, by fuming, or by dipping the object on which there may be prints in a solution.[44] Among chemicals in use are the following:

- Amido black is a dye sensitive to properties in blood and may be used with contaminated/visible prints involving blood. It has the capability to turn blood proteins to a blue-black color. It should not be used as a presumptive test for blood, because it also reacts to other things.
- Gentian violet is a dye used to develop purplish latent prints on the adhesive side of almost any kind of tape.
- Ninhydrin was formulated in 1910 and proposed for use in developing fingerprints in 1954; this chemical is used to develop latent prints on paper and cardboard, producing purplish prints (Figure 4-19).
- DFO (1, 8-diazafluren-9-one) functions similarly to ninhydrin but is about three times more sensitive in developing latent prints on paper. The developed red-colored prints are immediately visible but paler than those produced by ninhydrin. DFO prints fluoresce under FLS and laser illumination. Both DFO and ninhydrin may be used on paper, but DFO must be used first to get any fluorescence.
- Small-Particle Reagent (SPR) is used for developing latent prints that have been immersed in water, such as when a perpetrator has attempted to dispose of a firearm used in a crime by throwing it into a river or lake. It is also used to develop prints on dew- or rain-soaked cars; on surfaces covered with a residue, such as salt from being on or near the ocean; and on waxed materials, plastics, tile, and glass. Developed prints appear dark gray on a light surface and light gray on a dark surface. Although SPR can be sprayed on an object, immersion of the object for about 30 seconds in an SPR solution produces better results.

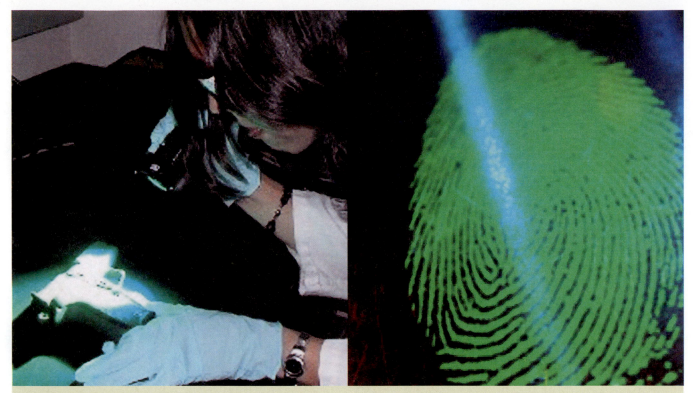

▲**FIGURE 4-18   Reflected ultraviolet imaging system**
The technician is holding a RUVIS SceneScope in her right hand, which is shaped a like a fat flashlight. The RUVIS operates on ultraviolet (UV) light and can locate objects that are naturally fluorescent. In this case, a .45 Colt semi-automatic pistol was dusted with fluorescent powder. This RUVIS has an attached camera, which photographed the fluorescing fingerprint on the pistol.
(*Left:* Courtesy HORIBA Jobin Yvon S.A.S., North Carolina Bureau of Investigation, State Crime Lab, Latent Evidence Section, *right:* Courtesy State of Utah Crime Lab)

- Rhodamine 6G is an excellent fluorescent chemical dye to use on metal, glass, leather, plastic, wood, and many other types of nonabsorbent surfaces. Rhodamine 6G may enhance latent prints already developed and also reveal others.
- After Super Glue fuming, Basic Yellow 40 can be effectively used on nonporous surfaces. It fluoresces well under alternative lighting. Ardrox and Basic Red 28 are also used following Super Glue fuming.

Cyanoacrylate (CA) or Super Glue Fuming

Super Glue fuming was developed in 1978 in Japan. The three factors associated with its rapid acceptance were ease of use, remarkable results, and low cost. The mechanics of

▶**FIGURE 4-19   Ninhydrin developed print**
Using ninhydrin is an excellent technique to develop latent prints on paper. In this case, a thumb print is raised on an envelope containing an extortion note. (Courtesy Wisconsin Department of Justice, Law Enforcement Services Division)

▲ Figure 4-20 Portable Super Glue fuming chamber
This portable Super Glue unit is being used to process a weapon and liquor bottles at the scene of a murder-robbery in New York City. Note that the chamber can be used in the field or in the laboratory. (© Seth Gottfried)

fluorescent powders and Super Glue fuming. Success has also been reported using combinations of these methods—for example, fuming followed by the use of fluorescent powders. There is no consensus method. Because of potential health threats to living victims, investigators need to be well-informed about the products they use. As bodies decompose, the likelihood of developing latent fingerprints on them is reduced.

Some authorities recommend after the medical examiner has released a body at the scene, it should be glue fumed to preserve any latent prints while the body is transported to the morgue. The body should not be refrigerated until after further latent print development efforts are completed. At the scene, there may be some indication of specific handling of a body by the suspect—for instance, placed in a pose or the victim's statement. Key target areas for finding latent prints on the victim are ankles, armpits, wrists, inner thighs, and neck. On living victims areas of redness are a key indicator of handling. Humidity and temperature levels can affect development efforts and charts are available to determine the optimum conditions for processing.[45]

COLLECTING AND PRESERVING LATENT PRINTS

Occasionally items such as beer cans or glasses that have condensation on them need to be processed for prints. Heat lamps or any other source of artificial heat should not be used to dry the object quickly. Such objects should be allowed to air-dry naturally. Similarly, articles that have been frozen and need to be processed for prints must be allowed to thaw and dry naturally. Whenever reasonable to do so, the actual item on which the print is located should be submitted for developing in the laboratory.

Once a print is found it should be photographed immediately with a rigid scale in view. The ruler allows a one-to-one, or actual-size, picture of the print to be made. This provides a permanent record of the print in the event that it is accidentally altered or destroyed while attempting to collect or transporting it.

Most latent prints are lifted with a clear strip of tape, 1½ inches to 2 inches wide, or with clear flap lifter after they have been developed with powders. One end of the clear tape is placed on the surface just before the latent print appears. Pressure is then applied to progressively lay the tape over the print, taking care not to leave air bubbles. If air bubbles are accidentally created, the tape should be carefully smoothed over to eliminate them. The tape may be left on the object if the object is to be submitted to the laboratory.

Alternatively, the pattern of the print is lifted by pulling up the tape, starting at one end and moving progressively to the other end. Now the powder that shows the print pattern is stuck to the sticky side of the tape. This tape is then laid back down on an appropriately colored

Super Glue fuming are fairly straightforward. Cyanoacrylate (CA) is heated in a high-humidity chamber. As the fumes condense, they develop white-colored latent prints in 5 to 15 minutes. The developed prints may be further enhanced with powders or soaked in chemicals that fluoresce under FLSs.

Super Glue fuming may be done by small Super Glue fuming wands, in small portable chambers (Figure 4-20) and in various sized chambers in the laboratory. On a larger scale, entire rooms and automobiles are processed using this method.

DEVELOPING LATENT FINGERPRINTS ON BODIES

The development of identifiable latent fingerprints on living victims and corpses has been accomplished using a variety of methods, including tradition, magnetic, and backing card. For example, assume that a latent print on a glass window is developed with dark powder.

MARKING AND IDENTIFYING PRINT LIFTS

When a latent print has been developed, lifted, and placed on a card, the card must be properly identified. Information recorded on the card should include the date, type of case, case number, address of the crime scene, name of the officer who made the lift, exact place of the lift, and type of object from which the print was lifted. Regardless of how well the latent print was developed and lifted, if the card is not properly marked with all the data required or if the fingerprint specialist is not furnished with the information required, the entire process may be wasted effort. In describing the exact place that the lift was made, it is sometimes helpful to draw a simple sketch of the object. The sketch should be made on the fingerprint card that is sent to the laboratory. The inclusion of corresponding numbers on both the lift and the sketch establishes the location of the latent print.

FORENSIC ODONTOLOGY

Forensic odontology has been defined as the intersection of dentistry and criminal law; it is a medical specialty relating dental evidence to investigation. The most common cases involve missing and unidentified persons (MUPs) cases, where unidentified human remains are found at a crime or death investigation scene.[46] In second place is the recognition, documentation, preservation, evaluation, interpretation, and comparison of bite mark evidence.

A forensic dentist may be able to make significant contributions to the following types of cases:

1. a head is found or there is an otherwise unidentifiable body;
2. a decomposing, burned, or skeletonized body is found;
3. sexual assault, child/elder abuse, domestic violence, and homicide cases involving aggressive and/or defensive bite marks. More rarely, bite marks may be self-inflicted as part of a staged crime.[47] Although bite marks are most frequently found on skin and in human tissue, they may also be located on pencils, styrofoam cups, food (Figure 4-21), and other objects.
4. identifying mass casualties of attacks and natural and industrial disasters—such as 9/11, the Indian Ocean tsunami (2004) that may have killed as many as 250,000 people, Hurricane Katrina (2005), and the Interstate 35 bridge collapse in Minneapolis (2007) (Figure 4-22). In Thailand, 75% of the 2004 tsunami victims were identified by forensic odontology;[48]
5. verifying a presumptive, or reasonably believed, identity—for example, Hitler, Eva Braun, and Mussolini during World War II and more recently al-Qaeda terrorists Abu Musab al-Zarqawi and Mohammed Atef.

IDENTIFICATION

Forensic odontology's normal approach to identifying MUPs is the comparison of postmortem or after-death dental remains with antemortem or predeath records, including written notes, radiographs/X rays, casts, bridges,

▶ **FIGURE 4-21**
Bite mark in food
A partially eaten "Moon Pie" bitten by one of the suspects in a double homicide. From the bite marks it can be determined that the individual making them had two non-equally protruding upper front teeth. Such information can play an important role in determining probable cause for arrest and/or search warrants.
(Courtesy Dr. Richard R. Souviron, DDS, ABFO, Chief Forensic Odontologist, Dade County Medical Examiner Department, Miami, Florida)

▲ **FIGURE 4-22   Identification of victims at disasters**
Cars and trucks lie in the wreckage of the I-35W bridge that spanned the Mississippi River in Minneapolis, Minnesota (August 1, 2007). Forensic odontology has been an invaluable tool in identifying the victims of disasters. (© AP Photo/The Minnesota Daily, Stacy Bengs)

fillings, and caps.[49] Morphological (shape and form) peculiarities of teeth can also help establish identity of MUPs.

Additionally, forensic dentists have established individual identity on the basis of "smiling photographs" (Figure 4-23). Some dentures are marked and can be traced to a particular owner, although the possibility that they were discarded at the scene must be eliminated. There is no set number of points required to establish a positive match; one unique feature may be sufficient.

The FBI maintains the National Dental Image/Information Repository (NDIR) on missing persons and unidentified remains and is adding dental information to the wanted persons file. Other sources of dental records include the military, health insurance carriers, local dentists, and community health clinics for indigent and low income persons and families. In some cases, it is useful to have a forensic artist prepare a likeness of the deceased, as he/she may have appeared in life, which can be done from as little as a skull. This image is placed in the news-

paper with a public appeal for assistance in making an identity. Any suggestions as to identity may be checkable against dental records.

Searches for dental records may not be productive, because (1) some number of individuals under the age of 30 have no dental decay, and (2) individuals with decayed or missing teeth may never have sought treatment. In either case, there are no records of antemortem dental restorations that can be compared with the postmortem dental features of a victim.

When human remains are discovered in remote areas, clandestine graves, abandoned buildings, or under similar circumstances, the bodies may be in very "rough" shape, and animal predation may require treating a larger area as a crime scene. However, teeth are the most durable part of the body, and dental evidence may play a key role in these types of investigations. The longer bodies have been left unattended, the greater the probability that teeth have fallen out or otherwise been dislodged from their normal place. Violence to the victim may have accomplished the same thing. "Rough" body scenes are unpleasant, and investigators should be sure that every precaution is taken to recover loose teeth and other evidence associated with the scene. The addition of a forensic anthropologist, skilled in methodically processing human remains sites, to the investigative team should be considered, especially at burial sites and when the victim's body is skeletonized.

DENTAL PROFILING

When there is an unidentifiable victim and there are no antemortem or predeath dental records, the forensic dentist can help narrow the population pool to which the deceased belongs by **postmortem (after-death) dental profiling** by providing a variety of useful observations:[50]

1. Some teeth give us an idea of racial characteristics—for example, Native Americans and Asians have deep grooves in the inner aspects of their upper front teeth, called shovel-shaped incisors.
2. Age at time of death estimate—through 13 years old an approximation of age accurate to within six months is possible; from 14 to 25 years old a one year plus or minus window is possible; after age 25, scientific testing is usually required to establish an approximate age.
3. Gender—the morphology of teeth does not vary by gender, but analysis of dental pulp and the cranium can provide gender identification. There is also research on using the geometric relationships of teeth to establish gender; this method has achieved accuracy rates of 84% in controlled testing.
4. Suggestion of social class by the presence or absence of various types of dental care.
5. Opinions about habits, such as pipe smoking and nail biting.

▲ **FIGURE 4-23** **Dental comparison**
The left photo shows upper and lower jaws of an unknown white male. Some bone loss (pyorrhea) and tobacco staining are evident. There were no fillings, decay, or missing teeth and no evidence of any dental treatment. The right photo is an enhancement and enlargement of a photo of the victim at his son's birthday party. His kidnappers/killers were sentenced to life terms. (Courtesy Dr. Richard R. Souviron, D.D.S., ABFO, Chief Forensic Odontologist, Dade County Medical Examiner's Department, Miami, Florida)

BITE MARKS

Investigators must be particularly alert to the possibility that bite-mark evidence exists, particularly when they are working sexual assault, child/elder abuse, and homicide cases. Female victims are most often bitten on the breast, buttocks, and legs during a sexual assault, whereas male victims are more likely to be bitten on the arms and shoulders. Bite marks on the arms and hands are usually defensive wounds caused when a person holds up his/ her arms to ward off an attacker.[51] Facial hair associated with bite marks may be transferred between attackers and victims; it should be collected consistent with the guidelines in the next major section, "Hair." In 99% of all violent rapes, victims are bitten at least once by their attacker (Figure 4-24).[52] The collection of bite mark evidence, when reasonably possible, should be left to a forensic dentist.

Bite marks may be mistaken for bruises, abrasions, indentions, or lacerations (Figure 4-25); most have an overall ovoid appearance. One or both arches of teeth may be present and there may be multiple, overlapping bites at the same location. Bite marks on skin should be processed quickly because they may be degraded by skin elasticity, the post mortem position of the body, and skin dehydration. Collecting bite mark evidence includes the following steps:

1. Document the bites using color photography; the shots should include general views establishing where the bites are on the victim, a medium-range photograph, and close-ups without and then with an American Board of Forensic Odontology (ABFO) #2 scale. Some labs request that the scales used be submitted with the evidence; in the absence of an AFBO #2, place two scales at right angles as close to the bite mark as possible without disturbing it. When possible, infrared and ultraviolet photos should also be taken.

2. Swab the *center* of each bite mark *twice* with a different sterile cotton applicator moistened with distilled water. Each swab should allowed to air dry and packaged in a paper envelop, sealed, and marked. Even if the prospects for collecting saliva seem

◄**FIGURE 4-24   Bite mark on breast and nipple**
Bite marks are often found on victims of sexual abuse, rape, and violence. It is not uncommon that the suspect bites the victim as part of the sexual sadist ritual. Here, a bite mark is reflected on the breast and nipple of a sexual assault victim. First swab the area for traces of the suspect's saliva, which may yield DNA evidence. Photograph the bite mark and follow other guidelines set forth by the ABFO relating to bite mark evidence collection and preservation. **(Courtesy Forensic Denistry Online)**

3. When the bite area is within reach of the victim's dentition, a cast of his/her teeth should be taken.
4. Impressions of the bite area can be made using dental grade silicon impression material.
5. If the victim is deceased, the medical examiner's office may remove the block of tissue containing the bite mark and preserve it in formalin. To maintain the size and contour of the bite mark, it is attached to a custom-made ring prior to the tissue being removed.[54]

Although bruises and bite marks change color as time passes, this process is not linear and unvarying. Statements about bruise color and age of the injury should be regarded warily because they are opinions unsupported by science. A 2010 study of the ability of forensic experts to date the age of bruises showed them to be unreliable; however, they were better in placing sequential photographs of bruises from the same subject in the correct chronological order. These photographs were taken from the time they appeared until they disappeared.[55]

remote, the procedure should be followed; in a rare case saliva was recovered from the skin of a victim submerged in a slow-running river for 5.5 hours.[53] If the bite mark is made *through* clothing, the clothing is also a potential source of saliva to be processed.

◄**FIGURE 4-25
Hand laceration by teeth**
Laceration at base of suspect's thumb area caused by victim's defensive bite. Suspect grabbed victim from behind, trying to gag her with his hand. **(Courtesy Los Angeles Police Department)**

Before collecting evidence from a suspect, the legal authority to do so must be established; normally this is done by search warrant, court order, or consent. A request for consent and sometimes a court order will alert suspects and/or their attorneys to a pending examination and may provide sufficient time for suspects to alter their dentition—for example, have all teeth pulled. Two search warrants should be obtained to (1) seize the suspect's dental records and (2) collect evidence from the suspect. The application for the search warrant should specify what evidence will be collected using what methods, including saliva swabbing for DNA if appropriate to the fact situation.

Collection of evidence from the suspect is the responsibility of forensic dentists or technicians working under their supervision, who should describe the protocols that will be used to the suspect. Elements of evidence collection include:

1. The suspect's dental records subsequent to, or in closest proximity to the date of the bite mark.
2. A complete set of photographs.
3. A clinical examination, to include identification of misaligned, broken, or missing teeth; a determination of how long teeth have been broken or missing; restorative dental work; evidence of trauma and surgery; maximum mouth opening; periodontal condition and any loose teeth. A dental chart is usually prepared.
4. Two impressions of the upper and lower arches of the suspect's teeth.
5. Sample bite marks in a wax—for example, aluwax, Styrofoam, or other ABFO-approved material; suspects should not be physically forced into providing a standard/reference sample.[56]

The process of comparing bite marks with a suspect's dentition includes analysis and measurement of size, shape and position of the individual teeth.[57] From the impressions, a life-sized study model of the suspect's dentition is produced. At the broadest level of comparison, if the arch and shape characteristics do not match, the suspect can immediately be excluded. Most comparison methods rely on the use of overlays. The use of laser imaging in bite mark comparisons is very promising, producing a high level of three-dimensional details.[58]

HAIR

Hair evidence is often found because both victims and suspects can transfer it to each other or the scene; hair is easy to locate and recover, and durable.[59] It may be found on ski masks abandoned by armed robbers, in the head and pubic hairs of assailants and victims, clutched in the hands of victims, on clothing, and numerous other places. Hair evidence is primarily associated with violent crimes.

Microscopic examination of hairs can determine whether the origin is a fiber wig, animal, or human. A number of useful conclusions are *possible* from the microscopic examination of human hair, such as the:

1. racial characteristics of the donor—that is, European, Asian, or African;
2. somatic or body area origin of the hair—for example, eyelashes, pubic, scalp, and beard;
3. manner in which it was removed—for instance, if hair has an anagen/active growth root it suggests forcible removal;
4. damage to the hair—for example, by putrefaction, blunt force trauma, or burned;
5. types of drugs ingested and how recently;
6. presence of hair contaminates, including blood, semen, soil, pet hair, and soil; contaminates *may* suggest an occupation—for instance, automotive spray paint particles might indicate working in a body shop;[60]
7. hair treatment, including bleaching, shampoo residues, and dyes;[61]
8. determination of whether known and questioned hair samples could have a common origin (Figure 4-26).

Most often, when a reference to DNA and investigation is made, it is in the context that individual identification can be established. This is true with nuclear DNA (nDNA), which is passed from both parents to their offspring. Thus, if a hair has its root, or other tissue attached, then establishing individual identity is possible from nDNA. However, when investigators have recovered only a hair shaft, it contains a different type of DNA, mitochondrial or **mtDNA,** which is inherited only from the maternal line. It is not possible to establish individual identity with mtDNA, because other people along the same maternal lines share it. There is also the possibility of a random match. In contrast, some mtDNA is so rare that it is seen only once even in very large DNA databases. MtDNA can be used to exclude suspects, establish that the victim is not from a particular lineage (or that he/she is), all of which helps to focus investigative effort.[62]

When collecting hair standards, at least 50 should be cut at the skin from various portions of the head to assure that all shades of texture and color have been properly sampled; this number should be doubled for deceased individuals, and they should be pulled.[63] At least 20 standard pubic hair samples should be cut at the skin surface from various regions on a live person; double that number and pull them from deceased. Standard hair samples can be placed in a clean envelope, which is sealed and labeled.[64] Pill boxes, glass vials, and other tightly sealed containers are also acceptable in many labs.

The collection of questioned hair samples requires a clean piece of paper to be placed under the area to be combed. All areas of the pubic or other area should be thoroughly combed to dislodge foreign hairs and other materials.[65] When the process is completed, place the

Photomicrograph of hair found inside a rape suspect's vehicle (*left*) is matched with a sample of hair from the victim (*right*). Note the darker shading of brown near the outside of each strand as a result of color added to the victim's hair. These types of peculiarities provide matches between the characteristics of hairs but not to the exclusion of a donor other than the victim. (Courtesy Texas Department of Public Safety)

comb on the paper, carefully fold it, and place the paper in an envelope. If samples are collected from several portions of the body, the comb should be changed between areas and each area packaged separately. Known and questioned samples should be packaged separately when submitted to the laboratory. The investigator should be present when qualified medical personnel collect samples. Before the process begins, the investigator should verify that the medical person understands the proper collection and packaging of samples.

Hair collection at the crime scene requires a different set of considerations regarding known and questioned samples:

1. Document by photos, the evidence log, and by diagram where the hairs were recovered.
2. Do not submit wet hairs to the lab; they should be allowed to air dry.
3. If they are firmly attached to an object, leave the hairs intact and submit the object.
4. When visible hairs are not firmly attached to an object or the object is too large to submit to the lab, carefully remove them with clean tweezers.
5. If hairs were possibly transferred to the victim's and/or suspect's clothing, keep their clothes apart. Package each article of clothing separately and submit to the laboratory separately.[66]
6. Do not overlook the potential probative value of animal hair; if a victim's pets were present at the time of the offense, samples should be pulled from them and handled in the usual manner.

BLOOD

Blood was class-characteristic evidence until the introduction of DNA analysis in the early 1980s. However, an initial study published in 2010 hints at the possibility that blood may have other important contributions to make. Blood samples from 195 people, from a few weeks to 80 years old were analyzed. The research reports the ability to identify age from blood, plus or minus 8.9 years.[67] However, even if confirmed, this capability may be five or more years away from common use. The identification of eye and hair color, skin pigmentation, height, and weight from blood analysis are also being explored.[68]

On average, an adult's body contains about 5 to 6 quarts of blood, and even small cuts can produce a lot of blood. At crime scenes, blood may be encountered in amounts ranging from small drops to large pools, in states ranging from fresh to dried, and in almost any place, including on floors, walls, ceilings, clothes, weapons, the suspect's and victim's bodies, and the exterior and interior of vehicles.

Because of the frequency with which blood is encountered and the fact that DNA analysis can provide individual identification (Table 4-1), officers need to be alert to locating and protecting this type of evidence. Moreover, they should wear appropriate PPE and take the other kinds of protective measures discussed in Chapter 3, "Investigators, the Investigative Process, and the Crime Scene."

THE APPEARANCE OF BLOODSTAINS

If blood at the crime scene is fresh and relatively uncontaminated, identifying it as blood is not difficult. If it is in some other condition, identifying blood merely by "eyeballing it" becomes increasingly difficult. Blood may appear as a rust-colored stain or have gray, black, green, or blue tints. It may also be mixed with earth, grease, paint, or other substances, making it difficult to see.

Very fine drops of blood can be located by viewing the surfaces concerned at an oblique angle close to the plane

TABLE 4-1	Sources of DNA Evidence	
EVIDENCE	**POSSIBLE LOCATION OF DNA ON THE EVIDENCE**	**SOURCE OF DNA**
Baseball bat or similar weapon	Handle, end	Sweat, skin, blood, tissue
Hat, bandanna, or mask	Inside	Sweat, hair, dandruff
Eyeglasses	Nose or ear pieces, lens	Sweat, skin
Facial tissue or cotton swab	Surface area	Mucus, blood, sweat, semen, earwax
Dirty laundry	Surface area	Blood, sweat, semen, vomit
Toothpick	Tips	Saliva
Used cigarette	Cigarette butt	Saliva
Stamp or envelope	Licked area	Saliva
Tape or ligature	Inside or outside surface	Skin, sweat
Bottle, can, or glass	Sides, mouthpiece	Saliva, sweat
Used condom	Inside or outside surface	Semen, vaginal or rectal cells
Blanket, pillow, or sheet	Surface area	Sweat, hair, semen, urine, saliva, dandruff
"Through and through" bullet	Outside surface	Blood, tissue
Bite mark	Person's skin or clothing	Saliva
Fingernail or partial fingernail	Scrapings	Blood, sweat, tissue

Source: *www.dba.Gov/Basics/Evidence_Collection/Identifying*, January 5, 2011.

of the surfaces. If the light is not strong or if the scene is dark, viewing the surfaces will be enhanced by shining a flashlight beam at the same oblique angle. Blood is naturally fluorescing and may be detected by the use of a FLS.

The drying time of blood depends on a number of factors, including whether it is on a porous or nonporous surface, its size and thickness, and the presence or absence of a fan or breeze. Higher temperatures hasten the drying time of blood, whereas increased humidity decreases it. Drying first appears at the edges of a bloodstain and works toward its center. A dried bloodstain will begin to pucker and crack from the edges inward after further drying. Thus, it is difficult to accurately estimate the age of bloodstains. Research has been carried out on dating the age of blood using changes in its chemical composition.[69]

USING BLOODSTAINS TO RECONSTRUCT THE CRIME

Bloodstains (known as blood spatter) may take many forms at a crime scene. These forms are not random but are produced by such factors as the type, location, and number of wounds inflicted; the type of weapon involved; movements by the victim while trying to escape, defend himself/herself, or attack the offender; changes in the location of the victim's body owing to its being moved by the offender or someone; and continuing postmortem violence to the body by the offender,

suggesting that the killer was in a state of rage and possibly knew the victim.

By studying bloodstain and spatter evidence, the investigator can learn significant facts that facilitate reconstruction of the crime. These facts include:

1. Direction in which blood droplets were traveling when they were deposited on the surface (Figure 4-27).
2. Distance from the source of the blood to the surface on which the droplets were found (Figure 4-28). An important fact to note concerning blood spatter is that blood droplets cannot exceed 4 feet in horizontal travel from a stationary point (for example, blood spatter from a direct gunshot wound); thus, the blood droplets in Figure 4-28 reflect vertical fall.[70]
3. Angle at which the droplets impacted (see Figure 4-29).
4. Direction and relative speed of blood trails.
5. Nature of the object used as a weapon.
6. Number of blows struck.
7. Relative locations of other persons, surfaces, and objects having droplets on them.
8. Sequence of events, if multiple events are involved.
9. Interpretation of blood-contact or blood-transfer patterns.
10. Estimation of the elapsed time for the event and the volume of bloodshed.[71]

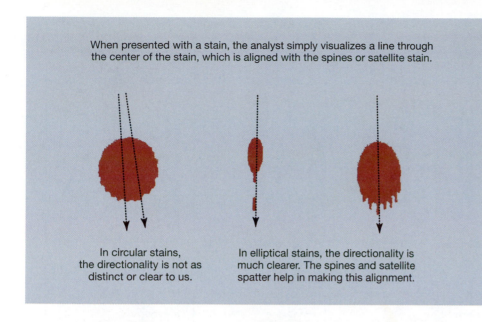

When presented with a stain, the analyst simply visualizes a line through the center of the stain, which is aligned with the spines or satellite stain.

In circular stains, the directionality is not as distinct or clear to us.

In elliptical stains, the directionality is much clearer. The spines and satellite spatter help in making this alignment.

◄**FIGURE 4-27**
Directionality of blood droplet
To visualize or demonstrate directionality in a droplet, the analyst simply draws a line down the long axis of the stain, splitting it into two equal parts. This line is oriented to the scallops, spines, or satellite stains. (Source: Tom Bevel and Ross M. Gardner, *Bloodstain Pattern Analysis: With an Introduction to Crime Scene Reconstruction*, 2nd ed. [Boca Raton, FL: CRC Press, 2002], p. 146. Used by permission.)

6in · 1ft · 2ft · 3ft · 4ft · 5ft · 6ft · 7ft

◄**FIGURE 4-28**
Distance between bloodstain and source
Increasing diameter of bloodstains as a function of increasing distance fallen by single drops of blood from fingertips onto smooth cardboard (Source: Stuart H. James and William G. Eckert, *Interpretation of Bloodstain Evidence at Crime Scenes*, 2nd ed. [Boca Raton, FL: CRC Press, 1998], p. 21. Used by permission.)

LOCATING BLOOD EVIDENCE

The places at which the investigator will find bloodstains are virtually unlimited. For example, if a criminal homicide occurred indoors, blood might be found not only on the floor but perhaps also on the walls or even the ceiling. Ordinarily when perpetrators of violent crimes get blood on their bodies or clothing, they will attempt to rid themselves of it immediately. In some instances, they may be so repelled by the sight of blood on their hands that they will impulsively wipe it on a piece of furniture, such as a stuffed chair; if the fabric is multicolored or sufficiently dark, the stain may escape detection by the unobservant investigator. They may also attempt to clean bloodied hands before leaving the scene by using such surfaces as the reverse side of a small throw rug or the undersides of cushions on a couch.

At bloody scenes it is not uncommon for the suspect to have left a shoeprint on some hard, smooth surface. In turn,

it is likely that some of the blood may be found in the cracks and crevices of the suspect's shoe soles. This is important evidence, because it can tie the suspect to the scene with great certainty, particularly if DNA evidence from the blood can positively link the suspect to the scene.

Another way of locating blood evidence is use of a presumptive or preliminary field test (Figure 4-30). **Luminol,** a water-based spray, locates trace amounts of blood within 30 seconds, creating a blue glow after the lights are turned out. Luminol's disadvantages are that the glow is short lasting; it doesn't differentiate between human and animal blood, and it reacts to copper, some alloys, and certain bleaches. **Hemident** also does not distinguish between human and animal blood. In the presence of blood, it produces a dark blue/green appearance within seconds. **Hexagon OBTI** (Figure 4-31) distinguishes between animal and human blood in two to three minutes; however, it also displays sensitivity to the blood of higher primates. To have legal significance, all three of these presumptive tests

▶ **FIGURE 4-29**

Impact angle and stain shape
The range of droplet shapes that result from the varying impact angles. The more elliptical the stain, the more acute the angle of impact. Round stains indicate that the impact angle was closer to 90 degrees. (Source: Tom Bevel and Ross M. Gardner, *Bloodstain Pattern Analysis: With an Introduction to Crime Scene Reconstruction*, 2nd ed. [Boca Raton, FL: CRC Press, 2002], Color Figure 2. Used by permission.)

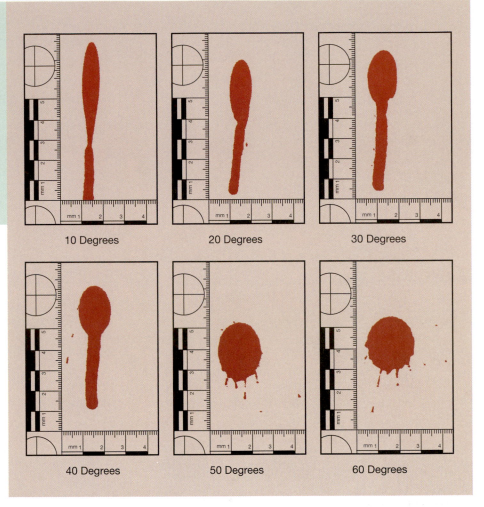

10 Degrees   20 Degrees   30 Degrees

40 Degrees   50 Degrees   60 Degrees

▲ **FIGURE 4-30   Use of BlueStar forensic**
Mop used by assailant in an effort to clean up blood from scene of an attack. The BlueStar reagent was sprayed on the mop, revealing presence of blood invisible to naked eye. (Courtesy BlueStar Forensics)

must be confirmed by more elaborate testing procedures in the laboratory. Some presumptive tests for blood may interfere with DNA analysis, and so investigators need to determine whether the one they are contemplating using does so.[72] If yes, the collection of blood samples from the scene should precede presumptive testing. Alternatively, a small blood sample can be collected and tested.

Occasionally, in an indoor homicide, the perpetrator will remove the body to an outdoor area to avoid discovery and then will return to the scene and attempt to eliminate all traces of the crime. Typically, this involves washing hands and scrubbing or mopping the floor on which the body had lain:

An aggravated assault occurred between two friends who mutually agreed to misrepresent it as an accident. When the victim appeared at the local hospital for

◄ **FIGURE 4-31 Hexagon OBTI**
Blood is placed in the white collection tube, followed by the addition of the reagent in the red-capped bottle at right. If the test is functioning properly, but there is no human blood detected, a single blue line appears in the window. Two single blue lines denote the presence of human blood. **(Courtesy BlueStar Forensics)**

treatment, the police were summoned owing to the nature of the wounds and their locations, which suggested to the doctor that they were not accidentally inflicted. Investigators went to the scene and were told the accident happened outside while barbecuing. Granted permission to look inside the house, they found fresh blood underneath the faucets at the kitchen sink. Trace amounts of blood were found on the recently mopped floor between the back door and the kitchen sink. The location of the blood evidence was particularly pertinent, because the people involved alleged that the "accident" had happened in the backyard while they were barbecuing and that they had gone directly to the hospital. Although a solid investigation was conducted, no prosecution resulted due to a lack of cooperation from the victim and witnesses.

Before handling any blood evidence, investigators must document its location and physical state (for example, fresh) by some combination of notes, diagrams, video recording, and photographs. Other details may be pertinent to record as well, such as the temperature, humidity, or existence of multiple severe wounds but little blood. The last condition suggests that the person was killed somewhere else or that an attempt was made to clean the victim and/or scene, an action possibly indicating that the perpetrator had an attachment to the victim.

Blood Samples from a Known Source

Only qualified medical personnel should collect blood samples from a person. The following guidelines apply:

1. Draw two 5-milliliter samples of blood in purple-stoppered tubes, the insides of which are coated with EDTA, a preservative used to prevent coagulation.

2. If drug or alcohol testing is to be done, collect a 10-milliliter sample in a gray-stoppered tube, which contains a sodium fluoride (NaF) preservative.

3. Identify each tube with the date, time, collector's name, case number, subject's name, location at which drawn, and evidence number.

4. Do not freeze blood samples; the tubes may break. Refrigerate them, and use cold packs, not dry ice, to pack them for shipment to the laboratory.

5. Pack the blood tubes in special bubble packs, or wrap them in the same type of material.

6. After sealing the outer container or box, label it "Keep in a Cool Dry Place," "Refrigerate on Arrival," and "Biohazard."

7. Submit the samples to the laboratory as soon as possible.[73]

Fresh or Dried Blood on a Person

If there is fresh blood, absorb it on a clean cotton cloth or swab. If the blood is clotting or has dried, use distilled water to moisten a cotton cloth or swab and then absorb the blood with the moist surface. Leave a portion of the cloth or swab unstained as a control or blank sample. Let the cloth or swab air dry naturally. Do not place it in direct sunlight or next to a heat source, and do not use a hair dryer on it. These actions could cause the evidence to begin decomposing, thus reducing or eliminating its evidentiary value. Wrap the evidence in clean, dry paper, or place it in an envelope with sealed corners; plastic or airtight containers should not be used.

Fresh Blood on Surfaces or in Snow or Water

The procedure for collecting fresh blood from most surfaces is the same as that previously described for blood on a person. However, when blood is in a filled bathtub or some other body of water or when it is on snow, a different approach is required. For blood in water, recover the sample from the thickest concentrations of blood and clots whenever possible. When gathering blood from snow, eliminate as much snow as possible from the sample. Freeze it in a clean, airtight container, and submit the sample to the laboratory as rapidly as possible.[74]

Fresh or Dried Bloodstains on Garments and Objects

Allow fresh bloodstains on garments to air dry naturally; then fold the clothing with the crusts intact. Do not fold clothing in a way that creases bloodstains, since the creases may cause them to become dislodged. As you fold the clothing, place clean paper between each layer. Usually, bloodstained garments are found at the crime scene or retrieved from a hospital's emergency room.

Fresh bloodstains on a small movable item, such as a weapon, lamp, or door, should also be allowed to air dry naturally. The item is then submitted to the laboratory for processing; pack the item in clean paper in such a way that the paper does not rub against the bloodstains, since rubbing could alter or eradicate the bloodstain pattern.

When bloodstains are on a large immovable object, they can be collected, if fresh, by using the cotton cloth or swab technique or by cutting a large sample from a dried stain. If there are multiple stains on the object, use a new cloth or swab each time you switch from one stain to another; likewise, thoroughly clean the scalpel, razor blade, or knife you are using to cut dried samples when you switch from one collection area to another. In some cases, it may be necessary to cut a section out of the immovable object and transport it to the laboratory; do not forget the need for a control or blank sample.

Other Considerations in Handling Blood Evidence

During warm weather, especially during daylight hours, blood evidence should not be locked in car interiors or trunks, because heat could rapidly degrade the evidence. If dried-blood evidence is not submitted to the laboratory immediately the garments, objects, and/or samples taken should be refrigerated.

LABORATORY DETERMINATIONS

Under ordinary conditions, laboratory examination of blood evidence can determine the following characteristics about the source of the blood:

1. species (human, dog, horse, and so on);
2. gender;
3. blood type and DNA profile;
4. use of drugs or alcohol by the blood source;
5. presence of certain types of illnesses (for example, venereal disease);
6. presence of carbon monoxide;
7. whether the source was a smoker.

The importance of such determinations was highlighted when labor leader Jimmy Hoffa disappeared in 1975. He had told people he was meeting that night with organized crime figures. It was thought that someone close to Hoffa betrayed him because of bloodstains found in that person's car. However, laboratory examination confirmed the person's statement that the bloodstains were from fish he was taking home. Hoffa was declared dead in 1982; his body was never found.

LIP COSMETICS, DNA, AND LIP PRINTS

Laboratories can differentiate between many types of lip cosmetics, and this information can destroy a suspect's alibi that the lipstick on his shirt was deposited there by his girlfriend when it is consistent with the victim's and inconsistent with the girlfriend's.[75] An unidentified victim's lip cosmetics will supply enough material for a DNA profile of him/her about 80% of the time.[76] Lip print comparisons presently lack scientific validity.

FIREARMS

Firearm evidence is commonly encountered and includes single- and double-action revolvers, semi-automatic handguns, rifles, scopes, shotguns, rim- and center-fire ammunition, bullets, shot pellets and slugs, shell cases, gunshot residues, clips and magazines, firing-pin impressions, and extractor and ejector marks. Moreover, there may be blood, tissue, and/or fingerprints on firearm evidence, making it even more important to a case. Investigators must acquire a broad, working knowledge of firearm evidence for three primary reasons: (1) the frequency with which they will encounter it; (2) the value of such knowledge in a combat situation:

A metropolitan police department had just completed transition to the .40 caliber, semiautomatic, 16-shot (15 magazine, plus 1 chambered) Glock Model 22. Two revolver wielding gunmen robbed a bar and ran out the back door, where they were confronted by a patrol officer walking the alley. Several quick shots were fired as all three men scrambled to get behind some type of cover. After several more shots were exchanged, the officer had fired six shots. One of the gunmen yelled "He's out of ammo, Let's get him!" They left their cover and rushed the officer, who dropped both of them.

and (3) your personal safety and that of others—never assume that a firearm is unloaded, no matter who brings or hands it to you; that assumption could get you or someone else killed:

It was late on the evening watch in a detective division and three investigators were sitting around talking. Two other investigators brought a man in who was not handcuffed and told him to sit down in front of a desk. One of them laid a revolver on the desk and said, "We're charging this guy with murder; watch him 'til we get back." A few minutes later, the suspect stood up, picked up the revolver, and killed himself in front of the three investigators.

LABORATORY DETERMINATIONS

The laboratory examination of firearm evidence may be able to provide answers to a number of important investigative questions.

1. Was This Bullet Fired from This Weapon?

Shotguns are smooth-bore weapons, but pistols and rifles have **rifling**. The **caliber** is the diameter of a bullet, whereas the **bore** (Figure 4-32) is the diameter of the barrel's interior between its opposing high sides, or **lands**. The low sides of the barrel's interior are called **grooves**. When a cartridge is fired, its bullet portion separates from it and passes through the barrel. Because the bullet's caliber is

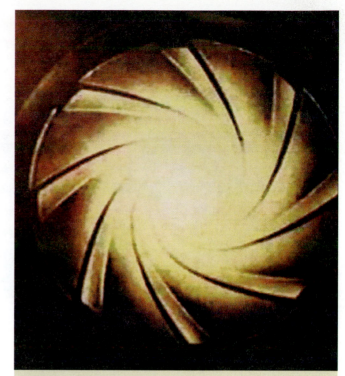

▲ **FIGURE 4-33 Barrel rifling**
Cross-section photograph of the barrel of a 9-mm pistol with traditional rifling. Note how the lands and grooves "twist" to the right, spinning the bullet as it is propelled through the barrel of the weapon. Rifling allows the bullet to be much more aerodynamic, improving the accuracy and stability of the bullet in flight. (Courtesy Forensic Training and Consulting, LLC)

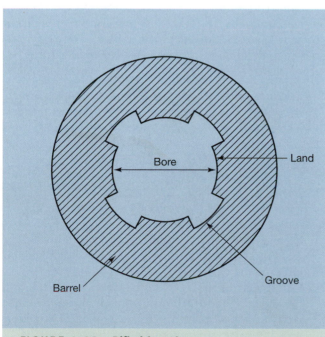

▲ **FIGURE 4-32 Rifled barrel**
Important features of a rifled firearm's barrel

somewhat larger than the bore, the rifling grips the bullet, causing it to rotate, usually in a right-hand direction. The rotation increases the range and accuracy of the bullet (Figure 4-33.)

This rotation also creates striations on the bullet. Marks are also left on fired bullets from manufacturer defects and the use of a firearm. The combination of these distinctive scratches creates a "signature" on a bullet as it passes down a rifled barrel. A bullet recovered from a body can be compared to one fired from a suspect's firearm in a laboratory (Figure 4-34). Identification, however, is affected by the condition of the gun and that of the bullet or fragments. Although it is ideal to have the firearm, bullets themselves can yield important data. By matching striations on bullets recovered at different crime scenes, investigators can tie together information from several cases; the combined data may produce new leads and result in the clearance of the case.

In some cases, the striations on a bullet recovered from a decomposed body can be negatively affected by the interaction between the bullet material and the body tissue.[77] Conversely, an older revolver whose cylinders do not properly align may sheer off a portion of the bullet when fired, creating distinctive markings. Other aspects

► **FIGURE 4-34**
Bullet comparison
A drug user murdered his supplier in order to "cancel" his debt and obtain additional drugs. This is a photomicrograph of the bullet recovered from the body (*left*) compared to a bullet fired from the murder gun (*right*) after the revolver was recovered from a river by police divers. (Courtesy Royal Canadian Mounted Police)

of how individual-class firearm evidence is produced are discussed later in this section.

2. What Else Can Be Learned from the Bullet?

A fired bullet yields evidence of the class characteristics of the weapon that fired it with respect to the number of lands and grooves as well as their height, depth, and width. The class characteristics of a firearm are the design specifications to which it was manufactured; weapons of a given make and model will have the same class characteristics. The individual characteristics of the bore are found in the striae along the fired bullet. Examination of a fired bullet will suggest the type of weapon from which it was fired, whether the bullet is a hard-nose or soft-nose projectile, and the pitch and direction of twist within the barrel. Additionally, if the fired bullet is recovered in sufficient size, it may be possible, through weighing and measurement, to determine its caliber. Since bullets are often recovered as fragments, the caliber may only be implied; for instance, the weight may rule out smaller calibers. Although it is possible to determine the caliber of the bullet, some caution must be taken with respect to determining the bore of the weapon from which it was fired, since a smaller-caliber bullet can be fired through a larger-bore weapon.

Fired bullets are ordinarily damaged on impact. In some cases, you can see fabric impressions on the bullet's nose that were made as the bullet passed through the victim's outer garment. Additionally, there may be minute traces of blood, tissue, bone, fabric, or other such materials (Figure 4-35). Great care must be taken by the investigator not to destroy or in any way alter such evidence. When the fired bullet is to be recovered from the victim, the investigator should alert the attending medical personnel, if there is any doubt about their familiarity with proper handling procedure, as to the

irreparable damage that can be wrought by the careless application of forceps or other such instruments in removing the bullet.

Note that it is ordinarily not possible to make a positive identification as to whether pellets were fired from a particular shotgun. However, in extraordinarily rare circumstances involving smooth-bore firearms, it may be possible to make an individual identification on the basis of gross defects in the barrel.[78]

3. What Determinations Can Be Made from Cartridge Cases?

In contrast to a bullet, which is typically acted on only by the barrel, a cartridge case is subject to a number of different forces that make marks on it, any of which can produce individual-class evidence. Such marks include:

1. Striations made on the outside of cartridge case as it is loaded into the chamber in preparation for firing; these striations may be caused by the action of the magazine or by the slide action of the firearm.
2. A firing-pin impression made on the base of the cartridge case, which is created when the weapon is fired (Figure 4-36).
3. Marks are left on the cartridge case as the exploding gases that propel the bullet forward force the casing outward against the chamber wall and backward against the breach face of the weapon (Figure 4-37). The breach face is the mechanism that holds the bullet in the chamber.
4. **Extractor marks** made when the case is pulled out of the chamber and **ejector marks** made when the case is "kicked out," both of which are associated with semiautomatic and automatic weapons.

Markings made on cartridges by self-loading pistols can vary somewhat over a series of discharges. In laboratory

▲ **FIGURE 4-36   Firing pin impressions**
(*Top*) Photomicrograph showing comparison of questioned and known firing-pin impressions of .22-caliber rim-fire cartridge cases. (*Bottom*) Photomicrograph showing comparison of questioned and known firing-pin impressions on .380-caliber center-fire cartridge cases. Note the significant differences between a rim-fire and a center-fire cartridge: on the center-fire cartridge, the pin must strike the center of the primer to ignite the powder; however, on the rim-fire cartridge, contact may be anywhere around the face of the cartridge. (**Courtesy Forensic Training and Consulting, LLC**)

▲ **FIGURE 4-35   Fabric traces in spent bullet**
In some cases, the fabric of the garment being worn by the victim can be found attached to the bullet. In this unique homicide, the fibers from the sweater of the victim (*top*) are found inside the flattened "mushroom" of the bullet (*bottom*) recovered from the body. (**Courtesy Forensic Training and Consulting, LLC**)

tests, the first and 250th cartridges fired by the same auto-loader were identifiable as being made by the same weapon, but some differences in individual characteristics were observed.[79] Visualization of fingerprints deposited on cartridge cases before the gun was fired can be problematic owing to discharge heat and friction, but prints may be recoverable.[80]

▲ **FIGURE 4-37 Breach-face markings**
Photomicrograph of the breach-face markings on two Speer 9-mm cartridge cases that were recovered at different locations at the scene of a murder. The victim was scheduled to testify in the trial of a drug dealer the next day. The murder is unsolved and under active investigation. (Courtesy Tennessee Bureau of Investigation)

What Miscellaneous Determinations Can Be Made by Examination of Firearms Evidence?

If a firearm is received at a crime laboratory several determinations beyond those mentioned may be possible. Does the weapon function properly, including safety features? Has it been modified to discharge in a manner other than designed, for example, for automatic fire? What was the shot trajectory? If the trigger pull on a weapon is of the "hair" nature, requiring only the slightest pressure to pull it, this would indicate that an accidental shooting was possible. Laboratory examination might reveal that a firearm is constructed—or malfunctioning—in such a way that it could discharge if dropped on its hammer, thereby giving more credibility to a claim that a shooting was accidental. Furthermore, even though invisible to the naked eye, obliterated serial numbers can sometimes be restored

by the laboratory, thus providing an additional investigative lead.

COLLECTING FIREARM EVIDENCE

A cardinal rule in handling weapons at the scene of a crime is that they should never be picked up or moved until they have been photographed and measurements have been made for the crime scene sketch. As in the case of many rules for criminal investigations and as discussed in an earlier chapter, there are several exceptions: (1) if rapidly deteriorating weather conditions, for instance, a driving rain/sleet/snow storm or quickly rising water, threaten the potential to recover fingerprint or DNA evidence from a firearm located outside, move it to a sheltered area; (2) at the scenes of aggravated assaults and murders, feelings run high, and there is a danger that an emotionally charged person may suddenly attempt to pick up a weapon and shoot another party; or (3) there may be some compelling safety need, such as un-cocking a weapon that is in potential danger of falling and discharging.

Following documentation, the process of collecting firearms evidence includes:

1. noting the position of the hammer and the slide, and safety, if applicable;
2. recording the description of rounds and empty chambers in a revolver (Figure 4-37);
3. removing cartridges from a revolver and packaging them individually;
4. noting for semi-automatic/automatic weapons whether there is a misfeed/jam, a chambered cartridge, an inserted magazine, and the number and description of each round in the magazine in their exact sequence;
5. removing any chambered round in a semi-automatic or automatic weapon and releasing the magazine—do not remove any cartridges from the magazine;
6. recording the serial number, not to be confused with patent or model numbers—to avoid manual transcription errors, some law-enforcement agencies and laboratories recommend dusting and lifting the serial number;
7. allowing any fresh blood on a weapon to naturally air dry;
8. placing metal objects recovered from water into a container filled with water from the same source.

In no case should a pencil or similar object be placed into the barrel of the gun to pick it up; this can dislodge evidence that may be in the barrel, such as tissue, blood, hair, or other trace evidence, and it can contaminate the barrel, thereby confusing the laboratory examiner.

To enhance the recovery of blood, tissue, and fingerprints, firearms evidence should be handled as little as possible consistent with the need to process it and "safe" the firearm. A victim is often the donor of blood and tissue on a firearm. Although a victim may grab a gun barrel and leave fingerprints, the more usual case is any fingerprints developed on a weapon or other firearms evidence are from the shooter, unless the victim's own gun has been used against him/her.

"Touch DNA" is a relatively new iteration in DNA analysis that involves skin cells rather than body fluids. When an assailant touches a weapon or rips the clothing from a rape victim, he/she may deposit some of his/her own outermost skin cells, which can establish individual identity. Requests for touch DNA examinations became so routine that some laboratories adopted a policy to conduct them only after all significant leads have been exhausted. Whether done in the field or the laboratory, the systematic swabbing of firearms evidence may produce blood, tissue, or touch DNA. Among the areas to which particular attention should be directed are serrated triggers, hammers, pistol grips, magazines, and safety mechanisms.

In rare situations it may not be possible to "safe" a firearm because of mechanical failure or damage, and in this case the laboratory should be contacted for guidance. The lab may recommend transporting the malfunctioning/damaged gun loaded, which is otherwise not done. Lacking such guidance, one can check with other resources, such as the local ATF office or a military installation.

MARKING AND PACKAGING FIREARM EVIDENCE

The FBI and many state crime laboratories do not recommend marking directly on firearms evidence. A gun should be tagged and placed in an approved firearms box. To secure the gun, place a strap over the barrel and another at the base of the hammer. Straps should never be placed inside the trigger guard. Magazines are another type of firearms evidence that is tagged. Smaller items—for example, cartridges and bullet fragments—should be placed separately in paper envelopes, sealed, and then put into a rigid container. Plastic wrapping or bags are not used with firearms evidence. If there is dried blood on any firearms evidence, a "Biological Hazard" sticker should be placed on the outside of the container.

TOOL MARKS

Tool mark evidence is commonly, but not exclusively, seen in burglaries at the point where a suspect attempted or achieved a forced entry. Figure 4-38 shows a case in which a pry bar was used as a murder weapon. In a rare case, a clod of soil at a gravesite had substantial details left by the digging tool. Later, when a suspect was identified, a mattock was found in the trunk of his car that

examiners concluded was used to dig the grave.[81] A mattock has a wooden handle of roughly 36–42 inches and a metal head, one end of which is a pointed "spike" and the other end looks like a hoe.

A **tool mark** is any impression, cut, gouge, or abrasion made when a tool comes into contact with another object.[82] When a tool and a softer surface come into contact with each other, the softer surface yields (Figure 4-39). The tool may create an impression in the softer surface, produce striations on it, holes through it, or cut/shear the item. Tools often leave microscopic markings that can be class or individual class characteristic evidence[83] (Figure 4-40). Additionally, contaminants on the tool and/or the surface affected may be transferred. Tools may simply require "elbow grease" to use or have a designed action, such as scissors or a bolt cutter. Tool mark examination includes locks and keys, for example, in an attempt made to open a lock with an unauthorized implement.

Tool mark examinations are conducted to:

1. identify the type of tool that made the mark or impression;
2. establish the action used to operate the tool;
3. specify the size and other characteristics of the tool;
4. identify unusual features—for example, a broken tip on a screwdriver;
5. establish whether two portions of a tool were ever commonly joined (Figure 4-41);
6. establish whether the evidence is suitable for comparison purposes;
7. determine whether "this" tool could have made "that" impression or mark. Alternatively, the examiner might report that the evidence is inconclusive or exclude the tool as a source for making an impression or mark.

In collecting evidence of tool marks, make every effort to obtain and submit the actual area for direct comparison. When this is not possible, a cast should be made. There are several good choices for casting tool marks, including Mikrosil. Tool marks should be photographed to establish their locations; however, the images have no forensic identification value. In no event should the investigator place a tool against a tool mark for size evaluation; doing so could lead to accidental cross contamination or result in the accidental destruction of evidence. When a tool is to be submitted to the crime laboratory for examination, the actual tool should be submitted; the making of test impressions or cuts is a function of qualified technicians in the laboratory. The importance of this last point is illustrated by the fact that under test conditions in the laboratory examiners found that when there was more than a 15-degree difference between the vertical angle at which a screwdriver was actually used and the comparison mark made in the laboratory, an improper finding of no identity from the same tool could result.[84]

► FIGURE 4-41
Fracture-match tool
While trying to pry open a window during an attempted burglary-rape, the suspect broke the kitchen knife he was using as a tool, leaving the end of the knife embedded in the window sill. The suspect was later found walking in a nearby park with the broken knife and handle in his pocket. A fracture match of the knife tip was made with the remainder of the knife handle. (Courtesy Albuquerque Police Department)

► FIGURE 4-42
A counterfeit marriage license
Note the differences between the "M" in "Robert M. Webster" and the "M" in "May," "March," and "Minister." Also, note the differences between the "3" and "4" in Webster's age and the same numbers elsewhere in the document. The differences in the type fonts as well as the gaps in the lines under the changed letters, left by whiting out the original entry, indicate a counterfeit document. (Courtesy Immigration and Naturalization Service, Forensic Document Laboratory)

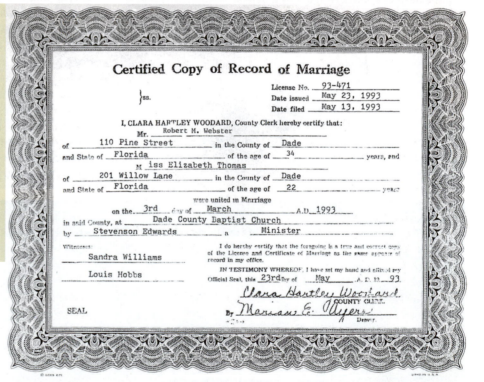

add his/her own initials, identifying number, and the date and time, and he/she should number the pages sequentially as they are completed.

2. Collect requested writings with the same class/type of writing instrument as was used in the questioned samples. If this is not known, use a black ballpoint pen. If the questioned is on lined paper, paper of the same size should be used to collect the known. As each signature or extended writing is completed it should be removed from the person's sight.

3. Nonrequested samples should be collected from existing documents created/signed closest to the time the questioned document was executed, because handwriting evolves over time. Among the sources for nonrequested samples are signatures on Miranda warnings; suspects' statement; notes to jailers; credit, employment, employment, insurance, and mortgage

applications; messages written on greeting cards given to others; and workers' compensation claims.

Nonrequested writings were not executed with the thought they would be scrutinized and therefore ordinarily are not disguised in any way. Disguised handwriting is problematic for document examiners, and it attracts more misleading and inconclusive rates of authorship opinions; one study concluded that the error rate for examiners in labeling a writing genuine or disguised was 4.3%.[89] A difficulty with nonrequested samples is locating sufficient high-quality signatures and extended writing material from the same time frame as the questioned samples.

Document examination is partially automated, using software such as CedarFox. Its capabilities include comparison of samples and searching handwriting databases to find potential matches, both of which must be confirmed by the examiner.[90]

LABORATORY DETERMINATIONS

In addition to the possibility of determining whether handwriting can be attributed to a particular person, laboratories *may* be able to:

1. Determine whether a document is authentic or counterfeit. In 1983, 62 volumes of diaries attributed to Adolph Hitler were purchased by a German publisher. Three handwriting experts concluded Hitler wrote them, although others disagreed. However, forensic analysis established the method used to produce the paper on which the diaries were written was not available until 1954, and the ink used was first manufactured in 1982.

2. Recover indented writing; if not visible to the eye, indented writings may be located by an electrostatic detection apparatus (ESDA).

3. Identify the class/type of the writing instrument, such as a ballpoint, felt-tip pen, or pencil.

4. Determine whether the inks of known and questioned samples have consistent characteristics—the Secret Service and the Internal Revenue Service maintain the International Ink Library with more than 9,500 samples.

5. Decipher charred, burned, or water-soaked documents.

6. Match the ends of cut/torn paper. A man handed a bank teller a note, "This is a robbery." He left

with money, but she retained the note. A week later, police executed a search warrant at the suspect's home, finding "This is a robbery" in indented writing on a pad. A portion of paper remaining in the pad also matched one end of the robbery note.[91]

7. Establish the source of paper through watermarks and other features.

8. Detect erasures, obliterations, and alterations to documents.

9. Determine whether one or more pages in a document were added subsequently to its original production.

10. Establish the relative age of a document.

11. Determine whether an office machine—for example, scanner, photocopier, typewriter, fax machine, or computer printer—is associated with a particular document. Often, the machine must have a defect or some unusual attribute to be distinguishable. However, there is substantial interest in developing "signatures" for scanners, printers, and digital cameras. One line of inquiry is looking at their intrinsic features to identify unique attributes; the alternative method is to embed microscopic codes, such as a serial number, on each page of output.

COLLECTING AND PACKAGING EVIDENCE

In many respects, all evidence collection is like the first rule of physicians: do no harm. Investigators should not attempt to reassemble torn or shredded documents; write on, trace, highlight, or underline portions of them; or make repairs to or fold them. Documents should be collected and processed using the following guidelines:

1. Wear gloves and use clean tweezers to handle documents.

2. Handle the documents as little as possible.

3. Use a transparent envelope if possible; otherwise, use a manila paper one.

4. Before placing the document in the envelope, fill out all required blocks of information on it and then slip it in the evidence and seal it.

5. Processing for latent prints and DNA is a laboratory responsibility.

6. Keep documents in a cool, low-humidity environment, out of the sunlight, until submitted to the lab.

| KEY TERMS

bore	dental stone	fluorescent powder
caliber	document	forensic light source
concentric fracture	ejector mark	forensic odontology
class characteristics	extractor mark	fracture match
CrimeShoe	fingerprint	grooves
cross contamination	fingerprint patterns	Hemident

Hexagon OBTI
impressions
individual characteristics
known source
lands
latent prints
latent/invisible prints
Luminol
minutiae

MtDNA
Paint Data Query
patent/contaminated/visible prints
plastic print
postmortem (after-death) dental
    profiling
questioned document
radial fracture
residue prints

rifling
SoleMate
Super Glue fuming
tool mark
Touch DNA
traditional powders
TreadMate
unknown (questioned) sources

REVIEW QUESTIONS

1. What are class and individual characteristics?
2. How are known and questioned sources different?
3. What procedures would you follow to take soil samples?
4. How do you cast a shoe impression using dental stone?
5. What is the proper way to collect loose paint chips at a crime scene?
6. Radial and concentric fractures are different in what way?
7. What are minutiae?
8. How are plastic prints formed?
9. You are assigned to dust for latent fingerprints on a white refrigerator door using a traditional powder. How should you do this?
10. Forensic odontology can be an asset in what five circumstances?
11. What conclusions are possible from the examination of hair?
12. What is Touch DNA?
13. How would you attempt to locate "hidden blood" at a crime scene?
14. A revolver is found near a body at an indoor crime scene. What procedures should be followed for processing the revolver?
15. How do you collect a tool impression in a door-frame where a prying-type action was used to gain entry in a burglary?
16. What is a questioned document?

INTERNET ACTIVITIES

The FBI and other federal agencies have been working for more than 20 years to advance forensic standards and techniques. One mechanism to achieve these goals has been the creation of scientific working groups (SWGs) and technical working groups (TWGs). Altogether, there are perhaps 15 SWGs and TWGs, whose membership include both federal and state/local law-enforcement agencies that have produced important publications. Visit SWGs and TWGs at *www2.fbi.gov/hq/lab/html/swg.htm*.

◄ Officers interview suspects arrested for possession of cocaine outside a house where a search warrant has been served. Interview questions focus on suspects' knowledge of the drug-related activities occurring inside the house.
(© A. Ramey/PhotoEdit)

5

INTERVIEWING AND INTERROGATION

In every criminal investigation process, interviewing and interrogation are among the most important means of obtaining needed information about a crime. Both require a combination of artistry and skill that must be cultivated and practiced. However, not all people who possess information needed by the investigator are willing to share it. This is true in both interviews and interrogations. Witnesses may have various motivations and perceptions that can influence their responses during an interview. Their motivations and perceptions may be based on either conscious choices or subconscious stimuli. In addition, gaining information from specific demographic groups such as the elderly, those who do not speak English, or persons with physical infirmities requires unique skills on the part of the investigator. Situational characteristics such as the time and place of the interview or interrogation may also create challenges to eliciting information about a particular case. Each of these conditions must be effectively addressed in both interview and interrogation settings. The successful interviewer or interrogator must fully understand the techniques of interviewing and interrogation and be able to evaluate the psychological reasons why people are willing or reluctant to impart information. In this chapter we also examine many other important elements in the interviewing and interrogation process, including witness protection, false confessions, and the most recent U.S. Supreme Court rulings regarding the admissibility of confessions and the most effective methods for **detection of deception.**

INTERVIEWS AND INTERROGATIONS: SIMILARITIES AND DIFFERENCES

The success of an interview or interrogation depends on a number of personal characteristics and commitments of the investigator. Planning for and controlling the events surrounding both interviews and interrogations are important but are generally viewed as more critical to the success of an interrogation. Establishing **rapport,** asking good questions, listening carefully, and keeping proper documentation are elements common to both forms of obtaining information. Table 5-1 illustrates the similarities between interviews and interrogations.

	TABLE 5-1	Similarities between Interviews and Interrogations
INTERVIEWS	**INTERROGATIONS**
Planning important	Planning critical
Controlling surroundings important	Controlling surroundings critical
Privacy or semiprivacy desirable	Absolute privacy essential
Establishing rapport important	Establishing rapport important
Asking good questions important	Asking good questions important
Careful listening	Careful listening
Proper documentation	Proper documentation

CHAPTER OUTLINE

Besides the difference in purpose between interviewing and interrogation, many other distinctions exist. Of paramount importance are the myriad legal requirements that pertain to interrogations but are absent in interviews. Because of the criticality of confessions and their use in obtaining convictions, it is not surprising that numerous legal guidelines and standards apply in interrogations that would not be needed in interviewing witnesses or victims; these are all discussed in greater detail later in this chapter. Also, it is far more likely that a hostile and adversarial relationship will exist between an interrogator and a **suspect** than between an interviewer and a **victim** or **witness.** The differences between interviews and interrogations are noted in Table 5-2.

OBJECTIVES OF INTERVIEWING

Interviews are conducted in criminal cases for the purpose of gathering information from people who have, or may have, knowledge needed in the investigation. The information may come from a victim or from a person who has no other relationship to the criminal activity other than being where he or she was. But interviewing is not a haphazard process consisting of a list of questions. It is a planned conversation with a specific goal.

The job of the investigator-interviewer is to elicit from the witness information actually perceived through one or more of the witness's five senses—sight, hearing, smell, taste, and touch. In any given case, any or all of a witness's senses may be involved. For example, in a case involving a drug-related killing, a witness may see the perpetrator pull the trigger, hear the victim scream, smell the pungent odor of marijuana burning, taste the white

TABLE 5-2	Differences between Interviews and Interrogations
INTERVIEWS	**INTERROGATIONS**
Purpose is to obtain information	Purpose is to test information already obtained
Minimal or no preinterview legal requirements; no rights warning	Extensive preinterrogation legal requirements; rights warning required
Cooperative relationship between interviewer and subject likely	Adversarial or hostile relationship between interrogator and subject likely
No guilt or guilt uncertain	Guilt suggested or likely
Moderate planning or preparation	Extensive planning and preparation
Private or semiprivate environment desirable	Absolute privacy essential

Source: John Fay, unpublished notebook, American Society for Industrial Security, Workshop in Criminal Interrogation (Jacksonville, FL: ASIS, 1991), p. A1-1.

powdery substance later identified as heroin, and touch the victim to feel for a pulse.

Because, as earlier suggested, witnesses report perceptions based on their own interests, priorities, and biases, obtaining accurate and sometimes even voluntary information is not as easy to obtain as it may first appear. Investigators must always be sensitive to any of the psychological, physical and environmental influences as well as the motivations affecting witness perceptions.

At the outset of the interview, the person to be interviewed must satisfy three requirements of being a witness: presence, consciousness, and attentiveness to what was happening.[1] Presence and consciousness are relatively easy to establish in the interview process; attentiveness is more difficult. Yet all three elements are important to establishing the accuracy of a witness's perception.

OBJECTIVES OF INTERROGATION

Interrogation as opposed to interviewing is designed to match acquired information to a particular suspect in order to secure a **confession.** Whereas interviewing is primarily for the purpose of gaining information, interrogation is the process of testing that information and its application to a particular suspect.

There are four commonly recognized objectives in the interrogation process:

1. to obtain valuable facts;
2. to eliminate the innocent;
3. to identify the guilty;
4. to obtain a confession.

As the investigator moves from the preliminary task of gathering valuable facts to the concluding task of obtaining a confession, the difficulty of acquiring information increases. That difficulty, however, is rewarded by an increase in the value of the information. Figure 5-1 illustrates these relationships. In attempting to obtain a confession from a suspect, the interrogator also gains information about the facts and circumstances surrounding the commission of an offense. In seeking such information, the investigator must be concerned with asking the basic questions that apply to all aspects of the investigative process: Who? What? Where? When? How? and Why?

QUALIFICATIONS OF INTERVIEWS AND INTERROGATORS

The effective interviewer or interrogator must be knowledgeable in the art and science of criminal investigation and know how to use psychology, salesmanship, and dra-

▲ **FIGURE 5-1   Objectives of interrogation**
(John Fay, unpublished notebook, American Society for Industrial Security, Workshop in Criminal Interrogation [Jacksonville, FL: ASIS, 1981], p. A2-1)

matics. Persuasiveness and perseverance are also essential to success. The interviewer or interrogator must make himself/herself easy to talk to. By the appropriate use of vocal inflection, modulation, and emphasis, even the Miranda warnings (discussed later in this chapter) can be presented to a suspect in a manner that does not cause the suspect to immediately assume a defensive posture. The words can be spoken without creating an adversarial atmosphere. The interviewer or interrogator must have a flexible personality and must be able to convey empathy, sympathy, anger, fear, and joy at appropriate times, but must always remain objective. The interviewer or interrogator must keep an open mind and be receptive to all information, regardless of its nature.

A positive, firm approach, an ability to inspire confidence, and knowledge of a broad range of topics of general interest all help establish dominance or control in an interview: Behavior—not words—that shows confidence, determines dominance.[2]

During an interrogation, the investigator must carefully evaluate each development while studiously avoiding the pitfall of underestimating the capabilities of the subject being interrogated. Screaming or shouting, belittling the subject or the information, sneering, and other such unplanned and uncontrolled reactions most often adversely affect the interrogation. The investigator must at all times maintain control of the interrogation without being openly domineering, by being a good active listener, by being serious, patient, and, most important, by being persistent and persuasive.[3] An ability to categorize the psychological and emotional traits being manifested by the suspect helps the investigator react in a manner that increases the possibility of conducting a successful interrogation, for it is the job of the interrogator to make it easy for a suspect to confess.

TIME, PLACE, AND SETTING OF INTERVIEWING AND INTERROGATION

Law-enforcement officers conduct interviews in a number of situations. The most common is the on-the-scene interview. Whether it is a routine traffic accident investigation or a major felony case, officers who respond to the scene should, at the earliest possible moment, seek out and identify individuals who may have knowledge of the event and whose information may contribute to the investigation. Such individuals, of course, include victims and other participants as well as uninvolved witnesses. Once witnesses have been identified, they should be separated from one another and, as much as possible, isolated from other people who may be loitering in the area (Figure 5-2). This prevents the witnesses from seeing or hearing irrelevant matters that may taint their actual knowledge. All witnesses should be interviewed as soon as practical, while their memory is still fresh, but this rule must be applied with discretion to take into account all circumstances.

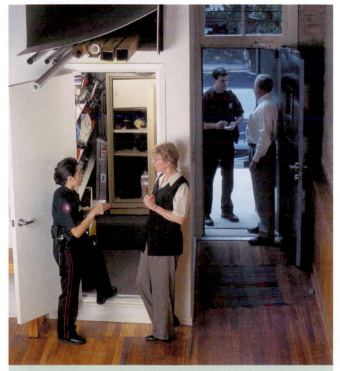

▲ **FIGURE 5-2   Police interview witnesses separately**
A domestic violence complaint called to 911 by a neighbor who heard these people screaming at each other and what sounded like heavy objects being thrown around, hitting walls and the floor, brought these officers to the scene. It turned out to be an argument, but neither party committed a domestic assault or battery. (© Bob Daemmrich/The Image Works)

Although convenience of the witness is important to a successful interview, the interviewer need not relinquish the psychological advantage in selecting the time and place of the interview. It is not a good practice, for example, to rouse a witness from bed in the middle of the night. However, there are certain psychological advantages to questioning a witness at a law-enforcement agency rather than in the witness's own home or office. A witness may feel in a better position to control the interview in familiar surroundings. The investigator cannot let this happen; he or she must be fair but always be in command of the situation.

After taking into account the factors of immediacy, privacy, convenience, and control, and weighing the importance of each in the context of the total circumstances, the investigator may decide to interview witnesses at their homes or places of business. As a matter of courtesy, the investigator should attempt to make an appointment to ensure convenience, particularly for professional and businesspeople. Others, such as salespeople, office workers, and laborers, may be interviewed during working hours with approval of their supervisors.

Privacy is of the utmost importance in conducting interviews (Figure 5-3). Distractions tend to have an adverse effect on the interview and its results. The interviewer should insist on as much privacy as possible, but the circumstances of on-the-scene interviews often have to be recognized as a fact of life for the investigator, who can be expected to perform only to the best of his/her ability in the given case. Similarly, investigators are often called on to canvass neighborhoods and interview residents. In these instances, investigators often are in no position to influence the conditions under which the interview takes place. Noisy children, blaring television sets, nosy neighbors, and similar factors must be accepted.

The physical and emotional states of the witnesses are important when one is conducting or determining whether to conduct an interview. Cold, sleepy, hungry, physically uncomfortable, or intoxicated people generally prove to be unsatisfactory witnesses.[4] Similarly, persons suffering noticeable emotional problems can give, at best, highly questionable information. Most investigators can recognize this state and wisely choose to wait until the witness becomes lucid before conducting the interview.

Reinterviewing witnesses should be avoided if the reinterview is likely to produce nothing beyond the information given in the initial statement. Reinterviewing tends to become less and less convenient for witnesses, even though they may be friendly and cooperative. There may also be a tendency for reinterviewed witnesses to feel that the investigator does not know his/her job or was not prepared during the initial interview. To avoid this problem, the investigator should first tell the witness that the purpose of the interview is not to rehash old information and should then explain what new

► FIGURE 5-3
Interviewing a witness
This woman saw a purse-snatching incident occur on a main street in this city about an hour before this photo was taken. She is with one of the investigating officers explaining what she witnessed, describing the man who grabbed the other woman's purse and ran, and giving a statement. (© Mike Karlsson/Arresting Images)

information is being sought. The investigator should ask for the information in a manner that does not elicit a repetition of the previous interview. But investigators should not hesitate to conduct follow-up interviews when necessary, whether there was lack of skill in obtaining an initial statement, new information has developed, or the time or setting of the initial interview did not elicit the full attention of the witness.

Unlike the interview, which may take place in any number of different locations and at various times—which may or may not be advantageous to the investigator—interrogation is a process controlled by the interrogator. The interrogator is in command of the setting and governs the number and kinds of interruptions. The most critical factor in controlling the interrogation is to ensure privacy and to guarantee that any distractions, planned or otherwise, are controlled by the interrogator. Privacy may be used as a psychological tool; the suspect may feel more willing to unload his/her burden of guilt in front of only one person.

THE INTERROGATION ROOM

The traditional interrogation room should be sparsely furnished, usually with only two chairs. There should be no physical barriers, such as tables or desks, between the investigator and the suspect. From the officer's standpoint, such barriers may create an unwanted feeling of psychological well-being on the part of the suspect.

If there is a table or desk in the room, the chairs should be corner to corner rather than on opposite sides. This arrangement permits the interrogator to move both chairs away from the table and eliminate the barrier (Figure 5-4).[5]

Proximity in an interrogation can also be important. The suspect and the interrogator should be close enough to touch without being too close, without having any object such as a chair or desk between them. "It seems, for example, that around 27 inches is the limit of proximity for white American middle-class males . . . If you move closer, people become uncomfortable . . . farther

▲ FIGURE 5-4   **Interrogation room**
Note that the table and chairs can be easily moved so the table does not separate the interrogator from the suspect.
(© Mike Karlsson/Arresting Images)

away than 27 inches, you can't read a person's face well."[6] There are, however, considerable differences in the comfort zones of various ethnic groups, and interrogators must make it a point to know as much as possible about the unique psychological and cultural characteristics of the individuals they are most likely to encounter both in interviews as well as interrogations.

The two-way mirror, although still a useful tool for allowing others to observe the interrogation, is widely known and may cause some subjects to refuse to cooperate in the interrogation. If a two-way mirror is to be used, it should be small and unobtrusive. As a standard practice, the interrogation room should be equipped with a video or audio system that includes a recording device, unless prohibited by state law. (The use of electronic recording in interrogation is discussed later in this chapter.)

Although the traditional interrogation room just described is designed to ensure control and domination over the interrogation because of its privacy, security, and aura of authority, this approach does not impress the habitual or experienced offender, who understands the rules and standards of conduct of the classical interrogation room. If the offender is skilled and intelligent, he/she not only can cope with the psychological influences such a setting is designed to foster but perhaps also can become the dominant force, or at least be on the same psychological level as the interrogator. When this occurs, the skills of the interrogator become even more important.

PREPARATION FOR THE INTERVIEW OR INTERROGATION

The success of the interviewer or interrogator and of the interview or interrogation is often determined by the time and dedication committed to preparing for the conversation. The interviewer must become familiar with the facts of the case under investigation and with the victim. To carry out the four objectives listed earlier, the interrogator must learn as much as possible about the offense, the victim(s), and the suspect through the process of collecting, assessing, and analyzing data and theorizing about the motivations and thought processes of the suspect. This begins the formulation of a profile that will then dictate the initial approach the interrogator will take on first contacting the suspect.

THE WITNESS

If the interview is to be conducted with a witness other than the victim, the interviewer should find out as much about the witness as possible before the interview. This includes learning about the witness's motivations and

perceptions and any barriers that might exist. In some cases it might be advantageous to determine if a witness has a previous criminal record.

THE OFFENSE

It is necessary that the interviewer know specifically what crime or crimes were allegedly committed. This knowledge includes a working familiarity with the elements of each offense and some understanding of the kind of information necessary to prove each. Accurate information on the date, time, place, and method of the crime—including tools used, points of entry and exit, method of travel to and from the scene, complete description of any property involved, weapons used, modus operandi, and physical evidence recovered—is essential. The interviewer should also obtain a full description of the crime scene and the surrounding area. In addition, any and all possible motives should be identified.

THE VICTIM

The interviewer should learn as much as possible about the victim's background, the nature of the injury or loss, attitudes toward the investigation, and any other useful information, such as the existence of insurance in a property crime case. If the victim is an organization or a business, a determination of any practices that would make the organization a criminal target could be extremely valuable. If relevant, the interviewer should determine whether the business is insured against losses.

THE SUSPECT

The interrogator must evaluate the circumstances surrounding the conduct of the interrogation and must begin to evaluate the suspect. An effective interrogator understands that a successful interrogation cannot be organized and compartmentalized into a neat, orderly, step-by-step package. Rather, it is a combination of personality, behavior, and interpersonal communication skills between the interrogator and suspect. It is made up of verbal processes and the way they are communicated, nonverbal actions including **body language,** and personality characteristics that together might be characterized as a psychological fingerprint.[7] Only by understanding the interaction of all these variables can the interrogator effectively evaluate the interrogation process as it will be initiated and as it will be modified during the interrogation.[8] To begin the preparation, the interrogator should review the offense report, statement of witnesses, laboratory reports, all file information pertaining to the suspect, and other related data. It is also essential that the interrogator know all the elements of the offense involved. Failure to possess this information may preclude obtaining a complete confession, which, by definition, must contain **admissions** by the suspect to the commission of each and every element of the crime.

▲ FIGURE 5-5
Investigator preparing for interview/interrogation
This investigator is reviewing her notes one last time to ensure she has all available information on and statements of witnesses, information and statements of the victim, lab reports, investigative materials, a knowledge of the elements of the offense, and as much information as is available about the probable suspect before beginning her interviews or interrogation. (© Spencer Grant/PhotoEdit)

WITNESSES: MOTIVATIONS, PERCEPTIONS, AND BARRIERS

There are many types of witnesses, and each has different motivations and perceptions that influence his/her responses during an interview. The motivations and perceptions may be based on either conscious choices or subconscious stimuli. The interviewer must learn to recognize, overcome, and compensate for these factors.

There is no way to categorize all personalities, attitudes, and other character traits. The variables are too numerous and individualized; the combinations are as complex as the human mind. Nevertheless, there are some basic groupings that can be mentioned:

- Some witnesses may be honest and cooperative and desire to impart information in their possession to the investigator. Despite these admirable qualities, however, the information may still be affected by other factors that influence all witnesses, such as age, physical characteristics, and emotions. It may be wise in most circumstances to interview this type of witness first to obtain basic information that can then be compared with later-acquired stories.
- Some witnesses may desire not to give any information in an interview regardless of what they know. Some may simply not want to get involved, while others may fear any contact with a law-enforcement agency, especially if they have had some earlier negative experiences with law enforcement. This is especially true of immigrants who have come from developing countries in which the police may have been corrupt. Others may not understand the significance of information they have, and some may not want to do anything that would aid law enforcement.
- Some witnesses may be reluctant to cooperate or be suspicious of the motives of the interviewer until a rapport is established and the investigator can assure the witness of his or her good intentions.

Because some witnesses may be deceitful and provide incorrect information, it is a basic principle that an investigator should never take a witness's explanation totally at face value but should obtain supporting information or evidence.

There may be other barriers that must be overcome in order to successfully interview someone who has knowledge of the circumstances under which a crime was committed. Language barriers, which may not initially be recognized as significant, may prevent the interviewer from obtaining any useful information; however, some people may be so talkative and provide so much information that their motives should be questioned, along

The investigation should reveal as much personal background information on the suspect as can be obtained (Figure 5-5). This information should include aliases, Social Security number, date and place of birth, education, marital status, employment history, financial history and current circumstances, prior offenses, past and present physical and mental health, any drug or alcohol abuse or addiction, relationship to the victim or crime scene, possible motive, biases and prejudices, home environment, sexual interests (if relevant), and hobbies. Additionally, the investigation and preparation for an interrogation should determine whether the suspect had the capability and opportunity to commit the offense and should confirm or disprove an alibi.

The interrogator should also obtain as much information as possible from other people involved to determine the suspect's attitude. This will enable the interrogator to anticipate levels of hostility or cooperativeness during the interrogation.

with the information they provide. A potential witness who may be under the influence of alcohol or drugs may or may not have information that could be used at trial; thus the condition of the witness is a major factor to be considered in assessing the value of any information obtained.

PERSONS WITH PHYSICAL INFIRMITIES

Interviewing an older person or any person with physical infirmities may present a unique set of challenges. The interviewer must have knowledge of and appreciation for the physical changes that may occur with aging and be able to effectively respond to those changes when conducting an interview.[9]

Visual Infirmities

Changes in vision that are related to aging vary widely from person to person. These changes are not strictly dependent on chronological age or general health, and excellent vision without glasses is sometimes maintained even in extreme old age. However, this last situation is an exception. About three-fourths of all older women and over half of all older men experience moderate to severe changes in visual functions. Those 65 or older account for half of all legally blind persons in the United States. The simple statistical probabilities are that an older person will have vision difficulties of one kind or another.

If the witness claims to have seen something, the investigator should ascertain if the witness had his or her glasses on, or contact lenses in.

Hearing Loss

Hearing loss resulting in a distortion of sounds generally is caused by changes in the inner ear. A person who suffers from a hearing loss must take advantage of every opportunity to use other skills in communicating, such as speech reading. Speech reading, often thought of as "lip reading," is the process of visually receiving cues from all lip movements, facial expressions, body posture, gestures, and the environment. Speech reading is a skill everyone has to a certain degree. It is only when hearing becomes impaired that this skill becomes important.

Interviewers will be able to communicate most effectively and interview hearing-impaired people by following these suggestions: (1) gain the person's attention; (2) speak to a person from a distance of 3–6 feet; (3) speak clearly; (4) control external noises as much as possible.

Competency of a Witness

The term *competency* refers to a witness's personal qualifications for testifying in court. Competency must be established before a witness is permitted to give any testimony. The witness's personal qualification depends on circumstances that affect his or her legal ability to function as a sworn witness in court. Competency has nothing to do with the believability of a witness's information.

Among the factors an investigator must evaluate in determining the competency of a witness are age, level of intelligence, mental state, relationship to individuals involved in the case, and background characteristics that might preclude the testimony of the witness from being heard in court. For example, in many jurisdictions, a young child cannot be a witness unless it can be shown that the child knows the difference between truth and imagination and understands the importance of being honest. Similarly, any person whose intelligence or mental state prevents him/her from understanding the obligation of telling the truth is not permitted to testify, regardless of the information he/she may possess.

Relationships among individuals involved in a case may also affect a witness's competency. Husbands and wives need not testify against each other, nor may attorneys testify against clients, doctors against patients, or ministers against penitents. Privileges vary by state. Background characteristics also may preclude a witness's testimony from being accepted in court. For example, some state laws forbid a convicted perjurer from testifying.

Possibilities such as those described in the preceding paragraphs mean the investigator must learn as much as possible about the witness before and during the interview.

RELIABILITY OF EYEWITNESS IDENTIFICATION

Eyewitness identification and other information provided by eyewitnesses to a criminal event are relied on heavily by both law enforcement and courts in the investigative and adjudication stages of our system of justice,[10] yet research indicates that eyewitness testimony is the most unreliable form of evidence and causes more miscarriages of justice than any other method of proof[11, 12] (Figure 5-6).

Research and courtroom experience provide ample evidence that an eyewitness to a crime is being asked to be something and do something that is not easily accomplished. Human perception is sloppy and uneven.[13] Existing research does not permit precise conclusions about the overall accuracy of the eyewitness identifications that are a common feature of criminal prosecutions, but research does lead us to conclude that identification errors are not infrequent.[14] Such errors are borne out by case studies in which the use of DNA evidence exonerated people who had been convicted on the basis of eyewitness identification.[15]

Many factors influence an individual's ability to accurately recognize and identify persons, and all of them depend on the circumstances under which the information is initially perceived and encoded, stored, and retrieved.[16] Eyewitness identifications take place in a

▲ **FIGURE 5-6** **Look-alikes**
Mistaken identifications led to the arrests of two innocent men: Lawrence Berson (*left*) for several rapes and George Morales (*right*) for a robbery. Both men were picked out of police lineups by victims of the crimes. Berson was cleared when Richard Carbone (*center*) was arrested and implicated in the rapes. Carbone was convicted. He later confessed to the robbery, clearing Morales.
(From Scientific American, 1974, Vol. 231, No. 6, Reprinted by permission)

social context[17] in which the witness's own personality and characteristics, along with those of the target observed, are as critical as factors relating to the situation or environment in which the action takes place.

Thus, human perception and memory are selective and constructive functions, not exact copies of the event perceived. The gaps will often be filled in by the observer in order to produce a logical and complete sequence of events. A person is motivated by a desire to be accurate as she/he imposes meaning on the overabundance of information that impinges on her/his senses, but also by a desire to live up to the expectations of other people and to stay in their good graces. The eye, the ear, and other sense organs are, therefore, social organs as well as physical ones.[18]

Agreeing with this theory of eyewitness perception, one observer notes:

Studies of memory for sentences and pictures indicate that when we experience an event, we do not simply file a memory, and then on some later occasion retrieve it and read off what we've stored. Rather, at the time of recall or recognition we reconstruct the event, using information from many sources. These include both the original perception of the event and inferences drawn later, after the fact. Over a period of time, information from these sources may integrate, so that a witness becomes unable to say how they know a specific detail. In the end they only have a single unified memory.[19]

The gender, age, expectations, intelligence, race, and facial recognition skills of the witness are factors that individually may or may not influence the eyewitness identification process but collectively or in combination with other variables are likely to have a bearing.[20] Facial attractiveness and distinctiveness, disguises, facial transformations, and the gender and race of the target (the person identified) are factors likely to influence identification.[21] Situational factors include such things as the presence of a weapon, exposure duration, and significance of the event in relation to all surrounding circumstances.[22]

Experts distinguish a number of factors that limit a person's ability to give a complete account of events or to identify people accurately. The following are among those factors:

- *The significance or insignificance of the event:* When an insignificant event occurs in the presence of an individual, it does not generally motivate the individual to bring fully into play the selective process of attention.
- *The length of the period of observation:* If ample opportunity is not provided for observation, the capability of the memory to record that which is perceived is decreased.
- *Lack of ideal conditions:* In situations where ideal conditions for observation are absent, the ability of the witness to perceive details is significantly decreased. Distance, poor lighting, fast movement, or the presence of a crowd may significantly interfere with the efficient working of the attention process.
- *Psychological factors internal to the witness:* A witness under stress at the time of observation may find this to be a major source of unreliability in his/her observations.

- *The physical condition of the witness.* If the witness is injured or intoxicated, this condition will affect his/her ability to provide complete and accurate information.
- *Lack of familiarity with members of another race or ethnic group.* Some of the most egregious cases of misidentification have occurred in those crimes which are interracial or interethnic in nature. These occur because in some cases the victim is not accustomed to dealing with members of the race or ethnic group of the assailant and is unable to distinguish important variation in facial characteristics. The more contact the victim has had with members of that race or ethnic group the less likely it is that a misidentification will occur.
- *Expectancy:* Research has shown that memory recall and judgment are often based on what psychologists term *expectancy*. This concept means that an individual perceives things in the manner in which he or she expects them to appear. For example, a right-handed eyewitness to a homicide might, in answer to a question and without positive knowledge, state the assailant held the gun in his right hand, whereas a left-handed person might say the opposite. Biases or prejudices are also illustrated by the expectancy theory, as is the classic problem associated with stereotyping.[23]

WITNESS INTIMIDATION

Citizens who witness or are victimized by crime are sometimes reluctant to report incidents to the police or to assist in the prosecution of offenders.[24, 25] Such reluctance may be in response to a perceived or actual threat of retaliation by the offender or his or her associates, or may be the result of more generalized community norms that discourage residents from cooperating with police and prosecutors. In some communities, close ties between witnesses, offenders, and their families and friends may also deter witnesses from cooperating; these relationships can provide a vitally important context for understanding witness intimidation. Particularly in violent and gang-related crime, the same individual may, at different times, be a victim, a witness, and an offender.[26] Historically, witness intimidation is most closely associated with organized crime and domestic violence, but has recently thwarted efforts to investigate and prosecute drug, gang violence and other types of crime.

FORMS OF WITNESS INTIMIDATION

Witness intimidation takes many forms, including:

- implicit threats, looks, or gestures;
- explicit threats of violence;
- actual physical violence;
- property damage;
- other threats, such as challenges to child custody or immigration status;
- confronting witnesses verbally;
- sending notes and letters;
- making nuisance phone calls;
- parking or loitering outside the homes of witnesses;
- damaging witnesses' houses or property;
- threatening witnesses' children, spouses, parents, or other family members;
- assaulting or even murdering witnesses or their family members.

Threats are much more common than actual physical violence and are in fact just as effective in deterring cooperation.[27] Although some witnesses experience a single incident of intimidation, it may also involve an escalating series of threats and actions that become more violent over time.[28] Other witnesses do not experience intimidation directly but rather believe retaliation will occur if they cooperate with police. Either way, they are deterred from offering relevant information that might assist the police and prosecutors. Particularly in communities dominated by gang and drug-related crime, residents have seen firsthand that offenders are capable of violence and brutality. Many witnesses also believe offenders will return to the community after relatively brief periods of incarceration or will be able to arrange for intimidation by others while they are incarcerated. In many cases the experience of actually having witnessed violence by the perpetrators or groups of individuals in the community lends considerable credibility to any threats and creates a general sense of fear that discourages cooperation with police.

RESPONSE STRATEGIES FOR ADDRESSING WITNESS INTIMIDATION

The following response strategies provide a foundation for addressing witness intimidation.

- *Form multi-agency partnerships.* The appropriate party to address the threat of witness intimidation may change as a case moves through the criminal justice system. For example, the police may be responsible for protecting or supporting witnesses at the outset a case, but the responsibility might later shift to the prosecutor when the case goes to trial.
- *Strengthen ties between police and the community.* Fostering cooperation of reluctant witnesses is a natural extension of community policing and community prosecution, which focus on engaging residents in preventing and responding to crime.[29] For example, mobile precincts can increase police visibility after a high-profile gang-related crime in an area where intimidation is likely to occur. Storefront precincts can increase the level of contact with residents and make it easier to provide encouragement and support.

- *Minimize the risk of witness identification when reporting crime or offering statements.* This is particularly true in neighborhoods where communitywide intimidation is a factor and residents may hesitate to cooperate with police at the scene of a crime, because they fear being labeled as an informant or a "rat." As a result, methods for reporting crime or offering witness statements that do not make cooperation obvious to observers are sometimes needed.[30]

- *Reduce the likelihood of contact between witnesses and offenders.* Most often, acts of intimidation are committed at a witness's home, workplace, or school, or during the normal course of the witness's daily activities. Minimizing the opportunities and avenues by which witnesses come into contact with offenders can reduce the incidence of intimidation. For example, wherever practical witnesses can alter their normal routines by varying the routes taken to work or school and making their schedules irregular and unpredictable.[31]

- *Transport witnesses to and from work and school.* Many witnesses feel vulnerable when traveling to and from work or school, or while attending to their business in the community. Police escorts during these times can deter offenders from making contact. However, such protection schemes consume significant police resources and may not be feasible for broad application.

- *Keep witnesses and defendants separated at the courthouse.* Other than at home, witnesses are most often intimidated in the courthouse, both while waiting to testify and while in the courtroom giving testimony. Not only must witnesses endure a face-to-face encounter with the defendant, but they may also be apprehensive about contact with the defendant's family and friends. Key danger areas include courthouse entrances, hallways, elevators, waiting areas, refreshment areas, and restrooms. Separate waiting rooms and entrances for witnesses and defendants can be useful.

- *Relocate witnesses.* Because it is unusual for offenders to travel outside their neighborhoods to intimidate witnesses, simply moving a witness to another location may effectively protect him or her from harm. Of course, the key to this strategy is to ensure that the new location remains confidential. Out of boredom, or because they are reluctant to sever ties with friends and family, the witnesses may unwittingly compromise the secrecy of their new locations.

DETERRING INTIMIDATORS

The following responses focus on actions that can be taken to deter intimidators.

- *Admonish intimidators.* When witnesses or victims tell police they are afraid or have experienced direct intimidation, police can visit the offender and his/her family and friends to caution them regarding their behavior and to explain the laws concerning witness intimidation and obstruction of justice. In court, judges should be vigilant about threatening gestures or actions and should admonish defendants or spectators who display such behaviors. Some jurisdictions educate judges about the types of courtroom intimidation that are exhibited by gang members, such as courtroom packing or wearing black.[32]

- *Request high bail and no contact orders.* In cases in which the risk of intimidation is significant, prosecutors can seek high bail to keep defendants in jail and away from witnesses. Where this strategy is used, bond hearings cannot be a mere formality; witness statements and risk assessments should be prepared in advance and presented in court. Prosecutors should seek release conditions that forbid contact with witnesses and victims and make sure that the consequences for violating such conditions are clearly articulated.

DOCUMENTING INTERVIEWS

Note-taking during an interview raises two primary concerns for the interviewer. First, it may occasionally be distracting or suspicious to a witness; witnesses may be reluctant to give information knowing it is being documented. Consequently, the investigator should tell witnesses that notes will prevent the need for subsequent interviews owing to lapses of the investigator's memory. This explanation usually reduces the reluctance of the witness. Second, the interviewer should avoid becoming preoccupied with taking notes, for this creates the appearance of inattentiveness. As important as notes may be, the interviewer should treat them as less important than conversation with the witness. Note-taking during the interview should be kept to a minimum, recording only salient details. As soon as possible after the interview, the investigator should complete the notes, before their memory wanes.

In many instances, witnesses should write or sign statements concerning the events of which they have knowledge. In many jurisdictions, law-enforcement officers are authorized to administer oaths so that such statements are sworn to or affirmed. The theory is that victims and/or witnesses are more inclined to be truthful if they are under oath and aware that charges of perjury could be lodged against them at a later date if they were determined to be lying.

The best form of documentation is electronic sound recording or a sound-and-visual recording of the interview.

TABLE 5-3	Comparison of Types of Interview Documentation	
TYPE	ADVANTAGES	DISADVANTAGES
Memory	Quick and easy	Limited absorption and recall
	Captures salient details	Most information lost shortly afterward
	Prevents need for reinterviewing	
Note-taking by interviewer	Sufficient in most cases	May distract or offend witness
	Captures salient details	May preoccupy interviewer, creating appearance of inattentiveness
	Prevents need for reinterviewing	
Handwritten or signed statements by witness	Useful if witness cannot testify	Request may be offensive to witness
	Can be used to impeach if witness changes story in court	Not necessary in routine cases
Electronic sound or sound-and-visual recordings	Relatively inexpensive	Not necessary except in the most important cases
	Some equipment portable	Generally not practical
	All information recorded in witnesses' own words	
	Does not rely on inaccuracies of memory or another's notes	
	Does not distract	
	Prevents unnecessary reinterviews	

Visual recordings are generally not practical when the interview is held anywhere other than at a law-enforcement agency, where equipment can be permanently situated. Audio recorders, however, are inexpensive, portable, and helpful in the majority of cases. The recorded interview has many significant advantages: all information is recorded in the witness's own words, details are not left to be recalled by human memory, concerns about detracting from the interview by note-taking are absent, interviewers may listen to the verbatim conversations over and over at a later time to be sure they have understood completely and accurately what was said, and the taped interview might avoid unnecessary reinterviews. The advantages and disadvantages of each type of documentation are shown in Table 5-3.

DOCUMENTING INTERROGATIONS

Documenting an interrogation consists of three main phases: note-taking, recording, and obtaining written statements. All three phases are geared to accomplishing two basic functions: first, retaining information for the benefit of the interrogator and the continued investigation and, second, securing a written statement or confession from the accused for later use as evidence in court.

THE USE OF ELECTRONIC RECORDINGS FOR INTERROGATIONS

The methods of keeping notes of interrogations is the same as described for interviews. Electronic recording of an interrogation is the best means of documentation. Audio, video, or a combination of both may be used, but case law and local requirements should be checked.

At present, 238 law-enforcement agencies in 38 states currently record custodial interviews of suspects in felony investigations. These agencies are located in every area of the United States and are quite diverse in size and individual practices. Following are some of the elements addressed in their respective policies as they relate to the use of electronic recordings for interrogation.[33]

- *Mandatory or discretionary:* Most agencies leave the recording decision to the discretion of the investigator in charge, although recordings are customarily made by the investigators in cases covered by discretionary policies.
- *When to begin recordings:* Most departments use either audio and/or video recording devices to record interrogations of persons under arrest in a police facility starting from the point when the *Miranda* warnings (discussed later in this chapter) are given until the interview is ended, with no intentional breaks or omissions in the recordings.
- *Crimes under investigation:* Most departments record only in "major" or "serious" felony investigations,

such as homicide, sexual assault, armed robbery, and other crimes against persons and those involving weapons. Many also record interviews in DUI, child abuse, and domestic violence investigations.

- *Equipment:* Some departments use multiple cameras from different views, while others use a single camera focused on the suspect.[34] Many departments are acquiring digital technology in order to improve picture resolution and conserve storage space.
- *Suspect's knowledge:* State eavesdropping laws govern whether suspects must be told they are being recorded. "One-party consent" laws allow the police to record without informing the suspects. "Two-party consent" laws require the police to obtain the suspects' consent. Most state laws permit police to record surreptitiously, although sophisticated suspects and repeat offenders may be aware without being told. Most departments inform suspects that the session will be recorded and/or place the recording equipment in plain view, although most of them are not required by state law to do so. Almost all investigators turn the recording devices off if the suspect declines to talk while being recorded.

BENEFITS OF RECORDING FOR POLICE OFFICERS AND PROSECUTORS

An electronic recording of suspect interviews has proven to be an efficient and powerful law-enforcement tool. Audio is good, but video is better. Both methods create a permanent record of exactly what occurred. Recordings prevent disputes about the investigator's conduct, the treatment of suspects and the voluntariness of statements they made. Investigators are not called on to paraphrase statements or try later to describe suspects' words, actions, and attitudes. Instead, viewers and listeners see and/or hear precisely what was said and done, including whether suspects were forthcoming or evasive, changed their versions of events, and appeared sincere and innocent or deceitful and guilty. An electronic record is law enforcement's version of instant replay.

Experience also shows that recordings dramatically reduce the number of defense motions to suppress statements and confessions. The record is there for defense lawyers to see and evaluate: if the officers conduct themselves properly during the questioning, there is no basis to challenge their conduct or exclude the defendants' responses from evidence. Officers are spared from defending themselves against allegations of coercion, trickery, and perjury during hostile cross-examinations.

The use of recording devices, even when known to the suspect, does not impede investigators from obtaining confessions and admissions from guilty suspects. When suspects decline to talk if recorded, the investigators simply turn the recorder off and proceed with taking handwritten notes.

Recordings permit investigators to focus on the suspect rather than taking copious notes of the interview. When investigators later review the recordings they can often observe inconsistencies and evasive conduct which they overlooked while the interview was in progress.

Electronic recording forces investigators to better prepare for conducting interrogations by:

- clarifying whether an interrogator missed something that requires further questioning;
- giving prosecutors a better understanding of cases, thereby fostering better charging decisions, plea-bargaining options, and case preparation;
- minimizing challenges by defense attorneys about the accuracy of the electronic recordings and the completeness of written confessions;
- reducing doubts about the voluntariness of confessions;
- jogging investigators' memories when they are testifying.

In addition, tapes can be reviewed and used as training aids for less experienced investigators who are attempting to develop their interrogation skills.[35]

THE WRITTEN STATEMENT

After the use of such recordings, the next-best form is a signed statement written in the first person by the suspect in his or her handwriting. Frequently, however, it is not possible to convince a suspect to prepare such a statement. Or perhaps the suspect cannot write.

Other forms in which statements may be admitted into evidence, listed in descending order of the credibility with juries, are these:

- a typed or handwritten statement by someone else that is signed in the accused's own hand;
- a typed or otherwise prepared statement that the accused does not sign but that is acknowledged in front of witnesses;
- the oral testimony of a person who was present and overheard the subject give a confession or admission.

In the last case, even though admissible, the testimony is likely to carry little weight with the jury. Table 5-4 lists the types of documentation in descending order of preference and the advantages and disadvantages of each.

The form and content of a written statement should include a heading, which incorporates the data identifying the circumstances under which the statement was taken, the body of the statement, and a verification. The statement should open with an indication of the time and place where it was taken, and an identification of the person giving the statement that includes his/her name, address, and age. The heading must also include a definite statement to the effect that the subject is giving the

TABLE 5-4	Comparison of Types of Confession Documentation (in Descending Order of Believability to Juries)	
TYPE	**ADVANTAGES**	**DISADVANTAGES**
1. Electronic video-audiotape or movie	May be required by legislative or judicial directive Shows all, including fairness, procedures, and treatment Easy to do Can be relatively inexpensive	May face legal constraints
2. Audio recording	Can hear conversations Can infer fairness	Some words or descriptions may be meaningless without pictorial support Necessitates identifying people and things involved
3. Statement written and signed in suspect's own handwriting	Can be identified as coming directly from suspect	Can't see demeanor or hear voice inflections Suspect may not agree to procedure
4. Typed statement signed by suspect	Signature indicates knowledge of and agreement with contents of statement	Less convincing than methods described above
5. Typed unsigned statement acknowledged by suspect	Contents of confession or admission are present Acknowledgment helps show voluntariness	Reduced believability of voluntariness and accuracy of contents
6. Testimony of someone who heard confession or admission given	Contents admissible	Carries little weight with juries

statement freely and voluntarily after having been appropriately advised of his/her constitutional rights.

The body of the statement, which acknowledges the subject's involvement in the crime under investigation, should, if possible, be phrased in the first person, allowing the suspect to include his/her own ideas in a free-flowing manner. However, if this is not possible or practical, then the question-and-answer format is permissible. The terminology used should include the words, grammar, idioms, and style of the person making the statement. The body of the statement should be arranged so that its content follows the chronological order of the subject's involvement in the case under investigation.

At the end, the statement should indicate that the suspect has read the statement or has had it read to him/her, that its contents and implications are understood, and that the suspect attests to its accuracy.

Other suggestions for the interrogator to keep in mind include:

- Each page of the statement should be numbered consecutively with an indication that it is page no. _____ of _____ pages. If the pages get separated, they can later be easily restored to order.

- The interrogator should ensure that each page is initialed by the subject. If the subject is unwilling to sign, the statement should be acknowledged by him/her. If the subject cannot write, another identifying mark may be used.

- On occasion an interrogator may encounter someone who says, "I'll tell you what I've done, but I'm not writing anything and I'm not signing anything." In such circumstances, the interrogator can explain that the suspect confessed, and the interrogator or some other person who heard the confession can go into court and testify about it. By preparing or signing a statement, the suspect protects himself/herself against the interrogator's testifying to something more damaging by changing the story in court (another good reason for electronic recording).

- If the suspect cannot read, the statement must be read to him/her, and the interrogator must ensure the suspect understands its contents before the suspect is allowed to attest to its accuracy.

- All errors in the statement should be corrected on the final copy and initialed by the suspect. The interrogator may accommodate the suspect by allowing small errors if this will help obtain the suspect's initials on each page of the statement.

- The interrogator should make sure the suspect understands all the words used in the statement. If some words are confusing, their meanings should be explained to the suspect and the suspect should be required to explain them back in front of witnesses in order to confirm this understanding.

- During the process of drafting and attesting to a statement derived through interrogation, there should be at least one additional witness who can testify to the authenticity of the statement and the circumstances under which it was obtained. After the suspect signs the statement in ink, the witnesses should sign their names, addresses, and positions.[36]

WHY PEOPLE CONFESS

It is human nature to talk. Most people cannot keep a secret. It has been estimated that 80% of all people will confess to a crime. There are two basic categories of people who tend to confess to crimes: (1) guilty parties who psychologically need to "get if off their chest" and (2) persons who are not guilty but who act under some urge to confess. It is to protect the latter category of people that some procedural safeguards are provided. For example, a conviction cannot be based solely on a confession. There must be some other independent corroborating evidence to support the conviction.

The psychological and physiological pressures that build in a person who has committed a crime or who suffers from feelings of guilt concerning any other type of conduct are best alleviated by communicating. Talking is the best means of communicating. Therefore, in spite of having been advised of certain protections guaranteed by the Constitution, some people feel a need to confess. Even confirmed criminals sometimes suffer from the same pangs of conscience as first-time offenders. However, fear of the potential punishments that await them contributes to their silence. Those who confess rarely regret it, for doing so gives them peace of mind. It permits them to look at themselves and life differently and to live with themselves. Most guilty individuals who confess are, from the outset, looking for the proper opening during an interrogation to communicate their guilt to the interrogator. The good interrogator will seek out and be able to recognize individuals who desire to confess and will approach the interrogation in such a way as to provide the accused with the proper opening and reason for the relief of the psychological and physiological pressures that have built up.[37] If it is human nature to talk, and if people cannot generally keep secrets, then the job of the interrogator is to make it easy for a suspect to confess.

FALSE CONFESSIONS

A false confession is an admission of guilt followed by a narrative statement of what, how, and why the confessor committed the crime. Over the years, confessions have been proven false in a number of ways, as when it is discovered that the confessed crime was not committed; when new evidence shows it was physically impossible for the confessor to have committed the crime; when the real perpetrator, having no connection to the defendant, is captured and implicated; and when DNA and other scientific evidence affirmatively establishes the confessor's innocence. Through these methods, and contrary to the widespread belief that people do not confess to crimes they did not commit, the pages of American history reveal large numbers of men and women who were wrongfully prosecuted, convicted, imprisoned, and sometimes sentenced to death on the basis of false confessions.[38]

Although many researchers have discovered large numbers of false confessions in recent years, it is not possible to project from these cases the frequency with which innocent people in general confess to crimes they did not commit. First, within the U.S. criminal justice system, the postconviction cases discovered by the Innocence Project[39] and others do not include the numerous false confessions that are disproved subsequent to arrest but before trial, those that result in a false guilty plea, those to minor crimes that attract no postconviction scrutiny, and those that involve juveniles in which confidentiality provisions are in place.[40] In a North American survey of 631 police investigators, respondents estimated from their own experience that 4.78% of innocent suspects confess during interrogation.[41]

Over the years, researchers have reported on numerous accounts of proven false confessions, producing a vast literature of case studies. As reported in books, newspapers, TV documentaries, and analyses of actual case files, these stories reveal false confessions occur with some unknown frequency, they share certain common features, and they seem more likely to occur in some types of people and under some conditions than others. From these descriptive analyses of specific instances and associations, one cannot draw conclusions about the causes of false confessions. Nevertheless, case studies of this nature have proven invaluable in the development of this area. By comparing and contrasting several known cases throughout history, for example, Kassin and Wrightsman[42] introduced a taxonomy that distinguished among three types of false confessions: voluntary, **coerced-compliant,** and **coerced-internalized.**

VOLUNTARY FALSE CONFESSIONS

Voluntary false confessions are those in which people claim responsibility for crimes they did not commit without prompting or pressure from police. Often this occurs in high-profile cases. For example, when Charles Lindbergh's infant son was kidnapped and killed in 1932, an estimated 200 people volunteered confessions. When "Black Dahlia" actress Elizabeth Short was murdered in 1947, more than 50 people confessed. In 2006 John Mark Karr confessed to the unsolved murder of JonBenet Ramsey. Researchers have not systematically studied these types of false confessions, in part because they are typically disproved at the outset by the confessor's ignorance and inability to furnish corroborating details about the crime. There are several reasons why innocent people might volunteer confessions, such as a pathological need for attention or self-punishment; feeling of guilt or delusions; the perception of tangible gain; or the desire to protect a parent, child, or someone else.

COERCED-COMPLIANT FALSE CONFESSIONS

In contrast, people may be induced to confess through the processes of police interrogation. In false confessions, the suspect capitulates in order to escape a stressful custodial situation, avoid physical or legal punishment, or gain a promised or implied reward. G. H. Gudjonsson[43] identified, based on a review of cases, some concrete initiatives for this type of confession, such as not being allowed to sleep, eat, make a phone call, go home, or, in the case of drug addicts, feed a drug habit. Like the results of classical forms of influence observed in psychological studies of conformity, compliance, and obedience to authority, this type of confession is an act of public capitulation and compliance by a suspect who knows he/she is innocent but perceives that the short-term benefits of confession (for example, being left alone, fed, or released) outweighed the long-term costs (for instance, a loss of reputation, conviction, and incarceration). This phenomenon was dramatically illustrated in the 1692 Salem witch trials, in which women confessed to witchcraft;[44] in *Brown* v. *Mississippi*, a classic case in which three black tenant farmers confessed to murder after they were whipped with a steel-studded leather belt; and in the infamous Central Park jogger case in 1989, in which five New York City teenagers confessed after lengthy interrogations, each claiming he expected to go home afterward. All the boys were convicted and sent to prison, only to be exonerated in 2002 when the real rapist gave a confession that was confirmed by DNA evidence.

COERCED-INTERNALIZED FALSE CONFESSIONS

Internalized false confessions are those in which innocent but vulnerable suspects confess and come to believe they committed the crime in question, a belief that is sometimes accompanied by false memories. Gudjonsson has argued that this kind of false confession results from "memory distrust syndrome," whereby people develop a profound distrust of their own memory that renders them vulnerable to manipulation from external cues.[45] Kassin likened this process of influence to the creation of false memories sometimes seen in psychotherapy patients. In both situations, an authority figure claims a privileged insight into the individual's past, the individual is isolated from others and in a heightened state of malleability, and the expert ultimately convinces the individual to accept a painful self-insight by invoking such concepts as dissociation or repression. The case of 14-year-old Michael Crowe, whose sister was stabbed to death, illustrates this phenomenon. After lengthy interrogations, during which Michael was misled by lies into thinking there was substantial physical evidence of his guilt, he concluded he was a killer: "I'm not sure how I did it. All I know is I did it." Eventually, he was convinced he had a split personality—that "bad Michael" acted out of jealous rage while "good Michael" blocked the incident from his consciousness. The charges against Crowe were later dropped when a drifter from neighborhood was found with the victim's blood on his clothing.[46]

RECOMMENDATIONS TO REDUCE THE POSSIBILITY OF FALSE CONFESSIONS

Given that false confessions do occur, even if rarely, police administrators need to ensure their investigators are properly trained in interrogation techniques that elicit the most accurate and truthful information from suspects. The following recommendations will do much to reduce the possibility of a false confession.[47]

- *Use police skill teams.* The teams should consist of seasoned interview specialists who, through training and actual interview experiences, possess the skills necessary to conduct successful critical interviews.
- *Provide mandatory police training.* Investigators must be made aware of the circumstances under which false confessions may be obtained. These include:
  —the suspect's desire to eliminate friends, relatives, and close associates from the investigative process;
  —the suspect's attempt to distract police from identifying other motives and/or suspects through a false confession, which is usually fraught with inconsistencies;
  —situations in which police officers provide too much information to the suspect, which the suspect may later repeat as part of a false confession. These include, among other things, the date and time of death, the location of the offense, the specific positioning of the body, wounds to the body, the instrumentation of death and so forth. Unless this kind of specific information has been released to the public by the media or through some other source, then only the police and the person(s) committing the crime should possess this kind of information.

- *Provide mandatory police training on special interview considerations in dealing with populations most vulnerable to false confessions.* These include juveniles, the mentally impaired, and individuals under the influence of alcohol and/or drugs.
- Police agencies that in the past have been involved in wrongful convictions based on false confessions should review existing policies and make the appropriate changes to eliminate the problem.
- Mandate that police conclude the interview by asking a series of questions that emphasize the voluntariness of the confession—that is, no coercion was used and the suspect was not under the influence of alcohol and drugs. Interviews should be concluded with questions that firmly establish the fairness and professionalism of the interviewing investigators. A simple yet very effective way to achieve this result is by asking such questions as: "Why did you decide to talk to me?" and "Why did you decide to talk to me now?"

ADMISSIBILITY OF CONFESSIONS AND ADMISSIONS

Before 1936 the only test for the validity and admissibility of a confession or admission was its voluntariness. However, the determination as to whether it was given voluntarily by the suspect was subject to very loose interpretation. There were no rules restricting the method by which law enforcement obtained "voluntary" statements. Physical violence, psychological coercion, empty promises, and meaningless guarantees of rewards were not considered objectionable procedures.

THE FREE-AND-VOLUNTARY RULE

The first notable incidence of U.S. Supreme Court intervention into interrogation practices came about in *Brown* v. *Mississippi*.[48] In this 1936 case, the Supreme Court held that under no circumstances could a confession be considered freely and voluntarily given when it was obtained as a result of physical brutality and violence inflicted by law-enforcement officials on the accused. The reaction to this decision by law enforcement was not unexpected. Many threw up their hands and claimed they could no longer function effectively because "handcuffs had been put on the police." However, as was true with many other decisions placing procedural restrictions on law-enforcement agencies, the police found they were able to compensate by conducting thorough criminal investigations.

Subsequent to the *Brown* decision, the Supreme Court, in a succession of cases, has continued to reinforce its

position that any kind of coercion, whether physical or psychological, would be grounds for making a confession inadmissible as being in violation of the **free-and-voluntary rule.** This includes such conduct as threatening bodily harm to the suspect or members of the suspect's family,[49] using psychological coercion,[50] engaging in trickery or deceit, or holding a suspect incommunicado. Investigators are also cautioned about making promises to the suspect that cannot be kept. All these practices were condemned in *Miranda* v. *Arizona* (discussed in much greater detail later in this chapter).[51] Despite the appearance that Miranda has eliminated all coercive techniques previously used in interrogations, this is not actually the case. What Miranda seeks is to abolish techniques that would prompt untrue incriminatory statements by a suspect. Thus, unlike physical coercion, psychological coercion, threats, duress, and some promises, the use of trickery, fraud, falsehood, and similar techniques are not absolutely forbidden. If such methods are not likely to cause an individual to make self-incriminating statements or to admit to falsehoods in order to avoid threatened harm, confessions or admissions so obtained are admissible.[52]

THE DELAY-IN-ARRAIGNMENT RULE

In 1943 the U.S. Supreme Court delivered another decision concerning the admissibility of confessions. Even though the free-and-voluntary rule was in effect in both the federal and state courts, another series of statutes seemed to have gone unheeded. Every state and the federal government had legal provisions requiring that after arrest a person must be taken before a committing magistrate "without unnecessary delay." Before 1943, if there was an unnecessary delay in producing the accused before a committing magistrate, the delay was merely one of a number of factors the courts were required to take into consideration in determining whether the confession was freely and voluntarily given.

The facts of **McNabb v. United States**[53] reveal that McNabb and several members of his family were involved in bootlegging. They were arrested after the murder of federal officers who were investigating their operation in Tennessee. McNabb was held incommunicado for several days before he was taken before a committing magistrate. He subsequently confessed, and the confession was admitted into evidence at his trial. He was convicted, but on appeal to the Supreme Court the conviction was reversed. The Court held that the failure of federal officers to take the prisoner before a committing officer without unnecessary delay automatically rendered his confession inadmissible. The significance of this case is that for the first time the Court indicated that failure to comply with this procedural requirement would render a confession inadmissible regardless of whether it was obtained freely and voluntarily. Thus, instead of examining the facts of the case to determine the voluntariness of the confession, the Court ruled, as a matter of law, that the procedural violation also rendered the confession inadmissible. The holding in the *McNabb* case was emphatically reaffirmed in 1957 by the Supreme Court in *Mallory* v. *United States*.[54]

As the mandate of the Supreme Court in the *McNabb* and *Mallory* cases had applicability only to federal prosecutions, the states were free to interpret their own statutes on unnecessary delay as they saw fit. Few chose to follow the *McNabb-Mallory* **delay-in-arraignment rule.** The majority have continued to require that there must be a connection between the failure of law enforcement to produce the accused before a committing magistrate without unnecessary delay and the securing of a confession.

INTERVIEWING AND INTERROGATION: LEGAL REQUIREMENTS

PREINTERROGATION LEGAL REQUIREMENTS

Preinterrogation legal requirements became of critical concern during the 1960s. As a result, the Supreme Court handed down a landmark decision that dramatically affected the conditions under which interrogations take place. The issue revolved around the Fifth Amendment protection against self-incrimination and the Sixth Amendment guarantee of the right to counsel, both as made applicable to the states through the due process clause of the Fourteenth Amendment.

MIRANDA V. ARIZONA

In *Miranda v. Arizona*[55] the Supreme Court, in a five-to-four decision, spelled out the requirements and procedures to be followed by officers when conducting an in custody interrogation of a suspect.

In March 1963, Ernest Miranda was arrested for kidnapping and rape. After being identified by the victim, he was questioned by police for several hours and signed a confession that included a statement indicating that the confession was given voluntarily. The confession was admitted into evidence over the objections of Miranda's defense counsel, and the jury found him guilty. The Supreme Court of Arizona affirmed the conviction and held that Miranda's constitutional rights had not been violated in obtaining the conviction because following the ruling from *Escobedo* v. *Illinois*[56] the year before, in which Escobedo's confession was ruled to have been improperly admitted because he asked to see his lawyer but was denied that right, Miranda had not specifically requested counsel. The U.S. Supreme Court, in reversing the decision, attempted to clarify its intent in the *Escobedo* case by spelling out specific guidelines to be followed by police before they interrogate persons in custody and attempt to use their statements as evidence. In clarifying the requirements of *Escobedo*, the Court felt compelled to include the Fifth Amendment requirements against self-incrimination in the decision. The guidelines require that after a person is taken into custody for an offense and before any questioning by law-enforcement officers, if there is any intent to use a suspect's statements in court, the person must first be advised of certain rights (Figure 5-7.) These rights include:

1. the right to remain silent;
2. the right to be told that anything said can and will be used in court;

THE EXPLANATION OF THE ADMONITION AND USE OR WAIVER OF YOUR RIGHTS	LA EXPLICACION DEL AVISO Y EL USO O NO DE TUS DERECHOS
1) You have the right to remain silent—you do not have to talk.	1) Tienes el derecho de quedar en silencio—no tienes que hablar.
2) What you say can be used, and shall be used against you in a court of law.	2) Lo que digas se puede usar y se usará en contra de ti en la corte de ley.
3) You have the right to talk with an attorney before you talk with us, and you have the right to have the attorney present during the time we are talking to you.	3) Tienes el derecho de hablar con un abogado antes de hablar con nosotros, y tienes el derecho de tener el abogado presente durante el tiempo que nosotros estamos hablando contigo.
4) If you do not have the funds to employ an attorney, one shall be appointed to represent you free of charge.	4) Si no tienes el dinero para emplear un abogado, uno sere fijado para que te represente, sin pagar.
5) Do you understand these rights as I have explained them to you, yes or no?	5) ¿Comprendes estos derechos como te los expliqué, si o no?
6) Do you want to talk to us about your case now, yes or no?	6) ¿Quieres hablar con nosotros de tu caso ahora, si o no?
7) Do you want an attorney present during the time we are talking to you, yes or no?	7) ¿Quieres un abogado presente durante el tiempo que estamos hablando contigo, si o no?

◄**FIGURE 5-7**
Warning-rights card in English and Spanish
(Courtesy Los Angeles County Sheriff's Department)

3. the right to consult with an attorney before answering any questions and the right to have an attorney present during interrogation;
4. the right to counsel. If the suspect cannot afford an attorney, the court will appoint one.[57]

SUSPECT'S RESPONSE: WAIVER AND ALTERNATIVES

It is common practice for the officer to ask the suspect if he or she understands the rights as they have been explained. If the answer is yes, then the officer may ask if the subject wants to talk with the officer. At this point, four alternatives are open to the suspect:

1. *The suspect may choose to remain silent,* not wanting even to respond to the officer's question. The courts have held that choosing to remain silent does not imply consent to be interrogated and no questions should be asked.
2. *The suspect may request counsel.* At that point, the investigator must not undertake any questioning of the suspect, for anything said will not be admissible in court. In *Edwards* v. *Arizona* in 1981, the Supreme Court held that no police-initiated interrogation may lawfully take place once the suspect has invoked the right to counsel unless, and until, an attorney has been provided or unless the defendant voluntarily begins to talk with the officers.[58] In **Minnick v. Mississippi** in 1990, the Supreme Court held that once counsel is requested, interrogation must cease; officials may not reinitiate interrogation without counsel being present, whether or not the accused has consulted with his or her attorney. The requirement that counsel be made available to the accused refers not to the opportunity to consult with a lawyer outside the interrogation room but to the right to have the attorney present during custodial interrogation. This rule is necessary to remove suspects from the coercive pressure of officials who may try to persuade them to waive their rights. The rule also provides a clear and unequivocal guideline to the law-enforcement profession.[59]

   The *Edwards* and *Minnick* lines of cases remained constant until the Supreme Court ruled in **Maryland v. Shatzer** in 2010. The facts involved an attempt by a detective to question Shatzer in 2003 about allegations that he had sexually abused his son. At the time Shatzer was in prison on an unrelated offense. Shatzer invoked his *Miranda* rights to have counsel present during the interrogation. The detective terminated the interview and the case was subsequently closed. Shatzer was returned to the general population. Another detective reopened the investigation three years later and attempted to interrogate Shatzer, who was still in prison. Shatzer

waived his *Miranda* rights this time and in 2006 made some inculpatory statements that were admitted at this trial for sexually abusing his son. Shatzer was convicted. After several appeals, which held the trial court was wrong to admit Shatzer's incriminating statements since he had previously asked for an attorney, the appeals courts held there was no exception once the request for an attorney had been made in accordance with the *Edwards* decision, since Shatzer was still being held in custody. The Supreme Court, however, agreed with the trial court, allowing the statements to be used against Shatzer. The Court reasoned that because Shatzer experienced a break in *Miranda* custody, lasting more than 2 weeks between the first and second attempts at interrogation, *Edwards* did not require suppression of his 2006 statements. The Court said that even though Shatzer was still in prison during the time between the 2003 and 2006 interrogations, he was in the general population, where he could have spoken with a lawyer during the 3-year break and was no longer in a police-dominated atmosphere on the sexual abuse case. Even though he was still in prison Shatzer resumed his "normal life."[60]

3. *The suspect may waive his or her rights and agree to talk with law enforcement without the benefit of counsel.* The waiver of rights is a sensitive topic for law enforcement, because it is the responsibility of law enforcement and the prosecutor to prove in court the waiver was validly obtained. A valid waiver must be voluntarily, knowingly, and intelligently given by the suspect. The burden is on the prosecution to prove that the suspect was properly advised of his or her rights, that those rights were understood, and that the suspect voluntarily, knowingly, and intelligently waived those rights before the court will allow the introduction of any incriminating testimony in the form of a confession. The waiver cannot be presumed or inferred. It must be successfully proved by the prosecution. Therefore, it is preferable for the investigator who secures a waiver of rights from a suspect to attempt to get the waiver in writing with sufficient witnesses to substantiate its voluntariness. Figure 5-8 is a sample waiver form. Most law-enforcement agencies also attempt to get individuals in custody to sign a rights waiver form as one more step to show a good faith effort to comply with the requirements of the *Miranda* ruling.

   However, a suspect who has waived his or her rights is free to withdraw that waiver at any time. If this occurs during questioning, the investigator is under a legal obligation to cease the interrogation at that point and either comply with the suspect's request for representation or simply cease the interrogation if the suspect refuses to talk.

YOUR RIGHTS

Date_____

Time_____

WARNING

Before we ask you any questions, you must understand your rights.

You have the right to remain silent.

Anything you say can and will be used against you in court.

You have the right to talk to a lawyer for advice before we ask you any question and to have him with you during questioning.

If you cannot afford a lawyer, one will be appointed for you.

Geauga County has a Public Defender. Before answering any questions, you have a right to talk with the Public Defender.

If you decide to answer questions now, without a lawyer present, you will still have the right to stop answering at any time. You also have the right to stop answering at any time until you talk to a lawyer.

Do you understand these rights? _____

Signed: _____

Witnesses:

_____

_____

WAIVER OF RIGHTS

I have read this statement of my rights and I understand what my rights are. I am willing to make a statement and answer questions. I do not want a lawyer at this time. I understand and know what I am doing. No promises or threats have been made to me and no pressure or coercion of any kind has been used against me.

Signed: _____

Witnesses:

_____

_____

Date: _____

Time: _____

FIGURE 5-8 Rights waiver form
(Courtesy Geauga County, Ohio, Sheriff's Department)

4. *The suspect may indicate a desire not to talk with the investigators.* At this point, law enforcement has no choice other than to refrain from attempting to interrogate the suspect concerning the events of the crime for which he/she has been arrested. In this event, the case must be based on independent evidence, which may or may not be sufficient to warrant prosecution. The U.S. Supreme Court's emphatic position on terminating interrogation once a suspect has invoked the right to remain silent was announced in 1975 in the case of *Michigan* v. *Mosley*.[61]

Since the responsibility is on the prosecution, supported by evidence provided by the investigators, to substantiate the voluntariness of the waiver and the propriety of the warnings given to the suspect, many law-enforcement agencies provide printed cards with the exact wording of the required warnings. They further recommend or require that when warnings are given they be read verbatim from the printed card. In this manner, the officer, when testifying in court, can positively state the exact words used in advising the suspect of his/her constitutional rights. Such a procedure avoids any confrontation with the defense as to the exact wording and contents of the *Miranda* requirements. But in 1989 in *Duckworth* v. *Eagen*, the Supreme Court held that it was not necessary that the warnings be given in the exact form described in the *Miranda* decision, provided the warnings as a whole fully informed the suspect of his or her rights.[62] This position was reaffirmed in a 2010 case *Florida* v. *Powell*.[63]

A person being subjected to **in-custody interrogation** often chooses not to answer any questions posed by law enforcement—or at least not until an attorney is present. When counsel is made available to the suspect before or during interrogation, it is almost universal practice for the attorney to advise the client not to say anything to the police. Therefore, the effect of the *Miranda* decision has been to reduce significantly the number of valid interrogations by law-enforcement agencies in this country today. For the most part, however, confessions obtained in compliance with prescribed rules are of better quality and are more likely to be admissible in court.

It must be impressed on investigators that the failure to properly advise a suspect of the rights required by *Miranda* does not invalidate an otherwise valid arrest, nor does it necessarily mean a case cannot be successfully prosecuted. Even in light of the line of court decisions indicating that *Miranda* warnings may not be required in all interrogation situations, good practice or departmental policy may require that all suspects in custody be advised of their rights.

IN-CUSTODY INTERROGATION

For investigators to understand the proper application of the *Miranda* requirements, it is essential they understand the meaning of in-custody interrogation. The *Miranda* case involved simultaneous custody and interrogation. Subsequent police actions revealed that all cases were not so nicely defined and the meanings of "in custody" and "interrogation" required clarification. Although it may be difficult to separate the custody from the interrogation in certain factual situations, the two concepts must be considered separately.

Custody

Custody occurs when a person is deprived of his/her freedom in any significant way or is not free to leave the presence of law enforcement. Analyses of case decisions show there is not yet a universally accepted definition of custody. Rather, case-by-case analysis is used to determine the applicability of the *Miranda* requirements (Figure 5-9).

MIRANDA AND MISDEMEANORS

The question of whether *Miranda* applies to misdemeanor arrests was the subject of controversy for many years. In 1984, the Supreme Court settled this issue. The Court ruled in *Berkemer v. McCarty* that *Miranda* applies to the interrogation of an arrested person regardless of whether the offense is a felony or a misdemeanor. The justices found that to make a distinction would cause confusion, because many times it is not certain whether the person taken into custody is to be charged with a felony or a misdemeanor.[64]

INTERROGATION AS DEFINED BY THE U.S. SUPREME COURT

For legal purposes, interrogation includes any express questioning or any verbal or nonverbal behavior by a law-enforcement officer that is designed to elicit an

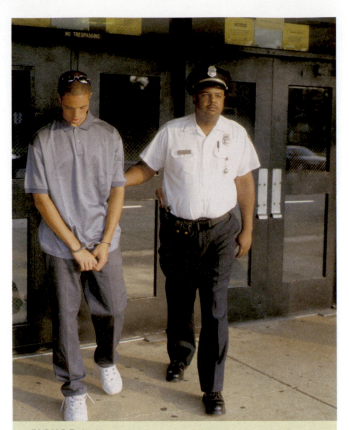
▲ **FIGURE 5-9**
Uniformed officer with handcuffed prisoner
In deciding when *Miranda* warnings are required, there is no universally accepted definition of "custody." In this, photograph, it is clear that this suspect is in custody between the officer leading him by the arm and the handcuffs; there is no doubt that the suspect is not free to leave. (© Cleve Bryant/PhotoEdit)

incriminating statement or response from the suspect of a crime. For many years following the *Miranda* ruling, there was considerable confusion over what constituted questioning or interrogation. For example, in a 1977 case the Supreme Court found that an impermissible interrogation occurred when an investigator delivered what has been called the "Christian burial speech" to a man suspected of murdering a young girl. While the suspect was being transported between cities, the investigator told the suspect to think about how the weather was turning cold and snow was likely. He pointed out how difficult it would be to find the body later. The investigator went on to say that the girl's parents were entitled to have a Christian burial for the little girl, who had been taken from them on Christmas Eve and murdered. Subsequent to this little speech, the suspect led the investigators to the spot where he had disposed of the body. The Supreme Court held this to be an interrogation within the scope of *Miranda*, even though direct questions had not been asked of the suspect.[65]

The Supreme Court faced the question of what constitutes interrogation for the first time in the 1980 case of *Rhode Island v. Innis*. In that instance a robbery suspect was arrested after the victim had identified him from photographs. The prisoner was advised several times of his constitutional rights and was being transported by three officers who had been specifically ordered not to question the suspect. During the trip, two of the officers were having a conversation about the case, and one commented how terrible it would be if some unsuspecting child found the missing shotgun (used in the robbery) and got hurt. The conversation was not directed at the suspect, nor did the officers expect a response from the suspect. However, the suspect interrupted the conversation and, after again being advised of his rights, led the officers to the shotgun. The Supreme Court stated the rule regarding interrogation as follows:

> We conclude that *Miranda* safeguards come into play whenever a person in custody is subjected to either express questioning or its functional equivalent. That is to say, the term "interrogation" under *Miranda* refers not only to express questioning, but also to any words or actions on the part of the police (other than those normally attendant to arrest and custody) that the police should know are reasonably likely to elicit an incriminating response from the suspect. The latter portion of this definition focuses primarily upon the perceptions of the suspect, rather than the intent of the police. This focus reflects the fact that the *Miranda* safeguards were designed to vest a suspect in custody with an added measure of protection against coercive police practices, without regard to objective proof of the underlying intent of the police.[66]

As a general rule, *Miranda* warnings need not precede routine booking questions that are asked in order to obtain personal-history data necessary to complete the booking process. As long as the questions are for that purpose and not a pretext to obtain incriminating information, *Miranda* warnings need not be given.[67]

MOST RECENT U.S. SUPREME COURT DECISION ON THE RIGHT TO REMAIN SILENT

On June 1, 2010 the U.S. Supreme Court's decision in the area of **Berghuis v. Thompkins** was decided and shines new light on issues surrounding both the invocation and waiver of the *Miranda* right to remain silent.[68, 69]

In *Berghuis*, Van Chester Thompkins was arrested in Ohio for a shooting that occurred approximately one year earlier in Southfield, Michigan. While in custody, Thompkins was questioned by two detectives in a police interview room. At the beginning of the interrogation, the detectives presented Thompkins with a general set of *Miranda* warnings.[70]

To make sure Thompkins could understand English, one of the detectives asked Thompkins to read a portion of the warnings out loud, which he did. Thereafter, the detective read the rest of the warnings to Thompkins and asked him to sign the form, indicating that he understood his rights. Thompkins refused to sign the form, and the officers began interrogating Thompkins. "At no point during the interrogation did Thompkins say he wanted to remain silent, did not want to talk to the police, or wanted an attorney."[71]

With the exception of some minor verbal responses and limited eye contact, Thompkins remained silent for most of the 3-hour interview. Approximately 2 hours and 45 minutes into the interrogation, one of the detectives asked Thompkins if he believed in God. Thompkins said he did. The detective then followed up by asking Thompkins if he prayed to God. Thompkins said, "Yes." The detective then asked, "Do you pray to God to forgive you for shooting that boy down?" To which, Thompkins answered, "Yes." Thompkins refused to make a written statement, and the interrogation ended.[72]

COURT PROCEEDINGS

Thompkins filed a motion to suppress the statements he made during the interrogation and claimed his Fifth Amendment right to remain silent had been violated. The trial court denied the motion, and Thompkins's admission was used against him at trial. Thompkins was convicted of first-degree murder and sentenced to life in prison without parole.

Thompkins appealed.[73] The Michigan Court of Appeals rejected the *Miranda* claim, and the Michigan Supreme Court denied review. Thereafter, Thompkins filed a petition for a writ of habeas corpus in the U.S. District Court for the Eastern District of Michigan that was likewise denied. The U.S. Court of Appeals for the Sixth Circuit reversed the district court ruling in favor of Thompkins.[74] However, for the reasons set forth herein, the Supreme Court reversed the judgment of the Sixth Circuit Court of Appeals and found no *Miranda* violations.

RIGHT TO REMAIN SILENT—INVOCATION

In filing his motion to suppress the statements he made during the interrogation, Thompkins first argued he had invoked his right to remain silent by not saying anything for the first 2 hours and 45 minutes of the interrogation. If, in fact, he had invoked his right to remain silent, it is undisputed the officers would have been obligated to stop questioning.[75] However, Justice Kennedy, in writing the majority opinion, explained that Thompkins's mere silence in the face of questioning was not clear and unambiguous invocation of his right to remain silent.[76] The Court noted that, unlike its earlier ruling in *Davis* v. *United States* regarding the invocation of the *Miranda* right to counsel, it never had defined whether an invocation of the right to remain silent must be unambiguous. In *Davis*, the defendant initially waived his *Miranda* rights and was interrogated for 90 minutes before saying, "Maybe I should talk to a lawyer." The Court held that if a subject is unclear, ambiguous, or equivocal in requesting a lawyer, officers can ignore the reference and proceed with the interrogation.[77]

In *Berghuis*, the Court acknowledged "there is no principled reason to adopt different standards for determining when an accused has invoked the *Miranda* right to remain silent and the *Miranda* right to counsel at issue in *Davis*. . . . Both protect the privilege against compulsory self-incrimination . . . by requiring an interrogation to cease when either right is invoked." Moreover, the Court explained there are no practical reasons for requiring that an invocation of the right to silence be clear and unambiguous. Namely, "an unambiguous invocation of *Miranda* rights results in an objective inquiry that 'avoid[s] difficulties of proof and . . . provide[s] guidance to officers on how to proceed in the face of ambiguity.'"[78] Accordingly, *Berghuis* does for the invocation of the right to silence what *Davis* did for the invocation of the right to counsel—it mandates that an invocation of either *Miranda* right must be clear and unambiguous to be effective.

RIGHT TO REMAIN SILENT—WAIVER

Thompkins next argued that absent an invocation of his right to silence, his statements still should be suppressed because he never adequately waived his right to silence. Two portions of the original *Miranda* decision seem to tilt the scale in Thompkins's favor on this issue. First, the *Miranda* Court said, "a valid waiver will not be presumed simply from the silence of the accused after warnings are given or simply from the fact that a confession was in fact eventually obtained."[79] Additionally, "a heavy burden rests on the government to demonstrate that the defendant knowingly and intelligently waived his privilege against self-incrimination. . . ."[80]

However, the Supreme Court has clarified its position with respect to the waiver since the *Miranda* decision. The impact has been to keep *Miranda* focused on the right to refrain from speaking and to consult an attorney. As the Court in *Berghuis* noted: "The main purpose of *Miranda* is to ensure that an accused is advised of and understands the right to remain silent and the right to counsel. . . ."[81] Thus, "if anything, our subsequent cases have reduced the impact of the *Miranda* rule on legitimate law enforcement while reaffirming the decision's core ruling that unwarned statements may not be used as evidence in the prosecution's case in chief."[82]

DETECTION OF DECEPTION

Identifying deceit is so difficult that repeated studies begun in the 1980s show that most people—including judges, attorneys, clinicians, police officers, FBI agents, politicians, teachers, mothers, fathers, and spouses—are no better than chance (50–50) when it comes to detecting deception.[83, 84] It is disturbing but true. Most people, including professionals, do no better than a coin toss at correctly perceiving dishonesty. Even those who are truly gifted at detecting deception (probably less than 1% of the general population) are seldom right more than 60% of the time. Consider the countless jurors who must determine honesty or dishonesty, guilt or innocence, based on what they think are deceptive behaviors. Unfortunately, those behaviors most often mistaken for dishonesty are primarily manifestations of stress, not deception.[85] There is simply no single behavior that is indicative of deception—not one.[86]

This does not mean we should abandon our efforts to study deception and observe for behaviors that, in context, are suggestive of it. But a realistic goal is to be able to read nonverbal behaviors with clarity and reliability.

THE CRITICAL ROLE OF THE COMFORT/ DISCOMFORT EQUATION IN DETECTING DECEPTION

Those who are lying or are guilty and must carry the knowledge of their lies and/or crimes with them find it difficult to achieve comfort, and their tension and distress may be readily observed. Attempting to disguise their guilt or deception places a very distressing cognitive load on them as they struggle to fabricate answers to what would otherwise be simple questions.[87]

The more comfortable a person is when speaking with investigators, the easier it will be to detect the critical nonverbal discomfort associated with deception. The goal is to establish high comfort during the early part of any interaction or during the period of time characterized as "rapport building." This helps to establish a baseline of behaviors during that period when the person, hopefully, does not feel threatened.

ESTABLISHING A COMFORT ZONE FOR DETECTING DECEPTION

In pursuing the detection of deception investigators must be aware of their impact on the actions of suspects being interrogated and recognize how their behavior will affect the other person's behavior.[88] How the investigator asks the question (accusingly), how the investigator sits (too close or not close enough), how the investigator looks upon the person (suspiciously), will either support or disrupt the suspect's comfort level. It is well established that if a person's personal space is violated, he/she will have a tendency to act nervous. In addition, if a person is questioned in a prosecutorial tone, this will very likely negatively intrude on the questioning process.

DEFINING SIGNS OF COMFORT

Comfort is readily apparent in conversations with family members and friends. It is easy to sense when people are having a good time and are comfortable. While seated at a table, people who are comfortable with each other will move objects aside so that nothing blocks their view, and over time, they may draw closer so they do not have to talk as loudly. Individuals who are comfortable display their bodies more openly, showing more of their torsos and the insides of their arms and legs (they allow ventral access or fronting). In the presence of strangers, comfort is more difficult to achieve, especially in stressful situations such as a formal interview or a deposition. This is why it is so important for the investigator to create a comfort zone from the very outset and to facilitate beneficial interaction with the person to be questioned.

When we are comfortable, there should be *synchrony* in our nonverbal behavior. The breathing rhythm of two comfortable people will be similar, as will the tone and pitch of their speech and their general demeanor. If a person is standing while talking to someone, leaning to the side with his/her hands in pockets and feet crossed, most likely the person he/she is talking to will do the same. By **mirroring** (called isoparaxis) another person's behavior, he/she is subconsciously saying "I am comfortable with you" (Figure 5-10).

In an interview setting or any situation in which a difficult topic is being discussed, the tone of each party should mirror the other's over time if there is synchrony.[89] If harmony does not exist between the people involved, synchrony will be missing, which will be discernible: they sit differently, talk in a different manner or tone, or at the least their expressions will be at odds, if not totally disparate. Asynchrony is a barrier to effective communication and is a serious obstacle to a successful interview or discussion.

Obviously, displays of comfort are more common in people speaking the truth; because there is no stress to conceal and no guilty knowledge to make them uncomfortable.[90] Thus, the investigator should still be looking for signs of discomfort—when they occur and in what context—to assess for possible deception.

SIGNS OF DISCOMFORT IN AN INTERACTION

We all show signs of discomfort when we do not like what is happening to us, when we do not like what we are seeing or hearing, or when we are compelled to talk about things we would prefer to keep hidden. We display discomfort first in our physiology, owing to arousal of the limbic brain.[91] Our heart rate quickens, we per-

▲ **FIGURE 5-10 Isoparaxis (mirroring)**
Here is an example of isoparaxis: both people are mirroring each other and leaning toward each other, showing signs of high comfort. (Joe Navarro, with Marin Karlins, *What Every Body is Saying* [New York: Harper Collins, 2008], p. 212)

spire more, and we breathe faster. Beyond the physiological responses, which are autonomic (automatic) and require no thinking on our part, our bodies manifest discomfort nonverbally. We tend to move our bodies in an attempt to block or distance ourselves from the source of our discomfort. We rearrange ourselves, jiggle our feet, fidget, twist at the hips, or drum our fingers when we are scared, nervous, or significantly uncomfortable.[92] We have all noticed such discomfort behaviors in others—for example, at a job interview or being questioned about a serious matter. These actions do not automatically indicate deception but do indicate that a person is uncomfortable in the current situation for any number of reasons.

When the investigator is attempting to observe discomfort as a potential indicator of deception, the best setting is one that has no objects (such as furniture, tables, desks, or chairs) between the person being observed and the investigator. Movements of the lower limbs are particularly revealing. Thus, if a person is behind a desk or table, the investigator should try to move it or get the individual to move away from it, because such an obstacle will block the vast majority (nearly 80%) of the body surfaces that need to be observed. In fact, the investigator should watch for the deceptive individual using obstacles or objects to form a physical barrier between the investigator and him/her. The use of objects is a sign that an individual wants distance, separation, and partial concealment, because the subject is being less open—which goes hand in hand with being uncomfortable or even deceitful. When it comes to questioning someone, the investigator can obtain more nonverbal clues while standing rather than sitting.

Other clear signs of discomfort seen in people during a difficult or troubling interview include rubbing the forehead; covering the throat; difficulty swallowing; clearing the throat; coughing; covering or twisting the mouth; biting or licking lips; yawning and sighs; itching and rubbing the nose, mustache, or beard; tugging at the ears or covering the ears; pulling the hair or grooming it; flushing of the skin or becoming extremely pale; squeezing the face; rubbing the neck; and stroking the back of the head with a hand. People may show their displeasure with the process by rolling their eyes in disrespect, picking lint off themselves (preening), or talking down to the person asking the questions—giving short answers, becoming resistant, hostile, or sarcastic, or even displaying microgestures with indecent connotations such as giving the finger.[93]

When making false statements, liars will rarely touch or engage in other physical contact with the investigator. Since touching is more often done by the truthful person for emphasis, such distancing helps to alleviate the level of anxiety a dishonest person is feeling. Any diminution of touching observed in a person engaged in conversation, especially while listening to or answering critical questions, is more likely than not indicative of deception.[94]

When observing a person's face for signs of comfort or discomfort, investigators should look for subtle behaviors such as a grimace or a look of contempt.[95] Also, they should check to see if the person's mouth is quivering, which is a clear indication of nervousness and discomfort. Any facial expression that lasts too long or lingers is not normal, whether a smile, a frown, or a surprised look. Such contrived behavior during an interview is intended to influence the investigator's opinion and lacks authenticity. Often when people are caught doing something wrong or lying, they will hold a smile for an unusual period of time. Rather than being an indication of comfort, this type of false smile is actually an indication of discomfort.

On occasion, when we do not like what we are hearing, whether a question or an answer, we often close our eyes as if to block it. The various forms of eye-blocking mechanisms are analogous to folding one's hands tightly across the chest or turning away from those with whom we disagree. These blocking displays are performed sub-

consciously and occur often, especially during a formal interview, and are usually related to a specific topic. Eyelid flutter is also observed at times when a particular subject causes distress.[96]

All these eye manifestations are powerful clues as to how information is registering or what questions are problematic for the recipient. However, they are not necessarily direct indicators of deceit. Little or no eye contact is *not* indicative of deception.[97] As a matter of fact, predators and habitual liars actually engage in greater eye contract than most individuals and will lock eyes with the person they are communicating with. Research clearly shows that psychopaths, con artists, and habitual liars will actually increase eye contact and consciously employed it, because they are aware it is so commonly (but erroneously) believed by many that looking someone straight in the eye is a sign of truthfulness.

However, there are cultural differences in eye contact and eye-gaze behavior that must be considered in any attempt to detect deception. For example, individuals belonging to many groups of people, such as Latinos, Asians and people from the Middle East, are often taught to look down or away when being questioned by individuals in a position of authority. This behavior is considered to be a gesture of respect and deference.[98]

Head movements can also be revealing. If a person's head begins to shake either in the affirmative or in the negative as they are speaking, and the movement occurs simultaneously with what they are saying, then the statement can typically be relied on as being truthful. If, however, the head shake or head movement is delayed or occurs after the speech, then most likely the statement is contrived and not truthful. Although it may be very subtle, the delayed movement of the head is an attempt to further validate what has been stated and is not part of the natural flow of communication. In addition, honest head movements should be consistent with verbal denials or affirmations. If a head movement is inconsistent with or contrary to a person's statement, it may indicate deception. While typically involving more subtle rather than exaggerated head movement, this incongruity of verbal and nonverbal signals happens more often than we think. For example, someone may say, "I didn't do it," while slightly nodding his/her head in the affirmative.

During discomfort, the limbic brain takes over, and a person's face can conversely either flush or lighten in color. During difficult conversations, the investigator may also see increases in perspiration or breathing, an accelerated pulsation of the carotid artery, and the person noticeably wiping away sweat or trying to control her/his breathing in an effort to remain calm. Any trembling of the body, whether of the hands, fingers, or lips, or any attempt to hide or restrain the hands or lips (through disappearing or compressed lips), may be indicative of discomfort and/or deception, especially if it occurs after the period of normal nervousness should have been dissipated.

However, indications of nervousness do not necessarily mean deception. The following case illustrates this point.

In a Florida case several years ago a suspect whom the investigators accused of sexual assault and murder was interrogated for 16 hours and eventually confessed. The statement was later suppressed by the judge and the charges were dropped. The suspect had become a prime suspect, because his face flushed and he appeared embarrassed during an initial interview, a reaction interpreted as a sign of deception. Investigators did not know the suspect was a recovering alcoholic with a social anxiety disorder that caused him to sweat profusely and blush in stressful social situations. These same characteristics that could have been interpreted as being signs of guilt in this case were characteristics of a person responding to extreme stress.[99]

A person's voice may crack or may seem inconsistent when being deceptive; swallowing becomes difficult as the throat becomes dry from stress and the person begins to swallow hard. These problems can be evidenced by a sudden bob or jump of the Adam's apple and may be accompanied by the clearing or repeated clearing of the throat—all indicative of discomfort. However, these behaviors are indicators of distress, not guarantees of deception. For example, many honest people who testify in court display these behaviors simply because they are nervous and not because they are lying. Even after years of testifying, many law-enforcement officers still acknowledge they get nervous on the witness stand. Thus it is important to remember that signs of tension and stress need to be deciphered within the context in which they are occurring.

PACIFYING BEHAVIORS

Although pacifiers, which are physical behaviors we use to calm ourselves, are not alone definitive proof of deception (since they can manifest in innocent people who are nervous), they do provide another piece of the puzzle in determining what a person may be truly thinking.

Reading Pacifying Nonverbal and Interpersonal Interactions

- *Expect some pacifying behaviors.* A certain level of pacifying behavior is normal in everyday nonverbal displays; people do this to calm themselves as they adapt to an ever-changing environment. Pacifying behaviors take many forms. When

stressed we might soothe our necks with a gentle massage, stroke our faces, or play with our hair. This is done automatically. Our brains send out the message "please pacify me now," and our hands respond immediately, acting in a way that helps make us comfortable again. Sometimes we pacify by rubbing our necks or our lips from the inside with our tongue, or we exhale slowly with puffed cheeks to calm ourselves. If a stressed person is a smoker, he/she will smoke more, if given the opportunity. If the person chews gum, she/he will chew faster. All these pacifying behaviors satisfy the same requirement of the brain—that is, the brain requires the body to do something that will stimulate nerve endings, releasing calming endorphins in the brain so that the brain can be soothed. As a general rule, men prefer to pacify by touching their face; women prefer to pacify by touching their clothing, jewelry, necklace, and neck.

- *Get a clear view.* To assure that no pacifying behavior will be missed, have nothing blocking the total view of the person. If, for example, the person pacifies by wiping his/her hands on his/her lap, the investigator would want to see this—which is difficult to observe when there is a desk in the way.

- *Expect initial nervousness.* Initial nervousness in the questioning process by the police is normal. For example, if an innocent person is being told by the police that he/she is considered a suspect in a murder or rape investigation, one would certainly expect a certain level of nervousness.

- *Get the person to relax first.* As questioning progresses, individuals should eventually calm down and become more comfortable. In fact, a good investigator will make sure this happens by allowing the person to relax before asking questions or exploring topics that might be stressful.

- *Establish a baseline.* Once a person's pacifying behaviors have decreased and stabilized to normal (for that person), the investigator can recognize that pacifying level as a baseline for assessing future behavior.

- *Look for increased use of pacifiers.* As the interview or conversation continues, it is normal for pacifying behaviors to increase (spike) in their frequency, particularly when they occur in response to a specific question or piece of information. For example, if a person is questioned about a crime and starts to ventilate his collar (a pacifier), that means that specific inquiry has caused a sufficient amount of stress to make the brain require pacification. This indicates the issue needs to be pursued further. The behavior does not necessarily mean that deception is involved but simply that the topic is causing the interviewee stress.

- *Ask, pause, and observe.* Good investigators, like good conversationalists, should not engage in staccato-fashion type questioning. Unfortunately, some false confessions (discussed earlier in this chapter) have been obtained because of sustained staccato-like questioning, which causes high stress and obfuscation and nonverbal cues. Innocent people have been known to confess to crimes and have even provided written statements in order to terminate a stressful interview when excessive or inappropriate pressure is applied.[100]

- *Keep the interviewee focused.* Investigators should keep in mind that many times when people are simply talking and telling their side of the story there will be fewer useful nonverbals used than when the investigator controls the scope of the topic. Pointed questions elicit behavioral manifestations that are useful in assessing a person's honesty.

- *Chatter is not truth.* One mistake made by both novice and experienced investigators is to equate talking with truth. When the person being questioned is talking, investigators tend to believe them. When the person is reserved, it is assumed they are lying. During conversation, people who provide an overwhelming amount of information and detail about an event or a situation may appear to be telling the truth; however, they may really be trying to obfuscate the facts or lead the conversation in another direction.

- *Stress coming in and going out.* A person with guilty knowledge will present two distinct behaviors in sequence. When asked a difficult question such as "Were you involved in the murder of your wife?" The first behavior will reflect the stress experienced when hearing the question. The person will subconsciously respond with various distancing behaviors including foot withdrawal (moving him away from the investigator) and may lean away or may tighten his jaw and lips. This behavior will be followed by the second set of related behaviors, pacifying responses to the stress that may include signals such as neck touching, nose stroking, or neck massaging as he ponders the question or answer.

- *Isolate the cause of the stress.* Two behavior patterns in series—the stress indicators followed by pacifying behaviors—have traditionally been erroneously associated with deception. This is unfortunate, because these manifestations need to be explained more simply as what they are—indicators of stress and stress relief—not necessarily dishonesty. No doubt someone who is lying may display these same behaviors, but individuals who are nervous also show them.

SPECIFIC BEHAVIORS TO CONSIDER IN DETECTING DECEPTION

Following are some specific behaviors to consider when one is attempting to determine if a subject is being deceptive.

- *Lack of emphasis in hand behaviors:* As noted social psychologist Aldert Vrij and others have reported, a lack of arm movement and a lack of emphasis are suggestive of deception.[101] Any sudden reduction in or change in movement reflects brain activity. When arms shift from being animated to being still, there is a reason, be it dejection or (possibly) deception.

  Deceptive individuals will tend to display less steepling of the fingers. The investigator should look for the white knuckles of the individual who grabs the chair armrest in a fixed manner as though in an "ejector seat." Many criminal investigators have found that when the head, neck, arms, and legs are held in place with little movement and the hands and arms are clutching the armrest, such behavior is very much consistent with those who are about to deceive, but again, it is not definitive (Figure 5-11).

- *Swearing to the truthfulness of assertions:* Interestingly, as individuals make declarative statements that are false, they will avoid touching not only other people but also objects, such as a podium or table. It is almost unheard of for a person who is lying to yell affirmatively, "I didn't do it," while pounding his/her fist on a table. It is not at all unusual for individuals who are not being truthful to immediately invoke the name of God and say such things as "I swear to God," or perhaps even invoke their children by making statements such as "if I'm lying may my children die or lose their eyesight," or some other ridiculously desperate plea to convince the interrogator they are not lying. The same psychological motivation for swearing is involved in the use of such expressions as "I have a spotless record" and "I am a very religious man, I couldn't do anything like that." Expressions of this type are frequently used by guilty subjects in an effort to lend forcefulness or conviction to their assertions of innocence. Also, what usually happens in this case is that there may be very weak, non-emphatic statements and gestures that are equally mild. People who are being deceptive lack commitment and confidence in what they are saying. Although their thinking brain (neocortex) will decide what to say in order to mislead, their emotive brain (the limbic system—the honest part of the brain) simply will not be committed to the ruse and therefore will not emphasize their statements using nonverbal

▲ **FIGURE 5-11   Flash frozen**
Sitting for long periods in a chair, as though flash frozen in
an ejector seat, is evidence of high stress and discomfort.
(Joe Navarro, with Marin Karlins, *What Every Body is Saying* [New York:
Harper Collins, 2008], p. 227)

▲ **FIGURE 5-12   The rogatory position (palms up)**
The palms-up, or "rogatory," position usually indicates that
the person wants to be believed or wants to be accepted. It is
not a dominant, confident display. (Joe Navarro, with Marin Karlins,
What Every Body is Saying [New York: Harper Collins, 2008], p. 228)

behaviors (such as gestures). The sentiments of the
limbic brain are hard to override.

- *The rogatory position:* When people place their out-
stretched arms in front of their bodies, with palms
up, this is known as the *rogatory* (or "prayerful")
display (Figure 5-12). Those who worship turn
their palms up to God to ask for mercy. This
behavior is also seen in individuals who say something that they want you to believe. When a person makes a declarative statement, note whether
the hands are palms up or palms down. During
regular conversation in which ideas are being discussed and neither party is vehemently committed
to a particular point, the investigator can expect to
see both palms-up and palms-down displays.

However, when a person is making a passionate and
assertive declaration such as "You have to believe me, I
did not kill her," those hands should be face down (Figure 5-13). If the statement is made palms up, the individual is supplicating to be believed, and such a
statement should be highly suspect. Although this interpretation is not definitive, any declarative statement
made with palms up should raise serious questions
about the truthfulness of the statement being made. People who are telling the truth do not have to plead to be
believed; they make a statement, and it stands.

USE OF TECHNOLOGICAL INSTRUMENTS TO DETECT DECEPTION

POLYGRAPH

The first workable polygraph is attributed to John Larson
(1892–1983) in 1921. Its use spread relatively quickly in
policing circles, and since then it has been improved a

▲ **FIGURE 5-13   Palms-down position**
Statements made palms down are more emphatic and more confident than statements made with the palms up, in the rogatory position. (Joe Navarro, with Marin Karlins, *What Every Body is Saying* [New York: Harper Collins, 2008], p. 229)

number of times, such as by adding the use of computer scoring (Figure 5-14). The primary purpose of a **polygraph** examination is to determine if victims, suspects, and informants are being truthful or untruthful about what they say. The polygraph is an adjunct to, but never a substitute for, other methods of investigation. Other common objectives for polygraph examinations are determining the reliability of informants, eliminating suspects, and narrowing the scope of an investigation. Research on the accuracy of the polygraph varies, roughly from 64% (laboratory studies) to 98% ("real world" use). Such differences may in part be attributable to laboratory protocols in which one group is told to lie about a mock crime scene or other event and the other group tells the truth. When people are not in real jeopardy for lying they may not have the same physiological responses as those who are lying to avoid criminal culpability for a felony.

Polygraphs record indicators of a person's cardiovascular pattern and fluctuations, respiratory patterns and fluctuations, and changes in skin resistance or sweat on the fingertips. The three most common findings by an examiner are no deception indicated, deception indicated, and inconclusive.

A supervisor's approval is required before an investigator can have a person examined by a polygraphist. The investigator is obliged to work with the examiner in a number of ways, such as:[102]

1. Providing the examiner with the information obtained in the investigation that supports and justifies the use of the polygraph.
2. Giving the polygraphist copies of incident, supplemental, and other relevant documents.

▶ **FIGURE 5-14**
Polygraph examination
Note that a blood-pressure cuff is attached to the subject's right upper arm; two pneumograph tubes are stretched across the chest and abdomen; and metal plates are attached to the index and ring fingers. Readings from these sources are displayed on the examiner's screen at the left side of this photograph.
(© Anna Clopet/Corbis)

3. Calling attention to evidence that the subject does not yet know the police have.

4. Making available background information on the subject, including criminal history and possible motives.

5. Advising of statements made by the subject to victims and witnesses, as well as alibis provided.

6. Giving news articles and other general information about the case.

7. Helping the examiner arrange for a sign-language interpreter or translator, as necessary.

8. Not trying to plan the procedures to be used, which is the purview of the examiner.

9. Not interrogating the suspect just before the examination.

10. Ensuring that persons authorized to be with the subject are present (for example, attorneys, parents, or legal guardians).

11. Promptly advising the examiner if the subject is going to be late or has cancelled.

▲ **FIGURE 5-15**
Computerized voice stress analysis system (CVSA)
Newly developed and released second-generation computerized voice stress analysis system (CVSA II) displayed on a laptop computer. (Courtesy National Institute for Truth Verification)

COMPUTER VOICE STRESS ANALYSIS

Computer Voice Stress Analysis (CVSA) was originally developed in 1988 by the National Institute for Truth Verification (NITV) and grew out of the Vietnam-era Psychological Stress Evaluator (PSE), which was used to differentiate between suspected Viet Cong and civilians. Around 1,600 police departments use the CVSA. The CVSA is small, easily portable, and, unlike the polygraph, does not require any attachments to the subject.

Basically, the CVSA notes microvariations in the audible and nonaudible portions of speech. As with the polygraph, reports of its accuracy have varied—for example, one laboratory study found that it was not significantly better than random chance, whereas NITV cited a number of studies showing much higher rates. Here, too, the earlier comments about the absence or presence of real jeopardy affecting the studies' outcomes apply.

The NITV spent many years and invested tremendous resources to develop an automated system to accurately quantify CVSA patterns with the goal of removing any subjectivity in evaluating CVSA charts. A new scoring algorithm has been developed and field tested in state and local law-enforcement agencies across the country. The charts under this new CVSA II (Figure 5-15), which was released in January 2007, reflect whether deception is or is not indicated. Field evaluations are showing a 96% accuracy rate for the new system, with a false positive rate of less than 1%.[103]

admission
Berghuis v. *Thompkins*
body language
coerced-compliant
coerced-internalized
computer voice stress
   analysis (CVSA)
confession
delay-in-arraignment rule

detection of deception
eyewitness identification
free-and-voluntary rule
in-custody interrogation
Maryland v. *Shatzer*
McNabb v. *United States*
Minnick v. *Mississippi*
Miranda v. *Arizona*
mirroring

polygraph
proximity
rapport
suspect
victim
voluntary false confession
witness
witness intimidation

| REVIEW QUESTIONS |

1. What are the similarities and differences between interviews and interrogations?

2. What are the four commonly recognized objectives in the interrogation process?

3. What are the qualifications of interviewers and interrogators?

4. What should an interrogation room look like?

5. What steps should an investigator take in order to prepare for an interview or interrogation?
6. Why is eyewitness testimony so unreliable?
7. What are the forms that witness intimidation can take?
8. What can the police do to deter individuals who would be inclined to intimidate witnesses?
9. What are the advantages of using electronic recordings for interrogation?
10. There are two basic categories of people who tend to confess to crimes. What are they?
11. Three categories of false confessions were discussed. What are they?
12. What recommendations were made to reduce the possibility of false confessions?
13. What was the first notable incident of U.S. Supreme Court intervention into interrogation practices by nonfederal law-enforcement officers?

14. What requirements are imposed on law-enforcement personnel by *Miranda* v. *Arizona*?
15. What are the facts and the significance of the U.S. Supreme Court case involving *Maryland* v. *Shatzer* in 2010?
16. What is the significance of the U.S. Supreme Court decision in the case of *Berghuis* v. *Thompkins*?
17. In the discussion of detection of deception a number of body positions were discussed: isoparaxis, flash frozen, rogatory position and the palms-down position. What is the significance of each of these positions as it relates to the detection of deception?
18. What types of measurements are employed by the polygraph and computer voice stress analysis to detect deception?

INTERNET ACTIVITIES

Much debate surrounds the fairness and effectiveness of eyewitness identification in police lineups. Go to *www.eyewitness.utep.edu/consult04A.html* and read the summary of the whitepaper regarding evaluating lineup fairness. What two aspects of lineup fairness should investigators consider? How similar to one another should the members of the lineup be?

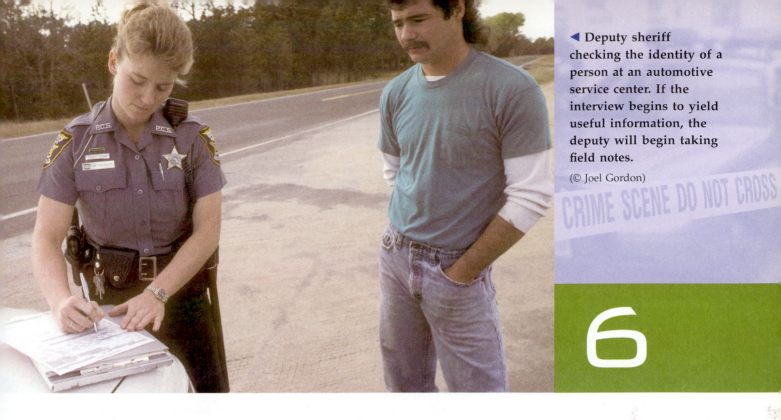

◄ Deputy sheriff checking the identity of a person at an automotive service center. If the interview begins to yield useful information, the deputy will begin taking field notes.

(© Joel Gordon)

CRIME SCENE DO NOT CROSS

6

FIELD NOTES AND REPORTING

1. Understand the importance of field notes.
2. List the six interrogatory investigative questions.
3. Understand formats for basic incident reports.
4. Explain techniques involved in writing effective reports.

5. Summarize the report approval and disposition processes.
6. Explain the purpose of follow-up investigation and supplemental reports.

Taking field notes and writing reports is considered a necessary evil by most law-enforcement officers and investigators. These tasks are not the most exciting or pleasurable parts of the profession. Yet, it cannot be overemphasized how important it is to perform these duties at the highest levels of accuracy and completeness.

This chapter examines several aspects of the field-note-taking and report-writing processes. After discussing field notes and the basic and primary questions that need to be asked in an investigation, it addresses the importance of completing well-prepared incident/offense reports. Incident-report formats vary among law-enforcement agencies. Despite the variation, however, there are common elements that should be included in all reports.

It is considered a standard practice that investigators should gain as much information as possible when arriving at the crime scene. Even facts and details that seem unnecessary at first may later prove to be highly valuable to the investigation. But this practice must be tempered with the following caution:

> determinations must be made as early as possible in the investigative process of what the case is about and what potential criminal charges may be filed, followed by what information the prosecutor will need to file formal charges, what the elements of the offense are, and, also important, what the prosecutor needs to prove a case. Equipped with this information, the first responders and follow-up investigators can pursue and focus on the investigation so that they can separate the important from the "nice to have" or superfluous information. Such an approach is appreciated by prosecutors.

FIELD NOTES

Field notes play a significant role in every criminal investigation. They provide a short written record of events, times, places, suspects, witnesses, and other information and are used as the basis for preparing incident/offense reports. The importance of taking effective and complete notes in every investigation, regardless of the offense, should not be underestimated. Because field notes are more reliable than a person's memory, they can be used as a source of specific facts and details that otherwise might be forgotten. Detailed field notes also reduce the need to recontact victims and witnesses regarding information that was overlooked or questions that were not asked in the initial contact. Finally, it is not uncommon for officers to testify in court several months or years after the conclusion of a particular investigation. Comprehensive field notes can not only help to refresh the

investigator's memory but also to strengthen his/her court testimony.

Field notes are the shorthand written record made by a police officer from the time she/he arrives at the scene until the assignment is completed. Field notes are more reliable than an officer's memory. It is probably easy to remember what you had for breakfast this morning, but what about your lunch five months ago?[1] Often an officer responds to several calls before he/she has time to write an incident/offense report on an earlier call. Even during that short time, some important details can be forgotten. The only way to prevent the possibility of lost information is to prepare thorough field notes.

Field notes are the primary information source for preparing the incident/offense report. Because the first-responding officer is usually the person who writes any incident report required by the situation, field notes are important, because they contain the information that forms the content of the incident report. Moreover, other

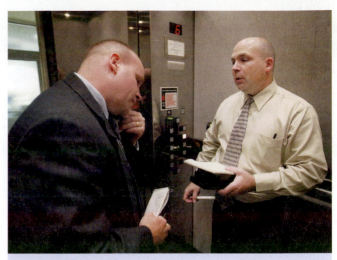

▲ **FIGURE 6-1**

Homicide investigators sharing information from their field notes

These investigators have just finished interviewing neighbor residents in an apartment building where a homicide occurred. The investigators are discussing the information gleaned from their interviews. One investigator is conferring on a cell phone with a third colleague in an effort to join the pieces of the event into a whole story. (© James D. DeCamp/ Columbus Dispatch)

officers who also responded may have taken actions or seen and heard things that are of investigative significance and for which there needs to be an investigative record. They will rely on their own field notes to write reports that supplement the incident report. Well-taken, detailed field notes are the wellspring for good incident reports.

Detailed field notes may reduce the need to recontact the parties involved. Once in a while, victims and witnesses get annoyed and even angry when they are recontacted by an officer who obviously didn't take good field notes when he/she talked to them earlier and therefore cannot complete the incident report without additional information. Comments such as "Weren't you listening to me?" or "You couldn't be very interested in my case, or you would have asked about this when you talked to me the first time" can be avoided by taking thorough notes. The follow-up investigator faces the possibility of similar comments when recontacting victims and witnesses: "Didn't you talk to the officer who took the report?" "With you guys, it looks like the left hand doesn't know what the right one is doing." Although follow-up investigators may be required by departmental policy to make such contacts, sometimes they may have to do so because of shortcomings in the incident report. (For more on this point, see Chapter 7, "The Follow-Up Investigation and Investigative Resources.")

Field notes can be used to defend the integrity of the incident/offense report. When an officer is testifying in a case for which he/she wrote the incident report, the officer can refer to field notes for assistance in recollecting the events. Most often, cases come to trial months or years after the incident report is written, so it would be rare for a testifying officer to remember everything about the event and all its details. In court, field notes are an indication of an officer's thoroughness as an investigator. Moreover, if at trial an officer is asked what sources of information were relied on in preparing the incident report, the notes add to the credibility of the report (Figure 6-1).

GUIDELINES FOR NOTE-TAKING

There are six main guidelines for taking notes:

1. Listen attentively, without interrupting the person who is speaking.
2. Intervene if the speaker is losing focus; bring the person back to the topic as gently as possible.
3. Review all specifics in your notes with the person providing the information.
4. Allow time for the person to consider the information you have stated and to verify it, correct it, or add information.
5. Add and/or correct information as needed.
6. Verify all changes in your notes with the speaker.[2]

NOTE-TAKING EQUIPMENT

Officers typically use small loose-leaf and spiral-bound notebooks for their field notes. Through experience they learn which sizes and types best suit the way they work.[3] Most officers use a ballpoint pen to write their notes. If you are going to write on the front and back of pages, do not use a heavy ink, as it "bleeds" through to the other side of a page, and you will not be able to use that side for note-taking. Number the pages separately for each case, and use some kind of case identifier, such as the case number, on each page so that the pages can be put back in order if they are accidentally separated. Officers should place a departmental business card, or duplicate its information, on the inside of the notebook used for field notes.

Entries in the notebook should be made on a chronological basis. If you are using a loose-leaf notebook, remove the pages when they are filled, place them in a sealed envelope with the covered time period noted on the outside, and insert new blank pages. If you are using a spiral-bound notebook, place the entire notebook in a sealed envelope and start with a new one. Too often, first-responding officers and investigators think it is all right to discard their field notes after they prepare the incident report. This is not a good idea. Frequently, in a later court proceeding, the officer/investigator will be asked to explain where or from whom he/she got the information contained in the incident report. If all the information and its sources are not contained in the incident report, the field notes made at the time of the investigation can often provide reliable answers to the questions asked.

Officers/investigators should not use case notebooks to record personal information such as a list of groceries to buy on the way home. Should such information mistakenly end up in the notes the officer/investigator takes to court, it can be used to embarrass the note-taker. The defense attorney has the right to inspect whatever the witness is using to refresh his/her memory and ask questions to insure that the witness is using the notes only to refresh memory, not to recall information totally forgotten. If the witness does not prepare for trial by studying the notes and case file beforehand, such a situation will become clear very quickly once the witness starts to testify.

SIX INTERROGATORY AND BASIC INVESTIGATIVE QUESTIONS

To gather needed information, first-responding officers and follow-up investigators should phrase all questions beginning with the six interrogatories—who, what, where, when, how, and why. Although no single set of questions can meet the investigative needs in all types of crime, following this format should provide the needed information for the officer/investigator to understand the chronological order of events as they occurred and to enable the preparation of a well-written and thorough incident report. Here are some examples of typical questions:

1. **Who**
   —was the victim?
   —discovered the crime?
   —reported the crime?
   —took the victim to his or her present location?
   —does the suspect associate with?
   —was last seen with the victim?
   —last saw the victim?
   —may be with the suspect when he/she is arrested?
   —are the witnesses connected with or related to?
   —had a motive and the means of committing the crime?
   —completed the crime scene entry and other logs?
   —processed the scene?
   —took what evidence where?
   —else may have heard, smelled, touched, or seen anything of investigative value?

2. **What**
   —crime was committed?
   —actions did the suspect take?
   —methods did the suspect use?
   —do witnesses know about the crime?
   —evidence is there?
   —tools or weapons were used?
   —actions did you take?
   —further action is needed?
   —information may victims and witnesses be withholding?
   —does the victim claim was stolen?
   —parts of the victim's account of the event match that of any witnesses, the appearance of the scene, and the physical evidence?
   —information (and evidence of what types) do you need to clear the crime?
   —knowledge, skills, or strength was needed?
   —other units or agencies are involved or need to be notified?
   —is the case about?
   —are the potential charges?
   —information does the prosecutor need to file formal charges or seek a grand jury indictment?
   —are the elements of the offense?
   —does the prosecutor need to prove the case?

3. **Where**
   —was the crime discovered?
   —was the crime committed?
   —were any tools, evidence, or recovered property found?
   —was the victim when the crime was committed?
   —is the victim now?
   —were the witnesses?
   —did the suspect go?
   —does the suspect frequent, live, and work?
   —is the suspect now?
   —was the suspect arrested?
   —was the evidence marked?
   —is the evidence stored?
   —might other witnesses be located?

4. **When**
   —were you dispatched, and when did you arrive?
   —was the crime discovered?

—was the crime committed?

—was the victim last seen?

—did help arrive, and what type was it?

—was the suspect arrested?

—did the suspect decide to commit the crime?

5. **How**

—was the crime committed?

—did the suspect get to and from the scene?

—did the suspect get the information needed to commit the crime?

—were tools and weapons obtained?

—was the arrest made?

—much injury was done to the victim?

—much damage was there to any premises involved?

—much money was taken, and what type of valuables?

—difficult was it to carry off the property that was stolen?

—is the suspect described by the victim and witnesses?

—closely do the descriptions of victims and witnesses match and diverge?

6. **Why**

—was the crime committed?

—were particular tools or weapons used?

—was the crime reported?

—was there a delay in reporting the crime?

—were the victim or witnesses reluctant to talk?

—were the victim or witnesses so quick to identify the suspect?

—am I uncomfortable with the victim's account and description of the suspect?

INCIDENT REPORTS

Despite the fact that **incident reports** are a crucial source of investigative information, writing them is often not a popular duty. One of the authors says that report writing "is not the favorite indoor sport of law-enforcement officers." The significance of this jest has serious implications. An incident report, like an investigative report, must tell a story. It must be written in such a manner that someone reading that report can understand what happened and can know the answers to the questions who, what, where, when, how, and why. Along with his/her memory, an officer/investigator must use the field notes taken to tell the story of the events. There are two indispensable elements of reports: (1) accuracy and (2) clear communication of the meaning that the writer intended.

More than a few excellent investigations have been wasted by an officer's failure to fully document what was done and not done. The case history that follows indicates the importance of recording all aspects of an investigation:

A burglary in progress was reported at a one-story doctor's office. As two officers moved to cover the building, a suspect was seen leaping from an office window carrying a small flight bag. The suspect ran from the scene, followed by one of the officers. He attempted to scale a fence. In the ensuing struggle, the suspect fell on the far side of the fence, breaking his arm. During treatment at a hospital, the suspect told the officer, in front of medical personnel, that he was going to claim his arm had been broken during questioning. He further indicated this would be an attempt to discredit the police, as he had only recently been released from the state prison and feared that such an immediate second violation would cause the court to invoke a stringent sentence upon conviction. Because many arrested people state that they are going to claim the police violated their civil rights, the officer regarded it as little more than a commonplace occurrence. Even though they did not relate directly to the investigation, the suspect's remarks and the identity of the persons witnessing them were included in the report as a matter of thoroughness. Subsequently, when the FBI investigated the matter of a possible violation of the suspect's rights, the allegation was easily refuted by corroborating statements from the medical personnel identified in the police officer's report.

A well-prepared incident report based on a thorough investigation of an offense can promote the rapid apprehension of the suspect, thus preventing further crimes and making the recovery of property more likely. The report also serves as the official memory of the department so that anyone who needs access to the file after the reporting officer or investigator is no longer available, can make sense of the report and the event.

Incident reports serve important operational and administrative purposes. When their data are combined, useful crime analysis reports can be produced, personnel assignments in the department can be properly aligned with the actual workloads, and geographic information system (GIS) data can produce informative maps showing, for example, where robberies with certain types of characteristics are being committed.

FORMATS FOR INCIDENT REPORTS

Although the exact layout for incident reports varies from one jurisdiction to another, all incident report forms have a "face" with blank spaces that must be filled in by the officer conducting the preliminary investigation. He/She enters basic case information in the blanks, such as information about the type of crime committed; the complainant, victim, witnesses, and offenders; and other details. Figure 6-2 shows a basic incident report.

CRN 01-____-____-_____

Athens-Clarke County Police
INCIDENT REPORT

Press Hard - Multiple Copies   Press Hard - Multiple Copies

Page 1 of ___
ORI - GA0290100
Revised 0900

From Date	From Time	To Date	To Time

☐ Complainant ☐ Victim No. ___ ☐ Witness No. ___
Desires Personal Information Not Be Released

Department Title *Most Serious Criminal / Traffic / Ordinance Offense. See Table.*

Zone

☐ Downtown
☐ AHA
☐ Athens
☐ Winterville
☐ Bogart

Premise Type
☐ 1. Highway
☐ 2. Serv. Station
☐ 3. Conv. Store
☐ 4. Bank
☐ 5. Commercial
☐ 6. Residence
☐ 7. School/Campus
☐ 8. All Other

Case Status
☐ Active
☐ Inactive
☐ Arrest -Adult
☐ Arrest-Juv.
☐ Ex. Cleared
☐ Unfounded
Status Date

Incident Location - Common Name   Address: No., Dir., St., Suffix, Apt.

☐ Alcohol Related   **Type Of Drug(s)** ☐ Amphetamine ☐ Barbiturate ☐ Cocaine ☐ Hallucinogen
☐ Drug Related ☐ Heroin ☐ Marijuana ☐ Opium ☐ Methamphetamine ☐ Synthetic Narcotic
☐ Unknown ☐ Unknown ☐ Form: _____

Solvability Factors:
☐ M.O. Present ☐ Physical Evidence
☐ Property Traceable ☐ Witness

Suspect Can Be: ☐ Named ☐ ID
☐ Located ☐ Described ☐ Vehicle ID

Complainant Information ☐ Juvenile ☐ Victim

Last   First
Middle   Suffix
Address: No., Dir., St., Suffix, Apt
City, State   ☐ Athens, GA   Zip Code
Phone: Home   Work
Race   ☐ M ☐ F DOB

Victim Information ☐ Juvenile ☐ State Of GA ☐ A.C.C.
Last
First
Middle   Suffix
Address: No., Dir., St., Suffix, Apt
City, State   ☐ Athens, GA   Zip Code
Home   Work   Cell/Pager
Race   ☐ M ☐ F DOB
Alias/Street Name
Employer   Occupation
☐ County Resident ☐ Student School
☐ Can ID Suspect ☐ Will File Charges ☐ Medical Treatment
Hospital
Type / Extent Of Injury: ☐ Fatal Injury ☐ Broken Bones
☐ Gun/Knife ☐ Superficial Injury ☐ Sexual Abuse ☐ Other
☐ Property Damage/Loss ☐ Mental Abuse ☐ Threats

Witness 1 Information ☐ Juvenile
Last, First, Middle, Suffix
Address: No., Dir., St., Suffix, Apt
City, State   ☐ Athens, GA   Zip Code
Phone: Home   Work
Race   ☐ M ☐ F DOB

Witness 2 Information ☐ Juvenile
Last, First, Middle, Suffix
Address: No., Dir., St., Suffix, Apt
City, State   ☐ Athens, GA   Zip Code
Phone: Home   Work
Race   ☐ M ☐ F DOB

Offender 1 Information ☐ Juvenile
Last
First
Middle   Suffix
Address: No., Dir., St., Suffix, Apt
City, State   ☐ Athens, GA   Zip Code
Home   Work   Cell/Pager
Race   ☐ M ☐ F DOB
Alias/Street Name
Employer   Occupation
☐ County Resident ☐ Student School
OLN   State
Height   Weight   **Stranger To Stranger?**
                        ☐ Yes ☐ No
Eye Color: ☐ Black ☐ Brown ☐ Blue ☐ Green
☐ Hazel ☐ Gray ☐ Other____
Hair Color: ☐ Blonde ☐ Brown ☐ Black ☐ Red ☐
☐ Gray ☐ Salt&Pepper ☐ Other____
Offender's Vehicle Description   ☐ Vehicle Searched
Tag   Year   State
Veh. Year   Make
Model   Style
Color-Top   Color-Bottom

☐ **Incident Recorded**   ☐ **Hand cuffed**
Tape No.   ☐ D. L.   ☐ B. B.

Burglary Factors For Incident/Offense No.____
Forced Entry? ☐ Kicked ☐ Heavy Object
☐ Yes ☐ No ☐ Pushed ☐ Lock Tamper
☐ Unknown ☐ Pry Tool ☐ Cutting Tool
Point Of Entry? ☐ Front ☐ Rear
☐ Door ☐ Window ☐ Side
☐ Roof ☐ Wall ☐ Basement
☐ Attic ☐ Other ☐ Unk ☐ Move A/C
Point Of Exit? ☐ Same As Entry
☐ Other
Structure Was: ☐ Occupied ☐ Unoccupied

Attached Documents:
☐ Incident/Offense Continuation
☐ Persons Form   ☐ Juvenile Complaint
☐ Domestic Violence ☐ Property / Vehicle
☐ GCIC ☐ ABR ☐ Victim Notification

Incident /Offense 1   Code Section
☐ Attempted ☐ Committed
Title
Assault Factors   **Weapon Type**
☐ Assault ☐ Theft ☐ DV   ☐ Gun ☐ Other
☐ Sexual ☐ Mental Subject ☐ Knife/Cutting Tool
☐ Hate Crime ☐ Unknown   ☐ Hands/Fists/Etc.
Weapon Description
Offense Status ☐ Active ☐ Inactive
☐ Unfounded ☐ Arrest ☐ Ex. Cleared
Involved Suspect No.(s)____ Victim No. (s)____
Murder Circumstance

Incident /Offense 2   Code Section
☐ Attempted ☐ Committed
Title
Assault Factors   **Weapon Type**
☐ Assault ☐ Theft ☐ DV   ☐ Gun ☐ Other
☐ Sexual ☐ Mental Subject ☐ Knife/Cutting Tool
☐ Hate Crime ☐ Unknown   ☐ Hands/Fists/Etc.
Weapon Description
Offense Status ☐ Active ☐ Inactive
☐ Unfounded ☐ Arrest ☐ Ex. Cleared
Involved Suspect No.(s)____ Victim No. (s)____
Murder Circumstance

Incident /Offense 3   Code Section
☐ Attempted ☐ Committed
Title
Assault Factors   **Weapon Type**
☐ Assault ☐ Theft ☐ DV   ☐ Gun ☐ Other
☐ Sexual ☐ Mental Subject ☐ Knife/Cutting Tool
☐ Hate Crime ☐ Unknown   ☐ Hands/Fists/Etc.
Weapon Description
Offense Status ☐ Active ☐ Inactive
☐ Unfounded ☐ Arrest ☐ Ex. Cleared
Involved Suspect No.(s)____ Victim No. (s)____
Murder Circumstance

Incident /Offense 4   Code Section
☐ Attempted ☐ Committed
Title
Assault Factors   **Weapon Type**
☐ Assault ☐ Theft ☐ DV   ☐ Gun ☐ Other
☐ Sexual ☐ Mental Subject ☐ Knife/Cutting Tool
☐ Hate Crime ☐ Unknown   ☐ Hands/Fists/Etc.
Weapon Description
Offense Status ☐ Active ☐ Inactive
☐ Unfounded ☐ Arrest ☐ Ex. Cleared
Involved Suspect No.(s)____ Victim No. (s)____
Murder Circumstance

Reporting Officer	Emp. No.	Report Date	Approving Supervisor	Emp. No.

▲ **FIGURE 6-2 Basic incident report**

(Courtesy Athens-Clarke County, Georgia, Police Department)

NIBRS-COMPLIANT INCIDENT REPORTS

For more than a decade, a voluntary program has been moving law-enforcement agencies away from the basic incident-report format and toward a detailed format that documents much more data about an offense. This program, the **National Incident-Based Reporting System (NIBRS),** was created as part of the **Uniform Crime Reports** and is administered by the FBI. It is in use in over 4,000 small and medium-size local law-enforcement agencies throughout the country, as well as a growing number of jurisdictions with populations in excess of 250,000. A large number of departments are working toward becoming NIBRS-compliant.

National crime reporting in the United States dates back roughly 70 years, to the time when the FBI began collecting and publishing annual "counts" of offenses in its Uniform Crime Reports (UCRs). Over the past 25 years, the desire for detailed, descriptive data about criminal offenses for crime analysis and other uses has necessitated a shift in incident-report formats. With this shift, which is still in progress, police agencies have started accumulating data about the relationship between victims and offenders, the role of drugs and alcohol in offending, and other factors. The availability of NIBRS data means that law-enforcement officials can more effectively allocate their resources to combat crime. Figure 6-3 reveals the level of detail in an NIBRS-compliant report, the last page of which is a continuation sheet for the chronological narrative. As computer technology continues to evolve, more and more of these reports are completed electronically (see "Computer-Generated Reports," below).

COMPUTER-GENERATED REPORTS

Since the 1980s, many law-enforcement vehicles have been equipped with **mobile computer terminals (MCTs)** (Figures 6-4 and 6-5). Although the terminals initially had limited capabilities and occasional reliability problems, MCTs have reduced demands on the overcrowded voice channels and enhanced officer safety. Technological advances continue to create new options and possibilities for the use of wireless systems in law-enforcement vehicles. Depending on the system and software used, current MCTs can do the following:

1. Provide consistently secure communications between 911 and law-enforcement units, and among law-enforcement units.
2. Allow officers to directly check important databases (rather than going through a dispatcher and waiting for a reply). They can access the National Crime Information Center (NCIC), as well as state and local systems. Officers can also receive information about newly wanted persons, including a facial composite likeness or mug shot. Outstanding warrants, court orders, stolen property inquiries, criminal

and driving records, mug-shot files, crime analysis reports, and GIS maps of crimes and other incidents may all be directly available to the officer.
3. Enable officers in the field to write incident reports electronically, with full access to spelling- and grammar-checking tools. In modest systems, the reports are saved to a disk, from which they are printed at the station.

In addition to using MCTs, some agencies are using **iPhones and iPads** (Figure 6-6). iPads are particularly useful in traffic enforcement; they print a hard copy of the citation for the violator and send a digital copy to the station.

Agencies using wireless technologies have experienced significant productivity gains as the systems reduce the amount of time officers must spend on paperwork. In general, the time gained per officer ranges from 2.5 to 4 hours per day.

HANDWRITTEN REPORTS

Despite the widespread use of MCTs, many officers still write all their reports by hand, because their jurisdictions cannot afford MCT technology, have not made its acquisition a priority item in their budgets, or believe that the technology's cost outweighs its benefits. In actuality, when the formats of handwritten and MCT-generated reports are compared, the differences can be so slight that it is difficult to distinguish between the two.

Hand writing reports is slower, and officers do not have the advantages provided by spelling and grammar checkers. Moreover, if officers make mistakes, sometimes the only solution is to rewrite the page up to the point of the error and then continue with the correct information. Although officers writing incident reports electronically also make mistakes, recovery is much easier, because it is a simple matter to insert additional words, sentences, and paragraphs.

COMMON ELEMENTS OF INCIDENT REPORTS

Incident-report contents vary, ranging from the essential data in a basic incident report to the more extensive information in an NIBRS-compliant report. However, certain elements are common to most reports. The importance of obtaining as much detailed and complete information as possible for inclusion in the incident report cannot be over emphasized.

Name

The full names of complainants, witnesses, and other parties must always be obtained. In the recording of proper names, the first time an individual is referred to in a report the sequence of names should be last, first, middle. When a person mentioned in the report is commonly known to acquaintances by some name other than the

STERLING HEIGHTS POLICE DEPARTMENT

ADMINISTRATION

OFFICER / #: | DATE: | TIME(S) OF INCIDENT: / | DATE(S) OF INCIDENT: / | INCIDENT #:

LOCATION OF INCIDENT: (Address or Block No.) | ARRIVAL TIME AND DATE: | AREA/SECTION | RELATED INCIDENT #:

REPORTEE: (Last, First, Middle) | DOB | PHONE (Home): ( )

ADDRESS: (Street, City, State, Zip) | PHONE (Business): ( )

OFFENSE

OFFENSE:
1. | 2. | 3.

OFFENSE STATUS: (Check only one per offense)
1.A ☐ ATTEMPTED　2.A ☐ ATTEMPTED　3.A ☐ ATTEMPTED
　C ☐ COMPLETED　　C ☐ COMPLETED　　C ☐ COMPLETED
Assist Agency

SUSPECT(S) USED: (Check as many as apply)
A ☐ ALCOHOL　　　D ☐ DRUGS
C ☐ COMPUTER EQUIP.　N ☐ NOT APPLICABLE

(For Burglary Only)
NUMBER OF
PREMISES ENTERED: _____
METHOD OF ENTRY:
F ☐ FORCEABLE　N ☐ NO FORCE

LOCATION OF OFFENSE: (Check Only One) (Enter Code Number for Offense #2 _____ #3 _____)

01 ☐ AIR/BUS/TRAIN TERMINAL
02 ☐ BANK/SAVINGS & LOAN
03 ☐ BAR/NIGHT CLUB
04 ☐ CHURCH/SYNAGOGUE/TEMPLE
05 ☐ COMMERCIAL/OFFICE BUILDING
06 ☐ CONSTRUCTION SITE
07 ☐ CONVENIENCE STORE
08 ☐ DEPARTMENT/DISCOUNT STORE
09 ☐ DRUG STORE/DR'S OFFICE/HOSPITAL
10 ☐ FIELD/WOODS

11 ☐ GOVERNMENT/PUBLIC BUILDINGS
12 ☐ GROCERY/SUPERMARKET
13 ☐ HIGHWAY/ROAD/ALLEY
14 ☐ HOTEL/MOTEL/ETC.
15 ☐ JAIL/PRISON
16 ☐ LAKE/WATER
17 ☐ LIQUOR STORE
18 ☐ PARKING LOT/GARAGE
19 ☐ RENTAL/STORAGE FACILITY
20 ☐ RESIDENCE/HOME

21 ☐ RESTAURANT
23 ☐ SERVICE/GAS STATION
24 ☐ SPECIALTY STORE (TV, FUR, ETC.)
31 ☐ SCHOOL
32 ☐ COLLEGE
33 ☐ REST AREA/ROADSIDE PARK
34 ☐ SCALE
88 ☐ OTHER
99 ☐ UNKNOWN

TYPE CRIMINAL ACTIVITY:
(Check Up To Three)
B ☐ BUYING/RECEIVING
C ☐ CULTIVATING/MANUFACTURING/PUBLISHING
D ☐ DISTRIBUTING/SELLING
E ☐ EXPLOITING CHILDREN
O ☐ OPERATING/PROMOTING/ASSISTING
P ☐ POSSESSING/CONCEALING
T ☐ TRANSPORTING/TRANSMITTING/IMPORTING
U ☐ USING/CONSUMING

TYPE WEAPON/FORCE INVOLVED: (Check Up To Three) (Enter A in Box if Automatic)
11 ☐ FIREARM (type not stated)
12 ☐ HANDGUN
13 ☐ RIFLE
14 ☐ SHOTGUN
15 ☐ OTHER FIREARM
20 ☐ KNIFE/CUTTING INSTRUMENT
30 ☐ BLUNT OBJECT
35 ☐ MOTOR VEHICLE
40 ☐ PERSONAL WEAPONS
50 ☐ POISON
60 ☐ EXPLOSIVES
65 ☐ FIRE/INCENDIARY
70 ☐ NARCOTICS/DRUGS
85 ☐ ASPHYXIATION
88 ☐ OTHER
99 ☐ UNKNOWN
00 ☐ NONE

ARRESTEE / SUSPECT

☐ ARRESTEE　☐ SUSPECT　SUSPECT CONNECTED TO OFFENSE NUMBER:　1.☐　2.☐　3.☐

#1: (Last, First, Middle) | ADDRESS: (Street, City, State, Zip)

DOB:
M ☐ MALE　W ☐ WHITE　A ☐ ASIAN
F ☐ FEMALE　B ☐ BLACK　U ☐ UNKNOWN
U ☐ UNKNOWN　I ☐ INDIAN
PHONE (Home): | PHONE (Business):

ARRESTEE WAS ARMED WITH: (Check Up To Two) (Enter A in Box if Automatic)
01 ☐ UNARMED　14 ☐ SHOTGUN
11 ☐ FIREARM,　15 ☐ OTHER FIREARM
　(type not stated)　20 ☐ LETHAL CUTTING INSTRUMENT
12 ☐ HANDGUN　　(e.g. Switchblade, Knife, etc.)
13 ☐ RIFLE　　30 ☐ CLUB/BLACKJACK/BRASS KNUCKLES

TYPE OF ARREST:
O ☐ ON-VIEW
S ☐ SUMMONED/CITED
T ☐ TAKEN INTO CUSTODY

ARREST CHARGE:

HEIGHT: ___'___" | WEIGHT: | EYES: | HAIR:

☐ ARRESTEE　☐ SUSPECT　SUSPECT CONNECTED TO OFFENSE NUMBER:　1.☐　2.☐　3.☐

#2: (Last, First, Middle) | ADDRESS: (Street, City, State, Zip)

DOB:
M ☐ MALE　W ☐ WHITE　A ☐ ASIAN
F ☐ FEMALE　B ☐ BLACK　U ☐ UNKNOWN
U ☐ UNKNOWN　I ☐ INDIAN
PHONE (Home): | PHONE (Business):

ARRESTEE WAS ARMED WITH: (Check Up To Two) (Enter A in Box if Automatic)
01 ☐ UNARMED　14 ☐ SHOTGUN
11 ☐ FIREARM,　15 ☐ OTHER FIREARM
　(type not stated)　20 ☐ LETHAL CUTTING INSTRUMENT
12 ☐ HANDGUN　　(e.g. Switchblade, Knife, etc.)
13 ☐ RIFLE　　30 ☐ CLUB/BLACKJACK/BRASS KNUCKLES

TYPE OF ARREST:
O ☐ ON-VIEW
S ☐ SUMMONED/CITED
T ☐ TAKEN INTO CUSTODY

ARREST CHARGE:

HEIGHT: ___'___" | WEIGHT: | EYES: | HAIR:

☐ ARRESTEE　☐ SUSPECT　SUSPECT CONNECTED TO OFFENSE NUMBER:　1.☐　2.☐　3.☐

#3: (Last, First, Middle) | ADDRESS: (Street, City, State, Zip)

DOB:
M ☐ MALE　W ☐ WHITE　A ☐ ASIAN
F ☐ FEMALE　B ☐ BLACK　U ☐ UNKNOWN
U ☐ UNKNOWN　I ☐ INDIAN
PHONE (Home): | PHONE (Business):

ARRESTEE WAS ARMED WITH: (Check Up To Two) (Enter A in Box if Automatic)
01 ☐ UNARMED　14 ☐ SHOTGUN
11 ☐ FIREARM,　15 ☐ OTHER FIREARM
　(type not stated)　20 ☐ LETHAL CUTTING INSTRUMENT
12 ☐ HANDGUN　　(e.g. Switchblade, Knife, etc.)
13 ☐ RIFLE　　30 ☐ CLUB/BLACKJACK/BRASS KNUCKLES

TYPE OF ARREST:
O ☐ ON-VIEW
S ☐ SUMMONED/CITED
T ☐ TAKEN INTO CUSTODY

ARREST CHARGE:

HEIGHT: ___'___" | WEIGHT: | EYES: | HAIR:

VEH.

IMPOUND Y OR NO | MAKE | MODEL | YEAR | COLOR | V.I.N. | LIC. ST. | LIC. YR. | LICENSE NO.

▲ FIGURE 6-3　**NIBRS-compliant incident report**
(Courtesy Sterling Heights, Michigan, Police Department)

STERLING HEIGHTS POLICE DEPARTMENT - Part Two

OFFICER / #:	DATE:	SUPERVISOR / #:	DATE:	INCIDENT #:

VICTIM

VICTIM #1: (Last, First, Middle) | PHONE (Home): | PHONE (Business):

ADDRESS: (Street, City, State, Zip) | DOB:

M ☐ MALE   W ☐ WHITE   A ☐ ASIAN
F ☐ FEMALE   B ☐ BLACK
U ☐ UNKNOWN   I ☐ INDIAN   U ☐ UNKNOWN

AGGRAVATED ASSAULT/HOMICIDE CIRCUMSTANCES:

01 ☐ ARGUMENT
02 ☐ ASSAULT ON LAW OFFICER
03 ☐ DRUG DEALING
04 ☐ GANGLAND
05 ☐ JUVENILE GANG

06 ☐ LOVERS' QUARREL
07 ☐ MERCY KILLING
08 ☐ OTHER FELONY INVOLVED
09 ☐ OTHER CIRCUMSTANCES
10 ☐ UNKNOWN CIRCUMSTANCES

20 ☐ CRIMINAL KILLED BY PRIVATE CITIZEN
21 ☐ CRIMINAL KILLED BY POLICE OFFICER
30 ☐ CHILD PLAYING WITH WEAPON
31 ☐ GUN-CLEANING ACCIDENT
32 ☐ HUNTING ACCIDENT
33 ☐ OTHER NEGLIGENT WEAPON HANDLING
34 ☐ OTHER NEGLIGENT KILLINGS

TYPE OF VICTIM: (Check Only One)

I ☐ INDIVIDUAL
B ☐ BUSINESS
F ☐ FINANCIAL
P ☐ POLICE OFFICER
O ☐ OTHER

G ☐ GOVERNMENT
R ☐ RELIGIOUS
S ☐ SOCIETY/PUBLIC
U ☐ UNKNOWN

JUSTIFIABLE HOMICIDE CIRCUMSTANCE:

01 ☐ Criminal Attacked Police Officer and that Officer Killed the Criminal
02 ☐ Criminal Attacked Police Officer and Criminal Killed by Another Police Officer
03 ☐ Criminal Attacked a Civilian

04 ☐ Criminal Attempted Flight from a Crime
05 ☐ Criminal Killed in Commission of a Crime
06 ☐ Criminal Resisted Arrest
09 ☐ Unable to Determine/Not Enough Information

VICTIM CONNECTED TO OFFENSE NUMBER

1. ☐
2. ☐
3. ☐

INJURY TYPE:

N ☐ NONE   F ☐ FATAL
B ☐ BROKEN BONES   M ☐ MINOR INJURY
I ☐ POSS. INT. INJURIES   O ☐ MAJOR INJURY
L ☐ SEVERE   T ☐ LOSS OF TEETH
    LACERATION   U ☐ UNCONSCIOUSNESS

RELATIONSHIP OF VICTIM TO SUSPECT: (For multiple suspect relationships enter suspect number(s) in space before box)

01 ☐ SPOUSE
02 ☐ COMMON-LAW
03 ☐ PARENT
04 ☐ SIBLING
05 ☐ CHILD

06 ☐ GRANDPARENT
07 ☐ GRANDCHILD
08 ☐ IN-LAW
09 ☐ STEPPARENT
10 ☐ STEPCHILD

11 ☐ STEP-SIBLING
12 ☐ OTHER FAMILY
20 ☐ ACQUAINTANCE
21 ☐ FRIEND
22 ☐ NEIGHBOR

23 ☐ BABYSITTEE (baby)
24 ☐ BOY/GIRLFRIEND
25 ☐ CHILD OF "BG" ABOVE
26 ☐ HOMOSEXUAL REL.
27 ☐ EX-SPOUSE

28 ☐ EMPLOYEE
29 ☐ EMPLOYER
30 ☐ OTHERWISE
31 ☐ VICTIM WAS SUSPECT
98 ☐ STRANGER
99 ☐ RELATIONSHIP UNKNOWN

Victim Residence

R ☐ Resident of the Community
C ☐ Resides in the County
S ☐ Resides in the State
O ☐ Out of state
U ☐ Unknown

WITNESS

NAME (Last, First, Middle):	ADDRESS (Street, City, State, Zip):	DOB	RESIDENTIAL PHONE:	BUSINESS PHONE:

PROPERTY

TYPE/ CODE	QTY	DRUGS	PROPERTY DESCRIPTION - INCLUDE MAKE, MODEL, SIZE, TYPE, SERIAL #, ETC. DRUGS - INCLUDE TYPE, QUANTITY, MEASUREMENT	VALUE	DATE RECOVERED Month/Day/Year
/					
/					
/					
/					
/					
/					
/					

TYPE PROPERTY LOSS/ETC.

0 NONE
1 STOLEN/ RECOVERED
2 BURNED
3 COUNTERFEITED/ FORGED
4 DAMAGED/ DESTROYED
5 RECOVERED
6 SEIZED
7 STOLEN
8 UNKNOWN

PROPERTY DESCRIPTION CODE TABLE: (Enter Number in Code Column Above)

01 AIRCRAFT
02 ALCOHOL
03 AUTOMOBILES
04 BICYCLES
05 BUSES
06 CLOTHES/FURS
07 COMPUTER HARDWARE/ SOFTWARE
08 CONSUMABLE GOODS
09 CREDIT/DEBIT CARDS
10 DRUGS/NARCOTICS
11 DRUG/NARCOTIC EQUIPMENT
12 FARM EQUIPMENT
13 FIREARMS
14 GAMBLING EQUIP.

15 HEAVY CONSTRUCTION/ INDUSTRIAL EQUIPMENT
16 HOUSEHOLD GOODS
17 JEWELRY/PRECIOUS METALS
18 LIVESTOCK
19 MERCHANDISE
20 MONEY
21 NEGOTIABLE INSTRUMENTS
22 NON- NEGOTIABLE INSTRUMENTS
23 OFFICE TYPE EQUIPMENT
24 OTHER MOTOR VEHICLES
25 PURSES/HANDBAGS/WALLETS
26 RADIOS/TVs/VCRs
27 RECORDINGS-AUDIO/VISUAL
28 RECREATIONAL VEHICLES

29 STRUCTURES-SINGLE FAMILY
30 STRUCTURES-OTHER DWELLINGS
31 STRUCTURES-OTHER COMMERCIAL BUSINESS
32 STRUCTURES-INDUSTRIAL/MANUFACTURING
33 STRUCTURES - PUBLIC/COMMUNITY
34 STRUCTURES - STORAGE
35 STRUCTURES - OTHER
36 TOOLS - POWER/HAND
37 TRUCKS
38 VEHICLE PARTS/ACCESSORIES
39 WATERCRAFT
77 PENDING INVENTORY
88 OTHER
99 SPECIAL

TYPE DRUG

01 = "Crack" Cocaine
02 = Cocaine
03 = Hashish
04 = Heroin
05 = Marijuana
06 = Morphine
07 = Opium
08 = Other Narcotics
09 = LSD
10 = PCP
11 = Other Hallucinogens
12 = Amphetamines/ Methamphetamines
13 = Other Stimulants
14 = Barbiturates
15 = Other Depressants
16 = Other Drugs
17 = Over 3 Drug Types
99 = Unknown

MEASUREMENT

WEIGHT
GM = Gram
KG = Kilogram
OZ = Ounce
LB = Pound

CAPACITY
ML = Milliliter
LT = Liter
FO = Fluid Ounce
GL = Gallon

UNITS
DU = Dosage Units/Items
NP = Number of Plants
XX = Not Reported

BIAS   Y ☐   N ☐   #1 [_____]   #2 [_____]   #3 [_____]

▲ **FIGURE 6-3** NIBRS-compliant incident report (*continued*)
(Courtesy Sterling Heights, Michigan, Police Department)

STERLING HEIGHTS POLICE DEPT.

INCIDENT NO.

▲ FIGURE 6-3   NIBRS-compliant incident report (*concluded*)
(Courtesy Sterling Heights, Michigan, Police Department)

proper name or an apparent derivation, the nickname should also be provided. The full names and badge numbers of other officers/investigators should be reported, including those from other agencies who participated in the investigation.

Race or Ethnicity and Sex

Race or ethnic extraction should never be documented in such a manner as to cast aspersion on a person. Ordinarily race is indicated by use of one of the following abbreviations: W (White), B (Black), H (Hispanic), A (Asian or Pacific Islander), I (American Indian or Native Alaskan), and U (Unknown).[4] Sex is always designated by F for female and M for male. The proper sequence is race/sex—for example, W/F.

Age

On entries requiring only a person's age, it should be indicated as of the last birthday. However, the first reference to the individual in the narrative portion of the

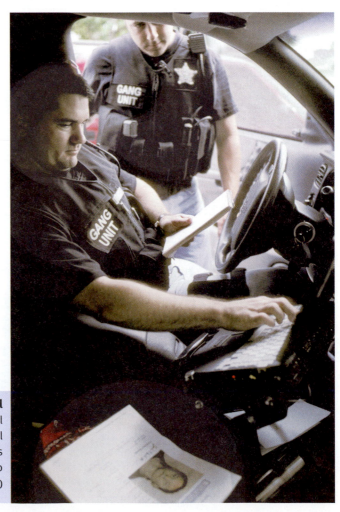

► FIGURE 6-4   **Officer using a mobile computer terminal**
This officer, with his partner observing, is checking several databases to verify the existence of a warrant for an individual and checking the person's photograph through the state's drivers licenses database before they go to a house a block away to make an arrest. (© Joel Gordon)

▲ **FIGURE 6-6**
A Seattle police officer uses an iPhone for a report while working in a park in downtown Seattle, Wednesday, March 3.
(© AP Photo/Elaine Thompson)

report should give the exact date of birth, if known. For certain parties, such as an unidentified deceased person or a suspect whose identity has not been established, age may be approximated or given in a narrow span of years—for example, "approximately 32 years" or "approximately 31–33 years."

Physical and E-Mail Addresses

This information is particularly important, because it helps investigators to find people for additional interviews or related procedures. Each residence and business address should show the street number and, when applicable, the apartment, suite, or room number. If this information is not immediately ascertainable, the general location should be described in sufficient detail to make its whereabouts known. When military personnel are involved, the location information should include serial numbers, unit designations, and ship or installation, if applicable. If a person is only visiting a location, both temporary and permanent addresses should be obtained. E-mail addresses have become so common that they should be included in the report.

Telephone, Cell-Phone, and Pager Numbers

The telephone numbers of an individual should always be obtained, including area code, residence number, business number, and any extension number. Additionally, officers should inquire about and record any cell-phone or pager numbers.

Personal Description

Minimally, the following points should be included: sex, race, age, complexion, hair and eye color, physical defects, scars, marks, tattoos, build, and the nature and color of clothing worn.

Property Description

Elements useful in describing property are make, model, serial number, color, and type of material from which constructed. Other types of information may also be pertinent. Using the case of a stolen car as an example, the presence of stickers, cracked windows, articles hanging from the mirror, or loud engine noise would be additional information useful in locating the vehicle, and, of course, make, model year, color, vehicle identification number, and license plate state and number.

Occupation

The occupation of a person may be of some importance to an investigation. In the case of a suspect, it may establish familiarity with the use of certain types of equipment or procedures associated with a particular function, such as banking. It may also lend further credibility to the statement of a witness:

A man exited from a restaurant as two suspects ran about 15 feet from the bank they had just robbed, entered a vehicle, and rapidly drove around the corner. Despite being presented with only a brief view of the car, the witness was able to give the police a fairly detailed description of it. At the trial, the defense was unsuccessful in casting doubt on the accuracy of the description, since the witness operated an automobile repair service.

Occupation is also useful in suggesting times when a person might be successfully and conveniently contacted by the investigator. An unemployed individual's ordinary line of work is to be given along with the notation "currently unemployed." College students or homemakers should be so designated. If the individual is employed, the occupation given in a report should be as specific as possible—for example, "brick mason" as opposed to "manual laborer."

Value

The value of property stolen may determine whether the offense is a felony or misdemeanor. For articles subject to depreciation, the fair market value should be used, unless the property is new or almost new, in which case the replacement cost should be used. On goods stolen from retail establishments, the merchant's wholesale cost, which constitutes the actual dollar loss, is the proper value to use. The value placed on nonnegotiable instruments such as traveler's checks or money orders should be the cost of replacing them; negotiable instruments, including bonds payable to the bearer, are valued at the market price at the time of the theft.

When the stolen property is subject to appreciation from the time of its acquisition by the owner—for example, limited-edition prints—the current fair market value is to be indicated.

The value of recovered stolen property ordinarily equals the valuation placed on it at the time of theft unless damaged, in which case it is to be established by the fair market value. In cases where the value of the stolen article is not readily ascertainable, the conservative estimate of the owner may be used.

Date

Many dates are used in a report, but officers/investigators must know what dates are most critical. Often, important dates needed by prosecutors to file formal charges are hard to find or are missing from reports. For example: it is more critical to know what date a motor vehicle was stolen rather than recovered. It is important to know what date a bad check was presented for payment or to be cashed (uttered) rather than the date it was returned from the bank and reported to law enforcement. In any investigation, learn which dates are most important to include in the report.

Time

For all official business, excluding general public and related information, most police agencies use the military system, or 24-hour clock, of hundred hours. Time runs from 0001 hours (12:01 A.M.) through 2400 hours (12 A.M.).

WRITING EFFECTIVE REPORTS: THE NARRATIVE

THE NARRATIVE

Almost always, there is more information to document than can fit on the face of an incident report. The additional information is entered in **narrative style** (Figure 6-7). There are a number of ways to organize the incident report to tell the story, but the narrative report generally makes the most sense if written in a chronological format beginning with the earliest thing that happened and progressing to the most recent fact or happening. The hardest part of writing a narrative is making sure that all the necessary information, including the smallest details, are transposed from the officer's/investigator's head and notes and recorded on paper. Doing a good job of report writing takes time, takes concentration, takes desire, and takes commitment. This sounds great on paper, but the realities of law enforcement often mean that an officer or investigator has calls backed up or a heavy caseload, and so the object is to write the shortest, most direct report possible. The belief is that very few cases ever go to trial, thus officers believe that the time and effort saved by writing short, direct reports are worth the risk. As we continue to point out in this chapter, the reality is that no one can predict which cases may later develop into something significant, where the quality of a report is critical. The account is written in the blank space on the reverse of the report's face or on a page referred to as "continuation," "investigative narrative," or "supplemental" (see Figure 6-7, a case that started as a missing-person report and turned into a criminal homicide investigation). Furthermore, even cases that are plea bargained require certain information to pass muster with the local prosecutor's office. It is of utmost importance that first-responding

Incident #   2002710051   Report Date: Wednesday, September 27, 2000
THERESA ANDREWS 23 YOA...5·7 BROWNISH RED HAIR 9 MONTHS PREGNANT.
COP ENTRY SENT OUT AT 16:51. 17:19 TELETYPE OHALLTERM SENT OUT. RIVERS WAS
CALLED AT 17:57

We received a call to go to 207 W. Riddle Ave. reference a missing person. Circumstances as stated by dispatch was that a female adult was missing from the home. It was reported that the husband came home from work, found the door open, his wife's belongings such as purse, keys, and cell phone at the residence. It was also reported that a person was to take a test ride in a vehicle for sale this morning.

Based on information given by dispatch I asked Detective Francis to accompany myself and Ptl. Wilmington to the residence. Upon arrival we were met by Mr . Andrews who was in the front lawn talking on a cell phone. He appeared to be upset but not frantic.

Upon speaking to him he stated that his wife paged him at work around 9:00 am this morning and told him that a lady was coming by to take a look and test drive their jeep that was for sale. The Pr stated that they have the jeep listed in trading times and were trying to sell the car. He stated that he tried to call back around noon or so and could not get an answer. He stated that he told her not to go with anyone, just get their driver's license and let them take a drive. Pr stated that upon arriving home he found the front door wide open. He stated that his wife's purse, house keys, and cell phone were in the house but she was gone as was the jeep.

The Pr described his wife as being 8 1/2 months pregnant and not feeling well. He stated that she has to be helped in and out of bed and that she had not been feeling well. Pr stated he had checked the hospital and was trying to phone the doctor to see if something had happened with the baby. The jeep was described as all black 1999 with soft top and Ohio Reg. CAB4351 and is a Wrangler type.

Ptl. Wilmington, Det. Francis and myself checked the interior of the house as well as the yard and garage area. No one was located. The house appeared to be very tidy with no signs of foul play or struggle. I instructed dispatch to place a COPS teletype, administrative teletype, and radio broadcast with the information. I also advised dispatch to enter Mrs. Andrews as missing as well as the vehicle.

▲ FIGURE 6-7   Portion of an investigative narrative

officers and follow-up investigators learn the minimum amount of information required by the prosecutor to enable her/him to do the basic filing of formal charges. It cannot be over emphasized that complaints by law-enforcement officers that prosecutors don't do a very good job are too often based on ineffective reports submitted by officers.

The incident report must also contain as much detail about the suspect as is known, including descriptive data, clothing, hair, complexion, language or accent information, and weapons displayed. All information from witnesses or other people interviewed, including details of the information provided, along with name and contact information needed by follow-up investigators and prosecutors, must be obtained. The report must include a listing of all evidence seized or found, with details about where it was found, by whom, who has control of it, how it was marked and recorded, and any other information necessary to protect the chain of custody.

If incidents reports are to serve the many uses to which they can be put, they must meet certain standards. Among the standards most usually cited are proper classification; complete, accurate, concise, objective, and fair information; and timely submission.[5] Keep the following guidelines in mind when you are preparing incident and investigative reports:

1. *Fill in all the blanks* on the incident report unless the information is not available or it is withheld, in which case this should be explained in the report. As discussed earlier, it is easier to get the necessary information at the scene than to try to recontact complainants and witnesses.

2. *Write the report in the first person,* using "I arrived at the scene at 1645 hours" as opposed to "Officer Morales arrived at the scene at 1645 hours." The reader of the report knows that Officer Morales wrote the report, and the officer's constant reference

to himself/herself in the third person (Officer Morales) is awkward. Although some departments require the use of the third person in reports, the trend in report writing is not to use it.

3. *Avoid unnecessary technical or legalistic jargon* such as "hereinafter," "point of fact," or "thereof," because you may convey a meaning that you do not intend or do not fully understand. Such jargon is a means by which your credibility can be attacked. Avoid writing statements of your own whose meaning you cannot fully explain. Certainly, if a suspect tells you, "I was abducted by aliens who implanted a control box in my head and they sent me commands to rob the pharmacy," you must faithfully record the statement even if you can't explain it—but the words are not your own.

4. *Write short sentences,* because they are less likely to be confusing to (or misunderstood by) readers, such as the prosecutor. A concise, "punchy" presentation of the facts makes it easier for the reader to "find the beef."

5. *Use short paragraphs* for the same reasons as those for writing short sentences.

6. *Support any conclusions you express with details,* because others who read the report, such as the prosecutor, need to know what facts shaped your thinking. Also, when a trial begins weeks, months, or even years later, you will have forgotten many facts. If you included them in the report, you will be able to refresh your recollection and provide convincing testimony.

7. *Don't repeat facts more than once,* unless doing so is required by your department's reporting format or policies. Duplication of entries wastes your time, and it creates the possibility that when you are distracted, tired, or in a hurry, your entries may conflict in some way with one another, calling your credibility into question.

8. *Check your spelling.* People who don't know you will form opinions of your capabilities on the basis of the reports you write and they read. Also, you are representing your department, so its reputation is on the line, because defense attorneys, judges, members of the news media, juries drawn from the community, and prosecutors read police reports. Misspelled words can change the meaning of a sentence or cause the meaning to be lost. Spell-checker software is an aid to accuracy, but it does not catch words that are spelled correctly but used inappropriately (for example, "E. Wazolewski took a write turn").

9. *Edit what you write.* Don't miss an opportunity to catch and correct your errors. Many people do this best when they read slowly and out loud, but you may find a system that works better for you. Taking the time to edit your report is more important than the system you use. If you are using a computer, editing is far easier than writing several successive handwritten drafts of a report. Moreover, the software includes a spell checker, thesaurus, and grammar checker.[6] Editing can also catch errors in the use of macros. Agencies using computer programs generally have pre-prepared macros that an officer/investigator can use to cover a certain point in the report that can be used as a generalization, such as, "the arrestee was searched incident to the arrest, and cocaine was found on his person." In fact, after being arrested for DUI, the routine search of the arrestee did NOT produce cocaine or anything else that violated the law. On the witness stand, the officer had to admit that that information was in a macro he used, but, clearly, he did not edit his report. That failure was not lost on the defense attorney or on the jury.

Not infrequently a new investigator will, if only at the subconscious level, attempt to impress those who will be reading the incident report by writing in an elaborate manner in order to display mastery of the English language. However, persons reading the report will learn much, or perhaps all, they will ever know about the investigation from what has been written. Therefore, it is essential to write in a clear and uncluttered style; the report must be written not only so that it can be understood but, more important, so that it also cannot be misunderstood.

The report must be completely accurate. No detail should be added or deleted; the potential or actual consequences of such deviations, however innocent the motivation, are considerable. For example, at the scene of an armed robbery, a young investigator was conducting interviews necessary to prepare the original report. One of the questions he asked the victim was "Have you ever seen the perpetrator before this happened?" The response was "Yes, he works on the loading platform of the grocery on Sixth Avenue." Out of a desire to provide as much detail as possible, the investigator supplemented this statement with information from the telephone directory, writing a portion of the interview in the following manner:

> The victim told the undersigned officer that the suspect works at Blake's Grocery Wholesale, located at 1425 Sixth Avenue, telephone number (813) 223-3291.

Later, the following exchange took place between the officer and the defense attorney in court:

Q Defense Attorney: *Officer, do you recognize this report?*
A Officer: *Yes, I do.*

Q Defense Attorney: *Did you prepare it?*
A Officer: *Yes, sir, I did.*

Q Defense Attorney: *Would it be fair to say that it represents your investigation?*
A Officer: *That is correct, sir.*

Q **Defense Attorney:** *Then, having conducted the investigation and having prepared the report, your testimony would be that it accurately and completely portrays your actions and what you learned?*

A **Officer:** *Yes, sir.*

Q **Defense Attorney:** *Would you read from page 2 of this report?*

A **Officer:** *"The victim told the undersigned officer that the suspect works at Blake's Grocery Wholesale, located at 1425 Sixth Avenue, telephone number (813) 223-3291."*

Q **Defense Attorney:** *Officer, the complainant in this case has already testified to the effect that she did not, in fact, tell you this. Why are you prejudiced toward the defendant in this case, and what else have you added to the report or subtracted from it in order to strengthen the state's case?*

Thus, a seemingly innocuous addition to a report reduced the credibility of the entire investigation. Clear communication and accuracy are the mainstays of effective reports. The absence of one diminishes the other.

In summary, the narrative is the most critical part of an incident/investigative report. It should tell a story from beginning—such as "Once upon a time"—all the way through to the end—"and they lived happily ever after." If the middle part of the story has holes in it, so the reader doesn't know how the story unfolds to get to the end, the report writer has failed to communicate what was intended.

SUPERVISORY REVIEW AND DISPOSITION OF INCIDENT REPORTS

By reviewing the reports written by subordinates, supervisors get a current picture of the quality of their officers' investigative efforts and report-writing skills. On the basis of such information, supervisors can give constructive feedback to subordinates, as well as make appropriate performance evaluations. To carry out this responsibility at the highest level, supervisors must carefully read their subordinate's reports for content, not just style and spelling. Supervisors must take the time to understand the investigatory process involved in the particular incident and make sure that the reports accurately address what is needed for a prosecutor to file charges and prove a case. With this knowledge, constructive feedback to subordinates has meaning.

In electronic systems, officers can often prepare reports while stopped between calls and routine. In such advanced systems, reports can be sent wirelessly to the supervisor. If the supervisor declines a report, it is sent back, with comments, to the officer, who resubmits it after addressing the comments.

▲ **FIGURE 6-8** **Report approval and disposition process**

The approval process for handwritten incident reports is much like that described for MCT-generated reports. Several times during the shift, the officer's supervisor will call to meet with him/her to review any completed incident reports. If a report needs additional information or clarification, it is returned to the officer. Once the report is completed to the satisfaction of the supervisor and is accepted, the supervisor makes a disposition, signs the report, and takes it to the station for appropriate disposition.

After approving an incident report, the supervisor must make a **disposition** of it. As depicted in Figure 6-8, any of the following dispositions may be made:

1. The case may be retained for further investigation by uniformed officers.
2. It may be unfounded (that is, the complaint is false).

3. The case may be inactivated due to a lack of leads.
4. It may be referred to plainclothes investigators.
5. The case may be completed and closed.

To some extent, a department's situation and policies affect the supervisor's decision about which dispositions to use. If the Uniform Division is seriously understaffed and officers have been reduced to being "report takers" because they do not have time to conduct thorough preliminary investigations, rarely will a case be retained for further investigation. By policy or the strong will of the investigations commander, the authority to unfound a case may be reserved for an investigation supervisor. In addition, because copies of incident reports may be routinely routed to an investigations supervisor, a uniformed supervisor who has inactivated cases only to have an investigations supervisor reactivate them may be slow about doing anything other than referring them to the investigations division, especially if the reactivations have at least occasionally resulted in the cases being successfully cleared. Regardless of the disposition, copies of all completed and approved reports are sent to the records keeping section of the agency.

FOLLOW-UP INVESTIGATION AND SUPPLEMENTAL REPORTS

Periodically during the follow-up investigation, supplemental reports must be initiated. Ordinarily, supplemental, or follow-up, reports should be written no less frequently than every 10 days, and the continuance of a particular investigation beyond 28 days should require supervisory approval to ensure proper use of an investigator's time. The purpose of writing follow-up reports is to keep the file current as new or corrected information is gathered. Additionally, specific acts or accomplishments might require individual supplemental reports, such as the activation or cancellation of a pickup order or BOLO, the issuance of a search warrant, the arrest of a suspect, the complainant's discovery that additional property was stolen that was not noticed as missing at the time the incident report was made, the recovery of all or part of the property taken, or a change in the title of the offense owing to improper classification on the original report—for example, a strong-arm robbery reclassified as a purse snatch.

Other circumstances under which supplemental reports are required include (1) when the offense is unfounded, (2) when it is exceptionally cleared, meaning that the police know who the perpetrator is but are unable to pursue the case further owing to circumstances beyond their control, such as the death of the only witness, and (3) when the case is inactivated. If the supervisor reviewing the incident report inactivates it because of insufficient leads to warrant follow-up investigation, then a supplemental report is not required. However, if some follow-up work is done, no promising leads are developed, and the case is then inactivated, the person assigned responsibility for it must complete a supplemental report to substantiate the basis for inactivation.

As a general concluding note, case files inactivated may in later months or years receive further investigative work that is productive. Therefore, it is of considerable importance that at each stage of report writing care is exercised in presenting all available information.

KEY TERMS

disposition (of incident report)
field notes
incident reports

iPad, iPhone
mobile computer terminal (MCT)
narrative style

National Incident-Based Reporting System (NIBRS)
Uniform Crime Reports (UCRs)

REVIEW QUESTIONS

1. Identify and briefly discuss four reasons why field notes are important.
2. What are the six interrogatory investigative questions?
3. Briefly discuss the operational and administrative uses of incident reports.
4. How would you characterize the difference between basic incident reports and those that are

NIBRS compliant? (Check the Internet for additional information on how these reports differ.)
5. How are MCTs and PDAs being used in law enforcement?
6. After a uniformed supervisor accepts a report, he/she must make a disposition of it. What are five dispositions that might be made?

1. Learn more about NIBRS at www.icpsr.umich.edu/ icpsrweb/NACJD/NIBRS/. Find out if your state has recently received any NIBRS grants. Read the brief report entitled, "Effects of NIBRS on Crime Statistics." How do NIBRS statistics differ from UCR data? What impact does NIBRS have on crime statistics? What factors need to be considered when one is comparing summary UCR statistics and NIBRS data?

2. Log onto your local, county, or state law-enforcement agency website and find out if the agency uses mobile computer terminals. If it does, in what capacity are they used? Are all patrol vehicles equipped with MCTs? Does the site provide any information on other data technology used by officers (PDAs, and so on)? If so, what?

7

THE FOLLOW-UP INVESTIGATION AND INVESTIGATIVE RESOURCES

CHAPTER OBJECTIVES

1. Describe the use of solvability factors.
2. Explain the preparation of a case file.
3. Discuss reinterviewing victims and witnesses.
4. Describe the purpose and use of NamUs.
5. Summarize NCIC files and capabilities.
6. Explain LeadsOnLine.
7. Identify behaviors in which investigators should not engage with informants.
8. State the purposes of physical surveillance.
9. Describe how a photo lineup should be conducted.
10. Identify three potential indicators of a staged crime.
11. Describe the intelligence cycle.
12. Summarize the use of facial recognition software by law-enforcement agencies.
13. Identify the ways crime analysts link crimes.
14. Explain the role of the scientific method in crime scene reconstruction.
15. Describe the four factors on which criminal profiling focuses.
16. Summarize geographical profiling.
17. Provide four examples of remote sensing.
18. Identify four ways investigators use the Internet.

Certain crimes, such as murder, rape, and child abuse, are always going to receive a follow-up investigation. To ensure that the use of investigative resources is warranted, other crimes are screened. Only those that have some promise for success receive a follow-up investigation. Investigators should be familiar with the numerous information sources and databases that are available to them. They should also have an understanding of special topics, such as conducting photo lineups and handling informants. These and related topics are covered in this chapter.

THE DECISION TO INITIATE A FOLLOW-UP INVESTIGATION

From Chapter 6, "Field Notes and Reporting," we recall that when an officer completes an incident report his/her immediate supervisor will review it and make one of several dispositions. The decision to inactive a case or refer it for further investigation is often made through the use of a case screening model, which requires the presence of sufficient solvability factors before a case can receive a follow-up investigation. **Solvability factors** are elements of information that have been demonstrated to correlate with higher probabilities of investigative success.

In some case screening models, solvability factors have different mathematical weights attached to them according to their potential to contribute to a successful investigation. These weights must total a certain number of points for a case to be referred for follow-up. In other models, the screener subjectively considers the solvability factors that are present and "other information" to make the decision. The solvability screening may be done by a patrol or investigative supervisor. Solvability factors usually include these questions:

- Is the suspect named?
- Can the suspect be identified?
- Is there a detailed description of the suspect?
- Is there significant physical evidence?
- Are other suspects named, identified, or described in detail?

- If a vehicle is involved, is there a license number or detailed description?
- Does the crime fit an established modus operandi or method of operation?
- Were deadly weapons displayed or used?
- To what extent was the victim physically harmed?
- What similarity is there to recently reported crimes?
- Will the victim be able to identify the suspect?
- Was traceable property taken?
- Are there reliable witnesses?
- Does the nature of the crime (for example, theft of explosives) necessitate a follow-up?
- Can a composite sketch of the suspect(s) be prepared?

THE FOLLOW-UP INVESTIGATION PROCESS

As a visual aid to follow-up investigators, some departments have checklists. Figure 7-1 is a "universal" checklist, meaning that it is not crime specific. Investigators draw a line through or enter Not Applicable or NA in portions of a universal checklist that are not applicable to a case they are handling. The steps involved in a follow-up investigation do not necessarily occur in an exact order. The specifics of each case will dictate how those steps actually unfold. For example, if a suspect is already in custody, the attempt to interrogate him/her will come much earlier than if an arrest is made much later. Generally, a follow-up investigation will include most of the following activities:

1. Departmental policies regarding follow-up investigation files vary but as a minimum require that a case file be prepared to organize the information that is immediately available—for example, the incident and supplemental reports. Over the course of an investigation the file will grow as lab reports, copies of checks, charge card records, and other data are received.

Some agencies require an **investigative plan (IP)** showing what lines of inquiry will be pursued and any special resources needed—for instance, the assistance of a surveillance unit. As the investigation progresses, many factors can cause IPs to be

► **FIGURE 7-1**
Universal follow-up investigation checklist
(Courtesy of Chief Lynn Rowe and
Lt. Rick Headlee, Springfield [Missouri] Police
Department)

Activity	Activity Description	Date Completed	Notes
1.	Autopsy/Crime Lab Reports		
2.	Bank Records Reviewed		
3.	Crime Vict. Notif. Record		
4.	Criminal Case Report Form		
5.	Department of Corrections		
6.	Department of Revenue		
7.	Identification Unit Rpts.		
8.	Intelligence Reporting		
9.	Interview Informants		
10.	Mandatory: Notify Victim		
11.	Medical Records		
12.	NCIC Criminal History		
13.	Neighborhood Canvass		
14.	Pawn Shop Records Check		
15.	Photographic Lineup		
16.	Phys. Evid./Property Disp.		
17.	Polygraph Examination		
18.	Search Warrant App./Exec.		
19.	Search Warrant Return		
20.	S.P.D. Records Check		
21.	State Fingerprint Record		
22.	State Probation & Parole		
23.	Stolen Property Files		
24.	Surveillance Conducted		
25.	Suspect Miranda/Interview		
26.	Suspect: P/C Item/Arrest		
27.	Witnesses Interviewed		
28.	Other:		
29.	Other:		
30.	Other:		
31.	Other:		

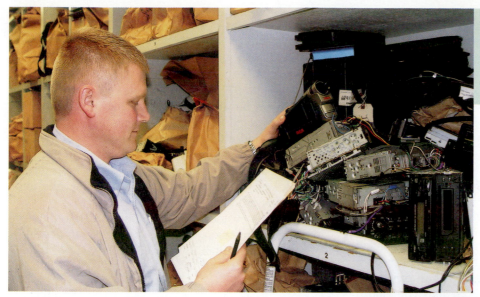

Investigator examining evidence in the property room
(Courtesy Chief Jack Lumpkin, Athens Clarke County (Georgia) Police Department)

revised, such as a newly identified witness who names a suspect or can describe where unrecovered physical evidence—for example, a handgun—is located. A case log may also be required, which is a chronological listing of what the investigator has done and the results.

Local prosecutors may have an effect on the paperwork for a follow-up investigation. For example, they may require a sheet that specifies the specific statutory crime to be charged, a list of each element needed to prove the crime, and the evidence supporting each element.

2. Read the offense report and any supplemental reports and become thoroughly conversant with them. As needed, contact or meet with the officer originating the report and those writing supplements to clarify information or resolve discrepancies. As a practical matter, this happens infrequently.

3. Get the criminal histories of named suspects. As appropriate, review the criminal histories of victims to assess the possibility for insurance fraud. "Victims" may file a false crime report to hide a theft they committed or to gain money by reporting a theft of something they never really had.

4. Obtain, as appropriate, the credit histories of key figures in the investigation.

5. Visit the crime scene if possible and review the visual documentation of the scene.

6. Review other incident reports that may be related.

7. Attempt to link suspects to other crimes by modus operandi (M.O.) analysis.

8. Examine the physical evidence (Figure 7-2) and review lab results as examinations are completed.

9. Contact victims and witnesses for in-depth interviews and search for other witnesses. If it has not already been done, conduct a neighborhood canvass (Figure 7-3). Review the names of people

▲ **FIGURE 7-3 Neighborhood canvass**
An Allentown Police Department Detective going door to door, canvassing residents in an effort to find witnesses to a shooting. If he develops information, he can immediately inform other investigators using the departmental radio in his left hand. (© Dennis Wetherhold, Jr.)

interviewed to determine whether any have criminal backgrounds or are known associates of criminal figures. Evaluate to determine if a "witness" may be involved in the crime or has potential to become an informant.

10. Assess the credibility of witnesses and also people who are unusually helpful:

In a case involving the abduction of two girls on a rural road, a person known to the police brought much appreciated coffee and sandwiches to the mobile command center several times. Finally, someone decided that giving him access to the command center was not wise, and as an afterthought they ran a records check on him. A prior record for child molestation existed, and the man confessed to the abductions. He also related that he used what he heard in the command center to keep ahead of the investigation and also fabricated a story about seeing a car with an out-of-state tag cruising the road the day of the abductions.

11. Delivering death notices is an occasional duty, and it requires the utmost compassion. Preferably the law-enforcement chaplin should accompany the investigator—failing that possibility, the family pastor or close friend, if their identities are known. Such notices should not be delivered to juveniles. If a juvenile is the only person available, or the intended message recipient is not present, a written message, with no other details, to call the department should be left. When called, the officer should return to the address and personally handle the notification. Serious injury notifications may also be necessary, and departmental policies and circumstances dictate whether those contacts must be made in person.

12. If not already done, arrange the preparation of a drawing/likeness of the suspect. Releasing the likeness and some details about the crime may be necessary to solicit public assistance, and this often requires the approval of the investigator's supervisor. Before any information is released, it should be carefully scrutinized to ensure that people are not endangered and that it does not hinder the investigative effort—for instance, by alluding to tactics or avenues of inquiry.

13. Reevaluate the case periodically, especially as new information is received.

14. Disseminate information about the crime and suspects within the agency as needed or secure the assistance of specialists—for example, profilers.

15. Coordinate with other jurisdictions if there are substantially similar methods of operation or the suspect may be, or is, involved with crimes elsewhere.

Significant and serial offenses may lead to the establishment of short-term departmental or multi-jurisdictional task forces by commanding officers.

16. Explore lines of inquiry and pursue leads by using databases available through a variety of international, national, regional, private organizations, and your own department. (These databases are covered in more detail later in this chapter.)

17. Identify and interview known associates of the suspect who may have information.

18. Obtain any documentary evidence—for example, bank statements, hotel records, telephone calls, and credit card charges.

19. Conduct a custodial interrogation to obtain a documented confession, identify any codefendants, and evaluate the suitability of the suspect as a confidential informant.

20. Talk to informants as needed.

21. Use specialized investigative procedures if appropriate (for example, physical and technical surveillance, polygraph and psychological stress examinations, and photographic and physical line-ups).

22. Prepare necessary affidavits, apply for, and execute search and arrest warrants and make the required "returns" to the court specifying what action was taken.

23. Identify, locate, and apprehend the suspect, if he/she is not already in custody.

24. Recover stolen property.

25. Determine if the suspect's auto or other property is subject to seizure under federal or state laws. If so, refer to initiate seizure and condemnation procedures when appropriate.

26. File supplemental reports on the progress of the investigation as required by departmental policy (for instance, case status and the release of any property to the victim or his/her family).

27. Keep all records well organized.

28. Keep victim/victim's family informed on any changes in the status of the case.

29. Meet with the prosecuting attorney.[1]

REVIEWING THE INCIDENT AND SUPPLEMENTAL REPORTS

The incident and supplemental reports may answer many of the follow-up investigator's initial questions, such as: (1) how, when, and where the crime was committed, including a chronological description of the events; (2) the victim's identity and if appropriate, his/her medical condition and statement; (3) the number of suspects, if any are in custody, whether they are in the jail or a hospital, and their descriptions or identities; (4) whether composite sketches of suspects at large have been prepared and distributed; (5) the words spoken by suspects during the commission of the crime, spontaneous statements made by them following their arrest, and any post-Miranda statements made by them to the arresting officer; (6) the identities and statements of witnesses and any conditions noted, such any degree of drinking or appearance of having been using drugs; (7) the nature and value of the property stolen; (8) the types of physical evidence seized; and (8) description of any vehicles involved or a copy of an impound report for vehicles seized.

JAIL BOOKING REPORT

The jail booking report is created when a subject is in-processed at a jail. This jail may be part of the investigator's agency, or it may be operated by another entity, such as the sheriff. The booking report is often computer generated and may have an incident report integrated into it, as well as a color photo; fingerprints; and description of the subject's health and medications; his/her mental state (for example, drunk or verbally or physically combative); medical treatment received while in custody; a full description of the subject, including scars, marks, and tattoos; criminal history; employment and home addresses; aliases used; and an inventory of the personal effects seized by jailers during the in-processing. In particular, the personal effects may provide useful information.

Among personal-possession items often found are matchbooks; Zig Zag paper; condoms; business cards for the subject (and from his/her associates or people he/she recently met); foreign currency; identity and credit cards in several different names; scraps of paper with telephone numbers on them; and various types of lists. Such items may suggest places the subject habituates or recently visited, suggest possible personal habits and associates, identify countries recently visited, or connect him/her to other crimes.

In one case, an investigator went to the jail to interview a subject arrested for stabbing a man in a bar. Among the subject's personal possessions was a real-estate card from a woman murdered several days previously. Although the man initially denied knowing the woman or being in the area where she was killed, he finally admitted to the crime after being confronted with the real-estate card.

VEHICLE IMPOUNDMENT REPORT

If a suspect is arrested while driving a vehicle, the vehicle is inventoried and towed to an impoundment lot. Articles that appear on the inventory list may or may not have a relationship to the case. Moreover, the impounding officer may not recognize their significance, as can be the case with

common tools that have been modified for use in burglaries. Thus, the impounding report should be carefully read. Under most circumstances, a follow-up investigator cannot search a car after it has been impounded without a search warrant issued on a showing of probable cause.

FIELD INTERVIEW/ INFORMATION REPORTS

A **field interview/information report (FIR)** is shown in Figure 7-4. Such reports are filled out when patrolling officers identify persons or vehicles that are suspicious to them but are not connected with any particular offense. These cards can establish whether a suspect was in the immediate area of a crime, how he/she was dressed at the time, what vehicle the suspect had access to, and who else was in the vehicle. On rare occasions, FIR cards have proved to be a suspect's best alibi witness.

TRAFFIC CITATIONS

As with FIR cards, traffic citations can link suspects to the vehicles they register and drive, as well as those to which they may have access. Access to the vehicles of others usually denotes a special relationship and may help identify girlfriends or boyfriends, criminal associates, relatives, or operators of particular kinds of businesses, such as used-car and scrap-metal firms. Traffic citations can also pinpoint where the operator was at a particular date and time. Occasionally, FIR cards are also written during traffic stops, so these two sources of information may be associated.

EXAMINING PHYSICAL EVIDENCE

The physical evidence should be viewed early in the investigation, because it may soon be forwarded to the crime laboratory for analysis. Actually seeing the evidence adds a level of specific understanding about each item of evidence as to its appearance, color, weight, damage done to it in the commission of the crime, modifications to weapons, and other matters. These observations may help the investigator make connections when he sees or hears a comment at a later stage in the follow-up.

REINTERVIEWING VICTIMS AND WITNESSES

Victims or their families should be contacted very early in the process. They often have questions about the status of the case, their rights, whether they need protection,

► FIGURE 7-4
Field interview/information
report (FIR) card
(Courtesy of Springfield, Missouri, Police
Department)

FRONT

SPRINGFIELD POLICE DEPARTMENT FIELD INFORMATION

Data:_____ Time: _____   FIR #: _____

Stopped/Seen at:_____ Beat: _____

Subject #1:

Name: _____ Address: _____

Sex:____ Race:____ Age:____ DOB:____ Hgt:____ Wgt:____ Hair:____ Eyes:____

Tattoos/Misc Description: _____

Subject #2:

Name: _____ Address: _____

Sex:____ Race:____ Age:____ DOB:____ Hgt:____ Wgt:____ Hair:____ Eyes:____

Tattoos/Misc Description: _____

Subject #3:

Name: _____ Address: _____

Sex:____ Race:____ Age:____ DOB:____ Hgt:____ Wgt:____ Hair:____ Eyes:____

Tattoos/Misc Description: _____

BACK

Vehicle Color (top/bottom): _____ Year: _____

Make: _____ Model:_____ Style: _____

License Number _____ License Year: _____ State: _____

Misc. Description: _____

Reason for stop: _____

List Suspicious Activity/Admitted or Known Criminal History/Gang Activity:

_____

_____

_____

_____

_____

_____

_____

Officer/ DSN: _____ Supervisor: _____
                          Signature   Initial

how a case gets processed through the criminal justice system, if they are eligible for victim's compensation for medical expenses or funerals, and, if they have been disabled by the crime, is there living assistance available to them. The investigator can answer some of these questions and then make sure the victims get linked to victim assistance entities, which may be state agencies. Some religious denominations also provide victims assistance on an ad hoc or other basis.

Recontacting victims and witnesses serves to confirm information in the incident or supplemental reports and to develop further information. Unfortunately, such contacts are sometimes met with questions such as "I already told the other cops everything I know. Why aren't you out looking for the guy that did this instead of bothering me with the same questions? Don't you cops talk to each other?" Experienced investigators let such frustrated comments politely roll off of their backs. "Look, I'm only trying to help you" has the potential to produce a downward spiral. It is better to "join" the victim or witness by using statements such as "I want to arrest the person that did this to you. In my experience sometimes victims or witnesses think of something else that is important, and rather than burden you with trying to find me, I thought it would be courteous for me to come to you." An often overlooked purpose of reinterviewing is to assess, if possible, the credibility of witnesses.

Before any reinterviewing is done, the investigators should carefully assess what a witness said he/she:

- saw—under what lighting conditions, at what distance, for how long, and was the witness wearing any needed glasses or contacts? A fair question to an 18-year-old witness would be "How do you know it was a '57 Chevy Impala?"
- heard—for example, "I heard him hitting her." What facts support that conclusion? Any auditory problems? Wearing a needed hearing aid?
- smelled—"The man who raped me was wearing Old Spice shaving lotion or cologne." A key question is "How do you know that odor?"
- touched—a blind person touches her mugger's face and reports it was unshaven with a short vertical scar above the left eye. The investigator might ask for other examples of her tactile sensitivity. If she reads Braille proficiently, it is likely to be very good. Blindfolded victims may also have useful tactile data: "I traced the letters GHS and the number 87 on a jacket while in the trunk of the car."
- tasted—for example, a hospitalized woman says that her last meal "tasted funny, like almonds," a sign of cyanide poisoning. How is she familiar with that taste?

LEADS

Some leads turn out to be "good," whereas others are simply "dry holes" and an unproductive use of time. The truth is that both kinds chew up resources and must be followed up, because often we can't accurately tell one from the other.

The fact that an incident report specifically names a suspect does not mean the person actually committed the offense or knows anything substantive about it. Victims can be mistaken about a person's name, report their suspicions as "fact," or attempt to cause problems for someone they don't like or have had difficulty with in the past. Or, their theory about how the crime was committed is simply wrong:

A burglary victim called an investigator to explain that she thought the offenders were two employees of a firm that the apartment complex had hired to do some work in her apartment. The described suspects, names unknown, had been given a key to her apartment in order to perform the necessary work. The burglary had been committed eight days later, and there had been no forced entry. The apartment manager, when contacted by the investigator, vouched for the men but had not directly supervised their work. The owner of the firm employing the men testified to their long-standing reliability and a lack of similar allegations in the past. A message was left for the suspects to contact the investigator. The suspects called back about a half-hour later and gave the investigator all the information requested and described the work done on the victim's apartment in detail. The investigator checked their backgrounds and concluded the men were not likely to have been the offenders and closed the investigation.

Major cases, such as the murder of a community leader or a robbery with a large "score," typically require the combined efforts of a number of investigators, who report to the supervisor responsible for the case. A key responsibility of the case supervisor is coordination of information, especially with respect to making sure that leads are prioritized and worked and that the results are disseminated to all team members. One way this can be done, by hand or on a computer, is by using a lead-assignment sheet log (see Figure 7-5).

USING DATABASES

The use of databases allows investigators to rapidly close off some lines of inquiry, encourage the continuance of others, and suggest new ones. The available databases are international, national, multistate, state/regional/local, as well as private. The ones identified here are illustrative and not exhaustive, and other capabilities are mentioned within crime-specific chapters.

INTERNATIONAL

One of the most frequently used databases of the International Criminal Police Organization (Interpol) is MIND/FIND, which determines whether passports, identity cards, and visas have been reported lost or stolen.

NATIONAL

The Bureau of Alcohol, Tobacco, Firearms and Explosives (ATF) has **Arson, Explosives, and Incident System (AEXIS),** which contains information on arson, bombs, and misuse of explosives, including incident characteristics that can be useful in determining patterns, trends, and motives. ATF also operates the National Integrated Ballistics Information Network (NIBIN). ATF's law-enforcement partners use Integrated Ballistic Identification Systems (IBIS) capabilities to acquire images of firearms evidence that are uploaded to NIBIN to determine if the evidence is related to other cases[2] (NIBIN is further discussed in Chapter 8, "The Crime Laboratory"). The Treasury Department's Financial Crimes Enforcement Network (FinCen) provides information and analysis to law-enforcement agencies with respect to money laundering.

When first operational in the 1970s, the Drug Enforcement Administration's (DEA) El Paso Intelligence Center (EPIC) focused on drug, alien, and weapons smuggling in the Southwestern states bordering Mexico. Now using advanced technologies, EPIC has an international focus. DEA's **National Drug Pointer Index (NDPIX),** which began operating in 1997, alerts participating agencies of investigative targets they have in common.

Launched in 2009, the **National Missing and Unidentified Persons System (NamUs)** is a database administered by the National Institute of Justice. Presently there are an estimated 100,000 missing person cases and more than 40,000 sets of human remains that have not been identified.[3] NamUs is a free web-based tool accessible to everyone, including law enforcement, coroners/medical examiners, victim advocates, and families and friends. Considerable data remains to be uploaded into NamUS; only 2,800 missing people have been entered and just 6,200 sets of human remains. The number of cases resolved using NamUs is not large, possibly because it is a great untapped resource for investigators: in 2010, only 1,100 law-enforcement agencies had registered to use it. Some cases have been resolved by family members. A woman's sister had been missing for 22 years. Using NamUs, she discovered that her sister had been murdered and dumped alongside a highway in another state. Authorities there were unable to identify her, and she was buried as a "Jane Doe" in a pauper's grave. The sister was able to make the identification based on unique unicorn and rose tattoos on her murdered sibling.

The Department of Homeland Security's (DHS) Homeland Security Information Network (HSIN) develops and shares information about domestic terrorism threats and incident management with its partners at the federal, state, local, tribal, territorial, private-sector, and international level; its principal function is the dissemination of information and Sensitive But Unclassified intelligence (SBU).[4]

The FBI maintains the **National Crime Information Center (NCIC),** which is the most comprehensive documented criminal justice information system in the country. Established in 1967, its structure has been periodically refined. NCIC has provided the information critical to solving high-profile cases, including the 1968 murder of Dr. Martin Luther King, Jr., which led to the arrest of James Earl Ray. NCIC was also instrumental in the arrest of Timothy McVeigh on the same day as the 1995 Oklahoma City bombing. The NCIC database consists of 19 files that are available continuously to those with approved access:

1. *National Sex Offender Registry File (1999):* contains records on individuals who are required to register in a jurisdiction's sex offender registry.
2. *Unidentified Person File (1983):* includes deceased persons, recovered portions of dismembered bodies, remains from disasters, and living persons unable to identify themselves, such as infants or Alzheimer's victims. It is cross-referenced to the Missing Persons File.
3. *Missing Persons File (1975):* covers individuals, including children, who have been reported missing to law enforcement, and there is a reasonable concern for their safety. It includes those absent who have a proven physical/mental disability or are senile; persons missing following a catastrophe; and those unemancipated under their state law, usually persons under 18 years of age. Some file information may be disclosed to the National Center for Missing and Exploited Children (NCMEC), a nongovernmental but federally funded private corporation.
4. *U.S. Secret Service Protective File (1983):* has records containing names and other information on individuals who are believed to pose a threat to the U.S. President or others afforded protection by the Secret Service.
5. *Protective Order File (1997):* has records on individuals against whom protective orders have been issued. A protective order may be temporary or final and is issued by a civil or criminal court to prevent harassing, threatening or violent acts against a person by another or regulates communication, proximity or contact with the protected person.
6. *Foreign Fugitive File (1987):* has records on persons wanted by a foreign country for a crime that would be a felony if committed in this country.

7. *Gang File (2009):* has records on violent gangs, their members, and associates; originally was part of a previous file established in 1995.

8. *Known or Appropriately Suspected Terrorist (KST) File (2009):* Emphasis for this file was added with a Homeland Security Presidential Directive (HSPD-6) in 2003; records on known or suspected terrorists are maintained; originally it was part of a previous file established in 1995.

9. *Immigration Violator File (1996):* covers criminal aliens who have been deported, as well as aliens with outstanding warrants for removal.

10. *Supervised Release File (1999):* contains records on individuals on probation, parole, and supervised release, as well as persons released on their own recognizance or during pretrial sentencing/deferred prosecution, which allows certain first-time offenders the chance to avoid a conviction by adhering to parole-like restrictions.

11. *License Plate File (1967):* includes information pertaining to unrecovered license plates that have been reported stolen. In two-plate states where only one plate has been stolen, the victim must agree not to use the remaining tag.

12. *Identity Theft File (2005):* contains descriptive and other information that law-enforcement personnel can use to determine if a person is a victim of identity theft or if the individual may be using a false identity.

13. *Vehicle File (1967):* has records on unrecovered stolen vehicles, vehicles involved in the commission of crimes, and those that may be seized based on a federally issued court order. Articles stolen from vehicles—for example, radios and CD players, are entered in the article file.

14. *Boat File (1969):* unrecovered stolen boats with unique identifying numbers may be entered in this file; "boat" includes jet skis, canoes, kayaks, and sail boards.

15. *Vehicle/Boat Parts File (1999):* has records for unrecovered component parts stolen from a vehicle or boat.

16. *Gun File (1967):* includes records of serially numbered weapons that are recovered (abandoned, seized, or found), missing, or are believed to have been involved in a felony.

17. *Securities File (1968):* has records on serially numbered stolen, embezzled, counterfeit, or used-for-ransom securities.

18. *Wanted Persons File:* has records of individuals who have an outstanding warrant. This file also contains records for juveniles who have been judged delinquent and who have escaped from custody or supervision or who have absconded while on probation or parole. There are also records on juveniles who were charged with committing an act of delinquency that would be a crime if committed by an adult and who have fled from the state in which

the act was committed. Agencies may also enter temporary felony want records into this file. Temporary felony want records allow a law-enforcement agency to take prompt action to apprehend a person suspected of committing a felony when circumstances prevent the agency from immediately obtaining a warrant.

19. *Article File (1967):* contains records on unrecovered articles that have a unique serial number or other unique personal identifying number. Included are lost public safety, homeland security, and critical infrastructure identification items, such as badges, credentials, smart cards, and "dog tags." Illustrations of other articles that may be entered are livestock, toxic chemicals, tools, sports equipment, and musical instruments. To be entered, articles must meet one or more of three criteria: (1) have a value of $500 or more—but office equipment, televisions, and bicycles may be entered regardless of their value; (2) regardless of value, the article being moved interstate, or the seriousness of the crime dictates entry; or (3) regardless of the value of any item, the total value of the items stolen exceeds $5,000.[5]

The effect of NCIC can be seen in the following examples:

> An officer noticed a man, with a small child in the front passenger's seat, driving his car too rapidly and weaving through traffic, causing other drivers to slam on their brakes. The officer stopped the vehicle and did a NCIC check on the driver. The subject was a registered sexual offender, who should not have been with a young child, was on parole in another state, and should not have left it.[6]

> A patrolling officer saw a pickup pulling a sailboat. The brake lights for the trailer were either not working or not hooked up. The officer stopped the truck with the intent of getting this deficiency corrected. The driver nervously handed over his license. The officer noticed a second driver's license on the dashboard of the pickup. Both photographs matched the driver, but there were different names and birth dates on them. An NCIC check revealed that both names were aliases used by the man. He had a criminal history and was wanted in connection with a series of boat thefts. In his patrol car, the officer received the suspect's real name, his mug shot, a photograph of his tattoo, and a photograph of, and other data on, the boat attached to the suspect's truck, which was stolen.

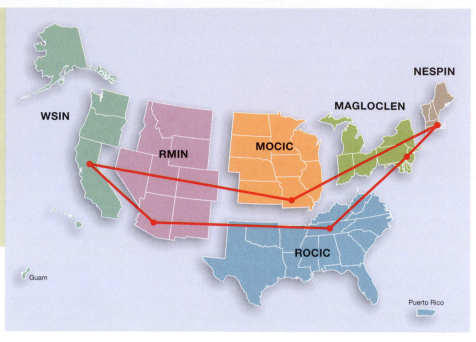

▶ **FIGURE 7-6**

RISS multistate centers
The members of RISS are the Western States Information Network (WSIN), the Rocky Mountain Information Network (RMIN), the Mid-States Organized Crime Center (MOCIC), the Regional Organized Crime Information Center (ROCIC), the Mid-Atlantic-Great Lakes Organized Crime Law Enforcement Network (MAGLOCLEN), and the New England State Police Information Network (NESPIN).

(Courtesy RISS)

The FBI also has other capabilities that support investigations. The purpose of the **National Center for the Analysis of Violent Crime** (NCAVC) is to provide behavioral-based analytical support to federal, state, local, and international law-enforcement agencies. The **Violent Criminal Apprehension Program (ViCAP)** is part of NCAVC and provides advice and support for a range of cases, including child abductions, serial, rapes and murders, and cyber-crime. NCAVC and ViCAP are further discussed in Chapter 9, "Injury and Death Investigation." The **Next Generation Identification (NGI) Program** is developing a fuller set of biometric data. Missing, unidentified, and wanted persons may be identified by the National Image/Information Repository (NDIR). Law Enforcement Online (LEO) is a free secure communications portal for law-enforcement officers, first responders, criminal justice professional, and antiterrorism and intelligence agencies around the world. It is one way to broadcast alerts, and it has distance-learning opportunities, a multimedia library, and 540 special-interest groups. The groups are a way to share your expertise and benefit from the expertise of other people.

REGIONAL INFORMATION SHARING SYSTEMS (RISS)

There are six multistate centers in RISS (Figure 7-6). Each of the six centers, funded by the federal government, can tailor its services to the investigative and prosecutorial needs of its member agencies. The core services of all centers are information sharing, analytic services, loan of specialized investigative equipment, confidential funds, training conferences, and technical assistance. RISS communicates over its secure intranet, RISSNET. The RISS National Policy Group consists of the Director and Policy Board Chairperson of each of the six centers. Law-enforcement agencies join their regional center based on its established application process.

Outside RISS, there are also a number of multistate databases, such as (1) the Alert-Emerging Threat Analysis Capability (ETAC), formed by a cooperative agreement between Missouri and Kansas law-enforcement agencies and governed by a Board of Directors consisting of one representative from each participating agency, and (2) the Western Identification Network (WIN), with Alaska, Montana, Oregon, Washington, Idaho, Nevada, Utah, and Wyoming as members of the consortium, as well as some local law-enforcement agencies in those states.[7] WIN was the first multistate Automated Fingerprint Identification System (AFIS) compact. AFIS, a capability pioneered by the FBI, uses high-speed computers to digitize, store, and compare fingerprint data and images. When possible matches are found, they are evaluated by expert examiners. The impetus for WIN came from (1) the recognition that people frequently moved among the member states and (2) smaller member states lacked the expertise and resources to create their own AFIS capability.

STATE AND LOCAL SYSTEMS

State information systems are robust; they contain files on over 100 million offenders. Simultaneously, they have some under-developed capabilities: only 19 state information systems accept photos of offenders' or wanted persons' scars, marks, and tattoos (SMTs).[8] State information systems include wanted, missing, and endangered persons; stolen property; driver's license and vehicle registration information; protective orders for juveniles and adults; state and local court information; Department of Corrections offender tracking; probation, parole, and supervised release data; prosecutorial information; and gang-related, juvenile justice, sexual-predator tracking, and other databases. Local systems serve a single jurisdiction, all the law-enforcement/criminal-justice agencies in a county, or a multicounty area.

NONPROFIT AND PRIVATE SOURCES

The Law Enforcement Intelligence Unit (LEIU) was formed in 1956 by 29 local and state law-enforcement agencies to exchange information about organized crime not available through normal police channels. LEIU originally excluded federal agencies, although that stance has been abandoned. In 2008, it changed its name to the Association of Law Enforcement Intelligence Units but kept its original acronym, LEIU. Its present focus is gathering, recording, and exchanging information about suspected or known criminal figures, groups, and businesses and terrorism.

Formed in 1966 as the Law Enforcement Teletype System (LETS) and incorporated as a not-for-profit in Delaware in 1973, LETS has morphed into the National Law Enforcement Telecommunication System (NLETS). Law-enforcement and other criminal-justice agencies use NLETS more than 1,000,000 times every day via 327,000 terminals.[9] In addition to providing secure channels for members' communication, NLETS also is a conduit for information and alerts flowing from the U.S. Department of Homeland Security (DHS). NLETS provides access to files from other states, such as those for wanted persons and concealed weapon permits; federal files, including the Federal Aviation Administration's (FAA's) aircraft registration data and tracking information; and the Canadian Police Information Centre (CPIC), which is similar to NCIC.

LeadsOnLine is a private subscription service used by more than 1,600 law-enforcement agencies. It provides access to transactions from thousands of reporting businesses, including scrap metal processors, secondhand stores, Internet drop-off stores, pawnshops, and eBay:

A husband listed a diamond ring for sale on Craigslist. A man made an appointment to come see the ring and along with several accomplices committed a home invasion robbery. While defending his son from violence the husband was killed. The invaders pawned the ring, which investigators located using LeadsOnLine, and the pawnshop records led them to the killers.[10]

Significant information about persons of interest is available for a fee from credit-reporting agencies such as Equifax, TransUnion, and Experian. Accurint for Law Enforcement (ALE) is an example of a group of high-end providers of information and information services that go beyond credit reports. Approximately 3,000 government entities use Accurint, which has access to 12 billion public records. It can quickly retrieve information about businesses and individuals, including current and former addresses, and links, such as to family members, neighbors, and associates. Among its capabilities is Person Alerts (PA); each time an individual who is a person of interest or fugitive appears in the database, the investigator is automatically notified.

Internet sites that can provide information about persons of interest are People Finder, Yahoo People Search, AnyWho, and BigFoot. The types of information vary somewhat from one site to another but include current and past addresses, possible relatives, birth dates, current telephone numbers, marriage and divorce information, litigation history, and e-mail addresses. WhoIs provides information about e-mail addresses both domestically and internationally.

Information about corporations can be obtained from each state's Secretary of State's Office. If a company uses a registered agent, some corporate information, such as officers, may not be available online, although some useful information about the corporation can be gleaned as a starting point. Dunn & Bradstreet can provide a Business Background Report, which provides summary coverage about the operations, history, and background of a company and its senior management; its Supplier Evaluation Report indicates the likelihood that a firm will cease doing business without paying its obligations in full or will seek debt relief under applicable federal and state laws.

Social network sites (SNS) are a category of websites that contain personal profiles and that may offer dating or other such services—for example, MySpace, FaceBook, MyYearbook, and Classmates. Legal restrictions apply to accessing some data, such as the names of people a victim was dating, but some useful information may still be gleaned from SNS files without a search warrant.

INFORMANTS

Informants provide information that is of investigative significance. They may expect to be paid or to receive consideration on charges pending against them or family members, or they cooperate for some other reasons. They may also be designated as confidential informants; some departments have adopted the term "cooperating individual" for them.

Law-enforcement policies generally identify activities that investigators should refrain from with informants. These includes socializing with them, becoming romantically involved, paying them without confirmation of the information, entering into a business relationship with them, accepting gifts, gratuities, or money from them, and loaning them money or accepting a loan from them. Policies also restrict who may be used as informants and determine whether prior special approval is required before they are used. Typically, restrictions apply to persons under 18 years of age, those who have been previously used and were not reliable, former drug-dependent individuals, and those on federal or state probation or parole (whose use as informants may require the approval of a judicial official).

An informant file, to which there is restricted access, consists of a recent photo of the informant, a complete informant sheet providing detailed information about him/her, copies of warrants and NCIC, and other items, including a criminal history, copies of cases in which the informant is a defendant, and debriefing reports following each meeting with him/her.

As a practical matter, some investigators run their own low-level informants, paying them out of pocket for their information or otherwise helping them. On the one hand, this is practical and works. On the other hand, an officer could be lured into a trap, and if he/she is killed, the department has to work the case in ignorance of the existence of the informant. Inexperienced investigators tend to contact informants too frequently or expect too much too quickly. To get inexperienced or lazy investigators "off their back," informants will "burn" them by knowingly giving them bad information. A more experienced investigator uses informants more judiciously:

A patrol officer passed a house in a rundown neighborhood near shipping docks. He heard screams and shouts through the screen door. Upon investigating he was told by a German seaman that "one of these whores stole my watch and wallet." Interviewing the woman alleged to be involved, the officer saw a small amount of marijuana on the bedside table. Several other "ladies" were also present in the house. The officer told the "mom" to have her "daughter" give the things back, which was done, and the seaman departed.

While talking to mom, the officer saw a picture of a boy on a table in the living room and asked about it. She proudly said it was her grandson, who lived with her and who was her "angel." The mom maintained a separate residence a few blocks away from her "office." The officer told the mom it would be regrettable if he had to arrest her, because the grandson would be placed in a foster home and be grown by the time she was released from prison. They reached an agreement.

Five months passed before the officer returned, seeking information about a local fugitive who had committed five burglaries of high-end jewelry stores. Three days later, based on mom's information, the suspect was arrested.

SURVEILLANCE

While some think of **surveillance** as "following," it actually means the continued observance of people, places, and things to obtain information of investigative significance. Most frequently surveillance is covert, although there may be occasions when it is made obvious in an attempt to spook subjects into making mistakes.

Surveillance is often broken into two types: physical and technical. Physical surveillance is personally done by one or more members of a surveillance team. Technical surveillance involves the use of various advanced technologies, including automatic vehicle tracking; pinhole cameras; acoustic, ultrasonic, and thermal image scanning; parabolic microphones; radio frequency (RF) bugs; and wiretaps. The balance of this section is devoted to physical surveillance.

PURPOSES OF SURVEILLANCE

Physical surveillance is carried out by people; it may be stationary/fixed/static or "rolling." At its simplest, it is done on foot, but it can also be done with cars, motorcycles, fixed-wing and rotary aircraft, boats, and rental apartments and offices. The purposes of surveillance include:

1. establishing the existence of a crime;
2. obtaining probable cause for a search warrant application;
3. apprehending suspects as they commit a crime;
4. identifying the associates of criminals and the places they frequent;
5. determining the reliability of informants;
6. providing protection for undercover officers and informants;
7. locating people, places, and things;
8. gathering intelligence about targets and premises prior to serving a warrant;
9. gathering intelligence on the activities of illegal groups and gangs;
10. preventing a crime by signaling police awareness of specific subjects.

PLANNING AND PREPARING FOR SURVEILLANCE OPERATIONS

Departmental policies and the applicable legal guidelines drive how the surveillance is conducted. In smaller agencies, investigators may have to do their own surveillance; in larger ones, there will be a unit with a title such as technical services to whom the work is "farmed out" or assigned.[11]

Planning the intelligence means making sure that the appropriate equipment is available (Figure 7-7) and safety and security measures are reviewed (Figure 7-8). Many investigators have been assaulted, wounded, and killed

Surveillance Kit Checklist

- Department two-way radio.
- Handheld portable radio with harness and fully charged spare battery.
- Mobile phone.
- Still camera with telephoto lens, adequate supply of film or other removable storage medium, and spare battery.
- Video camera with extra battery and removable storage medium.
- Stabilizing device, such as a portable tripod.
- Binoculars and portable infrared or thermal-imaging devices.
- Detailed road maps for the area.
- Compass or Global Positioning System receiver.
- Flashlight with extra batteries.
- Change of clothing with props, such as hats, to alter appearance, and other personal items, including toiletries.
- Food and water in a cooler.
- Cash, including coins to use at toll lanes requiring exact change, and toll passes.
- Extra set of car keys.
- Towels and glass cleaner.
- Equipment gear bag to hold preceding items.

◄ **FIGURE 7-7**
Surveillance kit checklist
(John T. Nason, "Conducting Surveillance Operations," FBI Law Enforcement Bulletin, Vol. 73, No. 5, May 2004, p. 3)

Safety and Security Measures

- During a mobile surveillance, do not take unnecessary risks to keep up with a subject speeding, running red lights, or otherwise driving recklessly.
- While stationary, keep the vehicle windows closed and the doors locked.
- Regularly scan rear view mirrors to observe anyone or any activity to the rear.
- Alert other team members to any suspicious or unusual persons or activity in the area.
- In high-crime areas and in hours of darkness, remain in a heightened state of alert.
- Position vehicle to enable a rapid response to assist others if needed.
- Ensure vehicle has emergency equipment lights, siren, and first-aid kit.
- Keep identification, weapon, and ballistic vest accessible.
- Know and use challenge, password, and other appropriate safety measures to prevent friendly fire situation from developing.
- When leaving a vehicle to go on foot surveillance, fully secure the vehicle and equipment inside.

◄ **FIGURE 7-8**
Surveillance safety and security checklist
(John T. Nason, "Conducting Surveillance Operations," FBI Law Enforcement Bulletin, Vol. 73, No. 5, May 2004, p. 6)

during operations, so risks must be assessed and the need for vigilance by all team members must be stressed. Additionally, all members of the team should be carefully briefed on such factors as:

1. The facts in the case.
2. Surveillance objectives.
3. Warnings about the subject, including any known drug use and possession of weapons.
4. The subject's previous experience with surveillance—whether he/she might be surveillance conscious and surveillance countermeasures may be used against the team.
5. Personal data about the subject, with photo, criminal history, associates, the vehicles of the subject and associates, locations the subject is known to visit, and whether the subject possesses unusual skills or abilities, such as being a martial arts practitioner or weightlifter.
6. Communication protocols for the team and descriptions of team members' roles (for example, photographer), and protocols for the keeper of the chronological surveillance log.
7. Before the surveillance, determination of which investigator should be sent into the area to assess conditions and to identify the "eye" or central observation point.

TERMINATION OF SURVEILLANCE OPERATIONS

There must be a periodic evaluation of whether a surveillance should be continued or terminated that includes the following considerations:

1. Have other cases arisen in which the use of surveillance is a better allocation of resources?
2. Is the operation providing important ongoing intelligence and evidence?
3. Does the continuation of the surveillance outweigh the increased risk of detection?
4. Can other investigative techniques or technical surveillance do the job at least as effectively?
5. Are there indicators that suggest threats to the team's safety?

GUIDELINES FOR CONDUCTING PHOTO LINEUPS, LIVE LINEUPS, AND FIELD SHOW-UPS

Eyewitnesses may be requested to see if they recognize anyone connected with the crime in one of three procedures: (1) a photo lineup, (2) a "live" lineup, and (3) a "show-up." Unlike the other two methods, one witness at a time views a single subject in a show-up. It is a technique that should only be used under the most exigent circumstances, because asking a witness to verify the identity of someone under law-enforcement control is inherently suggestive.[12]

The assigned investigator determines whether a case requires the use of a photo or live lineup and usually for all aspects of preparing them—for example, completion of a lineup creation form. That investigator also coordinates the process with witnesses, because they have some familiarity with him/her. The request to view a lineup should be kept factually neutral, such as "We'd like you to see a collection of photographs." Unless specifically asked by a witness, no mention of any suspect in custody should be made.[13] Several languages may be spoken in a community, and written witness instructions should be available in those languages. The investigator also needs to make sure that qualified language or American Sign Language (ASL) interpreters or other necessary accommodations are available. Sometimes the fact situation dictates whether a photo lineup or live lineup should be used:

A cab driver reported to the police that he had been robbed by one of his passengers. The cab driver made the report immediately after the suspect had fled on foot with the money. The driver reported that the suspect was a black male, approximately 25 years old, 6 feet 6 inches tall, 285 pounds, armed with a large nickel-plated type semiautomatic pistol. The man was wearing an orange shirt, blue jeans, and a white cowboy hat. Exactly $52.12 in cash had been taken.

Approximately 30 minutes after the crime was reported, the suspect was observed walking in the vicinity of the robbery by the same two officers who had taken the original report. The suspect was arrested by the police officers. A search produced a nickel-plated .45-caliber semiautomatic pistol and $52.12.

The investigator assigned to the case immediately knew that his only option was a photo lineup, because finding enough people for a live lineup who approximated the suspect in size, race, age, attire, and so forth would be very difficult.

In 2009 the Innocence Project released *Reevaluating Lineups: Why Witnesses Make Mistakes*. It identified numerous problems with existing photo, live, and show-up procedures and provided guidelines for using them in the future. Although these guidelines do not carry the weight of law by themselves, some states passed laws substantially mandating their use, and elsewhere many law-enforcement agencies adopted them. The processes described here are consistent with these "new" guidelines.

To avoid investigators giving subtle, unintended cues to witnesses, a "double blind" method of conducting photo and live lineups is now being widely used. The actual lineups are conducted by a trained lineup administrator who does not know who the suspect is or who the "fillers" are. In a photo lineup, fillers are photographs of people not believed to be involved in the crime. Administrators should be independent of the investigative unit—this is a good role for community volunteers and retired persons. The assigned investigator and anyone with knowledge of the suspect may not be in the same room as the lineup.

If several witnesses independently look at a lineup, the administrator may have some idea who the suspect is and potentially could unintentionally guide a witness to a particular identification, which is why such administrators require training. Alternatively, a different administrator could be used with every witness.

In addition to leading witnesses through a lineup procedure, the administrator has substantial record-keeping responsibilities. These often include, whether documented by video, audio, or in writing: (1) all identification and non-identification decisions, signed by the witness. If a signature is refused, the administrator records this fact and signs his/her own name; (2) the names of all persons present at the lineup and their affiliations; (3) the date, time, and location of the lineup; (4) the exact words used by the witness to identify the suspect; (5) the number of photos or individuals in the lineup; (6) the sources of all photographs or individuals used; (7) all photographs from a photo lineup; and in a live lineup, a photo or other visual recording of the lineup that includes all persons who participated in the lineup.[14] The administrator returns all photos and the result report to the assigned investigator. Depending on departmental policy and the results, the photos may be placed in the case file or the evidence room. After the lineup is completed, the investigator can be available to answer any witness's questions or to ask questions.

PHOTO LINEUPS

A **photo lineup** is a procedure in which a series of photographs are shown *sequentially* to a witness for the purpose of determining if he/she can identify the perpetrator of a crime. One practice is that as each photo is shown to a witness, he/she must make a decision about whether the person is the suspect before viewing the next photo. The

►FIGURE 7-9
Photo lineup form
(Garen Horst, Placer County California District Attorney's Office, 2010 Version, with some modifications)

PHOTO LINEUP FORM

Case No: _____   Place: _____

Date/Time: _____   Assigned investigator: _____

Administrator: _____   Witness: _____

Others present: _____

ADMONITION

The lineup administrator will show you a collection of photographs. Look at all six photos before making any comment. You do not have to identify anyone. It is just as important to clear innocent persons from suspicion as it is to identify suspects. Individuals may not appear exactly as they did on the date of the incident. For example, head and facial hair are subject to change. Do not attach any significance to differences in the characteristics of photos. The person who committed the crime may or may not appear in these photos. If you recognize any person in the photos as the suspect, tell the lineup administrator and sign on the number below identifying the suspect. The lineup administrator cannot give you feedback on any identification you make. If you make an identification, please do not discuss the case with other witnesses or the media or indicate to them in any way that you have identified someone. Regardless of whether an identification is made, law enforcement will continue to investigate the incident.

ACKNOWLEDGEMENT

I hereby acknowledge that I have read the foregoing admonition and understand it.

Witness: _____   Administrator: _____

1. _____   2. _____   3. _____

4. _____   5. _____   6. _____

STATEMENTS/COMMENTS: _____

_____

_____

Note: If an identification is made, ask the witness to state, in his/her own words, how certain he/she is of the identification. Record both identification and non-identification results in writing, including the witness' own words how sure he/she was.

second practice is to allow them to view all photos sequentially before any potential identification is made. There is some concern that allowing witnesses to see all photos sequentially before making a decision could contribute to some misidentifications, comparing photos a witness might point to the photo which *most appeared like the suspect*.

As a minimum, a photo lineup consists of six photographs—one of the suspect and at least five "fillers." Fillers are photographs of the same quality, size, shape, and type (black and white or color) of individuals who are similar in appearance—for example, sex, age, skin and hair color, facial hair, height, build, and other characteristics.[15] Although software may be able to make the background and lightening of photos similar, witness should be told not to attach any weight or significance to

such peripheral differences. Figure 7-9 is a Photo Lineup Form with instruction for witnesses, who are given the information individually in a private setting.

The photos are placed in the same position—for instance, middle of the page, in separate identical file folders that are numbered on the back for record keeping purposes and shuffled. The files are also shuffled before each new witness looks at them. The Innocence Project recommends having four blank files so the administrator doesn't know what the next file to be opened contains.[16]

If there are several witnesses, each is led separately through the process by the administrator. If there are multiple suspects, a separate photo lineup must be prepared for each suspect using different fillers; only one suspect can be in any single line up. If witnesses cannot be scheduled so they can be processed contemporaneously, without the opportunity for any personal contact with one another, a new photo lineup for each suspect must be prepared with different fillers for later witnesses. Even if a witness makes an identification, he/she should be guided to carefully consider any remaining photos. If a witness wants a second chance to view a photo lineup, wait at least 48 hours and then use another picture of the suspect wearing different clothes. If the posture of all the suspect and fillers is not standard, the suspect's picture should reflect him/her in a different posture. All new fillers must also be used.

Software is available to prepare a photo lineup and also produces the required recordkeeping documents. Because the computer selects the fillers, the investigator cannot be accused of selecting them in a manner that was intentionally biased against the suspect.[17]

LIVE LINEUPS

A **live lineup** is a process in which a series of "real people" are shown to an eyewitness to establish whether they can pick out the suspect (see Figure 7-10). All members of a lineup usually appear simultaneously, although there is some interest in sequential appearances. A suspect should be allowed to pick the order in which he/she appears. Requests from any attending defense attorney should be carefully considered and the request and its disposition documented by the administrator.

The suspect and at least four fillers are used, with the fillers selected on the same criteria as those used in a photo lineup. Some agencies prefer to use five fillers to make their photo and live lineup procedures parallel. If there are multiple witnesses, each one views the live lineup alone. The position of the suspect is changed in the lineup before each new witness to the same offense views it. If the witness has previously viewed a lineup involving a suspect and is asked to view another lineup with a second or subsequent suspect potentially involved in the same offense, the fillers must be entirely new each time.

The instructions to live lineup witnesses comport to those used in photo lineups, as does the need for the administrator to maintain strict neutrality. If any person in the live lineup is asked to perform a gesture, walk, or other movements, all others must individually do the same thing. The lineup administrator must be out of sight of the witness while conducting the lineup. The decision of the witness as to any identification must be conducted after the members of the lineup have left the room.

SHOW-UPS

When a crime occurs and fairly immediately thereafter officers stop a person suspected of being the perpetrator, they may lack probable cause to arrest him/her, but the offense is of such a severe or heinous nature that releasing the person may create a risk to public safety. Most **show-ups** involve a witness viewing one person stopped at or near the scene within a short time after the offense is committed.

If the victim is able or there is a witness, he/she might be taken separately to where the person in question is being briefly detained by the police. Most often this involves patrol officers. To view the person handcuffed in the backseat of a marked patrol car is tantamount to an accusation. Yet, having the person uncuffed, even if surrounded by officers, and standing near a marked patrol car, is only marginally better. It also raises concerns about officer safety and the possibility of escape. Show-ups in the field are problematic. If a warrant exists for some other offense, the person can be arrested, which will allow sufficient time to prepare a photo or live lineup.

The Innocence Project recommends that the person be taken to a neutral, noncriminal justice setting, to be viewed by the victim or a witness. All the cautions noted previously in this lineup section apply, except that only one person is viewed. Because a police investigatory stop and control of a person must be brief, there ordinarily will not be sufficient time to arrange a photo or live lineup that will sustain judicial scrutiny. Figure 7-11 is a show-up form; although it includes the use of an administrator, in some departments a patrol division supervisor or available investigator will fill this role.[18]

STAGED CRIME SCENES

Investigators should be open to the possibility that the offense they are investigating was staged. Staged crime scenes are not new. In the Bible, Joseph's brothers sold him into slavery and then dipped his robe in the blood of a goat they had killed to convince their father that Joseph had been devoured by a wild animal.[19] There are no official statistics on how often investigators encounter **staged crime** scenes, but there is some limited evidence that about 3% of all cases may involve some element of staging.[20]

One panel of experienced investigators concluded that the most common staged nonfatal crime was the false allegation of a sexual crime, followed by murder staged as a "burglary gone bad" or a robbery.[21] In part, the absence of statistics is due to the fact that when confronted with a staged crime scene, the police have simply unfounded the original report of a crime, reclassified it, or charged the person reporting it with filing a false report.

In recent years, some agencies have filed civil suits against the person falsely reporting a crime or staging a crime scene in order to recover costs of wasted investigative efforts. In addition to other charges that may apply to situations involving staged scenes, many states have

LIVE LINEUP FORM (Part 1)

Case No: _____   Date/Time: _____

Place: _____

Administrator: _____   Witness: _____

Others present: _____

ADMONITION

<u>WHY WE'RE HERE:</u> You were recently a crime victim or a witness to one. You will see a live lineup of five persons. There may be a person or persons in this lineup you recognize from the crime that brought you here today. The purpose of this form is to help you understand the lineup process and your role in it. Please carefully read all instructions. If you understand the instructions please sign at the bottom of this page. After you have seen the lineup, you will be asked to complete the other side of this form, which is about your experience in the lineup and sign it.

<u>PERSONS PRESENT:</u> An administrator will conduct the lineup. He/she is a "neutral" and doesn't know anything about the people in the lineup. The administrator cannot answer any questions related to them. Other people will be present who are not witnesses, however they are required to attend the lineup. If any of the other people present should ask you a question, you are not required to answer it.

<u>WHAT YOU WILL SEE:</u> You will be brought into a small, dimly lighted room (the lineup room). It has one-way glass separating it from the adjoining room. **While in the lineup room you cannot be heard or seen by anyone in the adjoining room no matter how close you get to the glass. You will be perfectly safe.** After you enter, the administrator will instruct you to look into the adjoining room. There will be five people who are similar in appearance and dress. They will be standing in a fully lighted room with their backs against a wall. There will be a number above each of them. Although you can see them, all they see is a mirror.

<u>WHAT YOU SHOULD CONSIDER:</u>

1. You are under no obligation to pick anybody from this lineup. Your only obligation is to be truthful. It is just as important to clear innocent persons from suspicion, as it is to identify suspects.

2. The **person** or **persons** involved in the crime **MIGHT or MIGHT NOT** be standing in the lineup.

3. Appearances can change over time (for example, head or facial hair may have grown or been cut, body weight may have been lost or gained, and height can be made to look different by slouching or standing very straight.

4. You might want to see the participants facing another direction. Please circle your choice below:

   Facing the wall   *Facing left*   *Facing right*

5. You might want to see the participants' gesture, walk, or make other movements. Please circle your choice below:

   Walk back and forth   Step closer to glass window   Any other movement, such as bend over at the waist or kneel down,

   please specify: _____

6. You might want the participants to repeat something you heard during the crime.
   Please write what you want them to say: _____

7. If you make an identification, neither the administrator nor others in the room can give you any feedback. Regardless of whether an identification is made, law enforcement will continue to investigate the incident.

<u>TAKE YOUR TIME:</u> Be sure to look carefully at each person and the number each is standing under. You may stand as close to the window or move back and forth as you want. **Remember, you cannot be seen or heard.** Again, if you want the lineup participants to do or say something, you only need to ask the administrator. When you are finished please inform the administrator and follow his/her instructions. If you have any questions or concerns, please talk with the administrator.

I hereby acknowledge and understand the foregoing admonition.

Signed: _____   Date: _____

▲ **FIGURE 7-10   Live lineup form (part 1)**
(Garen Horst, Placer County, California, District Attorney's Office, 2010 Version, with some modification)

LIVE LINEUP FORM (Part 2)

Case No: _____   Place: _____

Administrator: _____   Witness: _____

Others present: _____

Instructions: Please complete this form to the best of your ability, remembering the instructions that you were given. If you are unclear or uncertain about how to complete this form the administrator cannot tell you what to write. He/she can clarify the use of the form.
_____

On _____, 2010, I viewed a live lineup of five persons. They were numbered 1 through 5. There are three statements below. Each statement has a box next to it. I checked the one box that describes my thoughts about the lineup. I also personally filled out the information asked for in the statement I checked. If I am unable to identify anyone, I will write a few sentences explaining why. I understand this is not a shortcoming on my part, but a reflection of my best judgement.

☐ **I AM CERTAIN** that person number _____ was the person who (describe what he/she did during the crime):

_____

_____

_____

_____

_____

☐ **I AM NOT SURE,** but I think person number _____ was the person who (describe what he/she did during the crime):

_____

_____

_____

_____

☐ **I DID NOT RECOGNIZE ANYONE** in the lineup as being a person who was involved in the crime, because:

_____

_____

_____

_____

_____

YOUR LAST INSTRUCTION:
DO NOT DISCUSS THIS LINEUP IN ANY WAY WITH THE NEWS MEDIA. DO NOT DISCUSS THIS LINEUP IN ANY WAY WITH OTHER POTENTIAL WITNESSES, NOW OR IN THE FUTURE.

Signed: _____   Date: _____

▲ **FIGURE 7-10** Live lineup form (part 2) (*concluded*)

SHOW-UP FORM

Case No: _____   Place: _____

Date/Time: _____   Administrator: _____

Witness: _____

Others present: _____

ADMONITION

As a witness, you will be asked to look at a person or persons. You are not obligated to identify anyone. It is just as important to clear innocent persons from suspicion as it is to identify guilty parties. You should not conclude that the person or persons you see committed the crime simply because they are present. Please be advised that I cannot give you feedback on any identification you make. If you make identification, please do not discuss the case with the news media or other witnesses or indicate to them in any way that you have identified someone. Regardless of whether identification is made, law enforcement will continue to investigate the incident.

ACKNOWLEDGEMENT

I hereby acknowledge that I have read the foregoing admonition and understand it.

Witness: _____   Officer: _____

STATEMENTS/COMMENTS:

_____
_____
_____
_____

Investigator's note: If an identification is made, ask the witness to state, in his or her own words, how certain he or she is of any identification. Remember to record both positive identifications and non-identification results in writing, including the witness' own words how sure they are.

◄ **FIGURE 7-11   Show-up form** (Garen Horst, Placer County, California, District Attorney's Office, 2010 Version, with some modification)

laws dealing with fabricating false evidence and concealing, altering, or destroying evidence.

The essence of staging a crime scene is to misdirect investigators, usually away from the actual perpetrator. It may also be done for other reasons, such as protecting a family from embarrassment or financial hardship—for example, trying to make a suicide appear as an accident or a murder.[22] Most life insurance policies have a minimum waiting period, often two years, before suicides are covered. Assume that a man purchases a new life insurance policy, subsequently developed cancer, and commits suicide 23 months after the policy is issued. If his suicide is successfully staged as a murder, the family is financially protected.

Staging investigations focus on two questions: (1) what act is the staging intended to conceal, and (2) what was the motive for staging the crime, the determination of which usually leads to the perpetrator.[23] The staging motive is often one of self-preservation, to get away with the crime, or the previously mentioned avoidance of embarrassment or shame.[24]

Some staged crimes are so clumsy that they are immediately apparent. For example, a husband starts using meth and is secretly selling his wife's jewelry to buy it. To hide this fact, he breaks the window leading from the carport into the house to make it appear a burglary occurred. However, all the broken glass is on the carport—there is none on the inside of the house—meaning that the window was broken from the inside, not the outside. However, with so many crime investigation shows on television, people are learning more about police and laboratory capabilities and are becoming more sophisticated in staging scenes.

The first inklings of something being wrong may come from noticing that those who would seemingly be most affected by the crime, such as the murder of a spouse, display unusual behavior. Even allowing for the complexity of human behavior, when a surviving spouse treats the murder as an inconvenience, is only minimally distressed, or is even oddly undisturbed by it, investigators should be alerted. Stated somewhat differently, when there is an observable lack of congruence between the surviving spouse's affect and the murder, the cautious investigator wants to understand the reason for the gap.

Even when surviving spouses do not verbally express feelings of loss and despair to a significant degree, there are usually still nonverbal signs of distress—for instance, facial expressions, clutching their stomach, reaching for something to steady themselves or a chair to lower themselves into, moving their hands in circular motions as though they are trying to grasp the situation, and a mouth moving without the utterance of words suggest an inability to comprehend the loss.

In other staged situations, the investigator notes inconsistencies between the statements of the witness and the scene's physical evidence. These inconsistencies must be satisfactorily resolved, which may not be possible until the investigation gathers more information and receives the laboratory reports. Some staged crimes may be so successful that the case is closed and reopened only after the receipt of new information. For example, a new widow who came into a considerable amount of inheritance from the deceased is suddenly out partying continuously, immediately having an intense emotional relationship with someone, and cutting off contacts with the family's former friends and relatives, and rumors are surfacing about her previous affairs.

The best tool for identifying a staged crime is a thorough original and follow-up investigation. That documentation remains available and unchanging, needing only additional analysis.[25] Staged crime investigations profit from a logical process:[26]

1. Conduct a comprehensive and thorough review of the documented scene, which may be very time-consuming in violent crimes because of the abundance of evidence.
2. Carefully consider the victim's character, lifestyle, personal and professional associates, drug and alcohol use, normal hangouts, daily schedule and routines, physical condition, occupation, previous complaints to the police, and recent conversations with neighbors and friends. Is this information consistent with the scene and any behavior imputed to the victim; do any inconsistencies emerge that are significant?
3. Look at the incident from several perspectives. Does the reported sequence of events make sense—for example, why didn't the offender target the greatest threat first? Why did the greatest threat to the offender have the least amount of injuries? How did the husband escape a life-threatening injury or death while the assaults on his wife and children were fatal? Were the items taken from the scene valuable and easily removed, or did the offender take less valuable and odd items? Where were the stolen items before they were taken? How did the perpetrator know their location? Are the final positions of the bodies consistent with the location of

postmortem lividity (livor mortis), which is the settling of the blood to the parts of the body closest to the ground?[27] (Lividity produces a visible discoloration that is ordinarily reddish purple.
4. Identify and document in detail all possible indicators of staging.
5. Identify and document possible motives for the original act and for the staging. The person staging the scene is not someone who happened by and gratuitously changed things; it is almost always someone who knew the victim and had some association or relationship with him/her.
6. Determine who benefits from the original act and the staging.

COLD CASE INVESTIGATION

A **cold case** investigation, the most extreme form of a follow-up, is the reopening of an inactivated, unsolved case. "Cold" is a term that lacks precision, covering from months to many years. The most common type of cold case investigation is a murder or serial murders, followed by rapes.

Cold cases may have been inactivated because there were no more leads to pursue; forensic methods available now did not exist; more promising cases demanded attention; witnesses were reluctant to cooperate, were hostile, had vanished, died, or were murdered; and evidence was misplaced. Cases that are good candidates for reexamination are those that have some potential for overcoming these problems—for example, a new witness comes forward, or previously unrecovered evidence is located.

The work is challenging but has the potential to help families reach a resolution and to apprehend a significant predator. However, sometimes the victims or their families oppose a cold case investigation because they have "moved on" with their lives and don't want to revisit their painful past.

In 2001 the Los Angeles Police Department established a cold case unit, which started with 9,000 unsolved cases from the previous 20 years, most of which were not good candidates for activation; in the nine years that followed, approximately 100 offenses were solved.[28] Where staffing permits it, a dedicated staff of cold case investigators is believed to perform better than someone who is also carrying an active case load. The logic is that cold cases require a specialized type of investigation.

Like many other agencies, the Fayetteville (North Carolina) Police Department (FPD) had cold cases and resource constraints, and so they implemented an innovative solution pioneered by Professor Glover at St. Leo University, who involved students in reviewing cold cases. The FPD cold case unit consists of a supervising investigator from the police department and volunteers, including several retired and highly experienced investigators and

Professor Pauly, Methodist University, who had a long career in forensic investigation before becoming a faculty member. Carefully screened students who sign confidentiality agreements enter data to be analyzed by investigative software packages. The newly formed unit has not reported its first success.

INVESTIGATIVE SUPPORT AND ANALYTICAL TOOLS

FUSION CENTERS

Following 9/11, it was concluded that if the isolated parcels of information known about the terrorists and their activities before the attacks had been pooled and analyzed, the attacks may have been disrupted, mitigated, or prevented. As part of the overall response, fusion centers (FCs) were developed, staffed by multiple federal, state, tribal, and local agencies and private-sector entities (Figures 7-12 and 7-13). About 70 FCs are operational.[29] **Fusion**

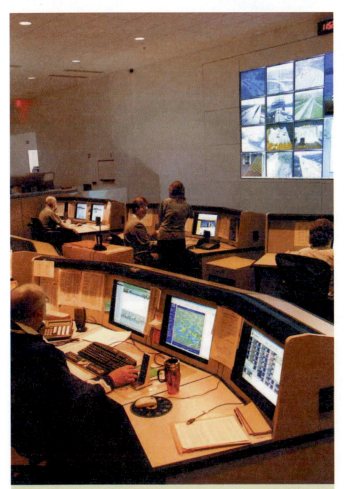

▲ **FIGURE 7-12   Fusion center**
(Courtesy Office of the Governor of Kentucky, Kentucky Office of Homeland Security)

is defined as turning information and intelligence into actionable knowledge; it is the fundamental process by which homeland security and crime-related information and intelligence are shared.

The essence of FCs is the constant merging, analysis, and dissemination of information and data from many disparate sources, including hospitals and the epidemiological monitoring capabilities of the Centers for Disease Control; this information is used both tactically and strategically for homeland security and crime-fighting purposes.

FCs have resulted in a convergence of crime analysis and intelligence to produce real-time, immediately actionable information. The concentration of information in FCs has alarmed civil libertarians concerned about abuses, and at the state level there is some sentiment that the federal government's intelligence contributions need to be more timely and substantial. It is predictable that issues will arise in an effort of such magnitude, and those issues deserve serious consideration.

INTELLIGENCE UNITS

Although many law-enforcement agencies have an intelligence unit, this unit's capabilities vary from simply trying to keep files current to using sophisticated analytical techniques. Depending on local capabilities and the fact situation, investigators may find no to considerable helpful information in local intelligence files.

Intelligence consists of pieces of raw information that when collected, evaluated, collated, and analyzed form meaningful and useful judgments that are both timely and accurate.[30]

In terms of categories of intelligence, there are at least four types:

1. *Indicative intelligence:* Focuses on emerging and new criminal developments.
2. *Tactical intelligence:* Immediately actionable and often results in arrests.
3. *Strategic intelligence:* Gathered and analyzed over time and usually confirms newly discovered patterns of criminal activity.
4. *Evidential intelligence:* Factual, precise information that can be presented in court.[31]

THE INTELLIGENCE/ANALYTICAL CYCLE

The **intelligence/analytical cycle** is driven by the needs of the client or end-user, who may be the commander of a task force working a serial murder case or the supervisor of an investigation unit trying to find a pattern in a string of violent convenience-store robberies. It is the end-user who specifies the types of information he/she wants, and it is the responsibility of the intelligence unit to make sure that the end-user understands both the possibilities and the limitations of the intelligence process and its

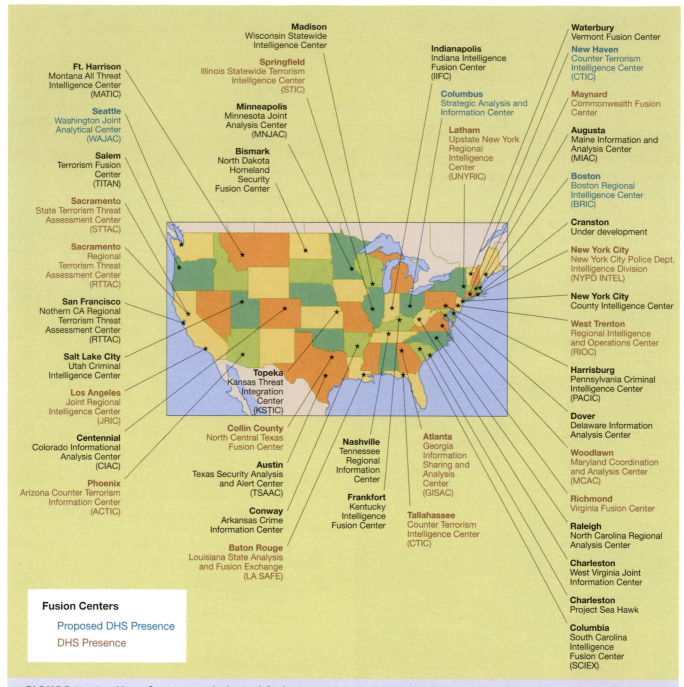

Madison
Wisconsin Statewide
Intelligence Center

Springfield
Illinois Statewide Terrorism
Intelligence Center
(STIC)

Minneapolis
Minnesota Joint
Analysis Center
(MNJAC)

Bismark
North Dakota
Homeland
Security
Fusion Center

Ft. Harrison
Montana All Threat
Intelligence Center
(MATIC)

Seattle
Washington Joint
Analytical Center
(WAJAC)

Salem
Terrorism Fusion
Center
(TITAN)

Sacramento
State Terrorism Threat
Assessment Center
(STTAC)

Sacramento
Regional
Terrorism Threat
Assessment Center
(RTTAC)

San Francisco
Nothern CA Regional
Terrorism Threat
Assessment Center
(RTTAC)

Salt Lake City
Utah Criminal
Intelligence Center

Los Angeles
Joint Regional
Intelligence Center
(JRIC)

Centennial
Colorado Informational
Analysis Center
(CIAC)

Phoenix
Arizona Counter Terrorism
Information Center
(ACTIC)

Collin County
North Central Texas
Fusion Center

Austin
Texas Security Analysis
and Alert Center
(TSAAC)

Conway
Arkansas Crime
Information Center

Baton Rouge
Louisiana State Analysis
and Fusion Exchange
(LA SAFE)

Topeka
Kansas Threat
Integration
Center
(KSTIC)

Nashville
Tennessee
Regional
Information
Center

Frankfort
Kentucky
Intelligence
Fusion Center

Atlanta
Georgia
Information
Sharing and
Analysis
Center
(GISAC)

Tallahassee
Counter Terrorism
Intelligence Center
(CTIC)

Indianapolis
Indiana Intelligence
Fusion Center
(IIFC)

Columbus
Strategic Analysis and
Information Center

Latham
Upstate New York
Regional
Intelligence
Center
(UNYRIC)

Waterbury
Vermont Fusion Center

New Haven
Counter Terrorism
Intelligence Center
(CTIC)

Maynard
Commonwealth Fusion
Center

Augusta
Maine Information and
Analysis Center
(MIAC)

Boston
Boston Regional
Intelligence Center
(BRIC)

Cranston
Under development

New York City
New York City Police Dept.
Intelligence Division
(NYPD INTEL)

New York City
County Intelligence Center

West Trenton
Regional Intelligence
and Operations Center
(RIOC)

Harrisburg
Pennsylvania Criminal
Intelligence Center
(PACIC)

Dover
Delaware Information
Analysis Center

Woodlawn
Maryland Coordination
and Analysis Center
(MCAC)

Richmond
Virginia Fusion Center

Raleigh
North Carolina Regional
Analysis Center

Charleston
West Virginia Joint
Information Center

Charleston
Project Sea Hawk

Columbia
South Carolina
Intelligence
Fusion Center
(SCIEX)

Fusion Centers

Proposed DHS Presence

DHS Presence

▲ **FIGURE 7-13** **Map of current and planned fusion centers**
(Todd Masse, Siobhan O'Neil, and John Rollins, Fusion Centers: Issues and Options for Congress [Washington, D.C.: Congressional Research Service, July 6, 2007], p. CRS-93)

techniques. As depicted in Figure 7-14, the backbone of the intelligence/analytical cycle is a continuous six-step process,[32] which is discussed next.

1. PLANNING AND DIRECTION

The intelligence/analytical process must be managed throughout, from identifying the focus of the intelligence effort to delivering the finished product to the police unit requesting it. As a practical matter, finished intelligence often creates new questions during the reevaluation stage, which starts the process all over again.

2. COLLECTION

Collection is the gathering and managing of raw data, which is then analyzed to produce the finished product.[33]

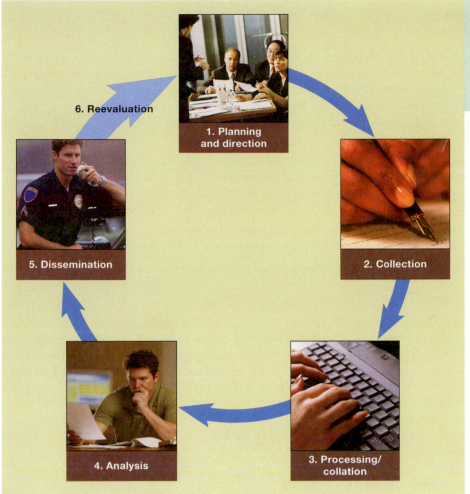

◄ **FIGURE 7-14**
The intelligence/analytical cycle
(U.S. Department of Justice, Department of
Homeland Security, and The Global Justice
Information Sharing Initiative, Fusion Center
Guidelines [Washington, D.C.: July 2005], p. 26)

3. PROCESSING

Processing converts raw information from all sources into a form that can be used by analysts.[34] This is accomplished by information management, which is the indexing, sorting, and organizing of raw data into files for rapid retrieval. It includes entering the data into a computer, checking the entries for accuracy, and collating paper files. One of the key considerations in processing is ensuring that the data-processing methods fit the analytical techniques that will be used.

4. ANALYSIS AND PRODUCTION

In the analysis and production step, the data that has been processed is translated into a finished intelligence product.[35] Analysts, who are subject-matter specialists (for example, organized crime, gangs, or terrorism), carefully scrutinize the data for timeliness, reliability, validity, and relevance. The role of the analyst is to combine the data and his/her analysis and judgment into a finished intelligence product that informs the end-user of the analyst's assessment of events and the implications of that assessment.

5. DISSEMINATION

The fifth element in the cycle is the dissemination of the finished intelligence report to the end-user who requested it.[36] The end-user can then make decisions or take actions on the basis of the intelligence provided.

6. REEVALUATION

It is crucial that the end-user provide feedback about the value of the intelligence so that there can be an ongoing cycle of improvement. Moreover, the finished intelligence report itself, the decisions made, and the actions taken all have the potential to create new questions that lead back to the first element, planning and direction, thus beginning a new intelligence/analytical cycle.

SURVEILLANCE CAMERAS AND FACIAL RECOGNITION SOFTWARE

Surveillance cameras (SCs) use continues to expand. In England, where there is an average of one surveillance camera for every 14 people, shoppers and workers are estimated to be caught on camera at least 300 times a

TABLE 7-1	Types of Crime Analysis
TYPE	**DESCRIPTION**
Tactical	Deals with recent offenses (for example, immediate to hours, days, or weeks) for the purpose of responding quickly to specific crimes; it provides uniformed officers and investigators with timely information (for instance, investigative leads) to guide their actions and apprehend offenders. Includes attempts to forecast where the next specific crime (such as burglary) will occur.
Strategic	Focuses on solving ongoing crime problems (months, quarters, or years) by matching police resources with crime, demands for service, and other variables.
Administrative	For police administrators, elected and appointed city and county officials, and others: analyzes crime and demographic, economic, geographic, and other factors on a long-range basis (quarterly, semiannually, or even multiyear) with respect to how they interact with one another. The information may be used in annual reports, policy-making, grant applications, and for other related purposes.

Synthesized from Crime Analysis Unit, "Types of Crime Analysis," Bernalillo County, New Mexico, Sheriff's Office, December 3, 2010, *www.bernco .gov*, and Crime Analyst, "Three Types of Crime Analysis," North Miami Police Department, December 3, 2010, *www.northmiamipolice.com*.

day.[37] In the United States there are 30 million SCs that record four billion hours of footage each week.[38] It is generally thought that people in this country are recorded 30 to 45 times daily. This footage can be "mined" to look for particular variables.

Malls may have hundreds of SCs inside and on the parking lots. They are also at ATMs, casinos, airports, downtown streets, "sit-down" and fast food restaurants, schools, dorms, grocery stores, football stadiums, and gyms, and they provide live monitoring of highway traffic. SCs are even in homes for security, although some also surreptitiously employ mini "nanny cams" to make sure their children are not being abused. Inevitably, SCs capture crimes in progress, providing investigative leads. Some retail giants, e.g. Target, quietly have established their own digital labs and work closely with investigators.

Facial recognition software (FRS) began being deployed by law-enforcement agencies during the 1990s. FRS has continued to evolve in terms of accuracy and the ways in which it is used. More advanced FRS can produce two- and three-dimensional facial images. Using advanced mathematical calculations, the face of an unknown person captured on camera can be compared to a known file photograph to make an identification. In 2010 the best-performing FRS had an error rate of 0.1 to 2.1%.[39]

FRS is being used by a growing number of states to ensure the identity of the person being licensed to drive. Some law-enforcement agencies compare SC photos of illegal activity with their departmental mug hot files. Impressionistically this procedure appears to have greater success with illegal check and credit card transactions at a counter. The subjects are relatively still in this setting, and there are multiple high-resolution images with which to work. FRS is also being used in homeland security efforts, such as at border-crossing stations. Some agencies have equipped patrol cars with facial recognition technology and digital cameras. During a two-year period, Pinellas County (Florida) Sheriff's Office deputies in the field correctly identified 295 people who had lied about their identity.[40] There is ongoing research to determine whether other likeness of suspects—for example, artist's sketches and composite drawings—can reliably be used with FRS.

CRIME ANALYSIS

Crime analysis is the process of using systematic analytical methods to acquire timely and pertinent information on crime patterns and trend correlations.[41] The three general types of crime analysis are summarized in Table 7-1. Commonly used methods to link crimes include:[42]

- *Trends:* **Trends** are general tendencies in the occurrence of crime across large geographic areas over extended periods of time. They arise when areas become more conducive or less conducive to a particular crime or crimes. Trends can be associated with shifts in demography; for example, as a neighborhood ages, its residents may be seen as soft targets for muggings and home-invasion robberies. Trends can also stem from the creation of new targets; for instance, the presence of a new shopping mall increases the opportunities for shoplifting and thefts from, and of, vehicles
- *Patterns:* If the same crime is committed repeatedly over a short period of time, sometimes, but not always, by the same offender, it is a pattern. For example, outside a five-star restaurant, a number of female patrons who are leaving alone have their purses snatched.
- *Series:* In a **series,** the same type of crime is committed over a short period of time, probably by the same offender. For instance, in an affluent, gated residential community of 73 houses, six burglaries occur in nine days.

◄ **FIGURE 7-15 Hot blocks**
One way to see areas of interest larger than a hot spot is to highlight *hot blocks*, or areas where many incidents cluster. In this GIS map, auto thefts or recoveries occurred in tight groups. In the map, red spots indicate clusters of car thefts, and blue clusters represent recoveries.

- *Sprees:* When the same type of offense is committed at almost the same time by the same offender(s) it is called a spree. An example is the vandalizing of cars by a group of kids who spray-paint license plates while walking through a neighborhood.
- *Hot spots:* A **hot spot** is a location where various crimes are committed on a regular basis, usually by different perpetrators. An example is a bar where underage drinkers are served, there are numerous fights, user-level drug sales take place, prostitution flourishes, and patrons are occasionally mugged, robbed, or carjacked in the parking lot (Figure 7-15).
- *Crimogens:* A **crimogen** is either an individually known offender who is responsible for a large number of crimes or one victim who reports a large number of crimes. Examples include a career criminal and a convenience-store operator who reports gas drive-offs, shoplifting, robberies, assaults, and even thefts of entire ATM machines.

Crime-analysis reports, depending on their intended use and sensitivity, may be distributed at staff meetings, shift briefings, the departmental intranet, or other method.

The policies of most law-enforcement agencies require feedback from the users of the products to help determine the effectiveness of the unit. The weight of the new emphasis on intelligence gathering and tight budgets has resulted in some law-enforcement agencies creating a Crime Analysis and Intelligence Unit, combining what have historically been separate functions.

CRIME SCENE RECONSTRUCTION

Reconstruction of past events is routine in law enforcement. The first officer at a domestic violence call listens to the parties involved, examines any injuries, looks at the scene were the violence allegedly took place, evaluates the credibility of statements made by the parties involved and any witnesses, and in consideration of all the information available at that time makes a decision on the proper handling of it.

In contrast, crime scene reconstruction (CSR) involves more complex events, takes place over a longer period of time, integrates data from more varied sources, and uses a rigorous methodology to reach conclusions. The Association for Crime Scene Reconstruction (ACSR)

► **FIGURE 7-16**
The scientific method and CSR

STEPS IN THE SCIENTIFIC METHOD	RECONSTRUCTION APPLICATION
1. State the problem	IQ: Was the victim approaching or going away from VMS when she was shot?
2. Gather the relevant data	Crime scene photographs and diagrams; medical examiner's report; lab reports: bloodstain pattern analysis, ballistics.
3. Form a hypothesis	Victim was going away from VMS
4. Predict what the hypothesis would indicate if true	It would contradict VMS's account of incident: victim attacked him with a knife in her hand; he shot her with SW revolver in self-defense at a range of 18″; she turned around, staggered down the hallway and collapsed.
5. Test of hypothesis	1. Victim found 13 feet from VMS's alleged shooting position, near end of "L" shaped hallway. 2. No blood evidence at the point victim was allegedly shot. 3. No back spatter blood on revolver or VMS's person/clothing. 4. Bullet's entry point was the victim's back, through her nightgown. 5. High-velocity bloodstain pattern indicates victim was shot approximately 9' from VMS's position. 6. Lab test concluded victim could not have been shot at distance claimed by VMS.
6. State the conclusion	Victim was shot moving away from VMS's position at a distance of approximately 9 feet.

defines CSR as "the use of scientific methods, physical evidence, deductive reasoning, and their interrelationship to gain explicit knowledge of the series of events that surround the commission of a crime." There are different approaches to CSR, but they share common perspectives:

- data defines the conclusion;
- the context in which evidence is found, as well as its analysis, provides objective data;
- consider human testimony cautiously;
- effective forensic examination produces more refined data;
- what happened is not the only question—its sequence is also important;
- use "reverse engineering" to work backward from the evidence to develop an understanding of what happened.[43]

The different CSR approaches also ask four basic questions as each item of evidence is being considered:

- What is it?
- What function does it serve?

- What does it tell about the timing and sequence of events?
- What interrelationships does it have with other items of evidence?[44]

The **scientific method** is at the heart of all approaches to CSR. The steps of the scientific method and their application to CSR are identified in Figure 7-16. This illustration addresses a single investigative question (IQ).

The six steps of the scientific method are easily followed in a controlled laboratory experiment where there can be a single test point of a hypothesis before a conclusion is reached. However, in investigation we develop multiple hypotheses, often at different times—such as the victim was seated when shot; the suspect gained entry through the victim's rear door; the first of three shots fired through the glass window came from the inside; and the suspect returned to the scene and mutilated the victim's body. These hypotheses are not collectively tested at a single point in time but intermittently throughout the investigation as the appropriate information—for example, autopsy reports, surveillance camera images, and lab

▲ **FIGURE 7-17   Specific crime scene reconstruction**
Suspect related he shot the victim from across the room. The
victim's yellow sweater and skin reveal the shot was fired
with the gun's muzzle in contact with the victim. There was
also "blowback" evidence on the pistol, blood and tissue,
from the victim. The physical evidence contradicts the
suspect's story. (Courtesy Forensic Training and Consulting, LLC)

that require answers; thus, the employment of the scientific method produces an ever-expanding and self-correcting body of knowledge related to the crime.[45] This expanding body of knowledge may also introduce thorny new problems that require entirely new hypotheses. Assume a man's body is found next to his car in the parking lot behind a bar. The car door is open, the keys are near the victim's hand, and the scene suggests he was about to enter or leave his car when he was shot once in the chest and head. One rear trouser pocket is semi-turned inside out, and there was no wallet. The investigator's initial impression was that a lone gunman killed the victim in a robbery gone bad. Later, the autopsy report arrived, and bullets from two different caliber handguns were recovered from the victim. Before reading any further, the investigator entertains several new possibilities: One shooter using two different weapons? Two shooters? One shooter scared off before taking anything, and quickly thereafter an opportunistic criminal took the wallet and finished the possibly conscious victim off? Found wounded and killed by a spurned lover, who then staged a robbery by taking the wallet?

Despite such thorny problems, CSR goes forward using the discipline of the scientific method, blending empirical knowledge, gained from observation and deduction, and rationalism, inductive thought and reasoning,[46] particularly critical thinking. At its heart, critical thinking is an unremitting intellectual process that rejects evidence and conclusions that lack sufficient proof; it does not allow, for example, assumptions to masquerade as facts.[47] Key skills associated with critical thinking include analyzing, synthesizing, and evaluating.

One approach to CSR is Event Analysis (EA) model of CSR. "*Incident*" is any situation a reconstructionist is asked to investigate; the term is neutral and avoids the implicit assumption that a crime has been committed. An incident includes all of the activity from its beginning to its end.[48] Incidents consist of macro components, "*events*"; these, in turn comprise a series of actions, "*event segments*," that are much like a series of time-phased photographs.[49] The primary focus of EA is to identify as many event segments as possible; each event segment is a mini-conclusion based on the verifiable data associated with it[50] (Figure 7-18).

The scientific method is designed to eliminate other explanations and cannot establish a final, "absolute truth." Scientific methods and statements are open to re-examination, particularly in light of new data and new analytical techniques. An allied example is the number of people who were convicted by eyewitness testimony but freed years later by DNA analysis. What this means in investigation is that at the end of using the scientific method we have eliminated the impossible and implausible and what is left is a valid possibility. CSR does not deal with the "why" of crimes; that is the purview of criminal profiling, discussed next in this chapter.

reports—becomes available (Figure 7-17). The testing, as well as the addition of new information, causes us to refine some hypotheses, discard others, and formulate new ones to test.

The scientific method is somewhat circular, because after we test a hypothesis, it often leads to new questions

▶ FIGURE 7-18
Illustration of event segment analysis

Case Situation:

Officers responded to call where a husband (TJM) returning home alone parked his BMW in the garage, closed the garage door, and entered the house through the door opening into kitchen. Although his wife was on an out-of-state trip, he expected his 17-year-old stepdaughter to be home. She was the only other person who would be in the house. He discovered "lots of blood" in her first-floor bedroom located in the home's west wing. TJM immediately went just outside the front door and used his cell phone to call 911. He did not reenter the house until arriving officers cleared it without finding anyone. The first arriving officer remained continuously with TJM, first outside the front door and later in the living room. Crime scene technicians arrived and began processing the scene. Soon thereafter, investigators reached the scene and 35 minutes later took TJM from the living room to the station, where he gave the statement used to describe this case situation.

Data Elements:

1. TJM brought BMW to scene.
2. TJM parked in garage.
3. TJM closed garage door.
4. TJM arrived alone at house.
5. TJM found blood in his stepdaughter's bedroom.
6. TJM immediately went outside the front door and called police on his cell phone.
7. First arriving officer stayed continuously with TJM, first outside the front door and later in the living room.
8. Other arriving officers searched but did not find anyone else in house.
9. Blood recovered from stepdaughter's room.
10. Visible blood droplets found on floor of master bathroom in home's east wing.
11. Blood found on inside of shower in master bathroom.
12. Blood found on rear bumper of BMW.
13. Blood found in trunk of BMW.
14. Blood noted in 5 and 9–13 above consistent with stepdaughter's DNA.

Event Segment:

Subsequent to stepdaughter's bleeding, TJM transferred her blood to the master bathroom and the BMW's bumper and trunk.

For detailed information about Event Analysis see Ross M. Gardner and Tom Bevel, *Practical Crime Scene Analysis and Reconstruction* (Boca Raton, Florida: CRC Press, 2009).

CRIMINAL PROFILING

Criminal profiling is also referred to by other terms, such as offender profiling and psychological profiling. It is the process of studying all available information related to a crime and developing a psychological portrait of the unknown offender. It has the potential to eliminate suspects, focus on one or several others, provide investigative leads, and be helpful in interrogations.

Profiling has a history of roughly 50 years. An early success involved "The Mad Bomber," who from 1940 until 1956 in New York City, with a "patriotic pause" during World War II, left over 30 bombs in public places. After reviewing the amassed evidence, psychiatrist James Brussels concluded:

He is a male, middle-aged, meticulous, largely self-educated, Slavic, Roman Catholic, has an Oedipal Complex, lives in Connecticut, and worked for Consolidated Edison or one of its subsidiaries. The police would have to publicize the profile to draw the man out, and when apprehended he will be wearing a buttoned double-breasted suit.[51]

Drawn out by the publicity, George Metesky wrote letters to newspapers, which unintentionally contained clues that ultimately led to his arrest in 1957. Remarkably, he was wearing a buttoned double-breasted suit, and other aspects of the profile were also correct. Conversely, the profiles of the Washington D.C. snipers who terrorized that area in 2002 with their random murders were substantially off-target. Profiling is not an exact science and relies to a degree on the training, experience, and judgment of the profiler.

The FBI led the modern development of profiling beginning in the 1970s. Along with continually refining the methodology, the FBI produced one of the most widely recognized concepts of profiling, the organized-disorganized offender model (Table 7-2). Although many offenders fit neatly into the organized or disorganized

| TABLE 7-2 | Crime Scene Differences between Organized and Disorganized Sexual Homicides |

ORGANIZED	DISORGANIZED
1. Offense planned; semblance of order before, during, and after the crime suggests aim of avoiding detection	Spontaneous offense, appears to be no plan to avoid detection
2. Victim frequently a targeted stranger in a location staked out by offender, to some extent victim is a target of opportunity; serial victims may share common characteristics, and offender may spend considerable time waiting for "right" victim	May know victim or select randomly, often familiar with location of crime
3. Personalizes victim	Depersonalizes victim; specific areas of the body may be selected for extreme violence; overkill or excessive force to face is often attempt to dehumanize victim
4. Offender may strike up conversation with victim as attempt to gain her confidence in order to capture victim without resorting to physical force	Minimal conversation aside from orders and directions
5. Scene reflects overall control	Scene random and sloppy, in great disarray
6. Demands submissive and compliant victim; may require certain reactions, e.g., fear and passivity during sexual activity	Sudden, overpowering violence to victim; offender uses a surprise blitz-style attack
7. Restraints used, e.g., ropes, chains, handcuffs, chemicals, belts, gags, blindfolds	Minimal use of restraints; victim killed quickly to avoid victim's getting the upper hand
8. Aggressive acts prior to death, weapon displayed, victim's life threatened	Any sexually sadistic acts follow death, e.g., mutilation of face, breasts, and genitals
9. Body hidden	Body left in view, often left in position killed
10. Weapons and evidence absent	Evidence and weapons often present, normally much physical evidence available
11. Transports victim or body, often using his or her vehicle	Body left at death scene

Source: Robert Ressler, Ann W. Burgess, and John E. Douglas, *Sexual Homicide: Patterns and Motives* (New York: Free Press, 1992), pp. 121–124, 131.

pattern, some of them reflect aspects of both patterns. A number of factors can lead to a mixed organized-disorganized crime: multiple offenders with different behaviors may be involved; a planned crime may deteriorate as unanticipated events unfold, such as being unable to control the victim; or the original motive may have been solely rape, but the victim's resistance (which may be successful) or the offender's changed emotional state may lead to murder. Youthful offenders or the offender's use of drugs and alcohol can also lead to a mixed scene.[52]

The FBI's Behavioral Science Unit continues to provide profiling services to other law-enforcement agencies. Profiling methods focus on the four factors that are briefly discussed below.

1. *Antecedent:* In this stage the profiler tries to understand the offender's mindset. What triggered the offender to commit the crime? Was he/she driven by fantasies about this victim, was it the characteristics of the victim and/or the location, was the situation attractive—for example, would have a longer time to spend with the victim, did he/she act opportunistically or was it planned? What does the lack of planning or the items brought to the scene suggest?

2. *Method:* Although offenders may vary in how they commit a crime, often there is a pattern to it. They enter the victim's residence in a particular way, within a time range, on a particular day or two of the week, overpowering victims with a blow from a blunt instrument, binding them in a certain way using the same material to restrain them—for instance, duct tape, abusing them in a specific way or sequence, and suffocating them with a plastic bag over their heads.

3. *Disposal:* What the offender does with the victim after the offense may form part of a modus operandi or suggest things about the offender. A raped woman might be left tied to the bed, forced into a closet, or ordered to shower and restrained again.

If there are multiple murder victims the bodies may be cleaned up and positioned in sexual or other poses, as was done by Florida's "Gainesville Ripper." Bodies that are dumped in a National Forest, industrial park, or a particular segment of a river may indicate a familiarity with the area. Leaving bodies where they will be quickly found suggests a need for recognition.

4. *Post-offense behavior:* There may be no observable post-offense behavior, or the offender may contact the news media to publish obscure clues or rage against how the police are characterizing him, or send taunting letters to the police.

Although profiling has been an asset in many significant violent investigations, it has some detractors who in one way or another regarded it as pseudo-science. It was severely criticized in 2010, characterized as never having been a scientific process and essentially based on common sense intuitions and faulty theoretical assumptions that appear to be consistent with educated guesses and wishful thinking.[53] A more moderate criticism was raised in 2009, which called for a higher level of scientific validity.[54] These criticisms have not gone unnoticed, and multiple research efforts have been completed and others are underway to strengthen the scientific base.

▲ **FIGURE 7-19**

Geoprofiling for illegal entries into the United States that resulted in criminal dispositions. The land of Mexico is to the left of the river (blue line); to the right is the United States. Note that the yellow line turns purple near the top of the image, showing an increase in elevation. Higher vertical lines portray more crossings made at that point. **(Courtesy Dr. Kim Rossmo, Center for Geospatial Intelligence and Investigation (GII), Texas State University, San Marcos)**

GEOGRAPHICAL PROFILING

Geographic information system (GIS) software provides the capability to superimpose various types of data on a map. For example, a law-enforcement administrator might want to see where traffic citations are being written versus where accidents frequently occur, which could lead to a refocusing of the enforcement effort. **Geographic profiling** is a specialty that rests on the premise that given a sufficient number of crimes, with adequate information suitable for analysis, a probabilistic map of the area in which the offender's residence is located can be calculated. The size of the area depends on the amount and quality of data. Geoprofiling has also proven itself useful in locating insurgents responsible for planting improvised explosive devices and in border security (Figure 7-19).

Although others had worked on geographic profiling, the term was coined by Rossmo, a former Detective Inspector with the Vancouver (Canada) Police Department. While studying for his doctorate, he conceived of the idea of using geographic profiling to target the residence of offenders and was the central figure in developing the first software package to be able to do this. As in the case of other recently developed investigative technologies, geoprofiling is in a state of transition as refinements are developed. It is not a perfect tool, and its capabilities can be decreased if the number of cases in a series are roughly less than 5 or the crime linkage is inaccurate.[55]

REMOTE SENSING

Remote sensing is the process of collecting and analyzing information about areas, objects, or events without being in contact with the focus of analysis.[56] Aerial surveillance was the first type of remote sensing; during the Civil War (1861–1865), officers were sent aloft in balloons to observe the disposition of enemy forces and report on what they saw. Some photographs were taken and used by commanders.[57] Today, aerial/visual sensing is conducted by manned space craft, satellites, rotary and fixed-wing aircraft, unmanned aerial vehicles (UAVs), and public surveillance cameras.

Aerial remote sensing can be used by law-enforcement personnel to detect illicit drug crops and clandestine labs, monitor airstrips, provide over-the-horizon (OTH) intelligence about drug smuggling boats and planes, quickly identify incipient forest fires, rescue lost hikers and mountain climbers, find airplane crash sites, locate fugitives and abducted persons, recover automobiles and other evidence from water systems, identify possible clandestine graves, as well as to provide investigative leads, the identification of suspects, and proof that the elements of a crime were committed.

Aerial surveillance platforms may be equipped with not only visual recording and transmitting capabilities but other sensor packages as well. Many police aircraft are equipped with Forward Looking Infrared Radar feet using metal detectors to search for items such as shell cases, projectiles, belt buckles, jewelry, buttons, and zippers. Advanced metal detectors with screens can show the depth of an item and estimate the probability that it is one type of artifact or another. (4) Radar-based through-the-wall surveillance (TWS) provides 3-D color images, including static objects and moving people, from a distance through walls as thick as 8 inches of concrete. This capability substantially reduces the danger to officers making high-risk entries into buildings to free hostages or apprehend violent offenders. Booby traps can also be identified, the number and locations of suspects determined, and other important tactical information provided. (5) Aquatic acoustic sensors can track boats smuggling drugs or weapons; and (6) smaller gamma-ray-based density meters can identify variations in the density of dashboards, tires, walls, and other surfaces. Such variations allow hidden compartments containing contraband to be identified, and larger gamma ray units can scan cargo (Figure 7-21).

TIME-EVENT CHARTING AND LINK ANALYSIS

Follow-up investigations often result in the accumulation of significant amounts of data. As a result, financial transactions, relationships, the importance of places,

(FLIR), which is a significant asset in tracking fugitives on foot at night through their heat signatures.

There are also numerous other remote-sensing capabilities, including (1) the use of canines to detect contraband and cadavers (Figure 7-20) and (2) ground-penetrating radar to locate clandestine graves, which is a process that is nondestructive to physical evidence. (3) Potential burial sites can be worked from the surface to a depth of several

▲ FIGURE 7-22   Time-event chart

▲ FIGURE 7-23   Link/association diagram
Organizations are in boxes. Solid lines indicate confirmed relationships. Dotted lines are suspected relations.

events, telephone calls, and other data can be obscured and their importance overlooked, resulting in an unnecessarily protracted or unsuccessful investigation. Software has automated creating a variety of charts, saving investigative effort for other uses. Two commonly used investigative tools are time-event charting and link analysis.

A time-event chart is shown in Figure 7-22; it depicts the major events involving an offender paroled from the state prison. Time is shown as intervals between major events. The actual dates for events could be added to the chart. For seven months, he made his regularly scheduled meetings with his parole officer. Three months later, an informant described him as a frequent crack user. Three weeks after that, the parolee robbed a tourist. Over the next 30 days, he committed three more robberies, each time progressing upward to a more lucrative target. The choice of a pharmacy as a target gave him both money and drugs, which are the same as money on the streets. If he is selling drugs, informants may know of it. The interval between robberies is growing shorter, and the parolee has become violent. It is possible that he is pulling jobs while high, so the potential for further violence is great. Figure 7-23 is a link chart showing the relationships between individuals involved in importing drugs.

THE INTERNET

The possibilities of the Internet have not escaped law enforcement, which has been quick to use it for investigative, administrative, and public information purposes. For investigative purposes, the police use the Internet in many ways, such as:

1. Appealing to the public for information about specific crimes, often through "crime-stopper" programs.
2. Requesting information about missing children and adults.
3. Posting federal, state, and local most-wanted lists. These lists may be limited to the "top 10," or there may be separate most-wanted lists, such as a list for the most-wanted violent felons or burglars.
4. Soliciting information about individuals who are wanted as fugitives.
5. Alerting the public about jail and prison escapees and requesting information if they are sighted.
6. Requesting information about the identities of unknown subjects ("unsubs").
7. Showing photographs of recovered stolen property so that the owners can identify and claim it.
8. Providing crime-mapping capabilities so that investigators can approach their work with better information and citizens can be informed.

KEY TERMS

Arson, Explosives and Incident System (AEXIS)
cold case
crime analysis
criminal profiling
crimogen
facial recognition software (FRS)
Field Interview/Information Report (FIR)
fusion
geographical profiling
hot spot
intelligence/analytical cycle

investigative plan
LeadsOnLine
live lineup
National Center for the Analysis of Violent Crime (NCAVC)
National Crime Information Center (NCIC)
National Drug Pointer Index (NDPIX)
National Missing and Unidentified Persons System (NamUs)
Next Generation Identification (NGI) Program

photo lineup
remote sensing
scientific method
series
show-up
social network sites
solvability factors
staged crime
surveillance
trends
Violent Criminal Apprehension Program (ViCAP)

REVIEW QUESTIONS

1. How are solvability factors used?
2. How do you prepare a case file?
3. Why are victims and witnesses reinterviewed?
4. NamUs provides what capabilities?
5. What is NCIC?
6. How can LeadsOnLine help an investigation?
7. What things should you not do with informants?
8. Why conduct physical surveillance?
9. How should a photo lineup be conducted?
10. What are three potential indicators of a staged crime?
11. What stages make up the intelligence cycle?
12. How is facial recognition software being used by law-enforcement agencies?
13. How do crime analysts link crimes?
14. Why is the scientific method important to crime scene reconstruction?
15. Criminal profiling focuses on what four factors?
16. What is geographical profiling?
17. What are four examples of remote sensing?
18. In what ways can the Internet be used by investigators?

INTERNET ACTIVITIES

1. Visit "FBI Next Generation Identification (NGI) Overview" and read about the FBI's new emphasis on biometrics (*http://biometrics.org/bc2010/presentations/DOJ/pender-FBI-Next-Generation-Identification-Overview.pdf.*)

2. Go to the Center for Geospatial Intelligence and Investigation, Texas State University to learn more about geoprofiling (*http://txstate.edu/gii*).

▶ The FBI crime laboratory is recognized as one of the most comprehensive and prestigious crime labs in the world. Since its inception in 1932, the FBI crime lab has provided valuable services for law-enforcement agencies at the state, county, and municipal level.

(PhotoDisc Collection/Getty Images)

8

THE CRIME
LABORATORY

CHAPTER OBJECTIVES

1. Define and distinguish forensic science and criminalistics.

2. Describe the importance of an investigator's understanding of crime laboratory capabilities.

3. List the three measures of effectiveness of crime laboratories and how they relate to the 2009 National Academy of Science (NAS) report on forensic science in the United States.

4. Distinguish the Frye test from the Daubert test, regarding the admissibility of scientific evidence.

5. Explain the role and the importance of DNA analysis in criminal investigation, and identify the latest technologies in DNA evidence investigation and data banking.

6. Highlight the process of fingerprint identification and comparison.

7. Describe AFIS, IAFIS, NGI, and NIBIN.

8. Discuss some of the problems currently associated with police crime laboratories.

A crime laboratory is a scientific organization with a dedicated mission of aiding the process of criminal justice. It provides this aid by answering, or helping to answer, the vital questions of whether a crime was committed, how and when it was committed, who committed it, and who could not have committed it. The criminal laboratory seeks answers to questions such as these through scientific analysis of material collected primarily from the scenes of crimes or from suspects.[1] Although there are hundreds of federal, state, and local crime laboratories throughout the United States, the range of services and personnel expertise within the laboratories varies among the organizations.

To understand the role of crime laboratories, one must understand their relationship to the scientific community and to the functions of the criminal justice system. There are two distinct activities involved in laboratory work. One is the gathering of evidence at the scene of a crime, which is done by evidence technicians or investigators. The second function is the scientific analysis of evidence, which occurs in the laboratory. The effectiveness of the second activity often depends on the efficiency with which the first operation is performed.

An important issue addressed in this chapter is an investigator's expectations regarding the function and responsibilities of a crime laboratory. Although the laboratory is one of the most valuable tools for a criminal investigator, he/she must be aware of its capabilities and limitations. It is not uncommon, for example, for an investigator to send evidence to a laboratory and delay the investigation until the laboratory results are received. Crime laboratories are not intended to replace field investigations. In addition, investigators are often not familiar with the types of evidence that are subject to laboratory analysis. Even the most minute and seemingly insignificant pieces of evidence may be subject to laboratory examination. If investigators are not aware of a laboratory's capabilities, critical pieces of evidence can go uncollected, unprocessed, and unused in substantiating guilt or innocence. Because the analysis of evidence is no better than the samples submitted, investigators play an important role in the success of scientific analysis.

The terms *forensic science* and *criminalistics* are often used interchangeably. **Forensic science** is that part of science applied to answering legal questions. It is the examination, evaluation, and explanation of physical evidence in law. Forensic science encompasses pathology, toxicology, physical anthropology, odontology (dental structure, development, and diseases), psychiatry, questioned documents, firearms, tool-mark comparison, and serology, among other fields. Recent technological advances have added molecular biology and genetics to this list.

One of the branches of forensic science, **criminalistics,** deals with the study of physical evidence related to a crime. From such a study, a crime may be reconstructed. Criminalistics is interdisciplinary, drawing on mathematics, physics, chemistry, biology, anthropology, and many other scientific endeavors. The late Paul L. Kirk, a leader in the criminalistics movement in the United States, once remarked: "Criminalistics is an occupation that has all of the responsibilities of medicine, the intricacy of the law, and the universality of science."[2]

CHAPTER OUTLINE

Introduction

Crime Laboratories

Measures of Crime Laboratory Effectiveness

Technologies

Handling Evidence in the Laboratory

ATF Forensic Science Laboratories

The FBI Crime Laboratory

Problems in Crime Laboratories

CRIME LABORATORIES

There are more than 400 federal, state, and local **crime laboratories** in the United States. The oldest crime laboratory in the United States was established in 1923. Fifty-five percent of the labs were established between 1968 and 1978, just after Supreme Court decisions limited police interrogations and while funds were available from the now defunct Law Enforcement Assistance Administration. Seventy-nine percent of the laboratories are within public safety and law-enforcement agencies; the remainder is distributed among medical examiners' offices, prosecutors' offices, scientific and health agencies, and other private and public institutions.[3]

Most crime laboratories have developed in response to a particular need in a community or region. The areas of scientific concentration in particular laboratories are based on those needs and also on the interests and skills of the people available. Not all crime laboratories have the same capabilities, owing to the availability of resources and the fact that some laboratories tend to emphasize and build up expertise in particular areas. The manner of collection of some types of physical evidence varies according to the type of test procedures the laboratory applies. Therefore, police investigators must familiarize themselves with the capabilities of the crime laboratories supporting their jurisdictions, as well as with the requirements of the national forensic science laboratories.[4]

As can be expected, almost all laboratories originated or were expanded to examine drugs (and, more recently, DNA), but the percentage of crime laboratories with the capability to examine other categories of physical evidence varies from 5% to 81%. In an effort to overcome some of the problems caused by varying specializations and concerns, and because of the absence of agreement on what should be the purpose, function, and services of crime laboratories, the **American Society of Crime Laboratory Directors (ASCLD)** was formed (Figure 8-1). This organization is a nonprofit professional society of more than 400 crime laboratory directors, managers, and supervisors from the United States and 17 other countries who have backgrounds as biologists, chemists, document examiners, physicists, toxicologists, and law-enforcement officers. The ASCLD is devoted to the improvement of crime laboratory operations through sound management practices. Its purpose is to foster common professional interests, management practices, information, and communication among its members and to promote, encourage, and maintain the highest standards of practice for crime laboratories. To carry out its purpose, ASCLD has established two additional entities.[5]

ASCLD/LAB, the crime laboratory accreditation program, is a voluntary program in which any crime laboratory may participate to demonstrate that its management, operations, personnel, procedures, instruments, physical plant, security, and personnel safety procedures meet certain standards. At the federal level, the ATF labora-

▶**FIGURE 8-1 ASCLD**
The ASCLD organization is dedicated to providing excellence in forensic science analysis through leadership in the management of crime laboratories; see *www.ascld.org.*
(Courtesy American Society of Crime Laboratory Directors)

AMERICAN SOCIETY OF CRIME LABORATORY DIRECTORS

"Excellence Through Leadership in Forensic Science Management"

tory system was the first to be accredited, and, the FBI laboratory, perhaps the most comprehensive crime laboratory in the world, received its accreditation a few years ago. This is not to imply that a laboratory is inadequate or untrustworthy if it chooses not to undertake this voluntary accreditation process.[6] Accreditation can be very time-consuming and expensive.

The National Forensic Science Technology Center (NFSTC) was established by ASCLD in 1995 and began operating in 1996. Its two primary functions are to help crime laboratories prepare for accreditation, especially laboratories whose primary focus is on DNA analysis, and to offer continuing education programs for crime laboratory personnel, including the support of college and university degree programs.[7]

THE MORGUE

One type of crime lab often forgotten is the morgue. A **morgue** is not just a place that houses the bodies of deceased persons; it is the critical element of the forensic process as the place where cause of death is determined. Experienced forensic pathologists conduct autopsies and analyze body fluids, tissues, and organs to produce information useful in an investigation when cause of death is questionable or when death has been caused by something other than a known disease.

DIGITAL CRIME LABS

As our society has become increasingly reliant on computers and the exchange of digital information, police have addressed the collection of the digital evidence through specialized crime laboratories staffed with highly trained technicians. Although many of the digital crime labs servicing the needs of local law enforcement have been federally operated by the FBI or the U.S. Secret Service, today most large police agencies also have digital forensics laboratories to help recover deleted or damaged files, restore hard drives, and collect digital information from almost any type of electronic device (for example, personal computers, laptops, cell phones, MP3 devices, iPods, digital cameras and camcorders, and PDAs (personal digital assistants). There are also 16 FBI-operated Regional Computer Forensic Labs (RCFL) throughout the United States that attempt to combine federal and local law-enforcement efforts in a more efficient and uniform manner in finding, extracting, and storing digital evidence and presenting it in court.[8]

There are three primary purposes for digital crime labs:

1. Examine and collect relevant digital evidence that may exist on personal computers in support of a crime. This activity is often associated with organized crime investigations involving vice, gambling, and drug trafficking. For instance, some of the most notorious vice cases involving U.S. Congressmen have developed from

examining seized computers in the brothels of high-paid madams. In a similar manner, narcotics officers have long used digital crime labs to discover patterns of contacts in large racketeering cases derived from e-mails sent from one courier to the next, supported by illegal payments and purchases involving off-shore accounts. More recently, police investigators have started seizing personal computers at the scenes of more traditional crimes. The following case study provides an insight into this methodology:

Ohio's Miami Valley Regional Computer Forensics Lab assisted the FBI Columbus Cybercrimes Task Force in the investigation of Michael Highman, 43, a middle-school teacher and boys' basketball coach at an area school. Highman was identified by the FBI as a user of a peer-to-peer sharing program through which pictures and videos could be downloaded on the Internet by other users. A search warrant was issued for Highman's home, and during their search investigators found a number of hidden computer storage devices. A hard drive was even concealed in his basement ceiling. The RCFL combed through Highman's electronic files and discovered nearly 200,000 images and videos of teenage boys engaged in various sexual acts. Most of the victims were between the ages of 14 and 17 and were depicted in sexual poses or engaging in sexual acts with other teenagers or older men. Highman's peer-to-peer capabilities allowed him to share his files and download additional pictures 24 hours a day. Particularly disturbing to parents was the finding that Highman had been photographing his basketball players shirtless and storing the files in his home. As a result of the work by these digital laboratories, Highman pleaded guilty and was sentenced to over 11 years in jail and 10 years of supervised release thereafter. Highman will have to register as a sex offender for the rest of his life. The ability of the digital forensics lab to find, extract, and preserve the evidence in this case ensured that Highman's network of child pornography can count no further victims.

2. Digital crime labs are also instrumental in securing evidence that directly involve computer crimes such as money laundering, possessing child pornography, embezzlement, fraud, and identity theft. In these cases, the computer and other devices become instruments of the crime, and police technicians and investigators work closely to analyze digital information as evidence of crime (Figure 8-2). (For more information relating to the computer as an instrument of the crime, refer to Chapter 17, "Computer Crime.")

▲ **FIGURE 8-2** **Digital crime lab**
A computer hard drive can provide vital evidence in some criminal cases. Computer crime technicians analyze digital evidence that may support everything from a murder case to a terrorist attack. (© Kim Kulish/Corbis)

3. Police crime labs have also been instrumental in preventing and investigating terrorist attacks in the United States. In fact, the USA PATRIOT Act (2001) was instrumental in developing federal and local efforts in establishing digital crime labs to investigate suspected terrorist activities on our homeland. The threat of terrorist attacks on the Internet aimed at destroying the critical infrastructure of our country poses a significant risk. Digital crime labs are often involved in potential or real "cyber terrorism" attacks that include everything from defacing governmental websites and spreading malicious viruses to thwarting attempts to take over air traffic control systems and damage major energy and telecommunication systems. (Again, refer to Chapter 17 for a more detailed description of crimes involving computers.)

EXPECTATIONS

It is not unusual to find situations in which investigators not acquainted with the services of the crime laboratory expect too much from scientific analysis. Popular culture has become a burden to bear for crime labs that are expected to run DNA tests or match ballistics evidence on a moment's notice, as their television counterparts on *CSI* do. Investigators may also expect the crime laboratory to provide a solution in every criminal case for this or other reasons. When investigators do not receive answers to the questions they pose through the submission of physical evidence, they are not only disappointed but more than occasionally also reluctant to use the technical assistance of the laboratory again.

To some extent, investigators must be selective in collecting and preserving evidence that they believe can be profitably submitted for scientific analysis to a crime laboratory. Always keep in mind that the laboratory was never intended to replace a complete field investigation. The function of the laboratory is to support the investigator and the primary line units of the police agency. The laboratory is sometimes capable of lightening the burden of the investigator, but it can never completely assume that burden. Too often, personnel collect evidence at the scene, send it to the laboratory, and then allow the investigation to stall until the laboratory report is received, expecting the laboratory to come up with some magical solution. This is an unrealistic expectation and largely results because the investigator does not understand what is and is not evidence subject to laboratory examination. The analysis of evidence can be no better than the samples submitted. The investigator therefore has a vital role to play in the success of laboratory examinations. James Osterburg, another criminalistics leader, summarizes why there is underutilization or total neglect of crime laboratories. What he said in 1968 is still largely true:

1. Lack of knowledge about how the laboratory can aid the criminal investigator.
2. Unfamiliarity with the more esoteric varieties of clue material, resulting in evidence not being preserved for examination.
3. Failure to collect physical evidence. This may be caused by a fear of cross-examination on some technical, legal, or scientific requirement that may be overlooked. It may be due to inadequate training or experience or to the overcautiousness of field investigators and the fear of destroying evidence.
4. Overrepresentation of laboratory capabilities.
5. Inconvenience to the investigator when there is no local laboratory available or backlogs are so great as to prohibit timely reports of laboratory results.[9]

This list is accurate and complete. The second and fourth points are especially important. If investigators do not know how the most minute or insignificant looking item can be processed at a properly equipped laboratory, critical pieces of material go uncollected, unprocessed, and unused in substantiating guilt or innocence. In addition, if the capabilities of a crime laboratory are overrepresented so that investigators, uniformed officers, prosecutors, and judges all believe it can produce results that it, in fact, cannot produce, these people eventually will underuse the laboratory. Too often scientists fail to keep justice personnel informed of the state of the art in forensic work.[10]

The laboratory can be an extremely valuable investigative tool if the field investigator uses it intelligently and understands its capabilities and limitations. The investigator must also assume responsibility for providing the laboratory with evidence that is properly collected, marked, and preserved so that laboratory analysis, to the effective limits of present technology, can be successful.[11]

MEASURES OF CRIME LABORATORY EFFECTIVENESS

After two years of listening to sworn testimony, independent research and investigative work, the Committee on Identifying the Needs of the Forensic Sciences Community at the National Academy of Sciences (NAS) issued a report (February 18, 2009) entitled, "Strengthening Forensic Science in the United States: A Path Forward."[12] The congressionally mandated report found that serious deficiencies in the nation's forensic science system existed. It called for significant reforms and new research focusing on the *effectiveness* of crime laboratories. Among the findings and recommendations discussed in the report were these:

- Rigorous and mandatory certification programs for forensic scientist are currently lacking, as are strong standards and protocols for analyzing and reporting on evidence.
- There is an absence of uniform, mandatory accreditation programs for crime laboratories and a gross shortage of adequate training and continuing education for laboratory practitioners; hence, some are accredited as with the ASCLD certification (previously mentioned), but others are not. The NAS report recommends that all crime laboratories should be *mandated* to seek accreditation which includes defined and documented levels of training and education for scientists and forensic specialists.
- There is a lack of autonomy and independence of crime laboratories; as a result, crime laboratories and police agencies should be fiscally and administratively separated. Crime labs should have strong and independent leadership away from any criminal justice agency.
- Many forensic science and crime laboratories are seriously underfunded, understaffed, and have no effective oversight; hence, special funding at both the state and federal level should ensure professional standards for personnel working within crime labs and enhance independent and evidence-based approaches to forensic science findings.
- The broader research community generally is not engaged in conducting research relevant to advancing the forensic science disciplines; thus, resulting court testimony from the forensic sciences is often flawed and unclear admitted through a case-by-case basis. Court testimony should be grounded in science. The committee concluded that two criteria should guide the admission of forensic evidence and testimony in court: the extent to which the forensic science discipline is founded on a reliable scientific methodology that lets it accurately analyze evidence and report findings (such as noted in fingerprinting and DNA analysis) and the extent to which the discipline relies on human interpretation that could be tainted by error, bias, or the absence of sound procedures and performance standards.

In addition to the findings and recommendations listed above, the NAS report found that there was no unified strategy for developing a forensic science research plan across agencies. In other words, state and federal agencies often had their own crime lab that not only duplicated effort and work but also produced relatively shoddy and untimely findings. The NAS report has had a significant and far-reaching ramification impacting the measures of crime lab effectiveness, including the traditional criteria of quality, proximity and timeliness as reflected in the following discussion.[13]

QUALITY

Quality is judged largely on the technical capabilities of the laboratory and the abilities of the personnel who staff the laboratory.

The technical capabilities of the scientific community affect how fully laboratories answer the questions posed by investigators. Although technical advances are developing rapidly, there are still limits on what science can do in analyzing and individualizing evidence. Unfortunately, because of these inherent technological limitations, crime laboratories may not receive the needed resources to expand or even deliver basic services.

Budget considerations largely determine the level of services that a crime laboratory can deliver. A lack of understanding of the extent to which efficient crime laboratory programs can contribute to the effectiveness of a law-enforcement agency has led many administrators to channel financial resources into more traditional kinds of law-enforcement operations.

"The most important resource in any crime laboratory is the scientific staff. Without an adequately trained, competent staff, the best organized and equipped laboratory will not be efficient."[14] Historically, there has been a shortage of qualified personnel with scientific backgrounds interested in working in a criminalistics laboratory. Many who are qualified shun police laboratory work, particularly on a local level, because private industry can offer much more attractive salaries.[15]

PROXIMITY

It is understood, if not accepted, that most law-enforcement agencies cannot afford to staff and maintain a crime laboratory (Figure 8-3). In light of this fact, however, police agencies that desire and will use the facilities of a crime laboratory should not be denied the opportunity to have such services at their disposal. Experience indicates that police investigators rarely seek laboratory and controlled substance verifications. One study showed that for every four requests cleared by a crime lab, one request went unworked by the end of a year's time.[19] Issues with funding, particularly in a struggling economy have left many labs understaffed, much to the chagrin of investigators and private citizens. Low staffing ratios, combined with the length of time it takes for processing or examining evidence, certainly affects timeliness. In one case, a DNA match in Montgomery County, Maryland, gave prosecutors the evidence that they needed to clear a violent rape from 1993. However, the laboratory was so backlogged that they were unable to process the detailed analysis of the match in time for trial. The suspect walked free as the state was forced to drop their case.[20] Notably, in 2010, a large proportion of the grant awards given by the National Institute of Justice were earmarked for "forensics, DNA, backlog reduction."

RESPONDING TO THE NATIONAL ACADEMIES OF SCIENCE (NAS) REPORT

The NAS report was sponsored by the National Institute of Justice at the request of Congress. It was authored by some of the nation's foremost scientists with expertise in physics, chemistry, biology, engineering, statistics, medicine, law and forensics, and was profoundly critical of forensic science and crime labs across the country. Millions of dollars have been spent on new programs and projects in an effort to dramatically increase the effectiveness of crime labs. For instance, the relatively new National Forensic Science Technology Center (NFSTC) originally developed in 1995 through a partnership with the American Society of Crime Laboratory Directors (ASCLD), has vaulted to national prominence to address training and accreditation needs. Some of their recent projects include:

- Quality documents program
- Laboratory auditing and accreditation computer-based workshops
- DNA laboratory auditing program
- The development of the Forensic Technologies Center of Excellence to include the National Forensic Science Technology Center, Marshall University Forensic Science Center, National Clearinghouse for Science, Technology and the Law, National Center for Forensic Science, and the Midwest Forensics Resource Center
- Various training programs on biological screening, crime scene investigation, pattern evidence, tire track and ten print, trace evidence, homicide investigation, and medical examiner/coroner death investigation

In addition to training and technical assistance, the NFSTC maintains several important data centers for forensic science. Originally developed in 2008 and launched in 2009, the National Missing and Unidentified Persons System (NamUs) is a publicly accessible, online system featuring searchable information for missing and unidentified cases nationally. (Refer to Chapter 7 for more discussion on NamUs.) Also founded in 2008, the Forensic Information Data Exchange (FIDEX) attempts to address the NAS report critical of a fragmented and non-coordinated forensic effort between criminal justice agencies and crime labs. FIDEX facilitates the sharing of information among forensic, investigative, evidentiary, prosecutors, law-enforcement agencies, crime laboratories, and the courts. And finally, the Forensic Innovation Center (FIC) developed in 2010 focuses on redefining forensic intelligence services through training team solutions and forensic knowledge partnerships.[21]

ADMISSIBILITY OF EXAMINATION RESULTS

In 1923, a federal court rendered a decision in the case of **Frye** v. **United States** that ruled inadmissible the results of a "deception test," an early version of the polygraph. The decision established a standard which provided that, for the results of a scientific technique to be admissible, the technique must be sufficiently established to have gained general acceptance in its particular field.[22]

Half a century later, the federal **rules of evidence** were adopted, which provide that if scientific, technical, or other specialized knowledge will help the trier of fact understand the evidence or determine a fact in issue, such evidence is admissible. The federal rules of evidence do not apply to the states, and several circuits continued to follow *Frye* rather than the federal rules. In 1993 the U.S. Supreme Court decided the case of **Daubert** v. **Merrell Dow Pharmaceuticals, Inc.** In that case, the Court said that the "general-acceptance" test of *Frye* is not part of the federal rules and, in fact, was superseded by the rules' adoption. The Court went on to say that the trial judge must make a preliminary assessment of whether the testimony of an expert provides an underlying reasoning or methodology that is scientifically valid and can properly be applied to the facts of the case. Many considerations will bear on the inquiry, including whether the theory or technique in question can be (and has been) tested, whether it has been subjected to peer review and publication, its known or potential error rate, the existence and maintenance of standards controlling its operation, and whether it has attracted widespread acceptance within a relevant scientific community. The Court went on to say that the inquiry is a flexible one and that its focus must be solely on principles and methodology, not on conclusions that they generate.[23]

Although *Daubert* applies only to cases in federal courts, a number of states have adopted the *Daubert* standard. Consequently, the application of *Daubert*, and its aftermath, has presented a challenge to crime laboratories to ensure that the standards imposed by the Court are followed in forensic examinations so that expert testimony and the results of examinations by crime laboratory personnel will be admissible, in both state and federal courts. In the most recent test of the *Daubert* standard, the 3rd Circuit Court of Appeals held in *United States* v. *Mitchell* that testimony be rigorously tested and excluded if compliance with requirements for ensuring accuracy in its application cannot be demonstrated.[24] (This case is discussed again later in this chapter.)

TECHNOLOGIES

The speed at which technological advances with forensic applications are developing, expanding, and evolving makes their description immediately obsolete. Computerization has increased speed and reliability of many of the processes formerly manually performed (Figure 8-5). Computer software is available to identify and track serial killers; produce aging progression, facial imaging, and other data to aid in the search for missing children; analyze hair to improve the detection of drug abuse, particularly after a long period of time has elapsed since the use of specified drugs; highlight fingerprints that were previously unrecognizable or undetectable on smooth surfaces with the use of laser technology; and digitally enhance photographs.

The critical role that investigative and forensic sciences play in the U.S. justice system, as well as the attorney general's interest in the rightful conviction of criminals and the exoneration of innocent persons, prompted a significant investment in improving efforts in these areas. This has been accomplished through management efforts of the Investigative and Forensic Sciences Division of the National Institute of Justice (NIJ) within the Office of Justice Programs (OJB) in the U.S. Department of Justice. The work has been coordinated with other bureaus in OJB and with the Federal Bureau of Investigation, the Drug Enforcement Agency, the Bureau of Alcohol, Tobacco, Firearms, and Explosives, the U.S. Secret Service, and the Departments of Defense, Commerce, and Energy.[25]

The National Institute of Justice has demonstrated the use of teleforensic technology as a means for communicating knowledge from forensic scientists in a crime laboratory to investigators at a crime scene. This joint project with NASA and the New York State Police has explored the use of NASA space technology and other remote sensing technologies for remote crime scene imaging. The main goal of this collaboration is to enable commercially available (and relatively inexpensive) products to transmit real-time, high-quality images and data from a crime scene to a lab where experienced technicians can help to focus and direct the investigation. It is envisioned that this technology will lay the groundwork for a time when forensic scientists can be on the scene of a crime without leaving their own laboratory, allowing them to point investigators to what evidence should be collected and how. The institute is developing a robot that can identify explosives and drugs and can be used to collect evidence at a crime scene. It is also developing a fluorescent imaging tool that will enable investigators to identify fingerprints or biological evidence under natural lighting conditions.[26] Private companies are developing numerous state-of-the-art tools to aid crime scene investigators and crime laboratories, including strong laser-directed light sources that will enhance the investigator's ability to detect and identify evidence.

Among the other forensic science projects in which the NIJ is involved is research to validate a procedure for determining the postmortem interval (the time between death and discovery of a body) by means of entomology; the development and validation of a ballistics-matching technology that uses three-dimensional images of bullets and cartridge cases; and a project with the Royal Canadian Mounted Police that will create a comprehensive firearms identification system database to be made available to law-enforcement agencies on CD-ROM. In addition, the institute is funding development of a computer-assisted procedure for handwriting analysis and comparison and is supporting a project for developing and validating a linguistic method of distinguishing authors of electronically created documents.[27]

The NIJ is heavily involved in many projects that aim to establish standards and protocols for DNA analysis, develop newer, faster, and more accurate DNA testing methods, and ensure that only accurate results are used as evidence in criminal trials.

▲ **FIGURE 8-5**

Computer technology and forensic science

New technologies that combine computer software with sophisticated scientific equipment have become powerful tools for analyzing evidence. (Texas Department of Public Safety, Garland Regional Crime Lab)

DNA ANALYSIS

Advances in technology have helped DNA testing to become an established part of criminal justice procedure. Despite early controversies and challenges by defense attorneys, the admissibility of DNA test results in the courtroom has become routine. In 2005, the last year that data was available as of this writing, crime laboratories in the United States received DNA samples from about 39,000 known- or unknown-subject cases. All 50 states, plus the District of Columbia, required that offenders convicted of certain crimes submit DNA samples. Most required that all felons submit samples.[28] In a 2007 survey, nearly 70% of prosecutors in jurisdictions with populations of more than 500,000 indicated that they used DNA evidence in felony cases. DNA was primarily used in cases involving sexual offenses, followed by a lesser number of murder and manslaughter cases, as well as aggravated assaults.[29]

Questions about the validity and reliability of forensic DNA test methods have been addressed, and for the most part validity and reliability are established. As a result of DNA testing, traditional blood testing and saliva testing have been rendered obsolete, because DNA is found in these substances and, in fact, is found in all body tissues and fluids.

Deoxyribonucleic acid (DNA) consists of molecules that carry the body's genetic information and establish each person as separate and distinct. Until recently, DNA was found primarily within the nuclei of cells in the chromosomes. DNA can now be extracted and processed from blood, tissue, spermatozoa, bone marrow, hair roots, saliva, skin cells, urine, feces, and a host of other biological specimens, all of which may be found at crime scenes. DNA has been recovered from fingerprints, cigarette butts, drinking cups, and hatbands and other articles of clothing.

DNA is generally found in cells that have a nucleus, hence the name **nuclear DNA.** However, some biological cells do not have nuclei, such as those forming fingernails, hair shafts, and teeth. What those cells do have is a more primitive form of genetic coding called **mitochondrial DNA (mtDNA),** found in the mitochondria, which are in the body of the cell. When a sperm and an egg join at conception, the new individual gets half of his or her nuclear genetic information from each parent. Conversely, mitochondrial DNA is inherited only from the mother. At conception, all of the new person's mitochondria come from the mother. Since mitochondrial DNA is passed directly through maternal relatives, it serves as a perfect identity marker for those relatives.[30] Indeed, the mitochondrial-DNA sequencing technique was originally developed by anthropologists to help trace human ancestors.

Identifying and Collecting DNA at a Crime Scene

DNA evidence may be found and collected from virtually everywhere at a crime scene, and only a few cells can be sufficient to obtain useful DNA information. DNA does more than just identify the source of the sample; it can place a specific person at a crime scene, refute a claim of self-defense, disprove a claimed alibi, and put a weapon in a suspect's hand. Consequently, the more an investigator knows about how DNA can be used, the more powerful a tool it becomes.[31]

Because samples of DNA are easily contaminated, extreme care should be taken while collecting samples. Several precautions are offered to maintain the integrity of the sample and the analysis:

- As discussed in Chapter 4, collecting biological DNA evidence in the field requires special considerations. The standard recommendation for collecting biological evidence is not to remove the stain from an object but rather to collect the object with the stain, provided that the stain can be adequately protected from contamination. If the entire object cannot be collected, then the next best way to gather such evidence is to remove the stain by cutting it out (for example, from a piece of carpet or clothing). On occasions when it is impossible to collect a stain by cutting it from the object, the two preferred methods of collection are (1) to use a dampened cotton swab (with distilled water) to collect the stain or (2) to use a clean instrument such as a razor blade to scrape the stain into a clean paper bindle. In both cases, the samples should be placed in a clean paper bag and allowed to air dry.[32]
- Wear gloves and change them often.
- If the sample is not completely air dried, it can be dried in the laboratory using a drying hood. Make sure the evidence is properly marked and the table below the drying hood is clean from contamination.
- Use disposable instruments, or clean instruments thoroughly before and after handling each sample.
- Use enough sample to optimize the chance of getting a clear result; however, consideration must be given to leaving a sufficient amount of sample so that a second test can be conducted by the defense. Avoid touching any area where it is believed DNA may exist.
- Avoid touching areas where the sample may exist or be placed. Avoid talking, sneezing, or coughing over evidence. Use physical face barrier protections whenever possible. Avoid touching your face, nose, and mouth when handling evidence and conducting analysis.
- Return evidence to new paper bags or envelopes. Label and store in the evidence room. Do not use plastic bags, and do not use staples to seal bags or envelopes.[33]
- For long-term storage, keep biological evidence in the freezer.[34]

DNA Technologies

In 1985 Alec Jeffreys and his colleagues in England first used DNA in a criminal case. Shortly thereafter, DNA evidence began making appearances in trials in the United States. Initially, DNA analysis required a fairly large sample, and the manual processing technique, called Restriction Fragment Length Polymorphism (RFLP), took up to 14 weeks, on average, to produce results. The RFLP system is slow but produces good results. Technological advancements have led to a polymerase chain reaction (PCR), which takes small samples of DNA and reproduces as many copies as are needed for adequate analysis. Short tandem repeats (STRs), which are even smaller pieces of the DNA helix (ladder), can be reproduced using PCR to generate multiple copies in an instrument called a *thermocycle*. With the PCR-STR process, it takes about 24 hours to extract DNA from an evidentiary sample and only 2 to 3 hours to type the DNA using automation. It works well on degraded samples and on analysis of old cases.[35]

Contamination

Just as contamination is an issue in the collection and packaging of evidence containing DNA, it is a very big issue in the handling of DNA during extraction and examination. It is also an issue that can affect the admissibility of, and credibility given to, DNA evidence in court. Coughing or sneezing while handling DNA evidence can cause contamination.

Population-Genetics Statistics

The effectiveness of DNA evidence in court depends on the ability of a witness to explain the probability that no other person, except an identical twin, has the same DNA type as that discovered on a crime scene sample that identically matches the DNA type of the defendant. Thus, the question is this: is it possible to individualize the identity of a person on the basis of an analysis of his or her DNA? The answer is yes and maybe. Although there are a number of ways geneticists can calculate the probability that no other person has the same genetic chart or "footprint" as the defendant, the question often arises as to what database of individuals is being used to calculate the probability (Figure 8-6). For example, if a Hispanic person is the defendant, would the probability that there would be another person with the same DNA sequence be any greater if the database used to compare DNA consisted of only Hispanics? Is this the fair way to determine probability? This is a simplified example of some of the issues being examined. In the end, the statistical probability derived by any method of calculation is an estimate.

Data Banking and CODIS

Today, all U.S. jurisdictions have legislation requiring the data banking of DNA evidence of convicted offenders. In some jurisdictions, DNA can be collected only from offenders convicted of sex-related crimes and homicides.

(1)

(2)

(3)

▲ **FIGURE 8-6   From blood sample to DNA "footprint"**
(1) Human biological evidence such as saliva, urine, semen, or blood is collected at the scene on cotton swabs, (2) the sample is then separated and blotted, and then (3) placed within the DNA Analyzer to determine the specific pattern or "footprint" of the sample. The electronic "footprints" are then digitally stored for comparative purposes, possibly against the DNA of a suspect, in the future. (Courtesy Utah Department of Public Safety, Bureau of Forensic Services)

In others, legislation has been expanded to allow for the collection of DNA specimens from all convicted offenders. This development has dramatically increased the workload of laboratories that are processing the material to establish the data banks.

In addition to individual-jurisdiction data banking, there is a national investigation support database, developed by the FBI, called the Combined DNA Index System (CODIS). CODIS is used in the national, state, and local index-system networks to link typing results from unresolved crimes with cases in multiple jurisdictions or persons convicted of offenses specified in the data-banking laws passed by the jurisdictions. By alerting investigators to similarities among unsolved crimes, CODIS can aid in apprehending perpetrators who commit a series of crimes. As of May 2007, the database contained over 4.5 million convicted-offender profiles and more than 177,000 unknown forensic profiles found at crime scenes.[36]

Today, DNA analysis is used for a variety of forensic purposes, from identifying victims of mass disasters (such as 9/11 and Hurricane Katrina) to tracing a person's ancestry. Each state collects a DNA sample and fingerprints from serious offenders such as persons convicted of rape and murder, but a few states have extended this practice to all arrestees, not just those successfully prosecuted for violent crimes. California, Florida, Louisiana, Texas, and Virginia are the five states with such legislative provision, and there are others focusing more on child predators and offenders associated with crimes against children.[37]

Standards, Testing, Research, and Developments

Laboratory accreditation by the ASCLD's accreditation board in all areas of forensic science requires that quality-assurance measures be in place at the laboratory. Quality-assurance standards have been developed for DNA analysis by the FBI's DNA Advisory Board. The National Institute of Standards and Technology has tested these performance standards for the various analysis techniques discussed earlier. The National Institute of Justice supported the development of criteria for external DNA proficiency training.

The NIJ is also supporting a five-year effort to fund research on, and develop technological enhancements to, the use of DNA in the criminal justice system. Projects include DNA chip technology that will make it possible to have portable DNA analysis equipment for use at crime scenes; mass spectrometry that offers great improvements in sample processing speed and throughput; and statistical modeling that facilitates producing acceptable statistical probabilities for use in court.[38]

New developments in DNA technologies now allow forensic scientists to produce genetic profiles from a mere six cells worth of genetic material. New "high-sensitivity" labs are now able to use DNA testing to solve crimes heretofore reserved for violent crimes such as homicide, rape, and assault where significant amounts of biological

evidence (for example, blood, hair, semen, saliva) were present. The first such lab, started in 2004 in New York City, concentrates on solving routine property crimes such as burglary, auto theft, and larceny. The concept behind "high-sensitivity" labs focuses on **low copy number DNA samples** (or samples that have fewer than 150 cells of genetic material) that result from minutia evidence (for instance, skin cells left on a smudged fingerprint, saliva traces on a cigarette butt, or perspiration droplets left on a window). The first use of such evidence came in 1999, when low-number DNA samples found on a weapon and other objects handled by a suspect helped solve a murder case being investigated by the Royal Canadian Mounted Police. Of course, the practice has become controversial, because no national standard for tests on such a small sample exists. Further, the admissibility in court of low copy number DNA analysis has not been tested. Yet, the potential for solving a wide range of crimes exists with this new technology, if not as the primary evidence against a suspect but perhaps even as a supporting part of the prosecutor's case.[39]

Familial or Kinship DNA Searches

As technology advances, so does the use of DNA. More recently, forensic investigators have begun using a practice called **"familial DNA searches,"** or **"DNA kinship searches,"** in investigating crimes. A familial DNA search is conducted when a DNA sample collected from a crime does not match any of the samples in the database. If this occurs, scientists can expand the search to see if the database contains any samples with similar patterns to the sample collected from the crime. Although each person's DNA is individually unique to that individual, family members will have similar DNA profiles. By expanding the search, forensic scientists are hoping that a relative to the potential suspect is in the system. The odds of finding a relative are high considering there are over three million DNA samples in U.S. state and federal databases and that a survey conducted by the U.S. Department of Justice found that 46% of jail inmates reported that they have at least one close relative who has been incarcerated.[40]

The use of familial DNA searches could have a huge impact on the justice system. If there are no known suspects for an offense, investigators will run any DNA samples collected from the scene through CODIS in hopes that the potential suspect is not in the system. Matches found this way are commonly called "cold hits." To date, there have been 30,000 cold hits using CODIS. If kinship DNA searches were used, the number of cold hits would surely increase. Forensic scientists claim that in a familial DNA search a parent/child relationship would be identified at the first lead 62% of the time, and 99% of the time the hit would be in the first 100 leads.[41]

Not everyone supports the use of familial DNA searches. Opponents believe DNA kinship searches cast suspicion on innocent family members who happen to be related to someone in the system.[42] Plus there is the concern of misuse by law-enforcement officials. A familial

DNA search often results in multiple hits, and forensic scientists state that it is the responsibility of the investigators to follow the leads with the highest degree of shared DNA makeup (those more likely to be a close relationship to the potential suspect). Others are concerned that the success of kinship DNA searches could lead to the creation of a universal or national database containing every citizen's DNA and fingerprints.[43]

Case Studies in Familial DNA

In 2000 Welsh police reopened the murder case of Lynette White. White had been fatally stabbed in 1988, and the case had gone unsolved for 15 years. In 2000 the police caught a break after reexamining the crime scene and finding blood spots on a skirting board that had been missed in the 1988 investigation. No exact matches were made when the DNA sample taken from the blood spots was run through the national database, but the system did find a similar DNA profile in the system. Both the sample from the crime scene and the sample in the system contained a rare form of a gene. The sample belonged to a 14-year-old boy who obviously could not be a suspect, considering that the crime took place six years before he was born. What police did have was a lead. There was a good possibility that the offender was related to the young man. After interviewing and taking DNA samples from the boy's family, police were able to make an exact DNA match to the boy's paternal uncle, Jeffrey Gafoor, who later confessed to killing White.[44]

On the morning of August 10, 1984, Deborah Sykes was abducted on her way to work. The 25-year-old woman was raped, sodomized, and stabbed to death. Police later arrested and charged Darryl Hunt, then 19, with Sykes's murder. Hunt claimed he was innocent, but he was sentenced to life in prison. Later, in 1990 and in 1994, DNA tests from semen found on the victim's body did not match Hunt's DNA (at the time of his trial, these more reliable tests were not available). In both 1990 and 1994, law-enforcement officials ignored these new findings. Eventually, further investigations of the DNA did find a close match to a man already in the system. Following this lead, police discovered that this man's brother, Willard Brown, had once attacked a woman not far from the place where Sykes had been killed. In December of 2003, when confronted with the DNA evidence, Willard confessed to murdering Sykes. That February, Darryl Hunt was released from prison after spending close to two decades incarcerated for a crime he did not commit.[45]

Successes

Even though DNA may be collected from a crime scene, it may not be submitted to a laboratory for a variety of reasons. Something may prevent further investigation on the case, or the DNA may not be needed to resolve the case. The backlogs and slow turnaround times previously discussed may also hinder investigations, but despite this, DNA evidence has proved to be a huge boon to the justice system by identifying and confirming a suspect, and by clearing or excluding others who may have been suspects.

For instance, a woman informed the FBI that she had overheard a man talking on a pay phone. The man said that he had killed a woman and buried her in the woods of a local park reserve. The local police were notified, and they located the badly decomposed skeletal remains of a person but could not find the victim's teeth. Since the medical examiner could not visually identify the person or use dental records for identification, she sent the remains to the FBI laboratory, where examiners removed DNA from the victim's bones and performed mitochondrial-DNA analysis. The results were compared to the DNA of missing persons in a national database. Law-enforcement authorities were able to identify the victim and later convicted her killer—the man on the pay phone.[46] Another example involved a threatening letter that was sent to a newspaper editor. The FBI swabbed the envelope flap and recovered some saliva cells, which were then typed using a DNA marker. The result was compared to a known suspect and was found to match.[47]

DNA can be extracted and analyzed from specimens that may be years or even decades old. In a case involving Kirk Bloodworth, who was found guilty of sexually assaulting and murdering a young girl, the verdict was based on an anonymous tip, identification from a police artist's sketch, eyewitness statements, and other evidence. He was later retried and again found guilty. But in 1993, more than eight years after his arrest, prosecutors compared DNA evidence from the victim's clothing to Bloodworth's DNA and found that the two did not match. He was subsequently released and then pardoned.[48]

THE INNOCENCE PROJECT

The Innocence Project, founded in 1992, is a nonprofit legal organization founded for the purpose of exonerating wrongfully convicted people through DNA testing. The use of DNA testing has forever changed the criminal justice system.[49] Before the use of DNA, forensic evidence relied on the comparison of hairs, particles, fibers, and blood types. As discussed in Chapter 4, blood types were determined from collected bodily fluids at a crime scene and compared with a potential suspect. Samples that were the same blood type suggested that the suspect *might be* the offender; however, conclusive statements indicating that the suspect *definitely* was the offender were not possible. As one would think, the practice of comparative blood typing is now considered outdated and has been replaced with DNA analysis. In the past five years, significant problems have arisen with the microscopic examination and comparison of hairs, fibers, and other microscopic evidence primarily because of the lack of sufficient reliability and the frequency of erroneous results.[50] The Innocence Project is especially interested in cases in which the defendant was convicted using what they consider "unreliable methods" and in cases in which the evidence was misrepresented or could have been subject to DNA analysis.

In recent years, the federal and some state governments have begun to allow incarcerated individuals who claim they are innocent to have access to DNA testing. In 2004 the federal Justice for All Act was created, which grants federal inmates access to DNA testing, and provides funding to similar state programs. By the end of 2010, 48 states had enacted legislation that permits inmates access to DNA testing. There are only two states that do not have legislation focusing on retesting of DNA evidence: Oklahoma and Massachusetts.[51]

Despite these improvements in legislative action and DNA technological access, there are still significant flaws in the process:

- Some courts will not consider newly discovered evidence *after* trial.
- Most of the new legislation fails to include adequate safeguards for the preservation of DNA evidence in the future.
- Several states do not allow individuals to appeal denied petitions for testing; therefore, the decision to retest is left to the appellate judges.
- A number of states fail to require full, fair, and prompt proceedings once a DNA testing petition has been filed, allowing the potentially innocent to languish interminably in prison.[52]

A Postconviction DNA Case

In the early morning hours of July 25, 1985, in Garland, Texas, a woman woke up to see a man standing over her bed with a knife. He then raped her and left. As he was leaving, the woman followed him to the patio door and believed she had gotten a good look at her attacker. She described her assailant as a young, white male, around 5'8", 140 pounds, blond, slim, very tan, and wearing beige pants and no shirt. The police suspected David Pope, but the victim was unable to identify him in a photographic line up. She did, however, pick him in a live lineup a month later. She also identified Pope in court as the man who raped her.

Evidence used against Pope in court included a knife found in the defendant's vehicle that resembled a knife stolen from the victim's house and a "voice print analysis" that matched Pope's voice to messages the attacker had left on the victim's answering machine in the weeks following the attack (voice print analysis is no longer used by the courts, because of reliability issues). Pope represented himself during the punishment phase of his trial and proclaimed his innocence. He stated that he had lived in the same apartment complex as the victim until the month before the attack, when he had been evicted. In the month of the attack, he had been living in his car on the apartment complex's property. He was convicted in 1986 for aggravated sexual assault and was sentenced to 45 years in prison.

In January 1999, an anonymous call to the Dallas County District Attorney's Office supported Pope's claim of innocence. The case was reopened, and the rape kit was submitted for DNA testing. The results not only proved that Pope was innocent, but the sample matched another person already convicted and serving time for rape. Pope was granted a pardon on February 2, 2001, *after* he had served 15 years.

Exonerated from Death Row

In 2007 Curtis Edward McCarty was exonerated after spending 21 years on death row in Oklahoma (Figure 8-7). He had been convicted of murdering and raping a woman in 1985. District Court Judge Twyla Mason Gray dismissed the charges after ruling that the evidence used to convict McCarty had been tainted by the questionable testimony of former police chemist Joyce Gilchrist. In her original notes, Gilchrist stated that the hairs and other biological evidence did not match McCarty; later she changed her notes, and in two trials Gilchrist testified that McCarty could have been the killer. In both trials he was found guilty and sentenced to death. The defense requested that the hairs be retested, but subsequently the hairs were lost.

▲ **FIGURE 8-7** **DNA errors**

Ex-police chemist Joyce Gilchrist stated that she always based her opinion on scientific findings and that she felt comfortable with her conclusions and testimony given to the court. Unfortunately, internal documents indicated otherwise. (*Left:* © AP Photo/Bernhard Grossruck, *right:* © AP Photo/Oklahoma Dept. of Corrections)

A judge has said that Gilchrist either destroyed or "lost" the evidence intentionally. In recent years, DNA has also proven that another person had raped the victim, not McCarty. McCarty is the 124th person to be exonerated from death row in the United States.[53]

Automated Fingerprint Identification System (AFIS)

In the mid-1970s in San Francisco, Miriam Slamovich, a concentration camp survivor, was shot point-blank in the face. She died a month later. On the bedroom window, her killer left a full, perfect fingerprint that became the object of thousands of hours of manual fingerprint comparisons over a 10-year period. When San Francisco installed an **Automated Fingerprint Identification System (AFIS),** the latent print from the Slamovich case was the first search made, and a hit was recorded in less than 6 minutes. The killer was in custody the same day.[54]

In August 1991, two pieces of paper allegedly handled by an unknown suspect in a Jacksonville, Florida, sexual-assault case were submitted to the Florida Department of Law Enforcement regional crime lab for analysis. A number of latent prints were developed on the paper and searched in the Automated Fingerprint Identification System without success. The unidentified latent prints were entered into the AFIS Unsolved Latent Fingerprint File (ULF) so that they could be searched against incoming fingerprint cards from current arrests throughout the state. In April 1994, an individual was arrested for auto theft and released. The fingerprint card taken at the time of the arrest was submitted to the department and searched against the ULF. On May 16, 1994, as a result of the reverse search (current fingerprint cards searched against the ULF), an identification was made. The offender was eventually located in New York and extradited to Florida. As a result of the AFIS search, blood was drawn from the suspect for comparison with semen samples obtained from the victim at the time of the offense almost three years earlier. There was a DNA match. In April 1995, the offender pled guilty to the sexual assault and was sentenced to 10 years in prison.[55]

Traditionally, fingerprints have been classified, filed, and searched according to the Henry Classification System. Technical searches of newly fingerprinted persons, conducted to determine if they have any prior criminal record, are labor-intensive but have been fairly productive. However, searches of latent fingerprints collected from crime scenes against a Henry system file have been so labor-intensive and unproductive that some jurisdictions don't even attempt them. Certainly, the larger the agency, the greater the problem.

In the early 1970s, the FBI and the National Bureau of Standards conducted feasibility research for establishing an automated fingerprint identification process. After a successful pilot study, the computers hit the market, and one of the most beneficial high-tech tools for law enforcement use in this century became a reality.[56]

AFIS allows law-enforcement agencies to conduct comparisons of applicant and suspect fingerprints with literally thousands or millions of file prints in a matter of minutes. A manual search of this nature would take hundreds of hours with little hope of success. The heart of AFIS technology is the ability of the computer equipment to scan and digitize fingerprints by reading spacing and ridge patterns and translating them into the appropriate computer language coding. The computer is capable of making extremely fine distinctions among prints, lending greater accuracy and reliability to the system.

The computer can map 90 or more minutia points (ridge endings, bifurcations, directions, and contours) for each finger. This number is high enough to individualize a fingerprint and distinguish it from all others. Latent prints normally do not have 90 minutia points, but matches usually can be made with as few as 15 or 20 minutia points. One agency reported a hit on 8 minutia points.

Technicians can computer-enhance fingerprints when preparing them for a search. This process enables an experienced technician to fill in missing or blurred portions of print fragments or to correct for breaks in patterns or ridges caused by burns or scars.

As noted, the computer translates patterns into mathematical computer codes. Thus, the computer is not comparing images of a suspect's prints against images of known prints; rather, it is conducting a mathematical search that can compare a subject print against file prints at a rate of up to 600 prints per second. Search time varies depending on such factors as preparation time, demographic data that are entered to limit the prints required to be searched, the size of the file, and the number of key factors, or matchers, being used to seek a match. A latent print can be searched against a file of 500,000 prints in about half an hour.

Although the accuracy of the AFIS system is 98% to 100%, this does not mean that the computer makes positive matches that frequently. In fact, the system never makes a final decision on identity. The system produces a list of possibles, called a *candidate list*. It is from this list that further determinations are made by a qualified fingerprint examiner.

The computer uses a scoring system that assigns points to each criterion used in the match. The technician sets a threshold score above which a hit is fairly well assured. The technician also sets the size of the candidate list. If any of the scores are high above the threshold, a hit may be likely. If all the scores on the candidate list are low, a hit is unlikely. Policy of the agency may dictate the placement of the threshold, thus limiting or enlarging the number of candidates. Time constraints and resources may be controlling factors in these determinations.

AFIS makes no final decisions on identity. A technician must make the final verification as to whether the system has obtained a hit. The computer assists but does not replace the fingerprint expert.

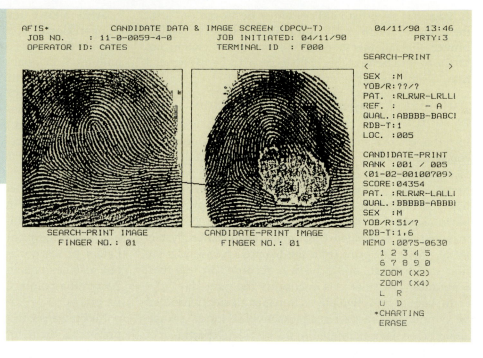

▶**Figure 8-8**

AFIS fingerprint comparison

This is an actual AFIS print. On the left is a file print several years old. On the right is a latent print left at the scene of a burglary. Even though a new scar is seen on the fingerprint on the right, AFIS was still able to match the prints. (Courtesy Dallas Police Department)

AFIS has two major duties. First is performing the functions of classifying, searching, and matching prints. Second is the storage and retrieval of fingerprint data. Data are stored on optical disks, thereby permitting side-by-side comparisons of search prints and file prints. Such comparisons are useful for verifying the data found in an AFIS search (Figure 8-8).[57]

In July 1999, law-enforcement agencies began to have access to the FBI's **Integrated Automated Fingerprint Identification System (IAFIS),** a national online fingerprint and criminal-history database with identification and response capabilities. IAFIS consists of three integrated segments: AFIS, the Interstate Identification Index (III), and Identification Tasking and Networking (ITN).

Here is how IAFIS works. A local agency must have a live-scan fingerprint terminal. If it does, it can scan the prints of a person who is arrested and electronically transmit the prints and mug shots, along with personal information about the arrestee, to the state's law-enforcement network for a fingerprint check. The same electronic prints and personal information are transmitted to the FBI fingerprint repository maintained by the Criminal Justice Information System (CJIS) Division in Clarksburg, West Virginia.

IAFIS is the largest biometric database in existence, housing 66 million fingerprints and criminal histories for subjects, plus 25 million civil prints. Information on tattoos, scars, and other physical characteristics is also stored in this massive database, which can handle 162,000 fingerprint submissions daily. Electronic criminal fingerprint submissions can be processed in 10 minutes, whereas electronic civil submissions are processed within an hour and 12 minutes.[58]

After going through several quality control checks, the information is run against those 66 million fingerprint records. If a match is found, it is verified by an examiner who manually compares the prints. If no match is found, the prints are then run through the AFIS system. Potential matches there are also examined for accuracy.

If no match is found in either the subject search or the fingerprint search, the record is added to the appropriate databases, an FBI identification number is assigned, and the submitting agency is notified of the search results and the assigned number.[59]

NEXT GENERATION IDENTIFICATION (NGI) PROGRAM

In 2010 the FBI launched a new, web-based platform to its special wanted persons database known as RISC-Repository for Individuals of Special Concern. This database houses information on suspected as well as wanted terrorists and organized criminals. The new program, known as Next Generation Identification (NGI), is driven by advances in technology that incorporate identification through a variety of biometric features unique to each individual. For instance, NGI not only scans IAFIS fingerprints on a known or wanted suspect, but also may check other biometric data collected on that person to include voice prints, palm prints, iris measurements, facial structure, or even an enhanced photo of an identifying tattoo (Figure 8-9). The primary purpose of the NGI program is to reduce error in the identification of suspects and individuals, as well as quickly and securely identify known suspects that may pose special risks.

▲ **FIGURE 8-9** **Next Generation Identification (NGI) program**
The FBI's new program that incorporates a variety of biometric data (other than just fingerprints) on known suspects, including palm prints, voice data, iris measurements, and facial structure. (For more information, *visit www.fbi.gov/about-us/cjis/fingerprints _biometrics/ngi/ngi2.*) **(Courtesy FBI)**

NATIONAL INTEGRATED BALLISTIC INFORMATION NETWORK PROGRAM

A joint program of the Bureau of Alcohol, Tobacco, Firearms, and Explosives (ATF) and the FBI, the **National Integrated Ballistic Information Network (NIBIN)** integrates all the elements of Ceasefire and Brasscatcher (both former ATF programs) and Drugfire (an FBI program) (Figure 8-10).

Just as each fingerprint is different, so a firearm leaves unique identifiable characteristics on expended ammunition. NIBIN compares images of ballistic evidence, both projectiles and casings, obtained from crime scenes and recovered firearms. As new images are entered, the system searches the existing database for possible matches. Hits are confirmed by a firearm examiner.

The system has amassed a large ballistic-image database filled with crime gun data submitted by local, state, and federal agencies throughout the country, and the intelligence information is available to all law-enforcement agencies. Since the inception of the system, partner agencies have achieved over 2,200 hits.[60]

◄ **FIGURE 8-10** **NIBIN system**
Just as individual fingerprints differ, each firearm leaves different, unique characteristics on expended ammunition. The national integrated ballistic information system network, developed by ATF and the FBI, compares images of ballistic evidence obtained at crime scenes to recovered firearms. Matches or "hits" are confirmed by a firearms examiner in the lab.

HANDLING EVIDENCE IN THE LABORATORY

HUMAN FACTORS

In handling evidentiary materials, laboratory personnel—scientists and technicians alike—have always been cautious not to disturb or ruin the viability of the materials for any possible examination that would later prove to be useful. Today, because of concerns over the transmission of hepatitis and the AIDS virus, the handling of evidence is of even greater concern.

Although a few laboratories may autoclave specimens, such sterilization with heat may tend to decrease the usefulness of the specimen for analysis purposes. Most laboratories, including the FBI, are merely extra careful in handling evidence involving tissue or body fluids. The procedure followed normally is to ask the agency sending the specimen for any factual information available on the subject so that a determination can be made as to whether the evidence was obtained from a person who may have been infected. In addition, scientists and technicians are instructed to keep their work areas clean, to clean those areas between conducting examinations, and to change and clean lab coats and gloves frequently.

INSTRUMENTAL ANALYSIS

The kinds of evidence subject to laboratory examinations are many and varied. For laboratory purposes, examinations generally fall into the following categories: chemical examinations, biological examinations, physical examinations, personal identification, firearm identification, documentary examinations, and photography.

In a textbook of this nature it is not practical to present a detailed discussion of the technical intricacies of various scientific instruments. However, it is appropriate to acquaint readers with some of the capabilities of instruments used in the scientific analysis of evidence. Table 8-1 presents some of the more sophisticated equipment currently being used in full-service crime laboratories. It excludes the more obvious or technical examination methods, such as many chemical analyses, fingerprint identification, firearm identification, physical and chemical documentary examinations, photographic techniques and equipment, microscopy, and DNA analysis; some of these methods were discussed earlier (Figure 8-11).

ATF FORENSIC SCIENCE LABORATORIES

The Bureau of Alcohol, Tobacco, and Firearms (ATF) of the U.S. Department of the Justice maintains five forensic science laboratories. The ATF National Laboratory was created by Congress in 1886. The ATF laboratories, in addition to analyzing alcohol and tobacco samples, conduct forensic examinations in support of the bureau's explosives, bombing and arson, and illegal-firearm-trafficking investigations, along with major case investigations of state and local authorities. In 2009 the ATF laboratories processed forensic examinations for 3,553 cases and imaged 187,283 bullets and casings for ballistics evidence.[61]

The laboratories hold the distinction of being the first federal laboratory system accredited by the ASCLD.[62] The majority of the examinations conducted by the laboratories involve chemical and physical examinations of explosives, firearms, and arson evidence, as well as the document, tool-mark, and latent-fingerprint examinations associated with those investigations.

The forensic laboratories are staffed by over 130 employees, most of whom are chemists, physical scientists, document analysts, latent-print specialists, and firearm and tool-mark examiners. The remainder are evidence technicians and clerical personnel.

Evidence collected at crime scenes of suspected arsons is examined to identify accelerants, incendiaries, and incendiary-device components. Evidence collected at explosion scenes is examined to identify explosives used, blasting caps, leg wires, fuses, timing mechanisms, energy sources, containers, wires, tapes, and various other component parts used to make the bomb. The laboratory system maintains liaisons with explosive manufacturers, who provide exemplars of new explosives products on the market.

Comparative trace-evidence examinations are conducted on materials including tapes, wires, glass, metals, soil, hair, paint, fibers, ink, paper, and wood to determine whether the materials could have a common origin and thereby associate a suspect with a crime.

Questioned-document examinations are conducted to identify handwriting on firearm transaction forms. In addition, examinations are performed to identify typewriters, copy machines, and cigarette tax stamps. Attempts are also made to decipher indented and obliterated writings.

The laboratories also perform a full range of fingerprint, firearm, and tool-mark examinations in support of agency investigations.

Firearm examinations involve primarily serial-number restoration, determination of the operability of weapons, comparison of metals in sawed-off barrels, and determination of the possible common origin of silencers seized from different suspects or locations (Figure 8-12). Gunshot-residue tests are conducted in shootings that involve law-enforcement officers. In addition, special tests to evaluate the performance of ammunition and weapons are occasionally done.

Tool-mark examinations generally involve evidence associated with bombings and arson. This includes examination of cut wires, torn tapes, drill holes, pipe

TABLE 8-1	Instrumental Analysis in the Crime Lab	
NAME OF INSTRUMENT	**PRIMARY USE**	**ADVANTAGES & WEAKNESSES**
Light Microscopy	Stereomicroscopes, polarizing microscopes, and comparison microscopes are widely used in trace evidence analysis.	Provides search and comparison of samples under magnification.
SEM—Scanning Electron Microscope	Based on principles similar to a light microscope; however, uses a stream of electrons to search for and view minute elements or samples.	Provides a detailed 3-D black & white image of the sample viewed; expensive.
Emission Spectrograph	Identification of metals and elements (e.g., sodium, tin, iron, copper) from the light emitted when each element is burned. Hence, rapid analysis from unknown substances can be developed; detection of traces of metallic impurities in residues such as oils and glasses.	Complete analysis of an unknown substance through one operation; requires only a relatively small sample for analysis.
Mass Spectrometer	Identifies unknown samples by creating profiles of the individual compounds and molecules of a substance.	Often used in expediting DNA analysis; sample is destroyed during analysis.
Visible Spectrophotometer	Compares dyes and coloring agents in materials such as hair, cloth, paint, and glass. Records the percentages of each color in a substance or sample.	Eliminates personal error in color comparisons; requires only a relatively small sample with a rapid analysis.
Infrared Spectrophotometer	Primarily identifies and compares inorganic materials such as plastics, rubber, paint, and and other chemical substances through the analysis of infrared energy passing through a substance.	Detects slight differences in the composition molecular arrangement of minute amounts of material.
Atomic Absorption Spectrophotometer	Determines quantitative and proportional concentrations of specific elements in materials through the analysis of a vaporized sample.	Very accurate and sensitive method of determining elemental concentration; relatively economical and rapid procedure.
Gas Chromatograph	(Figure 8-11) Separates and identifies gases or liquids from complex mixtures and solutions; often used to analyze narcotics, paints, plastics, inks, and petroleum-based products such as gas, oil, explosives, and accelerants. Often used in conjunction with the mass spectrometer.	Used in a wide variety of tasks through the analysis of volatile solids, high-boiling point liquids, and gases; sample is destroyed during analysis.
X-Ray Diffraction Spectrophotometer	Identifies and compares unknown crystalline substances through the diffraction of X rays.	Requires only a small amount of sample, and the sample is not consumed in the technique.

wrench marks, saw marks on wood and metal, and numerous other marks made by tools.

The bureau has four National Response Teams that respond to major bombings and arson disasters, nationally and internationally. The teams consist of highly trained investigators, forensic chemists, and explosives technology experts. The teams respond within 24 hours, collect evidence, and complete most laboratory examinations before leaving the crime scene.[63]

THE FBI CRIME LABORATORY

The **FBI Crime Laboratory** is one of the largest and most comprehensive forensic laboratories and is the only full-service forensic laboratory. It was established in 1932. Of importance to the investigator is the fact that the facilities of the FBI laboratory are available without charge to all

▶ **Figure 8-11**
Gas chromatograph
The gas chromatograph is used to separate and identify gases and fluids from complex mixtures and solutions. In criminal investigations, it is often used to analyze organic materials such as narcotics, explosives, and paints. (Courtesy Indiana State Police)

▲ **Figure 8-12**
Forensic examiner conducting firearm examination
In serious violent crimes such as armed robbery and homicide where a handgun is used, the crime lab firearms examiner often plays a major role. Frequently, he/she will be called on to examine recovered firearms in an effort to link suspects or their handguns to a particular crime. (Courtesy Indiana State Police)

state, county, and municipal law-enforcement agencies in the United States.[64] There are, however, some provisos concerning the submission of evidence for examination to the laboratory. The laboratory will not make examinations if any evidence in the case has been or will be subjected to the same type of technical examination by another laboratory or other experts. This policy is designed to eliminate duplication of effort and to ensure that evidence is received in its original condition, thereby allowing laboratory personnel to interpret their findings properly and ensure meaningful testimony and presentation of evidence in subsequent court cases.

To more effectively and efficiently use its current resources, the FBI laboratory has a policy not to accept cases from other crime laboratories that have the capability of conducting the requested examination. If such cases are submitted by other crime laboratories and there are no special circumstances to warrant the submissions, the cases will be returned unopened and unexamined. This policy should not be construed as lessening the FBI laboratory's continuing commitment to the scientific training of state and local crime laboratory personnel, and it does not limit the laboratory's acceptance of cases from other crime laboratories when special circumstances prevail.

Also, the FBI laboratory no longer accepts evidence from state and local law-enforcement agencies regarding property crime investigations unless the cases involve personal injury or the offenses were designed to cause personal injury.

In addition to doing analysis, the FBI furnishes the experts necessary to testify in connection with the results of its examination in either state or federal courts. Again, there is no charge to local law-enforcement agencies for this service.

The laboratory provides a comprehensive array of forensic services. Laboratory personnel conduct microscopic

◄ **FIGURE 8-13**
Forensic examiner conducting examination with a scanning electron microscope
One of the standard instruments in today's crime labs is the electron microscope. Typically, evidence such as hair, fiber, fabric, and rope undergoes microscopic examination in the crime lab. Many criminal investigations have been solved by lab personnel, with the help of an electron microscope, matching these types of physical evidence to materials found in the possession of a suspect.
(Courtesy Indiana State Police)

examinations of hair and fiber, fabric, tape, rope, and wool (Figure 8-13). Chemical examinations are conducted on many substances, often to supplement examinations conducted by other sections. Examinations are conducted on poisons (toxicology), paint, ink, tear gas, dyes, and flash and water-soluble paper, among others.

Mineralogy examinations are conducted on soils and combinations of mineral substances such as safe insulation, concrete, plaster, mortar, glass, ore, abrasives, gems, industrial dusts, and building materials.

Firearm examiners may be asked to determine if firearms are operating properly or to conduct gunpowder shot-pattern tests. Using the same basic principles of firearm examination, the identification of telltale marks left at crime scenes by punches, hammers, axes, pliers, screwdrivers, chisels, wrenches, and other objects can be made. The explosives specialist can analyze fragments of explosives to determine their original composition and possible sources of raw materials.

The metallurgy unit is called on to restore obliterated or altered numbers on such things as firearms, sewing machines, watches, outboard motors, slot machines, automobiles, tools, and other metallic items. Tests can show whether two or more pieces of metal are related, the possible cause of metal separation, and whether production specifications for metals have been met.

Handwriting examiners agree that no two individuals write exactly alike. Even though there may be superficial resemblances in the writing of two or more persons as a result of similar training, the complexity of writing is such that individual peculiarities and characteristics appear. These characteristics can be detected by a document expert, who then can arrive at a scientific opinion.

The FBI laboratory has also developed the ability to conduct forensic examinations on chemical, biological, and nuclear hazards. In 1996 the Hazardous Materials Response Unit was established in response to the threat of terrorism involving chemical, biological, and nuclear weapons (weapons of mass destruction—WMD), and to an expanding caseload of environmental crimes. After the horrific events of September 11, 2001, and the "anthrax cases" that closely followed, the FBI Lab greatly expanded its role in determining biological, chemical, and nuclear agents that may be used by terrorists. The laboratory works closely with the Centers for Disease Control in developing standardized protocols for handling and analyzing suspected WMD materials. As mentioned earlier, the laboratory has also developed the Computer Analysis and Response Team (CART) program, capable of conducting examinations in which information is extracted from magnetic, optical, and similar storage media and converted into a form usable to investigators or prosecutors. The CART team also has an integral role in preventing and investigating acts of sabotage and terrorism against American infrastructure (for example, telecommunications, computer, and transportation systems). Finally, the FBI's laboratory is leading the research and development efforts to improve and expedite DNA analysis methods and is one of the few laboratories conducting mitochondrial-DNA testing.

REFERENCE FILES

To aid examiners in their work, the FBI laboratory in 1932 established what is now one of the largest reference collections for helping solve cases. These files are of two types: standard reference files and collections, which contain known samples of items, generally of manufactured products, and reference files of questioned materials, which are composed of items actually arising from cases worked and which may form the basis for subsequent identification of individuals or their method of operation (MO). Many of these collections and reference files have been computerized to provide better and faster analyses and comparisons.

The Standard Ammunition File contains over 15,000 specimens of domestic and foreign manufacturers' samples. The Firearms Reference Collection contains over 3,500 handguns and 2,000 shoulder weapons and is used for identifying gun parts and locating serial numbers. The Reference Fired Specimen File contains test bullets and cartridge cases from weapons that have been in the laboratory.

The National Automobile Altered Numbers File is composed of selected specimens, including replica plastic impressions of altered vehicle identification numbers (VINs) found on stolen cars, trucks, and heavy equipment. The file helps investigators identify recovered stolen cars and link them with commercialized theft rings nationwide or other FBI-investigated cases. The National Vehicle Identification Number Standard File maintains standards of VIN plates from each factory of the major manufacturers of American automobiles. The file enables laboratory personnel to determine if a submitted VIN plate is authentic. In the event that bogus VIN plates are being prepared in an automobile factory, the factory as well as the particular machine used can be identified.

The Typewriter Standards File consists of original samples of typewriting from numerous styles of type made in this country as well as in foreign countries. The file permits classification of questioned typewriting on the basis of make and model. The Watermark Standards File is an index of watermarks and brands used by paper manufacturers and aids in tracing the source or origin of paper. Original samples of safety paper used for checks are the contents of the Safety Paper Standards File. These can be used to determine manufacturers. The Checkwriter Standards File is a collection of original checkwriter impressions and permits classification of questioned checkwriter impressions as to make and model. As an aid in determining the manufacturers of office copying machines (either photocopy or duplicator), the laboratory maintains the Office Copier Standards File.

The Shoe Print File contains photographs of designs used in soles and heels made by major U.S. manufacturers. The Tire Tread File, including wheelbase and tirestance information, is now in a database against which comparisons can be made. This replaces the blueprints, drawings, and photographs of tire-tread patterns, furnished by tire manufacturers, that used to form the basis of the reference file.

The National Motor Vehicle Certificate of Title File consists of original state motor vehicle certificates of title, manufacturers' certificates of origin, and vehicle-emission stickers. This file also contains photographic copies of fraudulent titles, statements, and stickers. The National Fraudulent Check File contains over 100,000 samples of checks, writings, and other documents. More than half of all checks examined are identified with other material in this file. The Anonymous Letter File consists of photographic copies of kidnap notes and extortion and threatening letters. The Bank Robbery Note File contains photocopies of writings of known bank robbers and holdup notes. The Pornographic Materials File includes pornographic materials submitted to the laboratory; it assists in determining the production and distribution sources of the materials. The Explosive Reference Files contain technical data, known standards of explosive items, and bomb components of commercial and military explosives and improvised explosive devices or homemade bombs.

Other files maintained by the FBI are the Automotive Paint File (which can identify makes and models involved in hit-and-run cases), the Hair and Fiber File, the National Stolen Coin File, Blood Serum Files, Safe Insulation Files, and the National Stolen Art File.

PROBLEMS IN CRIME LABORATORIES

The use of DNA analysis in criminal investigations has forever changed the criminal justice system. The use of DNA not only facilitates more accurate prosecutions in current cases but also supports the reopening of old unsolved, often cold, cases, to be reexamined and potentially solved; it also helps to prove or disprove inmates' claims that they are innocent. Significant legal limitations still apply to the use of DNA as part of a criminal investigation. Further, major concerns relate to the ethics and the training of the individuals who collect, process, and present DNA evidence in court. Human error is unpreventable, but negligence and the falsification of results is unacceptable and undermines the integrity of criminal justice discipline.

A number of forensic labs have fallen under investigation in recent years. For instance, in 2002, forensic lab technicians in New York City were caught "dry-labbing," or reporting results without actually performing any tests. And, in the last three years, there has been documented corruption and lack of supervision in the Houston, Texas, Police Crime Lab, resulting in the DNA section being closed for over two years.[65] Documented problems in Houston included poorly trained staff and intentional contamination of evidence. As a result, 413 cases had to be retested, because the evidence used to obtain convictions in criminal courts may have been flawed. An external investigation revealed that the serology and DNA work performed over a 12-year period (from 1980–1992) was unreliable.

Many of the problems found in crime labs can be traced to two causes: not enough funding and too close a relationship with the police. Underfunding is problematic because across the country many crime labs are backlogged with evidence that needs to be analyzed. The processing of backlogged evidence is sometimes rushed, resulting in human errors or blatant misconduct. The Massachusetts State Crime Lab reported that in mid-2007 it had more than 16,000 cases that needed to be retested and that some of the evidence was from cases as far back as the early 1980s. Even more alarming is the fact that the statute of limitations may have run out on a number of those cases. Having overly close ties to the police can potentially be a drawback, because the analysis of evidence must be objective and impartial. The job of lab technicians is to analyze evidence and present the findings, not necessarily to strengthen the prosecution's case. When the line between the two functions becomes blurred, the result can be an environment conducive to misconduct.

Human and analytical errors made in these laboratories often mean the difference between freedom for the guilty and incarceration of those who are innocent. Therefore, all people concerned must understand the extent of the existing problems within local, state, and federal crime laboratories.

LACK OF TRAINING

Continuing professional development is necessary for forensic scientists to remain current and to advance to an elevated level of expertise and responsibility. They are obligated to remain up to date in their field through specific and continued education and other developmental activities.[66] Unfortunately, few universities present degrees in forensic science, and even fewer provide certification for the operation of specific analytical instruments. Most chemists, biologists, geologists, and physicists prepare themselves for careers in forensic science by training under a person who is an experienced examiner and by studying independently.[67] Few defined or organized programs exist for the profession of forensic science. There are few minimum course requirements in terms of structured courses or core curriculum, since most educational requirements are determined by individual laboratories. In fact, in the last decade the number of forensic science academic programs has declined, and the ones that do exist have such low enrollment that support from universities is limited.[68] This situation is particularly surprising given the public interest in the subject created by the myriad popular crime-scene and forensics-oriented movies and television shows (for example, *Silence of the Lambs, CSI, The Profiler, Cold Case, Forensic Files*). This problem is further compounded by the fact that laboratory analysis and forensics require a rigorous background in the sciences (for instance, biology and chemistry) and not the social or behavioral sciences, where criminology and criminal justice students often study. As a result, many students who are interested in the wider subject matter simply do not have the technical and scientific background to enter the field. For those who are prepared properly, salary and benefits often do not match those in the scientific community, and so well-qualified individuals often choose to enter similar work in the medical or health fields.

Finally, although the formal education that scientists receive provides a foundation for learning and understanding the techniques of forensic science, for the most part, courts rely on additional training and years of experience in order to measure the actual knowledge and ability of the expert. The advancements in technology and sophisticated software used in crime laboratories across the country have created a gap between the skills of scientists and their ability to perform their tasks properly.[69] Many are not updated and trained to know how to use the new equipment appropriately, and as a result, many cases become flawed owing to the lack of training and contemporary knowledge.

LACK OF ACCREDITATION

Crime labs must identify a system for establishing its credentials as a forensic laboratory. As mentioned earlier, the primary credentialing organization is the American Society of Crime Laboratory Directors (ASCLD). Whenever a lab applies for accreditation, it has to meet certain requirements, which include the development and publication of a quality-control manual, a quality-assurance manual, a lab-testing protocol, and a program for proficiency testing. *Quality control* refers to the way a product, such as a DNA-typing result, is measured to make certain the product meets a specific standard of quality. *Quality assurance* refers to the actions taken by the laboratory to monitor and document the quality of work being performed. A *lab-testing protocol* is a technical manual that includes validation studies performed by the lab itself. Such a protocol sets forth standardized methodologies for performing routine tests in the laboratory. Last, *proficiency testing* monitors lab workers individually, as well as the laboratories as institutions. These tests determine whether or not lab workers are performing up to the specified standards of the institution.[70] Yet the fundamental problem with forensic science in crime labs is that, unlike clinical labs, forensic labs are unregulated by the government, allowing them to set their own standards. Forensic scientists do not have to establish competence by obtaining a license or certification. Therefore, a majority of crime labs do not seek accreditation (with the exception of New York, Texas, and Oklahoma, primarily reacting to a series of scandals within major crime labs within their states). In addition, accreditation rates are low for practicing forensic scientists, even though certification boards for all the major fields of forensics have been in existence for more than a decade.[71] According to ASCLD, of the 455 larger crime labs conducting forensic work, only 255 are accredited. Accreditation can cost a few thousand dollars for small operations and as much as $70,000 for the larger, multilaboratory operations. This price tag does not include the more significant costs associated with implementing new training programs and the equipment needed to meet current standards.[72]

Furthermore, most forensic scientists are not independent experts. About 80% of forensic scientists in North America are affiliated with prosecution or police agencies. Indeed, most forensic scientists work in police laboratories, and many are themselves law-enforcement officers, as are their superiors. This association has been known to create a sense of bias within the courtroom between forensic testimony and prosecution. Since the FBI, the police, and the crime lab have similar missions (to arrest, prosecute, and convict), the chance that forensic scientists' courtroom testimony will be unbiased by any other considerations becomes more unlikely.[73] Hence, accreditation alone does not ensure accurate, unbiased, and/or objective laboratory results. For instance in Oklahoma City, Oklahoma, a police chemist (Ms. Joyce Gilchrist, Figure 8-7) appears to have falsified evidence dating back as far as 1982. An internal police report detailed "compelling circumstantial evidence" that Ms. Gilchrist "either intentionally lost or destroyed" evidence from crime scenes. The most significant misconduct involved the case of a convicted man, sentenced to death for the murder of a police officer's teenage daughter in 1982. As a result, the Oklahoma State Bureau of Investigation and the FBI launched a review of nearly 2,000 cases—focusing first on 12 pending death row convictions and 11 cases in which death sentences had already been carried out. At least three current convictions, including the 1982 murder conviction, were reversed after DNA testing proved that the defendants were not guilty. In overturning the convictions, the Oklahoma Court of Criminal Appeals noted that even though Ms. Gilchrist was a highly educated and well-trained technician, her testimony was "terribly misleading, if not false."[74]

DNA CONTAMINATION

DNA technology can do astonishing things. Not only can DNA be used to identify criminals with amazing accuracy when biological evidence exists, but it can also be used to clear suspects and exonerate persons who have been mistakenly accused or convicted of crimes. However, the current federal, state, and local DNA collection and analysis system needs improvement. Numerous cases have emerged revealing faulty practices of forensic crime lab experts who mishandled DNA tests causing them to become contaminated and unable to be used.

Contamination is a concern for proper preservation of evidence. As we learned in Chapter 4, DNA evidence must be collected and packaged separately in individual containers, and each piece of evidence must be segregated from other evidence.[75] Unfortunately, some forensic scientists have tainted tests with their own DNA, in addition to throwing out evidence swabs, misreading results, fingerprinting the wrong suspect, and even cross contaminating different cases.

Washington's State Patrol crime lab was investigated in 2004 after wrongly accusing and sentencing a man for committing the rape of a 10-year-old girl. The forensic scientist working on the case simply botched the test, accidentally contaminating the child's clothing with DNA from another case he had previously been working on. The investigation revealed that forensic scientists contaminated tests or made other mistakes while handling DNA evidence in at least 23 cases which involved major crimes over the previous three years in that department. They were found to have tainted tests with their own DNA in 8 of the 23 cases and made mistakes in 6 other cases by discarding important evidence and by misreading results.[76] This is not the only such incident. Similar contamination was discovered in a December 2002 audit of the Houston Police Department Crime Lab, which noted analysts' lack of training, insufficient documentation of evidence, and evidence contamination. As a result, the Harris County District Attorney's Office has reviewed over 400 cases involving DNA evidence, and the Houston PD Crime Lab has remained closed.[77]

In 1997 U.S. Department of Justice documents obtained by the National Association of Criminal Defense Lawyers identified several examples of questionable practices in the DNA Unit of the FBI laboratory. These practices included the use of plastic pipettes used to extract DNA that had been dissolved in chloroform. However, chloroform also dissolves plastic pipettes, which could have contaminated the sample. Also, examiners commonly overexposed autoradiographs so that DNA bands appeared as football-shaped rather than as a line. This makes it difficult for an examiner to accurately locate the center of a band in order to analyze it. Some examiners would then move a band by hand for analysis, which could also have resulted in a contaminated misreading.[78]

SENTENCING MISTAKES AND POOR TRAINING

Josiah Sutton was tried and convicted in 1999 for rape. Although prosecutors had little to build the case on, since the victim was the only eyewitness and her recollection was faulty, they were able to get him convicted. Technicians from the Houston police crime laboratory had the rapist's DNA and told the jury that his was a solid match. They sent Sutton to prison to serve a 25-year term. After serving four years, new testing by the Houston crime laboratory showed that the DNA did not match Sutton's. He was released after spending four years of his life behind bars because of a mistake made by forensic examiners in a crime lab. The only reason his DNA was retested stemmed from a state audit and review conducted at the Houston crime laboratory. The audit found that technicians had misinterpreted data, were poorly trained, and kept poor records that did not meet specified levels of acceptance within the laboratory. They found that in most cases, they used up all available evidence, barring defense experts from refuting or verifying their results. They also discovered a leaky roof that had dripped so profusely that dozens of DNA samples of evidence had become contaminated with water.[79] Such mistakes not only harm the validity of evidence in cases, but they also cause citizens to lose confidence in law enforcement and the experts who work in the crime laboratories in their communities.

BACKLOG OF CASES

As previously discussed, public crime laboratories are overwhelmed by backlogs of unanalyzed DNA samples. As a result, these labs may become ill-equipped to handle the increasing arrivals of new DNA evidence and have no space to store the samples. The problems that emerge from the backlogs result in considerable delays in the administration of criminal justice.

Providing exact numbers for the number of backlogged cases in laboratories nationwide is a challenge, mostly because there is no universal definition of a backlog. The National Institute of Justice (NIJ) considers anything more than 30 days old to be backlogged, and by that definition nearly 75% of cases in crime labs would qualify.[80] Crime labs have two types of backlogs: case backlogs, in which DNA or other biological evidence is collected as potential evidence of a crime, and offender/arrestee backlogs, when samples are taken from convicted offenders and arrestees for review and uploaded to the FBI's CODIS system. Evidence that is stored in law-enforcement custody awaiting submission to a laboratory is not considered by NIJ as backlog.

Backlogs in crime labs are a simple function of supply and demand. Labs are simply unable to meet the increased demand for DNA analysis created by the following five factors:[81]

- *Increasing awareness:* Knowledge of the potential of DNA evidence to solve cases has grown exponentially among criminal justice practitioners and the general public alike
- *Property crimes:* The number of DNA submissions for property crimes has skyrocketed, and these types of crime are much more commonplace than violent crimes.
- *Scientific advances:* Advances that make it possible for tiny, trace amounts of DNA samples to be analyzed has led to more requests for DNA testing of guns and steering wheels to determine who may have last handled the object.
- *Cold cases:* Older and unsolved cases from the pre-DNA era are being opened and their samples submitted for testing in the hopes that usable information can be recovered.
- *Post-conviction testing:* Older, pre-DNA cases resulting in a conviction have been reopened so DNA testing can be done. The Innocence Project is a perfect example of this type of demand for testing.

Backlogs at crime laboratories are primarily the result of growing demand and limited resources. Crime laboratory analysts often have to work overtime and on weekends to complete analysis of backlogged cases, especially when the case is considered high profile. The time that it takes to process DNA cases in crime laboratories poses significant delays in many jurisdictions. State crime laboratories take an average of 23.9 weeks to process an unnamed suspect rape kit, and local laboratories average 30.0 weeks to process such tests. The cost to test these rape kits is estimated to be $1,100 per case, not accounting for additional overhead costs.[82]

In addition to problems with backlogging, both state and local labs reported that their main concern for their DNA programs was the lack of personnel. They expressed a need for supplemental funding for additional DNA staff and to increase current salaries to avoid the loss of skilled personnel within their laboratories to other potential employers willing to pay more money. Most labs also reported that although federal funding has played an important role in assisting with backlogged DNA cases, the amount of their overall budget funded through federal sources is minimal. Only 20.5% of state crime laboratories receive 50% or more of their funding from federal sources. Local laboratories receive only 4.5% from federal funding.[83]

Furthermore, postconviction DNA testing resulting in exoneration has caused many state legislatures to impose requirements for the indefinite storage of evidence used in crime convictions, although such requirements frequently become unfunded mandates passed down to local jurisdictions. Indeed, there have been reports of large metropolitan law-enforcement agencies who discarded potential DNA evidence in an attempt to create additional storage space for new evidence.[84] Therefore, evidence that could have possibly helped a victim is now gone forever and useless to future crime investigations.

SCANDALS AND MISTAKES WITHIN THE FBI CRIME LAB: THE MADRID BOMBING CASE

Another widely publicized incident relating to problems within crime labs involves the allegations made in 1995 by Frederic Whitehurst, a former FBI laboratory supervisory special agent who had worked for the lab since 1986. He alleged that over the course of several years, laboratory examiners had improperly testified outside their expertise, presented unacceptable evidence, perjured themselves, fabricated evidence, and failed to follow the appropriate procedures of the laboratory. He also said that he believed that FBI management retaliated against him for making those accusations.[85] Yet changes have been made within the FBI laboratory since Whitehurst blew the whistle on his coworkers. After intense investigation into his accusations, the FBI lab implemented a

▲ FIGURE 8-14   The Madrid bombing case

The FBI Laboratory error in matching the latent print (*left*) as that of Mr. Brandon Mayfield has cast doubt on the integrity of fingerprint evidence. Noting that the error print (*right*) was not rotated and cropped to match the corresponding latent print was a serious mistake that embarrassed the FBI as well as complicated the entire Madrid bombing investigation. (For more information on the technical aspects of this case, see *www.onin.com*.) (*Left:* © AP Photo/Don Ryan)

formal quality assurance plan and has since been accredited by the ASCLD.[86]

However, the most significant blunder to date in any crime lab within the United States occurred in March 2004 with the arrest of Portland, Oregon attorney, Brandon Mayfield. On March 17, 2004, the Spanish National Police provided the FBI with digital, electronically transmitted photographic images of latent fingerprints that were recovered from the plastic bag containing the detonator in the March 11 bombings in Madrid that killed 191 people and injured 2,000 others[87] (Figure 8-14). The FBI Lab in Quantico, Virginia, used the Automated Fingerprint Identification System (AFIS) to search for possible matches to the fingerprints. Mayfield's fingerprints were one of 20 candidates suggested for comparison by the system.[88] At least three FBI fingerprint specialists, including a supervisory agent with over 30 years of experience verified the identification of Mayfield as the suspect from the latent print on the plastic bag. One examiner testified that the latent print was "the left index finger of Mr. Mayfield."[89] It is not known whether the identification process was influenced by information pertaining to Mayfield's conversion to Islam or his activities as a lawyer in defending recent "terrorist" suspects before the match was officially declared.[90] However, what is known is that at some point in March or April, the FBI began "sneak and peak" and electronic surveillance of Mayfield under the Foreign Intelligence Surveillance Act (FISA) and the U.S. PATRIOT Act.[91] According to court documents, FBI agents began their surveillance of Mayfield two weeks after the attacks in Madrid, and, under a provision of the U.S. PATRIOT Act, they entered his home

without his knowledge—but aroused suspicion by bolting the wrong lock on their way out and leaving a footprint on a rug inside the house. During a later raid based on the fingerprint identification, the FBI seized computers, modems, safe deposit boxes, assorted papers, and copies of the Quran.[92]

On May 20, the Spanish National Police reported that they had identified the latent print in question as that of a different individual . . . an Algerian national living in Spain. As the information became conflicted between the two agencies, the FBI sent agents to Spain in order to recover the original latent print. To their surprise, the print had been destroyed.

Four FBI examiners with a combined total of 93 years of experience in latent print science reexamined and reanalyzed the latent print. The examiners concurred that the latent print had multiple separations (that is, it was divided by many lines of demarcation possibly caused by creases in the underlying material, multiple touches by one or more fingers, or both).[93] On the morning of May 24, 2004, utilizing information from this new evaluation by the four examiners, the FBI *reversed* its position on Mayfield and indicated that the print had no value for identification purposes, and Mayfield was subsequently released.

The ensuing investigation revealed that the FBI had originally sent examiners to Spain but that the investigators did not speak Spanish. Further, they never asked to see the original latent print. More problematic, if the print indeed had "no value for identification purposes," how could such a positive and previous identification to Mayfield be developed in the first place? After all, this was an international event with over 190 persons killed that focused on suspected terrorist links to al-Qaeda. It appears that the FBI violated one of the most basic rules of investigation: failing to maintain objectivity during scientific analysis and failing to compare the best evidence to samples found at the scene. Essentially, FBI fingerprint analysts drew much of their attention to Mayfield's past and relied on improper methodology to confirm the identification of a latent print to a suspect. As one expert indicated: "There were many discrepancies . . . and a competent (fingerprint) expert should have seen all the discrepancies."[94] The FBI's contention that the misidentification occurred as a result of problems with the quality of the digital image is in itself an indictment of the poor procedures followed by analysts. If the image was corrupted, then a positive identification should have never been made. Worst of all, this case has far-reaching implications concerning the scientific integrity of fingerprint identification, the acceptance of fingerprint evidence in court, and the scrutiny of crime laboratory personnel.

In a recent case, *United States* v. *Mitchell*,[95] the court concluded that latent fingerprint identification evidence, as produced by the FBI's procedures, met the requirements for admissibility established by *Daubert* v. *Merrell Dow Pharmaceuticals, Inc.* However, the FBI latent print unit's performance in Mayfield's case suggests that, notwithstanding *Mitchell*'s recognition of a valid scientific basis for fingerprint identification, the potential for error in the making of an identification requires that identification testimony be rigorously tested and excluded if compliance with requirements for ensuring accuracy in its application cannot be demonstrated.[96]

CODE OF ETHICS

The findings of forensic scientists are often the critical element in determining the guilt or innocence of an individual. The examination, which is the basis of the findings, must be conducted in accordance with the principles necessary to achieve an unfailing conclusion. Scientists must examine the subject matter as a whole, and their conclusions must be delivered under conditions that support their comprehension and use.

Different codes of ethics for forensic science have been adopted over the years. The American Society of Crime Laboratory Directors, the American Board of Criminalistics, and the Council for the Registration of Forensic Practitioners are all examples of organizations that have incorporated a specific code of ethics for forensic science.[97] An example of a code of ethics for forensic science can be found under the Preamble of the SAFS Ethics Committee, a pharmaceutical research group. It states that there is a requirement for forensic scientists to possess a comprehensible knowledge in the subject matter in which they are investigating. This requires them to have the necessary skills, background knowledge, and

forensic science judgment that can be directly applicable to issues at hand. Also, it is required that scientists conduct examinations in accordance with the principles of the scientific method by using state-of-the-art methodology. In addition, it is required that scientists employ enough safeguards necessary to assure control of the quality of the examination. These safeguards include the preservation of adequate materials to allow for reexamination if necessary and ample documentation to permit a reasonable evaluation of the protocol employed and a confirmation of the accuracy of the findings. Last, it is required that forensic scientists present their comprehensive presentation, whether verbal or written, in language that is understandable to counsel for the client, the court, and the jury.[98]

These ethics codes require competence, quality, training, and integrity on the part of forensic experts and managers working in every crime laboratory across the country. Forensic experts must be competent to take on tasks that are required in the assignments they receive. They are expected to perform their tasks to the best of their abilities, conducting themselves in a trustworthy and honest manner, especially when facing obstacles that may hinder their performance.

Unfortunately, scandal has become commonplace in a realm where science and integrity must be the hallmarks of competency. For example, a publicized report in Washington revealed how a crime lab chemist was caught snorting heroin on the job for months, stealing the drug from evidence he was testing. In addition, a review of two dozen crime lab disciplinary records in the state raised questions about the professionalism of some scientists on the payroll. It was discovered that in the past five years, a lab supervisor was caught viewing pornography on his office computer; another lab manager was fired because he sexually harassed female coworkers; and a DNA analyst was found sleeping on the job.[99] Another example of a lack of ethics focuses on the issue of proficiency tests. Crime lab workers must pass one test every year in each specialty to satisfy voluntary rules set by the American Society of Crime Laboratory Directors' Laboratory Accreditation Board. For instance, a Tacoma lab forensic scientist took a routine proficiency exam in September of 1998, in which his ability to interpret footprint evidence was tested. When accreditation inspectors visited the lab a year later, they could not find any record of the exam. They discovered that the scientist's supervisor had never reviewed the test or realized that the scientist had actually failed to correctly match all the footprints with the correct shoe.[100]

Unfortunately, stories such as these have become commonplace. A number of forensic crime lab examiners have failed to conduct themselves in an ethical manner, and it has become increasingly apparent that these mistakes can lead to even more detrimental problems over time. It is also apparent that justice cannot be served fairly under such circumstances.

KEY TERMS

American Society of Crime Laboratory
     Directors (ASCLD)
Automated Fingerprint Identification
     System (AFIS)
crime laboratory
criminalistics
Daubert v. *Merrell Dow*
     Pharmaceuticals, Inc.

deoxyribonucleic acid (DNA)
familial DNA search (DNA kinship
     search)
FBI Crime Laboratory
forensic science
Frye v. *United States*
Integrated Automated Fingerprint
     Identification System (IAFIS)

kinship DNA searches
low copy number DNA sample
mitochondrial DNA (mtDNA)
morgue
National Integrated Ballistic
     Information Network (NIBIN)
nuclear DNA
rules of evidence

REVIEW QUESTIONS

1. Define *forensic science*. What distinguishes it from criminalistics?
2. What difficulties are caused by an investigator not understanding the capabilities and limitations of crime laboratories?
3. What is the measure of effectiveness of crime laboratories and how do they relate to the 2009 National Academy of Science (NAS) report on forensic science in the United States?
4. What is the most important resource in a crime laboratory?
5. How important is DNA analysis in a criminal investigation?

6. What are AFIS, NIBIN, IAFIS, and CODIS?
7. What are the main areas of responsibility of the ATF laboratories?
8. What limitations are placed on the submission of evidence to the FBI laboratory?
9. What are the primary DNA analysis techniques that have been used since 1985?
10. Distinguish the *Frye* test from the *Daubert* test regarding the admissibility of scientific evidence. What is the importance of these two cases?
14. What are some of the major problems confronting police crime labs?

INTERNET ACTIVITIES

1. Visit the FBI website at *www.fbi.gov* and search for the crime laboratory. What services are provided to law enforcement by the lab? What are the primary missions of the FBI, and how does the crime lab support those missions? What are CART and CIRG? What are the primary forensic examinations performed by the lab? Finally, what is LEO, and how is it employed in reference to sharing forensic information among law-enforcement agencies?
2. Go to *www.crimelynx.com* and search for information about postconviction DNA cases under "Crime Policy Links." What is the most recent estimate of the number of convicted offenders who have been exonerated owing to DNA testing? Under what conditions can an offender request DNA testing?

Who pays for the testing? What occurs if the DNA tests are inconclusive? In your opinion, will the increasing popularity of postconviction DNA testing affect the nature of criminal investigations? Now go to *www.innocenceproject.com* and compare your information with that found on this website. Is there a difference?
3. Visit the Arizona Department of Public Safety Crime Lab at *www.azdps.gov/About/Organization/Technical _Services/Crime* and click on the DPS Crime Lab and Scientific Analysis Video. What qualifications and educational backgrounds are desired to work in a crime lab? What is EMSCOM, and how does it improve the effectiveness of the lab in responding to natural disasters or major terrorist attacks?

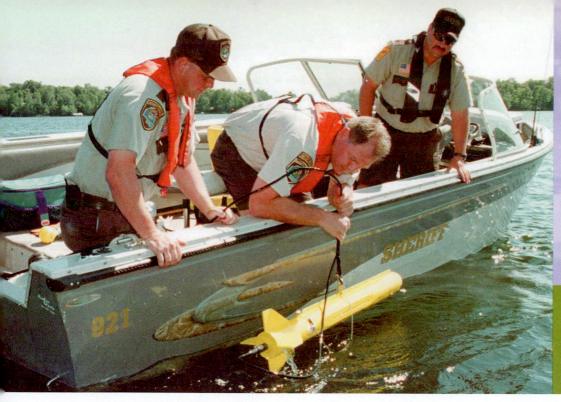

◄ Modern technology can often aid the investigation of accidental or felonious deaths. For example, the underwater search for missing bodies can be facilitated by sonar tracking devices such as the one shown in this photo from Hennepin County, Minnesota, where deputies are using a side-scan sonar unit to locate a body.

(© AP Photo/BrainerdDaily Dispatch, Steve Kohls)

9

INJURY AND DEATH INVESTIGATIONS

CHAPTER OBJECTIVES

1. Name the various legal definitions related to felony assaults and homicides.

2. Discuss the various stages of the medico-legal examination, including the autopsy.

3. Describe the various postmortem changes occurring at the time of death.

4. Recognize the potential evidentiary value of gunshot wounds, incised and stab wounds, lacerations, and defensive wounds.

5. Discuss the role of the forensic entomologist in determining time of death.

6. Identify the characteristics of strangulation wounds.

7. Describe wounds inflicted with a blunt object as opposed to those inflicted with a sharp-edged instrument.

8. Discuss information used by investigators to distinguish between homicides and suicides.

9. Be familiar with the methods and evidence involved in suicides.

10. Discuss the characteristics of various poisons and their associated manifestations.

11. Outline facts that need to be determined in the investigation of fire deaths.

12. Discuss serial murderers, their profiles, myths and misconceptions.

13. Understand the role of the National Center of the Analysis of Violent Crime (NCAVC) and the Violent Criminal Apprehension Program (ViCAP) in serial murder investigations.

The investigation of felonious injuries and criminal homicides can be the most important yet difficult responsibility assigned to a police investigator. First, these crimes are viewed as being among the most serious offenses committed in our society. The seriousness is reflected in all state statutes, which impose severe penalties for acts resulting in the grave bodily injury or death of a human being. Second, in the beginning stages of some homicide investigations, the inability to identify the decedent greatly complicates the investigative process and prevents it from moving forward. In all homicides, questions such as "Who were the victim's enemies?" and "Who would benefit most from the victim's death?" must be answered before any significant progress can be made in the investigation. Estimating the time of death also needs to be done early in the investigation. Third, criminal homicides, in particular, can generate a lot of media attention and public scrutiny for the department. Pressure to solve the crime from both inside and outside the police agency creates added strain on the criminal investigator.

For these cases, in particular, investigators may need to call on the assistance of experts in the scientific and medical fields. Investigators should create working relationships with specialists such as forensic pathologists, toxicologists, entomologists, and botanists, who can all provide useful assistance to the case. In short, the severity of these crimes warrants that investigators use all available resources in their investigations.

THE LAW

The various state statutes contain different names for **felonious assault**—such as aggravated assault, assault with intent to commit murder, and felonious battery—but all have one common legal element, namely, that the assault was committed for the purpose of inflicting severe bodily harm or death. In most such assaults, a deadly weapon is employed.

Police officials and members of the public often use the terms "homicide" and "murder" interchangeably. In fact, murder is only a part of the broad category of homicide, and **homicide** is divided into two broad classifications: nonfelonious homicide and felonious homicide. **Nonfelonious homicides** may be justifiable or excusable. **Justifiable homicide** is the necessary killing of another person in performance of a legal duty or the exercise of a legal right when the slayer was not at fault.

Excusable homicide differs from justifiable homicide in that one who commits an excusable homicide is to some degree at fault but the degree of fault is not enough to constitute a criminal homicide. There are two fundamental types of excusable homicide. The first involves death that results from misadventure. This is similar to what may be termed "accidental" death at the hands of another. **Misadventure** is death occurring during the commission of a lawful or an unlawful act when the slayer has no intent to hurt and there is not criminal negligence. An example of misadventure is the death of a person who runs in front of a moving automobile whose driver is unable to avoid the collision.

The second type of excusable homicide involves death that results from self-defense when the slayer is not totally without fault, such as someone who gets in a sudden brawl and has to kill to preserve his or her life.[1]

Felonious homicides are treated and punished as crimes and typically fall into two categories: murder and manslaughter. **Murder** is defined in common law as the killing of any human being by another with malice aforethought. Most states now provide for varying degrees of murder. **Manslaughter** is a criminal homicide that is committed under circumstances not severe enough to constitute murder but that cannot be classified as either justifiable or excusable homicide.[2]

THE MEDICO-LEGAL EXAMINATION

The **medico-legal examination** brings medical skill to bear on injury and death investigations. The medical specialist frequently called on to assist in such cases is the forensic pathologist. **Forensic pathology,** a subspecialty of pathology, is the study of how and why people die. To become a forensic pathologist, a physician first attends an approved pathology residency program and then attends three years in a strictly anatomic program or five years in a combined anatomic and clinical program. One or two additional years are devoted to studying the pathology of sudden, unexpected, natural death, as well as violent death, in an approved forensic fellowship training program (there are approximately 30 throughout the country). Most programs are centered in major cities that have a large number of deaths from various causes. The most important area of study for a forensic pathologist is death investigation, but some forensic pathology programs also include examination of the living to determine physical and sexual abuse. Physicians specializing in forensic pathology are ordinarily employed by some unit of government and are not in private practice.[3]

THE AUTOPSY

All violent and suspicious deaths require an **autopsy** to determine the time and precise cause of death.[4] The autopsy may also answer the following questions:

- What type of weapon was employed?
- If multiple wounds were inflicted, which wound was fatal?
- How long did the victim live after the injury?
- What position was the victim in at the time of the assault?
- From what direction was the force applied?
- Is there any evidence of a struggle or self-defense?
- Is there any evidence of rape or other sex-related acts?
- Was the deceased under the influence of alcohol or any type of drug?[5] (The actual analysis will be done by the toxicologist.)

Answers to all or even some of these questions increase the possibility of bringing the death investigation to a successful conclusion.

DEAD BODY EVIDENCE CHECKLIST

The following dead body evidence checklist will assist both the investigator and the medical examiner in systematically following all the steps necessary to be certain that no physical evidence is overlooked:

- Thoroughly photograph everything before moving or touching it.
- Collect fragile evidence on the body.
- Remove hair, fingernails and other trace evidence. Use toothpicks to collect evidence that might be under the fingernails if they are short. Place the items in waxed paper, bundle them, and place them in envelopes.
- Brush the head hair and the pubic region (if the body is unclothed). Hold butcher paper under the area being brushed.
- Remove trace evidence from the entire body's skin and clothing, including the face, hands, feet, legs, torso, pubic area, and neck, with Scotch tape or lint rollers. Use only frosted tape.
- Collect samples of pooled blood.
  —Use hemasticks to confirm it is actually blood.
  —Collect control samples (as close to the injured area as possible).
  —Use a cotton swab with one drop of distilled water on it. Place the swab in wax paper loosely, and then place it in an envelope.
- Collect exemplars from the following areas:
  —Environment (vegetation, soil, maggots, other)
  —Residence (carpet fibers, paint, misc. fibers, other)

—Vehicle (carpet fibers, seat fibers, roll the tires, VIN number, wheel base)

—Animals (hairs, bedding)

- Collect blood samples from the victim.
- Swab the bite mark areas.
- Swab the oral cavity.
- Collect exemplar hairs.
- The victim should be fingerprinted even if there is positive proof of identification.
- If circumstances dictate, palm prints and footprints should also be obtained. They may prove useful in matching prints that are later found in the suspect's home, business, car, or other location.
- Collection of the victim's clothing.

—If the clothing is damaged, the investigator should determine whether the damage is related to the assault or was caused by hospital or emergency personnel giving emergency treatment. When a determination is made of the cause of damage, it should be recorded in the investigation report.[6]

POSTMORTEM CHANGES AND TIME OF DEATH

A recurring problem in forensic medicine is the need to fix the time of death within the limits of probability. The longer the interval of time between death and the examination of the body, the wider will be the limits of probability. The longer the postmortem interval, the more likely it is that associated or environmental evidence will furnish more reliable data on which to estimate the time of death than will anatomical changes.[7]

It is necessary to be alert to the possibility that the postmortem interval (the time elapsed from death until discovery and medical examination of the body) may be preceded by a significant survival period (the time from injury or onset of the terminal illness or death). The survival interval is best established by evaluating the types, severity, and number of injuries present and the deceased's response to them, taking into account preexisting natural disease.

Establishing the times of an assault and death has a direct bearing on the legal questions of alibi and opportunity. If the suspect is able to prove that he/she was at some other location when the fatal injury was inflicted, then the suspect has an alibi and innocence is implicit. Conversely, if the time of a lethal assault coincides with the time when the suspect was known to be in the vicinity of the victim, then the suspect clearly had an opportunity to commit the crime.

ESTIMATING TIME OF DEATH

Many physico-chemical changes begin to take place in the body immediately or shortly after death and progress in a fairly orderly fashion until the body is fully decomposed. Each change has its own time factor or rate. The rates of development of postmortem changes are strongly influenced by unpredictable changes within the body and environmental factors. Consequently, the longer the postmortem interval, the wider is the range of estimate as to when the death probably occurred. In other words, the longer the postmortem interval, the less precise is the estimate of the time of death.[8]

ALGOR MORTIS (BODY COOLING)

After death, the body cools from its normal internal temperature of 98.6°F to the surrounding environmental temperature. Many studies have examined this decrease in body temperature, called **algor mortis,** to determine formulas that could predict its consistency. Unfortunately, because of numerous variables, body cooling is an inaccurate method of determining the postmortem interval. In general, however, evaluating a decrease in body temperature is most helpful within the first 10 hours after death. During this time, with a normal body temperature and at an ideal environmental temperature of 70° to 75°F, the body cools at approximately 1.5°F per hour, however the problem with using the 1.5°F-per-hour calculation is based on the assumption that the internal temperature is 98.6°F and the environmental temperature remains at a constant 70°–75°F. If a decedent's body temperature is higher than normal at the time of death because of an infection resulting in a fever, then the body temperature of 98.6°F cannot be used. Furthermore, the outside environment is rarely in the 70°–75°F range, and a body may actually gain heat if an individual expires outdoors during the summer, when temperatures may be greater than 100°F. Conversely, if a person expires in a 25°F environment, rapid cooling takes place.

Nonetheless, if body temperature is measured at a scene, it should be taken by the attending physician on at least two separate occasions before the body is moved. A rectal or liver temperature is the most accurate measurement. The environmental temperature should also be recorded. If these relatively simple procedures are followed, a very crude estimate of the postmortem interval can be made.[9]

Other factors that will affect the rate of cooling include:

- *The size of the body.* The heavier the physique and the greater the obesity of the body, the slower the heat loss.[10]
- *Clothing and coverings.* These insulate the body from the environment and therefore cooling is slower. It has been estimated that cooling of a naked body is half again as fast as when clothed.[11]
- *Movement and humidity of the air.* Air movement accelerates cooling by promoting convection and even the slightest sustained air movement is significant. Cooling is said to be more rapid in a humid rather than a dry atmosphere, because moist air is a better conductor of heat.

- *Immersion in water.* A cadaver cools more rapidly in water than in air, because water is a far better conductor of heat. For a given environmental temperature, cooling in still water is about twice as fast as in air and in flowing water about three times as fast.[12]

OCULAR CHANGES

In **ocular change,** the cornea becomes cloudy within 2 hours or less if the deceased dies with eyes open. If eyes are closed, it will be 12–24 hours. On the third postmortem day, the corneas become opaque. When gases begin to collect in the body, the eyes may bulge out of the eye socket, but when advanced decomposition sets in, the eyes become endopthalmic, or retracted into the socket.[13]

STOMACH CONTENTS

After a light meal, food will leave the stomach in 1–2 hours, a medium meal 3–4 hours, and a very heavy meal, 4–6 hours. Examination of the stomach contents may provide information not only about the time of death but also about what the person had eaten just before dying.[14]

RIGOR MORTIS

After death, the muscles of the body initially become flaccid. Within 1 to 3 hours they become increasingly rigid, and the joints freeze—a condition called **rigor mortis** (or postmortem rigidity or rigor) (Figure 9-1).

Rigor mortis is affected by body temperature and metabolic rate: the higher the body temperature, the more lactic acid produced and the quicker rigor occurs. For example, a person dying with pneumonia and a fever will develop rigor sooner than a person with normal body temperature. Similarly, if a person's muscles were involved in strenuous physical activity just before death, rigor develops much more quickly. The process is also retarded in cooler environmental temperatures and accelerated in warmer ones.

All muscles of the body begin to stiffen at the same time after death. However, muscle groups may appear to stiffen at different rates because of their different sizes. For example, stiffness is apparent sooner in the jaw than in the knees. Thus, an examiner must check to see if joints are movable in the jaws, arms, and legs.

A body is said to be in complete rigor when the jaw, elbow, and knee joints are immovable. This takes approximately 10–15 hours at an environmental temperature of 70°–75°F. A body remains rigid for 24–36 hours before the muscles begin to relax, apparently in the same order they stiffened.

A body remains rigid until rigor passes or until a joint is physically moved and rigor is broken. Consequently, in addition to indicating an approximate time of death, body position in full rigor can indicate whether or not a body has been moved after death.[15]

LIVOR MORTIS

Livor mortis (lividity, postmortem hypostasis) is a reddish purple coloration in dependent areas of the body due to accumulation of blood in the small vessels of the dependent areas secondary to gravity (Figure 9-2). Postmortem lividity is occasionally misinterpreted as bruising by people unfamiliar with this phenomenon.

Dependent areas resting against a firm surface will appear pale in contrast to the surrounding livor mortis,

◄**FIGURE 9-1   Rigor mortis**
This individual, who died of natural causes, had been dead for approximately 10 hours. Note the arms in the upright position—the result of rigor mortis. The body will remain rigid for 24–36 hours before the muscles begin to relax.

▶**FIGURE 9-2** **Livor mortis**
Livor mortis (lividity, postmortem hypostasis) is a reddish purple coloration in dependent areas of the body due to accumulation of blood in the small vessels of the dependent areas secondary to gravity. It is usually evident within 30 minutes to 2 hours after death, typically reaching its maximum coloration at 8–12 hours. Postmortem lividity is occasionally misinterpreted as bruising by people unfamiliar with this phenomenon.

owing to compression of the vessels in this area, which prevents the accumulation of blood. Thus, areas supporting the weight of the body, for example, the shoulder blades, buttocks, and calves in individuals lying on their backs, show no livor mortis but appear as pale or blanched areas. Tight clothing, for example, such as a brassiere, corset, or belt, which compresses soft tissues, may collapse the vessels, also producing pale areas.

Livor mortis is usually evident within 30 minutes to 2 hours after death. In individuals dying a slow, lingering death with terminal cardiac failure, livor mortis may actually appear antemortem (prior to death). Livor mortis develops gradually, usually reaching its maximum coloration at 8–12 hours. At about this time, it is said to become "fixed." Before becoming fixed, livor mortis will shift if the body is moved. Thus, if an individual dies lying on his/her back, livor mortis develops posteriorly (that is, on the back). If one turns the body on its face, blood will drain to the anterior surface of the body, now the dependent aspect. Livor mortis becomes "fixed" when shifting or drainage of blood no longer occurs, or when blood leaks out of the vessels into the surrounding soft tissue owing to hemolysis and breakdown of the vessels. Fixation can occur before 8–12 hours if decomposition is accelerated, or at 24–36 hours if it is delayed by cool temperatures. Thus, the statement that livor mortis becomes fixed at 8–12 hours is really just a vague generalization. That livor mortis is not fixed can be demonstrated by applying pressure to a dependent discolored area and noting the subsequent blanching at the point of pressure.

Although livor mortis may be confused with bruising, bruising is rarely confused with livor mortis. Application of pressure to an area of bruising will not cause blanching. An incision into an area of contusion or bruising shows diffuse hemorrhage into the soft tissue. In contrast, an incision into an area of livor mortis reveals the blood to be confined to vessels, without

blood in the soft tissue. Livor mortis is extremely important for three reasons:

1. When considered with other factors, it may help estimate the time of death.
2. It may indicate that the body has been moved after death. For example, if a body is found face down with lividity on the back, this would indicate the body has been moved. For this reason, the exact measurements, sketches, and photographs must be made at the scene before and while the body is being recovered.
3. The coloration of the skin may indicate the cause of death, as in the case of carbon monoxide poisoning, certain forms of cyanide poisoning, or extreme cold, when the color of the lividity is not purplish but cherry red.[16]

CADAVERIC SPASM

Cadaveric spasm refers to a kind of instant rigor mortis discussed earlier in this chapter. The same physiological changes occur except at a more accelerated rate. Cadaveric spasm is also commonly called "a death grip." It typically involves a decedent's hand tightly clutching a weapon, usually a gun, a knife, or a razor at the moment of death[17] (Figure 9-3).

DECOMPOSITION

In general, as rigor passes, skin first turns green at the abdomen. As discoloration spreads to the rest of the trunk, the body begins to swell because of bacterial methane-gas formation. The bacteria are normal inhabitants of the body. They proliferate after death, and their overgrowth is promoted in warm weather and retarded in cold weather.

◄ FIGURE 9-3   Cadaveric spasm
Cadaveric spasm is a term used to describe the instantaneous tightening of a hand or other body part at the time of death. Note the weapon clutched tightly in the left hand of this victim of a self-inflicted gunshot wound to the head.

◄ FIGURE 9-4
Advanced stages of decomposition
The individual shown here had been dead approximately two weeks in an unheated, unventilated room. Note the extreme discoloration and swelling of the facial area as well as the abdomen.

The different rates and types of **decomposition** a body undergoes depend on the environment (Figure 9-4). Bodies buried in earth, submerged in water, left in the hot sun, or placed in a cool basement appear different after the same postmortem interval. When a body is bloated, epidermal sloughing and hemoglobin degradation begin. Moreover, as bloating continues, air is forced from the skin. The increased internal pressure, caused by bacterial gas production, forces decomposed blood and body fluids out of body orifices by a process called *purging*. As the body undergoes skeletonization, the rate of tissue deterioration is dependent on environmental temperature. For example, a body exposed to a 100°F environmental temperature may completely decompose to a skeleton within a few weeks. In contrast, a body in a temperature of 65°F may not skeletonize for many months. In general, a body decomposing above ground for a week looks similar to a body that has been under water for two weeks or has been buried for six weeks. This generalization should serve as a reminder that an uncovered or naked body decomposes more rapidly than a covered or clothed one.

After a body is found, it is usually refrigerated until an autopsy is performed or a final disposition is made. Decomposition slows down or ceases if a body is refrigerated. When the body is exposed to room temperature, decomposition occurs rapidly. Recognition of this accelerated decomposition is particularly important if a person dies in a cold environment and is then moved to a warmer one.

Decomposition may not occur evenly throughout the body. For example, decomposition occurs more rapidly in injured areas. If a person is struck on the head and bleeding occurs only in that area, decomposition may be much more advanced on the head than on the remainder of the body. Fly larvae proliferate during summer, spring, and fall in warm, moist areas of the body such as the eyes, nose, and mouth. Larvae are attracted to injured areas, where they feed on exposed blood proteins and cause accelerated decomposition. Owing to the uneven decomposition, it is common to see skeletonization in only part of the body.[18]

FORENSIC ENTOMOLOGY

Entomology is the study of insects, and forensic entomology is the study of the insects associated with a dead body, which is used to determine the elapsed time since death. An analysis of the insects found on a homicide victim by a qualified **forensic entomologist** can also tell the investigators whether the body has been moved from one site to another, if it was disturbed after death, or the position and presence of wound sites, long after they are no longer visible as such to the naked eye. Insects can also be used in drug identification and the determination of the length of time of neglect.[19]

Insects are invariably the first witnesses to a crime, arriving within minutes or even seconds after death. There are two ways to use insects to determine time since death. The first method involves using dipteran (blow fly) larval development, and the second involves using insect succession over time (Figures 9-5 and 9-6).

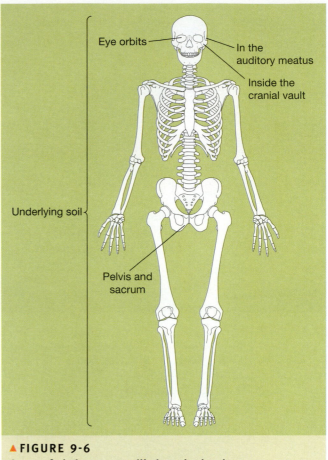

▲ **FIGURE 9-6**
Areas of skeleton most likely to harbor insects

▲ **FIGURE 9-5   Body area from which to collect insects**

The first method is used in the first hours, days, or weeks after death and can determine the time of death accurate to a day or less, or a range of days. The insects used in this method are those that arrive first on the corpse, that is, the calliphoridae or blow flies (diptera). These flies are attracted to a corpse very soon after death. They lay their eggs on the corpse, usually in a wound, if present, or in any of the body's natural orifices (Figure 9-7). Their development follows a set, predictable cycle, and each of these developmental stages takes a set, known time. This time period is based on the availability of food and the temperature. In the case of a human corpse, food availability is not usually a limiting factor. Insects are "cold blooded," so their development is extremely temperature-dependent. Their metabolic rate increases with increased temperature, which results in a faster rate of development, so that the duration of development decreases in a linear manner with increased temperature, and vice versa.

An analysis of the oldest stage of insect on the corpse and the temperature of the region in which the body was discovered allows an entomologist to determine the day or the range of days in which the first insects oviposited, or laid eggs, on the corpse. This determination, in turn,

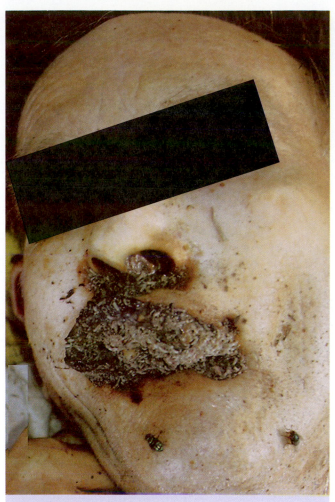

▲ FIGURE 9-7 Fly larvae
This individual had been dead for approximately four days. His body was found in the backyard by neighbors. During this period of time, temperatures had reached into the 90s. Note the fly larvae (maggots) in his nose and mouth.

leads to a day or a range of days during which death occurred. For example, if the oldest insects are seven days old, then the decedent has been dead for at least seven days. This method can be used until the first adults begin to emerge, after which it is not possible to determine which generation is present. Therefore, after a single blow fly generation has been completed, the time of death is determined using the second method, that of insect succession.

The highly decomposed and maggot-infested remains of two women were found in a bushy area. Two species of blow fly were collected, and an analysis of the oldest insect stage, together with data from the local

weather station, indicated they had died more than 11 days before discovery. Reluctant eyewitnesses were later brought forward during the police investigation and confirmed the date of death. The eyewitnesses were also able to identify the killer. However, because the eyewitnesses had not come forward earlier, it was possible the jury might doubt their word. This situation became more probable when two other people came forward saying that they had seen the victims alive and well and shopping in the mall only eight days before their bodies were discovered. This statement conflicted with the date of death identified by the two eyewitnesses and meant that the jury would have to make a subjective decision on who was lying and who was telling the truth. However, in this case, there was also the scientific, entomological evidence, which clearly indicated that the victims had died more than 11 days before discovery. This evidence refuted the testimony of the two shoppers and supported that of the two eyewitnesses. Therefore, the jury believed the earlier eyewitnesses, who were able to identify the killer. He was convicted of two counts of first-degree murder.

The second method of using insects to determine time since death is based on the fact that a human corpse, or any kind of carrion, supports a rapidly changing ecosystem. The body decomposes from the fresh state to dry bones in a matter of weeks or months depending on the geographic region. As the body decomposes, it goes through a predictable sequence of biological, chemical, and physical changes. Each of these changes is attractive to a different group of insects. Some insects, such as the blow flies, prefer to feed on the fresh body. Others prefer the remains a few days after death, while still others prefer the remains when they are dry. Some insects are not attracted to the body itself, but arrive to feed on other insects at the scene. Many species are involved at each decompositional stage, and each group of insects somewhat overlaps the ones adjacent to it. The insects that colonize a body are primarily species of flies (diptera) and beetles (coleoptera).

Therefore, with knowledge of the regional insect fauna and times of carrion colonization, the investigator can analyze the insect assemblage associated with the remains to determine a window of time in which death took place. This method is used when the decedent has been dead from a few weeks up to a year, or in some cases several years after death, with the estimated window of time broadening as time since death increases. It can also be used to indicate the season of death (for example, early summer). A knowledge of insect succession, together with regional, seasonal, habitat, and meteorological variations, is required for this method to be successful.

The partially skeletonized remains of a man were found in a wooded area close to a freeway in early spring. A large number of empty blow fly puparia were discovered with the remains, along with several groups of insects that are commonly later colonizers, including piophilidae and fanniidae, as well as a number of beetle adults and larvae. To analyze sequential insect evidence, the entomologist must have local data for the geographical region, habitat, and season, because there can be a great deal of difference between insect arrival and tenure in one region versus another. The species of insects present in this case indicated a minimum elapsed time since death of two months. However, since the body was found in very early spring, death must have occurred earlier than this. Large numbers of empty blow fly puparia indicated the earlier presence of many blow fly larvae, which would have been present only in warm weather. This fact indicated that death must have occurred before the previous fall, when numerous blow flies would have colonized the remains and gone through an entire life cycle, as evidenced by the empty puparia. It would also have allowed for the later colonizers to arrive by March. The onset of cold weather would have prevented additional blow fly colonization in winter, allowing some flesh to remain uneaten, which explained why the remains were only partially skeletonized. If the remains had not been discovered in early spring, blow flies from the upcoming summer would have completed the skeletonization process. Also, if the deceased had died earlier in the previous year, the body would have been entirely skeletonized before discovery. The insects, therefore, indicated that death had occurred in late summer of the previous year.

▲ **FIGURE 9-8   A bullet penetrating the skin**
The skin is pressed inward, stretched, and perforated in the stretched condition, after which it returns to its original position. The entry opening is smaller than the diameter of the bullet. Immediately around the opening is a contusion ring, because the bullet rubs against this part of the skin and scrapes the external layer of epithelial cells. (Courtesy Nucleus Medical Art Illustration, © 2007, *www.nucleusinc.com*, as depicted in Vernon J. Geberth's *Practical Homicide Investigation*)

EVIDENCE FROM WOUNDS

A basic knowledge of wounds is of great assistance to officers who are responsible for injury and death investigations. It helps them reach preliminary conclusions. The five most common types of wounds encountered by police officers in injury and death investigations are firearm wounds, incised wounds, stab wounds, puncture wounds, and lacerations.

FIREARM WOUNDS

When a bullet strikes a body, the skin is first pushed in and then perforated while in the stretched state. After the bullet has passed, the skin partially returns to its original position, and the entry opening is drawn together and is thus smaller than the diameter of the bullet. The slower the bullet speed, the smaller the entry opening. The bullet passing through the stretched skin forms a so-called contusion ring around the entrance opening as the bullet slips against the skin that is pressed inward and scrapes the external epithelial layers (Figure 9-8). The skin in the contusion ring becomes conspicuous by drying after some hours. In a favorable case, rifling marks on the bullet leave such a distinct mark in the contusion ring that the number of grooves in the rifling can be counted. The combined section of the contusion ring and entrance opening corresponds to the caliber of the bullet or exceeds it slightly. When a bullet strikes the body squarely, the contusion ring is round; when a bullet strikes at an angle, the ring is oval.

Along with the contusion ring, there is another black-colored ring, the "smudge ring," which often entirely covers the contusion ring (Figure 9-8). It does not contain any powder residues or contamination from the bore of the firearm but consists wholly of small particles originating from the surface of the bullet. The smudge ring may be absent in the case of clean-jacketed bullets or a bullet that has passed through clothing.

A bullet passing through the body forms a track that is usually straight but can also be bent at an angle in an unpredictable manner if the bullet meets or passes through a bone. Thus it is not possible to determine with certainty, from observation of the entrance and exit openings, in which direction the weapon was pointed when the shot was fired. The direction must be calculated by the pathologist from the results of the autopsy. The velocity of the bullet has a great influence on the appearance of the track: straight tracks indicate a high velocity, and bent or angular ones indicate a low velocity.

In gunshot injuries in soft parts of the body, especially in the brain, the bullet can produce a considerable explosive effect, which is greatest with unjacketed or soft-nosed bullets from large-caliber firearms. Such a bullet may split into several parts, each of which forms its own track, and thus there may be several exit wounds. When such a bullet strikes the head, large parts of the cranium can be blown away and the brain scattered around. A soft-nosed bullet that, before hitting the body, is split by striking against a hard object such as a tree branch can produce a number of irregularly shaped entrance holes.

A shot through the head is not always fatal. To be immediately fatal, the bullet must either produce a bursting effect or injure an artery of the brain or a vital brain center. A shot through the brain that is not immediately fatal does not always produce unconsciousness. Even when the heart has been perforated by a bullet, it occasionally happens that the injured person lives for several hours, retaining some capacity of movement.

It is often difficult to distinguish the exit wound from the entrance wound, especially from a shot at long range with a metal-jacketed bullet, assuming, of course, that the bullet passes through the body intact. In a favorable case, the exit wound may have a ragged appearance with flaps directed outward. To determine the direction of the shot with certainty in such a case, an autopsy is necessary. If the bullet was damaged by its passage through the body or if there was a bursting effect, it is generally easy to determine the exit wound, which is then considerably larger than the entrance wound and shows a star-shaped, ragged character, with flaps directed outward. Note, however, that in contact shots the entrance wound may be ragged and star-shaped. A bullet that ricochets may strike with its side, or obliquely, and produce a large and characteristic entrance wound.

Close and Distant Shots

It is very important to be able to estimate the distance from which a shot was fired. In many cases this fact is the only evidence available that can distinguish among suicide, a self-defense killing, manslaughter, or murder.

In practice, a distinction is made among *contact, close,* and *distant* shots. A **contact bullet wound** is made when the muzzle of the weapon is pressed against the body when the shot is fired. In a close shot, the distance of the muzzle is less than about 18 inches from the body (Figures 9-9 and 9-10), whereas a distant shot is one fired at a distance greater than 18 inches[20] (Figures 9-11 and 9-12).

In the case of a contact shot against an exposed part of the body, soot, metallic particles, and powder residues are driven into the body and can be found there during the autopsy. Blackening, caused by soot and powder, around the entry opening is often absent. A contact shot

▲ **FIGURE 9-9   Firearm discharge at close range**
Close shot, short distance. The diagram shows both incompletely burned powder grains and smoke deposits in the zone of blackening. The powder grains are concentrated immediately around the entrance hole. (Courtesy Nucleus Medial Art Illustration, © 2007, *www.nucleusinc.com*, as depicted in Vernon J. Geberth's *Practical Homicide Investigation*)

▲ **FIGURE 9-10   Close range gunshot wound**
This victim was first assaulted with a knife and then shot numerous times in the left side of the head. Note the blackened area around the bullet wound indicating direct contact or very close contact with the skin.

against a part of the body protected by clothing often produces a powder zone on the skin or in the clothes, and soot, powder residue, and fragments of clothing are driven into the track. In a contact discharge, the entrance wound differs considerably from an entrance wound in a close shot or a distant shot. When a contact shot is fired, the gases of the explosion are driven into the track but are forced out again and produce a bursting effect on the

▲ **FIGURE 9-11** **Firearm discharged from a distance**
Close shot, greater distance than in Figure 9-9. The diagram shows unburned powder grains, but no smoke deposits in the zone of blackening. (Courtesy Nucleus Medial Art Illustration, © 2007, *www.nucleusinc.com*, as depicted in Vernon J. Geberth's *Practical Homicide Investigation*)

▲ **FIGURE 9-12** **Distant shot**
When a bullet strikes a body from a distance, the skin is first pushed and then perforated while in the stretched state. After the bullet has passed, the skin partially returns to the original position, and the entry opening is drawn together and is thus smaller than the diameter of the bullet. The bullet passing into the stretched skin forms what is called a *contusion ring* around the entrance as the bullet slips against the skin that is pressed inward and scrapes the external epithelial layers.

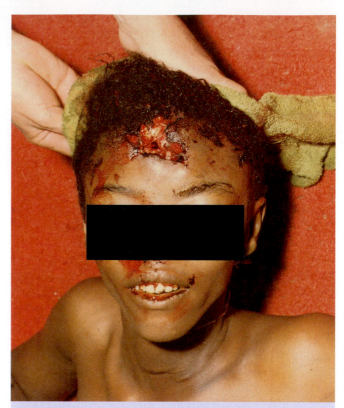

▲ **FIGURE 9-13** **Contact bullet wound**
Homicidal contact bullet wound to the forehead. Note the charring of the edges and the irregularly shaped tears of the skin owing to the undermining of the scalp. This contact bullet wound was made from a .38-caliber bullet against an exposed part of the body (in this case, the head). Soot, metallic particles, and powder residue are driven into the body and can be found during the autopsy.

skin and clothes. The entrance wound is often star-shaped with flaps directed outward (Figure 9-13).

A close shot produces a zone of blackening around the entrance wound of the track, either on the skin or on the clothes. Sometimes the flame from the muzzle has a singeing action around this opening, with hair and textile fibers curled up. The zone of blackening is formed of substances carried along with the explosion gases. When a cartridge is fired, the bullet is forced through the barrel of the weapon by the explosion gases. Only a small amount of the gas passes in front of the bullet. The combustion of the powder is never complete, even with smokeless powder and still less with black powder, and the explosion gases therefore carry with them incompletely burned powder residues, the amount of which decreases as the distance increases. Thus, in a close shot, a considerable amount of incompletely burned powder residue is found on the target. In addition to carrying this residue, the gases also carry impurities from the inside of the barrel, consisting of rust (iron), oil, and particles rubbed off the bullet. Metallic residues from the percussion cap and cartridge case also occur in the gases of the explosion. If the shot is fired at a right angle to the body, the zone of blackening is practically circular; if it is fired obliquely, the zone is oval. The extent of the zone of blackening is often difficult to determine by direct observation, and it is often better to photograph it, using infrared-sensitive material, which intensifies the zone of blackening so its extent is more easily determined. The zone of blackening gives valuable information for determining the distance from which a shot was fired, which may be an important factor in deciding between murder and suicide. It is important that comparative test shots be fired with the same weapon and same type of ammunition as those used in the actual crime.

Close shots with black powder show marks of burning up to a distance of 4–6 inches and a distinct deposit of powder smoke up to 10–12 inches. Dispersed grains of powder embedded in the target may be detected even at a distance of 3 feet. In distant shots, none of the characteristics of a close shot can be detected.

Powder residues occur on the object fired at in the form of incompletely and completely burned particles. A careful microscopic examination should precede any chemical examination, as it is often possible to establish in this way the shape and color of unburned powder particles and to distinguish many kinds of powder.

Black powder, which consists of potassium nitrate, sulfur, and charcoal, is identified by the presence of potassium and nitrate in the entrance wound. Smokeless powder consists chiefly of nitrocellulose or of nitrocellulose with nitroglycerine and is identified by the presence of nitrite, which can be detected by various microreactions. The grains of smokeless powder are generally coated with graphite and occur in many forms (for example, round or angular discs, pellets, and cylinders).[21]

High-Velocity Rifle Wounds

The difference in the size of the wounds and damage done between handgun bullets and rifle bullets, especially those of a large caliber, can be considerable. For example, Figure 9-14 depicts an individual who was shot in the head one time by a police swat team member. The officer was armed with a .308 Remington 700 rifle. The subject had barricaded himself in a motel room while holding a hostage. He was shot in the head after he made the fatal mistake of slightly opening the door to the motel room and pointing his rifle in the direction of a police SWAT team member. The rifle the decedent was holding is depicted on the left side of his body.

Shotgun Wounds

A shotgun is a smooth-bore, shoulder-fired firearm and is typically used to fire multiple pellets, rather than a single slug. The most common gauges with their corresponding bore diameters are as follows:[22]

- The pellets fired range in size from 0.08 inch for a No. 9 shot to 0.33 inch for 00 Buck.
- A "wad," which may be either paper or plastic, lies between the shot pellets and the powder. Most modern shells use plastic wads.
- A shotgun shell can contain anywhere from a couple of hundred pellets to nine for 00 Buck, to one large lead slug.

Entrance Wounds. From contact to 12 inches, there is a single round entrance 0.75–1 inch in diameter. The edge of the wound shows an abrasion ring. As the distance between muzzle and skin increases, powder tattooing appears. Powder blackening is most prominent at less than 12 inches. Powder tattooing is considerably less dense than it is in pistol wounds.

When pellets are discharged at between 3 and 6 feet of range, the single entrance wound widens to 1.5–2 inches in diameter and shows "scalloping" of the edges. At about 6 feet, the pellets begin to separate from the main

◄ **FIGURE 9-14**
High-velocity rifle wound
This individual was shot in the head one time by a police swat team member. The officer was armed with a .308 Remington 700 rifle. The subject had barricaded himself in a motel room while holding a hostage. He was shot after he made the mistake of opening the motel room door and pointing his rifle at a member of the police SWAT team.

▶**FIGURE 9-15**
Close-range wound from a 12-gauge shotgun
In shotgun entrance wounds, the characteristics of the wound vary based on the distance between the muzzle and the skin. For example, from contact to 12 inches, the edge of the wound shows an abrasion ring. As the distance increases, powder tattooing appears. This photo shows that powder tattooing is considerably less dense than it is in pistol wounds.

mass of pellets. Beyond 10–12 feet, there is great variation in the spread of the pellets (Figure 9-15).

The Wad. At close ranges, the wad will be propelled into the body through the large single entrance wound. Beyond 10–15 feet, the wad will have separated from the pellets and will not enter. However, it may mark the body. The gauge of the shotgun and the size of the pellets can be obtained from the wad and pellets, respectively. On occasion, a plastic wad may be marked by the choke or irregularities at the end of the barrel, making ballistic comparison possible.

Range Determination. Range determinations can be made later if the size of the shotgun pattern was described at autopsy and duplicated on paper. The same weapon with the same type of ammunition must be used in duplication of the pattern if accurate results are desired. Range formulas do not work.

X-ray patterns of the shot in the body are useless for range determinations, as are patterns on the body in which the shot first struck the target.

The size of the shot pattern on the body depends primarily on the choke of the gun. The type of ammunition and barrel length are secondary factors. The size of the pellet pattern is independent of the gauge of the shotgun, and an increase in gauge just increases the density of the pattern.

Exit Wounds. Shotgun pellets rarely exit except when used as instruments of suicide in the region of the head.

Gunshot Residue (GSR)

Gunshot residue (GSR) analysis is used to determine if a subject may have fired a weapon, handled an object—for example, a victim's shirt, with primer residue on it, or been in the vicinity of a firearms discharge.[23] "Primer" is the igni-

tion component of a cartridge. Examination is done by analyzing particles characteristic of primer residues on a subject's hands, face, or clothing. Of primary interest to analysts are antimony, barium, and lead. The Scanning Electronic Microscope (SEM) is commonly used for analysis.

As approximations, GSR remains on hands for 3 hours, faces for 8 hours, and nasal cavities for 48 hours.[24] If there are multiple exposures to GSR, a determination cannot be made as to which person fired the weapon or his/her relative position to the gun when discharged. Nor does GSR analysis reveal the muzzle to target distance. There is some evidence that a person could enter a room *after* a shot was fired and acquire GSR.[25]

GSP particles dissipate with normal activity and should be collected as quickly as possible, although they are longer lasting on suicide and murder victims because of this lack of activity. Gunshot Residue Collection Kits are commonly used for this purpose

If safe and otherwise possible to do so, the suspect's hands should not be handcuffed in the rear, because GSR may be wiped off. Visually inspect the suspect's hands for smudges, taking a photograph of any noted. Do not fingerprint the suspect before collecting samples. The investigator should wash his/her hands and wear latex-type gloves.

Open a container and remove the round disc, which is shaped like a shoe polish applicator, except that its bottom has an adhesive surface. Press the adhesive side against one hand in the area of the back of the thumb, rubbing it there, on the web of hand between the thumb and index finger, and down the index finger, extending to the fingertip. Continue rubbing in this area until "stickiness" is lost." The disc is then replaced in the container and sealed and marked in the usual manner. The other hand and both sides of the face are processed using separate discs. The containers are then transmitted to the lab.

▲ **FIGURE 9-16   Incise wound inflicted with a knife**
The wound is narrow at the edge and gaping at the middle. Such wounds typically bleed a lot. Incise wounds are often inflicted with a sharp-edged instrument such as a knife or a razor. The wounds are sometimes found on the arms, face, and legs.

▲ **FIGURE 9-17   Multiple stab wounds**
Death from stab wounds generally results from severe damage to a vital organ, internal bleeding, shock, or secondary infection that may develop several days after the attack. The close proximity of these wounds indicates that the victim was unable to struggle to any sufficient degree. Even wounds inflicted with the same knife as depicted in this figure can be quite different in size and shape.

INCISED AND STAB WOUNDS

The **incised wound**—more commonly referred to as a "cutting wound"—is inflicted with a sharp-edged instrument such as a knife or a razor. The weapon typically employed in inflicting both incised and stab wounds is a pocketknife, although kitchen knives are also common. In comparison with shootings, fewer cutting assaults result in death, largely because the perpetrator's intention was to injure or disfigure rather than kill the victim. Cutting wounds are often found on the arms, face, and legs. Even in these "friendly" cuttings, as they are sometimes referred to, death may occur. When the victim does die from a cutting wound, it generally is found around the throat. The severity of most incised wounds is directly related to the shape and sharpness of the weapon, the part of the body being cut, and the amount of force used in striking the victim. The incised wound is typically narrow at the edges and gaping at the center, with considerable bleeding (Figure 9-16). The inexperienced investigator may conclude that a gaping incised wound was inflicted by a large cutting instrument. However, a small knife with a honed blade is capable of causing very severe wounds.

Most frequently, death is caused when a stab results in severe damage to a vital organ, internal bleeding, shock, or secondary infections that develop several days after the attack. Any of these factors may itself be fatal; they often occur in combination. The shape, size, and keenness of the blade all determine a wound's shape and depth, as does the manner in which the knife is thrust into and pulled out of the body. One noticeable aspect of multiple stab wounds is their different shapes when made with the same knife. The proximity of the wounds in a multiple-stabbing assault may be helpful in determining the actions of the victim before death. If the wounds are concentrated within a small region of the body, then there is a good possibility that the victim was immobilized at the time of the assault—that is, held down, asleep, or intoxicated (Figure 9-17).

PUNCTURE WOUNDS

At one time the weapon most frequently used in assaults resulting in **puncture wounds** was the ice pick. However, ice picks are neither used nor as readily available today as they once were. Leather punches and screwdrivers also are capable of producing puncture wounds, which are normally small and have little or no bleeding. Such wounds can be easily overlooked, particularly if they are in hairy parts of the body. Infliction of a puncture wound produces death in the same way as do stab wounds (Figure 9-18).

LACERATIONS

When used in an assault, clubs, pipes, pistols, or other such blunt objects can produce open, irregularly shaped wounds called **lacerations.** Such wounds bleed freely and characteristically are accompanied by bruising around the edges. There is not necessarily a relationship

▶ **FIGURE 9-18   Puncture wound**
This victim received multiple ice-pick stab wounds. Leather punches and screwdrivers are all capable of producing puncture wounds. Because there is often little bleeding, a single wound can easily be overlooked, particularly if it is on a hairy part of the body.

between the shape of the wound and that of the weapon employed. Occasionally, when considerable force is used in an attack, an impression of the weapon is left on the victim's skin. Most frequently, when death results from an assault in which lacerations were inflicted, the cause is severe head injuries. Laceration wounds may be inflicted accidentally, as in the case of an intoxicated person who falls and strikes his/her head against a curb or step. In some instances, circumstances may appear more suspicious:

Checking the back doors of businesses at about 9:30 P.M., an officer found the proprietor of a jewelry store dead at the open rear entrance to his store. He had sustained a large laceration on his forehead and had bled considerably. At first, it appeared that a murder had taken place during a robbery or burglary. Careful processing of the scene yielded traces of blood and one small skin fragment from the brick wall near the rear entrance.

It was established that nothing was missing from the business. The medical examiner found the cause of death to be a heart attack. The head laceration contained minute traces of brick. Thus a reconstruction of events showed that as the owner was closing his business, he suffered a heart attack and convulsions, striking his head against the brick wall. The lacerations he suffered made it look as though he had suffered a fatal head wound.

The severity, extent, and appearance of injuries due to blunt trauma depend on the amount of force delivered to the body, the amount of time over which the force is delivered, the region struck, the amount (extent) of body surface over which the force is delivered, and the nature of the weapon. If a weapon deforms and/or breaks on hitting the body, less energy is delivered to the body to produce injury, since some of the energy is used to deform and/or break the weapon. Thus, the resultant injury is less severe than would have been the case if the weapon did not deform and/or break. If the body moves with the blow, this increases the period of time over which the energy is delivered and decreases the severity of the injury.[26]

For any given amount of force, the greater the area over which it is delivered, the less severe the wound, because the force is dissipated. The size of the area affected by a blow depends on the nature of the weapon and the region of the body. For a blow by a weapon with a flat surface, such as a board, there is a diffusion of the energy and a less severe injury than that caused by a narrow object—for example, a steel rod—delivered with the same amount of energy. If an object projects from the surface of the weapon, then all the force will be delivered to the end of the projection, and a much more severe wound will be produced. If a blow is delivered to a rounded portion of the body, such as the top of the head (Figure 9-19), the wound will be much more severe than would be the case if the same force is delivered to a flat portion of the body, such as the back, where there will be a greater area of contact and more dispersion of force.[27]

▲ FIGURE 9-19
Lacerations resulting from a pistol whipping
This victim was pistol whipped to death by an armed robber. This assault resulted in numerous lacerations to the head. Such wounds bleed freely and characteristically are accompanied by bruising around the edges. There is not necessarily a relationship between the shape of the wound and that of the weapon employed.

DEFENSE WOUNDS

Defense wounds are suffered by victims attempting to protect themselves from an assault, often by a knife or club. These wounds are commonly found on the palms of the hands, the fingers, and the forearms (Figure 9-20). In the most aggravated form, defense wounds resulting from a knife may even result in one or more fingers being severed.

▲ FIGURE 9-20 Defense wounds
This victim received severe defense knife wounds on the hands while trying to stop his assailant from stabbing him to death.

STRANGULATION WOUNDS

Ligature Strangulation

In **ligature strangulation,** the pressure on the neck is applied by a constricting band that is tightened by a force other than the body weight. Virtually all cases of ligature strangulation are homicides. Females predominate as victims. Suicides and accidents are rare. The mechanism of death is the same as in hanging, namely, occlusion of the vessels that supply blood and thus oxygen to the brain. Consciousness is lost in 10–15 seconds.[28]

Ligatures used range from electric cords (Figure 9-21), neckties, ropes, and telephone cords to sheets, hose, and

◀ FIGURE 9-21
Ligature strangulation
The pressure on the neck is applied by a constricting band that is tightened by a force other than the body weight. Virtually all cases of ligature strangulation are homicides. The victim in this photo died as a result of strangulation by use of an electric cord.

undergarments. The appearance of a ligature mark on the neck is subject to considerable variation, depending on the nature of the ligature, the amount of resistance offered by the victim, and the amount of force used by the assailant. The ligature mark may be faint, barely visible, or absent in young children or incapacitated adults, especially if the ligature is soft (for example, a towel) and removed immediately after death. If a thin ligature is used, there will be a very prominent deep mark encircling the neck. Initially, it has a yellow parchment-like appearance that later turns dark brown.

In ligature strangulation, in contrast to hangings, the ligature mark usually encircles the neck in a horizontal plane often overlying the larynx or upper trachea. When a wire or cord is used, it usually completely encircles the neck. There may be a break in the furrow, however, usually at the back of the neck, where a hand has grasped the ligature and tightened it at that point. Aside from the ligature mark, abrasions and contusions of the skin of the neck are usually not present. They may occur, however, if the assailant places his/her hands beneath and around the ligature and twists it, tightening it around the neck, or if the victim claws at the neck in an attempt to remove the ligature or relieve the pressure. If there is more than one loop of the ligature around the neck, there may be bruising of the skin if the ligature pinches the skin between two loops.

▲ **FIGURE 9-22   Death by manual strangulation**
This victim died as a result of manual strangulation. Note the crescent-shaped fingernail marks on the center of the throat along with bruising on the sides of the neck, indicating that the assailant attacked from behind.

Manual Strangulation

Manual strangulation is produced by pressure of the hand, forearm, or other limb against the neck, compressing the internal structures of the neck. The mechanism of death is occlusion of the blood vessels that supply blood to the brain. Occlusion of the airway probably plays a minor role in causing death, if any at all.

Virtually all manual strangulations are homicides. One cannot commit suicide by manual strangulation, since as soon as consciousness is lost, pressure is released and consciousness is regained.

In most cases of manual strangulation, the assailant uses more force than is necessary to subdue and kill the victim. Hence, marks of violence are frequently present on the skin of the neck. Usually, there are abrasions, contusions, and fingernail marks on the skin (Figure 9-22).

Although in most manual strangulations, there is evidence of both external and internal injury to the neck, in some cases there is no injury, either externally or internally. For example, one medical examiner reported seeing three women in a three-month period who had been manually strangled. The first woman showed absolutely no evidence either externally or internally; the second showed congestion of the face with fine petechiae of the conjunctivae (discussed later in this chapter) and skin of the face, but no evidence of injury to the neck, either externally or internally; and the third victim showed the classic evidence of injury: abrasions and

scratches of the skin with extensive hemorrhaging into the muscles of the neck. All three women were killed by the same individual. All three had blood alcohol levels above 0.30. The modus operandi of the perpetrator was to meet a woman in a bar, buy her liquor until she was extremely intoxicated, and then go off with her and have intercourse. He would then strangle her. At the time he strangled them, the women were unconscious due to acute alcohol intoxication, so a very minimal amount of pressure was necessary. He would place his hand over their necks and push downward, compressing the vessels of the neck. In the last case, the individual regained consciousness and struggled, with the resultant injuries. The perpetrator admitted having killed a number of other women in the same way over previous years in a number of states.

In manual strangulation, the victims are usually female. When they are male, they are often highly intoxicated. In all manual strangulation cases, a complete toxicological screen should be performed.

SUICIDE

For the investigator, a major concern in an apparent suicide case is to make certain that the death was self-induced and not the result of a homicide. In some cases, the investigator finds overwhelming evidence to this effect at the scene. In other cases, important information about the victim's behavior before death can be obtained from relatives, friends, coworkers, and employers. **Suicide** is often committed for the following reasons:

- ill health or considerable pain;
- severe marital strife;
- a recent emotionally damaging experience, such as an unhappy love affair, separation, or divorce;
- financial difficulties, including the threat of a much lower standard of living or failure to meet some significant and past-due financial commitments;
- perceived or actual humiliation;
- remorse over the death of a loved one;
- guilt for an act of one's own doing for which he/she cannot forgive him-/herself;
- revenge, frequently by adolescents who have serious difficulties with parents or spurned lovers and want to punish them and make them feel guilty about whatever difficulty preceded their death.[29]

These factors are far from all inclusive, but the investigator will find a significant number of suicides associated with them. Conversely, if there is an apparent suicide and thorough scrutiny fails to produce a solid motive, then the investigator's suspicion should be aroused. Thus, in all apparent suicides the possibility of a criminal homicide should never be lightly discarded.

METHODS AND EVIDENCE OF SUICIDE

Nine methods are most commonly employed in suicides: shooting, hanging, ingesting sleeping pills and other pharmaceuticals, drowning, cutting and piercing, ingesting of poisons, inhaling gases, jumping from high places, and intentionally crashing an automobile.[30]

Although all of these can be simulated in the commission of murders, there are important differences in physical evidence that distinguish suicides from murders.

Gunshot Wounds

It is sometimes difficult to determine whether a **gunshot wound** was self-inflicted or resulted from the actions of an assailant. However, there are certain indicators that may be helpful in reaching a conclusion. One of these is the location of the wound and the trajectory of the projectile on entering the body. The most common method of committing suicide with a firearm involves the victim placing a handgun to the temple and firing a shot. If there is no exit wound it will be difficult for the investigator to determine the precise angle at which the projectile entered. This information will eventually be obtained during the autopsy, but it may be several days before one is performed. However, in the meantime, the investigator must make some preliminary determinations. The following case illustrates some of the points discussed thus far.

A man telephoned the police hysterically, reporting that his wife had just shot and killed herself. When the police and an ambulance arrived, the victim was dead of a bullet wound in her upper left temple. The husband was holding the gun with which he alleged his wife had shot herself. He stated that he had arrived home from work just before the incident but that neither his wife nor their three preschool-age children had been there. His wife had arrived home a short while later, and she had been drinking heavily. When he questioned her about the whereabouts of their three children, she told him they were at his mother's home. A heated argument then followed about her neglect of their children, her drinking, and her seeing other men. According to the husband, his wife then slapped him in his face, and he slapped her back. At that point, she walked over to a nearby desk drawer, where he kept a revolver. She removed the revolver from the desk drawer, placed the barrel against her head, fired a single shot, and fell to the floor. No one else was home at the time this incident occurred.

The following set of facts was revealed by the medical examiner's autopsy report:

- The bullet entered the upper left portion of the head, traveled downward through the brain, and continued downward through the victim's body, coming to rest in her chest.
- There were no powder burns present around the gunshot wound.
- Death occurred immediately.
- If the wound had been self-inflicted, the victim would have been holding the weapon in her left hand, at least 2 feet from her head, and would have used her thumb to pull the trigger.

The relatives of both the victim and her husband provided the police with the following information:

- To their knowledge, the victim had not been despondent, nor had she ever previously attempted or discussed suicide.
- The victim and her husband had been having serious domestic difficulties, because she was seeing other men, spending the house money on liquor, and not properly caring for their three young children.
- Both parties were known to have assaulted each other in domestic disputes in the past.
- The victim was right-handed.

These facts tended to indicate the victim's death was not a suicide but a criminal homicide. An interrogation of the husband confirmed what the facts suggested—namely,

▶ **FIGURE 9-23**
Suicide by shotgun
This individual placed a 12-gauge shotgun against his right temple and pulled the trigger. As can be noted, there are scorch marks around the entry wound near the right ear. Shotgun wounds to the head, especially those involving large-gauge shotguns, generally result in enormous damage to the head.

that he was not telling the truth. The husband related that he had been truthful about the events leading up to the argument, but after his wife slapped him, he had angrily knocked her to the floor, removed the revolver from the desk drawer, and gone back to his wife, who was now on her knees. Standing over her, he fired a single shot into her head. After shooting her, he became frightened and fabricated the story of his wife's suicide.

This case demonstrates the importance of two factors in the investigation of an alleged suicide. The first is the importance of the location of the wound on the body and its trajectory on entering the body. Second is the presence or absence of evidence indicating that the victim was predisposed to committing suicide.

Suicide by Use of a Shotgun

The use of a shotgun to commit suicide can result in enormous physical damage, especially if the gun is discharged into the head (Figure 9-23).

Hanging

Certain misconceptions associated with suicidal hangings can lead to erroneous conclusions. The first is that the victim's neck gets broken and, second, that the feet are suspended off the floor. Although both of these conditions may occur, they are exceptions rather than the rule. The first misconception is related to the circumstances of legal executions by hanging. In legal executions, the procedures involved in inflicting death are intended to result in the neck being broken. This is accomplished by the use of a specific type of noose and a gallows with a trap door through which the person will drop some predetermined distance before being abruptly stopped. However, in a suicidal hanging, even

when the feet are suspended, the neck is rarely broken, because the fall is not long enough to cause the severe jolt necessary to break the neck (Figure 9-24)

It is also fairly common in suicidal hangings for the victim's feet or even the knees to be touching the ground. Occasionally, the victim is found in a sitting position. Finding victims in these positions often creates suspicion, because it is difficult for inexperienced investigators to understand how anyone could remain in these positions while slowly choking to death. They might improperly conclude the victim first was rendered unconscious or was killed and placed in the hanging position. It is more likely, however, the victim did not slowly choke to death but rather first tied the rope around some supporting device and then around his/her neck. Pressure was then applied by the victim either by crouching down, if in a standing position, or leaning forward, if in a sitting position. This initial pressure painlessly cuts off the flow of blood to the brain, which results in unconsciousness. When unconsciousness does occur, the full weight of the body is then applied to the noose, whereupon all oxygen is cut off to the brain and death follows. There is very little physical pain associated with suicides of this type. If one considers that many suicidal hangings occur in victims' homes, then it is logical to expect the feet not to be suspended above the floor, because few household objects are strong enough to hold the weight of a fully suspended body or one that has fallen several feet from a chair or table.

Livor mortis is most pronounced in the lower portion of the arms and legs and around the face, lips, and jaw. There may be some variations in the location of the discoloration, depending on the position of the body. When death occurs in this manner, one frequently finds petechial hemorrhaging in the eyes, caused when small blood

▲ **FIGURE 9-24   Suicidal hanging**
This suicide victim has been in this hanging position for approximately three weeks. The body is in an advanced stage of decomposition; the mosslike substance on the body is dried body fluids. The victim has used a ligature-type device wrapped around a beam in the attic to suspend his body.

▲ **FIGURE 9-25   Petechial hemorrhaging in the eye**
The victim of a suicidal hanging. In suicidal hangings, investigators often find what is referred to as a petechial hemorrhaging in the eyes of the deceased. This is a result of the small vessels in the eye bleeding because of an increase in blood pressure caused by the compression around the neck.

vessels in the eye bleed because blood pressure increases in response to compression around the neck (Figure 9-25).

Occasionally, hangings are accidental, not suicidal. The individual may have himself in a modified hanging position while masturbating and accidentally fall, slip, and knock over the object on which he is standing, resulting in an accidental death, known as autoerotic death or sexual asphyxia; the intent is sexual rather than suicidal. In these cases, the genitals are exposed, and semen may be present. (Chapter 10, "Sex-Related Offenses," provides an in-depth explanation of autoerotic death.) The presence of feces and urine is common because of the total relaxation of the bladder and bowel muscles at the time of death.

Sleeping Pills and Other Pharmaceuticals

Sleeping pills and other pharmaceuticals have for many years been a common means of committing suicide. However, some deaths resulting from the ingestion of sleeping pills or tranquilizing drugs may be accidental, not suicidal. The investigator has an obligation to determine whether the death was accidental or suicidal. Cer-

tain types of medication, such as barbiturates, when mixed with alcohol have a synergistic effect, which increases the potency of the drug beyond its normal strength. One should not be too quick to decide that the death is a suicide until the investigation is completed and some evidence is available to support this conclusion. In such cases, the investigator should seize as evidence any remaining medication and its container. Frequently, the container identifies the medication, the drugstore dispensing it, and the physician prescribing it. There is always the possibility that the medication was purchased or obtained illegally, thus complicating the investigative process. As in all apparent suicides, the investigator should conduct interviews of relatives, friends, and neighbors who may be able to provide background information about the victim.

Drowning

The majority of drowning incidents are either accidental or suicidal, but some are homicidal. Three questions must be answered in apparent drowning cases before any final conclusions can be reached: Was the cause of death drowning, or was the victim first killed and then placed in the water? If the cause of death was drowning, did it take place in the water where the body was recovered, or was the victim drowned elsewhere and then placed in the water where found? Was the victim conscious when placed in the water? Answers to these questions can be obtained by external examination of the body by the investigator and an internal investigation of the body by

▶ **FIGURE 9-26** **Drowning victim**
This individual died from an accidental drowning. Note the pink foam extruding from his nose and open mouth.

a physician. External signs to indicate that the victim was alive and conscious when entering the water include:

- objects clutched in the hand, such as grass or bottom soil commonly found in water;
- fingernail marks on the palms of the hands;
- white, pink, or red foam extruding from the nose and open mouth (Figure 9-26);
- livor mortis most marked in the head and neck, because the body settled with these parts in a dependent position.[31]

An internal examination by a physician serves to establish whether death occurred by drowning. The following evidence may be found in drowning cases:

- The chest cavity and the lungs are distended and soggy, with fine foam in the trachea and bronchi.
- The heart is flabby, with its right side dilated and filled with dark red fluid. The blood is unclotted and usually hemolyzed owing to the absorption of the drowning fluid into the system.
- The mastoid cells of the ear have hemorrhaged.
- In deep-water drowning, air embolisms may have formed in the blood.
- There may be water in the stomach and duodenum.
- Algae and other marine particles may be found in the stomach and adhering to the sides of the air passages.

In removing the body from the water, the investigator may notice considerable damage to portions of the victim's body, especially around the head and face. This should not cause the investigator to conclude prematurely that the victim was the object of foul play. Some bodies of water contain many rocks and shells; a free-floating body that is subject to strong currents can be repeatedly slammed into and dragged across such objects, causing severe damage, especially to the forehead, knees, tops of the feet, and backs of the hands. In addition, if the water is rich with fish, crabs, and other marine life, these, too, can cause damage. It is not unusual for the lips, ears, and nose to be at least partially eaten away. The extent of damage from objects or marine life in the water varies; understanding what can result from their presence minimizes the possibility of premature conclusions. But the investigator must also not prematurely conclude that all damage resulted after the body was placed in the water. The medical examiner can help draw conclusions about the actual nature of wounds (Figure 9-27).

Cutting and Piercing Instruments

The instruments ordinarily employed in suicides by cutting are razor blades, knives (Figure 9-28), and occasionally glass. One of the common characteristics of suicides inflicted by these instruments is the presence of hesitation marks. Hesitation marks are a series of lesser wounds inflicted by the victim in the general region of the fatal wound, often the wrists, forearms, or throat. In certain throat cuttings, it may be possible to reach a conclusion about whether the injury was self-inflicted or resulted from an assault. If a wound is self-inflicted, it tends to be deep at the point of entry and to shallow out at its terminus, which is near, or slightly past, the midline of the throat. In homicidal throat cutting, the wound appears deep from the start to the terminus. It is not unusual for a victim to inflict a series of severe cuts on different parts of the body to ensure death. The reasons vary, sometimes involving the influence of alcohol or hallucinogenic drugs. The prior ingestion of alcohol or drugs may have been a planned prelude to the act of self-destruction.

▲ **FIGURE 9-27**
Decomposition and marine life damage to an immersed body
Damage sustained by the victim in this photograph occurred while the victim was immersed in water. Note that the ears and eyelids are completely missing, and there is extensive damage to the nostrils and lips. These areas are among the first parts of the body to be attacked by marine life.

▲ **FIGURE 9-28   Suicide by knife**
This photo depicts an individual who took his life by stabbing himself in the abdomen with a knife.

Self-inflicted wounds can be surprisingly brutal and tend to make people disbelieve they were self-imposed. This is particularly true when mutilation of the sexual parts is involved. In one case, a 28-year-old man used a single-edged razor blade to cut off his penis. When questioned by paramedics, the man said: "It's just been eating away at me for so long, and when I thought about it, I heard voices saying 'Do it, do it.' I was just angry at myself. I had it all planned out and I did it."[32]

Poisons

The ingestion of liquid **poisons** is sometimes clear from outward signs on the body. Powerful caustic lyes or acids may produce vomiting once the liquid reaches the digestive tract. There is considerable damage to lips, tongue, and mouth, and there may be blood in the vomitus, along with pieces of the esophagus and stomach. Usually, death does not occur rapidly, and victims may employ another means of suicide to stop the excruciating pain (Figure 9-29).

Cases of suspected poisoning frequently pose very difficult problems to the police investigator and to the medical examiner. Many poisons produce symptoms similar to those of certain diseases, a fact that can complicate determination of whether a crime has been committed. However, if there is any reason to suspect poisoning, the investigation must proceed along the lines of a possible homicide, suicide, or accidental death until death due to natural causes is established.[33] To compound the problem, suicides and accidental deaths by poisoning are sometimes very difficult to distinguish from homicide. Alcohol, when consumed with certain medications, may result in an accidental (possibly suicidal) death by respiratory failure. An example is the combination of barbiturates and alcohol; when the alcohol level in the blood reaches about half the lethal dose, most individuals lose consciousness and thus stop breathing. But with the addition of a stimulant, such as an amphetamine, this effect may not occur, and individuals may drink a lethal dose of alcohol before they fall into a coma.

Actually, poisoning is now rarely used in homicides, because modern laboratory techniques can readily detect most poisons, thus unmasking an intended homicide. But when it is the method, a wide variety of poisons may be used (Table 9-1).

Characteristics of "Ideal" Poisons. There are certain elements that characterize an "ideal" poison, including:

- *Being odorless, tasteless, and colorless*—This allows for the administration of the poison to the intended victim while providing no warning signs that the victim can detect by the normal bodily senses of smell, taste, and sight.
- *Being readily soluble, preferably in water*—This allows for easy administration in normal foods and drinks that the victims might eat or drink.

►**FIGURE 9-29**
Ingestion of a caustic drain cleaner
This victim committed suicide by ingesting a strong caustic drain cleaner. On ingestion, vomiting was induced, thereby causing severe burns to the nose, chin, and chest area.

- *Having a delayed onset of action*—This allows for a time period in which the poisoner can attempt to create an alibi.
- *Being undetectable*—Certainly the more exotic the poison the more likely it will not be detected in more routine toxicological analyses.
- *Having a low-dose lethality*—Less of the toxic material needs to be administered. It is much easier to distribute a pinch of a substance than to distribute a pound.

- *Being easily obtained, but not traceable*—The poison will leave no investigative trail that would lead to the poisoner.
- *Being chemically stable*—This makes it easy to store the poison without loss of potency.[34]

Role of the Crime Scene Investigator in Suspected Deaths by Poisoning Cases. Even though the crime scene investigators seldom can identify the chemical compound that caused the death, they should be alert to the

TABLE 9-1	Poisons and Associated Physical Manifestations
TYPE OF POISON	**SYMPTOM OR EVIDENCE**
Caustic poison (lye)	Characteristic burns around lips and mouth of victim
Carbon monoxide	Victim's skin takes on an abnormally bright cherry-red color
Sulfuric acid	Black vomit
Hydrochloric acid	Greenish-brown vomit
Nitric acid	Yellow vomit
Silver salts	White vomit turning black in daylight
Copper sulfate	Blue-green vomit
Phosphorus	Coffee-brown vomit with an onion or a garlic odor
Cyanide	Burnt almond odor in air, cherry-red lividity color
Ammonia, vinegar, Lysol, etc.	Characteristic odors
Arsenic, mercury, lead salts	Pronounced diarrhea
Methyl (wood) alcohol, isopropyl (rubbing) alcohol	Nausea and vomiting, unconsciousness, possibly blindness

Source: Richard H. Fox and Carl L. Cunningham, *Crime Scene Search and Physical Evidence Handbook* (Washington, D.C.: Government Printing Office, 1985), p. 126.

general range of possibilities and the potentially hazardous environmental factors that may be connected with a poisoning.

Regardless of the nature of the incident—homicide, suicide, or accident—the symptoms of death by poison are the same. The field investigator should attempt to determine if the victim had any of the symptoms—-vomiting, convulsions, diarrhea, paralysis, rapid or slow breathing, contracted or dilated pupils, changes in skin color, or difficulty in swallowing—just before death. These symptoms are general manifestations of systemic poisoning. They do not provide proof of poisoning but can be meaningful in relation to other evidence. Someone who observed the victim just before death provides the best source of information concerning his or her symptoms. If no witness is available, the investigator must rely all the more on physical evidence from the crime scene.

The investigator should collect all available information concerning the activities of the victim during the last three days of life. Information on what types of medication were taken, when the last meal was eaten, and where it was eaten can be very important in determining the type of poison involved. Medical history may indicate that death was due to natural causes.

The **toxicologist** is concerned with the identification and recognition of poisons, with their physiological effects on humans and animals, and with their antidotes. Crime laboratories usually provide some toxicological support but vary considerably in the amount and type that they can furnish. However, full toxicological support is always available through a combination of hospital, medical examiner, coroner, and criminalistics laboratories. Crime laboratories can direct police to local facilities.

If the investigator suspects that poison was ingested, a diligent search should be conducted for the container. In suicides and accidental poisonings, the container frequently is close at hand. Even though a container appears empty, it should be processed for fingerprints, packaged, marked, and forwarded to the laboratory for examination. Additionally, any other object that could reasonably relate to the poisoning should be collected, such as unwashed dishes and glasses, wastebasket contents, envelopes, and medicine containers.

Opiate-Overdoses

Drugs are classified into different groups based on their origins and effects on the human body. The opiate class of narcotics, which includes morphine, heroin, and oxycodone, are commonly referred to as downers because of their sedative-like effects. With the exception of alcohol, opiates account for the largest portion of drug-related hospital admissions.[35]

Police agencies often identify fatal drug overdoses as accidental deaths, but being aware of and alert to the indicators of a drug overdose before entering a crime scene enables investigators to more effectively conduct their investigation.

Victims of an opiate overdose often exhibit specific characteristics. For example, victims may have a "foam cone," tinged orange or red with blood, around their nostrils and mouth, which is the most common characteristic of such an overdose. Opiates act as a central nervous system depressant, causing a decrease in heart rate and breathing. This slowing causes fluids to gather in the lungs, inhibiting the life sustaining exchange of oxygen and carbon dioxide. Essentially, victims drown in their own pulmonary fluids. As the fluids gather, victims may expel these fluids, mixed with gas bubbles, which then forms the foam cone. Autopsies of opiate overdose victims often reveal that death resulted from pulmonary edema, a swelling of the lungs with a pooling of fluids inside them.[36]

Because of this lack of oxygen, extremities, as well as the lips and tongue, frequently turn blue. Pupils may be constricted to a pinpoint. Many heroin users inject the drug into their body with a needle, a practice known as mainstreaming. Consequently, they also may have needle or track marks, generally found on their arms. Chronic users often damage the blood vessels in their arms to such a degree that they resort to injecting the heroin into their legs, eyelids, or between their toes. Others also attempt to mask the needle marks by injecting into a tattoo.[37] Although only an autopsy can determine the exact cause of death, investigators and first responders can use these characteristics to initially determine that the death likely resulted from an opiate overdose.

Gases

The gas most frequently involved in medico-legal investigations is carbon monoxide. When a death does result from this gas, it is generally accidental or suicidal. Carbon monoxide is found in automobile exhaust fumes and improperly ventilated space heaters in homes. In a death caused by auto emissions, the individual may have started the engine of the vehicle in the garage after closing the garage door or may have extended a flexible hose from the exhaust pipe into the vehicle and then closed the windows.

When death occurs from carbon monoxide poisoning, the victim's skin takes on an abnormally bright cherry-red color because of the reaction of the red blood cells to the gas. The red blood cells have a very high affinity for carbon monoxide molecules (approximately 250 times greater than for oxygen), absorbing them rapidly, thereby making the red blood cells incapable of absorbing oxygen and rendering them dysfunctional in the life-sustaining process. Death generally occurs when the red blood cells have reached a saturation level usually above 40%, although this varies; the level sometimes goes higher before death results if the victim is asleep, owing to the body's reduced oxygen needs (Figure 9-30).

Jumping from High Places

The major question to be answered in death resulting from jumping is whether the victim voluntarily leaped or was thrown or pushed. Often, there are suicide notes, witnesses

▶ FIGURE 9-30
Carbon monoxide death
This victim died accidentally from carbon monoxide poisoning resulting from an improperly ventilated space heater. Note the abnormally bright cherry-red color resulting from the reaction of the red blood cells to the gas and the pale area in the back region. This results because this area was resting against a firm surface and compressing the vessels in this area, which prevents the accumulation of blood.

who can provide this information, or background information that indicates previous suicide attempts or a predisposition toward suicide.

The Suicide Note

Research indicates that suicide notes are not left in most suicides. One study revealed certain facts about persons who do and do not leave notes. Generally, there are no differences between the two groups in age, race, sex, employment, marital status, history of mental illness, place of suicide, reported causes or unusual circumstances preceding the act, medical care and supervision, or history of previous suicide attempts or threats. However, the note-writers differed from the non-note-writers in the methods used to kill themselves. The note-writers used poisons, firearms, and hanging more often as a means of death than did the non-note-writers.[38]

GENDER DIFFERENCES IN SUICIDAL BEHAVIOR

Studies of suicide in the United States indicate that the suicide rate is higher for men than for women, whereas the attempted suicide rate is higher for women than men. Some evidence suggests that there are differences between men and women in the methods employed to commit suicide: women prefer barbiturates and poisons; if women do use a firearm, the fatal wound is frequently in the body rather than the head. It has been suggested that these methods are used because they are not disfiguring and because women are often more concerned about their appearance after death than are men. It is not unheard of for a woman to leave a note to her female friends or relatives specifying in detail the clothing and jewelry she wants to wear in her open casket and at her funeral, along with details relating to facial cosmetics.[39]

In contrast, some males kill themselves where their bodies will not be discovered by family members, such as in the woods or some other isolated area. These types of suicides can create investigative problems, especially if a note is not written. For example, if a passerby should come upon the body and steal the gun used in a suicide as well as valuables from the suicide victim, the police may initially believe the death was a murder and robbery rather than suicide.

FIRE DEATHS

Frequently, human remains of **fire deaths** are found at the scene of a fire. Properly examined, these remains may provide important data to the investigator about the facts surrounding the fire and the cause of death. Investigators should ask these questions:

- Was the decedent accidentally killed by the fire (whether or not the fire was caused by arson)?
- Was the decedent deliberately killed by the fire?
- Was the decedent already dead when the fire occurred?

To answer these questions, investigators should determine certain facts. These facts are outlined in the remainder of this section.[40]

COORDINATION AND COOPERATION

Coordination of, and cooperation between, police and fire investigators are of paramount importance in the successful investigation of any questioned fire. As with other forms of physical evidence at a fire scene, a body should never be moved until fully examined at the scene, unless

◄ FIGURE 9-31
Third-degree burns
This individual was driving a truck when it caught on fire. He leaped from the truck, but the burn injuries he had sustained would eventually prove fatal. The area of his face, hands, and abdomen are classified as third-degree burns. The cause of his death was listed as thermal injuries.

there is some possibility that the person is still alive or there is danger of further destruction of the body if it remains where it is. Also, because a dead human being is probably the most complex and rapidly changing type of physical evidence at a crime scene, cooperation between medical personnel (preferably forensic pathologists) and investigators is essential. This coordination should extend from the scene of the fire to the medical facility where the postmortem examination is conducted.

DEGREES OF BURNING

Burns are medically classified into four types. The extent of burns may provide information about the proximity of the body to the point of origin of the fire, the length of time the body was exposed to the fire, and the intensity of the fire.

First-degree burns are superficial and limited to the outer layers of skin. Although the burned area is red and swollen, blisters do not form and peeling may follow. Second-degree burns involve blistering and the destruction of the upper layers of skin. They occasionally cause scarring in living victims. With third-degree burns, the entire thickness of the skin (epidermis and dermis) is destroyed. In living victims with third-degree burns, pain is usually absent as nerve endings are destroyed; scarring results, and skin grafting is usually necessary (Figure 9-31). Fourth-degree burns completely destroy (char) the skin and underlying tissue.

IDENTIFICATION OF REMAINS

Because fire destroys human tissue, identification of the remains may be especially difficult. Yet because identification of a decedent is a key factor in any questioned

death investigation, an orderly, sequential approach must be used in the identification process. The six means that follow should be considered in sequence, from the "best" identification tools to the "worst":

- Fingerprints
- Dentition
- DNA printing
- Scars, marks, or tattoos on the exterior of the body
- Anatomical abnormalities or artificial appliances used to replacements hips or knees inside the body
- Identification, jewelry, and clothing on the body

SCENE CONSIDERATIONS

As with any physical evidence, burned bodies must be sketched, measured, and photographed in place and in relation to other evidence at the scene of the fire. The actual location of the body may be crucial to the investigation. Determination as to whether the decedent was a smoker is important for establishing what caused the fire and whether he/she was alive at the time of the fire.

EXAMINATION OF THE EXTERNAL BODY

The body of the deceased should be examined in detail both at the scene and again at the morgue. Significant areas for examination include those discussed next.

SIGNS OF TRAUMA

Any sign of injury to the external body should be carefully noted, sketched, and photographed. The use of a five-power magnifying glass (as a minimum) is required, because fire obscures signs of injury.

Skull Fracture

Another factor that may be misconstrued is the discovery that the victim's skull is fractured. Care must be taken to determine whether the fracture is implosive or explosive. An implosive fracture may have been caused by a fall, may be evidence of a previous felonious assault or homicide, or may result from a collapsed structural member. The exact cause will be determined at autopsy and evaluated during the follow-up investigation. An explosive fracture, however, is usually a natural consequence of fire. The extreme heat may cause the fluids in and around the brain to boil and expand. The resulting steam produces pressure sufficient to cause an explosive (pressure-release) reaction. The fracture(s) that result usually follow the natural suture lines of the skull. In extreme cases, the cranium may burst, causing the expelled brain and skull matter to form a circular pattern around the head. This is more common in children than in adults: the fontanel, or membrane-covered opening between the uncompleted parietal bones, is the weakest point in a fetal or young skull. The resulting circular pattern (0–12 inches from the skull) is significant when compared with the type of splattering that might result from a shotgun blast or high-order explosion.[41]

Blistering and Splitting Skin

The inexperienced investigator may be somewhat apprehensive in attempting to evaluate the effects of heat and flame on the skin of the victim. The medical investigator is in the best position to render a judgment in this area.

The formation of blisters (vesicles) is part of the body's natural defense system. The exact distinction between antemortem and postmortem blistering can be made only at autopsy. There are, however, certain signs that a medical investigator can use in developing a hypothesis. Postmortem blisters are generally limited in size and may contain only air or air mixed with a small amount of body fluid. Antemortem blisters are larger in size and contain a complex mix of body fluids. The precise determination of the fluids requires microscopic analysis. A blister surrounded by a pink or red ring can be considered to have occurred before death; the reddish ring is the result of an antemortem inflammatory reaction.

In some instances, temperatures may not have been sufficiently high to produce blistering. Likewise, if the skin is burned off or otherwise heavily damaged, blistering will not be evident.

The heat and flames of the fire also cause the skin to shrink or tighten and ultimately split. The splitting or lesions may be seen on the arms, legs, and torso. At first glance, one could misinterpret this condition, coupled with pugilistic attitude (described shortly), as indicating defense wounds.

In some cases, a seriously burned person survives the fire and is removed to a burn center. In an effort to save the person, the medical staff at the center may attempt to duplicate the natural splitting of the skin with a surgical technique known as an escharotomy. This technique is used to help foster circulation and to prevent the onset of gangrene. Should the burn victim die some time after the fire, these splits should not be misinterpreted as fire-induced.[42]

Noncranial Fractures

If enough heat is applied, bones shrink, warp, and fracture. Determining whether fractures were caused by a trauma or heat requires painstaking examination.

Pugilistic Attitude

The so-called pugilistic attitude of the body is a natural result of the dehydrating effect caused by the heat from the fire and is not related to the cause or manner of death. The arms and legs will be drawn into a posture resembling that of a boxer (Figure 9-32).

More often than not in fire deaths, a forensic pathologist who is an expert on burned bodies may have to be summoned.

EXAMINATION OF THE INTERNAL BODY

After the body has been closely examined, sketched, and photographed, an internal examination of it should be conducted by a forensic pathologist. Investigators should attend this procedure to get information about the facts, to correct discrepancies in data (such as measurements), and to recover evidence from the body. Significant areas for examination are as follows.

Soot, Other Debris, or Burning in the Air Passages

These findings may indicate that the decedent was breathing while the fire was burning.

Pulmonary Edema

A frothy substance in the lungs may result from irritants breathed in during a fire.

Epidural Hemorrhages

Hemorrhages above the tough membrane covering the brain (the dura mater) and under the skull may occur at the rear of the head due to heat. These hemorrhages should not be mistaken for the hemorrhages associated with blunt-force injuries.[43]

Internal Injuries

All internal injuries should be closely examined, measured, and photographed, with samples taken by the pathologist for later microscopic examination.

Foreign Objects

Any foreign objects found in the body, such as bullets, should be recovered as evidence by the investigator.

Because these objects are frequently small and difficult to locate, X-ray examination of the body before internal examination is recommended.

Toxicologic Examination

The pathologist should take samples for later examination by a toxicologist. Toxicologic results may be of extreme importance to the investigation.

Alcohol

Alcohol in blood indicates whether the decedent was incapacitated at the time of the fire and thus unable to escape. A finding of high levels of alcohol raises questions for the investigator about the decedent's habits.

Other Drugs

Indications of other possibly incapacitating drugs may provide new leads. The possibility of drug interactions—barbiturates with alcohol, for example—should also be considered.

Carboxyhemoglobin

Carbon monoxide (CO) is an odorless, colorless gas present at hazardous levels in all structural fires. Carbon monoxide asphyxiation (usually above 40% saturation) is probably the most common cause of death in fires. As previously discussed, CO causes the cherry-red color of postmortem lividity (as well as that of internal organs and muscle tissue).

Presence of Other Chemicals

Chemicals given off by burning materials may indicate the accelerant of the fire, as well as offer evidence that the decedent was breathing them in at the time of the fire.

MOTIVES IN FIRE DEATHS

In fire deaths, the following motives should be kept in mind by investigators:

- Destruction or mutilation of the body to conceal the identity of the decedent.
- Destruction or mutilation of the body to conceal the true cause or manner of death.
- Incineration of the body with homicidal intent.
- Incineration of the body to collect on an insurance policy. For example, a decedent may have committed suicide but have an insurance policy prohibiting collection after death by suicide. Beneficiaries may burn the body to indicate accidental death by fire.
- Suicide with an accelerant.
- An attempt by a suicide victim to hide the cause of death.
- A victim trapped in a building burned by an arsonist or by accident.

SERIAL MURDER

In the past 30 years, multiple definitions of **serial murder** have been used by law enforcement, clinicians, academicians, and researchers. Previous definitions of serial murder specified a certain number of murders, varying from two to ten victims.[44]

This quantitative requirement distinguished a serial murder from other categories of murder (that is, single, double, or triple murder).

Most of the definitions also required a period of time between the murders. This break-in-time was necessary to distinguish between a mass murder and a serial murder.

Serial murder required a temporal separation between the different murders, which was described as: separate occasions, cooling-off period, and emotional cooling-off period.

Generally, mass murder was described as a number of murders (four or more) occurring during the same incident, with no distinctive time period between the murders. These events typically involved a single location, where the killer murdered a number of victims in an ongoing incident (for example, the 1984 San Ysidro McDonald's incident in San Diego, California, resulted in James Oliver Huberty killing 21 people; the 1991 Luby's Restaurant massacre in Killeen, Texas, where George Jo Hennard killed 23 people; in 2007, the murder of 32 persons at Virginia Tech in Blacksburg, Virginia by Seung-Hui Cho; and the murder of 8 people in Manchester, Connecticut, in 2010 by Omar S. Thornton).

DEFINING SERIAL MURDER

There has been at least one attempt to formalize a definition of serial murder through legislation. In 1998 a federal law was passed by the United States Congress, titled: Protection for Children from Sexual Predator Act of 1998. This law includes the following definition of serial killings.

The term "serial killings" means a series of three or more killings, not less than one of which was committed within the United States, having common characteristics such as to suggest the reasonable possibility that the crimes were committed by the same actor or actors.

Although the federal law provides a definition of a serial murder, it is limited in its application. The purpose of this definition was to set forth criteria establishing when the FBI could assist local law-enforcement agencies

with their investigation of serial murder cases. It is not intended to be a generic definition for serial murder.

The lay public tends to refer to all multiple murders as serial killers, this however is not correct. For example, if two of more murders are committed by an offender or offenders at one time without a cooling-off period, this is typically referred to as a "spree murder." According to the definition, a lack of a cooling-off period marks the difference between the spree murder and the serial murder.

Also, unlike serial murderers, spree murderers are generally either killed or seriously wounded by the police at the scene of their multiple homicides or are wounded and taken into custody. It is also fairly common for them to kill themselves at the scene of the crime, generally with a self-inflicted gunshot wound to the head. Thus, although these murderers are every bit as destructive as serial murderers, they do not create the same long-term investigative difficulties as do serial murderers.

Serial murder is a relatively rare event, estimated to constitute less than 1% of all murders committed in any given year. However, there is a macabre interest in the topic that far exceeds its scope and has generated countless articles, books, and movies. This broad-based public fascination began in the late 1880s, after a series of unsolved prostitute murders occurred in the Whitechapel area of London. These murders were committed by an unknown individual who named himself "Jack the Ripper" and sent letters to the police claiming to be the killer.

These murders and the *nom de guerre* "Jack the Ripper" have become synonymous with serial murder. This case spawned many legends concerning serial murder and the killers who commit it. In the 1970s and 1980s, serial murder cases such as the Green River Killer, Theodore Robert (Ted) Bundy (Figure 9-33), and BTK sparked a renewed public interest in serial murder,

▶ **FIGURE 9-33**
Serial killer Theodore Robert (Ted) Bundy
This photo depicts a forensic dentist obtaining dental impressions from serial killer Theodore Robert (Ted) Bundy in conjunction with the murder of two Florida State University female students. Bundy's dental impressions were compared with bite marks left on the body of one of the victims. The marks were positively identified as his. Bundy, who was suspected of killing as many as 100 women, was subsequently executed in the state of Florida. (Courtesy Sheriff Ken Katsaris, Leon County Sheriff's Office, Tallahassee, Florida)

which blossomed in the 1990s after the release of films such as *Silence of the Lambs*.

MYTHS AND MISCONCEPTIONS ABOUT SERIAL KILLERS

The relative rarity of serial murder combined with inaccurate, anecdotal information and fictional portrayals of serial killers has resulted in the following common myths and misconceptions regarding serial murder.

Serial Killers Are All Dysfunctional Loners

The majority of serial killers are not reclusive or social misfits who live alone. They are not monsters and may not appear strange. Many serial killers hide in plain sight within their communities. Serial murderers often have families and homes, are gainfully employed, and appear to be normal members of the community. Because many serial murderers can blend in effortlessly, they are often overlooked by law enforcement and the public as indicated in the following cases:

- *Robert Yates* killed 17 prostitutes in the Spokane, Washington, area, during the 1990s. He was married with five children, lived in a middle-class neighborhood, and was a decorated U.S. Army National Guard helicopter pilot. During the time period of the murders, Yates routinely patronized prostitutes, and several of his victims knew other victims. Yates buried one of the victims in his yard, beneath his bedroom window. Yates was eventually arrested and pled guilty to 13 of the murders.
- *The Green River Killer, Gary Ridgeway*, confessed to killing 48 women over a 20 years in the Seattle, Washington area. He had been married three times and was still married at the time of his arrest. He had been employed as a truck painter for 32 years. He attended church regularly, read the Bible at home and at work, and talked about religion with co-workers. Ridgeway also frequently picked up prostitutes and had sex with them throughout the time period in which he was killing.
- *The BTK killer, Dennis Rader*, killed 10 victims in and around Wichita, Kansas. He sent 16 written communications to the news media over 30-year period, taunting the police and the public. He was married with two children, was a Boy Scout leader, served honorably in the U.S. Air Force, was employed as a local government official, and was president of his church.

Serial Killers Are All White Males

Contrary to popular belief, serial killers span all racial groups. There are white, African-American, Hispanic, and Asian serial killers. The racial diversification of serial killers generally mirrors that of the overall U.S. population. For example:

- *Charles Ng*, a native of Hong Kong, China, killed numerous victims in Northern California, in concert with Robert Lake.
- *Derrick Todd Lee*, an African-American, killed at least 6 women in Baton Rouge, Louisiana.
- *Coral Eugene Watts*, an African-American, killed 5 victims in Michigan, fled the state to avoid detection, and murdered another 12 victims in Texas, before being apprehended.
- *Rafael Resendez-Ramirez*, a native of Mexico, murdered 9 people in Kentucky, Texas, and Illinois, before turning himself in.
- *Rory Conde*, a Columbian native, was responsible for killing 6 prostitutes in the Miami, Florida area.

Serial Killers Are Only Motivated by Sex

All serial murders are not sexually based. There are many other motivations for serial murders including anger, thrill, financial gain, and attention seeking. For example:

- In the Washington, D.C., area serial sniper case, *John Allen Muhammad*, a former U.S. Army Staff Sergeant, and *Lee Boyd Malvo* killed primarily for anger and thrill motivations. They were able to terrorize the greater Washington, D.C., metro area for three weeks, shooting 13 victims, killing 10 of them. They communicated with the police by leaving notes, and they attempted to extort money to stop the shootings. They are suspected in a number of other shootings in 7 other states.
- *Dr. Michael Swango*, a former U.S. Marine, ambulance worker, and physician, was a health care employee. Although he was convicted of only 4 murders in New York and Ohio, he is suspected of having poisoned and killed 35 to 50 people throughout the United States and on the continent of Africa. Swango's motivation for the killings was intrinsic and never fully identified. Increasingly, Swango kept a scrapbook filled with newspaper and magazine clippings about natural disasters, in which many people were killed.
- *Paul Reid* killed at least 7 people during fast-food restaurant robberies in Tennessee. After gaining control of the victims, he either stabbed or shot them. The motivation for the murders was primarily witness elimination. Reid's purpose in committing the robberies was financial gain, and some of the ill-gotten gains were used to purchase a car.

All Serial Murderers Travel and Operate Interstate

Most serial killers have very defined geographic areas of operation. They conduct their killings with comfort zones that are often defined by an anchor point (for example, place of residence, employment, or residence of a relative). Serial murderers will, at times, expand their activities outside their comfort zone, when their confidence has grown through experience or to avoid detection. However, very few serial murderers travel interstate to kill.

The few serial killers who do travel interstate to kill fall into a few categories including:

- itinerant individuals who move from place to place;
- homeless individuals who are transients;
- individuals whose employment lends itself to interstate or transnational travel, such as long-distance truck drivers or those in military service.

The difference between these types of offenders and other serial murderers is the nature of their traveling lifestyle, which provides them with *many* zones of comfort in which to operate.

Serial Killers Cannot Stop Killing

It has been widely believed that once serial killers start killing, they cannot stop. There are, however, some serial killers who stop murdering before being caught. In these instances, there are events or circumstances in the offenders' lives that inhibit them from pursuing more victims. These include increased participation in family activities, sexual substitution, and other diversions. For example:

- *BTK killer, Dennis Rader,* murdered 10 victims from 1974 to 1991. He did not kill any other victims before being captured in 2005. During interviews conducted by law enforcement, Rader admitted to engaging in auto-erotic activities as a substitute for his killings.
- *Jeffrey Gorton* killed his first victim in 1986 and his next victim in 1991. He did not kill another victim and was captured in 2002. Gorton engaged in cross-dressing and masturbatory activities, as well as consensual sex with his wife in the interim.

All Serial Killers Are Insane or Are Evil Geniuses

Another myth is that serial killers have either a debilitating mental condition, or they are extremely clever and intelligent.

As a group, serial killers suffer from a variety of personality disorders, including psychopathy, antisocial personality, and others. Most, however, are not adjudicated as insane under the law.

The media has created a number of fictional serial killer "geniuses" who outsmart law enforcement at every turn. Like other populations, however, serial killers range in intelligence from borderline to above-average levels.

Serial Killers Want to Be Caught

Offenders committing a crime for the first time are inexperienced. They gain experience and confidence with each new offense, eventually succeeding with few mistakes or problems.

While most serial killers plan their offenses more thoroughly than other criminals do, the learning curve is still very steep. They must select, target, approach, control and dispose of their victims. The logistics involved in committing a murder and disposing of the body can become very complex, especially when there are multiple sites involved.

As serial killers continue to offend without being captured, they can become empowered, feeling they will never be identified. As the series continues, the killers may begin to take shortcuts when committing their crimes. This often causes the killers to take more chances, leading to identification by law enforcement. It is not that serial killers *want* to get caught; they feel they *can't* get caught.

CAUSALITY AND THE SERIAL MURDERER

Following the arrest of a serial killer, the question is always asked: how did this person become a serial killer?[45] The answer lies in the development of the individual from birth to adulthood. Specifically, the behavior a person displays is influenced by life experiences, as well as certain biological factors. Serial murderers, like all human beings, are the product of their heredity, their upbringing, and the choices they make through development.

Causality can be defined as a complex process based on biological, social, and environmental factors. In addition to these factors, individuals have the ability to *choose* to engage in certain behaviors. The collective outcome of all of these influences separates individual behavior from generic human behavior. Since it is not possible to identify all the factors that influence normal human behavior, it is not possible to identify all the factors that influence an individual to become a serial murderer.

Human beings are in a constant state of development from the moment of conception until death. Behavior is affected by stimulation received and processed by the central nervous system. Neurobiologists believe that our nervous systems are environmentally sensitive, thereby allowing individual nervous systems to be shaped throughout a lifetime.

The development of social coping mechanisms begins early in life and continues to progress as children learn to interact, negotiate, and compromise with their peers. In some individuals, the failure to develop adequate coping mechanisms results in violent behavior.

Neglect and abuse in childhood have been shown to contribute to an increased risk of future violence. Substance abuse can and does lead to increased aggression and violence. And there are documented cases of people who suffered severe head injuries and ultimately became violent, even when there was no previous history of violence.

It is generally agreed that *there is no single identifiable cause or factor that leads to the development of a serial killer.*

Rather, there are a multitude of factors that contribute to such development. The most significant factor is the serial killer's personal decision in choosing to pursue his/her crimes.

However, the following observations have been made by social scientists who study this particular type of criminal:

- Predisposition to serial killing, much like other violent offenses, is biological, social, and psychological in nature and is not limited to any specific characteristic or trait.
- The development of a serial killer involves a combination of these factors, which co-exist in a rare confluence in certain individuals. They have the appropriate biological predisposition, molded by their psychological makeup, which is present at a critical time in their social development.
- There are no specific combinations of traits or characteristics shown to differentiate serial killers from other violent offenders.
- There is no genetic template for a serial killer.
- Serial killers are driven by their own unique motives or reasons.
- Serial killers are not limited to any specific demographic group, such as sex, age, race, or religion.
- For the majority of serial killers who are sexually motivated by erotized violence during their development, violence and sexual gratification are inexplicably intertwined in their psyche.
- More research is needed to identify specific pathways of development that produce serial killers.

SERIAL MURDER AND THE NCAVC

If a serial murderer confines his/her activities to a single community or a small region, local police are in a good position to see emerging patterns. But because some serial murderers cover many miles in a short period of time, the FBI has developed the **National Center for the Analysis of Violent Crime (NCAVC),** which is designed to form a partnership among federal, state, and local law-enforcement agencies in the investigation of potentially related, unsolved violent crimes. NCAVC combines law-enforcement techniques, behavioral science principles, and data processing to help any law-enforcement agency confronted with unusual, bizarre, particularly vicious, or repetitive crimes.

Following are the types of offenses and incidents reported to NCAVC for analysis:

- Sexually oriented murder or assault by mutilation or torture, dismemberment, violent sexual trauma, or asphyxiation
- Spree murder (a series of indiscriminate murders or assaults, all committed within hours or days—for example, a series of sniper murders)
- Mass murder (four or more murders in a single incident)

- Robbery murder and nonfatal robbery with extreme violence
- Murder committed during the commission of another felony
- Kidnapping: fatal, with injury, or for ransom
- Murder of a hostage
- Murder for hire, contract murder, syndicate execution
- Murder of a law-enforcement officer
- Political or other assassination
- Terrorist or nationalistic murder
- Drug-related murder
- Gang murder
- Missing person with evidence of foul play
- Unidentified dead body when the manner of death is classified as a homicide[46]

NCAVC can analyze every unsolved murder in the United States, identify the existence of serial patterns, and link cases together. It then notifies the individual local agencies that have similar murders, and they in turn may establish investigative contact among themselves. NCAVC emphasizes that the primary responsibility for investigating cases lies with the state and local authorities.

NCAVC also conducts research on violent crimes and trains local officers in analytic techniques. It is located at the FBI Academy in Quantico, Virginia, where it is administered by the Behavioral Science Unit. The FBI Academy was chosen as the site because it is a national law-enforcement training center with vast resources for research and many capabilities for providing investigative support.

VICAP CRIME REPORT

When a violent crime remains unsolved for a period of time, the local law-enforcement agency provides details about it on a special **Violent Criminal Apprehension Program (ViCAP)** reporting form.[47] This form is submitted to the nearest FBI field office, which reviews it and forwards it to NCAVC. Following are examples of several murder cases solved with the assistance of ViCAP.

In 2001, a ViCAP crime analyst reviewed a state police publication that mentioned a bag of human bones found by hunters in a seaboard forest of an eastern state. The victim was a white male, about 40–60 years old, and between 5´, 7" and 5´, 9" tall. His cause of death was blunt-force trauma to the head. Recovered with the remains was a 14-carat gold ring with engraved letters. Authorities had no leads for identification of the remains.

The ViCAP crime analyst searched the database using the physical description of the victim and made an additional search, thinking that the letters engraved in the ring might be the initials of a name. A possible match was made with a July 1998 case in which three people were reported missing from a mid-western state. The report was made by a fourth member of the family, a son who waited a week before reporting his mother, father, and sibling as missing persons. Law-enforcement personnel had exhausted all investigative leads.

Authorities in the eastern and mid-western states contacted each other. In January 2001, ViCAP learned that forensic odontology had identified the bones in the bag as those of the father missing from the mid-western state. The letters in the recovered ring represented the maiden name of the missing mother and the name of the missing father.

ViCAP learned that a suspect who was identified and charged with the murder turned out to be the son who made the report in the mid-west. The remains of his mother and sibling have not been located.[48]

In 1999 a series of homicides occurred in Texas. Early in the series, the cases were presented as murders in the victims' homes. Female victims were sexually assaulted, blunt-force trauma was the cause of death,[49] and items of value were stolen from the homes.[50] The murder scenes were close to railroad tracks, sometimes only a few feet away.

In May 1999, personnel from the command post in Texas called ViCAP with information about three of the murders. One of the ViCAP crime analysts remembered a case from Kentucky in which railroad tracks were prominently mentioned. The analyst searched the database and quickly found the case in Kentucky: a male was killed along a pair of railroad tracks. The cause of death was blunt-force trauma.[51] His male companion was sexually assaulted and left for dead. ViCAP relayed information concerning the Kentucky rape/homicide to the command post in Texas. Subsequent DNA examinations linked the Texas cases with the Kentucky case.

An itinerant freight train rider was identified as the suspect in the series of cases.[52] He was apprehended by authorities on July 13, 1999, when he surrendered at the border in El Paso, Texas. Charged with nine murders—two in Illinois, one in Kentucky, and six in Texas[53]—the subject was tried, convicted, and sentenced to death. In July 2000, he confessed to the 1997 murders of two teenagers on a railroad track near Oxford, Florida.[54] The male victim's body was found on March 23, 1997; the female victim's body was not found until July 2000, when authorities, following the killer's directions, found her skeletal remains wrapped in a blanket and jacket.[55]

While confessing to the two murders in Florida, the subject said he once killed a woman in a southeastern state, somewhere along railroad tracks. She was an old woman, hanging her wash on the line, and he killed her inside her house. He did not provide more details.

KEY TERMS

algor mortis	gunshot wound	National Center for the Analysis of
autopsy	homicide	Violent Crime (NCAVC)
cadaveric spasm	incised wound	nonfelonious homicide
contact bullet wound	justifiable homicide	ocular change
decomposition	laceration	poisons
defense wound	ligature strangulation	puncture wound
excusable homicide	livor mortis	rigor mortis
felonious assaults	manslaughter	serial murder
felonious homicide	manual strangulation	suicide
gunshot residue (GSR)	medico-legal examination	toxicologist
fire deaths	misadventure	Violent Criminal Apprehension
forensic entomologist	murder	Program (ViCAP)
forensic pathology		

REVIEW QUESTIONS

1. What are the various categories of felony assaults and homicides?
2. What are the purposes of an autopsy?
3. What is algor mortis, and how does it help to determine the time of death?
4. Livor mortis is important for three reasons. What are they?
5. What is cadaveric spasm?
6. Briefly describe the typical entrance and exit gunshot wound.

7. Describe an incised wound, stab wound, and laceration.
8. What are defense wounds, and where are they most commonly found?
9. How is death produced by manual strangulation?
10. What are the most common reasons for committing suicide?
11. Which misconceptions are associated with suicidal hangings?
12. Why are poisons rarely used in homicides?
13. Discuss the differences in the suicidal behavior of men and women.

14. In regard to human remains at the site of a fire, what three broad questions should investigators keep in mind?
15. What are the common motives in fire deaths?
16. What are the myths and misconceptions about serial killers?
17. What role does the National Center for the Analysis of Violent Crime play in assisting local law-enforcement officers in apprehending serial killers?

INTERNET ACTIVITIES

1. A special forensic entomology website at *www.forensicentomology.com* has been created to assist in the education of crime scene technicians, homicide investigators, coroners, medical examiners, and others involved in the death-investigation process. This site assists in answering these questions: What do the insects of forensic importance look like? What are the proper methods of their collection? How can communications between the police and the forensic entomologist be enhanced?

2. As the twentieth century progressed, so did technology and the scientific sophistication of toxicology. Thus, the use of poison as a weapon also needed to evolve in order to remain covert and evade detection. The website *www.porfolio.mvm.ed.ac.uk/studentwebs/session2/group12/20th.htm* helps address these questions: What historical changes have occurred in the use of poisons to commit homicide? Which older types of poison are still popular? What new types are being used? How have advances in technology helped make poison more detectable in the body?

► Jennifer W., rape victim, is consoled by her fiancé during the sentencing of Timothy Mobly in Reno, Nevada. The investigation of sex-related offenses is one of the most sensitive matters undertaken by the police and is given high priority. These offenses involve not only physical but also psychological injury.

(© AP Photo/Debra Reid)

10

SEX-RELATED OFFENSES

This chapter discusses how to best interview sexual-assault victims, which can be a most delicate and challenging task for the criminal investigator. The investigator must obtain all the necessary information, yet do so with respect and concern for the victim. It is absolutely imperative that the investigator does not in any way pass judgment on the victim, which would result in revictimization. In this chapter we focus primarily on sexual assaults that are typically directed toward postpubescent adult females and discuss the considerable amount of physical evidence that is often available when sex crimes are committed. We also discuss two specific categories of victims that need special attention—namely, deaf victims of sex assault and elderly victims of sexual assault. Both categories of victims present some unique interview challenges to investigators. In addition, homosexual lifestyles and homicide investigations within this community have some unique characteristics that are important for investigators to understand in order to solve such cases. This chapter concludes with a discussion of autoerotic death (sexual asphyxia) and the value of conducting psychological autopsies in such cases.

THE LAW

The term **sex-related offenses** covers a broad category of specific acts against adults, children, males, and females. **Rape** or **sexual battery** is legally defined as the crime of a person's having sexual relations with another person under the following circumstances: (1) against a person's consent; (2) while the person is unconscious; (3) while the person is under the influence of alcohol or drugs; (4) if the person is feeble-minded or insane; (5) if the person is a child who is under the age of consent as fixed by statute.

SEX-RELATED INVESTIGATIONS

Rape is generally considered a woman-centered issue, but growing awareness has led to a rise in reports of homosexual male rape. In general, society places a greater stigma on male rape victimization. Fear, shame, and this stigmatization still prevent a large number of male victims from reporting their experience. Whether the victims are male or female, the offenders are over-whelmingly male, but it is certainly possible for a female to perpetrate rape.[1]

When police and medical examiners are confronted with a dead body, they are obviously not able to interview the deceased victim to obtain an explanation for what has occurred. Investigators must rely on their initial impression of the scene, such as the state of the victim's clothing, positioning of the body, items found, and the presence or absence of injuries related to sexual activity (for example, bite marks, hickeys, direct genital or oral injury), in deciding whether sexual activity or attempted sexual activity was related to the cause of death. The investigator must be mindful, however, in weighing the significance of the presence of sexual evidence. Although the victim may have engaged in sexual activity with another person before death, the intercourse might not be related to the cause of death.

In the case of a homicide involving a female victim, investigators often question whether a rape has taken place. However, the possibility of rape must also be raised when the homicide victim is male; this is especially true when a male child is involved. Currently, the U.S. Department of Justice estimates that about 1 out of every 10 rape victims over the age of 12 is male and that fully half of all underage sexual-abuse victims are male.[2] Sex is a major motivator and modifier of human behavior. Therefore, a determination of sexual activity may be of great value not only in a rape-murder case but also in natural, suicidal, and accidental deaths. Careful observation of the scene and the body may indicate a need for a rape investigation. Even if sexual intercourse does not seem to have any direct bearing on the cause of death, it may explain motives or the timing of death or simply provide a check on the veracity of a suspect or witness. The following cases illustrate these points:

A 53-year-old businessman was found dead in a motel room. There was no evidence of foul play. The bed was in slight disarray, with one of the pillows on the floor. The bed covers were bunched in an unusual position. The body on the floor was dressed in a shirt, loosened tie, trousers, underclothes, and socks. Shoes were neatly laid out next to a chair, and a jacket was on the back of a chair. Examination of the contents of the deceased's trouser pockets revealed the usual items, except for a pair of female panties. The autopsy revealed that the decedent had a massive heart attack; also, no vaginal cells were found on the penis. A logical reconstruction of the events preceding death suggested sexual foreplay with a female, in the course of which a wrestling match ensued during which the man took the woman's panties and then suffered a heart attack.

Although establishing the absence of sexual intercourse in this case did not significantly add to the medical solution of the problem, it did explain why the victim was found at a motel when he was supposedly having lunch.

A furnace repairman was found dead, slumped over the front seat of his van. There was no evidence of foul play, and the medical examiner was not called to the scene. Observation at the morgue revealed that there were peculiar parallel linear abrasions over the victim's knees, tearing of the overalls at the same region, and no underwear. His boots were reversed and loosely laced. Penile washings were positive for vaginal cells. Further investigation disclosed that he had visited a woman at 7 in the morning under the pretext of cleaning her furnace and had been stricken by a heart attack during intercourse. The woman hastily dressed him and dragged him across the back alley to his truck, not realizing that his underwear was neatly tucked under her bed.

A 15-year-old girl's body was found in a vacant lot. The absence of clothing on the lower body suggested sexual intercourse immediately before or at the time of death. Faint abrasions were present on the back of the neck, and marked hemorrhages were present in the eye. The medical examiner believed that this was a case of rape-murder. The autopsy confirmed recent sexual intercourse. The scratch on the back of the neck, however, proved to be superficial, and there were no deeper injuries. Reconstruction of the events immediately preceding death confirmed that the girl had had sexual intercourse with her boyfriend (who lived nearby), in the course of which (according to the boyfriend's testimony) the girl started making choking noises. She reported pain in her chest but said that it was going away. The boyfriend resumed intercourse. The girl started making even more violent noises. He assumed these to be related to her having an orgasm. After intercourse, he noticed the girl was motionless and unresponsive. After a few minutes, he decided she was dead and became very scared. He escaped from the scene and told investigators he had not seen his girlfriend on the night of her death.

INTERVIEW OF THE RAPE VICTIM

The interview requires intimate communication between a police officer and a victim who has been physically and psychologically assaulted. However, the investigative nature of the interview represents only one dimension of the officer's responsibility. By conducting the interview tactfully and compassionately, the officer can avoid intensifying emotional suffering. At the same time, the cooperation of the victim is gained, and the investigative process is thereby made easier.

As mentioned earlier, the investigator must not in any way pass judgment on the victim. The rape investigation is only the beginning of a long judicial-legal process often referred to as "the second rape" by victims and rape counselors.[3] Statements such as "She was where at what time that night?!" or "With that outfit, she was practically begging for it!" transfer blame from the perpetrator to the victim and leave the victim feeling just as helpless and abused emotionally as she was physically during the attack. There is no place for judgmental attitudes or predispositions such as these in a rape investigation.[4]

Although they may at first numb themselves to the trauma and try to go on as if nothing had happened, nearly all women who have been raped experience emotional or psychological disturbance to some degree. Victims generally at some time experience fear, insecurity, anger, depression, aversion to sexual contact, and feelings of loss of control. These feelings may last for months or even years after the assault.[5]

Rape victims frequently exhibit signs of posttraumatic stress disorder (PTSD) and, as a consequence, may experience alternating feelings of rage and helplessness. Flashbacks may leave victims overwhelmed and unable to function in mind and body.[6] (See Chapter 12, "Human Trafficking," for a more detailed discussion of PTSD.)

The investigator must be sensitive to the psychological state of the victim. Insensitivity can have two bad effects. First, from a practical standpoint, it might diminish the ability or the willingness of the victim to cooperate in the investigation. Second, it might cause serious psychological aftereffects. Certain steps make the interview less painful for the victim and more effective for the investigator.[7]

Interview Procedures and Investigative Questions

The attitude of the officer is extremely important and makes a lasting impression on the victim. As long as the investigator is confident the complaint is not a false rape allegation (discussed later in this chapter) the initial interview of the victim should not be excessively long. It is frequently best to obtain only a brief account of events and a description of the perpetrator for the pickup order. Rapid placement of the pickup order is essential. Unless the circumstances of the offense make it unwise to delay the investigation, the detailed interview should be conducted the following day, when the victim has calmed down. When threats have been made against the victim, protection should be provided. The interview should be conducted in a comfortable environment with absolute privacy from everyone, including husbands,

boyfriends, parents, children, friends, and anyone else personally associated with the victim. Without privacy, the victim's reluctance to discuss the details may be significantly reinforced.[8]

There is some question about whether the investigator interviewing the victim should be male or female. Some argue that a female victim feels more at ease in discussing the details of the assault with another woman. Others argue that an understanding male may help the victim to overcome a possibly aversive reaction to men, especially if the victim is relatively young or sexually inexperienced. The major criterion, regardless of whether the investigator is male or female, is that the person has the ability to elicit trust and confidence from the victim while possessing considerable investigative ability. Many police departments have moved toward male-female teams in rape investigation.[9]

In interviewing the victim, the investigator may find that the victim uses slang terms to describe the sex act or parts of the body. This is likely done because the victim does not know the proper terminology. At some point the investigator may find it necessary to use slang terms to interview the victim; however, in today's world, investigators must protect themselves from allegations of insensitivity or professional misconduct. Delicately employed proper terms can be used immediately after a victim's slang usage. This in no way demeans the victim's intellect; rather it conveys an image of professionalism to which most victims respond positively.

When the victim has had an opportunity to compose herself/himself, the investigator should make inquiries into the following areas.

TYPE AND SEQUENCE OF SEXUAL ACTS DURING AN ASSAULT

To determine the motivation behind a rape, the investigator must ascertain the type and sequence of sexual acts during the assault.[10] This task may be made difficult because of the victim's reluctance to discuss certain aspects of the crime out of fear, shame, or humiliation. Often, however, investigators can overcome a victim's reluctance with a professional and empathic approach. It has been found that although interviewers are likely to ask about vaginal, oral, and anal acts, they often do not ask about kissing, fondling, use of foreign objects, digital manipulation of the vagina or anus, fetishism, voyeurism, or exhibitionism by the offender.[11] In a sample of 115 adult, teenage, and child rape victims, researchers reported vaginal sex as the most frequent act, but they also reported 18 other sexual acts. Repetition and sequence of acts are infrequently reported. Most reports state that the victim was "raped," "vaginally assaulted," or "raped repeatedly."

By analyzing the sequence of acts during the assault, the investigator may determine whether the offender was acting out a fantasy, experimenting, or committing the sexual acts to punish or degrade the victim. For example, if anal sex was followed by **fellatio** (oral sex—mouth to penis), the motivation to punish and degrade would be strongly suggested. In acting out a fantasy, the offender normally engages in kissing, fondling, or cunnilingus (oral sex—mouth to female genitals). If fellatio occurs, it generally precedes anal sex. If a rapist is experimenting sexually, he is moderately forceful and verbally profane and derogatory. Fellatio may precede or follow anal sex.[12]

Verbal Activity of Rapist

A rapist reveals a good deal about himself/herself and the motivation behind the assault through what the rapist says to the victim. For this reason, the investigator must elicit from the victim everything the rapist said and the tone and attitude in which the rapist said it.

A study of 115 rape victims revealed several themes in rapists' conversations, including "threats, orders, confidence lines, personal inquiries of the victim, personal revelations by the rapist, obscene names and racial epithets, inquiries about the victim's sexual 'enjoyment,' soft-sell departures, sexual put-downs, and taking property from another male who was with the victim at the time of the rape."[13]

Preciseness is important. For example, a rapist who states "I'm going to hurt you if you don't do what I say" has threatened the victim, whereas the rapist who says "Do what I say, and I won't hurt you" may be trying to reassure the victim in order to gain compliance without force. A rapist who states "I want to make love to you" has used a passive and affectionate phrase and may not want to harm the victim physically. But a statement such as "I'm going to fuck you" is much more aggressive, hostile, and angry. Compliments to the victim, politeness, expressions of concern, apologies, and discussions of the offender's personal life, whether fact or fiction, indicate low self-esteem in the offender. In contrast, derogatory, profane, threatening, or abusive language suggests anger and the use of sex to punish or degrade the victim.

When analyzing a rape victim's statement, the interviewer is advised to write down an adjective that accurately describes each of the offender's statements. For example, the interviewer might record "You're a beautiful person" (complimentary); "Shut up, bitch" (hostility); "Am I hurting you?" (concern). The interviewer then has better insight into the offender's motivation and personality.

Verbal Activity of the Victim

The rapist may make the victim say certain words or phrases that enhance the rape for him. By determining what, if anything, the victim was forced to say, the interviewer learns about the rapist's motivation and about what gratifies him. For example, a rapist who demands such phrases as "I love you," "Make love to me," or "You're better than my husband" suggests the need for affection or ego-building. One who demands that the victim plead or scream suggests sadism and a need for total domination. If the victim is forced to say things that are demeaning, the offender may be motivated by anger and hostility.

Sudden Change in Rapist's Attitude during Attack

The victim should be specifically asked whether any changes were observed in the attitude of the rapist during the time they were together. The victim should be asked whether the rapist became angry, contrite, physically abusive, or apologetic and whether this was a departure from his previous attitude. If the victim reports such a change, she should be asked to recall what immediately preceded the change. A sudden behavioral change may reflect weakness or fear. Factors that may cause such sudden behavioral changes include a rapist's sexual dysfunction, external disruptions (a phone ringing, noise, or a knock on the door), the victim's resistance or lack of fear, ridicule or scorn, or even completion of the rape. An attitudinal change may be signaled verbally, physically, or sexually. Because the rape can be stressful for the rapist, how he reacts to stress may become important in future interrogations, and knowing what caused the change can be a valuable psychological tool for the investigator.

In attempting to determine the experience of the rapist, the investigator should ask the victim what actions the offender took to protect his identity, to remove physical or trace evidence, or to facilitate his escape. It may be possible to conclude from the offender's actions whether he is a novice or an experienced offender who may have been arrested previously for rape or similar offenses. Most rapists take some action, such as wearing a mask or telling the victim not to look at them, to protect their identity. But some go to great lengths to protect themselves from future prosecution. As with any criminal act, the more rapes a person commits, the more proficient he becomes in eluding detection. If a person has previously been arrested because of a mistake and later repeats the crime, he/she is not likely to repeat the same costly mistake.

The offender's experience level can sometimes be determined from the protective actions he takes. Novice rapists are not familiar with modern medical or police technology and take minimal actions to protect their identity. Some wear a ski mask and gloves, change their voice, affect an accent, or blindfold and bind their victims. The experienced rapist's modus operandi can indicate a more than common knowledge of police and medical developments. The rapist may walk through the victim's residence or prepare an escape route before the sexual assault, disable the victim's telephone, order the victim to shower or douche, bring bindings or gags rather than using those available at the scene, wear surgical gloves during the assault, or take or force the victim to wash items the rapist touched or ejaculated on, such as bedding and the victim's clothing.

Theft during Rape

Almost without exception, police record the theft of items from rape victims. All too often, however, investigators fail to probe the matter unless it involves articles of value. But knowing about the items stolen may provide information about the criminal and aid in the investigative process. In some cases, the victim initially may not realize that something has been taken. For this reason, the victim should be asked to inventory items.

Missing items fall into one of three categories: evidentiary, valuables, and personal. The rapist who takes evidentiary items—those he has touched or ejaculated on—suggests previous rape experience or an arrest history. One who takes items of value may be unemployed or working at a job providing little income. The type of missing items may also provide a clue as to the age of the rapist. Younger rapists have been noted to steal such items as stereos or televisions; older rapists tend to take jewelry or items more easily concealed and transported. Personal items taken sometimes include photographs of the victim, lingerie, driver's licenses, and the like. These items have no intrinsic value but remind the rapist of the rape and the victim. A final factor to consider is whether the offender later returns the items to the victim, and if so, why. Some do so to maintain power over the victim by intimidation. Others want to convince the victim that they meant her no harm and want to convince themselves that they are not bad people.

Rapists often target their victims beforehand. A series of rapes involving victims who were either alone or in the company of small children—who would not be able to defend them or effectively intervene—is a strong indication that the offenders had engaged in peeping or surveillance. They may have entered the residence or communicated with the victims earlier. For this reason, the investigator should determine whether the victims or their neighbors, before the rape, experienced:

1. calls or notes from unidentified persons;
2. residential or automobile break-ins;
3. prowlers or peeping toms incidents;
4. feelings of being watched or followed.

Frequently, rapists who target their victims have prior arrests for breaking and entering, prowling, peeping, or theft of women's clothing.

Delayed Reporting

If the victim has delayed making a complaint, the investigator should establish the reason. It may be that the victim was frightened, confused, or apprehensive. However, delays of several weeks or months reduce the likelihood of apprehending the suspect and tend to weaken the state's case should a trial be held. Nevertheless, such a complaint must be investigated in the same way as all other similar complaints, until or unless it is substantiated or considered unfounded. When a case is determined to be unfounded, that generally means either the crime was not committed or the case lacked the necessary legal elements for the specific crime. In some cases, the prosecutor will decide not to seek prosecution because of a lack of medical evidence, intoxication of the victim, a previous relationship between the victim and the suspect, or because the victim is too embarrassed or too upset to cooperate.[14]

DEAF VICTIMS OF SEXUAL ASSAULT

Sexual-assault victims who are deaf face unique issues not encountered by the hearing.[15] Thus investigators distinguish these people's experiences as sexual-assault victims from other sexual-assault victims. For example, when a deaf woman reports a sexual assault, she will often encounter stereotypes about being both a sexual-assault victim as well as being deaf. Also, like other rape victims she often has feelings of guilt and embarrassment because of the social stigma frequently attached to rape. These feelings can be compounded owing to the small and generally close-knit nature of the deaf community, which can contribute to a hesitancy to report a sexual assault. In addition, the closeness of the deaf community can compromise a victim's anonymity and erode privacy. Many deaf victims of sexual assault perceive a lack of support within the deaf community, particularly if the perpetrator is also deaf. Consequently, deaf victims can experience a profound sense of isolation.[16]

Another impediment to deaf victims seeking help is the lack of awareness about deafness and deaf culture among hearing people. Many view deafness from a medical perspective, focusing on hearing deficits rather than viewing deaf people as members of a linguistic and cultural community. In fact, many deaf women do not view themselves as disabled but rather as having a culture and a way of communicating not recognized by the dominant hearing culture.

RELUCTANCE TO REACH OUT

Many deaf victims may be reluctant to reach out to agencies that serve sexual-assault victims because most of the providers are hearing and do not have systems for effectively communicating with deaf people. For example, deaf sexual-assault victims cannot count on service agencies having access to a TTY (teletypewriter), much less a staff member who knows how to operate it. Even if a social service or law-enforcement agency has an interpreter, deaf victims, like hearing victims, may be reluctant to divulge intimate details to yet another stranger.

Some deaf victims of sexual assault also believe they cannot rely on interpreters to accurately represent their words and experiences. Service agencies that do not have qualified interpreters on site often use the victim's family or friends to assist in interviews, which can further inhibit a sexual-assault victim's candor.

IMPROVING POLICE RESPONSE

Deaf victims who were interviewed in a study conducted in Minneapolis, Minnesota, several years ago had varied opinions on how helpful police could be after a sexual assault. Although most said they regarded law enforcement as a resource, few had actually called the police after they were victimized. Many related frustrating experiences when dealing with the police department, including 911 call-takers who could not operate a TTY machine and police officers who mislabeled a deaf person as drunk or mentally ill or who misread body language as aggressive when a deaf person was simply moving closer to lip-read.

Service providers and deaf community members agreed that law enforcement must improve its methods for communicating with the deaf community, whether they are victims, witnesses, or suspects. They also suggested that police officers need training, interpreters, and more clearly defined agency policies. For example, in a research project involving the Minneapolis Police Department it was found that the department had policies for locating interpreters, but its officers knew very little about determining if a person was deaf or how to communicate with him or her in the field.

Despite these challenges, the Minneapolis Police Department is considered a model for other jurisdictions when it comes to serving the deaf community.

ELDER SEXUAL ABUSE

As an increasing percentage of our population grows older, we are beginning to see an increase in the number of **elder sexual abuse.** In some cases, sexual assaults are being inflicted by intruders who make unauthorized entry into nursing homes or assisted-living facilities, and in other cases these abuses are being inflicted by home providers, nursing-home staff, and in some cases nursing-home residents.[17]

SIGNS AND SYMPTOMS OF SEXUAL ABUSE

Emotional symptoms of anxiety and depression with accompanying feelings of fear and confusion are not uncommon complaints of the elderly. The cause of the distress may not be known, but the elder is treated for the symptoms. Unless a thorough inquiry is made, a sexual assault, either acute or chronic, may be missed.

Also, because there are often delays in the reporting of the abuse, elder victims of sexual assault are less likely to have a complete sexual-assault examination.

ASSISTED-LIVING FACILITIES

Assisted-living facilities generally provide different shifts of staff, check on residents over a 24-hour period and meals and cleaning services are often provided. It is generally believed that an elder living in an assisted-living facility is in a protected environment and has safety features in place; however, this is not always the case. Unfortunately, sometimes access into the facility is not tightly controlled, thereby allowing sexual predators easy access to the patients. The following case illustrates this.

A 41-year-old man entered the unsecured door of an assisted living facility and raped an 83-year-old woman in her room. The woman reported she was awakened to the man being in her room and that he stated, "Don't scream or I am going to kill you." She further stated that he held her down and assaulted her, taunting her and ordering her to use profanity. She refused. After the assault, the man ran into a facility employee and asked her to help him find a friend who he said worked at the facility. He then put his hand over her mouth and wrestled her to the ground, grabbing her checkbook. He escaped, and the employee called 911. The police arrived at 2:45 A.M. and found the perpetrator a few blocks away. When shown videos of himself at the facility, he admitted he entered the premises to sexually assault someone. The victim's son reported that his mother's personality changed after the attack. She moved out of the facility to be closer to him but became withdrawn and reclusive, which was exactly the opposite of her pre-assault personality characteristics.

NURSING HOMES

Three common nursing-home sexual-abuse victim profiles include these: (1) physically disabled older resident; (2) cognitively impaired resident; and (3) physically impaired younger resident. The physically disabled older resident has no cognitive or mental impairment but requires assistance with mobility. The assistance may be short term, such as needing rehabilitation following surgery, or long term, as for residents with complications from a stroke. The cognitively impaired resident has a primary diagnosis of Alzheimer's disease or other dementia, and the physically impaired younger resident may have a physical impairment owing to a chronic neuromuscular disorder, such as multiple sclerosis or amyotrophic lateral sclerosis (ALS, or Lou Gehrig's disease), or an impairment as a result of trauma from a motor vehicle accident or other severe head injury.

Nursing homes are, for the residents, precisely that—a home in which the staff functions as the residents' caregivers (in both a literal and figurative sense). The nursing home and its staff are perceived as "safe," and violations represent a more profound betrayal of trust than do violations committed outside the sanctity of the nursing home.

The sexual victimization of older adults in nursing homes is under-recognized and under-reported. Even when an incident is identified as earlier suggested, reporting is delayed and treatment and postrape services are often inadequate.[18] Furthermore, prosecution of these crimes is fraught with problems related to poor-quality evidence because of delays in reporting. Older adults residing in nursing homes often require assistance with basic activities of daily living such as bathing, dressing, and feeding because of physical and cognitive impairments. These disabilities make an individual dependent on others and as a result make the older person an easy target for a sexual predator.[19]

Resident-on-Resident Sexual Abuse

The issue of elder sexual activity is sometimes addressed in policy manuals of nursing homes with a section on the sexual rights of the elderly. Unfortunately, in some nursing homes, nursing home staff are said to ignore the pleas for help by resident females. The cases in this category generally involve elderly women who have tried to reject the sexual advances of elderly males who, in most cases, preyed on many elderly victims. In such cases, there is no history of a developing relationship but rather of a predatory style.

EARLY RECOGNITION AND DETECTION

Early recognition and detection of abuse and reporting of cases means knowing the physical and behavioral indicators of sexual abuse in the elderly, being able to ask the right questions of the elder and to report all suspected cases to the proper agency (for example, law enforcement, protective services, and/or hospital for forensic services). There are two major barriers that mitigate the need to report elder sexual abuse. The first barrier is the victim's reluctance to report the incident, which may occur because she is too frightened or embarrassed. In other cases, the offender may be a domestic partner, a situation often noted in domestic violence cases. In such situations, the elder may fear being sent to a nursing home and losing his or her independence and/or financial base from the partner. Thus, a plan needs to be worked out with the elder that will not jeopardize her/his financial security. This can be done by identifying the resources and social support available to help the elder remain in the home. This may require talking with law enforcement and/or the prosecutor regarding charges that can be brought against the offending partner.

The second barrier in reporting elder sexual abuse is that of disbelief. Caregivers, staff, and family may believe the elder is fantasizing, in a cognitive disorganized state, or making up a story. As with all ages of victims, staff need to take seriously all reports of sexual abuse. It will be up to experts in the area of elder sexual abuse to determine the credibility of the allegation and up to the prosecutor as to the viability of the case in the criminal justice system. Even if the prosecutor does not find adequate evidence to make the case, the elder should be respected and receive therapy services.

INTERVIEWING ELDER VICTIMS OF SEXUAL ABUSE

The following therapeutic tasks are important to develop trust with the elder in order to do an accurate assessment of the complaint of sexual abuse.

- Tell the senior what to expect. Talk slowly and clearly. Advise victims they will be going to a hospital for an examination and for collection of evidence.
- Assess the victim's sensory abilities. Can the victim hear and see people? A quiet and well-lighted area should be used, and the investigator's/staff person's face should be well in line of vision of the elder. If there are sensory problems, learn how the elder adjusts to the deficit by asking him/her or the family or caregivers.
- Observe the victim's demeanor. Is the victim quiet, crying, angry, or in distress? Ask how the victim is feeling and if he/she has any questions about what is going to happen. Allow adequate time for the elder to express his/her emotions.

SIGNS OF PHYSICAL TRAUMA

- *Signs of physical trauma* include observable objective evidence of injury such as bruises, abrasions, lacerations, and/or bleeding. The elder and accompanying family members need to be told that a comprehensive physical assessment will be conducted by the forensic examiner observing injury to the elder's general body condition, and a separate genital examination will be conducted. Evidence of intentional injury is sought by asking the question as to how the injury occurred. Accidental injury needs to be ruled out. For example, nursing-home staff have described genital bleeding as the result of "rough peri-care" (which involves cleaning of urinary and/or rectal orifices). This may or may not be accidental, and such assertions need medical verification.
- *Symptoms of physical trauma* include an indication of trauma provided by the elder. For example, the elder may say she was slapped or held by her

throat, but no observable injury can be noted. This, too, should be noted as part of the forensic record.

- *Signs of emotional trauma* include observable signs such as crying, rocking, hands shaking, flushed appearance, signs of perspiration. Elders may try to hide their feelings by being very quiet, guarded, or controlled in their demeanor.

WHY WOMEN DO NOT REPORT RAPE TO THE POLICE

Studies have shown that many women are reluctant to report rape to their local police. The reasons most often given include:

- Lack of belief in the ability of the police to apprehend the suspect.
- Worries about unsympathetic treatment from police and discomforting procedures.
- Belief that they were somehow at fault for the rape.
- Embarrassment about publicity, however limited.
- Fear of reprisal by the rapist.[20]
- Apprehension, as a result of television programs or newspaper reports, of being further victimized by court proceedings.

Unfortunately, some complaints about the criminal justice system's treatment of rape victims are justified. In many jurisdictions, efforts are being made to correct deficiencies. Many corrections have come about through legislative changes.[21] In other instances, women's groups have worked with local police departments to educate the public, especially women, about the crime of rape and to correct much of the misinformation that may be transmitted via television programs and other news media.

The failure of victims to report rapes has serious implications, because without such information, the effectiveness of the police in protecting other women is considerably diminished. A case in point occurred a few years ago in San Francisco:

A young woman who was raped turned first to her friends for help and comfort, then sought aid from a local Women Against Rape group. No one encouraged her to make a police report; she was indecisive and did nothing. Several days later, she read a news account describing a rape similar to her own. She immediately notified the police and learned the rapist had attacked three other women. With the additional information she provided, the police located and arrested the rapist by the end of the day.[22]

FALSE RAPE ALLEGATIONS

During the past several years, police agencies have been more selective in assigning personnel to rape investigations. They are now more sensitive to the emotional trauma experienced by victims. However, although the vast majority of rape complaints are legitimate, investigators must remain alert to the possibility of false rape complaints.

In the rape investigation, officers have a responsibility both to the legitimate victims of rape and to men who are falsely accused of rape. There are no hard-and-fast rules to guide the investigator to the truth, but experienced investigators generally find it by carefully questioning all parties involved and scrutinizing the circumstantial and physical evidence. Investigators should conduct a complete check on the background of the victim and all suspects. If the victim is a prostitute or promiscuous, this fact should be considered in the search for the truth. But once it is evident that the legal elements for rape are present, the victim's character should be disregarded. The following case shows the importance of the victim's background in rape complaints.

An 18-year-old woman reported that she had been walking past a vacant house at night when three young men whom she knew leaped from behind some bushes and dragged her, kicking and screaming, into the house. She claimed that she resisted. While two men held her down, each took turns having sexual intercourse with her. When the last one had finished, they fled. She went to a nearby store and called the police.

The officer assigned to the case had reservations about the validity of the victim's complaint for the following reasons:

- The occupant of the house next to the vacant house said that he had heard no screams even though his house was only 20 feet away and his windows were open.
- Sand examined in the area where the men supposedly had leaped from behind the bushes was undisturbed, although there were a number of shoe impressions in the sandy patch leading into the house.
- The woman's clothing showed no indications of a struggle.
- The interior of the house was examined, and a large piece of cardboard was found on the floor in a back room. The woman stated that she had been forced to lie on this while the men raped her. There was a considerable amount of dirt on the floor near the cardboard, but, except for some shoe impressions, there were no tracks that would indicate that

a person had been dragged through the house and to the cardboard.

- A physical examination administered at the hospital indicated the victim had recently had sexual intercourse, but there were no injuries or other traumas. As a result of additional information provided by the alleged victim, the investigator assigned to the case went to the suspects' known hangout, a nearby candy store. The candy store owner reported that he knew the victim, and she had voluntarily left the candy store with the three suspects earlier in the evening.

The manager said the girl frequently came into the candy store to pick up men; he said he had been told by patrons she was a prostitute who took her customers to an abandoned house nearby to have sexual intercourse. The manager was asked to call the police if any of the men returned. The following day one of the young men, who had heard that the police were looking for him, voluntarily came to police headquarters. He said he and two other young men had agreed to pay the girl $1 each for her sexual services, to which she agreed. They were directed by her to a nearby abandoned house, and each had sexual intercourse with her. When they finished, they refused to pay her, and one of the men stole her brand-new shoes (which she had just purchased and was carrying in the original box) to give to his girlfriend. The victim was reinterviewed and admitted she had lied to the police because she was angry with the men for cheating her out of the money they had agreed to pay her and because they also had stolen her new shoes. She was subsequently arrested and charged with making a false crime report and plead guilty. She was sentenced to 30 days in jail.

Had the victim actually been sexually assaulted, her background would have been irrelevant.

Occasionally, women falsely report that they have been raped as an attention-getting device. The following case illustrates this point.

A woman whose husband was a long-distance truck driver and frequently away from home reported to police that a house painter, who had responded to her home to apply for a painting job she had advertised in a local paper, had raped her. Because of the detailed information she gave the police, they were able to arrest the man. A lineup was conducted at police headquarters, and she positively identified the painter as the man who raped her. He was then charged with rape and bound over to the local district court. He spent three days in jail before being bonded out. Several

days later, the woman had second thoughts, contacted the prosecutors, and confessed that she had fabricated the rape story in order to get her husband to stay home and pay more attention to her. She was subsequently charged with and convicted of perjury.

She was sentenced to 180 days in jail and two years' probation. Further, she was ordered by the court to apologize to the man in the local newspaper and in radio advertisements. The man who was arrested lost his part-time job as a painter and had to employ a lawyer; his children in school were confronted by other children who said "Your dad's a rapist." His wife was too embarrassed to go to town, and his 18-year-old daughter quit high school because of the way she was treated. The accused man was also fired from his primary job as a driver after being arrested. Even though he had been cleared of the charges, there was still a stigma associated with his arrest.[23]

Some inexperienced investigators are not suspicious of false allegations because of the victim's age. This complacency is an error, as the following case illustrates.

A 65-year-old great-grandmother reported that a 19-year-old neighbor had raped and robbed her in her home. The woman advised police she had invited the young man over for a cup of coffee. After a while, he told her he wanted to have sexual intercourse with her. She refused his request, whereupon he slapped her in the face and told her he would kill her great-grandson, who was asleep in a nearby bedroom, unless she had sexual intercourse with him. The woman said she agreed because of her concern for her great-grandson's safety. She went into her bedroom, disrobed, and had sexual intercourse with the man. When they were finished, he demanded she give him some money and again threatened to injure the child if she failed to comply with his wishes. She gave him money, and he left.

The police pickup order was broadcast for the man. The woman was questioned and admitted she had invited the young man to her home and had suggested they have sexual intercourse; he had agreed. When they were finished, he demanded money from her. She refused. He then slapped her in the face and he threatened her great-grandson. The woman said she became frightened and gave the man her rent money. Because she now had to explain to her husband why the rent money was gone, she made up the rape complaint. However, even though the rape complaint was unfounded, a robbery had occurred.

Although there is always the possibility that a rape accusation is false, the investigator must remember that, according to the FBI's *Uniform Crime Report,* in 47% of all forcible-rape cases, sufficient evidence is present to make an arrest.[24] These are simply the cases in which evidence conclusively points to a particular offender. There are a large number of cases where a rape has clearly occurred, but no specific offender can be determined from the evidence. Furthermore, there are cases in which police investigators simply find no evidence that a crime has taken place. Even in these cases (which police often dismiss), it is still possible that a rape has occurred. The following story illustrates this point.

On arriving home late one evening and before going to bed, a 30-year-old woman living alone checked all the windows and doors to be certain they were locked. After checking them, she went to bed. Shortly thereafter she was awakened by a man in her bed; he held a knife to her throat and warned her not to make any noise or attempt to resist or he would kill her. The man then proceeded to rape the woman. After raping her, he ordered her to go to the bathroom and to douche. After douching, she was instructed to flush the toilet. The suspect then fled by the front door. When the police arrived, they could find no signs of forced entry into the home. When the woman was examined at the hospital, there was no evidence of sexual intercourse or the presence of semen. The police thought the woman had fabricated the incident because of the absence of forcible entry into the home or any physical evidence of sexual intercourse. The case was classified as unfounded. Two months later the man was arrested for another rape in the same general area where the first rape had occurred. The police found in his possession a number of keys; with the cooperation of his family members, it was determined that one of the keys was for a home the family had been renting several months before. This was the same home in which the first victim had been raped. The owner of the home had failed to rekey the lock after the family moved out and the new tenant moved in. The rapist merely retained the key and used it to enter through the front door and commit the rape.

THE VICTIM AND PHYSICAL EVIDENCE

Rape investigations usually begin when the victim either places a call to report the rape or takes herself to a hospital. The report may be filed moments after the incident occurred, or it may be days or weeks later. In either case,

▲ **FIGURE 10-1 Bagged hands**
This victim of rape and murder had her hands bagged at the crime scene in order to avoid loss of any possible physical evidence on her hands or under her fingernails.

the investigator must remember that the victim is a walking crime scene. Certain investigative procedures must be followed to ensure that physical evidence on the victim's person is not lost or accidentally destroyed.[25]

For example, when the victim is deceased and it is not practical or possible to process the victim's hands and fingernails at the crime scene, it is best to bag the hands (Figure 10-1). After the body is transported to medical examiner's office, the hands and fingernails can be processed for physical evidence.

INSTRUCTIONS TO THE VICTIM

The officer responding to a reported sexual assault should make a great effort to ensure that any evidence that may be on the victim is secure. Once evidence is destroyed, it cannot be retrieved. Attending to the victim's well-being is unquestionably the primary concern; if she is in immediate need of medical attention, attending to that need is the officer's first responsibility. However, a well-trained officer will tactfully find a way to meet the victim's physical and psychological needs while preserving potentially useful and incriminating evidence. For instance, the officer should encourage the victim not to shower or douche (assuming she has not already done so) and should urge her not to change clothes. These actions cause the loss of hair and body fluids such as blood and semen that could be analyzed at the crime lab and used to corroborate the victim's testimony as well as lead to the identification, prosecution, and conviction of the perpetrator.

The victim should also be advised not to alter the scene of the crime. Even the location of body fluids and hairs can be telling, and such routine actions as flushing the toilet may mean a loss of crucial evidence (for example, in cases where the perpetrator used a condom and dropped it into the toilet.)[26]

SEMEN AND HAIR AS EVIDENCE

As was discussed in considerable detail in Chapter 4, "Physical Evidence," semen that contains sperm and hair that has the root attached can now be identified through DNA typing as coming from a specific individual. Thus, it is absolutely essential that appropriate samples be collected and preserved from the victim and the suspect. Note that the presence of semen is not evidence that a rape occurred, nor does its absence mean a rape did not occur. For example, because rapists sometimes experience sexual dysfunction, the examining physician may find no semen during the pelvic examination. In interviews of 133 convicted rapists, 50 (37%) admitted some sexual dysfunction. Of the rapists, 23 stated that they were unable to achieve an orgasm during the sex act; 22 experienced difficulty in achieving and sustaining an erection; and 5 experienced premature ejaculation.[27]

Note that the terms "semen" and "sperm" are not synonymous. **Semen** is a grayish-white fluid, produced in the male reproductive organs, that is ejaculated during orgasm. In liquid form, it has a chlorinelike odor; when dried, it has a starchlike consistency. **Sperm** are the tadpolelike organisms that are contained in, and travel through, semen to fertilize the female egg. This distinction is important, because the laboratory examinations and tests employed to search for each are quite different. Thus, if a rape was committed by a male who is sterile (having no sperm in his ejaculate), then semen but not sperm may be present. Note that DNA typing is conducted on the sperm, not the semen. The physician examining the victim for sperm in the vagina therefore aspirates the vagina—removes fluids with a suction device—and microscopically examines them for sperm. The motility of sperm in the vagina is short, measured in hours rather than days; motility decreases to zero in about 3 hours. Menstruation may prolong motility to 4 hours. If large numbers of highly motile sperm are aspirated from the vagina, one may conclude that sexual intercourse had occurred 1 to 2 hours before the examination. If a few motile sperm remain, one may conclude that sexual intercourse occurred within 3 hours of the examination. Nonmotile sperm may be found in a living female in small numbers up to 48 hours after sexual intercourse. Nonmotile sperm have been found in dead bodies for up to several hours after death.[28]

When sperm cannot be found, a second test may be employed to identify the presence of acid phosphatase. Acid phosphatase, an enzyme, is a component of the liquid portion of semen. The test should be conducted by experienced crime laboratory personnel and interpreted with care. Routine hospital laboratory techniques are not applicable to this type of examination and may be errone-

ously interpreted as significant. Only strong reactions should be considered evidence of semen, because mild positive reactions have been noted with vegetable matter, feces, and many other types of organic substances. Experiments have been conducted to determine the persistence of a significantly positive reaction to the acid phosphatase test over variable lengths of time following sexual intercourse. In the living, acid phosphatase may be lost from the vagina after 12–40 hours.

INFORMATION FOR THE EXAMINING PHYSICIAN/SEXUAL-ASSAULT NURSE EXAMINER

The medical personnel responsible for examining the victim should be provided with all the available facts before the physical examination.

Usually, certain hospitals in a community are designated as the ones to which rape victims are taken for a physical examination. These hospitals frequently have both specially trained staffs and the necessary technical facilities. Under no circumstances should a male investigator be present in the hospital room when a female victim is being physically examined. If a male investigator believes that some physical evidence may be adhering to the victim's body, he should instruct the examining physician to collect such evidence and turn it over to him. The collection of physical evidence in this manner must conform to all guidelines for preserving the chain of custody.

COLLECTION OF THE VICTIM'S CLOTHING

The victim's clothing should be collected as soon as possible. If she is still wearing the clothes worn during the incident, she should undress over a clean cloth or large paper mat so that any evidence that may be dislodged from her clothes is not lost. Even if the victim was forced to disrobe before the sexual attack, it is possible that hair, semen, or fibers from the suspect's clothing have been deposited on her clothing. Each article of clothing should be placed in a separate container, properly labeled, and stored for later analysis. The victim may then be photographed before redressing to document any evidence of physical abuse.[29] Underpants should not be the only item of a victim's clothing recovered, because they often offer only limited physical evidence and are likely to be contaminated with other stains, such as vaginal secretions or urine, that interfere with the laboratory examination. Other garments, such as the dress, slip, or coat, may be of greater value in providing physical evidence. The evidence most frequently obtained from the victim's clothing consists of fibers from a suspect's clothing and loose pubic hairs. If the assault occurred in a wooded or grassy area, there will often be soil, seeds, weeds, and other vegetation adhering to the victim's clothing.[30]

The following actual case, which occurred before the advent of DNA typing, illustrates the importance of a careful search for physical evidence:

The partly dressed body of a 16-year-old female was discovered by two young boys traveling through a wooded area. The victim's slacks and underpants were pulled down around her ankles, and her brassiere was pulled up around her head. A check of the missing-persons file revealed that a female fitting her description had been reported missing by her parents 18 hours earlier. The body was later identified as the missing female.

The victim's body was removed from the scene in a clean white sheet and transported to a local hospital. The medical examination of the victim revealed that she had died from a fatal brain injury after being struck repeatedly with a blunt object. In addition, she had a large bruise on her right cheek, also caused by a blow from a blunt object, possibly a fist. The examination of the deceased's person and clothing yielded the following:

- Her clothing.
- Pubic-hair samples.
- Blood samples for typing.
- Grease stains on the inside of her thighs. The grease was initially deposited on the suspect's hands after he used an automobile master cylinder that had been on the floorboard of his car to batter the victim unconscious.
- A single human hair clutched in her hand, mixed with considerable dirt, leaves, twigs, and so forth.
- No semen was found either in or on her body, clothing, or in the immediate area.

Physical evidence also was obtained from the crime scene:

- Tire impressions.
- Samples of soil, leaves, weeds, and other vegetation.

A suspect who had been the last person seen with the victim and who also had an arrest record for a similar offense was taken into custody, and his vehicle was impounded. The vehicle's entire interior, including steering wheel, dashboard, door panels, seats, floor mats, and visor, was removed, as were all four wheels. These items were transported to the crime laboratory along with all the evidence collected from the victim and the crime scene. A pair of blood-stained trousers and hair samples were obtained from the suspect. The results of the laboratory examination revealed:

- The victim's brassiere had several fibers caught in the hooks, which were identical to those of the terrycloth seat covers in the suspect's car.

- The grease stain on the victim's thighs was compared with the grease found under the dashboard and near the ignition switch in the suspect's vehicle and found to be identical. An examination of the ignition switch revealed that the car could be started only if someone reached under the dash and crossed the ignition wires; thus, when the suspect tried to start his car, he deposited grease from the master cylinder onto the ignition switch.
- The single hair found in the victim's hand was similar in all characteristics to that of the suspect.
- Samples collected from the victim's hair at the morgue were similar to those recovered from the floorboard of the suspect's vehicle.
- Fibers from the victim's underpants were identical to fibers recovered from the suspect's vehicle.
- A tire impression at the scene matched a tire on the suspect's vehicle.
- Debris collected from the scene matched debris recovered from the interior of the suspect's car and dirt extracted from the rims of the wheels of the suspect's car.
- Human blood was found on the steering wheel of the suspect's car, but the presence of various contaminants prevented the blood from being typed accurately.
- Because the suspect had soaked his trousers in cold water overnight, blood typing was impossible.

The suspect confessed to murdering the victim after abducting her from a teenage dance, although his confession was not needed in view of the physical evidence. As previously indicated, he identified the murder weapon as an automobile master cylinder, which he had disposed of after the crime. It was never located. He killed the victim after she had violently resisted his efforts to assault her sexually.

Examination of most hair, fiber, debris, and tire or shoe prints at the scene can narrow the field. Analysis of these materials, however, will most often yield evidence characteristic of class (discussed in considerable detail in Chapter 4, "Physical Evidence"), not individualized results. However, the preponderance of class-characteristic evidence, coupled with the particulars of the case, made a compelling argument against the suspect.

THE ROLE OF THE INVESTIGATOR IN SECURING THE RAPE SCENE

It is the criminal investigator's job to collect, catalog, and store physical evidence for later analysis in the laboratory. As soon as possible, the investigative unit should take photographs of the scene of the crime, including the specific area where the rape is believed to have occurred, the area around the rape, and the areas around the entrances, exits, and general perimeter of the facility where the rape occurred (if it occurred indoors). After this is done, various methods may be used to gather evidence for laboratory testing. Evidence recovery methods may include naked-eye searches, the use of oblique light to spot hair and fiber on the surface of furniture or other surfaces, the use of ultraviolet light to illuminate fibers, careful vacuuming of selected small areas, adhesive lifts, combing or brushing, scraping under the fingernails and certain other surfaces, the use of blue light to detect semen, and the use of lasers.[31]

INCIDENCE OF ERRORS IN THE COLLECTION OF EVIDENCE

Physical evidence in a case is often the decisive factor in determining guilt or innocence. Developments in DNA technology over the last 25 years have added a new dimension to rape investigation. Currently, DNA analysis combined with careful hair and fiber analysis can "describe the clothes worn by the criminal, give an idea of his stature, age, hair color, or similar information" and thereby significantly limit the officers' search for a suspect.[32] With the exception of identical twins, no two persons have the same DNA structure. A good DNA sample can now be analyzed to identify with forensic and legal certainty any individual whose DNA structure is known.[33]

However, DNA testing is only as good as the investigative techniques used to gather the evidence. As items are collected, the investigator must carefully label the items and store them in such a way that they are preserved intact and uncompromised for later laboratory analysis. Current laboratory technology is accurate to such a degree that defense lawyers have little to challenge other than the chain of custody of the evidence and any possible contamination. Keeping careful records of the chain of custody of the evidence and protecting the evidence from contamination are crucial both for preserving the sample itself so that it can be analyzed and for ensuring that conclusions drawn from the analysis of the sample cannot be challenged in court.[34]

COLLECTING SAMPLES FOR DNA ANALYSIS FROM SUSPECTS

In the past, the only acceptable method for obtaining DNA analysis from a suspect was to obtain a vial of his blood. This, however, requires that he first agree to the procedure, sign a form, and then be transported to a local hospital to have his blood taken. This delay often resulted in the suspect changing his mind about the procedure. When this happened, a court order was the only way to obtain blood; however, there might not be sufficient probable cause for a court order to be issued, and so the police would be left with a suspect and no way to obtain his DNA for analysis.

This was a problem the New York City Police Department (NYPD) faced several years ago. They presented this problem to the forensic biology unit of the New York City Medical Examiner's Office, which was responsible for analyzing and documenting all DNA evidence in New York City. The medical examiner's office had a simple and acceptable solution. They recommended taking a buccal swab (described below) from the suspect while in custody in lieu of obtaining blood. Several other methods (discussed in greater detail on the following page) for obtaining DNA evidence can be used by investigators to legally collect evidence against suspects that can definitely link them to particular crimes through their DNA or can exonerate those who are under suspicion.[35]

Legal Criteria

To obtain voluntary DNA evidence from a suspect, a signed authorization should be obtained. Suspects and others whose DNA evidence is needed in an investigation have a legal right against self-incrimination and cannot be forced to provide DNA samples for analysis. A consent form was used by the NYPD after consultation with the Manhattan District Attorney's Office for those suspects who were willing to voluntarily provide a DNA sample for analysis.

Buccal Swab

The skin cells on the inside of the mouth continually break up and fall into the saliva, which is normally swallowed or spit out. These skin cells provide a perfect opportunity for the collection of DNA. The unique genetic code that is associated with particular skin cells is exclusive to one individual and is the same genetic code that appears throughout that person's body (blood, organs, sperm, hair, and so on). Items required for a buccal swab include:

- two sterile cotton swabs in their original wrappers (medical swabs generally come in packages of two sealed in a paper wrapper);
- paper envelope;
- latex gloves;
- wet paper towel.

The procedure is as follows:

- The process should be explained to the suspect to ensure that DNA is collected correctly the first time.
- Latex gloves should be worn by the investigator to prevent contamination (with his/her own DNA).
- The cotton swabs should be removed from the wrapper and given to the suspect.
- The suspect should then vigorously rub the inside of the mouth (cheek area) for 30 seconds.
- The swab should then be placed in the envelope and left open to allow the swab to dry, because moisture can contaminate cells.

- When the swabs are dry, the envelope should be sealed.
- Do not lick the envelope when sealing it; instead, use a wet paper towel to moisten the glued surface of the envelope flap.
- The envelope should be signed, dated, and the time recorded. Other pertinent information, such as the suspect's name and the case number, should be placed on the envelope.
- The envelope should be hand-delivered to the laboratory for testing.[36]

Surreptitious Collection of DNA from Suspects

The simplest and easiest way to obtain DNA samples is from saliva. For example, in 1974 the Buffalo, New York, Police Department had investigated a rape and stabbing of a woman, and the case had gone unsolved. Information was recently received indicating that a possible suspect might be a 60-year-old man who was married to the step-sister of the victim of the rape and murder. In an effort to obtain DNA samples, the Buffalo Police Department surreptitiously followed the man, and when he spit on the sidewalk the officers collected the samples. They were analyzed, and DNA from samples matched the semen samples collected from the victim. He was arrested and charged with the crime.

The same applies to a discarded coffee cup, used napkin or tissue, or half-eaten piece of food, all of which can be used to obtain DNA evidence. If such items are discarded by a suspect, they can be legally seized, provided, of course, they are discarded in a public place or a facility to which the police have access. If they are discarded in a place to which the police do not have access, permission or a search warrant is required for their removal. If any questions regarding the legality of seizing items for DNA analysis arise, the local prosecutor should be consulted for guidance. If a suspect is at a police facility, the investigator can offer the suspect a cigarette (forgetting for a moment about the no-smoking ban in the building), a cup of coffee, a soda, a sandwich, and so forth. The investigator must be certain not to touch the items; the suspect must be the only one who handles them. Skin cells from the inside of the mouth fall out onto the lip and are then recoverable from cigarette butts, coffee containers, soda cans, napkins, and so on. An empty, clean ashtray and a wastebasket must be available to the suspect. When the object is discarded, it may be collected for analysis. To prevent contamination, the investigator must be certain to wear latex gloves while handling such objects.[37]

Seizing a Suspect's Clothing for DNA Evidence

Clothing may contain evidence that can be connected back to the victim. If a suspect is under arrest, his cloth-

ing can be seized as evidence, provided of course he is arrested wearing the same clothing and has not washed them. In a hospital setting, the staff can be helpful by providing medical scrubs for a suspect to wear if his clothing is seized. If a suspect is not in custody, however, and the evidence such as blood or semen is not visible, a search warrant will probably be required to seize the clothing. In either event, local prosecutors should be conferred with about the legality of seizing clothing before proceeding. Items must be seized in a manner that assures that they will be admitted into court as evidence.[38]

Searching for DNA Evidence under Court Order: The Search Warrant

If a search warrant is obtained and evidence for DNA analysis is sought, the warrant/order should request the seizure of any item on which DNA might be found. Under some circumstances, judges may feel this definition of possible evidence is too broad. In those cases, specific items suspected of containing the suspect's DNA should be listed on the warrant for seizure. Typical items that would appear on a search warrant include: bloodstains, bedsheets (where semen stains might exist), cigarette butts, the suspect's toothbrush (if appropriate), and the suspect's comb (if appropriate). Any additional items found that may contain DNA will require the warrant to be amended before seizure.[39] Investigators should work with their prosecutors' offices as well as magistrates to be certain they comply with the necessary legal procedures to amend a search warrant when the need to do so arises.

SEXUAL-BATTERY EXAMINATION

Most hospitals or crisis centers responsible for the collection of evidence from sex-offense victims have developed sexual-battery examination kits. (See Figures 10-2 and 10-3 for a detailed description of the contents of these kits.)

CONDOM TRACE EVIDENCE

Manufacturers produce condoms using a variety of materials, both natural and synthetic. Each manufacturer has its own formula, which may vary even among its different brands.[40] Some condoms are made from lamb membranes, and one manufacturer recently introduced a model made from polyurethane plastic. Still, latex rubber condoms have, by far, the largest share of the market, perhaps because they cost considerably less. In addition to the basic materials they use to produce condoms, manufacturers also add other substances, known as **exchangeable traces** that comprise particulates, lubricants, and spermicide.

► FIGURE 10-2
Sexual-assault victim exam kit contents

Sexual assault victim exam kit contents

1. Collection vial—for urine.

2. Collection vial—for blood.

3. Pubic hair combings specimen envelope—used in the collection of possible foreign material in the pubic hair of the victim.

4. Head hair combings specimen envelope—used in the same way as pubic hair combings, but for hair on the head of the victim.

5. Vaginal smear slides—used in the collection of semen fluid for DNA evidence deposited by the assailant in the vagina of the victim. One slide is used for the vaginal area and the other is used for the specimen taken from the cervix of the victim.

6. Smear slides—used to collect DNA (seminal fluid) from other areas where the perpetrator's DNA may be found on the victim such as those resulting from the anal or oral penetration of victim.

7. Swabs—used in the collection of seminal fluid for DNA evidence that the perpetrator may have left on the victim (anal, oral, or other areas).

8. Vaginal swabs (4)—used to collect seminal fluid for DNA evidence of the perpetrator.

9. Cervical swabs (2)—used to collect seminal fluid from the cervix for DNA evidence of the perpetrator.

10. Saliva standard swabs—used to collect DNA evidence of the perpetrator from the victim's mouth.

11. Buccal swab—used to collect the victim's DNA.

12. Extra swabs—to collect possible semen from the perpetrator wherever it may be found on the victim.

13. Extra swabs—used to collect saliva left by the perpetrator from areas that may have been bitten, licked, or kissed.

14. Underwear specimen bag.

15. Genoprobe—used to screen for chlamydia and gonorrhea. This is taken at the time of evidence collection.

The same kit is used to collect evidence with male victims, but the differences are in the genoprobe that is used in the physical areas of the body from where the evidence is collected. Instead of vaginal swabs, penile swabs are used as well as anal or penile cultures for gonorrhea.

Source: This kit was created by the Florida Department of Law Enforcement and is provided to personnel who are responsible for gathering physical evidence from sexual assault victims. The contents depicted in photograph in Figure 10-3 were provided by Robyn Royall and Linda Brown, Sexual Assault Victim Examination Program, Pinellas Park, Florida.

EXCHANGEABLE TRACES

Particulates

Condom manufacturers add finely powdered particulates to prevent a rolled-up latex condom from sticking to itself. Particulates found in different brands include cornstarch, potato starch, and lycopodium (a powder found in plants), as well as amorphous silica, talc, and other minerals. In the laboratory, forensic scientists use several different techniques to characterize these particles and compare them with those obtained from other condom brands.

Lubricants

Sexual assailants prefer lubricated condoms, probably for the same reason they use petroleum jelly—that is, to help facilitate their crimes.[41] Many condom brands contain a liquid lubricant, which may be classified as either "wet"

or "dry." Both types of condom lubricant have an oillike consistency, but wet lubricants are water-based and/or water-soluble, whereas dry lubricants are not. Although many different manufacturers use the same dry lubricant, the viscosity grades sometimes differ. The forensic laboratory can recover these silicone oils easily from items of evidence and possibly associate them with a condom manufacturer. Wet lubricants may contain either polyethylene glycol or a gel made from a combination of ingredients similar to those found in vaginal lubricants. Forensic examination can associate specific formulations with particular condom brands, despite their similarities to other products on the market.

Spermicide

Both wet- and dry-lubricated condoms also may contain the spermicide nonoxynol-9. Its recovery and detection, along with lubricant ingredients and particulates,

▲ FIGURE 10-3   Sexual-assault victim exam kit contents

can help show condom use and indicate the specific brand.

THE VALUE OF CONDOM TRACE EVIDENCE

Condom trace evidence can assist investigators in several ways. It can help prove corpus delicti, provide evidence of penetration, produce associative evidence, and link the acts of serial rapists.

In Proving Corpus Delicti

Traces associated with condoms can help prove **corpus delicti,** the fact that a crime has occurred. This evidence can support the claims of either the victim or the accused. For example, the U.S. military can prosecute personnel diagnosed as HIV-positive for aggravated assault if they engage in unprotected sex, even if it is consensual. If servicemen accused of aggravated assault claim that they did in fact wear a condom but it broke or slipped off, condom trace evidence can support that claim.

In Providing Evidence of Penetration

Condom traces found inside a victim can provide evidence of penetration. In many jurisdictions, this evidence raises the charge to a higher degree of sexual assault.

In Producing Associative Evidence

Recovered condom traces may correspond to those found in a certain brand or used by a particular manufacturer. An empty packet of this particular brand found near the crime scene, especially if it bears the suspect's fingerprints, provides a strong association between the suspect and the crime. Unopened condom packages of the same brand found on the suspect, in his car, or at his residence also would help tie the suspect to the crime.

In Linking the Acts of Serial Rapists

People tend to be creatures of habit, and sexual criminals are no exception. A serial rapist likely will use the same brand of condom to commit repeated acts. Moreover, repeat offenders whose DNA profiles have been stored in a computer data bank may be likely to use a condom when committing subsequent crimes. Along with other aspects of his modus operandi, traces from the same condom brand or manufacturer found during several different investigations can help connect a suspect to an entire series of assaults.

GUIDELINES FOR EVIDENCE COLLECTION

Investigators need not make any drastic changes in their usual procedures in order to include the possibility of condom trace evidence. The following guidelines will assist criminal investigators and medical examiners in collecting this valuable evidence.[42]

At the Crime Scene

First and foremost, investigators must wear powder-free gloves to protect themselves from blood-borne pathogens and to avoid leaving particulates that may be similar to those contained in some condom brands. After collecting the evidence, they should package the gloves separately and submit them with the evidence so that the forensic laboratory can verify that the gloves did not leave behind any particulates.

At the crime scene, investigators should make every effort to locate any used condom and its foil package. If a condom is recovered, the traces from the victim on the outside and the seminal fluids from the assailant on the inside will have the greatest evidentiary value.

If investigators find an empty packet, they first should try to recover any latent prints from the outside. The inside of the package will probably not contain prints, but it may contain lubricant, spermicide, and particulate residues. Investigators should wipe the inside with a clean cotton swab. The traces on this swab will serve as a standard for comparison with traces recovered from the victim and the suspect.

With the Victim

In addition to providing general information about the crime, victims may be able to supply valuable details about the condom and its wrapper. They may recall the brand itself or other important details, including the condom's color, shape, texture, odor, taste, and lubrication.

After obtaining facts about the condom, investigators should ask victims about their sexual and hygienic habits, which might account for traces not attributable to the crime. A comprehensive interview would include the following questions:

- Has the victim recently engaged in consensual sex?
- If so, was a condom used? A vaginal lubricant? What brand?
- Does the victim use any external or internal vaginal products (anti-itch medications, deodorants, douches, suppositories, and so on)?
- If so, what brands?

These questions assume an adult female victim. Investigators must modify the interview to accommodate male or child sexual-assault victims.

With the Suspect(s)

Investigators also should question the suspect about the condom. A cooperative suspect will reveal the brand, tell where he purchased it, and describe how and where he disposed of both the condom and the empty packet. An uncooperative or deceitful suspect may claim he does not know or cannot remember, or he may name a popular brand but be unable to describe the condom or the packet in detail.

Legal Considerations

When investigators know or suspect that a sexual offender used a condom, they must remember to list condoms on the warrant obtained to search the suspect's possessions. The search of a suspect's home may reveal intact condom packets, but if investigators have not listed condoms on the search warrant, they will not be able to seize this valuable evidence.

RECORD OF INJURIES

A careful record should be made of the victim's injuries and be included in the report. Photographs of the victim's injuries serve two purposes. First, if a suspect is arrested and tried for the offense, the photographs tend to corroborate the victim's account of the attack. Second, the injuries may be of an unusual nature—bite marks, scratches, or burns from cigarettes—and may provide data valuable for developing the suspect's MO. In some cases, the injuries are readily visible to the investigator. In other cases, the injuries are concealed by the victim's clothing. The examining physician can provide details of injuries not readily noticeable. Color photographs should be taken if the victim has sustained visible severe injuries. If the injuries are in a location that requires the victim to disrobe partially or completely to be photographed, it is essential that a female police officer (not a male officer) or some other female officially associated with the police department or the hospital be present. If possible, a female police photographer should photograph the victim's injuries.

DRUG-FACILITATED SEXUAL ASSAULT

The U.S. Department of Justice has estimated that over 430,000 people in this country are victimized by sexual assault each year and that three out of four victims are acquainted with their attackers. Many of the women who report being raped by an acquaintance also report unusual symptoms such as blacking out and having hazy or no memories about the attack. Sexual offenders' increasing use of **date-rape drugs,** such as Rohypnol and gamma hydroxybutyrate, as tools of submission accounts for much of the complexity surrounding these cases.

Congress has responded to the growing use of date-rape drugs by passing the Drug-Induced Rape Prevention and Punishment Act of 1996, an amendment of the Controlled Substance Act. The law imposes a prison term of up to 20 years on anyone convicted of giving any controlled substance to another person without his or her knowledge, with the intention of committing a sexual assault.

Law-enforcement personnel can contribute to the successful prosecution of drug-facilitated sexual-assault cases by recognizing the symptoms of drugging, the availability and toxicology of widely used substances, and the range of delivery methods.[43]

DRUGS OF CHOICE

As already indicated, the two drugs that are most commonly used by sex offenders to facilitate their crimes are Rohypnol and gamma hydroxybutyrate.

Rohypnol

Rohypnol, also known as flunitrazepam, belongs to a class of drugs called benzodiazepines. It produces a spectrum of effects similar to those of diazepam (Valium), including skeletal muscle relaxation, sedation, and a reduction in anxiety. Of these effects, the sedative and hypnotic effects are the most important. Flunitrazepam is considered to be approximately 8–10 times more potent than Valium. The effect or "high" may last from 7–12 hours or longer after the dose. With pills or "hits" readily available for prices ranging from $2–$5, Rohypnol is extremely sought after. Street names include "roofies," "R-2s," "roach-2s," "trip and fall," and "mind erasers."

This fast-acting drug can be ground into a powder and easily slipped into food or drink. It can take effect within 30 minutes, and symptoms may persist for up to 8 hours.[44] Symptoms of Rohypnol intoxication include sedation, dizziness, visual disturbances, memory impairment, and loss of consciousness and motor coordination.[45] These effects may be compounded, and made potentially lethal, by alcohol. It is traceable in a person's urine for 48–96 hours after ingestion and in blood for only 12 hours.

The drug is easily obtained on the black market, through the Internet, and in other countries. A significant amount of Rohypnol makes its way to the United States from Mexico and Colombia. The recent notoriety of Rohypnol as a date-rape drug has prompted manufacturers to create a tablet that is more difficult to dissolve in liquid and that will turn a drink blue. Unfortunately, the original colorless, dissolvable tablets are still widely available (Figure 10-4).

Many victims of drug-induced sexual assault are targeted at parties, clubs, and bars. Members of the high

▲ **FIGURE 10-4 Rohypnol**
The drug Rohypnol is commonly used by sex offenders to facilitate their crime. It produces effects such as skeletal muscle relaxation, sedation, and a reduction in anxiety. The drug can be easily slipped into food or drink and can take effect within 30 minutes. It is often present in cases of date rape. (© 2005 www.streetdrugs.org)

school- and college-age populations are especially vulnerable to perpetrators of drug-induced sexual assault. The following case, which occurred in Prince William County, Virginia, illustrates this point.

Two 15-year-old girls were forcibly raped after unknowingly ingesting Rohypnol. During the trial, prosecutors dubbed this drug the "new stealth weapon" on the basis of its odorless and tasteless properties. Commonly known as the "date-rape drug," it dissolves rapidly when placed in a carbonated drink, making it virtually impossible for unsuspecting victims to detect. Once in the victim's system, it quickly produces physical as well as mental incapacitation. Approximately 8–10 times stronger than Valium, Rohypnol's sedative effect occurs within 30 minutes after ingestion. The main side effect is amnesia, but it also produces an intoxicated appearance, impaired judgment, impaired motor skills, drowsiness, dizziness, and confusion.

Prince William County's investigation revealed that in the late afternoon, the two young girls were taken willingly to an adult's apartment, having been reassured that they would be returned home after they saw the apartment. Once at the apartment, they were offered a soft drink. They both drank a Mountain Dew and started to feel "weird," as one victim put it, within about 30 minutes. Neither victim could remember what occurred over the next 9 hours.

The first victim woke up, disoriented, on the couch in the early morning hours. She went to the bathroom and noticed "hickeys" on her neck that had not been present the day before. She could not remember having sexual contact with anyone. She then went to look for the second victim, whom she found asleep on a pull-out bed. Once awakened, she, too, was disoriented. The second victim noticed a "hickey" on her inner thigh but did not remember engaging in any sexual contact. During the subsequent interviews, the men present in the apartment admitted having sexual intercourse with the victims but said it was consensual.

Three white tablets, marked "RH" were recovered from one of the men. These tested positive for Rohypnol. Both victims were seen by a sexual-assault nurse examiner. The internal genital findings were consistent with nonconsensual sexual assault.

After a jury trial, the defendant was found guilty of rape, distribution of a Schedule IV drug to a minor, and contributing to the delinquency of a minor. The co-defendant was found guilty of contributing to the delinquency of a minor.[46]

Gamma Hydroxybutyrate

Gamma hydroxybutyrate (GHB) (also known as "Grievous Bodily Harm," "gamma-OH," "liquid ecstasy," "georgia home boy," and "goop"), is another central nervous system depressant that is used to perpetrate sexual assaults. It is a clear liquid, slightly thicker than water, and can easily be mixed into food or drinks. As with Rohypnol, ingestion of GHB can lead to a variety of symptoms, such as an intense feeling of relaxation, seizures, loss of consciousness, coma, and even death.[47] The effects can be felt within 10–20 minutes after ingestion. A coma can occur within 30–40 minutes. The drug is traceable in a person's blood for only 4–8 hours and in urine for 12–15 hours (Figure 10-5).

It is often marketed as an antidepressant and a body-building and weight-control supplement. In addition, the Internet abounds with recipes for homemade GHB. The drug's intoxicating effects have led to its increasing popularity at parties and nightclubs,[48] where in some cases it becomes the tool of sexual offenders. The following two cases illustrate this point:

At a party several years ago in Detroit, three men slipped GHB into a 15-year-old female's soft drink with the intention of raping her. She lapsed into a coma and died the next day. The three men were convicted of involuntary manslaughter in connection with her death.

▲ **FIGURE 10-5 Gamma hydroxybutyrate (GHB)** This drug is a central nervous system depressant that produces a euphoric and hallucinatory state. Generally ingested orally after being mixed in a liquid, reaction to the drug is usually rapid, and an overdose results in unconsciousness that can occur within 20 minutes, and a coma within 30–40 minutes. GHB can be tasteless, colorless, and odorless, which makes it easy to add unobtrusively to beverages by individuals who want to intoxicate or sedate others. (© 2005 www.streetdrugs.org)

Over a two-year period several years ago, two men had been drugging women with GHB at "raves" and night-clubs. After the Los Angeles Sheriff's Department received complaints and had sufficient evidence to obtain a search warrant, officers uncovered more than 2,000 photographs of unconscious, naked women being assaulted and in sexually explicit poses. Many of the victims were unaware they had been violated until they identified themselves in the photographs, and many of the women in the photographs have yet to be identified. The men were convicted of over 50 counts of rape and sexual assault. One of the men received a 77-year sentence; the other was sentenced to 19 years.

MALES AS RAPE VICTIMS

People tend to think that only females are the victims of date rape or stranger rape. However, that is an incorrect assumption. For example, several years ago, a man was arrested and charged in Tampa, Florida, with raping seven men. The suspect is alleged to have given the men

GHB in their drinks. According to the affidavit filed by the Drug Enforcement Administration, the suspect is accused of having purchased the date-rape drug on the Internet from Canada. Most of the victims were picked up in local bars, but in one case the victim and rapist met on an American online chat room.

OTHER DATE-RAPE DRUGS

Rohypnol and GHB are only two substances used to facilitate rape. A host of other depressants and benzo-diazapines can debilitate sexual-assault victims. Valium, Ambien, temazepam, Flexeril, Xanax, and Benadryl are all drugs that may be legitimately obtained but then appropriated for illicit purposes. Five teenage girls who were raped at a party went to the authorities with strong suspicions that they had been drugged. Each victim tested positive for Valium. Two men were later convicted on five counts of rape in connection with the incident.[49]

EVIDENCE COLLECTION AND PROCESSING

Because victims may be unaware, or may only suspect, that an assault has occurred, law-enforcement personnel have the critical task of gathering as much physical evidence as they can as quickly as possible.

Investigators should be trying to look for specific types of evidence that have been present in other cases. Drug-related evidence may be found in the glasses from which the victim drank, containers used to mix drinks, and trash cans where these items were discarded. In one case, traces of GHB were found in the box of salt that was used to make margaritas. GHB is often carried in small bottles, such as eyedropper bottles, and is frequently administered in sweet drinks, such as fruit nectars and liquors, to mask its salty taste.

Recipes for making GHB have been found on an offender's computer. In several cases, rapists who use drugs to incapacitate their victims also photograph or videotape them. These pictures led to the identification of additional victims of the same offenders.[50]

Dispatchers or call takers should be trained to recognize the signs and symptoms of drug-facilitated rapes. Call takers should be prepared to handle calls in which victims are confused, incoherent, or unclear about what may have happened, and they should keep victims on the phone until an officer arrives. In addition to the standard instruction that the victim should not bathe or discard the clothes she was wearing, it is imperative to advise the victim not to urinate until she has been transported to a medical facility for an examination and there has been a proper collection of her urine. Because many drugs exit the system within hours, a urine sample should be the first order of business as soon as a sexual assault is suspected. Treating all sexual assaults as possibly drug-induced ensures consistent evidence collection of urine in

every case. However, it is important to get a victim's consent before drug screening is conducted.

Many laboratories are not equipped to do proper screening for the types of drugs used in sexual assaults. For an adequate drug screen, the laboratory test should include a screen for benzodiazapines, muscle relaxants, sleep aids, antihistamines, cocaine, marijuana, ketamine, opiates, and other substances that can depress the central nervous system. However, even though a laboratory might have the capacity to test for all these substances, its tests may not be sensitive enough to detect the minute amounts that can trigger criminal prosecution. For instance, most laboratories can detect 50–200 nanograms of Rohypnol per milliliter of urine, but even 10 nanograms per milliliter is sufficient for the purposes of an investigation, and it is recommended that GHB should be detected as low as 1 microgram per milliliter.[51]

THE INVESTIGATION

Law-enforcement officers cannot rely on forensic toxicology reports alone, because the drugs may already have left the victim's system by the time evidence collection is initiated. The victim may delay contacting police because of embarrassment, guilt, or lack of knowledge regarding the incident. In many cases, it may take a victim time to piece together the events that led to the blackout period. The investigator should remain objective and open-minded when interviewing the victim. A victim's inability to offer a clear and detailed account of the assault may be quite frustrating for the investigating officer, but he/she should always remember that the "not knowing" is even more frustrating and traumatic for the victim. It is quite normal for a victim of drug-induced sexual assault to have significant gaps in her memory and incomplete facts regarding the incident.

Accounts from any people at the scene of the suspected drugging can be very valuable for corroborating any unusual behavior or identifying possible suspects. These witnesses may also be useful in determining who escorted the victim from that location and what statements the suspect made about the victim. They may also provide leads to more evidence.

Inquiring about the victim's level of alcohol consumption before the incident and ascertaining the victim's typical reactions to alcohol may help clarify whether the symptoms resulted from drugging or from "normal" intoxication. Parents, roommates, or other persons residing with the victim can assist in establishing the victim's state of mind and behavior after the incident and in piecing together a time line of events.

EVIDENCE

When the investigation reaches the point at which a search warrant can be obtained for a suspect's residence, car, or place of work, the following items should be included in the search warrant:

- packages of Rohypnol and other drugs;
- bubble envelopes and other types of packaging that indicate receipt of a drug shipment;
- cooking utensils;
- precursors and reagents;
- prescriptions (from the United States and other countries), especially for sleeping aids, muscle relaxants, and sedatives;
- liquor bottles, mixers, and punch bowls (in which drugs may have been mixed with liquor);
- glasses, soda cans, bottles, and any other containers that might contain drug residue;
- video and photo camera equipment;
- photographs or videotapes of the victim;
- pornographic literature;
- Internet information on Rohypnol and GHB recipes;
- computers and computer disks.

HOMOSEXUAL LIFESTYLES AND HOMICIDE INVESTIGATION

In some but certainly not the majority of cases, the appearance, dress, and demeanor of some homosexuals fit the exaggerated *effeminate* and *butch* gestures and dress occasionally used by lesbians and gay men. These individuals are highly visible within the general population owing to these attributes. Also, some male and female homosexuals might dress as bikers and other macho types, depending on what role they assume in their sexual exploits. These lifestyles represent specific subcultures within the subculture of homosexuality.[52]

In addition, many male homosexuals engage in brief, causal sex with multiple partners, unlike lesbians, who are more likely to have a monogamous relationship. Some male homosexuals participate in what is called **cruising,** as they seek out a homosexual pick-up or partner for a brief sexual encounter.

A number of **gay bars** cater to different segments of the homosexual community. For instance, there are lesbian bars, leather bars, business-suit bars, drag bars, and dancing bars. These locations provide gays and lesbians, who have a specific orientation, a place where they can be themselves. However, other establishments exist exclusively for cruising opportunities, which make multiple sexual encounters convenient and easy. Such encounters occur in back rooms and stalls, and patrons can participate in various sexual activities privately with a partner or publicly while other patrons stand around and watch. It is not uncommon for some of the more active patrons to have several sexual encounters throughout the evening. They engage in furtive eye contact, staring, smiles, suggestive bodily movements, and wearing apparel, which signal an interest in participating in a particular sexual encounter. Often they wear a particular color handkerchief in the back pocket. For example, wearing a dark blue handkerchief in the left rear pocket indicates the person prefers anal intercourse and is a giver. If it's in the right rear pocket, the person is a receiver.[53]

In fact, **straight gays,** as some homosexuals refer to themselves, speak of these extreme types of gays as "queer queers." In general, they resent these extreme types and usually avoid social contact with them, because they believe it casts all homosexuals in a bad light. However, for homicide investigators to investigate homosexual murders effectively, they must be able to break through these various subcultures in a nonthreatening and nonjudgmental manner in order to be able to effectively open up lines of communication.

INTERPERSONAL VIOLENCE-ORIENTED DISPUTES AND ASSAULTS

Male homosexual homicides involving interpersonal violence often present patterns of injuries that can best be described as overkill. These injuries are usually directed to the throat, chest, and abdomen of the victims. It has been suggested, but not empirically proven, that the assaults to the throat takes place because of the sexual significance of the mouth and throat in male homosexual sex acts. There may also be certain **psychosexual wounds** present in homosexual and heterosexual homicides. For example, this may include the cutting of the throat, stabbing wounds to the throat and chest, the slashing of the abdomen, and attacks to the genitalia. These types of injuries are indications of a sexual motive. The psychological significance in an attack to the throat in male homosexual homicides could possibly manifest the destruction of this **substitute sex organ** that engulfs the penis. Anal intercourse is often thought to be the most prevalent sexual behavior between homosexual men. However, one study found that fellatio (mouth to penis oral sex) was the most common mode of sexual expression.[54]

Although most of these interpersonal violence-oriented scenarios involve male participants, there are similar cases of extreme sexual violence involving female victims engaged in a lesbian relationship. One particularly vicious case involved the brutal sexual torture and mutilation murder of a 12-year-old girl in Indiana. The victim, whose first name was Shanda, was killed because she had begun a lesbian relationship with a young girl who had previously dated another lesbian named Melinda. Melinda talked three other teenage girls into helping her kill Shanda. Shanda was taken to a remote location where she was stripped then physically and sexually assaulted. The pathologist later reported findings which indicated numerous multiple insertions had been made into the victim's anus. She was strangled, stabbed, and hit in the head with a tire iron. Her tormentors then poured

AUTOEROTIC DEATHS/ SEXUAL ASPHYXIA

Autoerotic deaths/sexual asphyxia occasionally occur as a result of the masochistic activities of the deceased. Typically, this form of death involves a white male who is found partially suspended and sometimes dressed in women's clothing (Figure 10-8). In other cases, the individual may be found completely nude (Figure 10-9). This type of death involves a ligature around the victim's neck, which is suspended from a fixed point usually within easy reach of the decedent. In such cases, there is no indication of suicidal intent, and the death often surprises friends, relatives, and associates. Usually the decedent has no history of mental or sexual disorder.

Individuals who regularly engage in this practice (but, obviously, do not die) report that the pressure from the ligature around their neck reduces oxygen to the brain and thereby heightens the sense of pleasure they receive from the orgasm.

Death is attributable to asphyxia. The most common method is neck compression; more exotic forms involve chest compression, airway obstruction, and oxygen

▶ **FIGURE 10-8**
Autoerotic death (sexual asphyxia)
Deaths from accidental asphyxia (asphyxiation) occasionally occur as a result of the voluntary activities of the deceased. The manner of death is described as autoerotic death or sexual asphyxia. The victim, most often a white male, is sometimes dressed in female clothing, as is the case in this photograph. The individual may bind his hands behind his back in such a way so that the binding mechanism can easily be released. Unfortunately, the person sometimes waits too long to release the binding mechanism, lapses into unconsciousness, and dies.

▶ **FIGURE 10-9**
Autoerotic death (sexual asphyxia)
The victim in this photograph was found completely nude. Before death he was viewing pornography and very likely masturbating. Unfortunately, before he had the opportunity to reduce the pressure from the collar around his neck, he lapsed into unconsciousness and died.

exclusion with gas or chemical replacement. Neck compression is illustrated in the first case that follows, and chest compression in the second.

A 33-year-old government employee was found in a rented motel room. He was in an upright position, and his feet were resting on the floor. A T-shirt around his neck suspended him from a room divider. He was attired in a skirt, sweater, brassiere padded with socks, panties, panty hose, and high heels. In the room were two suitcases. One contained men's trousers, shirts, socks, and undergarments. The second contained a knit sweater, skirt, slip, panties, bra, panty hose, and high heels. Investigators determined that he was married, had two preschool children, had recently been promoted in his job, and was well thought of by his associates.[57]

The victim was a 40-year-old commercial airline pilot who was married and the father of two small children. On his day off, he left home, telling his wife that he was going to target practice. A fisherman discovered him a short time later, crushed against the left rear fender of his 1968 Volkswagen in a large turnaround area at the end of a secluded road. The left door was open and the motor was running. The steering wheel was tied with a rope in an extreme left-turn position and the automatic transmission was in low gear. The tire tracks indicated that the automobile had been moving in concentric circles. The body was held against the car by a heavy link chain and was totally nude except for a chain harness. The harness had a moderately tight loop around the neck and was bolted in front. The chain passed down the sternum and abdomen and around the waist to form a second loop. From the waist loop, strands of chain passed on each side of the testicles and into the gluteal fold and were secured to the waist loop in the small of the back. A 10-feet length of chain was attached from the waist loop to the rear bumper and had become wound around the rear axle five times. It is not known whether he jogged behind the car or was dragged; however, when he tired of the exercise, he approached the car intending to turn off the motor. In doing so, the chain became slack and the back tire rolled over it, causing the chain to become wound onto the rear axle. The trunk of the car contained his clothing and a zippered bag holding locks, bolts, chains, and wrenches. A lock and key were on the ground beside the body, and another lock was found 20 feet from the body.[58]

Airway obstruction is illustrated in the following case:

The victim, a middle-aged male, was discovered dead in his apartment. He was totally nude and held to a pole that had been fitted into his apartment floor. Several black leather belts had been permanently affixed to the pole. These belts supported the victim from the neck, waist, and legs. Leg irons connected his ankles, handcuffs dangled from one wrist, and a gag was over his mouth. The belt around his neck was so tightly buckled that it lacerated his neck. On removal of the gag, it was found that he had placed so much paper in his mouth that he had been asphyxiated. Evidence of masturbation was also present.

The following is a case of oxygen exclusion with gas replacement:

A 50-year-old dentist was discovered dead in his office by an assistant. He was lying on his stomach, and over his face was a mask that he used to administer nitrous oxide to his patients. The mask was connected to a nitrous oxide container and was operational. His pants were unzipped, and he was thought to have been fondling himself while inhaling the gas.

Each of these cases was ruled accidental, and each occurred while the victim was involved in autoerotic activities. Although the motivation for such activity is not completely understood, asphyxia appears to be the cardinal feature of the act: "A disruption of the arterial blood supply resulting in a diminished oxygenation of the brain . . . will heighten sensations through diminished ego controls that will be subjectively perceived as giddiness, light-headedness, and exhilaration. This reinforces masturbatory sensations."[59] In autoerotic deaths, there does not appear to be a conscious intent to die, although the danger of death may well play a role. The masochistic aspect of this activity is evidenced by the elaborate **bondage** employed. Another masochistic practice associated with sexual asphyxia is the practice of infibulation, or masochism involving the genitals. The fantasies of the individuals who engage in sexual asphyxiation are heavily masochistic, involving such thoughts as one's own "penis being skewered with pins; being tied up in an initiation rite; being the leader of an imperiled group; and being raped by cowboys."[60] Evidence of the fantasy involvement may be found in the form of diaries, erotic literature, pornography, films or photographs of the individual's activities, or other such paraphernalia.

It appears that this phenomenon is quite rare among females, but the following case illustrates that it does occur.[61]

(a)

This case involved a 17 year-old girl who was originally thought to have committed suicide but in fact was an autoerotic asphyxiation. Her body was found in the basement of a single-family home occupied by her family. The victim was home alone at the time of the incident. The area the victim selected was secluded from the rest of the home. There was no evidence of any break-in or entry. The victim's brother found her hanging from a wire noose, which had been affixed to a rusty metal clothes rod. There was a white towel wrapped around the victim's neck, which would have formed a padding between the wire and her neck. She was nude from the waist up and was wearing a pair of black sweat pants. A wet T-shirt was observed approximately 6 feet away and appeared to have been discarded by the deceased. A white 5-gallon bucket was observed lying on its side near the area where the deceased was found. Forensic examination of the bucket revealed latent prints, which were later identified as belonging to the right foot of the deceased, the material on the deceased's hands turned out to be rust from the metal pipe to which the wire had been affixed (Figure 10-10).

(b)

▲ **FIGURE 10-10** **Female victim of autoerotic death**
(a) This victim reported as a suicide was actually an autoerotic fatality. She had been standing on a plastic bucket, which slipped out from under her feet. She was found hanging from an electrical wire fastened into a noose. (b) Close-up showing padding. The presence of the padding was a crucial factor in the analysis of this case.

THE PSYCHOLOGICAL AUTOPSY

Occasionally the medical examiner or police investigator is confronted with a death and must determine if it is the result of autoerotic or suicidal intent. For resolving questions about the death, there is a technique employed called the **psychological autopsy,** described as follows.

Resolution of unexplained death has long been of concern within law-enforcement agencies and for the past quarter century, an object of inquiry within the mental health specialties. The term "autopsy" is usually associated with postmortem examination of human remains to determine the cause of death. The psychological autopsy is an analytical statement prepared by a mental health professional based on the deceased's thoughts, feelings, and behavior.

Its specific purpose, therefore, is to form a logical understanding of death from tangible physical evidence, documented life events, and intangible, often illusive, emotional factors. To accomplish its purpose, the psychological autopsy is structured to address three questions: What was the deceased like? What occurred in his/her life that could have been stressful? For example: marital or relationship problems; business failures; problems with parents; school problems; drug or alcohol addiction, and so on. What were his/her reactions to those stresses? To accomplish this understanding, structured interviews are conducted with friends, relatives, teachers, and business associates of the deceased in the hope of developing psychological motivation for the death and pinpointing patterns of life-threatening behavior.[62]

KEY TERMS

autoerotic death	fisting	sado-masochism (S&M)
bondage	gamma hydroxybutyrate	semen
bondage and discipline	(GHB)	sexual asphyxiation
(B&D)	gay bar	sexual battery
coprolangia	hustlers	sexual self-mutilation
corpus delecti	inserters	sex-related offenses
cruising	male prostitutes	sodomy
date-rape drugs	psychological autopsy	sperm
elder sexual abuse	psychosexual wounds	straight gays
exchangeable traces	rape	substitute sex organ
fellatio	Rohypnol	urolangia

REVIEW QUESTIONS

1. Briefly discuss the major factors that should be considered in interviewing rape victims.
2. Why is it important to understand the differences between deaf victims of sexual assault and hearing victims?
3. What are the therapeutic tasks that must be developed with elders in order to do an accurate assessment of their complaint of sexual abuse?
4. What are some of the major reasons that women do not report rape?
5. Why do women sometimes make false rape allegations?
6. Why is the discovery of semen, sperm, and hair valuable in rape investigations?
7. Why is the absence of semen fairly common in rape cases?
8. What items are needed to complete a buccal swab?
9. What items can be surreptitiously collected in an effort to obtain DNA from suspects during questioning?
10. What are condom exchangeable traces composed of?

11. How can condom trace evidence be of value in linking acts of serial rapists?
12. What are the effects of Rohypnol and gamma hydroxybutyrate?
13. When laboratories conduct drug screening tests in order to identify drugs that might have been used in sexual assaults, which types of drugs should they screen for?
14. In the investigation of a possible drug-facilitated sexual assault, what kinds of evidence should be collected?
15. Male homosexual homicides involving interpersonal violence often present patterns of injuries that can best be described as overkill. In what ways does this overkill manifest itself?
16. What factors should indicate to the investigator that a death may have resulted from accidental sexual asphyxiation?
17. What is a psychological autopsy?

INTERNET ACTIVITIES

1. Visit the Rape Victim Advocates Web site at *www.rapevictimadvocates.org*. This site provides a discussion on the phases and concerns experienced by victims of rape trauma syndrome. In addition, it presents an overview of males as rape survivors—a topic not frequently addressed.
2. According to victimization studies, more than 430,000 sexual assaults occur annually in the United States. This site, *www.ncrjs.org/pdffiles1/jr000243c.pdf*, answers questions about what we have learned

from the victims of sexual assault. Questions include: What have victims taught us? How are victims prevented from detecting threats to their safety? How are victims inhibited from exercising self-defense? In what ways do rapists appear to present themselves as rescuers? In what ways does the victim's inability to recall what happened affect the system's response? In what ways is drugging a unique form of trauma? How does being able to forget compare with being unable to remember?

ASSAULTS AGAINST CHILDREN

The most common cause of child deaths is physical abuse, often perpetrated by the parents. The clinical term commonly used to describe physically abused children is the **battered-child syndrome.** Abuse of children takes various forms, from minor assaults to flagrant physical torture. Many times these injuries cannot or will not be explained by the parents, or the story seems inconsistent with the injuries received. For example, bruises in various stages of healing generally vary in color. Thus, one should be suspicious of an explanation of such injuries as being caused by a fall from a bike. Intentional injuries tend to occur most frequently on the face, back, ribs, buttocks, genitals, palms, or soles of the feet. Although abusers use a wide variety of instruments, the two most common are belt and electric cord (Figure 11-1).

The possibility of abuse should be considered for any child exhibiting evidence of bone fracture, subdermal hematoma, soft-tissue swelling, or skin bruising; for any child who dies suddenly; or for any child when the degree and the type of injury are at variance with the history given regarding the occurrence of the trauma.[1] Bruises, in particular, are the most common signs of physical abuse. In a systematic review of studies comparing the patterns of bruising among normal and abused children, Maguire and associates[2] identified a number of patterns distinguishing accidental bruises from nonaccidental bruises. Primarily, they found that bruises indicative of physical abuse were not located on bony prominences, such as knees and elbows, but rather on the head, chest, abdomen, and hands. Moreover, the bruises among physically abused children were more likely to be clustered,

▲ **FIGURE 11-1**
Boy beaten with the buckle end of a belt
One of the most common instruments used to physically abuse children is the belt. While the leather portion of a belt can inflict significant pain, the buckle end can cause serious injuries to young children, as is depicted in this photo.
(Courtesy Tampa Police Department)

greater in size, observable during all seasons as opposed to warm months, and documented among children less than 3 years of age. Note, however, that bruising may also be a manifestation of an underlying medical condition (for example, leukemia);[3] therefore, investigators should consider bruises in a broader context to include the child's medical history and environmental factors.

BURN INJURIES AND CHILD ABUSE

Although general awareness of the magnitude of child abuse is increasing, deliberate injury by burning is often unrecognized. Burn injuries make up about 10% of all

◄ **FIGURE 11-2**
Infant scalded with hot water
This infant was scalded with hot water by his mother as punishment for not responding to toilet training. Such unreasonable and absurd expectations are not uncommon for certain types of abusive parents. (Courtesy Tampa Police Department)

child-abuse cases, and about 10% of hospital admissions of children to burn units are the result of child abuse. In comparison with accidentally burned children, abused children are significantly younger and have longer hospital stays and higher mortality rates. Child burn victims are almost always under the age of 10, with the majority under the age of 2.[4]

Children are burned for different reasons. Immersion burns may occur during toilet training, with the perpetrator immersing the child in scalding water for cleaning or as punishment (Figure 11-2). Hands may be immersed in a pot of scalding hot water as punishment for playing near the stove, or a person may place a child in a hot oven as punishment or with homicidal intentions.

Inflicted burns often leave characteristic patterns of injury that fortunately cannot be concealed. Along with the history of the burn incident, these patterns are primary indicators of inflicted burns versus accidental ones. Findings in response to the following questions can raise or lower the index of suspicion, as well as help to determine whether a burn was deliberately inflicted:

- Is the explanation of what happened consistent with the injury? Are there contradictory or varying accounts of the method or time of the "accident" or other discrepancies in the witnesses' descriptions of what happened?
- Does the injury have a clean line of demarcation, parts within or immediately around the injured area that are not burned; a burn pattern inconsistent with the injury account; or any other typical characteristics of an inflicted burn? Are the burns located on the buttocks, the area between the child's legs, or the ankles, wrists, palms, or soles?
- Are other injuries present, such as fractures, healed burns, or bruises?

- Are the child's age and level of development compatible with the caretaker's and witnesses' account of the injury?
- Was there a delay in seeking medical attention? (Less serious burns may have been treated at home.)
- Does the caretaker insist there were no witnesses to the injury incident, including the caretaker?
- Do those who were present seem to be angry or resentful toward the child or each other?
- A detailed history, including previous trauma, presence of recent illnesses, immunization status, and the status of routine medical care, is critical, as is careful documentation of the scene of the injury, including photographs and drawings. To investigate a burn injury, the investigator should do the following:
  —Stay focused on the facts, and proceed slowly and methodically.
  —Ask questions, be objective, and reenact the incident.
  —Treat each case individually.

The incidence of further injury and death is so high in deliberate burn cases that it is critical for all concerned persons to be aware of the indicators of this form of child abuse.

TYPOLOGIES OF BURNS

Children may incur various types of burn injuries. A burn may be classified by how severe, or "deep," it is or by how the injury occurred. It is essential to have an understanding of the different grades of burn severity and to recognize the cause of a burn by observing the patterns that are evident when a child's skin comes into direct contact with hot objects or liquid. An informed analysis of burn cause and severity is fundamental in ascertaining whether a child's injury is deliberate or accidental.

MEDICAL CLASSIFICATION OF BURN SEVERITY

Physicians primarily categorize burns as having either partial thickness or full thickness (Table 11-1). Only an experienced medical practitioner can determine how deeply a burn has penetrated the skin, but there are some features of partial- and full-thickness burns that can be observed immediately after the incident:

- Patches of reddened skin that blanch with fingertip pressure and then refill are shallow partial-thickness burns. Blisters usually indicate deeper partial thickness burning, especially if the blisters increase in size just after the burn occurs.
- A leathery or dry surface with a color of white, tan, brown, red, or black indicates a full-thickness burn. The child feels no pain, because the nerve endings have been destroyed. Small blisters may be present but will not increase in size.

Investigators must develop good rapport with medical personnel, including both the hospital staff workers involved with the case and emergency medical technicians (EMTs). The EMTs, especially, can provide a wealth of information owing to the fact that they were probably the first persons to see the child's injuries. Also, an experienced social service investigator can provide valuable information regarding family history and any observed patterns of abuse.

Several factors affect the severity of a burn. A child's age plays a part in how severely the child is injured by a particular incident. For example, an adult will experience a significant injury of the skin after 1 minute of exposure to water at 127°F, 30 seconds of exposure at 130°F, and 2 seconds of exposure at 150°F. A child, however, will suffer a more severe burn in less time than an adult will, because children have thinner skin. As such, a young child's skin will be severely harmed even more rapidly and by less heat than will an older child's skin.

Furthermore, certain parts of the body have thinner skin, including the front of the trunk, inner thighs, bottom of forearms, and inner-arm area. Thicker-skinned areas include the palms, soles, back, scalp, and back of the neck. Given the same cause, burns incurred in thinner-skin areas tend to be more severe than burns incurred in areas protected by thicker skin.

CAUSES OF BURN INJURIES

The severity of a burn is also directly influenced by the circumstances that caused the burn:

- Scald burns occur when the child comes into contact with hot liquid.
- Contact burns occur when the child encounters a hot solid object or flame.

Scald Burns

Scald burns are the most common type of burn injury to a child. They are caused by hot liquids—hot tap water, boiling water, hot drinks such as tea or coffee, and thicker liquids such as soup or grease. Scald burns may occur in the form of spill/splash injuries or as immersion burns. Most deliberate burns are scald burns caused by immersion in hot tap water (Figure 11-2).

Spill/Splash Injuries. **Spill/splash injuries** occur when a hot liquid falls from a height onto the victim. The burn pattern is characterized by irregular margins and nonuniform depth. Ascertaining the area of the skin where the scalding liquid first struck the victim is the key to determining whether a burn is accidental or nonaccidental. Water travels downward and cools as it moves away from the initial contact point. When a pan of water is spilled or thrown on a person's chest, the initial contact point shows a splash pattern. The area below this point tapers, creating what is called an "arrow-down" pattern. This pattern is more commonly seen in assaults on adults than in assaults on children.

If the child was wearing clothing at the time of injury, the pattern may be altered. This is why it is important to determine whether clothing was worn and, if possible, to retain the clothing. Depending on the material, the water may have been against the skin longer, which would

TABLE 11-1	Classification of Burns
CLASSIFICATION	**CHARACTERISTICS**
First degree	Partial-thickness burns: • Erythema (localized redness) • Sunburn-like • Not included when calculating burn size • Usually heal by themselves
Second degree	Partial-thickness burns: • Part of skin damaged • Have blisters containing clear fluid • Pink underlying tissue • Often heal by themselves
Third degree	Full-thickness burns: • Full skin destroyed • Deep red tissue underlying blister • Presence of bloody blister fluid • Muscle and bone possibly destroyed • Require professional treatment
Fourth degree	Full-thickness burns: • Penetrate deep tissue to fat, muscle, bone • Require immediate professional treatment

result in a deeper injury and pattern. A fleece sleeper, for instance, will change the course of the water and hold the temperature longer in one area as opposed to a thin, cotton T-shirt.

Questions to ask in a scalding-injury investigation include these:

- Where were the caretakers at the time of the accident?
- How many persons were home at the time?
- How tall is the child? How far can he or she reach?
- Can the child walk, and are the child's coordination and development consistent with his or her age?
- How much water was in the pan, and how much does it weigh?
- What is the height to the handle of the pan when the pan is on the stove (or counter or table)?
- Was the oven on at the time (thus making it unlikely that the child could have climbed onto the stove)?
- Does the child habitually play in the kitchen or near the stove? Does the child usually climb on the cabinets or table?
- Has the child been scolded for playing in the kitchen? For touching the stove?

It is unusual for a child to incur an accidental scald burn on his or her back, but it has happened. As in all burn investigations, factors other than location of the burn must be considered before concluding that the injury was nonaccidental. Deliberate burning by throwing a hot liquid on a child is usually done either as punishment for playing near a hot object or in anger. However, the child may have been caught in the crossfire between two fighting adults and then been accused of having spilled the liquid accidentally.

Immersion Burns. When a child falls or is placed into a tub or other container of hot liquid, **immersion burns** result (Figure 11-3). In a deliberate immersion burn, the depth of the burn is uniform. The wound borders are very distinct, sharply defined "waterlines" with little tapering of depth at the edges, and there is little evidence that the child thrashed about during the immersion, indicating that the child was held in place. Occasionally, there may be bruising in the area of the soft tissue where the child was being forcibly held.

Only children with deliberate immersion burns sustain deep burns of the buttocks and/or the area between the anus and the genitals. The motivation for this type of injury generally involves punishment for failing to toilet train or for soiling of clothing. Dirty diapers or soiled clothing may be found in the bathroom. The water in the bathtub may be deeper than what is normal for bathing an infant or child and may be so hot that the first responding adult at the scene is unable to immerse his/her own hand in it.

▲ **FIGURE 11-3   Immersion burn**
This child was forcibly immersed in a tub full of hot water by her mother. Note the end of the immersion line near the knees. In this case, the child's legs were placed in water hot enough to cause significant blistering. The mother who was in the process of divorcing the child's father became angry with her when she caught the child talking to the father on the phone. **(Courtesy Tampa Police Department)**

Several key variables must be observed in investigating immersion burns:

- *The temperature of the water:* Variables that must be taken into account include the temperature of the water heater, the ease with which it can be reset, and recent usage of water.
- *The time of exposure:* This is an unknown that can sometimes be estimated from the burn pattern and its depth.
- *The depth of the burn:* Several days may need to pass before the true depth of the burn can be determined.
- *The occurrence of "sparing":* There may be areas within or immediately around the burn site that were not burned.

When a child's hand is forced into hot water, the child will make a fist, thus "sparing" the palm and discounting the statement that the child reached into the pan of hot water for something. A child whose body is immersed in hot water will attempt to fold up, and sparing will show as creases in the abdomen. Curling up the toes when the foot is forced into a hot liquid will spare part of the soles of the feet or the area between the toes. The area where the child was held by the perpetrator will also be spared. These flexing actions prevent burning within the body's creases, causing a striped configuration of burned and unburned zones, or a "zebra" pattern.

Deliberate immersion burns can often be recognized by one of the following characteristic patterns:

- *Doughnut pattern in the buttocks:* When a child falls or steps into a hot liquid, the immediate reaction is to thrash about, try to get out, and jump up and down. When a child is held in scalding hot bathwater, the buttocks are pressed against the bottom of the tub so forcibly that the water will not come into contact with the center of the buttocks, sparing this part of the buttocks and causing the burn injury to have a doughnut pattern.
- *Sparing the soles of the feet:* Another instance of sparing occurs in a child whose buttocks and feet are burned but whose soles have been spared. If a caretaker's account is that the child was left in the bathroom and told not to get into the tub, and that the caretaker then heard screaming and returned to find the child jumping up and down in the water, the absence of burns on the soles of the child's feet is evidence that the account is not true. A child cannot jump up and down in hot water without burning the bottoms of the feet.
- *Stocking- or glove-pattern burns:* Stocking and glove patterns are seen when feet or hands are held in the water. The line of demarcation is possible evidence that the injury was not accidental.
- *Waterlines:* A sharp line on the lower back, or in some cases the legs, indicates that the child was held still in the water. A child falling into the water would show splash and irregular-line patterns. The waterline on a child's torso, for example, indicates how deep the water was at the time of the incident.

Contact Burns

Contact burns occur when a child's skin comes into contact with a flame or a hot solid object. A contact-burn injury may be caused by a curling iron, steam iron, cigarette or lighter, fireplace, stovetop burner, outdoor grill, or some other hot implement. When a hot solid object touches a child, the child's skin is "branded" with a mirror image of the object. Flame burns are a much less common cause of deliberate injury. When they do occur, they are characterized by extreme depth and are relatively well-defined as compared with accidental flame burns.

When a child accidentally touches a hot object or the object falls on the child, there is usually a lack of pattern in the burn injury, since the child quickly moves away from the object. However, even brief accidental contact, such as falling against a hot radiator or grate, can cause a second-degree-burn imprint of the pattern of the object.

Distinguishing Nonaccidental from Accidental Contact Burns. Nonaccidental burns caused by a hot solid object are the most difficult to distinguish from accidental injuries. Cigarette and electric steam iron burns are the most frequent types of these injuries. Cigarette burns, especially multiple burns on the child's feet, back, or buttocks, are unlikely to have been caused by an accident; therefore, they are more suspect than individual burns in the area of the child's face and eyes, which can occur accidentally if the child walks or runs into an adult's lit cigarette held at waist height. Accidental burns are usually more shallow, irregular, and less well defined than are deliberate burns.

Purposely inflicted "branding" injuries usually mirror the objects that caused the burn (such as cigarette lighters and curling irons) and are much deeper than the superficial and random burns caused by accidentally touching these objects. Most accidental injuries with hot steam or curling irons occur when the hot item is grasped or falls. These are usually second-degree injuries that are randomly placed, as might be the case when a hot electric steam iron strikes the skin in multiple places as it falls. It is important to know where the iron was—for example, was it on an ironing board or a coffee table at the child's height?

Another source of accidental burns is contact with items that have been exposed for prolonged periods to hot sun. Pavement in hot sun, which can reach a temperature of 176°F, can burn a child's bare feet; however, such burns are not likely to be deep. A child placed in a car seat that has been in a car in the sun can receive second- and even third-degree burns. Full-thickness burns have also resulted from contact with a hot seat-belt buckle.

The following key questions will help in determining whether contact burns are accidental or nonaccidental:

- Where is the burn injury, and could the child reach the area unassisted?
- Does the child normally have access to the item (such as a cigarette lighter) that caused the injury?
- How heavy is the item, and how strong is the child? For instance, is the electric steam iron a compact, travel-size one that a small child could lift or a full-size home model that might be too heavy to lift?
- Is there any sparing that would be significant to the injury?
- How was the item heated, and how long did it take for the item to become hot enough to cause the injury?
- Is the injury clean and crisp, with the distinctive pattern of the object, or is it shallow or irregular, as from a glancing blow? Several cleanly defined injuries, especially on an older child, could indicate that the child was held motionless by a second perpetrator while the first perpetrator carefully branded the child.
- Are there multiple burns or other healed burns?
- Has the child been punished before for playing with or being too close to the hot object?

UNEXPLAINED CHILD FATALITIES

For those who work in law enforcement, there are few incidents that will affect them more than responding to the death of a child. Officers are trained to deal with mass shootings, decomposing bodies, and gruesome vehicle accidents, and yet many law-enforcement officers find any one of those incidents far preferable than showing up on the scene where a child has died. Unfortunately, child death is a reality that most officers will have to face at some point in their career. These types of calls are certainly traumatic for all involved, and are often less straightforward than other types of homicides or unexplained deaths. Because of the emotion and confusion involved in child death cases, law-enforcement officers—even well-meaning and well-educated ones—often make mistakes that can affect the outcome of an investigation.

Not all child fatalities that police come across are homicides, obviously. More often than not, a child fatality is easily identified as accidental—such as a drowning or a pedestrian-vehicle incident—whereas others will be quickly attributed to natural causes. But other times, it's either not obvious why or how a child dies—or it is all too clear that they have suffered either acute or chronic maltreatment at the hands of an adult. Nonetheless, law-enforcement officers must understand that ALL sudden and unexplained child deaths must be investigated thoroughly, because the consequences of improperly investigating such an incident mean that subtle clues can be missed or evidence can be misread, and a case that should have been treated as a homicide might be overlooked. Or, in other cases, a conclusion of homicide may be unwarranted. And finally, as we saw in the JonBenet Ramsey case, investigative focus may be attributed to parties that were not responsible for the death of the child, wasting valuable time that could be spent tracking the individual or individuals truly responsible. Any one of these scenarios is, of course, objectionable to law enforcement, and it is up to first responders to set the investigation on a course that will avoid any of these outcomes.

Sudden and unexplained child deaths are, according to the Office of Juvenile Justice and Delinquency Prevention, any death that involves a child who was not under the care of a physician for a known illness or disease. The death can be from either natural or unnatural causes, including: natural diseases such as flu or cancer; unsafe sleeping environments; trauma; accidental poisoning; homicide; and Sudden Infant Death Syndrome, or SIDS.[5]

SUDDEN INFANT DEATH SYNDROME

Although **sudden infant death syndrome (SIDS)** is a medical phenomenon, not a crime, a lack of knowledge about its elements can cause individuals involved in its investigation to erroneously conclude they have a criminal homicide.

Health professionals in the past had limited contact with SIDS families, because SIDS rarely occurs outside the home. A few babies have died of SIDS while hospitalized, but the usual case involves a baby who is brought to the hospital emergency room and is pronounced dead on arrival. As a result, many physicians and nurses have had little knowledge of SIDS.[6]

What Is Sudden Infant Death Syndrome?

Simply defined, SIDS (also often referred to as *crib death*) is the sudden and unexpected death of an apparently healthy infant that remains unexplained after the performance of a complete autopsy. On the average, 2 of every 1,000 infants born alive succumb to SIDS, and it is the leading cause of death among infants 1 week to 1 year of age.

In the majority of instances, the baby is apparently in good health prior to death and feeds without difficulty. Although there may be evidence of a slight cold or stuffy nose, there is usually no history of serious upper respiratory infection. In most cases, the infant is placed in a crib to sleep and is found dead several hours later.

Most SIDS deaths occur between November and March. Sudden changes in temperature may trigger SIDS. The risk of SIDS appears to be highest in crowded dwellings; in infants of young mothers; in males; in nonwhites regardless of socioeconomic status; in families of lower socioeconomic status regardless of race; and in premature infants. Twins have an increased risk of SIDS, which is likely a consequence of their low birth weight and premature birth. SIDS occurs in both breast-fed and bottle-fed babies. Most victims are between the ages of 1 and 6 months, with the highest frequency of occurrence between 2 and 4 months.

Characteristics of SIDS Victims' Appearance

- Usually normal state of nutrition and hydration
- Blood-tinged, frothy fluids around mouth and nostrils, indicative of pulmonary edema
- Vomitus on the face
- Diaper wet and full of stool
- Bruiselike marks on head or body limbs (postmortem pooling or settling of blood in dependent body parts)

Autopsy Findings

- Some congestion and edema of the lungs
- Petechial hemorrhages in thymus, heart, and lungs
- Minor evidence of respiratory tract inflammation

Misconceptions about SIDS

- *Aspiration, choking:* The babies do not inhale or choke on their feeding.
- *Unsuspected illness:* Particularly if the baby had a cold, the parents may feel guilty about not having

observed the child immediately after the events. However, only C. B.'s father had witnessed all the actual events. C. B. was eventually referred to Children's Hospital.

While in the hospital, C. B. had no clinical apnea or monitor alarms. Most of the time, she appeared happy and playful. However, when anyone attempted to touch her face, she became hysterical and combative. Over time, both the medical and nursing staffs began to suspect that C. B.'s parents were responsible for her apnea.

Local police and child protection services were notified, and C. B. was placed in a room with covert audiovisual surveillance. On the third day of monitoring, the video recording clearly showed C. B.'s father producing an apneic event by smothering her. Mr. B. was seen picking up the sleeping child, placing her prone on the bed, and forcing her face into the mattress. C. B. awoke and struggled to escape, wildly kicking her legs. Mr. B. continued until C. B.'s struggling stopped and she appeared limp and unconscious. Then he repositioned her on the bed and called for help. A nurse entered the room, stimulated her, and administered supplemental oxygen.

C. B.'s parents were confronted by a physician, nurse, and police officer. Mr. B. adamantly denied smothering C. B. He was subsequently arrested and removed from the hospital.

Mr. B. was a 27-year-old, unemployed, semiliterate laborer in good health. He was actively involved in C. B.'s day-to-day medical care and was clearly the dominant parent. He also became very knowledgeable about the mechanics of the various county and hospital welfare systems. Officials described him as "demanding and manipulative." During C. B.'s hospitalizations, the family lived in a hotel adjacent to the hospital with room, board, and radio pagers provided by the hospital. Throughout C. B.'s hospitalization, Mrs. B. was passive and deferred all medical decisions to her husband.

When they first arrived in Minnesota, the family had received emergency financial assistance and was closely monitored by local social service agencies. Four years earlier, Mrs. B. had allegedly been assaulted and raped. Two months prior to C. B.'s monitored episode, Mrs. B. was evaluated at a local emergency room for a "hysterical conversion reaction."

Following the incident at Children's Hospital, Mr. B. was taken to the county jail, and upon viewing the video, he admitted smothering C. B. He was charged with felonious, third-degree assault. The judge ordered a psychiatric examination. Mr. B. received a 10-month sentence in a local workhouse and 5 years' probation. Also, he was to have no contact with his daughter and no unsupervised contact with any child in the future.[17]

INVESTIGATIVE GUIDELINES

- Consult with all experts possible, including psychologists.
- Exhaust every possible explanation of the cause of the child's illness or death.
- Find out who had exclusive control over the child when the symptoms of the illness began or at the time of the child's death.
- Find out if there is a history of abusive conduct toward the child.
- Find out if the nature of the child's illness or injury allows medical professionals to express an opinion that the child's illness or death was neither accidental nor the result of a natural cause or disease.
- In cases of hospitalization, use covert video surveillance to monitor the suspect.
- Determine whether the caretaker had any medical training or a history of seeking medical treatment needlessly. MSBP is often a multigenerational condition.

THE ROLE OF THE PHYSICIAN IN CHILD-ABUSE CASES

The problem the investigator often encounters is that the victim is either too young to explain what has occurred or too intimidated to cooperate. In injuries or deaths of young children, investigators find radiologists (physicians who specialize in the interpretation of X rays) especially helpful. It is common for abused children to be brought to the hospital emergency room by their parents or relatives, who tell hospital personnel that the child was injured in a fall or some other accident. When there is a discrepancy between the characteristics of the injury and the explanation, X rays can be useful in determining whether the injuries were accidental. X rays of the entire body reveal not only the presence of fractures and other injuries to joints and bones but also the existence of older injuries in various stages of healing.

Careful questioning of the persons bringing the child to the hospital may be sufficient to confirm the need for a complete investigation. The following facts about child abuse are helpful in such questioning:

- In many cases, only one of a number of children in the family is chosen as the target of abuse, and frequently that child was conceived or born extramaritally or premaritally.
- The marital partner tends to protect the abusive parent through denial of the facts.
- Occasionally, an abusing father also assaults his wife, but more frequently he restricts the gross abuse to a child.
- In over half the cases in which child abuse results in hospitalization, there was a preceding incident of abuse of equal severity.

- Not infrequently the battered child is taken to a different hospital after each abuse in order to conceal the recurrence of injuries.[18] However, with the mandatory reporting of all suspicious child abuse injuries to the proper authorities and the computerized storage of previously reported events, it has become increasingly difficult for this ploy to work.

The families of battered children range across the entire socioeconomic spectrum. The investigator cannot assume that an injured child who comes from what appears to be a "good home" is not the victim of child abuse.

In cases where medical examination is inconclusive but abuse is strongly suspected, interviewing becomes even more significant. The rule is to leave no source unexamined. To fail to do so places the abused child back into a defenseless position in which further injury or death could occur. The interviewing of baby sitters, neighbors, teachers, and others must be conducted sensibly and sensitively. The aim is not to "get the person who did it," because there may not in fact have been an abuse incident; instead, the primary objective is to get the information so that if there has been abuse, the child can be protected.

CHILD SEXUAL EXPLOITATION

The sexual exploitation of children is a particularly heinous offense in our society. The primary areas of child sexual abuse include child molestation, child pornography, and sex tourism. Sex tourism often involves visiting foreign countries for the purposes of acquiring sexual activities with children, but there is recent evidence that as many as 600,000 children may be involved in child prostitution in the United States.[19] (Chapter 12 focuses on human trafficking and child sex slavery and provides greater insight into this growing problem.)

CHILD MOLESTATION

For purposes of discussion, Kenneth V. Lanning, supervisory special agent of the Federal Bureau of Investigation, divides child molesters into two categories—namely, situational and preferential.[20]

Situational Child Molesters

The **situational child molester** does not have a true sexual preference for children but engages in sex with children for varied and sometimes complex reasons. For such a child molester, sex with children may range from a once-in-a-lifetime act to a long-term pattern of behavior. The more long term the pattern is, the harder it is to distinguish from preferential molesting. The situational child molester usually has fewer numbers of different child victims. Other vulnerable individuals, such as the elderly, sick, or disabled, may also be at risk of sexual victimization by him or her. For example, the situational child molester who sexually abuses children in a daycare center might leave that job and begin to sexually abuse elderly people in a nursing home. The number of situational child molesters is larger and increasing faster than that of preferential child molesters. Members of lower socioeconomic groups tend to be overrepresented among situational child molesters. Within this category, the following four major patterns of behavior emerge: regressed, morally indiscriminate, sexually indiscriminate, and inadequate (Table 11-2).

Morally Indiscriminate. The morally indiscriminate pattern characterizes an increasing number of child molesters. For such an individual, the sexual abuse of children is simply part of a general pattern of abuse in his life. He

TABLE 11-2	Situational Child Molesters			
	REGRESSED	**MORALLY INDISCRIMINATE**	**SEXUALLY INDISCRIMINATE**	**INADEQUATE**
Basic Characteristics	Poor coping skills	User of people	Sexual experimentation	Social misfit
Motivation	Substitution	Why not?	Boredom	Insecurity and curiosity
Victim Criteria	Availability	Vulnerability and opportunity	New and different	Nonthreatening
Method of Operation	Coercion	Lure, force, or manipulation	Involve in existing activity	Exploits size, advantage
Pornography Collection	Possible	Sadomasochistic; detective magazines	Highly likely; varied nature	Likely

Source: Kenneth V. Lanning, *Child Molesters: A Behavioral Analysis for Law Enforcement Officers Investigating Cases of Child Sexual Exploitation*, 3rd ed. (Arlington, VA: National Center for Missing and Exploited Children, 1992), p. 10. Reprinted with permission of the National Center for Missing and Exploited Children (NCMEC). Copyright 1986, 1987, and 1992, NCMEC. All rights reserved.

is a user and an abuser of people. He abuses his wife, friends, and coworkers. He lies, cheats, or steals whenever he thinks he can get away with it. His primary victim criteria are vulnerability and opportunity. He has the urge, a child is there, and so he acts. He typically uses force, lures, or manipulation to obtain his victims. He may violently or nonviolently abduct his victims. Although his victims frequently are strangers or acquaintances, they can also be his own children. The incestuous father (or mother) might be a morally indiscriminate offender. He frequently collects detective magazines or adult pornography of a sadomasochistic nature. He may collect some child pornography, especially that which depicts pubescent children. Because he is an impulsive person who lacks conscience, there is an especially high risk that he will molest pubescent children.

Regressed. A regressed offender usually has low self-esteem and poor coping skills; he turns to children as a sexual substitute for the preferred peer sex partner. Precipitating stress may play a bigger role in his molesting behavior. His main victim criterion seems to be availability, which is why many such offenders molest their own children. His principal method of operation is to coerce the child into having sex. This type of situational child molester may or may not collect child or adult pornography. If he does have child pornography, it will usually be the best kind of evidence from an investigative point of view and will often include homemade photographs or videos of the child he is molesting.

Sexually Indiscriminate. The sexually indiscriminate pattern of behavior is the most difficult to define. Although the previously described morally indiscriminate offender often is a sexual experimenter, the sexually indiscriminate individual differs in that he appears to be discriminating in his behavior except when it comes to sex. He is the "try-sexual"—willing to try anything sexual. Much of his behavior is similar to, and most often confused with, that of the preferential child molester. While he may have clearly defined sexual preferences—such as bondage or sadomasochism, he has no real sexual preference for children. His basic motivation is sexual experimentation, and he appears to have sex with children out of boredom. His main criteria for his victims are that they be new and different, and he involves children in previously existing sexual activity. Again, one must realize that these children may be his own. Although much of his sexual activity with adults may not be criminal, such an individual may also provide his children to other adults as part of group sex, spouse-swapping activity, or even some bizarre ritual. Of all situational child molesters, he is by far the most likely to have multiple victims, be from a higher socioeconomic background, and collect pornography and erotica. Child pornography will be only a small portion of his potentially large and varied collection, however.

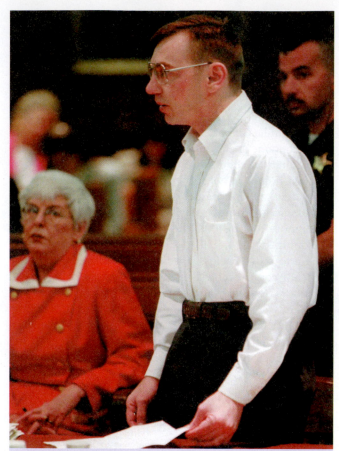

▲ **FIGURE 11-7** **Convicted murderer pleads for life**
This photo shows Jesse Timmendequas, a convicted child murderer, at the penalty phase of his trial. At this point in the trial, he apologized for his actions and begged to have his life spared. (© AP Photo/Jeff Zelevansky/Pool)

Inadequate. The inadequate pattern of behavior includes persons suffering from psychoses, eccentric personality disorders, mental retardation, and senility. In layperson's terms, the inadequate individual is the social misfit, the withdrawn, the unusual. He might be the shy teenager who has no friends of his own age or the eccentric loner who still lives with his parents. Although most loners are harmless, some can be child molesters and, in a few cases, even child killers (Figure 11-7). This offender seems to become sexually involved with children out of insecurity or curiosity. He finds children to be nonthreatening objects with whom he can explore his sexual fantasies. The child victim could be someone he knows or could be a random stranger. In some cases, the victim might be a specific "stranger" selected as a substitute for a specific adult (possibly a relative of the child) whom the offender is afraid of approaching directly. Often his sexual activity with children is the result of built-up impulses. Some of these individuals find it difficult to express anger and hostility, which then builds until it explodes—possibly against their child victims. Because of mental or emotional

TABLE 11-3	Preferential Child Molester		
	SEDUCTION	**INTROVERTED**	**SADISTIC**
Common Characteristics	Sexual preference for children; child pornography or erotica	Sexual preference for children; child pornography or erotica	Sexual preference for children; child pornography or erotica
Motivation	Identification	Fear of communication	Need to inflict pain
Victim Criteria	Age and gender preferences	Strangers or very young	Age and gender preferences
Method of Operation	Seduction process	Nonverbal sexual contact	Lure or force

Source: Kenneth V. Lanning, *Child Molesters: A Behavioral Analysis for Law Enforcement Officers Investigating Cases of Child Sexual Exploitation*, 3rd ed. (Arlington, VA: National Center for Missing and Exploited Children, 1992), p. 10. Reprinted with permission of the National Center for Missing and Exploited Children (NCMEC). Copyright 1986, 1987, and 1992, NCMEC. All rights reserved.

problems, some might take out their frustration in cruel sexual torture. The inadequate molester's victims, however, could be elderly persons as well as children—anyone who appears helpless at first sight. He might collect pornography, but it will most likely be of adults.

Preferential Child Molesters

Preferential child molesters have a definite sexual preference for children. Their sexual fantasies and erotic imagery focus on children. They have sex with children not because of some situational stress or insecurity but because they are sexually attracted to and prefer children. Although they can possess a wide variety of character traits, they engage in highly predictable sexual behavior. Their sexual behavior patterns are called *sexual rituals* and are frequently engaged in even when they are counterproductive to getting away with the criminal activity. Although preferential offenders may be fewer in number than situational child molesters, they have the potential to molest large numbers of victims. For many of them, their problem is not only the nature of the sex drive (attraction to children) but also the quantity (need for frequent and repeated sex with children). They usually have age and gender preferences for their victims. Members of higher socioeconomic groups tend to be overrepresented among preferential child molesters. More preferential child molesters seem to prefer boys rather than girls. Within this category, at least three major patterns of behavior emerge: seduction, introverted, and sadistic (Table 11-3).

Seduction. The seduction pattern characterizes the offender who engages children in sexual activity by "seducing" them—courting them with attention, affection, and gifts. Just as one adult courts another, the pedophile seduces children over a period of time by gradually lowering their sexual inhibitions. Frequently his victims arrive at the point where they are willing to trade sex for the attention, affection, and other benefits they receive from the offender. Many seduction offenders are simultaneously involved with multiple victims, operating what

has come to be called a child sex ring. This may include a group of children in the same class at school, in the same scout troop, or in the same neighborhood. The characteristic that seems to make the seduction molester a master seducer of children is his ability to identify with them. He knows how to talk to children—but, more important, he knows how to listen to them. His adult status and authority are also an important part of the seduction process. In addition, he frequently selects as targets children who are victims of emotional or physical neglect. The biggest problem for this child molester is not how to obtain child victims but how to get them to leave after they are too old. This must be done without the disclosure of the "secret." Victim disclosure often occurs when the offender is attempting to terminate the relationship. This child molester is most likely to use threats and physical violence to avoid identification and disclosure or to prevent a victim from leaving before he is ready to "dump" the victim.

Introverted. The introverted pattern of behavior characterizes the offender who has a preference for children but lacks the interpersonal skills necessary to seduce them. Therefore, he typically engages in a minimal amount of verbal communication with his victims and usually molests strangers or very young children. He is like the old stereotype of the child molester in that he is more likely to hang around playgrounds and other areas where children congregate, watching them or engaging them in brief sexual encounters. He may expose himself to children or make obscene phone calls to them. He may use the services of a child prostitute. Unable to figure out any other way to gain access to a child, he might even marry a woman and have his own children, very likely molesting them from the time they are infants. He is similar to the inadequate situational child molester, except that he has a definite sexual preference for children and his selection of only children as victims is more predictable.

Sadistic. The sadistic pattern of behavior characterizes the offender who has a sexual preference for children but who, in order to be aroused or gratified, must inflict psychological or physical pain or suffering on the child victim. He is aroused by his victim's response to the infliction of pain or suffering. Sadistic molesters typically use lures or force to gain access to their victims. They are more likely than other preferential child molesters to abduct and even murder their victims. There have been some cases where seduction molesters have become sadistic molesters. It is not known whether the need to perform sadistic acts developed late or was always there and surfaced late for some reason. In any case, it is fortunate that sadistic child molesters do not appear to be large in number.[21]

Interviewing Molested Children

Common sense and formal research agree that children are not merely miniature adults. We know, for example, that children develop in stages during which they acquire capacities for new functions and understanding. Adults, for the most part, attempt to speak to and treat children in accordance with their capabilities. We do not ordinarily expect children to understand or function on a par with adults.[22]

When children become victims or witnesses of violence or sexual abuse, however, they are thrust into an adult system that traditionally does not differentiate between children and adults. As one attorney has said:

> Child victims of crime are specially handicapped. First, the criminal justice system distrusts them and puts special barriers in the path of prosecuting their claims to justice. Second, the criminal justice system seems indifferent to the legitimate special needs that arise from their participation.[23]

What are some of the reasons for the problems that arise when children are called to participate in criminal proceedings? The first reason is the children's immaturity with regard to physical, cognitive, and emotional development. The second reason involves unique attributes of the offense of child sexual abuse, particularly when the perpetrator is a parent, parent substitute, or other adult having a trusting or loving relationship with the child. The third reason is our limited understanding of children's capabilities as witnesses. These three factors affect children's ability to comply with the expectations of our judicial system and inform our entire discussion of interviewing molested children.

Developmental Issues. Three developmental issues are important when allegations of sexual abuse arise.[24] First is the child's developmental level relative to other children in his or her age group. Knowing this information will dictate the nature of questioning to which the child

can reasonably be expected to respond. It will also help place the child's observable reactions to victimization in an appropriate context.

Second is the child's developmental level with regard to sexuality. Normal preschoolers, for example, express curiosity about the origin of babies and mild interest in physical differences between the sexes. While it is not unusual for young children to engage in self-stimulatory behavior or exhibitionism, intercourse or other adult sexual behaviors are quite rare.[25]

Third is the child's ability to respond adequately to interviews and to testify in court. Those who work with young children should be aware of the following principles:

- Children think in concrete terms.
- Children do not organize their thoughts logically. They often include extraneous information, and they have trouble generalizing to new situations.
- Children have limited understanding of space, distance, and time. A child may not be able to say at "what time" or in "what month" something occurred but may be able to say whether it was before or after school, what was on television, or whether there was snow on the ground.
- Children have a complex understanding of truth and lying.
- Children see the world egocentrically. Because they believe that adults are omniscient, they may expect to be understood even when they have answered questions only partially.[26]
- Children have a limited attention span.
- Children may have varying degrees of comfort with strangers.

These kinds of cognitive limitations are common among young children. Older children tend to exhibit different, yet equally challenging, developmental patterns.[27] For example, although preadolescents have fairly sophisticated language capabilities, they may use words or phrases they do not fully understand. The emergence of sexuality and concern with sexual identities during preadolescence make these youngsters particularly vulnerable to disruption when they are sexually abused. As they enter adolescence, they tend to become very self-centered and have strong needs for privacy and secrecy. It is common for preteens and teenagers to express their feelings through the arts or physical activity or by acting out in inappropriate or socially unacceptable ways.

Some researchers have specifically explored the developmental aspects of children's understanding of the legal system.[28] Not surprisingly, they have found that older children have more accurate and complete knowledge of legal terminology (for example, court, lawyer, jury, judge, and witness) as well as a better grasp of certain basic concepts of American justice. The researchers caution that children's understanding of the legal system is not only limited but sometimes faulty, so child witnesses may

◀FIGURE 11-8
Anatomically detailed dolls
Interviewing children who either have been sexually abused or have witnessed sexual abuse creates challenges for investigators. One tool that often assists investigators is the use of an anatomically detailed doll with all body parts, including genitals, present. Although there is some disagreement among experts as to the overall usefulness of these dolls, many law-enforcement agencies still use them. (Courtesy Eymann Anatomically Correct Dolls, Sacramento, California)

behave in ways that appear counterintuitive or inappropriate to the context.

For example, an interview with a child may begin by requesting identifying information: name, age, school, grade, home address. But young children may misinterpret these initial questions as meaning they are under suspicion or arrest.[29] Also, because they do not understand the different roles and obligations of all the people who interview them, children do not understand why they must tell their stories repeatedly to the police, social workers, doctors, prosecutors, and, ultimately, the court. While this repetition may be simply exasperating for some children, others may relive the traumatic event each time, and still others may assume the story is already known and omit important details in subsequent interviews. Some children may feel protected by the presence of the judge, but others may be intimidated.

To correct these problems, researchers recommend that attorneys, judges, and investigators choose their words with care when questioning child witnesses.[30] Some believe that targeted instruction for children who may serve as witnesses, possibly in the form of a "court school," would be helpful as well.[31] Many prosecutors and victim advocates take children for a tour of the courtroom and introduce them to some of the key players before their scheduled court date. Critics contend, however, that such precautions may induce unnecessary apprehension for children who ultimately are not called to testify. At a minimum, interviewers would be wise to explain thoroughly the nature and purpose of each interview or court appearance before the child is questioned.

An additional problem in interviewing children who may be victims of sexual molestation centers on the delicate issue of body parts and techniques for achieving accurate communication. One of the most common methods involves the use of anatomically detailed dolls.

Anatomically Detailed Dolls. When anatomically detailed dolls (male and female dolls with all body parts, including genitals; Figure 11-8) were first introduced in the late 1970s,[32] they were widely hailed and almost universally adopted by child-serving professionals as an important advance in techniques for communicating with troubled children. Congress (in the Victims of Child Abuse Act of 1990) and eight states[33] have enacted legislation expressly permitting the use of anatomically detailed dolls as demonstrative aids when children testify in court, and many appellate courts have upheld the use of such dolls.[34] The use of dolls at trial appears limited, however: courtroom observations of child sexual-abuse trials in eight jurisdictions revealed only one use of dolls per jurisdiction over the course of a year, with one exception where dolls were used in three of the four cases observed.[35]

Yet even as the dolls' value as demonstrative aids in court has gained widespread acceptance, their use in investigative interviews to arrive at a finding of sexual abuse that is later presented in court as expert opinion has been sharply criticized. At the core of the controversy is the extent to which anatomically detailed dolls may suggest sexual behaviors even among children with no history of abuse. Improper use of the dolls, and unsupported inferences about children's behavior with them, can imperil the search for truth.

Proponents of anatomically detailed dolls maintain that, when properly used, the dolls can facilitate and enhance interviews with children.[36] Dolls can help in the following ways:

- They can help establish rapport with the interviewer and reduce stress. Most children relate well to dolls. The dolls can have a calming effect and make the interview room appear less formal and more child-oriented.
- They can reduce vocabulary problems. Interviewers can use the dolls to learn a child's sexual vocabulary before questioning the child about the alleged abuse.
- They allow the child to show what may be difficult or embarrassing to say. Anatomically detailed dolls can be an invaluable aid to children who are unable or unwilling to verbalize what happened to them.
- They can enhance the quality of information. Dolls may help interviewers gather information without resorting to leading or protracted questioning to overcome children's reluctance to describe sexual acts.
- They can establish competency. Interviewers can use the dolls in a general way to demonstrate the child's mental capacity and ability to communicate.

Many critics fear, however, that anatomically detailed dolls could have adverse effects, whether by provoking horror or alarm at the sight of genitalia or by eliciting apparently sexualized responses, even among children who have not been sexually abused. Even some appellate courts have raised the issue that interviewing children with anatomically detailed dolls may contaminate their memory.[37] Research offers little support for these contentions, however. For example, one study of "nonreferred" children (that is, children with no history or current allegation of sexual abuse) found that although they did play more with undressed dolls than with dressed dolls, the children's primary activity was, in fact, dressing the dolls.[38] Others report that nonreferred children do examine the genitalia and orifices of anatomically detailed dolls, but only rarely do they enact sexual behaviors.[39] Of course, some proportion of nonreferred children may have experienced some form of undetected sexual abuse.

Related to this controversy is the fact that professionals in this field have yet to reach consensus on "proper" use of anatomically detailed dolls. A number of questions remain unanswered:[40]

- How "correct" in their appearance must the dolls be? Some respondents to a survey by Boat and Everson[41] revealed using Barbie dolls, Cabbage Patch dolls, and homemade stuffed dolls with varying degrees of accuracy in their representation of genitalia. Does the presence or absence of certain details influence children's behavior with the dolls? Must the dolls also be matched by age and racial features to the child and alleged perpetrator?
- When and how should the dolls be used to assist an investigation? Should the dolls be available to children at the start of the interview, or should they be introduced only after the child falters in responding to traditional questioning? Who should undress the dolls, and how should this activity be incorporated into the interview?
- How many sessions with a child are necessary before drawing conclusions about the child's behavior with the dolls?
- Should other adults be present during the interview?
- How many dolls should be available?

The answers to these questions vary with the professional orientations of the people who are asked. Clinicians' responses are more likely to reflect concerns for the children's well-being; legal professionals, on the other hand, express concern for the potential effects of certain practices when revealed in court. From the courts' perspective, it is probably least objectionable to:

- Introduce the dolls only after the child has verbally disclosed some abuse, or as a last resort to assist reluctant children.[42]
- Allow children to choose from a variety of dolls (rather than present only two to represent child and perpetrator).[43]
- Offer the child minimal or no instruction in use of the dolls.
- Incorporate information gathered from doll interviews with other data to provide a complete assessment.[44]

Similar recommendations would apply to use of other props, such as puppets or artwork.

Asking Leading Questions.
Professionals who interview children who are suspected of having been sexually abused are caught in a perilous dilemma. In the words of two well-known clinicians:

> In the best of all possible worlds, it would be advisable not to ask children leading questions. . . . But in the best of all possible worlds, children are not sexually assaulted in secrecy and then bribed, threatened, or intimidated not to talk about it. In the real world, where such things do happen, leading questions may sometimes be necessary.[45]

As with the anatomical dolls, leading questions are widely used as a courtroom technique to assist child witnesses,[46] but they are seriously challenged when used in investigative interviews. There is, however, a grain of truth to the argument that children can be led, coached, or even "brainwashed" by the interview process, and interviewers would be wise to reexamine their methods in light of our growing experience in the courts.

Briefly, the defense argument rests on the social psychological theory of social influence. In essence, as it applies to child sexual-abuse cases, this theory holds that children's responses to questioning are heavily influenced by the perceived authority or power of the adult interviewers. When they are praised or otherwise "rewarded" for disclosing elements of abuse, children learn what the interviewers want to hear. In other words, children answer to please adults.[47]

Furthermore, to continue this argument, the effect of social influence is magnified in child sexual-abuse cases, because the children are typically interviewed repeatedly by several different adults, each of whom contributes to the child's expanding story by infusing—and reinforcing—new information. Ultimately, according to one of the leading defense experts:

In situations where a child will eventually testify, the memory will consist of a combination of recall and reconstruction influenced by all of the interrogations, conversations, and sexual abuse therapy that have occurred during the delay. The longer the delay, the greater the possibility of social influence and the more the memory may consist of reconstruction rather than recall.[48]

Challenges based on this theory have successfully undermined prosecution of several highly publicized cases, including the well-known McMartin Preschool case.

In one study, 72 children age 5–7 underwent physical examinations. Half received external examinations of their genital and anal areas; the other half were examined for scoliosis (curvature of the spine). Within one month of the exam, the children were interviewed about the event using open-ended questions, anatomically detailed dolls, and specific and misleading questions. The results of this study were both illuminating and provocative. Specifically:

- The majority of children who experienced genital and anal touching did not report it, either in response to open-ended questions or when asked to demonstrate with the dolls.
- All but 5 (of 36) disclosed touching in response to specific questions (for example, "Did the doctor touch you here?").
- Only 3 (of 36) girls who received scoliosis examinations incorrectly reported genital or anal touching; only 1 of those provided additional (incorrect) details.

In sum, based on the total number of questions asked: "When all of the chances to reveal genital/anal contact were considered, children failed to disclose it 64% of the time, whereas the chance of obtaining a false report of genital/anal touching was only 8%, even when leading questions were asked."[49]

Children's Reactions to Victimization

There are few in our society who would argue that child sexual abuse does not cause serious problems for its victims. The burgeoning research on this subject suggests that the effects of victimization on children can be far-reaching, negative, and complex. In one study that compared 369 sexually abused children to 318 nonabused children, a number of factors emerged to distinguish the two groups.[50] The sexually abused children were significantly more likely to demonstrate:

- poor self-esteem;
- aggressive behaviors;
- fearfulness;
- concentration problems;
- withdrawal;
- acting out;
- need to please others.

Another study compared sexually abused children to two groups of nonabused children: one from a psychiatric outpatient clinic and the other from a well-child clinic. The researchers found that the sexually abused children were more similar to the psychiatric outpatients than to the normal children.[51] Sexually abused children displayed significantly more behavior problems (particularly sexual behaviors) and fewer social competencies than did normal children.

Sexually Abused Child Syndrome. Early attempts to describe a "sexually abused child syndrome" were quickly discarded as lacking a foundation in empirical research. Today, however, some of the leading researchers and clinicians in this field are moving toward consensus on behavioral indicators of child sexual abuse. The results of a nationwide survey of professionals experienced in evaluating suspected child sexual abuse revealed high levels of agreement concerning the following factors:[52]

- The child possesses age-inappropriate sexual knowledge.
- The child engages in sexualized play.
- The child displays precocious behavior.
- The child engages in excessive masturbation.
- The child is preoccupied with his or her genitals.
- There are indications that pressure or coercion was exerted on the child.
- The child's story remains consistent over time.
- The child's report indicates an escalating progression of sexual abuse over time.
- The child describes idiosyncratic details of the abuse.
- There is physical evidence of abuse.

Note, however, that these indicators represent a broad constellation of behaviors that are frequently seen among sexually abused children as a group. Owing to the many forms sexual abuse may take and the variations in individual coping methods and personalities, every child will exhibit a different set of behaviors subsequent to abuse. Thus, a child who experienced a single abusive incident may well be consistent with his or her story over time. Conversely, a child who experienced several years of abuse by a close relative may seem to contradict his or her story over time, depending on the attitudes expressed by family members or the manner in which he or she is questioned. In other words, there is no single array of behavioral indicators that definitively identify a sexually abused child.

The Risk of False Allegations

A recent spate of highly publicized sexual-abuse allegations has caused the public to recoil and question the limits of credulity. These allegations tend to fall into two categories: alleged sexual abuse of preschool children in day-care facilities, sometimes including bizarre and ritualistic elements; and sexual abuse allegations arising in the context of divorce and custody or visitation disputes. Such cases have caused many observers to question the veracity of child-sexual-abuse reports.[53]

Researchers have attempted to determine the percentage of unsubstantiated cases that can actually be attributed to false reports. The most comprehensive of these studies analyzed all reports of suspected sexual abuse filed with the Denver Department of Social Services (DSS) several years ago. All 576 reports had been investigated by the DSS Sexual Abuse Team and designated either "founded" (53%) or "unfounded" (47%). With the assistance of DSS caseworkers, the researchers applied clinical judgments to the case files and reclassified these reports, using the following categories:

- *Founded cases:*
  Reliable accounts
  Recantations of reliable accounts
- *Unfounded cases:*
  Unsubstantiated suspicions
  Insufficient information
  Fictitious reports by adults
  Fictitious reports by children

The last two categories, "fictitious reports by adults" and "fictitious reports by children," included deliberate falsifications, misperceptions, confused interpretations of nonsexual events, and children who had been coached by adults. On reclassification by the researchers, 6% of the total cases (34 allegations) were found to be fictitious. Of those, only 8 allegations had been made by 5 children, 4 of whom had been substantiated victims of abuse in the past.[54]

In a second phase of this study, the researchers examined 21 fictitious cases that had been referred to a sexual-abuse clinic for evaluation over a 5-year period. Of these allegations, 5 had been initiated by the child and 9 by an adult; in 7 cases the researchers could not determine who had initiated the charge. Custody or visitation disputes

were ongoing in 15 of these cases: in 1 child-initiated case, in 7 adult-initiated cases, and in all the "mixed" cases.[55]

Another study examined 162 consecutive sexual-abuse cases seen at a children's hospital over a 10-month period. Twenty-five of those cases involved allegations against a parent, and 7 of those (28%) involved a custody or visitation dispute. The disputed cases were less likely to be substantiated than cases without such conflict, but they were nevertheless substantiated more than half the time.[56]

Other studies have approached the relationship between custody disputes and false allegations from a different perspective, beginning with cases that are referred to clinicians for custody evaluations (rather than sexual-abuse diagnosis). These studies have found that a relatively high proportion of custody disputes involve false sexual-abuse allegations.[57] Note, however, that these studies depend on clinical populations (that is, troublesome cases that had been referred to a specialist for evaluation or diagnosis). Findings are based on a small number of cases, and, furthermore, the decision to label a report "fictitious" is based on clinical judgment: there is no objective, definitive measure of "truth." Because of these limitations, such studies cannot generalize to a conclusion that sexual-abuse allegations associated with custody disputes are necessarily false.[58]

In fact, sexual-abuse allegations arising from divorce and custody disputes appear to be quite rare. One study that attempted to quantify this phenomenon found that in most courts, about 2–10% of all family court cases involving custody and/or visitation disputes also involved a charge of sexual abuse. As an alternative way of framing the magnitude of this problem, sexual-abuse allegations occurred in the range of approximately 2–15 per 1,000 divorce filings among the courts that were studied. Based on data from seven jurisdictions, 105 of 6,100 cases (or less than 2%) of custody or visitation disputes involved sexual-abuse allegations.[59]

Research also suggests that sexual abuse in day care is no more common than it is within families. Extrapolating from 270 substantiated cases in 35 states over a three-year period, researchers estimated that 500 to 550 actual cases occurred in that period, involving more than 2,500 children. On the basis of the total of 7 million children attending day-care facilities nationwide, the researchers calculated that 5.5 of every 10,000 children enrolled in day care are sexually abused. This compares to an estimated 8.9 of every 10,000 children who are sexually abused in their homes. The conclusion: the apparently large number of sexual-abuse cases reported in day care "is simply a reflection of the large number of children in day care and the relatively high risk of sexual abuse to children everywhere."[60]

Emotional Reaction to the Pedophile

Because many investigators are parents, they react strongly to the pedophile. However, for legal and pragmatic reasons, such feelings must never be translated into physical or verbal abuse. Physical abuse by police is unlawful and should result in criminal and civil charges. Verbal abuse or open expressions of revulsion minimize the possibility of obtaining the suspect's cooperation and, perhaps, of obtaining a much-needed voluntary statement. The following case illustrates this point.

A 5-year-old girl told her mother that the man next door had taken her into his home, removed her underpants, placed his penis between her legs, and rubbed her vagina with it. After putting her underpants back on, he had sent her home. The mother called the police, but when they arrived the child was very hesitant to repeat the story.

Careful handling of the interview by the officer provided enough information to justify probable cause for an arrest, although the suspect denied the offense. Supplementing the child's statements were those of neighbors who had seen the man taking the child into his house, where she had remained for about 10 minutes.

The child was taken to the hospital and given an examination. The examining physician could find no injuries, semen, or pubic hair. The victim's clothing was normal in appearance. The situation at this juncture was a shy young child who probably would not be a good witness, an absence of physical evidence, a suspect who denied the charges, and witnesses who saw the child enter the suspect's house but saw no molestation. A voluntary statement was imperative if a successful prosecution was to result.

The suspect was interrogated and at first denied the charges. But when confronted with the child's and the neighbors' statements, he admitted molesting the child in the manner she described. He said that he had been drinking heavily at the time and attributed his actions to intoxication. The suspect agreed to give a full statement under oath to the state prosecutor.

Before the suspect was sworn in, the prosecutor was advised by the investigator, outside the presence of the suspect, the facts in the case. The prosecutor requested that the suspect be brought into his office. In an angry voice, he told the suspect, "If that had been my little girl, you son of a bitch, I would have broken your goddamned neck." The prosecutor then asked the suspect if he would like to make a statement. The suspect replied, "I have nothing to say to you." Subsequently, the suspect pleaded guilty to contributing to the delinquency of a minor, a misdemeanor.

The reason for this misdemeanor rather than the felony charge was insufficient evidence. The prosecutor was not new to this job, and he had an excellent reputation. Unfortunately, what he had done was identify the victim with his own daughter, who was about the same age as the molested child.

▲ FIGURE 11-9
Accused pedophile awaits the start of trial
Eric Franklin Rosser, who had been on the FBI's 10-most-wanted list, is shown here after his arrest. He is being prosecuted for his alleged involvement in child prostitution and pedophilia. He was arrested in Bangkok, Thailand.
(© Reuters/Corbis)

CHILD PORNOGRAPHY

Kenneth V. Lanning, supervisory special agent of the Federal Bureau of Investigation, divides what the pedophile collects into two categories: child pornography and child erotica.[61] **Child pornography** can be behaviorally (not legally) defined as the sexually explicit reproduction of a child's image and includes sexually explicit photographs, negatives, slides, magazines, movies, videotapes, and computer disks. In essence, it is the permanent record of the sexual abuse or exploitation of an actual child. To legally be child pornography, it must be a visual depiction (not the written word) of a minor (as defined by statute) that is sexually explicit (not necessarily obscene, unless required by state law). Child pornography can be divided into two subcategories: commercial and homemade.

Child erotica is a broader and more encompassing term than child pornography. It can be defined as any material, relating to children, that serves a sexual purpose for a given individual. Some of the more common types of child erotica include toys, games, drawings, fantasy writings, diaries, souvenirs, sexual aids, manuals, letters, books about children, psychological books on pedophilia, and ordinary photographs of children. Child erotica might also be referred to as pedophile paraphernalia. Generally, possession and distribution of these items does not constitute a violation of the law.

For investigative purposes, child erotica can be divided into the categories shown next.

Published Material Relating to Children

Examples of this include books, magazines, articles, or videotapes dealing with any of these areas:

- child development;
- sex education;
- child photography;
- sexual abuse of children;
- sexual disorders;
- pedophilia;
- man-boy love;
- personal ads;
- incest;
- child prostitution;
- missing children;
- investigative techniques;
- legal aspects;
- access to children;
- detective magazines;
- "men's" magazines;
- nudism;
- erotic novels;
- catalogs;
- brochures.

Listing of foreign sex tours, guides to nude beaches, and material on sponsoring orphans or needy children provide investigators with information about access to children. Detective magazines saved by pedophiles usually contain stories about crimes against children. The "men's" magazines collected may have articles about sexual abuse of children. The use of adult pornography to lower inhibitions is discussed elsewhere in this book. Although the possession of information on missing children should be carefully investigated to determine possible involvement in abduction, most pedophiles collect this material to help rationalize their behavior as child "lovers," not abductors. Personal ads include those in "swinger" magazines, video magazines, and newspapers, and may mention "family fun," "family activity," "European material," "youth training," "unusual and bizarre," "better life," and so on. Erotic novels may contain stories about sex with children but without sexually explicit photographs. They may contain sketches or drawings. Materials concerning current or proposed laws dealing with sex abuse; arrested, convicted, or acquitted child molesters; or investigative techniques used by law enforcement are common.

Unpublished Material Relating to Children

Examples include items such as these:

- personal letters;
- audiotapes;
- diaries;
- fantasy writings;
- manuscripts;
- telephone and address books;
- pedophile manuals;
- newsletters and bulletins;
- directories;
- adult pornography;
- financial records.

Commercial Child Pornography

Commercial child pornography is pornography that is produced and intended for commercial sale. Because of strict federal and state laws today, there is no place in the United States where commercial "child" pornography is knowingly openly sold. In the United States, it is primarily a cottage industry run by pedophiles and child molesters. The commercial child pornography still being distributed in the United States is smuggled in from foreign countries—primarily by pedophiles. The risks are usually too high for the strictly commercial dealer. Because of their sexual and personal interests, however, pedophiles are more willing to take those risks. Their motive goes beyond just profit. Commercial child pornography is still assembled and is much more readily available in foreign countries. United States citizens, however, seem to be the main customers for this material. Some offenders collect their commercial child pornography in ways that make it appear to be homemade child pornography (for example, by taking photographs of pictures in magazines; cutting up pictures and mounting them in photo albums, with names and descriptive information written below; or putting homemade labels on commercial videotapes). If necessary, highly experienced investigators and forensic laboratories can be of assistance in making distinctions between homemade and commercially produced child pornography.

Homemade Child Pornography

Contrary to what its name implies, homemade child pornography can be as "good" as, if not better than, the quality of any commercial pornography. The pedophile has a personal interest in the product. "Homemade" simply means it was not originally produced primarily for commercial sale. Although commercial child pornography is not openly sold anywhere in this country, homemade child pornography is continually produced, swapped, and traded in almost every community in the United States. While rarely found in "adult" bookstores, child pornography is frequently found in the homes and offices of doctors, lawyers, teachers, ministers, and other apparent pillars of the community. There is, however, a connection between commercial and homemade child pornography. Sometimes homemade child pornography is sold or winds up in commercial child pornography magazines, movies, or videos. The same pictures are reproduced and circulated again and again. With rapidly increasing frequency, more and more of both commercial and homemade child pornography is in video format. This actually increases the odds of finding child pornography in any investigation.

The law-enforcement investigator must realize that most of the children in prepubescent child pornography were not abducted into sexual slavery. They were seduced into posing for these pictures or videos by a pedophile they probably know. They were never missing children. The children in child pornography are frequently smiling or have neutral expressions on their faces, because they have been seduced into the activity after having had their inhibitions lowered by clever offenders. In some cases, their own parents took the pictures or made them available for others to take the pictures. Children in pubescent or technical child pornography, however, are more likely to be missing children—especially runaways—being exploited by morally indiscriminate pimps or profiteers. In contrast to adult pornography, but consistent with the gender preference of most preferential child molesters, there are more boys than girls in child pornography.

In understanding the nature of child pornography, the law-enforcement officer must recognize the distinction between technical and simulated child pornography. The Child Protection Act of 1984 defines a *child* as anyone under the age of 18. Therefore, a sexually explicit photograph of a 15-, 16-, or 17-year-old girl or boy is *technical child pornography*. Technical child pornography does not look like child pornography, but it is. The production, distribution, and, in some cases, possession of this type of child pornography could and should be investigated under appropriate child pornography statutes. Technical child pornography is an exception to much of what we say about child pornography. It often is produced, distributed, and consumed by individuals who are not child molesters or pedophiles; it is openly sold around the United States; and it more often portrays females than males. Because it looks like adult pornography, it is more like adult pornography.

However, sexually explicit photographs of 18-year-old or older males or females are not legally child pornography. But if the person portrayed in such material is young looking, dressed youthfully, or made up to look young, the material could be of interest to pedophiles. This is *simulated child pornography*. Simulated child pornography looks like child pornography, but it is not. It is designed to appeal to the pedophile but it is not legally child pornography because the individuals portrayed are over 18. This illustrates the importance, and sometimes the difficulty, in proving the age of the child in the photographs or videotapes.

Uses of Child Pornography Collections

Although the reasons why pedophiles collect child pornography and erotica are conjecture, we can be more certain as to how this material is used. Studies and police investigations have identified certain criminal uses of the material.

Child pornography and child erotica are used for the sexual arousal and gratification of pedophiles. They use child pornography the same way other people use adult pornography—to feed sexual fantasies. Some pedophiles only collect and fantasize about the material without acting out the fantasies, but in most cases the arousal and fantasy fueled by the pornography is only a prelude to actual sexual activity with children.

A second use of child pornography and erotica is to lower children's inhibitions. A child who is reluctant to engage in sexual activity with an adult or to pose for sexually explicit photos can sometimes be convinced by viewing other children having "fun" participating in the activity. Peer pressure can have a tremendous effect on children; if other children are involved, the child might be led to believe that the activity is acceptable. When the pornography is used to lower inhibitions, the children portrayed will usually *appear* to be having a good time.

Books on human sexuality and sex education, as well as sex manuals are also used to lower inhibitions. Children accept what they see in books, and many pedophiles have used sex education books to prove to children that such sexual behavior is acceptable. Adult pornography is also used, particularly with adolescent boy victims, to arouse them or to lower inhibitions.

A third major use of child pornography collections is blackmail. If a pedophile already has a relationship with a child, seducing the child into sexual activity is only part of the plan. The pedophile must also ensure that the child keeps the secret. Children are most afraid of pictures being shown to their friends. As such, pedophiles use photographs taken of the child as blackmail. If the child threatens to tell his or her parents or the authorities, the existence of sexually explicit photographs can be an effective silencer.

A fourth use of child pornography and erotica is as a medium of exchange. Some pedophiles exchange photographs of children for access to, or phone numbers of, other children. The quality and the theme of the material determine its value as an exchange medium. Rather than paying cash for access to a child, the pedophile may exchange a small part (usually duplicates) of his collection. The younger the child and the more bizarre the acts, the greater the value of the pornography.

A fifth use of the collected material is profit. Some people involved in the sale and distribution of child pornography are not pedophiles, they are profiteers. In contrast, most pedophiles seem to collect child erotica and pornography for reasons other than profit. Some pedophiles may begin nonprofit trading, which they pursue until they accumulate certain amounts or types of photographs, which are then sold to commercial dealers for reproduction in commercial child pornography magazines. Others combine their pedophiliac interest with their profit motive. Some collectors even have their own photographic reproduction equipment. Thus, the photograph of a child taken with or without parental knowledge by a neighborhood pedophile in any U.S. community can wind up in a commercial child pornography magazine with worldwide distribution.

Child Pornography, the Internet and the Law

Over the past decade, several important laws have been proposed and adopted to deal with the issue of child sexual exploitation on the Internet. For example, the *Child Protection and Sexual Predator Punishment Act of 1998* specifically addressed the issues of online sexual victimization of children. The law prohibits the transfer of sexually explicit material to minors, and increases penalties for offenses against children. Furthermore, the act amends the *Child Abuse Act of 1990* by requiring online service providers to report evidence of child pornography offenses to law-enforcement agencies. In 1998 Congress enacted the *Protection of Children from Sexual Predators Act*, which established three new criminal offense areas:

1. use of interstate facilities to transmit information about a minor;
2. transfer of obscene materials to or from minors;
3. definition of sexual activity to include the production of child pornography.

This important and landmark legislation also helped establish the Morgan P. Hardiman Child Abduction and Serial Murder Investigative Resource Center (CASMIRC), tasked with improving the coordination of major violent crimes involving children. CASMIRC also provides on-site consultation and advice for state and local agencies as well as operational support to any law-enforcement agency confronted with a child abduction, mysterious disappearance of a child, child homicide, serial murder, or expansive child pornography case. There are numerous state laws that also prohibit the possession, manufacturing, distribution, and sale of child pornography. In almost all instances, simple possession is a felony. Federal law on possession of child pornography also outlines the sexual exploitation of children prohibiting people from using children in the production of any sexually explicit material. Emphasis on the prosecution of child pornography has become a priority for federal authorities presumably because of the explosion of such activity via the Internet.[62] In the last decade, federal prosecutions for child pornography possession nearly tripled nationwide, and in some states, more child porn cases were filed than

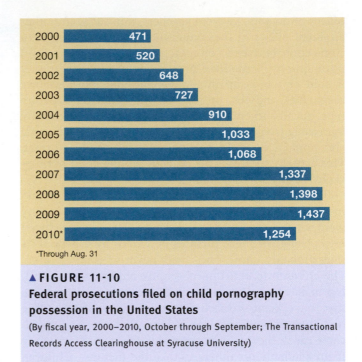

Year	
2000	471
2001	520
2002	648
2003	727
2004	910
2005	1,033
2006	1,068
2007	1,337
2008	1,398
2009	1,437
2010*	1,254

*Through Aug. 31

▲ **FIGURE 11-10**

Federal prosecutions filed on child pornography possession in the United States

(By fiscal year, 2000–2010, October through September; The Transactional Records Access Clearinghouse at Syracuse University)

traditional federal crimes such as mail and wire fraud and bank robbery. See Figure 11-10.

SEX TOURISM

Child pornography is closely tied to another form of child sexual exploitation—that of **sex tourism.** Sex tourism, which is also a by-product of sex trafficking, is defined by the United Nations as "tourism organized with the primary purpose of facilitating the effecting of a commercial-sexual relationship with a child."[63] Nearly half of sex tourism cases were closely connected to child pornography.[64]

Sex tourism allows pedophiles, mostly men,[65] to either arrange a trip through a travel agency that specializes in sex tours, or arrange travel themselves to an area known for child prostitution and child sex trafficking. Some of these travel agencies are virtual, or Internet based, and can be found among networks of child pornographers. Others hide behind the front of commercial travel agents. For example, Big Apple Oriental Tours, located in New York City, was discovered to have taken clients to nightclubs in the Philippines, Thailand, and Cambodia, where tour guides actually negotiated fees and sexual acts on behalf of their clients.[66] However, many pedophiles simply travel to areas known for lax law enforcement and bustling child sex industries to pick and choose for themselves.

Locations recognized for being sex tourism destinations generally are poverty-stricken nations with unstable economies and political structures.[67] In Thailand, for example, the government estimates that 10,000 children are involved in the commercial sex industry; however, nongovernmental agencies believe that the number is as high as 800,000. Growth in the demand for young boys in the area is attributed almost entirely to the sex tour industry.[68] Thailand is hardly the only destination for sex tourists, however. Other countries with abundant opportunities for child sex tourists include Mexico, India, Indonesia, Nepal, the Philippines, Cambodia, China, and Colombia.[69] Surprising to many people, the United States is also a popular destination for sex tourists seeking children, with Las Vegas and New Orleans serving as hot spots for affluent pedophiles.[70]

Approximately 24–25% of the world's sex tourists are American, thus constituting the largest concentration from any one country.[71] Some individuals travel with the singular intent of abusing children, whereas many are situational abuses and engage in the practice opportunistically while on business trips or family vacations.[72] Regardless of the intent, American law specifically forbids the practice of sex tourism. Federal statutes under Chapter 18, Sections 23 and 24 of the U.S. Code prohibit traveling across state lines or into the United States for the purpose of engaging in any illicit sexual conduct (which includes any commercial sex act with a person under 18). These statutes also prohibit an American citizen or national from engaging in illicit sexual conduct outside the United States. A violation of this law can result in a 30-year maximum sentence. The law does not require that the citizen have traveled outside the country with the intent of engaging in illicit sexual conduct in a foreign country. In 2003 the Protect Act, signed into law by President George W. Bush, reinforced these provisions.[73] The Department of Homeland Security has also developed the "Operation Predator" initiative to combat child exploitation, child pornography, and child sex tourism, with Immigrations and Customs Enforcement acting as the primary investigative agency. The United States has also funded global programs that conduct major public awareness and deterrence campaigns aimed at sex tourists, including Internet messages, pamphlets at international airports and public service announcements.[74]

Nevertheless, sex tourism is a difficult crime to investigate, prosecute, and prevent. The actions of foreign governments can implicitly encourage the industry[75] by directly targeting sex tourists or refusing to assist in the investigations of such crimes.[76] Owing to the nature and location of sex tourist crimes, federal investigators generally assume jurisdiction over these types of cases rather than local law enforcement.

USE OF THE COMPUTER AND THE INTERNET IN CHILD PORNOGRAPHY

Computers have become a pervasive part of daily life. Unfortunately, the ubiquity of the computer, and by extension the Internet, is an asset to the child pornographer (Figure 11-11). Child pornographers use personal computers to create, distribute, and catalog pornographic depictions of children and to widen their net of victimization.

Many child pornographers are compulsive record keepers, and for them the computer as a cataloging tool is electronic gold. While most people might use computers to

◄ **FIGURE 11-11**
Child pornography
Customs agent Donald Daufenbach shows off some of the computers seized in a child pornography raid. Many cybercrime investigators work in multi-agency task forces that focus on child porn and cases involving adults soliciting children for sex, so-called traveler cases. (© AP Photos/Douglas C. Pizac)

track a bank balance or store family vacation photos, law-enforcement investigations have determined that child pornographers use computers to organize and store photographs and movies that graphically depict scenes of sexual exploitation of children.

Child pornographers can acquire additional material through instant contact with other pedophiles. Chat rooms, bulletin boards, newsgroups, instant messaging, and e-mail are just some of the means child pornographers currently use to communicate with other pedophiles. Once he has made contact with willing cohorts, a pedophile can electronically exchange photographs, movies, and other depictions of child pornography. In a matter of seconds, a child pornographer may send or receive child pornography to or from almost anywhere in the world. Web cams have even made it possible to broadcast and receive live, real-time images of child molestation and pornography.

In addition, the home computer provides tools that make it easy to store and retrieve names and addresses of accessible victims. This library of victims can be developed with great ease and efficiency by way of referral from the pedophile's perverse network of colleagues.

Also, pedophiles can use computers to directly establish a rapport with children. Adolescent boys who spend a great amount of their time online are at particularly high risk of this type of contact. Again, using chat rooms, e-mail, and instant messaging, the pedophile may pose as an adolescent to gain the trust of the child. He may then indirectly victimize the child by sharing with him or her sexually explicit information or material. He may further attempt to obtain the child's phone number or whereabouts in order to engage in face-to-face contact and direct sexual victimization.

Desktop publishing holds unique possibilities for child pornographers. Like any other small publisher, pedophiles that use child pornography as a profit-making business can produce high-quality prints with relative ease. They can collect, record, "publish," and distribute pornographic material either as hard copy or as an electronic file. They can also create false or doctored graphic images of children in pornographic positions. The question then arises: are such false images punishable by law?

In the United States, Title 18, Section 2252, of the U.S. Code, commonly known as the Child Pornography Prevention Act (CPPA), deals with this aspect of child pornography and the Internet. The CPPA makes it a crime to sell, possess with intent to sell, download, or produce child pornography or any visual depiction that is intended to *represent or resemble* child pornography. This includes material "transported, by any means, including by computer, if (i) the producing of such visual depiction involves the use of a minor engaging in sexually explicit conduct; and (ii) such *visual depiction* is of such conduct."[77]

We must reiterate that there does not have to be an actual child involved in the making of such pornography for it to be legally punishable; there must be merely the presence of the "visual depiction" of a child. This stipulation assumes that there are harmful secondary effects associated with virtual child pornography—namely, as mentioned earlier, that pedophiles may use graphic depictions of child pornography to seduce children to join in the "fun."[78]

The movie *Traffic* contains a scene in which an underage character enacts having sex with a drug dealer. Under the CPPA, this scene would, in legal terms, be viewed as child pornography. For this reason, the Free Speech Coalition, an adult trade organization, has challenged the CPPA claiming that it is overly vague and violates First Amendment free speech rights.[79] A federal district court ruled against the Free Speech Coalition in 1997, but the 9th Circuit reversed that decision in late 2001, and the reversal was upheld by the Supreme Court in Spring 2002.[80]

Unfortunately, owing to the anonymous nature of the Internet and the sheer volume of Internet activity, transactions involving child pornography are often difficult for government agencies to track. As discussed in Chapter 17, "Computer Crime," however, some investigators are taking advantage of the anonymity of the Net by posing as minors in order to identify pedophiles. Once a pedophile has been discovered, his records of his computer activities can frequently be used as incriminating evidence. Furthermore, under strictly regulated circumstances, investigators may be able to track the Internet activity of pedophiles through various watchdog programs.[81]

Child pornography is often found in computer files on hard drives. Whenever such a condition may exist, it is important to remember the special techniques of investigating technologically based crime and retrieving digital images as evidence. (For a more thorough discussion of digital forensics and the investigation of child pornography involving computers, refer to Chapter 16, "Computer Crime.")

Currently, 50% of Internet child pornography cases call for investigation abroad.[82] The recent upsurge in worldwide child pornography prevention and detention agencies lends credence to the notion that child pornography on the Internet cannot be tackled by one country alone but has to be dealt with globally.[83]

INTERNET CRIMES AGAINST CHILDREN

With the popularity of the Internet in homes and schools, and particularly with the advent of social networking sites such as MySpace and Facebook, child pornography is no longer the only threat to children on the Internet. Cyberenticement through social sites, instant messaging, e-mail communications, and gaming connections can lure an unsuspecting child into sexual contact with a pedophile. In addition, online advertisers, such as Craigslist,

▲ **FIGURE 11-12   Online Solicitation**

(© NBC Newswire)

NBC's popular show *To Catch a Predator* takes a vigilante approach to catching, embarrassing, and arresting men who solicit underage boys and girls in Internet chat rooms. The show, attracting up to 7 million viewers per episode, has partnered with a private watch dog group known as Perverted Justice to pose as youngsters in chat rooms. The decoys often engage in highly sexualized conversation with adults attracted to them by screen names that suggest youth and innocence. If the adult solicits an in-person meeting, the decoy gives them an address where police are stationed outside and cameramen lie in wait for the ambush. Often, the adult will come into the home, and engage in light banter with a decoy chosen because he or she looks underage. At that point, the decoy leaves the room under the pretense of getting a drink, or changing clothes. The show's host, Chris Hansen, and his cameramen descend on the hapless predator, peppering him with questions about why he would solicit a child for sex. More often than not, the adult has a number of predictable excuses at hand, including "I thought he/she was 18" or "I've never done this before." Most deny that they are there to have sex with the purported minor. Hansen will subsequently present a transcript of the graphic instant messaging chat, making for truly squirm-worthy television. Once the predator leaves the home, law enforcement descends, making an arrest or citation related to the online solicitation. The show is certainly compelling enough to watch, but critics charge that the show is ethically questionable for its vigilante techniques, blurry lines between justice and law enforcement, and issues of entrapment. This has been further strengthened after the suicide of a Texas man who was caught and taped for the show. Perhaps as a result, *Dateline* is moving away from the subject of child predators, using Hansen's trademark trapping to lure in con men and identity thieves. However, the show has certainly left its mark on national consciousness, bringing Internet-enabled exploitation to the front of the minds of parents and potential victims.

(Sources: *Dateline NBC* website: www.msnbc.msn.com/id/10912603/; B. Stelter, "To Catch a Predator Is Falling Prey to Advertisers' Sensibilities," *The New York Times,* August 27, 2007.)

are also presenting opportunities for child prostitution and solicitation. Although only a small percentage of the nation's youth experience online solicitation for sexual purposes, the prospect is a frightening one to parents and law enforcement officers (Figure 11-12).

Most of the youth exposed to online solicitations were girls between the ages of 14 and 17. Profiles of those soliciting children sexually show that they tend to be men more than 70% of the time, and about 43% of these men are over the age of 18.[84] About 75% of the time, the person soliciting the child asked to meet them in person.[85]

As a result of the nearly 30 million children[86] on the Internet today, parents, law-enforcement officials, and even website managers are taking steps to ensure that online solicitations do not result in a criminal act against a child. The Internet Crimes Against Children (ICAC) Task Force Program was developed in response to these issues and provides resources to local and state law enforcement agencies to "enhance their investigative response to offenders who use the Internet, online communication systems, or other computer technology to sexually exploit children."[87] Investigations of online predators by law enforcement using undercover techniques appears to be making an impact. In a study examining arrests of online predators, researchers found that 87% of arrests of online predators in 2006 involved undercover investigators posing as youth. However, it should also be noted that arrests of online predators accounted for only 1% of all arrests for sex crimes against children in 2006.[88]

Websites such as MySpace have also joined in the investigation of online crimes against children. In April of 2007 the attorney generals of eight states (Connecticut, Georgia, Idaho, North Carolina, Ohio, Pennsylvania, Mississippi, and New Hampshire) drafted a letter to the popular social networking site calling on them to do more to remove pedophiles that were registered as users on the site. This followed reports of seven Connecticut girls being sexually assaulted by men they met on MySpace, and as many as 100 reports of some type of criminal activity perpetrated by adults who used the site to contact children.[89] The issue was further called into question after a *Wired News* reporter cross-indexed a number of user profiles with sex offender databases and found 744 convicted sex offenders on the site.[90] By July of 2007 MySpace announced that it had found and deleted nearly 29,000 profiles linked to sex offenders.[91]

The Internet—although providing limitless educational and entertainment possibilities to children—is clearly a means for predators to exploit children in a variety of ways. Internet crimes against children can include child pornography, communications involving sex trafficking and tourism, and even harassment among peers. Although law enforcement officers can pose as children in Internet chat rooms in an effort to lure sex offenders, the process is time-consuming. The best tool to protect children from Internet crime is parental education and involvement. The more a child is supervised while on the Internet, the less likely he or she is to be a victim of exploitation.[92]

BULLYING AND CYBERBULLYING

For generations, bullying has been seen as an ugly rite of passage for children and teenagers. In schools across the country, students were forced to endure daily abuse that included name calling, social exclusion, taunts, intimidation, pranks, and even physical violence. Teachers and parents were either unaware of the problem or simply unable to stop the bullying from occurring. However, what was once seen as fact of life is now considered to be a crime in many jurisdictions. Law enforcement is increasingly becoming involved in investigations of bullies and cyberbullies as the result of high profile bullying cases that have changed the way we think about this behavior.

Bullying is defined as "aggressive behavior or intentional harm by an individual or group repeated over time that involves an imbalance of power."[93] It can be verbal,

physical or even psychological in nature and can have devastating effects on its victims. Studies show that male victims of bullying are more than five times more likely to be moderately to severely depressed and four times more likely to be suicidal, whereas bullied girls are more than three time more likely to be moderately to severely depressed and eight times more likely to be suicidal.[94] In 2009 an 11-year-old Massachusetts boy named Carl Hoover committed suicide after being extensively bullied; the following year, 15-year-old Phoebe Prince killed herself after being tormented by female classmates jealous over her relationship with a school football player. And 2010 was also marked by a spate of suicides by young men who were mercilessly taunted for either being gay or being perceived by their peers as being homosexual. The result of these heartbreaking incidents has been increased legislation related to bullying; 44 states now have anti-bullying legislation on the book.[95]

Of those 44 states, 30 of them specifically address cyberbullying in their legislation.[96] **Cyberbullying** is defined as using the Internet, cellular phone, or other technology to harass another person. Facebook has become a popular venue for cyberbullying, allowing bullies to spread rumors and post unflattering photographs of victims as well as use chat and messaging features to send hurtful communications. Other types of cyberbullying include posting private videos on YouTube or other video hosting sites in an effort to humiliate the subject and using telephone text messaging to send photos or disparaging messages.

Police involvement in bullying cases is still fairly limited. For the most part, legislation addressing bullying or cyberbullying requires schools to adopt policies to address the issue and mentions nothing about law-enforcement intervention. But obviously if the bullying is physical in nature, police may be involved as they would in a simple assault. Furthermore, many states have separate laws regarding using electronic means to harass another person. For example, Wisconsin's statute 947.0125 prohibits unlawful use of computerized communication systems, which therefore classifies cyberbullying as a Class B misdemeanor and punishes it with a fine up to $1,000, or imprisonment for up to 90 days, or both. Though this issue is still evolving, the best thing that law-enforcement officers can do to help victims is be aware of the statutes within their state, and understand the seriousness of the effects of bullies on their victims.

CHILD ABDUCTION

Although high-profile news stories might perpetuate the notion that child abductions are often perpetrated by strangers, research indicates that most abductions are perpetrated by family members; in fact it is estimated that stranger abductions associated with a high risk of victim mortality account for only a small number of cases annually (for example, between 200 and 300 cases). This is in stark contrast to the presumably hundreds of thousands of cases involving family members. Moreover, when a child goes missing, it is often the case that the child has run away or been abducted by a non-custodial parent.[98]

THE PARENTAL INTERVIEW

Parents must be interviewed separately from each other and from other family members and reporting parties. Responding officers may feel reluctant to conduct separate interviews of the parents because of their emotionally escalated state. Conversely, if the parents do not appear particularly concerned about the child's absence, the officers may not view separate interviews as necessary. While they cannot determine what a parent's "normal" reaction to a missing child would be, officers must remain objective and realize that a family member may later become a suspect if the child has been abducted. They must balance this objectivity with empathy and support if the parents are in a state of emotional crisis. Most importantly, officers must ensure that they interview parents individually, preserve potential evidence, and document each parent's demeanor and attitude throughout the interview.

During the parental interview, officers should quickly compile accurate physical characteristics of the child, such as his or her appearance, age, and clothing, and should obtain recent photographs and videotapes. Officers should attempt to include full criminal- and psychiatric-history checks of all family members who had access to the child, as well as acquire a local agency history of any prior abuse or neglect calls to the home. In separate interviews of family members, responding officers should question whether the child's absence shows a significant deviation from established patterns of behavior.[99] However, further exploration into the victimology of the missing child can answer this question.

VICTIMOLOGY OF THE MISSING CHILD

To understand whether the child's absence is consistent with established patterns of behavior, officers first must understand the child's normal actions before the disappearance. Officers should use the following guidelines for assessing the personality of the missing child.[100]

- Develop and verify a detailed time-line of the child's last known activities up to the time the child was last seen or reported missing.
- Determine habits, hobbies, interests, and favorite activities.
- Identify normal activity patterns, and determine the victim's known comfort zone. Officers should assess the child's survival skills, ability to adapt to new or strange circumstances, and intellectual

maturity. Did the child frequently travel alone? Did the child have a routine where independent travel occurred on a regular basis (for example, riding a bike to school)? What fears and phobias did the child exhibit? For example, if the child was afraid of the dark, the probability of leaving voluntarily at night is low. Similarly, if the missing child was afraid to travel without a favorite item, such as a toy or security blanket, and the item remains in the house after the disappearance, the child may not have left voluntarily.

- Note any recent changes in behavior or activity patterns and any unusual events and stressors. Officers should explore any motivations for leaving. How does the child normally deal with stressful situations? Have any recent traumatic or stressful events caused such a prompt departure? Have any abuses occurred within the residence or family? Officers also should determine whether there were any recent changes in sleeping and eating patterns that would indicate stress.
- Identify and separately interview family members, close friends, schoolmates, teachers, coworkers, and other significant individuals. The FBI's National Center for the Analysis of Violent Crime has created a general assessment form for distribution to family members and associates that can assist in police officers' efforts to understand the child's personality.[101]
- Determine any history of alcohol and other drug use. Does the child have any particular medical conditions or allergies? If so, are the child's medications for the existing conditions still in the house? The presence of medications that the child needs may indicate an involuntary departure.
- Identify and interview boyfriends and/or girlfriends; determine normal dating patterns, including sexual activity. If the missing child is a postpubescent female, are there pregnancy and abortion issues? If so, officers should consider contacting local pregnancy, health, and abortion clinics. Also, officers should familiarize themselves with department policy and legal issues concerning confidentiality if they find the missing child at such a clinic. Obtain and review any personal writings, diaries, drawings, and schoolwork, including any entries into a personal computer or interaction with online systems or services. A critical item often overlooked in the missing-child call is the presence or absence of journals or diaries. Besides the obvious insights that diaries may provide into the child's state of mind, the presence or absence of any written communication can prove relevant. A child who consistently and regularly has expressed thoughts and feelings in writing might not depart voluntarily without leaving some form of written communication for people left behind.[102]

Similarly, calendars or schedules indicating planned events may provide insight into the child's possible motivation for staying or leaving.

- Determine any history of running away, discontent with home life, or ideas of suicide. Has the child disappeared voluntarily on prior occasions? If so, officers should note the last time the child ran away and the length of time missing. Did the child go to friends, other family members, or a runaway shelter? Officers should determine what enabled the child to run away successfully or, conversely, what prevented the child from sustaining a long-term absence. What happened that prompted the child's departure in previous absences? Officers should determine whether the child exhibited any runaway tendencies (for example, staying out all night), threats to leave, or other behaviors that violated clear directives from parents or caregivers. Officers also should determine the existence of any prior suicide attempts or gestures by the child and consider the possibility that the child has disappeared as a result of a self-inflicted injury.

These observations will assist officers in crafting the child's victimology, which will indicate whether the child had the motivation and capability of leaving voluntarily. If the victim assessment suggests that these two factors do not exist, officers must consider the possibility that an abduction has occurred.

Similarly, abductions of toddlers also occur primarily for emotion-based reasons. These cases typically lack planning, are impulsive, and frequently involve the mother's boyfriend or ex-boyfriend as the perpetrator.[106] Because toddlers typically are in the constant care of a caregiver, there is little opportunity for strangers to access them. Additionally, sexually motivated abductions are infrequent among this age group, possibly because of their increased mobility and independence which make them difficult to control.[107]

ABDUCTION PATTERNS

Experts in the field have noted patterns in familial and non-familial perpetrated abductions within victim-specific age groups. For example, newborn and **infant abductions** (that is, the taking of a child less than 1-year-old) occur, by definition, for reasons not typically associated with kidnappings, such as a desire for money, sex, revenge, or custody, which are considered traditional motives in kidnapping cases.[103] Although little research exists on the topic of infant abductors' motivation, it is suggested that these crimes are either emotion-based or motivated by maternal desires.[104] By way of general background, infant abductors usually are women, who account for 141 of the 145 cases analyzed. Offenders whose ages were verified ranged from 14- to 48-years-old, with an average age of 28. Race was determined in 142 cases: 63 offenders were white, 54 were black, and 25 were Hispanic. To gain further insight into infant abductors and the crimes they commit, members of the FBI's National Center for the Analysis of Violent Crime (NCAVC) interviewed 16 abductors; 105 offenders in this analysis had abducted infants in 10 different states. Nine of the abductors targeted hospitals directly: 5 approached the infant's residence: and 2 chose other locations. Although none had committed a violent crime before, 4 killed the infant's mother before stealing her baby.

Although emotion-based abductions also occur among preschool-aged children, this age group is at an increased risk of sexually motivated and profit-based abductions compared to infants and toddlers. Owing to their physical and emotional development, caregivers generally allow them greater autonomy which can increase their accessibility to strangers and acquaintances. In this age group, sexually motivated offenders are typically male, an acquaintance of the victim, and have access to the child's yard or neighborhood. Acquaintances also are associated with profit-based abductions which generally occur in the context of crimes against older, related victims, such as a parent.[108]

Child abductions most commonly are observed among elementary and middle school children where the victimization rates nearly triple.[109] Motives for abductions within this age group shift from emotion-based, as seen among younger age groups, to sexually driven crimes. Generally, the perpetrators are male, acquaintances or strangers, and target female victims. Younger children in this category tend to be abducted near their home, whereas older children often are abducted from more distant locations.[110]

The risk of sexually motivated abductions decrease as children become of high school age. In this case, emotion- and profit-based crimes are more prevalent. This may be due to the fact that high school-aged children have money and other valuable possessions and are exposed to high-risk activities, such as drug use and abusive relationships. Emotion-based abductions typically resemble adult domestic violence cases, often times involving a female victim and the boyfriend as the perpetrator. In contrast, profit-based abductions frequently pertain to drugs: victims tend to be male, and offenders are generally strangers and acquaintances.[111]

CHECKLIST FOR LAW ENFORCEMENT

The following checklist describes the most important steps that law enforcement can take as the investigation begins. The order of the steps is likely to vary depending on individual circumstances.

- Issue a BOLO (Be On the Look Out) bulletin to be broadcast to local law-enforcement agencies alerting them to the missing child, and send a teletype locally or regionally.

- Implement the **AMBER Plan,** which is a voluntary partnership between law enforcement and broadcasters to activate the bulletins in the most serious child abduction cases. (This plan is discussed in greater detail shortly.)
- Immediately enter the child's name into the National Crime Information Center (NCIC) registry of missing persons. There is no waiting period for entry into NCIC for children under age 18.
- Request the National Center for Missing and Exploited Children (NCMEC) fax the child's picture to law-enforcement agencies throughout the country.
- Inform the **FBI Child Abduction and Serial Murder Investigative Resource Center (CASMIRC)** of the case or ask for assistance if there is a chance the abduction was predatory.
- Notify the local FBI field office in case additional services and support are needed.
- Notify the state missing children's bureau and request additional services if needed.
- Secure the crime scene—for instance, the location outside a home where the child might have been abducted—and the child's bedroom. The officers who respond initially to the call must evaluate the contents and appearance of the child's room and retrieve the child's used bedding, clothing, and shoes and place them in clean bags to be used as scent articles. Also retrieve the child's toothbrush, hairbrush, and other items that might contain DNA evidence. Protect footprints in dust, mud, or snow to preserve the scent. Determine if personal items are missing, and interview the last persons known to have seen the child.
- Request tracking dogs or a helicopter equipped with an infrared or a heat-sensitive device (to detect heat emitted from the body) if needed after the residence, yard, and surrounding areas have been searched unsuccessfully.
- Advise airlines, airports, bus and taxicab companies, subways, ferries, and ports of the disappearance as necessary and distribute posters of the missing child.
- Revisit various "hot spots" or checkpoints at the same time of day and/or same day of the week following the disappearance to see if any eyewitnesses can be uncovered.
- Contact the neighborhood watch to see if anything suspicious was reported.
- Check the daily log of parking and traffic tickets and traffic stops to see if anything relates to the child's disappearance.
- Check the convicted sex offender registry to find out if a potential suspect lived or was ever stopped by the police in the area.
- Collect and review local newspapers in hopes of possible clues or leads to aid in the search. Check out local regional events and activities—such as carnivals, county fairs, festivals, sports events, and

▲ **FIGURE 11-13   AMBER alert**
An AMBER alert is displayed on a highway messaging sign increasing the opportunity for a member of the public to find the missing/kidnapped child. (© AP Photo/Nati Harnik)

music concerts—and want ads for hired help in search of leads regarding the predator and/or any witnesses to the disappearance.
- Establish a procedure for handling extortion attempts, if needed.
- Contact neighboring jurisdictions to find out if incidents of a similar nature have occurred there.[112]

AMBER ALERT PLAN

The AMBER Alert program is a voluntary partnership between law-enforcement agencies, state transportation officials and radio, television and Internet broadcasters to activate an urgent news bulletin in child abduction cases (Figure 11-13). Broadcasters use the Emergency Alert System, formerly known as the Emergency Broadcast System, to air a description of the missing child, the suspected abductor, and any vehicles involved in the abduction. The program was first introduced after the kidnap and murder of 9-year old Amber Hagerman of the Dallas-Fort Worth area and is now established in all 50 states.

How Does the AMBER Alert Work?

Once law enforcement is notified of an abducted child, they must determine whether the case meets the criteria set forth in the AMBER alert plan. The national AMBER Alert Coordinator, affiliated with the U.S. Department of Justice Office of Justice Programs, has recommended the following criteria:

- There is reasonable belief by law enforcement that an abduction has occurred.
- The law-enforcement agency believes that the child is in imminent danger of serious bodily injury or death.

- There is enough descriptive information about the victim and the abduction for law enforcement to issue an AMBER alert to assist in the recovery of a child.
- The abduction is of a child 17 years old or younger.
- The child's name and other critical data elements, including the Child Abduction Flag, have been entered into the National Crime Information Center system (NCIC).

If these criteria are met, alert information is put together and faxed to radio stations designated as primary stations under EAS. These stations then send the same information to area radio, television, and cable systems where it is broadcast to millions of listeners. Radio stations interrupt programming to announce the alert, and television and cable stations run a "crawl" on the screen with a picture of the missing child.[113]

Time Factors

How long does a runaway child typically stay away from home, and how does the passage of time influence the classification of a missing-child case? The California Department of Justice's Missing/Unidentified Persons Unit has reported the following trends in runaway returns:

TIME FRAME	RUNAWAYS RETURNED
Within 7 days	50%
7–14 days	30%
14–30 days	17%
More than 30 days	3%

These statistics indicate that the majority of runaway children cannot sustain an absence of more than two weeks from home. In general, the longer the absence, the greater the likelihood that an individual has abducted the child or that the child has fallen victim to a violent crime. If the child has a history of running away, officers should determine the length of time the child remained missing during previous absences. If the time length of the current absence grossly exceeds that of previous absences, officers should consider the current disappearance a deviation from normal behavior patterns.

Responding officers should note the amount of time that transpired between when the child was last seen and when the parents or guardian alerted authorities. While 24 hours or more may indicate apathy or neglect, this time frame also may reflect the common misconception that an individual must be missing for 24 hours before law enforcement can respond. The responding officers should construct a time line identifying the parents' activities during this interval. The time line highlights family dynamics and clarifies the parents' potential role in the child's disappearance.[114]

SEX OFFENDER REGISTRATION AND NOTIFICATION

In 1994 Congress passed the **Jacob Wetterling Crimes Against Children and Sexually Violent Offender Registration Act.**[115] The act required that states create sex-offender registries within three years or lose 10% of their funding under the Edward Byrne Memorial program.[116] Offenders who commit a criminal sexual act against a minor or commit any sexually violent offense must register for a period of 10 years from the date of their release from custody or supervision. All 50 states have sex-offender registration.[117]

Although sex-offender registration requirements vary according to state laws, some common features exist in registries throughout the country. In most states, the state criminal justice agency or board (for example, the state police or state bureau of investigation) maintains the state's registry. Sex offenders, both juveniles and adults, register at local law enforcement or corrections agencies, which then forward the information to the state's central registry. Registry information typically includes the offender's name, address, date of birth, Social Security number, and physical description, as well as fingerprints and a photograph. In addition, Iowa requires information about the sex-offense conviction that triggered the registration, and at least eight states collect samples for DNA identification.[118]

Most state laws require that offenders register only if their convictions occurred after the law's effective date, although some states, such as Minnesota, require that offenders register after they are charged with a sexual offense.[119] Offenders receive notice of the registration requirement from the court or registry agency. In Iowa, offenders can contest the registration requirement by filing an application for determination with the State Department of Public Safety.

In essence, the Jacob Wetterling Act gave states the option of releasing information about registered sex offenders to the public but did not require that they do so. This changed in 1996 when Congress amended the act to require that states disclose information about registered sex offenders for public safety purposes. This legislation became known as **Megan's Law,** in memory of Megan Kanka.[120]

U.S. Department of Justice guidelines allow states considerable discretion in determining the extent and manner of notification when warning the public about sex offenders living in the community. All states now have community notification laws.[121]

The most basic form of notification, sometimes referred to as *passive notification,* allows citizens to access registry information at their local law-enforcement agencies. In Iowa, citizens must complete a request form at their local police or sheriff's department and provide the name of the person being checked and one of three identifiers: address, date of birth, or Social Security number. If the agency finds the person's name on the registry, it can release certain information about the offender; however, federal guidelines prohibit states from releasing the identities of victims. Employers also may check potential employees.

In addition to allowing passive notification, a number of states permit government agencies to disseminate information about registered sex offenders to vulnerable individuals and organizations. Using this process, known as *active notification,* officials may choose to notify prior victims, landlords, neighbors, public and private schools, child-care facilities, religious and youth organizations, and other relevant individuals or agencies. Most officials reserve community-wide notification for only the most dangerous sex offenders. Community-wide notification usually involves using the media and public forums such as neighborhood associations and other community meetings.

The Pam Lychner Sexual Offender Tracking and Identification Act of 1996[122] established a national sex-offender database, which the FBI maintains.[123] This national tracking system gives law-enforcement authorities access to sex-offender registration data from all participating states. The Lychner Act also requires that the FBI register, and verify the addresses of, sex offenders in states that have not met the minimum compliance standards set forth by the Jacob Wetterling Act, although this may change.[124]

CRIME IN SCHOOLS

Sixty-five years ago, surveys of public school teachers indicated that the most pressing classroom problems were tardiness, talkative students, and gum chewing.[125] Far more serious complaints are currently heard from teachers, administrators, and students—about the presence of drugs, gangs, and weapons on campus and the threat of assault, robbery, theft, vandalism, and rape.[126]

According to the popular media, such as *Time* magazine and *U.S. News and World Report,* the problems in our nation's schools may be paralyzing the system.[127] In an effort to develop a systematic procedure for threat assessment and intervention in school violence cases, the FBI's National Center for the Analysis of Violent Crime (NCAVC) conducted an in-depth review of 18 school shootings. Because of confidentiality issues, the shooting cases studied were not identified. The study analyzed the shootings from a behavioral perspective and resulted in the development of the threat assessment intervention

model. The model outlines a procedure for evaluating a threat and the person making the threat so that an accurate assessment can be made of the likelihood that the threat will be carried out.

THREAT ASSESSMENT

A threat is an expression of the intent to do harm or act out violently against someone or something. A threat can be spoken, written, or symbolic—for example, motioning with one's hands as though shooting at another person.

Threat assessment rests on two critical principles: (1) that all threats and all threateners are not equal and (2) that most threateners are unlikely to carry out their threats. However, all threats must be taken seriously and evaluated.

In NCAVC's experience, most threats are made anonymously or under a false name. Because threat assessment relies heavily on evaluating the threatener's background, personality, lifestyle, and resources, identifying the threatener is necessary so that an informed assessment can be made—and so that charges can be brought if the threat is serious enough to warrant prosecution. If the threatener's identity cannot be determined, the evaluation will have to be based on the threat alone. That assessment may change if the threatener is eventually identified: a threat that was considered low risk may be rated as more serious if new information suggests the threatener is dangerous; conversely, an assessment of high risk may be scaled down if the threatener is identified and found not to have the intent, ability, means, or motive to carry out the threat (Figure 11-14).

Motivation

Threats are made for a variety of reasons. A threat may be a warning signal, a reaction to fear of punishment or some other anxiety, or a demand for attention. It may be intended to taunt; to intimidate; to assert power or control; to punish; to manipulate or coerce; to frighten; to terrorize; to compel someone to do something; to strike back for an injury, injustice, or insult; to disrupt someone's or some institution's life; to test authority, or to protect oneself. The emotions that underlie a threat can be love, hate, fear, rage, or desire for attention, revenge, excitement, or recognition.

Motivation can never be known with complete certainty, but understanding motive to the extent possible is a key element in evaluating a threat. A threat reflects the threatener's mental and emotional state at the time the threat is made, but it is important to remember that a state of mind can be temporarily but strongly influenced by alcohol or drugs or by a precipitating factor such as a romantic breakup, failing grades, or conflict with a parent. After a person has absorbed an emotional setback and calmed down, or when the effects of alcohol or drugs have worn off, his or her motivation to act on a violent threat may also diminish.

▶ **FIGURE 11-14**
Students and faculty flee from school after shooting
Recently, a number of the nation's high schools have experienced situations in which students have brought guns to school and killed or wounded many people. The FBI's National Center for the Analysis of Violent Crime (NCAVC) has conducted an in-depth review of 18 school shootings. From this analysis, they have developed a threat assessment model to help prevent school violence. (© Mark Leffingwell/AFP/Getty)

Signposts

In general, people do not switch instantly from nonviolence to violence. Nonviolent people do not "snap" or decide on the spur of the moment to meet a problem by using violence. Instead, the path toward violence is an evolutionary one, with signposts along the way. A threat is one observable behavior; another may be brooding about frustration or disappointment or fantasizing about destruction or revenge in conversations, writings, drawings, and the like.

Factors in Threat Assessment

Specific, plausible details are a critical factor in evaluating a threat. Details can include the identity of the victim or victims; the reason for making the threat; the means, weapon, and method by which it is to be carried out; the date, time, and place that the threatened act will occur; and concrete information about plans or preparations that have already been made.

Specific details can indicate that substantial thought, planning, and preparatory steps have already been taken, suggesting a higher risk that the threatener will follow through on the threat. Similarly, a lack of detail suggests that the threatener may not have thought through all the contingencies, has not actually taken steps to carry out the threat, and may not seriously intend violence. He or she may merely be "blowing off steam" over some frustration or be trying to frighten or intimidate a particular victim or disrupt a school's events or routine.

Details that are specific but not logical or plausible may indicate a less serious threat. For example, a high school student writes that he intends to detonate hundreds of pounds of plutonium in the school's auditorium the following day at lunchtime. The threat is detailed, stating a specific time, place, and weapon, but the details are unpersuasive. Plutonium is almost impossible to obtain, legally or on the black market. It is expensive, hard to transport, and very dangerous to handle, and a complex high-explosive detonation is required to set off a nuclear reaction. No high-school student is likely to have any plutonium at all, much less hundreds of pounds, nor would a student have the knowledge or complex equipment required to detonate it. A threat this unrealistic is obviously unlikely to be carried out.

The emotional content of a threat can be an important clue to the threatener's mental state. Emotions are conveyed by melodramatic words and unusual punctuation—"I hate you!!!!!" "You have ruined my life!!!!" "May God have mercy on your soul!!!!"—or in excited, incoherent passages that may refer to God or other religious beings or may deliver an ultimatum.

Though emotionally charged threats can tell the assessor something about the temperament of the threatener, they are not a measure of danger. They may sound frightening, but no correlation has been established between the emotional intensity in a threat and the risk that it will be carried out.

Precipitating stressors are incidents, circumstances, reactions, or situations that can trigger a threat. The precipitating event may seem insignificant and have no direct relevance to the threat, but nonetheless it becomes a catalyst. For example, a student has a fight with his mother before going to school. The argument may be a minor one over an issue that has nothing to do with school, but it sets off an emotional chain reaction that leads the student to threaten another student at school that day—possibly something he has thought about doing in the past.

The effect of a precipitating event obviously depends on predisposing factors: underlying personality traits, characteristics, and temperament that predispose an adolescent to fantasize about violence or act violently. Accordingly, information about a temporary "trigger" must be considered together with broader information about underlying factors, such as a student's vulnerability to loss and depression.

Personality Traits and Behavior

- *Leakage:* "Leakage" occurs when a student intentionally or unintentionally reveals clues to feelings, thoughts, fantasies, attitudes, or intentions that may signal an impending violent act. These clues can take the form of subtle threats, boasts, innuendos, predictions, or ultimatums. They may be spoken or conveyed in stories, diary entries, essays, poems, letters, songs, drawings, doodles, tattoos, or videos.[128] Leakage can also occur when a student tries, at times deceptively, to get unwitting friends or classmates to help with preparations for a violent act (for example, the student asks a friend to obtain ammunition for her because she is "going hunting").

- *Low tolerance for frustration:* The student is easily psychologically bruised, insulted, angered, and hurt by real or perceived injustices done to him or her by others and has great difficulty tolerating frustration.

- *Poor coping skills:* The student has little, if any, ability to deal with frustration, criticism, disappointment, failure, rejection, or humiliation. His or her response is typically inappropriate, exaggerated, immature, or disproportionate.

- *Lack of resiliency:* The student lacks resiliency and is unable to bounce back even when some time has elapsed since a frustrating or disappointing experience, a setback, or a put-down.

- *Failed love relationship:* The student may feel rejected or humiliated after the end of a love relationship and cannot accept or come to terms with the rejection.

- *"Injustice collector":* The student nurses resentment over real or perceived injustices. No matter how much time has passed, the "injustice collector" neither forgets nor forgives the wrongs the people he or she believes are responsible. The student may keep a hit list with the names of people who have wronged him or her.

- *Signs of depression:* The student shows symptoms of depression such as lethargy, physical fatigue, a morose or dark outlook on life, a sense of malaise, and loss of interest in activities that he or she once enjoyed.

- *Narcissism:* The student is self-centered, lacks insight into others' needs and/or feelings, and blames others for failures and disappointments.

The narcissistic student may embrace the role of a victim to elicit sympathy and to feel temporarily superior to others. He or she displays signs of paranoia and assumes an attitude of self-importance or grandiosity that masks feelings of unworthiness.[129] A narcissistic student may be either very thin-skinned or very thick-skinned in responding to criticism.

- *Alienation:* The student consistently behaves as though he feels different or estranged from others. This sense of separateness reflects more than in just being a loner. It can involve feelings of isolation, sadness, loneliness, not belonging, and not fitting in.

- *Dehumanization of others:* The student consistently fails to see others as fellow humans. He or she characteristically views other people as "nonpersons" or objects to be thwarted. This attitude may appear in the student's writings and artwork, in interactions with others, or in comments during conversation.

- *Lack of empathy:* The student shows an inability to understand the feelings of others and seems unconcerned about anyone else's feelings. When others show emotion, the student may ridicule them as being weak or stupid.

- *Exaggerated sense of entitlement:* The student constantly expects special treatment and consideration and reacts negatively if he or she doesn't get that treatment.

- *Attitude of superiority:* The student has a sense of being superior and presents himself or herself as smarter, more creative, more talented, more experienced, and more worldly than others.

- *Exaggerated need for attention:* The student shows an exaggerated, even pathological, need for attention, whether positive or negative, no matter what the circumstances.

- *Externalization of blame:* The student consistently refuses to take responsibility for his or her own actions and typically faults other people, events, or situations for any failings or shortcomings. In placing blame, the student frequently seems impervious to rational argument and common sense.

- *Masking of low self-esteem:* Although the student may display an arrogant, self-glorifying attitude, his or her conduct often seems to veil underlying low self-esteem. The student avoids high visibility or involvement in school activities, and other students may consider him or her a nonentity.

- *Anger-management problems:* Rather than expressing anger in appropriate ways and circumstances, the student consistently tends to burst out in temper tantrums or melodramatic displays or to brood in sulky, seething silence. The anger may be noticeably out of proportion to the cause or may be redirected toward people who had nothing to do with the original incident. The anger may come in unpredictable and uncontrollable outbursts, and it may be accompanied by expressions of unfounded prejudice, dislike, or even hatred toward individuals or groups.

- *Intolerance:* The student often expresses racial or religious prejudice or intolerant attitudes toward minorities or displays slogans or symbols of intolerance through such means as tattoos, jewelry, clothing, bumper stickers, or book covers.

- *Inappropriate humor:* The student's humor is consistently inappropriate. Jokes or humorous comments tend to be macabre, insulting, belittling, or mean.

- *Manipulation of others:* The student consistently attempts to con and manipulate others and win their trust so that they will rationalize any signs of his or her aberrant or threatening behavior.

- *Lack of trust:* The student is untrusting and chronically suspicious of others' motives and intentions. This lack of trust may approach a clinically paranoid state. The student may express the belief that society has no trustworthy institution or mechanism for achieving justice or resolving conflict and that if something bothersome occurs, he or she has to settle it in his or her own way.

- *Closed social group:* The student appears introverted. He or she has acquaintances rather than friends or associates only with a single small group that seems to exclude everyone else. Students who threaten or carry out violent acts are not necessarily loners in the classic sense, and the composition and qualities of peer groups can be important pieces of information in assessing the danger that a threat will be acted on.

- *Change of behavior:* The student's behavior changes dramatically. His or her academic performance may decline, or the student may show a reckless disregard for school rules, schedules, dress codes, and other regulations.

- *Rigid and opinionated outlook:* The student appears rigid, judgmental, and cynical, voices strong opinions on subjects about which he or she has little knowledge, and disregards facts, logic, and reasoning that might challenge these opinions.

- *Unusual interest in sensational violence:* The student demonstrates an unusual interest in school shootings and other heavily publicized acts of violence. He or she may declare his admiration for those who committed the acts or may criticize them for "incompetence" or failing to kill enough people. The student may explicitly express a desire to carry out a similar act in his or her own school, possibly as an act of "justice."

- *Fascination with violence-filled entertainment:* The student has an unusual fascination with movies, TV shows, computer games, music videos, or printed materials that focus intensely on themes of violence, hatred, control, power, death, and destruction. He or she may repeatedly watch one movie or read one book with violent content, perhaps involving school violence. Themes of hatred, violence, weapons, and mass destruction recur in virtually all the student's activities, hobbies, and pastimes. The student spends inordinate amounts of time playing video games with violent themes and seems more interested in the violent images than in the game itself. On the Internet, the student regularly searches for websites involving violence, weapons, and other disturbing subjects. There is evidence that the student has downloaded and kept material from these sites.

- *Negative role models:* The student may be drawn to negative, inappropriate role models such as Hitler, Satan, or others associated with violence and destruction.

- *Behavior relevant to carrying out a threat:* The student appears to be increasingly occupied with activities that could be related to carrying out a threat (for example, spending unusual amounts of time practicing with firearms or visiting violent websites). The time spent on these activities has noticeably begun to exclude normal everyday pursuits such as doing homework, attending classes, going to work, and spending time with friends.

CLASSIFICATION OF THREATS

Types of Threats

Threats can be classified into four categories:

1. A direct threat identifies a specific act against a specific target and is delivered in a straightforward, clear, and explicit manner: "I am going to place a bomb in the school's gym."

2. An indirect threat tends to be vague, unclear, and ambiguous. The plan, the intended victim, the motivation, and other aspects of the threat are masked or equivocal: "If I wanted to, I could kill everyone at this school!" While violence is implied, the threat is phrased tentatively—"If I wanted to"—and suggests that a violent act *could* occur, not that it *will* occur.

3. A veiled threat is one that strongly implies but does not explicitly threaten violence: "We would be better off without you around anymore." Such a statement clearly hints at a possible violent act but leaves it to the potential victim to interpret the message and give a definite meaning to the threat.

4. A conditional threat warns that a violent act will happen unless certain demands or terms are met: "If you don't pay me one million dollars, I will place a bomb in the school." This type of threat is often used in extortion cases.

THE ROLE OF LAW ENFORCEMENT

In the vast majority of cases, whether to involve law enforcement hinges on the seriousness of the threat: low, medium, or high.[130]

- *Low level:* A threat that has been evaluated as low level poses little danger to public safety and in most cases would not necessitate law-enforcement investigation for a possible criminal offense. (However, law-enforcement agencies may be asked for information in connection with a threat of any level.) Appropriate intervention in a low-level case would involve, at a minimum, interviews with the student and his/her parents. If the threat was aimed at a specific person, that person should be asked about his/her relationship with the threatener and the circumstances that led up to the threat. The response—disciplinary action and perhaps a referral for counseling or some other form of intervention—should be determined according to school policies and the judgment of the responsible school administrators.
- *Medium level:* When a threat is rated as medium level, the response should in most cases include contacting the appropriate law-enforcement agency, as well as other sources, to obtain additional information (and possibly reclassify the threat into the high or low category). A medium-level threat will sometimes, though not necessarily, warrant investigation as a possible criminal offense.
- *High level:* Almost always, if a threat is evaluated as high level, the school should immediately inform the appropriate law-enforcement agency. A response plan, which should have been designed ahead of time and rehearsed by both school and law-enforcement personnel, should be implemented, and law enforcement should be informed and involved in whatever subsequent actions are taken in response to the threat. A high-level threat is highly likely to result in criminal prosecution (Figure 11-15).

INVESTIGATING SCHOOL VIOLENCE

When investigating threats of violence in schools, listen carefully to witnesses in order to correctly identify the level of the threat and subsequently take appropriate action. Key questions include:

- Who made the threat?
- To whom was the threat made?
- Under what circumstances was the threat made?
- Exactly what words were said?
- How often were threats made?[131]

On some occasions, undercover juvenile informants can be used by police to gain insight in a school where threats have been received or plots of violence are suspected.[132] However, this practice is usually discouraged, since it places juveniles in a very precarious and potentially dangerous position. Some jurisdictions forbid the practice; others have developed very sophisticated guidelines regulating the use of a confidential informant who is under 16 years of age.

Ascertaining who made the threat or committed the act is often the least difficult part of the investigation due to the fact that juvenile perpetrators frequently use their crimes as a way of getting attention. Also, a young criminal often lacks the experience, sophistication, and self-control needed to adequately avoid detection (Figure 11-16).

and other persons likely to come into contact with human trafficking victims. The task forces themselves receive a week of intensive training. The Federal Bureau of Investigation has provided comprehensive antitrafficking training to agents attending the annual civil rights conference, including changes in the law, victim services, and suggested victim interview techniques. The Department of Homeland Security (DHS) mandated human-trafficking training for all officers and agents of U.S. Customs and Border Protection and made a web-based human-trafficking course available to officers and agents of U.S. Immigration and Customs Enforcement (ICE). Additionally, ICE offices nationwide hosted trainings reaching more than 6,000 federal, state, and local law-enforcement officials.

TRAFFICKING VERSUS SMUGGLING

There are key differences between the crimes of trafficking and smuggling. **Smuggling** occurs when someone is paid to assist another in the illegal crossing of borders. This relationship typically ends after the border has been crossed and the individual has paid the smuggler a fee for assistance. If the smuggler sells or "brokers" the smuggled individual into a condition of servitude, or if the smuggled individual cannot pay the smuggler and is then forced to work that debt off, the crime has now turned from smuggling into human trafficking. The key distinction between trafficking and smuggling lies in the individual's freedom of choice. A person may choose and arrange to be smuggled into a country, but when a person is forced into a situation of exploitation whereby their freedom is taken away, he/she is then a victim of human trafficking. Central to the distinction is the denial of the victim's liberty[4] (Table 12-1).

WHEN SMUGGLING BECOMES TRAFFICKING

The following two actual cases are examples of smuggling that turned into trafficking.[5]

A young woman was invited to come to the United States by family friends and told she could work for them as a housekeeper; they agreed to pay her $100 a week. She was provided with fraudulent documents and departed to the United States with her new employer. She knew this was illegal, but she needed the money and was willing to take the risk. At this point she was, in fact, smuggled into the United States, because she left willingly with full knowledge that she was entering the United States illegally.

However, upon arriving in the United States, she was kept in isolation, given a place to sleep in the basement, and told not to speak to anyone or she would be turned over to the Immigration Service. She was never paid for her work and felt she had no one to turn to for help. She was restricted from leaving the house, threatened with deportation if she attempted to talk to anyone, and forced into involuntary servitude. At this point she became a victim of trafficking.

A husband and wife in the United States convinced their relatives in India to allow their daughters to travel to the United States to receive an education. The husband and his wife were the aunt and uncle to the girls, and they promised the girls' parents they would provide

| TABLE 12-1 | Differences between Trafficking and Smuggling |

TRAFFICKING	SMUGGLING
• Is not voluntary; one cannot consent to being trafficked or enslaved	• Is voluntary; an individual typically contracts to be taken across border
• Entails forced exploitation of a person for labor or services	• Ends after the border crossing
• Need not entail the physical movement of a person	• Fees are usually paid in advance or upon arrival
• Can occur domestically, where citizens are held captive in their own country	• Is always international in nature
• Is a crime against the right of each person to be free from involuntary servitude	• Is a crime against the nation's sovereignty

Source: *The Crime of Human Trafficking: A Law Enforcement Guide to Identification and Investigation*, International Association of Chiefs of Police (2006), p. 4.

housing and support for the girls. In order for the girls to receive a student visa, their aunt and uncle enrolled the girls in school. The girls were granted student visas and allowed to enter the U.S. to receive an education.

Once the girls arrived in the United States, their aunt and uncle immediately told them they would not be attending school. The aunt and uncle never intended to have the girls attend school and enrolled them only for the purpose of fraudulently obtaining entry visas. At this point, the girls had unwittingly been smuggled into the United States through the use of visa fraud.

During the next several weeks, the girls were locked in a basement and continually told that if they tried to leave they would be arrested for their involvement in the visa fraud. Eventually their uncle took the girls to local hotels, where they were made to clean rooms and provide janitorial services. The girls were never paid for their work, all their identification had been taken away, and they were continually reminded that they could be arrested for their involvement in visa fraud. Because the girls were being held against their will through coercion and intimidation, and were being forced to work for no pay, they had become victims of trafficking.

FORCED LABOR, INVOLUNTARY SERVITUDE, PEONAGE, AND DEBT BONDAGE

While some trafficking victims are forced to work in the sex trade (discussed later in this chapter) many others are forced to perform other types of labor, such as domestic servitude, factory work, or agricultural work. Trafficking victims commonly experience physical and psychological abuse, including beatings, sexual abuse, food and sleep deprivation, threats to themselves and their family members, and isolation from the outside world.[6]

A trafficked victim may be subjected to various conditions of modern day slavery, such as forced labor, involuntary servitude, debt bondage, or peonage. Trafficking victims can be either foreign nationals or natives.

Under U.S. law, persons are placed in conditions of **forced labor** if they are forced to work against their will through actual or implied threats of serious harm, physical restraint, or abuse of the law.[7] If they are forced to work through physical force or threats of physical force, they are victims of *involuntary servitude*.[8] A person is subjected to **peonage** if that person is compelled by force, threat of force, or abuse of the law to work against his/her will in order to pay off a debt.[9] If the value of

a person's work is never reasonably applied toward payment of the debt, the person has been subjected to *debt bondage*.[10]

The term "forced labor" is also often used to describe all these forms of modern slavery.[11]

ESTIMATED NUMBERS OF VICTIMS

The hidden nature of forced labor and trafficking makes it extremely difficult to calculate the actual numbers of victims, but some estimates do exist. For example, the International Labor Organization (ILO) estimates that at least 12.3 million people are victims of forced labor at any given time, 2.4 million of whom toil in forced labor as a result of trafficking.[12] The U.S. Department of State estimates that 14,500 to 17,500 people are trafficked into the United States each year.[13] However, these numbers do not include the many individuals trafficked within U.S. borders. The Human Rights Center at the University of California, Berkeley estimates that at least 10,000 people are working as forced laborers at any one time in the United States.[14]

TYPES OF VICTIMS

Worldwide, women and children suffer disproportionately from trafficking. Poverty, gender discrimination, illiteracy and low levels of education, regional conflicts, and a lack of job opportunities affect women in great numbers. Such conditions pressure women to migrate and make them particularly vulnerable to trafficking by unscrupulous recruiters or employers who, through force, fraud, or coercion, place women in job situations to which they did not consent and from which they cannot freely escape. Accordingly, an estimated 80% of trafficking victims worldwide are women and children.[15]

In the United States, victims of trafficking are almost exclusively immigrants, and mostly immigrant women.[16] The average age of trafficking victims in the United States is 20.[17] In the United States, immigrant women and children are particularly vulnerable to the deceptive and coercive tactics of traffickers because of their lower levels of education, inability to speak English, immigration status, and lack of familiarity with U.S. employment protections. Further, they are vulnerable because they often work in jobs that are hidden from the public view and unregulated by the government.

TYPICAL CHARACTERISTICS OF TRAFFICKERS

Traffickers, usually a recruiter or the actual employer, compel their victims to accept a job through various forms of deception, coercion or physical force. Traffickers deprive their victims of the ability to consent and use physical force or psychological, legal, or economic coercion to trap their victims in forced labor situations from which they cannot escape.

victim and, as will be seen later, from the victim's presence. This element of the crime is satisfied once the robber has possession of the property; until possession has occurred, only an attempt has taken place.

CARRYING AWAY

Once the element of taking has been satisfied, the robber must then carry away the property. This element can be satisfied simply by showing that the accused totally removed the article from the position that it formerly occupied. It is not necessary to show that any great distance was involved in the carrying away.

PERSONAL PROPERTY

The object of the robbery must be personal property as opposed to real estate or things attached to the land. Again, as in larceny (discussed in greater detail in Chapter 14), any tangible property and some forms of intangible property represented by tangible items, such as stocks and bonds, gas, electricity, minerals, and other such commodities, can be objects of robbery.

ANOTHER

The property taken must belong to another, not to the accused. This again relates to the first element of taking. If the taking is trespassory—illegal—then the property must be the rightful property of someone other than the robber.

INTENT TO DEPRIVE PERMANENTLY

Robbery is a crime of specific intent and requires that the prosecution establish, in court, that the defendant, at the time of taking the property by force or threat of force from the victim or the victim's presence, did, in fact, intend to deprive the victim of the use and enjoyment of that property permanently. In most cases, this fact can be concluded from the facts and the circumstances surrounding the case, but in specific-intent crime cases, juries are not permitted to assume this particular fact. Thus, the police officer's investigation must be geared to establishing this as an essential element of the crime. The fact that force or the threat of force was used to secure the property from the victim is often enough to convince a jury of the accused's intent to deprive permanently.

USE OF FORCE, FEAR, OR THREAT OF FORCE

This element of the crime requires that the force or threat of force be directed against the physical safety of the victim rather than his or her social well-being. Thus, for example, a threat to expose some information that would be embarrassing to the victim unless a certain amount of money is paid does not satisfy this element of the crime. Proof that force was used or, at the very least, that threats were made such that the victim feared imminent bodily harm, is essential for successful prosecutions of robbery cases. However, the force used to separate the victim from his or her property in robbery need not be great.

When the victim of a robbery is seriously injured, there is usually little difficulty in convincing the investigator or the jury that force was used. However, difficulties may arise in the case of a victim who claims to have been robbed under the threat of force when no actual injury occurred. In this case, the skill of the investigator in determining the facts of the case becomes crucial to successful prosecution.

There are also more subtle situations in which the investigator must know legal requirements as well as investigative techniques. The typical purse-snatching case is an illustration. Often, the force element of the crime of robbery can be satisfied only by determining whether the victim attempted to resist the force used and, if so, the extent of that resistance. It is generally accepted by courts that a woman who puts her purse next to her on the seat of a bus without keeping her hand on it or loosely holds it in her hand is not the victim of robbery if someone quickly grabs the purse and runs. In these cases, the woman has not resisted. However, if she were clutching the bag tightly and someone managed to grab it from her after even a slight struggle, sufficient force and resistance would have occurred to constitute robbery. A good rule for the investigator to follow in cases of uncertainty is that the removal of an article without more force than is absolutely necessary to remove it from its original resting place constitutes larceny. If any additional force, no matter how slight, is used, it is then robbery, provided the object is taken from the presence or person of the victim. The property does not have to be held by the victim physically or be on his or her person. It merely has to be under the victim's control. "Control" in this sense means the right or privilege to use the property as the victim sees fit. Neither is it necessary or essential that the property be visible to the victim when the crime is committed.

When force is not used but a threat to the physical well-being of the victim is indeed made, it is not necessary that the victim actually be frightened to the point of panic. It is enough that the victim is reasonably apprehensive and aware of the potential for injury.

OVERVIEW: THE OFFENSE, THE VICTIM, AND THE OFFENDER

In terms of weapons used, a firearm is used in 40% of the incidents, a knife or other cutting instrument in 8% of the cases, and "some other weapon" in another 10% of reported robberies; the remaining 42% of the incidents are **strong-armed,** meaning no weapon was used.[1] An illustration of the use of "some other weapon" is the robbery of a convenience store by a man using a hypodermic needle filled with what he claims is AIDS-contaminated blood.

Together, this data reveals that approximately 6 of every 10 robberies are armed, and the balance are strong-armed. Armed robbers often carry two or more weapons. Because of this, officers must continue to exercise great caution when approaching a suspect who has thrown a weapon down.

About one-third of all robberies result in a physical injury to the victim.[2] Females are about 10% more likely to be injured than are males; Caucasians and African-Americans face nearly the same prospects for being injured.[3] Robbery is basically a stranger-to-stranger crime: 71% of the time the robber and the victim do not know each other.[4] About 60% of all robberies are committed by a single offender.[5] This factor tends to make robbery investigations more difficult: if the sole offender can keep his or her mouth shut, does not attract attention to him-/herself or run with other criminals, and does not get a bad break, the offender can be hard to catch. Although a small number of victims fight back in some way, in 82% of robberies it is the offender who initiates violence.[6]

The objective of the confrontation between robber and victim is to get the victim's immediate compliance. In most situations, the mere showing of a gun will accomplish this. One offender reports: "Sometimes I don't even touch them; I just point the gun right in front of their face. I don't even have to say nothing half the time. When they see that pistol, they know what time it is."[7] A victim who hesitates or is seen as uncooperative may or may not get a warning.

Other robbers are less "tolerant" and when faced with uncooperative victims, they shoot them in the leg or the foot. However, for some offenders, injuring the victim is part of the thrill, the "kick" of "pulling a job." What type of violence is used and when it is used may form part of an identifiable modus operandi (MO). Such an MO can tie together several robberies, and the combined information from various investigations often produces significant investigative leads.

There is no question that being under the influence and committing robberies are intimately related. Victims believe that 28% of those robbing them are high on drugs and/or alcohol.[8] Some offenders use alcohol to lessen their apprehension about getting caught. Robbery is basically an intraracial crime; in one study, blacks said that they were robbed by blacks 80% of the time, and whites said that they were robbed by whites 75% of the time.[9] Nationally, among those apprehended for robbery, 90% are males, 54% are blacks, and 19% are under the age of 25.[10]

Although no robbery is routine to victims, many cases are fairly straightforward to investigators. Some robberies, however, stand out because of unusual circumstances, as the following incidents illustrate:

> A lone robber held up a bank and made off with $600. As police were chasing him, the robber crashed the stolen Chevrolet Suburban he was driving. It burst into flames, and the money burned up. Now being pursued on foot by a police officer, the robber tossed off his plaid jacket and escaped. The police found a napkin with a name and a telephone number in the jacket. With the bank's surveillance photos in hand, the police confronted the man identified on the napkin. In turn, he identified the robber as someone whom he had been letting sleep on his couch. An arrest was subsequently made in the case.[11]

> Two thugs were cruising in a residential area looking for someone to rob. They spotted two men playing pool in an open garage. Blissfully unaware that the two men were off-duty police officers, the thugs approached them and placed a gun to one officer's head, and the officer began to struggle. The second officer pulled a weapon and shot both offenders.[12]

> A teenage boy robbed a convenience store at knife-point around 1:30 in the morning, taking money and merchandise and fleeing on foot. The police solved the case by following the offender's shoeprints in the freshly fallen snow straight to his home.[13]

Despite such variations, three styles of robberies—the ambush, the selective raid, and the planned operation—can be classified according to the amount of planning conducted by the perpetrators. The **ambush** involves virtually no planning and depends almost entirely on the element of surprise. A prime example is robberies in which victims are physically overpowered by sudden, crude force and in which "scores" are generally small.[14] The lack of planning does not mean, however, that there is no premeditation.

The **selective raid** is characterized by a minimal amount of casual planning. Sites are tentatively selected and very briefly cased, and possible routes of approach and flight are formulated. Scores vary from low to moderate, and several robberies may be committed in rapid succession.

The **planned operation** is characterized by larger "scores," no planned use of force, less likelihood of apprehension, and careful planning.

TYPOLOGY OF ROBBERIES

In addition to knowing the broad profile of the offense, the investigator must also be familiar with various types of robberies, such as the following.

VISIBLE STREET ROBBERIES

Approximately 5 of every 10 robberies happen on the street.[15] In 93% of the cases, the victim is alone[16] and typically on the way to or from a leisure activity within 5 miles of his or her home,[17] such as patronizing a night-club or restaurant:[18]

> I'd watch people in bars and follow them. One time, I followed this guy and grabbed his tie and swung it down to the ground. And, uh, he hit his head, and that's when I took the money and ran.[19]

The victim is three times more likely to be confronted by a single perpetrator than by multiple perpetrators.[20] Youthful robbers are particularly likely to commit strong-armed robberies—also referred to as **muggings**—in which no weapons are involved and in which they suddenly physically attack and beat the victim, taking cash, jewelry, wallets, purses, and other valuables. As discussed earlier, purse snatching may or may not be a robbery. If a woman is carrying a purse loosely on her open fingers and someone grabs it and runs and she then experiences fear, robbery is not an appropriate charge, because the fear did not precede the taking. But if the same woman sees or hears someone running toward her and in fear clutches her purse, which is then ripped from her by the perpetrator, a robbery has occurred. If apprehended, the suspect would likely be charged with some degree of larceny, depending on the value of the object(s) being stolen. The penalty for larceny is generally much lower than that for the crime of robbery, and in many states if a firearm is used during the commission of a robbery the penalty is even more severe than for unarmed robbery.

Street robberies usually involve little or no planning by the perpetrators, who may have been waiting in one place for a potential victim to appear or walking around looking for someone to rob on the spur of the moment.

Because street robberies happen so quickly and often occur at night in areas that are not well lighted, victims often have difficulty providing anything more than a basic physical description. The description may be even more limited if the victim is injured either by a weapon or by a beating in a sudden, overpowering mugging.

Spontaneous street robbers may "graduate" to jobs that involve a certain amount of planning. For example, they may stake out ATMs or banks. In the case of ATMs, they may have decided that they are going to rob the first "soft-looking" person who is alone and driving an expensive car. In the case of banks, they may rob someone on the street whom they have watched long enough to know that the person is going to the bank to make a cash deposit or to use the night depository. Although people sometimes commit robberies for excitement or to be "one of the guys," for the most part they do it to get the money, which often goes to pay for drugs.

USE OF SURVEILLANCE CAMERAS TO PREVENT STREET ROBBERIES

The use of surveillance cameras to monitor the streets to prevent robberies and other crimes is becoming increasingly common. For example the Paterson, New Jersey, Police Department makes extensive use of surveillance cameras in their city. Currently they are using 18 surveillance cameras installed in high-crime areas throughout the city. The cameras can be moved to other locations within two hours as needed. They are also monitored around the clock by a police officer (Figure 13-1).

The monitoring officer can zoom in on a particular image as needed. These images are also recorded, so in the event something is missed officers can go back and replay the video for a closer examination. The cameras have captured several robberies in progress as well as drug transactions. The police department also reports observing drugs and weapons being discarded as police officers approach the suspects. The officers monitoring the surveillance cameras can inform officers at the scene what they have observed and direct them to areas where any contraband may have been discarded. The cameras have been characterized by one high-ranking police official as having one officer walking multiple beats.[21]

CARJACKINGS

During the 1960s, many cars were stolen as temporary transportation by youthful offenders who used them for "joyriding" and then abandoned them. In many states, the criminal statutes recognized both a felony auto theft

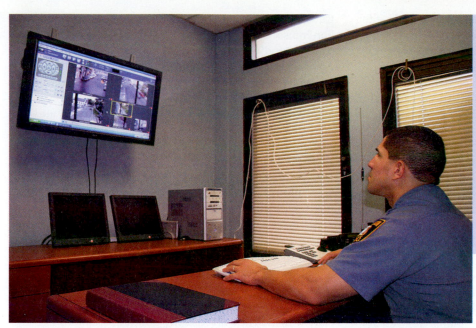

◀**FIGURE 13-1**

Use of surveillance cameras to prevent robberies

A Paterson, New Jersey, police officer is monitoring simultaneously 18 high-crime areas by the use of surveillance cameras. Each camera pans on a time sequence, produces high-quality video, and also allows the monitoring officer to zoom in on a particular location. The cameras can be moved to a new location within two hours. (Courtesy Lt. Anthony Trainer, Paterson, New Jersey Police Department)

and a misdemeanor joyriding charge. Around 1970, there was a shift to stealing cars for their parts and an increase in stealing cars for resale here and abroad, after they had been "repapered," meaning that the vehicles were given new, false identities.

In conventional auto thefts, the car is removed surreptitiously, and there is no contact between the thief and the vehicle's owner. Before 1990, if an offender used a weapon to confront an owner and steal the person's car, the crime was simply classified as a robbery. But in 1990, with the number of such incidents increasing, the term **carjacking** was coined in Detroit to describe the growing numbers of this potentially violent type of confrontation between offender and victim.[22]

One explanation for the increase in carjackings is that such crimes are the result of too much success in the antitheft-device market, including tracking devices such as Lojack, the Club, computer chips in ignition keys, and motion sensors. A second explanation is that there is a widespread supply of potential victims, no skill is required, no inside information is needed, and the need for planning is minimal.

In terms of location, the most common places for carjackings to occur are at the victim's home, gas stations, ATMs, car washes, parking decks, shopping-center parking lots, convenience stores, restaurants, bars, offices, train stations, apartments, public transportation parking lots and at traffic-control signs and signals.

Carjackers tend to operate in small groups of two to five perpetrators. The modus operandi used is to quickly separate the person from the car. In some instances, doing so may be as quick and violent as using a brick to shatter the driver-side window of an occupied car and manhandling the occupant out of the vehicle. Mothers with children are particularly vulnerable when confronted by offenders who

threaten to harm the children if the keys to the car are not given up immediately. One method of carjacking involves accidentally bumping the victim's car from the rear; when the driver gets out to investigate, one perpetrator pulls a gun, takes control of the victim's car, and flees, followed by his or her accomplices in the "bumper car." Another tactic is to use several cars to "box in" the target vehicle and then slow down gradually until it is stopped and the victim can be dealt with. Some carjackers target victims who drive into high-crime areas to buy drugs; some watch expensive cars in parking lots and then carjack them because they believe the victims are more likely to have jewelry and cash that can also be taken.

According to the FBI, the primary motives for carjacking are to acquire transportation away from the crime scene after robbing the driver, to get to and from another crime, such as another robbery or a drive-by shooting, to sell the car for cash, to trade it for drugs,[23] and to acquire temporary transportation. Whenever a carjacking takes place, the potential for a more serious crime exists.

Carjacking may also be a tool used by perpetrators to execute other crimes, which can lead to murder. For example, in one case a woman was carjacked and then forced into another car by the offenders. She was taken to a different location and raped. Later, she was forced to make several ATM withdrawals. Over the next several days, she was further abused and then executed by being slowly strangled with a coat hanger by one of the perpetrators while the others taunted her and cheered the executioner.

HOME-INVASION ROBBERIES

Home-invasion robberies (HIRs) typically target the person, rather than the residence, often selecting women and senior citizens.[24] Invaders often follow potential targets from shopping centers to their homes. They may enter the residence through an unlocked door or window, talk an unsuspecting victim into opening the door, or simply force the door open.

In some cases, the targets are "fingered," or identified, by others who pass information on to the invaders for drugs or money. Such offenders will also use deceit to gain entry into a residence. Home invaders may pose as police officers, water department employees, florists delivering bouquets, motorists who have "just struck your parked car," natural gas and electric company representatives, and "supervisors checking on your newspaper delivery service," to name just a few. The following case describes one such incident:

> Two men knocked on the door of a home and asked to use the telephone. After gaining entry by this ruse and casing the place, they decided the home was worth robbing. They returned that afternoon, forced their way in, severely beat the couple—who were in their late seventies—and left with valuables and the victims' pickup truck.[25]

AUTOMATIC-TELLER-MACHINE ROBBERIES

Automatic teller machines (ATMs) were introduced in the early 1970s, and their use has grown at a staggering rate since then. Today, there are approximately 12 billion ATM transactions annually.[26] At one point, robberies at these locations were so publicized that critics referred to ATMs as "magnets for crime" (Figure 13-2). However, the ATM robbery rate has dropped from 1 robbery per 1 million transactions during the 1990s to its present 1 per 3.5 million transactions.[27] A combination of factors account for this drop, including locating ATMs where customers have a high visibility of their surroundings, using landscaping of 24 inches or less in height, and keeping the ATM areas well-lit at night.[28] In addition, customers are becoming knowledgeable about self-protection measures and are adopting them. Despite such realities, public fear of being victimized at or near an ATM is substantial.

The ATM robbery victim is typically a lone woman who is using the machine between 8 P.M. and midnight.[29] To minimize the time spent with the victim and to avoid having to pressure the victim to make a withdrawal, many offenders simply wait until the transaction is completed before they pounce. Others confront the victim before the transaction, forcing her or him to make large withdrawals. Many victims report that they never saw the robber coming.

Offenders are most likely to work alone and are typically armed. They are usually about 25 years of age and tend to position themselves near an ATM, waiting for a likely victim to appear.[30] In addition to taking the cash and any valuables the victim has, offenders may carjack the victim's vehicle to flee the scene.

TAXICAB ROBBERIES

Taxi drivers have a higher homicide victimization rate than any other occupation in the United States and are also at great risk for robbery.[31] This is due to a combination of factors related to the nature of their job, including:

- having contact with a large number of strangers or people they do not know well;
- often working in high-crime areas;

▶ **FIGURE 13-2**
Automatic teller machines: natural target for robberies
Automatic teller machines are very popular today as a means of obtaining on-the-spot cash. At one point, robberies at these locations were so frequent that critics referred to ATMs as "magnets for crime." Placing ATMs in highly visible areas and improving surrounding lighting has led to a decrease in this form of robbery over the last few years. (© Syracuse Newspapers/David Lassman/Image Works)

Robbery prevention sign on taxicab
Left photo depicts the typical location of a robbery prevention sign on a cab. Right photo provides a close-up of what the potential would-be robber would see upon approaching or entering the cab. The safety deposit box referred to in the photo is actually a heavy-gauge steel box bolted to the cab floor with a slot on top into which bills can be inserted. The box can be opened only by a key kept at the taxicab garage.

THIS VEHICLE IS EQUIPPED WITH A SAFETY DEPOSIT BOX DRIVER DOES NOT HAVE A KEY AND ONLY CARRIES $5 IN CHANGE

- usually carrying cash with them in an unsecured manner and handling money as payment;
- usually working alone;
- often going to, or through, isolated locations;
- often working late at night or early in the morning.

These risk factors, among others, have been mentioned in a number of studies of workplace homicide and violence in general.[32]

Crime-Prevention Strategies for Robbery of Taxi Drivers

Although the cab companies or individual drivers must be the ones to implement the crime-prevention strategies suggested below, crime-prevention specialists in the police department can be proactive and work with cab companies to assist in operationalizing some of these recommendations.

- *Provide physical barriers to separate drivers from passengers:* Bullet resistant screens or partitions should be installed, because they make it more difficult for robbers to carry out the robbery.
- *Record activity with security cameras in the cab:* Police and prosecutors can use the images to help identify and catch offenders and increase the evidence available for prosecution and conviction.
- *Use of an alarm to call for help:* Can be used to signal someone at a central location (taxi company or police station) if they are having trouble or they can be a "trouble light" on the vehicle itself that cannot be seen by the passengers. Alarms must be designed so that they can be triggered easily through the pressing of a toggle switch at the driver's foot, on the steering wheel, or on the radio itself.
- *Keep track of vehicle locations with automatic vehicle location (AVL) systems:* With global positioning satellite (GPS) systems, all that is required is the triggering of an alarm and the monitoring of that alarm signal by someone who can send help.
- *Put trunk latches on the inside of vehicle trunks as well as near drivers:* This feature is designed to reduce

the potential harm to drivers who may be locked in the trunk following the robbery incident. Trunk latches also permit drivers to open trunks without getting out of the cab, which may prove useful late at night if the driver does not think it is safe to exit the cab.

- *Eliminate cash payments:* Drivers should be encouraged to use payment systems that are cashless. These include:
  —Credit or debit cards.
  —Accounts accessible though mobile phones.
  —Accounts for regular customers, such as those used by restaurants, hospitals, and social services. (Authorized passengers merely sign the bill.)
- *Drop money off:* Drivers should be encouraged to drop off cash during their shifts. They can drop the cash at home, at cash machines, or at dispatching offices where the money can be secured until their shift is concluded. However, dispatching offices holding drivers' cash must be made secure against robbery as well.
- *Keep money locked up or out of sight:* Drivers can put money in a locked safe in the cab (Figure 13-3). If a safe is used it should be advertised on both the exterior and the interior of the cab. In addition, drop-off routines must be varied to prevent robbers from staking out drop-off locations and carrying out hold-ups as drivers leave their cabs.
- *Control who gets in:* Drivers can use a number of techniques to control who gets into their cabs by:
  —Keeping doors locked while drivers are waiting for the next fare.
  —Keeping windows rolled up enough to prevent someone from reaching in.
  —Limiting the number of passengers.
- *Find out the destination before moving:* One rule of thumb cited repeatedly is to determine passenger's destination "up front." It is seen as a sign of potential trouble if the passenger refuses to give a

destination at the beginning of the trip or changes destinations while en route.

- *Share destination information with others:* Drivers should keep as many people informed of their whereabouts as possible, especially where cameras or GPS systems are not used.
- *Limiting where the cab will make a drop off:* Drivers should be wary of making a passenger drop off in a dark, isolated, or out-of-the-way location, because these do not permit surveillance by others or allow the driver to see if someone is lurking at the destination.
- *Limit injury when a robbery occurs:* Taxi drivers are frequently advised to cooperate with those trying to rob them by handing over their money and not fighting back. Similarly, drivers should keep an extra key in a pocket to allow them to use their cab if the robbers have taken their keys. This is particularly important if they have been abandoned in a remote location and have no way of contacting the police or their dispatcher.

CONVENIENCE-STORE ROBBERIES

Convenience stores account for about 6% of all reported robberies. These stores do a great deal of business in cash, are often open 24 hours a day, have numerous locations, and typically offer little or no protection from robbers. Thus, it is not surprising that convenience-store workers are among the occupational groups having the highest risk for workplace violence.[33]

Specific Actions That Can be Taken by Retailers to Reduce Convenience Store Robberies

- *Maximize natural surveillance:* Employees should have an optimal view of the entrance and interior of the store.
- *Have multiple employees on duty during high-risk periods:* Businesses that remain open between 11 P.M. and 5 A.M. should use at least one of the following crime-reduction measures: two or more employees, bullet-resistant safety enclosures, a security guard, or a pass-through window to conduct business.[34]
- *Control access:* A consistent finding of studies involving the interview of convenience store robbers is that escape routes are a key factor to their target selection. Eliminating or at least limiting potential escape routes by using fences or landscaping is highly recommended.
- *Establish territoriality:* Stores in high-crime areas should discourage loitering as well as maximizing the existing lighting and design of their parking areas.
- *Train employees:* Training should include how to behave during a robbery had how to avoid violence.

- *Use cash-control procedure:* One 10-year study of convenience store robbers found that "80% of potential robbers can be deterred if a convenience store limits the amount of money kept in its cash register and this fact is conspicuously posted on the front door of the business."[35]
- *Install cameras and alarms:* The presence of CCTV monitors, clearly visible near cash registers, as well as signs that state surveillance equipment is in use, have been found to have some deterrent effect by increasing the robber's risk of identification.[36]

Police Robbery Prevention Recommendations for Convenience Stores

- *Provide robbery prevention and awareness training:* Police are in a prime position to guide businesses in crime prevention. They are typically the first point of contact after a robbery and can be particularly helpful to small businesses that may have limited access to other programs and must therefore rely more heavily on police to guide them in developing robbery prevention strategies.
- *Inspect convenience stores for compliance with robbery prevention measures:* Police might assume responsibility for regularly inspecting convenience stores to determine whether they have adopted either mandatory or voluntary robbery prevention measures.
- *Enforce prohibitions on loitering outside convenience stores:* Police should enforce loitering or trespassing statutes or ordinances that prohibit loitering (and panhandling) in order to keep opportunistic offenders away from potential victims.[37]
- *Conduct robbery stakeouts:* Police departments need considerable resources to be able to sustain the number of officers needed to await possible robberies in various locations over a long time. Unless there is specific information that a robbery is likely to occur, a stakeout will not be set up. However, if a stakeout is set up police officers must work with store employees to carefully plan out the tactics that will be employed if a robbery should occur. This is so because in the event a police officer does confront an armed suspect there is the potential for a shooting to occur. Therefore the clerk on duty must be carefully informed about what course of action to take in the event a robbery occurs.
- *Increase police patrols:* Because it takes a relatively short time to complete a convenience store robbery, the chances of thwarting one by increased patrols is not highly likely. However, if the decision is made to increase patrol, it must be based on a careful analysis of the patterns of convenience store robberies in a particular jurisdiction. On occasion, clear patterns do develop where a particular segment of a community is targeted. In such cases, the police may decide to saturate the area with marked patrol units in the hope of dissuading

individuals to commit the robbery. This in turn raises the possibility that the robbers will decide to move to another geographical area or even another police jurisdiction to commit robberies. In other cases, the police may decide to assign additional unmarked units to a particular geographical area that can respond very quickly if a robbery alert is activated in their area.

TRUCK-HIJACKING ROBBERIES

In the United States, cargo theft may be responsible for losses of $10 billion to $12 billion a year.[38] If so, the only crime category with a higher dollar loss is health-care fraud. The estimate for cargo-theft losses includes both cargo theft and truck hijacking. It is believed that hijacking accounts for a significant percentage of total cargo-theft losses, but because crime statistics on it are not kept, no one knows what the percentage really is. As cargo theft through hijacking has increasingly been recognized as a significant crime problem, there have been calls to gather statistics for it in the National Incident Based Reporting System (NIBRS). The FBI office in Long Beach, California, estimates that cargo-theft losses in that region are $1 million per day.[39] It should also be noted that truck hijacking is not a uniquely American problem. For example, in Argentina, truck hijackers are referred to as *piratas del asfalto* ("asphalt pirates").

The fact that accurate statistics are needed has not discouraged law-enforcement agencies from making important moves to combat this crime problem. Large agencies, such as the New Jersey State Police, have created Cargo Theft and Robbery Investigative Units, while others have adopted the use of multiagency task forces and Cargo Criminal Apprehension Teams (Cargo CATs). Additionally, specialized law-enforcement groups, such as the Western States Cargo Theft Association, exist to supply training and to exchange information on this subject.

Truck hijacking is committed by experienced armed robbers acting on inside information. Because transporting goods by truck generates a substantial written record, there are many points at which insiders can learn the nature of a cargo and when it will be moved. Many truck hijackings happen in or near large cities, because it is easy to dispose of the goods there. If there is a seaport, the goods taken may also be quickly on their way to a foreign country within hours. The contents of some hijacked trucks are off-loaded to another truck or several smaller trucks and may be in several other states by the time the investigation is getting started. Hijackers take what is valuable, with a preference for cargoes that are easy to dispose of and hard to trace. Examples include loads of clothing and high-tech equipment components, which may each have a value of $500,000 or more.

A number of truck hijackings involve collusion on the part of the driver with those committing this specialized form of robbery. The driver may be bribed or given some portion of the cargo for his or her personal use. In a variation of this, hijackers give drugs to drivers and provide them with women and then coerce the drivers into cooperating by threatening to cut off their supply of drugs and women, to give a spouse photographs of the driver's liaisons with other women, or to expose the driver's use of drugs to employers.

Drivers of rigs may be confronted at roadblocks, or "detours," set up by hijackers. They may be forced from the road or accosted by the hijackers as they enter or leave truck rest stops. Some drivers have been tricked into stopping to help a "disabled" motorist. In more brazen moves, hijackers may invade truck parks, seize or kill security personnel, and take the trucks that they have targeted.

BANK ROBBERY

Although this portion of the chapter focuses primarily on bank robberies, many of the investigative and crime-prevention suggestions set forth herein (some of which have already been discussed) can also be applied to large retail businesses, small convenience stores, jewelry stores, appliance stores, and so forth. This includes methods of escape, escape routes, target selection, and robbery prevention.[40]

Distinguishing Professional and Amateur Bank Robbers

Bank robberies and, for that matter, most robberies do not appear to be well-planned offenses committed by professional criminals; instead, increasing evidence suggests that many bank robberies are spontaneous and opportunistic crimes that are often acts of desperation.[41–48]

Because most bank robberies are committed by solitary, unarmed, and undisguised offenders, they can be considered the work of amateurs rather than professionals. In contrast, it is the less common armed bank robberies that more often involve multiple offenders and the use of disguises.[49–51] Distinguishing bank robberies as the work of amateur or professional robbers provides important insight about the risks or robbery in selecting crime-prevention strategies most likely to be effective.

To a great extent, bank robbers can be classified as amateur or professional based on known characteristics of the robbery—the number of offenders, use of weapons and disguises, efforts to defeat security, timing of the robbery, target selection, and means of getaway (Table 13-1).

Method of Escape

The method of escape further distinguishes amateur from professional robbers. Cars are not the sole means of escape; many offenders escape on foot or even by bicycle, at least initially.

Getaway vehicles are more prevalent when there are two or more offenders: 72% of robbery teams use vehicles, which reflects some degree of planning.[52] In contrast, 58% of solitary robbers escape on foot. Two factors

	TABLE 13-1	Distinguishing Professional and Amateur Bank Robbers	

	PROFESSIONAL	**AMATEUR**
Offenders	• Multiple offenders with division of labor • Shows evidence of planning • May be older • Prior bank robbery convictions • Travels further to rob banks	• Solitary offender • Drug or alcohol use likely • No prior bank crime • Lives near bank target
Violence	• Aggressive takeover, with loud verbal commands • Visible weapons, especially guns • Intimidation, physical or verbal threats	• Note passed to teller or simple verbal demand • Waits in line • No weapon
Defeat Security	• Uses a disguise • Disables or obscures surveillance cameras • Demands that dye packs be left out, alarms not be activated, or police not be called	
Robbery Success	• Hits multiple teller windows • Larger amounts stolen • Lower percentage of money recovered • More successful robberies • Fewer cases directly cleared • Longer time from offense to case clearance	• Single teller window victimized • Lesser amounts stolen • Higher percentage of money recovered • More failed robberies • Shorter time from offense to case clearance, including same-day arrests • Direct case clearance more likely
Robbery Timing	• Targets banks when few customers are present, such as at opening time • Targets banks early in the week	• Targets banks when numerous customers are present, such as around midday • Targets banks near closing or on Friday
Target Selection	• Previous robbery • Busy road near intersection • Multidirectional traffic • Corner locations, multiple vehicle exits	• Previous robbery • Heavy pedestrian traffic or adjacent to dense multifamily residences • Parcels without barrier • Parcels with egress obscured
Getaway	• Via car	• On foot or bicycle

Courtesy Deborah Lamm Weisel, *Bank Robbery*, U.S. Department of Justice, Office of Community Policing Services, 2007.

discourage solitary robbers from using vehicles: without an accomplice to drive the vehicle, it must be parked and quickly accessible to the robber; further, solitary robbers typically select targets that are convenient, such as those close to their residence making a car unnecessary. In contrast, professional bank robbers appear willing to travel farther than other robbers, perhaps because there are fewer banks than other types of commercial targets or because banks tend to be clustered geographically and are open for fewer hours.[53, 54]

Escape Routes in Target Selection

Because many bank robberies are the work of amateurs, it may appear that robbers randomly select targets. They do not. Instead, robbers select targets primarily based on their concern with getting away from the robbery quickly.

Although much effort to reduce bank robbery has focused on bank interiors and security measures, most bank robbers do not feel they are at risk of apprehension during the commission of the crime. Instead, robbers assume there will be easy access to cash and that the robbery will be completed quickly. Thus, robbers for the most part are relatively unconcerned about alarms and cameras, neither of which will slow their escape.

A robber's choice of target is shaped by two escape features: the type of transportation available and the ease and number of escape routes.[55-63] Because offenders prefer choices during flight, they tend to select targets that have more than one escape path.

Solitary offenders typically cannot escape in a vehicle because of the logistics of parking and retrieving a vehicle. Thus, solitary offenders typically escape on foot.

In contrast, multiple offenders typically escape in a vehicle—often stolen just before the robbery to reduce the likelihood that the vehicle has been reported stolen by the owner.

BANK ROBBERY PREVENTION

Following are some of the actions banks can take to reduce the likelihood of robberies and minimize their losses.

- *Limiting cash access:* Cash in banks is available at teller windows—the most frequent target of robbers—and safes. Most banks have cash management policies, such as removing cash from the teller drawers when it reaches a predetermined amount, a fairly common practice among convenience stores as well. Some banks use vacuum systems to quickly and efficiently remove cash from teller drawers.

- *Using dye packs:* Exploding **dye packs** are widely used by banks to prevent stolen money from being used. Dye packs stain both the robber and the cash, preventing use of the money and aiding in the detection of the robber. Many dye packs are supplemented by tear gas, which is triggered by an electromagnetic field near the bank exit door. When the tear gas explodes, the robber is effectively immobilized (Figure 13-4).

- *Slowing the robbery:* Because bank robbers want the crime to proceed quickly, some banks have adopted strategies that are intended to slow the pace of the robbery. A slow robbery may increase the suspect's perception of risk and will sometimes cause the robber to abandon the crime.[64, 65] For example, interior obstacles such as revolving doors and customer service counters can slow the robber's escape; timed safes and withdrawal limits on cash-dispensing machines can further extend the duration of the robbery.

- *Employing greeters:* Bank employees known as greeters welcome customers and reduce the anonymity of a would-be robber; this face-to-face interaction may discourage a robbery before it occurs. Greeters should be trained to be alert to suspicious behavior. They are more likely to discourage amateur robbers than professional robbers.

- *Use of security guards:* There is disagreement regarding the effectiveness of bank security guards.[66–68] Guards are expensive, and they may also create an environment that makes customers fearful. Some research suggests that guards reduce the risk of bank robbery.[69–71] However, some studies also suggest that the presence of the armed guards increases the risks of violence during a robbery.[72–74]

- *Warning likely offenders:* Bank robbers tend to overestimate the amount of money they will get from a robbery, to underestimate the likelihood of arrest, and to be unaware of the sentences they face if convicted. Thus, some banks and trade associations have developed publicity campaigns designed to educate would-be offenders about the low take,

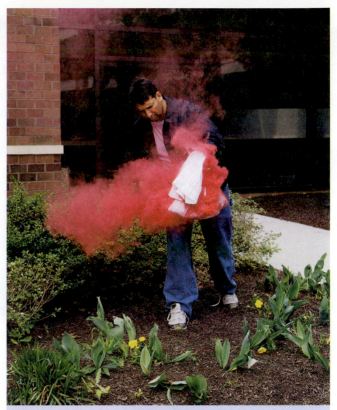

▲ **FIGURE 13-4 Exploding dye packs**
Exploding dye packs are widely used by banks to prevent stolen money from being used. When they explode, the dye packs stain both the robber and the cash, thereby preventing use of the money and aiding in the detection of the robber. Many dye packs are supplemented by tear gas that is triggered by an electromagnetic field near the bank exit door. When the tear gas explodes, the robber will be effectively immobilized. **(Courtesy 3SI Security Systems)**

high capture rate, and other perils of a career in bank robbery.[75]

- *Using tracking devices:* Some banks conceal electronic **tracking devices** with the robbery money, thus aiding police in locating offenders. Tracking devices use low-voltage transmitting microchips with transponders. However, tracking devices are intended to increase the chance of apprehending offenders, so they are not likely to prevent robberies from occurring.

- *Using bait money:* **Bait money** is cash with sequential serial numbers that are recorded by the bank. When the money reenters circulation, police track its use in hopes of locating the suspect. Bait money is already widely used by banks.

- *Offering rewards:* Some banks actively publicize "most wanted" bank robbers, displaying their surveillance photos and offering rewards for information leading to their capture. Banks use

► FIGURE 13-5

Bank surveillance camera

A bank surveillance camera captures the image of a man who has just entered the bank for the purpose of committing a robbery. He concealed a gun inside his hat. The man had entered the bank earlier in the day to case it for a robbery. At that time he was observed by an alert bank teller who had previously seen a bank surveillance photograph of the man which had been shown to her by law-enforcement officials several days before. The bank surveillance photo shown to her was of a man who had previously committed a bank robbery. She recognized the man and the police were contacted. The police then staked out the bank parking lot. The man returned several hours later, committed the robbery, exited the bank, entered his car at which time he and his companion were arrested.

(Courtesy Arlington, Texas Police Department)

websites, local silent witness programs, and tip lines to publicize crimes and to seek out offenders. There are also national tip organizations that coordinate information about highly mobile robbers.

- *Upgrading electronic surveillance:* Bank surveillance cameras are in widespread use: 98% of robbed banks have interior surveillance cameras. However, cameras do not appear to reduce robberies. Many bank robbers are not deterred, because they simply do not believe they will be caught. Others believe that cameras can be thwarted with a disguise or by covert behavior or that cameras can be disabled, such as with spray paint; or they simply do not think about cameras at all.[76–78] However, sometimes electronic surveillance can have unanticipated benefits. For example, one alert employee in a Texas bank noticed a man hanging around the bank lobby and thought she recognized him from a photograph she had been shown several days before by law-enforcement officials. The picture of the individual, who had held up other banks, was being shown to bank employees in the general area. The individual did not stay in the bank very long, but when he left the alert bank employee contacted the police who then started to surveil the bank parking lot. Several hours later the man returned to the bank. His partner remained in the car while he walked inside the

bank to commit the robbery. Once again, his image was captured by the surveillance camera, depicted in Figure 13-5. The man can be seen concealing what would turn out to be a gun in his hat. The police were not able to prevent the robbery, but once the man exited the bank and entered the getaway car, police officers were able to converge in their vehicles and to place both men under arrest. Thus, one possible strategy for bank robbery prevention could be to obtain bank surveillance photographs of individuals who committed bank robberies and show them to bank employees in the same general area in order to alert them to what the potential robbers look like. As it turned out, the individual and his partner confessed to robbing seven other banks in a half dozen nearby towns.

- *Rapidly activating alarms:* Although alarms lead to the arrest of bank robbers in only about 6% of crimes, there is evidence that prompt activation increases apprehension rates. Some bank employees do not activate alarms until after the robber has left the premises. This is so because of safety concerns about the employees and customers in case the police trapped the robber inside the bank thus creating a potential hostage situation and violence. In other cases, the delay might be due to panic or to comply with instructions made by the robber.

- *Installing bandit barriers:* The FBI recommends that banks install bullet-resistant glass **bandit barriers** between tellers and customers. Such devices are also becoming fairly common in convenience stores, especially those that operate 24 hours a day and are in high-crime areas (Figure 13-6).[79] Although most of these are permanent installations, some bandit barriers "pop up" when activated by tellers or when an object crosses the counter.

- *Installing access control vestibules:* Access control vestibules—also known as man-catcher vestibules or man-traps—are a specialized form of access control device. These devices can be used to scan potential customers for weapons before they access the bank interior; others are designed to be manually activated by tellers.

- *Hardening targets:* Banks have employed a wide variety of **target-hardening strategies** that are designed to make the bank interior appear inhospitable to would-be robbers. These include revolving doors, increased distance between entrances

and teller stations, higher teller counters, queuing and other physical barriers, and single-door entrances and exits.[80–82]

- *Consider the possibility of an inside job:* When a bank robbery does occur, investigators should consider the possibility of the robber having received assistance from someone inside the bank. One interesting case occurred recently in the Atlanta, Georgia, area. A Bank of America was held up by two young women identified as the "Barbie Bandits." These two young women, who would eventually be identified as Heather Johnston and Ashley Miller, both 19, were photographed by a bank security camera and subsequently identified by people who recognized them when their pictures were shown on local television (Figure 13-7). Their arrest and the subsequent investigation led to the arrest of two additional accomplices—namely, a convicted drug dealer, Michael Darrell Chastang, 27, and a Bank of America teller, Benny Allen III, 22. The four had conspired to commit the theft and divided the money after the crime was committed.

RESPONDING TO THE SCENE

In route to the scene of a robbery call, the officer must ensure that all information available from the dispatcher has been obtained, including the answers to the following questions: What is the exact location of the offense, including the type of business? Is the offense in progress? How many suspects are involved? What type of and how many weapons were displayed? What description of the suspect is available? By what method and in what direction did the suspect flee? What is the description of the means of transportation used by the suspect?

In approaching the scene, the officer must be alert for several possibilities:

- The dispatcher may provide information on the suspects' escape, such as their direction in fleeing from the scene and whether they were on foot or in a vehicle.
- Information about the target, MO, suspects, vehicles, weapons used, and other factors in recent robberies may help the responding officer recognize the suspects if they are moving away from the scene on the street along which the officer approaches, even if the dispatcher cannot supply any specific information other than the nature of the crime.
- The fleeing suspects may, as the officer approaches them on the way to the scene, abruptly turn off, fire at the officer, or otherwise suddenly reveal themselves.

The primary tactical objectives of officers responding to a robbery call are public safety, officer protection, and tactical control of the scene. Secondary objectives include conducting the preliminary investigation, apprehending perpetrators, and recovering property. Arriving at the scene unobserved by the suspects facilitates the achievement of both primary and secondary objectives. It also allows tactical control and the element of surprise to pass from the robbers to the police. Units assigned to a robbery call should plan and coordinate the actions to be taken at the scene. Because the perpetrators may have police scanners, care should be taken with respect to radio transmissions. Arriving officers should not give away their exact positions and should refer to buildings by prearranged letter designations

(for example, "the A building").[83] They can never assume that the robber(s) have left the scene; for example, robbers have been known to hide near or at the scene, seeking to escape detection. Responding units should approach separately on streets parallel to that on which the robbery occurred or is occurring, using emergency lights but not sirens. The use of emergency lights permits more rapid progress through traffic. The reason for not using a siren is that the sound may panic suspects near or at the scene, triggering violence or hostage taking. It is believed that 9 out of 10 hostage situations that develop out of robberies occur because of a too visible first-responding officer.[84]

However, remember that most states require a police vehicle responding in an emergency mode to have both its emergency lights and siren activated. Thus, when the tactically correct decision is made to deactivate the siren, the officer's driving must be adjusted accordingly, because now the motoring public no longer has the benefit of "hearing" the approaching police vehicle and being able to yield to it.

At a distance of three to five blocks from the scene in an urban area and much farther in rural settings,[85] the emergency lights should be turned off to avoid possible detection by a lookout. The police officer should begin to smoothly decelerate, thus avoiding engine noise, squealing tires, or "emergency" stops that could give away the police car's arrival.

The first officer on the scene must quickly "size up" the area to gather any possible intelligence, including location of the robbers, lookouts, and escape vehicles. The locations of the perpetrators are particularly important given the fact that such criminals may have automatic and other weapons—which they are willing to use. Actually identifying the **lookouts** may be difficult; two officers in New York, for instance, were killed by a lookout disguised as a nun.[86] The officer should leave his or her car quietly and move—unobserved—to a protected position to watch, where possible, two sides (for example, north and east) of the building. One of these sides should be the exit most likely to be used by the robbers. Moving unobserved does not necessarily imply moving quickly. Running into position may invite passersby to "rubberneck," giving away the officer's location.[87] Before moving to any position, the officer should make sure the background of that position, when viewed from the perpetrators' positions, does not silhouette him or her.[88] The officer in the second unit should take the same precautions as the first in moving into position. The second officer's responsibility is to cover the two remaining sides (for instance, the south and the west). Both officers should keep their vehicles and portable radios at low volume to avoid being detected. The primary and backup officers should be sure that their positions in the lines of fire do not endanger each other.

Also, when moving into their respective unobserved positions, officers must not get inside of, that is, between, any possible lookouts and the robbery scene. Such a position would leave them vulnerable to fire from several sides.

Both in approaching the scene and at the scene, officers should avoid action, physical, or situational stereotyping.[89]

ACTION STEREOTYPING

Action stereotyping occurs when the officers' expectations are set to see one thing, which closes their minds to other eventualities. For example, the responding officer may expect the suspect to come rushing out of the store, hop into a car, and speed away. Although this may be the case, there are also other possible behaviors:

Two robbers who confessed to over 20 "quick mart" robberies had been apprehended during a police surveillance. While being interrogated, the pair revealed that they had come close to being caught on several occasions when responding units arrived at the scene very quickly. They said they had escaped apprehension at those times by simply walking away in a normal manner. This proved to be an embarrassment for one officer who remembered the pair walking past his car. This officer said that they just appeared to be "normal" citizens and that there was nothing extraordinary about them.[90]

PHYSICAL STEREOTYPING

Physical stereotyping is an officer's expectations that the robber will look like a particular type. Such stereotypes may allow the suspect to escape or be fatal to officers:

An officer entered a convenience store in response to an alarm; his gun was drawn, but he started to put it away when he didn't see anything out of the ordinary. As he approached the two clerks behind the counter, the younger one yelled a warning: the other "clerk" was an armed robber whose appearance—he was 60 years old—did not fit with the officer's stereotype of a robber.[91]

Another aspect of physical stereotyping is that investigators may have difficulty believing witnesses' descriptions. For example, we expect bank robbers to be relatively young adults and vigorous. However, in northern Colorado nearly a decade ago, an 82-year-old man known as the "salt-and-pepper bandit" was arrested for a string of bank robberies; in another case, a 105-pound 70-year-old woman donned a black plastic bag as a disguise and robbed a bank, declaring, "There's a bomb here; give me the money, no bells, no sirens."[92]

SITUATIONAL STEREOTYPING

In **situational stereotyping,** the officers' previous experience with, and knowledge of, a particular location increases their vulnerability:

A silent alarm went off at a bar; the call was dispatched, and as the assigned unit drove toward the bar, the two partners joked about the inability of the owner to set the alarm properly, since he was continuously tripping it accidentally, creating frequent false alarms. The officer operating the police car parked it in front of the bar, and as the two officers began to saunter casually up to the front door of the bar, two suspects burst out with guns in hand and began shooting. Miraculously, neither officer was hit. One of the suspects was wounded and arrested at the scene; the other one escaped and was not apprehended until several weeks later.

Returning to some earlier points: although the suspects may be observed fleeing the scene or may reveal themselves in some manner to the officer assigned to respond to the call, such encounters do not take place with any regularity. In addition, deviating from the assignment to become engaged in a "pursuit," instead of proceeding directly to the call, is often unproductive. In such instances the "suspect," especially one driving an automobile, may merely be acting in a suspicious manner because he or she may have committed some minor traffic violation and is fearful that the officer is going to write a traffic citation. The officer actually assigned to the robbery call should not normally deviate from the assignment without significant reason; the officer's responsibility is to get to the scene and to get accurate, detailed information for the preliminary pickup order or BOLO as rapidly as possible. When the officer does this, more resources are then brought to bear on the offense, and the likelihood is reduced that other officers may unknowingly stop armed suspects for what they think is only a traffic violation.

If not assigned to the call as the primary or backup unit, other officers should not respond to the scene. Instead, they should patrol along a likely escape route such as entrances to expressways. They should avoid transmitting routine messages, because the primary unit will need to transmit temporary pickup orders or BOLOs concerning the offense.

If available, helicopters have the potential of being helpful in robbery investigations when a good description of the vehicle in which the robbers fled is included in the BOLO. Helicopters can cover territory rapidly. Flying at 500 feet, a helicopter provides observers accompanying the pilot with an excellent observation platform. Approximately 75% of all pursuits aided by a helicopter are successful.[93]

FOLLOW-UP ROBBERY INVESTIGATIVE PROCEDURES

To standardize the ways in which robberies are investigated, departments should have a standard operating procedure (SOP) that deals specifically with this crime. It is also extremely important that both the responding officer(s) and follow-up investigator are thoroughly familiar with this procedure. The specifics of the Robbery SOP naturally vary from jurisdiction to jurisdiction because of the sizes of communities and the number of investigative specialists that are available. However, we have attempted herein to provide a broad model from which an investigative procedure can be developed by an agency irrespective of its size or the number of investigative specialists it has.[94]

INITIAL INVESTIGATION

Although it may not always be possible, an on-duty investigator (preferably one who works robberies) should be available to respond to the scene of all reported robberies. If, however, a police department does not normally have investigators respond to the scenes of all robberies, then certain criteria must be set forth. They should respond when:

- requested by a uniform supervisor;
- a victim or witness has been seriously injured;
- a suspect has been apprehended;
- a suspect has been identified;
- victim(s) have been tied up or incapacitated for an extended period of time;
- large sums of money or property have been taken;
- the robbery has occurred inside a residence;
- a carjacking has occurred;
- leads with a high solvability factor are present and will be lost by a delayed response.

Specific Responsibilities for the Robbery Investigator

- Assume responsibility for the investigation.
- Ensure that proper preliminary investigative action has been taken by uniformed personnel, and take additional steps as necessary.

- Interview victim(s) and witness(es) in detail.
- Collect physical evidence.
- Canvass the area and document the names and addresses of all persons interviewed and include a summary of their observations.
- Determine if identifiable property has been taken (serial number, bait money, and so on), and ensure that this information is entered into the National Crime Information Center (NCIC).
- Determine if a cell phone has been taken, and identify the cell number, subscriber, and carrier information.
- Display photographs of known offenders and suspects to the victim(s) and witness(es). Request that they respond to the Robbery Bureau to view photographic files if necessary. If identification is made: have the victim(s) and witness(es) sign and date all photographs identified. Number and initial those photographs shown with the identified photograph(s) and preserve them as evidence for court presentation by placing them in an envelope sealed with evidence tape in the case file.
- Obtain notarized identification statements from individuals who are visitors or when the investigator believes that such a statement will enhance the possibility of prosecution.
- Follow up all available leads to a proper conclusion before terminating the initial investigation.
- When the investigation leads to the identification of a suspect, make record checks before obtaining an arrest warrant. It must be determined that the suspect was not incarcerated at the time of the offense.
- If verification of custody or detention dates is made, make a computer printout part of the case file. In instances where confusion exists concerning the subject's confinement, verification must be obtained from the appropriate governmental agency. When received, this information will be documented in the investigator's report.
- Discuss the case with the state's prosecutor and obtain an arrest warrant(s) in a timely manner.
- When applicable, consult appropriate federal law-enforcement agencies (for example, FBI, ATF, and so on) regarding the potential for filing federal charges against the suspect(s).
- If the subject is at large, and an arrest warrant has been issued, conspicuously display all relevant information along with a photograph at key locations within police headquarters. Also distribute wanted fliers to uniform patrol officers as well as other investigators.
- Upon notification that a wanted subject has been taken into custody outside the police jurisdiction, the applicable supervisor shall evaluate the case and, if appropriate, request that Robbery Bureau personnel be utilized for the extradition. If Robbery Bureau personnel are not used, the lead investigator shall

coordinate any investigative activity that is necessary immediately upon return of the subject and before the subject is booked into the jail.

- Review and analyze all reports prepared in the preliminary phase.
- Reinterview victim(s) and witness(es) if it appears there may be information that was not obtained owing to incomplete questioning or insufficient recall of the event. Occasionally, witnesses will remember some detail and not go to the "trouble" of looking for the police department's listing. Therefore, the investigator should leave a card with his/her name and departmental phone number.
- Return to the crime scene at exactly the same time of day the offense was committed and attempt to locate additional witnesses; at the same time, reconduct the neighborhood check. When conducting a neighborhood check, officers must be certain to record the names of all witnesses interviewed in order to avoid any type of duplication with other investigators who may be assisting on the case. In the event that possible witnesses are not at home, this, too, should be recorded to ensure that they are contacted later. It is imperative that every person who was in a position to have possibly witnessed the crime be contacted and interviewed.
- Make an attempt to tie the offense to other robberies, because the combined information from several offense reports may result in sufficient detail to identify the perpetrator.
- Review any pertinent departmental records, reports, or database.
- Seek additional information from other sources (for example, uniformed officers, informants, other investigators, other agency investigations, or informational/intelligence bulletins).
- Review the results of laboratory examinations.
- Determine the involvement of subject(s) in other crimes.
- Prepare the case for presentation to the Prosecutor's Office.
- Assist in the prosecution as required.

False Robbery Report

A file check should be made of the victim's name in case the person has a history of making crime reports. For instance, certain types of businesses—such as economy gasoline stations and convenience grocery stores—may not conduct even a minimal background investigation of employees. Given the availability of cash and long periods of isolation during the night hours, an untrustworthy employee will occasionally pocket cash for personal gain and cover its absence by claiming a robbery was committed. A file check on the complaining witness may suggest such a pattern. For example, one of the authors, who was a robbery investigator, routinely checked the police records

of robbery victims. In one instance, he found that a clerk employed at a convenience store, who regularly changed jobs, had allegedly been the victim of an armed robbery three times at three different convenience stores during an 18-month period, and in each case the suspect reportedly had the same identical physical description, said the same exact words when demanding the cash, and carried the same type of firearm. Naturally, this caused considerable suspicion, and when the victim was confronted with this string of "coincidences" he was unable to explain how it occurred and adamantly denied he was stealing the money. He was asked to take a polygraph examination to verify the authenticity of these robberies but refused. His employer was notified of the pattern of previous robberies as well as his reluctance to cooperate, and he was subsequently dismissed from his job.

The following represent two additional examples of false robbery reports.

Two teenage clerks were shot in a robbery at a Quick Mart convenience store. Despite the clerk's wounds, investigators were suspicious about the incident. After further questioning by the police, both "victims" admitted they made up the story about being robbed to conceal their theft of $400 and shot each other to make it look more convincing.[95]

A woman told officers that a laughing man put a gun against her 2-year-old daughter's head and robbed her at an ATM. The victim also reported that no one else was around the ATM when the incident happened at 7:52 A.M. Investigators initially thought it was highly unlikely that nobody else was at the ATM around the time of the alleged robbery. They checked the transactions at the ATM and found that a man had used the ATM just 4 minutes before the robbery and did not see anyone matching the robber's description. Moreover, the man did not immediately leave the ATM after he had finished his transaction. Based on this evidence, it was established that the woman had made up the story because she wanted some attention.[96]

GENERATING A LIKENESS OF A SUSPECT

The likeness of a suspect should be created and distributed as rapidly as possible. There are a number of methods available to create a likeness. One of them is through the use of a police artist (Figure 13-8). Several software programs can be used to generate suspect likenesses, including Sirchie's ComPhotoFit Plus Color[97] (Figure 13-9).

▶ FIGURE 13-8
Facial likeness of a robbery suspect created by a forensic artist along with a police mug shot showing the resemblance
The photo on the left depicts a facial reconstruction completed by Police Artist Gil Zamora, working with a robbery victim. The photo on the right depicts the police mug shot of the robbery suspect at the time he was arrested. As can be seen, the similarities are remarkable. (Photos courtesy of police artist Gil Zamora and Lt. Rick Martinez. San Jose California Police Department)

▶ FIGURE 13-9
Sirchie's ComPhotoFit Plus Color
The composite facial reconstruction photo on the left is a computer-generated composite sketch of a robbery suspect. The photo on the right, which is remarkably similar, depicts the photo of the suspect at the time he was booked into the county jail. The facial reconstruction was made with Sirchie's ComPhotoFit Plus Color. (Courtesy Laurie A. Ward, Crime Scene Administrator and Sheriff Grady C. Judd, Jr. Polk County Sheriff's Office, Bartow, Florida.)

KEY TERMS

action stereotyping
ambush
bait money
bandit barriers
carjacking
dye packs

home-invasion robbery (HIR)
lookouts
muggings
physical stereotyping
planned operation
robbery

selective raid
situational stereotyping
strong-armed robbery
target-hardening strategies
tracking devices
trespassory

REVIEW QUESTIONS

1. What are the elements of the crime of robbery?
2. Give a profile of visible street robberies.
3. When is purse snatching a robbery?
4. Give three explanations for the increase in carjackings.
5. Discuss how home invaders operate.
6. What are the two occupations in which a person has the greatest danger of being the victim of a violent crime on the job?
7. How are drivers confronted in truck-hijacking robberies?
8. Discuss the characteristics that distinguish professional from amateur bank robbers.
9. Discuss the multiple techniques that can be employed in bank robbery prevention.
10. Explain action, physical, and situational stereotyping.
11. Why is it important to have a standard operating procedure for robbery investigations?
12. Why should a file check be made of the victim in a robbery case?

INTERNET ACTIVITIES

1. Most large police agencies in the United States have robbery investigation units. Find several such agencies in your region. What is the total number of officers assigned to these units? What are the units' functions and responsibilities? Is there information concerning the numbers of robberies that are investigated and/or cleared? Is any robbery prevention information provided? Websites such as *www.officer.com* provide information to both local and international police agencies.
2. Go to the website *www.forensicartist.com* and learn more about how forensic artists generate the likenesses of people through age composition, composite drawing, and facial reconstruction.

▶ After determining no one was home, two burglars broke into a home through the rear entrance. They removed more than $100,000 in valuables. The homeowner's surveillance camera captured one of the burglars carrying a signed and framed Michael Jordan basketball jersey.

(Courtesy Ft. Lauderdale Police Department)

14

BURGLARY

The two most striking aspects of burglary are its frequency and economic impact. In 2009 burglaries averaged one every 14.3 seconds.[1] There were an estimated 2,199,125 burglaries reported, and, although the number reflects a 1.3% decrease compared to 2008, victims suffered an estimated $4.6 billion in lost property. The average loss per burglary was $2,096.[2] In spite of the reduction in the number of burglaries, the offense accounted for 23.6% of the estimated number of property crimes committed in 2009.[3] The clearance rate for burglaries was a low 12.5%, and only 299,351 people were arrested for burglary in 2009.[4] Thus, burglary is a crime of major importance and concern. Because such items as credit cards and checks may be taken in burglaries, the offense tends to spawn subsequent or secondary crimes, such as frauds and forgeries. Investigating these crimes can sometimes lead back to the identity of the burglars; to illustrate, during the breaking and entering of a convenience store, "scratch-off" lottery tickets were stolen. When the burglar attempted to cash in a few winners at another convenience store, he was videotaped by the security camera. After placing his picture in the newspaper the police quickly learned his identity, and the man was arrested. Burglaries also have the potential to turn into violent crimes, for example, when home owners or workers return unexpectedly.

Many homes and businesses have alarms, but the alarms may be affected by improper installation, faulty equipment, or user errors. Unfamiliarity with the system or not allowing for roaming pets results in 10%–25% of all automatic alarm calls being false ones; if all false alarms were eliminated, the result would be 35,000 officer days per year being available nationally to redirect toward genuine problems.[5] Many jurisdictions have responded to this situation by allowing one free false alarm and then charging the owner for subsequent false alarms on a flat-fee or escalating-the-charge basis for each subsequent false alarm.

People often think of burglaries as involving just homes and businesses, other structures may also be covered by many state burglary laws, including recreational vehicles, railroad cars, houseboats, airplanes, and automobiles.[6] Some states also have created a **coin-operated machine burglary** charge to cover vending machines outside of businesses. Unlike other types of burglaries, this offense is typically a misdemeanor; in states that lack such an offense category, the charge is for larceny, with the level of offense being determined by the value of the property stolen.

Various aspects of burglary are summarized in Table 14-1. Most burglaries are through a door rather than a window. In general, commercial establishments are attacked at the rear at night, whereas homes are mostly victimized during the day at the front door. There is some evidence that, as the geographical distance between burglaries shortens, the likelihood of there being a serial offender increases; this is true, respectively, for residential and nonresidential burglaries.[7] When the same home is burglarized a second time shortly after 30 days from the initial incident, it

Commercial burglaries are also committed through other points of entry, such as skylights and chopping a hole in a roof. In certain situations, such as strip malls, burglars will break into one business and then enter the others by knocking through connecting walls. As ATMs have become more widely available, such businesses as convenience stores have been broken into by people driving stolen vehicles as large as dump trucks through the glass doors. Once inside, burglars can grab an ATM and some store goods and be gone in 2–7 minutes. Day burglaries of homes tend to follow a pattern: the owners are often at work or running errands, and neighbors are used to seeing delivery people, campaign workers, and others approach front doors. So, seeing someone at a front door is not an abnormal occurrence that compels attention. Furthermore, front doors are often recessed, limiting visibility; burglar alarms are often not set; and many front doors can be quickly kicked in, facilitating the burglar's quick entry and exit.

Burglars may work alone—as illustrated by the Spiderman case discussed later in this chapter—or in organized groups or gangs. There are numerous cases of professional people becoming burglars, and burglars can be roughly categorized as professional and amateurs by their level of skill. Many juveniles and teenagers commit burglaries, including those involving cars. One study concluded that prolific burglars also shoplift, perhaps to supplement their income, to obtain goods they cannot get through their burglaries and to "lay low" when the risk of burglarizing may be perceived as too high.[9]

When police officers respond to a burglary-in-progress, officers must be alert when approaching the scene, both

may be by the same offender seeking to steal items left behind during the first offense—for example, something too big to take, or perhaps the first time the burglar did not know a fence, or perhaps he/she came back to steal items the resident bought as replacements (for example, televisions or video equipment) for losses in the first burglary.[8]

| TABLE 14-1   Burglary Facts |

Type of Premises Attacked

Residential	72.6%
Nonresidential	27.4%

Types of Attacks

Forcible Entry (e.g., used pry bar to break glass and enter)	61.0%
Unlawful Entry (e.g., through open door or window)	32.6%
Forcible Attempt	6.5%

Time of Attacks	Residential	Nonresidential
Day	37.2%	9.1%
Night	20.2	11.6
Unknown	15.1	6.7

Cases Cleared (Arrests and Exceptionally Cleared): 12.7%

Arrested Offender Demographics

Race	Gender	Age	
White 66.5%	M 85.1%	Under 15	6.9%
Black 31.7	F 14.9	Under 18	25.3
All Other 1.8		18 & over	74.7

Source: FBI, Uniform Crime Reports 2009, issued in 2010. See *www.fbi.gov/UCR/CIUS 2009*, Tables 41, 42, and 43, and Burglary definition page.

to protect themselves and to avoid rushing past look-outs or burglars driving calmly from the scene. At the scene, officers may have to tactically clear the building before their investigation can begin. This should never be attempted until adequate backup and specialized units, such as Canine, have arrived. During the preliminary investigation, officers have to consider the possibility of a crime staged for filing a false insurance claim; in particular, when there are fires at scenes, officers may need specialized assistance to determine if the fire is accidental or coincidental, set by the burglars to destroy evidence, or arson. In the end, a burglary is a burglary, but officers should examine each scene while being alert to all possibilities. The number of safe burglaries has lessened as we've progressed into a "cashless society," but officers still need to have a basic understanding of them to prevent the accidental destruction of evidence.

Burglars sell much of what they steal to support their lifestyle or trade the merchandise for drugs, tips from insiders about new burglary opportunities, or sex. Thus, as police try to recover stolen property, they come into contact with criminal fences and must check pawnshop records, local sales ads, swap meets, and eBay-type outlets.

THE OFFENSE AND OFFENDERS

From humans' earliest times, thieves existed and committed what we recognize as burglaries. The elaborate tombs of the Egyptian pharaohs, designed to send the rulers into the next world in splendor, contained magnificent treasures. They also contained elaborate security features to protect those riches. Yet they were often plundered by thieves of that time.

The nature of burglary has stayed the same over time, but *how* it is committed constantly changes, largely as an influence of technological advances and architectural design. For example, now virtually extinct in the United States are such specialized methods of burglary as entry through coal chutes—because people in this country heat mainly with electricity, natural gas, and even solar power. As municipalities began requiring the use of fire escapes, they were appended to the outside of apartment buildings. This created a new method of burglary—the "step-over." Although people would place bars or other barriers over apartment windows by the fire escape, they would neglect to protect other windows. The step-over artist would go up a fire escape to the apartment to be hit and then step over from the fire escape to the ledge of a window that was unprotected. As interior fire escapes became more common, the opportunities to be a step-over artist gradually declined, although they certainly still exist. A slight variation on the step-over method is still in practice: parents send children as young as five years old to do the step-over and then open the apartment door from the inside to let in the parents, who plunder the premises.

In the last 20 years, a method of burglary that has gained in popularity is one in which the offenders steal a car and drive it through the front door of a gun, jewelry, or other type of store. Once inside, they quickly grab what they can, exit, get picked up by a confederate (who is often operating another just-stolen car), flee the scene, and then abandon the stolen car. This method is essentially an aggravated case of the well-known **smash-and-grab,** in which a perpetrator throws a brick or concrete block through the plate-glass window of a jewelry store, seizes what can immediately be reached, and then gets away from the scene as quickly as possible.

Some targets selected for burglaries require more than just crude force; they demand a high level of skill and daring. A former Army paratrooper who stole some $6 million in cash, jewelry, and credit cards was dubbed "Spiderman" by investigators, because he specialized in burglarizing high-rise apartments—a total of 132 of them—before he was apprehended (Figure 14-1). To reach his targets, Spiderman would climb as many as 30 stories

▲ **FIGURE 14-1 The Spiderman burglar**
Man arrested as Spiderman gives a media interview at jail. His attorney is the man wearing the white coat, and a reporter takes notes in the background. Investigators claim that $6 million was taken during Spiderman's "career." (© AP Photo/Wilfredo Lee)

on the *outside* of the buildings—without any climbing equipment.[10] Initially, investigators had difficulty even considering this method of approaching the target, because its use seemed too improbable.

Some burglaries require careful planning and coordination. For example, thieves stole merchandise from parked Susquehanna Railroad freight cars four times in three months, netting as much as $100,000. The men used 30-inch bolt cutters to force entry into the cars. Once inside, the merchandise was "selected," and walkie-talkies were then used to summon gang members driving gutted vans, which were then used to haul the loot off. To stay ahead of the police, the ring monitored a police scanner. After surveillance of the tracks failed to produce any results, officers were pulled off of that assignment, and the burglars went back to work. However, a man walking his dog at 9:30 P.M. spotted the men on top of the freight cars and alerted police, who were able to make arrests at the scene.[11]

Although some burglars prefer to work alone to maximize profits and to avoid the possibility that their partner(s) will "roll over on them" if arrested by the police on burglary or other charges, others work in gangs. These gangs vary in composition (for example, from juveniles, to members or affiliates of organized crime, to those having ethnic or foreign ties). In one particular crime wave involving a Tennessee burglary gang, investigators were sure juveniles were involved because of the nature of the items being taken, but they were nevertheless shocked to later learn that the two members of this "gang" were both less than 13 years old. The MO was for the 12-year-old boy to boost the 10-year-old girl through a broken window, and she would then open the door and let her "partner" into the home.[12]

In Chicago in another case, a long-time burglar, with reported mob connections, operated his "crew" for 30 years. When the leader was arrested, more than $2,000,000 in jewelry and stolen property was found in his home. A member of the crew virtually signed his presence at burglaries by always taking expensive Lladro porcelain figurines and adding them to his personal collection. Part of the "formula" used so successfully by the gang for decades was that after spotting a potential victim, they would bribe a public official to run the mark's auto tag so they could immediately know where he/she lived, after which they would begin to accumulate information before making their move. The gang was also successful in identifying restaurant owners who skimmed money from their businesses and accumulated large sums of cash in home safes.[13]

In the New York City area, 52 men from Colombia operated the "Codewise Crew" burglary ring, committing 6–12 burglaries a day. The gang operated in groups of three members, spotting residences that looked easy and striking in the mid-afternoon when families were often not home. Lookouts would communicate with the inside man, advising him of detection threats. The men would meet at a bar in the morning and later go pull their burglaries. Ultimately, the gang's downfall occurred when some members got reckless about how they operated, leading to their arrest.[14] Another illustration of a major crime gang/group with foreign ties is Yugoslavian, Croatian, and Siberians (YACs). YACs have operated along the Eastern seaboard, specializing in burglarizing ATMs in supermarkets, which may have $100,000 in them at any time, and the safes of buildings thought to have large amounts of cash on hand, such as bars and restaurants.[15]

Although burglars are often thought to be poor and uneducated, relying on that profile may cause investigators to overlook professionals who are also burglars.

A former police officer pleaded guilty to 16 felony counts involving a string of residential and commercial burglaries he committed while on duty. Just a month before entering his plea, the 18-year law-enforcement veteran was granted a disability pension after experts testified at his retirement hearing that he suffered from an obsessive-compulsive disorder that led to his pathological gambling.[16]

A church organist was arrested for committing three burglaries of churches and synagogues in which religious items of gold and silver valued at $25,000 were stolen. Following his arrest, the suspect confessed to having burglarized 500 such places, taking articles worth $2.5 million. There was little hope that any of the stolen property would ever be recovered, since it was believed to have been melted down and sold. Police were led to the suspect when a drifter was arrested for disorderly conduct. In the drifter's duffel bag, religious articles were found. He admitted having stolen them from the suspect, who had provided him with shelter for the night.[17]

Although burglars may be classified according to a number of variables, such as preferences for premises to be attacked and types of property that they will, or will not, take, the most useful classification is skill. Conceived as a continuum, the two extremes would be the amateur burglar and the professional. The largest number of burglars would be clustered toward the less-skilled end of the continuum, with progressively fewer toward the skilled end.

Professional burglars may commit only a few offenses per year, going for the bigger "scores," as in the following cases:

The FBI, working with Brazilian police officials, recovered three Norman Rockwell paintings valued at over $1 million. Nearly 25 years earlier, they were stolen from the Elayne Galleries in St. Louis Park, Minnesota. No one knows how the Rockwells ended up in Brazil. The thieves have never been caught.[18]

Space Coast Credit Union employees came to work on a Monday morning to find a hole in the roof over the vault and more than $100,000 missing. The police had responded to the alarm that went off at 12:30 and 1:30 Sunday morning, but they could not see the roof from the parking lot or the highway, nor could they find anyone with a key to the premises so that they could check inside. Several months before, a bank was successfully attacked using the same method of operation. In that case, the burglary was described as "the biggest financial loss in our city."[19]

However, professional burglars can also be quite active, committing a large number of offenses:

Members of a burglary ring were arrested for committing some 1,000 burglaries over a three-year period. They selected shops, businesses, and fast-food restaurants that would have anywhere from several thousand to $75,000 on hand. The targets included McDonald's, Pizza Hut, Burger King, and Dunkin Donuts.[20]

Although many professional burglars may commit only a few offenses a year, they are of considerable interest to investigators because of the large value of cash or property taken and their intimate knowledge of sophisticated fencing systems, which are often detected, and therefore investigated, only following the apprehension of a professional. In addition to the big score, the hallmark of the professional is the thorough planning that precedes each burglary. Professionals usually refuse to place themselves in jeopardy for anything other than sizable gains and do so only after weeks or even months of painstaking study of the target selected. Knowing exactly what they want in advance, professionals do not ransack premises. Thus, if they have employed surreptitious methods of entry, articles taken may not be missed for some time. Working nationally, or at the very highest professional level, internationally, this type of burglar often operates for long periods of time without being arrested.

When arrested, such burglars are usually released without being charged owing to a lack of physical evidence, coupled with their own skill in responding to the questions of investigators. When operating in elegant hotels or apartment buildings, the professional will use a businesslike appearance and manners to talk his way out of a situation. Should an occupant return unexpectedly, the burglar may pull out forged credentials identifying him as the building's security officer and say he found the door ajar and was just beginning his investigation. Or he may pretend to be drunk, ask for directions to some similarly numbered room, and stagger away acting confused.

However, if these or similar ploys fail, or if the burglar's real intent is apparent, the professional will employ violence if necessary to escape:

A well-known cardiologist was shot to death when he walked into the burglary of his home in a fashionable section of Washington, D.C. The police arrested a man who was alleged to be a "superthief" for the crimes. Upon searching the suspect's swank suburban home, the police found some $4 million worth of stolen property. It took the police 472 man-hours and 400 legal-size pages to count, tag, and describe the property. The 18-foot truck in which the seized property was transported away contained 51 large boxes and two smelters that were believed to have been used to melt down precious metals.[21]

Amateur burglars often operate on the basis of impulse or react to suddenly presented opportunities. Such burglars tend to work not only in one city but often in a relatively small segment of it. Amateurs may cruise in cars looking for businesses to victimize, prowl hotels seeking unlocked doors, or try to locate doors whose locks can be easily slipped using a credit card. While amateurs may occasionally enjoy a relatively big score, it is the absence of preplanning that sharply differentiates them from professionals. If they are narcotics addicts, amateurs must often work four or more days per week, committing several offenses each day, in order to support their habits. Even if they are not addicts, this may still be necessary to support their lifestyles. Frequently using sheer force to enter, amateurs crudely ransack businesses or residences to find anything of value. Occasionally, unlike their discerning professional counterparts, they take costume jewelry in the belief that they have found something of considerable value. When confronted by an unexpectedly returning business owner or occupant of a residence, amateurs may become immediately violent, and secondary crimes, such as murder or rape, unintended in the original offense, can occur. Finally, amateur burglars often have lengthy records and are frequently in and out of jail.

THE LAW

The crime of **burglary** generally consists of the following elements: (1) breaking and (2) entering (3) a dwelling house or other building (4) belonging to another, (5) with the intent to commit a crime therein. The common-law crime of burglary necessitates that the act be committed in the nighttime. This element has been deleted in a number of state statutes.

Burglary and related offenses are classified as crimes against the habitation, dwelling, or building itself; no force need be directed against a person. The breaking element may be satisfied through acts that constitute a breaking into, a breaking out of, or a breaking within. Generally, the slightest force used to remove or put aside something material that makes up a part of the building and is relied on to prevent intrusion, for example, doors or windows, constitutes breaking. This element can be satisfied whether accomplished at the hands of the perpetrator, through the use of some inanimate object like a brick, or by the participation of an innocent third party. Similarly, the element of entry is satisfied once the slightest intrusion has taken place by the perpetrator, an inanimate object, an animal, or an innocent third person.

The character of the building at which the breaking and entering takes place largely determines the type of offense committed. The most serious offense is often breaking and entering of a dwelling house, that is, a place used by another person as a residence. The nature of the dwelling itself is not determinative but, rather, the manner in which it is used. Hence, a hotel room can be considered a dwelling house.

The other major ingredient controlling the nature of the crime is the intent with which the perpetrator unlawfully breaks and enters the building. The more serious the crime intended to be committed after entry, the more serious becomes the breaking and entering itself. Thus, breaking-and-entering which is done with the intent to commit a felony carries a higher sentence in many states.

APPROACHING THE SCENE AND INITIAL ACTIONS

When responding to a burglary-in-progress call, uniformed officers should drive rapidly while avoiding excessive noise, such as the dramatic but unnecessary use of the siren. The last several blocks to the scene should be driven at lower speeds for two reasons. Doing so eliminates the possibility that the squealing tires of the police vehicle will give the perpetrators, if still on the scene, the advantage of crucial seconds of warning. Additionally, lower speeds allow opportunity for observation. A vehicle driving away from the vicinity of the scene may be seen and its description and license plate number noted as a possible investigative lead. Under such conditions,

late-model, expensive cars, such as Cadillacs and Lincolns, should not be discounted. Burglars often select these, not only because of the large amounts of equipment and stolen property such cars can hold but also because they recognize that the police often behave respectfully to the occupants of these vehicles, because of the implied social status.

When dispatched to a burglary-in-progress call, the uniformed officer working alone should attempt to coordinate his/her arrival time and position with the backup unit. This will enable the officers to secure the building immediately. One unit can arrive positioned so it can watch two sides of the building—for example, the north and east sides—while the other unit can observe the west and south sides. When a two-officer unit is dispatched to a burglary-in-progress call, the operator of the police vehicle should drop his or her partner off in a position to view two sides of the building and position the vehicle to allow observation of the remaining two sides. When working alone, if it is necessary to begin checking the exterior of the building immediately, the uniformed officer should drive around it to determine whether there is a readily observable break. If this is not possible, the officer should check rapidly, but cautiously, on foot. When a flashlight is used during hours of darkness, it should be held away from the body, because the suspect is most likely to aim at the light source if firing at the officer. If a point of entry is established, under no circumstances should an officer attempt to enter, as entering would needlessly expose him or her to extreme danger. Most burglars prefer to be unarmed because, in many states, breaking and entering while armed is a more serious offense than an unarmed breaking and entering. However, occasionally burglars are armed and willing to use their weapons to avoid apprehension:

A woman whose home overlooked the back of a shopping center saw two people break into a dress shop through the rear door. She called 911, who gave the call out as a burglary in progress, subjects on the premises. A motorcycle officer who was returning to the station at the end of his shift heard the call, which was assigned to a patrol unit, and swung by to back them up because he was close to the scene. The woman, still connected to 911, gave a running account of what happened. The motorcycle officer arrived first and pointed his motorcycle lights at the rear door. Instead of maintaining his position and waiting for assistance, he walked up to the door—fully silhouetted by his own lights. As he stood in the doorway, he was shot three times and collapsed. As the officer lay dying, one of the perpetrators stood over him and emptied his pistol into him. This death should not have occurred. It was caused because the officer used a tactically unsound procedure and because he encountered armed subjects willing to shoot it out with the police. Both subjects were arrested at the scene. Follow-up investigation revealed that they had a major incentive to use deadly force against the police—they were wanted on murder charges in two other states.

The fact that no point of entry is determined by riding or walking around the building does not mean that a forcible entry has not occurred. Whenever possible, the roof should be checked, particularly vents and skylights. Even if there is an alarm sounding, there may not be a burglary. Alarms frequently malfunction, particularly during inclement weather. However, officers must never become complacent about checking premises with a reputation for false alarms. If a breaking and entering has occurred, additional cars, if available, should be brought into the general area. Burglars often park their vehicles some blocks from the building to be attacked, and the perpetrator may not yet have had time to flee the area. "Lovers" parked in the general area should not go overlooked by the police. Burglars often use couples as lookouts or have their girlfriends remain in the car while they commit the offense. The perpetrator may have reached the car but have been unable to flee the immediate area; the use of a "just parked lovers" story may allow him to escape detection.

If a burglary has been committed and the police department has a canine unit, the uniformed officer at the scene should request its presence before entering the building. The alarm servicing company ordinarily sends a representative to the scene fairly rapidly to provide officers with access to the building. If there is no alarm, then the owner must be contacted either from information usually posted on the door or from other sources. Before beginning the crime scene search, officers must thoroughly check the building to ensure that the burglar is not hiding on the premises. To achieve the proper degree of caution, the building check should be conducted as though it were known that the burglar was still there.

Figure 14-2 is a **burglary investigation checklist;** it makes no distinction between the tasks associated with initiating the incident report and those associated with the follow-up investigation, so that the entire scope of investigative tasks can be seen at once.

INVESTIGATIVE CONSIDERATIONS AT THE SCENE

Caution must be exercised to avoid the accidental destruction of physical evidence while attempting to make a determination of whether the burglar is still in the building. Officers should be sensitive to the possible presence of physical evidence but not act in a manner that might jeopardize the most important thing—the officer's safety. If gross physical force has been used in gaining entry, the point of attack is easily established (Figure 14-3). However, one cannot assume that it is also the point of exit. Often burglars will break into a building at a particular point and then leave by opening a door. Where gross physical force is used, the point of attack is of particular importance because examination of it may yield the types of physical evidence discussed in Chapter 4, "Physical Evidence." In combination, the determination of the points of attack and exit will suggest the avenues of approach and flight traveled by the perpetrator, which also must be explored for the possible presence of physical evidence. Officers must be particularly attentive for unusual signs that may be of investigative value. Juvenile burglars commonly commit destructive acts of vandalism (Figure 14-4). Also, age may be suggested from the choices of what is taken and what is left behind:

When I started hustling . . . didn't know much, like what crap be really worth and how to get bills for it . . . at first alotta stuff I just leave back . . . just grabbed things for me . . . like a nice coat or small crap you can just walk with and sell quick for cash . . . like a gun . . . main thing for me was getting some bills so I could high-cat around and get stuff . . . Nike shoes. I couldn't walk around with no stereo or TV . . . had to leave the big stuff.

The sudden removal of trophies or other prized possessions by their owner from a business or residence, followed by a burglary for the purpose of committing arson, should raise certain questions in the investigator's mind. Further, the weight or dimensions of property taken in a burglary may suggest, if only roughly, the number of people involved in the offense. Articles or tools left behind, combined with other specifics of the crime, may be useful in the identification of an MO.

Many commercial establishments keep check imprinters on their premises. A not uncommon occurrence is for a burglar to gain entry to a commercial building, tear several checks from the company checkbook, imprint them, and cash them the next day. Thus, it is of particular importance to have the proprietor ensure that no checks have been taken. Normally, when a burglar employs this practice the checks will be taken from the very rear of the book or from several different series in order to lessen the likelihood of detection.

TABLE 14-2	Home-Burglary Victimizations by Amount of Loss

AMOUNT OF LOSS	PERCENTAGE OF BURGLARIES
No loss	1.2%
Less than $50	10.5
$50–$99	4.2
$100–$249	14.4
$250–$499	11.7
$500–$999	11.3
$1,000 or more	30.8
Not known/not available	15.9

Source: Bureau of Justice Statistics, *Criminal Victimization in the United States—2007.* Washington, D.C.: U.S. Department of Justice, December 2007; Internet edition without page numbers, Table 85. Most recent statistics as of December 2010.

are not intrinsically significant. However, to many households, even relatively small losses are devastating. Moreover, when you consider the residual feelings of the victims, there is another type of loss: victims feel as though their privacy has been violated. They often struggle psychologically afterward to regain a sense of security in their own homes.

Many burglars are amateurs in the sense that even though they may commit the crime numerous times, they often act on impulse, driven by the need for money:

> Usually when I get in my car and drive around I'm thinking, I don't have any money, so what is my means for money? All of a sudden I'll just take a glance and say, there it is, there's the house! . . . Then I get the feelin', that very moment that I'm moving then.[33]

Some burglars report that "legitimate" financial emergencies are the only reason they resort to breaking in:

> Usually what I'll do is a burglary [or a couple of them] if I have to . . . helps get me over the rough spot until I can get it straightened out. Once I get it straightened out, I just go with the flow until I hit a rough spot where I need the money again . . . The only time I would go and commit a burglary is if I needed money at that point in time. That would be strictly to pay light bill, gas bill, rent.[34]

Although such cases clearly exist, burglaries are more often committed for other reasons:

> I might find somebody with some good crack . . . while I'm high I say damn I want me some more of that good shit. Go knock a place off, make some more money, go buy some more dope.[35]

> I use the burglary money for gifts for young ladies— flowers or negligee or somethin'. Some shoes . . . put them shoes on, them pumps . . . then watch 'em dance nude.[36]

> See I go steal money and go buy me some clothes . . . See, I like to look good. I likes to dress . . . own only one pair of blue jeans 'cause I like to dress [well].[37]

> Burglary is excitin' . . . it's just a thrill to going in undetected and walking out with all their shit . . . like going on a treasure hunt.[38]

From these quotes, it can be seen that burglars tend to commit their crimes for four broad reasons: (1) keeping themselves and their families fed, clothed, and sheltered; (2) keeping the party going; (3) keeping up appearances so that they can look better off financially than they are; and (4) keeping adventure in their lives.[39]

Whereas amateur burglars act on impulse, the more professional burglars are, the less likely they are to take chances. They develop information on their own or pay tipsters for it. They may simply cruise well-to-do neighborhoods looking for opportunities or follow expensive cars to their homes. Once they have identified a preliminary target, they begin a "workup," watching the house until they have become familiar with the people who live there, their daily routines, the absence or presence of alarms and dogs, views of possible attack points from other homes in the area, and the frequency of private and public police patrols.

One way of developing information on their own is simply to read the newspapers. Wedding announcements often reveal that a couple will honeymoon in another city or country and then reside in whatever community. With a little effort, burglars can often find out the couple's address and burglarize the home, stealing wedding gifts and other items, while the victimized partners are blissfully enjoying their honeymoon. Other types of announcements that might provide similar opportunities include funeral arrangements and gala charity events or parties, which many wealthy people can be expected to attend. Butlers and maids can get lists of the people attending such events. Tipsters—sometimes called "spotters," "fingermen," "noses," or "setup people"—provide another source of information that can be used in selecting homes for burglaries. For example, insiders at cruise ship operations can provide passenger lists. Medical personnel know when patients will be in their offices for appointments. Workers in various occupations such as telephone installers and flower delivery workers, enter numerous homes legitimately and have the chance to size up opportunities. Coworkers know when their bosses are going on vacation. Insurance office personnel know which homes' contents have been heavily insured and which may have special riders attached for silverware or other valuables. Armed with such information, professional burglars reduce the risk of apprehension and increase the probability of "making a nice haul."

Homes are burglarized during the day because that's when the occupants are most likely to be gone—working, attending school, or running errands. The same generally holds true with many neighbors, who might otherwise witness the attack. Burglars do not want to attract attention to themselves, but they also do not want a confrontation with an occupant. If they have learned the home's telephone number, they will call to see if anyone is there. While an answering machine encourages some burglars, it makes others leery of going ahead, fearing that someone is home and using the machine to screen the calls.

Alarms and dead-bolt locks are a deterrent to amateur burglars but not to more professional ones. Residential burglars usually do not have to carry an assortment of tools because so many targets are "soft." Often, they carry little other than workman's gloves and a large screwdriver or small pry bar (Figure 14-9). If they cannot easily effect entry at the front door, they will try to enter through the garage—which is ideal because they are out of sight—or a rear window. Most home burglars go straight to the bedroom, because that's where most people keep small valuables, such as jewelry, cash, furs, and guns. The master bathroom is also where most people keep their prescription drugs. As their experience builds up, burglars will begin to check the "clever" places where people hide their valuables, including in freezer compartments and behind towels in linen closets. If they have an accomplice, they will call him or her to bring the vehicle into which televisions, DVD/Blu-Ray Players, stereo systems, tools, and other valuables are loaded. Table 14-3 shows the seven types of property most commonly taken in burglaries.

▲ **FIGURE 14-9   Pry marks on residence's front door**
Pry marks left on the front door frame of a residential burglary. This is a general orientation photograph; close-up photographs of the marks with a ruler alongside them would also be taken. The positions of the pry marks would also be documented by notes and a sketch, using precise measurements. Ideally the marks would be cut from the door frame to be able to make comparisons with tools that may subsequently be found in the possession of a subject arrested for the crime. Failing that, they could be cast using Mikrosil, Silmark, or some similar putty. The drying times for putty varies, most drying in 5–8 minutes in normal temperatures and 12–15 minutes when very cold. (Courtesy Chief Rick Boren and Sgt. Doug Shafer, Columbus (Georgia) Police Department)

CAR, RV, AND TRAILER BURGLARIES

In most states, breaking into cars, recreational vehicles (RVs), and trailers constitutes a burglary. **Car burglars** tend to be juveniles, teenagers, and young adult offenders. Many entries by these offenders are done by simply opening unlocked car doors; others involve breaking a window to reach inside and take whatever is available.

TABLE 14-3	Property Most Frequently Taken from Homes with Reported Losses	
PROPERTY		**PERCENTAGE OF CASES**
Portable electronic and photographic gear, jewelry, clothing, and other personal effects		42.5%
Household furnishings		12.8
Tools, machinery		12.1
Cash		11.1
Purse, wallet and credit cards		6.5
Bicycles and their parts		4.2
Firearms		2.2

Bureau of Justice Statistics, *Crime Victimization in the United States, 2007 Statistical Tables*. Washington, D.C.: U.S. Department of Justice, December 2007, Table 84. Most recent statistics as of December 2010.

Unlocked trunk releases are also pulled and items in the trunk stolen. Some street-wise suspects carry a spark plug with them, which when thrown hard easily breaks a car window. Additional "tools" include tire irons, slim jims, or other pry-bar type instruments, hammers, door lock punches, or whatever is handy, such as portable signs and rocks.

Typical items taken include visible change, wallets left in the center console and purses left on the floor board, car electronics, CDs, speed detectors, laptops, cameras, and cellular phones. Juveniles and teenagers often do more damage than is necessary in removing dashboard electronics. When valuable, but larger items, such as golf clubs, are left behind, the lack of a vehicle to transport them out of the area and/or the inability to sell them quickly also suggests youthful offenders. People of all ages on drugs commit auto breaking-and-enterings (B&Es), stealing items that they can quickly convert to cash to support their drug use. Wherever cars are parked, they can become a target. Apartment complexes, sorority and fraternity houses, and mall, mass transit, campus, and employee parking lots offer plentiful targets that allow offenders to quickly commit a larger number of car burglaries. Cars that are burglarized on railroad cars and new car sales lots tend to suggest more experienced car burglars. In most jurisdictions, car burglaries increase sharply around Christmas time, when shoppers leave many packages in plain view in their vehicles.

Modest pop-up campers may cost in the $5,000–$10,000 range, whereas RVs can top out at $1.5 million. Burglaries at dealerships tend to focus on electronics, and often the damage to the RVs is greater than the amount of the property stolen. Many RV burglaries occur at RV storage sites and along interstate and major state highways, because those routes are typically used by travelers. Pop-ups are often attacked in state or national parks when the owners are away hiking, photographing, hunting, or fishing. High-end RVs often have safes where the owners keep valuables and sometimes surprisingly large amounts of cash. High-end RVs have also been the target of home invasion–style robberies.

In addition to apprehensions made by patrol officers viewing crimes in progress, such crimes are often foiled or solved by reviewing surveillance data, targeting repeat offenders, owners returning unexpectedly to their vehicles, perpetrators bragging about their success, juveniles displaying their goods to classmates at school, suspects stopped for traffic offenses with the stolen property in plain view in the rear seat, and the use of "bait cars" by police.

INVESTIGATING CRIMINAL FENCES AND OTHER OUTLETS FOR STOLEN PROPERTY

Criminal **fences** or receivers are persons who knowingly purchase stolen property at a fraction of its cost and then resell it at a considerable profit (but still at a "really good" price) to the consumer. Fences usually buy at 10%–20% of an item's actual cost or may simply set a flat price for the goods—for example, $700 for a particular year, make, and model of car. How "hot" the goods are and how quickly they can be safely resold are also factors in setting the price. When confronted with someone who bought property that later turned out to be stolen, officers must determine whether the purchaser acted in good or bad faith. Among the indicators of a buyer's lack of good faith are

1. paying a price below that of a "good bargain";
2. purchasing from persons who are not known to them;
3. buying from persons whom they don't know how to recontact;
4. accepting items without a receipt;
5. buying property that bears an obliterated identification number or from which the number has been removed;
6. purchasing articles that have unusual property control numbers on them, such as those identifying the owner as a state agency;
7. having a past history of receiving stolen property;

The most basic notion of a fence is that after committing a burglary or another crime (for example, hijacking a truckload of clothing), the thief takes the merchandise (for instance, a television) to the fence and says, "How much will you give me for it?" Although this approach is still used, fencing has become considerably more complicated, and there are numerous types of fences,[40] as shown by these examples:

- *Amateurs fences,* who usually do fencing intermittently, have limited resources and may buy stolen goods for resale to friends, as gifts to girlfriends, or for their own personal use.
- *Store owners and individuals,* who often buy only the goods for which they have placed an order with the thief or only from a thief who works for them relatively full time. Such thieves may also work as freelancers or as members of gangs, some of which are ethnically based, in multistate areas.

Theft of luxury clothing items, such as leather coats and upscale designer-label clothing, is a growth industry. The property may be stolen in burglaries or some other type of crime, including "mopping," another term for shoplifting. The clothing is then sold to fences or underground boutiques. Inside one drab family residence in Queens, police uncovered over $500,000 in stolen clothes. Said one detective, "The inside of this place looks like Macy's."[41]

Pakistani owners of a convenience store also led a three-state ring of thieves. They recruited 200 professional shoplifters and illegal Pakistani immigrants with promises of a better life and plenty of money to send home. Members of this group stole over-the-counter cosmetics, computers, DVD players, jet skis, pharmaceuticals, and anything else they could get their hands on. The merchandise was taken to a warehouse where it was repackaged and sent to coconspirators in two different states and in Pakistan. Competition to "bring in the most" was intense. One thief, enraged that another thief had brought in more than he had, hired thugs to beat up the higher-performing member of the gang. Gang cohesion was also reduced when some members "skimmed" some items for themselves, reducing the "take" for the rest of them. As investigators "rolled" individual gang members, the investigation snowballed, resulting in the eventual recovery of $450,000 in cash and $1.6 million in stolen goods.[42]

- *Professionals,* who have substantial bankrolls, do business with a select clientele known by them or reliably referred to them, may work for long periods without being caught, and usually have several locations at which to store their purchases.
- *Occasional or opportunistic fences,* who normally conduct their businesses legally (for example, as garages or **pawnshops**) but who from time to time "turn a deal" (Figure 14-10).
- *Providers of illicit goods and services,* such as those who trade drugs and access to prostitutes for stolen merchandise.

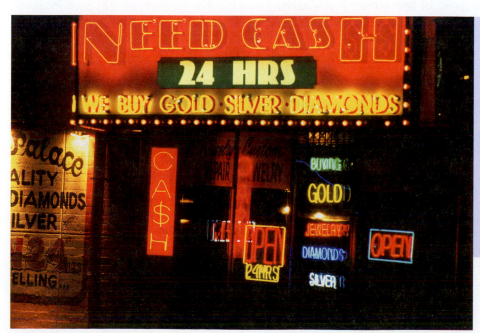

◀**FIGURE 14-10**
Pawnshops: Legitimate businesses or fencing operations?
Fences are persons who knowingly purchase stolen property for a fraction of its cost and then resell it at a considerable profit. Pawnshops suffer a continuing image problem from the illegal conduct of fencing by some of its operators. Most, if not all, jurisdictions have enacted statutes and ordinances in an effort to regulate how pawnshops conduct their business. (© Randy Faris/Corbis)

▶ **FIGURE 14-11**
Police raid uncovers stolen bicycles and other property
A police raid on a fencing operation in an inner-city neighborhood recovered a great deal of stolen property, some of which the police are inventorying in this picture. The operators of the fence paid for stolen goods with cash, drugs, and access to prostitutes.
(Courtesy Major Tolbert and Lt. Richard Zapal, Savannah Chatham Metropolitan Police Department)

- *Technology-proficient fences,* who do their business on the Internet. Some of these "fences" are the thieves themselves:

Two career thieves who may have committed as many as 100 burglaries in Massachusetts and New Hampshire sold approximately $30,000 worth of their booty on eBay. They had another $70,000 in stolen property that they also planned to sell there when police arrested them.[43]

Many fences can operate for long periods of time without being detected because they are often "invisible" until some situation creates the need for police to take a closer look at individuals and/or locations (Figure 14-11). Outlets for stolen property include swap meets, flea markets, for-sale advertisements in local newspapers, secondhand furniture stores, eBay and other Internet outlets, and overseas venues, often in third-world countries. In some instances, knowledge about fencing operations comes to the police under more unusual circumstances:

Two men approached a police sergeant with an offer of a $25,000 cash bribe in return for destroying physical evidence that tied them to a robbery. They were given some items and appeared satisfied with having bought themselves a cop. However, the officer was actually working the two men with the knowledge and support of his department and the local FBI field office. Ulti-

mately, the two men and their associates were linked to warehouse burglaries and container thefts that totaled more than $3 million in stolen goods, and they had acted as fences for stolen laptop computers.[44]

From a policy viewpoint, the police know that the more the receiver markets can be disrupted or eliminated, the greater the likelihood that there will be some reduction in burglary and other offenses, whose profits depend on the availability of these illicit markets. Plainclothes officers quietly visit swap meets, flea markets, and other likely outlets, looking for known burglars or their associates offering merchandise for trade or sale. Such locations may be good candidates for the use of facial recognition software. Articles being offered are examined for possible signs of being stolen, such as missing or newly attached serial numbers. Arrested burglary offenders are always asked, "What did you do with the stuff you took?" When squeezed between facing almost certain prison time and giving their fences up, some will barter the information for a more lenient sentence. Because drug users usually steal to support their habits, whenever they are arrested, they are going to be asked, "What can you give me?" Their answers to this question may help identify drug dealers, fences, and other types of offenders.

Once in a great while, such questioning may yield a professional, big-time fence, but more frequently this is not the case. Professional fences usually screen their customers carefully and have worked with them over a period of years. Moreover, an arrested offender knows that by giving up a big-time fence, he/she will risk getting "wacked" for talking. Thus, the more usual case is that offenders try to get away with giving up "little fish."

Once a suspected fence is detected, officers work the case, investigating to confirm or disconfirm the fencing operation. When this is accomplished, officers attempt to broaden the case and apprehend more than just the offenders in front of them. This often entails both physical and electronic surveillance to identify the places fences frequent and who their associates are. An undercover officer may then be assigned to begin frequenting these places, covertly gathering additional information and/or attempting to develop a relationship with the fence and his/her associates. This method is also used when active burglars are targeted for arrest and surveillance is initiated. At some point, arrest and search warrants will be issued. When multiple locations and perpetrators are involved, raids executing the warrants should be conducted simultaneously to prevent offenders from slipping away.

As an industry, pawnshops suffer a continuing image problem from the illegal conduct of some operators. When the illegality was perceived as a serious problem, state statutes and local ordinances were enacted to regulate their shops' conduct, and this has reduced the number of pawnshops acting as fences. Usually these laws require that the pawnshops provide the names and addresses, and in some instances fingerprints, of persons pawning property, along with a full description of the property. In some locations, all secondhand dealers of property must provide the same type of information. In both instances, this must ordinarily be done within 24 hours of each transaction. Because of the temptations created by the high profits that can be gained by buying and selling stolen property, pawn and other second-hand dealers are closely scrutinized. State investigative agencies and many individual agencies maintain pawnshop databases to monitor secondhand merchandise transactions:

While entering information in the database, an officer working with the burglary squad noticed that a subject had sold an expensive loose diamond to a local used-jewelry store. She also noticed that the subject had previously sold expensive jewelry to the same business. In the sale that had attracted the officer's attention, the subject had received $10,400 for the diamond. On the transaction slip from the jewelry store, it was noted that the seller lived in a nearby jurisdiction and worked as a plumber, so the officer contacted the police department there to find out if any high-priced jewelry thefts had occurred. She was not successful there, but ultimately she found a department in the area where investigators had noted a pattern in which the subject did plumbing jobs, and subsequently there would be missing jewelry from the homes he had worked in. Eventually, the diamond, actually valued at $63,000, was matched with a victim's ring from which the plumber had pried it.[45]

In another case, the same officer noted that the home of one of the department's employees had been burglarized, resulting in the loss of a camera, zoom lens, and credit card. While processing transaction slips, she found a pawnshop that had taken in the camera and zoom lens, along with a diamond ring and bracelet, which had been purchased with the stolen credit card. Investigation revealed that the subject selling the articles to the pawnshop had an extensive criminal background and lived within a few blocks of the employee. On the basis of this and other evidence, he was arrested and the property recovered.[46]

Police **sting operations** are an effective means of combating fences, identifying active criminals, penetrating criminal organizations, and recovering property. In a typical sting, officers set up a legitimate-appearing "front" business in which they slowly develop a reputation as being fences. As all transactions are videotaped, a great deal of intelligence is gathered that can be used in their current investigation or in collateral ones. Alternatively, the officers may do business in a different type of setting and use a warehouse located elsewhere to store the stolen property:

An FBI agent, a cooperating witness, and participating local departments ran a fencing operation out of a Brooklyn social club. The "drop" for the merchandise was a warehouse they had rented at another location. This undercover operation resulted in the indictments of 39 individuals on charges of selling stolen property, drug trafficking, gun dealing, and loan-sharking. Over $5 million in property was recovered, including a hijacked truckload of designer gowns valued at more than $1 million.[47]

In Chapter 7, "The Follow-Up Investigation and Investigative Resources," the enhanced capabilities of NCIC 2000 were discussed. The NCIC databases are of great importance for investigators, particularly since images of stolen property have been added. This new capability enhances the opportunity to recover stolen property.

THE INVESTIGATOR'S CRIME PREVENTION ROLE

While at the scene of a burglary, investigators should tell the victims the precautions they can take to decrease the likelihood of their being "hit" again.

▶ FIGURE 14-12
Sample office security checklist
(Source: Courtesy Bolen Industries, Hackensack, New Jersey, with modification)

	Yes	No
1. Do you restrict office keys to persons who actually need them?	☐	☐
2. Do you keep complete, up-to-date records of the disposition of all office keys?	☐	☐
3. Do you have adequate procedures for collecting keys from terminated employees?	☐	☐
4. Do you restrict duplication of office keys, except for those specifically ordered by you in writing?	☐	☐
5. Do you require that all keys be marked "Do not duplicate" to prevent legitimate locksmiths from making copies without your knowledge?	☐	☐
6. Have you established a rule that keys must not be left unguarded on desks or cabinets, and do you enforce that rule?	☐	☐
7. Do you require that filing-cabinet keys be removed from locks and placed in a secure location after opening cabinets in the morning?	☐	☐
8. Do you have procedures that prevent unauthorized personnel from reporting a "lost key" and receiving a "replacement"?	☐	☐
9. Do you have some responsible person in charge of issuing all keys?	☐	☐
10. Are all keys systematically stored in a secured wall cabinet either of your own design or from a commercial key-control system?	☐	☐
11. Do you keep a record showing issuance and return of every key, including the name of the person, the date, and time?	☐	☐
12. Do you use telephone locks or access codes to prevent unauthorized calls when the office is unattended?	☐	☐
13. Do you provide at least one lockable drawer in every secretary's desk to protect personal effects?	☐	☐
14. Do you have at least one filing cabinet secured with an auxiliary locking bar so that you can keep business secrets under better protection?	☐	☐
15. Do you leave a night light on?	☐	☐
16. Do you record all equipment serial numbers and file them in a safe place to maintain correct identification in the event of theft or destruction by fire?	☐	☐
17. Do you shred all important papers before discarding them in wastebaskets?	☐	☐
18. Do you lock briefcases and attaché cases containing important papers in closets or lockers when not in use?	☐	☐
19. Do you insist on identification from repair people who come to do work in your office?	☐	☐
20. Do you deposit incoming checks and cash each day so that you do not keep large sums in the office overnight?	☐	☐
21. Do you clear all desks of important papers every night and place them in locked fireproof safes or cabinets?	☐	☐
22. Do you frequently change the combination of your safe to prevent anyone from memorizing it or passing it on to a confederate?	☐	☐
23. When working alone in the office at night, do you set the front-door lock to prevent anyone else from getting in?	☐	☐
24. Do you have the police and fire department telephone numbers posted and handy?	☐	☐
25. Do you check to see that no one remains in hiding behind you at night if you are the last to leave the office?	☐	☐
26. Are all windows, transoms, and ventilators properly protected?	☐	☐
27. Do you double check to see that all windows and doors are securely locked before you leave?	☐	☐
28. Are all doors leading to the office secured by heavy-duty, double-cylinder, dead-bolt locks?	☐	☐
29. If your office is equipped with a burglar alarm system or protected by a guard service, do you make sure the alarm equipment is set properly each night?	☐	☐
30. Do you have a periodic security review by a qualified security expert or locksmith?	☐	☐
31. Are computer access codes and/or selected files password-protected on a need-to-know basis?	☐	☐
32. Are all computer disks and tapes containing sensitive, client, or secret information maintained under controlled conditions during the day and locked securely at night?	☐	☐

REDUCING THE RISK OF COMMERCIAL BURGLARY

Many of the suggestions provided in the next section for preventing residential burglaries also apply to businesses. In addition, operators of businesses should be told to prevent easy access to their roofs by securing all vents and roof openings; to use security-providing locks, frames, and doors properly; to light the exterior of the building; to use, if feasible, an alarm system and surveillance camera; to use a money chest rather than a fire-resistant safe; and to set the safe in concrete in open view at a place that can be lighted at night. Completion of the office security checklist in Figure 14-12 serves two purposes: It provides the owners with useful information about how to improve their security, and it may provide important investigative leads, particularly if a surreptitious entry is involved.

REDUCING THE RISK OF RESIDENTIAL BURGLARY

To protect their residences as well as businesses, when appropriate, occupants should do the following things when they are on vacation or otherwise away:

1. Stop delivery of mail and newspapers, or arrange for a neighbor to pick them up daily.
2. Arrange for a special watch on their premises by patrol officers.
3. Use timers to turn on lights and radios at various times to make it look like the residence is occupied.
4. Ask reliable neighbors to immediately report any suspicious activity to the police.
5. Ask a trusted neighbor to come over occasionally and change the position of drapes, blinds, and other things.
6. Put up "Beware of Dog" signs, or if they really have a dog, ask someone to take care of it in the home whenever feasible.

For day-to-day security, occupants can take other actions that will help them avoid being burglary victims or, if they are victimized, will help reduce their losses:

1. Create an uninviting target: use motion-sensor lights, purchase an alarm system, use dead-bolt locks on solid doors mounted in steel frames, and place locks on windows.
2. If possible, avoid placing valuables where they can be seen through windows.
3. Cut plants low around doors and windows so that burglars can't conceal themselves while breaking in.
4. Grow thorny plants around places where someone might attempt to force an entry.

5. Don't leave ladders or tools lying around in the yard or clothes on an outside line—a thief who initially may have thought of just taking them will see the greater opportunity they create.
6. Don't tell strangers about your comings and goings.
7. Don't allow strangers to use your telephone, and don't give your correct number to anyone who claims they are calling by mistake; instead, ask the caller whom he/she was trying to reach at what number. Baby-sitters and children should be instructed to do the same thing.
8. Don't keep spare keys in the usual places—under the mat, over the door, and in flower pots. Burglars know these places.
9. Don't go out to run a quick errand without locking all doors, including garage doors.
10. Engrave valuables with special identifying numbers. Alternatively, mark them with small translucent decals that have your special identification data on them. These microdots are about the size of a speck of pepper and are virtually invisible to the naked eye.
11. Keep strong control over your keys. It may be helpful to leave them for service workers or give them to maids, but at the cost of greater risk exposure.
12. Don't leave notes on the door saying where you have gone or when you will be back.
13. Get to know your neighbors; they'll be more likely to respond faithfully to requests to "watch my place while I'm gone."
14. When new snow is on the ground, back out of your driveway and pull back in several times; do the same walking in and out of your door. This makes it harder for burglars to figure out if you are home.
15. To enhance recovery of your property if you are victimized, take pictures of valuables and record makes, models, and serial numbers of your property.

KEY TERMS

amateur burglars	coin-operated machine burglary	professional burglars
ATM attacks	fences	safe
burglary	loiding	smash-and-grab
burglary investigation checklist	pawnshops	sting operations
burglary tools	picking	theft of luxury
car burglars	possession of burglary tools	

REVIEW QUESTIONS

1. Describe the dimensions of the crime of burglary.
2. What is the profile of persons arrested for burglary?
3. How are professional and amateur burglars distinguished?
4. What are the elements of the crime of burglary?
5. What considerations are important in approaching the scene of a burglary?
6. How are attacks on ATMs committed?

7. The text noted that black home owners and younger people are victimized more frequently than others. What are some possible explanations for this?
8. What signs at a burglary scene may suggest juvenile perpetrators?
9. How are fire-resistant safes and money chests differentiated?
10. What special actions are required if there are explosives at a burglary scene?

11. How do burglars get their information?
12. With respect to the possible illegal receiving of stolen property, what are some indicators of the absence of good-faith purchasing?
13. Explain two investigative approaches to locating fences.
14. What measures can home owners and business operators take to lessen their chances of being burglarized?

INTERNET ACTIVITIES

1. The two most famous burglaries in American history are usually referred to by one word, "Watergate." What were these burglaries about, and what was their ultimate importance?
2. To learn how different police agencies across the country are attacking burglary problems go to

www.cops.usdoj.gov (the Community Oriented Policing Services [COPS] website), click on "Resource Information Center (RIC), and enter "burglary" in the search field.

In 2008, store surveillance video captured a Florida woman shoplifting. Police investigators later discovered that the woman was part of an extensive shoplifting ring comprising approximately 18 family members. The group allegedly stole more than $100 million worth of merchandise over a five-year period.

(© AP Photo/Bedford, N.H. Police Department)

15

Larceny/Theft and White-Collar Crime

This chapter deals with two groups of crimes: larceny/theft and white-collar crime. The traditional definition of larceny/theft is the unlawful taking and carrying away of the tangible personal property of another with the intent to permanently deprive that person of his interest in the property. **Tangible personal property** means things that have both a physical existence that can be touched and intrinsic value—such as jewelry, lawn mowers, cameras, laptop computers, televisions, furniture and clothing, and collectibles such as coins and civil war uniform buttons.

In contrast, **intangible property** has value, but it is more abstract—such as stocks, bonds, checking and saving accounts, and other types of financial instruments, as well as patents and copyrights. State statutes have historically addressed the theft of intangibles through specific statutes, which supplemented the existing larceny statutes. Larceny essentially incorporates the elements of the crime of robbery, except the element of the use of force, threat, or fear is not included (see Chapter 13, "Robbery"). Additionally, although robbery is a face-to-face crime, the law does not require that the victim of a larceny be present at the time of a crime. However, the victim may be present as illustrated by purse snatching, pickpocketing, and an owner driving home from work in time to see a stranger pick up his daughter's bicycle from the lawn of his home, toss it in the back of a SUV, and drive away.

Larceny/theft is often divided into **grand larceny** and **petit or petty larceny;** the former is a felony and the latter a misdemeanor. The difference between the two is the value of the property stolen, which varies by state; the dividing line between the two is often that if the value of the property stolen is $1,000 or more, it is a felony. In some states, larceny/theft statutes are divided into grades or classes of offending, such as Class A, Class B, and so on; the gradations of offenses are usually based on the amount of loss to the victim, and the legal penalties are tied to the grade or class of the theft.

Many states have also enacted specifically titled larceny/theft statutes that reflect special aspects of their economy, such as "timber theft or fraud," or special problems, for example, "transit fare evasion, identity theft" or "organized retail theft" to distinguish between prosecutions that are aimed at rings of professional shoplifters causing significant losses and that have more serious penalties versus those directed at the teenager who "lifts or boosts" a CD, tube of lipstick, or shirt (Figure 15-1) and is charged with "theft from retail merchants," a lesser shoplifting offense.

CHAPTER OUTLINE

The term *white-collar crime* was coined in 1939 by sociologist E. H. Sutherland. His white-collar criminals were characterized by respectability and higher social status, which they used to commit more complex offenses such as **fraud** and **embezzlement,** as opposed to street crimes. Now, almost 70 years later, the U.S. Department of Justice defines **white-collar crime** as nonviolent, illegal activities that rely on deceit, deception, concealment, manipulation, breach of trust, subterfuge, or illegal circumvention. Note that Sutherland's definition was based on the characteristics of the offender versus the present orientation of white-collar crime being the characteristics of the actions taken by the offender.[1] There is no set of laws titled "white-collar crime." It is a construct, useful for how we think about such crimes, but offenders are often charged with larceny/theft crimes, such as theft by fraud. Many of these crimes are investigated and prosecuted at the federal level. For instance, the FBI investigates theft crimes that involve the transportation of stolen property across state lines, the U.S. Postal Inspectors investigate mail and wire fraud, and the U.S. Secret Service investigates fraudulent credit cards and checks drawn upon payment and financial systems of the United States. In addition, the Secret Service is charged with the enforcement of counterfeiting and fraud statutes aimed at preserving the integrity of United States currency, coin, and financial obligations.

▲ **FIGURE 15-1 Theft from retail merchant**
Teenage shoplifter takes one last look around before concealing merchandise in her backpack. (© Benelux)

Statistically, pickpockets are not a large problem in the United States; the crime accounts for only about one-half of 1% of all larceny/thefts, but losses are still serious to victims. Abroad, pickpockets flourish in all major cities, such as Rome, Beijing, Bangkok, Paris, Berlin, and London. In foreign countries, tourists lose not only their valuables but often their passports, which interrupts their vacations while they seek to get a replacement. The crime flourishes where people congregate at peak hours, such as transportation centers, along crowded streets, and at sporting events.

Children as young as five and six years old are trained as pickpockets in some foreign countries. There are schools in South America from which, in order to graduate, the would-be pickpocket must "lift" items from all the pockets of a mannequin dressed in a three-piece men's suit. Each pocket is guarded with a bell that cannot ring if the "student" is to pass. Pickpockets may work alone, although a "crew" of three is common: one distracts the mark (for example, drops something, bumps him/her, or feigns a medical emergency or accident), another takes the valuables, which are immediately handed to a third accomplice, who quickly slips away. A seasoned operator can take the wristwatch off your arm without you realizing it; in Oslo, Norway brazen pickpockets even lifted the wallet of the Chief of Police. Some very skilled pickpockets morph over to shoplifting expensive jewelry because of the higher values. Investigators should exercise caution when arresting pickpockets, a small number of whom turn violent when apprehended. They should also be on-guard for assaults from previously unnoted accomplices.

Most victims had exposed valuables, such as their wallet, within the 30 minutes before their victimization; pickpockets study the crowd and carefully select their target. Women are more likely to be victimized than men are, whereas men are more likely to be the perpetrators. Secondary crimes included credit card fraud and withdrawals from the victim's ATM account, because the victim's personal identification number (PIN) was written down in the wallet.[2]

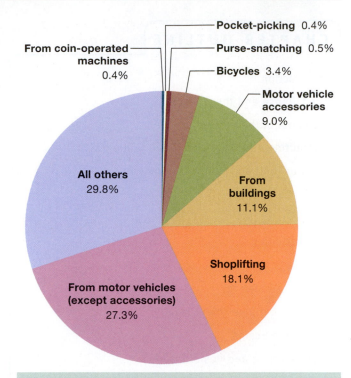

▲ **FIGURE 15-2** **Larceny-theft distribution, 2009**
(Uniform Crime in the United States, 2009 [Washington, D.C.: FBI, 2010], *www2.fbi.gov/ucr/cius2009/documents/index.htm*)

THE OFFENSE AND THE OFFENDER

Although the number of larcenies decreased by 9% in 2009 estimates, a larceny/theft occurs every 5.0 seconds, a rate of nearly three times that for burglary,[3] and the average loss is $864.[4] This crime bears a low clearance rate; only 21.5% are resolved by arrest of exceptional means.[5] A little over half of all larceny/thefts were of items valued at $200 or below.[6] Larceny/theft is often an opportunistic act; fishing rods and tool boxes are taken from open beds of pickup trucks parked at a Sam's Club, or a thief loitering at an airport notices that someone waiting for a flight is distracted and takes her purse, carry-on luggage, or laptop. Many items are taken from motor vehicles or acquired through shoplifting tactics as indicated in Figure 15-2. Overwhelmingly, these offenses are committed by young, white males.

Because small items of low value are often stolen and there are frequently no leads, many larceny/theft cases are simply inactivated after the incident report is taken, and they receive no investigative follow-up. This fact accounts for the reality that the recovery in property in larceny/theft is low; in only 3.7% of all such cases is at least some property recovered. However, 4.7% of the time all of the property is recovered, often from offenses with larger losses and significant leads.[7]

ELEMENTS OF THE CRIME

Although the traditional definition of larceny is still operative in some states, others have eliminated the distinction between the theft of tangibles and intangibles and created more comprehensive larceny/theft statutes to cover both types of losses. Such statutes drop the former "tangible personal property of another" and use "property

of another," to cover the loss of a wide range of things, such as stocks and bonds, services—such as electricity, natural gas, television cable, high-speed Internet access, tickets to the symphony and sporting events, lawn mowers, paintings, hotel rooms and rental cars, computer software and information files, cash and jewelry. To illustrate, in some states the failure to return a rental car within 72 hours of the agreed-on time in the lease is evidence of intent to commit larceny/theft.

The person from whom the property is taken in a larceny/theft need not own it and may simply be the custodian of it. Although he/she is the victim of the crime for reporting purposes, if the property is recovered it is returned to the owner. If there is no recovery, the owner receives the fair market value from his/her insurance company.

The broader larceny/theft laws recognize that the taking may be accomplished in a variety of ways, such as:

1. **theft by trick,** such as con games and swindles;
2. **theft by receiving stolen property,** meaning knowingly receiving and disposing of property he/she should have known or knew was stolen;
3. **theft by deception**—for example, the removal of a price sticker from one item for sale and replacing it with a less expensive sticker;[8]
4. **theft by fraud,** illustrated by the unauthorized use of another's credit card, using someone else's medical insurance card or Social Security number to get benefits, and "pump and dump" stock schemes,

whereby a stock is heavily promoted—after the stock runs up in price, its promoters dump it;

5. **theft of services,** covering such things as "skipping out" on hotel, restaurant, and bar bills, or illegally connecting or reconnecting an electrical meter.

In states with comprehensive larceny/theft laws, the crime of embezzlement has often disappeared, because the language of the larceny/theft law usually provides a means to bring charges for that conduct, often by a crime titled **theft by conversion.** Where it remains, the elements of embezzlement are the same as the traditional larceny charge, with the addition that a person who has been entrusted with something of valuable converts it to their own purpose or use in contravention of his/her legal obligation.

SHOPLIFTING AND ORGANIZED RETAIL CRIME (ORC)

SHOPLIFTING

In the United States, **shoplifting** produces losses of $33.1 billion annually with an average loss of $120.[9] Security experts calculate that for every $40 dollars stolen, only one dollar of merchandise is recovered. A significant problem is that there is no single profile of a shoplifter; they can be ordinary people or professional thieves.[10] Slightly more men (55%) than women (45%) shoplift, although women take higher-value items, juveniles account for roughly 33% of all cases.[11] These types of offenses are most likely to occur on Saturdays (18%) and Fridays (15%), and 60% of all cases occur between noon and 6:00 P.M.[12] There are also seasonal variations in shoplifting, with spikes in activity just before students go back to school in August, before Christmas, Easter, and when schools are letting out for summer. There are five types of shoplifters: (1) kleptomaniacs or those who have a compulsion to steal; (2) amateurs, who steal on impulse or because of peer pressure; (3) professionals, who are the least numerous but produce the largest losses; (4) drug users, who steal to support their habit, often selling what they take to criminal fences; and (5) "desperate straits" people, such as vagrants or the homeless and mothers who cannot afford items for their babies.

Retail establishments combat shoplifting by a combination of prevention strategies, such as sales staff greeting customers to make them feel singled out, posting signs about prosecuting shoplifters, placing expensive items in locked cases, putting on display only one of a pair of items, keeping aisles uncluttered to facilitate observation, roving employees and uniformed security officers, using electronic tags, and placing dummy surveillance cameras in plain sight. In recent years, "clamshell blisters" have gained popularity. This type of packaging seals a product in a clear plastic container, which allows 360-degree visibility of the product and is difficult to open. Retailers also use a strategy of apprehension that involves the use of observable, real surveillance cameras, "spy cameras" (for example, inside of clocks, smoke detector sprinklers, and heads of mannequins), observation ports, and the use of store security to work the floor. *Source tagging* is used widely—merchants place a small insert between the pages of a book or in a package of tools; the tag emits a narrowband radio frequency that triggers an alarm if the item has not been scanned.

Investigators working a shoplift detail should be alert for customers in a retail establishment who (1) avoid contact with sales personnel; (2) pick up a small item and wander about the store because they may finally palm it, and leave; (3) "have their heads on swivels" to assess their opportunity to steal; (4) wear baggy clothing or coats in weather not requiring it; (5) distract sales personnel or serve as shields so their partner can take and conceal items; (6) make repeated trips to fitting rooms, sometimes to wear store merchandise out under the clothes they wear; and (7) carry large handbags or push strollers in which items can quickly be concealed.

Theft by employees includes such activities as the removal of products, supplies, merchandise, money, data, information, and intellectual property.[13] Estimates vary across studies, but roughly 50% of all shoplifting is done by employees. The annual cost of embezzlement and employee theft is between $20 and $90 billion and upward of $240 billion if thefts of intellectual property are included; it is believed that 30%–50% of all business failures are caused by embezzlement and employee theft.[14]

ORGANIZED RETAIL CRIME (ORC)

Shoplifting has long suffered from the misperception that it is "small-time crime." Yet, its previously noted annual losses of $37.4 billion dwarf the combined annual losses of burglary ($4 billion) and motor vehicle theft ($7.9 billion).[15] Recognition of such facts has led to important new initiatives in combating shoplifting and other crimes against retailers. In 2006 legislation was signed creating an Organized Retail Theft Task Force at the FBI and mandating the creation of a public database on retail theft. A related database already exists, the National Retail Federation's (NRF) Retail Loss Prevention Intelligence Network (RLPIN), which was designed with the assistance of the FBI and other law-enforcement agencies.

Two terms that have emerged recently are **organized retail theft (ORT)** and **organized retail crime (ORC).** ORT refers to the problem of significant losses to retailers caused by crews or rings of often mobile professional shoplifters. ORC has emerged as a broader term and includes not only professional shoplifters but also other associated problems such as thefts from merchandise distribution centers, truck hijacking, credit card fraud, counterfeit goods, and the fences and other outlets for stolen merchandise.

Target is one of the largest retail stores in the United States, operating more than 1,700 stores in 49 states nationwide and employing more than 350,000 people. Target has focused their attention on organized retail crime (ORC) by developing a specialized investigative model. The Target model focuses on forensic evidence in four primary areas:

- clarification of images from video;
- photographic comparisons;
- suspicious and suspect vehicle identification;
- latent fingerprint identification and comparison with other crimes involving Target.

After a meticulous and time consuming investigation comparing criminal activity in multiple states via their real-time investigative process, the Target investigative team discovered a string of broken X-Box and PlayStation 3 game consoles that were fraudulently returned to retail stores in multiple locations. The team discovered a sophisticated and well-organized ring of criminals that were purchasing new game consoles at retail stores, removing the working hard drives, replacing them with broken hardware and counterfeit serial numbers, and returning the malfunctioning systems for a full refund. They then sold the new machines through various online auction websites. The Target team was able to positively identify the thieves actively working in several states. Criminal felony indictments eventually stopped the multimillion-dollar ORC ring.[16]

▲ FIGURE 15-3   Gang tattoos
(© Yuri Cortez/AFP/Getty Images)

ORC offenders range from independent, loosely tied together crews to more organized entities, including traditional crime families to the ultraviolent transnational gangs such as Mara Salvatrucha (MS-13). While some ORC groups may essentially specialize in crimes against retailers, others, like MS-13, have diverse interests, including alien, drug, and gun smuggling. One MS-13 leader has called for gang action against volunteer border patrol groups, such as the Arizona Minutemen, because that state is often a gateway into the United States from Mexico for their activities. Some ORCs run by persons with ties to Middle Eastern countries wired "profits" to Jordan, Egypt, and Palestine, where they were allegedly used to finance terrorist organizations such as Hamas and Hezbollah; tracing the money once it reaches unfriendly foreign countries has proven difficult, but it seems clear that some ORC profits are used to finance terrorism.[17]

Some of the most violent organizations, MS-13 members have long worn their numerous tattoos with pride (Figure 15-3). However, continued pressure from federal, state, and local investigators has resulted in a number of indictments and convictions of the easily identifiable gang members. Consequently, some MS-13 leaders have quietly encouraged members to be less ostentatious with the tattoos.

ORC offenders are known to have paid illegal immigrants, the homeless, and drug addicts to steal items for them (for example, $1.00 for each can of baby formula). Because some of the people in these categories might shoplift on their own, it is difficult for investigators to know exactly what they are dealing with when they make some shoplifting arrests. Yet, it is important to try to find out not only from a case investigation standpoint but also because of the potential national security implications.

Some ORC operations have their own warehouses chock full of stolen goods, which are sold through controlled convenience stores and neighborhood stores, flea markets, and other outlets, as well as shipped to unsuspecting wholesalers. Some stolen goods have expiration dates ("use by" or "use before") on them, such as diabetes-testing and teeth-whitening strips, batteries, baby formula, condoms, pharmaceuticals, and food products. The public health is endangered when expiration dates on stored stolen products are altered to make them marketable. This endangerment also exists when other items, such as frozen dinners, are allowed to thaw and then are refrozen or stored at improper temperatures before being sold.

COPPER AND OTHER PRECIOUS METAL THEFT

As the price of copper rises above $4.00 per pound, the number of thefts from electrical companies, construction sites, utilities, telephone lines, cell towers, air conditioners, transformer units, and even catalytic converters in newer model cars also dramatically increases (Figure 15-4). Copper and other precious metal (for example, platinum, gold and silver alloys, zinc) thefts have become so prolific that in 2008 the FBI developed a specific intelligence report focused on the theft of copper as a major threat to critical infrastructure within the United States.[18] According to the report, the theft of copper and other precious metals is conducted by individuals as well as organized transnational groups that work independently and in loose association with large fencing operations and the sale of contraband. The theft of these metals is spurred by several important factors:

- Since 2001 the price of commodities (especially copper) has dramatically climbed from $1 per pound to over $4 per pound on the Comex division of the New York Mercantile Exchange. As a result, the number of thefts as well as the monetary loss from such thefts has skyrocketed across the country.
- The trade and sale of copper is poorly regulated and is fueled by supply and demand at a global level. With robust economies and national building programs, the countries of China and India have spiked the demand for copper. Thieves can easily sell raw copper to metal shops and recyclers capitalizing on these higher spikes in price.
- There is little means to associate stolen raw copper to a specific crime scene. Therefore, even if large caches of copper wire or gold alloy are located and found, tying these products to a specific case is almost impossible.
- The theft of copper and other precious metals is relatively new, and various database development, focused task-force operations, and laws designed to capture important scrap-metal transactions have only recently been implemented by local and federal law-enforcement agencies to curb the problem.

One of the newest and most important scrap-metal tracking systems developed to assist law enforcement is the LeadsOnline Metal Theft Investigative System (MTIS). The electronic reporting system records important seller information that is collected by recyclers and scrap-metal dealers—such as an image of the driver's license and vehicle of the seller, type and quantity of the metal sold, digital images of fingerprints, and, of course, pictures of the seller as well as the metal being sold.[19] The MTIS is being used in several areas (New York City, Dallas, San Francisco, and the entire State of Arkansas) with more than 3,000 law-enforcement users and is bolstered by recent state legislation that requires all scrap-metal dealers and pawn shop owners to report large-quantity copper

▲ **FIGURE 15-4   Copper theft**
Transformers contain approximately 50 lbs. of copper with the potential to yield $200 of profit if sold to a scrap-metal dealer. (© Ultimate Group, LLC/Alamy)

and precious metal sales to the police. The MTIS is compatible with NCIC and is an official eBay partner, and serves as an important means to investigate copper and other precious-metal thefts across multiple jurisdictions.

INVESTIGATIVE POINTS

When investigating a larceny/theft, investigators should consider the following strategies.[20]

- Gather a detailed list of the stolen items, including serial numbers and photos.
- Assess the modus operandi compared to other crimes within close geographic proximity.
- Examine other reports and field interviews for suspicious individuals, vehicles, and activity in the area.
- Check pawn shops and chop shops.
- Obtain and review surveillance video.
- Collect intelligence by carefully questioning arrestees charged in unrelated offenses after Mirandization and obtaining information on the offense for which they are charged.
- If the stolen property is a cell phone, laptop, or iPad, it may be tracked via GPS.

IDENTITY THEFT AND FOLLOW-ON CRIMES

Identity theft, which began to emerge as a problem in the 1990s, has been called the "crime of the new millennium."[21] The normal daily activities of consumers include purchasing tickets and merchandise online, cashing checks, using credit and debit cards, and renting videos—all of which result in information being shared. At all points where personal data is collected, processed, or stored, there are opportunities for identity theft.[22] Identity theft may be the fastest growing crime of any kind in our society. In 2009 almost 8 million Americans were victimized by this crime with combined individual costs and losses to businesses placed at nearly $50 billion.[23] The person whose identity is stolen is one victim; the businesses that suffered losses owing to the criminal use of the stolen identity represent another group of victims. Estimates of the cost to individual victims to clear their names vary, but sources maintain that it requires as few as 24 to as much as 600 hours of effort and from $80 to $1,500 worth of lost earnings to correct credit and other related problems. Over 1,300 victims have been the subjects of criminal investigations, arrests, or wrongful convictions.[24]

Identity crimes involve two types of criminal acts: (1) identity theft and (2) the **follow-on crimes** that occur, such as credit card and check fraud.

HOW IDENTITY THEFT OCCURS

Abundant opportunities exist for identity thieves to get the personal information of people they victimize. Among methods used to obtain data are these:

1. Stealing wallets and purses containing identification, bank, credit, membership, and other types of cards.
2. Stealing mail, which provides bank and credit statements, preapproved credit offers, Social Security numbers, and other personal data. Some thieves follow mail carriers at a distance and then steal from mailboxes that appear to have just had a large stack of mail delivered. Alternatively, they might cruise affluent neighborhoods looking for raised red flags on mailboxes and stealing outgoing correspondence.
3. Going to the Post Office and completing a change of address form to divert mail to another location.
4. Rummaging through the victims' trash, or the trash of businesses, to "mine" for personal data—a practice described as **dumpster diving.**
5. Fraudulently obtaining the victim's credit report by posing as a potential landlord or employer.
6. Stealing personal identification from the victim's home.
7. Opportunistically using information from lost wallets and purses.

8. Family members, relatives, roommates and acquaintances misappropriating information.
9. Stealing personal data assistants (PDAs) and smartphones, such as Blackberries and iPhones, and laptops and tablets; this area may become more significant in the future, because more than one spyware virus for PDAs and smartphones are known to exist.
10. Obtaining personal information by hacking into home and business computers or by such tactics as downloading spyware programs. (Identity thieves posing as a legitimate business duped an Atlanta-area company out of personal information for perhaps as many as 400,000 people nationally.[25])
11. Stealing information from employers, medical and insurance offices, student records, and other locations or bribing corrupt employees to provide the victims' personal data.
12. Scamming victims out of personal information on the Internet is done by a technique known as **phishing.**[26] Two common phishing scams are sending an e-mail to potential victims that appears to be from a legitimate source, such as eBay, AOL, Yahoo, Best Buy, Wells Fargo, a credit card company, or a bank, and asking that they update their account information data. The second method involves using an e-mail to notify victims they have won a prize, such as the Canadian or Netherlands Lottery, but need to pay a processing fee to receive it, thereby tricking the victims into completing an accompanying credit form.[27]

There are numerous variations on these two methods. One is an e-mail promising a free credit report subject to the recipient completing a personal information form. A second method is an e-mail from the U.S. Internal Revenue Service offering an $80 credit if they will participate in an online satisfaction survey, Form IR-2007-148, which also requires the disclosure of personal information.

Any time a possible victim reports an unsolicited e-mail contact from the IRS it is a phishing attack, because the IRS neither initiates unsolicited contacts that way nor does it ask for passwords and other related information. Other bogus forms falsely attributed to the IRS include IR-2007- ending in 49, 75, 104, 109, or 116. Victims should be directed not to open attachments associated with such e-mails and to report the attack to *phishing@irs.gov*. Since this mailbox was established in 2006, more than 30,000 taxpayers have reported 400 separate phishing incidents.
13. **Shoulder surfing,** or watching and listening from a nearby location as victims identify themselves and use credit cards or write checks or are punching in their long-distance calling-card numbers.[28]
14. Using technology, such as skimmers, to obtain personal data. **Skimmers** are pager-sized data collection devices that cost roughly $300. These are attached

How debit card skimming works

Here are some of the ways thieves steal bank information from ATMs and point-of-sale debit card readers:

Switch the entire device
Thieves replace the entire card-reading device with their own, then recover the machine after it's filled with customers' data.

Install a card skimmer
Thieves insert a device into an existing machine—a skimmer—that reads account info from users' cards; this device may transfer that info wirelessly.

Install a new keypad
Thieves install their own keypad over the existing one, enabling them to capture personal identification numbers as users enter them.

Install a camera
Thieves install a tiny camera that enables thieves to see PINs as they are entered on the keypad; a transmission antenna sends the information wirelessly.

Store card reader

Thief's card reader

Card skimmer

Thief's key pad

Hidden micro camera

This is an ATM as it would normally appear. Note the concave card slot built into the machine's face.

A magnetic card reading device over the card slot could catch users unaware, and such devices are getting more sophisticated.

How to protect yourself:

• ATMs at banks may be safer than those at gas stations and stores since banks have more experience in providing security.	• Credit card transactions provide more security because you have more time to dispute questionable charges.	• Don't use an ATM or payment machine if the equipment appears altered, such as if there's glue residue around the keypad or card slot.	• Feel the keypad or card slot to see if they are raised, suggesting thieves have inserted an extra layer of equipment.	• Jiggle the card as you withdraw it from the slot; the movement might shake loose a card skimmer.	• As you enter your PIN, cover the keypad with your other hand.	• If you're having trouble using an ATM, don't accept help from strangers.	• Check your bank statements regularly for suspicious activity.

▲ **FIGURE 15-5   How debit card skimming works**

(Identitytheft911, Wells Fargo Bank, Los Altos [Calif.] Police Department, *San Jose Mercury News; Dallas Morning News*, October 20, 2010, p.21a.)

to the telephone line running between a business's legitimate card swipe and a telephone jack. During what appears to be a normal transaction, the skimmer reads and stores the data, which is retrieved later by the user. There are also portable skimmers through which waiters and clerks can run victims' cards while they are in the back of the restaurant. More difficult to detect is "skimmer bug" software that can be inserted into point-of-sale terminals. These bugs store the data read in the terminals' circuitry, and then the modem is used to send the data to the thieves' computers. Some banks have found dispensers filled with bank pamphlets attached to the side of their ATMs. What they discovered is that these thief-placed dispensers actually contain miniature cameras that record the names, debit card numbers, and codes of ATM users[29] (Figure 15-5).

15. Employing *card trappers*. One example of this involves attaching a false card slot to the front of the ATM. As legitimate users enter their codes, shoulder surfers wait nearby or use binoculars or a camera with a telephoto lens to get the accounts' access codes. Unable to retrieve their cards, custom-

ers leave the ATM, and the thieves have both the access codes and the ATM cards.[30]

16. Picking up discarded computers. From these, thieves recover sensitive files between 33% and 50% of the time.[31]

17. Sending a fraudulent letter and IRS-like form to nonresident aliens who have earned income in the United States. The form is an altered version of IRS Form W-8BEN, "Certificate of Foreign Status of Beneficial Owner for United States Tax Withholding." This form asks for many types of personal information and account numbers and passwords. United States citizens receive a similar phony IRS Form, W-9095, the intent of which is also identity theft.

18. An innovative and novel twist on sending a letter from the IRS, is the new scam-letter from the FBI that informs the recipient that they have been the "victim" of a fraud and that the FBI is investigating their case. The unsuspecting individual is then asked for important personal information on which further fraud and theft scams can be conducted. These letters can be received via e-mail or the postal mail and can be quite elaborate (Figure 15-6).

THE FBI *FEDERAL BUREAU OF INVESTIGATION*

OFFICIAL NOTICE

FBI Headquarters in Washington, D.C.
Federal Bureau of Investigation
J. Edgar Hoover Building
935 Pennsylvania Avenue, NW
Washington, D.C. 20535-0001
Tel: 203-413-1789
http://www.fbi.gov/libref/directors/directmain.htm

Attn: Beneficiary,

This is to officially inform you that it has come to our notice and we have thoroughly investigated with the help of our Intelligence Monitoring Network System that you are having an illegal Transaction with Impostors Claiming to be Mr. Tito Mboweni Republic of the Reserve Bank Governor Of South African,Maria Ramos ABSA Bank CEO ,Christo Luus General Manager ABSA BANK, none officials of ABSA Bank, FNB Banks, Dr. Mamphela Ramphele FNB, Kevin Chaplin,Dr Danny Jordan CEO of the 2010 fifa world cup,Dr Irvin Khoza: Chairman, 2010 fifa organization committee, Joseph S. Blatter Fifa President, Chief Competitions Officer Derek Blanckensee, Chief Security Officer Linda Mti, Chief Financial Officer Farouk Seedat, Chief Communications Officer Richard Mkhondo, Chief Operations Officer Nomfanelo Magwentshu, Chief IT & T Officer Phumlani Moholi, Chief Marketing and Commercial Officer Derek Carstens, Chief Transport and Logistics Officer Skhumbuzo Macozoma,are Impostors claiming to be the Federal Bureau of Investigation. During our Investigation, we noticed that the reason why you have not received your Payment is because you have not fulfilled your Financial Obligation given to you in respect of your Contract/Inheritance Payment.

Therefore, we have contacted the Federal Ministry of Finance on your Behalf and they have brought a solution to your problem by coordinating your payment in total USD$11,000.000.00 in an ATM CARD which you can use to withdraw money from any ATM MACHINE CENTER anywhere in the world with a maximum of $4000 to $5000 United States Dollars daily. You now have the lawful right to claim your fund in an ATM CARD. Since the Federal Bureau of Investigation is involved in this transaction, you have to be rest assured for this is 100% risk free it is our duty to protect the American Citizens, European Citizens, Asian Citizen and UK. All I want you to do is to contact the ATM CARD CENTER Via email for their requirements to proceed and procure your Approval Slip on your behalf which will cost you $300.00 only and note that your Approval Slip which contains details of the agent who will process your Transaction.

CONTACT INFORMATION
NAME: Mrs. Michelle Isaac
EMAIL: mrsmichelleisaac@yahoo.cn
Telephone Numbers: + 27 730-385-679

Do contact Mrs. Michelle Isaac of the ATM CARD center with your details:
FULL NAME:
HOME ADDRESS:
TELL:
CELL:
CURRENT OCCUPATION:
BANK NAME:

So your files would be updated after which he will send the payment Information's which you'll use in making payment of $300.00 via Money Gram

▲**FIGURE 15-6   Scam-letter**
A scam-letter can be very sophisticated. Note the "official notice," the seal of the FBI taken from their website, and the picture of Robert Mueller. Most interesting is the "note" attached to the letter that informs the receiver to forward any "impostors" to the official FBI "ATM Card Center."

Transfer for the procurement of your Approval Slip after which the Delivery of your ATM CARD will be affected to your designated home Address without any further delay. Mrs. Michelle Isaac will reply you with the secret code (3898 ATM CARD).

We advice you get back to the payment office after you have contacted the ATM SWIFT CARD CENTER and we do await your response so we can move on with our Investigation and make sure your ATM SWIFT CARD gets to you. Thanks and hope to read from you soon.

FBI Director Robert S.Mueller III.

Robert S. Mueller, III
Director
Since *September 4, 2001–Present*

Note: Do disregard any email you get from any impostors or offices Claiming to be in possession of your ATM CARD, you are hereby advised only to be in contact with Mrs. Michelle Isaac of the ATM CARD center who is the rightful person to deal with in regards to your ATM CARD PAYMENT and forward any emails you get from impostors to this office so we could act upon and commence investigation.

▲ **FIGURE 15-6** Scam-letter (*concluded*)

19. Calling a home and telling the person that because he or she failed to come to court as required by "the jury duty summons sent to their residence" that the judge is going to issue a bench warrant for his/her arrest. When the panicked recipient of the calls insists no such summons was sent, the "Clerk of the Court" says "perhaps there has been a mistake, let's verify some information" and gets enough personal information to commit identity theft.

20. Offering "debt consolidation" services by phone, promising the unwary that by working with the holders of their credit cards, they can immediately get up to 50% of their debt immediately forgiven, and the one remaining monthly payment "will be less than 20% of the total you are paying now; all I need to get you started right now is your credit card numbers."

21. In yet another scheme, scammers are stealing Social Security numbers assigned to children who do not have bank accounts. The stolen Social Security numbers are then used to develop phony credit profiles, credit cards, bank accounts, and identification. Thieves run up huge debts that will never be paid off. These schemes unfortunately are quite successful and go undetected for long periods of

time, until the rightful owner of the Social Security number applies for credit; if that person is a child, it may be years before the scheme is ever detected.

The U.S. Department of Education's (USDOE) Office of Inspector General reports that some students are receiving calls from people falsely claiming that they represent USDOE and offering them scholarships or grants. This financial assistance can be immediately obtained for a $249 processing fee that the student can pay with their credit card number. The USDOE does not charge a processing fee for financial assistance.[32]

FOLLOW-ON CRIMES

Once armed with enough stolen personal identification data, the process of identity theft is executed and follow-on crimes are committed by:

1. Calling credit card companies, asking them to change the address "your" bill is mailed to and quickly running up charges on accounts. The victim

may be unaware of any problems for a month or more. This practice is called **account takeover.**

2. Opening up new, fraudulent, credit card accounts using the victim's name, banking information, Social Security information, and other data. The first hint of trouble for a victim may be when a card company or collection agency calls because the "account" is in serious arrears.

3. Establishing new accounts for wireless telephone service, which go unpaid.

4. Opening bank accounts on which they write worthless checks.

5. Using counterfeit checks and debit cards to drain victims' banking accounts.

6. Purchasing cars by taking out loans using the victim's name, defaulting on payments and then fleeing with what is now a stolen vehicle.

7. Using the victim's identity if involved in an automobile accident, stopped for a traffic violation, or arrested by the police. If released by the police or

bonded out of jail following an arrest, they don't show up for any required court appearance and an arrest warrant is issued in the victim's name.[33]

8. Fraudulently obtaining other types of identification, including passports, drivers' licenses, Department of Defense cards, and Social Security numbers.

9. Committing mail, investment, telemarketing, and Social Security frauds.

From the preceding list, three main patterns of identity theft can be established: (1) financial identity theft, when the thief uses the information for financial gain; (2) criminal identity theft, whereby the imposter provides someone else's name to law-enforcement officers issuing a traffic citation or conducting a criminal investigation; and (3) identity cloning, which permits the thief to establish a "new life."[34] In Chapter 7, the use of visual link analysis software was discussed and an application of it shown. Figure 15-7 demonstrates the use of this technique applied to an identity theft. In terms of main patterns of identity

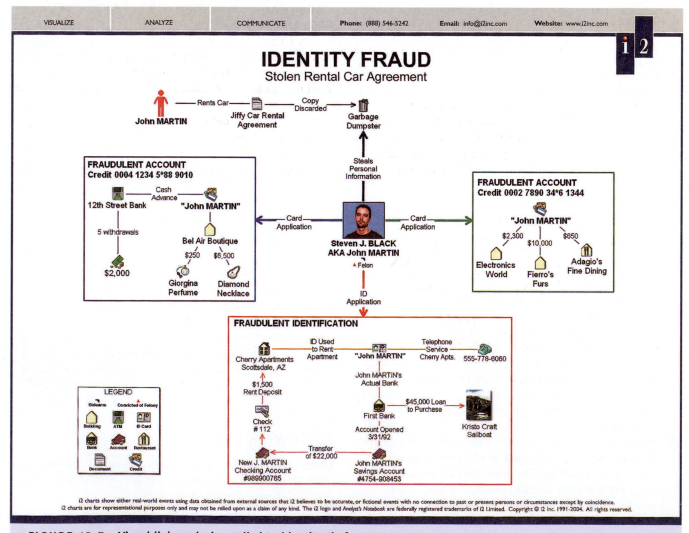

▲ **FIGURE 15-7   Visual link analysis applied to identity theft case**

theft, the thief, Steven Black, is involved with two patterns: (1) financial identity theft and (2) establishing a "new life."

INVESTIGATION OF IDENTITY THEFT AND FOLLOW-ON CASES

From an investigatory view, the co-entwining of identity theft and follow-on crimes almost invariably means investigating multiple crimes, with a number of victims. Additionally, these crimes may be committed in many different jurisdictions, requiring careful case coordination and information sharing among the investigative agencies involved. All states and the District of Columbia have specific identity theft statutes;[35] Federal jurisdiction comes from United States Code, Title 18, Section 1028, The Identity Theft and Assumption Deterrence Act of 1998. This means there is often joint jurisdiction in identity theft cases. Depending on the nature and the specifics of the case, federal agencies with which state and local investigators may work include the FBI, the Secret Service, the Social Security Administration, the Post Office, and Homeland Security. In deciding whether there will be federal or state jurisdiction, one consideration will be the level of seriousness and extent of harm, with the most flagrant cases often becoming the responsibility of the jurisdiction with the most substantial criminal penalties.

Figure 15-8 summarizes how personal information is obtained by identity thieves. Note that the "big three," which account for more than 50% of cases, are lost/stolen wallet, checkbook, or credit card; friends/acquaintances/relatives with access; and corrupt employees with access

to the information. Unless the available information dictates otherwise, the big three may initially provide fruitful avenues for the investigation. Eighty-five percent of victims report that their first realization about the theft comes from a negative contact[36] (for example, a credit card company soliciting payment of past due amounts) or a collection agency. This means investigators are responding to calls where victims are angry, confused, and worried about their financial futures and personal reputations. Another immediate difficulty for the investigator is that most identity thefts and the follow-up crimes come to light only one to six months after they began,[37] meaning that victims' recollections about how and when the identity theft occurred may not be very helpful and that documentary evidence is of vital importance in working the case.

Figure 15-9 is an identity theft and follow-on crimes checklist, with emphasis on the unique types of determinations which need to be made.

CREDIT CARD FRAUD

The link between identity theft and credit card fraud was established earlier in this chapter. However, there are also other types of credit card frauds. Altogether these frauds create losses of $2 billion globally according to the Federal Trade Commission. Credit card fraud is particularly prevalent in this country because Americans hold 71% of all credit cards issued worldwide.[38] Credit card fraud has become so lucrative that some organized crime rings and drug dealers have shifted their "careers" to engage in it because it is simple to execute and quickly

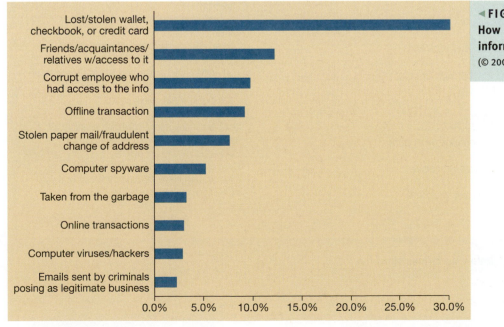

▶FIGURE 15-8
How was victim's personal information obtained?
(© 2005 Javelin Strategy & Research)

Completed	Task
	How did victim become aware of identity theft?
_____	Fraudulent charges on credit card bill(s)
_____	Received bills for accounts not opened
_____	Found irregularities in credit report
_____	Contacted by creditor demanding payment
_____	Denied a loan
_____	Sued for debt victim did not incur
_____	Not receiving bills from legitimate accounts
_____	Received legal filing, such as bankruptcy
_____	Denied employment
_____	Driver's license suspended for violations not committed
_____	Incident report completed naming victim as suspect
_____	Victim advised of warrant or arrested
_____	Other (specify): _____
_____	What date did victim become aware of ID theft?
_____	When reported? Explain any gaps.
_____	When did the first fraudulent activity begin?
_____	What is the presently known chronology of fraudulent activities?
_____	Assign victim the responsibility for describing in as much detail as possible activities associated with all fraudulent activities.
_____	What is the full name, address, birth date, and other identifying information that the fraudulent activities were committed under?
_____	What documents and identifying information were stolen or compromised? If known, when?
_____	Credit card: list banks, contact information, and account numbers.
_____	ATM card: contact information and account numbers.
_____	Get voided check or checking account number, bank info, and contact information.
_____	Brokerage and/or stock account numbers: who holds accounts, contact information.
_____	Passport: obtain all relevant information, including country issuing.
_____	Driver's license or license number; state issuing.
_____	State identity card: number, state issuing.
_____	Social Security card or number, get number.
_____	Birth certificate (identify state and locality issuing), number.
_____	Resident alien green card or other documents, get all particulars.
_____	Bank and other account password/secret word, such as mother's maiden name.
_____	Other (specify).
_____	Unknown.
	To the best of the victim's knowledge, what crimes have been committed?
_____	Use of victim's actual credit cards or numbers without authorization?
_____	Opening new credit card accounts in victim's name?

Completed	Task
_____	Opening utility/phone accounts in victim's name?
_____	Unauthorized withdrawals from victim's bank accounts?
_____	Loans taken out in victim's name?
_____	Access to/withdrawals from securities/investments accounts?
_____	Obtaining government benefits in victim's name?
_____	Obtaining employment in victim's name?
_____	Obtaining medical services or insurance in victim's name?
_____	Committing crimes attributed to victim?
_____	Check fraud?
_____	Passport/Visa fraud?
_____	Other (specify).
	To assist in pinpointing when and by whom ID was stolen or compromised, determine whether in the last 6 months if:
_____	Victim carried social security daily.
_____	Kept PINs and passwords in wallet or purse.
_____	Had mail stolen. What? When? Get any reports.
_____	While away, mail kept at Post Office/collected by someone else.
_____	Traveled on business or pleasure outside of home vicinity. When? Where?
_____	Mail diverted by forwarding request to Post Office or in a way unknown to the victim.
_____	Expected new credit card which did not arrive. Get particulars. Issuer contacted by victim? Report made?
_____	Garbage was stolen or gone through.
_____	Left stamped payment bills in unlocked mailbox.
_____	Service providers (maids, delivery, electricians, etc.) in home.
_____	Placed documents with personal information in garbage without shredding—e.g., envelopes with victim's name on them, bank statements, payroll stubs.
_____	Placed pre-approved credit cards and "convenience" checks in garbage without shredding.
_____	Threw ATM and credit card receipts away without shredding.
_____	Shared PIN and password information with someone else.
_____	Home/office/car burglarized? When? Reported? If not, why?
_____	Checkbook, wallet, purse stolen.
_____	Provided personal information to service providers—e.g., blood collection agency, financial adviser, took out auto/health/life insurance. Identify, get details.
_____	Copy of credit report issued to someone claiming a legitimate business interest or using victim's name.

continued

▲ FIGURE 15-9   Identity theft/follow-on crimes checklist

Completed	Task	Completed	Task
_____	Victim authorized a business to obtain credit report information. Which? When?	_____	What information does the victim have about the suspects?
_____	Some personal information was available on the Net—e.g., genealogy or school reunion site.	_____	Run records checks on suspects identified by victim.
_____	Gave personal information to telephone solicitor, telemarketer, "government worker" working door-to-door, charitable organization, entered contest, or to claim prize supposedly won.	_____	Have the victim list all banks which have legitimate accounts, identify accounts which have fraudulent activities.
_____	Made legitimate purchase, but clerk was out of sight with card during transaction.	_____	Have the victim list all legitimate credit card companies and banks which have issued credit cards, identify those with fraudulent activities.
_____	A new credit card account was just opened by the victim.	_____	Have victim specify all legitimate utility company accounts, identify those with fraudulent activities.
_____	Victim's home/property was refinanced.	_____	Have victim identify all legitimate loans, leases, and mortgages, list those with fraudulent activities.
_____	Victim provided information to obtain lease.		
_____	Victim opened new utility account(s).	_____	Have victim list all merchants with whom he/she has a store credit account—e.g., pharmacies and department stores. List all fraudulent activities.
_____	Victim applied for occupational or other license or permit.		
_____	Victim took out new loan or finished paying one.	_____	Have victim list all financial institutions where fraudulent accounts were opened.
_____	Victim applied for government benefits.	_____	Victim should list all fraudulent documents obtained in his/her name.
_____	Victim was featured in local paper, industry publications, on Internet, school site.		
_____	Online purchases were made using victim's credit card.	_____	Provide assistance to the victim by suggesting he/she contact the three major credit reporting companies, Equifax, TransUnion, and Experian, as well as financial institutions, the Department of Motor Vehicles, Social Security, and other entities. Victim should do this immediately by phone and follow up within 48 hours with letters, asking for return receipts.
_____	Released information to family member/friend.		
_____	Over the past 6 months, what purchases did the victim make from which sites, when, and for what merchandise?		
_____	Have the victim list all persons, businesses, nonprofits, or others to which he/she provided Social Security number.		
_____	Does the victim have his/her Social Security number imprinted on checks?	_____	Provide any agency ID Theft Victim Assistant packages available. This information should include web addresses, such as the one at the Federal Trade Commission, which provides detailed guidance and sample forms and letters to use. Advise victim to log and carefully file all correspondence and return receipts from the Post Office.
_____	Get a list of all places such checks were tendered.		
_____	Has victim or others written his/her Social Security and driver's license numbers on checks tendered?		
_____	List all such instances.		
_____	Are identity crimes affecting the victim's business?		
_____	Whom does the victim identify as possible suspects? For what reasons?		

(Source: This information was adapted from content on an undated "Identity Theft" compact disk prepared by the Secret Service, United States Postal Inspection Service, and the International Association of Chiefs of Police.)

▲ **FIGURE 15-9   Identity theft/follow-on crimes checklist (*concluded*)**

profitable.[39] Figure 15-10 illustrates a credit card fraud which simply involves the illegal use of the victim's credit card account.

The quickest exact growing sector of credit card fraud may be the counterfeiting of credit cards; the continuing availability of new technologies has helped counterfeiters produce exact replicas of bona-fide cards, including the so-called "hidden" security features, such as holograms, used by legitimate credit card issuers.[40] One source of the necessary equipment is the Far East; another is corrupt vendors. A Canadian vendor was arrested for supplying equipment to thieves and terrorist organizations as part of a multimillion dollar credit and debit card ring.[41] In the advanced payment scheme, the accounts created by credit cards that were obtained through yet-to-be detected thefts, identity theft, or counterfeiting are overpaid by the "card holder," with a bad check. The money is then quickly withdrawn by a cash advance before the check clears the bank. There are also other scams associated with credit cards. In the advanced fee scheme, a person with poor credit pays in advance to have their record "repaired." Other variants of advanced fee schemes involve victims paying by credit card to have a company find them new jobs, work-at-home employment (such as stuffing envelopes), scholarships, and low-cost car or other loans. These offers may appear in newspaper ads, be delivered by the postal service, or appear in the victim's e-mail inbox. Once victims have been taken in by a credit card or other type of fraud, criminals compile lists with their names to sell to other defrauders, including those who contact the victims with an offer to recover their lost assets.

▲ **FIGURE 15-10** **Visual link analysis applied to credit card fraud**

(© i2 Incorporated, 1991–2004. All rights reserved.)

CHECK FRAUD

Check fraud (Figure 15-11) is the forgery, alteration, counterfeiting, or knowing issuance of a check on an account that is closed or has insufficient funds to cover the amount for which the check is written.[42] People may innocently "bounce" a check because of nonsufficient funds owing to a math error in their checkbook or mistiming a deposit. Investigation and prosecution rarely happen, because the check is made good, and the necessary fees are paid.

Others write checks they know are no good and cannot cover; people leaving one state for another may write a bad check because they think there is no consequence; and others write checks on accounts they or others have closed. **Check kiters** open accounts at several banks, knowingly, issuing a check that overdraws their account at Bank 1 and then depositing a check in that account from their Bank 2 account to cover the first worthless check.

This process is repeated with ever-increasing amounts until the scheme falls apart because it cannot be continued indefinitely. An employee with the standing authority to issue checks may sign unauthorized checks or forge the manager's or owner's signature. Among the signs that an employee in a position of trust such as bookkeeper or business manager may be or is committing check based crimes are these:

1. checks made payable to the business or to cash by customers are deposited in an account the employee controls;
2. replacement checks to the employee are issued when there is no need to do so, for example, the original check was not lost;
3. payroll advances to the employee are not subtracted from the next paycheck;
4. there is no documentation explaining why checks are made payable to "Cash" or what happened to them;

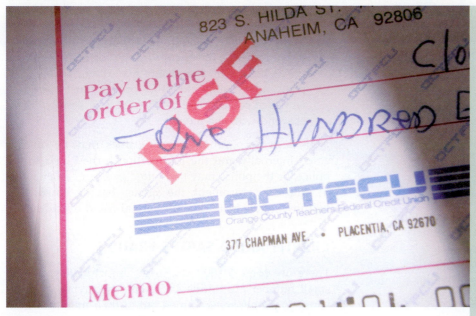

5. the employee is reimbursed for unexplained expenses;
6. the employee keeps promising to show the business owner the bank statements, but it never seems to happen;
7. vendors and suppliers are complaining about slow and late payments.

Altogether, check fraud produces losses of some $24 billion annually,[43] and in addition to the practices previously described, others involve more sophisticated techniques. In one, an individual learns that he/she has gotten a job applied for online, which offers "signing bonuses" of $2,500 or more to "new hires." The "new employer" advises the "employee" that by mistake a larger amount in the $19,000 to $50,000 range has been sent to the employee, who is instructed to keep the signing bonus but wire the remaining funds to the employer, often at a European location. Of course, the job doesn't really exist, and the check sent by "mistake" is fraudulent. Because the "new employee" deposited the check originally, it is his/her responsibility to make it good. A wrinkle on this technique is when someone shows up to buy a car or other large-ticket item with a counterfeit cashier's check from a bank or a credit union that was "made out for too much," and the unsuspecting seller not only gives the buyer a check for the difference but also allows the suspect to drive off with the car, which may be quickly sold, creating an additional profit for the suspect. Very good counterfeit checks can be produced by using around $10,000 to purchase a computer system and software. It is estimated that counterfeit checks account for about $1 billion in annual losses.

Checks can be altered by washing them in commonly available chemicals and then dried with little damage to the checks. This process removes ink from the check. The checks can then be scanned into a computer, many copies can quickly be printed, and the checks cashed for the amounts desired by the "payees," who are in on the scheme and may be using identification obtained through identity theft.

Listed below are some of the indicators that a check has been altered or counterfeited:

- There is no perforated edge; most checks should have perforation on one edge.
- The routing and fractional routing numbers are inconsistent and/or do not match the location of the bank listed on the check.
- The check contains spots or stains.
- The word "VOID" appears.

COUNTERFEITING

Although we most often associate counterfeiting with currency, there is a vast range of other types of counterfeiting, including stamps, checks, bonds, and securities, as well as ski lift, sporting event, rodeo, and concert tickets. None of these are just-emerging crimes; the 1966 Beatles concert in Cleveland was plagued with this problem.

Gangs counterfeiting Universal Product Codes (UPC) have been operating a number of years. UPC codes help with inventory control and proper pricing at the point of sale where cashiers scan in the price. In particular Wal-Mart, Lowe's, and Home Depot have been hard-hit, with

Wal-Mart's losses reaching $1.5 million.[44] The modus operandi was to counterfeit UPCs in large numbers at print shops or by using personal computers, enter the stores and affix these UPCs over real ones, thereby lowering the price of the item that would be scanned in at the point of sale:

A kitchen faucet worth $169 would suddenly wear a UPC code indicating the price to be $39 or a lighting fixture's price would shift from $249 to $55.[45] Later the same day at a different location for the same retailer, another person would show up—with the phony UPC removed—and get a refund for the actual amount; doing this several times per day easily netted $1,000 to $1,500 daily. False identifications were presented at the refund counter, including English or Irish passports.[46]

FRAUDS, SCAMS, AND CONS

The economic turndown and resulting recession since 2008 has heralded a new wave of frauds, scams, and cons. While the largest of these frauds involved investment and "Ponzi" schemes (discussed later in this chapter), a notable rise in not only the individual number but also the financial losses associated with fraud has been reported.[47] Losses ranged from a few hundred dollars attributed to classic charity cons to over $150 million dollars associated with the largest Medicare fraud in history.

VENDOR FRAUD

Virtually every unit of government and business are dependent on outside vendors who supply such things as office supplies, equipment, vehicles, merchandise for retail, and consulting services. Vendor fraud costs businesses more than $400 billion in losses annually. Among the fraudulent practices used by vendors are these:

1. Bidders colluding to set bids at a higher than warranted price per unit and bidders concealing they are insolvent or have a record of defaulting on their bids.
2. Providing employees in the procurement office with cash and other types of bribes, such as trips in exchange for being the winning bidder.
3. Substituting lower-costing or counterfeit goods to fulfill the terms of a bid.
4. Consultants or contractors overstating the number of days worked or the amount of materials required to do the job.
5. Submitting bogus invoices for office supplies or other goods in the hope they will be paid.

6. Bogus Yellow Page advertising. In the minds of most people the "Yellow Pages" are legitimate ads in the local telephone directory; however, because the phrase was never copyrighted or registered others can use it. Fraudsters may offer "yellow page" advertising and either produce just a few one-page copies for the subscribers or simply abscond with the money.

In large corporations, these crimes may be investigated internally and the information turned over to the police, or the police may be invited in at an earlier stage. In units of government, the agency having jurisdiction will investigate instances of criminal fraud by bidders.

CHARITY AND DISASTER FRAUDS

There are some 70,000 charities. Unfortunately, a very small number are frauds and create two types of problems: (1) people are scammed out of their money and do not get a tax deduction, and (2) public confidence in charities is undermined, making it harder for legitimate charities to raise funds for important causes. Sham charities are skillful at their pitches, using words that suggest good causes; included are terms such as veterans, hunger, children, and orphans. They also often use names that are similar to those of legitimate charities and religious organizations. These pitches are made in person at homes, with buckets at intersections, through the mail, and Internet solicitations. In the aftermath of the 9/11 attacks (2001), the earthquakes in Turkey (2004), the Indian Ocean Tsunami (2004), and Hurricanes Katrina (2005) and Earl (2010), sham charities used the tragic events to line their pockets.

INSURANCE FRAUD

Insurance frauds can be **hard fraud** or **soft fraud**.[48] Hard fraud is when someone deliberately fakes an injury, accident, theft, arson, or other loss to illegally collect from insurance companies.

Virgil made a car collision insurance claim, stating that he had been trying to avoid a deer and crashed into a wall. The insurer deemed the car a total loss, and the claim was paid. Later, the insurance company learned that Virgil's son Brian was driving the car even though he was not covered by the policy. Both were arrested on one felony count of insurance fraud.[49]

In contrast, soft fraud, also called opportunity fraud, involves normally honest people who tell "little white lies" and collect reimbursements to which they are not entitled, as in the case when the value of the items reported stolen in burglary is overstated. Too, insurance companies have been known to scam insurers by charging them more than is warranted or declaring bankruptcy and going out of business when faced with a flood of claims they cannot pay following a natural disaster. Other types of insurance frauds are discussed next.

Arson Fraud

Chapter 19, "Arson and Explosives," addresses arson fraud. Here, a case is offered because it illustrates the point that such frauds can go tragically wrong.

> Helen hired two local teenagers to "torch" her Tampa restaurant, Gram's County Kitchen, so she could collect insurance money. However, fumes from the gasoline the teenagers poured in the restaurant accidentally ignited, causing an explosion. One died and the other was permanently scarred.[50]

Automobile Fraud

One source of automobile fraud is staged accidents, which include the **swoop and squat,** the **drive down,** and the **paper accident.** In the swoop and squat, a car quickly cuts in front of a legitimate motorist, hits the brakes, and creates a rear-end collision for which repair and fake medical claims can be made (Figure 15-12). The drive down involves waving to another driver to go ahead and make a turn in the intersection or elsewhere and then driving into the car, making it appear that the struck vehicle is at fault. Paper accidents are exactly that: no

accident has taken place. Collusion is required by a body shop operator, who may even provide a wrecked car for the adjuster to inspect. By only filing for the cost of repairs, which are not done, the amount paid by the insurance is not out of line and therefore not scrutinized closely. Naturally, the insured and the body shop owner split the money for the repairs. Owners who cannot make their car payments, which often involve luxury cars, arrange to have them stolen, and the insurance pays for the car. Then the car is sent to a chop shop. The owner protects his/her credit record and receives some money from the chop shop profit. To make false claims of injuries in accidents believable, the collusion of a doctor is necessary. In one very aggressive case, a chiropractor had "runners" out scouting for accidents and recruiting people to his practice, where false treatment bills were submitted to insurers and false medical records were created to submit to insurance companies.

HEALTH-CARE AND MEDICARE FRAUD

Annual health-care costs are estimated to be $2.2 trillion; the magnitude of spending is a magnet for fraud.[51] Estimates of the dollar loss attributable to fraud range from 3%–14% of annual expenditures.[52] The most commonly affected agencies in health-care fraud are two federal programs: (1) Medicare, which provides comprehensive care for the disabled and people 65 or older, and (2) Medicaid, a provider of services for low-income people.[53]

Perhaps the most common health-care fraud scheme is billing for services never provided. This is done by making claims for services, equipment, and tests not actually rendered, by filing claims for tests on patients who had, but did not show up, for appointments or by using

◄**FIGURE 15-12**
The classic "swoop and squat" auto accident fraud occurs when the perpetrator rapidly pulls in front of a car and then hits the brakes. The victim vehicle then rear-ends the other car, after which significant medical and auto damages are claimed. The victims of these types of crimes often drive more expensive makes, such as Mercedes-Benz, BMW, Porsche, Cadillac, and the like.
(© Christof R. Schmidt/F1 Online/Photolibrary)

patient information to file entirely fictitious claims.[54] Other fraud methods used by medical providers:

1. Filing duplicate claims.
2. "Upcoding" or using billing codes for more expensive tests or longer office visits than actually occurred.
3. "Unbundling charges," which is the practice of charging separately for each component of service. This produces a greater claim than if the service was properly billed as one single charge.
4. Misrepresenting the diagnosis in order to get paid for services not covered by the health plan or to charge for costly tests not actually provided.
5. Performing unnecessary tests;[55] a Massachusetts orthopedic surgeon routinely gave patients potentially harmful X rays and steroid injections they didn't need so he could falsely bill Medicaid. In less than three years, one patient was X rayed 74 times and given steroid injections on 112 occasions.[56]
6. Billing using the names of people who are deceased.
7. Charging for home health aide visits which were not made.

Others involved in health-care fraud are employers and employees. Employers may enroll employees who are actually not eligible in plans or change the dates of employment or termination to expand the dates of coverage. Members enrolled in health plans may alter the documents they submit in order to get a greater reimbursement than they are entitled to or to let someone else use their plan identification to obtain services.[57] An often overlooked effect for many types of medical fraud is that a person may end up with a false medical history, which may affect their ability to get life insurance or alter how they are subsequently treated medically.

Schemes to defraud the Medicare system are not limited to unscrupulous employees and medical providers. In 2009 alone, federal investigators uncovered over 2,000 cases of healthcare-related fraud[58]—with a portion of these perpetrated by organized criminal enterprises. In 2010 investigators exposed a massive fraudulent billing scheme perpetrated by an Armenian-American organized crime ring known as the Mirzoyan-Terdjanian Organization. The scam, dubbed "Diagnosis Dollars," involved more than 73 individuals working in conjunction across the United States to defraud the system out of $163 million dollars. The group not only opened over 120 fake clinics, they also stole the identities of Medicare beneficiaries and healthcare providers, frequently opening bank accounts in the names of the doctors whose identities were stolen.[59] To date, it was the largest Medicare fraud scheme ever perpetrated by a single criminal enterprise and represents the vulnerability of not only Medicare, but other American financial systems (for example, Social Security, State welfare programs, food stamp programs, unemployment systems) that may be compromised from an organized attack (Figure 15-13).

The Mirzoyan-Terdjanian Organization represented a very sophisticated and select group of high-level criminal from the former Soviet Union. The primary leader, Armen Kazarian was identified as a leading member of the "Vory v Zakone," a term that means "thief-in-law" and refers to members of the Russian organized crime cartel composed of former members of the secret police and intelligence agency (KGB) of the Soviet Union, popularized by the 2007 hit movie, *Eastern Promises*.

The Food and Drug Administration (FDA) identifies another type of health-care fraud: "It is the deceptive promotion, advertising, distribution, or sale of articles represented as being effective to diagnose, prevent, cure,

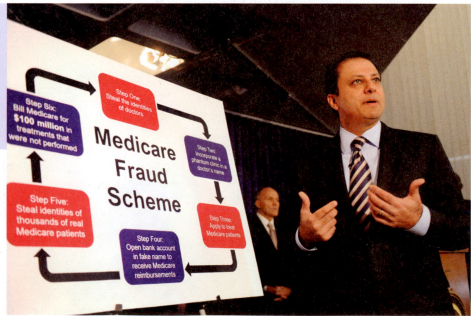

▶**FIGURE 15-13**
Investigators discuss the complexities of the largest Medicare fraud in history, resulting in the arrest of 73 individuals, some connected to the "Vory v Zakone" or Russian Mafia. (© New York Daily News Archive/Getty Images)

treat, or mitigate an illness or condition, or provide a beneficial effect on health, but has not been scientifically proven safe and effective for such purposes."[60] Products identified as such by the FDA may also cause serious health problems. Some of these products are counterfeit drugs with no therapeutic value; others claim they can produce rapid weight loss, or cure skin cancer, Alzheimer's disease, rheumatism, hardening of the arteries, diabetes, improve virility, and eliminate gangrene and prostate problems.

WORKERS COMPENSATION FRAUD

The most common worker compensation fraudulent claim is when people falsely claim that they were injured on the job. They may have actually been injured while away from the job, faked the injury while working, or have an actual injury about which they report exaggerated symptoms. In New York, 18 people, including several teachers and a chiropractor, were arrested for defrauding the workers compensation system out of $550,000, because they were seen working other jobs while receiving benefits.[61] In addition to state workers compensation agencies being defrauded, cases may also involve insurance companies providing disability coverage.

MORTGAGE FRAUD

An array of fraudulent practices related to the real estate and mortgage industry have also been recently exposed. According to the Federal Bureau of Investigation, mortgage fraud schemes typically involve misrepresentations, false statements, or exclusions related to the property or the prospective buyer. These often take form as inflated appraisals, false loan applications, kickbacks, and straw buyers which are manifested in reverse mortgage and foreclosure rescue schemes, illegal property flipping, builder bailout scams, and air loans.[62]

Investigators are often made aware of these schemes through Suspicious Activity Reports (SAR) provided by federally funded banks and other financial institutions. The information in SARs can supply officials with leads to direct their investigations.[63] Additionally, the Federal Bureau of Investigation created the Financial Intelligence Center (FIC) to boost investigations of alleged mortgage fraud. Through the use of various technologies and data exploitations tactics, the FIC provides analyses of intelligence and financial databases.[64] Task forces comprised of federal, state, and local law-enforcement agencies also exist in "high-threat" locations and are utilized in the effort to combat mortgage fraud schemes.[65]

HOME IMPROVEMENT AND REPAIR FRAUDS

Common home improvement and repair scams include unneeded roofing, gutter, plumbing, chimney, or other repairs or replacements; paving driveways with a thin surface that quickly cracks; using materials and methods that do not meet local building codes; substituting cheap paint for higher-quality paint; not replacing rotted or missing decking when roofing; charging for more expensive shingles or for more bundles of shingles than were actually used, or not replacing valley gutters and shingles in places that are hard for the owner to see; using whitewash instead of paint; and "free" home, furnace, or other inspections that turn up "serious problems." Often, the "inspector" causes the damage that needs to then be repaired. These scams are usually worked going door-to-door using high-pressure sales and scare tactics, particularly with older people. Mention may be made that they just finished a job "nearby" and have leftover materials so "I can make you a good deal." Representations will be made that "we are having a sale and I can knock 20% off of the bottom line," although the actual price is never specified. The "vendor" usually refuses to provide a written estimate or contract and evades giving information about the location of his business. Natural disasters, including tornados, hurricanes, floods, and mud slides often bring out packs of repair scammers who prey on people desperate to get their lives back in order.

These scam artists often ask for a down payment or the whole amount and are never seen again; do the work in a substandard manner or not at all; or urge the victim to make temporary repairs that are poorly done when more substantial work is needed, only worsening a problem.

The Federal Trade Commission recommends dealing only with licensed and insured contractors, checking references and consumer affairs agencies for complaints about the vendor, getting recommendations from family, friends, and coworkers who have used contractors, not doing business with door-to-door solicitors, obtaining several bids from reputable contractors, and not using homes as financing collateral because owners may end up losing them.

INTERNET FRAUDS AND SCAMS

The fastest growing area of theft and larceny involves the myriad of frauds and scam on the Internet. These range from the common, unsolicited Nigerian 419 scams and "lottery winner" e-mails that almost everyone who has ever used the Internet has received, to the more sophisticated auction frauds that now threaten legitimate corporations such as eBay, PayPal, and Western Union. According to the Internet Crime Complaint Center (IC3) website, complaint submissions increased 33% in 2008 and estimates for 2009 approach another 30% increase from the previous year. The Internet Crime Complaint Center (IC3) is a unique partnership between the FBI, the National White Collar Crime Center (NW3C), and the Bureau of Justice. Its primary purpose is to serve as a vehicle to receive, develop, and refer criminal complaints regarding the rapidly growing area of cybercrime.[66] Cybercrime is specifically addressed in Chapter 17; however, this section discusses the various larceny and fraud crimes stemming from Internet use.

IC3 reports that **auction fraud** (including nondelivery of merchandise and/or payment) was by far the most reported Internet offense in 2008 and 2009, accounting for over 58% of referred complaints. Auction fraud involves the misrepresentations of a product advertised for sale through an Internet auction site or the nondelivery of products purchase through an Internet auction site.[67] These types of crimes commonly fall within three broad categories:

- **Overpayment fraud** targets the seller. A seller advertises a high-value item—such as a car or a computer—on the Internet. A scammer contacts the seller to purchase the item, then sends the seller a counterfeit check or money order for an amount greater than the price of the item. The purchaser asks the seller to deposit the payment, deduct the actual sale price, and then return the difference to the purchaser.

- **Wire-transfer schemes** start with fraudulent and misleading ads for the sale of high-value items being posted on well-known online auction sites. When buyers take the bait, they are directed to wire money to the crooks using a money transfer company. Once the money changes hands, the buyer never hears from them again.

- **Second-chance schemes** involve scammers who offer losing bidders of legitimate auctions the opportunity to buy the item(s) they wanted at reduced prices. They usually require that victims send payment through money transfer companies, but then don't follow through on delivery.[68]

Many of these auction frauds are committed by perpetrators living in a foreign country, such as South Africa or Romania. Consumers should exercise extreme caution when the seller posts the auction as if he resides in the United States, but then responds to the victim outside the United States. The perpetrators almost always request that funds be wired directly to him or her via Western Union, MoneyGram, or bank-to-bank wire transfer to addresses outside the United States. These services have virtually no recoverable recourse and sadly, provide dead-end leads for local police investigators. Finally, consumers should be wary if the deal "sounds too good to be true." Unfortunately, it usually is! Local police investigators should make sure that the victim files a complaint with the IC3, as well as provides security alerts to eBay or PayPal, if those sites were involved. Each provides a strong security alert and fraud prevention program as well as a list of "tips" for would-be buyers.[69] A common auction fraud report, filed in August 2010 is as follows:

I was sold a stolen vehicle on eBay. The seller indicated that he had recently moved to South Africa to start a new business and that he "had to sell his relatively new Beemer" for $10,000. I thought it was a great deal, so I wired the money to the seller (in South Africa) after checking him out on the Internet. He indeed had a number of business listed worldwide and a new one on his website in South Africa. I sent the money via Western Union, because I did not want to pay the state sales tax and I figured that the deal would go through, since the car was being shipped from Houston and I lived in Dallas, not even two hundred miles away. When I received the "bill of sale" on the vehicle, it was from one of the seller's businesses and not in his personal name. The problem was . . . of course . . . when the vehicle arrived, so did the police who informed me that the 2008 BMW was stolen and had to be impounded. I guess the deal was too good to be true![70]

Internet Gambling and Lottery Scams

While the Unlawful Internet Gambling Enforcement Act was passed in 2006 by Congress, essentially making all forms of gambling via the Internet illegal, a number of underground Internet sites still exist. The sites are "offshore," meaning that they are hosted in foreign countries, making enforcement very difficult. Further, the extent to which some of these sites are honest also appears to be an open question, as so many are beyond the reach of gaming regulatory agencies and American law enforcement.

Most Internet frauds involving gambling are usually based on phony letters announcing you as a winner (Figure 15-14). In these types of scams, the victim is notified of his/her "winnings" and is requested to provide confidential information on which false identifications are developed and/or more sophisticated identification theft schemes are placed into motion.

Nigerian 419 and Black Money/ Wash-Wash Schemes

The **Nigerian advanced fee scam** begins with a potential victim getting an unsolicited fax, e-mail, or letter that purports to be from a current or former Nigerian governmental official or a relative of such. The recipient is told that a "confidential source has recommended the contact." The con takes its name from Chapter 42, Section 419, of the Laws of the Federation of Nigeria and Lagos, which deals with advanced fee frauds. Millions of U.S. dollars are available through an over-invoiced deal with the Nigerian national Petroleum Company, the recovery of unclaimed insurance money, money from a dead or defeated former government official, or other such spin.

From: POWERBALL NOTIFICATION <pabet4us@yahoo.co.uk>
Date: October 23, 2010 12:57:16 PM EDT
To: undisclosed recipients
Subject: Check Your E-mail

FROM THE DESK OF THE PROMOTIONS MANAGER
POWERBALL LOTTERY E-GAMES PROMOTIONS,
Accredited Claim Agent-
29 Colmore Row,
Birmingham, B3 2EW
United Kingdom
www.powerball.com

23th October, 2010.

Attn: Lucky Winner,

RE: AWARD WINNING EMAIL NOTIFICATION!!!

We wish to notify and congratulate you on the selection of your email ID as the jackpot winning entry in the Powerball E-Games Promotions, being the inaugural edition of our new e-lottery program. Your email ID identified with winning No. 10, 17, 18, 26, 43, 47 and was selected among the winning email ID's in the draws held today using the latest version of the Computer Random Selection System (CRSS) from the 50,000 promotional entries submitted by our international software support/affiliate companies.

You have been awarded with the jackpot promotional cash prize of $1,000,000.00 (One Million United States Dollars Only) credited to Reference Numbers PB/EGP/60961/OV. You will join the other two winners from Nigeria, Your payment will be made through our Nigerian payment center, since we have two winners already from Nigeria. Your winning cash prize has been transferred into an ATM VISA CARD to curtail the risk of carrying huge amount of money around. You shall receive your winning cash prize as an international ATM VISA Card which you shall cash in your country. To immediately process the claims of your prize award, please contact your assigned claims agent:

Name: Mohammed Hakim Ali
E-mail: mohammedhakim1949@hotmail.com
TEL: +2348060850444

To facilitate the claims of your winnings, you are advised to provide the claims officer assigned to you with the following details for processing the payment of your winnings:

Name:
Address:
Telephone Number:
Email Address:
Occupation:
Nationality:
Social Security Number:
Bank Name:
Bank Address:
Account Number:
VISA or MASTERCARD Bank:
Account Number:
Reference Number:
Award Prize Amount:

Once again, congratulations from all our staff on your promotional prize winning

Patricia Riley (Mrs.)
Coordinator; Powerball E-Games Promotion.

▲ **FIGURE 15-14   Internet "winners" notification**
Note the important and confidential information requested from this unsolicited e-mail.

▶ **FIGURE 15-15**
Partially cleaned $100s in the Nigerian "wash-wash" advanced fee scheme
(© Eduardo Munoz/Reuters/Corbis)

The letter writer wants the victim's help in investing in the United States and will pay handsomely for it, up to 30% of the "total." Another 10%–15% of the money will be set aside to pay for miscellaneous expenses in getting the money transferred. The victim provides personal information, including bank account numbers to facilitate the movement of funds from Nigeria to this country. The personal information is not immediately abused; later it may be sold or employed in another type of fraud. The victim is pressured into sending money to cover unanticipated costs, which continues as long as the victim sends money. The money requests to the victim are accompanied by official-looking government and bank documents with embossed seals and verification stamps, all of which are counterfeit or phony.

"Wash-wash" (Figure 15-15) is what Nigerian cons call the black money scheme, also an advanced fee scam. It may be run in conjunction with a 419 or as a stand-alone con. The con reports that the dollars he is trying to get into this country have been treated with a chemical that turned them black, disguising their true value; in order to be able to wash the $100 bills clean so they can be used, special, expensive chemicals must be bought, and the victim must pay for them. A meeting is set up outside the United States, to avoid the higher risk of arrest. The victim flies there to actually see the money that will be "cleaned and divided." The meeting is conducted in a hotel room or other location. The con has a specially treated bill that is black, and he uses the "small amount of special cleaning chemicals he has left" to demonstrate the process, and the bill is partially cleaned. This process is actually very cheap and on the order of a sleight-of-hand trick. The victim advances several thousand dollars to buy the chemicals; but then, the vial is "accidentally left in a cab or broken." So, the victim advances more money. This is repeated as many times as the victim pays up and then the fraudsters disappear, allegedly to get the chemicals themselves.[71]

OTHER FRAUDS: PIGEON-DROP AND BANK-EXAMINERS CONS

Confidence games are practiced by individuals who understand human nature, gain the mark's trust by being good listeners, and through smooth talking, set the hook, and run the scam. As many as 70% of con games may be run against the elderly, who are often very trusting. Among the most enduring con games are the pigeon-drop scheme and the bank-examiner scheme.

The **pigeon drop** is run in many variations; commonly, two cons operate it. The first one strikes up a conversation with the mark on a street filled with shops or at a mall. The job of the first con is to make a "quick connection" with the mark and gain his/her confidence; they talk about the mark's family or whatever is comfortable. The second con approaches with a story of having just found an envelope filled with a lot of money and asks them if it belongs to them. When the envelope is opened, there will be some paperwork suggesting that it came from drug sales or other illegal activity. After asking the first con and the mark what should be done with the money, the mark is lead to the conclusion that all three should share it. Because there is no identification in the envelope, the money cannot be returned, and there is no real harm because the person who lost the money is dishonest. The two cons, quickly joined by the mark, talk about all the things they could do with the money. One of the cons calls his/her employer, who is an "attorney."

| TABLE 15-1 | Internet Scams in 2009 |

SCAM	TYPE OF SCAM	DESCRIPTION
"Hitman Scam"	E-mail extortion	An e-mailer claims to have been sent to assassinate a victim, but the victim would be spared if he/she wires money overseas.
Astrological reading scam	Spam or pop-up message	A victim receives a free reading but is enticed into paying for a full reading to learn about something favorable about to happen.
Economic stimulus scam	Telephone call and online	A recorded phone message that sounds like President Barack Obama directs victims to websites requiring online applications and $28 in fees to receive a large sum of stimulus money.
Job site scam	Online	Victims are persuaded to provide personal information or copies of payroll checks only to find their bank account drained.
Fake pop-ups for antivirus software	Online	Victims click on fake pop-up ads warning them about threatening viruses on their computers and end up downloading malicious computer codes or viruses.

Source: *2009 Internet Crime Report* (Washington, D.C.: U.S. Department of Justice, 2010) and "Dallas Summit Target Cyber Crime," *The Dallas Morning News*, May 2, 2010, p. 18A.

The attorney advises that the money be put in "his firm's" trust account while a due diligence search is made to find the owner of the lost money. Additionally, the mark and the two cons are to provide a sum of money, as a show of good faith until the found money can be distributed, which will also be placed in the mythical trust account. After the mark withdraws his good faith money, the lawyer may take the group to lunch and take control of all of the money. The victim—the pigeon—has thus lost all the money he withdrew from the bank.

The **bank-examiner con** often begins with a call to the mark's home in which the caller identifies himself as a bank examiner who relates there is some apparent wrongdoing at the bank, and the assistance of the mark is solicited in finding out who it is. The mark is asked to withdraw some money from his/her account and then to meet the examiner at a nearby location. The bank examiner may be accompanied by "Sgt. Jones," who flashes a badge and praises the mark for his help. The bank examiner gives the mark a counterfeit cashier's check to replace the funds withdrawn but asks him/her not to deposit it for the week it takes to complete the investigation. By then, the scam has been run several times in that community, and the con men are long gone before the mark finds out that the check is bogus.[72]

Pigeon-drop and bank-examiner frauds are often started via the Internet. Unsolicited e-mails and other communications are transacted between the victim and the con through e-mail as well as the telephone. Clearly, the ubiquitous nature of the Internet has aided in new and various forms of scams that will undoubtedly continue to evolve over the years. Table 15-1 reveals recent variations of scams via the Internet.

VICTIMS OF FRAUD: SENIOR CITIZENS

Senior citizens are particularly susceptible to being the victims of a variety of fraud schemes, including Medicare fraud, telemarketing and funeral scams, counterfeit prescription drugs, Internet scams and cons, and phony reverse mortgages. For instance, many senior citizens are new to the Internet and unaware of the potential for fraud and scams associated within its use. They often come from a social genre that "trusted" their neighbor and believe that the government "protects" them from criminal predators. They often believe that scams and cons are relatively rare and that most people are honest in their business dealings. These are characteristics of the "greatest generation," who fought in World War II and who believe that most people are basically honest and technology is well-regulated . . . criminals are often viewed as street thugs that involve themselves in relatively minor crimes like shoplifting and other thefts. Most senior citizens polled continue to believe that violent crime is relatively rare in our communities and that the police can prevent most crime.[73]

From the perspective of a scammer, senior citizens are ideal victims for a number of reasons. First, they generally have good credit and a sizable savings. Second, elderly victims are not as likely to report being a victim

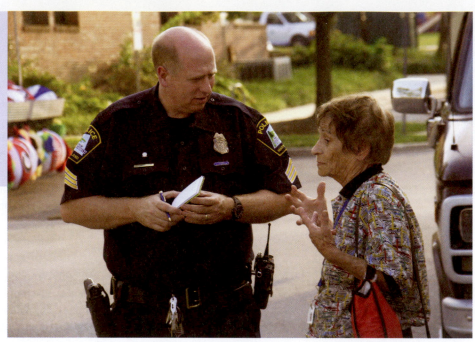

▶ **FIGURE 15-16**
Senior citizens are often the victim of scams and cons
Federal and local police are trying to better educate senior citizens through individual workshops, Senior Citizen Police Academies, and general e-mails and postal mailings focused on fraud prevention. (© Tom Carter/Index Stock Imagery/Photolibrary)

of fraud because they may not realize they were conned; if they do acknowledge their victimization, they may not report it, owing to embarrassment or shame. Third, even if they were to report the crime, some senior citizens can be poor witnesses, based on their limited ability to recall information. Moreover, a significant time lapse between the scam and discovery of the crime makes details of the event more difficult to remember.[74] Senior citizens account for a large amount of the victims to frauds and cons—so much so, that the FBI has focused considerable attention on educating senior citizens in an attempt to lower their victimization (Figure 15-16).

MONEY LAUNDERING

Criminals want to launder money to avoid prosecution, increase their profits, avoid seizure of their accumulated wealth, evade paying taxes whenever possible, and appear legitimate.[75] In laundering cases prosecuted, 60% of the money came from embezzlement or fraud, 17% involved drug trafficking, and 7% involved racketeering or customs charges.[76] **Money laundering** is the illegal practice of filtering "dirty" money or ill-gotten gains through a series of transactions until the money is "clean," appearing to be proceeds from legal activities. The United States Criminal Code defines money laundering as the concealment of the source and/or the destination of money, which has usually been gained through illegal activities.[77] Worldwide money laundering activity is estimated to be $1 trillion each year.[78] Money launderers have access to all the speed and ease of modern electronic finance to move funds globally. Thus, substantial cooperation and information sharing among law-enforcement agencies are

essential to identify the sources of illegal proceeds, trace the funds to specific criminal activities, and confiscate criminals' financial assets.[79]

At the risk of oversimplifying a complex subject, money laundering involves three distinct steps: (1) **placement,** (2) **layering,** and (3) **integration** (Figure 15-17).[80]

PLACEMENT

Placement is the process of placing unlawful proceeds into legitimate financial institutions or systems. Transactions are kept to $10,000 or less to avoid triggering the requirements of the federal Bank Secrecy Act (BSA, 1970). The BSA obligates institutions to report single transactions exceeding $10,000 to the U.S. Department of Treasury's Financial Crimes Enforcement Network (FinCen). FinCen is one of the Treasury's primary agencies to establish, oversee, and implement policies to prevent and detect money laundering. It also provides intelligence and analytical support to law enforcement. With FinCen's leadership, a meeting of financial intelligence units (FIUs) was held in 1995 in Brussels. An outgrowth of this meeting was the formation of the Egmont Group, which is an international network of FIUs dedicated to information sharing and coordination.

The BSA also requires a report when one entity makes multiple deposits exceeding $10,000 in a single day. In 1996, under regulatory authority granted by the Annunzio-Wylie Money Laundering Act (1992), the U.S. Treasury adopted a rule requiring banks and other depository institutions to report to FinCen any *suspicious* activities involving $5,000 or more.

Placement is often done by **smurfing,** or making multiple deposits of cash or buying multiple bank drafts,

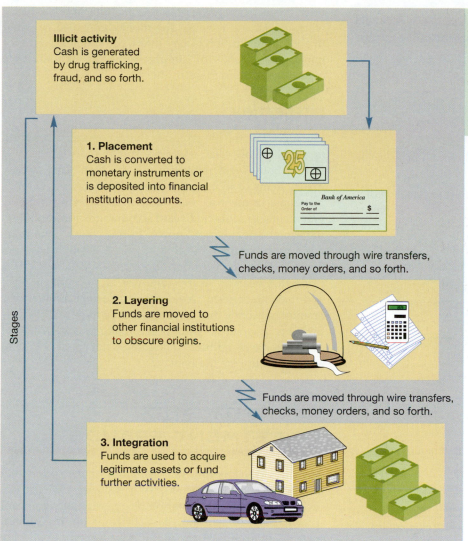

Stages

Illicit activity
Cash is generated by drug trafficking, fraud, and so forth.

1. Placement
Cash is converted to monetary instruments or is deposited into financial institution accounts.

Bank of America
Pay to the
Order of
$

Funds are moved through wire transfers, checks, money orders, and so forth.

2. Layering
Funds are moved to other financial institutions to obscure origins.

Funds are moved through wire transfers, checks, money orders, and so forth.

3. Integration
Funds are used to acquire legitimate assets or fund further activities.

◄**FIGURE 15-17**
Money laundering: Placement, layering, and integration
(United States General Accounting Office, *Money Laundering: Extent of Money Laundered Through Credit Cards Is Unknown* [Washington, D.C.: 2002], p. 7)

which are checks issued by one bank against funds deposited in that bank that authorize a second bank to make payment to the entity named in the draft. One or more individuals conduct these transactions, often at multiple financial institutions. Other methods include buying money orders or travelers' checks at one institution, depositing them at another and using cash to buy chips at a casino, participating in gambling activities, and then cashing in the chips for a casino check. As a general matter, casinos withhold federal income tax at a 25% rate on winnings above $5,000. Placement has also been facilitated by bribing bank officials to ignore FinCen reporting requirements (which is increasingly difficult) by purchasing entire banks and operating them as part of a criminal enterprise and using "safe haven" **off-shore accounts** in some 60 nations that advertise "untraceable" financial services. These nations include the Cook Islands, Egypt, Guatemala, and Ukraine. In these jurisdictions, launderers may buy a "shelf company" that has been registered for years and open accounts into which illegal funds are deposited. Laws in the Seychelles Islands provide immu-

nity to depositors from all outside criminal charges, even if it is known the money came from criminal acts. The only government requirement is that investors not engage in illegal activities in the Seychelles Island chain.[81]

Another method of placement is the Colombian **black market peso exchange (BMPE)**.[82] Colombian drug dealers export drugs to North America and Western Europe. Sales of drugs produce vast amounts of money in the currency of the countries in which the drugs are sold. The drug cartel contacts a peso broker, who will give it pesos for the currency held in foreign countries for roughly 80 cents on the "dollar." The cartel thus has its money, and the BMPE must now pick up the money and get it placed into the banking systems of the respective countries. In the final phase, the broker advertises to Colombian importers that they have foreign funds available to buy goods from other countries. On behalf of importers, the BMPE purchases goods from foreign manufacturers whose goods are shipped to the Caribbean or a South American country. These goods are then smuggled into Colombia to avoid expensive tariffs. Once the goods are

TABLE 15-2	Indicators Associated with Accounts Used for Money Laundering

1. Smurfing

2. Unusual underlying business plan

3. Account holder's wealth atypical for his/her profile

4. Unusually high rates of return for low-risk business activity

5. Reactivation of dormant account, often with increasingly large deposits

6. Questionable, unrealistic, or conflicting explanation of business plan or account activity; account holder has lack of knowledge about the field his/her business is in

7. Unnecessarily complex transactions

8. Disbursement of funds by several checks when one would do

9. Account holder has criminal record or suspicious associates

10. Account holder has defensive stance when asked about account activity

11. True beneficiary of account is deliberately concealed

12. Last-minute changes in fund transfer instructions

13. Account holder is discovered to use false/stolen identification

14. Account revenue is atypical for size and nature of business

15. Funds transferred to personal or relative's accounts

16. Account behavior changes without explanation

17. "Tidy" or rounded sums used to pay for commodities

18. Business lacks normal documentation

Source: No author, *FIUs* (Financial Intelligence Units) in *Action: 100 Sanitized Cases*, London: Egmont Group, 2000, drawn from a 170-page document.

sold, the broker is paid in pesos, which are then deposited into a legitimate banking system.

Money from illegal sources also still gets laundered in the traditional way. Front businesses—such as bars, restaurants, night clubs, and vending machine companies—and illicit source funds are commingled with legitimate revenue, with taxes being paid on all of it. These front businesses may be owned by criminals or be ones that they control. Indications of accounts being used for money laundering are summarized in Table 15-2.

LAYERING

Layering involves converting the funds placed into other assets or moving them to other financial institutions, the purpose of which is to further distance the funds from

their illegal source; these assets include bonds, stocks, works of art and jewelry. The money may also be wired to another institution to pay into a controlled account for non-existent goods or simply move through multiple other accounts anyplace in the world.[83]

INTEGRATION

In integration, the illegal funds that have been placed and layered are now clean and are virtually indistinguishable from wholly legal money. They are then used to buy luxury items or to invest in legitimate business ventures, real estate, or other sectors.[84] Both in the layering and integration phases some credit card accounts are used, although the actual extent is not known. In this country, the practice appears limited, but it is practiced through off-shore banks.[85] These banks offer anonymous ATM and credit cards that bear no user name, just an account number, and that can be used worldwide; there is no limit on the amount of money that can be withdrawn daily. The cards must be "preloaded" or deposits made to cover 200% of anticipated expenditures. The money not spent is held in a trust account by the bank.

SECURITY AND INVESTMENT FRAUDS

Securities fraud is any manipulation or deception that affects the purchase or sale of a security and usually includes the misrepresentation or omission of significant information. In general, a security is an investment instrument from which an investor expects to derive financial benefit through the efforts of others.[86] Illustrations include stocks, bonds, and other financial instruments. The two primary laws governing the securities industry and protecting investors are the Securities Act of 1933 and the Securities Exchange Act of 1934, both of which have been amended through the years.[87] In addition to these federal laws, each state has statutes and regulations pertaining to securities transactions, and the various stock and commodity exchanges also have regulatory requirements.[88]

In the 1987 movie *Wall Street*, the character Gordon Gekko soothingly intones at a stockholders' meeting, "Greed is good," which seemed to become the order of the day for some individuals and corporations. In 1990 Michael Milken, the "junk bond king," pled guilty to securities fraud and related charges and paid a fine of $600 million, thereby avoiding the more serious charges of racketeering and insider trading.

Formed by a merger of two companies in 1985, energy trading company Enron quickly soared owing to the deregulated energy markets, becoming the seventh largest corporation in this country. By 2000, Enron had filed for bankruptcy, brought down by some five years of using car thefts—totaling a mere $17.6 billion in losses.[91] Put another way, the dollar loss for all property crimes in 2007 represented only a fraction (about 20%) of the total loss suffered by investors from the Madoff scheme! Even if 2007 was an "off year" for crime, to get a realistic picture of the magnitude of this crime: Bernie Madoff's fraud would essentially equal the monetary losses from all conventional property crimes against U.S. citizens for three years![92] There has been some retribution and repayment of loss since 2008. Madoff pled guilty and was sentenced to 150 years in prison, and in December 2010 federal authorities revealed that many Madoff's victimized clients may regain about half of their losses as a result of seized property and assets by the federal government.[93]

Bernie Madoff's investment fraud was brought to light the same year that was fictional character, Gordon Gekko reappears in the sequel, *Wall Street: Money Never Sleeps;* in this movie, Gekko hawks his new book entitled, "Greed is Good!" The cynical nature and devastation of monetary loss from Bernie Madoff's investment fraud provide the backdrop to the movie, which highlights one of the oldest and most successful cons: the Ponzi Scheme.

PONZI/PYRAMID SCHEMES

Carlos "Charles" Ponzi formed the Security Exchange Company in Boston in 1919 and promised to double people's investments in the company within 90 days (Figure 15-19). For early investors, this actually happened, because he used the deposits of subsequent investors to pay for the money doubling of previous investors. Eventually the scheme collapsed, because recruitment of new investors could not be sustained. Ponzi was arrested, convicted, and imprisoned for various crimes. This type of investment fraud is still practiced today and is referred to as a **Ponzi scheme, pyramid scheme,** or endless **chain scheme.** The ruse is based on "greed" and attempts to lure would-be investors into a program that promises or guarantees extraordinarily high returns. As in the initial Ponzi fraud, the scheme actually appears to be working in the beginning, as investors receive monetary "returns on investment," however; these returns are not based on profits from a working corporation or stock fund, but rather from new investors entering the program. The entire scheme fails when additional investors cannot be enticed into the scheme. It is usually at this time that the fraud becomes apparent as the perpetrator suddenly vanishes, taking all of the remaining investment money. Sudden stock market downturns and a slowing economy also quickly reveal Ponzi schemes as investors withdraw their money from the program, causing a rapid acceleration of payout and revealing the fraudulent nature of the scheme. This is precisely why so many Ponzi and pyramid schemes have come to light in the past few years, as the U.S. Stock Market dipped to its lowest point in decades in 2008 and the U.S. economy

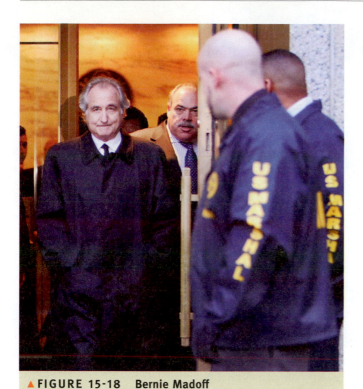

▲ **FIGURE 15-18 Bernie Madoff**
Madoff pled guilty to a federal indictment alleging that the former securities broker dealer carried out one of the largest Ponzi schemes, defrauding his clients out of an estimated $64 billion. He pled guilty in June 2009 and was sentenced to 150 years in prison. (© AP Photo/Kathy Willens)

accounting methods that concealed massive losses, leading to a downward estimate of its net value by $1.1 billion. The scandal caused thousands of employees to lose their retirement savings and resulted in massive losses to investors. Its activities led to the conviction of some Merrill Lynch and Arthur Anderson officials, prison terms for some Enron officials, one of whom pled guilty to conspiracy to commit money laundering and conspiracy to commit wire fraud. The Board of Directors paid a $168 million fine to settle charges that they failed to adequately protect investors.

In 2008 federal officials investigated and arrested former NASDAQ chairman, Bernie Madoff, on charges of securities fraud (Figure 15-18). Madoff operated an asset management firm that, for decades, used the funds from new clients to pay profits and redemptions to existing clients. Often using his social networks to attract new investors, Madoff eventually defrauded his clients out of $64 billion, representing the largest investment fraud in history.[89] The number of dollars lost in the fraud is mind boggling! To place this number into perspective, compare the dollar loss in the preceding year, according to the 2007 FBI Uniform Crime Report.[90] According to the FBI, there were 9.8 million crimes against property in the United States in 2007, which included about 2.2 million burglaries, 6.6 million larcenies, and about 1.1 million

▲ FIGURE 15-19   *Ponzi schemes*

Carlo Ponzi (1882–1949) immigrated to the United States, where he swindled thousands of investors out of millions of dollars. He was deported to his native Italy in 1934 and at one point worked for the dictator Mussolini. In 1949 he died penniless in Brazil. The scam he developed is timeless; in 2007 Norman Hsu was charged with defrauding investors out of at least $60 million in a massive Ponzi scheme and with making illegal political contributions. (© Bettmann/Corbis)

continues to suffer a major recession. Table 15-3 lists some of the more infamous cases within the last few years. To would-be investors, the best adage may again well be, "if it sounds too good to be true, it usually is!"

As with most frauds, there are numerous variations in the Ponzi and pyramid routines. For example, these schemes may be run as "gifting clubs" or "women empowering women" programs. Eight new participants, called *givers*, are recruited, and each "gifts" the "receiver," who is the person at the head of the pyramid, with $2,000. When the receiver has $16,000 in hand, the pyramid splits, and the eight new participants move upward in the pyramid, each hoping eventually to become the receiver; to do so requires each of them to recruit new entry-level givers.

New participants in pyramid schemes are often required to sign confidentiality agreements requiring them not to discuss the specifics or the names of participants and attesting that they were not promised anything for participating in the program (although each is led to believe that they all will become receivers). As the following sections indicate, Ponzis can be run in many different ways.

PUMP AND DUMP SCHEMES

The U.S. Securities and Exchange Commission describes **pump and dump** schemes, which are also called "hype and dump manipulation," as involving the touting of a company's stock through false and misleading statements to the market place often by using the Internet.[94] After distributing favorable, but false, information to drive up the price of the stock (the pump), the price of the stock rallies by its being bought. The pump or hype may include urging potential investors to "buy now before it is too late," suggestions that the recommendation is based on "inside" knowledge, or that an "infallible" economic model identified the stock.[95]

The pump is often done with microcap stocks, issued by the smallest companies, over half of which have capitalizations of less than $1.25 million.[96] Thus, "microcap" means companies that have micro capitalizations. Microcap stocks are traded in the over-the-counter (OTC) market, which has no listing standards. This is in sharp contrast to the great amount of information on companies whose stocks are traded on the major exchanges. Therefore, detailed, accurate information about the company is usually not available for victims who need such data in the face of a pump hustle.

AFFINITY FRAUD

Affinity fraud is run on groups of people who share some affinity to one another, such as religious, ethnic, and professional groups and groups whose members have a high sense of friendship and trust in one another.[97] The scammers often recruit the most respected members of the group to help promote the program, which offers "guaranteed returns." The use of such members makes it easier to recruit victims, and when it is apparent that the group has been defrauded, it may choose not to report the victimization to spare the respected member and the group embarrassment. The investment fraud can be run as a Ponzi scheme or as one of many other iterations:

 African-American groups were approached by a company that was portrayed as being successful and having more than $36 million in assets, when in fact it had a negative net worth of more than $27 million. The company promised to insure all investments made, and make a 30% tax-free return. Eventually, groups were conned out of $52 million before the company was stopped; the defendant later pleaded guilty to conspiracy to commit securities fraud.[98]

The stock market plunge in September and October, 2008, revealed a number of Ponzi and Pyramid type frauds and schemes are listed here.

	R. ALLEN STANFORD	SHAWN MERRIMAN	NICHOLAS COSMO	ARTHUR NADEL	STEPHEN WALSH, PAUL GREENWOOD	WEIZHEN TANG	RAY M. WHITE	MARVIN RAY COOPER
Age	58	46	37	76	62, 64	50	50	32
Location	Texas and Antigua, West Indies	Aurora, CO	Hauppauge, Lake Grove and Queens, NY	Sarasota, FL	Sands Point, NY, North Salem, N.C.	Toronto	Mansfield, TX	Honolulu, HI
Company or companies	Stanford Financial Group, Stanford International Bank and others	Market Street Advisors	Agape World, Agape Merchant Advance	Scoop Management, Scoop Capital and others	Westridge Capital Management, WG Trading Investors and others	Oversea Chinese Fund, WiWin Capital Management and others	CRW Management	Billion Coupons, Billion Coupons Investment
Alleged length	At least 1999–09	1994–09	2004–09	1996–09	2006–09	2009–09	2007–09	2007–09
Amount raised from investors/clients	More than $8 billion	$17 million–$20 million	$370 million	$60 million	At least $553 million	$50 million–$75 million	At least $10.9 million	More than $4.4 million
Number of investors/clients	About 50,000	At least 38	More than 1,500	More than 100	Universities, public pension and retirement plans	More than 200	More than 250	At least 125 (many members of the deaf community)
Personal expenses	At least $1.6 billion in personal loans	Masterpieces by Rembrandt, Rubens, and other artists	Jewelry, hotel and limousine bills, youth baseball league	More than $1 million in wire transfers to private accounts	Homes, horse farm, collectible Steiff teddy bears	NA	Real estate and car-racing activities	Flying lessons, $1 million home, computer equipment

Source: Court filings by federal prosecutors and records from the Securities and Exchange Commission, Commodity Futures Trading Commission, FBI and U.S. Postal Inspection Service. Web Bryant, "Economic Troubles Reveal Plague," USA Today, April 17, 2009, p. B-1.

PAY PHONES/ATM MACHINE INVESTMENTS

Another type of investment fraud involves coin-operated, customer-owned telephones (COCOTs) or ATMs,[99] which investors "purchase" at $5,000–$7,000 each. They are then "leased" back to a management company for five years; the company collects rental fees from telephone companies or banks, maintains the machine, and pays the investor monthly profits. The profits promised are a 12.5%–15% annual return.[100] These offers usually come from life insurance agents or other persons not licensed to sell securities, and the investment is not properly registered. This type of investment is inherently risky, because the companies making the offers often have weak balance sheets; the realistic downside is that companies cannot provide the services promised, the phones or ATMs are never purchased, or the investment offer is actually being run as a Ponzi scheme.[101] This type of fraud became so prevalent that 26 states acting in concert took legal action on behalf of 4,500 investors who lost an estimated $76 million.[102]

ONE-YEAR CALLABLE CERTIFICATES OF DEPOSIT

The stock market has been volatile in recent years, and many older investors have fled it looking for more stable investments, such as certificates of deposit (CDs). CDs issued by local banks insured by the Federal Deposit Insurance Corporation (FDIC) have long been a trusted investment, because they are covered for losses up to $100,000. In purchasing a CD, the buyer agrees to invest a fixed amount for a fixed time. In return, the issuing entity agrees to pay the purchaser interest at regular intervals.[103] In addition to banks, CDs are now sold by national and regional brokerage firms and independent sales people or "deposit brokers." These brokers can sometimes negotiate a higher interest rate for their customers on the promise of bringing a certain sum of money to the bank.[104]

Unscrupulous sellers of CDs often trumpet the higher rates of interest to be paid but do not explain to investors about the terms used, thus misleading them. For example, a **one-year callable CD** has a "one-year call provision," meaning that the entity issuing the instrument can choose to call (terminate it by redeeming) a CD before its maturity date. The option to call a CD is with the bank and not with the investor. However, investors typically may not understand this language or are misled about its meaning, thinking that after a year of earning interest they can terminate their investment and use the money any way they want. Not only can they not do so, penalties for early withdrawal may amount to 25% or more. There are numerous cases across the country of investors in their 90s being sold CDs by unscrupulous entities that do not mature for 20–30 years. In addition to selling people unsuitable investments, these "brokers" may not be working with an FDIC institution but acting as the agent

for other investors, or the investor is not told that they own only a portion, and not all, of the CD. Moreover, some CD programs are operated as pyramid schemes, with the early investors receiving "Ponzi payments."

PROMISSORY NOTES

A **promissory note** is essentially a short-term written I.O.U. that promises to pay its holder, the investor, the fixed amount invested plus a fixed amount of interest at some specified date in the future.[105] Although promissory notes can be legitimate investments, those that are mass-marketed, sold door-to-door, or promoted on the Internet or through telemarketing are often scams, which amount to some $300 million annually. Most promissory notes have to be registered as securities with the Securities Exchange Commission and in the states where they are to be sold, but notes with maturities of nine months or less may be exempt from being registered. Therefore, when notes are not registered and mature in nine months or less, it is another sign that a scam may be in the offering instead of a great investment opportunity. Legitimate corporate promissory notes are not usually sold to the general public, but to sophisticated buyers who conduct a due diligence search before investing.[106]

The fraudsters recruit a sales staff with lucrative commissions ranging from 20%–30%; frequently, life insurance agents known and trusted in the community are recruited for this role.[107] These agents do not have a license to sell securities and rely solely on the information their employer provides, which later turns out to be false or misleading.[108] Enticed by promises of a 15% or 20% return on an "insured, guaranteed, no risk investment" and dealing with someone who is familiar to them, few victims ask any tough questions.[109] The pitch may include statements that reinforce the notion that this is a no risk investment, there is substantial collateral, and the investment is insured against loss. The money raised by the promissory notes may be needed to "open oil wells that were capped years ago because they were unprofitable to operate then, but new technology now makes it profitable to bring them on line." The notes may also be associated with activities such as "bringing out new products, funding a new television show, helping a real estate company acquire prime land for development, modernizing a Mexican gold, Colombian emerald, or South African diamond mine, or financing an e-commerce venture."

The fraudsters may simply take the money and run, leaving their unwitting sales agents to face charges, or operate the investment fraud as yet another variation on a Ponzi scheme. Promissory note fraud is also run as a type of affinity fraud.

PRIME BANK NOTES

International defrauders invented the prime bank note investment scam, which promises extremely high yields in a relatively short period of time.[110] They claim to have special access to investments that are usually "limited to only the very wealthy." The yields promised range from 5% per month to hundreds of percent annually. Victims are told that their money will be pooled to trade in prime bank notes, prime bank guarantees, prime bank debentures, letters of credit, bank purchase orders, zero coupon bonds, or other official sounding instruments.[111] Victims believe that such instruments can be purchased for a steep discount and then quickly resold for a substantial profit. They may also be advised that the profits are so vast that the International Money Fraud or the Federal Reserve Bank requires that a certain percentage of it be spent for charitable relief in third-world countries or elsewhere, which adds respectability to the pitch. The funds are actually sent to overseas banks in Geneva, London, or elsewhere. From there, they are transferred to off-shore institutions, where they are laundered, and the victims' money disappears. As is frequently the case in many types of frauds, this one can also be operated as a Ponzi scheme. Although individual investors are frequently victims, units of government are sometimes reeled in by the scheme—for example, the city of Clovis, New Mexico, lost $3.5 million in a prime note investment fraud.

VIATICAL SETTLEMENTS

Viatical settlements were developed during the 1980s, in part to help dying AIDS patients pay their bills; their life insurance policies were bought by investors for less than the face value of the policy, and the investors had their money returned and a profit made upon the death of the insured.[112] Later, the practice was extended to others, especially the elderly. Because some people live longer than their medical diagnosis suggests is possible, and because new treatments are constantly developed that extend the life of the insured, this is a risky venture even when operated legitimately.[113]

Viatical settlement frauds are conducted in many guises—for example:

The National Medical Funding Company placed ads in gay publications soliciting terminally ill patients to sell their life insurance policies. The company never bought the policies; instead, they used the information from applicants to fabricate phony viatical contracts, which were then sold to Arizona investors as fully insured 12- to 16-month investments that paid 14% or more. As investors started complaining about bounced checks and payments that never arrived, the fraud was identified, with investors losing $13 million.[114]

TELEPHONE SCAMS

Unrelated to telemarketing fraud are three scams related to telephone billing, such as: (1) 1-900 and foreign exchange numbers, (2) the Mexican collect call scam, and (3) cramming.

1-900 AND FOREIGN EXCHANGE NUMBERS

Scammers will leave a telephone message or send an e-mail from someone offering to engage in phone sex, telling the recipient they have won a prize (which may end up being only a few dollars), telling them that a family member is sick, or some other bogus message. The return number may be a 1-900 (pay for service calls, some of which may be legitimate), 809 (Dominican Republic), 284 (British Virgin Islands), 876 (Jamaica), or some other three-digit code.[115] While international calls normally require a "011" prefix, calls to the just-identified countries, Canada, and some other Caribbean countries do not. The recipients think they are making a domestic long-distance call, but they are actually being connected to a number outside the United States and are billed at international call rates. Return callers often have to wade through automated menus and hear "dentist office" music to keep them on the line. These scams average $35 per call or more, which appears on the victims' telephone bills. Victims' vulnerability can be greatly reduced if they determine what country the three-digit prefix designates.

MEXICAN COLLECT CALL SCHEME

The Mexican collect call scam originated in that country, preys upon Hispanic consumers, and is basically a reverse of the scheme just described. The telephone rings and a voice, using the correct names of family members, says this is an emergency collect call, and the caller accepts the charges only to discover a stranger is on the line talking about something entirely different.

CRAMMING

It is entirely legal for phone companies to bill consumers for certain types of services as part of their regular telephone bill. **Cramming** is the practice of placing unauthorized, misleading, inaccurate, or deceptive charges on the victims' telephone bills, which may be accidental but is often intentional. Categories of cramming include voicemail, long-distance service, paging, Internet access, memberships, and pornography. Worldwide, pornography is a $97 billion industry, $13 billion of which is earned in the United States; a full 25% of all search engine requests involve pornography.[116] It did not, however, become a major industry simply by providing "free pornography." One source of its revenue is cramming—for example, visitors to some porn sites read that they can "download" movies for free; but the next month there is a charge on their telephone bill. Similarly, another common "cram" used in the porn industry is to request age verification through a VISA or MasterCard number. However the following month, there is a charge on their card for access to the porn website. There is virtually no recourse, since many of these sites are hosted in foreign countries. Much worse, the billing continues on a month-to-month basis until the victim contacts their credit card company. Yet in other cases, the "good" credit card numbers are sold to others and the fraud continues. The victim is forced to close their account and in the most vicious of cases, the victim's credit history is diminished for nonpayment of services.

TELEMARKETING AND POSTAL FRAUDS

Many of the types of frauds discussed earlier in this chapter can be run as telemarketing and postal frauds. These two mediums of communication are a means of reaching massive numbers of potential victims quickly. Table 15-4 identifies the top 10 telemarketing frauds, a number of which were discussed earlier in this chapter. Note that many of these top 10 telemarketing schemes are variations on advance fee frauds. It is estimated that consumers lose $40 billion to telemarketing annually, and one out of six consumers is cheated each year.

In the postal or mail fraud content that follows, some scams not already covered are described. Remember that these can also be run by other means, such as telemarketing. Included in postal scams are real estate, franchise scams, unsolicited merchandise, fees for normally free services, and phony inheritance cons. The top five postal frauds are (1) free prize schemes, (2) foreign lotteries, (3) pyramids scams, (4) investment frauds, and (5) work-at-home cons.[117]

LAND FRAUD

Offerings to sell parcels of land arrive in the mailboxes of potential victims, describing wonderful land on which

| | **TABLE 15-4** | **Top 10 Telemarketing Scams** | | |

NUMBER	SCAM	PERCENTAGE OF ALL COMPLAINTS	AVERAGE LOSS
1	**Fake Check Scams** Consumers paid with phony checks for work or items sold, instructed to wire money back. These have been the #1 telemarketing scam reported two years running.	58%	$3,854.78
2	**Prizes/Sweepstakes** Requests for payment to claim prizes that never materialize.	14%	$6,601.40
3	**Advance Fee Loans** False promises of business or personal loans, even if credit is bad, for a fee upfront.	5%	$1,583.02
4	**Lotteries/Lottery Clubs** Requests for payment to claim lottery winnings or get help to win, often foreign lotteries.	3%	$8,417.61
5	**Phishing** Calls or e-mails pretending to be from a well-known source, asking to confirm personal information.	2%	$149
6	**Magazine Sales** Con artists misrepresent cost of subscriptions or pretend to be the publisher offering renewals.	1.5%	$118.79
7	**Credit Card Offers** False promises of credit cards, for a fee, even if credit is bad.	1.5%	$292.58
8	**Scholarships/Grants** Scammers falsely promise to help get scholarships or government educational grants, for a fee.	1.4%	$532.28
9	**Buyers Clubs (not travel or lottery)** Charges for memberships in discount buying clubs consumers never agreed to join. This is the first time Buyers Clubs have appeared in the top 10 telemarketing list since 2004.	1%	$99.35
10	**Nigerian Money Offers** False promises of riches if consumers pay upfront to transfer money to their bank accounts. This once popular scam has not made an appearance in our top 10 telemarketing list since 2002.	1%	$1,687.50

Source: National Fraud Information Center, 2010.

to build vacation cabins or retirement homes or even just to hold as a "prime investment." The letters and brochures are slick and the language is glowing. Potential buyers should check with other brokers in the area or see if there are complaints against the person or company making the offer. This may simply be a version of an advanced fee scheme, or the land is worth very little because it is far from utility connections or cannot be built on without enormous costs because it is on the side of a steep ridge or mountain. Once they purchase the land, victims cannot resell it for even a fraction of what they paid for it.[118]

FRANCHISE CONS

Franchise offers arrive in the mail touting fast food or quick printing business opportunities that require a substantial investment. These offers mention brand names, such as FedEx/Kinko's or McDonald's, which are familiar to people or "soon to be very big in this area of the country." Using the cover of appearing to be a legitimate business opportunity, con men drain money from victims for application and other fees and then disappear.[119]

UNSOLICITED MERCHANDISE

People may receive gifts in the mail they didn't request, such as key chains, return address labels, and pens. Accompanying the gift is a postcard that suggests the sender's affiliation, such as recording for the blind, scholarships for students, and after-school programs. Money may not be directly solicited by the postcard, but many people send a check, thinking of it as payment for the gift or a small donation. Recipients of unsolicited merchandise have several alternatives: (1) if unopened, they can return it to the sender, which the Post Office does for free; (2) if opened and the contents are unattractive, throw them away, and (3) if opened and the merchandise is attractive, keep it without any obligation.[120] If recipients elect either of the last two options, they may get a high-pressure call or even a visit. In both cases, they should hang up, or not talk to the visitor or allow him/her inside the home. They are under no obligation to pay for unsolicited merchandise.

FEES CHARGED FOR NORMALLY FREE SERVICES

Many services are available for free from the government or other legitimate organizations. A mail come-on hopes that you are unaware of these services and offers to provide them for a fee. Victimization schemes include child-support collection, unclaimed income tax refunds, and filing for property tax exemptions, all of which are run as advanced fee frauds.[121]

MISSING RELATIVES

One of the cruelest frauds is the **missing person fraud,** which plays on victims' hopes of locating a missing loved one. The con men read the newspapers and visit official police sites where there are Internet postings soliciting information about missing persons, including personal information and the circumstances surrounding the disappearance. The fraudsters send a letter in which they pose as "people recovery specialists," offer phony credentials as former FBI, CIA, or other governmental agents, tout their national and international contacts, provide false accounts of successes, including recovering people from cults, and mention their access to special databases.

Once the offer is accepted, preliminary information is gathered by telephone, an advance fee is required, a face-to-face meeting is scheduled, and the fraudsters are never heard from again. Alternatively, they may come back with some vague information, which to follow up on involves some costs that require an additional sum of money.

PHONY INHERITANCE SCHEMES

Everybody fantasizes about winning the lottery or inheriting some money from a distant relative. Con men know this and fuel our fantasy with letters delivered to our mailboxes from **"estate locators"** or **"research specialists,"** which purport to be efforts "to locate the heirs of a substantial sum of money." These letters are, like other mail frauds, sent out in the thousands to unwary recipients who are asked to pay $30 or more for an "estate assessment."[122] This scam may also ask for personal information as the first step in an identity theft.

KEY TERMS

account takeover	check kiters	franchise offer
affinity fraud	cramming	fraud
auction fraud	drive down	grand larceny
bank-examiner con	dumpster diving	hard insurance fraud
black market peso exchange	embezzlement	identity theft
(BMPE)	estate locators	intangible property
chain scheme	follow-on crime	integration

Motor vehicle theft is one of the most significant issues facing law enforcement today. In 2009 there was one motor vehicle theft every 39.7 seconds.[1] The number of motor vehicle thefts in the United States has been decreasing since 2000. With the collapse of communism and the opening of free-market economies in eastern Europe, auto theft has become an enormous problem. This, coupled with the increase in fraudulent insurance claims and other factors, has created a real challenge for law enforcement. In addition, investigating motor vehicle thefts can be difficult, and in some cases very complex, for several reasons.

When investigating vehicle theft, officers must determine the reason for the theft. Vehicles may be stolen temporarily, for example, for use in the commission of other crimes such as robberies or drive-by shootings, after which the vehicles are abandoned. Often, the stolen vehicle is not reported as such, because it is considered secondary or incidental to the robbery or drive-by shooting. Other reasons for theft can include joyriding, professional theft, and fraudulent schemes.

Professional thieves use a variety of means such as chop shops, stripping, salvage switches, and export to other countries to dispose of stolen vehicles. Once a vehicle has been chopped or stripped, trying to identify particular stolen vehicles and/or parts can be extremely difficult. However, this seemingly formidable task has been made easier in part by the creation of standardized vehicle identification number systems. Finally, investigators are often faced with situations where the perpetrators are not strangers or professional thieves but the owners themselves.

Given limited law-enforcement resources and an economically difficult time, vehicle theft may not be considered a top priority. Nonetheless, investigators have many major resources and organizations at their disposal. This chapter provides an overview of several of these resources, such as the National Insurance Crime Bureau and the American Association of Motor Vehicle Administrators, as well as the information they can provide. Although motor vehicle theft is the main topic of this chapter, also addressed is the theft of other high-value items, such as heavy equipment; commercial vehicles and cargo; marine vehicles; and aircraft and avionic equipment. We also discuss prevention programs that can help minimize the theft of motor vehicles and other items.

MOTOR VEHICLE THEFT

The number of motor vehicle thefts in the United States for 2009, as reported by the FBI, was 794,616, with a national loss of $5.2 billion in vehicle value. Of the total thefts, 72.1% were automobiles. Although 56.8% of stolen vehicles are later recovered, only 12.4% of the cases are cleared by law-enforcement agencies. Of these cases cleared by arrest or exceptional means, 14.7% were under 18 years of age, 82.3% were male, and 61.1 % were white.[2]

Other statistics for 2009: The average value of vehicles stolen was $6,505. The number of reported thefts decreased by 17.1% from the previous year,[3] 35.7% when compared with 2005 figures,[4] and 31.5 % when compared with 2000 figures.[5] Although these decreases look significant, some of the change could be caused by changes in reporting procedures, changes in crime classifications at local levels, more or fewer agencies reporting their statistics for central processing, or a variety of other reasons. Despite the decreased numbers, motor vehicle theft remains a problem of national concern.

MISCELLANEOUS STATISTICS AND NOTES

- According to the National Insurance Crime Bureau, there were 60,763 motorcycle thefts in the United States in 2008; 18,422 motorcycles were recovered, resulting in a recovery rate of 30%.[6]
- National and international rings, particularly those in cities near ports, export vehicles to countries all over the developing world, where they can be sold for three or more times the price for which they are sold in the United States.
- Since the collapse of communism in eastern Europe, the theft of motor vehicles has skyrocketed. More than 2 million vehicles are stolen annually in Europe. Many are illegally exported to developing countries, particularly in the Middle East.

- The theft of airbags and the resale of stolen salvaged airbags is still a major problem. One company that insures about 20% of the cars in the United States annually pays out over $10 million because of stolen airbags. Several states have enacted legislation that is largely ineffective because there is no national system in place to identify and respond to this problem. The National Insurance Crime Bureau (NICB) has been spearheading a drive to develop strategies for attacking this problem.
- Heavy-truck and tractor-trailer thefts are on the increase. The insurance industry annually pays out over $18 million because of commercial-vehicle theft, excluding cargo losses. California and Florida have the highest number of tractors stolen, while California, Texas, and Florida are ranked as the top three for trailer theft.

Auto Theft—Myths

- Auto theft happens to other people, not to me.
- Auto theft is a victimless crime. Insurance companies pay the costs.
- Most of the vehicles stolen are new models, so I don't need to worry if my car is a couple of years old.
- Most stolen vehicles disappear forever, because they are either exported or cut up into pieces.
- When an auto thief is caught, punishment is severe.

Auto Theft—Facts

- It is estimated that in 20%–30% of auto thefts, the operator has left the keys in the car.
- Everyone with comprehensive insurance pays for auto theft and fraud through increased premiums, even if he/she never has a vehicle stolen. According to the National Insurance Crime Bureau, consumers pay $300 per year just for insurance fraud.[7]
- Punishment for auto theft is not swift and sure.
- The theft of older-model cars is prevalent. For example, in 2007 the National Insurance Crime Bureau reported the top 10 most stolen vehicles in the United States were model years 1989–2004.[8]
- Everyone's tax dollars pay the cost of fighting auto theft, including the costs of components of the criminal justice system.
- Auto theft is not a victimless crime. Insurance does not pay for the victim's insurance deductible, work loss, inconvenience, emotional trauma, and time loss (estimated to average more than 40 hours, which include making telephone calls; filling out police reports; purchasing a replacement vehicle; completing insurance claim forms; and dealing with licensing and registration problems, vehicle inspection, and repairs, which may take many weeks if parts have to be ordered).[9]

▲ FIGURE 16-1   Thief breaks car window
The professional car thief is motivated by high profits and relatively low risk of apprehension. These thieves use a variety of means for entering locked cars, including breaking windows to open locked doors. The professional thief can break into a car, start it, and drive away in as little as 20 seconds. (© Premium Stock/Corbis)

TYPES OF THEFT

Motor vehicle thefts generally fall into one of four categories: temporary theft, joyriding, professional theft, or fraud.

Temporary Theft

The term **temporary theft** is not used to imply that the crime is not serious but to distinguish joyriding from something more ominous. Of growing concern are the thefts of vehicles specifically for use in the commission of other crimes such as robberies or drive-by shootings, after which the vehicles are abandoned. These thefts are on the increase and, when reported, are often recorded only as the underlying crime rather than also as a motor vehicle theft, thereby skewing the actual theft figures.

Joyriding

Joyriding is most often engaged in by teenagers—15–19 years old—who steal a car simply to drive it around before abandoning it. Among the reasons teenage joyriders cite for the thefts are that joyriding makes them feel important, powerful, and accepted among their peers; it's fun and exciting; they did it on a dare; it relieves boredom and gives an adrenaline rush; they don't feel like walking; they want to impress girls; to make money by stripping cars and selling the parts; to get even with parents, or to escape family problems; and it was done as part of a gang membership or initiation. Since many youngsters are not professionals, they fre-

quently target vehicles that are easy to steal and generally lack any antitheft devices. The large number of apprehensions in this age category may be due to the arrests of joyriders.

Professional Theft

In **professional theft** (Figure 16-1), the car thief is motivated by very high profits and generally low risk. The profits to be gained are second only to those from drugs. Anyone who has ever purchased a replacement part for a car is aware that the cost of replacing all the parts of a vehicle is much higher than the original cost of the entire vehicle. The professional can often sell the parts of a stolen car for up to five times the original assembled value. Considering what the thief "paid" for the vehicle, the profit margin is substantial.

However, professionals do have costs in operating their "businesses." It is not infrequent for professional thieves to employ and train youths to steal cars. Often a youth is paid a set amount, several hundred to several thousand dollars, for each theft. The amount varies depending on the make, model, and year of the vehicle. There are even "training schools" in some areas of the country where juveniles and young adults are taught how to steal cars, trucks, motorcycles, and other vehicles. The professional thief, for example, can break into a locked, high-priced car, start it, and drive it away in as little as 20 seconds.

Fraud

Although certain types of theft involve fraud perpetrated on innocent purchasers, the major category of **vehicle fraud** as described here does not actually involve the theft of vehicles by professionals or even strangers. The various types of vehicle fraud are generally committed by the owner or someone acting on behalf of the owner, with the underlying purpose of profiting at the expense of an insurance company.

The NICB estimates that anywhere from 15% to 25% of all reported vehicle thefts involve some type of fraud and that a vast majority of them involve fraudulent insurance claims. Insurance crime is an enormous problem, and its true magnitude is almost impossible to pinpoint. The associated crimes of identity theft and credit card fraud, both of which have reached epidemic proportions, make the fraud problem even more complex.

In addition, some insurance experts estimate that between 16 and 35 cents of every dollar in premiums paid by the public for motor vehicle insurance is used to pay fraudulent claims or to fight fraud. The NICB says that if the amount of insurance claim fraud and vehicle theft occurring in the United States represented a corporation, it would rank in the top 25 of the Fortune 500 and be called a growth industry. In addition, insurance fraud is on the rise, because it is an easy crime to successfully commit. Insurance companies, even those with highly qualified special investigation units whose function is to investigate suspected cases of fraud, must be concerned about potential liability resulting from lawsuits if someone is wrongly accused or a claim is wrongly denied. The fact that insurance companies are believed to have a great deal of money—deep pockets—makes these companies even more susceptible to civil suits and potential liability and, in turn, even more cautious.

Fraudulent auto-theft claims are not the only type of fraud to which the insurance industry is subjected, but they account for a significant part of the overall fraud. Fully 10% of all property and casualty claims are either inflated or outright fraud. Estimates are that fraudulent insurance claim payouts are $100 billion annually. This amount fluctuates, since it is well recognized that fraud increases as the economy worsens.

METHODS OF OPERATION— THE PROFESSIONAL

To turn a profit, professional thieves use a variety of means to dispose of stolen motor vehicles. Among the most common are chop shops, quick strip, salvage switches, export, and cloning.

Chop Shops

Very simply, a **chop shop** is a place where stolen vehicles are disassembled for resale of their parts (Figure 16-2). The operators and employees of chop shops cut stolen motor vehicles apart with torches, power saws, and other tools, sometimes in as little as 8–9 minutes. They alter or dispose of the parts that are potentially traceable and sell the untraceable parts to repair shops or salvage yards.

▲ **FIGURE 16-2   Interior of a chop shop**
A chop shop such as the one pictured here is a place where stolen vehicles are disassembled for resale of their parts. Stolen vehicles are cut apart in as little as 8 minutes in these chop shops. Parts are then sold to repair shops or salvage yards. Sometimes the repair shop operator is in collusion with the thief or the chop shop. (Courtesy National Insurance Crime Bureau)

Sometimes the parts buyers are unsuspecting. Often, the salvage yard or repair shop operator is in collusion with the thief or the chop shop. In fact, a chop shop may well direct the theft of a specific type of motor vehicle in order to "fill an order" for a specific part needed by a repair shop or salvage yard.

A modification of the typical chop-shop operation is as follows:

> Thieves steal a car, disassemble it carefully so that the parts are not damaged, have the remainder conveniently recovered and disposed of through a salvage sale, buy the salvage, reassemble the vehicle with all its original parts, and sell the vehicle, which has already been classed as a recovered theft and is no longer considered stolen.

Quick Strip

In a **quick strip,** a vehicle is stolen and stripped mainly for valuable accessories such as seats, stereos, car phones, and tires. These items are attractive to thieves because they normally do not contain any identifying numbers, thus making them difficult to identify and easy to dispose of.

Salvage Switch

Generally, a **salvage vehicle** is one that has been damaged or wrecked to such an extent that the cost of repairing it is beyond its fair market value. Thus, its primary value in the legitimate market comes from the sale of its undamaged parts. To the criminal, however, the value of a salvaged vehicle is far greater than its parts. The real profit is made after the criminal buys the salvage, provided it is accompanied by the certificate of title and the vehicle identification number (VIN) plate. Often the offender does not even want the vehicle and leaves it at the salvage yard from which it is purchased or disposes of it elsewhere. The thief then steals a vehicle identical to the wreck, changes the VIN plate, and sells the stolen vehicle, with a matching title, to an innocent purchaser or to a purchaser who is offered such a "good" price that no questions are asked. Through the **salvage switch,** the thief is able to disguise and dispose of stolen vehicles in the legitimate market.

Export

Vehicles manufactured in the United States are extremely popular in other countries. The sale of American-manufactured vehicles can also be highly profitable. Vehicles manufactured in other countries for sale in the United States are also stolen for export. Buyers in foreign nations often pay double the purchase price for quality cars, some of which is due to high tariffs. The NICB estimates that 13% of all vehicles stolen in the United States are illegally exported.[10] Mexico and Central and South

American countries are among the most popular but certainly not the exclusive destinations for stolen U.S.-manufactured vehicles. It has been estimated that as many as 20,000 stolen or embezzled cars, trucks, buses, motorcycles, and other vehicles are transported into Mexico each year. This amounts to 6.6%–10% of the estimated number of stolen vehicles exported each year.

Contributing to this problem are the limited, although effective, controls exercised by Mexican customs and the few effective controls exercised by the United States over southbound traffic entering Mexico. The volume of traffic going into Mexico makes it almost impossible to inspect and investigate all vehicles. Many stolen vehicles are also taken to Canada. Some are resold, but many are exported to their final destinations. Exports account for a growing percentage of unrecovered stolen vehicles, and the problem is even greater in port cities.

With the collapse of communism and the opening of free market economies in eastern Europe, auto theft has grown to become an enormous international problem. According to Interpol, auto theft has become the second largest source of terrorist funding.[11]

Cloning

Vehicle cloning is a crime in which stolen vehicles receive the identity of nonstolen, legally owned vehicles of the same make and model. This is accomplished by counterfeiting labels, stickers, VIN plates, and titles to make the stolen car look legitimate. Illicit profits from vehicle cloning in the United States are estimated by the NICB to be in excess of $12 million each year. Many high-priced, luxury vehicles are objects of cloning.[12]

Cloning is not confined to the United States. Many offenses have occurred in Mexico, Canada, and the United Kingdom. Exportation of legitimate vehicles is also used by professional thieves to clone vehicles. Once exported, the VIN number and other counterfeit indicia appear on stolen, cloned vehicles titled and registered in one or more states. These vehicles are referred to as being "reborn." Often, multiple copies of the counterfeit indicia will appear on stolen vehicles and, unless the vehicles are thoroughly inspected by trained investigators, these stolen vehicles are almost impossible to identify as being fraudulent. Many of the stolen, cloned vehicles are then exported to such popular destinations as Eastern Europe, Russia, the Caribbean, the Dominican Republic, Central and South America, and the Far East.[13] The NICB says that cloned vehicles are also used to facilitate drug trafficking, money laundering, and for transportation to and from crime scenes by organized crime.[14]

Many of the fraudulent theft schemes described in the next section apply equally to the cloning of a vehicle.

FRAUDULENT THEFT SCHEMES

Fraudulent auto-theft claim schemes fall into three major categories: false-vehicle schemes, in which no vehicle exists or the vehicle is not owned by the criminal; false-theft schemes; and inflated-loss-theft schemes.

False-Vehicle Schemes

False-vehicle schemes are particularly prevalent where insurance companies are lax or have ineffective programs to verify the existence of a vehicle before issuing an insurance policy. As a general rule, this type of fraud is planned well in advance of obtaining insurance coverage. The criminal purchases a policy that has a provision covering loss by theft. In fact, the vehicle does not exist except on paper, has already been salvaged, or does not belong to the person who buys the insurance. Most often, the vehicle insured is a recent model. Some time later (generally within three months, to hold down the cost of the insurance coverage purchase) a theft report is filed with a law-enforcement agency, and a claim is made to the insurance company.

Several modifications of the salvage switch, described earlier, are illustrative of false-vehicle schemes. Once a salvaged vehicle is purchased, insurance coverage is obtained. After a short time, a theft-loss claim is filed for the vehicle, which, of course, was in "excellent condition."

In some jurisdictions, a **salvage title** may be issued. This does not necessarily prevent false-theft claims on salvage; it merely channels the process in a different direction. One way the criminal avoids the problems associated with the issuance of salvage titles is by **washing,** or laundering, the title. This is done by fabricating the sale of the vehicle and transferring the title to an alleged purchaser in another state that does not issue salvage titles or does not carry forward a "brand" on the title issued by another state. The "buyer" then obtains a clean title in that state and transfers it back to the insured either directly or through several other people or businesses to make it appear to be a legitimate transaction. Then, with a clean title, the insured files a theft claim.

In another technique, the salvage buyer falsifies the necessary support documentation so that it shows the salvage vehicle as being completely rebuilt or restored and thereby obtains a "clean," or regular, title. The thief may not even bother to get a clean title; upon filing a claim for the alleged theft, he/she may simply contend that the vehicle was rebuilt or restored but was stolen before the insured could file the necessary paperwork to obtain a nonsalvage title.

In still another version of the salvage switch, the VIN plate may be attached to a rented or borrowed car of the same make and model and, along with the certificate of title, may be presented to and inspected by an agent of the company from which coverage is sought. After the policy is issued, the salvage vehicle VIN plate is removed and the vehicle is returned to the person or company from which it was borrowed or rented.

Presenting a counterfeit or stolen certificate of title or manufacturer's certificate of origin (MCO) as the basis for having a policy issued on a **"paper vehicle"** or on a stolen vehicle with a concealed identity is another technique for defrauding insurance companies through the filing of false-vehicle claims. A manufacturer's certificate of origin is the original identification document issued by a vehicle's manufacturer, somewhat like a birth certificate. It accompanies the vehicle through its delivery to a new car dealer until it is first sold to a retail purchaser, after which the MCO is surrendered to the jurisdiction issuing the first certificate of title in the name of the retail purchaser.

A variation on the counterfeit- or blank-title scheme is the altered title, whereby the criminal manages to conceal the existence of a lienholder who may have already repossessed the vehicle because of missed payments. A theft report is then filed along with the fraudulent insurance claim.

It is not uncommon to find the following scenario in a fraudulent claim on a false vehicle:

Henry Johnson owns a late-model full-size car. The vehicle is paid for and Johnson has the title in his possession. Johnson decides to sell the car. After he has it advertised for a few days, he receives a satisfactory offer from a person who pays cash and takes the car to another state to have it titled and registered. Johnson signs the title over to the buyer, who takes possession of the vehicle and drives it to his own state of residence. The next day, Johnson, claiming he can't find his car title, applies for a duplicate title in his own state. The title is issued and is branded with the word "duplicate." Although it may take several weeks to receive the duplicate title, the process may still be faster than it takes for the buyer's home state to issue a new title to the buyer and send the original of Johnson's title back to his state for official cancellation. Upon obtaining the duplicate title, Johnson files a theft claim with his insurance company and surrenders the duplicate title to the company in exchange for the theft-loss payment. After learning of the scam, the insurance company goes looking for Johnson and finds that all the information he provided was false, and he has disappeared not only with the insurance money but also with the money he made from selling the vehicle. Normally, the issuance of a duplicate title renders the original or any previously issued duplicate void, but this fact was unknown to the buyer of Johnson's car or to the buyer's home state, where he applied for a title in his own name.

False-Theft Schemes

As opposed to the many different fraudulent schemes in which no vehicle exists, in a **false-theft scheme,** the vehicle does exist and is in fact owned by the person who has

obtained the insurance policy. The primary reason why an owner would file a phony theft-loss is generally either to avoid liability for some conduct that resulted from the use of the vehicle or to reduce or avoid some financial loss. The specific motivation leading to the filing of the fraudulent claim may exist at the time the policy coverage is obtained or may result from circumstances that develop later.

Among the vast number of motivations—and there are as many motivations as there are false claims—for filing false theft-loss claims are these:

- To cover or avoid personal responsibility for a hit-and-run accident. The owner reports the car stolen (before the police come to question him or her) and subsequently files an insurance claim.
- To replace an old vehicle that just doesn't look good or drive smoothly any longer.
- To replace a "lemon" that can't be sold for a decent price.
- To obtain money for another vehicle that is in need of repair or replacement.
- To avoid loss of the vehicle without receiving any financial gain—for example, through repossession caused by a default of payments or in response to a court order to transfer the title to a former spouse after a divorce.
- To end costly car payments or repair bills.
- To avoid the hassle of selling.
- To obtain a more favorable interest rate on a car loan.
- To break a restricting car lease.

As noted at the outset of this chapter, fraud may be committed by the insured acting alone or with another person or persons. When a vehicle owner conspires with others, the fraud is often referred to as an "owner give-up." Examples of both solo and give-up false-theft schemes include these:

- The vehicle is abandoned and later reported stolen (Figure 16-3).
- The vehicle, which may have been previously damaged or had some major mechanical defects, is reported stolen. Shortly afterward, it is recovered, and the insured claims that the damage or defects were caused by the theft.
- The vehicle is sold to an out-of-state buyer, and then a duplicate certificate of title is applied for and used to file the claim—just as in the Johnson scenario, reported earlier.
- The vehicle is not stolen but is hidden before the theft report and before the claim being filed. After the loss is paid, the vehicle can be returned to use, stripped, sold, chopped for parts, taken out of state, or otherwise disposed of.
- The vehicle is dumped in water, a method of causing damage that is increasing in use. This is often referred to as car dunking or vehicle dumping.

▶**FIGURE 16-3**
Vehicle abandoned in false-theft scheme
Vehicle owners have been known to file false theft reports on their cars, often to avoid liability for some conduct associated with the vehicle or to reduce or avoid financial loss. The owner typically attempts to abandon the vehicle in a location beyond the scope of a general search conducted by the police. (© Chinch Gryniewicz, Ecoscene/Corbis)

Such vehicles generally cannot be repaired economically even if recovered.

- Vehicle burying is another way that owners dispose of unwanted vehicles—for example, an employee at the Charlotte/Douglas International Airport in North Carolina was charged with insurance fraud after police unearthed his car from the ground at a remote, wooded edge of the airport. After his attempts to sell the car met with no success, the insured, who worked as a landscaper at the airport, decided to use a backhoe to dig a pit and bury his car inside. He then reported the car stolen in order to collect an insurance settlement.[15]

- Vehicle arson is another form of fraud that is planned beforehand and is motivated by a desire to collect on an insurance policy either to make a profit or to solve a financial problem. (Vehicle arson will be covered in more detail later.)

Inflated-Theft-Loss Schemes

In contrast to the preceding schemes, in the **inflated-theft-loss scheme** the vehicle actually exists, actually belongs to the insured, and actually is stolen. The fraud occurs when the insured makes a false claim concerning the physical or mechanical condition of the vehicle when it was stolen; actually causes some damage or removes some parts on recovery of the vehicle but before it is inspected by the insurance company; claims there were expensive parts on or improvements made to the vehicle before it was stolen; or, if no follow-up inspection is conducted by the insurer, claims certain damage occurred that actually did not happen.

One frequently used scam has the insured enter into a conspiracy with a repair shop, after a stolen vehicle is recovered, to allege that damages were caused during the theft. The damages do not exist. The vehicle is immediately "repaired" before the insurance appraiser has the opportunity to inspect the vehicle, and the repair shop insists that the insurer accept the repair bill, possibly using a photo of a wrecked vehicle of the same make and condition as the vehicle "before repair." A spinoff of this basic scenario has the repair shop show the appraiser an actual wrecked vehicle in its possession of the same make and model as the insured's car.

The inflated-theft-loss claim also extends to vehicle contents. The claimant alleges the vehicle contained valuable clothes, cameras, golf clubs, and other "new" items of considerable value when it was stolen.

Defrauding the Owner and the Insurer

Sometimes the owner is not involved in the fraud, and both the owner and the insurer become victims, as illustrated in the following example:

An individual leases a vehicle from a rental company and, during the rental period, reports the vehicle stolen to both the police and the rental company. Shortly after, the renter again calls the police and reports that the vehicle was recovered, using some excuse such as his coworker took it to the store or he forgot where he parked it the night before because he had had too much to drink. Consequently, the police never enter the "stolen" report into the National Crime Information Center (NCIC). Conveniently, the renter fails to notify the rental company, which assumes that the law-enforcement agency entered the theft into NCIC. The thief may have several days' or longer use of the vehicle before the victims can put the whole story together.

Some vehicles are exported by owners for the purpose of filing and collecting on fraudulent theft claims.

> Another type of export fraud occurs when a vehicle owner makes multiple copies of proof-of-ownership documents to present to the Bureau of Customs Enforcement officials and exports his or her vehicle. After the vehicle arrives at its foreign destination, the VIN plate is removed and mailed back to the owner, who steals a car of the same make and model, switches the VIN plate, and, using the additional copies of ownership documents, exports the stolen vehicle. This is another variation of cloning.

As illustrated by the preceding examples, people who engage in insurance fraud are limited only by their imaginations. They are able to change tactics as quickly as law-enforcement agencies and the insurance industry devise methods for combating current fraud schemes.

THEFT OF HEAVY CONSTRUCTION EQUIPMENT

Heavy construction equipment (or, simply, **heavy equipment**) is commonly referred to as **off-road equipment**. The National Crime Information Center (NCIC) received 16,291 reports of commercial equipment thefts in 2006, with annual loss estimates as high as $1 billion. The recovery rate is only 28%. Insurance claims have been increasing at an annual 10%–20% rate for the past decade. The national average for a used piece of construction equipment is $135,000. The states with the highest theft rates are Texas, California, North Carolina, and Florida. California, Texas, and Florida have the highest recovery rates.[16]

Off-road equipment is stolen for the following reasons: its high value, a demand for the equipment, low security, low risk, and high rewards.[17] Thieves may steal on order, for stripping, or for export. One offender was caught with a notebook filled with photographs he had taken of machinery on various farms. When interrogated, he stated he had roamed the countryside obtaining the photographs in the notebook. The notebook was then used as a "sales catalog" when meeting with prospective buyers and as a means of instructing thieves working with him as to exactly what equipment from a particular location was to be taken. This arrangement made it possible for the equipment to be consigned or sold before it was even stolen, minimizing the amount of time that the equipment was in the thieves' hands and therefore their risk.

The theft of off-road equipment and the investigation of the thefts cause numerous problems for owners, manufacturers, and law-enforcement agencies. Title or registration generally is not required for such equipment, and owners have traditionally resisted such requirements for several reasons. They fear that the title and registration records could be used to levy taxes on expensive items of property and that such a financial burden would have to be passed on to their consumers. Further, they believe that registration requirements would impede their ability to move the equipment rapidly and freely around the country.

Owners are also victimized by the problem of inventory control. Construction equipment is often spread over several miles of job site or over several job sites and may be left idle for days or weeks at a time in isolated areas. Thus, when the professional thief is overcome by the irresistible temptation, it is often days before the theft is noticed and reported to the police.

Another issue that compounded the construction equipment theft problem until recently was the fact that off-road equipment, unlike conventional motor vehicles, had no standard, permanently affixed identification number. Historically, each manufacturer had its own system of identification, and the numbering systems could vary from 4 to as many as 15 alphanumeric digits. On January 1, 2000, the 237 manufacturers of heavy equipment throughout the world (including the big four U.S. manufacturers—Case, Caterpillar, Deere, and Ford) began using a standardized 17-character **product identification number (PIN)** on all new equipment models[18] (Figure 16-4). The definition of "new model" will not necessarily change by calendar year. Consequently, it will take a few years before the standardized 17-character PIN becomes uniformly applied.

In at least one instance, the PIN is now more difficult to counterfeit than has been the case in the past. The new PIN plate on Caterpillar equipment is laser-engraved on black anodized aluminum and has a bar code and a microprinted security feature—the PIN number.[19]

Heavy equipment is also easily stolen; a single key may be used to start all models produced by a particular manufacturer, and where key locks are in place, the machinery can be jumped by placing a pocket knife or screwdriver across the electrical posts on the starter. Although manufacturers offer antitheft devices, they are costly items that add substantially to the base price of the equipment.

The unfamiliarity of most law-enforcement officers with the nature, identity, and terminology of construction and farm equipment is among the principal problems faced by law enforcement. Few agencies have anyone with the expertise to identify specific machines or to locate and interpret identification numbers (Figure 16-5).

▶ FIGURE 16-4
Product identification removed from stolen piece of construction equipment
The Product Identification Number (PIN) had been removed from this piece of construction equipment and, following its recovery, an NICB special agent was able to identify the unit by other partial numbers so it could be returned to its rightful owner. (Courtesy National Insurance Crime Bureau)

▶ FIGURE 16-5
Illustrations of heavy construction equipment

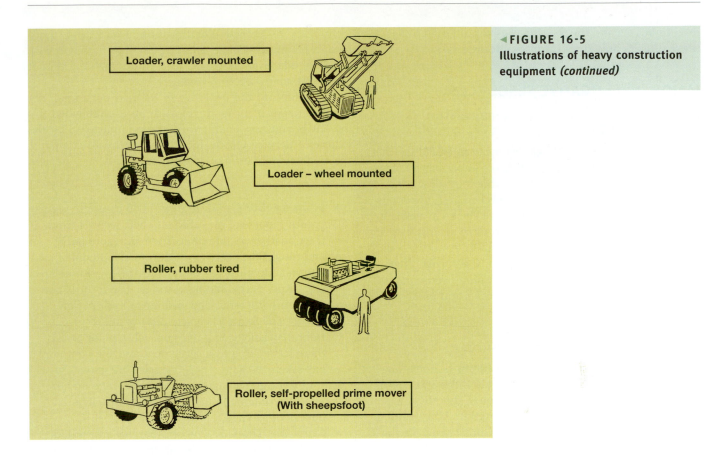

COMMERCIAL-VEHICLE AND CARGO THEFT

The insurance industry pays out about $18 million every year because of **commercial-vehicle theft.** It is difficult to convert this figure to the number of vehicles stolen, because commercial-vehicle theft data is incorporated into the overall motor vehicle theft statistics. Suffice it to say, the number is significant and rising. Additionally, it is estimated that the actual number of cargo thefts is 20% more than reported.

The theft of cargo from, or in, commercial vehicles—is a rapidly growing criminal enterprise. Although not a separate crime in itself, **cargo theft,** in the United States, is estimated as accounting for as much as $25 billion in direct merchandise losses each year.[20] As an aside, cargo theft is just one aspect of a larger problem called *cargo crime*, which also includes smuggling, counterfeiting, and product piracy. Total direct merchandise losses from all cargo crime are estimated as approaching $60 billion per year.[21] The products most vulnerable to cargo crime, in general, and cargo theft, in particular, are assembled computers, computer components and software, electronic products, cigarettes, and fashion apparel, packaged foods, appliances, and seafood.

In January 2010 the FBI announced that a cargo-theft data element was adopted in the national uniform crime reports program. This means state and local agencies need to begin capturing and reporting this date to the FBI. The new program called Cargo Net provides that state UCR programs will have 18–24 months to implement needed software changes to begin collecting the data on the state level.[22]

INVESTIGATIVE TOOLS AND TECHNIQUES

Vehicle theft investigation is a fairly technical and sophisticated specialty. An effective investigator needs experience and expertise. Despite the fact that vehicle theft may not be among the offenses receiving the highest priority for the allocation of limited resources by a law-enforcement agency, there are thousands of specialists in the United States and elsewhere whose expertise is available to any investigator or street officer needing assistance. Often, these resources are just a telephone call away.

In any specialized investigative field, one is not born an expert and cannot become an expert without extensive training and experience. So it is with vehicle thefts and related crimes. Individuals who possess the expertise, such as highly skilled investigators, cannot assume that uniformed officers with general policing responsibilities have any knowledge about the field beyond their limited exposure in an academy setting. Thus, if investigators are anxious for patrol officers to perform some initial investigative tasks, the investigators should offer to teach those officers how to perform the desired tasks.

MAJOR INVESTIGATIVE RESOURCES

Automatic License Plate Recognition Systems (ALPR)

Automatic License Plate Recognition Systems (ALPR) can be installed in law-enforcement vehicles or at permanent locations on streets or highways. The technology allows thousands of vehicle license plates to be checked in short periods of time, limited only by the number of vehicles available to check. The ALPR checks each license plate against lists of stolen cars (with license plates), BOLOs, Amber Alerts, and others. The City of Long Beach, California, after a couple of years checked almost 7.5 million license plates. They recovered over 1,000 stolen vehicles and made over 200 arrests.[23]

National Insurance Crime Bureau

The **National Insurance Crime Bureau (NICB)** is not a law-enforcement agency that investigates auto thefts and arrests offenders in the traditional sense. Rather, the NICB is an information-gathering and dissemination body and a law-enforcement assistance agency. In this regard, its special agents do investigate professional theft rings and other auto-theft cases in conjunction with local, state, and federal law-enforcement agencies.

Beginning in 1912 with the efforts of a few individuals representing different insurance companies that joined forces to disseminate information on stolen motor vehicles, the cooperation gradually spread and evolved into several independent regionalized and, later, national groups. This growth limited communication and interaction. Duplication of efforts and costs, along with the creation of considerable confusion among law-enforcement officials in deciding whom to contact for information, led to the initial consolidation of all existing auto-theft information agencies and organizations into the National Automobile Theft Bureau (NATB) in 1912. In 1965 the NATB was completely nationalized and centralized.

Late in 1991 a merger took place between the NATB and the Insurance Crime Prevention Institute (ICPI), and on January 1, 1992, the National Insurance Crime Bureau was formed. The NICB now has approximately 150 investigative field agents working with another 800 fraud investigators who work for individual insurance companies.

The NICB is not a government organization. It is a not-for-profit organization operated by, funded by, affiliated with, and serving approximately 1,000 associated insurance companies nationwide. It supports engineering, research, and experiments aimed at reducing vehicle theft and fraud and is a recognized national voice for law enforcement and the insurance industry on legislative matters.

The NICB assists in the identification of vehicles and helps educate law-enforcement officers in investigative techniques of vehicle identification, fraud, and theft. Online Insurance Crime Training for Law Enforcement, including material on vehicle theft fraud, can be found at *www.nicbtraining.org.*

In addition to the expertise of its field personnel, the computerized records developed and established by the NICB, and now maintained and administered by the Insurance Service Office, Inc. (ISO), a private company, are invaluable investigative aids. These database services include:

- *Insurance theft file:* More than 1,000 insurance companies report stolen vehicles. Theft records from the Canadian Automobile Theft Bureau (CATB) and most European countries are also maintained and include all types of vehicles, off-road machinery, boats, parts, and accessories. The records contain full ownership and insurance information.

- *Salvage file:* Salvage vehicle reports are received from insurance companies on vehicles for which there has been a loss settlement and the company has taken the title. These vehicles are generally sold through salvage pools or to salvage buyers. The file contains information on both sellers and buyers of salvage.

- *Export file:* The U.S. Customs Service and others send copies of export declarations for entry into the system. The information aids in the detection of illegal exports and of fraudulent theft reports on exported vehicles in cases where a subsequent stolen vehicle report is filed.

- *NCIC mirror image and purge file:* All active and inactive theft records on vehicles and boats housed in NCIC are also contained in the mirror image file. In addition, vehicle theft records purged from NCIC since 1972 for a variety of reasons are provided to NICB on a daily basis and are entered into the system as a permanent record. The file is an important and time-saving tool for law enforcement.

- *Information-wanted file:* When a purchaser skips out on payments to a finance company that has purchased physical-damage insurance on the vehicle from one of the NICB sponsoring member companies, the information is made available to law-enforcement agencies investigating the vehicle as a suspected stolen unit.

- *Inquiry file:* When a law-enforcement agency makes an inquiry on a vehicle for an investigation, any subsequent information received or any inquiry on the same vehicle from another person or agency will be passed on to the original inquirer.

- *Shipping and assembly file:* This file holds the shipping and assembly records for most automobiles; light-, medium-, and heavy-duty trucks; semitrailers; motorcycles; and snowmobiles produced for sale in the United States and Canada.

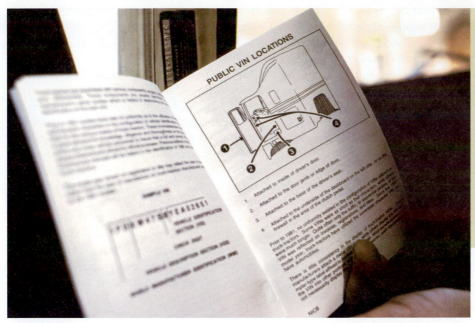

◄ **FIGURE 16-6**
The Passenger Vehicle Identification Manual
One of the most important investigative tools used in vehicle theft cases is the Passenger Vehicle Identification Manual. Published by the National Insurance Crime Bureau, this booklet contains useful information, including an explanation of vehicle identification numbers, the federal motor vehicle theft prevention standards, and VIN plate attachment and location. (© Joel Gordon)

- *Impound file:* An increasing number of states are now collecting and reporting impound records to NICB for entry into this file. The file helps clear many stolen records and is a valuable investigative tool.
- *VINASSIST:* This NICB program, provided to law-enforcement agencies at no cost, defines, edits, evaluates, and corrects vehicle identification numbers, a process that greatly aids law enforcement in positively identifying specific recovered motor vehicles.
- *All-claims database:* With this database, claims filed against participating member insurance companies can be compared to detect possible fraudulent claims, including auto theft–related insurance fraud.

The NICB is organized into nine geographic areas, with its headquarters in the Chicago suburb of Palos Hills, Illinois, serving as the Area 1 office. The other offices serving major metropolitan and surrounding locales are in Seattle; Los Angeles; Dallas; Tampa; Washington, D.C.; New York; Columbus, Ohio; Hartford, Connecticut; and Chula Vista, California.[24]

Since 1919 the NICB or its predecessor, the NATB, has annually published the *Passenger Vehicle Identification Manual* (Figure 16-6), which contains the following information:

- federal motor vehicle theft prevention standards;
- explanation of vehicle identification numbers;
- VIN plate attachment and location;
- federal safety certification labels;
- passenger vehicle and light-duty truck VIN structure;
- motorcycles and all-terrain vehicle VIN structure;
- general information on snowmobiles and boats;
- vehicle shipping and assembly record information.[25]

Every five years, the NICB also publishes the *Commercial Vehicle Identification Manual*, which contains the following information:

- world manufacturer identification codes;
- model year identifier;
- truck-tractor identification;
- commercial-trailer identification;
- off-road equipment identification.[26]

In 2010 the NICB published *Heavy Equipment Identification Manual*, which contains:

- product identification number locations;
- types of construction equipment.[27]

Insurance Bureau Canada (IBC)

Known formerly as the Canadian Insurance Crime Prevention Bureau, the Insurance Bureau Canada has been functioning since 1923 but became an independent division within the Insurance Council of Canada on January 1, 1998. It is to Canada what NICB is to the United States. IBC is supported by over 90% of private-property and casualty insurers. Within the organizational structure of IBC are found the Canadian Automobile Theft Bureau (CATB) and the Canadian Police Information System, the sister organization of NCIC. IBC is headquartered in Toronto, Ontario. It has four regional offices, located in Innisfall, Alberta; Toronto; Montreal, Quebec; and Halifax, Nova Scotia.[28]

International Association of Auto Theft Investigators

Another resource available to the investigator is the International Association of Auto Theft Investigators (IAATI) and its regional affiliated chapters, which are located in many parts of the world, including Europe and Australia. With a current membership of almost 3,800 representing more than 35 countries, IAATI was formed in 1952 for the purpose of formulating new methods to attack and control vehicle theft and fraud. Its members represent law-enforcement agencies, state registration and titling agencies, insurance companies, car rental companies, the automobile manufacturing industry, and other interested groups. International and regional training seminars are held throughout the year. As with many such organizations, it is a great network of specialists all willing to assist any investigator or officer who requests help.

State Organizations

Many states have organizations consisting of auto-theft investigators who meet regularly to exchange intelligence information and learn new methods of combating the problems of theft and fraud.

National Crime Information Center

Another valuable resource for the investigator is the FBI's National Crime Information Center (NCIC). Online inquiries can be made to NCIC's vehicle or license plate files to check on records for stolen vehicles, vehicles wanted in conjunction with felonies, stolen component parts, and stolen license plates. In addition, a request can be made for an off-line search, which is a tool designed to assist an investigator by providing lead information. For example, an investigator attempting to track a stolen vehicle that is known to be traveling across the country can request an off-line search to see if any stolen inquiries had been made within a specific time frame on that vehicle. A hit would identify the time and location from which the inquiry was made, thus providing a lead to locating the vehicle.

The original NCIC system held more than 40 million records in its 17 databases and processed more than 2 million transactions a day, but it was more than 30 years old. An updated, new-generation system, NCIC 2000, was implemented in July 1999. It has all the advantages of the old system plus impressive new capabilities such as image processing, whereby mug shots, other photographs, signatures, and identifying marks can be electronically submitted; single-finger fingerprint matching, including storing and searching for right-index fingerprints; a linkage field, whereby multiple records concerning the same criminal or the same crime can be automatically associated; and several new databases, including the Convicted Persons on Supervised Release Database, the Convicted Sexual Offender Registry, and the SENTRY file of persons incarcerated in federal prisons. These can all be accessed through NCIC 2000.[29]

The NCIC databases can be used for many different purposes. For instance, through the linkage function, an inquiry on a gun can also identify a wanted person or a stolen car. Since vehicle information can be included in the Convicted Sexual Offender Registry, a traffic stop with an inquiry on the license plate may identify an individual as a registered sexual offender.[30]

Special Investigative Units

In the mid-1970s Kemper Insurance Company created the first special investigative unit (SIU) for insurance companies. Its primary purpose was to investigate potentially fraudulent auto-theft claims. There are more than 800 SIU investigators employed in the insurance industry working fraud claims. Approximately 80% of the insurance companies now have SIUs. The agents and units work with and train insurance adjusters to detect oddities and "red flags" indicating potential fraud. The SIUs also work closely with law enforcement by lending assistance in investigations—providing computer information, claims histories, and statements of insureds made under oath.

The priorities of the NICB agents primarily assigned to fraud cases changes as new problems arise. The current priority is Medicaid Fraud.[31]

AAMVANET

The AAMVANET computerized communication network links state and provincial agencies on matters of highway usage and highway safety. The system was initiated by and for the **American Association of Motor Vehicle Administrators (AAMVA)**. The AAMVANET corporation, a subsidiary of AAMVA, is working with the FBI to coordinate efforts to create the **National Motor Vehicle Title Information System (NMVTIS)**. Beginning in 1992, AAMVANET developed the prototype for NMVTIS. Through NMVTIS, any inquiry receives a complete and up-to-the-minute history of a vehicle, including whether it was reported stolen, salvaged, or exported or is otherwise incapable of being the subject of a new transfer. In addition to inquiry capability, the system prevents the laundering of titles between states for the purpose of removing brands such as those that appear on salvage, flood-damaged, rebuilt, or unrepairable vehicles. Currently, with the exception of Illinois, all states are either fully operational, partially online, or providing data by batch.[32] The ultimate goal of the developers is to provide a system whereby a potential purchaser of a used vehicle will be able to inquire about the status of the vehicle before making a final commitment to purchase.

Government Agencies

In virtually all state governments, organizations or entities exist that possess information of value to investigators. Specifically, motor vehicle and driver's license offices, insurance fraud investigative units, and fire and arson investigative units may provide valuable information or assistance.

Manufacturers

Manufacturers are one of the most important resources an investigator can cultivate and turn to for assistance, particularly as they relate to the content and location of numbers on vehicles or parts. Domestic and foreign automobile manufacturers are generally most supportive of an investigator's inquiries, as are the Harley-Davidson Motorcycle Company and the John Deere, Case, and Caterpillar companies, which manufacture construction and farm equipment. This list is not meant to be exhaustive. Help will generally be given by any manufacturer when requested.

North American Export Committee

In an effort to stem the tide of stolen vehicles being exported from the country, the NICB, U.S. and Canadian Customs, Royal Canadian Mounted Police, Insurance Bureau Canada, and Miami-Dade Police Department in Florida, along with other law-enforcement agencies, the insurance industry, and other interested parties, established the North American Export Committee in 1995. The committee investigates ways in which the exporting of stolen vehicles could be slowed without impeding commerce at port facilities.

Shipments of vehicles occur in two ways—some vehicles are rolled on and then rolled off a ship, and some are shipped in containers. These are quite different concepts requiring entirely different approaches. U.S. Customs is charged with the responsibility of checking the paperwork on vehicles to be exported, and the paperwork must be received by Customs three days before a vehicle can be shipped. Only limited resources are devoted to this responsibility, however, because Customs is more concerned about property coming into the country and about commodities, other than vehicles being exported. Customs' role has become even more limited after 9/11. It was moved from the Treasury Department to the Department of Homeland Security and was reorganized. Customs inspectors are now part of the Bureau of Customs and Border Protection (CBP), whereas the law-enforcement agents are part of the Bureau of Immigration and Customs Enforcement (ICE). Either Customs or local law-enforcement checks the paperwork, physically examines as many of the vehicles as possible, and enters the VINs into a computer that transmits all those checked to databases with NICB, NCIC, OCRA (Mexican law-enforcement database), a rental car database, and a motor vehicle liens database. Overnight, the list is run against the export, stolen, salvage, and VIN verification files of NICB and the other databases. The next morning, an exceptions report is available to the submitting agencies so that the "trouble messages" (problems) can be checked out before the vehicles are shipped. At the Port of Miami, trouble messages occur on approximately 20% of the exports. Such electronic reporting is now used at 80 ports in the United States.[33]

Containerized vehicles present a different set of problems. There are over 8 million containers exported from the United States in a year. No manifest is going to acknowledge that a container has one or more stolen vehicles. Checking a container, even if it meets a predetermined set of conditions called a profile, is hot, sweaty work—the unloading and reloading take hours—and it interferes with commerce. Stolen vehicles are usually found in the front or middle of a container, with goods packed all around them. To make enforcement more productive, an efficient, effective, and economic method of looking inside containers had to be found.

Science Applications International Corporation developed a device that examines and photographs the contents of a container as it is passing through a gamma ray. In mid-1998, the corporation, in cooperation with the Miami-Dade County Multi-Agency Auto Theft Task Force and on behalf of the North American Export Committee, tested this equipment for a 90-day period at the Port of Miami in what is called the **Stolen Auto Recovery (STAR) System** (Figure 16-7). Before the 90 days were up, more

◄FIGURE 16-7
Stolen vehicle recovered through gamma-ray scan
This stolen vehicle was located when the container in which it was found passed through a gamma-ray scan at the Port of Miami. The container's manifest reported its contents as household goods. (Courtesy Miami-Dade Auto Theft Task Force)

1980	A	1995	S	2010	A
1981	B	1996	T	2011	B
1982	C	1997	V	2012	C
1983	D	1998	W		
1984	E	1999	X		
1985	F	2000	Y		
1986	G	2001	1		
1987	H	2002	2		
1988	J	2003	3		
1989	K	2004	4		
1990	L	2005	5		
1991	M	2006	6		
1992	N	2007	7		
1993	P	2008	8		
1994	R	2009	9		

▲ FIGURE 16-13   Vehicle model year
(National Insurance Crime Bureau)

▲ FIGURE 16-14
General Motors VIN plate with bar code
(IAATI-SE newsletter, 1997)

▲ FIGURE 16-15
Federal Safety Certification Label with bar code
(IAATI-SE newsletter, 1997)

they have a 17-character standardized VIN. If **gray-market vehicles** are brought into this country legally, a bond for each must be posted with Customs and Border Patrol (CBP) until such time as the appropriate modifications have been made to bring the vehicle into compliance with the U.S. Environmental Protection Agency (EPA) emission control requirements and the safety standards promulgated by the U.S. Department of Transportation

(DOT). When these steps have been accomplished and the modifications approved, the federal government will issue a replacement VIN plate that conforms with the 17-character standard.

Many vehicles are found operating on the streets and highways of this nation before, or without conforming to, the legal conversion requirements for gray-market vehicles. The operation of these vehicles is unlawful, and they are subject to seizure by CBP. The frequency of such seizures and the ability to ensure compliance with the EPA and DOT regulations are, of course, a direct function of the resources devoted to the programs and the priorities established. Not unlike state and local agencies, federal law-enforcement programs also suffer from limited resources. In some years, the number of gray-market imports has approached 100,000 vehicles.

The nonconforming VIN on a gray-market vehicle is sometimes nothing more than a Dymotape label stuck on the left-side dash and visible through the windshield. Often such a VIN is on a plate riveted in the appropriate place, but its construction does not satisfy the accepted format requirements. Learning the proper appearance and configuration of the accepted VIN format will aid investigators not only in identifying gray-market vehicles but also in detecting altered VINs.

Attempts to Conceal the Identity of Vehicles

Salvage switches, cloning, defacing, or altering numbers are among the many ways of concealing the identity of a vehicle, thus making it difficult for even a trained investigator to accurately identify a vehicle.

Why is concealing a vehicle's identity so important? Simply put, if a vehicle cannot be positively identified, it cannot be proven that the vehicle was stolen, when it was stolen, or from whom it was stolen. Thus, one who is in possession of such a vehicle cannot be prosecuted as a thief. Even the most careful thief has extreme difficulty totally concealing the identity of a stolen vehicle.

Although it does happen, total inability to identify a vehicle is rare if the investigator doesn't hesitate to call on his/her own or others' knowledge, training, and experience. Knowing how and when to call on outside resources is important to the successful investigation. NICB special agents and other highly qualified law-enforcement officers know how and where to look for clues to a vehicle's identity.

The public VIN on the dash is not the only number that identifies a specific vehicle. The VIN may be stamped in several different places on the vehicle's body, frame, or component parts. The location of some of these secondary numbers is not a big secret, but others, referred to as **confidential VINs,** are stamped into frames or bodies in places supposedly known only to the manufacturer and to law-enforcement agencies and officers who are specialists in vehicle identification and auto-theft investigation, such as NICB special agents. Various other parts such as engines and transmissions will be given an identification number when manufactured, but, because they are distinct component parts, often manufactured in different locales from the final assembly plant, the numbers may be totally different from the VIN. However, documents created and maintained by the manufacturer, and provided to NICB, can be checked to determine the VIN of the vehicle in which the part was installed.

Other parts or components of a vehicle manufactured or subassembled elsewhere may be designed to fit a specific vehicle. In such cases, the part may have a serial number that is related to, but not identical to, the VIN. It may have a number that is a derivative of the VIN or that's formed from parts of the VIN, the same way a T-top may need to be matched to a vehicle of a specific body type denoted by the sixth and seventh characters of the VIN and the six-digit sequential number. Numerous combinations are possible and plausible; again, this is where the manufacturer's records become indispensable (Figure 16-16).

The numbers often used to match parts so as to foster accurate assembly of a vehicle may be written on components with pen, pencil, chalk, marking pen, or crayon. It does not matter what they are written with, as long as there are numbers that can lead an investigator to the end result of positively identifying a vehicle. Frequently, the various components subassembled elsewhere in the same plant or shipped from other plants will be accompanied by production order forms or written orders containing the VIN or a derivative number, which matches the parts for assembly. After the parts are matched and assembled, the production form has no use and may be left in some nook, cranny, or crevice of the assembly. If the investigator knows where to look, such a document may often be found and thus lead to vehicle identification.

Federal Safety Certification Label

All cars distributed in the United States since 1970 must have a **federal safety certification label.** This sticker, in addition to the required certification statements, also contains the vehicle's VIN. If the sticker is removed, it leaves behind a "footprint" that often shows the word "void." Obviously, if the correct sticker is in place and the correct public VIN shows through the windshield, the VINs should match.

The shape and size of the labels, as well as the materials from which they are constructed, vary among manufacturers. More common among domestic manufacturers is a paper label covered with a clear Mylar-type plastic.

The label is bonded to the vehicle with a mastic compound. Construction is such that the label should be destroyed if removal is attempted. Some foreign manufacturers construct the certifying label out of thin metal and attach it with rivets. In either case, security against removal and replacement is not absolute. However, investigators are encouraged not to use the VIN on the safety certification label as absolute proof of vehicle identification. The federal safety sticker will be located on the driver's door or on the doorpost and, in recent years, also includes a description of the vehicle and VIN on a barcode.

Federal Legislation

In an effort to reduce auto theft by easing the process of vehicle identification, Congress enacted the **Motor Vehicle Theft Law Enforcement Act** of 1984. Title I of the law requires that manufacturers place additional permanent identification numbers on up to 14 major parts of certain car lines. The car lines are selected every year for each manufacturer by the National Highway Traffic Safety Administration

▲ **FIGURE 16-17**   **Components requiring marking**
(Courtesy of 3M Corporation)

AUTO MANUFACTURERS NAME	VIN LABEL	RDOT LABEL
Ford/US		R Ford DOT
Audi		Audi R DOT
Ford/Germany		R Ford DOT
Mercedes Benz		R DOT MERCEDES-BENZ
Porsche		R DOT
VW		R DOT
Renault		R ◇ DOT
Ferrari		R DOT
Maserati		R DOT
Saab		R SAAB DOT
Nummi/US		UNITED MOTOR R DOT
Honda		R H DOT
Isuzu		R DOT
Mazda		MAZDA R DOT
Mitsubishi		R DOT
Subaru		R DOT
Toyota		TOYOTA R DOT

▲ **FIGURE 16-18**
Original- and replacement-part labels for selected manufacturers
(Courtesy of 3M Corporation)

(NHTSA), the federal agency charged with setting the standards for the administration of the law. The car lines chosen each year for **parts marking** are those designated as high-theft lines. The parts requiring the additional identification are the major parts that are normally most sought after in a chop-shop operation and include: the engine; transmission; both front fenders; hood; both front doors; front and rear bumpers; both rear quarter panels; decklid, tailgate, or hatchback (whichever is applicable); and both rear doors (if present) (Figure 16-17).

The numbers must either be inscribed on the designated parts or be printed on labels attached to the parts. Labels must tear into pieces if removed; if completely removed, they must leave a "footprint," which becomes visible through certain investigative techniques such as using an ultraviolet light. The standards apply to the major parts of the designated new car lines and to replacement parts for the same car lines. The new-part labels must have the manufacturer's logo or other identifier printed on them and must use the full 17-character VIN for identification (Figure 16-18); if, however, a VIN derivative of at least 8 characters was being used to identify the engine and transmission on a particular covered line on the effective date of the law, that practice may continue. The identifier on covered replacement parts must carry the manufacturer's trademark, logo, or other distinguishing symbol, the letter "R" to reflect replacement, and the letters "DOT" (Figure 16-18). The labels are to be affixed to the part on a surface that is not normally exposed to damage when the part is installed, adjusted, removed, or damaged in an accident. When the part is removed from the vehicle, the label or inscription must be visible without disassembling the part.

The law limits the application of the requirements to no more than 14 production car lines for any one manufacturer, and the costs to the manufacturer for compliance cannot exceed $15 per vehicle, excluding the costs of marking the engine and transmission.

There is an exemption in the law, called a "black-box" exemption, which allows NHTSA to exempt from compliance with the standards up to two car lines per year for any single manufacturer if the vehicle line is equipped by the manufacturer with a standard equipment antitheft device determined by NHTSA to be as effective in deterring and reducing vehicle theft as would be compliance with the parts-marking requirements of the theft prevention standard.

The intent underlying the passage of the law, the promulgation of standards, and the marking of original and replacement parts was to reduce auto theft by ostensibly making it more difficult for the thief to conceal the identity of major parts, by providing fewer significant parts that would be untraceable, and by making it easier for law-enforcement investigators to identify stolen parts.

Having determined that the parts-marking program initiated in 1984 was effective, Congress passed the Anti-Car Theft Act of 1992, which continued and extended the program. The 1992 legislation also called for the U.S. Attorney General to conduct an initial evaluation, in 1997, of the effectiveness of the program in inhibiting chop-shop operations and deterring motor vehicle theft, with the objective of extending the parts-marking program to all lines (makes and models) by the end of 1997. The study recommended continuance of the program. The act required a long-range review of the program in 1999. In addition to evaluating whether chop-shop operations were affected and theft had been deterred, the study was to determine whether the black-box exemptions were an effective substitute for parts marking in substantially reducing motor vehicle theft.

The act also required repair shops to check the VIN on all parts against a national file. Previously, this was the NCIC stolen-vehicle file, but the FBI, by direction of the act, established the National Stolen Parts Motor Vehicle Information System (NSPMVIS). Other provisions of the law made armed carjacking a federal crime; doubled the maximum penalty for importing, exporting, transporting, selling, or receiving a stolen vehicle; and directed U.S. Customs to spot-check vehicles and containers leaving the country.

To carry out the study mandate of the 1992 legislation, the Attorney General directed the National Institute of Justice to commission a study on the effectiveness of the parts-marking program. The report, released in 2000, concluded that the available evidence warrants application of the parts-marking standard to all motor vehicle lines. The decision was, in large measure, based on estimates and the absence of negative information. The study estimated that parts marking costs manufacturers about $5 per vehicle.[40] The study also concluded that 33–158 fewer cars are stolen per 100,000 marked cars because of parts marking.[41] The research was unable to establish whether antitheft devices installed in vehicles were an effective alternative to parts marking.[42]

Manufacturers urged the Attorney General not to expand the program, but the Attorney General listened to law-enforcement investigators who identified four ways that parts marking provides assistance. First, thieves often remove, alter, or obliterate the VIN plate and other numbers, but as long as one part number remains intact, the vehicle can be identified; this enables the owner to be identified and facilitates proving that the vehicle was stolen and securing an arrest. Second, auto-theft investigators in many jurisdictions have been given authority to seize parts or vehicles when markings have been removed or destroyed. Third, the absence of markings causes investigators to inquire further, and such investigations often lead to larger stolen-vehicle cases. Fourth, in jurisdictions requiring inspections of rebuilt vehicles before issuing a new certificate of title, a determination can be made as to whether stolen parts are being used in the rebuilding process.[43]

VIN Editing and Reconstruction

In any investigation, even when it appears that the VIN has not been altered or defaced, the investigator must check the validity of the identifying numbers. Using the worksheet in Figure 16-12 will verify the correctness of the check digit only as compared with, and calculated from, the other 16 characters. A VIN edit computer program available at many law-enforcement agencies and state motor vehicle regulatory offices can readily determine if the entered VIN is "good." If the VIN is invalid, computer programs can analyze the available information and at least narrow the valid possibilities of a correct VIN. Such programs replace what formerly was a long drawn-out manual process accomplished by checking manufacturers' records. VINASSIST, available from NICB, is one such program and is currently being used by over 10,000 insurers and law-enforcement agencies. As noted earlier, the program edits, evaluates, and corrects vehicle identification numbers.

VIN Restoration

The restoration of manufacturers' serial numbers altered or obliterated from metal is a process that can be performed by an investigator with the proper material at hand (Figure 16-19). There is no mystery involved in number restoration as long as the investigator is willing to do the necessary preparation and has the patience to await results that are often slow in developing.

When a die is struck on metal, the molecules beneath the die are compressed, and it is on these compressed molecules that the restoration mediums are applied. The type of metal surface dictates which of the three primary methods of restoration—heat, acid, or acid and electricity—should be used. In the heat process, an oxygen-acetylene torch is used on cast iron only. An electrolytic process in which 5–6 volts of electricity at 2–3 amps are used in conjunction with a solution of hydrochloric acid is generally used on steel. For the etching of aluminum, one solution of potassium hydroxide and a second of hydrochloric acid and mercuric chloride are applied using a cotton or fiberglass swab.

Regardless of which type of surface is involved and which restoration process is used, the surface must be unusual residue or materials, old tires, matches, or any other item that may be related to the case. Samples should be taken of soil, which may contain evidence of flammable liquids. When found, each item should be photographed before being moved, and then it should be properly packaged and marked as evidence.

An inspection of the salvage must be completed for information on the origin and possible motive for the fire. Generally, investigators inspect the burnt automobile before contacting the owner, and the inspection is made as soon after the fire as possible. The inspection starts where the fire apparently originated. In accidental fires, this will normally be the part of the vehicle that is the most badly damaged from the intensity of the heat. Accidental fires usually spread in diminishing degrees from the point of origin according to prevailing conditions. Conditions include direction and velocity of wind and/or materials on which flames feed, such as gasoline in the tank, woodwork, or other similarly flammable parts of the vehicle. When there are significant variations in these patterns, arson emerges as a possibility. Arson fires started with flammable materials usually show intense heat in more than one place. The investigator should carefully note the extent of the fire and its path. This information may prove valuable in the later questioning of the owner or witnesses.

The car also should be inspected for the removal of equipment such as stereo, heater, air horns, fog lights, and so forth. Notice should also be made of other irregularities such as old tires on new cars or missing spare tires.

Inspection of the Fuel System

The investigator should determine whether the cap to the gas tank was in place at the time of the fire. Sometimes gasoline to start the fire is siphoned from the tank, and the cap is carelessly left off. If the cap is blown off, it will show effects of an explosion. The drain plug in the bottom of the tank should be checked. In addition, if it was removed or loosened before the fire, there might be evidence of fresh tool marks, especially pliers' marks, on it.

The gas lines should be examined for breaks between the tank and the fuel pump. Breaks should be examined for tool marks. Some arsonists disconnect the line below the tank to obtain gasoline to start the fire and fail to replace the line.

Gasoline to start the fire is sometimes obtained by disconnecting the line from the fuel pump and running the starter. If the fuel pump is melted, there should be evidence of fire on the sidepans. If the fuel pump was disconnected to allow the gasoline to run out and then be set on fire, there may be carbon deposits inside the gas line at the fuel pump.

The investigator should establish whether parts of the fuel pump are missing. If key parts of the fuel system are missing, and the owner says that the vehicle was running at the time of the fire, then there is strong reason to suspect arson. This is true regardless of whether the vehicle is equipped with a mechanical pump in a low-pressure carbureted system or an electric pump in a high-pressure fuel-injected system.

Inspection of the Electrical System

A short circuit in the electric wiring is the most common excuse offered for automobile fires. The chances of a modern automobile's burning up from a short in the wiring are negligible. Engineers have virtually eliminated this hazard. If a fire in fact did start from malfunctions in the electrical system, there generally is enough evidence to substantiate it.

The wires near where the fire started should be inspected. If the wires are not melted completely, a short can be located. A short melts the strands of wire apart and causes small beads of melted wire to form on the ends. Wires that are burned in two have sharp points. If the fire started in an electrical system, the system must be close to a flammable substance for the fire to spread. If a fire started from a short while the motor was running, the distributor points will be stuck or fused.

Inspection of the Motor, Radiator, and Parts Under and Near the Hood

The only possible place for an accidental fire to start at this location is around the fuel pump or carburetor and at the wiring. Any evidence of a fire on the front lower part of the motor not attributable to these parts indicates the use of flammables. If lead is melted from any lower or outside seams of the radiator, this is strong evidence of flammables. The fan belt does not usually burn in an accidental fire.

Gasoline on the motor sometimes causes the rubber cushions for the front of the motor to show evidence of fire. This evidence does not occur in accidental fires.

The radiator should also be checked. A badly burned lower right corner indicates that the gas line from the fuel pump to the carburetor was disconnected, the starter was run to pump out gasoline through the fuel pump, and then the gasoline was set on fire.

Inspection of the Body

The body of the car is usually so badly burned as to afford little evidence. However, signs of the intensity of heat sometimes point to the use of an inflammable. An excessive amount of flammable material may run through the floor of the car and burn underneath, causing oil or gasoline soot to form on the underside of the car. An examination should be made for this soot. If the hood was raised during the fire, the paint on the top panels may be blistered but not be burned off where the two panels touched. If the wind was blowing from the rear of the car to the front, the paint should be burned for almost the length of the hood. The radiator core will be burned, but there will not have been enough fire at the rear of the car to do much damage to the gasoline tank. If the paint on the hood is burned only an inch or so from the rear toward the front, this would indicate that the wind was blowing from the front of the car toward the rear, in which case the gasoline tank may be badly damaged but the radiator will be intact.

CONTACT WITH THE OWNER

An investigation must be made of the car owner for evidence of intent, motive, and opportunity, and the owner must be questioned to establish his or her knowledge of the fire and to verify information. Before interviewing the owner, the investigator should learn as much as possible about him/her. This information may prove quite useful during the interview. The importance of preplanning the interview cannot be overemphasized. The more facts the investigator has available, the greater the probability of a successful clearance or later conviction.

Information should be obtained from the owner about the details of the purchase, such as date, cost, trade-in, down payment, amount of mortgage due, payments past due, name of salesperson, and so forth. The investigator should also inquire about the general condition of the car at the time of the fire and ask about defects, mileage, presence or absence of unusual equipment, and recent repairs.[45]

PREVENTION PROGRAMS

Each year new and innovative approaches to the prevention and the detection of crime and the apprehension of offenders are developed. Some of these are related to investigative techniques, whereas others are high-tech equipment developments that are designed to reduce the vehicle theft problem or assist law-enforcement officers in their efforts. Other strategies are available to reduce the incidence of fraud.

AUTO THEFT

Law-enforcement officers and agencies in a number of jurisdictions now rely on integrated communications and computer networks of the FBI, state, and local police to identify and locate stolen vehicles. One unique system uses a small device called a micromaster, which is installed at random in a vehicle's electrical system. The micromaster is a microprocessor-controlled transceiver with its own unique code.

If a vehicle is stolen, the owner reports the theft to the local police in the usual way. The owner also tells the police that the vehicle is equipped with a micromaster. The police then announce through normal channels and the National Crime Information Center that a micromaster-equipped vehicle has been stolen. A computer then activates a transmitter that sends a signal with the stolen vehicle's own code. (The present system can manage up to 8 billion discrete micromaster codes.) The signal activates the micromaster's transceiver, and starts sending a signal identifying it as a stolen vehicle. The activation and tracking of the micromaster signal is under the control of

law-enforcement authorities. They have a homing device or, more recently used, GPS tracking system that gives them information about the location of the car. The system also allows police officers to identify micromaster signals and determine whether the stolen car has been involved in a crime.[46] LoJack is probably the best known system in use. Some of these tracking systems rely on signal relay towers, whereas others use a satellite-enhanced global positioning system (GPS) method of tracking. The law-enforcement vehicles are equipped with tracking computers that bring up street maps that pinpoint the location and direction of travel within a very close proximity.

Many vehicles are now being manufactured with anti-theft locks, starter disengagement systems (called *ignition kill switches*), and various other devices in an attempt to reduce the attractiveness of a particular model to the thief. Some of these are models that qualify for the black-box exemption to the labeling standards established under the guidelines of the Motor Vehicle Theft Law Enforcement Act of 1984.

In recent years, a number of private concerns have begun marketing antitheft devices that can be used effectively on older vehicles. It should be noted at the outset that no device can absolutely prevent motor vehicle theft, and one should look askance at any product or brand of product that is represented to be an absolute theft preventive.

Theft deterrent devices are of two types—passive or active. With a **passive system,** the driver does not need to do anything to activate the system, though he or she may be required to do something to deactivate the system. An **active system** requires that the operator do something every time the vehicle is driven or parked.

Audible alarm systems may be either passive or active and may be effective if anyone pays attention when an alarm is activated. Because some systems activate easily when someone passes the vehicle, a strong wind blows, or lightning strikes half a mile away, many people pay little attention, beyond a passing glance, to a vehicle with an alarm blaring. Escape from the vicinity of the noise is more important than determining if a theft is occurring. The alarms are treated more as an annoyance than as a theft deterrent.

A boot is an active device installed under a front tire that prevents the vehicle from being moved until the boot is removed. Other active devices can key lock the transmission or the brakes.

Many communities have instituted decal "alert" programs that provide decals for vehicles registered with the local law-enforcement agency and authorize any law-enforcement officer to stop the vehicle and question the driver if the vehicle is observed on the streets during certain hours (such as 2 A.M. to 6 A.M.).

A fuel shut-off device, which blocks the fuel line, may be activated by removal of the ignition key or by the throwing of a switch.

A case-hardened steering-column ignition lock that cannot be removed using a conventional slide hammer or lock puller can be effective, as can a case-hardened steel protective cap that fits over the ignition lock to prevent extraction of the ignition lock cylinder. The cap fastens to a steel collar that fits around the steering post and over the ignition lock. The ignition key fits through a slot in the cap.

Several manufacturers install a microchip or transponder in the ignition key that must be electronically read when inserted into the ignition in order for the vehicle to start. Early versions of some of these systems had only a few combinations, which could easily be defeated if a thief could procure a set of masters with all the combinations. However, General Motors' PASS-KEY III and Ford's Passive Anti-Theft System (PATS), as well as the newer systems on many other domestic and foreign-made brands, use much more advanced and sophisticated electronic systems that are deterring theft.

General Motors' OnStar system uses GPS to track vehicles whose drivers need assistance. OnStar can now slow down a stolen vehicle. The Stolen Vehicle Slowdown (SVS) service is an enhancement to the normal stolen vehicle assistance program offered by OnStar. When an OnStar equipped vehicle is stolen, OnStar can provide the vehicle's exact GPS location to law enforcement. They would also notify law enforcement if the slowdown service is available. When law enforcement has sight of the stolen vehicle, the OnStar operator can flash the lights of the car to verify that law enforcement has the correct vehicle. If necessary, law enforcement can request a slowdown. OnStar will then send a signal to the vehicle that causes the throttle input to be ignored. As a result, the vehicle will start slowing down to idle speed. All other systems of the vehicle continue to act normally.[47]

A steel or an alloy post, rod, or collar may attach to the steering wheel, which can be extended and locked in place. The device prevents the steering wheel from making full rotations. This type of active device can be an effective deterrent to theft if used properly, but it is obviously ineffective if the operator of the vehicle forgets or considers it an inconvenience to install it each time the vehicle is left unattended.

VIN etching is a process that helps identify vehicles recovered by the police after a theft has occurred. As noted earlier, thieves often attempt to conceal the identity of stolen vehicles by grinding numbers. When the VIN is permanently etched, using acid, on all the vehicle's windows, the identifying numbers are often overlooked by the thief or require that the thief remove all the window glass to prevent identification, a major task a thief may not be willing to undertake.

Some programs focus on the responsibilities of vehicle owners to do their part in preventing vehicle theft. The Michigan affiliate of the American Automobile Association implemented a law providing that if a car is stolen and the keys are anywhere in the passenger compartment, the owner, in addition to absorbing his or her insurance deductible, also absorbs an extra $500 plus 10% of the value of the vehicle. The total amount is deducted from the amount of the insurance payment made on the theft loss claim. The responsibilities of owners are also reflected in a survey initiated by the NICB that consists of scoring answers to some questions and taking necessary preventive actions on the basis of the total score. This is called a *layered approach to theft deterrence* (Figure 16-22).

Some other prevention techniques include these:

- If a lighter receptacle is used for a radio, telephone, or radar detector, remove the item when leaving the vehicle and reinsert the lighter. Thieves look for empty receptacles.

▶ **FIGURE 16-22**
The layered approach
(Courtesy of National Insurance Crime Bureau)

❶ Location

City population	Points
Over 250,000	8
250,000 to 100,001	6
100,000 to 50,001	4
50,000 to 10,000	2
Under 10,000	0

❷ Vehicle style

Vehicle owned	Points
Sports car	5
Luxury car	4
Sport-utility	4
Sedan	3
Passenger van	1
Station wagon	0

❸ Vehicle age

Age of vehicle	Points
0 to five years	1
Six to eight years	2
Nine-plus years	0

❹ Bonus point

Add 1 point to your score if you live near an international port or border.

Your score tells how many layers of protection your vehicle needs. For example, if your vehicle scored a 4, the chance of theft is considered low and it should have a first layer of protection. If your vehicle scored a 12, it should have first, second and third layers. The scores:

Layer 1 (0 to 4 points)

Common sense—Remove keys from the ignition, lock the doors, close all windows, park in lighted areas.

Layer 2 (5 to 10 points)

Visible or audible deterrent—Steering wheel locks, steering column collars, theft-deterrent decals, tire locks, window etching.

Layer 3 (11 to 14 points)

Visible immobilizer— Smart keys, fuse cutoffs, kill switches, and starter, ignition or fuel disablers.

Layer 4 (15 to 16 points)

Tracking systems

- Always lock the vehicle and remove the keys.
- Lock valuables in the trunk. Do not leave personal identification or credit cards in the vehicle.
- Do not leave a vehicle running while unattended.
- Photocopy registration and insurance papers and carry them on your person, not in the glove compartment.
- Park in a garage or in a well-lighted, heavily traveled area.
- When parking at a curb, turn the wheels toward the curb and use the emergency brake. This makes the vehicle harder to steal.
- Do not hide spare keys in or on the vehicle.
- Write the name of the owner and the VIN in crayon under the hood and in the trunk.
- Drop business cards down window channels into door interiors. This will make later identification easier.

Theft of vehicles from new- and used-car dealers is not a new phenomenon. Sometimes the dealership knows a vehicle is missing, such as when a vehicle taken on a test drive is not returned. Other times, if an inventory is large, a vehicle may be stolen overnight and not missed for several days. Employee theft is also a problem. Key control is an essential crime prevention practice for a dealership. Keys should be kept in a locked cabinet with only a few people having access. Keys that are out for demonstration or sales purposes must be monitored. Controls should be so tight that no one can take a key and get a duplicate made. Customers should never be allowed to test-drive a vehicle without a salesperson going along. Display lots should be well lighted, and barriers should be erected that permit access and good observation from outside but are sufficient to deter theft at night and when the dealership is closed. Officers who are familiar with the concepts of crime prevention through environmental design should be consulted.

CAR RENTALS

Car rental companies are generally knowledgeable about motor vehicle theft and techniques of prevention, but an investigator would be wise to understand some basics. In daily rental, the company is handing over the keys of a car to a person no one in the company has seen before or knows anything about. The rental agreement should be completely filled out, and the picture and information on the renter's driver's license should be carefully checked to make sure it matches the description of the person to whom the vehicle is being rented.

Rental companies generally require a credit card even for a cash rental. This not only serves as a good indication that the customer is a responsible person but also helps ensure that the contract will be paid. The employee of the rental company should make sure the credit card is current and check it against the driver's license to make sure the same name is on both documents.

Theft of rental vehicles generally occurs when a vehicle is not returned after it has been rented. At least one national rental company is in the process of installing tracking systems, as described earlier, which are traceable using radio-wave or GPS systems.

HEAVY EQUIPMENT

Tiny transponders that act as identification devices are now available. The device can be glued anywhere on the vehicle. Some agencies are experimenting with injecting the transponder into tires of construction equipment. If attempts are made to completely conceal or alter a stolen vehicle's identity, a receiver can accurately distinguish the vehicle from all others.

Owners of construction equipment are also encouraged to take the following actions:

- Use security devices such as ignition locks, stabilizer arm locks, and fuel shut-off valves.
- Record all product identification numbers, and participate in equipment identification programs.
- Photograph all equipment, paying particular attention to unique features such as dents, decals, and scratches, to aid in later identification.
- Leave equipment in well-lighted and fenced areas at job sites and equipment yards.
- Know the location of all construction equipment at all times.
- Keep law enforcement informed about where equipment is located and how long it will be maintained in a particular location.
- Take extra precautions on weekends. Most equipment thefts occur between 6 P.M. on Friday and 6 A.M. on Monday.
- Do not leave keys in any equipment that uses keys, and lock all machines that can be locked when not in use.
- Immediately report suspicious activity (such as a stranger taking photographs of equipment) to law-enforcement officials.

Other methods of reducing or preventing theft of off-road equipment are available. Programs are available through private enterprise whereby heavy equipment can be registered, with each piece being assigned its own identification number. The equipment is "decaled" with its own number welded on at several locations. Should a law-enforcement officer become suspicious, the dispatcher can call a toll-free number and remain on the line as the company calls the owner to verify the location of the equipment.

FRAUD

The prevention of fraud can best be accomplished by knowing some things about both the insured and the vehicle. "Know your insured" is always sound advice for an insurance agent. Getting good identification on the person, learning why the person selected a particular agent or agency, and finding out how the insured learned of the agent or agency can all be useful in helping to determine whether the act of insuring is legitimate. Knowing about the insured vehicle is equally important in the fight against fraud.

Perhaps the most profound fraud prevention effort ever initiated is the preinsurance inspection program, particularly when photographs are required. Deceptively simple in concept and application, it is amazing that fewer than half a dozen states have even considered, much less adopted, mandatory legislation. The concept requires that before a vehicle can be insured, it must be physically inspected by a representative or an agent acting on behalf of the insurer.

A simple inspection requirement can immediately eliminate or substantially reduce two of the most prolific tactics in committing insurance fraud. First, it virtually eliminates the false-vehicle theft, which is normally based on insuring a "paper," or "phantom," car—in other words, a vehicle that does not exist—and subsequently reporting it stolen in order to file against and recover on an insurance policy. Second, a well-written preinsurance report can substantially reduce fraudulent claims about theft of expensive equipment on a vehicle or claims that damage actually present before issuance of the policy occurred when the substandard vehicle either was involved in a reported accident or was stolen.

Photographs supporting an inspection report make the program particularly effective, and color photographs are even more revealing. Photographs can show the exact condition of a vehicle at the time a policy was issued so as to dispel fraudulent damage claims filed later. It is recommended that at least two photographs be taken from diagonal corners so that one picture shows the front and one side of the vehicle and the other photo shows the rear and other side. These two photos will eliminate false damage claims, but there remains the question of proving that the photos are of the insured vehicle and not simply one of the same year, make, and model. To resolve this concern, a few of the jurisdictions having inspection programs require that a third photograph be taken of the federal motor vehicle safety certification label (often called the EPA label), which is usually found on the left door. This label contains, among other information, the vehicle identification number, which, as noted earlier, is the specific identifier for that vehicle as distinguished from all other vehicles. This reverifies the number contained in the written report, thus avoiding or explaining inadvertent omissions or the accidental transposition of numbers.

An inexpensive instant-developing camera and film can be used for the program. In 1977 New York became the first state to enact legislation mandating photographic inspection before the issuance of insurance policies. The program initially required that two photographs be taken from a 180-degree angle, but the law was amended in 1986 to require the third photo of the federal motor vehicle safety certification label. Massachusetts was the next state to adopt a preinsurance inspection program. Legislation followed thereafter in New Jersey and Florida, although not all these states have equally effective legislatively mandated programs. In addition to these states, two insurance companies have their own photographic inspection programs. Neither GEICO nor State Farm will insure a noninspected vehicle.

Is the program effective? Although it is difficult to measure how much crime (insurance fraud) is deterred by a photo inspection program, it has been estimated that in the state of New York, reduction in costs and in insurance fraud claims has saved well over $100 million, and these savings have been passed on to insurance buyers through premium reductions. Although insurance premiums have not actually been reduced in New York, the overall increase in premiums in that state has amounted to less than half the national average.[48]

ODOMETER FRAUD

One of the most costly consumer frauds of modern times is **odometer fraud,** also known by various other names, including odometer tampering, rollbacks, and clocking. The National Highway Traffic Safety Administration (NHTSA) estimates that over 3 million cars are clocked each year and that the cost of this fraud to American consumers surpasses $3 billion annually.

The most susceptible vehicles to odometer tampering are those that are relatively new with exceptionally high mileage. Of the total number of passenger cars sold in the United States each year, approximately half are sold to car rental or leasing companies or to others for business use. Each year, at least 4 million of these late-model high-mileage cars are replaced. Those that are taken off lease or are no longer used for business purposes find their way into the used-car market.

The reason for odometer rollbacks is to increase the value of used vehicles on the market. Obviously, a car with fewer miles should bring a higher price than one with high mileage. It has been conservatively estimated that on a small or intermediate-size car, the sales value increases $50 for each 1,000 miles that the odometer is set back; in larger vehicles, the value increases to around $65 per 1,000 miles the odometer reading is reduced. Thus, a late-model car that is clocked from 70,000 miles to 30,000 miles can increase its value to the seller by $2,000 to $2,600. This amounts to a nice additional profit for persons inclined to indulge in such deceitful conduct.

Besides the obvious profits to the seller of clocked vehicles, the costs to the purchaser can be even greater in the form of potential unanticipated safety problems and increased repair costs. Since cars are generally the largest purchase made by people after the cost of a home, the condition of a car and the anticipated costs for repair and maintenance figure prominently in the decision of whether to buy a particular car. But when the odometer has been clipped, mileage is not a dependable guide for estimating potential maintenance costs, since such a vehicle will be more costly to maintain and more likely to need expensive repairs. If the purchaser-owner is unable to afford the higher costs, the quality of maintenance and repairs may suffer, along with the safety and roadworthiness of the vehicle.

Because of the proliferation of this fraud, most states have created some type of investigative unit to deal with odometer tampering by accepting complaints from citizens and determining if there is any basis for enforcement action. In addition, there are national and federal agencies and organizations actively engaged in enforcing laws and trying to prevent odometer and title fraud. NHTSA has an odometer fraud investigation arm. They work on multiple state large-volume cases. The Department of Justice attorneys prosecute the cases investigated by NHTSA. The National Odometer and Title Fraud Enforcement Association comprises investigators from the member states, NHTSA investigators, federal prosecutors, and interested auctions and dealers. State investigators can be most helpful in local investigations.

When examining a late-model low-mileage vehicle that is suspected of being clocked, the investigator should check for extensive wear on the brake pedal, the driver's seat, and the seals around the trunk. Does the extent of wear conform to the claimed mileage? A check should be made for service stickers on the door, on the doorpost, and under the hood. If present, a date and odometer reading may be present; missing stickers may suggest tampering. The odometer wheels should be in alignment, should not rotate freely, and should not be scratched or nicked. Any of these conditions may be indicative of a rollback and warrant further inquiry. The investigator should order a vehicle history file through the state's motor vehicle titling agency and then check with each successive owner (including individuals, dealers, and auctioneers), obtain all odometer disclosure statements, piece together an odometer history, and attempt to determine if there has been a rollback. If a rollback seems likely, the investigator should determine the possessor of the vehicle when it was clocked. Standard investigative techniques should then be applied.

Title fraud is as big a part of the odometer rollback problem as is the act of clocking. Title alteration, discarding of title reassignment forms to complicate the tracing of ownership, manufacturing of false reassignments, and title laundering are criminal acts that violators often engage in to support and cover up odometer rollbacks.

To mandate better record keeping, reduce the opportunity for odometer tampering, and assist law enforcement in the investigation of cases, Congress enacted the **Truth in Mileage Act** in 1986. This act, along with amendments made in several subsequent years, attempts to improve the paper trail of odometer readings by requiring more tightly controlled documentation and recording of odometer readings each time that ownership of a vehicle changes. The law attempts to close loopholes that permit the inception of fraudulent title schemes and to reduce the incidence of title washing between jurisdictions by requiring all states to adhere to strict record-keeping criteria, thus avoiding schemes to create confusing paper trails that intentionally avoid jurisdictional boundaries of courts and law-enforcement agencies.

MARINE THEFT

Marine theft is a serious problem to the boating community (Figure 16-23). It includes the theft of boats, boat trailers, outboard motors, jet skis, and all equipment associated with boating or water activities. Marine theft is a "shadow crime." It is real but difficult to define because of the lack of accurate statistical information. The main reporting mechanism, the *Uniform Crime Report* (UCR), compiled and reported annually by the Federal Bureau

◄ **FIGURE 16-23**
Marine police on lookout
Marine theft, which includes theft of boats, trailers, and all associated equipment, is a serious problem in the boating community. In communities that have extensive waterways, local police often have a marine patrol unit that provides routine patrol and investigates theft of marine equipment. (© Bonnie Kamin)

of Investigation, enters the theft of an outboard motor in the burglary index, the theft of a boat trailer in the vehicle file, and other related thefts in different categories. As a result, the magnitude of the marine theft problem is hidden in other crime indexes. Marine insurance theft data are similarly disjointed because there are many types of policies—home owners', business, inland marine, yacht—that provide coverage for marine equipment. Nevertheless, it is estimated that nationwide losses resulting from marine theft exceed $250 million annually.

The majority of thefts occur from homes, businesses, or dry storage facilities. A boat and outboard motor on a boat trailer can be stolen in a matter of seconds by a thief who simply backs up to the trailer, hooks up, and drives away. Although locking mechanisms are available for boat trailers and may deter the amateur thief, such devices are easily overcome by the professional.

Theft by water is accomplished simply by towing the boat away with another boat or by starting the motor and driving away. Boats powered by outboard motors, under 25 horsepower, usually do not have keyed ignition switches. However, even on larger boats, a dozen master keys will start virtually any marine motor, whether outboard or inboard.

Approximately 87% of all boats stolen are under 20 feet in length. Of these, boats of 16 feet and less constitute 65% of the thefts. The National Crime Information Center reports over 27,000 boat thefts entered into the computer system. Law-enforcement experts agree that most thefts are not investigated thoroughly (if at all) because of the difficulty investigators experience understanding marine equipment identification numbers and the lack of available ownership information.

Because of the absence of accurate statistical data, law enforcement is somewhat hampered in its efforts to address the problem. Consequently, there is a general lack of knowledge about marine theft and a resulting lack of commitment of resources to address the problems. In many agencies, marine theft reports are assigned to the auto theft or burglary unit and are treated as low-priority items.

Why are boats stolen? The number-one reason is profit. Marine theft is a high-profit, low-risk crime. Most often, a boat, motor, and trailer are stolen and sold as a package at a fair market value. To reduce the possibility of identification, some organized theft rings operate a chop shop, switching stolen motors, trailers, and boats or selling them separately.

There is also a lucrative market for the exportation of stolen outboard motors. In Central and South America, a used outboard motor will sell for more than a new motor in the United States. In addition, as in auto theft, insurance fraud may be involved in 25% or more of the reported marine thefts.

The increase in marine theft has often been linked by the media to drug trafficking. Experts tend to disagree. If, in fact, 87% of the boats stolen are under 20 feet in length, it is unlikely that these are being used for drug trafficking. Boats 30 feet and longer could very well be involved in drug trafficking, but such thefts constitute only 3% of the problem. Of course, larger boats are also targets for professional thieves because of their high value. However, there may be some legitimate linkage between the theft of outboard motors and the drug problem. A 300-horsepower outboard motor, which retails for over $15,000, can be sold without any ownership documents.

Most small boats are stolen not by professionals but for the personal use of the thief or, occasionally, for joyrides. This is particularly true in the theft of personal watercraft. Approximately 20% of all boat thefts involve personal watercraft stolen by juveniles for their own use. Only occasionally are boats stolen to be used as transportation in other crimes, such as burglary of a waterfront home or business.

HULL IDENTIFICATION

Effective November 1, 1972, the Federal Boating Safety Act of 1971 required boats to have a 12-character **hull identification number (HIN).** Before this, boat manufacturers assigned whatever numbers were needed for their own production records. The HIN was subsequently codified by federal regulation. The promotion of boating safety was the original purpose for the HIN. It enabled the U.S. Coast Guard to identify "batches" of boats produced by a manufacturer that failed to meet certain production standards. This consumer protection function soon became secondary after titling and registering authorities began using the HIN assigned to a boat to identify ownership in much the same manner as the VIN is used for a motor vehicle.

Although manufacturers are required to affix each HIN to the outside of the boat's transom in a "permanent manner" so that any alteration or removal will be evident, in reality this is rarely enforced. Many manufacturers attach the HIN using a plastic plate pop-riveted to the transom. This can be easily removed and replaced with a false HIN. Some manufacturers of fiberglass boats place the HIN on the outer layer of the gelcoat using a "Dymo label"–type device during the molding process. However, this can easily be scraped or gouged out by a thief with a screwdriver or knife. A professional thief will replace the removed HIN with automotive body filler that often matches the color of the gelcoat. Then, by stamping a false HIN into the body filler, it appears that the HIN was affixed by the manufacturer and the alteration often goes undetected. An additional problem occurs when the Coast Guard allows a manufacturer to alter a HIN on any boat that remains in inventory by changing the production dates or model year to reflect a newer model year. Even for an experienced marine investigator, it is difficult to recognize whether a HIN was altered to cover a theft or modified by a manufacturer to reflect a newer model year.

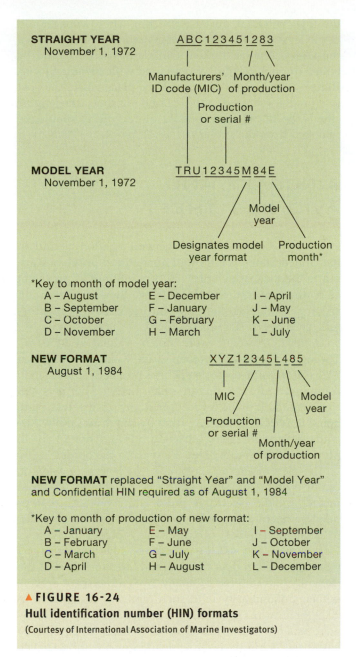

▲ FIGURE 16-24
Hull identification number (HIN) formats
(Courtesy of International Association of Marine Investigators)

The first three characters of the HIN are the manufacturer's identification code (MIC), assigned to each manufacturer by the Coast Guard. Since 1972, over 13,000 MICs have been assigned. Many codes have been reassigned after the original company went out of business. Because of this, it is very difficult even for the most experienced marine investigator to remain familiar with all the manufacturer's codes. In addition, large conglomerates such as Mercury Marine and Outboard Motor Corporation have purchased many boat manufacturers and used manufacturer's identification codes assigned to the parent corporation for multiple boat lines.

The middle five characters of the HIN are used as production numbers or serial numbers assigned by the manufacturer. Although the letters "I," "O," and "Q" cannot be used, any other letter can be used in combination with numbers. These "production" numbers can and often are repeated on a monthly basis for an entire year. Whereas the automobile VIN has a 30-year uniqueness and a check digit to avoid unintentional or deliberate omission of numbers and intentional or unintentional transposition of numbers, the HIN does not yet have these features.

TITLE AND REGISTRATION ISSUES

There are approximately 12 million pleasure boats in the United States. Roughly 160,000 of these are federally registered by the Coast Guard and are referred to as "documented." Ownership and financial disputes over **documented vessels** can be resolved in the federal courts. The remainder of the pleasure boats are registered and/or titled by each state, except Alaska, in which registration issues are regulated by the Coast Guard.

Over 30 states require that boats be titled, but only a few states require the titling of outboard motors. Even in titling states, many boats are exempted by being less than a specified length or powered by less than a specified horsepower of motor. More than half the titling programs are administered by wildlife or natural resource agencies. The remainder are operated by motor vehicle agencies.

Many jurisdictions that title boats do not have computerized ownership records or do not retain the information for more than one year. The boat registration or title files in only a few states can be accessed using the National Law Enforcement Telecommunications System (NLETS). The inability of an investigator to obtain ownership information in a timely and efficient manner makes boat theft investigation very difficult.

NCIC BOAT FILE

As noted earlier, over 27,000 stolen boats are included in the NCIC system, under the title "Boat File." The Boat File, one of the 17 NCIC 2000 files, records information on stolen boats, boat trailers, and boat parts. Information in the file is retrievable on an online basis by entering the registration or document number, the hull identification

Figure 16-24 shows the three different HIN formats approved by the Coast Guard. The straight-year and model-year formats were used from November 1, 1972, until August 1, 1984, when a new format replaced them. The only differences between the three formats are the last four characters. In the straight-year format, the last four characters reflect the calendar month and year of production. In the model-year format, the ninth character is always the letter "M" followed by the model year and a letter indicating the month of production. The newer format, optional starting January 1, 1984, and mandatory as of August 1, 1984, uses the ninth and tenth characters to reflect the calendar month and year of production and the eleventh and twelfth characters to represent the model year.

number, or the assigned NCIC number. Unless otherwise removed or located, information in the Boat File is maintained for the balance of the year of entry, plus four years. The exception to this is records that have no boat hull identification number or other number assigned by the owner that can be used for identification purposes. These remain in the file for only 90 days after entry.

The boat theft problem may be much greater than what the NCIC statistics display. There is no mandate requiring that boat thefts be entered into NCIC and, because of the difficulty of reporting, many thefts are not entered. According to marine theft experts, new edits installed in the NCIC Boat File in late 1993 contained errors, causing valid entries to be rejected and further discouraging the entry of stolen boat information by law-enforcement agencies. Another major flaw in the system is that NCIC does not enter all the Coast Guard–assigned manufacturer's identification codes and, in some cases, has assigned codes that are not those recognized by the Coast Guard.

INVESTIGATIVE RESOURCES

Marine theft investigations are often complex and time-consuming. With the difficulty in obtaining ownership information, the tens of thousands of boat manufacturers, and the lack of computerized theft information, the success of an investigation is often predicated not on what the investigator knows but on whom he or she knows to contact for assistance. A major resource is the International Association of Marine Investigators. This organization has over 2,000 members who network with other law-enforcement officers and agencies and insurance investigators throughout the United States, Canada, Europe, the Caribbean, and Central and South America. The organization holds an annual training seminar on marine theft issues.

PREVENTIVE MEASURES

There are several ways a boat owner can lessen the possibility of marine theft. For example, one individual who used to make his living by stealing boats and reselling them recommended that any boat with an electric starter should have a toggle switch that shuts off the electrical system when in the off position. The switch can be located under the dash or behind a panel. Typically, when a thief attempts to start the boat and cannot, the thief assumes that it is malfunctioning and gives up the effort to steal it.

To discourage theft, a boat owner may want to remove a vital engine part when the boat is left unattended. Trailered boats are more easily stolen than boats in the water. The best way to protect boats on trailers is to keep them out of the sight of thieves. They should be parked behind a house or behind or inside a garage where they cannot be seen from the street.

Owners should never leave boats where they will tempt a potential thief. If a boat appears difficult to steal, the thief will seek an easier victim. The owner should never leave the keys or the registration on board when the vessel is not attended. Outboard motors should be bolted through the hull and secured with clamping locks. If the owner is to be away from the place where the boat is stored for an extended period of time, the engine should be disabled or one or more wheels should be removed from the trailer.

AIRCRAFT AND AVIONICS THEFT

With approximately 225,000 general-aviation aircraft in the United States, the theft of aircraft and burglary leading to the theft of avionics are certainly not as prevalent as motor vehicle theft. Nonetheless, they are significant criminal problems that law-enforcement investigators may encounter[49] (Figure 16-25).

In 2009, 7 aircraft were stolen, valued at $150,000. Through the end of October, 2010, 5 aircraft, valued at $225,000, have been stolen. These numbers sound small compared to the 56 aircraft stolen in 1991, but it is still significant.[50] It is believed that many of the thefts are going to Mexico and being used by the drug cartels. Aircraft owners are being strongly advised not to fly to Mexico and preferably stay away from the border.

The theft of aircraft electronic equipment, or **avionics,** can be a highly lucrative enterprise for thieves. Avionics include all the electronic radio and navigation equipment on board an aircraft—easily valued at over $10,000 in even the smallest aircraft. Many pieces of avionics look similar and can be accurately identified only by referring to the model number and/or name. Part of the difficulty encountered by many law-enforcement officers is their unfamiliarity with such pieces of equipment. In 2009 there were 34 aircraft burglaries in which 97 items were stolen worth $312,000. As of October 31, 2010, there have been 24 burglaries in which 47 items worth $126,000 were stolen.[51]

There are many reasons for equipment burglaries. One of the prime reasons is the lack of security at airports and the indifference on the part of many sales outlets regarding the identification and sources of used equipment. In addition, although most avionics contain stickers and plates identifying the manufacturer, model number, part number, and even the serial number, these are often easily removed and in some cases are just stick-on labels.

Most modern avionics are designed to be easily removed from the aircraft panel to facilitate frequent repair and maintenance of the equipment. Stolen avionics are often resold through the used-parts market or to persons who need the items and are willing to overlook the source of such reasonably priced equipment.

Much of the stolen avionics equipment is exported to other countries. Some is resold using counterfeited

◄ **FIGURE 16-25**
Stolen aircraft crashes into bank building
The theft of aircraft in the United States is a relatively rare event. However, breaking into an aircraft to steal electronic parts is relatively simple, since both door locks and ignition locks on many private planes can easily be picked. Thefts of aircraft are most likely to occur at airports that are poorly lit and unattended at night. The aircraft in the picture was stolen by a juvenile from a small airfield and ultimately crashed into a downtown bank building. (© Chuck Sutnick/Tampa Fire Rescue/Getty Images)

VIN labels and VIN plates. Other equipment is switched so that the stolen equipment is never discovered, as illustrated by the following example: A thief will identify the type of equipment desired in a specific aircraft at a specific airport. The thief or thieves will then locate the same type of equipment in another aircraft at another airport. At the time of theft, the electronic equipment will be removed from the first aircraft and placed in the second aircraft after the second aircraft's equipment has been removed. The equipment from the second aircraft is then sold on the market; normally, the owner of the second aircraft doesn't even know the equipment is missing because the same material, stolen from the first aircraft, has been installed in his or her craft. The theft of equipment from the first aircraft is reported, but it is never recovered because it is already comfortably installed in aircraft number two.

RESOURCES

An investigator who is unfamiliar with aircraft and aircraft thefts should not hesitate to obtain assistance from those who have the necessary expertise. It is advised that before undertaking a significant investigation, an investigator should visit a local airport, contact airport management, aircraft companies, flight schools, and so forth, to learn basic information about aircraft, avionics, and the theft of both. The Aviation and Crime Prevention Institute located in Hagerstown, Maryland, is an excellent source of assistance and support for law-enforcement officers involved in the investigation of aviation theft.[52] The mission of the institute is to reduce aviation-related crime through information gathering, communication with law enforcement and the public, and education programs in theft prevention and security awareness.

THEFT TECHNIQUES

The techniques thieves use to steal aircraft and burglarize aircraft for the avionics equipment are not that much different from, and most frequently parallel to, those used for stealing automobiles. Of course, if theft of the aircraft is the objective, it is unlikely that the thief will gain access by smashing a window. Indeed, smashing a window is generally not necessary. Perhaps the weakest security point of any aircraft is its locks. Most aircraft manufacturers use a limited number of key combinations, and a single key may open many aircraft of the same make. Occasionally, one manufacturer's key will open an aircraft of a different manufacturer.

Both door locks and ignition locks can easily be picked, and generally there are no antitheft devices on aircraft. Many of the more expensive aircraft don't even use ignition keys, so the only requirement for the thief is to enter the cabin.

Many of the techniques used to cover the theft of aircraft are similar to the processes used to conceal the theft of motor vehicles. The following illustrates a salvage switch involving aircraft: A thief decides on the type of aircraft desired and then purchases a total wreck of a similar aircraft from a junkyard. Rather than the certificate of title and VIN plate that come with a motor vehicle, the wrecked aircraft comes with its VIN plate and log book (a document required by the Federal Aviation Administration [FAA] that records the aircraft's history and repair record). The thief then steals (or has stolen) an aircraft of the same year, make, and model; switches the VIN plate; and installs the log book. After the thief adapts the registration markings and ensures that colors match the wrecked aircraft, the salvage switch is complete.

Thefts of aircraft are most likely to occur at airports that have poor lighting and are unattended at night, especially if they have little or no security, have no control tower, and perhaps are not even fenced.

AIRCRAFT IDENTIFICATION

Aircraft have the same basic identification information as do motor vehicles. The major difference is that aircraft are regulated under a federal licensing system, whereas motor vehicles are regulated under state licensing systems. All aircraft are identified by a registration number, which is similar to a license plate number; a VIN; and make and model. The U.S. registration numbering system is part of a worldwide system under which each country has a letter and/or number code. In the United States, the code begins with the letter "N." Consequently, all U.S.-registered aircraft display an N number.

Most registered aircraft receive their N numbers when they are manufactured. It is possible for the purchaser of a used aircraft or of an aircraft currently being built to request a special N number. Such requests are processed by the FAA.

The N number is found on each side of the aircraft or on the vertical tail in large or small letter and numeral combinations. In some cases, such as on older aircraft, the N number may be displayed on the underside of one wing and the topside of the opposite wing. Helicopters have the N number displayed under the nose or undercarriage.

Most aircraft have a small plate on the instrument panel with the plane's N number on it. An investigator can look at the plate and determine whether the plate number matches the N number displayed on the exterior of the aircraft. If the plate is missing, further investigation is warranted.

Although each aircraft has a VIN, manufacturers design their own numbering systems, and the location of a VIN plate varies depending on the make. For example, on Cessna aircraft the VIN plate is found on the doorjamb; the door must be open to see the plate. The VIN plate on most single-engine and small twin-engine Beechcraft planes can be found on the right side above the wing flap; large Beechcraft planes have the VIN plate inside the main-cabin entry door frame. On Piper aircraft the VIN plate is usually found on the lower side of the tail on the aircraft's body.

As in any attempt to identify a vehicle, a vessel, or aircraft, the investigator should understand the construction process well enough to know whether and where to look for identifiers. When aircraft are built, many of the parts are subassembled elsewhere in the plant, and such subassemblies are marked with the VIN number in Magic Marker or pencil so that the aircraft can later come together at the main assembly point. If the plate is missing, the investigator should look under seats, under carpeted areas, in inspection panels, and elsewhere for ID numbers relating to the VIN.

When trying to locate a VIN plate in aircraft other than those previously mentioned, the investigator should look in some of the most common locations, such as on the doorjamb on either side of the plane, on the lower tail section on either side of the plane, on the body where the main wing is attached, near the nose wheel, or on the lower body. In other words, when in doubt, the dedicated investigator will look over the entire aircraft in an attempt to find the attached plate, which will provide make, model, and VIN information.

THEFT PREVENTION TECHNIQUES

Following are a few examples of the theft-deterrent devices available and the actions an aircraft owner can take, some without cost, to reduce the chance of theft of the aircraft or the avionics.

- There are a number of alarm systems on the market, and some even have a pain generator, a second piercing alarm inside the cockpit that is most aggravating to the human ear.
- Ignition kills, which require entry of a security code into the control panel in the cockpit, are available. If the pilot fails to get the code right after a specific number of tries, the engine-starting circuits are disabled and, in some cases, a siren will sound.
- There should be a prearranged password known only to crew members and the airport operator. Thus, a person who calls and directs that the plane be prepared for flight must know the password in order to get the plane readied. This technique has prevented the theft of many aircraft.
- A wheel-locking device, or "boot," prevents the plane from being towed or from moving under its own power.
- More secure locks can be installed.
- Airplanes should be parked at night at airports that are well lighted, fenced, and otherwise provided with security. Window covers should be used to conceal avionics.
- Avionics equipment should be checked to ensure that it is the manufacturer-installed equipment. Each piece should then be marked with a dot, paint, engraving, or scratch, and a detailed inventory should be made and recorded.
- Propeller chains and locks are available.
- Instrument panels can be equipped with a locking bar or locking cover.
- Flight operations personnel at airports should be given a list that identifies each crew member and other persons permitted to be around the plane or to authorize service over the phone.
- Airport authorities should have a central point of contact available 24 hours a day.
- Vital aircraft records should not be kept in the aircraft.

KEY TERMS

active system (theft deterrent)
American Association of Motor Vehicle
    Administrators (AAMVA)
Automatic License Plate Recognition
    System (ALPR)
avionics
cargo theft
chop shop
commercial-vehicle theft
confidential VIN
documented vessel
false-theft scheme
false-vehicle scheme
federal safety certification label
gray-market vehicle

heavy equipment
hull identification number (HIN)
inflated-theft-loss scheme
joyriding
marine theft
Motor Vehicle Theft Law Enforcement
    Act (1984)
National Insurance Crime Bureau
    (NICB)
National Motor Vehicle Title Information
    System (NMVTIS)
odometer fraud
off-road equipment
"paper vehicle"
parts marking

passive system (theft deterrent)
product identification number (PIN)
professional theft (of vehicle)
quick strip (of vehicle)
salvage switch
salvage title
salvage vehicle
Stolen Auto Recovery (STAR) System
temporary theft (of vehicle)
title fraud
Truth in Mileage Act (1986)
vehicle fraud
vehicle identification number (VIN)
VIN plate
washing (of title)

REVIEW QUESTIONS

1. Describe a chop-shop operation.
2. How does a salvage switch work?
3. Distinguish false-vehicle, false-theft, and inflated theft-loss schemes.
4. What is a "paper" vehicle?
5. How is a certificate of title "washed"?
6. What are some of the factors contributing to the theft of off-road equipment?
7. What is the National Insurance Crime Bureau, and what functions does it perform for law enforcement?
8. Why is vehicle identification the most difficult and time-consuming task faced by an investigator in an auto theft case?
9. Why do vehicles have a standardized identification numbering system?
10. What was the purpose behind passage of the Motor Vehicle Theft Law Enforcement Act of 1984?
11. Describe the three basic methods for restoring vehicle identification numbers.
12. Describe some of the principal investigative steps in determining whether a vehicle fire is an accident or arson.
13. Describe the workings and benefits of a photographic preinsurance inspection program.
14. What is odometer fraud, and why is it a significant offense?
15. Discuss the nature and seriousness of marine theft.
16. What are avionics, and why is avionics theft prevalent?

INTERNET ACTIVITIES

1. Check the web to see if your state has law enforcement and/or insurance organizations that specialize in the investigation of motor vehicle and other related thefts. What types of investigative services do they provide? Are auto theft statistics available for your state? Does the site have auto theft prevention information? If you were a criminal investigator, what other information do you think should be available on the site?

2. Learn more about the export of stolen motor vehicles and other items by logging on to the U.S. Customs site at *www.cbp.gov* and the North American Export Committee site at *www.naexportcommittee.org*. The latter website also has several related links to insurance fraud and vehicle theft prevention.

▶ Cyber criminals have many advantages. They can strike anyplace in the world without face-to-face contact with their victims.
(© Frederik Skold/The Image Bank/Getty Images)

17

CYBERCRIME

Computer-assisted crimes, such as identity theft and stalking, were discussed in Chapter 14, "White Collar Crime and Larceny." In such crimes the computer is a tool used to assist in the commission of the offense. **Cybercrime** differs from computer-assisted crime in that the computer itself is the target.

This chapter explores the conditions that had to exist before cybercrime could emerge; offenders and offenses; the differences between traditional crime and cybercrime; cybercrime tools and services; the types of computer intrusions that make cybercrime possible; and other related topics.

CHAPTER OUTLINE

CYBERCRIME: AN OVERVIEW

Cybercrime is more profitable than illegal drug trafficking.[1] In 2009 worldwide costs to consumers and businesses exceed 1 trillion dollars,[2] 8 billion of it occurring in the United States, where 20% of online consumers were victimized in a single year.[3] Their median loss was $575.[4]

There were two prerequisites for the emergence of cybercrime: (1) computers had to be commonplace, and (2) they had to be linked in a network. The first electronic computer was built in 1942, and the first personal computer (PC) was the Kenbak-1, introduced in 1971,

although fewer than 50 were ever built. Radio Shack began selling the TRS-80 in the late 1970s; IBM jumped into the PC market in 1981; and the Apple Macintosh appeared three years later. Joseph Licklider, in 1962, conceived of what is now called the Internet, with his idea of a "Galactic Network." A rudimentary form of the Internet, ARPANET, was publically demonstrated in 1972, the same year Ray Tomlinson developed e-mail. In those early years the Internet was largely used only by the government and universities. However, the rapid development of the PC market and the commercialization of the net in the early 1990s quickly led to a worldwide network; the first online service provider for consumers was Delphi (1992). Presently, over 200 million Internet searches are performed daily.[5]

The satisfaction of the two prerequisites set the stage for a new breed of criminals who (1) didn't have to leave the comfort of their homes to commit crimes; (2) were invisible/anonymous, avoiding the dangers of personal contact with their victims; (3) could strike anywhere in the world; (4) were enabled to approach thousands of potential victims simultaneously; (5) executed crimes that victims might never detect or be too embarrassed to report; (6) committed crimes that might be discovered only much later, hampering investigations; (7) stood to reap profits far beyond those associated with conventional crimes; and (8) didn't have to worry about fencing tangible stolen property—for example, televisions and cars—because what they stole was intangible property—for instance, they looted checking, savings, and casino accounts.[6] Figure 17-1 illustrates some of the differences between traditional and cybercrime techniques.

Traditional criminal techniques

Burglary: Breaking into a building with the intent to steal.

Deceptive callers: Criminals who telephone their victims and ask for their financial and/or personal identity information.

Extortion: Illegal use of force or one's official position or powers to obtain property, funds, or patronage.

Fraud: Deceit, trickery, sharp practice, or breach of confidence, perpetrated for profit or to gain some unfair or dishonest advantage.

Identity theft: Impersonating or presenting oneself as another in order to gain access, information, or reward.

Child exploitation: Criminal victimization of minors for indecent purposes such as pornography and sexual abuse.

Cybercrime

Hacking: Computer or network intrusion providing unauthorized access.

Phishing: A high-tech scam that frequently uses unsolicited messages to deceive people into disclosing their financial and/or personal identity information.

Internet extortion: Hacking into and controlling various industry databases (or the threat of), promising to release control back to the company if funds are received or some other demand satisfied.

Internet fraud: A broad category of fraud schemes that use one or more components of the Internet to defraud prospective victims, conduct fraudulent transactions, or transmit fraudulent transactions to financial institutions or other parties.

Identity theft: The wrongful obtaining and using of another person's identifying information in some way that involves fraud or deception, typically for economic gain.

Child exploitation: Using computers and networks to facilitate the criminal victimization of minors.

▲ **FIGURE 17-1** **Comparison of traditional and cybercrime techniques**

(No author, *Cybercrime: Public and Private Entities Face Challenges in Addressing Cyber Threats* [Washington, D.C.: General Accountability Office, June 20007], p. 6)

CYBERCRIME TOOLS AND SERVICES RELATED TO THEFT AND FRAUD

Cybercrime tools and services are being mass marketed on the Internet. They are found on publicly accessible web forums, such as Internet Relay Chat (IRC); the major vendors are principally located in Russia, Eastern Europe, and Malaysia.[7] Sellers and buyers also communicate by ICQ software (pronounced "I seek you"). Table 17-1 summarizes three major categories of cybercrime tools and services related to theft and fraud.

Buying malicious tools and services on the Internet from anonymous vendors in foreign countries has resulted in many would-be cybercriminals being scammed and left empty handed. These "wannabes" are in no position to complain to anyone about their losses, and "honest" malicious tools and services vendors, referred to as "verified sellers,"[8] stand to lose potential sales if their industry is generally seen as fraudulent. As a result, independent "guarantors" often act as the middlemen in the sales process for 3–5% of the selling cost, ensuring that the exact terms of the contract are met.[9] Guarantors hold the buyer's money, verify that the software works as advertised, and then transmit the money to the vendor and the product to the buyer.

TABLE 17-1	Cybercrime Tools and Services	
TOOLS/SERVICES	**DESCRIPTION**	**PERCENTAGE OF MARKET SHARE**
Malicious Software	Ready to run crimeware is often purchased on the Internet— e.g., viruses, worms, and spyware. Cost ranges from less than $10 for a simple virus to over $5,000 for advanced capability programs. The Trojan horse is the most commonly sold malicious software at approximately $750 per copy. (Malicious software is discussed later in this chapter.) Some sites offer free downloads of older versions of malicious software that may be useable or that places a virus on the downloader's computer.	39
Cybercrime Services	Examples include distribution of spam and pop-up messages, and denial of service attacks to shut down websites.	34
Stolen Data	Includes bank, savings, checking, credit card, PayPal, iTunes, and casino account numbers; user names and passwords; identity documents—for example, data from scanned passports—are also available to assume new identities or engage in fraud. Offenders may use or sell data "harvested."	27

Source: Bill Chu, Thomas J. Holt, and Gail Joon Ahn, "Examining the Creation, Distribution, and Function of Malware On-Line," (Washington, D.C.: U.S. Department of Justice, March 2010), pp. 7–8, with some changes and additions.

OFFENDERS AND OFFENSES

Not so long ago, computer enthusiasts hacked into computers out of curiosity or for excitement. Now, the overwhelming motive is for financial gain. Hackers/crackers who use their skills to illegally make money are called **"black hatters";** those who use them for good—for example, for identifying security risks in computer systems and notifying corporations and other entities of their vulnerability—are designated as **"white hatters."**

Cybercrime is a major source of profit for some transnational criminal organizations (TCOs).[10] During the first six months of 2010, cyberattacks increased from 60 million to nearly 180 million.[11] Hong Kong Triad groups are funding the academic education of some members to acquire degrees in computer science, software engineering, and information systems in order to commit lucrative cybercrimes.[12] Al Qaeda is also acquiring cybercrime expertise to fund its operations.[13]

The triads are in competition with other TCOs, including well-educated members of groups in Russia and Eastern Europe; this competition is so keen that recently the black market price for stolen credit card numbers has dropped from 7$ to 10$ to 1$.[14] **"Carders"** are cybercriminals who primarily profit from selling stolen credit card numbers. MasterCard International reported that in a single year more than 40 million consumer credit card numbers were accessed by hackers.[15] In 2011 Sony reported that sensitive information was stolen from 102 million user accounts.

In cases for which perpetrator data is available, 76% of cybercriminals are male, and most range in age from 14 to 30 years. Hackers are often described as "antisocial loners," which is not very useful for investigators. More helpful is Table 17-2, a taxonomy or classification scheme that categorizes cybercriminals by type, characteristics, motivation, and skill. This table is not a fixed hierarchy of offenders, but it does provide a framework for thinking about the capabilities and threats posed by different cybercriminals. To a degree, Table 17-2 is limited in that it represents "pure" categories, when in fact cyberoffenders may be active in several different categories. Table 17-3 summarizes data about cybercrime perpetrators and complainants. It suggests that offenders have a preference not to victimize people living in the offenders' own state.

COMPUTER INTRUSIONS

Computer intrusions are accomplished by the use of malware, a term derived from combining *mal*icious and *software*. **Malware** is intended to (1) deny use of computers; (2) covertly gain control over computers, for example, through the use of a Remote Administrator Tool (RAT);

| **TABLE 17-2** | **Taxonomy of Cybercriminals** | | |

TYPE	CHARACTERISTICS	MOTIVATION	SKILL LEVEL
1. Novice	• Limited computer/programming skills • Use software ("tool kits") written by others, e.g., SpyEye, IcePack, XRumer, and KanBe, which cost from $700 to several thousand dollars • Referred to as "script kiddies" or "script bunnies" • Commit simple cybercrimes, e.g., virus attack	• Thrill seeking • Ego enhancement • Prove themselves to others • Collect "trophies"	Low
2. Cyberpunks	• Higher skills than novices • Can write some of their own programs • Better understanding of systems they attack • Deface web pages, send spam • Many engage in account data thefts, cyberfraud	• Media attention • Financial gain	Moderate
3. Internals/Insiders	• Often information technology (IT) professionals • Represent greatest risk because in position of trust • Historically have triggered great losses • Inflated sense of their importance/value • Have strong sense of entitlement	• Typically revenge • Feel slighted, e.g., not promoted • Disgruntled, seek to "right" a "wrong" done to them	High
4. Petty Crooks	• Some are making transition from novice or street to cybercrimes • Not interested in notoriety/attention, keep low profile • May work to obtain requisite skills, e.g., attend technical school • May show a progression in skill or interest over time, such as moving to professional criminals category	• Greed, financial gain • In small number of cases may act out of revenge, e.g., former employer, ex-girl/boyfriend	Moderate
5. Virus Writers	• Often in transition to some other category • Age of VWs varies • Stop or shift to another category during mid- to late-20s	• Mixed motives • Motives may be similar to novices and petty criminals	Very high
6. Old Guard Hackers	• Generally have no criminal intent • However, disregard for others' property may cause operational interruption or other losses • Enjoy technical challenge of hacking • Write but generally do not use tool kits they sell to novices	• Curiosity • Need for challenges	Very high
7. Professional Criminals	• Some number are well trained former intelligence operatives—Russia, Eastern Block European countries and some Asian gangs • Crime is their career field • Seldom arrested; convicted even less often • Choose lucrative targets, e.g., banks, casinos, intellectual property (e.g., games, movies, recipes) • Fully exploit the potential of the Internet as a crime tool • Apolitical, will commit national security espionage for profit, even against their own governments • "Guns for hire," if the price for accepting a "project" is right • High tolerance for risk	• Money and financial gain • Life-style attractive	Very high

CONTINUED

| TABLE 17-2 | CONTINUED |

TYPE	CHARACTERISTICS	MOTIVATION	SKILL LEVEL
8. Information/ Espionage Warfare	• Targets are defense industry corporations to nations • Disrupt, destabilize, corrupt, exploit, or otherwise compromise operational capabilities, e.g., production schedules, satellites, military unit communications, and data integrity/reliability • Theft of national security information, e.g., stealth capabilities of aircraft and submarines, weapons in development • May be conducted, or sponsored by corporate competitors, a national government, or contracted with professional criminal gangs	• Highly trained, skilled, and experienced, • May be very patriotic • Profit motivation may be primary	Highest

Source: Markus Rogers, "A Two-Dimensional Circumplex Approach to the Development of a Hacker Taxonomy," *Digital Investigation*, Vol. 3, Issue 2, 2006, pp. 98–100, with some changes and additions.

| TABLE 17-3 | Cybercrime Perpetrators and Complainants per 100,000 People |

RANK	STATE	PERPETRATORS PER 100,000 PEOPLE	RANK	STATE	COMPLAINANTS PER 100,000 PEOPLE
1	District of Columbia	116.00	1	Alaska	485.91
2	Nevada	106.73	2	New Jersey	166.74
3	Washington	81.33	3	Colorado	143.21
4	Montana	68.20	4	Nevada	135.75
5	Utah	60.22	5	District of Columbia	131.90
6	Florida	57.28	6	Oregon	124.18
7	Georgia	56.99	7	Maryland	121.67
8	Wyoming	56.40	8	Arizona	121.01
9	North Dakota	51.01	9	Washington	120.56
10	New York	48.10	10	Florida	116.25

Source: No author, *2009 Internet Crime Report* (Washington, D.C.: Internet Crime Complaint Center, the National White Collar Crime Center and the Bureau of Justice Assistance, 2010), pp. 7 and 9.

(3) secretly access or intercept computer data; and (4) subvert the operation of computers for personal profit. Many of the techniques discussed in this section are being adapted for attacks on smartphones.

Although malware is often for a single purpose, the clear trend of cybercriminals is to use multipurpose or **"blended threat" malware** —for example, the ABC Virus, which includes spyware, control from remote sites, and data theft capabilities. Malware may be transmitted with downloaded images, a "spoofing" e-mail, which appears to come from a legitimate source, such as a bank; Valentine's Day and Christmas cards; files saved on CDs and flash drives that are shared with other users; fake free security software offers; "You have won an instant $100" messages; bogus news, storm, or sports reports; or by other means discussed in this chapter, such as drive-bys. This section addresses common malware intrusions; there is some inherent overlap in these categories—for instance, an infostealer Trojan horse can also be categorized as spyware.

1. *Botnets:* A **"herder" ("botmaster")** uses malware to hijack hundreds to tens of thousands of computers and is able to remotely control them all, including the ability to update the malware and to introduce other programs such as spyware. Hijacked computers are called **zombies** (robots, or **bots**). The malware creating the bot "lies low," waiting for commands from the herder and thus is difficult for security software to detect.

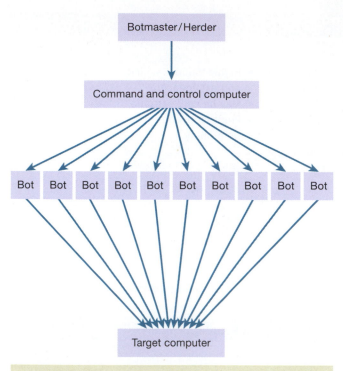

▲ **FIGURE 17-2   Typical botnet**

A **botnet** is a network of zombies or bots (Figure 17-2). The Georgia Institute of Technology estimates that globally 15% of all computers may be zombies.[16] The herder makes money from repeatedly selling clandestine botnet access to others to use for pop-up advertising or other purposes, at an average cost of 37 cents per week for each zombie.[17] A herder with 10 weekly clients for a botnet with 10,000 zombies could gross $1.9 million annually.

Computers are often hijacked by what appear to be legitimate e-mail messages. A growing method is **"drive-bys,"** which occurs as a user-unintended side-effect of visiting a website; Drive-bys are made possible by exploiting web browser vulnerabilities. For example, a person on Facebook sees a video on YouTube that friends might be interested in and sends the link to them. When the friends click on the link, the malware is surreptitiously installed. A variation of this involves seemingly innocent celebrity websites that are actually malicious; click on one, and a drive-by occurs. In 2009 Jessica Biel was the most dangerous celebrity site to visit; in 2010 it was Cameron Diaz; visits to celebrity websites creates a 10% chance of being a drive-by victim.[18]

2. *Viruses:* At any one time there may be as many as 16,000 viruses floating around. The *primary purpose* of a **virus** is to replicate as many times as possible and to cause as much mischief or damage as possible. A number of programs provide a good level of security from infection, including Norton, Anti-Virus, McAfee, Intego, and Kaspersky.

A virus is an unauthorized software program that is surreptitiously inserted into an executable program on a single computer.[19] When a user launches the infected program, the virus looks for other executable programs in which to place a copy of its malicious code. Thus, the typical virus requires human intervention to spread itself. The user may spread the virus to other computers—for example, if it has attached itself to outgoing e-mail. Infected computers may run slower and slower as more programs are infected. The viruses can also reformat a hard drive, causing the loss of all data, or odd/taunting messages may appear on the screen.

Polymorphic and metamorphic viruses are similar in that they each make changes to their replicants to hide from security software, but they do so differently. A **polymorphic virus,** such as Virut, encrypts its replicant into an alternate form, but it must then decrypt itself back into its original form to execute. In contrast, a **metamorphic virus** completely rewrites itself each time it reproduces. No metamorphic replicant or "child" looks like its parent.

Worms are considered a variant or subclass of viruses and therefore are substantially similar to them. The key difference between the two is once inserted into a computer, a worm can distribute itself across the Internet without any action by the computer user because it is self-contained and does not have to be part of another software program.

One of the most famous worms was the e-mail that appeared in 2000 with the tag line of "I Love You." When recipients clicked on its "love letter" attachment, the virus was installed. Originating in the Philippines, this worm affected 10% of all Internet users in nine days by sending itself automatically to everyone on each infected computer's contact list. It is estimated that this virus created losses of $15 billion.[20]

The software security firm Sophos estimates that an unprotected computer connected for the first time to the Internet has a 40% chance of getting a worm within 10 minutes; that risk reaches 94% after an hour.[21]

In 2010, just two years after it was discovered, the Conficker worm had infected 7 million computers. Its encryption code is so sophisticated that only a small number of people would have the skill to write it; moreover, Conficker is adept at reappearing even after some antivirus packages have eliminated it.[22]

3. *Time, logic, and e-mail bombs:* A **time bomb** is programmed to "go off" at a particular time or date, such as April Fool's Day, Halloween, or Friday the 13th. A **logic bomb** is "detonated" when a specific event occurs—for example, all personnel records are erased when an electronic notation is made that a particular person was fired. **E-mail bombs** are

intended to overwhelm a person's e-mail account by surreptitiously subscribing it to dozens or even hundreds of mailing lists. Alternatively, 10 knowledgeable people might be able to collectively send 650,000 e-mail messages in an hour to a single user's account. In such circumstances, the Internet service provider usually suspends the use of the e-mail account, disrupting the ability of the victim to use it. Such a circumstance is called a **denial of service (DoS)** attack.

On a larger scale, a botnet herder can use all of his/her zombies to overwhelm even the largest servers, in a **distributed** (across the botnet) **denial of service (DDoS)** attack. DDoSers are also referred to as **flooders,** and their known corporate victims include Yahoo!, Amazon, and CNN. In 2007 Tallinn, Estonia, decided to relocate a Soviet-era monument from the center of the city to the suburbs. Two days of rioting by ethnic Russians was followed by DDoS attacks against Estonian agencies. Many believe that the attacks were conducted by or on behalf of the Russian government.

DDoS threats can also be used for extortion. Russian gangs successfully extorted millions of dollars from 50 online casinos and betting businesses in 30 different countries by threatening such attacks; the profitability from remaining online 24 hours a day was greater than the extortion paid by the victims.[23]

4. *Ransomware:* Also known as a cryptovirus, **ransomeware** holds the data on a computer or the use of the computer hostage until a payment is made

(Figure 17-3). Ransomware encrypts the target's files—for example, through a CryZip Trojan—and the attacker tells the victim to make a payment of a specified amount to an E-Gold, a Yandex, or a WebMoney account to receive the decryption key.[24] Alternatively, the attacker requires the victim to prepay for a certain value of goods with a specific business in a foreign country. The goods are used or traded by the attacker, or the "business" may simply exist on paper and the attacker receives the ransom from the sale of it.

Ransomware encryption methods are too sophisticated to be easily cracked, and pressure is placed on the victim by the notification "For every 30 minutes that goes by without full payment, one file will be deleted."[25] Although ransomware attacks have been aimed primarily at businesses, individual personal computer users have also been victimized with the demanded payment in the $200–$300 range.

Movieland, also known as Moviepass.tv and Popcorn.net, allegedly puts displays or plays music on a computer that cannot be closed or turned off. Movieland's creators claimed the "users" did not pay the required $29.95 for the program after the trial period, and users state that their systems were being held hostage.[26]

5. *Dead drop:* To avoid personal contact, intelligence agents use a location called a **dead drop** or drop zone to leave and pick up messages. Similarly, some cybercriminals prefer to distance themselves from incriminating files; they use another computer or server, a virtual dead drop, sometimes

called an egg drop or drop zone, on which to store the data they have stolen.[27] The attackers sell the data or use it to commit cybercrimes themselves.

6. *Trojan horse:* There are numerous platforms for delivering **Trojan horses.** One way is to offer what appears to be legitimate software program with a title that mimics a well-known package that many users may try, such as a free download of a "Web Accelerator." The Trojan horse piggybacks on the Web Accelerator download. In another version, a pop-up appears on the screen with "Yes" and "No" buttons to answer the question "Do You Want to Optimize Your Internet Access?" No matter which button is pushed, the Trojan horse is downloaded. Another pop-up that functions in the same manner is a window that offers some type of a browser plugin.

Symantec, a leading antivirus company, recognizes three categories of Trojans: (1) backdoor, with a primary purpose of establishing the opportunity for remote access at some later time; (2) downloader, with the main goal of facilitating the downloading of some other type of software, most usually additional malware; and (3) infostealer, with an objective of stealing information, such as account names, numbers, and passwords.[28]

7. *Spyware:* **Spyware** is a broad term that sometimes is used to mean the same thing as malware but more narrowly is thought of as a surveillance tool, such as the infostealer form of a Trojan horse. Webroot, an antivirus software company, audited 19,480 businesses in 71 countries and found an average of 19 pieces of spyware.[29] Crimes involving stolen passwords result in losses of $2.75 billion annually.[30]

A keystroke logger, referred to as a keylogger, may be the most common form of spyware. As shown in Figure 17-4, a **keylogger** secretly "harvests" every keystroke that a computer user makes and thus steals sensitive data for profit.

Keyloggers may be hardware or software. KeyGhost makes a hardware version that is roughly the size of a small thumb and is easily installed. The keyboard cord is plugged into the keylogger, which in turn is inserted into the back of the computer. There are two families of keylogger software: (1) ZeuS, Zbot, and Wsnpoem, whose attack channel is spam e-mails that trick users into opening them, and (2) Limbo2 and Nethel, which are downloaded as a drive-by when users visit a malicious website.[31] There are over 200 unique programs designed to steal passwords via keylogging.[32]

Some spyware is relatively benign, learning what sites a user visits on the Internet to shape marketing strategies. However, an accumulation of benign spyware slows down a computer's speed.

8. *Rootkits:* In many computer operating systems (OSs), the "root" is a "superuser" account for sys-

▲ **FIGURE 17-4** **Keylogger attack**

tem administration. A "kit" is the malware introduced into the computer. A **rootkit** gives an attacker "super powers" over computers—for example, the ability to steal sensitive personal information.

Rootkits—for instance, TDSS—are considered the most sophisticated type of malware and are quickly emerging as the largest intrusion threat to computers.[33] There are at least five different "flavors" of rootkits. A common one, after being introduced into a computer, alters the OS so that it can remain hidden indefinitely. Rootkits do not replicate or ordinarily do not cause damage to files.

9. *Scareware:* A **scareware** attack often starts with a pop-up message on your screen, "Virus Activity Detected!" claiming that your computer has a virus—and for $19.95 you can download antivirus software to fix the problem (Figure 17-5). The unwary user who buys the software thinks the problem is resolved, but the software is really useless and delivers malware, and the vendor sells the user's credit card number. In 2010 a new method of delivering scareware, using a bogus update to the Firefox web browser, was discovered in England.

INVESTIGATION OF CYBERCRIMES

FEDERAL EFFORTS

The FBI and the United States Secret Service (USSS) play prominent roles in investigating computer assisted and cybercrimes. The FBI has a four-fold mission in this area: (1) to stop those behind the most serious computer intrusions and the spread of malware; (2) to identify and thwart online sexual predators who use the Internet to meet and exploit children and those who produce, possess, or share child pornography; (3) to counteract operations that target U.S. intellectual property, endanger national security or competitiveness; and (4) to dismantle national and transnational organized criminal enterprises engaging in Internet fraud.

The USSS has broad jurisdiction to investigate computer crimes, including unauthorized access to protected computers, identity theft, DDoS attacks involving disrup-tion of e-commerce or extortion, and distribution of malware. The USSS has established Electronic Crimes Task Forces (ECTFs) (Figure 17-6) in approximately 20 cities across the country, bringing together the expertise of federal, state, and local agencies and representatives from industry and the academic community. The mission of ECTFs is the prevention, detection, mitigation, and aggressive investigation of attacks on the United States' financial institutions and critical infrastructures.

Many federal agencies participate on ECTFs and lead or serve on other investigative task forces (TFs) spread

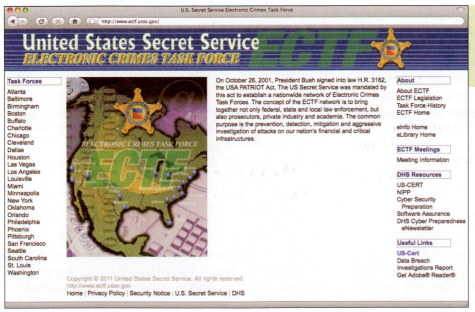

◀ **FIGURE 17-6**
Website for the United States Secret Service Electronic Crimes Task Force

across the country. Among the federal agencies participating in these efforts are United States Attorney's Offices, the FBI, United States Postal Inspection Service (USPIS), and the U.S. Immigration and Customs Enforcement (ICE). The Social Security Administration (SSA) participates in approximately 100 such TFs. Many of these TFs are aimed at specific computer assisted crimes, such as identity theft, advance fee schemes, and exploitation of children.

STATE AND LOCAL EFFORTS

Computer/cyber/high-technology/electronic crime units are commonly found in all larger municipal and county agencies, although their mission, expertise, and capabilities vary widely. As departmental size decreases, so does the probability that such units exist. These "poor cousins" and larger agencies both face barriers to establishing and growing an effective computer-, cyber-, or electronic-crimes unit, because: (1) the needs for, and benefits of, an electronic crimes unit are not well understood; (2) many local agencies cannot alone afford to provide adequate office space, purchase the necessary hardware and software, or dedicate and train the staff required; (3) administrators are reluctant to engage in the hard and uncertain work of recruiting qualified information technology partners from industry and the academic community; (4) support for such units is often nonexistent or low, especially for administrators who are trying to meet more basic service delivery needs; (5) the inability to fully staff such units means that where they do exist, their mission may be restricted to a few crimes—for example, identity theft, child pornography, online child predators, cyberbullying and stalking, and non-delivery of merchandise ordered online—because the "unit" consists of a single officer; (6) it is difficult to retain trained and experienced officers; (7) existing laws may be inadequate; and (8) prosecutorial expertise may be lacking.[34]

Of necessity, many local agencies depend on the computer-crime expertise of their state investigative agency, state police, or state patrol. These state agencies are often staffed with a combination of officers trained in computer-crime investigation and civilian information technology specialists. In addition to a staff located at headquarters, qualified personnel are usually located within troop commands or other geographical districts. These agencies also operate TFs, as do State Attorney Generals and local prosecutors. A number of local agencies have also cooperated in founding their own units, the services of which are shared.

LEGAL CONSIDERATIONS

Federal laws pertaining to computer-assisted and cyber-crimes are comprehensive, although the corresponding state statutes vary in their sophistication and breadth. As with other types of crime, investigators must be thoroughly familiar with the applicable federal and state laws. In particular, knowledge of the federal Electronic Communications Privacy Act (ECPA) of 1986 and its subsequent amendments is essential. ECPA violations may result in criminal charges being brought against officers, personal civil liability, and the suppression of evidence. Therefore, investigators should be guided by their department's policies and those of the local prosecuting authority.

CONSENT SEARCHES

Search and seizure were discussed in Chapter 2, "Legal Aspects of Investigation." Consent searches are revisited here within the personal computer-crime context, because unlike warrant applications there is no judicial official screening to guide investigators' actions when a consent search is sought in the field.[35]

Whenever reasonably possible, investigators' should seek a warrant. However, many times a request to search on the basis of consent may be a sound, even prudent, course of action, because a consent search does not require probable cause. To avoid conflicting accounts that may arise later, the party granting consent should execute a written consent form (Figure 17-7) prepared by the local prosecuting authority. When the examination of a computer system is contemplated, the consent form should specify in broad terms that computer and other electronic evidence may be searched. Computer case law continues to evolve, and the discussion here is for general information and is not a guide to authoritative practice.

The general rules for **consent searches** is that the police can rely on a person's *actual authority* to consent to a search or the *apparent authority* of such other parties they reasonably believe can grant a search of the premises—for example, an adult guest who has "the run of the household" while the owners are absent.[36]

The consent must be freely and voluntary given; police threats such as "Let us look at your computer files or we'll arrest your girlfriend and take away your children" will nullify the consent.[37] Different fact situations determine whether investigators can conduct a consent search:

1. If the persons with actual or apparent authority to consent are not native English speakers and appear to lack meaningful comprehension, the burden is heavier on the government to show the consent was voluntary.[38] It must be demonstrated *before* the search that such persons comprehended the situation well enough to understand the action to which they consented.

2. The extent of a consent search is limited by the subject and scope of the consent—for example, consent to "search the computer in my son's room" does not extend to household computers located elsewhere.

CONSENT TO SEARCH FORM

I, _____, presently residing at _____ have been informed of my right to refuse to consent to a search. I have not been promised anything nor have I been threatened in any manner. My consent is given freely and voluntarily. I have been advised that I can modify or withdraw my consent at any time.

I authorize and consent to a search of the _____ located at _____ by _____ and such other personnel as he/she shall designate, including any containers of each and every kind.

The officer(s) are authorized by me to seize and take custody of any notes, letters, pages, papers, records, materials or other property, including computers, together with all of their components, related processing and internal and external storage devices, scanners, routers, printers, display monitors, modems, and any and all accessories and property the officers believe to be pertinent to their investigation.

The officer(s) are authorized by me to search for and seize electronic data within the authority, consent, and scope given above. The officer(s) may use any means to search any or all files, including deleted, encrypted, and password protected files.

I also authorize the officer(s) to remove to another place(s) they deem appropriate any property, equipment, or other material related to their investigation, to sort out, read, examine, analyze, evaluate, test, and reproduce it. I also authorize these actions by those the officer(s) may designate to perform them.

Date: _____   Time: _____

Signature of Consenting Party: _____

Witness Signature: _____

Witness Signature: _____

◄**FIGURE 17-7**
Consent to search form oriented toward personal computers
Source: Priscilla Adams, Consent Searches (Oxford, Mississippi: National Center for Justice and the Rule of Law, University of Mississippi Law School, 2010), p. 6 with modifications.

In *United States v. Stierhoff* (549 F.3d 19, 2008) a defendant suspected of stalking signed a broadly worded consent form for the Rhode Island State Police to search the room he rented as a residence and in which his computer was located. Over $140,000 in cash and financial records in the room suggested the possibility of a separate tax evasion case. When investigators began examining his computer, Stierhoff verbally narrowed his consent to the files containing his "love poems." However, the police also opened a file labeled "Offshore," which deepened their suspicions about tax evasion. Later that night, investigators, with a separate consent form from Stierhoff, searched the defendant's storage unit and found more evidence of tax evasion. The Internal Revenue Service was notified. Stierhoff was later convicted at separate trials of stalking and failure to pay taxes on over $1 million during a four-year period. His lone "victory" was that both the tax evasion trial and appeal courts agreed that the evidence from the "Offshore" file was not admissible. This case illustrates that consent may be modified or withdrawn at any time.

United States v. Wong (334 F.3d 831, 2003) shows the importance of being patient and using a warrant when possible. The investigation of a murder led to the seizure of a computer under warrant. The investigator later obtained a search warrant to have it forensically examined for graphic files pertaining to the case. Child pornography was found, which the court held was a plain view exception to the Fourth Amendment.

3. When a person is asked for permission to search personal computers in a home, his/her mere silence does not rise to consent. If investigators falsely tell a person "we have a warrant to search your computer" the fruits of the search are not admissible.

4. Consent to enter a home does not constitute authority to conduct a search. A nonverbal gesture to "come in" is sufficient to enter the premises. Although mere entry does not authorize a search, investigators can act on plain view offenses—for example, child pornography pictures or drugs lying on a table.

5. Among those who cannot give law-enforcement officers consent to search private living areas for computers or other purposes are landlords and apartment managers. Under some rental agreements they may be able to enter and inspect for an agreement violation—for instance, if a nonpermissible pet is on the premises, if the tenant is given reasonable notice, if the manager does so at a reasonable time and conforms to other related provisions of the agreement. If evidence of a crime is observed—for instance, credit-card-making machines or computers being used to produce counterfeit currency—the manager's information can form the basis of probable cause for a search warrant. However, if the manager's intention is actually to "get the goods" on tenants and is essentially acting as a law-enforcement officer, the evidence will be inadmissible.

Dormitory, sorority, and fraternity managers, and usually medical and administrative staff with respect to a patient's room, cannot give consent when there is a reasonable expectation of privacy.[39] Hospital security personnel responsible for protecting a patient's possessions, such as a laptop, do not appear to have a right to surrender them to investigators. Hotel managers cannot normally give consent to search private rooms, although they can if tenants have terminated their occupancy or eviction proceedings have been completed.

6. Spousal and domestic partner search consents for domiciles may be valid depending on the circumstances. If a spouse or partner is absent, consent by the other is usually approved by the courts. Even so, the courts have imposed restrictions; in *Trulock* v. *Freeh* (275 F.3d 391, 2002) a housemate consented to a search of the computer she shared jointly with her boyfriend; both accounts on the computer were password protected. The police found incriminating evidence in the boyfriend's account, but the court refused to admit the evidence on the basis that the use of a password created a reasonable expectation of privacy by him.

If, however, the password is on a "sticky note" attached in plain view to the computer or has been shared with others, the courts may not be deferential to a claim of privacy. Encrypted files might create a privilege similar to password protected files. Short of password protection, defendants may claim an expectation of privacy based on instructions such as "no one is to use my computer except me" or keeping it locked up when not in use.

If both spouses or partners are present and one affirmatively objects and the other consents, any search is unconstitutional (*Georgia* v. *Randolph* 547 U.S. 103, 2006). Under Randolph, the nonconsenting party must be physically present and immediately challenge any qualified co-occupant who consents.[40]

In *U.S.* v. *Groves* (530 F. 3d 506, 2008) the question arose whether police could strategically plan to avoid the presence of a potentially nonconsenting cotenant. Groves was a convicted felon who did not consent to a search of his residence, shared with a live-in girlfriend. Three weeks later, knowing Groves was at work, the police revisited the Groves domicile and were granted entry by the girlfriend. The court held the search was constitutional because Grove was not "objecting at the door," and the police had no role in removing him from it.

7. Parents ordinarily have unlimited authority to consent to searches over the dissent of their children who are under 18 years old and living at home, because there is a recognized hierarchy in the family. However, if juveniles have created "private space," such as footlockers to which only they have a key, a right to privacy claim might be raised. If their children are older than 18 years, a parent may in some circumstances be able to give consent. However, if children are older than 18, pay rent, and have asserted their right to deny access to their room, the courts have held that parents' consent to search that private space is not valid.

8. Montana appears to be the only jurisdiction that has clear guidance as to whether a minor child can consent to a search of their parent's home; a child there who is 16 years or older may be able to authorize a search in the absence of both parents. Elsewhere, the fact situation will guide whether children can do so. As the Supreme Court noted, no one "would reasonably expect an eight-year-old to be in a position to authorize anyone to rummage through his parents' bedroom."[41] The authority of minors to consent to a search of their parents' home and computers has no "bright line" test.

A search warrant is a better option than relying on the uncertain authority of a child. Nonetheless, *before* acting on a child's consent, investigators' should pursue a rigorous line of inquiry to determine if it is *reasonable* to believe such authority is valid. The courts will closely scrutinize the basis on which the police acted on the consent of children, including their, age, maturity, physical and mental state, intelligence, education, and the instructions their parents gave them—for example, "don't let anyone in the house unless it's an emergency."

9. The courts have held differently on whether a computer-repair person may allow the police access to a computer being repaired that has evidence on it. Some states have laws requiring computer-repair services to report crimes they detect—for example, credit card fraud.

In *United States* v. *Grimes* (244 F.3d 375, 2001), the defendant's wife brought her husband's computer to a repair shop with the complaint that it wouldn't boot up. Subsequently, the repairman called the wife and reported that there were a lot of image files, and he recommended deleting some of them, which the wife authorized. In the process of determining which files might be deleted, 17 pornographic images were discovered and reported to a local detective, who looked only at the 17 images and did not request that the repairman examine the remaining image files. The 17 files were copied on a floppy and given to an FBI agent, who patiently obtained a warrant to seize the computer, which was held to be lawful by the court.

10. Those on parole or probation may have their releases based on conditions creating diminished Fourth Amendment rights that approximate consent. In *United States* v. *Herndon* (501 F.3d 683, 692, 2007) a warrantless search of a probationer's computer was upheld, based on reasonable suspicion that he had violated the terms of his probation. Herndon's release prohibited him from using the Internet, and he was required to allow his probation officer to search his computer at any time for such use. After Herndon told his probationer officer he was using the Internet to look for a job, the officer drove to his residence and searched an external hard drive, finding child pornography. The court upheld the search, noting that Herndon's privacy rights were "dramatically reduced" by the terms of his release and the government's legitimate interest in preventing his recidivism.

11. *Routine* searches at border crossings or other points of entry into or departure from this country do not require a warrant, probable cause, reasonable suspicion, or consent. In *United States* v. *Arnold* ((523 F.3d 941, 946, 2008) the court ruled that reasonable suspicion was not required to search a laptop or other personal electronic devices, because it was a nondestructive intrusion akin to searching luggage. This decision did not address border searches involving password protected or encrypted files.

   More intrusive *nonroutine* searches of people that involve their dignity and privacy—for example, strip and body-cavity searches—require a degree of reasonable suspicion; destructive searches—for instance, cutting open panels in a car to look for drugs—fall into this category also.[42]

12. Although outside the scope of consent searches, it is noted that inventory searches that discover evidence of a crime are admissible if the searches are conducted pursuant to a departmental policy that is uniformly followed in similar cases and the inventory has a legitimate non-investigatory intent—for example, protection of the property of an arrestee. However, because the intent is to protect tangible personal property, it is unlikely that the examination of the files on a computer inventoried from the trunk of an impounded vehicle would pass judicial scrutiny.

THE CRIME SCENE

COMPUTER AND PERIPHERAL EVIDENCE

Evidence related to computer-assisted and cybercrimes is subject to the same fundamentals of crime processing that were discussed earlier. Important evidence may be associated with many items, including tablets, computer notebooks and laptops, desktops, rack systems, and main frames, as well as external hard drives, printers, scanners, compact disks, flash drives, memory card readers, web cameras, and wireless access points and network servers. The existence of a wireless network should alert investigators to the possibility that evidence may also be located on devices located away from the primary crime scene, such as in another room or a garage.

Search warrants may be issued to cover both the seizure of the targeted computers and peripherals and the actual digital forensic examination of them, or separate search warrants may be used.

CRIME SCENE PROCESSING

If the resources are available, trained and experienced computer investigators are the best choice for processing a cybercrime scene. In many jurisdictions this option may not exist, and so the first responding officer will have that responsibility. In all instances, investigators must be sure of their legal authority to search and any applicable limits.

This section is not a definitive guide to processing computer crime scenes, which is properly covered by in-service training covering a full range of situations, such as searching corporate computers that may hold trade secrets and other confidential information. It does provide a perspective on common situations, but a department's policy is the definitive source for action.

Securing and Evaluating the Scene

1. Remove and exclude all persons from the area where evidence is to be collected.[43] Do not accept advice or assistance from "volunteers" whose actual motive may be to destroy evidence or misdirect the investigation.

2. If a wireless system is involved, direct non-investigative personnel to stay in a particular room until the possibility of potential evidence in rooms beyond where the computer is located is determined. If several persons of interest and/or suspects are present, they should be placed in separate rooms.

3. If a computer and other devices are off, leave them off. If they are on, do not move them, press any keys, check for DVDs, or click the mouse, because changes or damage to evidence may be triggered. If the computer is on but the screen is blank, *very slightly* move the mouse to see what information is displayed.

4. If the computer's power state cannot be immediately determined, look and listen for indications that it is on—for example, fans running, drives spinning, and light-emitting diodes (LEDs), and observe the monitor to see if the machine is on, off, or in a sleep mode.

5. If the computer is on, check the display for signs that files are being deleted or overwritten, such as the words *delete, format, remove, destroy, copy, move,* or *wipe.* Also check the monitor for signs that the computer is being remotely controlled. In all these cases, the immediate disconnection of power is recommended.

6. If the destruction of evidence is not a concern, the immediate disconnection of power is not recommended, because information, data, and images of apparent evidentiary value may be seen on the screen and photographed—for instance, financial documents, child pornography, identities of coconspirators/other suspects, text documents, chat rooms used. In such cases, assistance from investigators qualified to capture volatile data is essential.

7. If no destructive processes are running and if there is no information of evidentiary value on the screen, remove the power cord from the back of the computer.

8. Do not attempt to examine the computer's contents. This is highly technical and specialized work that should be undertaken only by qualified personnel.

Preliminary Interviews

In addition to other information, the following should be established:

1. Who owns the computers? For example, the homeowner, a renter, or a business?

2. Who uses the computer and its related devices? What are their login names, user account names, and instant messaging screen names?

3. What are the passwords for any password-protected accounts, and are any files encrypted? Whose accounts are these?

4. What e-mail, personal web, or social networking websites, such as MySpace and Facebook, accounts exist, whose are they, and what passwords are used?

5. What data-access restrictions, destructive devices or software, or automated applications are in use?

6. For wireless networks, where is all accessible equipment located?

7. Who provides the Internet service?

8. Whose name is on the Internet bill, and who actually pays the bill?

9. How is the Internet accessed? For example, cable, modem, Digital Subscriber Line (DSL), Wi-Fi, or T-1 leased service, which normally involves 20 or more people online simultaneously.

Documenting the Scene

1. Both in the report and by video and photography identify the location, type of devices, their condition, and power status. Get views of all sides, including the backs, where cables are attached.

2. Record all activity and processes visible on the monitor.

3. Note all devices physically connected to the computer as well as the same for wireless components. Record their serial numbers, the content of "sticky notes" attached to them, and related written information.

4. Note the condition and power status of the computer's network access.

5. Document, photograph, and sketch all wires, cables, and devices connected to, or inserted in, the computer.

6. Tag every cable as to where each end was attached.

7. Document and photograph every wireless device in the locations at which they were found.

8. Document and photograph the locations of related evidence, such as printed pages of Internet addresses, financial records, images, and computer code, GPSs/maps/directions, electronic money transfers, books on hacking, software packages, lists of computers accessed and dead drops, credit card information, reproductions of signatures, checks and money orders, diaries and calendars, mail in victims' names, cash, fictitious identification, passwords and information on encryption and steganography. ("Steg" or "Stego" has been used for thousands of years. Historically, steg means writing in a cipher or code so that only the sender and the recipient know what the message means. In the context of computers, steg means hiding a file in a larger file so that others are not aware of its presence or meaning.)

Collecting and Transporting Evidence

The following steps should be followed when collecting and transporting computers and related devices:

1. Remove batteries from laptops and place tape over the power switch on all computers and associated devices. Disk-drive trays should also be taped closed.

2. Place all digital evidence in **antistatic packaging;** do not use regular plastic bags or other containers that can produce static electricity and condensation, both of which can damage or destroy evidence. Antistatic bags and packaging is often colored—for example, pink or light blue—to distinguish them from regular evidence bags, and they may have bubble wrap built into them to protect evidence. If antistatic bags or packaging are not available, wrap the evidence in sturdy manila/kraft paper.

3. Each computer and peripheral should be placed in a separate container to avoid cross-contamination. In some investigations, examining them for DNA evidence may become an important possibility.

4. Carefully pack all evidence to prevent it from being damaged from shock and vibration while being transported.

5. Keep digital evidence away from magnetic fields—for instance, those produced by radio transmitters and magnetically mounted emergency lights. Other transportation hazards include prolonged exposure to heated seats, hot car interiors and trunks, and static electricity produced by shuffling feet on carpets. Prolonged exposure to cold and humidity are also threats.

6. Regular procedures for handling other types of evidence, such as maintaining the chain of custody, should be carefully followed.

KEY TERMS

antistatic packaging
black hatters
blended threat malware
bot
botmaster
botnet
carder
computer-assisted crime
consent search
cybercrime
dead drop

denial of service (DoS) attack
distributed denial of service (DDoS)
    attack
drive-by
e-mail bomb
flooder
herder
keylogger
logic bomb
malware
metamorphic virus

polymorphic virus
ransomware
rootkits
scareware
spyware
time bomb
Trojan horse
virus
white hatters
worms
zombies

REVIEW QUESTIONS

1. How are computer-assisted and cybercrimes contrasted?
2. What two prerequisites were fulfilled before cyber-crime could emerge?
3. What six advantages do cybercriminals have over traditional criminals?
4. What is malware?
5. How do black hatters and white hatters differ?
6. What is a botnet?
7. What is the primary purpose of a virus?
8. How are DoS/DDoS attacks carried out?

9. What is a drive-by?
10. How are scareware attacks executed?
11. Is there a difference between polymorphic and metamorphic viruses?
12. What is ransomware?
13. What are the basic components of a keylogger attack?
14. What are the general rules for a consent search?
15. What are major points of securing a computer crime scene?

► In addition to the loss of life and destruction caused by Hurricane Katrina, one of its lingering consequences has been the spontaneous development of unpermitted dump sites for millions of tons of debris along the Gulf Coast.

(Photo courtesy of the Louisiana Department of Environmental Quality)

18

AGRICULTURAL, WILDLIFE, AND ENVIRONMENTAL CRIMES

CHAPTER OBJECTIVES

1. Discuss the connection between crime in the agricultural environment and cities.

2. Explain how fluctuations in the economy have some effect on what is stolen from farms and ranches.

3. Discuss the prevalence of timber theft.

4. Explain how horses and cattle rustlers operate.

5. List and describe five major methods of marking horses and cattle for identification.

6. State four major threats to wildlife.

7. Describe how drug production in agricultural areas is linked to cities.

8. Summarize measures to prevent rural and agricultural crimes.

9. Distinguish between situational and professional poachers.

10. Outline the bear-poaching problem.

11. Understand techniques used to investigate wildlife crimes.

12. List and describe the characteristics of hazardous waste.

13. Discuss methods of investigating environmental crimes.

INTRODUCTION

Conventional wisdom says that crime is fundamentally a big-city problem. However, the cost of rural and agricultural crimes is estimated at $5 billion annually.[1] Roughly, one in five farms is located in Metropolitan Statistical Areas (MSAs), which leads to an overstatement of urban crime and an understatement of agricultural/rural crime.[2] There are also many connections between agricultural/rural crime and our cities. The composition of farm labor has changed, with many workers now living in urban areas. Some of them return at night to steal from their employers, or they tip off criminals as to where they can make valuable scores. Thieves run out interstate highways to raid softer targets and return to their cities to dispose of their loot with local fences. Stolen farm machinery passes through big city ports as it is sent abroad for sale, often to South America; as few as 12 hours may pass between the time the machinery is stolen and the ship sails. Wheeled tanks of **anhydrous ammonia,** a nitrogen fertilizer, are stolen from farms and used in the production of methamphetamine, which is sold in urbanized areas, as is marijuana grown in national forests and other public and private lands. Livestock investigation is unfamiliar territory for many investigators, who may not recognize various aspects of livestock identification, breeds, scars, marks, tattoos, and brands. Some poached game ends up on the menus of city restaurants. Theft of, and vandalism to, archaeological resources (Figure 18-1) reduces our enjoyment of national parks and forests and the heritage we leave subsequent generations. Historically, many horses rustled in this country were sold to slaughterhouses, and the meat products were shipped abroad from urban ports for human consumption, often in Europe and Asia. By early 2007 a patchwork of state legislation and court rulings had eliminated domestic processing of horses for human consumption, although the exportation of horses to Canada and Mexico for that purpose remains a loophole.

Environmental crimes, such as those involving the illegal treatment, storage, transportation, and disposal of hazardous waste, are often out of the spotlight but nonetheless are of crucial importance. These crimes are not only a significant threat to public health; they also affect outdoor recreation and wildlife. The purpose of this chapter is to call attention to the nature and extent of crimes against agriculture, wildlife, and the environment and to provide information regarding their investigation.

DIMENSIONS OF AGRICULTURAL, WILDLIFE, AND ENVIRONMENTAL CRIMES

Ranchers, farmers, and others living in rural places are often the victims of thefts, including thefts of livestock, tack, pesticides, tractors, dirt bikes, all-terrain vehicles, drip lines, stock trailers, plants and timber, tools, hay, grains and citrus, irrigation pipes, and sprinkler heads. Some variation in what is stolen is accounted for by fluctuations in the economy. For example, when freezes kill oranges and grapefruit or droughts kill avocados, prices rise on the remainders, because there are fewer of them, and so thieves looking for an easy buck steal them.[3] Annual losses owing to avocado theft amount to $12 to $15 million.[4] Lone **"night pickers"** may opportunistically steal from orchards and groves after dark, farm hands may throw a few sacks in the trunk of their cars to "supplement their wages," or entire crops may be picked clean in a single night by a well-organized ring. One grower reported that a tour bus stopped so people could pick fruit from his trees.

Copper theft has been in vogue for several years, because the price for scrap copper surged to approximately $4 per pound owing to a building boom in Asia; rural thieves, often methamphetamine users, stripped farm pumps, plaques from graveyards, and wires from phone lines and gutted air conditioners and catalytic converters from cars for a quick buck.[5] In Kern County, California, there were 213 copper thefts in a single year; in addition to lost time and damaged crops, each water pump replaced cost a farmer from $3,000 to $10,000.[6] A van quickly loaded with stolen grapes creates a loss of $3,000 or more to a vineyard;[7] a grower loaded two trucks with 88,000 pounds of almonds valued at $260,000, which were stolen by "nutnappers" the night before the nuts were to be driven to market.[8] In Florida, state and county parks are being plundered of palmetto berries, which are offered by herbal companies for baldness and enlarged prostates. The thieves, often illegal immigrants from Mexico and Guatemala, are organized; they are dropped off by a truck and picked up later in the day.[9] The "pickers" are paid a dollar a pound for the berries and may be able to collect up to 150 pounds a day.[10]

Reported losses due to livestock theft are $19.7 million annually;[11] this crime is believed to be at least 50% underreported, so losses may actually be in the $40 to

► FIGURE 18-1

Damage to archaeological resources
Ancient Native-American petroglyphs on the Wind River Reservation that have been damaged by gunfire. Previous photographs taken over a period of decades show that such vandalism and destruction is a continuing problem at this site. The Wind River Reservation is home to the Eastern Shoshone and Northern Arapaho peoples. (Courtesy Floyd Phillips, Bureau of Indian Affairs)

$50 million range. Horse rustling may amount to 40,000 to 55,000 head annually. Beef and calf production is a $35.7 billion industry, yet there are no definitive numbers of heads of cattle stolen each year.[12] Special Rangers for the Southwestern Cattle Raisers Association recovered more than 3,716 head of cattle, 144 horses, 18 saddles, and 10 trailers, altogether valued at $4.8 million, in a single year.[13]

There are also less common thefts associated with livestock. In Maryland, burglars entered an out building and took $75,000 worth of bull semen that had previously been collected from about 50 bulls and kept frozen in individual 5-inch straws with the bulls' names on them.[14] A barn was burglarized in California to take $30,000 worth of the genetically engineered rBST hormone in filled syringes, which is used to increase milk production in dairy cows; investigators believed the syringes would be sold on the black market to unscrupulous dairy farmers.[15]

Private and public lands are being invaded by stealthy fossil hunters, who are also described as **bone rustlers.** Depending on the type, a complete dinosaur skeleton may command $500,000 or more. In South Dakota, thieves dug up the graveyard of rhinoceros-like mammals called *titanotheres* and made off with 18 skulls, each worth $5,000.[16] In one national forest, park rangers marked fossils at several different sites with chemicals invisible to the unassisted eye. By inventorying these areas over a six-week period, they learned that 32,000 pounds of fossils had been stolen. One of the most successful fossil-poaching investigations was a joint local, state, and federal effort dubbed "Operation Rockfish," named after a fossil common in southwest Wyoming. A

Lincoln County Sheriff's Department pilot noticed new holes in the ground in and around Fossil Butte National Monument. First suspecting that toxic chemicals were being dumped, he invited several federal agents to fly with him. On-the-ground investigation revealed that fossils were being stolen and sold both in the open and on black markets, some for prices in excess of $10,000. Nationally, Operation Rockfish resulted in the recovery of $7 million worth of stolen fossils. Although petrified wood can be obtained legally from some sources, because of its great beauty it is being stolen from federal lands to make countertops and furniture.[17]

Our national and state lands are also victimized by plant poachers, whose targets vary as market conditions shift. Several years ago matsutake mushrooms, which grow in the northwest, reached $30 per pound; by 2007 prices had fallen to $3–$5 per pound, reducing much of the incentive for wholesale poaching. Although ginseng roots are cultivated, the wild variety growing in hardwood forests commands substantial prices. The roots are used in Asian medicine and also sold domestically with the reputed effect of reducing cholesterol and blood sugar levels, enhancing memory, and fighting colds and other conditions. Kentucky gathers more wild ginseng than any other state, a crop worth $8 million; about 50% of it is poached.[18] The prices paid pickers in good years may reach $365–$800 per pound; it is sold to overseas brokers for as much as $2,000 per pound.[19] The theft of saguaro cacti for landscaping purposes in the southwest is episodically a problem (Figure 18-2), as is the occasional theft of quaking aspen trees from the western mountains; but recently the red-flowered ocotillo plant has been in greater favor with thieves, because

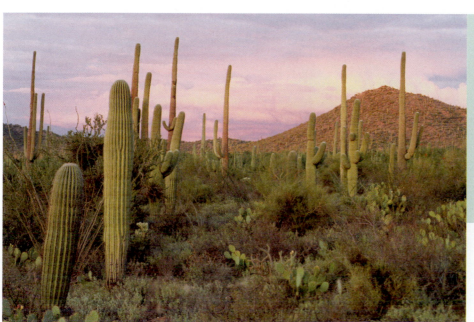

◀ **FIGURE 18-2   Saguaro cacti**
The theft of saguaro cacti from national lands in the West is a continuing problem. Saguaros grow very slowly; after 10 years they may be only 4–6 inches tall. They reach maturity in about 150 years and may live another 50 years beyond that, reaching a height of about 45 feet. Consequently, saguaro thefts amount to stealing part of our national heritage. (© Jo MacDonald/Corbis)

▶ **FIGURE 18-3   Ocotillo plant**
Like the saguaros, these plants are prized for landscaping and thrive in loose to stony soil in open areas that are well drained. They occur naturally in the southwest and Mexico in desert areas below 5,000 feet. Their blood-red blooms appear in March and April. Ocotillos ordinarily grow to 15–20 feet in height with a corresponding width of roughly 10–15 feet. (© David Muench/Corbis)

many can be stolen with low risk of detection. Depending on their size, ocotillo plants retail for $150–$5,000 (Figure 18-3).[20]

TIMBER THEFT

Forest economists believe that thieves are stealing trees worth $1 billion annually and that 1 in every 10 trees is cut down illegally.[21] Large areas don't have to be cut down to create serious losses (Figure 18-4). In Pennsylvania, a prime black cherry tree, valued for making furniture, can bring $6,000.[22] Because of their beautiful swirl grain, curly maple trees in Washington are being poached to make guitars and other musical instruments.[23] On a larger scale, two Wyoming men were charged with stealing 8,439 trees valued at $100,000 from Medicine Bow National Forest; the clear-cutting operation could result in fines of $500,000.[24] Unlike thieves who must sell what they steal to fences for pennies on the dollars, thieves

▶ **FIGURE 18-4
Illegal cutting of trees**
A Federal Bureau of Land Management Ranger discovered that 17 old-growth juniper trees had been illegally cut and removed from the Badlands Wilderness Study Area (WSA) in Oregon. Such trees grow so slowly that they are considered a nonrenewable resource: a juniper tree with a 3-feet diameter takes 1,000 years to reach that size. The juniper stumps with the yellow evidence cone at the right were part of the multiple crime scenes involved with the thefts.

(Courtesy Federal Bureau of Land Management)

◄FIGURE 18-5
Timber theft crime scene
A Mason County Deputy Sheriff examines the work of maple tree thieves. In their haste to turn their contraband into cash, tree thieves may abandon tools and other important physical evidence. (© Mark Harrison/Seattle Times)

involved in **timber theft** get full value. In some urban areas, particularly along parkways and expressways in the month leading up to the Christmas holiday, Christmas-type trees "disappear" as motorists cut them down and cart the trees home to decorate. To combat such thefts, some cities chemical-coat trees that are likely targets, causing them to smell "awful." Another coating has an unnoticeable odor until it starts to heat up, and then it "smells worse than cat urine."

Investigations into the illegal cutting of timber involve a full range of investigative techniques (Figure 18-5). Examination of crime scenes continues to result in the discovery of evidence of paint transfers and tool marks on wood debris left behind by suspects. These marks and paint transfers result from the use of axes, wedges, and splitting mauls and serve to tie a suspect to a crime. Examination of tool marks on wood is based on established principles: tone can identify a suspect tool by the mark it leaves on a surface. In several cases, containers left at the scene of a timber theft have been processed and fingerprints developed. These fingerprints have been useful in identifying and placing suspects at the scene. In addition, casts of both shoe and tire impressions that were later identified as belonging to particular suspects and vehicles have been found at some crime scenes.[25] Increasingly, DNA is proving important as key evidence in many of the types of crimes discussed in this chapter, including plant and tree thefts, livestock rustling, and fish and wildlife poaching.

Although the crime scene examinations at the site of timber thefts are important, they are supplemented by the long process of interviewing potential witnesses to the crime, conducting investigations to develop witnesses, and checking possible outlets where forest prod-

ucts might be processed or sold. To conduct investigations concerning timber sales, law enforcement officers must become familiar with the variety of terms and techniques pertaining to a timber sale, from its inception to the eventual purchase.

THEFT OF AGRICHEMICALS

Agrichemical is a broad term whose meaning encompasses a variety of products used on farms, including pesticides, fertilizers, and herbicides. As a rule of thumb, fertilizers are not a target of theft because of their bulk and relatively low cost. In contrast, pesticides and herbicides can be costly; even a truckload may be worth thousands of dollars. The exact type of agrichemical taken varies by geographic region, depending on what the predominant crop is. Currently, anhydrous ammonia, mentioned earlier in this chapter, is the agrichemical of choice for thieves. Agrichemical theft from farmers may have crested in about 2000, owing to operators buying only the quantities they could immediately use and employing more stringent security measures when they were even briefly stored.

Because the theft of agrichemicals may take the form of any of several different criminally chargeable acts, it would be possible for investigators in different parts of the same agency to be working on various activities by the same ring without knowing it. For example, the hijacking of a truck might be worked on by robbery investigators, the burglary of a dealership by the property section or burglary investigators, while personnel assigned to the ranch and grove unit might be working on the theft of pesticides from a local farmer. Although one ring might not exhibit a wide range of criminally chargeable behaviors, these behaviors may be sufficiently different to cause the fragmentation of investigative information.

To be effective in the investigation of agrichemical thefts, the investigator must become familiar with the legal supply channels and the principal agrichemicals that are used in his or her region. In particular, note that the same basic chemical or formulation may be sold by several different manufacturers under different product names. For example, atrazine is manufactured and sold by Ciba-Geigy as AAtrex for use as a corn herbicide. Imagine the difficulty created for an investigation if a victim reports the theft of "50 gallons of atrazine," and the information is entered into police records that way—but the victim was using "atrazine" as a synonym for "AAtrex."

Finally, a few farmers steal agrichemicals or buy them at "bargain prices" from thieves. Once the agrichemicals have been used, the manufacturers' containers are burned, and so the detection of the criminals who received the stolen property is difficult. One method of identifying farmers who are possible illegal receivers of agrichemicals is to determine whose purchasing patterns through legal supply channels are inconsistent with their crop needs.

LIVESTOCK AND TACK THEFT

It is ironic that we can land people on the moon and safely return them, but the old crime of rustling remains a problem (Figure 18-6). Although new and often sophisticated methods of rustling are now used, the object of attack—livestock—remains the same, as do the motivations: profit and food.

Livestock refers to cattle, horses, sheep, goats, hogs, mules, jackasses, and other such species. **Tack** refers to saddles, bridles, harnesses, and related equipment. Certain generalizations can be made with respect to livestock and tack thefts:

- Most livestock thefts are committed by persons who have been or are currently employed in some aspect of a livestock business. One significant exception to this broad observation is that in economically hard times, rural areas adjacent to urban centers experience more thefts; thus the physical evidence suggests that the motivation was food rather than profit. Such so-called **freezer crimes** typically involve only one or a few head of cattle, and when they are butchered at the scene, it is often in a manner that reflects only a crude understanding of the process.[26]

- It is common for livestock to be stolen, transported, and disposed of before the theft is discovered. Whereas the theft of horses may be discovered in a day to two weeks, theft of range cattle may go undetected for months.

- Except for small roadside slaughters committed as freezer crimes, livestock is stolen to be sold for economic gain. The excellent interstate systems that cross the country lend themselves—like the famous trails of frontier days—to transporting the stolen livestock rapidly for sale in states other than the one in which the theft took place.

- Because horse owners are typically very attached to their animals, their theft often creates very emotional situations.

- Horse thieves also tend to be tack thieves.

Many law-enforcement agencies, particularly sheriffs' departments, have created specialized investigative units

▶ **FIGURE 18-6   Stolen horses**
Acting on a tip that rustlers in remote Nevada were driving wild horses from land belonging to the Pyramid Lake Paiute tribe, investigators located a hidden corral and released the horses back into the wild. (© AP Photo/ Debra Reid)

or designated a particular individual as the agency's specialist in such matters.[27] Regardless of whether the investigator works as part of a specialized unit or as the sole specialist, he/she must have or develop an expertise in the various aspects of livestock identification, including breeds, markings, blemishes, scars, marks, tattoos, and brands. In short, to be effective, the investigator must be able to speak "livestock."

The heaviest burden in livestock investigation often falls on the uniformed officer who takes the original offense report, because such an officer may have no knowledge, or only rudimentary knowledge, of livestock and the applicable special laws.[28] Police agencies can help compensate for this lack by adopting forms

similar to those shown in Figures 18-7 and 18-8 and by providing training in their use. When such forms are not used, a good guide to follow is that an animal is property and can be described as any other type of property can, although the language may be unfamiliar to the investigator. In such situations, the frank acknowledgment of a lack of familiarity or expertise can elicit a systematic and detailed description from the owner. Subsequent to the taking of the original offense report, the progress of an investigation often hinges on the mutual assistance, cooperation, and free exchange of information given by ranchers, feedlot operators, stock auctions, farmers, sale yards, livestock associations, and other entities.

▲ FIGURE 18-8 Horse identification form
(Courtesy of Kern County, California, Sheriff's Department)

CATTLE RUSTLING

The majority of cattle-rustling thefts are committed by one or two people who take the animal for their own use.[29] The usual method of operation is to drive to an isolated area, locate an animal, shoot it, and either butcher it there or load the carcass into a vehicle and butcher it at home. Butchering the animal at the scene means the thieves must spend more time there, but it avoids the problem of having to dispose of unused remains later. Sometimes the thieves shoot the animal and then drive to a place where they can watch to see if anyone comes to investigate. If no one comes, they return to butcher the animal. Since the rustlers often work at night, they can see the headlights of approaching vehicles for some distance, giving them ample time to depart the area. Freezer-crime rustlers are difficult to apprehend, because they must be caught when they are committing the act or

while they are transporting the carcass or meat. Surveillance methods that work well in urban areas are usually difficult to execute in rural areas. Given this, rural surveillance success depends on:

- topography of the area;
- availability of cover for concealment;
- number and position of access roads;
- size of the area containing the cattle.

One method for successful surveillances is for investigators to select an area that is attractive to thieves and well suited for surveillance.[30] Ranchers should be requested to move cattle into the area selected by the investigator. The rancher must not allow employees or other persons to learn that an operation is being set up. If other people are involved in moving the cattle to the area selected, they should be given a fictitious but plausible reason for the move—for example, a change of pasture is needed, a tally must be taken, there is going to be a veterinary inspection, or brands must be checked.

Vehicles coming out of isolated areas should routinely be visually inspected for signs of blood on the rear bumper or trunk areas.[31] Because rustlers are invariably armed with some type of firearm, extreme caution must be used when approaching suspicious vehicles. Panicky suspects, who might not otherwise think of assaulting a peace officer, may do so impulsively. In addition to having firearms, this type of rustler will also often be carrying butcher knives and ropes.

In contrast to the modest equipment usually employed by the freezer thief, professional rustlers use more sophisticated means to commit their crimes, such as light planes or helicopters to spot vulnerable herds and watch for patrolling officers. The thieves coordinate their movements with walkie-talkies, and "dirt-bike cowboys" herd the cattle to where they will be killed and butchered, often by the use of chain saws. Refrigerated trucks with meat-processing equipment inside quickly transform the rough-butchered cattle into salable products.[32] Professionals may also have a full array of forged documents, such as a bill of sale and counterfeit U.S. Department of Agriculture inspection stamps. The professional rustling operation can be very profitable. Thirty head of cattle can be taken from the range, loaded onto a truck, and butchered in the truck; the waste is dumped off the road, and the 60 sides of beef are illegally stamped and delivered. The dressed or hanging weight in the meat cooler is roughly 300 pounds per side. This means that 60 sides of stolen beef can be sold to an unwary or unscrupulous butcher for a profit of roughly $15,000 to $17,000 for a night's work.

As a general matter, peace officers have a right to stop any conveyance transporting livestock on any public thoroughfare and the right to impound any animal, carcass, hide, or portion of a carcass in the possession of any person whom they have reasonable cause to believe is not the legal owner or is not entitled to possession.[33] To transport cattle legally, certain written documents may be required, such as:

- bill of sale;
- certificate of consignment;
- brand inspector's certificate;
- shipping or transportation permit.[34]

Because these provisions vary by state, every investigator must know:

- what documentation is required for lawful transportation (for example, a "horse-hauling permit");
- what the investigator's precise authority is in such matters;
- how to handle violations of law.[35]

Equipped with such knowledge, the investigator is better prepared to deal with issues related to transportation violation or a possible theft. Although the applicable state law may permit the officer to impound livestock or meat, there are several less drastic alternatives. Under unusual conditions or when only slight suspicion exists, investigators may elect to get a full description and identifying information about the driver and the rig and its contents. Other information essential for a useful follow-up inquiry is the origin and destination of the trip. If suspicion is more pronounced, specialists may be requested to come to the scene of the stop. Such specialists may come from the investigator's own agency, another local department, the state police or state investigative agency, or the Marks and Brands Unit of the state's department of agriculture. If the investigator is sufficiently confident that a shipping violation or theft exists, he/she can make the arrest and impound the load. Live animals can be delivered to the nearest feedlot or sales yard, and meat can be placed in refrigeration storage. Such situations require that officers in the field have a basic working knowledge of the applicable laws and exercise sound judgment. They are not required to be experts in such matters, and their general investigative experience is a substantial asset in making an evaluation of the situation.

HORSE RUSTLING

There is not a great deal of variation in how horse rustlers operate. If the horse is in a corral, the thief will park a vehicle and trailer nearby, walk up and take the horse, load it in the trailer, and drive off.[36] Because such thefts usually occur during the hours of darkness, the rustler can be several hundred miles away before the theft is discovered. When horses are in a pasture, the task of stealing them is only slightly more difficult. The thief walks into the pasture with a bucket of grain. One or more of the horses will usually approach him, and because they are herd animals, if one approaches, others are also likely to follow along. The theft then proceeds in the same fashion as a corral theft.

One tactic commonly used by horse rustlers is to knock down the corral or pasture fence after loading up the trailer with horses and chase any remaining horses down the road. The owner will think that the horses got out on their own, and it may be several days before he/she realizes that some horses were stolen. Thus, even if there is no clear evidence of a theft, the investigator should not assume that the horse just strayed off; at least, a lost report should be initiated. If the horse is later discovered to have been stolen, the incident can be reclassified.

TACK THEFT

Tack is equipment that is used with horses; the most common items are saddles, bridles, and horse blankets.[37] Of all stolen tack, approximately 80% is saddles—which often have base prices in excess of $2,000 each. Unfortunately, tack is not always marked for identification, making tracing a very difficult proposition. A specialized

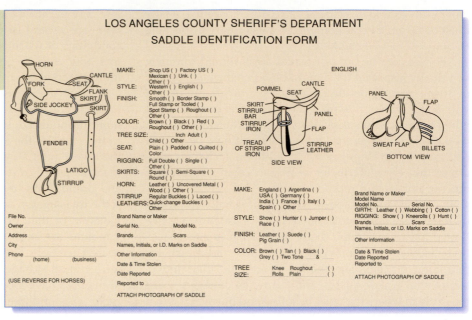

▶ **FIGURE 18-9**
Saddle identification form
(Courtesy of Los Angeles County, California,
Sheriff's Department)

reporting form (Figure 18-9) is a very useful investigative aid. Some owners have injected microchips, which are about the size of a grain of uncooked rice, in their saddles to facilitate recovery if they are stolen.

LIVESTOCK IDENTIFICATION

The purpose of **livestock identification** is to establish that a particular animal is the property of a specific owner. Methods of livestock identification continue to change. In times long past, some ranchers would supplement their brands with wattles. They were formed by pinching skin on the animals' neck or jaw, and cutting most, but not all of it off; the hanging portion was the wattle. In more recent years, ear cropping has largely fallen away, because it is expensive to do and not easy to read by the uninitiated. In the wake of the 9/11 attacks, concern about terrorists deploying pathogens to attack livestock and crops has been a driving force in the formation of the **U.S. Department of Agriculture's National Animal Identification System (NAIS),** the framework for which was announced in 2004.

Presently, NAIS participation is voluntary from a federal perspective. Under NAIS, all agricultural animals would receive a 15-digit Animal Identification Number (AIN), which ultimately could track them from cradle to grave. The national security and public health interest is compelling; every time an animal is sold, its AIN and owner information become part of a database that could quickly and accurately pinpoint where disease outbreaks occur, whether triggered by terrorists or nature, such as mad cow disease. Although program guidelines are unfolding, AINs could be established by bar-coded ear tags or microchips implanted under the skin.

In general, people are more willing to use a wider range of identification methods on cattle than they are on their horses. Cattle are commonly branded, and there are a lot of brands: over 26,000 different ones in Utah alone, some of which date back to 1847.[38]

Brands are combinations of numbers, letters, marks, and shapes that establish a unique identification and must be registered with the state before they can be used. The state agencies approving a brand application are often located with the department of agriculture and have a name such as "Brands and Inspections." In some states, brands must be in a specific location on the animal, whereas in others there is some flexibility. As shown in Figure 18-10, there are three ways to read brands. Treated as a separate category are picture brands, which simply mean what they represent Figure 18-11.

There are five major methods of marking horses and cattle for identification:[39]

1. *Hot-iron:* Hot-iron branding is a method of identification that has been used in this country for nearly 400 years. It is simple to use; an "iron" is heated in a fire and then the end bearing the brand is impressed on the upper hip of the animal, producing a permanent, hair-free shape in the hide that duplicates the face of the branding iron.

2. *Tattoos:* When used on horses, the tattoo is applied to the inside of the top lip; on cattle, the inside of the ear is tattooed near the mid-vein. Tattoos should always be placed in either the right ear or the left ear, or in both ears, but should be consistent for an entire herd.

3. *Freeze brands:* Freeze branding uses liquid nitrogen or dry ice and alcohol to supercool the iron. When it is applied to a hide, it kills cells that produce hair pigments, and so white hair grows back. On

Top to Bottom	Left to Right	Outside to Inside
Bar H	A cross	Circle K
2 bar X	Slash X	Diamond P
D hanging C	Double cross	Box M
Y lazy P	Diamond slash K	Triangle S
Rafter diamond	Lazy E, quarter circle E	Double circle, lazy K

Running W		Rising sun	
Ladder		Broken arrow	
Rocking R		Arrowhead	
Pitchfork		Frying pan	
Flying H		Shoe nail	

▲ FIGURE 18-11 Picture brands

light-colored cattle, white hair cannot be easily seen; when branding such cattle, one must apply the iron for a longer time, which leaves a permanent hairless brand.

4. *Ear tags:* Plastic ear tags can be bought prenumbered or blank so the rancher can use his/her own numbering system. Different colors and sizes of tags are available, and they can be read at a distance. The tags are placed through the ear of cattle at a point between the ear's second and third cartilage rib, to prevent them from being easily ripped out. But because these tags can be pulled out, many experts recommend that a second method of identification also be used. A non-electronic ear tag is the means selected by most ranchers and farmers to identify cattle.

5. *Electronic:* A microchip equipped with a radio transponder has Radio Frequency Identification (RFID) capabilities.[40] These chips may be injected, worn as part of ear tags, or embedded in neck collars. The information on the microchip can be read using a handheld RFID reader. If RFID-enabled ear tags are properly placed on cattle, they can be read with great accuracy as cattle move through properly positioned gates with readers.

DNA profiles of expensive horses and bulls are common as a theft deterrent, required by some breed associations and mandated by some insurance companies to prevent insurance scams (for example, a less-expensive horse is killed, and a claim is made for an expensive horse, which is sold, creating an additional source of "profit"). DNA can easily be obtained from animals by means of nasal swabs or mane or tail hair with the root attached.

PHYSICAL EVIDENCE

The processing of a crime scene where an agriculture-related theft has occurred is in many respects no different from the processing of any other crime scene. For example, when cattle rustling occurs, the perpetrators frequently cut the barbed wire or locks that secure a grazing area. The cut wire and lock will have tool marks on them from the cutting tool. In addition, if the suspect's clothing came into contact with any of the barbed wire at the scene, pieces of fiber may adhere to the barbs. Shoe or tire impressions found at the crime scene may later be linked to a specific suspect and vehicle. Soil samples collected at the crime scene may also prove to be valuable, linking evidence to a suspect with similar soil on his/her shoes or clothes or on the vehicle used to transport the cattle. DNA evidence is also playing an increasing role in livestock theft cases.

CRIME PREVENTION METHODS

Information about how to prevent rural and agricultural crimes can be obtained from a variety of sources, including sheriff's departments, county police, state investigative agencies, state departments of agriculture, county extension agents, and various associations. Although some techniques developed in urban areas can be readily applied to the farm, others would create costs disproportionate to the benefits that could reasonably be expected to accrue to the rancher or farmer. Consequently, the technology in this area is sometimes familiar, sometimes takes advantage of unique aspects of the rural environment, and is continuously in the process of changing and developing. The suggestions that follow are organized around the object of attack. In general, they are specialized and can be supplemented as necessary with more conventional strategies, such as the use of case-hardened padlocks.

FARM EQUIPMENT THEFT

- Participate in identification programs and keep photos of equipment.
- Do not leave unattended equipment in remote fields for hours at a time or overnight. If it is necessary to do so, disable the engine by taking a vital part, and use logging chains to secure other equipment. Even if such precautions are taken, equipment in remote areas should be hidden from view from roadways.
- Equipment is best protected, in descending order of preference, by positioning it as follows: secured in a locked building near the main house or an inhabited house; secured in a gated area that is kept locked and is close to the main or an inhabited house; secured in one or more ways and not visible from commonly traveled roads.
- Immediately report all suspicious activity, such as strangers taking photographs of equipment, to local enforcement officials.

TIMBER THEFT

- Post the property.
- Document its condition with date-stamped photographs.
- Check periodically to determine if any timber has been cut.

- Promptly report all losses.
- Take aerial photos of land.

AGRICHEMICAL THEFT

- End-users, whenever feasible, should buy only in quantities that they can readily use.
- If large-quantity purchases cannot be avoided, they should be stored in a locked, lighted building very close to the main house or an inhabited house. If possible, place a few geese or guinea hens inside as watch animals.
- Rural dealers should employ security personnel during the months when they have large inventories.
- Be suspicious of people offering unusually good buys on agrichemicals; the absence of a market helps deter thefts.

LIVESTOCK AND TACK THEFT

- Mark all livestock for identification; maximum deterrence is obtained when marks are readily visible.[41]
- Take a regular tally or count.
- Do not follow a set routine, such as going to the movies every Friday night, which would give a thief an advantage.
- Enter into cooperative arrangements with trusted neighbors to help watch one another's places.
- When possible, avoid leaving animals in remote pastures or on faraway ranges.
- Mark tack and keep it in a room that can be secured.
- Do not use "set guns" or "booby traps." They are often illegal and frequently injure innocent people or animals; surviving thieves have won damage suits because of such injuries.
- Keep photographic records of livestock and tack.

WILDLIFE CRIMES

Wildlife officers require many of the same types of knowledge and skills as do other peace officers, including knowledge of the laws of arrest, search, and seizure, and skills such as interviewing people, crime scene processing, and interrogating suspects. In addition, wildlife investigators need to know specialized laws pertaining to their field and to be able to recognize the species and gender of wildlife. They also must be able to master unusual skills, such as interpreting tracks and being able to follow a trail (Figure 18-12). Because many poaching incidents come to light only long after the event, when the remains of the animal are discovered, wildlife officers must be familiar with methods of cold case investigation. Such

▲ **FIGURE 18-12 Evidence of deer poaching**
In the course of a major poaching investigation, wildlife investigators seized these boots, whose soles had been carved to resemble cattle hooves. By using them, the poacher tried to lay down a false trail and mislead investigators. (Texas Parks & Wildlife Department © 2005, Photo by Earl Nottingham)

discoveries may come months later when the snow melts to reveal the remains of game or predatory animals dig up remains that were buried by poachers to conceal their crime.

The U.S. Fish and Wildlife National Forensics Laboratory in Ashland, Oregon, is a premier source of assistance for wildlife investigators, as is the Wildlife Forensic DNA Laboratory at Trent University in Canada. In cases of poaching, DNA profiles can tie together the remains of a deer found at the location where it was field-dressed, dried bloodstains collected from the back of a pickup, and meat packages found in the poacher's freezer.[42] This approach provides scientific evidence that is very strong and difficult to overcome in court.

Because wildlife investigators often patrol alone in the wild, they encounter individuals and small groups of people who may be difficult or even deadly to deal with, including survivalists, fugitives, radical environmentalists, paramilitary units, drug smugglers, and persons engaged in illegal activities on public lands, such as growing marijuana and operating clandestine drug labs.

MAJOR THREATS TO WILDLIFE

There are a number of major threats to our wildlife. Urban sprawl destroys animal habitats, as does the accidental or illegal release of chemicals, land erosion, and oil spills. Wildlife **poaching** is also a major threat; it is defined as the illegal taking or possession of game, fish, and other wildlife. Because poaching is a secretive crime committed in the wild, it is believed that wildlife investigators find only 1%–5% of all poached animals.[43]

Poaching makes it more difficult to reestablish game populations, as some states are trying to do with elk and bighorn sheep, threatens endangered species, reduces our enjoyment of being outdoors, and hampers the development of tourism. We don't know what poaching and the illegal trade in animals and animal parts cost annually, but it is believed to be in the billions of dollars annually worldwide.

Poachers and Poaching

Poachers can be categorized into two types: **situational poachers** and **professional poachers.** Most poachers are situational, some being motivated by opportunity and others by circumstance. A driver sees an elk on the road, frozen by the car's headlights. Impulsively, or after short deliberation, he opportunistically shoots the elk out of season. Some situational poachers kill to feed their families because of economic hardship. A few opportunistic poachers kill simply for the thrill of it (Figure 18-13).[44] Although fewer in numbers, professional poachers take much more game than do situational poachers, because they kill for profit.

There is almost a fixation on possessing world-class game trophies (Figure 18-14).[45] The dark side of this fixation results in very organized poaching and often involves unlicensed guides taking trophy seekers into areas closed for hunting, hunting out of season on public lands or on private lands for a fee, or using illegal hunting methods. Over a three-year period in Canada, rich "hunters," many of who were millionaires, rode in a helicopter until a moose was spotted. The chopper would touch down and a hunter would disembark. Once airborne again, the pilot would force the moose to run back toward the waiting hunter.[46] The use of aircraft for such purposes is periodically uncovered; 20 years ago an Alaskan admitted that all 37 Boone and Crockett Club's record book grizzlies that he had helped hunters bag were illegally herded to them using an airplane.[47]

Some of the impetus to poach comes from the fact that there are only a very limited number of big game tags available each year, which are usually distributed by a statewide lottery. For hunting bighorn sheep in New Mexico during 2006/2007, only 12 out of 7,382 hunters received tags through the lottery. Moreover, in Montana, a hunter who gets a bighorn sheep tag has to wait seven years before becoming eligible for the lottery again. In New Mexico, two bighorn sheep tags a year

▶ **FIGURE 18-13   Wolf killed**
Faced with this scene, a wildlife investigator is quickly led to two competing theories: this is a thrill kill, or a rancher shot the wolf to stop predatory attacks on his/her herd. A detailed examination of the scene, knowledge of local events and people, and the follow-up investigation established this as a thrill kill. Although infrequent, claims are sometimes made that an animal was killed in self-defense; this usually involves grizzly bears. If such a claim is reported promptly, an examination of the scene, particularly with an eye toward the distance between the person and the bear, is one key to making a determination of the claim's legitimacy. (Photo courtesy New Mexico Department of Game and Fish)

▶ **FIGURE 18-14   Poached trophy**
The investigation into this poaching of a bighorn sheep resulted in the recovery of the trophy part of the kill and the arrest of one subject.
(© Colorado Division of Wildlife)

are auctioned off to help manage that population. One of them alone brought in $177,500; the reason for the price is simple: most animals taken are Boone and Crockett record book class, and one year the biggest Rocky Mountain bighorn sheep taken in North America was in that state.[48]

There is a substantial Asian market for body parts from poached wild black and grizzly bears. Across the United States and Canada, the mutilated carcasses of bears are found with their gall bladders cut out and their paws chopped off. The gall bladders are thought to have special curative powers in traditional oriental medicine, and a single one may be sold for as much as $3,400 in South Korea, making it by weight more valuable than narcotics.[49] The sale of wild-bear bladders is illegal in China, and there are domestic bear "bile milking" farms.

◄ **FIGURE 18-15**
Poaching investigation
A Nevada Department of Wildlife game warden photographs a boot impression in the snow; note the ruler laid beside the impression to establish the scale. The boot impressions were thought to be made by "hunters" poaching chukars, a medium-sized game bird in the pheasant family. (© Brad Horn/The New York Times/Redux)

However, because wild-bear products are thought to be more potent, a lucrative black market flourishes for people willing to pay top dollar. Wild-bear-paw soup is a great delicacy in China, and a single bowl costs as much as $1,000.[50] At the end of their bile-producing days, farmed bears in China are slaughtered, but the soup from their paws is much less expensive.[51]

INVESTIGATIONS

Wildlife officers generally spend only about 20% of their time engaged in law-enforcement activities (Figure 18-15). The balance is spent teaching hunting, boating, and snowmobile safety courses to the public, staffing exhibits at fairs or other functions, participating in disaster/emergency preparedness training, and conducting surveys and censuses.

Information

Information is an essential commodity in combating poachers and in increasing investigations' rate of success. In some states, 80% of all poacher arrests come from leads from citizens. To assist wildlife officers in getting information, a number of states have established special programs, such as Citizens Against Poachers (CAP) and Turn in a Poacher (TIP).

Uniformed Patrol

Uniformed wildlife officers patrol in boats and cars to see if game is being taken out of season or by illegal means; they visit various sites to observe, to check licenses, and to examine the daily take. In addition to patrolling by car, they use airplanes during the day to locate hunters, trappers, and camps in remote areas. At night, aircraft can

also be useful in pinpointing places where it appears that artificial light is being used by poachers to take game, a tactic known as **jacklighting.** In both day and night uses of aircraft, the pilot or spotter relays information to ground units so that they can take appropriate action. In some instances, aircraft keep poachers from leaving an area under surveillance and direct wildlife officers in cars to intercept the poachers.

Intensive Hunting Patrols

Wildlife officers also employ intensive hunting patrols, especially during the opening weekends for various types of game such as pheasant, wild turkey, waterfowl, grouse, and deer. Intensive patrols tend to be concentrated in areas of high public use, especially those with a history of excessive violations.

Vehicle Check Stops

Vehicle check stops are strategically set up on carefully selected roads to check vehicles for bag limits, unplugged shotguns, and licenses and to determine whether necessary special stamps (for example, duck hunting) have been acquired.

Fishing Patrols

Fishing patrols (Figure 18-16) check to see that no protected or endangered fish, eels, crabs, lobsters, or other aquatic life forms are being taken, that aquatic species are taken only by legal means during the proper seasons and times of day, that legal limits are being respected, and that the proper licenses have been obtained. Wildlife investigators are also vigilant in determining the taking of sport and game fish by commercial fishing methods, such as through the use of seines and trotlines.

▶**FIGURE 18-16**
Fishing violation arrest
(California Department of Fish and Game photo
by Debra Hamilton)

▶**FIGURE 18-17** **Organized poaching ring**
Texas investigators arrest members of a highly organized poaching
ring that operated at night. The group was apprehended on a
private hunting preserve that specialized in having trophy deer to
hunt for a substantial fee. The poachers' equipment included
weapons with silencers, night-vision goggles, and GPS systems.
(Texas Parks & Wildlife Department © 2005, Photo by Earl Nottingham)

Resident License Verification

Despite the availability of a variety of databases, some
out-of-state hunters attempt to pass themselves off as
residents, primarily for two reasons: (1) the allocation of
tags for residents for bear, antelope, elk, and other species requiring tags is greater than for nonresidents, and
(2) they can save a great deal of money: in Idaho in 2008,
a combined hunting and fishing license and an elk tag
cost a resident $66.75 versus $472.25 for the nonresident.
It is a matter of false economy; the chances of "getting
away with it" are low, detection appears to be fairly
high, and penalties are stiff.

Covert Investigations

Covert investigations vary in their complexity. At the
simplest, a wildlife officer who could not approach an
area without being plainly visible for some distance may
dress as a trout fisher and work his way along a stream
watching for violations. Wildlife investigators also employ
sophisticated sting operations. In Texas, some ranchers
learned that their well-managed trophy deer herds were
targets for poachers (Figure 18-17). The ranchers normally charge $2,500–$10,000 for the right to hunt their
property legally. Undercover investigators agreed to take

poachers out at night or to hunt from roads on the
ranches. They received as little as $125 and a bag of mar-
ijuana from one "client." The sting operation netted dozens of arrests and broke the back of poaching for a
number of ranchers.

ENVIRONMENTAL CRIME

This planet—which our children and their children have
to live on—suffers from what we do to it. Rainforests
are being chopped down for timber. The entry of raw
(untreated) sewage into water systems threatens fish

populations. Worldwide, smokestack industries pour carbon dioxide into the air, polluting it and counteracting our efforts to combat the greenhouse effect and rising temperatures. Nuclear accidents render portions of countries uninhabitable. Swamps and marshes are disappearing at an alarming rate, along with their rich ecosystems. And toxins are dumped illegally. In fact, Native-American tribal lands in this country regard illegal dumping as one of the major problems facing them; for example, the Torres-Martinez Reservation outside Los Angeles identified 26 illegal dump sites across its 24,000 acres.

Although not all these events constitute environmental crimes, they do suggest that our planet is in distress. Therefore, we must enforce environmental laws.

THE LEGAL AND ENFORCEMENT FRAMEWORK

There are roughly 18 major federal environmental laws that form the basis for Environmental Protection Agency (EPA) programs. These laws deal with a number of issues, including chemical safety and site security, clean air and water, oil pollution, toxic-substance control, emergency planning, and environmental cleanup. Many states have substantially similar laws on some of these issues, and a number of local jurisdictions have enacted their own laws to combat environmental crimes. From this maze of laws, three patterns of enforcement emerge, regarding:

- acts over which only the federal government has jurisdiction;
- acts for which there is concurrent federal and state jurisdiction;
- acts for which there is unique state and/or local jurisdiction.

Individuals and businesses may be subject to criminal and civil fines for violating laws and consent decrees. Other sanctions that can be applied include the revocation of licenses and permits and the imposition of freezes on eligibility to receive federal grants.

The federal Resource Conservation and Recovery Act (RCRA) of 1976 and its subsequent amendments give the Environmental Protection Agency authority over hazardous waste from "its cradle to its grave." **Hazardous waste** may be solids, liquids, sledges, or byproducts of manufacturing processes. They may also be commercial products such as battery acid and household cleaning supplies. A waste is hazardous if it has one or more of the following characteristics (Figure 18-18):

- *Ignitability:* Wastes that can create fires, those that can readily catch fire, and friction-sensitive substances (for example, paints, degreasers, linseed oil, and gasoline)
- *Corrosiveness:* Wastes that are acidic and those capable of corroding metal objects such as drums and tanks (for instance, cleaning fluids, battery acids, and rust removers)

▲ **FIGURE 18-18   Characteristics of hazardous waste**
(Courtesy Environmental Protection Agency)

- *Reactivity:* Substances that are unstable under normal conditions and that can create explosions and/or toxic fumes, gases, and vapors when mixed with water (for example, sulphur-bearing wastes and cyanides)
- *Toxicity:* Substances that are harmful or fatal when ingested or absorbed and that, when improperly disposed of on land, may eventually pollute groundwater (for instance, mercury, certain pesticides, and lead)

PROVISIONS OF STATE RCRA LAWS

Many states have enacted laws that are very similar to the federal RCRA. Among the common provisions of these laws are these:

- Identification and listing of hazardous wastes
- Establishment of permit and license systems regarding various types of hazardous waste, including their treatment, storage, and disposal (T/S/D)
- A manifest or shipping-paper system that tracks hazardous waste from "its cradle to its grave"
- Identification of the responsibilities of the generators and the transporters of hazardous waste
- Requirements for hazardous-waste management facilities, such as proof of financial reliability
- Designation of enforcement authority and criminal penalties

In a typical case, hazardous-waste crime charges are brought against one or more individuals and/or corporations involved in any combination of the three major components of the waste cycle:

1. *Generating:* Among the companies engaging in activities that involve hazardous waste are chemical companies, which produce it as a byproduct of their legal activity; furniture and wood manufacturing companies working with various solvents and ignitable wastes, which must periodically be disposed of; and

▶**FIGURE 18-19**
Storage of hazardous waste under inadequate conditions
Properly identified hazardous waste improperly stored in deteriorated drums. The federal government and many states have enacted laws to protect against hazardous-waste violations that threaten both people and the environment. Treatment, storage, and disposal (T/S/D) violations are committed by companies that fail to follow specific guidelines, including those that identify proper conditions for storage of hazardous materials. (Courtesy Illinois Environmental Protection Agency)

vehicle maintenance operations, which involve lead-acid batteries, solvents, and heavy metal and inorganic wastes.

2. *Transportation:* This component involves the hauling away of hazardous waste from industrial sites. False manifests may be prepared to make the loads look less harmful, thereby allowing for inexpensive disposal of the waste. Tankers in poor condition may leak hazardous waste as they are driven along highways, and illegal disposal of hazardous waste also occurs when tankers deliberately discharge the waste in small amounts onto the road.

3. *Treatment, storage, and disposal(T/S/D):* **T/S/D crimes** are committed by companies that treat hazardous waste without a permit or treat it inadequately; store it without a permit to do so; improperly identify the nature of the waste or store it under inadequate conditions; discharge it into sewers; simply abandon it; mix it with regular waste for cheaper disposal; or store incompatible chemicals or amounts of chemicals above their permitted amount or concentration (Figure 18-19).

Hazardous-waste generators vary in the level of regulatory requirements that they are required to meet (Table 18-1). Regardless of generator status, all generators must comply with basic RCRA requirements, including the use of manifests to track waste shipments. Conditionally exempt small-quantity generators must obtain an EPA permit once they generate more than 100 kilograms of hazardous waste per month. In all cases, waste must be properly stored and labeled. The EPA's *universal waste* list identifies items thrown out in large numbers, including batteries, some lamps, obsolete pesticides, and thermostats. The T/S/D requirements for universal waste are less stringent and do not count against a generator's status.

The most frequent violators of hazardous-waste regulations and laws are the small generating firms. Companies in this group violate hazardous-waste laws to maintain their profitability by avoiding the cost of legal disposal. However, large companies (or their employees) that have violated state RCRAs or various federal environmental laws include such well-known businesses as Texaco, Ocean Spray Cranberries, Fleischmann's, Ashland Oil, B. F. Goodrich, and Kaiser Steel.

TABLE 18-1	**EPA Hazardous-Waste Generator Status**		
GENERATOR CATEGORY	**MONTHLY GENERATION RATE**	**MAXIMUM QUANTITY ACCUMULATION LIMIT**	**MAXIMUM TIME ACCUMULATION LIMIT**
Conditionally exempt small-quantity generator (CESQG)	Less than 100 kg	1,000 kg	None
Small-quantity generator (SQG)	100 to 1,000 kg	6,000 kg	180 days
Large-quantity generator (LQG)	More than 1,000 kg	No storage limit	90 days

Source: Environmental Protection Agency

Investigators must be alert to the fact that traditional crimes are also involved in acts that constitute environmental crimes. Examples of these include falsification of records and forgery—typically involving manifests and T/S/D records—and bribery of public officials, such as regulation inspectors and landfill operators, who accept money to certify that the hazardous waste was properly disposed of when it actually ended up being illegally dumped or abandoned.

INVESTIGATIVE METHODS

Patrolling officers should be alert for signs that indicate the possibility or presence of **illegal dumping of hazardous waste.** Some of these signs are similar to the signs of a mass chemical attack, but in illegal-dumping cases the scale is smaller. Among the signs to watch for:

- suspicious discharges into waterways;
- discolored and dying vegetation that is unusual for the season;
- unusual number of dead animals, fish, and/or birds;
- unusual and persistent odors;
- odors that are accompanied by uncomfortable sensations (for example, burning) affecting skin, eyes, and respiratory system;
- new activity by trucks at closed businesses or abandoned buildings or on secondary roads;
- tankers visiting waterways in which they might illegally dump their cargoes.

Officers should approach suspected hazardous-waste spills and toxic-waste sites with the wind at their backs and from the highest ground reasonably available. They should use binoculars to assess the scene in a standoff mode and notify their communications center as quickly as possible.

Leads on illegal hazardous-waste sites may be offered by disgruntled or former employees, occasionally by a current employee (who may have reservations about doing so because of the possibility of losing his/her job should the employer shut down); by home owners in the area of such sites; and by local pilots, boaters and fishers, competitors, building inspectors, and others. As in other types of investigation, the most immediate concerns are determining the reliability and the motive of the person bringing the information forward and assessing the public safety and health risks.

Surveillance is an excellent tool for gathering information, because it can establish illegal practices and the persons involved with them. Night-photography equipment is essential, and thermal imaging and nightscopes are very useful in investigating "midnight dumping." Satellite and aerial photographs of known hazardous-waste dumping areas can assist in locating the sites of additional illegal dumps and are useful in determining whether generators and disposal facilities are exceeding their legal or permit capacities.

For most environmental crimes, it is necessary to form a team to conduct the investigation. Access to an attorney or inclusion of one on the team is a must because of multiple, complex laws, consent decrees, and regulatory guidance. An attorney can be helpful in drafting or reviewing requests for search warrants, arrest warrants, and other legal documents. The team should also include people whose skills match the needs of the investigation, such as backhoe operators or hydrologists. Because of the dangers associated with hazardous-waste sites, investigators must wear PPE to protect themselves. Even when properly equipped, investigators can encounter unusual or unanticipated hazards (Figure 18-20). Specialized investigators from federal and state agencies are often available

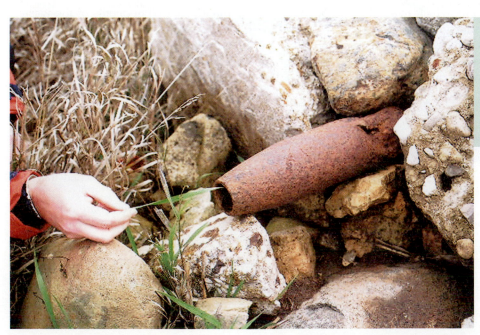

◀ **FIGURE 18-20 Unusual hazard**
An investigator from the Illinois Environmental Protection Agency uses a blade of grass to point at an artillery projectile found at a closed military instillation. (Courtesy Illinois Environmental Protection Agency)

to assist with complex investigations. The EPA's National Enforcement Investigations Center (NEIC) has multidisciplinary teams for conducting investigations, one of the leading forensic environmental chemistry laboratories, and an extensive library, all of which are available to federal, state, and local agencies.

KEY TERMS

agrichemical
anhydrous ammonia
bone rustler
brand
copper theft
freezer crime
hazardous waste

illegal dumping of hazardous waste
jacklighting
livestock
livestock identification
night picker
poaching
professional poacher

situational poacher
tack
timber theft
T/S/D crimes
U.S. Department of Agriculture National Animal Identification System (NAIS)

REVIEW QUESTIONS

1. In what ways are cities and agricultural crime linked?
2. Some variations in what is stolen from farms and ranches are caused by fluctuations in the economy. Theft of copper and anhydrous ammonia is a relatively recent trend. Why is this kind of theft happening, and how does it reflect fluctuations in the economy?
3. If you were going to make a public presentation on the subject of timber theft, what major points would you make?
4. Compare how horse and cattle rustlers operate. What are the differences and similarities?
5. What are four concerns with respect to conducting stakeouts in rural areas?
6. What is NAIS?
7. There are five major methods of marking horses and cattle for identification. If you used your horse casually, just for recreational enjoyment, which method would you use to identify your horse? Why?
8. In our national parks and other federal lands, there are at least 29 species whose existence is threatened by poaching. What are the other major threats to wildlife?

9. Hypothetically, what kinds of physical evidence might exist where cattle have been rustled?
10. Your friend has just bought 20 mostly timbered acres with a small house where she will live. She is concerned about "tree rustlers." What crime prevention suggestions can you give her?
11. What is the difference between situational and professional poachers? If you came upon a needy poacher who had just killed a deer to feed his family, would you "cut him some slack"? What if this person were a close relative?
12. Explain this statement: "One reason for poaching bighorn sheep is that there are only a very limited number of permits/tags available each year."
13. Why is information an "essential commodity" in investigating poaching?
14. Can you identify and describe the four characteristics of hazardous waste?
15. What are the three major components of the waste cycle?
16. What are three examples of T/S/D crimes?
17. What are six signs of illegal dumping of waste?

INTERNET ACTIVITIES

1. Do any sheriff's offices in your state have an agricultural or rural crime unit? What services do they provide?
2. What are some examples of livestock and crop theft in your state?
3. What species of wildlife are being poached in your state?
4. What types of environmental crimes are committed in your state? How serious are they? Who investigates them?

19

ARSON AND EXPLOSIVES INVESTIGATIONS

CHAPTER OBJECTIVES

1. Discuss the steps in the preliminary investigation of arson.

2. Define the various types of burn indicators.

3. Describe ignition devices that may be used in arson.

4. Assess several common motivations of arsonists for setting fires.

5. Explain the scientific methods used in arson investigation.

6. List several groups of people whom an arson investigator should interview.

7. List questions that investigators should ask in interviews and interrogations.

8. Discuss how legal entry can be made into a fire scene and how evidence may be legally obtained.

9. Describe the two types of major explosions, namely, mechanical and chemical.

10. Understand how improvised explosive devices (IEDs) work.

11. Outline the procedures for handling and investigating bomb threats.

12. Explain how to collect and preserve evidence at the bomb scene.

13. Discuss the unique features of a bomber's signature.

The crime of arson has increased dramatically in recent years. In 2008 there were 30,500 intentional fires that were set by arsonists, resulting in the deaths of 315 people and a dollar loss of $866 million. But this $866 million is only the tip of the iceberg when it comes to the total amount of money lost annually as a result of arson.[1] Fire services increases that cost by at least an extra $10 billion. Untold thousands of jobs are also lost when factories are burned for profit. Likewise, thousands of homes are lost each year, forcing home owners and tenants to relocate and often incur higher house and rent payments.[2]

Arson is an inherently difficult crime to detect and prosecute, in part because the motivations for and methods of committing arson vary widely. Some arsonists may be troubled juveniles who start fires with matches or cigarettes; others are professional arsonists, who frequently use timing devices and accelerants. Arson investigation also falls between police responsibility and fire department responsibility, an area that is too often not effectively covered. Both the police and the fire services can legitimately claim authority in arson cases, but each also may rationalize that the responsibility belongs to the other. Unfortunately, in most jurisdictions, neither is prepared to devote the resources needed to achieve identification, arrest, and conviction rates commensurate with other crimes. Arson investigators need more cooperation and better training. Administrative officials need to help, but in order to help they need to give the problem a greater share of their attention. Probably the most urgent step in controlling arson rates is for top fire and police officials and local, state, and national governments to recognize the magnitude of the problem and then provide the necessary resources to combat it.[3]

In the second half of this chapter, we discuss explosive investigations, which are in many respects quite different from arson investigations. We provide a detailed discussion of the different types of explosives used, and the techniques employed to detonate them. We also discuss improvised explosive devices (IEDs)—their contents, components, and the most common types of IEDs that have been employed or attempted to be employed in the United States and around the world. We also discuss serial bombers and the ways in which they leave specific "signatures" that can assist law enforcement in linking bombings.

in the middle of a bare concrete basement floor typically eliminates defective heating appliances or wiring. Points of origin sometimes are established by reconstructing furniture and walls, and replacing loose boards and doors. Neighbors and occupants can help describe how things were before the fire. The direction of heat flow then can be followed by checks for the deepest charring, indications of highest temperature, and the duration of heat. Temperatures are indicated by the condition of metal, glass, wood, plastics, and other materials. Because heat rises, a general rule is to look for the lowest point of deep char as the point of origin. This rule, however, has many exceptions.

After the area of origin has been established, the investigator should check for the level of origin by examining the bottoms of shelves, ledges, moldings, and furniture and all sides of the legs, arms, and framework of reconstructed furniture. The investigator also should clean the floor carefully at the point of origin, examining and moving all objects to one side. After this is done, the floor or rugs should be swept as clean as possible for examination of burn patterns (Figure 19-1).

The floor and lower areas of the room produce the most clues to the cause of the fire, because they are the living area. Most equipment and contents are near floor level, actions of occupants are conducted near floor level, and most materials drop there during a fire.

PRELIMINARY INVESTIGATION

Arson investigations entail several exceptions to fire-service training. For example, the fire service has taught firefighters that fire loss is less and public relations are better if they clean premises of debris, water, and so forth. However, if arson is suspected, firefighters should not disarrange the premises, especially at the point of origin. Moving debris, even window glass, may destroy valuable physical evidence.[4]

In nearly all cases, there is little additional loss if the area encompassing the point of origin is not cleaned out, because this area is usually the most heavily damaged by the fire, with little salvage possible. Often it is necessary during overhauling to move large quantities of acoustical tile, plasterboard, canned goods, cartons, and other items. If this material is beyond salvage, it is natural to throw it into the worst-burned area of the building. But this is probably the area the investigator will want to examine carefully, and such discards will have to be moved again. In the confusion, the fire's cause is likely to remain in doubt.

One effective way to determine fire causes is to determine the point of origin. For instance, a point of origin

WHERE AND HOW DID THE FIRE START?

Once the fire is out, the primary task is to begin examining what is left of the building for physical evidence that may indicate how the fire began.

The point of origin can be a clue to possible arson. For example, if two or more distinct points of origin are found, two or more separate fires probably were deliberately set. Also, if the fires started in the middle of a large room or in a closet, then the level of suspicion should go up sharply.[5]

TWO FACTORS NEEDED TO CAUSE A FIRE

During the investigation, one should remember that a fire always has two causes: a source of heat and material ignited. In checking for the fire cause at the point of origin, tone should use the **layer-checking technique.** Before any material is moved or shoveled out, the investigator should make notes and carefully examine the strata while working through to the floor. These layers often contain wood ash, plaster, melted aluminum, window glass, charred drapery fabric, and charred newspapers. They may give a picture of the sequence of burning. If, for example, charred newspapers were found beneath charred drapery fabric, this could indicate a set fire, particularly if

► **FIGURE 19-1**

Arson investigators at work
A team of arson investigators search the scene of a suspected arson. Arson investigators receive hours of specialized training to effectively conduct this type of investigation. They must be careful not to destroy potential evidence while sifting through soot and debris. (Courtesy Thomas Evans, Pinellas County, Florida, Sheriff's Office)

papers would not usually be in the area or if they were of different types of dates. Aluminum and similar alloys melt fairly early in a fire (at about 1,150°F), often splash or run over other material near floor level, solidify, and protect the material from further damage. Draperies and heavy curtains may burn free and drop on flammable liquid, preventing it from being completely consumed, especially if the liquid is heavy or not particularly volatile.[6]

ACCIDENTAL FIRES

Once the point of origin has been discovered, the next step is to determine how the fire started. Even though arson may be suspected, the investigator must first investigate and rule out all possible accidental or natural causes. Many courts have held that this elimination of accidental causes is a firm basis for an arson charge. Also, if the investigator is put on the witness stand, questions will likely be raised about the possibility of accidental causes. A failure to eliminate accidental causes could substantially weaken the prosecution's case.

Some of the more common accidental or natural causes of fire fall into these categories:

- *The electric system:* Fuses in which pennies have been inserted; broken or rotted insulation; overloaded circuits; defective switches; and improperly installed wiring.
- *Electrical appliances and equipment:* Defective electrical units with short circuits; overheated irons; and light bulbs covered by paper shades.

- *Gas:* Leaks in gas pipes; defective stoves and heating units.
- *Heating units:* Overheated stoves or steam pipes; clothing being dried too close to fireplaces or open flames; faulty chimneys; explosions from kerosene stoves; and overturned space heaters.
- *Sunlight:* The concentration of sun rays on bubbles in glasses, windowpanes, or convex shaving mirrors placed near combustible materials such as paper or rags.
- *Matches:* Children playing with matches, especially in enclosed areas such as closets or utility rooms.
- *Smoking:* The careless disposal of cigars, cigarettes, pipe ashes, and other lighted devices into trash cans in the home; individuals who fall asleep while smoking in bed or in a chair.

Indications of cigarettes in furniture or mattresses are heavy charring of the unit and the floor; a char pattern on furniture frames, heaviest on the inside; heavy staining and blackening of mirrors and window glass in the area, indicating a long, slow fire; a burning time of 1–4 hours; collapsing of part or all of the core springs. Lying flat on a padded surface, cigarettes usually char a small hole and burn out. If the cigarette is partially covered at the sides or bottom, a fire usually results in an hour or so. Cigarettes ignite foam rubber padding to about the same degree as other padding. With foam rubber padding, fire occurs a little faster, because smoldering rubber reaches an ignition temperature faster and burns with greater intensity.[7]

SPONTANEOUS HEATING AND IGNITION

There are a few fundamental causes of spontaneous heating, but the conditions under which these factors may operate are numerous. Nearly all organic materials and many metals are subject to oxidation, fermentation, or both and therefore have some potential for spontaneous heating.

Spontaneous heating is produced in three major ways: chemical action, fermentation, and oxidation (the most common way). For example, chemical-action heating occurs when unslaked lime and water or sodium and water are combined. Fermentation heating is caused by bacterial action. Here, moisture is a prime factor. The most dangerous materials are those subject to combinations, such as fermentation and oxidation with drying. Fresh sawdust over 10 feet deep is subject to fermentation heating but rarely reaches ignition temperature. In oxidation heating, rapid oxidation must take place in the presence of a good insulating factor and an oxygen supply. Oxidation takes place in oils containing carbon, hydrogen, and oxygen. This combination is mostly found in vegetable and fish oils and, to some extent, in animal oils.

The susceptibility to spontaneous heating is usually determined by drying time. Unadulterated hydrocarbons, such as mineral and petroleum oils, are not considered subject to spontaneous ignition.

Spontaneous ignition is rare in residences and small businesses. It is considerably accelerated by external heat such as sunshine, steampipes, hot air ducts, and friction from wind or vibration. Spontaneous ignition is rather mysterious, because of many unknowns. Therefore, it is often used as a catch-all explanation.

The usual time required to produce spontaneous ignition by oxidation or fermentation runs from several hours to several days or months. This form of ignition is characterized by internal charring of a mass of combustibles, and some of the remains of this material usually are found at the point of origin (if the firefighters have been careful and especially if fog was used), because it normally takes a considerable mass—several inches of fairly dense material—to create the factors necessary for spontaneous heating. Sometimes when material of the appropriate type is suspected and found to be deeply charred all the way through, investigators must satisfy themselves that external heat was not responsible. When not heated internally, sacks of meals, flour, and the like usually survive fire with only an inch or two of charring on the exposed surface.

Dust and polishing mops have often been accused of causing spontaneous ignition and probably have in some rare cases. Most fires originating near a mop in a closet or on a back porch are caused by a child playing with matches.[8] It is debatable whether the average mop would have enough bulk to provide the necessary insulation to raise the temperature to the ignition point, although with favorable conditions—such as a large mop, saturated with fast-drying oils, pressed in a corner with other brooms, and receiving outside heat from a steampipe or the sun's rays through a window—ignition could occur. During the several hours required for the material to ignite, it gives off very acrid odors. Linseed and similar oils are especially odorous. People in the area during that time usually would be aware of these odors.

BURN INDICATORS

Burn indicators are the effects of heat or partial burning that indicate a fire's rate of development, points of origin, temperature, duration, and time of occurrence, as well as the presence of flammable liquids. Interpretation of burn indicators is a principal means for determining the causes of fires, especially arson. Following are some of the burn indicators.[9]

ALLIGATORING

Alligatoring is the charring and cracking that gives wood the appearance of alligator skin. In the past, the appearance of the charring and cracking of wood has been given meaning by the fire investigation community beyond what has been substantiated by controlled testing. Contrary to previous and erroneous assumptions, the presence of large, shiny blisters (alligator char) is not evidence that a liquid accelerant was present during the fire or that a fire spread rapidly or burned with greater intensity. These types of blisters can be found in many different types of fires[10] (Figure 19-2).

DEPTH OF CHAR

Analysis of the depth of char is most reliable for evaluating fire spread, rather than for establishing specific burn

▲ **FIGURE 19-2 Alligatoring**
This is the charring and cracking that gives wood the appearance of alligator skin. (Courtesy Fire and Fraud Section, Aetna Casualty Surety Company)

Char base
Char layer
Pyrolysis zone
Pyrolysis zone base
Normal wood
Char depth

▲ FIGURE 19-3   Line of demarcation in a wood section
(Factory Mutual Engineering Corporation, Norwood, Massachusetts. Reprinted with permission.)

times or intensity of heat from adjacent burning materials. By measuring the relative depth and extent of charring, the investigator may be able to determine which portions of a material or construction were exposed the longest to a heat source. The relative depth of char from point to point is the key to appropriate use of **charring**—locating the places where the damage was most severe owing to exposure, ventilation, or fuel placement. The investigator may then deduce the direction of fire spread, with decreasing char depths being farther away from the heat source (Figure 19-3).

Depth of char is often used to estimate the duration of a fire. The rate of charring of wood varies widely depending on such variables as:

- rate and duration of heating;
- ventilation effects;
- surface area-to-mass ratio;
- direction, orientation, and size of wood grain;
- species of wood (pine, oak, fir, and so on);
- moisture content;
- nature of surface coating.[11]

BREAKING OF GLASS

If a pane of glass is mounted in a frame that protects the edges of the glass from the radiated heat of a fire, a temperature difference occurs between the unprotected por-tion of the glass and the protected edge. Researchers estimate that a temperature difference of about 158°F (70°C) between the center of the pane of glass and the protected edge can cause cracks that start at the edge of the glass. The cracks appear as smooth, undulating lines that can spread and join together. Depending on the degree of cracking, the glass may or may not collapse from its frame. If a pane of glass has no edge protection from the radiated heat or fire, the glass breaks at a higher temperature difference. Research findings suggest that fewer cracks are formed and the pane is more likely to stay whole.

Glass that has received an impact will have a characteristic "cobweb" pattern: numerous cracks in straight lines. The glass may have been broken before, after, or during the fire.

If flame suddenly contacts one side of a glass pane while the unexposed side is relatively cool, a stress can develop between the two faces and the glass can fracture between the faces. *Crazing* is a term used in the fire inves-tigation community to describe a complicated pattern of short cracks in glass arising from this condition. These cracks may be straight or crescent-shaped and may or may not extend through the thickness of the glass. While crazing is still a theory and has not yet been confirmed, research has established that it can be created by the rapid cooling of glass brought on by the application of water spray in a hot environment. Occasionally with small-size panes, differential expansion between the exposed and the unexposed faces may result in the pane's popping out of its frame.[12]

COLLAPSED FURNITURE SPRINGS

The collapse of furniture springs may provide the inves-tigator with various clues concerning the direction, dura-tion, or intensity of the fire. However, the collapse of the springs cannot be used to indicate exposure to a specific type of heat source or ignition, such as smoldering igni-tion or the presence of an ignitable liquid. The results of laboratory testing indicate that the annealed springs, and the associated loss of tension (tensile strength), are a func-tion of the application of heat. The tests revealed that short-term heating at high temperatures and long-term heating at moderate temperatures over 750°F (400°C) can result in the loss of tensile strength and in the collapse of the springs. The tests also revealed that the presence of a load or weight on the springs while they are being heated increases the loss of tension.

By analyzing furniture springs, the investigator can compare the differences between the springs and other areas of the mattress, cushion, frame, and so forth. Com-parative analysis of the springs can assist the investiga-tor in developing hypotheses concerning the relative exposure of various items or areas to a particular heat source. For example, if the springs at one end of a cush-ion or mattress have lost their tension and those at the other end have not, then hypotheses may be developed. The hypotheses should take into consideration other circumstances, effects (such as ventilation), and evidence at the scene concerning the duration or intensity of the fire, the area of origin, direction of heat travel, and the relative proximity of the heat. Areas characterized by the loss of tensile strength may indicate greater relative exposure to heat than do areas without the loss of strength.

Other circumstances and effects to consider are the loss of mass and material; the depth of char in a wood frame; and color changes, possibly indicating intensity, in metal frames. Comparative analysis should also include consideration of the covering material of the springs. The absence of material may indicate a portion closer to the source of heat, while the presence of material may indicate an area more remote from the heat source. The investigator should also consider the condition of the springs before the fire.[13]

Spalling is the breakdown in the surface tensile strength of concrete, masonry, or brick that occurs when exposure to high temperatures and rates of heating produces mechanical forces within the material. These forces are believed to result from one or more of these factors:

- moisture present in uncured or "green" concrete;
- differential expansion between reinforcing rods or steel mesh and the surrounding concrete;
- differential expansion between the concrete mix and the aggregate (this is most common with silicon aggregates);
- differential expansion between the fine-grained surface or finished layers and the coarser-grained interior layers;
- differential expansion between the fire-exposed surface and the interior of the slab.

Spalling of concrete or masonry surfaces may be caused by heat, freezing chemicals, or abrasion. It may be induced more readily in poorly formulated or finished surfaces. Spalling is characterized by distinct lines of striation and the loss of surface material, resulting in cracking, breaking, and chipping or in the formation of craters on the surface. Spalled areas may appear lighter in color than adjacent areas. This lightening can be caused by the exposure of clean subsurface material. Also, adjacent areas may tend to be sooted.

Spalling of concrete, masonry, brick, or painted surfaces (such as plaster) has often been linked to unusually high temperatures caused by burning accelerants.

Although spalling can result from high rates of heat release or a rapid change in temperature, an accelerant need not be involved. The primary mechanism of spalling is the expansion or contraction of the surface while the rest of the mass expands or contracts at a different rate. Another factor in the spalling of concrete is the loading and stress in the material at the time of the fire. Since high-stress or high-load areas may not be related to the fire, spalling of concrete on the underside of ceilings or beams may not be directly positioned over the origin of the fire.[14]

DISTORTED LIGHT BULBS

Heat can also have an effect on the glass of a light bulb. The investigator can examine the distortion of a light bulb, for instance, to determine the direction of head impingement. Bulbs over 25 watts expand toward the heat, and bulbs that are 25 watts or less pull inward on the side of the heat; the bulbs in Figure 19-4 demonstrate this phenomenon. The bulb in the middle is greater than 25 watts, and the bulb on the right is less than 25 watts.[15]

Interior pressure of gas on weakened glass, pushing the glass in the direction of the heat source

Bulb has vacuum, so distortion is pulled inward on side of heat source

Direction of heat source

◄ **FIGURE 19-4**
Distorted light bulbs
Heat can affect the glass of a light bulb, and the investigator can examine the distortion of a light bulb to determine the direction of the heat source. Bulbs over 25 watts expand toward the heat (middle bulb), and bulbs (right) that are 25 watts or less pull inward on the side of the heat.
(Courtesy of National Fire Protection Association, Inc., Quincy, MA)

TEMPERATURE DETERMINATION

If the investigator knows the approximate melting temperature of a material, an estimate can be made of the temperature to which the melted material was subjected. This knowledge may be of help in evaluating the intensity and duration of the heating, the extent of heat movement, or the relative rates of heat release from fuels.

When using such generic materials as glass, plastics, and white pot metals for making temperature determinations, the investigator must be aware of the wide variety of melting temperatures for these materials.

The best approach is to take a sample of the material and have its melting temperature ascertained by a competent laboratory, materials scientist, or metallurgist. Wood and gasoline burn at essentially the same flame temperature. The turbulent diffusion flame temperatures of all hydrocarbon fuels (plastics and ignitable liquids) and cellulosic fuels are approximately the same, although the fuels release heat at different rates.

The temperature achieved by an item at a given location within a structure or fire area depends on how much the item is heated. The amount of heating depends on the temperature and velocity of the airflow, the geometry and physical properties of the heated item, its proximity to the source of heat, and the amount of heat energy present. Burning metals and highly exothermic chemical reactions can produce temperatures significantly higher than those created by hydrocarbon- or cellulosic-fueled fires.

Identifiable temperatures achieved in structural fires rarely remain above 1,900°F (1,040°C) for long periods of time. These temperatures are sometimes called **effective fire temperatures,** because they reflect physical effects that can be defined by specific temperature ranges. The investigator can use the analysis of the melting and fusion of materials to assist in establishing whether higher-than-expected heat energy was present.[16]

FIRE SETTING AND RELATED MECHANISMS

It is the duty of an arson investigator to search the debris of a suspicious fire, particularly around the point of origin, to gather evidence pointing to the mechanism used by the fire setter in the arson effort.[17]

An arsonist may use the simplest of methods, a match and some paper, or elaborate mechanical or chemical methods. An **incendiary mechanism** may be mechanical or chemical, and consists of an ignition device, possibly a timing device, one or more "plants" to feed or accelerate the initial flame, and, frequently, "trailers" to spread the fire about the building or from plant to plant.

IGNITION DEVICES

Matches

Only juvenile arsonists and **pyromaniacs** seem to favor striking matches. Other fire setters want some delay, so they adapt the ordinary match to some timing mechanism. For example, several matches may be affixed to a lighted cigarette with a rubber band or tape, the heads of the matches set about halfway down the cigarette from its glowing end. In some cases, matches are laid alongside a cigarette. Books of paper matches are also popular. Because cigarettes will continue to burn when laid on their sides, they are effective ignition devices; the slow-burning cigarette allows the fire setter a few minutes to get away from the scene before the fire makes any headway.

Gasoline and Other Accelerants

Gasoline and other **accelerants** ("boosters" that speed the progress of a fire) are very popular with many different types of arsonists (Figure 19-5). The investigator should remember that gasoline and many types of liquid accelerants burn at about 3,000°F as opposed to ordinary combustibles, which burn at 1,600°F. If, for example, the investigator observes a metal door melted in a pile, gasoline was probably used as an accelerant because steel generally reaches its melting point at 3,000°F.

TELLTALE SIGNS OF ACCELERANTS

- Distinct burn/damage pattern
- Witness observations (smelling gasoline, and so on)
- Explosion
- Burns to the hands, face, legs, or hair of a suspect/witness
- Unnatural fire spread (downward, very fast, and so on)
- Flames appear suddenly in an entire room followed by heavy black smoke
- Bright yellow/orange flames with black smoke
- Flames seen burning directly from the floor
- Intense localized rusting/warping (especially to the undersides and lower portions) of metal appliances and metal objects within the suspected liquid burn-pattern area
- Light, moderate, and heavy floor burn patterns in puddle or trailer shapes corresponding to the original shape of the accelerant pool on tight or nonporous floors (burn patterns vary with the type of accelerant, surface texture, and ventilation)
- Gapping of wood or vinyl floor seams within the pour burn pattern that may be caused by a liquid accelerant burning inside the seam
- Rainbow-colored sheen on the surface of suppression water over the pour area
- Even height of smoke and heat patterns in the room of origin

▲ **FIGURE 19-5   Gasoline used as an accelerant**
These photographs depict in sequential order an incendiary device involving a plastic milk jug, a birthday candle, and gasoline. The cap of the milk jug was drilled to the proper size to hold the candle. As the candle burned it eventually fell into the gasoline and ignited the vapors at the level of the hole. The burning vapors then expanded which in turn intensified the fire. The delay time for the device was approximately 20–25 minutes. These photographs depict a test that was done before the upcoming trial of a person who allegedly used the device in the interior of a car, supporting investigators' suspicions that the car had been intentionally burned. (Courtesy Dave Crosbie, Burnsville, MN, Fire Department)

- Accelerant containers in or near the scene
- Increased burn damage pattern at the bottom of furniture, boxes, and so on, on the floor in the burn pattern
- Burn patterns
  —"Rundown" burn patterns on floor just below loose floorboards, board seams, or edge moldings
  —Localized staining on the underside of carpet padding

  —Pool-shaped, mottled, black-and-brown staining on a concrete floor with a tendency for the mottled portion to repel water—area may retain odor of accelerant
- Fire damage with no identifiable point of origin
- Wall burn patterns running from the floor seam upward, or appearing in corners
- Burned-out flooring beneath heavy appliances or furniture, which would usually protect the floor

- Localized "clean burn" areas on a wall, appliance, or similar vertical surfaces above the floor pattern where intense heat burned away soot deposits
- Sharp line of char demarcation in a cross section of wood stud or a sharp line of calcination (color change) in plaster or drywall—indicates rapid (rather than smoldering) heat buildup
- Window glass that has melted down like "ribbon candy" and has a clean interior face (little or no soot) on the side with the accelerant
- Spring annealing in furniture/bedding—sometimes results from liquid accelerant being poured on, or adjacent to, furniture
- "Inverted cone" burn/scald patterns on vertical surfaces with the pour pattern[18]

Chemicals

Various chemical combustions have been used to set fires. Saboteurs have used such means for years. Units that provide for an acid to be released on some combination of chemicals are favorite devices, with the acid releasing itself by eating its way through the cork or even the metal of its container. The time lag from setting to ignition can be estimated with some certainty by an arsonist with a little knowledge of chemistry.

Various rubber receptacles—such as hot water bottles, ice bags, or contraceptives—have been used for a phosphorus and water ignition device. A pinhole is made in the rubber container, allowing the water to seep out. Once it drains below the level of the phosphorus, ignition takes place. As this chemical ignites upon contact with air, a time lag is secured by controlling the amount of water and the size of the hole in the container.

Even the ordinary fire setter sometimes uses a chemical that ignites on contact with water. The device is activated by rain. Holes in a roof or a connection to the building's gutter system have been used to trigger such devices. Another device is used to divert the sewage line in a building. It is set up at night to trigger the next morning when the toilet is flushed for the first time.

Most chemical ignition units leave some residue, have a distinctive odor, or both. Debris must be analyzed at a laboratory if it is suspected that chemicals have been used as ignition devices. Fortunately, most arsonists do not know enough to use chemical ignition or timing devices, and the machinery and tools necessary for the construction of some of these devices are not always readily available. The devices usually are fairly simple. Most complex devices, in contrast, are used only in a time of war by enemy agents.

Gas

Although not commonly encountered, the combination of gas and the pilot light on the kitchen stoves of many residences is always a possibility. Illuminating gas rises to the ceiling, being lighter than air, and then slowly moves to floor level as it continues to escape. When it reaches a combustion buildup, it is close to the pilot-light level. An explosion, usually followed by fire, takes place. A candle placed in a room adjoining the kitchen has also been used as a means of ignition. Therefore, arson investigators must remember that although such explosions usually follow suicide attempts or accidents, arsonists may use an ordinary gas range as a tool.

In such cases, investigators should get help from an engineer at the local public utility. The time lag between the initial release of the gas and the explosion can be estimated from the size of the room involved, the number of openings, the type of gas, and related data. For example, a kitchen 10 by 15 feet with a ceiling 9 feet high equals a total volume of 1,350 cubic feet. When 71 cubic feet of gas are introduced into the room, the lowest limit of explosive range will have been reached. In a well-ventilated room, it is almost impossible to build up to this limit, but an arsonist seals off the room so that the gas builds up. In a fairly well-sealed room, a single burner left open on a kitchen gas stove will deliver enough gas to explode in about 5 hours. The oven jets will build up the same volume in 2 hours; an oven plus four burners, 30 minutes to 1 hour.

The widespread use of gas as an arson tool has been thwarted because of its smell. Neighbors usually detect the smell, call the police or the fire department, or break in themselves, ruining a carefully planned arson attempt.

Electrical Systems

Any wiring system, including doorbell and telephone circuits, can be used as a fire-setting tool. Ignition devices hooked to the wiring systems of buildings have been used throughout the country by arsonists. The time can be established by a study of the habits of those using the premises. Possibly a security guard switches on the light every hour while inspecting the various portions of the building, or employees turn on the lights at opening time, and so on.

Although a doorbell system can be used to trigger an ignition device, the bell may be rung by some chance visitor and the plans of the fire setter thwarted. Telephone timing devices have the same fault. A wrong number or an unexpected call can start the fire, possibly days ahead of schedule.

Electrical appliances have also been used to set fires. An open heater is placed close to a flimsy set of curtains, and an apparently accidental fire results. An electrical circuit is deliberately overloaded with several appliances until it heats up. Sometimes an accelerant such as kerosene is dropped into a switch box. In a few cases, a length of normal wiring is removed and lighter wire substituted so that it overheats and, without blowing the fuses, serves as an ignition device.

Investigators generally discover physical traces of electrical ignition devices after a fire.

Mechanical Devices

Alarm clocks were once a favored weapon of arsonists. With a simple alarm clock, some wire, and a small battery, a fire setter was "in business." But a search of the fire debris usually sent the arsonist to prison. Some arsonists used the lead hammer in the clock to break a glass tube that fed flammable matter to a fixed flame. This action pushed one container of chemicals into another, closing an electrical circuit. Some arsonists attached matches to the hammer, where they were pressed against an abrasive surface to ignite flammable material. The clock was activated by setting the alarm for a certain time. The weights in a grandfather's clock have been used in a similar manner.

Some mechanical devices are childish, some are worthy of a master craftsperson, and others are truly fiendish. Unfortunately for many of these ingenious incendiaries, their machines do not burn and can later be used in their prosecution.

PLANTS

A **plant** is the material placed around the ignition device to feed the flame. Newspapers, wood shavings, rags, clothing, curtains, blankets, and cotton waste are some plants. Newspapers are the most frequently used; cotton waste is used extensively in factory or industrial fires.

Accelerants are also usually part of the plant. Kerosene and gasoline are favored accelerants; alcohol, lighter fluid, paint thinners, and other solvents are also popular. However, any flammable fluid or compound may be used to accelerate the blaze.

TRAILERS

Trailers are used to spread the fire. A trailer is ignited by the blaze from the plant. It carries the fire to other parts of a room or building. Usually a trailer ends in a second plant, another pile of papers, or excelsior sprinkled with gasoline, kerosene, or some other booster. From the primary plant, the fire setter may lay four trailers to four secondary plants. Four separate fires thus result from one ignition device.

Rope or toilet paper soaked in alcohol or similar fluid, motion picture film, dynamite fuses, gunpowder, and other such substances have been used as trailers. Sometimes rags or newspapers are soaked in a fire accelerant and twisted into rope. Some arsonists use a liquid fire accelerant such as kerosene as a trailer by pouring a liberal quantity on the floor in a desired path.

MISSING ITEMS

Sometimes items that are missing from the fire scene can prove valuable. For example, does it appear that many of the building's contents, especially furniture, clothing, or valuable items, were removed before the fire? Were house pets removed? The moving of a pet to a kennel or the home of friends just before a fire should raise the suspicions of the investigator.

ARSON FOR PROFIT

Understanding the motive of the arsonist is extremely important if the investigation is to be successful. There are several common motivations among arsonists for setting fires. The motive behind committing arson for profit is economic gain, whether it be the enormous gain derived from inflating insurance coverage beyond the building's value or the limited economic gain derived from cutting one's losses before oncoming financial disaster.[19]

To decide where and how to begin the investigation, the investigator needs to determine whether the arson in question was due primarily to financial stress, to a fraud scheme (without much stress), or to a combination of some stress and the profitability of fraud.

FINANCIAL STRESS AS THE PRIMARY CAUSE

The home owner or business owner who decides to arrange an arson fraud may do so out of submission to financial stress. In general, two primary factors influence the insured person's decision to commit arson fraud: (1) the desire for financial relief and (2) greed—the desire for easily obtained financial assistance. One way to conceive of an arson-fraud scheme is to view it as the result of the interplay between these two factors. Experience in cases where owners have been caught in arson-fraud schemes indicates that the more extreme and immediately pressing the financial stress, the more desperate the insured becomes. Certainly, the number of insureds who are not persuaded to commit arson—no matter how severe their financial stress—is great, and the swelling bankruptcy court dockets reflect the prevailing honesty of most citizens. However, a rapidly developing situation of financial stress can place the insured in a position where he or she desperately examines all kinds of options both legal and illegal.

Perhaps we can understand the arson-fraud motive of a home owner who has just been fired or who faces a mortgage foreclosure (an event which has become endemic in recent years) and burns a home or business. It is important to conduct a search for evidence for those forms of stress. The investigator is likely to find a great deal about such matters in court papers associated with divorces, foreclosures, bankruptcies, and liens. Although it is not fully accepted as a rule of thumb, the more severe the financial stress of an insured, the more likely the person is to either personally set the fire or to involve a minimum number of people—usually a professional arsonist—in the crime.

Investigators often view real estate arson schemes as purely the result of the fraudulent motives of the owners. Actually, the motives for committing real estate arson split between those that are pure scams (discussed later) and those that result from the owner's or landlord's deteriorating financial position. Financial stress in the latter instance can result from any number of factors: strong net migration out of the neighborhood, a long and expensive backlog of code violation citations and fines, or a steady deterioration in the quality of the housing—sometimes by design of the landlords. Whatever the specific reasons, housing that no longer produces net income for the owner or landlord can help place the person (and perhaps the coinvestors) in a financially precarious position. The clues to determining whether the financial condition of a building or a real estate corporation would make arson-fraud attractive lie in the financial records of investment, income, and tax depreciation.

Short-Term Business Problem

The businessperson on the brink of insolvency faces financial stress that is more severe than the one who faces a short-term problem, such as a slack period in a seasonal business or an unforeseen problem of cash flow. Because of the regularity with which insurance settlements occur (when claims are not denied), the businessperson who selects arson can be fairly sure of having much of the money or all of it in hand within a short period of time. One reason to suspect that a short-term business problem, rather than a more serious one, led to the arson is the absence of creditors threatening to force the owner into bankruptcy, and thus the absence of a bankruptcy filing. An examination of the business's books enables the investigator (or accountant) to infer better whether the cash-flow problem was the likely motive for arson.

Desire to Relocate or Remodel. Arsons do occur in businesses that are subject to quickly shifting consumer tastes, and this type of arson-fraud scheme may be motivated by the desire of the owner to secure enough money to remodel or move. In this way, the insured feels able to keep up with changing tastes or to move to a more fashionable location with better market potential. Examples of businesses vulnerable to these trends are beauty salons, "theme" restaurants, and furniture stores. Frequently, such owners arrange for the arson because they realize that shifting tastes have caught them unprepared. However, an owner may also sense the onset of a new trend in its early stages and try to avoid financial distress and arrange for the arson to occur early enough to remodel or move by using the insurance proceeds. In cases in which an inventory no longer sells because of shifting tastes, a variety of internal business and supplier records can help establish whether this was the motive. In this type of arson for profit, as in many other types, the actual discomfort of financial distress may not be the motive as

much as the perception that the insured will soon be in such distress—unless he/she acts immediately.

Buildup of Slow-Moving Inventory. A short-term cash-flow problem can be caused by an unusually large buildup of slow-moving inventory. Although the inventory problem may not appear to the investigator to be a logical motive for the arson, this issue may be easier to understand if the investigator becomes familiar with what are normal or abnormal levels of inventory for a particular type of business, for certain periods of the year. If an inventory problem led to the arson, then the insured likely has filed a full and possibly even inflated claim to recoup the value of the allegedly destroyed inventory. For this reason, such documentation may point toward the motive but in itself be insufficient to establish the motive. The investigator should look also for multiple points of fire origin and the attempt to destroy all inventory.

Outmoded Technology. Several years ago, two of the largest arson-for-profit cases prosecuted in this country involved companies that failed to keep pace with the technological progress of their competitors. The arson frauds involving the Sponge Rubber Products Company and the Artistic Wire Products Company originated partly because the technologies for making the respective products had changed to more efficient, profitable forms. For whatever reasons, the owners had not kept pace. Where an industrial concern may be destroyed because of these technological problems, tell-tale signs of arson for profit are usually present. First, professional arsonists, even good ones, can rarely destroy a large industrial facility simply by burning it. Incendiary devices, sometimes involving explosives, may be required. Remnants and residues of these can often point to a "professional" arson job. Second, books and business records of the companies often reveal financial stress in ways such as corporate debt reorganizations as well as documented searches for new capital or drastic changes in marketing strategies before the arson. Third, since an owner involved in an industrial arson may claim that a labor-management grievance led to it, investigators should search for documentation on formally filed labor grievances, both with the local union and with state and federal regulatory bodies, in order to confirm or deny the validity of such a claim.

Satisfaction of a Legal or Illegal Debt

The businessperson or home owner whose property is destroyed by fire does not always broadcast clear signals of financial stress. One reason for this is that the source of the stress may not be apparent. It may not show up in the books of a business or in other indicators such as divorce or bankruptcy records. For example, if the owner incurred an illegal loan-sharking debt that the lender has called in, the tremendous pressure and threats of violence can make an incendiary fire an acceptable risk to the business owner. On many occasions, the owner either sets the fire or arranges for it to be set. In others, however, the loan shark sets it or has it set, knowing that the businessperson has fire and perhaps other (for example, business interruption) insurance in force.

Evidence of an illegal debt will be difficult to locate if the investigator follows only the "paper trail" from the insured to his or her business and personal records of transactions. If arson to satisfy an illegal debt is suspected, it is important for the investigator to seek out information on the owner's actions that led to the indebtedness—for example, a recent gambling junket, heavy betting during the sports season, or borrowing from a loan shark for a highly speculative venture that initially appeared to have enormous profit potential but later failed to meet expectations. When the trail leads to an illegal debt involving the insured but his or her denial of any involvement is convincing, the investigator should examine the possibility that the loan shark arranged the fire without the insured's knowledge or consent.

Purely Fraud Schemes as the Primary Motive

Many types of arson occur because of the actual or anticipated problem of financial stress; others result from schemes where there was not, and probably would not be, any financial problem. These types of arson-fraud schemes result from the planning and plotting of professional fraud schemers and their associates. Their objective is to defraud insurance companies, as well as banks and even creditors, of as much money as possible. Some of the common types of frauds encountered by investigators follow.

Redevelopment. In cases where a defined tract has been designated for receipt of federal redevelopment funds, owners and investors may stand to make more money if existing buildings on the tract are razed at no cost to themselves. Arson is a convenient vehicle, for although it may not destroy the building, the city or redevelopment authority will usually raze the remains at no cost to the owner, especially if the building is a safety hazard. Investigators who study tracts designated for redevelopment can often plot which blocks and even which buildings may burn as a result of redevelopment fraud schemes. Owners who decide to arrange this type of arson realize that if the building is only partly damaged, the adjusted insurance settlement may pay for repairs (which they do not want) but not for rebuilding. Therefore, in the interest of ensuring maximum destruction, professional arsonists are likely to be called on for their expertise.

Building Rehabilitation. To improve the condition of old or run-down dwellings, a variety of federal and state loan and loan insurance programs are available for housing rehabilitation. Certain unscrupulous owners, contractors, and others who know the "rehab" business realize that they stand to reap huge profits by obtaining funds to make repairs and then claiming that fire destroyed the rehabilitated unit. In most cases, the claimed repairs were not made, or they were only partially completed, or they were done with inferior (cheaper) materials. Therefore, in addition to reaping a profit from that portion of the loan that was not used to buy materials and pay laborers, this type of arsonist often files insurance claims for the full amount of the allegedly completed work. In addition to arson and insurance fraud, such persons commit a variety of frauds against the federal or state government that provides the rehabilitation program assistance. Financial records should indicate the cost of the work actually done.

Real Estate Schemes. In many core urban areas, the most common form of arson for profit involves the destruction of dilapidated multifamily housing. Because such housing is usually in an advanced state of disrepair, there may be little if any financial stress facing the owners. This is so because either the owner recouped the investment through depreciation of the building and through rent gouging or the owner recently purchased the building for a small fraction of the amount for which it was insured. The typical MO involves an owner purchasing the housing for a small cash-down payment, often accompanied by a large, unconventional mortgage. The owner then sells the building to another speculator (usually an associate) for an inflated amount, again with little money down and a large mortgage. Often the building is insured not only for the inflated, artificial value of the second sale but for the replacement value of the building, which is even greater. Then the building burns, the policyholder is almost routinely paid, and the speculating schemers split the proceeds according to a preset formula.

To reap the maximum profit from this type of scheme, the speculators often involve one or more kinds of specialists:

- Several arsonists, so that one arsonist will not know all the plans or be easily recognized because of repeated trips to the neighborhood
- A public insurance adjuster to help inflate the claim on the building
- A realtor who scouts around for "bargain" properties to buy
- An insurance agent who may be corrupted and who is helpful in insuring buildings far beyond what normal, reasonable underwriting standards would permit

This type of real estate–arson scheme is very lucrative, and its perpetrators realize that the greater the number of buildings burned, the greater the profits. Soon, another speculator, perhaps in league with a contractor or realtor, sees how "well" the first speculator is doing, and out of greed the latter begins the same type of arson scheme, creating a chain reaction. The idea spreads to still other speculators, and shortly an entire city can find itself in the midst of a real estate arson-for-profit epidemic.

Planned Bankruptcy. Although this variation of arson for profit is not encountered often, its incidence does seem to be growing. In a typical bankruptcy fraud, the owner establishes a business and buys quantities of goods on credit. The owner pays the first few creditors quickly and in cash in order to increase the volume of merchandise he or she can then buy on credit. The inventory is then sold, often surreptitiously through another company or to a fence, and then the business declares bankruptcy. Often the creditors are left with large numbers of unpaid bills. One way to satisfy them is by paying them off with insurance proceeds obtained after a "mysterious" fire in the business. Additional money is generated from such a fraud scheme because the owner represents in the fire insurance claim that substantial amounts of inventory were destroyed, when in fact merchandise was purposely moved out before the fire. Occasionally, a cheaper grade of merchandise is substituted in its place. Because the creditors are paid, their incentive to complain or report the probable fraud is reduced. Because the destroyed records of such inventory are hard to reconstruct, it is difficult to determine exactly what was destroyed in the fire, and hence its value. Also, since bankruptcy-fraud fires always seem to destroy the office and files where the books are kept, it is difficult for the investigator to reconstruct the flow of money into and out of the business, as well as the flow of merchandise.

ARSON GENERATED BY THIRD PARTIES

This is another broad category of arson for profit, where the beneficiary of the fire is not the owner-insured but a third party who arranges for the fire out of some economic motive. Because the insured is really the major victim here, rather than the culprit, the investigator must determine whether a third-party arson for profit did occur in order to avoid targeting the wrong individual. The following are some examples of major forms of third-party arson.

Elimination of Business Competition

This type of scheme is motivated by someone who seeks to create a business monopoly or at least to maintain a competitive edge. Businesses most prone to this type of arson are those that stand to suffer from too great a concentration of similar businesses in a limited geographic area. Examples include restaurants, taverns, and sex-oriented establishments (for example, topless bars, adult bookstores, and massage parlors), which need to generate a large volume of business in order to make a profit. Increased competition can pose an economic problem to similar businesses in a limited area, which can cause some or all of them a degree of financial distress. Consequently, the financial records of a burned business may indicate the existence of financial problems that could lead the investigator to the mistaken assumption that the owner arranged the fire in order to obtain relief from that condition. Actually, in this example, a competitor is more likely to set the arson in order to improve his or her business situation.

The following case illustrates the type of arson in this category.

A brand-new nightclub had recently been opened in fairly close proximity to an older nightclub. The new nightclub was highly successful and started to draw business away from the old nightclub. Two employees of the old nightclub thought they would take matters into their own hands and "torch" the new nightclub one night after it closed, in hopes that this would help get back some of the old club's customers. Sometime during the early morning hours these two individuals broke into the new nightclub and set out eight 2½-gallon cans of gasoline at strategic locations throughout the business. Three 12-inch pipe bombs were then inserted into three of the cans of gasoline. The fuses were lit, and the individuals quickly fled the business and drove away. Unbeknown to the would-be arsonists, the gasoline-soaked black powder could not be ignited. Thus, when the fuse finally made contact with the black powder, nothing happened. The following morning, when the business was reopened, the unexploded devices and cans of gasoline were found (Figures 19-6 and 19-7).

▲ **FIGURE 19-6**
Pipe bomb and gasoline found at nightclub
A pipe bomb intended to be used in conjunction with a can of gasoline. A hole was cut out of the top of the gasoline can between the handle and the lid to allow the bomb to be inserted into the can. The pipe bomb was immersed into the can. It was at this point that the gasoline saturated the inner workings and got the gunpowder wet, therefore making it impossible to ignite. (Courtesy Michael M. Gonzalez, Chief of Fire Investigation, Tampa Fire Department, Tampa, Florida)

▲ **FIGURE 19-7**
Internal view of pipe bomb found at nightclub
This photograph depicts the pipe bomb that was used in conjunction with the can of gasoline in Figure 19-6. Pipe bombs have been a favorite device of arsonists for years, owing to the inexpensive costs of the materials used to construct them. International and domestic terrorists have also used pipe bombs in their efforts. (Courtesy Michael M. Gonzalez, Chief of Fire Investigation, Tampa Fire Department, Tampa, Florida)

and were working in a companion business of the old club 260 miles away. Of course, the sudden departure of these individuals caused them to emerge as major suspects. Their fingerprints, which were on file, were compared with fingerprints found on the gasoline cans, and a positive fingerprint identification was made of both suspects. Unfortunately, the suspects had assumed that any fingerprints they left on the cans would be destroyed once the cans were ignited, so they failed to take any precautions to ensure their fingerprints were not left on the cans. They were subsequently arrested and convicted of attempted arson. An interesting sidelight to this was the presence of a handwritten number on one of the pipes. After checking with several local hardware stores in the general area of both businesses, the investigators determined that the number was actually the price of the pipe and had been handwritten on it by one of the hardware store employees (Figure 19-8). The employee who had written the number on the pipe was not able to make an identification of the individuals who had purchased it, but the possibility of an identification had to be considered by investigators.

Although this was not considered to be an organized crime–related arson attempt, the same category of arson is fairly common when an organized-crime figure maintains a financial interest in this type of business and either seeks a monopoly or offers to hire out his or her services to create the monopoly for a client or associates in that business. In either case, it is important to involve investigators who are familiar with organized-crime intelligence gathering and investigation when elimination of business competition is suspected as a motive for arson.

Extraction of Extortion Payments

The identity of the criminal who drives out competitors by burning them out may not be known to the victim. However, offenders who demand extortion payments to let someone remain in business will necessarily identify

During the initial investigation, it was suspected that at least one of the possible motives for this attempted arson was to eliminate competition with the older nightclub. Thus, the investigators focused their efforts on the owners and employees associated with the older nightclub. Several days after the attempted arson, an investigative inquiry was made at the nightclub, and it was determined that two employees had recently left town

◄ **FIGURE 19-8**
Handwritten evidence on a pipe bomb found at nightclub
The pipe bomb in question had the number 519 handwritten on it. This represented the price of the item when it was sold. Investigators were able to trace the pipe to a nearby hardware store and identified the clerk who had written the price on the pipe, which was $5.19. (Courtesy Michael M. Gonzalez, Chief of Fire Investigation, Tampa Fire Department, Tampa, Florida)

themselves (if only through their collectors) in order to effect timely payment. In this motive pattern, the arson may be a warning signal to a businessperson to "pay up or else," or it may be a signal to similar businesstypes to either pay or wind up like the burned-out victim. This pattern is similar to that found in the elimination of business competition, in that an organized-crime figure or someone who wants to appear to victims as such a figure (for example, a juvenile gang leader) is often behind this type of scheme. Investigators who suspect this motive should examine the possibility of extortion payments being demanded of similar businesses in the locality.

Labor-Management Grievances

Arsons in business establishments may be the result of an unresolved labor-management grievance for which the perpetrator felt there was insufficient redress or resolution. Investigators should be careful to distinguish whether this type of arson is part of a more regularized pattern of violent activity in the industry or whether it could have resulted from a lone disgruntled employee. It is important to approach the possibility of this motive pattern carefully, because it can occur in an industry that is feeling the effects of an economic downturn, and thus the management logically may be reluctant to accede to labor demands because of their cost. Therefore, the financial records of the business, as well as of the entire industry, may signal financial stress. In reality, the arson may have been caused by an employee unsympathetic to that economic condition. Investigators who suspect this motive pattern should examine the history of labor-management grievances in the business by reviewing records of complaints filed with state and federal labor regulatory agencies.

OTHER MOTIVES FOR ARSON

REVENGE-MOTIVATED ARSON

Revenge-motivated fires are set in retaliation for some injustice, real or imagined, perceived by the offender. Often revenge is an element of other motives. Concept of mixed motives is discussed later in the chapter. The primary motive of revenge can be divided into four subgroups.

Personal Revenge

The subgroup with a personal revenge motive, as the name implies, uses fire to strike at an individual owing to a personal grievance. This one-on-one retaliation may be a one-time occurrence and not the product of a serial arsonist. Triggering such retaliation may be an argument, a fight, a personal affront, or any of an infinite array of events perceived by the offender to warrant retaliation. Favorite targets include the victim's vehicle, home, or property possessions.

Societal Retaliation

Perhaps the most dangerous of the revenge-motivated arsonists is the one who feels he/she has been betrayed by society in general. This type of person generally suffers from a life-long feeling of inadequacy, loneliness, persecution, and/or abuse and strikes out in revenge against a society perceived to have wronged him/her. Such a person may suffer from a congenital condition affecting appearance or health. The targets are random and fire-setting behavior often escalates. All known cases involve serial arsonists.

Institutional Retaliation

Arsonists with retaliation against institutions in mind focus on such institutions as government, education, military service(s), medicine, religion, or any other entity reflecting and representing the establishment. Often these arsonists are serial arsonists, striking repeatedly at these institution(s). The offender, in such cases, uses fire to settle grievances with the institution and to intimidate those associated with it. Buildings housing the institutions are the most frequently selected targets.

Group Retaliation

Targets for group retaliation may be religious, racial, fraternal (such as gangs or fraternal orders), or other groups. The offender tends to feel anger toward the group or members of the group collectively, rather than anger at a specific individual within the group. The target may be the group's headquarters, church, or meeting place, or symbolic targets such as emblems or logos, regardless of what they are attached to. Arsonists motivated by group retaliation sometimes become serial offenders.[20]

DETECTION AND RECOVERY OF FIRE-ACCELERANT RESIDUES

Because flammable liquids flow to the lowest level, heat travels from this level up, and the charring on the bottom of the furniture, ledges, and shelves will be as deep as, or deeper than, the charring on the top.[21]

After a fire has been extinguished, the floor should be carefully cleaned. Many signs may be found there, such as charred, inkblot-like outlines of flammable liquids. A rug that appears charred all over may, when dried out and swept with a stiff broom, show a distinct pattern of the flammable liquid. This pattern occurs because the liquid is absorbed into the nap of the rug and burns more heavily. Flammable liquid usually soaks into the joints of wooden flooring, and as a result the joints will be heavily burned.

The baseboards and sills should be checked, because flammable liquid often runs under and chars them on the bottom. Corners of the rooms should also be checked, because few floors are perfectly level, and flammable liquid often runs into and burns out the corners. In most common household fires, the corners at floor level are least damaged. The depth of charring in the floor and ceiling should be compared. If the floor is charred as much as or more than the ceiling, this indicates a flammable material directly at floor level. In the average fire, the floor temperature is only about one-third that of the ceiling.

When gasoline or similar material is suspected to have been thrown on porches or buildings without basements, especially those with single constructed flooring, the soil beneath the burned area should be checked. The investigator should dig 1 or 2 inches into the earth and smell for the odor of flammable liquids. A vapor tester is better for this purpose, because flammables such as alcohol have little or no odor in cold, wet earth.

If recovered material is suspected of containing flammable liquids, it should be sealed in an uncoated metal paint can, not in plastic bags or plastic containers. Uncoated metal paint cans can be purchased at almost any hardware store. Plastic should never be used because it gives off hydrocarbons that contaminate the material. The container should be tightly sealed to minimize evaporation or contamination. Evidence tape should be used to ensure integrity of the chain of evidence. The container may also be marked for identification purposes with permanent ink. Before they can be analyzed, accelerant residues must first be separated from the ashes, wood, carpeting, or other material in which they are found. This extraction is usually accomplished by simple, steam, or vacuum distillation. These are listed in increasing order of efficiency, particularly for petroleum products, and increasing complexity of apparatus. Steam distillation and vacuum distillation are capable of extracting 65% of any gasoline from debris; for fuel oil, the efficiencies are 30% and 90%, respectively.[22]

ALTERNATIVE FUELS IN FIRE DEBRIS ANALYSIS

Alternative fuels are becoming more prominent on the market today and soon, fire debris analysts will start seeing them in liquid samples in fire debris samples.[23] Thus, crime lab analysts must have a basic knowledge of the composition and characteristics of this fuel and the unique properties it has that are different than traditional fuels used in the commission of arsons. Biodiesel fuel is one of the most common alternative fuels and is now readily available in many parts of the United States and around the world. Biodiesel is manufactured from vegetable oils and/or animal oil/fats. When present in the fire debris, the samples should be analyzed by the use of the gas liquid chromatograph,[24] discussed later in this chapter.

SCIENTIFIC METHODS IN ARSON INVESTIGATION

The presence of flammable liquids may establish arson and sometimes link a suspect to the fire.[25] The objection is sometimes raised that identifiable amounts of liquid fire accelerants rarely survive a fire, and efforts to detect them would be largely wasted. But arson investigators often find accelerant residues, and accelerants can survive fires. One expert, for example, performed the following experiment: He poured 2½ gallons of kerosene over furniture and rugs in one room of a wooden building, and 1 gallon of gasoline over straw in another room, and then he left a trail of gasoline as a fuse. The building was allowed to burn freely and completely. He was able to extract identifiable amounts (more than 1 milliliter) of both kerosene and gasoline from the debris.[26]

The areas most likely to contain residues of liquid fire accelerants—floors, carpets, and soil—are likely to have the lowest temperatures during the fire and may have insufficient oxygen to support the complete combustion of the accelerant. Porous or cracked floors may allow accelerants to seep through to underlying earth. Numerous instances have been recounted of the excellent retention properties of soil for flammable liquid.[27] Another place where accelerants may be discovered is on the clothes and shoes of a suspect.

Because each method of accelerant detection (including the human nose) has a threshold of sensitivity, another question that arises is the vapor concentration that is produced by accelerant residues. Some idea of the order of magnitude can be obtained from the experiment of two experts. They burned small (2-milliliter) samples of various accelerants for 30 seconds and then measured vapor concentrations ranging upward from 60 parts vapor per million of air—within the range of detection of currently available portable detectors and generally, but not always, well above readings produced by hydrocarbons from such things as burnt wood and burnt mattresses.[28]

Another way of looking at the potential vapor concentration is illustrated by the following hypothetical case: Suppose that a gallon of gasoline is used to accelerate a fire in a 15-by-15-by-8-feet room and that 1% (39 milliliters) survives the fire in cracks in the floor. (The residue would consist of higher boiling-point components, such as naphthalene.) The subsequent evaporation of 1 milliliter (3%) of the residue would produce an average vapor concentration of 2.7 parts per million throughout the entire room. Such a concentration can be detected with available equipment. Ventilation of the room, of course, dissipates the vapor and generally causes the vapor concentration to be highest at the points where the residues are located, a situation that can be used to advantage in locating evidence samples to be preserved for laboratory analysis.

DETECTION OF FIRE ACCELERANTS

Several types of portable equipment are available to the arson investigator for detecting residues of flammable liquids at fire scenes. Some of these use chemical color tests, catalytic combustion, flame ionization, gas liquid chromatographs, and infrared spectrophotometers and ultraviolet fluorescence. The sensitivities, limitations, advantages, and disadvantages of each of these are discussed next.

Olfactory Detection

The sensitivity of the human nose to gasoline vapor is about 1 part per 10 million. Gasoline is a complex mixture of chemical compounds, the proportions of which vary with the source of the crude oil and the type of process used in its manufacture. Benzene and other aromatic hydrocarbons, for example, may constitute from 0.1% to 40% of the mixture. Although no conclusive data on the sensitivity of the nose to gasoline are available, the sensitivity of the nose to benzene vapor is 0.015 parts per million. Assuming that 15% (or more) of gasoline vapor consists of aromatic hydrocarbons to which the nose is as sensitive as it is to benzene, then the sensitivity to gasoline is 1 part in 10 million (or greater). Thus, the nose is as sensitive as any of the currently available detecting equipment. But there are flammable liquids to which the nose is not sensitive. Another problem is the tendency of the nose to lose its sensitivity to an odor after prolonged or intense exposure to it. Further, the odor of fire accelerants may be masked by another strong odor, such as that of burnt debris. In fact, in one case an arsonist attempted to camouflage gasoline by mixing it with vanilla.[29] Finally, it may be impractical or impossible to search with the nose for accelerant odors along floors or in recessed areas.[30]

Increasingly, agencies are using specially trained canines for the detection of accelerants. They have proved to be quite effective. On occasion such dogs are even brought to the scene of the arson while the fire is occurring in the hopes that the dogs will be able to detect accelerants on individuals who may have set the fire and are in the crowd watching it.

Chemical Color Test Detectors

Chemical color tests may be used to detect both liquid accelerant residues and their vapors. Certain dyes indicate the presence of hydrocarbons by turning red. Dyes are less sensitive and less specific to flammable liquids than other available methods. Dyes also may interfere with laboratory identification of the accelerant. Hydrocarbon vapors can be detected by pumping a suspected sample through a glass container of reagent that changes color in the presence of hydrocarbons. The reported sensitivity of this method is on the order of 1 part per 1,000. Again, the method is less sensitive and less specific (reacting to hydrocarbons that are not fire accelerants) than others available. Its main advantages are low cost and simplicity.[31]

Catalytic Combustion Detector

The most common flammable vapor detector operates on the catalytic combustion principle and is popularly known as a sniffer, combustible-gas indicator, explosimeter, or vapor detector. A **catalytic combustion detector** is portable, moderate in cost, and fairly simple to operate. Vapor samples are pumped over a heated, platinum-plated coil of wire that causes any combustible gas present to oxidize. The heat from the oxidation raises the electrical resistance of the coil, and this change in resistance is measured electronically. A sensitivity (to hexane vapor) on the order of a few parts per million can be achieved with this method. Because oxygen is required for the operation of the detector, its sensitivity is reduced in oxygen-deficient areas, but these are unlikely to occur in arson investigations. (An internal source of oxygen could be fitted to a detector if required.) Another problem is the gradual loss of sensitivity when this type of detector is exposed to gasoline containing lead. Lead deposits form on the platinum catalyst and interfere with its operation.[32]

Flame Ionization Detector

In the **flame ionization detector,** the sample gas is mixed with hydrogen, and the mixture is burned. Ionized molecules are produced in the flame in proportion to the amount of combustible organic gases in the sample. (Pure hydrogen, air, and water vapor produce little ionization.) The degree of ionization is then measured by electrometer. The sensitivity of this method (to methane) is on the order of 1 part in 10 million. It is thus more sensitive but more complex and expensive than the catalytic combustion method.

Gas Liquid Chromatograph

The portable **gas liquid chromatograph (GLC)** adapted for field use (sometimes called the *arson chromatograph*) is one of the most common detectors in arson investigations. The sample gas is first separated into components on the basis of the speed with which they travel through a tube filled with packing material. The amounts of each component are then measured by either a catalytic combustion or flame ionization detector. The sensitivity ranges from a few hundredths of a part per million to a few parts per million, depending on the type of detector used. The main advantage is specificity because of the preliminary separation process. The main disadvantages are its size, weight, and cost. Also, the time required for the analysis of each sample is about 12 hours, a disadvantage in some situations. In addition, there is a setup time of about 1 hour. The operation of the gas chromatograph requires a certain amount of technical training.

Infrared Spectrophotometer

Infrared spectrophotometers can achieve high specificity to flammable liquids and high sensitivity (on the order of hundredths of a part per million). Infrared light of varying wavelengths is directed through the sample, and the amount of light passing through is plotted on a pen recorder. The recording is compared with those of known compounds to determine the identity of the sample. Because the chemical bonds in a compound determine how it absorbs infrared radiation, these recordings (called spectrograms) are unique for different compounds. However, evidence mixed with impurities must be purified before it can be successfully identified. In particular, since water vapor absorbs infrared light, it interferes with the identification of flammable vapors. This is a disadvantage in arson investigation, where water is commonly present. A final disadvantage is the high cost of this type of detector.

Ultraviolet Fluorescence

Ultraviolet fluorescence consists of illuminating the darkened fire scene with an ultraviolet lamp. Certain substances, including constituents of gasoline and its residue, absorb the ultraviolet light and release it as visible light. They appear to glow against the darkened background. The color of the glow is affected by exposure to heat, and so the method also can be used to locate the point of origin of a fire. The only equipment required is an ultraviolet lamp and a portable power supply. The sensitivity of the method appears comparable to that of other methods of detection. The main disadvantage of the method is that it requires extensive testing, particularly to identify fire accelerants to which it does not respond.[33]

INTERVIEWS

To establish possible motives and develop suspects, the arson investigator must interview people who might know about the fire and how it started. The following kinds of people may provide information.[34]

POSSIBLE WITNESSES

Prospective witnesses include tenants, businesspeople, and customers from the burnt building or surrounding buildings, as well as passersby such as bus drivers, taxi drivers, delivery people, sanitation workers collecting garbage, police patrols, and people waiting for buses and taxis.

Questions to Ask

Did you observe the fire? At what time did you first observe the fire? In what part of the building did you observe the fire? What called your attention to the building? Did you see any people entering or leaving the building before the fire? Did you recognize them? Can you describe them? Did you observe any vehicles in the area of the fire? Can you describe them? Can you describe the smoke and the color of the flame? How quickly did the fire spread? Was the building burning in more than one place? Did you detect any unusual odors? Did you observe anything else?

FIREFIGHTERS AT THE SCENE

Firefighters can be an invaluable source of information to arson investigators because of their technical knowledge and what they observe at a fire.

Questions to Ask

What time was the alarm received? What time did you arrive at the scene of the fire? Was your route to the scene blocked? What was the extent of burning when you arrived? Were doors and windows locked? Were the entrances or passageways blocked? What kind of fire was it? What was the spread speed of the fire? In what area(s) did the fire start? How near was the fire to the roof? Was there evidence of the use of an accelerant? Was any evidence of arson recovered? Did the building have a fire alarm system? Was it operating? Was there any evidence of tampering with the alarm system? Did the building have a sprinkler system? Did it operate? Was there any evidence of tampering with the sprinkler system? Was there anyone present in the building when you arrived? Who was the person in the building? Did that person say anything to you? Were there any people present at the scene when you arrived? Who were they? Did you observe any vehicles at or leaving the scene when you arrived? Can you describe them? Were there contents in the building? Was there evidence that contents had been removed? Was the owner present? Did the owner make a statement? What did the owner say? What is the fire history of the building? What is the fire history of the area?

INSURANCE PERSONNEL

The profit in many arson-for-profit cases is an insurance payment. Three people may be interviewed to determine if the profit centers on an insurance claim: the insurance agent or broker, the insurance adjuster, and the insurance investigator.

There may be restrictions on the amount of information insurance personnel can turn over without a subpoena, but the investigator should be able to determine enough to indicate whether a subpoena or search warrant would prove fruitful.

Questions to Ask the Agent or Broker

Who is the insured? Is there more than one person insured? Is the insured the beneficiary? What type of policy was issued? What is the amount of the policy? When was it issued? When does it expire? What is the premium? Are payments up-to-date? Have there been any increases in the amount of coverage? What amount? When did the increase take effect? What was the reason for the increase? Are there any special provisions in the policy (for example, interruption of business or rental income)? What are they, and when did they take effect? Does the insured have any other policies? Were there previous losses at the location of the fire? Were there losses at other locations owned by the insured?

Questions to Ask the Insurance Claims Adjuster

Did you take a sworn statement from the insured? Did the insured submit documents regarding proof of loss, value of contents, bills of lading, value of building, and the like? Did you inspect the fire scene? Did you inspect the fire scene with a public insurance adjuster? Did you and the public adjuster agree on the cost of the loss? Have you dealt with this public adjuster before? Has he or she represented this owner before? Has the insured had any other losses with this company? (If so, get details.)

Questions to Ask the Insurance Investigator

Were you able to determine the cause of the fire? Did you collect any evidence? Who analyzed the evidence? What were the results of the analysis? Was the cause of the fire inconsistent with the state of the building as known through an underwriting examination? Have you investigated past fires at the location? Have you investigated past fires involving the insured? What were the results of the investigations? Have you had previous investigations involving the public adjuster? Have you had prior investigations involving buildings handled by the same insurance agent or broker? What were the results of these investigations? Does this fire fit into a pattern of fires of recent origin in this area? What are the similarities? What are the differences? Have you taken any statements in connection with this burning? Whose statements did you take? What do they reveal?

Property Insurance Loss Register

The insurance industry maintains a modern computerized data bank, the **Property Insurance Loss Register (PILR),** to keep track of fire, burglary, and theft claims. PILR is a listing of everyone who has an insurable interest in fire claims and a listing of *only* the insureds in burglary and theft claims. Thus, PILR is one of the most effective routes for determining a repeated pattern of claim activity on the part of individuals and organized rings. Most insurance companies are members of PILR and routinely submit data, listing insureds and claim details, to the registry after fire and burglary losses. The information is immediately entered into the PILR data bank; should the name of an insured (or of a person with an insurable interest, in the case of fire losses) have been entered before, a "hit" will be reported to the

insurance company that submitted the entry. Hits can vary widely in significance, as shown by the following examples:

- *Probably insignificant:* A major landlord or mortgagee experienced a minor fire at another location 12 months before the immediate loss.
- *Inconclusive:* A home owner experienced a $4,000 burglary loss 18 months before the immediate fire loss.
- *Suspicious:* A business owner made two expensive burglary loss claims against two other insurers during the 12 months preceding the immediate, very suspicious fire loss under investigation. (Why is the owner having such bad luck, and why is he or she changing insurance companies so frequently?)
- *Highly suspicious:* A home owner or tenant experienced two expensive and suspicious fire losses at previous addresses during the 24 months before the immediate loss.
- *Probably incriminating:* An insured has made claims against two different insurers for the same immediate loss under investigation. There can be legitimate circumstances in which double claims are made; for example, the building and some of its contents may be insured by one carrier, while special inventory or equipment is insured by another.[35]

The insurance company that has made an entry is notified only when a hit occurs. Thus, the lack of a PILR response in the claim file may indicate either that there was no hit or that no entry was made. When obtaining the claim file, the investigator should ask the claims adjuster whether PILR entries were submitted and, if so, which individuals were listed on the entries. If no PILR entries were made or if the names of some of the possible suspects with an insurable interest were not included, the National Insurance Crime Bureau (NICB) can request PILR data if it is a party to the investigation.[36] If previous fire, burglary, or theft losses are reported by PILR, it then becomes possible to compare the claimed losses to see whether the same furnishings, inventory, or equipment were already reported lost, stolen, or destroyed. Likewise, PILR's records can be a means of constructing the "big picture" for an arson-for-profit conspiracy. By running the names of every possible suspect in one suspicious fire through PILR and/or the NICB's database, a dozen or more interrelated claims may be uncovered and used to develop evidence against the entire ring. In some states, model arson laws may allow the investigator to easily obtain the claim files for the previous losses from the insurance companies involved. In instances where such laws do not apply or where suspicious prior burglary claims are not covered by the laws, the NICB may be able to secure copies of the previous claims when it is a party to the investigation.[37]

OTHER WITNESSES CONCERNING FINANCES OF THE INSURED

A number of other people may have information on the finances of the owner, including business associates, creditors, and competitors. This information may indicate how the owner stood to profit from the burning.

Questions to Ask

How long have you known the owner/insured? What is the nature of your relationship with the owner/insured? Do you have any information on the financial position of the business? Is the owner/insured competitive with similar businesses? Have there been recent technological advances that would threaten the owner/insured's competitive position? Has there been a recent increase in competition that would affect the owner's/insured's position? Have changes in the economy affected the owner/insured's position? Has the owner/insured had recent difficulty in paying creditors? Has the owner/insured's amount of debt increased recently? Has the owner/insured lost key employees lately? Has the location where the owner/insured does business changed for the worse recently? Has the owner/insured increased the mortgage or taken out a second or third mortgage? Has the owner/insured had difficulty making mortgage payments? Do you have any other information about the owner's/insured's financial position?

NEWS MEDIA PERSONNEL

This category includes both the print and electronic media. Individuals affiliated with these groups may have noticed something of value to the investigator or perhaps have video footage of the fire and fire scene. For example, if the arsonist remained in the area after the fire and mingled with spectators, his or her presence may be captured on video and prove quite valuable in an investigation.

THE MEDICAL EXAMINER

The autopsy should reveal whether any victim found dead in the fire was dead or alive before the fire started and what the cause of death was. It is not uncommon for a person to be murdered and the scene made to appear as if the person had been killed by fire. (See Chapter 9, "Injury and Death Investigations," for a detailed discussion of fire deaths.)

INTERVIEWING A SUSPECT

The following questions are based on the assumption that the person to be interviewed is involved in arson for profit, that the investigator has enough evidence to make an arrest or to convince the subject that he or she is liable to arrest and that the subject is more valuable to the investigation in a cooperative role than as a defendant.

Questions to Ask the Suspect

What method was used to accomplish the arson? Specify whether what was used was an incendiary device, gasoline or another inflammable fluid, or some other means. If an incendiary device was used, be specific as to the type of device. Where did you obtain the incendiary device? If it was improvised, who made it? How much did it cost? Who paid for the incendiary device? Was it paid for by cash or check? If gasoline or another flammable fluid was used, where was it obtained? How much was obtained and used? Were any special techniques used in setting the fire (or causing an explosion) to avoid detection?

Questions to Ask the Torch, Specifically

Are you willing to cooperate in this investigation? How many other people are involved in the arson-for-profit scheme? How are they involved? What role does each person play in the scheme? Explain (in detail) how the scheme works. How did you first become involved in the scheme? How did you meet the other participants? Where did you meet the other participants? Are you still in contact with the other participants? How often do you see them? Where do you see them? What do you talk about when you meet with them? Would you be able to record your conversations with them? Are you willing to record your conversations with them? Would you be willing to introduce an undercover investigator into the group? Could you introduce an undercover investigator into the group without the other participants' becoming suspicious? How far in advance of an arson are you told about it? What role do you play in connection with the arson (torch, driver, fence, and so forth)? Are you willing to swear to an affidavit for a search warrant? Are you willing to testify before a grand jury? Are you willing to testify at trial? Do you have information on other arson-for-profit schemes?

INTERVIEWING THE TARGET AND THE OWNER

The target of the investigation may be an owner, a landlord, a fire broker, or the like. The interview should take place after obtaining the background information on the fire and after interviewing the individuals previously listed.

Questions to Ask the Target

Tell me in your own words what you know about this fire. When did you first hear of the arson? Who told you? Where were you and what were you doing before, during, and after the arson? Who was with you? Do you know who committed the arson? Do you have any knowledge of any previous fire at the building? Do you have any knowledge of any previous incidents of any kind and at any location owned or rented by the owner/occupant of the building? Do you know of any recent changes in insurance coverage? Do you know the owner of the arson property? Describe your relationship to the owner. Do you have any financial interest in the burned property?

Questions to Ask the Owner

Tell me in your own words what you know about this fire. How long have you owned the burned property? What was the purchase price? What was the total amount of the mortgage? Who is your insurance company? Agent? Broker? Public adjuster? How much insurance do you carry? Is there more than one policy on this property? On its contents? On rental or business interruption? Have you increased your insurance coverage on the property in the past year? If so, why and at whose suggestion? Have you ever received an insurance cancellation notice on this property? Where were you at the time of the fire? When did you first hear of the arson? Who told you? When were you last in the building? Was the building secured? If so, in what manner? Who else has access to, or keys, to the building? Who was the last person to leave the building? Do you have any knowledge that the sprinkler system or burglar alarm system was on and working? Indicate the name and address of all lienholders. What is the amount of each lien? What was the value of the inventory on hand immediately before the fire? Can you provide documentation for this value? Was any inventory removed from the premises before the fire? If yes, by whom and for what purposes? Where did it go, and why was it removed? Was any inventory removed from the premises after the fire? If yes, by whom and for what purpose? List the inventory removed and its value. Did you set the fire or cause it to be set? Do you know who set it?

INTERVIEWING A POTENTIAL INFORMANT WHO IS NOT A SUSPECT

Before interviewing a potential informant who is not a suspect, investigative efforts should be made to determine if the informant has any police record and, if so, if it could have any bearing on the reliability of the information provided. For example, if a potential informant was previously convicted of arson and perjury, then the investigator should be cautious about acting on that person's information.

Questions to Ask a Potential Informant

How are you currently supporting yourself? Do you have any pending prosecutions against you? Where? What are you charged with? Do you have any information about arson for profit in this city, county, state? How did you acquire this information? Do you know anyone engaged in arson for profit? What roles does that person play in the scheme? How do you know this? What is your relationship with this person or persons— loan shark, bookmaker, fence, other? Where does this person live, frequent? Who are his/her associates? Do you know them? Are they part of the scheme? Have you been asked to involve yourself in the scheme? In what way? Have any of these people talked freely to you about their activities? Have they talked in your presence? What was said? Can you engage them in conversation about past arsons? Future arsons? Would they be suspicious of you? Could you wear a concealed recorder during conversation? Could you introduce an undercover officer into the group? Would you be willing to testify before a grand jury? Would you be willing to testify at trial? Would you be willing to swear to an affidavit for a search warrant? What do you expect in return for your help?

THE ARSON SUSPECT

In some arson investigations, a single prime suspect may emerge and investigative efforts will be focused accordingly. However, in most cases, a number of suspects emerge, and merely establishing that one or more of them had a motive to set the fire is not proof enough for an arrest and conviction. The investigator must also determine which of the suspects had the opportunity and the means to commit the crime. This determination must be related to the background, personal characteristics, past activities, and financial status of each of the suspects. For example, 10 people may have had a chance to set the fire, but only 4 or 5 may have had a motive, and of this number, perhaps only 1 or 2 would risk an arson conviction for the expected profit or satisfaction.

In probing an arson fire, seldom does direct evidence link a suspect with a fire. Because arsonists tend to take elaborate precautions not to be seen near the fire, they are seldom caught in the act. It may be best for the investigator to concentrate on gathering circumstantial evidence and some provable facts from which valid conclusions can be drawn. For example, let us assume that a warehouse fire was ignited by a timing device— a slow-burning candle attached to some flammable material triggered 2 hours before the fire actually started. The owner, who is also a prime suspect, is identified but can prove his whereabouts at the time of the fire. However, he cannot prove where he was 2 hours before the fire. In addition, the structure was locked when the fire department arrived to fight the fire, and the owner is the only one with a set of keys. The owner also took a large insurance policy out on the warehouse a short time ago.

Although far more evidence would likely be needed to arrest and convict the owner, there is sufficient justification for focusing a considerable amount of the investigation in his direction. If some other evidence is found to link him more directly to the fire (say, candles and flammable material found in the trunk of his car), then the circumstantial evidence becomes significant.

PHOTOGRAPHING THE ARSON SCENE

STILL PHOTOGRAPHY

Photographing a fire scene can be a challenge. Adverse conditions—poor lighting, time constraints, inconvenient angles, and so forth—necessitate the use of camera equipment that is reliable and quick. High-end digital cameras for professionals are frequently the types that are used for this. The advantages of digital cameras are that the images can be immediately viewed, printed, and if necessary quickly transmitted and disseminated.

The photo session should take at least as long as the physical examination; however, it is not necessary to photograph every step. The investigator should follow the same path in photographing the structure as is followed in the physical examination—the path of the burn trail from the least to the greatest amount of damage. The photos are as important as the written report because they show what happened rather than merely telling what happened.

Ideally, the investigator should be concerned with photographing things and areas that show, in detail, what happened. For example, if there are severely darkened ventilation patterns out of a window or a door, the investigator should photograph them. The investigator should also photograph burn patterns at lower levels and those that show distinct lines of demarcation, melted or stained glass, areas where explosions occurred, broken locks, and areas where the electric service enters the building. If the investigator does not know what happened, detailed photos will help in assessing what took place.

In some cases, it is necessary to compile a panoramic view. This can be accomplished with a composite of several photos that are taped together to create a much larger overview. The area of the fire's origin should be photographed twice, first before the rubble is disturbed and then after the debris has been removed. Severe burn patterns should be documented, especially patterns that show how the fire burned. Burn patterns at the base of doors and underneath door moldings are a strong indication that flammable liquids were used. This is because a fire spreading of its own accord burns upward, not downward.

If clocks are present, the investigator should always photograph the faces of the clocks showing the times they stopped. Fires often cause interruptions in electricity, which means electrical clocks will usually stop within 10 minutes to an hour after the time the fire started. Knowing when the fire started is crucial to the case.

VIDEOTAPE

Another form of visual documentation is videotaping, discussed in Chapter 3, "Investigators, the Investigative Process, and the Crime Scene." Although the average fire investigation does not require videotaping, it should be done if the investigator reasonably believes that the case will involve litigation.[38]

EXPLOSIVES INVESTIGATION

Under the fire and explosion investigation definition, an **explosion** is a physical reaction characterized by the presence of four major elements: high-pressure gas; confinement or restriction of the pressure; rapid production or release of that pressure; and change or damage to the confining (restricting) structure, container, or vessel that is caused by the pressure release. Although an explosion is almost always accompanied by the production of a loud noise, the noise itself is not an essential element of an explosion.[39] The generation and violent escape of gases are the primary criteria of an explosion.

KNOW YOUR EXPLOSIVES

The earliest explosive was black powder or gunpowder, made of sulfur, charcoal, and potassium nitrate (also called saltpeter).[40]

Nitroglycerin came along a bit later. It has a greater energy density than black powder, but its sensitivity to shock makes it difficult to work with, and it is rarely used today for anything except as a vasodilator medication for individuals with heart problems who experience angina.

Alfred Nobel invented dynamite by combining nitroglycerin with sodium carbonate and diatomaceous earth. The latter ingredient is available at any garden nursery, made of ancient decomposed seashells. Dynamite was the first commercially viable explosive, and made Nobel wealthy enough to endow an annual prize for advancements in science and peacemaking.

Dynamite is usually formed into sticks and wrapped in paper. Over time, the nitroglycerine in the dynamite will "weep" or "sweat," forming unstable crystals on the wrappers. Proper storage of dynamite dictates the packages be turned periodically to prevent this.

Some people think trinitrotoluene or TNT and dynamite are the same things, but they are not. TNT starts with toluene, a common solvent used in model airplane glue, among other things. The explosive is produced by repeatedly nitrating it with nitric and sulfuric acids. TNT is more stable than dynamite, and can be poured (it melts at 176°F) into molds or combined with other explosives. It is the most common explosive used in conventional military munitions such as artillery and mortar shells.

TNT is the standard for measuring the destructive power of other compounds and weapons. The "Little Boy" atomic bomb dropped on Hiroshima in World War II was equivalent to about 15,000 tons (15 kilotons) of TNT. To provide perspective, a kiloton of solid TNT would be a cube measuring about 10 yards on each side. TNT is yellow, and skin that's in repeated contact with it turns the same color.

Terrorist bomb makers prefer plastic explosives. These are compounds containing one or more of the explosives already described, plus pentaerythritol tetranitrate (PETN) or RDX, plus wax or some other plasticizer. The resulting compound is a moldable, castable substance that can take almost any shape. PETN is a major ingredient of Semtex, while RDX is used in Torpex and C-4.

Umar Abdulmytallab (discussed in greater detail later in this chapter) stashed PETN in his underwear in December 2009 in his unsuccessful attempt to destroy Northwest Airlines Flight 253 on route from Amsterdam to Detroit. RDX was the primary explosive in the 2006 railroad bombings in Mumbai, India, and in the bombing of the Moscow Metro in March 2010.

Most, if not all, explosives developed since black powder have nitrate compounds as a base component. It is these nitrate molecules and ions that high-tech bomb "sniffers" (discussed later in this chapter) look for. Plastic explosives tend to be denser than other common materials carried by travelers, and the explosives are sometimes surrounded by wires, batteries, or electronics that complete the bomb. These are detectable with X rays and other visual scanning methods.

When these methods fail, or when the gadget locates a suspicious lump that might be a bomb, it must be examined visually or examined by a remotely operated device.

COMPUTERIZED TOMOGRAPHY

One method used to identify explosives is a CT scan. The "CT" stands for computerized tomography, which is a method for generating a three-dimensional image from multiple 2-D X-ray images captured from multiple angles.

Modern CT scanners use multiple emitters to fire X rays through an object to a sensor on the opposite side. The sensor records the gross structures it "sees" as well as the amount of energy received, giving an indication of the density of the material it passed through. The computer combines all of these images into one virtual object that appears on a computer display. The virtual object can be rotated on any axis and zoomed in or out to inspect details of interest.

Contraband objects with telltale shapes, like guns, are fairly easy to spot. The latest equipment stores data on densities of objects, both common and deadly, and uses X-ray diffraction to identify and display those in a telltale color. An operator at an airport or other high-threat location can pay closer attention to a container colored in red and determine whether it's plastic explosive or cold cream.

There are several limitations to CT as an explosives detector. The software that flags an explosive may give a false positive alert on something innocuous, like a child's Play-Doh. CT scanners are large—typically, the size of a small truck—and expensive.

SNIFFERS

Not all explosives detectors rely on the sense of sight. Some are called "sniffers" but do not exactly rely on the sense of smell. The more formal name for sniffers is Ion Mobility Spectrometry (IMS). This might be a blasphemy to an analytical chemist to call it a sniffer but it is much easier to say.

In an IMS instrument typically used for explosives detection, a sample is heated to produce a vapor, which is then ionized (ions are atoms or molecules containing an unequal number of protons and electrons, so they have a positive or negative charge) by a radiation source, something similar to smoke detectors in a house.

The ions move through a drift chamber and an electric field that causes them to separate by size, mass, and geometry. As the ions arrive at a detector at the far end of the drift chamber, those size, mass, and shape characteristics form a signature unique to the compound from whence they came. If the signature matches what the device is programmed to detect, similar to PETN, it sounds an alarm.[41, 42]

TYPES OF EXPLOSIONS

There are two major types of explosions: mechanical and chemical. These types are differentiated by the source or mechanism by which the explosive pressures are produced.

Mechanical Explosions

In **mechanical explosions,** the high-pressure gas is produced by purely physical reactions. None of the reactions involves changes in the basic chemical nature of the substances. The most commonly used example of a mechanical explosion is the bursting of a steam boiler. The source of overpressure is the steam created by heating and vaporizing water. When the pressure of the steam can no longer be confined by the boiler, the vessel fails and an explosion results.

Chemical Explosions

In **chemical explosions,** the generation of high-pressure gas is the result of reactions in which the fundamental chemical nature of the fuel is changed. The most common chemical explosions are those caused by the burning of combustible hydrocarbon fuels such as natural gas, liquified petroleum gas, gasoline, kerosene, and lubricating oils.

An example of a chemical explosion is the one that destroyed the Alfred P. Murrah Federal Building in Oklahoma City several years ago. In this case, the convicted and subsequently executed bomber, Timothy McVeigh, loaded a van with 4,000 pounds of ammonium nitrate (commonly used as a fertilizer) that had been soaked in fuel oil and detonated with high explosives. The destructive force of such a device is enormous. The explosion killed 167 people[43] (Figure 19-9).

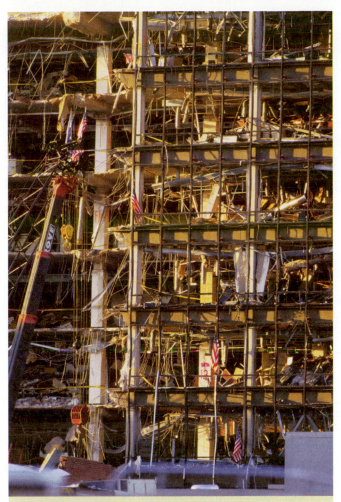

▲ **FIGURE 19-9**

Damage resulting from a chemical explosion

The effects of a chemical explosion that destroyed the Alfred P. Murrah Federal Building in Oklahoma City. The destructive force of this chemical explosion killed 167 people. Timothy McVeigh was eventually convicted and executed for committing the crime. (© Ralf-Finn Hestoft/Corbis)

IMPROVISED EXPLOSIVE DEVICES (IEDs)

An **improvised explosive device (IED)** is a combination of items or components that are neither designed nor produced to be used in conjunction with each other but, when placed together or assembled, constitute a mechanism that has the capability of exploding and causing personal injuries and property damage.[44] With this very broad definition, one can easily appreciate the fact that an IED can be constructed with almost any item that provides the two basic, overall components, namely: the main charge explosive and the fusing system. However, many devices employ additional components, such as an external concealment container, in which to hide the device from observation and discovery.

FACTORS AFFECTING IED CONSTRUCTION

There are four general factors that directly affect the construction of an IED. These are (1) the ingenuity of the builder, (2) the skill of the builder, (3) access to nonexplosive components, and (4) access to explosives. The ingenuity of the builder concerns the ability of individuals to design or plan for the construction of a device to accomplish their aims. Some may refer to this as inventiveness, cleverness, or cunning in devising a building plan to bring various explosive and nonexplosive components together in order to fashion a device.

BASIC COMPONENTS OF THE IED

As previously stated, IEDs have two very basic components, the main charge explosive and the fusing system. The main charge, either low or high explosive, can be combined with other materials to create a more lethal device. These materials include an incendiary to create an explosive-incendiary device or chemical, biological, or nuclear materials to fashion a weapon of mass destruction. Although most IEDs are not considered weapons of mass destruction, there has been an ever-increasing trend to use large vehicles to carry large quantities of explosives to their targets, thereby creating weapons which result in mass destruction. These large, vehicle-improvised explosive devices (LVIEDs) have been used in numerous truck bombings: in England and Northern Ireland during the 1980s and 1990s, in the 1983 marine barracks and French military compound bombings in Beirut, Lebanon, in addition to the 1983 and 1984 U.S. embassy bombings; the bombings of the U.S. embassies in Kenya and Tanzania in 1998; the first World Trade Center bombing of 1993; and the bombing of the Alfred P. Murrah Federal Building in Oklahoma City on April 19, 1995, discussed earlier in this chapter.

The fusing system is designed to provide the required stimulus or energy to cause the main charge to function or explode. Their construction can be as simple as a length of fuse to complex electronic systems and are of two types, namely electrical or mechanical. Fusing systems do not need to be complex in order to function and most are not. Indeed, the more complex the fusing system, the greater the chances it will not work as designed. However, of all the components used in the construction of the fusing system, one is essential—the initiator, which is any device that may be used to start a detonation or deflagration. These devices include the safety or cannon fuse, squibs, electric matches, igniters, percussion caps, detonators, and many improvised components. Essentially, the fusing system has but one function, to apply a stimulus to the initiator to enable it to function as the main charge.

▲**FIGURE 19-10**

Blast-type primary-effect explosive device, a cartridge of dynamite, and safety fuse

Primary effect by *blast* is suggested in the detonation of a high-explosive main charge constructed without a hard-cased container, such as a metal pipe, or added fragmentation. Although much fragmentation results, large vehicle improvised explosive devices (LVIED) are characteristic of blast-only bombs in which the intended results are casualties and destruction of property. (Thurman, James T. 2011. *Practical Bomb Scene Investigation,* Second Edition. Boca Raton, Fl: Taylor & Francis, fig. 3.1. Courtesy James T. Thurman)

▲**FIGURE 19-11**

Blast fragmentation effect explosive device and a pipe bomb with nails

Blast fragmentation devices may be constructed with either high or low explosives and may use a hard-cased container, such as a metal pipe or other suitable enclosure, or have fragmentation-shrapnel added to or around the main charge explosive. (Thurman, James T. 2011. *Practical Bomb Scene Investigation,* Second Edition. Boca Raton, Fl: Taylor & Francis, fig. 3.2. Courtesy James T. Thurman)

PRIMARY EFFECT BY TYPE OF IED

Improvised devices are constructed to provide a basic type of effect when they function. They are called *explosive–incendiary,* and *incendiary.* The explosive device is further divided into five subgroups of effects: blast, blast fragmentation, shaped charge, claymore charge, and platter charge. Although there may be collateral effects from the explosion of an IED, these generally are the desired effects intended by the builder. As such, following a bombing (not just an explosion), the investigator should seek to determine what type of effect the builder desired. This will help focus the investigation and provide investigative lead information, not only with regard to components at the scene, but also the follow-up field investigation.

Primary effect by blast is suggested in the detonation of a high-explosive main charge constructed without a hard-cased container, such as a metal pipe, or added fragmentation. Although much fragmentation results, LVIEDs are characteristic of blast-only bombs in which the intended results are casualties and destruction of property (Figure 19-10).

Blast fragmentation devices may be constructed with either high or low explosives and may use a hard-cased container, such as a metal pipe or other suitable enclosure, or have fragmentation-shrapnel added to or around the main charge explosive. These types of IEDs use the explosive to propel casualty-producing fragmentation and shrapnel throughout the scene. The addition of shrapnel—for example, nails—to the outside of a pipe bomb or to a cartridge of high explosives is highly suggestive of the intent and type of device (Figure 19-11).

A **shaped charge** is specifically designed and constructed to achieve a very specific end result: namely the blasting of a hole through metal and other types of hardened material. Owing to the use of high explosives, there may be very little of the shrapnel-charge container remaining at the scene. As such, the indication that a charge of this type was utilized may be based on two factors. The first is the target. Was the subject trying to gain access to something or some area? Second, is a hole either round or linear, present in/through the target? This is not to suggest for example that a huge hole in the side of a bank building was possibly caused by a shaped charge. Improvised shaped charges tend to be rather small, usually less than 6 inches in diameter, with most being 2–3 inches or less. However, a type of explosives effect, similar to the traditional shaped charge, needs to be clarified at this point. Specifically, the arrangement of explosives into a pattern, usually a semicircle, can produce an enhanced explosives effect on the target. This arrangement of explosives by Timothy McVeigh was done in his construction of the massive vehicle bomb that destroyed the Murrah Federal Building. Additionally, the damage to the *USS Cole* from the suicide bombing on October 12, 2000, in Aden, Yemen, may have been enhanced by the

◀ **FIGURE 19-12**

Effects of a claymore-type explosive charge consisting of nails directed toward a vehicle at a distance of approximately 15 feet

A claymore charge uses explosive energy to propel shrapnel in one primary direction. (Thurman, James T. 2011. *Practical Bomb Scene Investigation*, Second Edition. Boca Raton, Fl: Taylor & Francis, fig. 1.18. Courtesy James T. Thurman)

arrangement of the explosives into a shaped-charge configuration. In these types of incidents, no such shaping container is required.

A **claymore charge** uses explosive energy to propel shrapnel in one primary direction. Construction materials resulting from this type of device, in addition to the fuzing system, would logically include some type of container in which to contain the explosives and shrapnel. Most devices of this type employ high explosives rather than low explosives (Figure 19-12).

Although seldom used, improvised *platter charge* devices have been used to attack vehicles, especially armored vehicles. The detonation of a high-explosive charge propels a metal disk or platter towards the target, resulting in a hole, similar in size to the platter, in or through the target. Should the metal platter be made of brittle metal, the platter may fragment at the site of the explosion and create a claymore effect or when hitting the target with little or no penetration. Recoverable components may include the fuzing system and a container used to house the device and/or the mounting stand on which the device was aimed toward the target.

The *explosive-incendiary* device, in addition to blast or blast fragmentation damage, utilizes an explosive charge to initiate an incendiary material incorporated into the device. The incendiary usually provides a greater fireball, and hence an increased incendiary effect on the target. This type of device can consist of almost any type of container accommodating an accelerant, usually but not always, gasoline, in addition to the explosive main charge (Figure 19-13).

Incendiary devices, which may or may not explode from the initiation of the accelerant, do not contain explosives but consist of a container with an accelerant and fuzing system. The fuzing system may be as simple as a wick, which is lighted before it is thrown, or it may be hypergolic, spontaneous ignition reaction of two materials placed in contact with each other.

▲ **FIGURE 19-13**

Blast-incendiary effect explosive device, a pipe bomb, and a camp stove metal container with propane fuel

The explosive-incendiary device, in addition to blast or blast fragmentation damage, utilizes an explosive charge to initiate an incendiary material incorporated into the device. The incendiary usually provides a greater fireball, and hence an increased incendiary effect on the target. This type of device can consist of almost any type of container accommodating an accelerant, usually but not always, gasoline, in addition to the explosive main charge. (Thurman, James T. 2011. *Practical Bomb Scene Investigation*, Second Edition. Boca Raton, Fl: Taylor & Francis, fig. 3.3. Courtesy James T. Thurman)

► **FIGURE 19-14**
Underwear bomber
The improvised explosive device concealed in the underwear of Omar Farouk Abdlumutallab involved the use of a syringe in a soft plastic container filled with pentaerythritol tetranitrate which is a highly volatile, colorless crystal which is hard to detect. The device was strapped to his legs by a substantial portion of the explosive and was more than likely in a syringe filled with nitroglycerin which was converted into an electrical detonator. The device was intended to blow a large hole in the side of the plane and cause immediate decompression thereby tearing the aircraft apart. (Courtesy ABC News)

THE UNITED STATES AS A TARGET OF IEDs

One of the more sensational cases involving attempts to use IEDs in the United States in recent years occurred in May, 2010, on Broadway in New York City. At that time, an IED was left in a Nissan Pathfinder SUV right in the heart of downtown Manhattan. The device, which was found in the back seat, consisted of two red plastic five gallon gasoline containers, three canisters of propane gas, similar to those used for barbeque grills, fire crackers described as super grade M88s, sold legally in some states, and a 55-inch-long metal gun container weighing about 75 pounds, which contained 8 bags of nonexplosive grade fertilizer. With the bags the locker weighed in excess of 200 pounds. There was also a wire from the battery powered fluorescent clock that ran into the gun locker, where a metal pressure cooker pot contained many more M88s. The bomber planned to ignite the cans of gasoline which in turn would explode the propane tanks and then the fertilizer. (Apparently he was not aware the fertilizer he was using was a nonexplosive grade fertilizer).

The presence of the vehicle was first noted by a vendor selling T-shirts nearby who noticed the vehicle at the curb with its engine running and its hazard lights on. The man saw smoke coming from the vehicle and immediately notified a nearby New York City mounted police officer. The bomb never did explode and upon examination was characterized by bomb experts as amateurish.

A suspect was arrested a couple of days later. His name was Faisal Shazad, he was 30 years old, had been born in Pakistan and became a naturalized American citizen in 2009. After being arrested, he confessed to having planted the bomb, and also to having received his bomb making training in Pakistan by the Taliban. In 2010, after pleading guilty to all charges against him, he

was sentenced in federal district court in Manhattan to life in prison.

A second case involving the attempted use of an IED in the United States occurred in December, 2009. In this case the attempted use of an IED occurred on a Northwest Airlines flight that was approaching Detroit, Michigan. The terrorist in this case was a Nigerian national named Umar Farouk Abdlumutallab, a 22-year-old Nigerian national who have left behind a martyrdom statement in Arabic. It was believed that the attack was planned by the Yemen-based branch of Al-Qaida. This case, which was dubbed by the media as "the underwear bomber" involved the use of an improvised explosive device (Figure 19-14). The device involved the use of a syringe in a soft plastic container filled with PETN, which is a highly volatile, colorless crystal and is hard to detect if carried in the container. Part of the device was strapped to his legs but a substantial portion of the explosives was more than likely in a syringe filled with nitroglycerin which was converted into an electrical detonator. The idea was to blow a large hole in the side of the plane and cause immediate decompression, thereby tearing the aircraft apart. For reasons which have not yet been determined, he did not attempt to ignite the device until they were approaching Detroit at a much lower altitude. Explosives experts believe there was almost certainly a failure between the primary and main charge of the IED, which meant the PETN did not fully detonate. Speculation by aviation specialists are that if the IED had gone off it would have likely not caused sufficient damage to bring the plane down and although badly damaged it would have been able to make it to the airport. The attempted use of the bomb was spotted by passengers who saw smoke emanating from the seat occupied by the terrorist, at which time he was overpowered.[45]

INVESTIGATING THE EXPLOSION SCENE

The objectives of the explosion scene investigation are no different from those for a regular fire investigation: to determine the origin, identify the fuel and ignition sources, determine the cause, and establish the responsibility for the incident. A systematic approach to the scene examination is just as important in an explosion investigation as in a fire investigation—or even more so—because explosion scenes are often larger and more disturbed than fire scenes. Without a preplanned, systematic approach, explosion investigations become more difficult or even impossible to conduct effectively.[46]

The first duty of the investigator is to secure the scene of the explosion. First responders to the explosion should establish and maintain physical control of the structure and surrounding areas. Unauthorized persons should be prevented from entering the scene or touching blast debris remote from the scene itself because the critical evidence from an explosion (whether accidental or criminal) may be very small and may be easily disturbed or moved by people passing through. Evidence is also easily picked up on shoes and tracked out. Properly securing the scene also tends to prevent additional injuries to unauthorized and/or curious persons who may attempt to enter an unsafe area. As a general rule, the outer perimeter of the incident scene should be established at one and a half times the distance of the farthest piece of debris found. Significant pieces of blast debris can be propelled great distances or into nearby buildings or vehicles, and these areas should be included in the scene perimeter. If additional pieces of debris are found, the scene perimeter should be widened.

The investigator should establish a scene pattern. Investigation team members should search the scene from the outer perimeter inward toward the area of greatest damage. The final determination of the location of the explosion's epicenter should be made only after the entire scene has been examined. The search pattern itself may be spiral, strip/line, grid, zone/quadrant, or pie/wheel. (See Chapter 3, "Investigators, the Investigative Process, and the Crime Scene," for a detailed description of these patterns.) Often the particular circumstances of the scene dictate the nature of the pattern. In any case, the assigned areas of the search pattern should overlap so that no evidence is at the edge of any search area.

It is often useful to search areas more than once. When this is done, a different searcher should be used on each search to help ensure that evidence is not overlooked. The number of actual searchers will depend on the physical size and complexity of the scene. The investigator in charge should keep in mind, however, that too many searchers can often be as counterproductive as too few. Searchers should be briefed as to the proper procedures for identifying, logging, photographing, marking, and mapping the location of evidence. The location of evidence may be marked with chalk marks, spray paint, flags, stakes, or other marking means. After being photographed, the evidence may be tagged, moved, and secured.

Structures that have suffered explosions are often more structurally damaged than those burned in a fire. The possibility that a floor, wall, ceiling, roof, or entire building will collapse is much greater and should always be considered.

Explosion scenes that involve bombings or explosives have added dangers. Investigators should be on the lookout for additional devices and undetonated explosives. The modus operandi (MO) of some bomber-arsonists includes using secondary explosive devices specifically targeted for the law enforcement or fire service personnel who will be responding to the bombing incident.

LOCATING AND IDENTIFYING ARTICLES OF EVIDENCE

Investigators should locate, identify, note, log, photograph, and map any of the many and varied articles of physical evidence. Because of the propelling nature of explosions, the investigator should keep in mind that significant pieces of evidence may be found in a wide variety of locations, including outside the exploded structure, embedded in the walls or other structural members of the exploded structure, in nearby vegetation, inside adjacent structures or vehicles, or embedded in adjacent structures. In the case of bombing incidents or incidents involving the explosion of tanks, appliances, or equipment, significant pieces of evidence debris may have pierced the bodies of victims or be contained in their clothing.

The clothing of anyone injured in an explosion should be obtained for examination and possible analysis. The investigator should ensure that photographs are taken of the injuries and that any material removed from a victim during medical treatment or surgery is preserved. This is true whether the person survives or not. Investigators should note the condition and position of any damaged and displaced structural components, such as walls, ceilings, floors, roofs, foundations, support columns, doors, windows, sidewalks, driveways, and patios. Investigators should also note the condition and position of any damaged and displaced building contents, such as furnishings, appliances, heating or cooking equipment, manufacturing equipment, victim's clothing, and personal effects. Investigators should note the condition and position of any damaged and displaced utility equipment, such as fuel gas meters and regulators, fuel gas piping and tanks, electrical boxes and meters, electrical conduits and conductors, heating-oil tanks, parts of explosive devices, or fuel vessels.

Investigators should identify, diagram, photograph, and note pieces of debris that indicate the direction and relative force of the explosion. They should keep in mind that the force necessary to shatter a wall is more than that necessary to merely dislodge or displace it and that the force necessary to shatter a window is less than that necessary to displace a wall but more than that necessary to blow out a window intact. The greater the force, the farther pieces of debris will be thrown from the epicenter.

Investigators should log, diagram, and photograph varying missile distances and directions of travel for similar debris, such as window glass. Larger, more massive missiles should be measured and weighed for comparison of the forces necessary to propel them. The distance as well as the direction of significant pieces of evidence from the apparent epicenter of the explosion may be critical. The location of all significant pieces should be completely documented on the explosion scene diagram, along with notes as to both distance and direction. This enables investigators to reconstruct the trajectories of various components.

COLLECTING EVIDENCE AT THE EXPLOSION SCENE

After locating and identifying articles of evidence, the investigator begins the collection process. The collection of evidence at the explosion scene is a form of scene documentation that involves among other things the correct selection and use of containers in which to hold the evidence materials. The containers should be selected according to the type of evidence recovered and should afford sufficient protection to the materials that would permit their collection, storage, transport to the laboratory for examination, and subsequent use in any legal proceedings. Various containers depicted in this chapter can be used to contain evidence from bombing crime scenes.[47]

The containers are available in various sizes, depending on the size of the specimen and number of items of evidence to be placed in it. The items of evidence are collected and logged in depending on where they have been found at the scene—essentially, from which grid or designated collection area. In the grid collection method, (discussed in much greater detail in Chapter 3, "Investigators, the Investigative Process, and the Crime Scene"), all similar items of evidence from one grid can be placed into one container. However, this does depend on the quantity of materials in that grid and the type of laboratory examination to be requested on those items. Consider the container guides for collection of evidence materials in Figures 19-15 and 19-16. For instance, in one grid the search team finds evidence that will not have to undergo residue analysis. This evidence can be placed in a polyethylene Ziploc bag. In yet another grid, pipe fragments, logically ones containing the explosive main charge, are present, along with pieces of miscellaneous debris. Because the pipe fragments would require residue analysis, they would be placed in a metal can or a nylon bag and the other materials in a polyethylene Ziploc bag. The use of a nylon bag, can, or glass container for materials requiring residue analysis is necessary to retain the volatile residues and prevent them from permeating through the container. Regular polyethylene or paper bags are not suitable for volatile compounds. The properly heat-sealed nylon bag, such as that used for narcotics evidence, provides an adequate barrier to retain residues of most volatile explosives. Metal cans and glass containers can be used if nylon bags are not available. It should be noted that when using nylon to contain sharp objects, the sharp edges should be padded to prevent the material from puncturing the bag.[48]

As a general rule, individual items of evidence from the same grid are placed in separate containers. The use of separate containers places a great burden on the evidence custodian by having to account for and secure the many unnecessary containers. However, more than one container may be used if there is a large quantity of evidence received or for the reasons stated previously regarding the residue analysis.

Following the placement of evidence into a suitable container by a member of the search team, the container must be appropriately marked for its identification and accountability. This is effected by placing the following minimum details on the evidence container:

- name of the person finding the evidence;
- date;
- location where found;
- short description of the evidence;
- item number;
- case number and the evidence log number.

Other data, such as the specific street or area address, case number, time found, and so on, may be included, depending on the departmental policy. These data should be marked with a permanent marker and then covered with transparent tape to prevent their inadvertent removal. If nylon bags are used, most of which do not have a Ziploc closing feature, they must be heat-sealed to retain the residue vapors. Other containers, polyethylene and paper bags, cans, and glass should be closed and sealed with tamperproof evidence tape (this tape gives a visible indication when it is removed or altered). Evidence too large for a normal container, depending on the type, can be wrapped with plastic or paper or placed into a clean wooden box constructed for this specific purpose. Evidence accountability marking can be effected with the use of an evidence tag or label attached to the item or the container.

Depending on departmental policy and the complexity of the scene, the procedures for the collection and inventory by the evidence custodian vary. One method is to place the marked evidence containers on the ground or floor within the grid in which they were found; the evidence custodian then walks through the scene, places the evidence item number on each container with his or her initials, enters the item number and the descriptive data into the evidence log, and then collects the container. Or the evidence searcher who found and placed the evidence into the container takes the evidence and the evidence containers to the evidence custodian for entry into the evidence log, as the evidence is collected from each grid or a number of grids. In both methods, the custodian places the item number on the container with his or her initials and enters that number and descriptive data into a log. Preference may be given to the first procedure, in which the custodian, finder, and person placing the evidence into the container are the same individual. This assists in any legal proceedings, because only one person enters all the evidence into the court record, rather than all evidence searchers entering what they individually found. This streamlines the proceedings.

▲ FIGURE 19-15   Collecting evidence at the bomb scene
Evidence collection containers include, among others, (a) antistatic polyethylene bags, (b) biohazard bags, (c) paper bags, (d) metal cans, and (e) Ziplock polyethylene bags. (Thurman, James T. 2011. From *Practical Bomb Scene Investigation*, Second Edition. Boca Raton, Fl: Taylor & Francis, fig. 4.40a, 4.40b, 4.40c, 4.40d, 4.40e. Courtesy James T. Thurman)

The plotting of each item of evidence on the diagram is not required during the explosion scene investigations. However, should the team leader want selected items of evidence plotted, the plotting should be completed before the evidence is removed from the location where it was found. Therefore, during the evidence identification and collection stages, coordination must be effected between the team leader (who directs what items he or she wants plotted on the diagram and photographed) and the sketcher, photographer, and the evidence searchers or finders. Additionally, at this time the team leader may want to direct the sketcher to indicate, without identifying specific items of evidence with regard to their item numbers, the types of evidence in some or all of the search areas or grid zones. Again, this is not a specific item description but a generic designation of evidence that when reviewed on the diagram can provide a relative direction and extent of the type and quantity of evidence

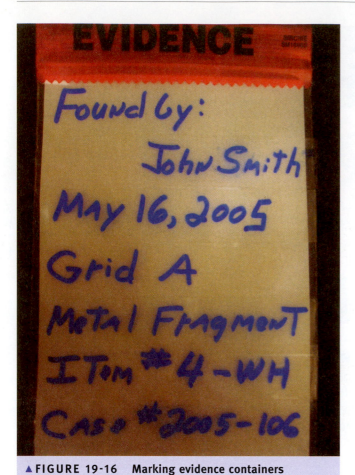

▲ FIGURE 19-16   Marking evidence containers
Evidence containers, regardless of their type, should include the name of the person finding the evidence, date and location where found, a short description of the evidence, case number, and the evidence log item number. The container should be sealed with tamperproof evidence tape. (Thurman, James T. 2011. From *Practical Bomb Scene Investigation*, Second Edition. Boca Raton, Fl: Taylor & Francis, fig. 4.41. Courtesy James T. Thurman)

or debris spread in specific areas of the scene. This is sometimes referred to as the "fan" effect: evidence emerging from the epicenter in a narrow arc and extending out into the scene in an ever-widening arc, or fan. The photographer may also document this fan effect.

If a bomb has been used, depending on the type of bomb components recovered, known standards or samples of materials (organic or indigenous to the scene) may be collected and inventoried. These materials include electrical components, switches and wiring, papers, boxes, and metal components from a vehicle or structure. These materials are collected from the scene when the bomb component fragments and paraphernalia may be similar to materials present in the target area at the time of the explosion. Also known as elimination or comparison samples, they are very useful in laboratory examinations by providing a "standard" of the materials at the scene and are used for comparison with the recovered evidence that

usually contains not only bomb components but also materials from the scene. By identifying those items as having been present when the bomb exploded one can exclude them as bomb components. As an example, in an explosion in a vehicle in which various types of electrical wires were identified and recovered during the scene investigation, the investigation team also collected a number of the electrical wires from the vehicle wiring harness and submitted them to the laboratory as "known samples." During the laboratory examinations of the debris, a comparison was conducted between the known wires from the vehicle and the recovered wires. This examination resulted in an association between some of the recovered and known wires, effectively eliminating the possibility of those wires having been a part of the bomb. The remaining wires were ultimately identified as being part of the electrical fusing system of the bomb. The laboratory examiners' job would have been more difficult without the known and comparison standards.

ANALYZING THE FUEL SOURCE

Once the origin, or epicenter, of the explosion has been identified, the investigator should determine what type of fuel was employed. This is done by comparing the nature and type of damage to the known available fuels at the scene.

The available fuel sources must be considered and eliminated until one fuel is identified as meeting all the physical damage criteria. For example, if the epicenter of the explosion is identified as a 6-feet crater of pulverized concrete in the center of the floor, escaping natural gas can be eliminated as the fuel. Chemical analysis of debris, soot, soil, or air samples can be helpful in identifying the fuel. For explosives or liquid fuels, gas chromatography, mass spectrography, or other chemical tests of properly collected samples may be able to identify their presence. (See Chapter 8, "The Crime Lab and Crime Scene Reconstruction," for a detailed discussion of instrumental analysis.)

Air samples taken in the vicinity of the area of origin can be used in identifying gases or the vapors of liquid fuels. For example, commercial "natural gas" is a mixture of methane, ethane, propane, nitrogen, and butane. The presence of ethane in an air sample may show that commercial natural gas was there rather than naturally occurring "swamp," "marsh," or "sewer" gas, which are all-methane.

Once a fuel is identified, the investigator should determine its source. For example, if the fuel is identified as a lighter-than-air gas and the structure is serviced by natural gas, the investigator should locate the source of gas that will most likely be at or below the epicenter, possibly a leaking service line or malfunctioning gas appliance. All gas piping—including that from the street mains or LP-gas storage tanks, up to and through the service regulator and meter, to and including all appliances—should be examined and leak-tested if possible.

Odorant verification should be part of any explosion investigation involving, or potentially involving, flammable gas, especially if there are indicators that no signs of leaking gas were detected by people present. Its presence should be verified.

SUSPICIOUS PACKAGES AND LETTERS

Note that items do not have to be delivered by a carrier. Most bombers set and deliver the bombs themselves. The following are precautions that should be followed when encountering a suspicious package or letter:

- If it was delivered by carrier, inspect for lumps, bulges, or protrusions, without applying pressure.
- If it was delivered by carrier, do a balance-check to determine if package is lopsided or heavy-sided.
- If there is a handwritten address or label from a company, check to see if the company exists and if it sent the package or letter.[49]

Any of the following characteristics could denote a suspicious package or letter:

- Packages wrapped in string—modern packaging materials have eliminated the need for twine or string.
- Excess postage on small packages or letters, which indicates that the object was not weighed at a post office.
- Any foreign writing, address, or postage.
- Handwritten notes, such as "To Be Opened in the Privacy of . . . ," "Confidential," "Your Lucky Day Is Here," and "Prize Enclosed."
- Improper spelling of common names, places, or titles.
- Generic or incorrect titles.
- Leaks, stains, or protruding wires, string, tape, and so on.
- Hand delivery or a "drop-off for a friend."
- No return address or a nonsensical return address.
- Delivery before or after a phone call from an unknown person asking if the item was received[50] (Figure 19-17).

USE OF ROBOTIC DEVICES IN MOVING AND DESTROYING DANGEROUS OBJECTS

Because handling suspicious packages can be quite dangerous to law-enforcement personnel, they have increasingly resorted to the use of robots to move and destroy such objects. The two photos shown depict dual-purpose robots. The first photo shows a robot designed to move potentially dangerous objects; the second depicts a robot

▲ **FIGURE 19-17 Warning! suspect letter and package indicators**
(U.S. Department of the Treasury, Bureau of Alcohol, Tobacco and Firearms)

▶ **FIGURE 19-18**
Robot for moving potentially dangerous objects
This photograph depicts a MAX BR-100 intrepid configured with arm turntable that allows 90° movement of the arm assembly. It permits law-enforcement personnel to safely remove a potentially dangerous device while minimizing danger to themselves and others who might be in the area. (Courtesy HDE Robotics Group, Inc., Fort Worth, Texas)

▶ **FIGURE 19-19**
Robot configured with a shotgun that is fired remotely
MAX TR 2000 Enhanced Technical Robot System configured with a Benelli 90 shotgun that is fired remotely. This device can be used to detonate a suspicious object or remove it from its existing location to a safer area. (Courtesy HDE Robotics Group, Inc., Fort Worth, Texas)

engineered to detonate a suspicious object (Figures 19-18 and 19-19).

BOMB THREAT STANDOFF

Law-enforcement officers should be aware of what the bomb-threat standoff distances are in order to maximize the safety for both uninvolved citizens as well as themselves. Figure 19-20 provides a detailed description of these distances along with other relevant information.

READING THE BOMBER'S SIGNATURE

Probably one of the earliest identified serial bomb builders in the United States was George Metesky, the "mad bomber" of New York City. Metesky terrorized New York City for 16 years with more than 30 pipe bombs between November 16, 1940, and his arrest in December, 1956. Not only did Metesky build devices that were similar to one

THREAT	THREAT DESCRIPTION	EXPLOSIVES CAPACITY[1] (TNT EQUIVALENT)	BUILDING EVACUATION DISTANCE[2]	OUTDOOR EVACUATION DISTANCE[3]
PIPE BOMB	5 LBS/ 2.3 KG	70 FT/ 21 M	850 FT/ 259 M
	BRIEFCASE/ SUITCASE BOMB	50 LBS/ 23 KG	150 FT/ 46 M	1,850 FT/ 564 M
	COMPACT SEDAN	500 LBS/ 227 KG	320 FT/ 98 M	1,500 FT/ 457 M
	SEDAN	1,000 LBS/ 454 KG	400 FT/ 122 M	1,750 FT/ 534 M
	PASSENGER/ CARGO VAN	4,000 LBS/ 1,814 KG	640 FT/ 195 M	2,750 FT/ 838 M
	SMALL MOVING VAN/DELIVERY TRUCK	10,000 LBS/ 4,536 KG	860 FT/ 263 M	3,750 FT/ 1,143 M

This card supersedes any previous undated versions 11/99

THREAT	THREAT DESCRIPTION	EXPLOSIVES CAPACITY[1] (TNT EQUIVALENT)	BUILDING EVACUATION DISTANCE[2]	OUTDOOR EVACUATION DISTANCE[3]
	MOVING VAN/ WATER TRUCK	30,000 LBS/ 13,608 KG	1,240 FT/ 375M	6,500 FT/ 1,982 M
	SEMI-TRAILER	60,000 LBS/ 27,216 KG	1,570 FT/ 475 M	7,000 FT/ 2,134 M

All personnel must either seek shelter inside a building (with some risk) away from windows and exterior walls, or move beyond the Outdoor Evacuation Distance.

Preferred area (beyond this line) for evacuation of people in buildings and mandatory for people outdoors.

All personnel must evacuate (both inside of buildings and out).

Building Evacuation Distance

Outdoor Evacuation Distance

Threat

[1] Based on maximum volume or weight of explosive (TNT equivalent) that could reasonably fit in a suitcase or vehicle.
[2] Governed by the ability of an unstrengthened building to withstand severe damage or collapse.
[3] Governed by the greater of fragment throw distance or glass breakage/falling glass hazard distance. Note that pipe and briefcase bombs assume cased charges which throw fragments farther than vehicle bombs.

◄ FIGURE 19-20
Terrorist bomb threat standoff
These two cards depict the terrorist bomb standoff distances that can be used as a guide for law-enforcement personnel. (Courtesy of U.S. Government Bookstore, 2007)

another, but he also often included a threatening letter to the local power company, Consolidated Edison, within the bomb. He also sent letters to various businesses, including Consolidated Edison and the police, signed with the initials "FP," which were later identified after his arrest as an acronym for "Fair Play." Metesky's case is strikingly similar to that of the most recent serial bomber in the United States, Unabomber Ted Kaczynski, who used the initials "FC," later identified as "Freedom Club," in his bombs[51] (Figure 19-21).

Serial bombers are associated with the term **bomber's signature,** which refers to an identifiable pattern or characteristic of using essentially the same or similar bomb construction components and construction, fabrication, and design techniques for multiple bombs. In other words, forensic examinations can establish a specific pattern of the use of materials and, in concert with the selection of targets, establish a direct link between different bomb-

ings, similar to being able to associate handwriting with specific components found in the possession of a subject with components used in one or more bombs. In other cases in which a device has been previously linked to a specific person, then that device can be associated with similar or other identical devices. It is far easier to establish that multiple devices were constructed with similar materials and construction techniques by unknown persons or groups rather than by an individual. When investigators establish a single source or person, the results of the intercomparison examinations usually reveal singularly specific materials or construction techniques that preclude participation of others in the building process.

Understanding and recognizing the bombers' signature are significant to the post-blast investigation. There are two primary ways of establishing or recognizing the bombers' signature: first, by the field investigator who sees a similarity between several bombings, and, second,

▲ **FIGURE 19-21 The bomber's signature**
Ted Kaczynski (The Unabomber) was responsible for
16 mailed and package bombs that killed three people and
injured 23 between 1978 and 1995 in attacks around the
country. Federal investigators knew some types of wires used
in the bombs were out of production. He always used stamps
long past their due dates and scraped the labels off batteries
to erase their serial numbers. Some of the bomb components
had markings indicating they had been taken apart and
reassembled repeatedly. He marked some components with
numbers, so when he disassembled and reassembled the
bombs he would not make any errors. He is presently serving
a life sentence in a federal prison after having been
convicted for his crimes. (© AP Photo/Elaine Thompson)

related investigation to form a whole picture, rather than
both remaining pieces of an unconnected puzzle.

SIMILARITIES BETWEEN BOMBINGS

Whenever the field investigator believes that there is an
association between multiple incidents and that possibly a
bomber's signature exists, this belief should be communicated to the laboratory. This is even more important if the
incidents are spread over a period of time, because it is
entirely possible that the same laboratory examiner who
received the first submission, say, from bombing #1, may
not be the same examiner who receives the evidence from
incident #2. Also, the evidence from multiple bombings
may have been provided to different laboratories. It is possible, however remotely, that forensic laboratories may not
associate similar devices if the possibility of association is
not drawn to their attention by the field investigator. However, laboratories do have searchable databases in place
that should preclude this oversight from occurring.

ASSOCIATION OF BOMBINGS THROUGH FORENSIC EXAMINATION

The second way in which multiple incidents may be associated with one another is through forensic examination
of devices. Most explosions, unless they are large or unless
the targets are considered significant by the media, are
usually not reported on a national or worldwide basis. As
such, it may not be possible for investigators from different parts of the country to know what types of devices
may have been used hundreds or even thousands of miles
away. Therefore, within federal laboratories, when multiple devices are received in the laboratory from different
parts of the country, possibly spanning weeks, months, or
longer, an association of componentry and fabrication
techniques may be effected through forensic examinations. It is noted that in this age of instant communication
and sharing of information by investigators and bomb
technicians, the likelihood of incidents and bomb-building
technology not being known from one part of the United
States to another is also remote. Additionally, as a direct
result of this sharing of bomb construction data between
state and municipal laboratories, associations between
multiple devices may be made in laboratories other than
the large federal laboratories.

It is possible to conclude that a person (or persons)
made multiple devices with just one point of comparison,
but this is rare indeed, just as it is sometimes possible to
make a latent fingerprint identification with only one,
exceptionally specific point of identification. In most
cases, the associations between devices/bombings are
effected with multiple points of identification. How many
are needed? It is impossible to provide an answer, because
every bombing series is different from another. However,
the more components used and the more specific the fabrication techniques used, the better the association.

by association of bombings through forensic examinations.
By associating two or more incidents, investigators can
focus by looking at the totality of information derived from
all the incidents, rather from each one individually. Essentially, by combining the investigative data investigators
may notice a pattern that can help identify a subject, which
would not have been possible by looking at the investigative leads from the incidents separately. One aspect of field
investigation data can supplement another lead from a

KEY TERMS

accelerant
alligatoring
blast fragmentation
bomber's signature
burn indicators
catalytic combustion detector
charring
chemical explosion
claymore charge
effective fire temperatures

explosion
flame ionization detector
gas liquid chromatograph (GLC)
improvised explosive device
incendiary device
incendiary mechanism
infrared spectrophotometer
layer-checking technique
mechanical explosion
plant

Property Insurance Loss Register
   (PILR)
pyromaniac
shaped charge
spalling
spontaneous heating
spontaneous ignition
trailer
ultraviolet fluorescence

REVIEW QUESTIONS

1. If arson is suspected, why should firefighters not alter the premises, such as by mopping up or overhauling the scene of the fire, especially at the point of origin?
2. What two factors are needed to cause a fire?
3. What is the layer-checking technique, and how can it assist in determining the cause and the origin of a fire?
4. What are some of the more common causes of accidental or natural fires?
5. What types of burn indications can be examined by the arson investigator to assist in determining whether a fire is accidental or incendiary in nature?
6. What are some of the most commonly used ignition and timing devices in the commission of arsons?
7. Why can items missing from the fire scene be as valuable as things remaining at the scene?
8. What are some of the most common motives for arson?
9. Why should uncoated metal paint cans (or similar containers), not plastic bags or containers, be used for the storage of material suspected of containing flammable liquids?
10. What are some of the advantages and disadvantages of olfactory detection in determining the presence of fire accelerants at the scene of a fire?

11. What types of individuals might be able to provide information relevant to the fire?
12. What is the purpose of the National Insurance Crime Bureau?
13. What are the two basic types of explosions? Briefly describe each.
14. What are the principal objectives of an explosion scene investigation?
15. What is the first duty of the investigator at the scene of an explosion?
16. What criteria should be employed in order to make a determination as to the types of containers that should be used for storage of evidence at the bomb scene?
17. What are the minimum details that should be placed on an evidence container?
18. Once the origin, or epicenter, of the explosion has been identified, the investigator should determine what type of fuel has been employed. How is this typically done?
19. What is the definition of an improvised explosive device (IED)?
20. What are the basic components of an improvised explosive device?
21. What does the term "bomber's signature" mean?

INTERNET ACTIVITIES

1. The Bureau of Alcohol, Tobacco and Firearms provides updates and statistics concerning arson and explosion incidents. Go to the bureau's website at *www.atf.gov*. Search the site for information on fire and explosion incidents for your state. The website also has information about arson and explosion training for police officers. What topics are covered in the training curriculum?
2. Many large police agencies and/or states have investigative units specializing in arson and bomb detection. Check several municipal and state police agencies in your region by using websites such as *www.officer.com* and *www.leolinks.com*. What are the functions and the responsibilities of these units? Under what conditions do they respond (arson investigation, bomb threats, and so on)? Are any statistics provided concerning the number of cases they have responded to and/or investigated?

► In 2010, Mexican authorities arrested Texas-born Edgar Valdez, a 37-year-old former football star, known as "La Barbie" for his blue eyes and blond hair, in Laredo, Texas. Within a fortnight of that arrest, Mexican authorities also arrested Sergio "el Grande" Villarreal, another major drug lord, severely hampering drug operations in Mexico.

(© Mario Guzman/epa/Corbis)

RECOGNITION, CONTROL, AND INVESTIGATION OF DRUG ABUSE

CHAPTER OBJECTIVES

1. Identify and describe several opium-derived drugs.
2. List and describe synthetic narcotics.
3. Identify and distinguish among stimulants, depressants, and hallucinogens.
4. Outline techniques used in investigating dangerous drugs and narcotics.
5. Assess the motives, methods, and management of drug informants.
6. Describe several sources of information for undercover officers conducting drug investigations.
7. Identify and describe the four major categories of drug-buy operations.
8. Discuss the legal exceptions to a search warrant.
9. Describe the process of identifying and conducting raids on clandestine labs.
10. Discuss drug evidence handling and potential security problems.

Currently, every major police department in the United States has assigned—with ample justification—a top priority to the control of drug abuse and related offenses. Most of the departments have narcotics or drug units that specialize in the identification, arrest, and prosecution of drug traffickers, ranging from low-level street dealers to leaders of organized-crime syndicates. As a result, most police agencies have allocated significant resources for narcotics officers, undercover agents, drug surveillance and recovery equipment, and agreements with drug informants. The illegal importation, manufacture, sale, and use of drugs, however, have increased more rapidly than the resources for combating them.

Explanations for the phenomenal growth of drug abuse abound in the literature on this subject. Many cite variables associated with socioeconomic and political conditions. Others suggest that the inability of some individuals to deal with personal stress and emotional problems has led to the increase in drug abuse. Regardless of the contributing factors, police must deal with the violation itself, not the motivations and human conditions that produce it.

This chapter focuses on the categories of drugs that are most commonly encountered by law-enforcement officers in their enforcement activities: opium-derived drugs, synthetic narcotics, stimulants, depressants, and hallucinogens. The procedures involved in narcotics investigations are also addressed. Most of the techniques used in investigating dangerous drug and narcotics cases are the same as those used in investigating other cases. The identification of the source of the drug and the risk factors in apprehending a drug suspect, however, make investigations of these cases unique.

Another aspect of drug and narcotics cases that makes the investigation process atypical is the use of drug informants. Drug informants can provide valuable information on various types of drug activity, but compared with informants used in other investigations, they are perhaps the most difficult to manage. Drug informants have different motivations for helping the police, such as fear of punishment for criminal acts, revenge against their enemies, money, repentance, or altruism. Regardless of the motivation, informants who have entered into agreements with police agencies should initially be screened carefully and then, subsequently, be monitored. The chapter concludes with discussions on clandestine laboratories, search warrants, evidence handling, and gangs and drugs.

DRUGS AND SCHEDULING

Officers and agents charged with investigation and interdiction of illegal drug activities are responsible for a vast array of information in order to properly carry out their duties. Although many facts about drugs never change, synthetic drugs provide opportunities for new formulations, higher potency, and more difficult identification by law enforcement. Further complicating the jobs of drug investigators is the fact that the flow of illegal drugs is constantly changing and adapting in response to law-enforcement practices, socioeconomic circumstances, market conditions, and availability of product. Therefore, those involved in drug interdiction must stay on top of current information regarding source countries and the types of drugs that may be encountered in the field by law-enforcement officers. Frequent updates are available from federal agencies, such as the National Drug Intelligence Center, which publishes drug identification guides with updated photographs and new information.[1] Before undertaking any drug investigation, investigators should also familiarize themselves with the street slang. Commonly used terms often change over time and are different in different parts of the country.

Up-to-date information about drug trafficking trends and common or emerging drugs is essential to the credibility of those working with informants or undercover. This type of information also helps law enforcement agencies target and prioritize investigations.

Title II of the Comprehensive Drug Abuse Prevention and Control Act of 1970, also known as the Controlled Substances Act (CSA), consolidated a number of laws related to the manufacture and sale of drugs. **Narcotics,** stimulants, depressants, hallucinogens, steroids, and chemicals that could be used in the illicit production of those drugs were classified by federal law as belonging to one of five schedules (Figure 20-1).

OPIATES

Several drugs are derived from the opium poppy (Papaver somniferum). Known as **opiates,** they include opium, morphine, heroin, codeine, and other drugs less well known.

OPIUM

One of the first drugs of abuse was **opium.** Its pleasurable effects were known to many ancient civilizations, including the Egyptians, as early as 1500 B.C.E. During the Renaissance in Europe, opium was employed in the treatment of hysteria, making it one of the early therapeutic agents in treating mental disorders.

In the seventeenth century, opium smoking spread throughout China, and opium dependence was recognized as a problem. Opium eating was known in the United States and England during the Revolutionary War. Opium was later used by eighteenth-century doctors to treat venereal disease, cancer, gallstones, and diarrhea and to relieve pain at childbirth.

Opium comes from the poppy plant, whose pod is carefully cut to allow a milky white fluid to ooze onto the surface of the pod. Thereafter, it air-dries into tan beads. It is then carefully scraped by hand and allowed to further air-dry, after which it turns a blackish brown color. Raw opium has a pungent odor and may be smoked, making the user appear sleepy and relaxed. Prolonged use creates both physical and psychological dependence. Raw opium is the source of morphine, heroin, and codeine (Figure 20-2).

MORPHINE

Morphine is obtained from raw opium; 10 pounds of raw opium yield 1 pound of morphine. A German named Sertner first isolated the substance in 1804 and a few years later named it "morphine" after the Greek god of sleep, Morpheus. The drug was later used in medicine in 1825 as a painkiller and is still used as such today. Morphine is one of the most effective pain relievers known to man.[2]

Schedule I

a. The drug or other substance has a high potential for abuse.

b. The drug or other substance has no currently accepted medical use in treatment in the United States.

c. There is a lack of accepted safety for use of the drug or other substance under medical supervision.

Examples: Heroin, LSD, marijuana.

Schedule II

a. The drug or other substance has a high potential for abuse.

b. The drug or other substance has a currently accepted medical use in treatment in the United States or a currently accepted medical use with severe restrictions.

c. Abuse of the drug or other substances may lead to severe psychological or physical dependence.

Examples: Morphine, cocaine, methadone.

Schedule III

a. The drug or other substance has a potential for abuse less than the drugs or other substances in schedules I and II.

b. The drug or other substance has a currently accepted medical use in treatment in the United States.

c. Abuse of the drug or other substance may lead to moderate or low physical dependence or high psychological dependence.

Examples: Anabolic steroids, ketamine, OxyContin.

Schedule IV

a. The drug or other substance has a low potential for abuse relative to the drugs or other substances in schedule III.

b. The drug or other substance has a currently accepted medical use in treatment in the United States.

c. Abuse of the drug or other substance may lead to limited physical dependence or psychological dependence relative to the drugs or other substances in schedule III.

Examples: Valium, Xanax.

Schedule V

a. The drug or other substance has a low potential for abuse relative to the drugs or other substances in schedule IV.

b. The drug or other substance has a currently accepted medical use in treatment in the United States.

c. Abuse of the drug or other substance may lead to limited physical dependence or psychological dependence relative to the drugs or other substances in schedule IV.

Example: Cough medicine with codeine, such as Robitussin AC.

◄ **FIGURE 20-1**
Federal schedule of controlled substance
21 United States Code, Section 812

◄ **FIGURE 20-2   Traditional method of gathering opium**
Historically, one of the first drugs to be abused was opium. Opium comes from the poppy plant. The poppy pod is cut to allow the milky, white fluid to come to the surface of the pod. After it is dried, it is hand scraped and allowed to be further air-dried after which it turns a blackish brown color. (© AP Photo/Adam Butler)

The use of morphine increased considerably with the invention of the hypodermic syringe by an Englishman around 1843. The syringe was introduced to this country about 1853 and was used extensively for wounded Union troops during the American Civil War. Some developed physical and psychological dependence, because doctors did not clearly understand the addictive nature of opiates until around 1870.

Morphine appears in tablet, capsule, and liquid forms, has no distinguishing color and provides the medical standards by which other narcotics are evaluated. It is usually administered by injection. The drug creates both physical and psychological dependence in the user, who feels euphoric and seems sleepy or relaxed. The pupils of the eyes may constrict.[3]

HEROIN (DIACETYLMORPHINE)

Heroin was developed in England in 1874, but it evoked little interest until about 1890, when it was found to be considerably stronger than morphine. Commercial production of heroin was begun in 1898 in Germany by the Bayer Company. Heroin was advertised as a cure for morphine dependence, but it was soon learned that heroin dependence was even more difficult to cure.

Heroin is an odorless, crystalline, white powder. It is usually sold in glassine paper packets, aluminum foil, or capsules. The darker the color, the more impurities it contains. Being about four to five times stronger than morphine, heroin is the principal drug of addiction among the opium derivatives. It is generally injected.

By the time the heroin reaches the addict, it often has been diluted considerably. Heroin reaching this country is perhaps 20%–80% pure. Deaths from overdoses are not uncommon and ordinarily occur because a dose was more pure than that to which the addict's body was accustomed. Addicts may also have a fatal allergic reaction to the drug or some substance used to "cut," or reduce, the purity level of the drug, such as powdered milk, sugar, or quinine. Such incidents have routinely been documented at emergency rooms, since hundreds of juveniles and young adults from around the country have been admitted for heroin overdoses and allergic reactions to the "cut" placed in snorted heroin, known as **chiva.**[4] Spanish for heroin, chiva (goat) hit the streets across America in the late 1990s, originating primarily from Colombia. It has a very high concentration level made from clandestine laboratories that normally process cocaine. In addition, the powders are cut with various substances, from ground-up metal, crushed wood, sand, and cyanide to strong nasal constrictors and/or stimulants such as ephedrine and caffeine. Allergic reactions to the "cut substances" have been attributed to hundreds of deaths, as well as to the exceptionally strong concentration of heroin causing accidental overdose. The numbers continue to rise as chiva use escalates along with a spike in smoking black tar heroin

▲ **FIGURE 20-3 Powder and black tar heroin**
On the street, heroin is most commonly observed in the powder form, ranging in color from dark brown to white, depending on cultivation location and the level of impurities in the sample. Black tar heroin is named for its characteristic dark color and sticky touch. It is often snorted, smoked, or ingested rather than taken through intravenous injection. Smugglers often transport heroin in concentrated amounts that are "stepped-on" or diluted before individual sales. (© Uwe Schmidt/Corbis)

(Figure 20-3) derived from chiva processing.[5] The fatal overdose is not always accidental. On occasion, addicts suspected of being police informers have been given "hot shots"—pure heroin—to eliminate them.

In addition to facing the perils of the law, withdrawal, and other aspects of addiction, the drug addict also faces the serious health problems associated with dirty needles. Many suffer STDs (sexually transmitted diseases) and hepatitis B. These are transmitted diseases, so people sharing needles with other drug abusers run the risk of injecting themselves with traces of blood from a disease carrier and thus becoming infected. Drug users who administer their drugs through intravenous injections and share their needles with others face the additional danger of contracting the human immunodeficiency virus (HIV) and subsequently acquired immune deficiency syndrome (AIDS).[6]

Colombia has become a major source of heroin production; the Drug Enforcement Administration (DEA) estimates that as much as 5% of the heroin in the United

States comes from Colombia. Although this percentage may not seem high in comparison to the amount of heroin imported from other countries, the rate of importation has grown enormously since the early 1990s.

Seizures of Colombian heroin by the DEA indicate that it is 80%–99% pure. It is usually a light brown or tan powder. The poppies are being grown in the mountains of the Cauca Province around Popayan. It is anticipated that within the next several years Colombia will become an even more important source of heroin in the United States, because existing organized crime cartels in Colombia have well-established routes developed from years of cocaine smuggling. The high-purity concentration of new heroin derivatives (chiva and black tar) from Colombia is a significant factor in recent heroin overdoses.[7] In Latin America, Mexico is also a chief exporter of heroin. Elsewhere in the world, Southeast Asia (mostly Myanmar) is a major supplier. However, Afghanistan sets the standard worldwide for heroin exportation. The country is responsible for a staggering 90% of the world's heroin production.[8]

Further, with the war in Afghanistan and its related political instability, significant exportation of heroin from the historical "Golden Crescent" area (Iran, Pakistan, and Afghanistan) is on the rise. For years under the Taliban rule in Afghanistan, opium poppy growing and production were severely limited. The offense was punishable by death, often accompanied by the confiscation of private property and land. The rule was often ruthlessly enforced by the Taliban government. Since the U.S. invasion into Afghanistan (in 2002) forcing the ouster of the Taliban government, opium poppy cultivation is again thriving.[9] Unfortunately, continued unrest and revolution are often ripe conditions for drug, gun, and human smuggling. These have been particularly interesting subjects with a strong financial nexus to terrorism. In Chapter 21 (Terrorism), we discuss the financing of terrorism from such sources.

"CHEESE" HEROIN

In the past few years the Dallas, Texas, Police Department has raised the alarm about a new and dangerous combination of drugs being used in the city Dallas. Called **"cheese" heroin,** it is a combination of heroin, approximately 8% (sometimes black heroin), and a large quantity of crushed Tylenol-PM® tablets. Teens have named the drug *cheese* because of its yellowish color (it is really tannish in color). It generally comes in powder form and is administered by snorting through the nose through a tube much in the same way that cocaine is often used (discussed later in this chapter). It costs approximately $2 per dose, turning the hardest of narcotics into a "gateway drug" for teenagers. The potency of the drug makes addiction imminent for its young users, and combined with its low price, cheese has quickly become a particularly worrisome substance for authorities and parents alike. Withdrawal symptoms often begin within six hours of use, and include:

- bloodshot eyes;
- runny/bloody nose;
- unexplainable cough;
- sleeping a lot;
- changes in behavior;
- disorientation;
- lethargy;
- hunger;
- severe headaches;
- chills;
- abdominal pain;
- muscle pain and anxiety so severe the user may return to using the drug regularly within one to three days.

Furthermore, the drug contains what can be a toxic level of acetaminophen. Acetaminophen overdoses can lead to liver damage or failure. However, the relative ease of overdose due to the purity of the heroin involved is the most likely cause of death or serious injury by this drug. Nearly 20 deaths in the Dallas area alone have been attributed to the drug since 2005, and police in places like New York City are beginning to see the effects of the drug, dubbed "starter heroin."[10] Most of the victims of fatal cheese overdoses died in their sleep after a night of partying and were found by their family members.

CODEINE

The alkaloid **codeine** is found in raw opium in concentrations from 0.7% to 2.5%. It was first isolated in 1832 as an impurity in a batch of morphine. Compared to morphine, codeine produces less analgesia, sedation, and respiratory depression. It is widely distributed in products of two general types. Codeine to relieve moderate pain may consist of tablets or be combined with other products such as aspirin; liquid codeine preparations for the relief of coughs (antitussives) include Robitussin AC, Cheracol, and terpin hydrate with codeine. Codeine is also manufactured in injectable form for pain relief.

Codeine is also a major ingredient in a popular concoction known by several different monikers, including **"drank,"** "purple drank," "Texas tea," or "lean." Originating from the hip-hop scene in Houston, Texas, the drink is a mixture of soda such as Sprite or Big Red, pieces of Jolly Rancher candy, and prescription cough medicine containing codeine and promethazine. Promethazine is an antihistamine, which is actually added to deter abuse of the codeine element of the drug by causing extreme weakness and sleepiness in large quantities. However, in the smaller quantities used for drank, it actually enhances the opiate effect. The result is a feeling of euphoria characterized by slow movement and motor skill impairment that causes the user to lean to one side.

The drink has been celebrated in rap culture, particularly by DJ Screw of Houston who died of a codeine overdose in 2000 and by popular artists Three 6 Mafia and Lil' Wayne. Drank is a fairly expensive cocktail, costing $40 to $80 an ounce, but is relatively easy to obtain across the Southern United States, especially in Texas and Florida.[11]

OXYCONTIN

Another powerful narcotic that is presently sold legally is **OxyContin.** This drug, which is usually prescribed for cancer patients, has pushed aside marijuana, cocaine, and other narcotics as the drug of choice for addicts and teenage abusers. The active ingredient in OxyContin is a morphinelike substance called oxycodone, which is also found in the prescription drugs Percodan and Tylox. But unlike those drugs, which need to be taken in repeated dosages, OxyContin is a time-released formulation that is effective for up to 12 hours. Experts say, however, that addicts can achieve an intensely pure high by crushing the pills and snorting or injecting them. A telltale piece of paraphernalia among adolescent users is a pill crusher, sold by drugstores to help elderly people swallow their medication.[12]

With the abuse of OxyContin on the rise, police in at least three states are reporting a record number of pharmacies being broken into. The homes of people with legitimate OxyContin prescriptions are being robbed, and home invasions are targeting the pills. These patients are often tracked down by relatives who know what is inside their medicine cabinets or by neighbors who hear them talk about their prescriptions. Illegal users are even accosting drugstore customers in parking lots on the hunch that they might be carrying this sought-after drug.[13]

In an effort to deal with this growing problem, the manufacturer of OxyContin has developed a tamper-proof pill containing a newly designed polymer.[14] This polymer makes the pill extremely difficult to crush for the purposes of snorting and injecting the drug, and when pill fragments are heated, it turns into a gel-like substance. Though the FDA has stated that the benefits of this "tamper proof" pill are limited, the new pill does offer a level of difficulty to the misuse of OxyContin that the FDA calls "advantageous" (Figure 20-4).

OTHER OPIUM DERIVATIVES

Other opium derivatives abused and stolen from pharmacies, hospitals, and physicians are Dilaudid, Papaverine, and Pantopon.

OPIATE OVERDOSES

The importation of heroin is of particular interest to lawmakers and law enforcement as a resurgence in heroin use among suburban teenagers has recently come about. South American drug lords strategically market the drug to a younger audience by stamping

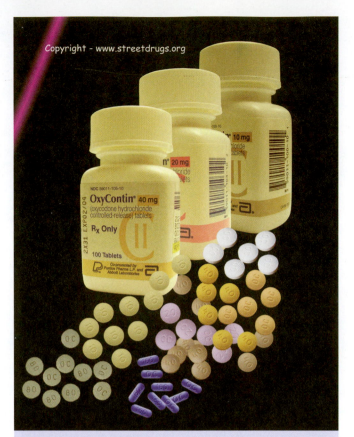

▲ **FIGURE 20-4   OxyContin**
OxyContin is a powerful narcotic that is sold legally. This drug is usually prescribed for cancer patients. There is some evidence that it is more popular among addicts and teenagers than is marijuana and cocaine. Addicts can achieve an intensely pure high by crushing the pills and snorting or injecting them. OxyContin is often the target sought in pharmacy burglaries. (© 2005 www.streetdrugs.org)

packets of the drug with recognizable and popular "brands" such as Prada and Chevrolet and have even used the popularity of such films as *Twilight* and pop stars such as Lady Gaga to promote their product and create a foothold in the teenage marketplace. Small bags of the drug sell for as little as $5, making the drug easily accessible for high schoolers and middle schoolers. The Drug Enforcement Agency reports that overdoses, common with the potent varieties of the drug, are on the rise (Figure 20-5). Charlotte, NC, for example, has experienced a five-fold increase in deaths from heroin overdoses as part of this new wave of popularity.[15] A significant rise in opiate overdoses has also been reported in Boston, New York, Miami, San Francisco, and Los Angeles. In fact, with the exception of alcohol, heroin and other opiates account for the largest portion of drug-related hospital admissions; they average approximately 300,000 per year.[16]

Victims of opiate overdose are often young, averaging 18–22 years of age and exhibiting specific character-

Opiate-Related Hospital Admissions
1996–2005

istics such as a "foam cone," tinged orange or red with blood, around their nostrils and mouth. Heroin and other opiates are powerful central nervous system depressants that essentially slow the body's ability to pump blood and breathe. Fluid often gathers within the lungs and the victim expels this pulmonary fluid with blood causing the "foam cone."[17] Other signs of an opiate overdose may include the common bluish tint from lack of oxygen and resulting swelling in the extremities, particularly in the lips, tongue, arms, and hands. Pupils may be constricted to a pinpoint, and many heroin users inject the substance into their veins. Look for bruising and varicose veins in the arms, the result of damaged and leaking blood vessels. Some users try to hide such use and inject in the legs, eyelids, rectal area, penis or vaginal areas, and in between their toes. Others also attempt to mask their needle marks by injecting into a tattoo. Although only medical personnel (or an autopsy in the case of death) can determine the problem, investigators can use these outward signs to initially determine an opiate overdose.[18]

SYNTHETIC NARCOTICS

Synthetic narcotics, though chemically related to the opium alkaloids, are produced entirely within the laboratory. A continuing search for a drug that kills pain but does not create tolerance and dependence has yet to yield a drug that is not susceptible to abuse.

MEPERIDINE (DEMEROL)

The commercial name for **meperidine** is Demerol, and it was the first synthetic narcotic. Next to morphine, it is probably the most widely used drug for the relief of intense pain. It is available in pure form and in combination products. The drug is administered by mouth or by injection; the latter is the more common method of abuse.[19]

METHADONE

Methadone is known by the commercial names Dolophine Hydrochloride and Methadone HCl Diskets. A heroin-dependent person can be treated with doses of methadone as a replacement for heroin. Methadone is manufactured in a solid form and administered orally. It's considered a "maintenance drug" and is used to maintain a heroin addict at a stable level of opiate use, protecting the addict from the incidental dangers of heroin use.

The beneficial properties of methadone are that it is longer acting than most opiates and addicts do not build up tolerance as fast as with heroin. Also, oral administration is less potentially hazardous than injection, since it significantly reduces the addict's risk for diseases such as hepatitis B, hepatitis C, and AIDS. On average, it takes about three weeks on methadone before a heroin addict completes the withdrawal stage and moves to the maintenance stage. However, it must be noted that the simultaneous use of methadone and heroin do not totally negate the physiological effect of the heroin on the user.

There is considerable controversy over the adoption of methadone maintenance programs. Critics argue that drug dependence is not cured. Proponents argue that it presents a cheaper way of supporting drug dependence and gets abusers out of crime and back to a conventional life. Proponents recognize that the programs need to include appropriate psychiatric help for overcoming the psychological dependence.[20]

STIMULANTS

Drugs falling into the **stimulants** group directly stimulate the central nervous system, producing excitation, alertness, wakefulness, and, in some cases, a temporary rise in blood pressure and respiration rate. The major stimulants abused are cocaine, amphetamines, phenmetrazine, and methylphenidate. The effects of an overdose are agitation, an increase in body temperature, hallucinations, convulsions, and possibly death. The withdrawal symptoms are apathy, long periods of sleep, irritability, depression, and disorientation.[21]

COCAINE

Cocaine is a naturally occurring stimulant that is extracted from the leaves of the coca plant (Erythroxylon coca).

The leaves of this western South American shrub have been chewed by Colombian, Bolivian, and Peruvian Indians since antiquity for religious, medicinal, and other reasons. Allegedly, the chewing of coca leaves has enabled the Indians to work in high altitudes and on inadequate diets. The chewing of the coca leaf, which continues to the present day, should not be confused with the use of the extracted drug, cocaine. Coca leaves contain only about ½%–1% cocaine; the cocaine contained within them is released more slowly, and the route of administration (oral) is different from that in most cocaine use[22] (Figure 20-6).

Because reports of native coca use generated considerable interest in Europe, efforts were made in the nineteenth century to isolate the purified psychoactive ingredient in coca leaves. When success was achieved in the 1880s, cocaine's potential value as a tonic, its general stimulant properties, its possible value for specific ailments, and its local anesthetic properties were explored. Its use as an anesthetic was particularly important because it could be used in eye surgery, for which no previous drug had been suitable. Cocaine also constricted blood vessels and limited bleeding in an anesthetized area. This property made it valuable for surgery of the nose and throat, areas that are richly supplied with blood. Although many of cocaine's uses as a therapeutic drug have been abandoned, it continues to be used as a local anesthetic.[23]

Illicit cocaine is sold as a white, translucent, crystalline powder, frequently adulterated to about half its volume. The most common adulterants are sugars (especially lactose and glucose) and local anesthetics (Lidocaine, Procaine, and Tetracaine) similar in appearance and taste to cocaine. Amphetamines, other drugs with stimulant properties, are also used. Given the high cost of cocaine, the temptation to adulterate at each level of sale is great. The combination of high price and the exotic properties attributed to it have contributed to cocaine's street reputation as the status drug.

Cocaine is most commonly inhaled, or snorted, through the nose. It is deposited on the mucous linings of the nose, from which it is readily absorbed into the bloodstream. Repeated use often results in irritation to the nostrils and nasal mucous membranes. Symptoms may resemble those of a common cold—that is, congestion or a runny nose. Users therefore often resort to cold remedies, such as nasal sprays, to relieve their chronic nasal congestion. They may be unable to breathe comfortably without habitually using a spray.

A less common route of administration for cocaine is intravenous injection. The solution injected may be cocaine or a combination of heroin and cocaine. This route of administration carries the dangers of any intravenous use. Furthermore, intravenous injection introduces unknown quantities of cocaine or cocaine and heroin directly and suddenly into the bloodstream, leaving body organs wholly unprotected from the toxic effects of the drug.

Cocaine deaths from intravenous injection are more numerous than from snorting, despite the greater prevalence of the latter method.

Freebasing

The practice of freebasing cocaine involves the dissolving of cocaine in a base solution, usually distilled water and calcium carbonate or lactose. The mixture is then shaken so that cocaine is dissolved completely. Several drops of ether are then added, and the mixture is shaken again. The cocaine is attracted to the ether, while the other additives are attracted to the base solution.

The ether-cocaine solution separates from the base (like oil and water), with the ether rising to the surface. An eyedropper is commonly used to suction off the ether-cocaine solution, which is then placed on an evaporating dish or crucible and allowed to evaporate naturally. This process can be accelerated by the use of a flame; however, this practice is extremely dangerous, because the ether is highly flammable.

The cocaine crystals are then scraped off the dish with a metal spatula, placed in a glass pipe or bong (water pipe), and smoked. The resultant high is alleged to be greater than that from simple snorting, although users remark that injection of the drug provides a more intense high than does freebasing.

The pleasant effects of freebasing begin to decrease in duration as usage increases, and users display changes in moods and irritability if a high cannot be maintained. As freebasing usage becomes chronic, a person can experience the same symptoms as a chronic nonfreebasing abuser of cocaine.

Crack or Rock Cocaine

A relatively inexpensive form of cocaine called **crack (rock) cocaine** has grown tremendously in popularity among cocaine users (Figure 20-7). The drug is made by mixing ordinary cocaine with baking soda and water and then heating the solution in a pot. The material, which is somewhat purer and more concentrated than regular cocaine, is dried and broken into tiny chunks that dealers sell as crack rocks. These little pellets are usually smoked in glass pipes and are frequently sold in tiny plastic vials. Rock cocaine is 5–10 times more potent than powdered cocaine; the high lasts about 5 minutes and leaves the user wanting more. According to mental health specialists, crack users are more likely to show serious psychiatric consequences, including intense paranoia, extreme depression, and often suicidal and even violent behavior. Part of the attraction to the dealer is the enormous profit that can be made by the sale of crack. For example, in Los Angeles an ounce of cocaine can sell for $1,000–$1,500. Since each ounce contains 28 grams, and each gram can produce up to six rocks selling for $25 each, the dealer can realize a profit of around $2,700.

COCA LEAF

Copyright - www.streetdrugs.org

▲ **FIGURE 20-6 Cocaine powder and leaves**
Leaves from the coca plant grown in South America are harvested and dried. The leaves are crumbled and mixed with high distillant chemicals that extract the cocaine from the plant material. The liquid chemicals are then evaporated causing the cocaine alkaloid to form into chunks or rocks. Cocaine is usually shipped in pressed kilo (2.2-pound) bricks of highly concentrated material. (© 2005 www.streetdrugs.org)

▲ FIGURE 20-7   Crack or rock cocaine
Crack, the smokable form of cocaine, provides an immediate "rush." This form of cocaine is relatively inexpensive and very popular among cocaine users. The drug is made primarily by mixing ordinary cocaine with baking powder and water and then heating the solution in a pot. The resulting crack rocks are purer and more concentrated than regular cocaine. (© 2005 www.streetdrugs.org)

AMPHETAMINES

Amphetamine, dextroamphetamine, and methamphetamine are so closely related chemically that they can be differentiated from one another only in the laboratory. These compounds resemble the natural body hormones of epinephrine and norepinephrine. As a result of this similarity, they can act directly, by mimicking the natural hormones in their effects on nerve endings, and/or indirectly, by causing increased release of the natural hormones. In either case, the **amphetamines** stimulate certain areas of the nervous system that control blood pressure, heart rate, and respiratory and metabolic rates, all of which are increased. Appetite is markedly decreased, and the senses are hyperalert. The body is in a general state of stress, as if it were extremely threatened or expecting a violent fight. This group of drugs artificially intensifies and prolongs such stimulation, keeping the body in a state of tension for prolonged periods of time.[24] Many different classes of people employ amphetamines in abusive quantities, including middle-aged businesspeople, housewives, students, athletes, and truck drivers. Government studies indicate that young people are the greatest abusers. Drivers take them to stay awake on long trips; students take them while cramming for exams; and athletes take them for extra energy and stamina.[25] When

the drug is prescribed, the dose frequently ranges between 2.5 and 15 milligrams per day. Abusers have been known to inject as much as 1,000 milligrams every 2–3 hours. Medical use of amphetamines is now limited to control of narcolepsy, appetite control, and control of hyperactivity in children.

PHENMETRAZINE (PRELUDIN), METHYLPHENIDATE (RITALIN), AND PEMOLINE (CYLERT)

Phenmetrazine is related chemically to the amphetamines, and its abuse produces similar effects. Like phenmetrazine, methylphenidate (Ritalin) is related chemically to amphetamines. It is prescribed for treatment of mild depression in adults and attention deficit disorder in children. Pemoline, like amphetamines, is a stimulant. These stimulants were developed and approved for marketing as a drug to be used in the treatment of hyperactive children.

CRYSTALLIZED METHAMPHETAMINE

Crystallized methamphetamine, better known as *crystal meth* and *speed* during the 1960s and 1970s, was originally taken as pills or injected.

Currently, the drug is most typically either injected or smoked using a glass pipe similar to those employed by crack cocaine users. Crystal meth first appeared in Hawaii, possibly via Korea, but has spread throughout the United States and has become particularly problematic in rural areas of Texas, Oklahoma, Missouri, Kansas, and Arkansas owing to the ease of manufacturing and the inherent availability of anhydrous ammonia from agricultural fertilizer.[26] The other ingredients for the drug, such as lithium (found in batteries), ether (found in antifreeze), and pseudoephedrine (found in cold medicine), are relatively easy to obtain, even with federal restrictions that limit the availability of pseudoephedrine to potential cookers. The **Combat Methamphetamine Epidemic Act of 2005** took several steps toward containing the pseudoephedrine problem by requiring that:

- medications containing pseudoephedrine must be either "behind the counter" or in lockbox displays requiring a key from store personnel at retail outlets;
- purchasers must show valid identification to the seller;
- sellers must maintain a log with the purchaser's signature, name, and address along with the quantity purchased;
- purchasers are limited to 3.6 grams of pseudoephedrine per day and 9 grams within a 30-day period—of that 9-gram total, no more than 7.5 grams can be purchased via mail order.[27]

However, despite the strict federal regulations, pseudoephedrine can still be obtained in large quantity often

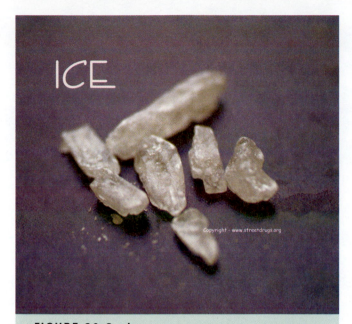

▲ **FIGURE 20-8** Ice

Made from powdered methamphetamine, "ice" is often observed as a crystalline substance. Users usually smoke ice, resulting in an intense high for as long as 12–14 hours. (© 2005 www.streetdrugs.org)

by using a network of "smurfers," or individuals who visit a number of different pharmacies or retail stores. Furthermore, guides to the manufacture of the drug can be found on the Internet and manufacturers can set up shop in motel rooms, abandoned houses or trailers, or even cars.[28]

Crystal meth, also known as *ice* and *glass,* owes its special appeal to several factors (Figure 20-8):

- A puff of crack cocaine buoys its user for approximately 20 minutes, but the high from smoking ice endures for 12–24 hours. It does, however, share crack's addictive properties, and it produces similar bouts of severe depression and paranoia as well as convulsions.
- Ice can be manufactured in clandestine speed labs, whereas cocaine must be extracted from the leaf of the coca plant, refined, and imported by smugglers at considerable risk.
- Because it is odorless, ice can be smoked in public virtually without detection.

In its solid form, the drug resembles rock candy or a chip of ice. When lighted in a glass pipe, the crystals turn to liquid and produce a potent vapor that enters the bloodstream directly through the lungs. Ice reverts to its solid state when it cools, thus becoming reusable and highly transportable.[29] One gram of crystal meth is enough for 15–20 hits, making it extremely cost effective to many users.

Crystal meth or "ice" production has several obvious hallmarks, owing to the fact that many of the ingredients can be found in discount stores. Large purchases of items containing ingredients required for crystal meth production, such as cough medicine and batteries, may indicate illicit activity. Furthermore, the use of anhydrous ammonia in the production of crystal meth produces a noxious odor that is noticeable by neighbors and visitors. Clandestine meth labs and special considerations for officers going into such labs are discussed later in the chapter.

Strawberry Quick Meth

Reports of candy-flavored methamphetamine are emerging around the nation, stirring concern among police and abuse prevention experts that drug dealers are marketing a new drug to younger people. According to intelligence gathered by the Drug Enforcement Administration (DEA) agents from informants, local police, and drug counselors, the flavored crystals have shown up in California, Idaho, Kansas, Minnesota, Missouri, Nevada, New Mexico, Texas, and Washington. The DEA has concluded that drug traffickers are trying to lure in new customers, no matter what their age, by making the meth seem less dangerous. Normally methamphetamine is a white or brownish, bitter-tasting crystalline powder that dissolves in water and that, as already indicated, is usually smoked or snorted. The new version looks like the "Pop Rocks" candy that sizzles in the mouth. Among the new flavors are Strawberry Quick, chocolate, cola, and other soda flavors (Figure 20-9). One DEA agent reported a red amphetamine that had been marketed as a powered form of an energy drink. **Strawberry Quick meth** is reportedly popular among new users who snort it because the flavoring can cut down on the drug taste. Teenagers who have been

▲ **FIGURE 20-9**
Strawberry-Colored Crystal methamphetamine
Crystals of methamphetamine, colored with a strawberry-flavored children's drink mix, are a prime example of the new line of drugs. (© AP/Wide World Photos)

taught that meth is bad may see this flavored version as less harmful. Law-enforcement officials have concluded that Strawberry Quick is definitely designed for the younger crowd. As methamphetamine's popularity has waned, drug dealers have found it necessary to create new ways to market it.

Strawberry Quick came to prominence in January 2007 after the Nevada Department of Public Safety issued a bulletin describing the type of meth discovered in their state. It certainly has spread to other states.[30]

Ya-Ba or Nazi Speed

Ya Ba, also known as *Nazi Speed,* is a highly pure methamphetamine pill originating from Southeast Asia. The brightly colored pills are candylike and often flavored (for example, cherry-red, grape-purple, white-vanilla), apparently to make them more appealing to young people. As could be predicted, ya-ba pills are fast becoming a favorite drug at all-night rave parties, since their high is much stronger and longer lasting than that of other club drugs such as ecstacy and gamma hydroxy butrate (GHB), a drug commonly used in the crime of date rape. (See Chapter 10, "Sex-Related Offenses," for a more detailed discussion.) Users generally take a pill orally or place it in foil, heat it, and inhale the smoke. The high commonly lasts up to 10 hours.[31]

METHCATHINONE

Methcathinone, called *cat* or *goob,* is a psychomotor stimulant with a chemical structure similar to methamphetamine.[32] Originally patented in Germany in 1928 and later used in the Soviet Union in the late 1930s and 1940s for the treatment of depression, methcathinone was all but unknown in the United States until 1957, when an American pharmaceutical firm received a patent for it and began animal studies to determine its potential as an appetite suppressant.

Because initial testing revealed that methcathinone was approximately one and a half times as potent as methamphetamine, clinical trials were never initiated and testing was discontinued. The formula for methcathinone languished in the archives of the pharmaceutical firm until 1989, when it was rediscovered and "liberated" by a college intern working for the firm. He shared the formula, and in 1990 a close friend set up a clandestine laboratory on the campus of Northern Michigan University (NMU) and attempted to develop a market for cat.

Although cat use did not take hold among the students at NMU, it rapidly found acceptance among the local population of Michigan's upper peninsula. The relative ease with which cat is manufactured made it readily available, and its use and abuse rapidly spread throughout the peninsula and northern Wisconsin.

Methcathinone first came to the attention of law enforcement in the winter of 1990, when the Michigan State Police in the peninsula purchased a sample of what was purported to be a "new" drug more powerful than crack. The substance was analyzed to be methcathinone, closely related to, but more powerful than, methamphetamine. In January 1991 the Michigan State Police seized the first clandestine methcathinone lab ever discovered in the United States, in a college dormitory room in Marquette, Michigan. Six months later, the DEA raided another methcathinone lab in Ann Arbor, Michigan. However, much to the surprise of law-enforcement authorities, methcathinone was not a controlled substance under either Michigan state law or federal statute.

On May 1, 1992, under the DEA's emergency scheduling authority, methcathinone was placed in Schedule 1 of the Controlled Substances Act. After a scientific and medical evaluation, this classification was made permanent on October 7, 1993.

The effects of methcathinone on the human body are very similar to those of methamphetamine. Cat is reported by users to induce feelings of omnipotence and euphoria, marked by increased energy. Other reported effects include relief from fatigue, increased self-assurance, acute alertness, hyperactivity, talkativeness, a sense of invincibility, confidence, and increased sexual stimulation.

Cat is usually a white or off-white powdered substance, very similar in appearance to methamphetamine. It is usually sold in gram quantities for $75–$100 and snorted in lines ranging from 1/10 to 1/4 of a gram. Because cat is usually sold in pure form, it reportedly can produce an immediate "rush," with a high that lasts 4–6 hours or more. There is typically a delay of 1–2 hours between dosages.

Users rapidly develop a tolerance for cat, requiring them to use larger amounts more frequently. Because cat destroys the sinus membranes, causing chronic nosebleeds and sinusitis, users may eventually resort to intravenous injection or oral ingestion.

Chronic cat use is characterized by binging. Addicts often go for days without sleep—eating very little, if at all—until they finally collapse. The onset of the "crash" occurs 4–6 hours after the last instance of use. Users often sleep for several days before beginning the cycle again.

Undesirable side effects reported by users include loss of appetite, weight loss, dehydration, stomachaches, profuse sweating, temporary blindness, deterioration of the nasal membranes, dry mouth, and an increased heart rate. Other side effects include anxiety, nervousness, depression, and hallucinations. The most consistently reported side effect—one with a serious implication for law-enforcement officers—is extreme paranoia. In one case, a cat abuser killed himself when he thought he was about to be arrested.

Symptoms of methcathinone intoxication can include profuse sweating, sweaty palms, increased heart rate, restlessness, increased body temperature, and uncontrollable shaking. Officers encountering suspected cat users should be particularly aware of withdrawal symptoms, which include irritability and argumentativeness. Other withdrawal symptoms include convulsions, hallucinations, and severe depression.

◄FIGURE 20-10 Khat
In the United States, khat use is most prevalent among immigrants from Somalia, Ethiopia, and Yemen. The drug is usually smuggled while wrapped in wet newspapers or banana leaves in order to keep the leaves moist, since khat's chemical composition begins to deteriorate quickly when the leaves are dried too fast. (© Simon Maina/Getty Images)

KHAT

Not to be confused with the previously described methcathinone (street name *cat*), **khat** (pronounced "cot") is a leafy import from a large flowering shrub that grows in northeast Africa and the southern Arabia peninsula. The active ingredients in khat are cathinone and cathine. Fresh khat leaves are a glossy brown color and contain an ingredient chemically similar to amphetamine. The cathinone in khat begins to degrade 48 hours after the plant has been cut. Thus, khat has to be refrigerated and kept moist or frozen to retain its potency for a longer period. Drying the leaves too fast causes the active ingredient (cathinone) to dissipate[33] (Figure 20-10).

The plant has been cultivated for centuries and is in widespread use today, primarily in Yemen, Somalia, and parts of Ethiopia and the Middle East. References to khat first appeared in the United States as American soldiers encountered rebels in Somalia, high on the drug during combat encounters. Ingestion of the drug does not impair motor skills but rather creates a mild, amphetamine-like euphoria that heightens the senses, self-esteem, and aggressiveness. The drug is also known as *Abyssinian Tea, African Tea*, and *African Salad*.

While khat is legal in countries such as the United Kingdom and Canada, it was recently classified as a Schedule I drug carrying penalties similar to heroin and cocaine in the United States. Khat is often transported into the United States from Europe, Canada, and North Africa wrapped in plastic bags or, as mentioned, in banana leaves to retain moistness. It is commonly sold by word of mouth or in ethnic specialty shops in cities such as Boston, Dallas, Houston, Los Angeles, Detroit, Buffalo, Philadelphia, Washington, D.C., and New York.[34]

DEPRESSANTS (SEDATIVES)

Depressants (sedatives) depress the central nervous system and are prescribed in small doses to reduce both restlessness and emotional tension and to induce sleep. The drugs most frequently abused are **barbiturates,** glutethimide, methaqualone, and meprobamate. Chronic use produces slurring of speech, staggering, loss of balance and falling, faulty judgment, quick temper, and quarrelsomeness. Overdoses, particularly in conjunction with alcohol, result in unconsciousness and death unless proper medical treatment is administered. Therapeutic doses cause minimal amounts of psychological dependence; chronic excessive doses result in both physical and psychological dependence. Abrupt withdrawal, particularly from barbiturates, can produce convulsions and death. Barbiturates are frequently nicknamed after the color of the capsule or tablet or the name of the manufacturer. The barbiturates most frequently abused are secobarbital and amobarbital,[35] which are among the short- and intermediate-acting barbiturates. The onset time is from 15 to 40 minutes, and the effects last for up to 6 hours.

GLUTETHIMIDE (DORIDEN)

When introduced in 1954, glutethimide was wrongly believed to be a nonaddictive barbiturate substitute. The sedative effects of glutethimide begin about 30 minutes after oral administration and last 4–8 hours. Because the effects of this drug last for a long time, it is exceptionally difficult to reverse overdoses and many result in death.

Glutethimide used with 16-milligram codeine tablets is one of the most popular pill combinations on the black market today. This combination gives a heroin-like effect and is known as *dors and 4s* or *Ds and Cs*. It is commonly taken by oral ingestion.

METHAQUALONE

Methaqualone was at one time very popular in the United States but has since been significantly reduced in the market. The drug was widely abused, because it was mistakenly thought to be safe and nonaddictive and to have aphrodisiac qualities. Methaqualone caused many cases of serious poisoning. When administered orally, large doses produce a coma that may be accompanied by thrashing or convulsions. It was marketed in the United States under various names, including Quaalude, Parest, Optimil, Somnafac, and Soper. Most methaqualones found on the street today are counterfeit and usually test as diazepam (Valium).

SPEEDBALLING

Speedballing is a slang term that refers to the simultaneous ingestion, usually through injection, of heroin (a depressant) and cocaine (a stimulant). The cocaine provides the user with a tremendous euphoric "rush," after which a drowsy or depressing sensation arises. An overdose of either drug can cause convulsions and death. Death by overdose using this type of drug mix was reportedly instrumental in the demise of several well-known rock musicians and celebrities, including Jimmy Hendrix, Janis Joplin, John Belushi, and River Phoenix.

HALLUCINOGENS

Hallucinogenic drugs, natural or synthetic, distort the perception of objective reality. In large doses, they cause hallucinations. Most of these drugs are processed in clandestine laboratories and have yet to be proved medically valuable. The effects experienced after taking hallucinogens are not solely related to the drug. They are modified by the mood, mental attitude, and environment of the user. The unpredictability of their effects is the greatest danger to the user. Users may develop psychological dependence but not physical dependence, so far as is known. The most commonly abused hallucinogens are PCP (phencyclidine), LSD 25 (lysergic acid diethylamide), mescaline (peyote), psilocybin, and psilocyn.

PHENCYCLIDINE (PCP)

Phencyclidine, commonly called **PCP,** in its pharmaceutically pure form is a solid white powder. Because the hydrochloride salt readily dissolves in water, and as a street drug is often adulterated or misrepresented as other drugs, its appearance is highly variable. It is sold in powder form and in tablets, both in many colors. Often it is placed on parsley or on other leaf mixtures to be smoked as cigarettes (joints).[36]

When misrepresented, PCP is commonly sold as THC (the main psychoactive ingredient in marijuana, which is rarely available on the street). But phencyclidine has also been sold as cannabinol (another marijuana constituent), mescaline, psilocybin, LSD, and even amphetamine or cocaine. Because of the variability in street names and appearance, and because PCP is sometimes found in combination with barbiturates, heroin, cocaine, amphetamine, methaqualone, LSD, and mescaline, users may be mistaken about its true identity. The mixture of marijuana and PCP has been thought to be common, but it has rarely been reported by street-drug analysis laboratories.

Significantly adding to the risk of using PCP, especially when it is taken orally, is the wide variability in purity of the street drug. Even when PCP is not misrepresented, the percentage of PCP has been found to be quite variable. Depending on how carefully PCP is synthesized, it may contain impurities, including potassium cyanide. Generally, samples represented as "crystal" or "angel dust" tend to be purer than those sold under other names or misrepresented as different drugs.

In addition to phencyclidine, over 30 chemical analogues, some of which are capable of producing similar psychic effects, can also be synthesized and may appear on the street. Thus the problems of identifying and tracking the use of PCP and related drugs is unusually difficult.

Phencyclidine is used legally in veterinary medicine to immobilize large animals. Although it was originally developed as an anesthetic for humans, it was later abandoned, because it produced psychological disturbances and agitation in some patients. PCP made its first illicit appearance in the United States in 1965 on the West Coast. At that time it rapidly developed a bad street reputation and had only limited popularity.

Because of its great variation in appearance, PCP is difficult to identify by sight. It is found in powder and tablet forms; on parsley, mint, oregano, or other leafy material; as a liquid; and in 1-gram "rock" crystals. When PCP is sold as a granular powder ("angel dust"), it may consist of 50%–100% phencyclidine. Sold under other names and in other guises, the purity varies from 10% to 30%; leafy mixtures contain still smaller amounts of the drug.

PCP is most commonly smoked or snorted. By smoking a leafy mixture on which the drug has been sprinkled, users can better regulate the dose. Because of the longer period before the drug takes effect and the greater purity, overdoses are probably worse when the drug has been taken orally.

The effects of PCP include feeling weightless, smaller, out of touch with the immediate environment, and dying or being already dead. Common signs of PCP use include flushing of the skin, profuse sweating, involuntary eye movements, muscular incoordination, double vision, dizziness, nausea, and vomiting. Another common indicator of PCP use is that the user has a desire to shed their clothes. Often times, police respond to a call similar to "a naked man running down the street," only to find that subject is high on PCP. Police officers report that individuals under the influence of PCP can be extremely violent and almost superhumanly strong.

METHYLENEDIOXY METHAMPHETAMINE

Methylenedioxy methamphetamine (MDMA or ecstasy) is a bitter white powder related to amphetamine and mescaline. It enjoys a high popularity among ravers and has now become a very common drug of abuse in the nightclub and party scene. The drug's popularity has grown at an alarming rate. Although it is difficult to say exactly how many people are experimenting with it, law enforcement officials consider ecstasy to be one of the most troubling illicit drugs because of its widespread use (Figure 20-11).

Many ecstasy users are drawn to the drug by its ability to reduce inhibitions, promote euphoria, produce light hallucinations, and suppress the need to eat or sleep. One pill's effects can last as long as 6 hours, but users build up a tolerance. An overdose can cause an accelerated heart rate, high blood pressure, aching muscle cramps, and panic attacks. According to many experts, ecstasy is psychologically addictive and can result in paranoia and psychosis.

The drug is manufactured to a large extent in laboratories in Belgium and the Netherlands. It can be created for as little as 50 cents, sold in the country of origin, and then smuggled into the United States, where it is sold for as much as $40 a pill. For the most part, Israeli organized-crime syndicates have been implicated as the main source of the drug's distribution in the United States. This so-called club drug has become increasingly popular among juveniles and is commonly used as a recreational drug at raves.[37]

LYSERGIC ACID DIETHYLAMIDE (LSD 25)

Lysergic acid diethylamide (LSD) is a semisynthetic compound produced from lysergic acid, a natural substance found in ergot fungus, a disease that affects rye and wheat. An average dose of 30–50 micrograms—about the size of a pinpoint—will take the user on a "trip" lasting 10–12 hours. Drops of the solution are taken on a lump of sugar or on blotted paper. Along with experiencing mental changes, the user may have dilated pupils, a lowered body temperature, nausea, goose bumps, profuse perspiration, increased blood sugar levels, and a rapid heart rate. Subsequent flashbacks are not uncommon.

Before 1972 there was no way to detect LSD in the body chemically. However, scientists at Collaborative Research, Inc., in Waltham, Massachusetts, developed a means for detecting it in small amounts in human blood and urine and for measuring the amount present. This discovery made it possible to study the distribution of LSD in the bodies of animals to determine the residual effect of the drug.[38] The DEA reports that LSD is making a comeback with juvenile circles and is also used frequently at raves.[39]

MESCALINE (PEYOTE)

The primary active ingredient of the peyote cactus is the hallucinogen **mescaline,** which is derived from the buttons of the plant. Mescaline has been used by the Indians of Central America and the southwestern United States for centuries in religious rites. Generally ground into a powder, it is taken orally. A dose of 350–500 milligrams of mescaline produces illusions and hallucinations for 5–12 hours. Like LSD, mescaline is not likely to produce physical dependence but may produce psychological dependence.

PSILOCYBIN AND PSILOCYN

Psilocybin and **psilocyn** are obtained from mushrooms generally grown in Mexico. Like mescaline, they have historically been used in Indian rites. They are taken

▲ **FIGURE 20-11   Ecstasy**
Ecstasy pills come in a variety of colors with unique markings, including shamrocks, stars, letters, and skull/crossbones, depending on where the drug was manufactured. The use of ecstasy is very popular in the nightclub and party scene. This drug has become increasingly popular among juveniles and is commonly used as a recreational drug at raves. (© 2005 www.streetdrugs.org)

▲**FIGURE 20-12** **Psilocybin**

Another popular drug among adolescent youth is psilocybin. The mushrooms are eaten, causing hallucinations, disorientation, impaired coordination, and confusion on the part of the user. Mushrooms covered in chocolate, as observed in this photo set, look like candy and are often found at raves. (© 2005 www.streetdrugs.org)

orally, or placed in tea, and their effect is similar to mescaline's, except that a smaller dose—4 to 8 milligrams—produces effects for about 6 hours. Psilocybin has also become a popular drug on the party scene and at raves (Figure 20-12).

FOXY AND 5-MEO-AMT

Foxy became a controlled substance via emergency scheduling by the Drug Enforcement Agency in the spring of 2003. This Schedule I hallucinogen is a synthetic compound with chemical properties similar to those of psilocybin and psilocin. The drug is found in powder form, which is then often used to fill capsules or create tablets. The tablets may be imprinted with graphics. Most often, the drug appears at clubs and raves and is used primarily by teenagers and young adults. Effects begin to manifest in the user within about 30 minutes, and they include visual and auditory hallucinations, extreme talkativeness, and decreased inhibitions. These effects peak between 1 and 2 hours after administration and can last 3–6 hours.[40]

More commonly called *AMT, alpha,* or *alpha-O,* 5-MeO-AMT shares many similarities with Foxy. Both have similar chemical properties, induce hallucinogenic effects, and are generally used within the club or rave scenes. Additionally, the powdered AMT may be dissolved in water and distributed onto blotter paper, sugar cubes, or candy. AMT is longer-lasting than Foxy, often producing hallucinations for up to 18 hours.[41]

KETAMINE

Ketamine hydrochloride is a synthetic drug that was developed in the mid-1960s and is an anesthetic agent that has

legitimate uses, mostly in veterinary medicine. Ketamine was used extensively in the Vietnam War because it is fast-acting and has a relatively short duration, making it a drug of choice for "battlefield medicine." However, it soon became obvious that many humans who were anesthetized with ketamine often became agitated and suffered hallucinations when they awoke. It has since been replaced as an anesthetic for humans by other, more efficient agents with fewer side effects.

Ironically, the side effects that made ketamine unpopular and unsafe as a legitimate medical drug have spawned its use in the illegitimate market. On the street, ketamine is called *Vitamin K, Special K,* or *K.* It has also been closely associated with the all-night rave party phenomenon. Ketamine causes hallucinations, excitement, and delirium similar to the drugs phencyclidine (PCP) and LSD; however, the effects are not as pronounced or as long in duration. Hallucinations caused by ketamine may last only an hour or two, but the intoxication-like effects of the drug may be noticeable for several hours. Because ketamine is an anesthetic, it may temporarily mask the feeling of pain. Users of ketamine can injure themselves and not know it.

Because ketamine is so difficult to produce, it is not manufactured in clandestine laboratories. Most of the ketamine abused today comes from stolen veterinary stock and is known by brand names such as Ketalar and Ketaset. The legitimate drug is usually supplied in vials of liquid, although it can be in the form of white powder or pills.

In liquid form, ketamine may be injected into a large muscle. This route allows for a slower absorption and longer duration than the intravenous route. In powder form, ketamine is usually snorted in the same manner as

▲ FIGURE 20-13 Ketamine

Ketamine hydrochloride is a synthetic drug developed in the mid-1960s as an anesthetic agent. Two of the street names used for this drug are Vitamin K and Special K. Ketamine causes hallucinations, excitement, and delirium similar to LSD or PCP. Because it is an anesthetic, it may temporarily mask pain—so much so that users can even injure themselves and not be aware of it. (© 2005 www.streetdrugs.org)

▲ FIGURE 20-14 Manicured marijuana and seeds

Note the smaller size of a marijuana cigarette compared to a regular cigarette on the left. The cleaned or manicured leaves of the marijuana plant are used to fill these "cigarettes." Low doses of the smoked drug tend to produce initial restfulness and a sense of well-being. Other effects include an alteration of sensory perceptions, including an illusory expansion of time and space. (Courtesy DEA)

cocaine. Both powder and liquid can be sprayed or sprinkled on vegetable matter and smoked or mixed with a drink. While it is not known if a person can become physically dependent on ketamine, tolerance and psychological dependence are distinct possibilities with frequent use.

The average street dose of ketamine ranges from 0.2 to 0.5 gram. The size and weight of the abuser, the desired effects, and the presence of other drugs in the abuser's system determine the ultimate effect. A vial of liquid ketamine is equivalent to approximately 1 gram of powder and sells for $100–$200. A 0.2-gram dose of powder, or a *bump*, commonly sells for $20. Ketamine may be packaged for sale in small plastic bags, aluminum foil, paper folds, or gelatin capsules.[42] Obviously, an abuser must also possess hypodermic syringes and needles to administer the drug by injection (Figure 20-13).

CANNABIS

MARIJUANA

Although classified as a mild hallucinogen, the Schedule I substance **cannabis** is often considered separately owing to its wide availability and popularity. Drugs obtained from the cannabis plant include **marijuana** and hashish. Marijuana is found in the flowering tops and leaves of the cannabis-sativa (also known as *hemp*) plant. The leaves of the plant always grow in odd numbers. The plant thrives in mild climates around the world, but the principal sources of import into the United States are Colombia, Mexico, and Jamaica. Its most common nicknames are *pot, reefer, grass, weed, Maryjane,* and *a joint.* Marijuana is made by crushing or chopping the dried leaves and flowers of the plant into small pieces. The cleaned or manicured leaves are then rolled into a cigarette and smoked, smoked in some other fashion, or mixed with food and eaten. The principal psychoactive substance is thought to be delta-9-tetrahydrocannabinol (THC), a chemical found nowhere else in nature. Most marijuana is found to have less than 5% THC, but improvements in horticulture and chemistry in the cultivation process have led to much more concentrated varieties. Hybrid varieties, such as those found in the potent sinsemilla strain of the plant, and plants grown in carefully controlled indoor operations may yield up to 20% THC[43] (Figure 20-14).

Although the effects of the drug vary among users, in many cases low dosages of marijuana produce an initial restfulness and well-being, followed by a dreamy, carefree state of relaxation and food cravings. Larger dosages can result in altered perceptions, impaired memory, and rapid changes of emotion. Effects of the drug are usually felt almost immediately by the user and may last several hours.

As of this writing, the Supreme Court was considering whether users who have doctor's approval and were permitted by state law to use homegrown marijuana to mitigate side effects from chemotherapy or symptoms of AIDS, cancer, glaucoma, and other medical conditions could be prosecuted by federal agents.[44] Currently, marijuana is not permitted for medical use, and those prescribing the drug are not protected from federal prosecution. However, the debate as to the medicinal uses of marijuana is ongoing. Perhaps the main reason for the unwillingness of the federal government to legalize marijuana for medicinal use is the drug's reputation as a "gateway" drug. The gateway theory states that the use of marijuana causes an eventual graduation by users to harder drugs such as cocaine and heroin. However, this idea is controversial. Several studies have recently disproved this association, but marijuana remains a Schedule I drug at this time.[45]

Marijuana Grow Houses

Marijuana grow houses are normal houses in residential areas that are converted for the purposes of growing marijuana. Large houses are often used, because they provide greater capacity for growing marijuana, but such operations may be found in any home, in any neighborhood.

To make a house suitable for cultivating marijuana, significant changes are made to the home's structure. High-intensity lighting is needed to grow the plants (which is costly), so many home grow operations bypass the electricity illegally, putting the neighborhood at risk of fire and electrocution. Combined with construction to provide water and ventilation for the grow operation, the house becomes uninhabitable for future residents. Unless major repairs are made, the house is ruined, and the property value of other houses in the area is lowered.

Marijuana grow houses often have links to criminal elements and organized crime. Individuals associated with grow operations have been found to carry weapons and may be considered dangerous. Also, there is a risk of increased violence and residual crime in neighborhoods associated with illegal activity. Marijuana grow houses are not only a police concern; they are also a public safety issue.[46]

What Are the Dangers?

There are many dangers associated with marijuana grow houses and problems that can result from having one in a neighborhood. These include:

- *Poisonous fumes:* Noxious fumes from the growing operation can build up inside the house or be vented outside (which affect the neighboring homes).
- *Fires:* Electricity is bypassed, by being diverted from neighboring homes. This increases the chance of fires starting owing to the amateurish rewiring jobs.
- *Electrocution:* People inexperienced with rewiring electrical systems may electrocute themselves, or people exposed to the wiring may be electrocuted.
- *Violence:* To protect distribution and production of marijuana, those involved in a growing operation may be armed, and have been known to carry out assaults or homicides.
- *Increased crime:* Marijuana from home grow operations are sold to children and other members of the community. The money raised from these sales is used to fund organized crime.
- *Booby traps:* Traps may be set by growers to protect their product from unauthorized persons entering the home or property. These traps can be life threatening and expose emergency responders (and others entering the property) to hazardous conditions.
- *Environmental damage:* Chemicals used in the grow operation are improperly disposed of by being drained into the ground and water system.
- *Hazard to children:* Children in the neighborhood are exposed to the dangers mentioned above, and may be sold marijuana. Police have found children living in or brought by their parents to the grow houses, exposing them to these hazards.[47]

What Are the Signs of a Marijuana Home Grow Operation?

There are a number of factors that may indicate the presence of a marijuana home grow operation. These include:

- Residents rarely appear to be at home and may be in the house only for brief periods of time (such as a few hours) before leaving. Despite this, radios or televisions may be left on all night, making it sound as if someone were there.
- Visitors behave strangely or visit at odd hours.
- Entry into the home is often made through the garage or side/back entrance, to conceal activities.
- Windows are boarded or covered up, preventing light from entering the house and concealing activities inside. The glare of bright lights may be seen escaping from the windows, and the windows may have a layer of condensation on them. Even though the windows are always closed, air conditioners never run.
- Equipment used in the growing operation (such as large fans, lights, plastic plant containers, and other items) is carried into the home.
- Sounds of construction or electrical humming from equipment may be heard.
- Exterior appearance of the property is untidy. There is little outside maintenance done (unshoveled snow, uncut grass, and so on), and garbage bags containing used soil and plant material may be discarded in areas surrounding the house. Mail delivered to the house may be left unchecked, so that flyers and junk mail pile up in the mailbox.
- Warning signs are posted in windows or around the outside the house. These may warn people to "Beware of the Dog" or that "Guard Dogs" are on the property.

Cash Value

The amount of money that marijuana grow houses generate is well into the billions. For example, recently the Riverside County, California Sheriff's Department conducted raids on nine houses and found a total of 14,000 plants with an estimated value of $60–$80 million.[48] This clearly is a very lucrative criminal enterprise (Figure 20-15).

HASHISH

A drug-rich resinous secretion from the flowers of the cannabis plant, **hashish** is processed by drying to produce a drug several times as potent as marijuana. The resin from the flowers is richer in cannabinols than the leaves and tops, and THC content is 5%–12%. (The leaves range from 0.27% to 4% in THC content.) Hashish is most commonly smoked in a small "hash pipe."

HASHISH OIL

The Middle East is the main source of hashish entering the United States. Liquid hashish, or **hashish oil,** is produced by concentrating THC. The liquid hashish so far discovered has varied between 20% and 65% THC. There is reason to suspect that methods are now being employed to make an even more powerful concentrate. The purity of the final product depends on the sophistication of the apparatus used.

Like other forms of the drug, liquid hashish can be used several ways. Because of its extraordinary potency, one drop of the material can produce a high. A drop may be placed on a regular cigarette, used in cooking, added to wine, and even smeared on bread. When smoked, a small drop of hashish oil is smeared inside the glass bowl of a special pipe with a flattened side. The user exhales deeply, tilts the bowl, and holds the flame from a match under the oil. In one inhalation, the smoker draws slowly on the pipe as the oil begins to bubble, continuing as it chars and burns.

There are many ways to produce hashish oil, but most clandestine operations use a basket filled with ground or chopped marijuana suspended inside a larger container, at the bottom of which is contained a solvent, such as alcohol, hexane, chloroform, or petroleum ether. Copper tubing or similar material is arranged at the top, and cold water circulates through it. The solvent is heated, the vapors rise to the top, they condense, and then they fall into the basket of marijuana. As the solvent seeps through the plant materials, the THC and other soluble chemicals are dissolved, and the solution drops back to the bottom of the container. Continued heating causes the process to recur. The solution becomes increasingly stronger until the plant material is exhausted of its THC.

SYNTHETIC MARIJUANA

Synthetic marijuana, otherwise known as **K2** or "spice," is actually a mixture of herbs and spices treated with a chemical additive and marketed as a type of incense. The substance contains synthetic cannabinoids, mimicking some of the effects of marijuana but also resulting in some nasty side effects. Popular among young adults as

Colombia	⬛ (purple)	Golden Crescent (Afghanistan, Pakistan, Iran)	⬛ (yellow)
Mexico	⬛ (orange)	Golden Triangle (Burma, Laos, Thailand)	⬛ (green)

▲ **FIGURE 20-17** **Global heroin trafficking patterns**

States has enacted measures to control many of the ingredients found in methamphetamine, Mexican labs have taken advantage of the lack of regulation on such items within their own country, as well as the ease of importing chemicals such as pseudoephedrine from Canada and the Middle East.[55] As a result, methamphetamine labs in Mexico have increased their capacity to export to the Southwestern United States in the past decade. Most methamphetamine trafficked from Mexico enters the United States via pedestrian couriers and both private and commercial vehicles, particularly through points of entry in Arizona, Texas, and California.[56] However, other more sophisticated means have also been discovered. For instance, in San Diego, California, a mile-long tunnel was discovered that led from a kitchen in a home in Tijuana, Mexico, to two warehouses in San Diego's Otay Mesa industrial district[57] (Figure 20-18). The cinder-blocked tunnel travelled under the U.S.-Mexican border and dropped 80–90 feet to a wood-lined floor, equipped with a rail system, ventilation and fluorescent lighting. The tunnel represented one of the most sophisticated in design and was used extensively for the transportation of heroin, cocaine, methamphetamines, and marijuana smuggling. The tunnel was also suspected to have been used to transport illegal aliens and human-trafficking victims exploited for sexual purposes inside the United States. (Refer to Chapter 12, "Human Trafficking," for more information on this subject.) As a

▲ **FIGURE 20-18**
Drug tunnel discovered in San Diego, California, in 2010
(© AP Photo/U.S. Immigration and Customs Enforcement)

result of this tunnel, the San Bernardino County Sheriff's Office, San Diego Police Department, Immigration and Customs Enforcement (ICE) and the Drug Enforcement Administration (DEA) have developed a new unit (The San Diego Tunnel Task Force) focused on the discovery of tunnels.

Mexico also exports nearly 7 tons of heroin a year into the United States. Black tar heroin, a powerful yet inexpensive variety of the opiate, is made exclusively in Mexico.[58] The drug is smuggled into the United States mostly via pedestrian couriers and commercial and private vehicles. The most common points of entry are in Texas, particularly at Laredo and El Paso, and California at San Ysidro.[59]

Drug Violence in Mexico

Mexico's prolific drug export business has had an increasingly violent effect on the country. Since Mexican President Felipe Calderon launched an offensive on drug cartels in 2006, more than 28,000 people have died in drug-related violence. Those killed include federal troops and police fighting an offensive against organized trafficking, politicians, cartel members who have run afoul of their own organizations, cartel members in conflict with other cartels, and scores of innocent bystanders. Calderon directly blames the United States for the turmoil and violence in his country, stating "The origin of our violence problem begins with the fact that Mexico is located next to the country that has the highest levels of drug consumption in the world."[60]

The hardest hit areas of Mexico are those in the northern border area, with Ciudad Juarez—just miles from El Paso, Texas—as one of the most notable. There are also high levels of violence in Michoacán and Guerrero states. Travel advisories to Mexico have been extended by the U.S. State Department for tourists as a result of the turmoil within the country. That turmoil has officials watching border states closely for an uptick in violence that may have spilled over the border. Authorities in Arizona and Texas have reported an increase in home invasions and abductions related to the Mexican drug trade, and bodies of cartel foes have been found over the border.[61] However, El Paso—one of the American cities closest to the chaos—was recently named the safest city in the United States.[62]

COLOMBIA

The country of Colombia, located in South America, has a political and environmental climate perfectly suited for the production and distribution of cocaine, heroin, and marijuana. Fertile valleys, which are generally removed from populated areas, are ideal for cultivation of opium poppies, marijuana plants, and coca leaves. Colombia also imports the coca plant, from Peru (the world's main source of the plant) and Bolivia for manufacture. Government corruption and political unrest in the country has created an atmosphere where clandestine cocaine production facilities can operate without fear of government intervention. These labs, in turn, are able to manufacture more cocaine than any other country in the world.[63] The drug is then generally delivered to Mexican traffickers for delivery into the United States through Texas, California, Arizona, and New Mexico. After the drug reaches the United States, it is transported to either Mexican or Colombian trafficking groups for distribution into markets such as Baltimore, Boston, Detroit, Newark, and Phoenix. Marijuana and heroin are transported similarly, often through complex maritime shipments to Mexico. Heroin may be shipped directly into the United States by couriers aboard commercial airline flights.[64]

THE GOLDEN CRESCENT

The Golden Crescent is the moniker adopted for three countries in Southwest Asia: Afghanistan, Pakistan, and Iran. Currently, these countries contribute a large percentage of the heroin imported into the United States, with Afghanistan holding a virtual monopoly on the heroin market. Afghanistan cultivates nearly 90% of the world's opium poppy supply, especially since war and political turmoil in the region makes opium one of the few viable and profitable crops.[65] Most of the crops, along with those from Pakistan and Iran, are exported into Turkey, where traffickers then use couriers to bring the drugs into the United States via commercial airlines. Most of these smuggled shipments are bound for New York and Chicago, where they are either sold locally or transported to other markets.[66] Pakistan and Afghanistan are also the largest producers of hashish.

THE GOLDEN TRIANGLE

Burma, Laos, and Thailand make up the area referred to as the Golden Triangle, known mainly for heroin and marijuana production. Thailand is also a major producer of methamphetamine. Drugs from this area are transported to the United States by Thai nationals, as well as Nigerian and Chinese traffickers. The main modes of transport include couriers on commercial flights, mail, and by concealment in cargo containers. Most of the shipments to the United States are bound for the East Coast, particularly to the Baltimore, Washington D.C., New York, and Chicago areas. Another route for drugs from the Golden Triangle into the United States is through the U.S./Canadian border, particularly at Detroit and Buffalo, New York.[67]

EUROPE

Western Europe remains the biggest producer of MDMA, or ecstasy. The DEA estimated that nearly 80% of the ecstasy coming into the United States came from Western Europe, particularly Belgium and the Netherlands.[68] This drug is often directly transported by couriers into major U.S. airports such as JFK International in New York and Los Angeles International.

DRUG INVESTIGATIONS

Narcotics investigations are particularly challenging to law enforcement because most investigations begin before a crime actually occurs. The goal of any narcotics investigation, then, is to establish that there is probable cause that an individual or group is breaking the law by using, manufacturing, or selling drugs. Once probable cause has been established by methods such as surveillance, informant use or undercover work, search warrants may be granted and arrests can be made.

GATHERING INFORMATION

Drug investigations must rely heavily on information from outside sources in order to develop a case. In fact, initiating a drug case depends on how well investigators can locate and identify leads that will strengthen their case against an identified target. Sources of information relevant to drug investigation targets can include telephone complaints, confidential informants, patrol officers, private sector sources, outside agencies, and internal police records.

Anonymous Tips

Anonymous tips can come from people with varying motives: relatives or neighbors may be concerned about a loved one's health or about their own safety if drug manufacture or other such activity is taking place near their home; the exgirlfriend or boyfriend of a drug dealer may turn them in for the sake of revenge; or a disgruntled customer may anonymously tip off police if he or she feels cheated by a dealer.

Telephone calls to law enforcement agencies are the most common form of anonymous tip. Because anonymous tipsters generally prefer to remain anonymous, great care must be taken by those who answer such phone calls to capture as much relevant information as possible. Narcotics investigators should train telephone operators to consistently ask specific information that will help to prioritize complaints. Narcotics complaints are different from others in that there is often no obvious victim or evidence that a drug crime has happened after it has been committed. It is therefore important that those taking telephone reports of a drug crime ascertain whether the information is more than hearsay.[69] When taking a telephone complaint about a drug crime, one should note whether the complainant has actually witnessed the crime that he or she is reporting. One should also note whether or not the complainant has personally been involved in a narcotics transaction with the person he or she is registering the complaint against and is willing to assist in the investigation or talk to police or prosecutors if necessary. If a complainant is merely reporting what he or she heard from a third party, the report will take a lower priority than one

from a caller who reports specific, first-hand information relating to drug manufacture or sale. However, any information that might corroborate an existing investigation should be a priority.

CONFIDENTIAL INFORMANTS

Although legitimate telephone or walk-in complaints from the public are valuable to drug investigators, they are relatively rare. Narcotics investigators have to rely heavily on the use of confidential informants, who generally know dealers, manufacturers, and users personally. Confidential informants are useful because they are able to gather information not usually available to law enforcement officers through their personal knowledge and familiarity with narcotics offenders. They are often able to gain first-hand and up-to-the-minute information about drug crimes that can be the basis of warrants for searches and arrests if properly corroborated by the investigator.[70] However, the ability of informants to gather such information often means that they are criminals themselves, making their motivations suspect and the management of such informants difficult. The career of a narcotics investigator often depends on how well he or she is able to recruit, develop, and manage informants. As a result, it is crucial that investigators understand motivations and types of informants.

INFORMANTS: MOTIVATIONS AND TYPES

Like most people, informants need motivation to produce. The more motivated they are, the more likely they are to apply themselves to the task at hand and remain committed to achieving success. Therefore, by identifying an informant's true motives, an investigator greatly enhances the potential success of an investigation. Initially, informants commonly voice a specific motive for providing assistance. However, as a case proceeds and a relationship with an investigator develops, other reasons may surface. Some of the more common motivational factors encountered by drug enforcement investigators are fear, revenge, money, repentance, and altruism.[71]

The most frequently encountered motivational factor may be the confidential informant's (CI's) fear of punishment for criminal acts. Severe criminal penalties tend to increase the number of persons wanting to cooperate with drug-enforcement authorities. Informants may also fear their criminal associates. Individuals wrongly accused by drug dealers of being informants may then become informants for self-preservation, money, or both.

Informants frequently cooperate with the government to seek revenge against their enemies. Jealousy may also prompt their acts of vengeance.

Some individuals provide information or services for money. These money-motivated informants, known as *mercenaries*, are usually the most willing to follow the directions of their handlers. Mercenaries frequently possess other motives as well.

Repentance can be a motivating factor. Informants often claim they cooperate in order to repent for past crimes. However, this is seldom their only motive for cooperating.

Some individuals are motivated by a sense of altruism. People with professional obligations or feelings of responsibility frequently provide information to the police. Examples of altruistic informants include airline ticket agents and private mail-service carriers.

Problem Informants

Some informants have personalities that make them difficult, if not impossible, to manage. These individuals may also have questionable motives for offering their services to a law-enforcement agency. Investigators who misjudge the true motives of informants experience tremendous control problems, which can create safety issues and place department resources and personnel in jeopardy. Therefore, investigators should avoid recruiting certain types of individuals, if possible.

Egotistical Informants

Egotistical informants, who are encountered frequently, may not have received positive reinforcement from their parents or schoolmates when growing up. Consequently, they seek positive feedback from their handlers as their primary reward. Investigators who provide this positive reinforcement motivate egotistical informants to continue supplying information. Unfortunately, these informants are often the hardest to handle, because their egos prevent them from relinquishing control of the investigation entirely to their handlers.

Informants with "James Bond Syndrome"

Some persons see their roles as informants as a way to have their lives imitate art. While working as informants, they imagine themselves in a police or spy drama. Sometimes they even attempt to orchestrate events to parallel a scene from a movie or novel. Frequently hard to handle, these informants often exaggerate their knowledge of criminal activity to enhance the likelihood of their becoming informants.

Wannabe Informants

Wannabe informants are people who, for whatever reason, failed to qualify for a law-enforcement position and now seek to become involved in law enforcement as informants. Because they lack criminal associates, these individuals usually cannot provide specific information about drug dealing. Therefore, they do not make good informants.

Perversely Motivated Informants

The most dangerous and disruptive informants in drug law enforcement are perversely motivated CIs. They offer their services in order to identify undercover agents; learn the department's methods, targets, and intelligence; or eliminate their own competition in drug sales. Sometimes criminal organizations instruct these individuals to infiltrate departments and learn whatever they can to assist the traffickers. These individuals may even provide genuine information about specific events as a decoy to divert resources from more significant trafficking activity.

Therefore, investigators must question all walk-in and call-in informants (that is, individuals who volunteer their services without prompting), because they may be, or have the potential to be, perversely motivated. After completing a thorough background investigation of CIs, investigators must constantly guard against providing more information than informants furnish in return. Furthermore, investigators should not discuss specific details of methods and techniques used during drug investigations with informants.

Restricted-Use Informants

In addition to problem informants certain other informants, by virtue of their criminal background or other status, pose special management challenges to both investigators and supervisors.[72] Department managers should carefully scrutinize these individuals before using them as CIs. Examples include juveniles, individuals on probation or parole, individuals currently or formerly addicted to drugs, felons with multiple convictions, and individuals known to be unreliable.

Investigators should not use these individuals as informants until a supervisor approves them. In fact, because these informants require special scrutiny, only senior investigators should handle them. Furthermore, investigators must constantly reevaluate the motives of these individuals.

DEPARTMENT POLICY

Agencies should not leave the management of drug informants exclusively to investigators. Formulating a written policy ensures consistency in the use and management of CIs and serves as a guide for inexperienced investigators.[73]

The policy should indicate which investigators may maintain informants, as well as who will supervise these CIs. In addition, the policy should clearly establish that informants are assets of the department, not of individual investigators. In this regard, management should both authorize and encourage investigators to share informants. Also, checks and balances must be in place to ensure that the policy is followed.

Policy concerning the management of confidential informants should establish procedures in several areas. These include creating and documenting informant files, debriefing and interacting with informants, and determining methods and amounts of payments for services rendered.

The Informant File

Investigators should formally establish files for CIs who regularly furnish information, as well as for those who expect compensation for information they supply. Informant files document investigators' interactions with CIs. In fact, investigators should not use any source that cannot be documented.

Although investigators should document their contacts with CIs, not everyone in the department needs to know an informant's identity or have access to informant files. Access should be on a need-to-know basis, including only the investigators and their supervisors who deal directly with the informant.

To further protect informants' identities, investigators should use code numbers in lieu of informants' names in investigative reports. Informants should keep the same number throughout their working relationships with the department.

The informant file should include information pertaining to the CI's vital statistics, such as physical description, work and home addresses, vehicles driven, contact telephone numbers, next of kin, and so forth. National Crime Information Center searches, performed before the informant is used and then systematically thereafter, ensure that the informant has no outstanding warrants. These records should be kept in the informant's file, along with the CI's photograph, fingerprints, and FBI and state "rap" sheets.

Establishing an informant file sends a not-so-subtle message to CIs that investigators document every encounter and verify all information that CIs supply. Such documentation may also deter a perversely motivated informant. In addition, informant files enhance the credibility of the department in the eyes of the court and the public, who view CIs as inherently unreliable and who may believe that the agency fabricated information. Therefore, every time an informant provides information concerning an actual or a potential criminal matter, the agency should include a written report detailing this information in the CI's file. The original report should remain in that file, and a copy should be maintained in the case file.

The department must also document what steps it takes to corroborate information provided by a CI. This is especially important when informants act unilaterally. As a matter of policy, all CI information should be verified regardless of the CI's past reliability.

Informant Debriefings

Each time investigators initiate investigations on the basis of information received from a CI, the designated handler should interview and debrief the CI in order to ascertain the informant's motive(s) and to advise the informant of the department's rules. For example, informants should know that they carry no official status with the department, that the department will not tolerate their breaking the law or entrapping suspects, and that the department cannot guarantee that they will not be called as witnesses in court.

At the end of the interview, the investigator should put this information in writing in an "informant agreement." This agreement should be signed by the informant, witnessed by the handler, and placed in the informant's file. Investigators should debrief their informants on a regular basis—for example, every 30, 60, or 90 days—to keep them active or, if necessary, to terminate their association with the department because of lack of productivity.

Investigator-Informant Contact Procedures

The department must establish investigator-informant contact procedures and train employees in their use. For example, the handler should meet with the informant in private, if possible, but always in the presence of another investigator. In fact, the department should either strongly discourage or prohibit investigators from contacting informants alone, especially if the officer plans to pay the informant. Meeting with or paying a drug informant alone leaves the officer and the department vulnerable to allegations of wrongdoing.

Although informant handlers often develop special working relationships with their informants, department policies should preclude contact with informants outside the scope of official business. Investigators must keep their relationships with CIs strictly professional. This is particularly important when the informant and the investigator are not of the same sex. Policies should also expressly prohibit such contact as socializing with informants and/or their families, becoming romantically involved with informants, conducting nonpolice business with them, and accepting gifts or gratuities from them.[74]

To ensure adherence to department policy, supervisors should review informant files regularly. In addition, they need to attend debriefings periodically to oversee the entire informant management process.

Finally, department administrators must establish procedures for investigating alleged policy violations by investigators or informants. Thorough investigations of this type maintain the integrity of the department by dispelling any notion that the department does not enforce its own policies.

Informant Payments

Payments to CIs can be divided into two distinct categories—awards and rewards. Awards take a monetary form. They are based on a percentage of the net value of assets seized during a drug investigation as a result of information provided by a CI. Advising the informant of the exact amount of the percentage at the beginning of the case provides incentive for the CI to seek out hidden assets that might otherwise go undetected.

However, because payments based on seized assets are not universally accepted in the courts, the investigator should consult the case prosecutor before promising a specific amount to the informant.

Rewards, however, do not represent a percentage of the value of the seized assets. Amounts are usually determined by the type and the quantity of drugs seized, the quality of the case produced, the number of defendants indicted, the amount of time and effort the CI exerted, and the danger faced by the CI during the course of the investigation. Unlike awards, rewards come directly from an agency's budget.

While an informant might receive money as a reward, many informants cooperate with law enforcement agencies to receive a reduced sentence for a pending criminal matter. Regardless of the form of compensation, the department's policy must address (1) the circumstances under which an informant qualifies for an award and/or reward, (2) who can authorize such payments, and (3) the conditions under which payments will be granted.

Although many informants receive substantial awards when they locate the assets of drug dealers, agency budgets may limit the dollar amount of rewards paid to informants. For this reason, investigators should exercise caution when explaining the payment policy to informants. They should avoid mentioning a specific dollar amount that the informant will receive. Otherwise, the informant may try to hold the department to that amount, regardless of future budgetary constraints.

In addition to providing awards and rewards, departments can reimburse informants for expenses incurred during an investigation. In fact, the department may want to reimburse the CI with small amounts of money beyond actual expenses as added incentives to continue working.

It is highly recommended that informants be paid only in the presence of witnesses, with the final payment being made after all court proceedings have been completed to help ensure the informant's presence at the trial. Once a payment is made, a record documenting the date, exact amount, and payer must be included in the CI file in anticipation of future court inquiries.

OTHER SOURCES FOR INFORMATION

Patrol officers are a valuable asset to narcotics investigators, and every effort should be made by investigators to foster a good relationship with them. Patrol officers have inherent advantages over investigators because they already have a routine presence in neighborhoods where drug activity takes place, allowing them to collect specific information without arousing suspicion. Furthermore, patrol officers are familiar with the layout of neighborhoods and, on occasion, specific houses or buildings, making them invaluable in planning surveillance or raids.[75] Patrol officers may also have unofficial informants who may be parlayed into formal informants for narcotics investigators. Because of the additional resources that they offer,

developing relationships with patrol officers is a sound strategy in drug investigations.

Information from Private Sector Sources

The private sector can provide a wealth of information valuable to drug cases about suspects and their behavior. Drug offenders tend to come into contact with a predictable group of private sector businesses, such as travel agents, car rental employees, hotel clerks, retail clerks, and pharmacists, who may volunteer information to investigators.[76] Travel agents can show investigators patterns of travel that may outline trafficking destinations. Retail clerks may be able to tell officers about customers who repeatedly purchase large quantities of the materials found in crystal meth. Realtors are often able to obtain floor plans for homes they have sold, aiding in the planning of raids or searches.

Telephone/cellular phone providers and Internet service providers are also valuable tools to investigators. Internet service providers can pull and track e-mails that may be pertinent to investigations. This generally requires a court order. Lists of telephone calls made from a phone must also be obtained via subpoena. This information is one of the most important tools available to a narcotics investigator as it allows them to track communications between drug offenders, leading to identification of other involved parties or triangulation of hiding places, clandestine labs, and the like.[77]

Outside Agencies

Outside agencies can also offer a wealth of information about a suspect in a narcotics investigation. Outside police agencies, such as the Drug Enforcement Administration (DEA), the Federal Bureau of Investigation (FBI), the Internal Revenue Service (IRS), Immigration and Customs Enforcement (ICE), and others, may have useful information or resources to offer investigators. For example, the IRS may be investigating a suspect on money laundering charges and could provide information pertinent to that suspect's drug activities. Investigators should keep in mind, however, that not all outside law-enforcement agencies are forthcoming with information that they have obtained about a suspect. Often, developing relationships with agents in organizations that an investigator has frequent contact with is a good way to obtain information that would not normally be shared with other agencies.

Many agencies use shared databases where information about ongoing cases, upcoming busts, and suspects is available at the click of a mouse. Police agencies may subscribe to such databases or may obtain access by way of task forces or other forms of interagency cooperation.

Internal Records

One of the best sources of information for investigations is the drug unit's own police department. Investigators should look for the following types of information when searching for intelligence on a suspect, criminal organization, or geographical area: police intelligence reports organized by suspect name, address, or type of criminal activity; incident reports that contain records of previous offenses; National Crime Information Center (NCIC) records, which contain in-depth information on a person's criminal history; field interview cards filled out routinely by patrol officers investigating criminal activity; traffic citations, which are helpful in obtaining physical descriptions and other identifiers; fingerprint files; arrest records; and warrant files, which include detailed information about a suspect or a physical location.[78]

SURVEILLANCE

Surveillance, defined as the "surreptitious observation of persons, places, objects, or conveyances for the purpose of determining criminal involvement,"[79] is an excellent tool used by narcotics investigators to gather information about a suspect. Surveillance is required to corroborate intelligence from informants, confirm criminal activity, obtain probable cause and to gather intelligence about a suspect's routines and behaviors that may be of use in planning apprehension.

Surveillance is an expensive and very time-consuming activity. It requires the efforts of multiple officers at a time, including a supervisor. Equipment required for surveillance, such as binoculars, cameras with telephoto lenses, communication systems, and night-vision devices is costly. Furthermore, officers may spend long periods of time trying to achieve the objectives of any surveillance operation. Anywhere from a few hours to a couple of weeks may be spent watching a subject, depending on the complexity of an investigation.

Before any type of surveillance begins, officers should have already gathered basic information about a suspect. Physical descriptions of the suspect and his or her vehicle are crucial, as well as descriptions of associates. The suspect's home and business address should be ascertained, in addition to the addresses of locations he or she frequents.

Once this basic information has been determined, investigators should scout out the locations where surveillance will take place. Investigators should map out the area, finding the best places from which to conduct surveillance. It is also a good idea to become familiar with the layout of the area, noting street names and traffic conditions to ensure maximum mobility. Officers should also determine what types of vehicles are more likely to go unnoticed in the area, and how they should dress so that they don't look suspicious or out of place while conducting surveillance.

Electronic Surveillance

Electronic surveillance is often used to supplement mobile and stationary surveillance and is also very useful as supporting evidence in court cases. However, electronic surveillance is also subject to a number of legal considerations because of its intrusive nature. Officers should familiarize themselves with case law relevant to electronic surveillance and always consult with prosecutors before utilizing these types of surveillance.

The most prominent method of electronic surveillance is wiretapping, using third-party eavesdropping devices placed on telephone lines to capture conversations. As often as wiretaps are seen as investigative tools on fictional law enforcement television shows, they are actually used as a last resort in many cases. They are very expensive and time-intensive. Furthermore, they are quite complex, legally speaking. In *Katz v. United States*, 389 U.S. 347 (1967), the United States Supreme Court held that wiretaps create an intrusion into a person's reasonable expectation of privacy and therefore constitute a "search and seizure" as defined by the Fourth Amendment to the Constitution of the United States. As a result, wiretaps require probable cause and a warrant to authorize the intrusion. However, they are a very useful tool in many complex investigations.

When an officer is a party to a conversation with a suspect, generally in cases in which undercover officers are being utilized, he or she can record the conversation without violating the suspect's reasonable expectation of privacy. Recording telephone conversations between an officer and a suspect is allowable then, as is use of a concealed microphone.

Pen registers are another means of telephone surveillance. These tools decode the dialed impulses on phone lines in order to record all numbers dialed from that phone. They record the date and time of all phone calls and thus are effective tools when the suspect routinely uses his/her phone to conduct drug transactions. However, the information gained is of little value unless investigators invest time into following up information obtained by the pen registers.

Video and Photo Surveillance

Known as *visual surveillance*, the use of both still and video cameras to corroborate audio surveillance and officer observation is important to drug investigations and their prosecution. When using still photography, investigators can use 35-mm or small digital cameras to document criminal activity. Although basic camera setups are sufficient, attachments such as telephoto lenses and night-vision equipment can enhance photographs. Date and time stamps on cameras may also be helpful for purposes of corroboration.

Video cameras provide a more complete document of surveillance activity than photographs do and can also be fitted with night-vision or infrared equipment for nighttime surveillance.[80]

Trash

Searching through discarded trash is another supplement to surveillance. Often suspects may discard documents or materials that are helpful to investigators trying to

◄ **FIGURE 20-19**
Drug dog in action
Canines provide an invaluable service to police officers in detecting the presence of drugs in clandestine places. They are often used during search warrant executions as well as during routine checks of international flights to detect smuggled drugs and paraphernalia. (© Daniel Munoz/Reuters/Landov)

establish probable cause. For example, crystal meth manufacturers often discard telltale signs that they are operating a meth lab, such as large quantities of empty blister packs that contained pseudoephedrine pills or battery packages. Investigators should take care to remain surreptitious when retrieving and going through a suspect's trash. *Trashing,* as it is sometimes called, does not require a warrant, because there is no expectation of privacy with discarded trash that is essentially in plain view for all to see.

UNDERCOVER OPERATIONS

Often portrayed by popular television and movies, undercover drug operations are actually used quite sparingly by law enforcement. These operations are very dangerous and can take a large toll on the personal lives of undercover officers. However, they are quite useful in identifying participants in drug conspiracies, whether they involve manufacturers, distributors, or users. Undercover officers can often predict which participants may be cooperative with law enforcement and are able to identify evidence for prosecution of drug crimes. They are often privy to locations of drugs or other evidence and usually know the locations of drug proceeds as well. The undercover officer is also very useful in determining the time and place appropriate for search and seizures and arrests[81] (Figure 20-19).

The officers selected for undercover work ultimately determine the success of the operation. They should be intelligent, reliable, confident, resourceful, and have good judgment and excellent communication skills. They should also have a solid knowledge base of the types(s) of drug they are investigating. Training is essential to the success of the undercover officer. Experienced undercover officers should always be the first choice for assignments, unless a less-experienced officer has a special skill required in the investigation that other officers do not (such as Spanish-language proficiency).[82]

Undercover operations may be as simple as a one-off purchase from a dealer or as in-depth as posing as someone who possesses a special skill needed by a drug trafficker, such as a truck driver or a pilot. The amount of preparation and back story needed will vary depending on the complexity of the operations. Smaller operations are the norm in drug investigations, and minimizing the contact between undercover officers and suspects is ideal, because the longer a suspect and officer have contact, the more likely it is that the officer will be discovered. Long-term undercover operations are expensive and dangerous, and generally are not used by local law enforcement entities.

Buying drugs from a suspect is the best means of gathering evidence about a drug operation. When an undercover officer develops a relationship with a suspect, he or she will generally have many opportunities to purchase drugs as evidence. Officers should have some type of monitored surveillance, such as a hidden microphone, ongoing throughout the transaction, allowing for corroboration as well as officer safety. This is a situation unique to drug investigations, because the officer is actually participating in the commission of a crime. This is lawful, provided that it can be shown that the suspect would have committed the act with or without the presence of the officer.[83] **Drug buy operations** by undercover officers generally fall under one of four categories.

Buy-Walk

These types of buys are usually made as part of an ongoing investigation whereby investigators attempt to make cases against distributors by working up the ladder to the source or merely attempting to gain the confidence of the seller. In buy-walk cases, the undercover officer purchases

►**FIGURE 20-20**
Undercover officer making an immediate narcotics arrest on the street
"Buy/Bust" operations are commonly used by the police to control drug traffic. Most often, they yield low amounts of drugs and cash but are designed to have an immediate impact on the visible trade in a specific area or neighborhood.
(© Bonnie Kamin/PhotoEdit)

drugs from the suspect but does not initiate an arrest after completion of the deal. The officer often makes multiple buys from the suspect. This method fosters a business relationship with the suspect and generates a number of investigative leads. Once the suspect feels comfortable with the officer, the officer may get an opportunity to identify places of residence and observe other associates.[84] Small, multiple purchases may be chemically analyzed for purity and for signatures that can be traced back to distributors. Furthermore, with each drug purchase, larger quantities may be negotiated in order to pinpoint the source of the drugs. One successful technique is to work up to requesting a quantity that the dealer is incapable of providing without traveling to his or her supplier and then conducting vehicle surveillance to identify the supplier.[85]

Buy-Bust

In the buy-bust, the undercover officer completes a drug buy, resulting in the immediate arrest of the seller (Figure 20-20). These operations generally take place only with small amounts of drugs or cash and are considered very dangerous to the undercover officer, owing to the proximity between the officer and the suspect when the arrest commences. Undercover officers should not be physically involved with the arrest and should in fact back away from the situation as much as possible once they have completed the transaction. This method is generally used in small cases, where conspiracies are not involved.[86]

Buy(Flash)/Bust

This is the most commonly used technique in undercover drug enforcement operations. The "flash" is a large quantity of money that an undercover officer shows to a sus-

pect without actually giving it to them. It serves as a guarantee that the undercover officer can pay for a large quantity of drugs upon delivery. This operation is very dangerous; undercover officers have been murdered for the flash money, which can range from $5,000 to $100,000. Following is a list of considerations essential to ensuring safe management of the buy(flash)/bust:[87]

1. Whenever possible, isolate the suspects and get them on neutral ground to do the transaction.
2. Do not allow the suspects to isolate the undercover officer. The best way to avoid this is by staying on neutral ground. The undercover officer should dictate the time and the place to the suspects.
3. Flash the money in an open location, isolating suspects from one another if possible. Do not flash the money twice in the same location.
4. Minimize the vulnerability of the undercover officer during the bust.
5. The undercover officer should always be armed.

Flash busts are very effective but must be carefully managed to ensure the safety and the integrity of the investigation. Informants should never be allowed to handle flash rolls, and if possible, two undercover officers should be used in these types of transactions. If one officer handles the money, he/she can leave as soon as the flash is completed, increasing the safety of both officers.[88] Flash busts require extensive training and a consistent policy on the part of police departments, and should only be attempted by experienced undercover officers.

Reverse Operations

The final type of undercover operation is the reverse operation. Reverse undercover operations are those in which the officer acts as the seller of the drug, in an effort to obtain probable cause against drug buyers. This type of operation is more controversial than the buy/busts previously discussed, because of the element of entrapment bound to be brought up in defense claims. Investigators must take care to show other evidence that the buyer was predetermined to commit the crime, with or without the presence of the officer.[89]

Undercover operations are far more complex than a few pages in a textbook can convey. Entire books have been written about the factors involved in such operations, and undercover officers receive careful and in-depth training to help them prepare for all levels of undercover work. Undercover work in narcotics investigation is a valuable tool but requires immense operational planning to be successful and safe.

Informant Purchases

A tool similar to undercover purchases of drugs involves confidential informants obtaining drugs via a controlled purchase. This usually occurs when use of an undercover officer would be impractical. If a peddler will sell only to an informant and not to an undercover officer, the informant must be searched before the sale to make sure that he/she has no narcotics already on his/her person. Officers should ensure that the informant has no money on him, except official funds with recorded serial numbers for the purchase. The informant should be wired with a hidden microphone in order to corroborate the transactions. Surveillance teams should monitor the informant constantly throughout the transaction, and the informant should go to a designated location immediately after the transaction in order to be searched. At that time, evidence should be recovered from the informant, and he or she should be thoroughly debriefed. Evidence obtained through "informant buys" is admissible in court, but the testimony of the informant may be required.

Drug Canines

Drug dogs are extremely useful to narcotics investigations; a positive alert by a canine can provide probable cause to further search a suspect. Dogs have a keen sense of odor, with nearly 30 times more olfactory cells than humans. When properly trained, canines can be used in a variety of settings to detect the presence of drugs. Drug dogs are usually used to provide passive alerts that drugs are present. This means that the dog either sits or uses some other signal (such as a bark) when the odor of drugs is detected. Canines can be used in vehicle examinations, freight examinations, consensual encounters between suspects and officers in homes, airports, businesses, bus stations, and storage facilities. Canines may also be used in limited person examinations.[90]

The Supreme Court ruled in *U.S. v. Place,* 462 US 696 (1983) that use of a drug canine to sniff property is not considered a search. However, use of a drug dog to sniff a person is less clear legally. Many courts have ruled that using canines to sniff a person for presence of drug odors requires reasonable suspicion and that random and suspicionless dog sniffs are not reasonable.[91]

Drug dogs differ from track-and-bite canines, which are taught to be aggressive upon apprehension of a subject. Drug dogs must never use aggression toward a suspect. Canines are a very expensive undertaking for a police department. They must be carefully trained, and a handler must be selected and trained. The training of a drug dog is ongoing and is critical to the admissibility to the any evidence obtained through its use.

Field Testing

A variety of field testing kits are available to law enforcement to give valuable clues about the identity of substances. Field tests can test for the presence of specific substances, including marijuana, cocaine, amphetamine, and heroin. Investigator kits usually include vials of chemicals in small pouches. When small samples of a substance are put into the pouch and then the chemicals in the vials are released, the mixture will produce certain colors. Those colors indicate the presence of controlled substances.[92]

Field tests are easy to perform. They are, however, only presumptive because they may produce false positives. Any drug that will be used as evidence must be positively identified by a qualified chemist. Additionally, a negative test does not preclude the possibility that another similar drug may be present.[93]

HIGH-INTENSITY DRUG TRAFFICKING AREA (HIDTA) PROGRAMS

HIDTA programs are an invaluable resource to narcotics investigations. HIDTA programs were created by the Anti-Drug Abuse Act of 1988 and provide federal assistance to better coordinate and enhance counterdrug law enforcement efforts of local, state, and federal agencies in areas where major drug activity occurs. Currently, there are 31 HIDTAs in the nation, including Puerto Rico and the U.S. Virgin Islands (Figure 20-21). HIDTAs are joint efforts of regional, local, and federal agencies, whose leaders work together to assess regional drug threats, to design strategies to combat those threats, and to develop initiatives to implement the strategies. Regional strategies include building multiagency task forces. HIDTA legislation also provides for investigative support centers in designated areas that create a communications infrastructure that can facilitate information-sharing between agencies.[94] For example, the Washington/Baltimore area HIDTA offers software for participating agencies that provides case management functions and also notifies agencies if another agency is collecting information on the same suspect. They also grant access to a number of databases that allow investigators to access law-enforcement records and financial information.[95] The North Texas HIDTA

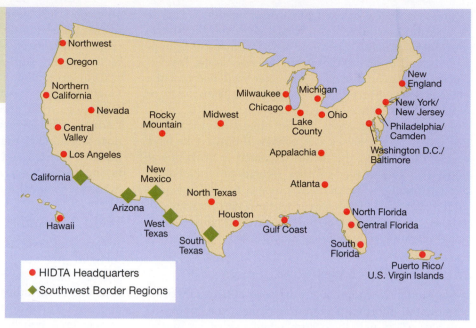

► **FIGURE 20-21**
High-intensity drug trafficking area—HIDTA task force locations
(Office of National Drug Control Policy; see *www.whitehousedrugpolicy.gov/hidta/*)

analyzes information from participating departments, and identifies major drug trafficking organizations, including patterns and trends of these organizations. The North Texas HIDTA's Investigative Support Center prepared 644 intelligence profiles and conducted over 10,000 database searches in 2002. That same year, the North Texas HIDTA seized 23 pounds of methamphetamine in the course of one investigation in the Dallas area, and indicted 24 participants in a crack-cocaine distribution ring in Denton, TX.[96]

HIDTAs are just one example of a task force in action. Each jurisdiction may have its own drug task forces, involving a variety of law enforcement or outside agencies, which are valuable to narcotics investigations. Investigators should take full advantage of these resources, when available.

SEARCHES, SEIZURES, AND WARRANTS

Drug investigations are useless without evidence. Therefore, it is vitally important that an investigator be knowledgeable of the latest legal guidelines that govern the search for, and seizure of, evidence. Case law in the United States provides literally thousands of decisions that affect how officers may handle searches and seizures. There are some major principles, however, that every narcotics investigator should be familiar with in order to present a legally sound case against drug criminals. Things that are commonly searched for and seized in drug crimes include the drugs themselves or other contraband; instrumentalities of a crime, meaning those items that are not necessarily illegal on their own but

that are used to carry out a crime; fruits of a crime, such as things bought with drug proceeds; and mere evidence of a crime.

PROBABLE CAUSE

The general requirements for searches and seizures of evidence or persons are a search warrant or recognized exception to the warrant requirement (to be discussed later) and probable cause. Probable cause to search and seize exists when "facts and circumstances in a given situation are sufficient to warrant a person of reasonable caution to believe that seize-able objects are located at the place to be searched."[97] Generally, a single fact cannot establish probable cause; it is usually several facts and circumstances taken together that do. Probable cause may also be established by hearsay, which is typically the case with informants. This information may be used as long it can be shown that the totality of the circumstances surrounding the information suggests that it is reliable. Information should be verifiable, and corroborating information is helpful in establishing probable cause.[98]

SEARCH WARRANTS

The search warrant is one of the most valuable tools available to a narcotics investigator. The warrant authorizes searches of homes, businesses, and automobiles of subjects and generally results in the arrest of multiple suspects, expediting the investigation and its closure.[99]

Searches require search warrants, or a recognized exception to a warrant in order to be legal. There are four requirements for the valid issuance of a search warrant. The first is that a neutral and impartial magistrate authorizes the warrant. The second requirement is that probable cause exists to search the place described in the warrant. Third, the warrant must be precise in describing both the places and persons to be searched and the items to be seized. Fourth, the warrant requires a supporting oath or affirmation by the requesting officer. Narcotics officers requesting a warrant should follow additional guidelines when requesting warrants, since so much of the information provided to law enforcement officers comes from confidential informants.

PAST RELIABILITY OF THE CONFIDENTIAL INFORMANT

The past reliability of the confidential informant is of considerable importance, especially when the effort to determine probable cause to obtain a search warrant is based exclusively on such information. One should consider the length of time the applicant has known the informant and the number of occasions on which reliable information was supplied. For example, how many times before did the confidential informant's information result in the seizure of contraband or paraphernalia on persons, on premises, or in vehicles, and how many of these offenses resulted in a conviction? To confirm that the confidential informant has been reliable, the officer should be prepared to cite specific instances of reliable information. Other considerations are the informant's familiarity with the type of offense involved in the affidavit and familiarity with paraphernalia used in connection with the offense.

INFORMATION SUPPLIED BY THE INFORMANT

Information to be considered in this area includes the date, time, and place of the meeting between police and the informant; the substance and content of the information; and the date, time, and place that the information was obtained.

The law-enforcement officer should try to elicit from the informant as many facts as possible that can be corroborated—for example, the telephone number and address of the suspect's residence, a physical description of the suspect, the occupation of the suspect, vehicles owned or operated by the suspect, a description of the vehicle and the tag number, and the time at which the suspect may be observed at the premises or within the described vehicle.

CORROBORATION OF THE INFORMATION SUPPLIED

All efforts should be made to corroborate information supplied by a confidential informant. In some instances, corroboration is a simple check of the accuracy of portions of the information, such as the suspect's address, associates, vehicle, hangouts, patterns of behavior, and criminal record. When information is corroborated, careful records should be kept, including the date, time, and method of corroboration. Some jurisdictions have found it useful to attach a mug shot of the suspect along with a photograph, diagram, or sketch of the property, vehicle, store, or other place to be searched.

There are also requirements for the valid execution of a search warrant. The first is that time limits set out in the warrant or by statute are observed. This requirement ensures that probable cause remains until the warrant is executed. Next, time-of-day limits should be observed. This means that officers should serve warrants at a reasonable hour, mostly because of safety and privacy concerns. Officers must knock and announce their presence before gaining entry to a home or business, unless an exigency exists. Another requirement states that police can not go beyond the terms spelled out in the search warrant. Finally, officers must leave an inventory of items seized with both the suspect and the judge who issued the search warrant.

THE EXCLUSIONARY RULE

This rule states that courts will exclude any evidence that is obtained in violation of the Fourth Amendment's provisions against unreasonable searches and seizures, no matter how pertinent it is to the case at hand. This includes *Fruit of the Poisoned Tree* items. This means that evidence recovered from constitutionally sound methods may be excluded if the initial action was proven to be illegal. For example, an officer may legally search a person incident to their arrest. However, if that initial arrest is later determined to be illegal, the items recovered during the postarrest search may be thrown out.[100] There are exceptions to the exclusionary rule, however. The first is the *Good Faith Exception*. This states that if officers act in reasonable reliance on a search warrant that is issued by a neutral magistrate but is ultimately found to be invalid, the evidence may still be used.[101] The second is the *doctrine of inevitable discovery*. This doctrine holds that evidence that would have been discovered with or without the illegal search or seizure is allowed into court.[102] The computer errors exception allows evidence to be admitted even though the search or seizure was based on an erroneous piece of information.[103]

WARRANTLESS SEARCHES

There are cases where warrants are not necessary, although these are each fairly narrowly defined by the courts. The first is the consent search. These types of searches are permissible without a warrant and without probable cause as long as consent has been voluntarily given by a person who has authority to give consent and that the scope of the search doesn't exceed the consent given. Narcotics officers should keep in mind that the scope of a consent search must be consistent with the nature of the consent given and that the consenter can place limitations on the search.

Vehicle searches are also exempt from the warrant requirement. This is a boon to narcotics officers, because many drug traffickers conceal drugs within their vehicles. The logic behind allowing warrantless searches of vehicles is that there is a reduced expectation of privacy in vehicles because they are mobile and used in public areas, their interiors are visible to the outside, and because vehicles are highly regulated by the government.

Vehicles also create an exigency in that they are inherently moveable. In other words, by the time a narcotics officer is able to write an affidavit and obtain a warrant, the vehicle may be gone. As a result, a narcotics officer may stop a car based on reasonable suspicion and then search that vehicle, including all passenger areas, containers, and the trunk when they have probable cause to believe evidence or contraband is contained.[104]

Vehicles that have been lawfully impounded may also be searched without a warrant, but the search may not be a pretense for further investigation. Searches of impounded vehicles are allowed for the safety of officers and the impounding agency, and as a result must take place within agency guidelines and procedures.

Open-field searches are another type of search that can take place without a warrant. The Supreme Court has held that open fields outside the curtilage surrounding buildings or homes are not constitutionally protected and are therefore allowable without a search warrant. There is no reasonable expectation of privacy in an open field.[105] This particular exception is useful to narcotics officers who might encounter marijuana fields in their investigations.

Another situation in which a search warrant is not required is an exigent situation known as the evanescent evidence exception. In this case, evidence is likely to disappear in the time it would take to get a warrant. In drug cases, this could involve drugs that may be flushed down the toilet in the time needed to secure a warrant. The evanescent evidence exception requires a rough approximation of probable cause and the evidence must be seized in a reasonable manner. Officers may also search without a warrant if there is a threat of a subject escaping in the time it would take to get a warrant, or if there is danger to a person's life.[106]

Plain-view searches may also be conducted without a warrant. Officers may confiscate evidence that they find in plain sight, which is a useful tool to narcotics officers. Often, drug paraphernalia that may be useful evidence are left in plain view. The Supreme Court has ruled that "objects falling in the plain view of an officer who has a right to be in the position to have that view are subject to seizure and may be used as evidence."[107] However, officers may not move other objects to gain a better view of evidence otherwise hidden from view, and the objects cannot be in a position where officers would have to dislodge or move it to examine it closely.

Stop-and-frisk searches are another example of the warrantless search. These are conducted in the interest of officer safety and/or crime prevention. To stop a suspect, the officer must have articulable facts and reasonable suspicion that criminal activity is afoot. For further procession to a frisk, which is essentially a pat-down of a suspect's outer clothing, there must be reasonable facts to suggest that the individual is presently armed and dangerous.[108] If the officer happens to come across drug paraphernalia during the frisk, that evidence would be admissible in court.

Finally, searches incident to arrest are allowable without a search warrant. In these cases, officers are allowed to search the area under the immediate control of the suspect, which is essentially their armspan.[109] In an automobile, this includes the entire passenger compartment of the vehicle, including the glove box if it is unlocked[110] (Figure 20-22). If the arrest occurs in the suspect's home, then the officers are allowed to make a protective search of the home to look for additional suspects. Plain view doctrine would apply in such a case.[111]

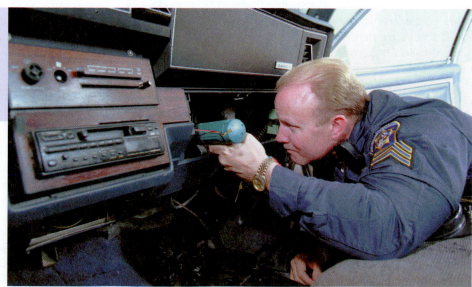

► FIGURE 20-22
Officer searching vehicle for drugs
Once the contraband has been detected by the dogs, an officer will thoroughly and painstakingly search the car. (© AP Photo/Rich Pedroncelli)

SEARCH PROCEDURES

Once a search begins, narcotics officers should survey the entire site and make a determination as to the best way to conduct the search, keeping the legal aspects of searches in mind. The leader of the search should establish a work station where paperwork can be filled out and evidence collected.

Searches should be careful, thorough, systematic, and within the limitations of the search warrant. Most drug searches permit the opening of packages, checking the insides of light fixtures, and looking in ceiling panels and other potential hiding places. Other places that should be checked are attics and crawl spaces; furnace ducts; plumbing access panels; furniture (including mattresses and boxsprings); dresser drawers; kitchen appliances; food containers; children's furniture and toys; and personal property such as cameras, storage sheds, garages, and other outbuildings. Each room should be subject to two separate searches by different individuals to ensure that all areas are covered. Drug criminals are extremely good at hiding money and drugs, making searching for drugs a skill that requires quite a bit of patience and experience.[112]

The following items are generally related to drug crimes and should be listed in the warrant and included in the search:[113]

1. drugs, in any quantity;
2. cash, which should be checked against money lists for buy money from undercover and controlled buys;
3. drug packaging and processing materials, such as plastic baggies, balloons, and so on;
4. drug paraphernalia;
5. weapons;
6. paperwork, which can include address books with drug contacts, personal correspondence, notes, telephone bills, and other records of possible drug transactions;
7. financial records;
8. computers;
9. keys (a key to a target location may prove a suspect's direct connection to it);
10. surveillance equipment;
11. other items specifically relevant to the investigation at hand.

Searches should be well documented, with photographs taken of evidence in its original place and with narratives detailing where evidence was found and who found it. The suspect and the warrant judge, as noted earlier, should receive a detailed inventory of anything removed from the location as evidence.

EVIDENCE HANDLING

Aside from the burglaries, larcenies, and other crimes committed because of narcotics, additional related problems sprout from the drug-culture vine. Some of these growths entwine the individual police officer and the overall police function. One offshoot, the handling and securing of narcotics and dangerous drugs after they are collected and seized, has emerged as an area of growing concern to police administrators for a number of reasons (Figure 20-23).

Once seized by the police, narcotic and dangerous-drug evidence requires protection so that it may be preserved in its original state until it is brought before a court or destroyed through a legal process. It is during this period that the greatest demands are placed on personnel of the law enforcement agency concerned. Narcotic and dangerous-drug evidence must be protected not only against loss and outside threats of incursion but, unfortunately, sometimes from internal theft as well.

◀ FIGURE 20-23 Drug seizures
Large seizures of drugs pose special problems and considerations for testing the concentration and holding of evidence for trial. In most cases, samples of the large seizure are tested, and only a small portion of the drugs are actually kept as evidence. Most courts allow a sample of the drugs to be admitted as evidence along with officer/agent testimony linking the sample with the confiscated seizure. The remaining drugs are then destroyed after testing. (© AP Photo/Davide Karp)

►**FIGURE 20-24**
Money and Drugs
During sophisticated investigations involving large-scale operations, it is not uncommon to seize huge caches of cash. Literally, millions of dollars are bartered each year in the drug trade, making for high-stake risks and potentially dangerous situations.
(© AP Photo/Nam Y. Huh)

Although relatively uncommon, there have been occasions when narcotic and dangerous drug evidence, as well as large caches of money, has disappeared from a "secure" area under the control and within the confines of a police agency (Figure 20-24). The following methods for handling drug evidence will go far in addressing this concern and minimizing its occurrence.[114]

There are two recognized methods for introducing narcotic and dangerous-drug evidence into the processing sequence immediately after it is seized and marked. Neither method omits any of the processing steps; the difference is found in the manner in which the sequential steps are arranged.

The first method (the laboratory-first method) requires that all seized evidence (after it is field tested, marked, photographed, weighed, and initially inventoried) be transported immediately to the laboratory for analysis. Drop boxes are provided in the laboratory for the deposit of evidence during periods when the facility is not operational. All seized narcotic and dangerous-drug evidence is taken directly to a room in the vicinity of the laboratory. This room, known as an inventory room or a display room, is specially equipped for inventorying narcotic and dangerous-drug evidence and is not used for any other purpose. Weighing scales, cameras, film holders, lighting equipment, evidence seals, evidence containers, appropriate forms, desks, typewriters, tables or counters, and necessary administrative supplies are maintained in the room. When not in use, the room is locked, and the keys (two) are retained in a secure location (normally, one key is kept in the laboratory and the other is controlled by the watch supervisor or desk officer). To achieve even greater control over inventory rooms, departments that

have a high volume of narcotic evidence are employing more sophisticated entry-control systems, including "entry" or "swipe" cards on a system that records the cardholder's identity and time of entry and departure. Video cameras may also be used to record all behavior in the inventory room.

After seizure of the evidence and while en route to police headquarters, the seizing officer requests a witnessing officer of supervisory grade (at least one grade above that held by the seizing officer) and a member of the laboratory staff (technician on duty) or a technician from the mobile laboratory unit, if available, to meet with him or her at the narcotic and dangerous-drug inventory room. When the supervisory official arrives at the inventory room, the seizing officer displays the material seized (the witnessing officer does not handle any of the evidence). After the evidence package has been marked and displayed in the manner best suited for a photographic inventory, the laboratory technician photographs the evidence (the photographer does not handle any of the evidence). When photographs of the evidence have been taken, the evidence is weighed and inventoried under the direct supervision of the supervisory officer. Appropriate forms are then completed and witnessed, and the evidence is sealed in containers or envelopes provided for that purpose.

After these steps have been accomplished, in company with the witnessing officer and the laboratory technician, the seizing officer carries the evidence to the laboratory drop box and deposits it therein. If the drop box cannot accommodate the evidence package, the laboratory evidence-room custodian or an alternate is requested to come to the laboratory, assume custody of the evidence, and store it in the laboratory evidence room. If the evidence is taken to the laboratory during normal operational hours, the drop box is not used; the evidence is turned over directly to the laboratory evidence custodian or alternate.

On completion of the analytical process by the laboratory, the evidence is delivered to the narcotic and dangerous-drug evidence room in the property room. Here, the evidence custodian assumes control of the evidence and provides for its preservation and subsequent processing as required.

In the second method (the evidence-room-first method), seized narcotic and dangerous-drug evidence, after being field tested, marked, photographed, weighed, and inventoried, is sealed in an appropriate container and deposited in a drop box or delivered directly to the evidence room in the property room. There are variations to the procedure; in some cases, certain intermediate steps (photographing the evidence, for example) are omitted or the initial processing (weighing, photographing, and inventorying) may be accomplished in the property room or evidence room. The single difference between the two methods is that in one the evidence is analyzed before it is stored, whereas in the other the evidence is taken directly to the narcotic and dangerous-drug evidence room (or to an adjunct depository), receipted, and then removed to the laboratory for analysis.

Of the two methods used for introducing narcotic and dangerous-drug evidence into the processing sequence, the laboratory-first procedure is preferred and should be followed whenever possible. The main advantage of this method is that it reduces actual handling of the evidence and decreases the number of custody transfer points. By first delivering the evidence to the laboratory, the evidence must undergo only one journey to the narcotic and dangerous-drug evidence room—that is, after analysis, rather than before and after. Consequently, the exposure of the evidence to various loss hazards is reduced and its security is enhanced.

It must be recognized, however, that establishment of the laboratory-first method depends on the existence of certain features that are not available to many law enforcement agencies. The laboratory-first method requires that a mobile laboratory unit or laboratory technician be on call for around-the-clock operation. Also, this method requires an easily accessible laboratory—preferably located in the same building housing the headquarters of the police agency itself.

PHARMACEUTICAL DIVERSIONS

The diversion of pharmaceutical drugs is considered an increasing problem within the drug enforcement community, especially with the popularity of narcotic drugs such as OxyContin. Health-care professionals are sometimes involved with the distribution of controlled substances from hospitals, clinics, pharmacies, and doctor's offices. In fact, the DEA has estimated that around 13,000 practicing physicians or pharmacists may be involved in the illegal diversion of drugs.[115] Investigation of these types of activities are difficult because doctors and other health professionals are usually seen as highly educated, productive members of society. Diversions are also easy to cover up. Careful records regarding controlled substances are required to be kept by doctors and pharmacists, but suspicious fires, break-ins, and robberies may act as covers for drug shortages or the destruction of records. Furthermore, many investigators are unfamiliar with the problem of diversion and how to deal with it.

Doctors and Diversion

There are generally four types of doctors who divert drugs. The first is the dishonest physician, who profits from the illegal sale of controlled substances. The second is the impaired doctor, who diverts drugs for his or her own use and addiction. The third type is the dated doctor. The dated doctor has been in practice for a number of years and may be willing to hand out drugs to anyone who appears to have a legitimate reason. These doctors are generally unwilling to conform to new rules and regulations about prescription drugs. Finally, there's the gullible physician who falls victim to scams by patients regarding prescription drugs. Gullible physicians are not considered criminals.[116]

Among the most common indications that a physician may be unlawfully diverting drugs are these:

- A physician places excessively frequent orders for narcotics.
- A physician picks up and pays for filled narcotics prescriptions from a pharmacy.
- A physician places an emergency call for a narcotic medication to a pharmacy and requests delivery. The deliverer is met by the physician and given a prescription for the drugs. In some instances, no patient exists, or if one does exist, the narcotics are retained by the physician, and other medication is substituted.
- A narcotics prescription is issued to a patient by a physician with instructions to have it filled and to return with the drug for administration. Substitute medication is then given to the patient.
- In narcotics records, a physician uses fictitious or deceased people's names and addresses.
- The physician frequently requests that a prescription for an alleged patient be taken to the pharmacy by a nurse, a receptionist, or a member of the family and be returned to the doctor personally.
- While other physicians are in the operating room or making hospital rounds, the addict-physician searches their vehicles or medical bags for narcotics.
- A physician obtains a key to the narcotics locker in a hospital and has a duplicate made.

- A physician may place an order for a patient in a hospital; when the drug is prepared by a nurse, the doctor takes it over and either uses a substitute syringe containing a placebo or administers only a small portion of the drug.

Nurses and Diversion

Nurses tend to be more likely to divert drugs for their personal use than to divert drugs for resale. Investigators may choose to deal with personal diversions far differently than they would diversions that are destined for resale.

CLANDESTINE DRUG LABORATORIES

Clandestine drug laboratories throughout the United States produce a variety of illegal drugs for sale and distribution. The processes used in production of these drugs range in their degree of sophistication from primitive to advanced. By the same token, those who operate such laboratories may range in expertise from the novice experimenter to the professional chemist. These factors alone can have a serious impact on the safety of the general public and on police and fire department personnel who may deal with these laboratories in enforcement and emergency situations.[117]

Raids conducted on clandestine drug laboratories are inherently dangerous, irrespective of the dangers associated with taking suspects into custody. The degree of danger is based largely on the types of chemicals that are typically used and the chemical processes employed. These dangers may be heightened by the operator's lack of expertise and experience and by the physical limitations and restrictions of the facility being used, as well as by weather conditions and other factors. Such dangers cannot be overemphasized. Major accidents resulting in loss of life have occurred during raids conducted on such facilities by those who are untrained, inexperienced, or careless in the dismantling, handling, transportation, storage, or disposal of the involved chemicals.

Normally, direct physical involvement with drug laboratories takes place during the execution of a search warrant on a suspect property. Under these circumstances, there is generally enough information to forewarn police officers about the nature of the operations and the types of chemicals that are most likely involved. Adequate safety precautions can thus be developed and employed. However, police officers may inadvertently encounter a laboratory operation while conducting other enforcement or investigatory operations. In such instances, unless there is imminent danger of loss of life, police officers and civilians alike should be restricted from entering laboratory premises. Clandestine laboratories typically employ processes using chemicals that are toxic, corrosive, caustic, and flammable. The laboratory environment may pose explosive toxic or carcinogenic risks that should be dealt with only by specially trained and equipped personnel.

IDENTIFYING LABORATORY OPERATIONS

Clandestine laboratory operations are typically identified in one of four ways. In some instances, fire departments responding to the scene of a fire or explosion find evidence of laboratory operations. Positive determinations, however, depend on the ability of emergency service personnel to recognize the type of substances and equipment typically used in such operations. Therefore, these personnel must be trained in identification of clandestine lab operations. Since fire departments should be close at hand during police raids of drug laboratories, responsible personnel from both agencies should develop a working relationship in dealing with problems that arise from these types of operations.

Evidence of drug laboratory operations may also be generated through informants. Laboratory operators who are attempting to establish operations in a new community often need to determine sources for the purchase of specific chemicals. Plans for development of a lab and related involvement of suppliers or distributors frequently are revealed by confidential informants and intelligence gathered from arrestees.

The community at large may also provide valuable tips on laboratory operations on the basis of observations of unusual activities or circumstances. Many drug labs operate in urban or suburban residential communities where citizens who are alerted to the common signs of laboratory operations can provide valuable information to the police. These indicators include:

- A residence where one or more individuals visit but where no one lives. Laboratory operators are generally cautious about the risks of fire, explosion, or contamination and attempt to limit their exposure and risk.
- Residences or other buildings that have sealed doors and windows, although they are not abandoned facilities.
- The presence of ventilating fans that operate irrespective of weather conditions.
- A strong ammonia or related odor.
- An unfurnished "residence."
- A "resident" who frequently goes outside for a cigarette or to get some air.

Although these circumstances do not prove the existence of an illegal drug manufacturing operation, several of these factors together may be suggestive enough to warrant establishment of low-profile police surveillance.

METH LABS

Meth labs have been around since the 1960s, when they were organized and operated by outlaw motorcycle gangs. To stop the spread of "clan labs," chemicals such as ether and ephedrine were restricted by the Chemical Diversion and Trafficking Act of 1988. Rogue chemical companies that sold to clan-lab precursors were prosecuted and put out of business by the DEA and other local, state, and federal law enforcement agencies.[118]

In the late 1980s and early 1990s, the biker manufacturers began to be edged out of the market by new and very violent methamphetamine manufacturers—the Mexican national methamphetamine organizations. Today, they dominate the meth manufacturing market. Their industrial-size labs are producing methamphetamine in mass quantities for distribution across the United States. This is evidenced by recent DEA operations that resulted in methamphetamine arrests in California, Texas, and North Carolina.

With the restriction of methamphetamine manufacturing chemicals, lab seizures started to decline in the late 1980s. Since then, however, the trend has been reversed with a vengeance, and lab seizures have started to skyrocket. One of the reasons for this increase is the Internet. Now all a methamphetamine manufacturer has to do is turn on his or her computer, point and click to find a recipe, and point and click again to find the chemicals. If the "meth cook" has any questions during the manufacturing process, he/she can simply visit one of the methamphetamine-manufacturing chat pages. These small "tweeker"-type labs are capable of making anywhere from ounce to pound quantities of methamphetamine. Size does not matter when it comes to clan labs; these small labs are just as dangerous for law enforcement officers as are the biker and Mexican national labs.

Meth labs can be broken down into six different styles:

- Biker or traditional;
- Mexican national;
- cold-cook;
- pressure cooker;
- hydrogenation;
- tweeker.

Chemicals used to manufacture methamphetamine are easily obtainable, even with chemical restrictions. Laboratory equipment used to manufacture methamphetamine runs the full spectrum from the scientific to the yard-sale purchase. Heating mantles, condensers, vacuum pumps, buchner funnels, and 22-liter reaction vessels are regularly seized at clandestine labs. Not wanting to attract attention of law enforcement, clandestine laboratory equipment manufacturers are turning to other types of clan-lab equipment. They now use pressure cookers, hot plates, mason jars, sun tea dispensers, nalgene containers, homemade compressed-gas cylinders, Pyrex bowls, sports bottles, microwave ovens, and other such material.[119]

A new method for producing meth without the elaborate laboratories traditionally associated with the drug has many law enforcement agencies concerned. Rather than complex systems of tubing, glassware, and burners, the new method requires only a 2-liter soda bottle, cold pills, and noxious chemicals. Manufacturers shake the bottle and the volatile reaction produces methamphetamines. Known as **shake and bake,** this new approach requires a much smaller amount of pseudoephedrine, allowing the manufacturer to slip under the radar and avoid the repercussions of the Combat Meth Act. Unlike the laboratory method, no flame is required to produce the drug and it can be made in a home, car, or even a space as small as lavatory stall.[120] This is particularly worrisome, because it allows meth addicts to make their own supply at home, instead of buying mass produced quantities from a dealer. As a result of this popular new method, meth arrests that had been declining ever since the Combat Meth Act was implemented are on the rise again.

Shake and bake scenarios are not only quick and easy for meth addicts to use, they are exceedingly dangerous. While there is no open flame, the chemical reaction taking place inside the 2-liter bottle is extremely violent and volatile. Opening the cap too soon, for example, can result in a huge flash fire causing extreme burns on unlucky addicts.

CATCHING COOKS: METH MONITORS

After the Combat Methamphetamine Epidemic Act of 2005 was enacted, the availability of ingredients used in the manufacture of methamphetamines became much more difficult to assemble. The legislation required pharmacies and retailers to limit access to, and record sales of, over-the-counter products containing pseudoephedrine, ephedrine, and phenylpropanolamine. However, the large paper log books used by many retailers initially were a cumbersome means of tracking manufacturers. Often—and particularly during cold and flu season where sales of those ingredients for legitimate purposes are highest—there were thousands of records to maintain, and the books presented a threat for identity theft for those who had to sign it. Furthermore, there was no way that pharmacies, retailers, or law enforcement could see whether or not those purchasing the medications were "smurfing"—that is, visiting a number of retail establishments in the area in order to obtain the quantity needed.

However, several companies have introduced database systems that allow retailers to enter information and identifiers for those purchasing pseudoephedrine medications. A pharmacy can enter in an individual's information into the database and determine immediately if he or she has already reached the limits proscribed in the Combat Meth Act at other locations. This also allows law enforcement to track suspects, recognize patterns, and develop leads to identify meth laboratories in real time. *Leadsonlabs.com* is one such database, and users of the software report that the ability to network

CONSPIRACY INVESTIGATIONS

A **conspiracy** is defined as two or more people entering into an agreement to violate the law with a commission of one or more overt acts in furtherance of the agreement. Drug investigators undertake conspiracy cases when they desire to get the leaders of a drug organization who may not handle drug transactions and would otherwise be too insulated from the day-to-day operations by associates operating further down the chain of command. The law of conspiracy makes it possible for each conspirator to be held accountable for the actions of anyone else involved.[121]

There are three main types of conspiracies. The first is the *chain conspiracy*. In a chain conspiracy, the investigator must show that a group of conspirators are all working toward a common goal, depending on one another to further the success of the scheme. Each participant must be aware that their success depends on each member of the conspiracy.

In the more complex *wheel conspiracy*, there is a central or primary conspirator called the *hub*. The hub makes an agreement with other conspirators, referred to as *spokes*. Each spoke is aware of everyone else's role in the scheme. All are bound together by the *rim*, which is a common agreement, tying each person to the conspiracy.

Finally, the *enterprise conspiracy* is defined by federal statutes. In this type of conspiracy, the enterprise may have a number of different criminal activities going on. These activities are called *racketeering* and include such things as drug violations, loan-sharking, mail fraud, bribery, counterfeiting, and obstruction of justice. The members of an enterprise do not have to be aware of one another's roles, and investigators have to show only that members have agreed to participate in the enterprise. Enterprise conspiracies in narcotics investigations must obviously include drug violations, as well as one other activity defined under racketeering.[122]

GANGS AND DRUGS

Street gangs, outlaw motorcycle gangs, and prison gangs are the main distributors of drugs in the United States. Currently, there are about 31,000 gangs and 850,000 active gang members in the country.[123] Gangs present numerous problems for narcotics investigators, because they are difficult to infiltrate. Their use of violence makes confidential informants scarce, and undercover operations are exceptionally risky to the officer.

Street gangs are located throughout the country in cities of various sizes and characteristics. Large, well-organized gangs are the most likely to be involved with drug trafficking, because their networks allow for the manufacture, sale, transportation, and distribution of drugs throughout the nation. These gangs are mostly involved with drugs such as cocaine, heroin, and marijuana. Violence is employed regularly within these gangs in an effort to control and expand distribution activities.

Outlaw motorcycle gangs are smaller than street gangs but are highly organized. The three main outlaw motorcycle gangs are the Hell's Angels Motorcycle Club, the Banditos, and the Outlaws Motorcycle Club. The primary drugs associated with outlaw motorcycle gangs are methamphetamine, marijuana, and cocaine. Like street gangs, outlaw motorcycle gangs have been known to use violence to further distribution activities.

Prison gangs are much smaller than street or outlaw motorcycle gangs and are aligned along racial or ethnic lines. The most prominent prison gangs include the Aryan Nation, Mexican Mafia, and Nuestra Familia. These gangs consist of a select group of inmates who are organized into a hierarchy and operate within prisons and on the streets to distribute cocaine, marijuana, methamphetamine, and heroin. These gangs are notoriously difficult to infiltrate and are considered extremely violent and dangerous.[124]

PARADIGM SHIFT

For decades, police have fought a "war against drugs," the efforts of which you have read about throughout this chapter. However, at this point in U.S. history, a paradigm shift in drug interdiction may be on the horizon. The Obama administration has begun to consider drug use in this country as a public health issue rather than as a strictly criminal one. Director of the Office of National Drug Control Policy R. Gil Kerlikowske has recently acknowledged that prevention and treatment (not interdiction and arrest) may be the only ways to effectively curb the problem of drug abuse and addiction. Thus federal funds are being earmarked for programs that fit under the prevention and treatment umbrellas versus police interdiction and arrest strategies.[125] These types of programs include training primary-care physicians to help them to identify patients with drug problems, funding for advanced-treatment facilities, and mentoring/prevention programs for children. These programs have little to do with the law-enforcement strategies addressed in this chapter, but they do herald changes that may affect the funding and implementation of such strategies.

Although a major shift in the fundamental strategies in which law enforcement addresses the issue of illegal drugs may be coming, it still remains doubtful that legalization (or decriminalization) of any drug will occur in the United States anytime soon. Although a few states have recently passed medical marijuana laws, in 2010 Californians voted against a measure that would completely legalize it, sending a clear message that drugs are still seen as a dangerous and destructive force in American society.

KEY TERMS

amphetamines
barbiturates
cannabis
cheese heroin
chiva
clandestine drug laboratories
cocaine
codeine
Combat Methamphetamine Epidemic
   Act of 2005
conspiracy
crack (rock) cocaine
crystallized methamphetamine
depressants (sedatives)
drank
drug buy operations

hallucinogenic drugs
hashish
hashish oil
heroin (diacetylmorphine)
HIDTA
K2
ketamine
khat
lysergic acid diethylamide (LSD)
marijuana
marijuana grow houses
meperidine (Demerol)
mescaline
meth labs
methadone
methaqualone

methcathinone
methylenedioxy methamphetamine
   (MDMA) (ecstasy)
morphine
narcotics
opiates
opium
OxyContin
phencyclidine (PCP)
psilocybin and psilocin
shake and bake
speedballing
stimulants
Strawberry Quick meth
surveillance
synthetic narcotics

REVIEW QUESTIONS

1. What major drugs of abuse are derived from opium?
2. What role does the drug methadone play in treating heroin addicts?
3. What are the acute and chronic effects of cocaine use?
4. What is freebasing?
5. According to the Drug Enforcement Administration, what are drug traffickers attempting to accomplish by introducing Strawberry Quick meth to the market?
6. What is methcathinone?
7. Why is the drug OxyContin so attractive to drug addicts?
8. What is speedballing?
9. What are some of the known side effects of PCP?
10. What are the signs of a Marijuana Grow House Operation?
11. What are the major exceptions to searching without a search warrant?
12. How are clandestine drug laboratory operations typically identified?
13. Which major factors should be considered when attempting to secure a search warrant solely on the basis of information supplied by a confidential informant?
14. What is a HIDTA?
15. Define a conspiracy, and give examples of conspiracy cases.
16. What are the two recognized methods for introducing narcotics and dangerous drugs into the processing sequence immediately after they are seized and marked?

INTERNET ACTIVITIES

1. The U.S. Drug Enforcement Agency website, *www.justice.gov/dea/index.htm*, provides a variety of statistics and information on drug trafficking and use in various countries around the world. For the most recent drug-trafficking intelligence, log on to the website and click "Law Enforcement—Threat Assessment" or "Law Enforcement—Major Operations." Find the most recent reports about Mexico. See how enforcement efforts have recently affected the drug cartels operating on the U.S.-Mexico border.

2. Find out about the changes in abused drugs commonly found on the party scene or at all-night raves. Visit the National Institute of Drug Abuse sponsored website, *www.clubdrugs.gov*, and browse the site for information pertaining to "club drugs" and teenagers. What new drugs are becoming popular among America's youth? How pervasive is inhalant abuse? What are the so-called club drugs?

► America's invasion of Iraq in 2003 and the continued war in Afghanistan have escalated violence against the United States. Terrorist incidents around the world and recent thwarted attacks by individuals operating inside the United States have generated great concern for law enforcement here.

(© Arif Ali/AFP/Getty Images)

21

TERRORISM

The events of September 11, 2001, were clearly the most horrendous and devastating terrorist acts ever to occur on U.S. soil. Few people would take issue with the proposition that 9/11 forever changed the lives of all Americans. The events of that day evoked a sense of national outrage, caused profound losses, and created a sense of vulnerability.

This chapter discusses various aspects of terrorism and their relation to the work of a criminal investigator. It opens with an overview of international terrorism and the international groups that have committed terrorist acts against the United States and its allies. There is specific focus on Middle Eastern groups, since they pose perhaps the greatest threat against America. Increasingly, Middle Eastern groups are recruiting terrorists from American soil, and these "home-grown" terrorists represent an emerging threat to national security. The chapter then turns to an examination of domestic terrorism and its perpetrators, including right-wing and left-wing domestic groups. Right-wing terror groups, along with extremist groups, are responsible for high-profile incidents in the past, such as the Oklahoma City bombing in 1995. Current political and economic climates have many experts worried that terror acts from such groups may see a resurgence. The next section addresses the financing of terrorism, with a focus on drug, arms, and human smuggling, credit card and charities fraud, and theft. This is followed by a discussion of several U.S. national agencies charged with the task of gathering information on terrorism, terrorism prevention and investigation, and counterterrorism.

Although federal agencies are clearly important in assessing the threat of future terrorist acts, the role of criminal investigators at both the state and the local law-enforcement levels should not be underestimated. The remainder of the chapter outlines the ways that criminal investigators can assist in the fight against terrorism. Confronting terrorism is not an occasional or a seasonal venture; it is an ongoing responsibility. Now, more than ever, criminal investigators must be prepared to encounter and handle terrorist-incident crime scenes.

The world and the United States are not strangers to terrorism. The first U.S. plane hijacking occurred in 1961, when Puerto Rican Antuilo Ortiz, armed with a gun, diverted a National Airlines flight to Cuba, where he was given asylum.[1] A rebel faction in Guatemala assassinated U.S. Ambassador John Mein in 1968 after forcing his car from the road. Black September terrorists struck in Munich at the Olympics in 1972 and the following year killed U.S. Ambassador Cleo Noel in the Sudan. The Baader-Meinhof group and the Popular Front for the Liberation of Palestine (PFLP) seized a French airliner in 1976 and flew the 258 passengers to Uganda, precipitating the Entebbe hostage crisis. In 1979 the Italian Prime Minister was kidnapped and killed by Red Brigade members; the U.S. Embassy in Tehran was seized by Iranian radicals; and Mecca's Grand Mosque was taken over by 200 Islamic terrorists who took hundreds of pilgrims hostage, an incident that left 250 people dead and 600 wounded. Today our newspapers highlight the almost daily occurrences of suicide bombers in Israel, new plots of violence against airliners in London, and the gruesome beheadings of innocent civilians by the Shiite al-Mahdi Army in Iraq. For example, the National Counterterrorism Center indicates that over 11,000 terrorist attacks occurred throughout the world in 2008. Although the number of attacks decreased from 2007, the acts resulted in a substantial number of deaths and injuries. A majority of these victims were Muslim and living in Afghanistan, Iraq, and Pakistan.[2]

Nevertheless, across the United States, people are wondering if the September 11, 2001, attacks were harbingers of the future or anomalies. They were not anomalies: the United States is opposed by international and domestic terrorist groups, and the likelihood of additional incidents is quite real. Together, globally and locally, police have to be smarter and work harder using better tools to eliminate, disrupt, minimize, and investigate terrorist attacks.

INTERNATIONAL TERRORISM

"**International terrorism** involves violent acts or acts dangerous to human life that are the violation of the criminal laws of the United States or any state, or that would be a criminal act if committed within the jurisdiction of the United States or any state. Acts of international terrorism are intended to intimidate a civilian population, influence the policy of a government, or affect the conduct of a government. These acts transcend national boundaries in terms of the means by which they are accomplished, the persons they intend to intimidate, or the locale in which perpetrators operate."[3] The FBI further defines terrorism as the unlawful use of force or violence against persons or property to intimidate or coerce a government, the civilian population, or any segment thereof, in furtherance of political or social objectives. It is impossible to discuss all of the groups around the world now labeled "terrorist"; however, it is important to give a brief description of those groups that pose the most significant threat to the United States. Many originate from the Middle East, where anti-American tensions have recently escalated, primarily because of the wars in Afghanistan and Iraq. For that reason, this discussion focuses on groups stemming from that area.

RADICAL ISLAM

Radical Islam has long been a component of terrorist activity throughout the world (Figure 21-1). Groups with ties to radical Islamic beliefs have been at the forefront of the news since the late 1970s, when the Islamic revolution in Iran reached its peak and led to the capture of the U.S. embassy in Tehran. Terrorist organizations that lay claim to radical Islamic beliefs, whether from the Sunni tradition (making up over 92% of the Islamic world) or the Shi'ite tradition (centered primarily in Iran), have garnered widespread press attention over the past 30 years, particularly since al-Qaeda claimed responsibility for the September 11, 2001 attacks.

Radical Islamic groups are generally characterized by a belief that is not shared by mainstream Muslims: violence is a means to an end. These radical groups believe that Western culture poses an imminent threat to the sanctity of the Muslim religion, corrupting morals and threatening to overtake the Muslim way of life. Western interventions in Israeli/Palestinian affairs and in Iraq have served as prime examples of Western "colonialization" in the minds of Muslim terrorist groups, further fueling their resolve to take action against the United States and its allies.[4] Since the September 11th attacks, several attempted and completed terrorist acts perpetrated by radical Islamists have occurred on U.S. soil. Most notably, the country was stunned when Army Major Nidal Hasan shot and killed 13 people at a U.S military base in Fort Hood, Texas, in November 2009. Colleagues of Nidal reported that he appeared to be fixated on the notion that the military equated with a war on Islam. Thirty-two additional individuals were also injured in that incident.[5] More recently, federal authorities arrested Faisal Shahzad for attempting to detonate an explosives-filled SUV in New York City's Time Square. Shahzad later admitted that he received explosives training in Pakistan

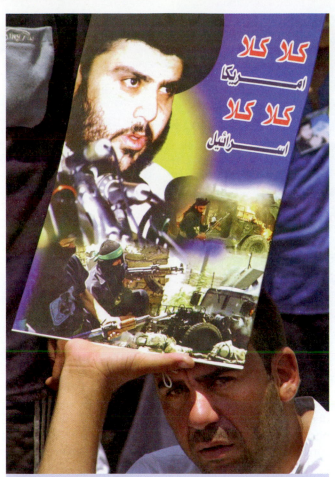

▲ **FIGURE 21-1   Radical Islam**
The Mahdi Army is a militia force created by Iraqi Shi'ite cleric Muqtada al-Sadr in 2003. It rose to international prominence in April 2004, when it began the first major armed confrontation against the U.S.-led forces in Iraq. Since that time is has been actively engaged in using IEDs (Improvised Explosive Devises or roadside bombs) against U.S. forces as well as malicious beheadings of Iraqi police officers and civilians. (© AP Photo/Mohammed Uraibi)

and would have attempted to set off another bomb in New York City had he not been arrested.[6]

Some factions that help compose three major radical and fundamentalist movements within Islam pose a direct threat to the interests of the West, and specifically to the United States. They are discussed next.

The Wahhabi Movement

An Islamic orientation owing much of its basic ideology to the writings of Abd al-Wahhab (1703–1792),[7] who espoused a very conservative form of Sunni Islam. His teachings are commonly referred to as *salafi*, which fundamentally means adhering to the ways of the earliest Islamic generations. The basic concept of the **Wahhabi movement** is that the teachings of Islam were corrupted

after the time of the Prophet Muhammad. Much like the early Christian Inquisition during the twelfth and thirteenth centuries, the Wahhabis dealt harshly with those nonobservant of their Muslim traditions. Thus the early Wahhabi focus was internal, on other nominally devout Muslims. The Wahhabi tradition today is centered in Saudi Arabia, with followers primarily on the Arabian Peninsula, including Qatar and Yemen. It is a conservative, closed-society tradition that is intolerant of nonbelievers. Some believe this stance encourages violence against the West.

Many practitioners of Wahhabism prefer to be called *muwahhidun* (unifiers of Islamic practice) or *salafists*. There is no single approach to salafism, which in part accounts for the variety of orientations associated with it, such as: (1) the *shumuliyas*, who believe that religion, politics, and government are inseparable; (2) the *wasatiyyans*, who are reformers/moderates but not necessarily anti-Western and entertain ideas about how to simultaneously accommodate some Western values with those of Islam; and (3) the Islamic revivalists/fundamentalists, which includes the Muslim Brotherhood and radical Jihadist Salafism.

The Muslim Brotherhood

The **Muslim Brotherhood** movement was formed in 1928 as an Egyptian youth organization and grew into a political party by 1939, influenced by the writings of Hasan al-Banna (1906–1949) and Sayyid Qutb (1906–1966) in Egypt.[8] Building on the tenets of Wahhabism, al-Banna believed that the Islamic faith is not just a religion, but an all-encompassing way of living and governing. As such, its focus included not only a rejection of the secularization of Islam but a renunciation of Western colonialization and the modern views and values that often accompanied it throughout the Middle East. The Muslim Brotherhood supports the use of violence to return the entire Middle East to its original and purest form of Islam under the rule of the Shari'a, the first books of the Holy Koran. The term **jihad** is interpreted as an obligation for all Muslims to engage in a "holy war" against the West.

The Muslim Brotherhood has a past history of attempted and successful assassinations of Arabic leaders, including Egyptian President Anwar-al-Sadat (1918–1981), who was seen as too moderate following his 1979 signing of peace accords with Israel. Some of its members helped found al-Qaeda, have been elected to parliamentary seats throughout the Middle East, and have established banks, including one in the Bahamas in 1988 that helped finance terror activities worldwide. Brotherhood members have fought with al-Qaeda in Afghanistan against the Russians and in support of radical Muslims in Kashmir, Chechnya, and Iraq.

Jihadist Salafism

This is the radical branch of **Salafism,** whose ideology rocketed during the 1980s and 1990s as a direct result of the Soviet-Afghan War (1980–1989). It embraces a strict,

▶**FIGURE 21-2 Jihad**
For nearly 1.3 billion people, Islam is a religion of discipline and peace. However, radical elements within Wahhabism and Jihadist Salafism promote violence and jihad against the United States, modernization, and the West in general. (© AP Photo/Ali Fraidoon)

literal interpretation of Islam combined with an emphasis on jihad as a holy war against all Western influences in the Middle East (Figure 21-2). This is the ideology of the al-Qaeda and Jemaah Islamiah terrorist groups. More interestingly, it is the newly adopted perspective of new radical groups sympathizing with al-Qaeda and fighting U.S. troops in Iraq and Afghanistan, such as Abu Musab al-Zarqawi's Tawhid and Jihad (holy war) group.

Although al-Zarqawi was killed in June 2006, his group continues to plague American soldiers. Other groups, such as Harkat al-Mujahedeen and the Lashkar e-Taiba, are especially active in Afghanistan, particularly as American involvement in that country continues to escalate.

RADICAL ISLAMIC GROUPS

Radical Islamic groups and their history, goals, leaders, tactics, and operational methods were for the most part unknown to state and local investigators before 9/11. However, the new imperative is to master such knowledge. Sun Tzu, who lived around 400 B.C.E., observed that "if you are to win a war, you must know your enemy."[9] Of necessity then, the first part of this chapter deals with who terrorist enemies are, their history, what they want, what they've done, and why they are a threat to us. With this overview, the subsequent portions of the chapter dealing with responses to terrorism and its investigation assume greater meaning. Although there are several Islamic terrorist organizations that are active, the following groups pose the most significant, dangerous, and continued threat to U.S. interests.

Al-Qaeda

Al-Qaeda ("the base") is easily the most recognized and feared of all radical Muslim terror groups. The group has its basis in the mujahedin, or "holy warriors," who fought against the Russians when they invaded Afghanistan in 1979. During the 1970s Afghanistan's leaders were dependent on the Soviet Union for economic and political support. As a result, Islamic movements in Afghanistan were suppressed in favor of Soviet Marxism. When the pro-communist government faltered in the late 1970s, Russia invaded in a doomed attempt to prop it up.[10] The invasion caused Afghanistan's tribal and religious leaders to abandon their infighting and band together to resist the Russians. The U.S. government, eager to undermine the Soviet Union's power, offered assistance in the form of funding and personnel. The result was a jihad against the Soviet Union, fought by a coalition consisting of Afghans, Central Intelligence Agency operatives, and scores of young Arab men, drawn from places such as Saudi Arabia, who were eager to fight for Islam.[11]

One such Saudi citizen was Osama bin Laden, who came from a wealthy family and who had studied civil engineering before arriving in Afghanistan. He set up the organization known as "the base," or *al-Qaeda*, in order to track the movements of fighters and money coming into the Afghan resistance. The United States and Saudi Arabia both applauded the efforts of bin Laden, whose efficiency and strategic knowledge led Afghan fighters toward victory. Soviet troops withdrew from Afghanistan in 1989, and bin Laden returned, victorious and a hero, to Saudi Arabia, where he rejoined his family.[12] Bin Laden quickly came into disfavor with the Saudi Arabian government as a result of his vocal opposition to the Saudi alliance with the United States during the first Gulf War. He fled Saudi Arabia and returned briefly to Afghanistan in 1991, finally settling in Sudan in 1992, a country that welcomed his arrival.[13] It was there that bin Laden stepped up his sponsorship of training camps for fundamental Islamic young men, particularly those who subscribed to Jihadist Salafism.[14] Because of these and other activities, the Saudis revoked his citizenship in 1994, and his family, at least publicly, disowned him.

Following the 1993 World Trade Center bombings, American interest in bin Laden escalated, although he denied involvement in the attack. The United States was also interested in his training camps in Sudan, believing that graduates from bin Laden's schools were responsible for attacks on U.S. forces in Somalia and Riyadh. Sudan, acting under pressure from the United States and Egypt, finally expelled him in 1996.[15]

Bin Laden again returned to Afghanistan, where the Taliban, a strict Muslim faction, had united Afghanistan under their harsh rule. The Taliban offered sanctuary to bin Laden and benefited greatly from his wealth. In return, bin Laden and his al-Qaeda organization were protected and allowed to recruit hundreds of followers in his pursuit of jihad against the United States.

The goals of the jihad were to drive U.S. forces out of the Arab peninsula, overthrow the pro-Western Saudi government, thereby liberating the holy sites Mecca and Medina, and support radical Islamic groups throughout the world. By the late 1990s al-Qaeda's training camps were turning out hundreds of "graduates" annually.[16]

In 1998 al-Qaeda made its first strike against the United States. A suicide bomber drove a truck into the U.S. embassy compound in Nairobi, Kenya, killing 216 people and injuring over 4,500. Eight minutes later, another truck bomb detonated in Dar-es-Salaam, Tanzania, killing 11 and injuring over 100. The United States reacted by launching cruise missiles on the training sites in Afghanistan, attempting to kill bin Laden. As a result of the embassy bombings, bin Laden made his way onto the list of America's most wanted men.[17] He was also indicted for the attacks, along with 17 other al-Qaeda members.

The October 12, 2000, bombing of the *U.S.S. Cole* has also been attributed to al-Qaeda. Although bin Laden never formally took responsibility for the suicide attack, which killed 17 U.S. Navy personnel, the key suspect in the case told Yemini authorities that he and the suicide bombers were acting under the directions of Osama bin Laden.[18]

On September 11, 2001, planes hijacked by al-Qaeda cells crashed into the Twin Towers in New York City and the Pentagon. Aboard another hijacked flight, passengers unsuccessfully fought to retake the plane to prevent its use in another attack, resulting in its crash in rural Pennsylvania and the loss of everyone aboard. The United States promptly declared war against the terrorist groups responsible and went after bin Laden and his supporters in Afghanistan.

The subsequent wars in Afghanistan and Iraq have resulted in the killing or capture of hundreds of al-Qaeda fighters and operatives. Hundreds of documents linking al-Qaeda to the September 11 attacks have been found, and other documents suggest future plans to attack U.S. interests. By December of 2001 the Taliban rule in Afghanistan had been toppled. However, bin Laden and many of his closest cohorts within al-Qaeda were still at large.

Nearly a decade after the September 11 attacks, Osama bin Laden was finally located in a small town in Pakistan by ongoing intelligence operations. A small team of U.S. Navy commandos (Navy SEAL Team 6) approached the compound in an attempt to apprehend bin Laden, however a firefight broke out and bid Laden was killed. The body was taken into custody and subsequent DNA tests confirmed the identity of the body as that of Osama bin Laden (Figure 21-3). The core leadership of al-Qaeda had been destroyed in previous U.S. military actions in Afghanistan and Iraq, and the death of bin Laden only further depreciated the potential of the world's most notorious terrorist group. The leadership of al-Qaeda has now fallen to bin Laden's top lieutenant and personal cleric, Dr. Ayman al-Zawarahi.[19] America has become familiar with this new leader, and the many video tapes that deride the American "invasion" into Iraq and Afghanistan that he has presented to the public. In January 2006 an unmanned Predator drone guided by the CIA hit a house in the village of Damadola, in northwest Pakistan in an a attempt to kill al-Zawarahi. The missile destroyed the house and killed a dozen people, but al-Zawarahi was not among them. Although U.S. military actions have largely pushed al-Qaeda out of Iraq and fractured its Afghanistani presence, remnant elements of al-Qaeda still exist and a myriad of diverse "Jihadist fighters" still present a formidable enemy and credible threat to the United States, having set up operations elsewhere.

Al-Qaeda's activities in Somalia and Yemen have become a great concern to the United States in the past few years. On Christmas Day 2009 a 23-year-old Nigerian man named Umar Farouk Abdulmutallab was discovered with a bomb on a Northwest Airlines flight to Detroit. Abdulmutallab was unsuccessful in his attempt, but as details emerged about his motivations, homeland security officials became increasingly alarmed about what they had previously thought was just a regional outpost of al-Qaeda in Yemen. Abdulmutallab trained in Yemen, and a martyrdom statement by him was released by al-Qaeda's Yemeni operation. It is becoming clear that the Yemeni network has an international reach. The group has taken advantage of a weakened central government in Yemen, mobilizing an impoverished and angry population and establishing training camps in remote areas. U.S. intelligence officials have warned that a number of Americans have travelled to Yemen and disappeared, possibly to train in these camps.

Al-Qaeda is also expanding its presence in war-torn Somalia. The open borders, lack of central government, and emergence of Al-Shabab, a militant Islamic group, have all contributed to a hospitable environment for al-Qaeda operatives. Al-Qaeda fighters have moved to the

Deceased

▲**FIGURE 21-3** **Osama bin Laden**

Osama bin Laden was one of the most wanted persons in the world with a $25 million reward for his capture. However, in June 2011, bin Laden was finally located living inside a walled compound in Abbottabad, Pakistan. Elite members of the U.S. Joint Special Operations Command (Navy SEAL Team Six) attempted to secure bin Laden; a brief firefight ensued and bin Laden was killed. (http://www.fbi.gov/wanted/topten/usama-bin-laden) (*Left:* © AP Photo/U.S. Department of State, *right:* © Getty Images)

southern region of Somalia to train Al-Shabab fighters in al-Qaeda techniques.[20] These camps have become a magnet for foreign fighters coming from all over the Middle East and potentially even the United States. In 2010, 14 people (mostly located in Minnesota, home of the largest Somali population in the U.S.), were charged with providing financial support or recruits to Al-Shabab.[21] Their close ties to al-Qaeda continue to worry U.S. intelligence and law enforcement, afraid that Al-Shabab operations are merely another pipeline to terror against the United States.

Several cases have raised concerns about the extent to which al-Qaeda has new operatives functioning within the United States. In the last few years alone, investigators have uncovered a number of plots perpetrated by al-Qaeda affiliates living in the country. For instance, Oussama Abdullah Kassir was sentenced to life in prison in 2009 for operating a training camp in Bly, Oregon that was designed to provide Muslims with military-like jihad training. In addition, officials revealed that Kassir was also operating several terrorist websites.[22] The presence of al-Qaeda operatives in the U.S. was further substantiated when officials recently indicated that members of the group considered poisoning the U.S. food supply by putting ricin and cyanide in the food at restaurant and hotel buffets.[23]

Al-Qaeda has also been linked to numerous other terrorist organizations throughout the Middle East and Asia, such as Hizbollah, Al-Jihad, Harakat al-Mujahedeen, the Islamic Movement of Uzbekistan, HAMAS, the Chechens, and Jemaah Islamiayah; it is due partly to its wide reach that al-Qaeda remains powerful. Despite the fact that its power center has been disrupted in the past and hidden,

al-Qaeda communicates regularly with the Arab world through the media. Al-Queda continues to condemn U.S. involvement in Muslim affairs and urges jihad and violent terrorist attacks against the United States and its allies. The basis of their threat to the United States is in their ideology, past actions, continuing intent, and capability, and their financial resources help to make such plans a reality. In 2009 al-Qaeda leaders in Yemen boasted of their ability to defeat U.S. intelligence and airport security in an attempted bombing involving an American passenger jet.[24]

Jemaah Islamiyah

Jemaah Islamiyah (JI) began when two radical Indonesian clerics named Abdullah Sungkar and Abu Bakar Ba'asyir established a pirate (unauthorized) radio station in 1960, which advocated Shari'a, strict Muslim law. Subsequently, they opened an Islamic school, which taught a hard-line version of Salafi Wahhabism. Increasingly in conflict with their government, both men were arrested in 1978 and sentenced to four years imprisonment. The two men eventually fled to Malaysia, where they developed a large following of other refugee Indonesians. Two prominent radical Islamics, Riduan Isamuddin (a.k.a., Hambali) and Abu Jibril, became part of JI's leadership.[25] Together, the core group of four men preached jihad and the establishment of an Islamic republic across Malaysia, Indonesia, southern Thailand, and the southern Philippines[26] and were able to develop cells in these target countries.[27]

In 2000 JI carried out a series of bombings in Indonesia and Manila, resulting in the deaths of 27 people.[28] There were also plans for large-scale attacks against the United

States in Singapore and the Philippines, but these plans were foiled by the arrests of several key JI members. Angered by these circumstances, Hambali began to focus JI's efforts on smaller strikes against places frequented by Western tourists. This planning culminated in the 2002 bombing of a Bali nightclub. Two hundred and two people died in the attacks.[29] Although key leaders were subsequently arrested, JI's operations continued, thereby resulting in another fatal bombing in 2003. The networks established by JI throughout Southeast Asia have resulted in a seemingly strong backbone of Islamic terrorists who are willing to carry on JI's flight, with or without its original leaders. JI's dangerousness to the United States and its allies is due to its al-Qaeda-trained operatives, its strong network, good resources, and its ability to strike at "soft" targets.

Hizbollah

Hizbollah, or "the Party of God," was founded in 1982 in reaction to the Israeli invasion of Lebanon. This invasion was generally precipitated by continuing Palestinian military action from Lebanon in Northern Israel and more particularly by the unsuccessful assassination attempt on the life of Israel's Ambassador to the United Kingdom by the Abu Nidal organization. During the invasion, Israel battled Palestinian Liberation Organization (PLO), Syrian, and Muslim Lebanese forces, driving halfway across Lebanon to Beirut.

The roots of Hizbollah go back to the late 1970s, when hundreds of Shi'ite clerics and students were forced to leave Iraq and settle in Lebanon. These exiles recruited young militants and formed the Committee Supportive of the Islamic Revolution, which identified closely with the Shi'ite Muslim government in Iran. The group was also loosely associated with a Lebanese Shi'ite militia, known as Amal,[30] led by Nabih Berri.

The 1982 invasion of Lebanon by Israel damaged or destroyed more than 80% of the villages in southern Lebanon with 19,000 Lebanese killed and another 32,000 injured. The invasion caused a mass exodus from the southern areas of Lebanon, owing mostly to the total destruction of Lebanese agriculture by the Israelis. The exiles flooded into northern Lebanon, settling into refugee camps that were also occupied by displaced Palestinians. These refugee camps quickly became a hotbed of discontent against Israel and Western Zionist sympathizers, such as the United States. Militant groups such as Amal organized a Lebanese resistance front to fight the Israelis, but it wasn't until Iran sent 1,500 troops to the aid of the Lebanese fighters that the development of Hizbollah truly began. The Iranian fighters further fostered the desire among the Lebanese Shi'ites to model their government after Iran's, where Muslim clerics and disciples of the Ayatollah Khomeni ruled. The Shi'ites wanted the same for Lebanon.[31]

The final stage of Hizbollah's development occurred when a schism arose within Amal. Nabih Berrie (the leader of Amal) had begun to participate in a committee whose head was pro-Israeli. Others within Amal felt this was a manipulation conceived of by Americans who wished to water down Lebanese militancy. They also considered it a betrayal of Islam. As a result, the more radical Islam faction of Amal broke free and joined the smaller radical groups and the Iranian forces to establish the *Committee of Nine,* Hizbollah's first decision-making council. Hizbollah eventually absorbed all the smaller Shi'ite resistance groups, becoming a powerful force against the Israeli occupation.[32] Guerrilla attacks were conducted against the Israelis, which included the use of car bombs, sniper attacks, and suicide bombers.

Hizbollah's terrorist activity began to escalate. On April 18, 1983, a suicide bomber drove into the U.S. embassy in Beirut, Lebanon, killing 63 people, including the top-level American intelligence officials in Lebanon at the time.[33] On October 23, 1983, another suicide bomber drove at least 6 tons of dynamite into a U.S. Marine command center located at Beirut's International Airport, killing 241 Marine and Navy personnel (Figure 21-4). Twenty seconds later, another blast erupted at the barracks of a French military contingent. Fifty-eight French soldiers died in the attack. Hizbollah claimed responsibility for both attacks, claiming them to be retaliation for French and U.S. support of Christian governmental factions in the Lebanese civil war.[34]

U.S. troops were ordered out of Lebanon in early 1984 by President Ronald Reagan, a move that did not lead to a drop in the violence. Malcolm Kerr, President of the American University of Beirut (AUB), was assassinated on January 18, 1984; another American embassy bombing occurred on September 20, 1984, which killed 14 people;

▲ **FIGURE 21-4   Sayyad Hassan Nasrallah**
The head of Hizbollah in Lebanon; aside from involvement in the 1983 suicide bomber attack on the Marine barracks in Beirut which killed 241 Marines, Hizbollah is very active in the financing of various terrorist operations through trafficking of drugs, arms, and human beings. (© AP/Wide World Photos)

and kidnappings of Westerners by Hizbollah escalated. The rising toll of the dead and missing led the United States to stage a complete withdrawal from Lebanon, leaving only six diplomats in the country by November of 1984.[35]

Again, retreat by the United States did not mean an end to terrorist attacks against U.S. and Western interests. In 1985 TWA flight 847 was hijacked by Hizbollah affiliates, resulting in the death of one American on board. Hizbollah also claimed responsibility for the kidnappings of 18 American and British journalists and church officials, three of whom were killed, including Beirut Central Intelligence Agency (CIA) Station Chief William Buckley, who was held 19 days and then executed. In 1992 the Israeli embassy in Buenos Aires, Argentina, was bombed, killing 29 people. Although Hizbollah never directly claimed responsibility, they did release a surveillance tape of the embassy that overtly implied their responsibility. In 1994 a Jewish community center in Buenos Aires was bombed, killing 95 people. Hizbollah was also responsible for this act.[36]

In 2000 faced with mounting casualties, Israel ordered a complete retreat from Lebanon after nearly 18 years of occupation. This act served to legitimize Hizbollah not only in the Shi'ite community but also the Arab world at large. No other Arab group had been able to successfully drive Israel from occupied lands. Palestinians waging the current Intifada (or uprising) cite Hizbollah as a major inspiration in their battles. Furthermore, Hizbollah holds 12 seats in the Lebanese parliament and has built an extensive educational and social aid network within the Lebanese Shi'ite community.[37]

Although the 1994 Jewish community center attack in Buenos Aires is the last terrorist act directly linked to Hizbollah, the organization remains a risk to the United States and Israeli interests. Attacks against Israeli troops have continued in the Sheeba area, which Israel claims is a part of Syria and therefore not subject to withdrawal. Hizbollah forces claim that Sheeba is part of Lebanon and has continued to launch missile attacks against Israeli forces.[38]

Although initially dismissed because of the religious differences between the groups, evidence has been found linking Hizbollah to al-Qaeda. Leaders of both groups apparently met several times in the 1990s, and there is some evidence that the groups have been coordinating logistics and training for specific operations.[39] Investigators of a 2002 bombing of an Israeli-owned hotel in Mombasa that killed 16 people have found clues that point to such a collaboration. Materials and techniques used in the attack, formally blamed on al-Qaeda, are the same as those used by the Hizbollah suicide bombers in the attacks on the U.S. Marine barracks and embassy in the 1980s. Furthermore, the only claim of responsibility for the attack was made on Hizbollah radio. Also, missiles found after an attempt to shoot down an Israeli charter jet by al-Qaeda were identified as SAM-7s, used almost exclusively by Hizbollah fighters against Israeli targets.[40]

More recent intelligence also indicates that Hizbollah provided aid to al-Qaeda operatives fleeing Afghanistan at the end of 2001. Between 80 and 100 al-Qaeda fighters were given fake passports by Hizbollah, allowing their safe passage into Saudi Arabia and Yemen. Some 10 to 20 senior al-Qaeda commanders are believed to have settled within Lebanon since 2001, as well.[41] As a result, Hizbollah remains a designated foreign terror organization, classified as having a high activity level by the U.S. State Department. During his 2002 State of the Union address, President George W. Bush singled the organization out as a target of the U.S. War on Terror.[42]

In 2004 Hizbollah won nearly a quarter of the parliamentary seats in the Lebanese government and was largely responsible for starting the Second Lebanon War in July 2006 by firing rockets into northern border towns of Israel and capturing several IDF soldiers. The incident became an international topic of debate as over a thousand civilians were killed in the ensuing bombing and ground invasion by Israel. The war ended after a short but deadly 34 days, rendering Lebanon's infrastructure in chaos and parts of southern Lebanon uninhabitable because of unexploded cluster bombs. Hizbollah and Nasrallah emerged as "victors" against the Israeli forces and boasted that their armed forces were now much stronger than before, and much better armed with missiles supplied by Iran. Over a million people attended Nasrallah's speech in Beirut in late August 2006 declaring "victory" over the Zionist state. The war was something of a public relations disaster for Hizbollah, causing it to lose favor among many pro-Western Lebanese. However, it retains several seats in Lebanon's parliament and has ministers in the national unity government formed in 2009. Though the Bush administration classified Hizbollah as a primary target in the War on Terror, the Obama administration has recognized that it has evolved somewhat from a "purely a terrorist organization" to a more legitimate political operation, and has expressed hopes that it can tap into the more moderate elements of the organization.[43] However, many believe that Hizbollah remains one of the most dangerous terrorist organizations in the world, by virtue of their size, training, discipline, financing, and their arms cache. In March of 2009 retired chief of operations for the DEA Michael Braun stated that Hizbollah had become involved in the operation of Mexico's drug cartels.

Hizbollah's involvement in Mexico raises two separate issues: the first is that the organization is connected to drugs and arms trafficking, as well as money laundering in an effort to fund their objectives in Lebanon. In August of 2010 a major Hizbollah-connected drug trafficking organization in South America was targeted by a DEA operation, and officials say that currently Hizbollah is aligning itself with powerful Mexican syndicates who are responsible for nearly 90% of cocaine trafficking into the US.[44] The implications of a 2009 indictment in a New York federal court against alleged Hizbollah member Jamal

Yousef are quite telling: Yousef had a cache of weapons, including military rifles, rocket-propelled grenades, C-4 plastic explosives and surface to air missiles. He offered to sell those weapons to a narco-terror organization, the Revolutionary Armed Forces of Colombia (FARC), which we discuss later in this chapter. This case underscores the fact that Hezbollah maintains operations in Mexico and is a participant in arms and drug trafficking; Hezbollah is willing to join forces with narco-terrorist organizations that seek to destabilize American interests; and these weapons could have just as easily been smuggled into the United States for use in a terrorist plot.[45]

The second issue is that of immigration. Hizbollah relies on the same document traffickers and transportation experts that the Mexican drug cartels do to smuggle humans into the United States. In 2008 Salim Boughader Mucharrafille, a Mexican of Lebanese descent, was sentenced to 60 years in prison by Mexican authorities for smuggling 200 people, including Hizbollah supporters, into the United States. Others, including Mahmoud Yossef Kourani, have used the Mexican border to cross into the United States in order to generate support and resources for Hizbollah. Kourani was caught in Dearborn, Michigan, and pled guilty in 2006 to supporting the organization.

Currently, Hizbollah's presence in the United States is primarily limited to fundraising, technology purchases, recruiting, and arms smuggling. We will discuss the Holy Land Foundation and other fund-raising schemes later in the chapter, but it is worth noting that Hizbollah has a long history of fundraising in the United States. For example, the Hammoud brothers in North Carolina were purchasing large quantities of cigarettes in their state, which were cheaper than other states owing to lower taxes, and shipping them into states where taxes were much higher. By selling the cigarettes on the black market, the Hammouds were able to funnel millions back to Lebanon.

It should be noted that Hizbollah's presence in the United States is also one of intelligence-gathering and reconnaissance. Former CIA head James Woolsey told a Senate committee in February of 2009 that Hizbollah has identified 29 key targets in the United States and other parts of the "Western World" whose destruction would cripple Western civilization. Because their intelligence-gathering force is supplemented and trained by Iran's Ministry of Intelligence Service (MOIS), this is particularly worrisome.

Hizbollah maintains sleeper cells throughout the United States and Canada to carry out fundraising and reconnaissance activities, but do they pose a direct threat of a terrorist attack on American soil? The answer is quite possibly. The most likely trigger of a Hizbollah attack on America by sleeper cells is an American attack on Iran, Syria, or Lebanon. Continued tensions with Iran, an influential ally of Hizbollah, are in fact the greatest risk for such an attack.[46] Likely targets would include synagogues or other Jewish centers; civilian targets like malls or hotels; economic infrastructure such as banks or financial institutions; symbolic American landmarks; or other infrastructure like power or water supply. As such, continued monitoring of Hizbollah by United States intelligence and law enforcement organizations is essential to homeland security.

Palestinian Terrorist Groups

The current conflict between the Israelis and the Palestinians is a decades-old dispute regarding land rights that grows increasingly complex by the day. The issues arose with the creation of Israel in 1948, which eventually resulted in the loss of the Palestinian state and the displacement of the Palestinian people. This conflict is worsened owing to the two fundamentally different ideologies of both sides and a general unwillingness of both to compromise. The most dangerous manifestation of this conflict comes in the form of terrorist groups that are often willing to go to any length to draw attention to their cause. Palestinian terrorist groups, whether secular or grounded in Islamic fundamentalism, are known throughout the world for their extreme tactics (including suicide bombing) used against the Israelis and their supporters. These organizations focus their attacks on civilian and political targets within Israel, often in reaction to Israeli aggression upon Palestinians.

The Popular Front for the Liberation of Palestine (PFLP).

The PFLP is a Christian-led Marxist-Leninist group founded in 1967 by George Habash as a direct response to the Six-Day War of 1967. George Habash, code-named "al-Hakim," or "the doctor," is a Christian-Marxist Palestinian. Under his leadership, the PFLP essentially established the concept of skyjacking an airplane, back in the late 1960s. Their motivation was relatively benign: to make the world aware of the plight of the Palestinian people. Killing passengers and using skyjacked planes as weapons (for example, the attacks on September 11, 2001) were *not* PFLP tactics. However, PFLP did conduct other violent attacks aimed directly at Israel. For instance, in 1972, working in conjunction with the PFLP, Japanese Red Army terrorists killed 25 people at Lod (now Ben Gurion International Airport) in Haifa; and in 1976, during their last skyjacking attempt, PFLP terrorists died at the hands of Israeli Special Forces at the now famous Entebbe raid in Uganda. In recent years, and particularly after the retirement of George Habash in 2000 as leader of the PFLP, the group has been relatively quiet, responsible only for a few suicide bombings in the West Bank. And, after more than 50 years of involvement in various Palestinian terrorist groups, George Habash died of a heart attack in a hospital in Amman, Jordan on January 26, 2008. Habash was 81 years old at time of his death.

The Abu-Nidal Organization (ANO).

This organization was formed by Sabri al-Banna, code-named Abu Nidal (meaning "father of the Holy Struggle"). The group

► **FIGURE 21-5   HAMAS**
This group is responsible for over 90% of the suicide bombings in Israel, with most bombs being relatively crude homemade devices aimed at killing a relatively small number of people. (© AP Photo/ Enric Marti)

formed after it split from the Palestinian Liberation Organization as a result of perceived moderation on the part of Yassir Arafat in 1972. Al-Banna was strictly antimoderation and adhered strongly to the doctrine that Israel must be destroyed at any cost, branding Arafat, the PLO, and the rest of the al-Fatah as traitors. Al-Banna continued to launch international terrorist operations against Israeli interests and even struck at pro-Arafat groups and moderate Arab countries in his list of targets. The Abu Nidal organization has been financially backed by Syria, Libya, Iraq, and Iran.[47]

The Abu Nidal Organization has attacked more foreign and Arab interests than any other Palestinian terrorist organization to date, and at one point was considered the most dangerous group in the world, having been accused of killing or wounding nearly 1,000 people in 20 different countries. Over the past 30 years ANO attempted or carried out assassinations of Arab government officials and high-ranking PLO officers. This is one of the few Palestinian groups to have actually claimed an attack within the United States, having conducted a robbery in St. Louis, Missouri, in the mid-1980s. In August 2002 Sabri al-Banna's body was found in an Iraqi apartment with multiple gunshot wounds. Reports state that he committed suicide, but intelligence sources believe he was killed by Iraqis so Saddam Hussein could have access to the Abu Nidal Organizational network, which is still active, yet diminished, throughout the world.

The Palestinian Islamic Resistance Movement (HAMAS).

HAMAS, a radical fundamentalist organization, came to prominence as the foremost opponent of the Oslo peace accords following the first major Palestinian Intifada in the 1990s (Figure 21-5). The primary modus operandi of HAMAS is **suicide bombings** against civilian targets. HAMAS has been directly responsible for over 90% of the suicide bombings against Israel. The bombings have been notoriously ruthless, often aimed at inflicting the most civilian damage possible. For example, on March 27, 2002, in the Israeli resort of Netanya, a bomber blew himself up at a hotel, killing 28 Israelis who were celebrating Passover. This attack remains one of the most deadly HAMAS actions to date.[48]

Deconstructing the Suicide Bomber. For most Americans, trying to understand the motivation behind suicide bombing is very difficult. In our culture, such actions are often labeled unpredictable, irrational, and fanatical. However, a careful analysis of the phenomenon shows that suicide bombings are not spontaneous outbursts of emotion but rather calculated, strategic moves by a specific group for a specific purpose. Indeed, suicide bombers are actually trained in the actions. They undergo a relatively long period of indoctrination filled with group pressure, pep talks, organizational support, and personal commitment. Quite interestingly, suicide is strictly forbidden in the Holy Quran; however, when deemed by a religious edict to protect the Kingdom of Islam, suicide bombing serves as a means to an end. Some argue that the huge difference in might between Israel and the Palestinian people militarily gives legitimacy to the act, while others suggest that people who have little political power in the present or no hope for the future engage in the ultimate desperate measure.[49]

▲ **FIGURE 21-6 Shahid**
Suicide bomber wearing a satchel-style bomb of TNT wrapped with metal ball bearings and ignited by a simple finger push device. The bomber wears a jacket or coat over the deadly cargo upon entering a crowded café or night spot. (© AP/Wide World Photos)

Under the religious and ideological leadership of radical Islamic cleric, Sheikh Ahmed Yassin, people who engage in suicide bombing became a *shahid*, or martyr fulfilling a religious command. Most suicide bombers in Israel fit a specific profile: young men between 18 and 24 years old, born in relative poverty with little or no education and with no real understanding of the outside world or of the geopolitical issues surrounding the Middle East. For the most part, the shahid is a victim of some personal tragedy or event from the Israeli occupation in the West Bank or Gaza. This person seeks honor, praise, and financial reward for his family after the action has been completed, as well as the personal religious rewards of seeing the face of Allah and the temporal love and servitude of 72 virgins in heaven. Most suicide bombers in Israel kill themselves and two other individuals. They often walk less than two miles from their home before engaging in their deadly action. For the most part, their "weapon" is crude: TNT or dynamite wrapped with iron nuts and bolts, or metal ball bearings worn in a vest or around their waist (Figure 21-6). In a crowded café or on a bus, or in a shopping center, suicide bombers wreak havoc on their unsuspecting victims. However, on March 22, 2004, Yassin was killed by the Israeli Moussad returning from prayer services at a West Bank mosque. The radical leader was gone, and the number of suicide bombings in Israel dramatically decreased.

U.S. intelligence officials have consistently warned that HAMAS may strike U.S. interests or American gathering places in Israel and throughout the Middle East.

The report does not rule out attacks on American soil. The FBI has long suspected there are HAMAS sympathizers among Islamic extremists in the United States. Federal and local law enforcement officers are closely tracking thefts of explosives (like those used in HAMAS backpack bombs) and unusual sales of fertilizer, chemicals, and fuel that could be used to make a truck bomb.[50]

HAMAS' activities within the United States, much like Hizbollah, focus on recruiting and fundraising. American freedoms have allowed HAMAS to mobilize intellectual support for their cause in universities and via the Internet. This, in turn, allows for an increased flow of funds to HAMAS. As such, it is not in the best interest of HAMAS to "cause troubles in the American theater."[51] However, HAMAS leadership has sometimes countered that assertion with anti-American rhetoric. And like Hizbollah, American tensions with Iran are a major trigger for potential sleeper cell activation on American soil. Because Iran indirectly funds HAMAS, any attack or hostilities visited on that country by the United States could stimulate a HAMAS response. Furthermore, HAMAS has a history of independent cells that do not always fall in line with the parent organization. For example, a rogue cell broke an Israeli-HAMAS ceasefire in 2003. Such a cell could certainly instigate a terror operation within the United States based on a different set of motivations than HAMAS' "legitimate" organization.

HAMAS is clearly one of the most interesting groups in the Middle East. Although it has been responsible for the vast majority of suicide bombings and radical violence in Israel (particularly under the leadership of Yassin), it enjoys a favorable opinion among the Palestinian people. HAMAS has consistently tried to focus on helping the people within the occupied territories of the West Bank and Gaza, collecting millions of dollars in aid and rebuilding schools, mosques, and hospitals. In fact, in 2006 it was elected the governing body for the Palestinian territories of the West Bank and Gaza in Israel. Essentially, HAMAS is the government of the Palestinian Authority, and although they have recently denounced violence and suicide bombings, their motives and intentions still focus on the destruction of Israel.

OTHER ACTIVE INTERNATIONAL GROUPS

Aum Supreme Truth

Also known as *Aum Shinri-kyo*, the group gained infamy for releasing sarin nerve agent in the Tokyo subway system, killing 12 people and injuring up to 6,000. Established in 1987, the Aum aimed to take over Japan, and then the world. It adopted a view that the United States would initiate Armageddon by starting World War III with Japan. Control changed hands in 2000, and under Fumihiro Joyu, the Aum changed its name to Aleph and now claims to reject the teachings of its founder. Membership is 1,500 to 2,000.

Basque Fatherland and Liberty

Known by its Basque initials, ETA (Basque Homeland and Freedom), the group was founded in 1959 with the aim of establishing an independent, Marxist Basque homeland in the border area between Spain and France. The group has killed more than 800 people since the 1960s, and targets primarily Spanish officials. It finances activities through kidnapping, robbery, and extortion. Estimated membership is in the hundreds.

Kach and Kahane Chai

The Kach and Kahane Chai groups are Israeli terrorists whose goal is to restore the biblical state of Israel. Radical Israeli-American Rabbi Meir Kahane founded Kach. Kahane Chai, or "Kahane Lives," was founded by Binyamin Kahane following his father's assassination in New York in 1990. Both were declared terrorist groups by Israel in March 1994. The younger Kahane and his wife were murdered in a drive-by shooting in Israel on December 31, 2000. The Kahanes' groups protest against the Israeli government and harass and threaten Palestinians in Hebron and the West Bank. They receive support from sympathizers in the United States and Europe; their numbers are unknown.

Kurdistan Workers' Party

Founded in 1974 as a Marxist-Leninist insurgent group, the Kurdistan Workers' Party (PKK) is primarily composed of Turkish Kurds bent on forming an independent Kurdish state in southeastern Turkey. Turkish authorities captured Chairman Abdullah Ocalan in 1999, tried him, and sentenced him to death. Shortly thereafter, Ocalan announced a "peace initiative" in August 1999, ordering members to refrain from violence and to withdraw from Turkey. Members supported the initiative and publicly claim to use only political means to achieve the new goal of improving the rights of Kurds. There are 4,000 to 5,000 supporters, most in northern Iraq, and thousands of sympathizers in Turkey and Europe. Syria, Iraq, and Iran have harbored party members and offered limited funds. Turkey reports that over 30,000 people have died at the hands of PKK terrorists since 1984. In 2003, the Turkish government passed a special "Amnesty and Reintegration Act" giving partial amnesty to harden fighters and guerrillas in the Kurdistan Freedom and Democracy Congress (KADEK), formerly known as the PKK. This activity, as well as the U.S. war in Iraq has substantially quieted attacks from this group. As of early 2005, Ocalan had not been executed and is reportedly imprisoned on Imrali Island in a special facility.

Liberation Tigers of Tamil Eelam

Founded in 1976, Liberation Tigers is the most powerful Tamil group in Sri Lanka. Its aim is to establish an independent Tamil state. It began attacks on the Sri Lankan government in 1983 and relies on a guerrilla strategy that includes terrorism. One group, the Black Tigers, carries out suicide bombings and assassinations. The Tigers have some 8,000 to 10,000 combatants in Sri Lanka and control most of the northern and eastern coastal areas of Sri Lanka. In 2009 the group agreed to a cease-fire with the Sri Lanka military, however, some sporadic fighting continues to be reported.

National Liberation Army

Based in Colombia, this Marxist insurgent group formed in 1965 and is currently in a dialogue with the Colombian government. The group's 3,000 to 6,000 armed combatants engage in kidnapping, hijackings, bombings, extortion, and guerrilla war. Its strength lies mostly in rural and mountainous areas of north, northeast, and southwest Colombia.

Revolutionary Armed Forces of Colombia

The *Fuerzas Armadas Revolucionarias de Colombia* (FARC), established in 1964 by the Colombian Communist Party, is Colombia's oldest, largest, most capable, and best-equipped Marxist insurgency (Figure 21-7). It operates with impunity in many areas of the country. It engages in bombings, murder, kidnapping, extortion, hijacking, and guerrilla and conventional war against Colombian political, military, and economic targets. The majority of Colombia's 3,000 annual kidnappings are FARC operations. There are 9,000 to 12,000 armed members and an unknown number of supporters, mostly in rural areas. Cuba provides some medical care and political consultation.

Revolutionary Organization 17 November

A Greek radical leftist group established in 1975, it is named for the 1973 student uprising that protested Greece's military regime. It is against not only its government but also the United States, Turkey, and the European Union. It wants Greece out of the EU and NATO, and the Turkish military out of Cyprus. It's responsible for killing various U.S. officials and Greek public figures; its most recent victim, in June of 2000, was the British defense attaché.

Turkish Revolutionary People's Liberation Party/Front

Also called Dev Sol, this Marxist group formed in 1978 is virulently anti-American and anti-NATO. It finances activities through robbery and extortion. The Turks crippled Dev Sol in a series of attacks. Their size is relatively small, and police operation against the group has likely weakened its strength.

Sendero Luminoso

The "Shining Path" terror group of Peru, Sendero Luminoso is based on founder Abimael Guzman's belief in militant Maoist doctrine. Some 30,000 persons have died since Shining Path took up arms in 1980. Its stated goal is to replace Peruvian institutions with a communist

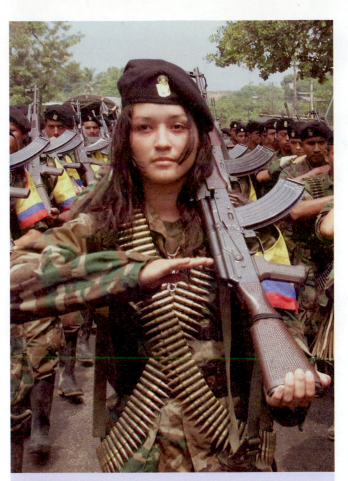

▲ **FIGURE 21-7**
Revolutionary Armed Forces of Colombia
FARC is one of the most successful Marxist organizations in the world, having derived significant income from the lucrative cocaine trade in Colombia. Many of the "soldiers" of FARC are female, and the average age is only 19. (© AP Photo/Ricardo Mazalan)

peasant revolutionary regime. Peruvian counterterrorist operations, arrests, and desertions in recent years have reduced membership to an estimated 100 to 200 armed militants.

The preceding groups have much closer ties than was thought previously, as revealed by international financial investigations that "follow the money trail" and by records originating in Afghanistan and Iraq.[52] For example, Khalid Ouazzani, a naturalized U.S. citizen, admitted to conspiring to provide material support and resources to al-Qaeda from August 2007 to February 2010. Ouazzani reportedly provided al-Qaeda with over $20,000.[53] Other cases have also indicated the extent to which naturalized U.S. citizens and American-born citizens are supporting terrorist groups materially. In 2010 federal investigators arrested two Minnesota residents for raising funds to promote the Somali-based terrorist organization al Shabab.[54] In fact, U.S. Attorney General

Eric Holder has warned that homegrown jihadists are feared the most because of their familiarity with the country and its infrastructures. Of the 126 people indicted on terrorist-related charges in the last two years, 50 were American citizens.[55]

OTHER INTERNATIONAL THREATS: MEXICO

The extreme violence in Mexico related to the drug trade in that country was discussed in Chapter 20. However, this is more than an issue of illegal narcotics trafficking. By the end of 2010 more than 30,000 Mexicans had died in drug-related violence since President Felipe Calderon began his campaign against the drug cartels in that country in 2006.[56] If you define terrorism as an act of violence, terror or intimidation to achieve a result, then certainly the violence in Mexico qualifies. And this violence has caught the attention of U.S. agencies tasked with preventing terrorism in the United States.

At the root of the violence are the drug cartels. There are seven major cartels in Mexico: Gulf, Los Zetas (who are infamous for mass beheadings); Sinaloa (currently, Mexico's most powerful cartel); Tijuana/Arrellano Felix; Juarez; Beltran Leyva; and La Familia Michoacana (Figure 21-8). The government fight against the cartels has served to splinter and destabilize them, moving them closer to the American border, and intensifying their violent and ruthless tactics to gain control of the lucrative drug market. In 2010 a new super cartel known as New Federation had emerged, the result of a collaboration of Sinaloa and Gulf cartels to fight the increasing dominance of Los Zetas.[57]

The violence visited on the Mexican people as a result of drug trafficking into the United States by these cartels is horrific enough, but American officials worry that the violence is not contained in Mexico. Interesting to note: El Paso, Texas—just a stone's throw from the most dangerous city in the world, Ciudad Juarez—was named one of America's safest cities by CQ Press in 2010. However, in other border areas, there have been several incidents of cartel-related violence that has directly affected the United States (Figure 21-9). Tucson, Arizona, has reported more than 700 cases related to Mexican drug cartels, including kidnappings, assaults, home invasions, and human smuggling.[58] Former Arellano Felix associates set up shop outside of San Diego, California, and perpetrated kidnappings and killings in an effort to gain a foothold in the marijuana market there.[59] And in March of 2010 a pregnant American consulate worker and her husband were shot to death in Ciudad Juarez, where they had been attending a birthday party. The husband of another consular employee was also killed.[60] As a result, consulate employees along the Mexican border have been allowed to relocate to American soil to avoid the violence. Other incidents include "pirate" attacks on a lake at the Mexico/Texas border, reportedly by members of the Zeta cartel. In May of 2010 bass anglers at the lake were accosted by boats of

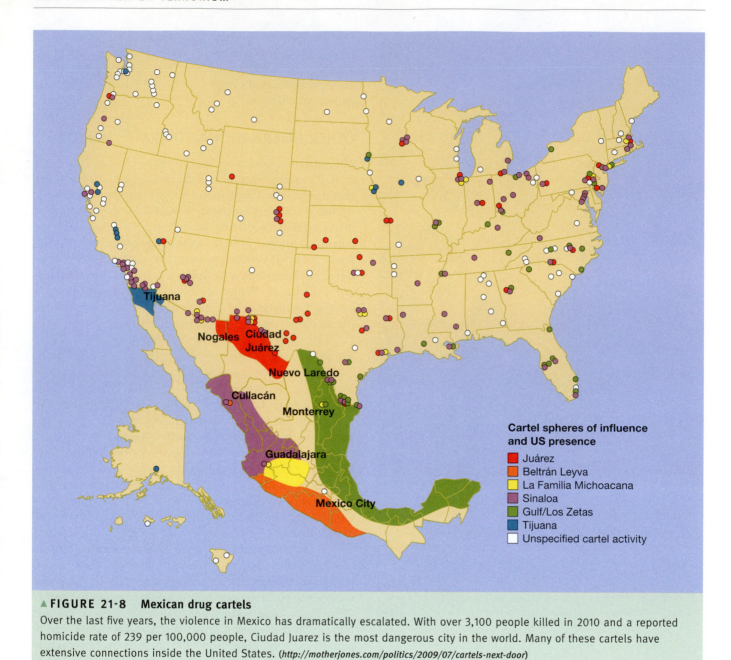

▲ **FIGURE 21-8 Mexican drug cartels**
Over the last five years, the violence in Mexico has dramatically escalated. With over 3,100 people killed in 2010 and a reported homicide rate of 239 per 100,000 people, Ciudad Juarez is the most dangerous city in the world. Many of these cartels have extensive connections inside the United States. (*http://motherjones.com/politics/2009/07/cartels-next-door*)

armed gunmen and robbed.[61] In September a man was shot and killed by what his wife described as pirates on the same lake. Mexico's lead investigator in the case was found beheaded a few weeks later.[62]

Yet another concern with the violence in Mexico was mentioned briefly in our discussions of Hizbollah. The Lebanese terrorist organization is apparently using drug cartel transit routes to enter the United States for the purposes of human smuggling and arms trafficking. Because the cartels' allegiance lies with those with the most money to offer, U.S. officials worry that al-Qaeda could also use these trafficking routes to infiltrate the United States.[63] Furthermore, the DEA posits that 60% of terrorist organi-

zations have some ties with the illegal drug trade.[64] Although no direct ties exist between other terror organizations and the Mexican cartels, it stands to reason that these partnerships would be incredibly foreboding for American security.

HOMEGROWN TERRORISM

For many years the United States government and its intelligence and law-enforcement arms have focused on terror threats from outside the United States. The men who hijacked the planes on 9/11 were all exports from

◀FIGURE 21-9
Terrorism and Mexico
The Mexican drug war has claimed more than 30,000 lives as the end of 2010; some are American citizens. (© Reuters/Tamaulipas' State Attorney General's Office /Landov)

other nations, sent here to perpetrate attacks. But it is becoming obvious that al-Qaeda has shifted its tactics to recruit terror operatives from right here in the United States. The organization, fractured by the ongoing U.S. war in Afghanistan and military presence in Iraq, may be less able to pull together a "spectacular" attack on the scale of 9/11. That attack required years of organization and planning from al-Qaeda, something they are less likely to be able to do with the constant relocation and turmoil they are currently faced with. Many experts feel that this means al-Qaeda may have begun a sea-change in their tactics, focusing on the recruit, indoctrination and support of "homegrown terrorists." Homegrown terrorists include those who plot to carry out attacks at home in the United States and those who provide material support to foreign terrorist organizations via financial, intellectual, or other means. Between September 11 and the end of 2009, a total of 46 cases of domestic recruitment and radicalization to jihadist terrorist groups were reported.[65] By the end of 2010 there had been several more high-profile terrorist stings involving domestic terrorists. Clearly, this is a disturbing trend that has commanded the attention of law enforcement, homeland security forces, and the general public.

WHO IS THE "HOMEGROWN TERRORIST"?

The majority of homegrown terrorists are American citizens, although others may be immigrants to this country. American citizens are particularly attractive recruits for a couple of reasons. First, they are able to travel quite extensively largely without questioning or investigation. This allows recruited jihadists the ability to fly overseas, travel to a terrorist training camp, and return without

raising any eyebrows, particularly if they take less direct routes. Second, they are also ideal candidates for jihadist organizations because of their innate knowledge of the English language, and of American cultural norms. This allows these individuals to blend into crowds, as well as to identify potential targets and weaknesses for terrorist organizations. Finally, open access to the Internet is another advantage to terrorist organizations who recruit Americans. This medium allows for easy radicalization via Internet propaganda; a sense of community or solidarity with people halfway around the world; and a means to communicate plot details. One of the more active and vocal examples of the Internet recruiter is Anwar al-Awlaki, an extremist English-speaking Muslim cleric based out of Yemen, who has been linked to many Muslim extremists including the Christmas Day bomber, Umar Farouk Abdulmutallab, and Major Nidal Hassan of the Ft. Hood shootings.

Immigrants to the United States who feel disenfranchised or disenchanted with their new homeland are also a target for jihadist recruiters. Several recent plots have involved immigrants or recent American citizens.

Prisoner radicalization is also a concern for United States law enforcement. The insides of prisons have long been a place where inmates converted to Islam, but increasingly, those inmates are identifying with jihadist beliefs. Violent inmate culture, a feeling of institutional and governmental oppression, and limited education combined with religious fervor makes prisoners easy targets for extremist recruiters. "Jailhouse Islam" has been cited as a factor in the radicalization of several homegrown terrorists, and officials have warned that the world's largest prison system could be a potential breeding ground for homegrown terrorists.[66]

ATTACKS FROM INSIDE THE UNITED STATES

Unfortunately, there have been a number of homegrown terrorists identified in the past few years. But fortunately, they have all been caught either before their plots were carried to fruition or because their plots failed. While this speaks to the tenacity of law enforcement and intelligence operations, it also points to the fact that the homegrown phenomenon is now a crucial concern in the war against terrorism. What follows are examples of some of these homegrown terrorists, their motivations, and their modus operandi in assisting jihadist organizations.

▲ **FIGURE 21-10** **Jihadist**
Abu Mansoor Al-Amriki, a jihadist born and raised in Daphe, Alabama. Al-Amriki trained with Somali terrorist organization Al-Shabab, which is linked to al-Qaeda. (© Newscom)

- Colleen LaRose, more commonly known as "Jihad Jane," is a U.S. citizen apprehended for conspiracy to provide material support to terrorists, conspiracy to kill in a foreign country, attempted identity theft and making false statements to a government official. LaRose had been exchanging emails for years attempting to recruit fighters for "violent jihad" in South Asia and Europe. Her U.S. citizenship and Caucasian appearance made her appealing to the Islamic extremists she had been in contact with. She had also made posts on various online message boards expressing sympathy with terrorists and expressing a desire to help in any way possible to help ease the suffering of the Muslim people in their "holy war." She planned to use her European looks to blend into the Swedish population, and to carry out the killing of a Swedish artist who depicted the face of Mohammed on a dog.[67]
- In November 2009 five young men from Virginia were arrested in Pakistan for attempting to join Jihadist terrorist groups, specifically al-Qaeda. They had been reported missing by their parents in Virginia on the advice of the local Muslim community after the men had traveled to the Middle East without informing their parents. The "Virginia 5" was reported to have been arrested in a safe house of an anti-India terrorist group in possession of Jihadist literature who were building schematics and maps of local areas. Officials believe they may have been in the planning stages of an attack.[68]
- Abu Mansoor Al-Amriki, or "The American," was born Omar Hammami in the small town of Daphne, Alabama, to his Syrian-born father and Caucasian Southern-Baptist mother (Figure 21-10). Al-Amriki has become the celebrity of the Al-Shabab group in Somalia, promoting Jihad and his group to youth through the Internet, video and hip-hop lyrics. He alone has greatly advanced the image of the violent Islamist insurgency group. Al-Amriki left the country several years ago for Somalia and has quickly moved through the ranks of Al-Shabab, now directing forces in the field, organizing attacks and developing strategy with other top al Quaeda officials. His role as a high profile recruitment tool is what makes him such a concern for U.S. law enforcement officials. He is able to connect to a younger generation through effective and attractive means like hip-hop lyrics, demonstrating Al-Shabab's attempt to recruit not only young foreign nationals but specifically English-speaking Americans and westerners.[69] Al-Amriki's influence is particularly worrisome, given that in June 2010 two Americans were stopped by FBI officials from boarding separate flights to Egypt to join Al-Amriki in Somalia.
- A North Carolina man, Daniel Boyd, along with six other individuals, was arrested in the summer of 2009 for operating a terrorism training camp in North Carolina. Daniel Boyd, a U.S. citizen, his two sons and four others had allegedly been training in their rural lakeside home for "violent jihad." Mr. Boyd had traveled to Afghanistan nearly 20 years earlier to train at terrorist camps in Pakistan and Afghanistan, and he fought the Soviets for three years before returning to the United States. It was reported that members of the group traveled to Israel in 2007 with the intent of joining the jihad movement but returned with no success. The seven men were charged with providing material support to terrorism.[70]
- In 2009 Major Nidal Malik Hasan, a psychiatrist for the United States army, killed 13 people and wounded 30 at Fort Hood, Texas, in a processing center for soldiers about to be deployed. Hasan was reportedly unhappy about the continuing wars in Iraq and Afghanistan and was afraid of being deployed to Afghanistan. Hasan showed many signs throughout his career in the Army of resistance to the war efforts in the Middle East, and he disagreed with American foreign policies

related to Israel and the Middle East. He had been in contact with Anwar al-Awlaki, as well.[71] Unfortunately, Hasan's behavior went largely unnoticed by the U.S. Army, who failed to connect the dots and predict potential terrorist activity before it was too late.

- The Times Square bomber, Faisal Shahzad, is another example of a U.S. resident who was radicalized, exposed to training overseas, and then used that training to plot an attack on U.S. soil. On May 1, 2010, Shahzad left a vehicle parked in Times Square that contained a large quantity of explosives. Fortunately, the devices inside the vehicle did not detonate, but smoke coming from the vehicle led to a quick response by authorities and an evacuation of a large swath of the tourist attraction. Shahzad had been living in the United States for 11 years and had even become a naturalized U.S. citizen in 2009. Shahzad was married with two children and by all accounts lived a normal life as a financial analyst with an MBA, living in a Connecticut suburb. In 2009 Shahzad lost his job and had become very committed to his religion. Shahzad had reportedly spent nearly five months in Pakistan where, according to him, he had been getting training from the Pakistan Taliban. The Pakistan Taliban claimed responsibility for the botched attack in Times Square.[72] Shahzad's terrorist activity seems to have been triggered, by many reports, after he lost his job, had his house foreclosed on, and was reportedly being sued by an energy company. After that he and his family made trips to Pakistan where his wife eventually stayed. Shahzad returned to the United States and rented a small apartment in a Connecticut suburb where he planned his attack. Shahzad was able to travel with ease for extended periods of time in foreign countries without raising suspicion. After the attempted Times Square attack, he was even able to purchase a single one-way ticket to Saudi Arabia in cash with no luggage checked. This is a prime example of how terrorist organizations can use U.S. citizens and residents to carry out their goals.

In late 2010 a few plots involving homegrown terrorist raised the alarms even higher. On November 28 Mohamed Osman Mohamud, a 19-year-old naturalized U.S. citizen from Somalia, planned to detonate explosives during a Christmas tree lighting ceremony in downtown Portland, Oregon. Mohamud was working with two people he thought were al-Qaeda agents, but he was in fact dealing with undercover FBI operatives. Mohamud submitted articles to extremist magazines and online publications, and confided to the undercover operatives that he wanted to wage war on America, and that the 9/11 attacks were "awesome."[73] A little over a week later, on December 9, another plot involving a U.S. citizen in Baltimore was foiled after he praised violent jihad on Facebook. Antonio Martinez, a 21-year-old construction worker, tried to blow up a U.S. military recruitment center. He, too, was working with undercover FBI operatives.[74] Much discussion from these two FBI-involved stings, as well as a similar plot in Dallas to blow up a skyscraper also involving the FBI, has revolved around the concept of entrapment. Some believe that without collaboration and active participation from undercover FBI agents, these attacks would have never come to fruition. However, the willingness of the participants to go so far as to push the trigger in these plots speaks to the fact that they felt strongly enough in their jihadist beliefs to kill hundreds, possibly thousands of American citizens on their own soil.

THE THREAT

With the uptick in homegrown terrorist incidents, it is obvious that this is the next phase of terrorism in the United States. Recent reports by the former heads of the September 11 Commission indicate that the government and law enforcement were slow to take this threat seriously and have failed to put strategies into place to deal with the issue.[75] Currently there is no federal agency specifically charged with identifying and preventing radicalization and related attacks. There are also no set legal or legislative procedures specific to the phenomenon, leading to problems like the accusations of entrapment leveled at FBI agents in the Portland, Dallas, and Baltimore cases discussed previously. The FBI has reached out to Muslim populations, particularly Somali immigrants, in an effort to identify potential extremists, and relies heavily on tips from vigilant citizens. However, experts warn that the "Americanization of al-Qaeda" is likely the biggest threat to homeland security in the coming years, and advises interagency cooperation and community outreach to stem the growth of the homegrown terrorist threat.

DOMESTIC TERRORISM

As defined by the FBI, **domestic terrorism** is the unlawful use, or threatened use, of violence by a group or an individual based and operating entirely within the United States or its territories, without foreign direction, committed against persons or property to intimidate or coerce a government, the civilian population, or any segment thereof, in furtherance of political or social objectives.[76] Its perpetrators can be divided into two groups: right-wing terrorists and left-wing terrorists.

RIGHT-WING TERRORISTS

Domestic **right-wing terrorist** groups often adhere to the principles of racial supremacy and embrace antigovernment, antiregulatory beliefs.[77] They may also cling to anti-abortion and survivalist views and the need for paramilitary training in "militias." In general, right-wing militias believe that inevitably there will be a "show-down" with the federal government, so they stockpile weapons and food. In contrast, patriot groups tend to be more focused on the overthrow and destruction of the federal government. There has been some movement toward "leaderless resistance," which is enacted by small groups autonomously. The Montana Freemen illustrate the antiregulatory attitude of some right-wing groups. They refused to register their cars or pay income taxes, filed liens on government property, established their own court system, announced rewards for the arrest of government officials, and forged financial documents such as money orders. A 960-acre farm was declared sovereign territory and named "Justus Township." The 21 armed freemen surrendered after being under siege from authorities for roughly 90 days in 1996.[78]

More traditional right-wing groups have included the Ku Klux Klan and the Neo-Nazi Party. Although these anti-Semitic and hate-oriented groups have continued to plague American society, they have been relatively quiet over the last five years, primarily owing to the success of civil litigation against specific groups brought about by the Southern Poverty Law Center, the focused attention given by law enforcement to such groups, and the natural death of several leaders within the movement.[79]

Domestic right-wing groups have been around for years, and have always thrived on insecurities about the economy and politics. The second wave of the Ku Klux Klan was born in the early 1900s out of fears that waves of immigrants and Southern migrants were taking industrial jobs from white Americans. We can see parallels to that in the modern economy, where tight jobs markets have ratcheted up tensions toward immigrant groups that are perceived as pushing Americans out of jobs. The multiracial makeup of the newest White House administration has further increased fears among white supremacist groups that white Americans will be marginalized.

A paradigm change in American politics has also increased anxiety toward the government. Health care reform has many Americans afraid of increased government intervention in their everyday lives, and rumors of planned gun control legislation have increased concerns among some parts of the population that Americans will be unable to defend themselves against an out-of-control government. Some legitimate political and economic concerns are feeding the rhetoric that is espoused by extremist groups, and as a result, both racist groups and antigovernment groups are experiencing a surge in interest among Americans feeling disenfranchised or fearful of what the future holds.

Fueling that interest is the availability of information about extremist groups on the Internet. Many of the groups have a web presence, either formally or informally, that allows people with similar views to feel connected to a legitimate cause. Stormfront is a white supremacist-themed site with message boards, news stories, content aimed at children, fundraising mechanisms, and even merchandise. Those who post on Stormfront can interact and connect with up to 40,000 other users per day and are treated to a host of links to other extremist groups on the World Wide Web. Furthermore, the advent of social networking sites such as Facebook and MySpace have enabled extremist groups to reach out to people who identify with their cause. These sites allow almost instantaneous communication between members, allowing conspiracy theories, rhetoric, and calls to action to reach an unprecedented audience in a matter of moments at any given time.

The Southern Poverty Law Center, which researches extremist and hate groups in America extensively, reports that there are currently 926 extremist groups operating in the United States. This number has nearly doubled in the past decade, a result of the "perfect storm" phenomenon.

It would be difficult to stay up to speed on all 926 of these groups, each of which can splinter and implode on a regular basis. White supremacists groups such as the National Socialist Movement, which is America's largest neo-Nazi organization, and Volksfront, which attracts a large following of young men, are among the most active and consistent extremist groups in the country. The most popular antigovernment militia groups, such as the Kentucky State Militia and the Michigan Militia, are also a regular presence among right-wing extremist organizations.[80] One of the most potentially violent of these is the Hutaree or Christian Warrior militia, based in eastern Michigan. Established in 2008, the group is heavily inclined to the paramilitary, training extensively for an "end times battle." Nine members of this group were indicted by a grand jury in Detroit for conspiring to murder police officers and civilians using explosives and firearms in a plot to replace all factions of the government.[81]

Extremist groups are not known for subtlety, which can be a boon to law-enforcement officials assessing everyday situations for potential extremist ties. Most white supremacists want to be identified as such, and thus have adopted a certain style and symbology that makes their beliefs clear to anyone who sees them. White supremacists and other racist extremists often tattoo these symbols prominently on their arms, neck, chest, back, and legs. As a result, men are often seen without shirts in order to give others the best view of their ideology. Hallmarks of racist extremism include the rune, which looks a lot like an upside-down peace sign; SS Bolts, which signify neo-Nazi beliefs and resemble two side-by-side lightning bolts; swastikas; the Iron Cross, which can identify National Socialist Movement sympathizers; and spider webs, which can identify racist convicts and are becoming tattooed more and more on people unaware of their meaning. The number 14 is a neo-Nazi favorite, as is 88, which is shorthand for "Heil Hitler." The acronyms "ZOG" (Zionist Occupied Government), "ROA" (Race

Over All), and "ORION" (Our Race Is Our Nation) are also white supremacist identifiers.

Names of white supremacist bands may also be featured as tattoos, bumper stickers, and T-shirts that identifies a person's extremist ideology. Many extremist groups have used music as a way to reach out to disaffected youth and as a highly effective recruiting tool. Some of the most popular extremist bands include Skrewdriver, Blue Eyed Devils, Bound for Glory, Rahowa, Extreme Hatred, Angry Aryans, Aggravated Assault, Nordic Thunder, Blood and Honour, Brutal Attack, Berserkr and Max Resist.

These symbols, numbers, band names, song lyrics, and acronyms can also crop up in graffiti found at the scene of a crime, sometimes tying what may seem like a simple incident of vandalism to a hate crime or terrorist threat.[82] Police officers should be aware of the most common signs and symbols of extremism as a matter of routine.

This became particularly clear in a 2010 incident where two officers in West Memphis, Arkansas, were killed by extremists and "sovereign citizens" Jerry Kane and his 16-year-old son Joe. Officers Brandon Paudert and Bill Evans noticed a white minivan with unusual license plates, and pulled it over. Jerry Kane argued with the officers before his son got out of the car and shot them with an AK-47. **"Sovereign citizens"** are right-wing extremists who believe that they get to choose which laws to obey and are independent of the rule of courts, law enforcement, the IRS, juries, and elected officials[83] (Figure 21-11).

Although we traditionally think of terrorists as those who perpetrate large-scale attacks on populations, extremists are considered terrorist threats as well. Right-wing and racist groups and individuals are using vio-lence to further their ideologies and political agendas, and they are increasing in frequency. In 2009 the mother of 23-year-old Richard Poplawski called police complaining that she wanted her son out of the house after an argument. She told dispatchers that Poplawski did have several weapons, but that information was never passed down to the first responders.

Officer Paul Sciullo III, Officer Stephen Mayhle and Officer Eric Kelly were gunned down by the young man, who had a history of violent behavior. Most unnerving was the revelation that he had been active on the Stormfront website in the months before his attack. Under his Internet monikers "Rich P" and "Braced for Fate," Poplawski had been posting about his fears that the economic crisis heralded a "Zionist occupation"; that the Obama administration was going to strip citizens of their right to bear arms; and that police would round up political dissenters and bus them to camps. His Stormfront and MySpace accounts also contained derogatory references to African-Americans, Hispanics, Asians, and Jews, as well as photographs of his tattoos, which have symbolic roots in white supremacy movements.[84]

Nativist movements are also on the rise. **Nativists** are extremist immigration opponents who go beyond advocating immigration policy and actually harass or confront immigrants. The Southern Policy Law Center estimates an 80% increase in these groups, which include various factions of the Minuteman Project and Federal Immigration Reform and Enforcement (FIRE) Coalition.[85] In 2009 Minuteman American Defense members in Arizona were accused of shooting and killing a Latino man and his 9-year-old daughter. These groups are also known for staging protests, propagating conspiracy theories (such as the Obama citizenship theory) and acting as vigilantes in immigration issues.

LEFT-WING TERRORISTS

Left-wing terrorists generally profess a revolutionary socialist doctrine and view themselves as protectors of the people against the "dehumanizing effects" of capitalism and imperialism.[86] They advocate revolution as the means of transforming society; from the 1960s to the 1980s, leftists were the most serious domestic terrorist threat.[87] Their demise as a threat was brought about by law-enforcement efforts and the fall of communism in Eastern Europe, which deprived them of ideological support.[88]

The traditional left-wing extremist was replaced in the 1990s by a right-wing opposite as the most dangerous domestic terrorist, but subgroups of the left have developed that are potentially just as dangerous as the right and arguably more economically destructive.[89] A resurgence of anarchist groups, including those associated with Anarchist International, have dramatically increased since September 11, 2001. Most of these groups are relatively small and confine their activities to "rallies" against what they see as incursions of the government into the

▲ **FIGURE 21-11 Death on the interstate**
A traffic stop turns deadly. Jerry and Joe Kane, who identified themselves as sovereign citizens, killed two Arkansas policemen. (© AP Photo/West Memphis Police Dept.)

▲ **FIGURE 21-15 Terrorists records**
Information about al-Qaeda and its allies being unloaded by FBI personnel. The boxes contain videotapes, maps, notebooks, and other documentary sources seized by military, intelligence, and law enforcement personnel in Afghanistan and brought to the United States for closer investigation. The proof for investigators in linking specific terrorist organizations to charities, foundations, and state sponsorship are often found in financial records, an often time-consuming and tedious investigative process that may yield an important conviction. (© AFP/Getty Images)

reach into Islamic society than giving is in Western cultures. It can also function as a form of income tax, educational assistance, foreign aid, and political influence. The Western idea of the separation of civic duty and religious duty does not exist in many Islamic cultures. Thus, charitable organizations take advantage of the Islamic sense of religious duty to raise significant amounts of money.[132] Another unique aspect of the Islamic faith that played a role in the difficulty of tracking expenses was the use of the system known as **hawala.** This system is based on individual trust, family relationships, and regional affiliation. It is an integral part of the economies of many countries in the Middle East and Southeast Asia. It is a method that has been used for centuries to transfer funds from one person or place to another without the issue of federal banking or monetary reporting systems.[133] Since hawala is based largely on trust, there is an absence of the traditional paper trail used in most forensic financial investigations (Figure 21-16). The difficulty for law enforcement is to promote regulation of the hawalas in order to prevent their abuse by terrorist organizations without harming the financial centers of the populations they serve. One approach being tried in the UAE is to require that hawalas be licensed and regulated.[134] It is not known how many hawalas operate within the United States, but many believe that they have existed in America since the 1980s. Based on a 1994 law, hawalas were supposed to register with the government, but no enforcement activity was ever created. Following 9/11, Congress quickly passed the USA PATRIOT Act, part of which requires that hawalas operating within the U.S. register with the Treasury department and report any suspicious activities.[135] Failure to comply with this law gives law enforcement a justification for investigation. This is similar to the tactic that resulted in the 1930 indictment and conviction of Chicago gangster Al Capone for tax evasion.[136]

of such a case often lies in providing financial records that prove knowledge and association with a terrorist group (Figure 21-15) as well as understanding charitable giving in Islamic cultures.

One of the five pillars of Islamic faith is known as *zakat,* or charitable giving. It is much broader in its

---

▶ **FIGURE 21-16**
Checklist of items common in an illegal hawala operation

- Spiral notebooks, scraps of paper, or diaries listing information for numerous financial transactions, which generally include the date, payer name, amount received, exchange rate, and payment method or remittance code
- An unusually high number of phone lines at a residence or business; short incoming calls and lengthy overseas calls
- Fax transmittal logs/receipts, which may contain name of sender, beneficiary, or a code
- Wire transfer receipts/documents
- Phone records/documents; multiple calling cards
- Multiple financial ledgers (one for legitimate transfers, one for criminal activity, and one possibly for settling accounts)
- Bank account information, particularly multiple accounts, under same name
- Multiple forms of identification (false ID for the subject and for several other individuals)
- Third-party checks
- Evidence of other fraud activity

(Adapted from Dean T. Olson, "Financing Terror," *FBI Bulletin,* Volume 76, Number 2, February 2007)

NATIONAL COUNTERTERRORISM INTELLIGENCE STRUCTURES

The National Infrastructures Protection Center (NIPC) is responsible for protecting and investigating unlawful acts against U.S. computer and information technologies and unlawful acts, both physical and electronic, that threaten or target critical U.S. infrastructures.[137] NIPC manages computer intrusion technologies, coordinates specialized training related to its spheres of interest, and supports national security authorities when unlawful attacks go beyond crimes and become foreign-sponsored events. Founded in 1998, NIPC is housed by the FBI. In addition to protecting national security information, NIPC is engaged in preventing and investigating **cyberterrorism,** the use of electronic tools to disrupt or shut down critical components of our infrastructure, including energy, transportation, and government operations. For example, massive thefts of credit card numbers and other such acts could do serious harm to the public's confidence in using e-commerce transactions.[138]

The U.S. PATRIOT Act of 2001 provides law enforcement with new, broadened electronic surveillance authority; using DCS 1000, an Internet surveillance program formerly designated as "Carnivore," the FBI can intercept e-mail messages. Other methods of communication that the PATRIOT Act allows surveillance of include digital pagers, wireless telephones, fax machines, and videoconferencing. Terrorists, child molesters, pornographers, drug traffickers, spies, money launderers, hostile governments, hackers, and nations waging information warfare against the United States all use these means of comunication.[139]

The Departments of Justice, Defense, Energy, and Health and Human Services, the Environmental Protection Agency, and the Federal Emergency Management Agency form the National Domestic Preparedness Office (NDPO). Established in 1998, it is responsible for assisting state and local authorities with the planning, equipment, and training (including health and medical support), needed to respond to weapons of mass destruction attacks.

The FBI Counterterrorism Center has steadily expanded since its creation in 1996. It operates on three fronts: international terrorism operations both within the United States and abroad, domestic terrorism operations, and counterterrorism measures at home and abroad.[140] The center is staffed by 18 participating agencies, including the Department of State, the Central Intelligence Agency, and the Secret Service.

OTHER CRIMINAL ACTIVITIES LINKED TO TERRORIST GROUPS

In addition to the major types of terrorist financing already mentioned, there are many smaller operations that raise funds. Some of these include selling baby formula on the black market for a significant markup, coupon scamming involving hundreds of stores,[141] and counterfeit goods including cheap copycat designer clothes, purses, and CDs.[142] Interpol has issued a report indicating strong links between terrorist organizations and intellectual property crime.[143] Even the music industry has its own dark side with the racist genre of "hatecore" music that is producing millions of dollars in profits, most of which goes to the neo-Nazi movement in Germany.[144] Each of these actions may not garner the attention that more high-profile actions like drug or weapons smuggling do, but each represents a part of the financial portfolio of many terrorist organizations.

The creation of the Department of Homeland Security represents one of the largest federal reorganizations since the modern Defense Department was developed in 1947. The 170,000-employee department absorbed the U.S. Coast Guard; the Immigration and Naturalization Service; the Customs Department; the Secret Service; much of the Bureau of Alcohol, Tobacco, and Firearms; the Federal Emergency Management Agency; the Border Patrol; and a host of other enforcement agencies.

Created in 2001 as an immediate response to the 9/11 attacks, the Department of Homeland Security (DHS) was established by President Bush to develop and coordinate the implementation of a comprehensive national strategy within the federal executive branch needed to prevent, respond to, and recover from terrorist acts within the United States (Figure 21-17). The DHS thus absorbed the U.S. Coast Guard; the Immigration and Naturalization Service; the Customs Department; the Secret Service; much of the Bureau of Alcohol, Tobacco, and Firearms; the Federal Emergency Management Agency; the Border Patrol; and a host of other enforcement agencies.

Among its responsibilities are facilitating the exchange of information across agencies, reviewing and assessing the adequacy of federal plans relating to terrorism, and increasing, as necessary, vaccine and other pharmaceutical stockpiles. The Department of Homeland Security also plays a significant role in intelligence gathering and analysis. The development of Homeland Security Operation Centers across the United States places significant emphasis on information and intelligence analysis.

INVESTIGATION OF TERRORIST ACTIVITIES

The role for local and state officers in combating terrorism has greatly expanded since 9/11. Terrorists may be operating alone, or in concert with sophisticated narcotics cartels, insurgent organizations in foreign countries, or state sponsors. In any event, they are often involved in criminal activity directly affecting state and local officers. Analysis of terrorist operations has revealed a pattern of activity—actions that typically precede major incidents. These *pre-incident indicators* have become a primary subject of training for law enforcement officers. Coupled with knowledge of

▶**FIGURE 21-22**
Identifying suspicious packages and envelopes

Some characteristics of suspicious packages and envelopes include the following:

- **Inappropriate or unusual labeling**
  ○ Excessive postage
  ○ Handwritten or poorly typed addresses
  ○ Misspellings of common words
  ○ Strange return address or no return address
  ○ Incorrect titles or title without a name
  ○ Not addressed to a specific person
  ○ Marked with restrictions, such as "Personal," "Confidential," or "Do not X Ray"
  ○ Marked with any threatening language
  ○ Postmarked from a city or state that does not match the return address

- **Appearance**
  ○ Powdery substance felt through or appearing on the package or envelope
  ○ Oily stains, discolorations, or odor
  ○ Lopsided or uneven envelope
  ○ Excessive packaging material such as masking tape, string, and so on

- **Other suspicious signs**
  ○ Excessive weight
  ○ Ticking sound
  ○ Protruding wires or aluminum foil

If a package or envelope appears suspicious, DO NOT OPEN IT.

Source: Centers for Disease Control and Prevention: Emergency Preparedness and Response, *www.bt.cdc.gov/agent/anthrax/mail/suspiciouspackages.asp*, accessed January 10, 2011.

weapons are not discussed in depth, because the use of these types of weapons would have a catastrophic national impact and fall squarely within the realm of national security and defense, not the police.[148]

In early 2011 the Washington, D.C., and Baltimore, Maryland, area was hit by a number of package bombs that resulted in the disruption of mail service, traffic jams, and some social chaos and disorder, but relatively minor physical damage and no serious injuries or deaths. However, the pattern of incidents reminded officials of past letters and packages that contained lethal biological agents[149] (Figure 21-22). Fire departments have extensive training, appropriate equipment, and experience in handling hazardous-material (HAZMAT) situations. Because of this, they, along with public health officials and other specialists, play major roles in processing biological and chemical threats and attack sites. In addition, the FBI has developed a number of Hazardous Materials Response Teams (HMRTs), which are situated in sensitive locations around the country. HMRTs are composed of special agents uniquely trained and equipped to collect evidence in hazardous environments. They are a crucially important part of the FBI's responsibility to investigate acts of terrorism involving weapons of mass destruction.[150]

LIMITED BIOLOGICAL ATTACKS: ANTHRAX

Biological agents include both living microorganisms and the toxins produced by organisms. Their effect on humans ranges from various degrees of illness to death. Compared with chemical agents, biological agents are generally slower-acting. Among the biological agents that could be used in a terrorist attack are smallpox, anthrax, plague, botulism, tularemia, hemorrhagic fevers, and Q fever.

Anthrax (Figure 21-23) is an acute infectious disease caused by a bacterium;[151] it has a one- to six-day incubation period, although in some unusual cases incubation may take as long as eight weeks. In nonwarfare situations, it most commonly occurs in hoofed animals, but it can also infect humans. There are three types of anthrax, each with its own means of transmission.

In *cutaneous anthrax*, a cut or abrasion in the skin allows the anthrax bacterium to enter the body. This type of anthrax develops fairly rapidly: the incubation period can be one to seven days but is usually two to five days. There is no latent period for its development. Starting as a raised itchy patch resembling the site of an insect bit, it progresses into a red-brown bump that becomes filled with fluid and may be accompanied by local swelling. This ruptures the skin, creating a painless ulcer 1–3 centimeters wide. At the center, a black area emerges, caused by dying flesh. The affliction may be accompanied by fever and sweating. The affected skin dries and falls off in one to two weeks, often leaving no scar.[152] Cutaneous anthrax can spread via the substantially clear fluid that oozes from the rupture site. Death is rare with appropriate antibiotic treatment, and even without it there is an 80%–95% recovery rate.[153]

▲ **FIGURE 21-23   Cutaneous anthrax on victim's arm**
Note the darker spot, which is an area of dying flesh. Anthrax is an acute infectious disease caused by a bacterium. It is one of the biological agents that terrorists could use in an attack against the United States. In cutaneous anthrax, a cut or abrasion in the skin allows the anthrax bacterium to enter the body. Death is rare with appropriate antibiotic treatment. (© CDC/Phil/Corbis)

results within 24 to 36 hours after the onset of respiratory distress. Therefore, it is important to begin antibiotic treatment early. The effectiveness of treatment started after the onset of significant symptoms is limited,[156] and mortality rates at this stage are estimated to be 90%–100%.

Inhalation anthrax is extremely unlikely to occur through person-to-person contact, so communicability is not a concern. The disease is spread by a deliberate act. Large amounts of high-quality, weapon-grade inhalation anthrax delivered in an aerosol form could produce horrific mass casualties. The Centers for Disease Control (CDC) recommends getting annual flu shots to facilitate early differential diagnosis because flu presents many of the same symptoms as does inhalation anthrax. There is a vaccination for the anthrax virus, but it is not yet available to the general public.

Biological Scene with No Overt Dissemination: Unopened Suspicious Letters and Packages

In the past, workers have died from handling unopened mail containing inhalation anthrax, so new precautions have been implemented to reduce the potential for receiving anthrax-tainted mail through the U.S. Post Office and other major carriers. For instance, guidelines have been issued to help spot suspicious mail, postal workers are being trained to identify such mail (Figure 21-24), and many post offices are using electronic beams to kill biological bacteria such as anthrax. However, even at a **biological scene with no overt dissemination**—such as one in which suspicious mail is unopened, the situation is well controlled, and there is no known dissemination of a biological agent—precautions are warranted:

1. If individuals at the scene are not symptomatic—which is the most likely scenario—extensive PPE (personal protection equipment) (Figure 21-25) and respiratory protection may not be needed.[157] The Centers for Disease Control recommends that the minimum level of respiratory protection for first responders at a biological-hazard site is the use of a half-mask or full-face-piece air-purifying respirator with particulate filters from N95 to P100.[158] Disposable hooded coveralls, shoe covers, and gloves are also warranted.[159] Currently, this equipment is not routinely carried in police cars. Therefore, wait for support specialists, such as a HAZMAT or public health team, if they are needed.

2. Control the scene and assess the threat (for example, is it credible?). If the threat is credible, let other responding officers know what the situation is; the 911 dispatch center will notify the appropriate federal, state, and local agencies, which, in turn, will determine whether they accept the threat as credible. Direct people to leave the room, and close windows and doors. Have all people from the room in which the suspicious mail was discovered

Intestinal anthrax is contracted by eating anthrax-contaminated meat that has been insufficiently cooked; it produces an acute inflammation of the intestines. Initial symptoms are nausea, vomiting (including vomiting of blood), fever, abdominal pain, and severe, bloody diarrhea. The incubation period is one to seven days.[154] The mortality rate is estimated to be 25%–75%;[155] the latter figure may indicate a lack of timely diagnosis and treatment.

Inhalation anthrax enters the body through the respiratory system; its usual incubation period is one to six days, but there have been a few latent cases that did not reveal themselves until six weeks after exposure. During the first one to three days after exposure, the physical symptoms are similar to those of a cold or flu; thus they are not very specific. They may include a sore throat, fever, fatigue, muscle aches, mild chest discomfort, and a dry, hacking cough. A period of brief improvement may follow, lasting from several hours to days. Then the symptoms return and quickly advance to severe respiratory distress, shock, and, typically, death. Death usually

► **FIGURE 21-24**
Suspicious mail
(United States Postal Service)

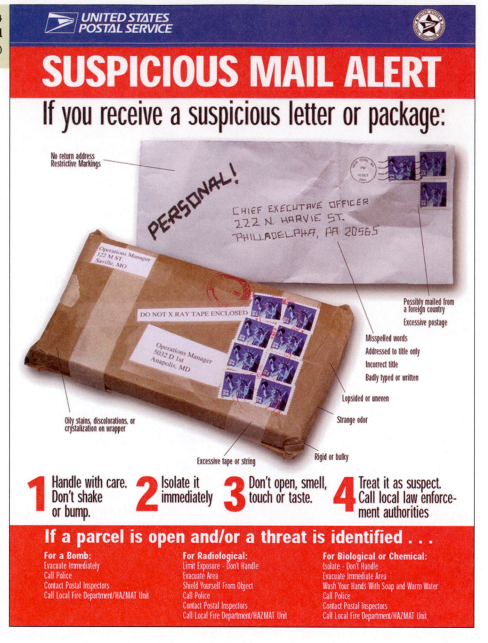

UNITED STATES POSTAL SERVICE

SUSPICIOUS MAIL ALERT
If you receive a suspicious letter or package:

No return address
Restrictive Markings

Possibly mailed from
a foreign country

Excessive postage

Misspelled words

Addressed to title only

Incorrect title

Badly typed or written

Lopsided or uneven

Strange odor

Rigid or bulky

Excessive tape or string

Oily stains, discolorations, or
crystalization on wrapper

1 Handle with care. Don't shake or bump.

2 Isolate it immediately

3 Don't open, smell, touch or taste.

4 Treat it as suspect. Call local law enforcement authorities

If a parcel is open and/or a threat is identified . . .

For a Bomb:
Evacuate Immediately
Call Police
Contact Postal Inspectors
Call Local Fire Department/HAZMAT Unit

For Radiological:
Limit Exposure - Don't Handle
Evacuate Area
Shield Yourself From Object
Call Police
Contact Postal Inspectors
Call Local Fire Department/HAZMAT Unit

For Biological or Chemical:
Isolate - Don't Handle
Evacuate Immediate Area
Wash Your Hands With Soap and Warm Water
Call Police
Contact Postal Inspectors
Call Local Fire Department/HAZMAT Unit

---

stay together in a room some distance away or, preferably, outside the building.

3. Allow only qualified emergency personnel to enter the scene.

4. You and other responders should not smell, shake, or handle the mail (except as necessary when seizing it as evidence).

5. The person handling the evidence should triple-bag the suspicious mail in heavy plastic evidence pouches; limit handling of it to an absolute minimum, and do not drop the mail. When sealing the pouches, avoid creating a puff of air that could spread pathogens. This is most likely to happen if the pouches are sealed too vigorously or if they are noticeably larger than the size actually needed.[160]

6. Mark "Biohazard" on each evidence pouch. Place the evidence in a rigid, leak-proof container, seal the container, and mark it "Biohazard." Repeat this process two more times. The evidence should then be taken by police courier to the appropriate public health laboratory.

7. Get the names of and locator information for everyone who was in the room, anyone who came into the room, and the primary handler of the mail. Determine how the mail traveled through the organization before it reached the point at which it was discovered. Consider the possibility of additional contaminated mail.

8. Do not conduct your preliminary investigation in or near the room where the suspicious mail was found.

◄ FIGURE 21-25   PPE
Officers use personal protection equipment with special sensing devices to make sure the air is free from potentially harmful chemical or biological agents before entering a building. (© Alex Wong/Getty Images) (Source: North Carolina State Bureau of Investigation)

9. Have the organization's health and safety officer advise persons who have been exposed to the biological threat about the precautions they should take and any follow-up health measures they should pursue.

10. Do not allow site decontamination to take place until the crime scene is released.

11. Inspect the ventilation system to see if it was tampered with, since other attack modes and agents could also be in operation.

12. Follow standard procedures for discarding disposable PPE items and for decontamination.

Biological Scene with Limited Dissemination: Opened and Easily Bagged Letters and Packages

A somewhat higher level of personal protection equipment (PPE) is required at a **biological scene with limited dissemination**—such as one in which dissemination occurs only through an opened letter or package—even if the situation is still fairly contained:

1. A full-face-piece respirator, giving facial coverage roughly from the hairline to the chin, with a P100 filter or air-purifying respirator (PAPR) with a high-efficiency particulate air (HEPA) filter and appropriate PPE are needed for safety.[161] Disposable hooded coveralls, shoe covers, and gloves are sufficient for this situation.[162]

2. Control the scene and assess the threat; communicate the facts to other responders. If the threat is credible, close windows and doors; direct people to leave the room immediately without taking anything with them or touching anything.

3. Ask the organization's health and safety officer to attend to the people who have been exposed and to consider turning off the ventilation system.

4. Proceed with your investigation along the lines outlined in the previous list.

CHEMICAL ATTACKS: MASS CASUALTIES

Chemical attacks may be accomplished with V agents, mustard gas, sarin, soman, and tabun. With some **chemical agents,** incapacitation of victims occurs in only 1 to 10 minutes. We have no experience dealing with mass casualties from a chemical-agent attack. Depending on the size of the jurisdiction, the nature of the chemical agent, the method of dispersal, the timeliness of any warning that might be given, weather conditions, and other factors, casualties could number in the hundreds of thousands or even higher. Atropine autoinjectors are available to the military, emergency first responders, and civilians for use as an antidote for most nerve gases. They should not be used on children, who require a pediatric dose. Within the context of what we presently understand, the actions discussed next are appropriate if a chemical attack occurs and produces mass casualties.

Initial Response to the Scenes

There may or may not be a warning before the attack; you must be on the alert for signs of danger when you patrol or are assigned to the scene of a possible chemical threat or to a **chemical attack scene.** If assigned to such a site, always approach with the wind at your back and from the high ground.[163] To achieve these favorable conditions, you may find it necessary to drive across open areas; remember, you are not restricted to driving on roads. Watch for the following signs of chemical attacks:

1. Lack of insects.
2. Birds falling from the sky, dying animals acting in an unusual manner, and dead animals.
3. Discoloration and withering of some types of grass, plants, shrubs, and trees. (These signs may become evident a few minutes to several days after the attack. The discoloration may be light or dark.)
4. Unexplained casualties, multiple victims, or victims with confused behavior, nausea, headaches, severe twitching, burning, or runny eyes, nose, or mouth, extremely small pupils, labored breathing, reddened or blistered skin, loss of bladder or bowel control, convulsions, or cardiac arrest.
5. Unusual liquid droplets with an oily film. (Liquids may be any of several colors—for example, clear, amber, or dark.)
6. Unexplained odors such as the smell from bitter almonds, freshly mown grass or hay, onions, sulfur, geraniums, garlic, mothballs, fruit, or fish. (Nerve gas has no odor.)
7. Vapor, mist, thin fog, or low clouds unrelated to the weather.
8. Unusual metal debris or unusual equipment such as abandoned sprayers and unexplained munitions.[164]

Protection Measures

1. The most important thing you can do is resist the urge to rush in and help. First protect yourself; put on the highest level-PPE you have, including respiratory protection, immediately. Control the scene and assess the threat. The greatest contribution you can make is keeping others advised of conditions. You must be prepared to operate in somewhat of a standoff mode. Use binoculars, if you have them, to assess the scene.
2. In the absence of appropriate PPE, turn off your car's air conditioner and ventilation system, make sure windows are completely shut, and work from inside the car. It is crucial that you protect your respiratory system. Even placing a cloth or your sleeve over your mouth is beneficial.
3. Inform other responders about the dangerous conditions, as well as the direction in which suspicious plumes and clouds are moving, the color and odor of such plumes and clouds, the scene condition, and the numbers, symptoms, and conditions of casualties.[165] Identifying the chemical agent or giving others sufficient information to do so is a high priority.
4. You will not be alone long; an integrated team will soon be there to help. Standing plans will immediately go into effect, and key federal agencies such as the Environmental Protection Agency (EPA), the Department of Defense (DoD), the Federal Emer-

gency Management Agency (FEMA), and the Centers for Disease Control (CDC) will handle tasks appropriate to their responsibilities regarding terrorist attacks. The FBI is designated as the lead federal agency for such incidents. At the same time, state and local terrorist plans, which are coordinated with the federal efforts, will go into effect. Fairly quickly, additional officers, public health officials, the fire department, and rescue and medical personnel will be arriving to help control the scene and to consider decontamination, triage, treatment, and transportation of living casualties.
5. Deny entry to the area to all but emergency responders.
6. Identify a staging area for responders.
7. Direct survivors to a single area; assure them that help is on its way.
8. Be alert to the possibility of secondary devices being present—for example, command-detonated car bombs to kill rescuers. Watch for suspicious people.

After emergency responders arrive at the chemical attack scene, these better-equipped and trained specialists will enter and work the "hot zone." Your responsibilities then will be to help maintain the scene perimeter and to write the incident/offense report. When you are relieved from duty at the scene, follow your agency's post-incident decontamination procedures.

Ideally, contingency planning, disaster preparedness drills, and the rapid arrival of an incident commander will relieve officers from the responsibility of making some of the decisions discussed earlier. If traffic or other conditions delay or prevent their arrival, officers must make the best decisions they can based on their training and experience, the available resources, and the situation.

TERRORISM AND THE FUTURE

In addition to the dangers already discussed, other types of terrorist acts are possible, including agroterrorism, threats to water supplies, and the use of high-energy radio frequency (HERF) and electromagnetic pulse (EMP) weapons. **Agroterrorism** is the deliberate and malicious use of biological agents as weapons against the agricultural and food supply industries.[166] HERF weapons direct a high-energy radio signal at particular targets, such as computers and networks. They are essentially Denial-of-Service weapons (Chapter 17). EMP bombs can destroy electromagnetic systems over a wide area when detonated.[167] Then, too, there is the possibility of a nuclear device or a much less sophisticated **dirty bomb** that renders an isolated area inhabitable for a period of time. Such dirty bombs involve combining nuclear waste from medical X rays or commercial, low-level nuclear material with high explosives, sending the radioactive material into the nearby environment.

Confronting terrorism is not an occasional or seasonal venture; it is an ongoing responsibility. With the help of allies, the United States has the capacity to significantly disrupt terrorist groups and their finances and operations. Information systems must be improved and the products shared; genuine teamwork across numerous agencies will ensure such progress. The United States must have the political will to be decisively and continuously engaged, and the public must help sustain the effort and provide information. The greatest untapped resource in the fight against terrorism is local public safety officers: they are an army of eyes and ears on the nation's streets, and the first line in preventing the next terrorist attack.

In assessing future terrorist threats, we must look at things that we didn't consider post-9/11. At that time, reeling from shock, homeland security consisted of looking for and identifying major plots against American interests. In the years following, many of those types of plots have been foiled, but, by and large, we may not have been seeing the forest for the trees. Homegrown terrorists have become a huge threat to American interests, as al-Qaeda was splintered by the wars in Afghanistan and now-discontinued operations in Iraq and have begun to reach out to disenfranchised and sympathetic, young, often first-generation Americans from Middle Eastern countries. New factions of al-Qaeda have sprouted in Somalia and Yemen, supplanting operations in more traditional locales. The escalating violence in Mexico presents new opportunities for terrorist organizations to utilize cartel routes into the United States. And even domestic, right-wing groups reacting to a paradigm shift in American politics and economics are an increased threat. Indeed, these challenges facing American law enforcement at all levels are, quite frankly, unprecedented in our nation's history.

KEY TERMS

agroterrorism
al-Qaeda
anthrax
biological agents
biological scene with limited
    dissemination
biological scene with no overt
    dissemination
chemical agents
chemical attack scene

cyberterrorism
dirty bomb
domestic terrorism
ecoterrorism
HAMAS
hawala
Hizbollah
international terrorism
Jemaah Islamiyah (JI)
jihad

left-wing terrorists
Muslim Brotherhood
narco-terrorism
nativist
right-wing terrorists
Salafism
sovereign citizens
suicide bombings
Wahhabi movement

REVIEW QUESTIONS

1. How does the FBI define *terrorism*?
2. What are the three major radical or fundamental movements within Islam?
3. How did Osama bin Laden vault to power in Afghanistan? Name some of the important terrorist incidents that al-Qaeda has conducted in the last decade.
4. What does *Hizbollah* mean?
5. What types of events are associated with the Palestinian group known as HAMAS?
6. Explain how the current political and economic climate has affected the resurgence of right-wing organizations.
7. What is ecoterrorism? Name two important special-interest groups associated with ecoterrorism that are active in the United States.

8. Discuss how the violence in Mexico relates to terrorism.
9. Assess the threats from domestic and foreign terrorists.
10. Discuss how terrorist organizations are financed. Give examples.
11. List several steps that every police agency and/or officer can do to help prevent terrorism.
12. What is anthrax, and how does it relate to terrorism?
13. List some of the signs that a chemical attack may have taken place. How can officers protect themselves from such attacks?

Circumstantial evidence can be considered analogous to links in a chain. Each link might be an unfortunate coincidence, but the greater the number of links, the more a jury is likely to infer guilt by joining the links into a chain of overwhelming circumstantial evidence.

Opinion Evidence

Witnesses ordinarily are not permitted to give their opinions or draw conclusions on matters about which they are testifying. Their function is to present the facts about which they have firsthand knowledge. It is within the province of the jury to determine the truthfulness of those facts and to draw whatever conclusions it believes are necessary. However, there are a few exceptions to that general rule. Everything a human being perceives through the senses is generally expressed in the form of a conclusion. It is difficult, if not impossible, to describe something perceived as an absolute fact without expressing it in the form of a conclusion. The only things on which a nonexpert may give opinion evidence are matters of description in which fact and opinion are so interwoven that they cannot be separated without losing most of their probative value. Matters of description in which a nonexpert may give an opinion include color, size, shape, speed, mental condition, identity, race, and language.

An expert is someone with special skills or knowledge not ordinarily possessed by others. The skills or knowledge may be acquired through experience, study, observation, or education. To be an **expert witness,** one need not necessarily have a formal education. The expert witness is permitted to interpret facts and give opinions about their significance; the lay witness may present only facts that are a matter of firsthand knowledge. The expert witness is called on to assist the jurors in understanding facts that they are ordinarily not sufficiently trained to understand, such as the results of medical examinations, chemical analyses, ballistics reports, and findings from questioned documents. Results of DNA analysis, for example, would certainly require the supporting testimony of an expert witness.

THE HEARSAY RULE

Most people have heard a story from several different sources and recognized how different the versions sound. Whether these alterations are caused by poor memory or deliberate attempts to spice up the truth is immaterial in a legal context. The fact that stories tend to be changed when they are repeated makes their reliability and truthfulness questionable. For this reason, the hearsay rule was created. **Hearsay** is derived from "heard say." Testimony in court that repeats what others were heard to say means testifying to a second version of what actually happened. The witness has no personal knowledge of the facts in question. Thus, the truth of the testimony depends on the truthfulness and the competence of the person from whom the information was heard rather than of the person testifying. For these reasons, the hearsay rule is perhaps one of the most important yet most confusing rules of evidence.

Inaccuracy, unreliability, and untrustworthiness are only some of the reasons why hearsay evidence is excluded. The inability of the judge and jury to observe the demeanor or conduct of the person who actually has firsthand knowledge of the information is another.

Other reasons for generally excluding hearsay rely on protections guaranteed in the Constitution. The Sixth Amendment guarantees a defendant the right to be confronted by the witnesses against him or her and the right to cross-examine those witnesses. Because the person with firsthand knowledge is not present in court, that person cannot be confronted or cross-examined by the defendant.

Hearsay is a version of the truth repeated in court by one who does not know whether the assertion is true. People may assert things lightly and casually out of court without being overly concerned about the truth; but they would likely be more careful about speaking truthfully in court, when an individual's life or liberty may be at stake and when they are testifying under oath.

The hearsay rule also excludes written statements by people not in the courtroom to testify. Because the writer's personal knowledge is in his or her head, writing that knowledge makes it secondhand information.

If the out-of-court assertion is being offered as evidence not to prove the truth of a matter but only to show that it was said, it is not hearsay and thus may be admissible. This is one of the rare occasions in which the hearsay rule would not be applicable. For example, a homicide victim may have made threats against the defendant. These threats can be repeated in court to show the defendant's state of mind when he/she killed the victim and to support a claim of self-defense. The truth or falsity of the threats is not the issue.

A second exception deals with reputation. The reputation of a defendant or a witness in a trial may be questionable. A third party may testify about what he/she has heard concerning another's reputation. Because an individual's reputation is representative not of actual character but, rather, of what other people think of that person, the truth of the reputation is immaterial. But the fact that such a reputation exists is admissible. For example, if the defendant presents evidence in a trial for assault that he/she is a calm individual, a witness may testify to having heard that the defendant is extremely short-tempered.

In these situations, evidence is offered to show only that the statements were made, not that they are true. Because the witness has personal knowledge, it is not hearsay, and because the statements are not offered for the truth of their contents, they are admissible.

The hearsay rule is based on the recognition that human beings have weaknesses and that the testimony of human witnesses provides the majority of evidence presented to juries in modern trials. Because we will continue to rely on the testimony of human beings as the principal source of information for trying cases, the law must continue to impose standards to ensure the most accurate and reliable testimony possible. Unequivocal application of the hearsay rule to all situations does, however, present certain injustices in our modern judicial system. For this reason, a number of specific exceptions to the hearsay rule have developed.

EXCEPTIONS TO THE HEARSAY RULE

The sheer number of exceptions often creates doubt about whether the hearsay rule has any merit. Among the many reasons for the existence of the hearsay rule, two stand out as the most critical: the unreliability and the untrustworthiness of declarations repeated under oath in court. Until March 8, 2004, the exceptions to the rule could be justified only if these two major drawbacks could be overcome. If the circumstances surrounding the hearsay evidence could ensure a high degree of trustworthiness and reliability, that evidence was admissible as an exception to the rule in order to minimize any injustice. Each exception had to meet many tests to satisfy the criteria of reliability and trustworthiness before it was admissible. Supreme Court decisions eliminated concern over the constitutional issues by holding that the exceptions did not violate the Sixth Amendment guarantees of confrontation and cross-examination,[2] and did not violate the due process guarantees of the Fourteenth Amendment.

In the 2004 case of *Crawford* v. *Washington*,[3] the U.S. Supreme Court decided that some hearsay evidence, that which contains "testimonial" statements, is inadmissible in a criminal prosecution if the original declarant who made the out-of-court statement is unavailable to testify unless the defendant had the opportunity to confront and cross-examine the witness in an earlier proceeding. Thus, with one decision, the Court unraveled many years of judicial precedents that justified many of the exceptions on the basis of trustworthiness and reliability. The Court, in overturning its previous decisions that found the exceptions did not violate those constitutional principles, is now saying that the Constitution does require confrontation and the opportunity for cross-examination if the hearsay evidence is a testimonial statement.

The question of what qualifies as a testimonial statement, was not answered by the Court when it said

> We leave for another day any effort to spell out a comprehensive definition of "testimonial." Whatever else the term covers, it applies at a minimum to prior testimony at a preliminary hearing, before a grand jury, or at a former trial; and to police interrogations. These are the modern practices with closest kinship to the abuses at which the Confrontation Clause was directed.[4]

Although it appears that the general consensus is that if it is conceivable an out-of-court statement might later be used in court against the defendant, it is testimonial and the *Crawford* decision does apply, but, since the *Crawford* decision, many thousand federal and state cases have been decided interpreting the application of the decision to differing factual scenarios and many of the decisions conflict with one another. As is typical for U.S. Supreme Court decisions, time and many court decisions, including more from the high court, will result in a clearer picture of the requirements for adhering to this change of philosophy.

Some hearsay exceptions apply in both civil and criminal cases; others apply only to civil or criminal cases. The following paragraphs discuss several exceptions applicable in criminal cases. In each case, note is made of whether the *Crawford* decision is potentially involved. It should be noted that examples of applications of *Crawford* to specific fact situations will serve no purpose at this point because of many different interpretations of *Crawford*'s applicability in the thousands of cases in state and federal courts.

Confessions

A **confession** is an acknowledgment by a person accused of a crime that he/she is guilty of that crime. To constitute a confession, the admission of guilt must incorporate all the elements of the crime and exclude any reasonable doubt about the possibility of innocence. Confessions are generally of two types. A judicial confession is an in-court confession made before a judge. A judicial confession can also take the form of a guilty plea. Judicial confessions do not fall within the hearsay rule, because they are in-court assertions of the truth of the matter asserted by the person directly involved.

Confessions made out of court fall within the hearsay rule. For such confessions to be admissible, they must meet the tests of admissibility and overcome the assumptions of unreliability and untrustworthiness.

The admissibility of a confession usually raises questions about constitutionality. First, it must be shown that the confession satisfies constitutional requirements of voluntariness. A confession that is obtained involuntarily certainly would not be admissible under modern law. Second, courts admit confessions as an exception to the hearsay rule on the theory that it is highly unlikely that a person will say something against his or her own interest unless it is true. Therefore, a confession tends to establish the reliability and trustworthiness of the truth of the matter asserted. People do not often deliberately make statements that jeopardize their own life or liberty unless those statements are true. Based on this assumption, the major objections to admitting confessions, as hearsay, are overcome. (See the discussion in Chapter 5, "Documenting the Interview and Interrogation.")

Since a confession is made by the defendant, confrontation and cross-examination are not an issue, and the *Crawford* decision is not applicable.

Admissions

One who makes an **admission** does not acknowledge all the facts surrounding the crime necessary to constitute guilt but does admit to certain facts or circumstances from which guilt may be inferred by the jury. For example, without confessing to the crime, an accused may admit having been at or near the scene of the crime at the time it occurred, having a motive to commit the crime against the victim, possessing the gun used in the crime, having foot impressions that match those found outside the window of the victim's house, and leaving town the day after the crime was committed. These admissions may be introduced in the trial by a witness who overheard the accused make these statements or in the form of a written document or electronic recording repeating these statements. They may be introduced for basically the same reasons as confessions are admissible. The contents of the admissions are certainly against the interest and welfare of the defendant and, like confessions, must have been made voluntarily to be admissible. If these factors exist, it is unlikely that a defendant would make such admissions unless they were true. Therefore, the courts allow the admissions on the basis that the principal objections to the hearsay rule—unreliability and untrustworthiness—have been overcome. Here again, the *Crawford* decision is not applicable for the same reasons that it does not apply to confessions.

Spontaneous and Excited Utterances

Human nature is such that speaking the truth is an instinctive reaction. Therefore, if one makes a spontaneous or excited utterance after something startling or unusual has happened, the utterance may be admissible as an exception to the hearsay rule when testified to by one who heard it made. It may be offered to prove the truth of the matter asserted. The spontaneity of the utterance and its declaration under startling and unusual circumstances lend credence to its reliability and trustworthiness. To illustrate, a 5-year-old girl, observing a playmate struck at a railroad crossing, was heard by a passerby to scream, "The engine runned over Billy!" The passerby was permitted to testify in court about what he had heard the girl say. If the little girl is available and qualified, she can be cross-examined as to what she said. Since a third person is testifying to what the girl said, it is most likely that the girl is unavailable for an acceptable reason. This is one of those instances when the applicability of *Crawford* has resulted in conflicting decisions.

It is under this exception that electronic recordings of 911 emergency calls are sought to be introduced. The impact of *Crawford* on the admissibility of 911 recordings have been extremely varied, even within a single jurisdiction and are evaluated on such things as the length of time after the occurrence before the 911 call was made. Was it the first call made? Where was the call made from? Was there a questionable underlying purpose of the call?

In other words, courts look to all the circumstances to determine if they think the caller had prosecution in mind when the call was made. If so, it could be considered "testimonial" and be excluded under *Crawford*.

Dying Declarations

A declaration concerning the facts and circumstances of the fatal injury made by the victim of a homicide who is about to die, expects to die, and does not hope to recover is admissible as an exception to the hearsay rule. The theory is that a person about to die has no reason to lie. Statements admissible under this exception must concern the injury inflicted to the declarant and are admissible only in the trial of the person charged with the declarant's death.

Former Testimony

Written or oral testimony in a hearing or trial falls within the hearsay rule if that testimony is sought to be introduced in a later judicial proceeding. For example, if a witness testifies against the defendant in a preliminary hearing to determine probable cause to hold the defendant for trial, the court record is not admissible in the later trial unless it meets the tests of the former-testimony exception to the hearsay rule. Because the testimony was given in a court under oath, it is presumed reliable and trustworthy and is admissible provided the two judicial proceedings involve the same defendant, who is charged with committing the same act, under the same circumstances. In addition, the witness who originally testified at the former hearing must be unavailable for testimony before the transcript of the hearing is admissible, and, to show that constitutional requirements have been satisfied, it must be proved that the defendant had the right to cross-examine the witness in the former hearing or trial. As the Supreme Court pointed out, this is one of the specific instances when the *Crawford* decision is applicable. The requirement that the defendant must have had the opportunity to cross-examine the declarant has been a long standing test to satisfy the reliability element of this exception to the hearsay rule.

EVIDENTIARY PRIVILEGES

Defendants and other witnesses have a right to have certain matters of communication barred from disclosure in court—for example, confidential communications between husband and wife, confidential communications between attorney and client, and grand jury proceedings that are confidential requirements of law are barred.

The **evidentiary privileges** may vary from state to state. Some are universally recognized as necessary and have existed since the early days of common law. Others exist only if the state legislature has created the privilege by statute. Some of the more common evidentiary privileges fall into four basic categories. The first might be called professional privileges and includes those that exist between attorney and client, physician and patient, priest and penitent, and journalist and informant. Government communications and information, state secrets, and matters of diplomacy are classified as political privileges. The third category is social privileges and includes confidential communications between husband and wife or between a guidance counselor and a child. Finally, judicial privileges include grand jury proceedings, communications among jurors deliberating a verdict, and the privilege against self-incrimination guaranteed by the Fifth Amendment.

All these privileges can be waived by the person against whom the evidence is to be used or who would suffer from its disclosure. Thus, an attorney cannot disclose evidence of a confidential communication between attorney and client unless so directed by the client. Likewise, a spouse cannot testify against a mate without the latter's express permission, unless the spouse is the victim of the mate's crime.

Although only confidential communications are excluded by the privilege, it is the relationship, not the communications, that is privileged. The theory underlying evidentiary privileges creates a balance between the disclosure of truth and the welfare of society. The assumption is that the public benefits more by protecting these relationships than it does by requiring disclosure of the truth to seek to convict one defendant.

WITNESSES

Until a few hundred years ago, witnesses appeared at a trial voluntarily. There were no legal means to compel attendance. With the advent of the rules of evidence, procedures had to be established for requiring the presence of people who possessed knowledge of the facts of the case. The **subpoena** is used for this purpose. It is a written order commanding the person named to appear in court at a specified date and time to testify, under oath, before a judicial tribunal, to facts within the witness's personal knowledge that are pertinent to the case. A *subpoena duces tecum* commands the individual to bring certain records or documents in his or her possession. Refusal to obey subjects the individual to punishment for contempt. Likewise, refusal to testify or answer specific questions may be grounds for contempt unless valid grounds exist, such as the self-incrimination protections guaranteed in the Constitution. People who possess firsthand knowledge have a duty, not a right, to appear in court.

In early common law, defendants had no right to call witnesses on their behalf. Therefore, the prosecution was required to call all witnesses having knowledge of facts, regardless of which side those facts favored. Today, the defense has an equal right to compel the attendance of witnesses. Hence, the state may use only those witnesses it chooses. Witnesses may also be called by the judge, but this power is rarely exercised.

Once in court, the witness's competence to testify must be ascertained. Competence of witnesses was discussed earlier in this chapter. If the witness is not insane, intoxicated, or excluded for other reasons, and if the testimony will not fall within any of the evidentiary privileges, he/she will be presumed competent to testify, though this must first be asserted by taking an oath or affirmation.

In common law, taking an **oath** was a process by which individuals swore to tell the truth on the basis of their sacred belief in a supreme being. Today, of course, the oath is still a recognized means of establishing a witness's competence, but it is no longer the only method. The affirmation is also used for people who refuse, for personal reasons, to take the oath. Because they are otherwise competent to testify, some guarantee that they will tell the truth is necessary. A witness may be declared competent if he/she understands and undertakes the obligation of an oath. This obligation is to tell the truth with a realization of the penalties for perjury. As long as the witness understands and undertakes the obligation, even without swearing to a supreme being, the witness is considered competent to testify. This process is called **affirmation.**

A declaration of a witness's competence in no way guarantees the credibility of the testimony. Credibility deals with believability, which, like the weight of any other evidence, is determined by the jury. Attitude, personality, appearance, hygiene, and general demeanor all affect a witness's credibility, along with the substance of the testimony.

THE INVESTIGATOR AS A WITNESS

The success or failure of a criminal investigation is often ultimately measured in terms of the quality and effectiveness of an officer's presentation of evidence to a court and jury. Because one aim of the entire process of criminal investigation is to bring about the apprehension and prosecution of violators of the criminal laws, the presentation of the case in court must be of paramount concern to the investigator from the moment of arrival at the crime scene. Inability to understand and appreciate this crucial role in the judicial process not only adversely affects the investigator's performance as a witness but also reflects on the investigator's overall professional effectiveness.

Every law-enforcement witness, whether a uniformed officer or criminal investigator, must become skilled at testifying on the witness stand. Preparation should include knowledge of the rules of evidence so that the officer not only can perform in the field more effectively but also can have a better understanding of courtroom procedures and the functions of the prosecution and the defense. To prepare a case adequately, the investigator must understand the rules of admissibility and the relevance of evidence collected. The best witnesses are those who have an understanding and appreciation of their role in the courtroom and their relationship to other participants in the judicial process.

Taking the Witness Stand

From the moment the law-enforcement witness enters the courtroom, people are forming opinions. The officer should walk naturally when approaching the witness stand, not look at or speak to the prosecutor, and not frown at the defendant. If the jury sees these expressions, it interprets them as signs of partiality. The law-enforcement witness should stand erect while being sworn in and, when permitted to be seated, should sit erect, facing the jury. The investigator should not continually cross his/her legs or fidget uncomfortably. Hands should be kept comfortably in the lap or on the arms of the chair.

Nervousness is natural for anyone who appears as a witness. Usually it disappears with experience. However, if the law-enforcement witness is properly prepared and answers all questions accurately and truthfully to the best of his/her knowledge, nervousness is minimized.

Eye contact and speaking voice are extremely important. Many authorities contend that the witness should maintain eye contact with the jury while answering questions rather than watching the prosecutor or defense attorney. But this skill must be developed. It is difficult for most people to look at the jury when responding to a question from an attorney who may be standing on the opposite side of the courtroom. If the jury cannot hear or understand what the witness is saying, the testimony is worthless. Witnesses should speak loudly enough for people in the back of the courtroom to hear clearly and understand what they are saying. Then they can be sure that the jury, the attorneys, and the judge also can hear them.

Answering Questions

The ability to answer questions under direct and cross-examination is usually developed through experience. The law-enforcement witness must answer without emotion or partiality. Sarcasm, witty remarks, or an attitude of "I'm out to get the defendant" must be avoided at all times. The good law-enforcement witness must be positive and firm in answering all questions and should readily admit not knowing an answer if this is the case. The witness who constructs an answer to avoid embarrassment jeopardizes the case for the prosecution. Even the slightest fabrication of testimony is perjury and is likely to be discovered on cross-examination. It should be remembered that to err is human. It is not impossible for law-enforcement witnesses to make mistakes in their testimony. Although it is slightly embarrassing, the witness should not hesitate to admit having made a mistake. This acknowledgment should be accompanied by an explanation. Even if the mistake is not discovered until after testimony is complete, the witness should immediately advise the prosecutor of the mistake so that the prosecutor will have the opportunity to correct it before the conclusion of the trial.

The requirement of being positive and firm in responding to questions also means that the witness must avoid the use of such expressions as "I think," "I believe," or "as I recall." It is difficult to avoid using expressions such as these, because they are part of everyday usage of the English language, but in court they can raise questions as to the definitiveness of the officer's testimony and can be a factor in the degree of credibility given to the testimony by the jury.

There are two basic methods by which witnesses are examined. The narrative technique allows the witness to tell the facts in his/her own words as they are known to be, in response to a question such as "Now tell us what you found at 1234 Elm Street." This technique is used if the examiner knows the witness well and has confidence that the witness will relate only relevant, unobjectionable matters. The advantage of the narrative technique is that it permits the witness to relate details chronologically and make them clearer to the jury. The obvious disadvantage is that an inexperienced witness may ramble, give objectionable or irrelevant testimony, or expose the jury to tainted evidence, potentially causing a mistrial. Hence, prosecutors use this technique sparingly.

Usually attorneys use the question-and-answer technique for examining witnesses. They ask a single, pointed question and receive an answer to it. When the question-and-answer technique is used, the law-enforcement witness should hesitate momentarily before answering. This allows time for the opposing attorney to raise any objections. It also gives the witness an opportunity to digest the question to make sure it has been clearly understood. If not, the witness should ask that the question be repeated as many times as necessary. If the question does not make any sense after several repetitions, the witness may ask that the question be phrased in different terms. The witness should not volunteer information.

Courtesy and respect are important qualities of an effective witness. The judge should always be addressed as "Your Honor." The witness's language should be intelligible and understandable to the jury. Police witnesses should deliberately avoid the use of slang and words unique to the police service, for these may not be understood by the jury. Profanity should not be used in the courtroom unless the witness is repeating a direct quote. If such is the case, the officer should not hesitate in repeating the exact words used during the investigation.

Occasionally a yes or no answer may be demanded of a witness, particularly on cross-examination. Sometimes such an answer is not an appropriate response to the question. If this occasion arises, the witness should not be pressured into an inaccurate response for the sake of brevity. The witness is always permitted to qualify answers and should persist in this right, if necessary asking the judge for permission to qualify the answer. But if the question can be accurately answered with a simple yes or no, the witness should respond accordingly.

Cross-Examination

The purpose of cross-examination is to ensure that testimony given under direct examination has been accurate and truthful. Through cross-examination the attorney attempts to impeach witnesses called by the opposing side. **Impeachment** is the process of discrediting or contradicting the testimony of the witness to show that the witness is unworthy of belief. It is designed to weaken or destroy the effect of the testimony presented under direct examination and thus to destroy the credibility of the witness in the eyes of the jury. Cross-examination tests the reliability of the witness by attempting to detect whether testimony was intentionally slanted or whether an error or misstatement was made.

The five basic methods for attacking the credibility of a witness are these:

1. showing that the witness's previous statements, personal conduct, or conduct of the investigation is inconsistent with the witness's testimony in court;
2. showing that the witness is biased or prejudiced for or against the state or the defendant because of a close relationship, personal interest in the outcome of the case, hostility toward the opposing party, or similar biases;
3. attacking the character of the witness—revealing previous criminal convictions or other irrefutable characteristics that would render testimony unworthy of belief;
4. showing the witness's incapacity to observe, recollect, or recount owing to mental weakness, a physical defect, influence of drugs or alcohol, or the like;
5. showing that the witness is in error, that the facts are otherwise than as testified.

Cross-examination tactics used by attorneys vary widely, but they fall into two basic categories. Browbeating or belligerent cross-examination is designed to put the witness under pressure to provoke an unprofessional reaction. The attorney may ask a series of questions rapidly in an attempt to confuse the witness and force inconsistent responses. The attorney may try to reverse the witness's words or may continually repeat the same questions in an attempt to elicit inconsistent or conflicting answers.

The cross-examiner who assumes a friendly, condescending role attempts to lull the witness into a false sense of security to bring about less caution in listening to and answering questions. Once the witness's guard is down, the cross-examiner often resorts to leading questions. Leading questions suggest the answer desired. Although leading questions are not permitted in direct examination, they are permitted in cross-examination.

Another danger that should be avoided in cross-examination involves questions regarding whether the officer has talked with anyone about the case. Law-enforcement witnesses often have the impression that this kind of question is designed to attack their integrity by attempting to show that they discussed the details of the case with the press or others in an attempt to create prejudice toward the defendant. In fact, discussing the case with the prosecutor before the trial is perfectly permissible. If the officer answers no to the question and this later turns out to be false, his/her credibility suffers. Likewise, if the witness responds no to the question, "Did the prosecutor tell you how to testify?" the answer is only partly complete. Obviously, the prosecutor generally has instructed the witness to testify to firsthand knowledge of facts and to tell the truth. But the question is designed in such a manner as to imply that an affirmative response means the prosecutor told the witness exactly how to answer each question. The best way of handling this type of situation is to respond, "Yes, I talked with the prosecutor about the case. The prosecutor advised me to relate the facts about which I had firsthand knowledge."

Use of Notes and Reports on the Stand

It is permissible for witnesses to use notes and reports to help refresh their memory while testifying; the human mind can retain only so much information. The witness is not and cannot be expected to remember minute details such as dates and numbers that are of lesser importance than the major facts of the case. However, the witness should constantly be aware of the proper use of notes and reports and the ramifications of their use.

There are two reasons why a witness may refer to notes and reports. The first is a need to remember a particular fact in question. In this case, the officer does remember the case and is permitted to use the notes and reports to help recall minor details. This use of notes and reports is perfectly permissible. However, if the officer's references to the notes and reports are necessitated by an inability to remember anything about the events preceding the trial, the consequences of referring to notes and reports are entirely different.

In the rules of evidence, using notes and reports simply to refresh the memory is referred to as *past recollection refreshed*. As indicated, this is permissible but should be used with restraint, because it may indicate a lack of pretrial preparation. When notes or reports are used by a law-enforcement officer in direct examination, the defense attorney has an absolute right to examine those notes and reports and test the witness's memory before allowing the witness to continue testifying under direct examination. This is done to ensure that the witness is, in fact, testifying from memory.

In the event that the witness cannot remember the facts of the case but uses the notes or reports as the sole basis of testimony without any independent recall, the term applied is *past recollection recorded*. In this instance the oral testimony of the law-enforcement officer becomes worthless, as the knowledge is entirely based on the notes or reports. Should this occur, the prosecutor most

gamma hydroxybutyrate (GHB) A central nervous system depressant used to perpetrate sexual attacks; mixed into a victim's food or drink, can induce relaxation or unconsciousness, leaving the victim unaware of the attack; can also cause seizures or death.

gas liquid chromatograph (GLC) A portable device that separates a sample gas into measurable components; used to detect residues of accelerants at fire scenes.

geographic profiling An investigative strategy in which the locations of a series of crimes (or, sometimes, the scenes of a single crime) are used to determine the most probable area of the offender's residence.

Girard, Stephen Bequeathed $33,190 to Philadelphia to develop a competent police force. In 1833, the city passed an ordinance creating America's first paid daytime police department.

Goddard, Calvin A U.S. World War I veteran and physician, he is widely considered to be most responsible for raising firearms identification to a science and for perfecting the bullet-comparison microscope.

Goddard, Henry One of the last Bow Street Runners, who in 1835 made the first successful identification of a murderer by studying a bullet recovered from a murder victim. In the case, a bullet mold with a noticeable defect was found at the suspect's home; this defect corresponded to a defect found on the recovered bullet.

gray-market vehicles Vehicles purchased abroad and shipped to the United States; may require modifications to meet U.S. emission control and safety standards.

grooves In a firearm's rifled bore, the low cuts that separate the higher lands.

Gross, Hans Austrian prosecutor who wrote the first major book on the application of science to investigation in 1893.

group cause homicide Involves two or more people with a common ideology, who sanction an act committed by one or more of the group's members that results in another person's death.

H

hacker's dictionary A software program that provides unauthorized access to computer systems by generating millions of alphanumeric combinations until it finds one that matches a password.

hacking or cracking The process of gaining unauthorized entry into a computer system.

hallucinogenic drugs Natural or synthetic drugs that distort perception of objective reality and, in large doses, cause hallucinations; can lead to unpredictable effects based on user and environment.

hard and soft insurance frauds Hard fraud is when a person fakes an injury, loss, accident, theft, arson, or other loss to illegally collect from an insurance company. Soft frauds are when people tell "little white lies" to increase the amount of an actual loss for which they will be compensated by their insurer.

hashish A natural hallucinogen, derived from resinous secretions of the cannabis plant, that is more potent than marijuana; sold in soft lumps and usually smoked in a small hash pipe.

hashish oil An extremely potent hallucinogen, derived by distilling THC from marijuana, that produces a high from a single drop; smoked in a cigarette or glass-bowled pipe, or ingested in food or wine.

hazardous wastes Solid, liquid, sludge, and manufacturing by-product wastes that are ignitable, corrosive, reactive, and/or toxic; may pose a serious threat to human health and the environment if improperly managed.

hearsay Testimony by a witness that repeats something which he or she heard someone say out of court and which the witness has no personal factual knowledge of; inadmissible in court.

heavy equipment Heavy construction equipment; usually does not require a title or registration. Also called *off-road equipment*.

Hemident A reagent used in preliminary or presumptive field tests to check for the presence of blood.

Henry system Devised by Edward Henry, the fingerprint classification system that facilitated the use of fingerprints in criminal identification; adopted in England in 1900 and today used in almost every country.

hepatitis B (HBV) and hepatitis C (HCV) Viruses present in blood (and, for HBV, other bodily fluids) that attack the liver and can lead to death; a health hazard at scenes where bodily fluids are exposed.

heroin (diacetylmorphine) An opiate that is much stronger than morphine and often causes death due to its purity or diluents; an odorless, crystalline white powder, which is usually sold diluted and is injected.

home-invasion robbery (HIR) A crime in which one or more offenders deliberately enter a home to commit robbery; characterized by gangs who target individuals rather than residences and use violence to terrify and control their victims.

homicide The killing of a human being by another human being; can be felonious or nonfelonious.

hot spots A location where various crimes are committed on a regular basis, usually by different offenders. Also called a *hot dot*.

hull identification number (HIN) Identification number assigned to boats.

human immunodeficiency virus (HIV) The blood-borne pathogen, also present in other bodily fluids, that can progress into AIDS, which reduces the body's defenses against diseases and leaves victims vulnerable to infections from which they die; a health hazard at scenes where bodily fluids are exposed.

hypercompliance In hypnosis, the situation in which the desire to please the hypnotist or others leads the subject to provide information that does not reflect his or her actual memories.

hypersuggestibility In hypnosis, the subject's heightened degree of suggestibility, which creates the possibility of the hypnotist's influencing the subject, intentionally or inadvertently, to give false information.

hypnosis A state of heightened awareness in which subconscious memories may surface that can be of help to an investigation.

I

identity theft The assumption of another person's identity for use in fraudulent transactions that result in a loss to the victim; accomplished by acquiring personal information about the victim (e.g., date of birth, address, credit card numbers).

immersion burns Burns on the skin that occur when part or all of the body falls into, or is placed into, a tub or other container of hot liquid.

impeachment In a trial, the process of discrediting or contradicting the testimony of a witness to show that he or she is unworthy of belief.

incendiary mechanism A fire-starting mechanism that consists of an ignition device, possibly a timing device, one or more plants to accelerate the flame, and, often, trailers to spread the fire; can be mechanical or chemical.

incest Broadly, any sexual abuse of a minor by an adult who is perceived by the minor to be a family member; also, under some statutes, sexual activity between closely related adults.

incident report The first written investigative record of a crime, usually compiled by the uniformed officer assigned to the call, who conducts the preliminary investigation.

incised and stab wounds Wounds inflicted with a sharp-edged instrument such as a knife or razor; typically narrow at the ends and gaping at the center, with considerable bleeding. Also called *cutting wounds*.

in-custody interrogation The legal condition under which the *Miranda* warnings are required, although case decisions vary on the definitions of "custody" and "interrogation."

indicative intelligence Information pertaining to emerging and new criminal developments; may include fragmentary or unsubstantiated information, as well as hard facts.

individual characteristics Characteristics of physical evidence that can be identified as coming from a particular person or source.

inductive reasoning The thought process that moves from specific details to a general view; e.g., the facts of a case are used to arrive at a logical explanation of the crime.

infant abduction The taking of a child less than one year of age by a nonfamily member; classified by the FBI as kidnapping, although the motive is usually to possess the child rather than to use the child as a means for something else (e.g., money, sex, revenge).

inflated-theft-loss scheme An insurance fraud in which the owner of a stolen vehicle reports a greater financial loss— based on alleged current value, damage, or stolen parts— than is the case.

infrared spectrophotometer A device that identifies samples by recording the amount of infrared light that passes through them; used to detect residues of flammable-liquid accelerants at fire scenes.

Integrated Automated Fingerprint Identification System (IAFIS) Maintained by the FBI, a national online fingerprint and criminal-history database with identification and response capabilities; may be accessed by local law enforcement agencies.

intelligence/analytical cycle A five-part process designed to produce usable information for the client.

international terrorism The use or threatened use of violence against persons or property by a group (or an individual) whose operations transcend national boundaries and are done to further political or social objectives.

interrogation A conversation between an investigator and a suspect that is designed to match acquired information to the suspect and secure a confession.

interrogatory questions Who? What? Where? When? How? And Why?

interviewing The process of obtaining information from people who have knowledge that might be helpful in a criminal investigation.

investigative psychology A criminal-profiling approach based on interpersonal coherence, significance of time and place, criminal characteristics, and the offender's criminal career and forensic awareness.

investigator An official who gathers, documents, and evaluates evidence and information in the investigation of a crime.

iodine A dye used in developing latent prints on porous (particularly paper) and nonporous surfaces; one of the oldest and most proven means of locating prints.

J

Jacob Wetterling Crimes against Children and Sexually Violent Offender Registration Act A 1994 federal act requiring that states create and maintain registries of sex offenders. See also **Megan's law.**

jail booking report A document containing complete personal information about a suspect, including a photograph, fingerprints, and a list of the suspect's personal property at the time of booking.

joyriding The theft and use of a motor vehicle solely to drive it, after which it is abandoned; usually committed by teenagers.

judicial notice An evidentiary shortcut whereby the necessity of formally proving the truth of a particular matter is eliminated when that truth is not in dispute.

justifiable homicide The necessary killing of a person in the performance of a legal duty or the exercise of a legal right when the slayer is not at fault.

K

ketamine A synthetic hallucinogen that produces hallucinations, excitement, and delirium of less intensity and shorter duration than the effects of PCP and LSD; sold as liquids, tablets, or white powder, and injected, smoked, or ingested in a drink.

kinesics The relationship between body language (limb movements, facial expressions, and so on) and the communication of feelings and attitudes.

Kirk, Paul A biochemist, educator, and criminalist; wrote *Criminal Investigation* in 1953; helped to develop the careers of many criminalists.

known samples (1) Standard or reference samples from known or verifiable sources; (2) control or blank samples from known sources believed to be uncontaminated by the crime; (3) elimination samples from sources who had lawful access to the crime scene.

L

lacerations Wounds inflicted by blunt objects such as clubs, pipes, and pistols; typically open and irregularly shaped, bruised around the edges, and bleeding freely.

lands The high sides in a firearm's rifled bore.

laser illumination A method of developing latent prints in which lasers are used to illuminate a crime scene, causing otherwise-undetectable fingerprints to fluoresce when viewed through a special lens.

latent/invisible prints Fingerprints created when friction ridges deposit body perspiration and oil on surfaces they touch; typically invisible to the naked eye.

Lattes, Leone Made a key discovery in forensic serology in 1915, which permits blood typing from a dried blood stain.

Law Enforcement Online (LEO) Maintained by the FBI, an intranet system through which enforcement officers can communicate, obtain critical information, and participate in educational programs and focused dialogs.

layer-checking technique In arson investigation, the process of examining the strata of debris, working through to the floor; may indicate the sequence of burning.

left-wing terrorists Terrorists who usually profess a revolutionary socialist doctrine and view themselves as protecting the people against capitalism and imperialism.

LEO *See* **Law Enforcement Online.**

letter of transmittal In the context of criminal investigation, it is the letter which accompanies physical evidence to the crime laboratory; its elements include the identity and locator information of the submitting individual, the case facts, examinations requested, and other related information.

lifted-prints log A written record of lifted-prints evidence that contains the same type of information as that listed in the evidence recovery log.

lifters Various materials and devices used to "lift" evidence, especially fingerprints and footwear prints, from a surface and preserve it; include flap, electrostatic, rubber-gelatin, and clear-tape lifters.

ligature strangulation Pressure on the neck applied by a constricting band that is tightened by a force other than body weight; causes death by occluding the blood vessels that supply oxygen to the brain.

lineup A procedure in which a number of similar-looking persons, including the suspect, are shown simultaneously or sequentially to a witness who may be able to identify one of them as the perpetrator; can also be conducted with photos.

link analysis he process of charting or depicting temporal and other data gathered during a criminal investigation to uncover and help interpret relationships and patterns in the data.

livestock Farm and ranch animals raised for profit.

livor mortis Soon after death, a purplish color that appears under the skin on the portions of the body that are closest to the ground; caused by settling of the blood.

Locard, Edmond Researcher interested in microscopic evidence; all crime sense today comes under the presumption of Locard's Principle—that there is something to be found.

logic bomb A computer program that uses illegitimate instructions or misuses legitimate instructions to damage data structures; operates at a specific time, periodically, or according to other instructions.

loiding The act of slipping or shimming, by means of a celluloid strip or credit card, a spring-bolt lock that does not have an antishim device.

lookout Accomplices of a robber who watch for police and may provide armed backup for the offender.

lysergic acid diethylamide (LSD) A semisynthetic hallucinogen that produces mental changes lasting up to 12 hours; taken as drops on a sugar lump or blotted paper, was popular in the 1960s and is now making a comeback among juveniles.

M

macroscopic scene The "large view" of a crime scene, including things such as locations, the victim's body, cars, and buildings.

manslaughter A criminal homicide that is committed under circumstances not severe enough to constitute murder but that cannot be classified as justifiable or excusable.

marijuana A natural hallucinogen, derived from certain hemp plants, that produces a dreamy, carefree state and an alteration of sensory perceptions; in the form of crushed dried leaves and flowers, it is smoked or eaten in food.

marine theft The theft of boats, boat trailers, outboard motors, jet skis, and all equipment associated with boating or water activities.

mechanical explosions Explosions in which a high-pressure gas is produced by purely physical reactions; commonly caused by steam (e.g., the bursting of a steam boiler).

media statement Information released to the news media; must not prejudice the suspect's right to a fair and impartial trial.

Megan's law An amendment to the Jacob Wetterling act, legislation requiring that states disclose information about registered sex offenders to the public.

meperidine (Demerol) A synthetic narcotic that in illicit use is usually injected but can be taken orally; the first synthetic opiate.

mescaline A natural hallucinogen, derived from the peyote cactus, that produces hallucinations for up to 12 hours; ground into a powder and taken orally.

meth labs Illegal laboratories that manufacture methamphetamine; range from industrial-size organizations to oneperson tweeker labs, with prevalence skyrocketing due to the availability of "recipes" and chemicals via the Internet.

methadone A synthetic narcotic used to maintain a heroin addict at a stable level of opiate use during and after withdrawal from heroin; administered orally, thus reducing dangers from injection.

methaqualone A strong depressant that can cause poisoning and convulsive comas; removed from the legal U.S. market; street versions are usually counterfeit.

methcathinone A psychomotor stimulant chemically similar to methamphetamine but more potent, often producing extreme paranoia; usually a white or off-white powder that is sold pure and snorted. Also called *cat* and *goob*.

methylenedioxy methamphetamine (MDMA) or **ecstasy** A hallucinogen that produces reduced inhibitions, euphoria, light hallucinations and can result in paranoia and psychosis; sold as a white powder, with usage increasing alarmingly.

Metropolitan Police Act (1829) An act of Parliament that created the London Metropolitan Police, the first centralized, professional police force in Britain, which soon became the international model of professional policing.

microscopic scene A crime scene viewed in terms of specific objects and pieces of evidence associated with the crime, such as knives, guns, hairs, fibers, and biological fluids.

minutiae The characteristics of friction ridges on palms, fingers, toes, and soles of the feet.

Miranda* v. *Arizona The 1966 case in which the Supreme Court established that law enforcement officers must advise a person of his or her constitutional rights before beginning an in-custody interrogation.

mirror To match a person's words, actions, and mannerisms in order to eliminate communication barriers, foster trust, and create the flow of desired information.

misdemeanor A violation of the criminal code that is less serious than a felony; often punishable by imprisonment for no more than one year and/or a fine of no more than $500.

missing person frauds A particularly cruel type of advancedfee scam. Cons gather information on missing persons and then contact relatives explaining how they might be able to find the person for an up-front fee.

mitochondrial DNA (mtDNA) DNA found in the mitochondria of a cell; inherited only from the mother, it thus serves as an identity marker for maternal relatives.

mobile data terminal (MDT) An electronic system in a police car that provides features such as secure communication with 911, and among police units, direct access to national and local databases, and computer functions (e.g., e-mail, Internet access, computing, word processing).

money laundering The process of making illegally obtained money seem legitimate by filtering it through a business and falsifying the business's accounts and invoices.

morgue A crime lab that determines cause of death; when the cause is questionable or is other than a known disease, conducts analyses that produce investigative information.

morphine An opiate in tablet, capsule, and liquid form (but usually injected) that produces euphoria, drowsiness, and relaxation; provides the medical standards by which other narcotics are evaluated.

Motor Vehicle Theft Law Enforcement Act (1984) Federal legislation requiring that manufacturers place permanent identification numbers on major parts of certain car lines.

mugging *See* **strong-armed robbery.**

Mulberry Street Morning Parade Instituted by Chief Detective Thomas Byrnes in New York City in the late 1800s, an innovative approach to criminal identification in which all new arrestees were marched each morning before detectives so that the detectives could make notes and later recognize the criminals.

Munchausen syndrome by proxy (MSBP) A psychological disorder in which a parent or caretaker attempts to elicit medical attention for himself or herself by injuring or inducing illness in a child.

N

narrative style In incident reports, the officer's written chronological account of events at the crime scene from the time he or she arrived until the assignment was completed.

National Center for the Analysis of Violent Crime (NCAVC) Operated by the FBI, an organization that provides investigative and operational assistance to agencies dealing with violent crimes; consists of the BEA, CASMIRC, and VICAP.

National Crime Information Center (NCIC) The FBI's online system of extensive databases on criminals and crime; available to federal, state, and local agencies.

National Incident-Based Reporting System (NIBRS) An FBI program for crime reporting that features a detailed report format documenting far more data than does a basic incident report; involves voluntary participation, but made mandatory by some states.

National Institute-Based Reporting System The FBI's *Uniform Crime Reporting System (UCR)* began in 1929 and its focus is on reporting the types and numbers of crimes.

National Integrated Ballistic Information Network Program (NIBIN) A joint program of the ATF and the FBI, a computerized database of crime gun information that stores images of ballistic evidence (projectiles and casings), against which new images are compared for identification.

National Motor Vehicle Title Information System (NMVTIS) Under development; a computerized database that will include complete histories of vehicles in all states and will prevent title laundering between states.

NCAVC *See* **National Center for the Analysis of Violent Crime.**

NCIC *See* **National Crime Information Center.**

neighborhood canvas A systematic approach to interviewing residents, merchants, and others who were in the immediate vicinity of a crime and may have useful information.

neuro-linguistic programming (NLP) An approach used in interviewing and interrogating that emphasizes establishing rapport, through mirroring, as a means of improving communication and thus obtaining useful information.

NIBRS *See* **National Institute-Based Reporting System.**

ninhydrin A chemical used in developing latent prints on paper and cardboard; produces purplish prints, making it unsuitable for use with money.

NMVTIS *See* **National Motor Vehicle Title Information System.**

nuclear DNA DNA found in the nucleus of a cell; inherited from both the mother and the father.

O

oath A formal attestation in which a witness swears to tell the truth on the basis of his or her belief in a supreme being and acknowledges a realization of the penalties for perjury; a means of establishing a witness's competence.

odometer fraud The crime of rolling back a vehicle's odometer so that it shows a lower mileage than is the case, and obtaining or altering paperwork to support the fraud. Also called *odometer tampering, rollback,* and *clocking.*

off-road equipment Heavy construction equipment and farm equipment.

off-shore accounts Accounts in so-called safe-haven foreign banks, often operated by small island-nations which promise untraceable financial services.

one-year callable certificates of deposit Unscrupulous sellers tout these certificates of deposit (CDs) (which trumpet high rates of interest), but mislead or do not explain to investors about the actual terms of the investment.

opiates Drugs derived from the opium poppy (e.g., opium, morphine, heroin, codeine).

opium An opiate in the form of blackish-brown, pungentsmelling beads of dried fluid, which are smoked; produces drowsiness and relaxation and is the source of morphine, heroin, and codeine.

organized/disorganized offender patterns A criminalprofiling approach in which offenders are categorized as organized or disorganized on the basis of personal and crime scene characteristics. Mixed organized-disorganized crimes reflect aspects of both patterns.

Osborn, Albert In 1910, wrote *Questioned Documents,* still considered one of the definitive works on document examinations.

OxyContin A powerful narcotic consisting of oxycodone, a morphinelike drug, in a time-release formulation that, when crushed and snorted or injected, produces an intense heroinlike high; the latest drug of choice among addicts and teenage abusers.

P

packet sniffers Computer programs designed to monitor network communications and selectively record sensitive information (e.g., passwords, credit card numbers); used by hackers and, with a court order, by the FBI.

palo verde seedpod case A 1992 murder case in Phoenix, Arizona in which DNA analysis of plant evidence was used for the first time in criminal proceedings to help secure a conviction.

"paper vehicle" A vehicle that does not exist but is insured on the basis of a counterfeit title or manufacturer's certificate of origin so that it can later be reported stolen.

paralanguage Characteristics of speech—such as volume, pitch, tone, and tempo—that communicate, often unconsciously, meanings and attitudes of the speaker that may not be evident in the words themselves.

parts marking The process, mandated by law, of attaching VIN labels to the major parts of vehicles in high-theft lines.

passive system (theft deterrent) A type of vehicle antitheft device which activates automatically but may require that the driver do something to deactivate the system.

Peel, Robert *See* **bobbies.**

peremptory challenge The limited number of race and gender-neutral challenges each side has in a criminal case to excuse a juror for any other reason.

personal cause homicide Homicide motivated by a personal cause, which ensues from interpersonal aggression. The slayer and the victim(s) may not be known to each other.

personal protection equipment (PPE) Equipment and clothing designed to protect individuals at high-risk crime scenes from injury and infection.

phencyclidine (PCP) A hallucinogen in powder (angel dust), tablet, liquid, leafy mixture, and rock-crystal forms that produces unpleasant effects and can cause extreme violence and strength; as a street drug, often adulterated and misrepresented, yet usage is increasing notably.

phishing E-mails or letters soliciting personal and account information with which the collector can commit identity fraud or sell the information to someone who will commit that crime.

photographic log A written record listing the photographs taken at a crime scene and detailing who took them, where and when they were taken, and under what conditions.

photographing The primary means of documenting a crime scene.

phreakers People who misuse telephone systems through a variety of fraudulent methods that make it seem as if long-distance service and airtime are being legitimately purchased.

physical stereotyping Occurs when an officer expects that the robber will fit a preconceived description; can result in the escape of a suspect or harm to the officer.

pigeon drop con Another old, but effective scam in which one con strikes up a conversation with someone on the street. Another con approaches them with a bag of money, which is from some illicit source, which he/she just found. After talking about what they could do with the money, one of the cons calls his/her boss, an "attorney" who meets them. The attorney says they will be able to keep the money after they do a reasonable search for the owner, but that "good faith money" must be put up. After the mark puts up his/her money, the cons disappear with it.

PIN *See* **product information number.**

Pinkerton, Allan Formed the Pinkertons in 1850 along with Edward Rucker; the only consistently competent detectives in the United States for over 50 years.

placement, layering, and integration The three main phases of laundering money from illicit sources so it can take on the appearance of legitimate income.

plaintiff In a civil case, the party that was allegedly wronged and that files the lawsuit.

planned operation A robbery that involves careful planning and no planned use of force; has less likelihood of apprehension and generates a large score.

plant In arson, the material placed around the ignition device to feed the flame.

plastic prints Prints created when fingers touch moldable material, such as newly painted surfaces, the gum on stamps, putty, and the sticky side of adhesive tape.

poaching The illegal taking or possessing of game, fish, and other wildlife.

"police spies" In early nineteenth-century England, a derogatory term used in reference to plainclothes detectives; coined by persons who feared that the use of such officers would reduce civil liberties.

polygraph A mechanical device that records physiological changes that occur in a person while he or she is being questioned, with deviations from normal readings indicating deception; can be used only with subject's voluntary consent. Also called a lie detector.

Ponzi/pyramid fraud Basically this involves recruiting people who are promised great returns on their money. The early investors are paid with the money from later investors. The scheme always collapses because the recruitment of investors cannot be sustained and the cons will ultimately steal the funds for their personal use.

Popay, Sergeant Dismissed from London's Metropolitan Police in 1833 for infiltrating a radical group and advocating the use of violence after he acquired a leadership position. Today, we would call Popay's call for violence entrapment.

positive match In DNA analysis, an identical match of a suspect's DNA with that found on evidence at the crime scene.

power-assertive rape-murder A series of acts in which the rape is planned but the murder is an unplanned response of increasing aggression to ensure control of the victim. The acts within the rape assault are characterized by forceful aggression and intimidation.

power-reassurance rape A planned single rape attack followed by an unplanned overkill of the victim. Motivated by an idealized seduction and consequent fantasy, the killer focuses on acting out a fantasy and seeks verbal reassurance of his sexual adequacy.

preferential child molester A person who molests children because he or she has a definite sexual preference for children.

preliminary investigation The process undertaken by the first officer (usually a patrol officer) to arrive at the scene of a crime; includes assessment, emergency care, scene control, a BOLO, scene determination, incident report, and, sometimes, evidence procedures.

preponderance of evidence The burden of proof in civil cases; requires only that the evidence presented by one side be seen by the jury as more believable than the evidence presented by the opposing side.

primary scene The location at which the initial offense was committed.

probable cause A condition in which an officer has suspicion about an individual and knowledge of facts and circumstances that would lead a reasonable person to believe that a crime has been, is being, or is about to be, committed.

procedural criminal law That branch of criminal law that defines what can and cannot be done with, or to, people.

product identification number (PIN) PIN stands for product identification number.

professional theft (of vehicle) The theft of a vehicle to fill a specific order or to resell the parts.

promissory notes Essentially short term I.O.U.s which promise to pay its holder, the investor, the fixed amount invested, plus a fixed interest at some future specified date. While these may be operated legally, many such investments are simply frauds and the money disappears.

proof The combination of all the evidence in determining the guilt or innocence of a person accused of a crime.

Property Insurance Loss Register (PILR) An insurance industry database that lists the insureds in burglary and theft claims and everyone with an insurable interest in fire claims; detects repeated patterns of claim activity.

proximity The amount of space between the participants in a conversation—neither too close, which causes discomfort, nor too far apart, which causes a loss of connectivity.

psilocybin and psilocin Natural hallucinogens, derived from certain mushrooms, that produce hallucinations for about 6 hours; taken orally.

psychological autopsy An analysis of a decedent's thoughts, feelings, and behavior, conducted through interviews with persons who knew him or her, to determine whether a death was an accident or suicide.

pump and dump A scheme where glowing, but false, information about a stock is widely distributed, often through the Internet, and the rapid buying of it "pumps" the price of the stock up. Once pumped, the fraudsters "dump" the stock for a quick profit.

puncture wounds Wounds inflicted with piercing instruments such as leather punches, screwdrivers, and ice picks; typically small, with little or no bleeding.

pyromaniacs Arsonists who lack conscious motivation for their fire setting.

Q

quick strip (of vehicle) The process of removing from a stolen vehicle valuable parts (e.g., seats, stereos, tires) that have no identifying numbers and thus can be easily sold.

R

radial fracture lines Lines that move away from the point of impact in a glass window.

rape or sexual battery The crime of having sexual relations with a person against her or his will; with a person who is unconscious or under the influence of alcohol; or with someone who is insane, feeble-minded, or under the age of consent.

rape-murder Murder that results from or is an integral part of the rape of the victim; either an unplanned response (of increasing aggression or panic over sense of failure) or a planned act (of revenge or sadism).

rapid response deployment or quick action deployment (QUAD) An intervention approach in which patrol officers are trained in the principles and tactics of rapid deployment for critical incidents so that responding officers can take action immediately rather than wait for a SWAT team.

rapport In interviews and interrogations, the harmonious relationship with the witness or suspect that must be established by the investigator to foster trust and meaningful communication.

rebuttal In a trial, the optional process in which the prosecution, after the defense has closed its case, presents new evidence or calls or recalls a witness; it occurs at the discretion of the prosecution.

re-cross-examination In a trial, the requestioning of a witness initially called by the opposing party.

redirect examination In a trial, the requestioning of a witness by the party that called the witness.

reflected ultraviolet imaging system (RUVIS) Lighting and imaging system in which ultraviolet light applied to undetected fingerprints is "bounced" back, highly intensifying the prints.

refurbishment fraud A practice in which working components from damaged or returned items (e.g., a computer) are used in the construction of new items or are resold as new items.

revenge-motivated arson Fires set in retaliation for some injustice, real or imagined, that is perceived by the offender.

rhodamine 6G An excellent fluorescing chemical for enhancing developed latent prints and revealing others; used on metal, glass, plastic, wood, and other nonabsorbent surfaces.

rifling The lands and grooves in the rifled bore of a firearm.

right-wing terrorists Terrorists who usually espouse racial supremacy and antigovernment or antiregulatory beliefs; they often hold antiabortion and survivalist views and call for paramilitary training in "militias."

robbery The crime of taking and carrying away the personal property of another by means of force, fear, or threat of force, with the intent to permanently deprive the owner of its use.

rogues' gallery Instituted by the New York City Police Department in 1857, a display in which photographs of known offenders were arranged by criminal specialty and height for detectives to study so that they might recognize criminals on the street.

Rohypnol A benzodiazapine used to perpetrate sexual attacks; mixed into a victim's food or drink, can induce sedation, memory impairment, or unconsciousness, leaving the victim unaware of the attack. Also called *flunitrazepam.*

root kits Exploit packages that enable computer-system intruders to maintain the highest level of access by installing back doors and secret accounts and altering logs and basic system services.

rough sketch A drawing made at the crime scene; not drawn to scale, but indicates accurate dimensions and distances.

rules of evidence Federal evidentiary rules which state that scientific, technical, or other specialized knowledge is admissible if it will help the trier of fact understand the evidence or determine a fact at issue.

S

safes Locked receptacles for protecting valuables; classified as fire-resistant safes (offering protection from fire but minimum security) or money chests (providing security and reasonably good protection from fire).

salami slice A computerized-theft technique in which dollar amounts are automatically rounded down and the difference is diverted to the perpetrator's special account.

salvage switch A method of disguising a stolen vehicle whereby the title and VIN plate of a salvage vehicle are transferred to an identical stolen vehicle, which can then be sold in the legitimate market.

salvage title The title issued to an insurance company after it has paid a total-loss claim; remains with the vehicle until it is destroyed.

salvage vehicle A vehicle that has been damaged to such an extent that the cost of repairing it is more than its fair market value.

scald burns Burns on the skin caused by contact with hot liquids, either through spills/splashes or immersion; most common type of burn injury to children.

Scotland Yard The original headquarters of the London Metropolitan Police, so-called because the building formerly housed Scottish royalty. Since 1890, the headquarters have been located elsewhere, but have been still known as New Scotland Yard.

search The process of looking for evidence of a crime.

search and seizure The process of looking for evidence of a crime and taking that evidence into the custody of a law enforcement agency.

search warrant Written authorization by a judge allowing law enforcement officers to look for specified items of evidence of a crime in a specified place.

secondary scenes The locations of all events subsequent to, and connected with, the event at the primary scene.

selective raid A robbery that involves a minimal amount of casual planning and may be repeated several times in rapid succession.

semen A grayish-white fluid produced in the male reproductive organs and ejaculated during orgasm; has a chlorinelike odor and dries to a starchlike consistency.

series A crime characteristic in which crimes of the same type are committed over a short period of time, usually by the same offender.

sex offenses Crimes related to sexual activity; classified as serious (e.g., rape), nuisance (e.g., voyeurism, exhibitionism), and mutual consent (e.g., adultery, prostitution).

sexual homicide In sexual homicide, a sexual element (activity) is the basis, or the sequence of, acts leading to the death.

shaken-baby syndrome (SBS) Severe intracranial trauma caused by the deliberate application of violent force (shaking) to a child.

Shoeprint Image Capture and Retrieval System (SICAR) Computer software that classifies, archives, and identifies shoeprints.

shopping cart fraud A computer crime in which the offender selects purchases at an online store, saves a copy of the purchase page and lowers the prices, and then submits the altered page and continues the checkout process.

shoulder surfing When identity thieves stay close enough to people using their credit cards, pins, telephone calling cards, and writing checks that they can gather sensitive identity information.

situational child molester A person who molests children because the opportunity exists to do so or because of his or her inadequacy, regressed personality, or desire for experimentation; does not have a sexual preference for children.

situational stereotyping Occurs when an officer's knowledge and experience with a location creates the expectation that the present situation will be the same as past situations; increases the officer's vulnerability.

sketching The process of drawing a crime scene using rudimentary methods; sketches made can be "rough" or "smooth."

skimmers Data collection devices through which credit cards are passed. When used illegally, they are employed to obtain the credit card numbers used by customers so credit card and/or identity theft can be committed.

small-particle reagent (SPR) A chemical used in developing latent prints on objects that have been immersed in water, dew- or rain-soaked cars, surfaces covered with a residue such as ocean salt, waxed materials, plastics, tile, and glass.

smooth bore A bore without rifling; characteristic of most shotguns.

smooth sketch A finished sketch of the crime scene, often drawn to scale using information contained in the rough sketch.

smurfing A method associated with money laundering. Multiple deposits of cash are made at different accounts in different banks or bank drafts are bought; the transactions are kept under $10,000 to avoid the bank rendering a required report of the transaction to federal authorities.

snow print wax An aerosol wax sprayed on footwear impressions in snow to tint the highlights so that the impressions can be photographed before being cast.

solvability factors Used to screen and evaluate the information in an offense/incident report to determine if there is sufficient information to warrant a follow-up investigation. Such factors include whether suspects are named, the existence of significant physical evidence, the use or display of deadly weapons, and similarities to recently reported crimes.

spalling The breakdown in the surface tensile strength of concrete, masonry, or brick that occurs when exposure to high temperatures and rates of heating produces mechanical forces within the material.

speedballing The simultaneous ingestion of heroin (a depressant) and cocaine (a stimulant); produces a euphoric rush followed by a drowsy or depressing effect. Can cause convulsions and death.

sperm Tadpolelike organisms that are contained in, and travel through, semen to fertilize the female egg.

spill/splash injuries Burns on the skin that occur when a hot liquid falls from a height and splashes onto the body.

spontaneous heating An increase in temperature that results from a natural process; caused by chemical action, fermentation, or oxidation.

spontaneous ignition The catching afire of materials subjected to spontaneous heating; usually requires several hours to several months of oxidation or fermentation.

sprees A crime characteristic in which crimes of the same type are committed at almost the same time by the same offender.

STAR *See* Stolen Auto Recovery System.

stimulants Drugs that directly stimulate the central nervous system, producing excitation, alertness, wakefulness, and, sometimes, a temporary increase in blood pressure and respiration rate; in overdose, can cause hallucinations, convulsions, and death.

sting operations In combating fences, this is a tactic in which undercover officers pose as fences in a "front" business to gain information. Such operations have proven to be an effective means of identifying criminals, penetrating criminal organizations, and recovering property.

Stolen Auto Recovery System (STAR) A method of examining and photographing the contents of shipping containers, by means of gamma rays, while they are entering a port or being loaded onto a vessel; used to identify stolen vehicles being shipped abroad.

stop and frisk A limited pat down of the outer clothing of a person encountered by a law enforcement officer when the person is acting suspiciously, and the officer, concerned about safety, seeks to determine if the person has a weapon.

strategic intelligence Information gathered and analyzed over time that usually confirms new or recently discovered patterns of criminal activity.

striae Tiny furrows made by the action of a tool on an object's surface (e.g., marks left on a door's hinge from an attempt to force the door open with a pry bar).

strong-armed robbery A robbery in which the perpetrator attacks and beats the victim but no weapons are involved.

subpoena A written order commanding a particular person to appear in court at a specified date and time to testify as a witness.

substantive criminal law That branch of criminal law dealing with the elements that describe and define a crime.

sudden infant death syndrome (SIDS) The sudden and unexpected death of an apparently healthy infant, usually during sleep, the cause of which has yet to be determined.

superglue fuming The process of heating cyanoacrylate in a high-humidity chamber so that the condensing of the resultant fumes develops any latent prints.

surrebuttal In a trial, the process in which the defense, after a rebuttal by the prosecution, presents new evidence or calls or recalls a witness; permitted only if the prosecution conducts a rebuttal.

surreptitious entries Burglaries in which no apparent force is used and thus a point of entry or exit cannot be established; may indicate loiding, picking, an unlocked door, a perpetrator with authorized access, or an occupant-staged crime.

surveillance The secretive and continuous observation of persons, places, and things to obtain information concerning the activities and identity of individuals.

swoop and squat One of several varieties of auto fraud. In this version, a person suddenly swoops in front of the car you are driving and hits his/her breaks, causing you to rear-end them. The person then claims medical injuries were caused by you and your insurer usually pays the "victim."

synthetic narcotics Narcotics that are chemically related to opiates but that are produced entirely within laboratories; primarily used as painkillers.

T

tack The equipment used with horses (e.g., saddles, bridles, horse blankets).

tactical intelligence Information that implies immediate action and can lead to arrests or the collection of additional information; may be derived from surveillance, informants, and intelligence analysis.

telephone record analysis time-event charting An intelligence technique in which telephone records are compiled and analyzed to obtain information on the relationships between the subscriber and the numbers called.

testimony A witness's oral presentation of facts about which he or she has knowledge.

threat assessment The process of determining the risk level posed by a threat and whether law enforcement should be called in and a criminal prosecution pursued; includes evaluation of the threatener.

title fraud For motor vehicles, any act that involves altering, laundering, or counterfeiting a title or title reassignment form; often engaged in to support and cover up odometer rollbacks.

T-men Agents of the Bureau of Internal Revenue (which enforced Prohibition), so-called because the bureau was part of the Department of the Treasury.

tool mark Any impression, cut, gouge, or abrasion made when a tool comes into contact with another object.

totality of the circumstances In determining the applicability of the *Miranda* warnings, an approach that takes all the circumstances into consideration, rather than imposing a strict interpretation based on formal procedures.

trace evidence Evidence that is extremely small or microscopic in size or is present only in limited amounts.

trace evidence vacuum A vacuum which gathers small (even microscopic) evidence at the crime scene. Examples of evidence gathered by it include hairs and fibers.

traced forgery Created by tracing over a genuine signature, commonly found on fraudulent (questioned) documents such as contracts, checks, and monetary instruments.

tracing evidence Evidence that helps identify and locate the suspect.

traditional powders The basic powders, available in a number of colors, that have been used for decades for developing latent fingerprints.

trailer In arson, any substance used to spread the fire from the plant to other parts of a room or building.

trends A general tendency in the occurrence of crime across a large geographic area over an extended period of time.

Trojan horse Any computer program that is altered or designed to perform an unwanted or malicious function while appearing to perform a routine or benign function.

Truth in Mileage Act (1986) Federal legislation that requires more tightly controlled documentation and recording of odometer readings each time ownership of a vehicle changes.

T/S/D crimes Any illegal acts involving the treatment, storage, and disposal of hazardous wastes.

tuberculosis A chronic bacterial infection, spread by air, that usually infects the lungs and can lead to death if untreated; a health hazard for anyone in contact with high-risk individuals such as drug addicts and homeless persons.

tumbling The illegal altering of a cellular phone's microchip so that its access codes change after each call, making it difficult to trace the fraudulent user; done through a personal computer.

U

ultraviolet fluorescence A technique in which a darkened fire scene is illuminated with an ultraviolet lamp so that certain substances glow; used to detect residues of accelerants and to locate the point of a fire's origin.

unbundling A medical fraud technique in which each component of service is separated and billed separately, creating a higher charge than if properly billed as a single category of service.

unknown or questioned samples (1) Recovered crime scene samples whose sources are in question; (2) questioned evidence that may have been transferred to an offender during the commission of a crime and may have been taken away by him or her; (3) questioned evidence recovered at multiple crime scenes that associates a particular tool, weapon, or person with each scene.

upcoding A type of medical fraud in which patients and insurers are billed for longer office visits than occurred, or are billed for more expensive tests which were never done.

V

vehicle canvass A systematic approach to documenting every vehicle in the immediate vicinity of a crime as a means of locating the suspect's vehicle.

vehicle fraud Any fraudulent activity involving motor vehicles; includes theft of vehicles, fraud perpetrated on purchasers of vehicles, and fraud committed by owners (or persons acting on their behalf) against insurance companies.

vehicle identification number (VIN) The 17-character identification number assigned to every car manufactured or sold in the United States.

venire The large panel of potential jurors from which a trial jury will be picked.

viatical settlements Though some viatical settlements are operated legally, many are scams. An example of a viatical settlement is when people's life insurance policies are bought for less than face value. The seller thus has access to cash and the buyer makes a profit on the difference between the face value of the policy and the amount paid to the insured.

VIN *See* **vehicle identification number.**

violation In some states, this is a minor transgression of the law, often punishable by a fine of no more than $250 (e.g., littering).

Violent Criminal Apprehension Program (VICAP) FBI unit whose mission is to facilitate cooperation, communication, and coordination between law enforcement agencies and to provide support in their efforts to investigate, identify, track, apprehend, and prosecute violent serial offenders.

virus A malicious program that is secretly inserted into normal software or a computer's active memory and runs when the host runs; causes effects ranging from annoying messages and deletion of data to interference with the computer's operation.

Vollmer, August Often thought of as an administrator, Vollmer's other contributions are towering: he helped John Larson develop the first workable polygraph in 1921 and established in Los Angeles in 1923 America's first full forensic laboratory.

Vucetich, Juan Worked on the use of fingerprints in Argentina. In 1894, he published his own book on the subject, *Dactiloscopia Comparada.*

W

washing (of title) The process of fabricating a vehicle's sale to a purchaser in a jurisdiction that does not issue salvage titles or carry title brands forward, thereby obtaining a clean title on the vehicle.

weight (of evidence) The amount of believability a jury gives to the testimony of a witness or the presentation of an item of evidence.

West case A 1903 incident in which two criminals with the same name, identical appearances, and nearly identical measurements were distinguished only by fingerprints, thus significantly advancing the use of fingerprints for identification in the United States.

white-collar crime Any illegal act committed by concealment or guile, rather than physical means, to obtain money or property, avoid payment or loss of money or property, or obtain business or personal advantage. While these may be operated legally, many such investments are simply frauds and the money disappears.

witness A person who has firsthand knowledge regarding a crime or who has expert information regarding some aspect of the crime.

worm A malicious program that attacks a computer system directly, rather than infecting a host program; spreads rapidly through the Internet or e-mail.

Chapter 1

1. Material on the evolution of criminal investigation is drawn, in part, from Thomas R. Phelps, Charles R. Swanson, Jr., and Kenneth Evans, *Introduction to Criminal Justice* (New York: Random House, 1979), pp. 42–55.
2. T. A. Critchley, *A History of Police in England and Wales*, 2nd ed. (Montclair, NJ: Patterson Smith, 1972), p. 34.
3. Ibid.
4. A. C. Germann, Frank D. Day, and Robert J. Gallati, *Introduction to Law Enforcement and Criminal Justice* (Springfield, IL: Charles C. Thomas, 1970), pp. 54–55.
5. Melville Lee, *A History of Police in England* (Montclair, NJ: Patterson Smith reprint, 1971), p. 240.
6. Thomas A. Reppetto, *The Blue Parade* (New York: Free Press, 1978), p. 26.
7. Ibid., pp. 26–28.
8. Ibid., p. 29.
9. James F. Richardson, *The New York Police* (New York: Oxford, 1970), p. 37.
10. James D. Horan, *The Pinkertons* (New York: Bonanza Books, 1967), p. 25.
11. Ibid., p. 23.
12. Ibid., p. 25.
13. Jurgen Thorwald, *The Marks of Cain* (London: Thames and Hudson, 1965), p. 129.
14. Reppetto, *The Blue Parade*, p. 258.
15. Thorwald, *The Marks of Cain*, p. 129.
16. Reppetto, *The Blue Parade*, p. 257. There seems to be some dispute over whether there was ever any real threat and, if so, whether Pinkerton or the New York City Police actually discovered it.
17. Ibid., pp. 257–258.
18. Ibid., p. 258. Reppetto asserts that as a military analyst Pinkerton was a failure. His overestimates of enemy strength may have made General McClellan too cautious, resulting in McClellan's dismissal by President Lincoln.
19. Ibid.
20. William J. Bopp and Donald Shultz, *Principles of American Law Enforcement and Criminal Justice* (Springfield, IL: Charles C. Thomas, 1972), pp. 70–71.
21. Thorwald, *The Marks of Cain*, p. 131.
22. Reppetto, *The Blue Parade*, p. 259, notes that in two separate instances a total of eight Reno gang members arrested by the Pinkertons were subsequently lynched. In the first instance, three gang members reportedly were taken from Pinkerton custody.
23. Thorwald, *The Marks of Cain*, p. 131.
24. Ibid., p. 263.
25. Clive Emsley, *Policing and Its Context 1750–1870* (New York: Schocken Books, 1983), p. 106.
26. Augustine E. Costello, *Our Police Protectors* (Montclair, NJ: Patterson Smith, 1972 reprint of an 1885 edition), p. 402.
27. Richardson, *The New York Police*, p. 122.
28. Bopp and Shultz, *Principles of American Law Enforcement and Criminal Justice*, p. 66.
29. William J. Mathias and Stuart Anderson, *Horse to Helicopter* (Atlanta: Community Life Publications, Georgia State University, 1973), p. 22.
30. Thorwald, *The Marks of Cain*, p. 136.
31. Ibid.
32. Reppetto, *The Blue Parade*, p. 263.
33. Ibid., p. 267.
34. Ibid., p. 278.
35. Ibid., p. 282.
36. Ibid., p. 283.
37. Richard Saferstein, *Criminalistics* (Englewood Cliffs, NJ: Prentice Hall, 1977), p. 5.
38. Jurgen Thorwald, *Crime and Science* (New York: Harcourt, Brace & World, 1967), p. 4.
39. Thorwald, *The Century of the Detective*, p. 6.
40. Ibid.
41. Ibid., p. 7.
42. Ibid., p. 9.
43. Ibid.
44. Ibid., p. 10.
45. Ibid., p. 12.
46. Ibid., pp. 83–84.
47. Anthony L. Califana and Jerome S. Levkov, *Criminalistics for the Law Enforcement Officer* (New York: McGraw-Hill, 1978), p. 20; also see Frederick R. Cherrill, *The Finger Print System at Scotland Yard* (London: Her Majesty's Stationery Office, 1954), p. 3.
48. Ibid.
49. Cherrill, *The Finger Print System at Scotland Yard*, p. 2.
50. Califana and Levkov, *Criminalistics for the Law Enforcement Officer*, p. 20.
51. Cherrill, *The Finger Print System at Scotland Yard*, p. 4.
52. Thorwald, *The Century of the Detective*, pp. 14–16.
53. Ibid., p. 18.
54. Ibid.
55. Ibid., p. 32.
56. Ibid., p. 33.
57. Saferstein, *Criminalistics*, p. 4.
58. Thorwald, *The Marks of Cain*, p. 81.
59. Thorwald, *The Century of the Detective*, p. 58.
60. Ibid.
61. Ibid., p. 60.
62. Ibid., p. 62.
63. Thorwald, *The Marks of Cain*, p. 138.
64. Ibid.
65. Ibid.
66. Ibid., p. 139.
67. Ibid.
68. Saferstein, *Criminalistics*, p. 281.
69. Thorwald, *The Century of the Detective*, p. 88.
70. Ibid.
71. Ibid., p. 87.
72. Ibid., p. 88.

73. Richard Saferstein, *Criminalistics: An Introduction to Forensic Science,* 5th ed. (Englewood Cliffs, NJ: Prentice Hall, 1995), p. 384.
74. Tod W. Burke and Walter F. Row, "DNA Analysis: The Challenge for Police," *The Police Chief,* Oct. 1989, p. 92.
75. Saferstein, *Criminalistics,* 5th ed., p. 383.
76. "British Police Use Genetic Technique in Murder Arrest," *The Atlanta Constitution,* Sept. 22, 1987, p. A3.
77. David Bigbee et al., "Implementation of DNA Analysis in American Crime Laboratories," *The Police Chief,* Oct. 1989, p. 86.
78. Saferstein, *Criminalistics,* 5th ed., p. 384.
79. Bigbee et al., "Implementation of DNA Analysis," p. 86.
80. The account of the role of DNA in solving the Mann-Ashworth murders is drawn, in part, from Clare M. Tande, "DNA Typing: A New Investigatory Tool," *Duke Law Journal,* April 1989, p. 474.
81. This information is from Ricki Lewis, "DNA Fingerprints: Witness for the Prosecution," *Discover,* June 1988, pp. 44, 46.
82. Bigbee et al., "Implementation of DNA Analysis," p. 88.
83. This account is drawn from several sources: Jim Erickson, "Tree Genes: UA Professor's DNA Work Helps Convict Killer," *The Arizona Daily Star,* May 28, 1993, Metro/Region Section, p. 1; and Tim Henderson, "Report on Analysis of Palo Verde Samples," University of Arizona, April 14, 1993.
84. Saferstein, *Criminalistics,* 5th ed., p. 438.
85. Ibid., p. 30.
86. Thorwald, *The Marks of Cain,* p. 161.
87. Ibid.
88. Thorwald, *The Century of the Detective,* pp. 418–419.
89. Ibid., p. 419.
90. Thorwald, *The Marks of Cain,* p. 164.
91. Ibid.
92. Thorwald, *The Century of the Detective,* p. 434.
93. Alex J. Goddard et al., "High-Resolution Imaging of Latent Fingerprints by Localized Corrosion on Brass Surfaces," Journal of Forensic Sciences, Vol. 55, No. 1, January 2010, pp. 58–65.
94. Paul R. Wolpe, Kenneth R. Foster, and Daniel D. Langleben, "Emerging Neurotechnologies for Lie Detection: Promises and Perils," *The American Journal of Bioethics,* Vol. 5, No. 2, 2005, pp. 39–49.
95. Melissa Littlefield, "Constructing the Organ of Deceit: The Rhetoric of fMRI and Brain Fingerprinting in Post-9/11 America," *Science, Technology, and Human Values,* Vol. 34, Issue 3, May 2009, pp. 365–382.

Chapter 2

1. Neil C. Chamelin, Vernon B. Fox, and Paul M. Whisenand, *Introduction to Criminal Justice,* 2nd ed. (Upper Saddle River, NJ: Prentice Hall, 1979), p. 236.
2. Ibid.
3. Ibid., pp. 236–237.
4. 110 U.S. 516 (1884).
5. Ibid., pp. 237–238.
6. Ibid., p. 238.
7. Ibid., p. 242.
8. Wayne LaFave, *Arrest: The Decision to Take a Suspect into Custody* (Boston: Little, Brown, 1965), pp. 3–4.

9. *Terry* v. *Ohio,* 392 U.S. 1 (1968).
10. 129 S.Ct. 695; 172 L.Ed.2d 496 (2009).
11. See, for example, Section 901.15, Florida statutes, for these and other circumstances when arrest by an officer without a warrant is lawful.
12. The majority of this section is taken verbatim from Neil C. Chamelin, Vernon B. Fox, and Paul M. Whisenand, *Introduction to Criminal Justice,* 2nd ed. (Upper Saddle River, NJ: Prentice Hall, 1979), pp. 244–246.
13. 232 U.S. 383 (1914).
14. *Elkins* v. *United States,* 364 U.S. 206 (1960).
15. 338 U.S. 25 (1949).
16. 367 U.S. 643 (1961).
17. 374 U.S. 10 (1963).
18. *Jones* v. *State,* 895 So.2d 1246
19. *Hudson* v. *Michigan,* 126 S.Ct. 2159 (2006).
20. *Muehler* v. *Mena,* 544 U.S. 93, 125 S.Ct. 1465 (2005).
21. *United States* v. *Robinson,* 414 U.S. 218 (1973).
22. 395 U.S. 752 (1969).
23. 494 U.S. 325 (1990).
24. *Maryland* v. *Buie,* 108 L.Ed.2d 276 (1990).
25. Ibid., p. 277.
26. Ibid., p. 283.
27. 267 U.S. 132 (1925).
28. *Chambers* v. *Maroney,* 399 U.S. 42 (1970).
29. 527 U.S. 465 (1999).
30. *Husty* v. *United States,* 282 U.S. 694 (1931).
31. 453 U.S. 454 (1981).
32. 75CrL 177 (U.S. 2004).
33. 129 S.Ct. 1210; 173 L.Ed.2d 485 (2009).
34. 553 U.S. 164; 128 S.Ct. 1598; 170 L.Ed.2d 559 (2008).
35. *United States* v. *Halloway,* 290 F.3d 1331 (C.A. 11) (Ala.) (2002). See also *Johnson* v. *United States,* 333 U.S. 10, 14–15 (1948), listing situations falling within exigent circumstances exception.
36. 387 U.S. 294 (1967).
37. *United States* v. *Holloway,* 290 F.3d 1331 (C.A. 11) (Ala.) (2002).
38. *Brigham City* v. *Stuart,* 126 S.Ct. 1943 (2006).
39. 130 S.Ct. 546; 175 L.Ed.2d 410 (2009).
40. 392 U.S. 1 (1968).
41. 508 U.S. 366 (1993).
42. *Hiibel* v. *Sixth Judicial Circuit Court of Nevada,* 124 S.Ct. 2451 (2004).
43. Ibid., pp. 2457–2458.
44. *Wong Sun* v. *United States,* 371 U.S. 471 (1963).

Chapter 3

1. Portions of the information on the preliminary investigation are drawn from several sources, including Technical Working Group on Crime Scene Investigation, *Crime Scene Investigation: A Guide for Law Enforcement* (Washington, D.C.: U.S. Department of Justice, January 2000), pp. 11–17, National Institute of Justice, *Crime Scene Investigation: A Reference for Law Enforcement Training* (Washington, D.C.: National Institute of Justice, June 2004), pp. 7–51, and the authors' experiences.
2. "Mysterious Poet Assailant Proves to Victimize Herself," *Atlanta Journal and Constitution,* Oct. 3, 1981, p. A3.
3. Henry C. Lee, Timothy Palbach, and Marilyn T. Miller, *Crime Scene Handbook* (San Diego, CA: Academic Press, 2001), pp. 2–3.

4. Ibid., p. 4.

5. Ibid.

6. Ibid., pp. 4–5, from which the content of this point is summarized.

7. Barry A. J. Fisher, *Techniques of Crime Scene Investigation,* 6th ed. (Boca Raton, FL: CRC Press, 2000), p. 46, with some restatement.

8. Ibid., p. 32.

9. Some of the points in this paragraph are restatements from *Crime Scene Investigation,* pp. 19–23.

10. Jeffrey Dailey and Lou Martin, "Smart Briefs: Digital Evidence," National Institute of Justice, July 2005. Ninety-two percent of small/rural agencies used digital cameras, and 56% used digital recorders. In addition to documenting crime scenes, digital cameras can be used for other purposes, such as making mug shots.

11. Some of the points in this paragraph are restatements from *Crime Scene Investigation,* pp. 19–23, with additions by the authors and suggestions from reviewers of the 10th edition, Spring 2010.

12. Information in the three sections on releasing information to the news media has been drawn from various policies SOPs. For example, see Kansas City (Missouri) Police Department, Procedural Instruction 06-9, "Media Contacts and Interactions," August 22, 2006, and Madison (Wisconsin) Police Department, Policy Manual, 3-600, "News Media Relations," 2003.

13. Bill Berkeley, "Wrong Assumptions Ruined Probe," *Atlanta Journal and Constitution,* Feb. 17, 1982, pp. A1, A13.

14. "But Some Have Ins and Outs," *St. Petersburg* (Florida) *Times,* Feb. 24, 1979, p. A1.

15. "Man Accused of Shipping Self to Bank," *Atlanta Journal and Constitution,* May 10, 1979, p. A18.

16. John Lester, "Forensic Expert Uses Tiny Clues to Solve Crimes," *Tampa Tribune,* Sept. 9, 1992, pp. 1–2.

17. "Real Estate Agent Pleads Guilty to 5 'Lock Box' Thefts," *Washington Post,* Sept. 12, 1978, p. B5.

18. No author, HIV Transmission, Centers for Disease Control and Prevention, March 25, 2010, p. 1. www.cdc.gov/hiv/resources/qa/transmission.htm.

19. Minnesota Department of Health, "Facts on AIDS: A Law Enforcement Guide," pp. 1–2, *www.health.state.mn.us/divs/idepc/diseases/hiv/factsonaods.html,* accessed November 11, 2010.

20. Centers for Disease Control, "HIV Transmission," March 25, 2010, *www.cdc.gov/hiv/resouces/qa/transmission.htm.,* no page number.

21. Ibid.

22. Ibid.

23. Ibid.

24. South Dakota Risk Management Bulletin, Issue #45, "State Employee Blood-Borne Pathogens Procedures," February 5, 2010.

25. S. T. Mast, G. D. Woolwine, and J. L. Gerberding, "Efficacy of Gloves in Reducing Blood Volumes Transferred during Simulated Needle Stick," *Journal of Infectious Diseases,* 1993, Vol. 168, No. 6, pp. 1589–1592.

26. Hepatitis B Foundation, "Hepatitis B Basics," *www.hepb .org,* 2010, no page numbers.

27. Ibid.

28. Centers for Disease Control, "Hepatitis C," *www.cdc.gov/hepatitis/hcv,* June 2010, no page numbers.

29. Ibid.

30. World Health Organization (WHO), "Tuberculosis," *www .who.int/factsheets/fs104/en,* no page numbers, accessed November 14, 2010.

31. Centers for Disease Control, Fact Sheet: Trends in Tuberculosis, 2009, *www.cdc.gov/tb/publications/factsheets/statistics/tbtrens.htm,* no page numbers, 2009.

32. WHO, Tuberculosis.

33. C. Winston, "Decreases in Reported Tuberculosis Cases-United States, 2009," *Morbidity and Mortality Weekly Report,* Vol. 59, No. 10, May 31, 2010, pp. 289–294.

34. Ibid., p. 7.

35. California Commission on Peace Officer Standards and Training, "Basic Course Workbook Series: Learning Domain 30, Preliminary Investigation," Version 2 (Sacramento, CA: 2001), pp. 2–14, with some additions.

36. Sioux Falls (South Dakota) Police Department, Policy 1202, Photographic Evidence/DIMS, April 1, 2009, pp. 1–2.

37. This section is taken with restatement from Kim Waggoner, ed., *Handbook of Forensic Services* (Washington, D.C.: Federal Bureau of Investigation, 2007), pp. 179–180.

38. Ross M. Gardner, *Practical Crime Scene Processing* (Boca Raton, Florida: CRC Press, 2005), p. 163. This is an excellent work and should be in the library of any serious professional because of the numerous "hands on" details it provides.

39. Ibid., p. 171.

40. These four views are identified in Ibid., pp. 166–169. Although they have been well documented for years, Gardner does a crisp job of delineating between views and methods of fixing.

41. Tacoma Police Department, Forensic Services Policy and Procedures Manual, "Crime Scene Diagramming," May 11, 2004, p. 3.

42. Gardner, September 1, 2007 e-mail and attachment to Charles Swanson, handwritten note on manuscript he reviewed.

43. Gardner, *Practical Crime Scene Processing,* p. 171.

44. Ibid., 172.

45. Ibid., pp. 173–174.

46. Ibid., pp. 174–175.

47. Ibid., p. 178.

48. Forensic Services Policy and Procedures Manual, p. 4.

49. Gardner, *Practical Crime Scene Processing,* p. 178.

50. Mike Byrd, "Unearthing New Technology in Crime Scene Responses with Forensic Mapping," (*www.Crime -Scene-Investigation.net//Forensic Mapping.HTML*), undated, p. 4.

51. Gardner, *Practical Crime Scene Processing,* pp. 181–183.

52. Ibid., p. 188.

53. Kent J. Buehler, "The Role of Archaeological Techniques in Forensic Settings" (Norman: University of Oklahoma, College of Arts and Sciences, *Oklahoma Archaeological Survey Newsletter*), Vol. 23, No. 1, July 2003, p. 1.

54. Gardner, *Practical Crime Scene Processing,* p. 188.

55. Ibid., p. 190.

56. This section is taken from Wade, ed., *Handbook of Forensic Services,* pp. 7–11.

Chapter 4

1. National Institute of Justice, *Crime Scene Investigation: A Reference for Law Enforcement Training*, NCJ 200160 (Washington, D.C.: Government Printing Office, June 2004).
2. Richard Saferstein, *Criminalistics*, 7th ed. (Upper Saddle River, NJ: Prentice Hall, 2001), p. 65.
3. Ibid., p. 64.
4. Federal Bureau of Investigation, *Handbook of Forensic Science* (Washington, D.C.: Government Printing Office, 1978), p. 2.
5. Technical Working Group on Crime Scene Investigation, *Crime Scene Investigation: A Reference for Law Enforcement* (Washington, D.C.: U.S. Department of Justice, June 2004).
6. Ibid.
7. Catriona MacDonald, et al., "Discrimination of Soils at Regional and Local Levels Using Bacterial and Fungal T-RFLP Profiling," *Journal of Forensic Sciences*, September 14, 2010, early online publication.
8. Kim Waggoner, *Handbook of Forensic Services* (Washington, D.C.: Federal Bureau of Investigation, 2007), p. 132.
9. Raymond Murray and John Tedrow, *Forensic Geology* (New Brunswick, NJ: Rutgers University Press, 1975), pp. 17–19.
10. Ibid., p. 23.
11. M. Horrocks and K. J. Walsh, "Pollen on Grass Clippings: Putting the Suspect at the Scene," *Journal of Forensic Sciences*, 2001, Vol. 46, No. 4, pp. 947–949.
12. Murray and Tedrow, *Forensic Geology*, p. 25.
13. Missouri State Highway Patrol, Forensic Service Handbook (MSHP: Jefferson City, Missouri, June 2007), p. 30.
14. *Handbook of Forensic Services*, pp. 132–133.
15. Ibid., p. 133.
16. K. Steck-Flynn, "Analysis and Collection of Soil Samples," See *www.crimeandclues.com/soil_analysis.htm* (August, 2007).
17. For example, see J. LeMay, "The Documentation of a Large Outdoor Crime Scene with a Large Number of Footwear Impressions," *Journal of Forensic Identification*, Vol. 60, No. 6, 2010, pp. 738–747.
18. Barry A. J. Fisher, *Techniques of Crime Scene Investigation*, 6th ed. (Boca Raton, FL: CRC Press, 2000), p. 251.
19. Ibid.
20. No author, Footwear and Tire Track Evidence, Imprimus Forensic Services, LLC, 2008, p. 1, *www.imprimus.net/crime_scene_footwear_and_tire_track_evidence_class.html*.
21. Tom Adair, Footwear Impression Evidence, Evidence Technology Evidence, Vol. 8, No. 6, November/December 2010, p. 10.
22. Ibid., pp. 10–11.
23. S. Wiesner, T. Tsach, and Y. Shor, "A Comparative Research of Two Lifting Methods: Electrostatic Lifter and Gelatin Lifter," *Journal of Forensic Sciences*, November 15, 2010, online early publication, accessed December 23, 2010, no page numbers. This unreplicated study compares the gelatin and ESDL methods. The "superior sequence" was electrostatic lifting followed by the use of a gelatin lifter.
24. Missouri State Highway Patrol, Forensic Service Handbook, p. 21.
25. Fisher, *Techniques of Crime Scene Investigation*, p. 254.
26. Waggoner, *Handbook of Forensic Services*, p. 126.
27. Ibid., pp. 124–125. This section is drawn with restatement and added information from this source.
28. B. B. Christy, "The Use of the PDQ Database Along with Other Resources to Provide Vehicle Information for Hit and Run Fatalities in Virginia," Trace Evidence Symposium, poster session, August 15, 2007. Accessed December 21, 2010, *http://projects.nfstc.org/trace/docs/Trace%20Presentations%20CD-2/christy.pdf*.
29. Waggoner, *Handbook of Forensic Services*, p. 101.
30. In this paragraph and the next two, some points are drawn, with restatement and additions, from No author, North Carolina State Bureau of Investigation, *Evidence Guide* (Raleigh, N.C.: State Bureau of Investigation, January 2010) pp. 40–42 and No author, *Evidence Handling and Laboratories Capabilities Guide* (Richmond, Virginia: Virginia Department of Forensic Service, February 2010), pp. XI-25–XI-27.
31. No author, Texas Department of Public Safety, *Physical Evidence Handbook* (Austin, TX: Texas Department of Public Safety, July 9, 2010), p. PEH-02-05, 6 of 12.
32. No author, *Submissions Manual* (Kingston, RI: Rhode Island State Crime Laboratory University of Rhode Island, December 1, 2006), p. OP SM 1-1-01, 24.
33. Maureen Bottrell, "Forensic Glass Comparison, Forensic Science Communications," Vol. 11, No. 2, April 2009, no page number. Accessed December 19, 2010.
34. Waggoner, *Handbook of Forensic Services*, pp. 70–71.
35. Mignon Dunbar and Terence M. Murphy, "DNA Analysis of Natural Fiber Rope," *Journal of Forensic Sciences*, January 2009, Vol. 54, Issue 1, pp. 108–113.
36. Robert C. Chisnall, "Knot Tying Habits, Tier Handedness, and Experience," *Journal of Forensic Sciences*, 2010, Vol. 5, Issue 5, pp. 1232–1244.
37. Although the fingerprints of twins may have a high degree of similarity, variations still occur that make identification possible. C. H. Chin, et al., "Fingerprint Comparison I: Similarity of Fingerprints," *Journal of Forensic Sciences*, 1982, Vol. 27, No. 2, pp. 290–304.
38. Saferstein, *Criminalistics*, p. 397.
39. Ibid., p. 401.
40. Brian Yamashita and Mike French, "Latent Print Development," pp. 7-8–7-11, in Scientific Working Group on Friction Ridge Analysis, Study, and Technology (SWG-FAST), *The Fingerprint Sourcebook* (Washington, D.C.: National Institute of Justice, September 2010). The sourcebook has several chapters that are not yet completed. Accessed December 26, 2010.
41. Ibid., p. 7-4.
42. Fisher, *Techniques of Crime Scene Investigation*, p. 117.
43. Yamashita and French, *Latent Print Development*, p. 7-5.
44. A. J. Brooks, "The Search for Latent Prints When an Offender Wears Gloves," *Fingerprint and Identification Magazine*, 1972, Vol. 53, No. 12, pp. 3–7, 15–16.
45. James Osterburg and Richard H. Ward, *Criminal Investigation* (Cincinnati: Anderson Publishing, 1992), p. 109. For general information on the subject, see S. Clark, "Chemical Detection of Latent Fingerprints," *Journal of Chemical Education*, July 1993, Vol. 70, No. 7, pp. 593–595.
46. William Sampson and Karen L. Sampson, "Recovery of Latent Prints From Human Skin," *Journal of Forensic Identification*, Vol. 55, No. 3, May/June 2005, no page numbers. Accessed December 22, 2010. This paragraph is drawn, with restatement and additions, from this source.

47. C. Michael Bowers, "Who Is a Qualified Forensic Dentist?" in C. Michael Bowers, ed., *Forensic Dental Evidence* (Boston: Elsevier, 2011), p. 30.

48. Ibid., p. 32; from which these first four points are taken.

49. Panarat Thepgumpanat, "Thai Tsunami Forensic Centre Produces First IDs," Reuters, January 18, 2005, *www.alertnet.org.*

50. C. Stavrianos et al., "Applications of Forensic Dentistry: Part I," *Research Journal of Medical Sciences*, 2010, Vol. 4, Issue 3, p. 179.

51. I. A. Pretty and D. Sweet, "A Look at Forensic Dentistry—Part 1: The Role of Teeth in the Determination of Human Identity," *British Dental Journal,* April 14, 2001, Vol. 190, No. 7, p. 362.

52. C. Michael Bowers, "Recognition, Documentation, Evidence Collection, and Interpretation of Bite Mark Evidence," in C. Michael Bowers, ed., *Forensic Dentistry: A Field Investigator's Handbook* (Academic Press: Burlington, MA: 2004), p. 106.

53. A. J. Freeman, D. R. Sennn, and D. M. Arendt, "Seven Hundred Seventy Eight Bite Marks: Analysis by Anatomic Location, Victim, and Biter Demographics, Types of Crimes, and Legal Disposition," *Journal of Forensic Sciences*, November 2005, Vol. 56, Issue 6, pp. 1436–1443.

54. D. Sweet and G. Shutler, "Analysis of Salivary DNA Evidence from a Bite Mark on a Body Submerged in Water," *Journal of Forensic Sciences,* September 1999, Vol. 44, Issue 5, pp. 1069–1072.

55. No author, *Physical Evidence Handbook* (Madison, WI: State Crime Laboratories, 8th edition, 2009), p. 73.

56. M. L. Pilling et al., "Visual Assessment of the Timing of Bruises by Forensic Experts," *Journal of Forensic and Legal Medicine,* April 2010, Vol. 17, Issue, 3, pp. 143–149.

57. Bowers, "Recognition, Documentation, Evidence Collection, and Interpretation of Bite Mark Evidence," pp. 123–124.

58. A. van der Velden, M. Spiessens, and G. Williams, "Bite Mark Analysis and Comparison Using Image Perception Technology," *The Journal of Forensic Ondonto-Stomatology,* Vol. 24, No. 1, June 2006, p. 14.

59. See S. A. Blackwell et al., "Three-Dimensional Comparative Analysis of Bitemarks," *Journal of Forensic Sciences* May 2009, Vol. 54, Issue 3, pp. 658–661.

60. Karen A. Lanning et al., "Scientific Working Group on Materials Analysis Position Paper on Hair," *Journal of Forensic Sciences,* September 2009, Vol. 54, Issue 5, p. 1198.

61. Ibid., p. 1199.

62. On dyed hair, see Julie A. Barrett, Jay Siegel, and John V. Goodpaster, "Forensic Discrimination of Dyed Hair Color," *Journal of Forensic Sciences,* March 2010, Vol. 55, Issue 2, pp. 323–333.

63. Lanning et al., "Scientific Working Group on Materials Analysis Position Paper on Hair," p. 1198.

64. Waggoner, *Handbook of Forensic Services,* pp. 159–160.

65. Ibid., p. 160.

66. Ibid., p. 160.

67. No author, "Evidence Submission Guideline #6: Forensic Fiber and Hair Evidence Analysis" (Indianapolis: Indianapolis-Marion County Forensic Services Agency, October 2, 2008), pp. 2–3.

68. D. Zubakov et al., "Estimating Human Age from T-Cell Rearrangements," *Current Biology,* Vol. 20, Issue 22, November 23, 2010. Accessed December 30, 2010.

69. Jack Ballantyne, *Determination of Age (Time Since Deposition) of a Biological Stain* (Washington, D.C.: U.S. Department of Justice, May 2009), p. 2. This is a project final report and not an official government publication.

70. Ibid., p. 2.

71. Edward Hueske, *Practical Analysis & Reconstruction of Shooting Incidents* (Boca Raton, FL: CRC Press, 2006), p. 226.

72. Henry C. Lee, Timothy Palmbach, and Marilyn T. Miller, *Crime Scene Handbook* (San Diego: Academic Press, 2001), p. 282.

73. S. Shanan et al., "Evaluation of Six Presumptive Tests for Blood: Their Specificity, Sensitivity, and Effect on High-Molecule-Weight DNA," *Journal of Forensic Sciences,* January 2007, Vol. 52, Issue 1, pp. 102–109.

74. Waggoner, *Handbook of Forensic Services,* pp. 45–46.

75. Ibid., p. 48.

76. Megan Zellner and Lawrence Quarino, "Differentiation of Twenty-One Glitter Lip Glosses by Pyrolysis Gas Chromatography/Mass Spectroscopy," *Journal of Forensic Sciences,* Vol. 54, Issue 5, pp. 1022–1028.

77. For example, see Laurance G. Webb, "Recovery of DNA for Forensic Analysis from Lip Cosmetics," *Journal of Forensic Sciences,* 2001, Vol. 46, Issue 6, p. 1474.

78. O. C. Smith, L. Jantz, H. E. Berryman, and S. A. Symes, "Effects of Human Decomposition on Striations," *Journal of Forensic Sciences,* 1993, Vol. 38, No. 3, pp. 593–598.

79. See R. Thomas, "Contribution to the Identification of Smooth Bore Firearms," *International Criminal Police Review,* 1974, Vol. 28, No. 280, pp. 190–193.

80. Aylin Saribey, Abigail Hannam, and Celik Tarimci, "An Investigation into Whether or Not Class and Individual Characteristics of Five Turkish Manufactured Pistols Change During Extensive Firing," *Journal of Forensic Sciences,* September, 2009, Vol. 54, Issue 5, pp. 1068–1072.

81. John W. Bond and Chuck Heidel, "Visualization of Latent Fingerprint Corrosion on a Discharged Brass Shell Casing," *Journal of Forensic Sciences,* July 2009, Vol. 54, Issue 4, pp. 892–894.

82. Michael D. Clark, "Tool Identification from a Clod of Soil from a Grave," *Journal of Forensic Sciences,* January 2011, Vol. 56, Issue 1, pp. 241–243.

83. Saferstein, *Criminalistics,* p. 441.

84. Benjamin Bachrach et al., "Statistical Evidence of the Individuality and Repeatability of Striated Tool Marks: Screwdrivers and Tongue and Groove Pliers," *Journal of Forensic Sciences,* March 2010, Vol. 55, Issue 2, pp. 348–357.

85. H. S. Maheshwari, "Influence of Vertical Angle of a Tool on Its Tool Mark," *Forensic Science International,* 1981, Vol. 18, No. 1, pp. 5–12.

86. Saferstein, *Criminalistics,* p. 453.

87. *Evidence Handling and Laboratories Capabilities Guide,* p. ix–2.

88. E'lyn Bryan, "Questioned Document Examination," *Evidence Technology Magazine,* May/June 2010, Vol. 8, No. 3. Accessed January 10, 2011, p. 1, with additions.

89. *Evidence Handling and Laboratories Capabilities Guide,* p. ix–2.

90. Carolyne Bird, Bryan Found, and Doug Rogers, "Forensic Document Examiners' Skill in Distinguishing between Natural and Disguised Handwriting Behaviors," *Journal of Forensic Sciences,* September 2010, Vol. 55, Issue 5, pp. 1291–1295.

91. Yong Shin, *Technology Transfer of Forensic Document Analysis System: Final Report* (Washington, D.C.: U.S. Department of Justice, September 2010), p. 4. This is a project final report and not an official government publication.

92. Tim Harlow, "St. Anthony Man Pleads Guilty to Bank Robbery Charge," *The Star Tribune* (Minneapolis), November 7, 2008.

Chapter 5

1. Marshall Houts, *From Evidence to Proof* (Springfield, IL: Charles C. Thomas, 1956), pp. 10–11.

2. John E. Hess, *Interviewing and Interrogation for Law Enforcement* (Cincinnati: Anderson, 1997), p. 33.

3. Ibid., pp. 81–84; Charles L. Yeshke, *The Art of Investigative Interviewing* (Boston: Butterworth-Heinesmann, 1997), pp. 56–68.

4. Paul B. Weston and Kenneth M. Wells, *Criminal Investigation: Basic Perspectives* (Englewood Cliffs, NJ: Prentice Hall, 1970), p. 151.

5. Hess, Interviewing and Interrogation for Law Enforcement, p. 84.

6. William Hart, "The Subtle Art of Persuasion," *Police Magazine*, January 1981, p. 10.

7. Stan B. Walters, *Principles of Kinesic Interview and Interrogation*, 2nd ed. (New York: CRC Press, 2003), p. 2.

8. Yeschke, *The Art of Investigative Interviewing*, pp. 25–40, 113–134.

9. New York City Police Department, *Student's Guide—Social Science 1998*, pp. 4–7. This discussion of the process of aging was provided by the New York City Police Department.

10. Brian L. Cutler and Steven D. Penrod, *Mistaken Identification: The Eyewitness, Psychology, and the Law* (New York: Cambridge University Press, 1995) p. 6.

11. Ibid., p. 7.

12. Robert L. Donigan, Edward C. Fisher, et al., *The Evidence Handbook*, 4th ed. (Evanston, IL: Traffic Institute, Northwestern University, 1980), p. 205.

13. Robert Buckhout, "Eyewitness Testimony," *Scientific American*, Dec. 1974, Vol. 231, No. 6, p. 23. Also see Elizabeth F. Loftus, Edith L. Greene, and James M. Doyle, "The Psychology of Eyewitness Testimony," in *Psychological Methods in Criminal Investigation and Evidence*, David C. Raskin, ed. (New York: Springer, 1989), pp. 3–45; Hunter A. McAllister, Robert H. I. Dale, and Cynthia E. Hunt, "Effects of Lineup Modality on Witness Creditability," *Journal of Social Psychology*, June 1993, Vol. 133, No. 3, p. 365.

14. Cutler and Penrod, *Mistaken Identification*, p. 112.

15. Janet Reno, "Message from the Attorney General," Introduction at the National Institute of Justice, Office of Justice Programs, Eyewitness Evidence: A Guide for Law Enforcement (Washington, D.C.: U.S. Department of Justice, Oct. 1999), p. iii.

16. Siegfried Ludwig Sporer, Roy S. Malpass, and Günter Koehnken, *Psychological Issues in Eyewitness Identification* (Mahwah, NJ: Lawrence Erlbaum, 1996), p. 23.

17. Cutler and Penrod, *Mistaken Identification*, p. 113.

18. Buckhout, "Eyewitness Testimony," p. 24. See also Steven Wallace, "The Puzzle of Memory: Reflections on the Divergence of Truth and Accuracy," *The Florida Bar Journal*, October 2005, pp. 24–28.

19. Elizabeth Loftus, "Incredible Eyewitness," *Psychology Today*, Dec. 1974, Vol. 8, No. 7, p. 118.

20. Sporer, Malpass, and Koehnken, *Psychological Issues*, pp. 26–29.

21. Ibid., pp. 34–35.

22. Ibid., pp. 36–39.

23. Buckhout, "Eyewitness Testimony," pp. 24–26.

24. Kelly Dedel, "Witness Intimidation," *Problem-Oriented Guides for Police Problem-Specific Guides Series No. 42*, (Washington, D.C.: U.S. Department of Justice, Office of Community Oriented Policing Services, 2006), pp. 2–30. (This discussion was adapted from this source.)

25. In this chapter, the term *witness* is used to refer both to victims and to bystanders who could provide information to police. The term *victim* is used to denote the victim of the initial crime.

26. C. Johnson, B. Webster, and E. Connors, *Prosecuting Gangs: A National Assessment*, NIJ Research in Brief Series (Washington, D.C.: U.S. National Institute of Justice, 1995).

27. P. Finn and K. Healey, *Preventing Gang and Drug-Related Witness Intimidation*, NIJ Issues and Practices Series (Washington, D.C.: U.S. National Institute of Justice, 1996); R. Elliott, "Vulnerable and Intimidated Witnesses: A Review of the Literature," *In Speaking Up for Justice* (London: Home Office, 1998).

28. N. Fyfe and H. McKay. "Police Protection of Intimidated Witnesses: A Study of the Strathclyde Police Witness Protection Programme," *Policing and Society* 10, no. 3 (2000a): 277–299.

29. J. Tomz and D. McGillis, *Serving Crime Victims and Witnesses*, 2d ed. (Washington, D.C.: U.S. Department of Justice, National Institute of Justice, 1997).

30. Elliott, "Vulnerable and Intimidated Witnesses"; Finn and Healey, *Preventing Gang and Drug-Related Witness Intimidation*.

31. C. Gaines, "Witness Intimidation," *United States Attorneys' Bulletin* 51, no. 1, (2003): 5–10.

32. K. Healey, *Victim and Witness Intimidation: New Developments and Emerging Responses*, Research in Action Series (Washington, D.C.: U.S. National Institute of Justice, 1995).

33. Thomas P. Sullivan, "Police Experiences with Recording Custodial Interrogations," *Northwestern University School of Law* 1 (Summer 2004): 4.

34. See the discussion of camera angles in G. Daniel Lassiter et al., "Criminal Confessions on Videotape: Does Camera Perspective Bias Their Perceived Veracity?" *Current Research in Social Psychology* 7, no. 1 (2001), at www.uiowa.edu/~grpproc/crisp/crisp.7.1.htm.

35. Sullivan, "Police Experiences with Recording Custodial Interrogation," pp. 5–10.

36. See Timothy T. Burke, "Documenting and Reporting a Confession: A Guide for Law Enforcement," *FBI Law Enforcement Bulletin*, Feb. 2001, Vol. 70, No. 2, pp. 17–21.

37. Fred E. Inbau and John E. Reid, *Criminal Interrogation and Confessions* (Baltimore: Williams & Wilkins, 1962), p. 1.

38. Saul M. Kassin, "The Psychology of Confessions," *Annual Review of Law in Social Science* 4 (2008): 194–196. (This discussion was adapted with permission from this source.)

39. The Innocence Project is a national litigation and public policy organization dedicated to exonerating wrongfully

40. Kassin, "The Psychology of Confessions."

41. S. M. Kassin et al., "Police Interviewing and Interrogation: A Self-Reporting Survey of Police Practices and Beliefs," *Law and Human Behavior* 31 (2007): 381–400.

42. S. M. Kassin and L. S. Wrightsman, "Confession Evidence," in *The Psychology of Evidence and Trial Procedure*, eds. S. M. Kassin and L. A. Wrightsman (Beverly Hills: Sage, 1985), pp. 67–94.

43. G. H. Gudjonsson, *The Psychology of Interrogations and Confessions: A Handbook* (Chichester, UK: Wiley, 2003).

44. C. F. Karlsen, *The Devil in the Shape of a Woman: Witchcraft in Colonial New England* (New York: Vintage, 1989).

45. S. M. Kassin, "Internalized False Confessions," in *Handbook of Eyewitness Psychology: Vol. 1: Memory for Events*, eds. M. Toglia, J. Read, D. Ross, and R. Lindsay (Mahwah, NJ: Erlbaum, 2007).

46. S. A. Drizin and B. Colgan, "Tales from the Juvenile Confession Front: A Guide to How Standard Police Interrogation Tactics Can Produce Coerced and False Confessions from Juvenile Suspects," in *Interrogations, Confessions and Entrapment*, ed. G. D. Lassiter (New York: Kluwer Acad., 2004), pp. 127–162.

47. Thomas P. O'Connor, *False Confessions* at the 115th IACP Conference held in 2008 in San Diego; the Police Investigative Operations Committee, the Police Image and Ethics, and the Forensics Committee adopted a resolution supporting research of wrongful convictions and recommended that Congress support and fund efforts to review and develop recommendations to reduce and eventually eliminate wrongful convictions. (This discussion is based on these recommendations.)

48. 297 U.S. 278 (1936).

49. *Payne* v. *Arkansas*, 356 U.S. 560 (1958).

50. *Miranda* v. *Arizona*, 384 U.S. 436 (1966).

51. Ibid.

52. Donigan et al., *The Evidence Handbook*, pp. 47–48. See also *Frazier* v. *Cupp*, 394 U.S. 731 (1969); *Oregon* v. *Mathiason*, 429 U.S. 492 (1977).

53. 318 U.S. 332 (1943).

54. 354 U.S. 449 (1957).

55. *Miranda* v. *Arizona*, 384 U.S. 436 (1966).

56. *Escobedo* v. *Illinois*, 378 U.S. 478 (1964).

57. 384 U.S. 436 (1966).

58. 451 U.S. 477, 101 S.Ct. 1880 (1981).

59. 498 U.S. 146 (1990).

60. 559 U.S. ___. 130 S. Ct. 1213 (2010).

61. 423 U.S. 96, 96 S.Ct. 321 (1975).

62. 492 U.S. 195, 109 S.Ct. 2875 (1989).

63. 130 S.Ct. 1195, 175 L.Ed.2d 1009 (2010).

64. 82 L. Ed. 317 (1984).

65. 430 U.S. 387 (1977).

66. 446 U.S. 291, 100 S.Ct. 1682 (1980).

67. *United States* v. *Clark*, 982 F.2d 965, at 968 (6th Cir. 1993).

68. Jonathan L. Rudd, "You Have to Speak Up to Remain Silent: The Supreme Court Revisits the *Miranda* Right to Silence," *FBI Law Enforcement Bulletin* (September 2010): pp. 25–31.

69. *Berghuis* v. *Thompkins*, 560 U.S. ____ (2010).

70. *Id.* "Notification of Constitutional Rights and Statement (1) You have the right to remain silent. (2) Anything you say can and will be used against you in a court of law. (3) You have the right to talk to a lawyer before answering any questions and you have the right to have a lawyer present with you while you are answering questions. (4) If you cannot afford to hire a lawyer, one will be appointed to represent you before any questioning, if you wish one. (5) You have the right to decide at any time before or during questioning to use your right to remain silent and your right to talk with a lawyer while you are being questioned."

71. *Id.*

72. *Id.*

73. Thompkins also filed a motion for a new trial claiming ineffective assistance of counsel. This motion was likewise denied and followed the appeal regarding alleged *Miranda* violations to the U.S. Supreme Court.

74. The Sixth Circuit Court also ruled in favor of Thompkins on the ineffective-assistance-of-counsel claims.

75. *Miranda* at 446. In *Michigan* v. *Mosley*, 423 U.S. 96 (1995), the Court explained that when a subject invokes his right to silence, all questioning must cease. However, the Court further held that the invocation of the right to remain silent does not mean that police never may resume questioning. Indeed, in *Mosley*, the Court held that the police had scrupulously honored the suspect's Fifth Amendment rights when a different officer questioned the subject in a different location about a different crime after 2 hours had elapsed since the subject invoked his right to remain silent. (Note, this differs from an invocation of the right to counsel, wherein officers would not be allowed to reinitiate contact after merely the passage of time. See *Edwards* v. *Arizona*, 451 U.S. 477 (1981) and *Maryland* v. *Shatzer*, 559 U.S. ___ (2010).

76. Justice Kennedy delivered the 5–4 opinion of the Court, in which Chief Justice Roberts and Justices Scalia, Thomas, and Alito joined. Justice Sotomayor filed a dissenting opinion, in which Justices Stevens, Ginsberg, and Breyer joined.

77. *Davis* v. *United States*, 512 U.S. 452 (1994).

78. *Berghius.*

79. *Miranda*, at 475.

80. *Id.*

81. *Davis*, at 460; *Moran* v. *Burbine*, 475 U.S. 412, at 427 (1986).

82. *Dickerson* v. *United States* – 530 U.S. 428 (2000), 443–444.

83. Joe Navarro, with Marin Karlins, *What Every Body Is Saying* (New York: HarperCollins, 2008), pp. 207–229. (This discussion and accompanying references were adapted with permission from this source. The copyright holder for this book is Joe Navarro and HarperCollins Publishers.)

84. C.V. Ford, *Lies!, Lies!!, Lies!!! The Psychology of Deceit* (Washington, D.C.: American Psychiatric Press, Inc., 1996), p. 217; P. Ekman, *Telling Lies: Clues to Deceit in the Marketplace, Politics, and Marriage* (New York: W.W. Norton & Co., 1991), p. 162.

85. P. Ekman and M. O'Sullivan, "Who Can Catch a Liar?" *American Psychologist* 46 (1991): 913–920.

86. Ekman, *Telling Lies*, pp. 187–188.

87. Ibid., pp. 162–189.

The opening fragment before note 40: "convicted people through DNA testing and reforming the criminal justice system to prevent future injustice; available from *www.innocenceproject.org/*."

88. Ekman, *Telling Lies*, pp. 170–173.

89. R. B. Cialdini, *Influence: The Psychology of Persuasion* (New York: William Morrow and Company, Inc., 1993), pp. 167–207.

90. Ekman, *Telling Lies*, p. 185.

91. In the study of nonverbal communications, the limbic brain is where the action is—because it is the part of the brain that reacts to the world around us reflexively and instantaneously, in real time, and without thought. For that reason, it gives off a *true* response to information coming in from the environment (D. G. Myers, *Exploring Psychology,* 2nd ed. (New York: Worth Publishers, 1993), pp. 35–39. Because it is uniquely responsible for our survival, the limbic brain does not take breaks. It is always "on." The limbic brain is also our emotional center. It is from there that signals go out to various other parts of the brain, which in turn orchestrate our behaviors as they relate to emotions or our survival (J. LeDoux, *The Emotional Brain: The Mysterious Underpinnings of Emotional Life* [New York: Touchstone, 1996], pp. 104–137). These behaviors can be observed and decoded as they manifest physically in our feet, torso, arms, hands, and faces. Since these reactions occur without thought, unlike words, they are genuine. Thus, the limbic brain is considered the "honest brain" when we think of nonverbal (D. Goleman, *Emotional Intellligence* [New York: Bantam Books, 1995], pp. 13–29.

92. G. de Becker, *The Gift of Fear* (New York: Dell Publishing, 1997), p. 133.

93. Ekman, *Telling Lies*, pp. 101–133.

94. D. J. Lieberman, *Never Be Lied to Again* (New York: St. Martin's Press, 1998), p. 24.

95. Ekman, *Telling Lies*, pp. 158–169.

96. J. Navarro and J. R. Schafer, "Detecting Deception," *FBI Law Enforcement Bulletin* (July, 2001): 9–13.

97. A. Virj, *Detecting Lies and Deceit* (Chichester, UK: John Wiley & Sons, Ltd., 2003), pp. 38–39.

98. R. R. Johnston, "Race and Police Reliance on Suspicious Non-Verbal Cues," *Policing: An International Journal of Police Strategies & Management* 20, no. 2 (2007): 280–281.

99. Saul M. Kasin and Gisli H. Gudjonsson, "True Crimes, False Confessions," *Scientific American Mind* 16 (June 2005): 24–31.

100. S. M. Kassin, "A Critical Appraisal of Modern Police Interrogations," in *Investigative Interviewing: Rights, Research, Regulation,* ed. Tom Williamson (Devon, UK: Willian Publishing, 2006): 207–228.

101. Virj, *Detecting Lies and Deceit*, pp. 25–27.

102. These points are found on the website for the American Association of Police Polygraphists, p. 2, January 21, 2005; see *www.policepolygraph.org/standards.htm*.

103. Based on information supplied by Captain John P. Slater (Ret.), Law Enforcement Training Coordinator, National Institute for Truth Verification, 2007.

Chapter 6

1. Michael Biggs, *Just the Facts: Investigative Report Writing* (Upper Saddle River, NJ: Prentice Hall, 2001), p. 16.

2. California Commission on Peace Officer Standards and Training, Basic Course Workbook Series, *Investigative Report Writing* (Sacramento: Office of State Publishing, 1999), pp. 2–12, is the source of several of these points

3. Biggs, *Just the Facts*, pp. 16–19, with some restatement by the authors.

4. U.S. Equal Employment Opportunity Commission, Standard Form 100, Rev. 3-97, "Employer Information Report EEO-1, 100–118," Instruction Book, *www.eeoc.gov/stats/jobpat/e-1instruct.html*, Nov. 14, 2001.

5. Allen Z. Gammage, *Basic Report Writing* (Springfield, IL: Charles C. Thomas, 1966), pp. 13–14. These points remain valid even today; for example, see California Commission, *Investigative Report Writing*, pp. 4–21.

6. These points are drawn from Paul L. Godwin, "Painless Report Writing," *Law and Order*, Feb. 1993, pp. 38–40, with some additions by the authors.

Chapter 7

1. Information in this section is derived from the authors' experiences, as well the Springfield (Missouri) Police Department, SOP 402.8, "Criminal Investigations," September 30, 2010.

2. Bureau of Alcohol, Tobacco, Forearms and Explosives, Fact Sheet, National Integrated Ballistic Information Network (Washington, D.C.: BATF, February 2010), p. 1.

3. No author, National Missing and Unidentified Persons System (NamUS), accessed November 29, 2010, *www.NFSTC.org/programs/ManUs*.

4. Department of Homeland Security Exhibit 300 Public Release BY10/A&O-Homeland Security Information Network (HSIN), 2010.

5. Drawn from Stephen Morris, Deputy Assistant Director, FBI, Statement before the House of Representatives, Subcommittee on Crime, Terrorism, and Homeland Security, January 21, 2010 and NCIC Files, accessed November 28, 2010, *www.fbi.gov/about-us/cjis/ncic_files*.

6. Stephanie L. Britt, "NCIC 2000," FBI Law Enforcement Bulletin, July 2000, Vol. 69, No. 7, p. 14. This example and the one which follows are both drawn from this p. 14.

7. The information on WIN is drawn from Chelsea S. Keefer, "The Western Identification Network: A Multi-State AFIS," *The Police Chief*, Vol. 77, No. 5, May 2010, *www.PoliceChiefMagazine.org*, and No author, Western Identification Network Service Strategy, January 2008, *www.WINID.org*.

8. No author, *Survey of State Criminal Justice History Information Systems, 2008* (Washington, D.C.: Bureau of Justice Statistics, October 2009), introduction, pp. 3–4.

9. James X. Dempsey, *Overview of Current Criminal Justice Information Systems* (Washington, D.C.: Center for Democracy and Technology, 2000), p. 102.

10. LeadsOnLine, *www.LeadsOnLine.com/main/default.aspx*, accessed November 28, 2010.

11. Information in this section is derived from the authors' experiences, as well as Savannah-Chatham Metropolitan Police Department, Standard Operating Procedure (SOP) 2-01, "Criminal Investigations," April 4, 2004, and Springfield (Missouri) Police Department, SOP 402.8, "Follow-up Investigations," Dec. 1, 2002.

12. No author, *Reevaluating Lineups: Why Witnesses Make Mistake*s (New York: Cardozo School of Law, Yeshiva University, 2009), p. 14

13. Best Practices Committee, Lineup Guidelines (New York State District Attorneys Association, May 17, 2010), p. 2.

14. See Virginia General Assembly House Bill Number 207, introduced January 13, 2010.
15. *Reevaluating Lineups,* Appendix, p. 4.
16. Lineup Guidelines, p. 19.
17. Ibid., p. 3.
18. For example, see Dallas (Texas) Police Department 304.01, Eyewitness Identification, August 4, 2009.
19. Robert R. Hazelwood and Michael R. Napier, *International Journal of Offender Therapy and Comparative Criminology,* 2004, 48: p. 744. On this topic also see Brent E. Turvey, "Staged Crime Scenes: A Preliminary Study of 25 Cases," *Journal of Behavioral Profiling,* December 2000, Vol. 1, No. 3, pp. 1–9 and W. Jerry Chisum and Brent E. Turvey, *Crime Reconstruction* (New York: Applied Press, 2007), pp. 441–480.
20. Hazelwood and Napier, p. 746.
21. Ibid., p. 755.
22. Ibid., pp. 754–755. On this point, also see J. E. Douglas and C. M. Munn, *Crime Classification Manual* (New York: Lexington Books, 1992), p. 251.
23. Hazelwood and Napier, pp. 746–747.
24. Ibid., pp. 747–751.
25. Ibid., p. 756.
26. Ibid., p. 756, from which several of these points are taken with change and additional comment.
27. Harper J. Douglas and C. Munn, "The Detection of Staging and Personation at the Crime Scene," in A. Burgess, J. Douglas, and R. Ressler, eds., *Crime Classification Manual* (New York: Lexington Books, 1992), with restatement from p. 253.
28. Radell Smith, "LAPD Cold Case Unit: 100 Down and Thousands to Go," Examiner.com, December 5, 2010, *www.examiner.com/Criminal-profiles-in-national/lapd-cold-case-unit-100-down-and-thousands-more-to-go.*
29. Robert W. Taylor and Amanda Russell, "The Failure of Police Fusion Centers and the Concept of a National Intelligence Sharing Plan," Caruth Police Institute, Dallas Texas, prepublication draft received December 3, 2010, p. 5.
30. Marilyn B. Peterson, Bob Morehouse, and Richard Wright, *Intelligence 2000* (Law Enforcement Intelligence Unit and International Association of Law Enforcement Intelligence Analysts, 2000), p. 7.
31. Chandler, Arizona, Police Department, General Order D-23, "Criminal Intelligence," Aug. 7, 2001, pp. 2–3.
32. There is nothing magical about six steps. Some authorities say there are four steps and others as many as seven. Virtually all models agree on the sequence of steps.
33. Iowa Department of Public Safety, *www.state.ia.us/government/dps/intellcycle.htm,* November 19, 2001, pp. 2, 6.
34. Porter, "The Intelligence Production Cycle," p. 3.
35. Ibid.
36. Ibid.
37. No author, "George Orwell, Big Brother is Watching You," *London* (England) *Evening Standard,* March 31, 2007.
38. James Vlahos, "Surveillance Society: New High-Tech Cameras Are Watching You," *Popular Mechanics,* October 1, 2009, p. 1, *http://popularmechanics.com/technology/military/4236865.*
39. No author, NEC Press Release, January 20, 2010, "NEC's Face Recognition Technologies Ranked No. 1 by the NIST in All Participating Categories," p. 1. *http://nec.co.jp/press.*
40. No author, National Institute of Justice Press Release, November 13, 2007, "Facial Recognition Technology," p. 1. *http://ojp.usdoj.gov/nij/topics/biometrics/facial-recognition.htm.*
41. Steven Gottlieb, Sheldon Arenberg, and Raj Singh, *Crime Analysis from First Report* (Montclair, CA: Alpha Publishing, 1994), pp. 13–24. Although an older citation, this source remains highly regarded. Also see Victor Goldsmith, ed., *Analyzing Crime Patterns: Frontiers of Practice* (Thousand Oaks, CA: Sage, 2000), and Karim H. Vellani and Joel Nahoun, *Applied Crime Analysis* (Boston: Butterworth-Heinemann, 2001).
42. Massachusetts Association of Crime Analysts, "Crime Analysis," www.macrimeanalysts.com/aboutca.html, Oct. 18, 2001.
43. Ross M. Gardner and T. Bevel, "Theoretical and Practical Considerations in Crime Scene Reconstruction," *Journal of Forensic Identification,* Vol. 57, No. 6, p. 894.
44. Ibid., p. 899.
45. Ross M. Gardner and Tom Bevel, *Practical Crime Scene Analysis and Reconstruction* (Boca Raton, Florida: CRC Press, 2009), p. 18.
46. Ibid., p. 18.
47. W. Jerry Chisum and Brent E. Turvey, *Crime Reconstruction* (Academic Press: Burlington, MA, 2007), p. 107.
48. Gardner and Bevel, p. 37.
49. Ibid., pp. 37–38.
50. Ibid., p. 38.
51. "New York's Mad Bomber," *njnj.essortment.com/madbomber_rwid.htm,* December 3, 2001, pp. 1–2.
52. John E. Douglas, Ann W. Burgess, and Robert K. Ressler, *Crime Classification Manual* (San Francisco: Jossey-Bass, 1992), pp. 133–134.
53. Christopher Devery, "Criminal Profiling and Criminal Investigation," *Journal of Contemporary Criminal Justice,* Vol. 26, Issue 4, November 2010, pp. 393–409.
54. Louis B. Schlesinger, "Psychological Profiling: Investigative Implications from Crime Scene Analysis," *Journal of Psychiatry and Law,* Spring 2009, Vol. 37, Issue 1, pp. 73–84.
55. Hong Jiang Chu et al., "Geographic Profiling Methods: Improvement and Combination," *Applied Mechanics and Materials,* Vol. 34–35, October 2010.
56. Robert Sanderson, *Introduction to Remote Sensing,* New Mexico Space Grant Consortium, New Mexico State University, undated.
57. The first balloonist photograph is credited to a Frenchman in 1858, Felix Tournachon; the oldest surviving photograph from a balloon was by James Wallace Black, who took an aerial shot of Boston in 1860.

Chapter 8

1. Florida Bureau of Law Enforcement, "Crime Laboratory," unpublished document, 2007, p. 2.
2. Paul L. Kirk, "The Ontogeny of Criminalistics," *Journal of Criminology and Police Science,* 1963, Vol. 54, p. 238.
3. Joseph L. Peterson, Steven Mihajlovic, and Joanne L. Bedrosian, "The Capabilities, Uses, and Effects of the Nation's Criminalistics Laboratories," *Journal of Forensic Sciences,* 1985, Vol. 30, No. 1, p. 11.
4. Richard Fox and Carl L. Cunningham, *Crime Scene Search and Physical Evidence Handbook* (Washington, D.C.: U.S. Department of Justice, 1985), p. 1.

5. Statement of Kevin L. Lothridge, President, American Society of Crime Laboratory Directors, National Forensic Science Technology Center, before the House Judiciary Committee, Subcommittee on Crime, May 13, 1997.

6. Ibid.

7. *www.nfstc.org/aboutus.htm* (graciously supplied by NFSTC)

8. Kevin Rayburn, "U of L Teams with FBI, Other Agencies to Stop Digital Crime," *University of Louisville News,* KY, November 3, 2006, *http://php.louisville.edu/news/news.php?news+727* (accessed September 1, 2007).

9. James W. Osterburg, *The Crime Laboratory* (Bloomington: Indiana University Press, 1968), p. 3.

10. Marc H. Caplan and Joe Holt Anderson, *Forensics: When Science Bears Witness,* National Institute of Justice (Washington, D.C.: Government Printing Office, Oct. 1984), p. 2.

11. For a discussion of working relationships between police investigators and crime laboratory personnel, see Joseph L. Peterson, *The Utilization of Criminalistics Services by the Police: An Analysis of the Physical Evidence Recovery Process,* Law Enforcement Assistance Administration, National Institute of Law Enforcement and Criminal Justice (Washington, D.C.: Government Printing Office, March 1974).

12. National Research Council of the National Academies of Science, *Strengthening Forensic Science in the United States: A Path Forward* (Washington, D.C.: The National Academies Press, February 2009).

13. Sara Frueh, "Badly Fragmented Forensic Science System Needs Overhaul; Evidence to Support Reliability of Many Techniques is Lacking," *News from the National Academies,* February 18, 2009.

14. National Advisory Commission on Criminal Justice Standards and Goals, *Police* (Washington, D.C.: Government Printing Office, 1973), p. 303.

15. See Kenneth S. Field, Oliver Schroeder, Jr., Ina J. Curtis, Ellen L. Fabricant, and Beth Ann Lipskin, *Assessment of the Forensic Sciences Profession: Assessment of the Personnel of the Forensic Sciences Profession,* Vol. II, National Institute of Law Enforcement and Criminal Justice, Law Enforcement Assistance Administration, U.S. Department of Justice (Washington, D.C.: Government Printing Office, March 1977), pp. I-4–I-9.

16. National Advisory Commission, *Police,* p. 302.

17. Ibid.

18. Peterson, *Utilization of Criminalistics Services,* p. 6.

19. American Society of Crime Laboratory Directors. *180-Day Study: Status and Needs of United States Crime Laboratories,* May 28, 2004, p. iii.

20. Candace Rondeaux and Ernesto Londoño. "As Requests for DNA Tests Soar, So Do Lab Backlogs," *Washington Post,* July 15, 2007.

21. For more information regarding the National Forensic Technology Center (NFSTC), see *www.nfstc.org.*

22. 293 Fed. 1013 (D.C. Cir. 1923).

23. 507 U.S. 904 (1993).

24. *United States* v. *Mitchell,* 365 F. 3d 215 (3rd Circ. 2004).

25. Office of Justice Programs and Office of Community Orientated Policing Services, National Institute of Justice, *A Resource Guide to Law Enforcement, Corrections, and Forensic Technologies* (Washington, D.C.: U.S. Department of Justice, May 2001), *www.ncjrs.org,* p. 53.

26. Ibid., p. 57.

27. Ibid., pp. 57–58.

28. Matthew Durose, "Census of Publicly Funded Forensic Crime Laboratories, 2005," *Bureau of Justice Statistics Bulletin,* July 2008.

29. Jeffrey M. Prottas and Alice A. Noble., "Use of Forensic DNA Evidence in Prosecutor's Offices," *Journal of Law, Medicine and Ethics,* Summer 2007, pp. 310–315.

30. *www.fbi.gov/kids/dna/dna.htm,* July 17, 1998.

31. National Commission on the Future of DNA Evidence, National Institute of Justice, "What Every Law Enforcement Officer Should Know about DNA Evidence," pamphlet (Washington, D.C.: U.S. Department of Justice, no publication date).

32. Theresa F. Spear, "Sample Handling Considerations for Biological Evidence and DNA Extracts," California Department of Justice, California Criminalistics Institute.

33. Ibid.

34. T. Spear, "Sample Handling Considerations for Biological Evidence and DNA Extracts," and T. Spear and N. Khoshkebarr, "Analysis of Old Biological Samples: A Study on the Feasibility of Obtaining Body Fluid Identification and DNA Typing Results," California Department of Justice, California Criminalistics Institute.

35. Notes from the seminar "Supporting Your Case Using DNA Evidence," Altamonte Springs, Florida, Aug. 23–24, 2001.

36. See *www.fbi.gov/hq/lab/codis/clickmap.htm.*

37. Ronald Bailey, "Criminal Kinship: Slouching Toward a DNA Database Nation," *Reason Magazine,* May 19, 2006. *www.reason.com/news/show/116487.html.*

38. Office of Justice Programs and Office of Community Orientated Policing Services, *A Resource Guide,* pp. 56–57.

39. Shaila K. Dewan, "New York Works on a Better DNA Trap to Catch Burglars," *The New York Times,* May 26, 2004, p. 1 and p. 23.

40. Frederick R. Bieber, Charles H. Brenner, and David Lazer, "Human Genetics: Finding Criminals through DNA of Their Relatives," *Science,* Vol. 312, No. 5778 June 2, 2006, pp. 1315–1316.

41. Ibid.

42. Ibid.

43. Ronald Bailey, "Criminal Kinship."

44. Ibid.

45. Ker Than, "Family DNA Helps Cops Catch Criminals," *Live Science,* May 11, 2006, and William J. Cromie, "Catching Criminals through Their Relatives' DNA; Finding Genetic Needles in Database Haystacks," *Harvard University Gazette.* May 11, 2006, *www.news.harvard.edu/gazette/daily/2006/05/11-dna.html.*

46. *www.fbi.gov/hq/org/dnau/htm*

47. Ibid.

48. Office of Justice Programs, *National Institute of Justice Journal* (Washington, D.C.: U.S. Department of Justice, Dec. 1997), pp. 17–19.

49. Cromie, "Catching Criminals."

50. The Innocence Project, *http://innocenceproject.org/,* November 15, 2010.

51. Ibid.

52. Ibid.

53. Ibid.

54. Scott Cooper, "Judge Releases McCarty; Rips Former Chemist," *OKC News*, May 11, 2007.

55. Thomas F. Wilson, "Automated Fingerprint Identification Systems," *Law Enforcement Technology*, Aug.–Sept. 1986, p. 17.

56. Florida Department of Law Enforcement, *Criminal Justice Information Systems Newsletter*, May 1995, p. 1.

57. Kenneth R. Moses, "A Consumer's Guide to Fingerprint Computers," *Identification News*, June 1986, p. 6.

58. *www.fbi/gov/about-us/cjis/fingerprints_biometrics/iafis/iafis*

59. Much of the material in this section is drawn from Thomas F. Wilson and Paul L. Woodward, *Automated Fingerprint Identification Systems: Technology and Policy Issues* (Washington, D.C.: U.S. Department of Justice, 1997).

60. Federal Bureau of Investigation, *CJIS* (a newsletter for the criminal justice community), 1999, Vol. 3, no. 2, pp. 1–3.

61. *www.atf.gov/publications/factshetts/factsheets/factsheets-facts-and-figures.html*

62. *www.atf.treas.gov/labs*

63. *www.atf.treas.gov/explarson*

64. *www.fbi.gov/labs*

65. *www.fbi.gov/lab/report/labhome.htm*

66. Roma Khanna and Steve McVicker, "'Troubling'" Cases Surface in Report on HPD Crime Lab," *Houston Chronicle*, July 17, 2007, and Mike Glenn, "Police DNA Lab under the Microscope," *Houston Chronicle*, July 11, 2006.

67. *Education and Training in Forensic Science: A Guide for Forensic Science Laboratories, Educational Institutions, and Students,* National Institute of Justice, June 2004, p. 25.

68. Richard Saferstein, *Criminalistics: An Introduction to Forensic Science,* 6th ed. (Upper Saddle River, NJ: Prentice Hall, 1998), p. 17.

69. Randolf Jonakait, "Forensic Science: The Need for Regulation," *Harvard Journal of Law and Technology,* Spring 1999, p. 6.

70. Saferstein, *Criminalistics,* p. 243.

71. Paul Gianelli, "Crime Labs Need Improvement," *Issues in Science and Technology,* 2003, p. 2.

72. Ibid., p. 3.

73. Robert Tanner, "Crime Labs under a Microscope: Miscues Lead to Calls for Changes in Forensic Labs," *Washington Post,* July 27, 2003, p. 2.

74. John F. Kelly and Phillip K. Wearne, Tainting Evidence: Inside the Scandals of the FBI Crime Lab (Denver: Free Press, 2003), *www.bioforensics.com/conference/Examiner%20Bias/Tainting%20Evidence.pdf* (accessed March 15, 2011).

75. "Document Says Police Chemist Falsified Evidence," *Dallas Morning News,* April 21, 2004, p. 2A.

76. Barry Fisher, *Techniques of Crime Scene Investigation,* 6th ed. (Boca Raton, FL: CRC Press, 2000), p. 15.

77. Ruth Teichroeb, "Rare Look Inside State Crime Labs Reveals Recurring DNA Test Problems," *Seattle Post Intelligencer,* July 22, 2004, p. 2.

78. "Chief Hopes Computers Restore Faith in Crime Lab," *Dallas Morning News,* p. 4A.

79. Jack King, "DOJ Aware of Problems in FBI's DNA Lab," *NADCL News Release,* p. 1–2.

80. Matthew Durose. "Census of Publicly Funded Forensic Crime Laboratories, 2005," *Bureau of Justice Statistics Bulletin,* July 2008.

81. Mark Nelson. "Making Sense of DNA Backlogs—Myth vs. Reality," *National Institute of Justice Special Report,* June 2010.

82. Nicholas P. Lovrich, Travis Pratt, Michael Gaffney, Charles Johnson, Christopher Asplen, Lisa Hurst, and Timothy Schellberg, "National Forensic DNA Study Report," February 2004, p. 3. See *www.ojp.usdoj.gov/nij/pdf/dna_studyreport_final.pdf.*

83. Ibid., p. 63.

84. Ibid., p. 4.

85. Ibid., p. 17.

86. United States Department of Justice, "Background to the OIG Investigation," *FBI Labs Report,* March 1997, p. 1.

87. Ibid., p. 4.

88. Excerpted from an affidavit filed by FBI Special Agent Richard K. Werder in support of an arrest warrant for Brandon Mayfield. The warrant was signed by U.S. District Judge Robert Jones on May 6, 2004.

89. The AFIS system analyzed the print against a widely accepted 45-million fingerprint database yielding 20 possible matches.

90. Excerpted from testimony of Mr. Ken Moses, FBI Forensic Identification Services, May 19, 2004 (*U.S. v. Brandon Mayfield*).

91. Steven T. Wax and Christopher J. Schatz, "A Multitude of Errors: The Brandon Mayfield Case," *The Champion,* Sept./Oct. 2004, National Association of Criminal Defense Lawyers,*www.nacdl.org.*

92. Ibid.

93. Associated Press, "FBI Apologizes to Lawyer Held in Madrid Bombings," *MSNBC.com,* May 25, 2004.

94. Excerpted from the motion to dismiss material witness filed in U.S. District Court, Oregon on May 4, 2004.

95. Alan John Bayle, as quoted in Wax and Schatz, "A Multitude of Errors: The Brandon Mayfield Case." Note that Bayle's finding of fundamental error by the FBI analysts was consistent with the view held by the Spanish police authorities regarding the print.

96. *United States* v. *Mitchell,* 365 F.3d 215, 244-47 (3rd Circuit, 2004).

97. Excerpted from Wax and Schatz, p. 8. See also *Kumho Tire Co., Ltd.* v. *Carmichael,* 526 U.S. 137 (1999), criticizing purported expert's application of his methodology.

98. Peter Barnett, *Ethics in Forensic Science: Professional Standards for the Practice of Criminalistics* (Boca Raton, FL: CRC Press, 2001), p. 163.

99. H. Dale Nute, "An Ethical Code for Forensic Science," *www.southernforensic.org/ethics%20code.htm* (accessed August 10, 2010), pp. 2–3.

100. Teichroeb, "Oversight for Crime Lab Staff," p. 2.

Chapter 9

1. Neil C. Chamelin and Andrew Thomas, *Essentials of Criminal Law* (Englewood Cliffs, NJ: Pearson/Prentice Hall, 2009), pp. 116–130.

2. Ibid.

3. Jay Dix and Robert Calaluce, *Guide to Forensic Pathology* (Columbia: University of Missouri, 1998), p. 3.

4. Wisconsin Crime Laboratory, *Criminal Investigation and Physical Evidence Handbook* (Madison: Department of Justice, State of Wisconsin, 1968), p. 10.

5. John J. Horgan, *Criminal Investigation* (New York: McGraw-Hill, 1974), p. 292.

6. This information was obtained at *www.crime-scene-investigator.net/deadbodyevidence.html.*

7. James L. Luke, "The Estimation of Time of Death in the Early Postmortem Period," *The American Journal of Forensic Medicine and Pathology* 17, no. 3 (September 1996): 270.

8. Ibid.

9. Dix and Calaluce, *Guide to Forensic Pathology,* pp. 35–36.

10. Cyril J. Polson, David J. Gee, and Bernard Knight, *The Essentials of Forensic Medicine,* 4th ed. (Oxford: Pergamon Press, 1985), p. 11.

11. Keith Simpson and Bernard Knight, *Forensic Medicine,* 9th ed. (London: Butler & Tanner Ltd., 1988), p. 9.

12. I. Gordon, H. A. Shapiro, and S. D. Berson, *Forensic Medicine: A Guide to Principles,* 3rd ed. (Edinburgh: Churchill Livingstone, 1988), p. 18.

13. Johnnie Bennett, *Introduction to Forensic Science;* available at *http://bennettkids.homestead.com/autopsies.html.*

14. Ibid.

15. Dix and Calaluce, *Guide to Forensic Pathology,* pp. 33–34.

16. Francis E. Camps, ed., *Gradwohl's Legal Medicine,* 3rd ed. (Bristol: Wright and Sons, 1976), p. 83.

17. For a more detailed discussion, see Ask Dr. Baden at *www.hbo.com/autopsy/baden.*

18. Dix and Calaluce, *Guide to Forensic Pathology,* pp. 38–40.

19. Gail S. Anderson, Forensic Entomology, British Columbia, Canada, Simon Fraser University, School of Criminology, 2005. (This discussion was specifically developed by Dr. Anderson for this chapter. She is also a court-qualified expert and may be contacted at ganderso@sfu.ca.)

20. Vernon J. Geberth, *Practical Homicide Investigation* (Boca Raton, FL: CRC, 2006), pp. 325, 327.

21. Barry A. J. Fisher, *Techniques of Crime Scene Investigation* (New York: Elsevier, 1992), pp. 452–458. This discussion was adapted with permission from this source.

22. The information on shotgun wounds was obtained from material developed by Vincent J. M. DiMaio, M.D., Medical Examiner, Dallas County, Texas.

23. For a comprehensive view of the scientific literature on GSR see Oliver Dalby, David Butler, and Jason W. Birkett, "Analysis of Gunshot Residue and Associated Materials: A Review," *Journal of Forensic Sciences,* July 2010, Vol. 55, Issue 4, pp. 924–943.

24. No author, *Physical Evidence Collection Manual* (Boise: Idaho State Police, January 25, 2008), p. 10, accessed January 6, 2011, *www.isp.idaho.gov.forensic/documents/evidencepackaginghandbookupdated1-25-08_000.pdf.*

25. Lubor Fojtasek and Tomas Kmjec, "Time Periods of GSR Particles Deposition after Discharge-Final Results," *Forensic Science International,* October 2005, Vol. 153, Issue 2/3, pp. 132–135.

26. Dominic J. DiMaio and Vincent J. M. DiMaio, *Forensic Pathology* (New York: Elsevier, 1989), p. 87.

27. Ibid.

28. Ibid., pp. 231–243.

29. Jacques Charon, *Suicide* (New York: Scribner's, 1972), p. 56.

30. Ibid., p. 39.

31. Lemoyne Snyder, *Homicide Investigation* (Springfield, IL: Charles C. Thomas, 1973), p. 228.

32. Donna Newson, "Doctors Perform Rare Surgery," *Tampa Tribune,* July 25, 1980, pp. A1, A10.

33. Richard H. Fox and Carl L. Cunningham, *Crime Scene Search and Physical Evidence Handbook* (Washington, D.C.: Government Printing Office, 1973), pp. 124, 126. This discussion of poisons was taken from this source.

34. John Harris Trestrail, III, *Criminal Poisoning* (Totowa, NJ: Humana Press Inc., 2000–2001), p. 29.

35. Todd F. Prough, "Investigating Opiate-Overdose Deaths," *FBI Law Enforcement Bulletin,* April 2009; available from *www.thefreelibrary.com/Investigating+opiate-overdose+deaths-a0197673510.*

36. U.S. Department of Health and Human Services, Substance Abuse and Mental Health Services, *wwwdasis.samhsa.gov/webt/information.htm.*

37. Werner U. Spitz, ed., *Spitz and Fisher's Medicolegal Investigation of Death* (Springfield, MA: Charles C. Thomas, 1993).

38. J. Tuckman et al., "Credibility of Suicide Notes," *American Journal of Psychiatry,* June 1960, No. 65, pp. 1104–1106.

39. David Lester, *Why People Kill Themselves* (Springfield, IL: Charles C. Thomas, 1972), p. 36.

40. Z. G. Standing Bear, *The Investigation of Questioned Deaths and Injuries—Conference Notes and Outline* (Valdosta, GA: Valdosta State College Press, 1988), pp. 78–82.

41. John J. O'Conner, *Practical Fire and Arson Investigation* (Boca Raton, FL: CRC Press, 1993), pp. 160–161.

42. Ibid.

43. Camps, *Gradwohl's Legal Medicine,* p. 358; Lester Adelson, *The Pathology of Homicide* (Springfield, IL: Charles C. Thomas, 1974), p. 610; Richard Lindenberg, "Mechanical Injuries of the Brain and Meninges," in Spitz, *Spitz and Fisher's Medicolegal Investigation of Death,* pp. 447–456.

44. *Serial Murder: Multi-Disciplinary Perspectives for Investigators* (Washington, D.C.: U.S. Department of Justice, Federal Bureau of Investigation, 2005), pp. 8–9. (This discussion was adapted from this source.)

45. Ibid., pp. 11–12.

46. National Center for the Analysis of Violent Crime, Behavioral Science Unit, FBI Academy (Quantico, VA: 1985), p. 5.

47. ViCAP Crime Analysis Report Form used by the FBI for profiling, 1999.

48. Eric W. Witzig, "The New ViCAP," *FBI Law Enforcement Bulletin,* January 16, 2003.

49. David McLemore, "Aliases, Trainhopping Obscure Suspect's Trail," *Dallas Morning News,* June 17, 1999, sec. A1, p. 16.

50. Pauline Arrillaga, "Town Copes after Slayings by Suspected Rail Rider," *Dallas Morning News,* June 11, 1999, sec. A., p. 29.

51. *Supra* note 12, sec. A., p. 17.

52. Michael Pearson, "Railroad Killer," *Associated Press,* June 22, 1999.

53. Mark Babineck, "Railroad Killer," *Associated Press,* July 2000.

54. "Railroad Killer," *Associated Press,* July 2000.

55. Ibid.

Chapter 10

1. Bureau of Justice Statistics, "Number of Victimizations and Victimization Rates for Persons Age 12 and Older, by Type of Crime and Gender of Victim," *www.ojp.usdoj.gov/bjs/pub/pdf/cvus9901.pdf,* 1999.

2. Ibid.

3. Robert Spaulding and David Bigbee, "Physical Evidence in Sexual Assault Investigations," in Robert Hazlewood and Wolbert Burgess, eds., *Practical Aspects of Rape Investigation: A Multidisciplinary Approach,* 3rd ed. (New York: CRC Press, 2001), pp. 261–277.

4. Rebecca Campbell and Sheela Raja, "Secondary Victimization of Rape Victims: Insights from Mental Health Professionals Who Treat Survivors of Violence," *Violence and Victims,* 1999, Vol. 14, No. 3.

5. Karen Carlson, Stephanie Eisenstat, and Terra Ziporyn, "Rape," *The Harvard Guide to Women's Health* (Cambridge, MA: Harvard University Press, 1996), pp. 526–527.

6. Karen Carlson, Stephanie Eisenstat, and Terra Ziporyn, "Posttraumatic Stress Disorder," in ibid., pp. 495–496.

7. *Interviewing the Rape Victim: Training Key 210* (Gaithersburg, MD: International Association of Chiefs of Police, 1974), p. 1.

8. Ibid.

9. Morton Bard and Katherine Ellison, "Crisis Intervention and Investigation of Forcible Rape," *Police Chief,* May 1974, Vol. 41, No. 5, pp. 68–74.

10. This discussion and accompanying references came from R. R. Hazelwood, "The Behavior-Oriented Interview of Rape Victims: The Key to Profiling," *FBI Law Enforcement Bulletin,* Sept. 1983, pp. 13–15.

11. L. L. Holmstrom and A. W. Burgess, "Sexual Behavior of Assailants during Rape," *Archives of Sexual Behavior,* 1980, Vol. 9, No. 5, p. 437.

12. Ibid., p. 427.

13. L. L. Holmstrom and A. W. Burgess, "Rapist's Talk: Linguistic Strategies to Control the Victim," *Deviant Behavior,* 1979, Vol. 1, p. 101.

14. C. LeGrande, "Rape and Rape Laws: Sexism in Society and Law," *California Law Review,* 1973, p. 929.

15. Lauren R. Taylor and Nicole Gasken-Laniyan, Study Reveals Unique Issues Faced by Deaf Victims of Sexual Assault, 2007, U.S. Department of Justice: Office of Justice Programs, National Institute of Justice, pp. 24–26.

16. J. Obinna, S. Krueger, C. Osterbaan, J. M. Sandusky, and W. DeVore, *Understanding the Needs of the Victims of Sexual Assault in the Deaf Community,* final report submitted to the National Institute of Justice, Washington, D.C.: February 2006 (NCJ 212867), *www.ncjrs.gov/pdffiles1/nij/grants/212867.pdf.*

17. Ann Wolbert Burgess, Robert A. Prentky and Elizabeth B. Dowdell, "Sexual Predators in Nursing Homes," in *Practical Aspects of Rape Investigation,* 4th ed., Robert R. Hazlewood and Ann Wolbert Burgess, eds. (Boca Raton, FL: CRC Press, Taylor & Francis Group, 2009), pp. 484–499. (This discussion of elder sexual abuse was adapted with permission from this source.)

18. U.S. General Accounting Office, *Nursing Homes: Complaint Investigation Processes Often Inadequate to Protect Residents* (No. 6AO/HEHS-99-80) (Washington, D.C.: Health Education and Human Services, 2002).

19. A. W. Burgess, E. B. Dowdell and R. A. Prentky, "Sexual Abuse of Nursing Home Residents," *Journal of Psychosocial Nursing* 38, No. 6 (June) 2000: 10–18.

20. Queens Bench Foundation, *Rape Victimization Study* (San Francisco, 1975), pp. 81–87; E. L. Willoughby and James A. Inciardi, "Estimating the Incidence of Crime," *Police Chief,* 1975, Vol. 42, No. 8, pp. 69–70; President's Commission on Law Enforcement and the Administration of Justice, *Task Force Report: Crime and Its Impact* (Washington, D.C.: Government Printing Office, 1967), p. 80; Eugene J. Kanin, "False Rape Allegations," *Archives of Sexual Behavior,* 1994, Vol. 23, No. 1, pp. 81–90.

21. The state of Florida repealed its previous statute, Forcible Rape and Carnal Knowledge 794, replacing it with a new statute, titled Sexual Battery 794. The new law provides for various penalties for sexual battery depending on the amount of force used and the injuries sustained by the victim. In addition, the statute provides that specific instances of previous sexual activity between the victim and any person other than the defendant cannot be admitted into evidence.

22. Queens Bench Foundation, *Rape Victimization Study,* p. 86.

23. "Vicious Lies and Apologies," *St. Petersburg Times,* July 30, 1990, pp. A1, A4.

24. "Crime in the United States: 2000 Uniform Crime Reports," *www.fbi.gov/ucr/cius_00/00 crime3.pdf.*

25. Spaulding and Bigbee, "Physical Evidence in Sexual Assault Investigations."

26. Ibid.

27. A. N. Groth and A. W. Burgess, *Rape, a Sexual Deviation,* paper presented to the American Psychological Association Meeting, Washington, D.C., Sept. 5, 1976, p. 4.

28. J. H. Davis, "Examination of Victims of Sexual Assault and Murder," material developed for a homicide seminar offered by the Florida Institute for Law Enforcement, St. Petersburg, Florida, 1965.

29. Ibid.

30. Arne Svensson and Otto Wendel, *Techniques of Crime Scene Investigation* (New York: American Elsevier, 1973).

31. William Watson, "Forensic Serology and DNA Analysis," lecture given at the University of North Texas, 2001.

32. Joe Nickell and John Fischer, *Crime Science: Methods of Forensic Detection* (Lexington: University Press of Kentucky, 1999).

33. Watson, "Forensic Serology and DNA Analysis."

34. Spaulding and Bigbee, "Physical Evidence in Sexual Assault Investigations."

35. Thomas B. Carney, *Practical Investigation of Sex Crimes* (Boca Raton, FL: CRC Press, 2004) p. 55. (Reprinted with permission.)

36. Ibid., p. 55.

37. Ibid., p. 57.

38. Ibid., pp. 57–58.

39. Ibid., p. 58.

40. Robert D. Blackledge, "Condom Trace Evidence: A New Factor in Sexual Assault Investigations," *FBI Bulletin,* May 1996, pp. 12–16. This discussion was adapted from this article.

41. R. D. Blackledge and L. R. Cabiness, "Examination for Petroleum-Based Lubricants in Evidence from Rapes and Sodomies," *Journal of Forensic Sciences,* 1983, Vol. 28, pp. 451–462.

42. R. D. Blackledge, "Collection and Identification Guidelines for Traces from Latex Condoms in Sexual Assault Cases," *Crime Laboratory Digest,* 1994, Vol. 21, pp. 57–61.

43. Tamantha Chapman, "Drug-Facilitated Sexual Assault," *Police Chief,* June 2000, pp. 38–39.

44. Bureau of Justice Statistics, *Violence against Women: Estimates from the Designed Survey* (Washington, D.C.: U.S. Department of Justice, Aug. 1995).

45. Hoffman-LaRoche, Inc., "Rohypnol Fact Sheet"; Drug Enforcement Administration, "Intelligence Report (Rohypnol)," July 1995.

46. A. G. Gardiner, Jr., "Rohypnol: The New Stealth Weapon," *Police Chief*, April 1998, p. 37.

47. Drug Enforcement Administration, "Fact Sheet (GHB)," Aug. 1998; Food and Drug Administration, "Training Bulletin," Office of Criminal Investigations, San Diego, CA.

48. Executive Office of the President's Office of National Drug Control Policy, "Gamma Hydroxybutyrate (GHB) Fact Sheet," Oct. 1998.

49. Chapman, "Drug-Facilitated Sexual Assault," p. 41.

50. Nora Fitzgerald and K. Jack Reilly. *Assessing Drug Facilitated Rape.* The U.S. Department of Justice, Office of Justice Programs, National Institute of Justice. April 2000, p. 14.

51. American Prosecutors Research Institute, *The Prosecution of Rohypnol- and GHB-Related Sexual Assaults* (Alexandria, VA: April 1999).

52. Vernon J. Geberth, *Practical Homicide Investigation: Tactics, Procedures, and Forensic Techniques* (Boca Raton, FL) CRC Press, 2006, pp. 500–509.

53. Ibid. For a more detailed discussion regarding this topic see Table 15.1: Standard Color Codes for Homosexual handkerchiefs, p. 501.

54. R. Crooks and K. Baur, *Our Sexuality*, 4th ed. (Redwood City, CA: Benjamin/Cummings, 1990), pp. 317, 324, 332–333, 340.

55. Edna Hendershot, Alverd C. Stutson and Thomas W. Adair, "A Case of Extreme Sexual Self-Mutilation," *The Journal Forensic Sciences* 55, No. 1 (January 2009), pp. 245–246.

56. Readers who are interested in viewing the photographs of the self-mutilation injuries may do so by referring to Hendershot et al., ibid. p. 246.

57. R. R. Hazelwood, *Autoerotic Deaths* (Quantico, VA: Behavioral Science Unit, FBI Academy, 1984).

58. J. Rupp, "The Love Bug," *Journal of Forensic Science,* 1973, pp. 259–262.

59. H. L. P. Resnick, "Eroticized Repetitive Hangings: A Form of Self-Destructive Behavior," *American Journal of Psychotherapy,* January 1972, p. 10.

60. R. Litman and C. Swearingen, "Bondage and Suicide," *Archives of General Psychiatry,* July 1972, Vol. 27, p. 82.

61. Vernon J. Geberth, *Practical Homicide Investigation,* 4th ed. (Boca Raton, FL: CRC Press, 2006), pp. 375–377.

62. N. Hibbler, "The Psychological Autopsy," *Forensic Science Digest,* Sept. 1978, Vol. 5, pp. 42–44.

Chapter 11

1. C. J. Flammang, *The Police and the Unprotected Child* (Springfield, IL: Charles C. Thomas, 1970), p. 90; Harold E. Simmons, *Protective Services for Children* (Sacramento, CA: General Welfare Publications, 1968), p. 45.

2. S. Maguire, M. K. Mann, J. Sibert, and A. Kemp, "Are There Patterns of Bruising in Childhood Which Are Diagnostic or Suggestive of Abuse? A Systematic Review," *Archives of Disease in Childhood,* 2005, Vol. 90, pp. 182–186.

3. H. Dubowitz and S. Bennett, "Physical Abuse and Neglect of Children," *Lancet,* 2007, Vol. 369, pp. 1891–1899.

4. Phylip J. Peltier, Gary Purdue, and Jack R. Shepherd, *Burn Injuries in Child Abuse* (Washington, D.C.: U.S. Department of Justice, 1997), pp. 1–9.

5. D. Finkelhor and R. Ormrod. "Homicides of Children and Youth," *Juvenile Justice Bulletin.* Office of Justice Programs, Office of Juvenile Justice and Delinquency Prevention, October 2001, *www.ncjrs.gov/pdffiles1/ojjdp/187239.pdf.*

6. *A Resource Handbook: Sudden Infant Death Syndrome* (Tallahassee, FL: Department of Health and Rehabilitative Services, 1978), pp. 1–2. Much of the information dealing with SIDS was taken from this source.

7. Ann L. Ponsonby, Terrence Dwyer, Laura E. Gibbons, Jennifer A Cochrane, and You-gan Wang, "Factors Potentiating the Risk of Sudden Infant Death Syndrome Associated with Prone Position," *New England Journal of Medicine,* Aug. 1993, Vol. 329, No. 6, p. 373. The scientists conducted the study (58 infants with SIDS and 120 control infants) and perspective cohort study (22 infants with SIDS and 233 control infants) in Tasmania. Interactions were examined and math analyses done with a multiplicative model interaction.

8. J. L. Emery and J. A. Thornton, "Effects of Obstruction to Respiration in Infants with Particular Reference to Mattresses, Pillows, and Their Coverings," *BMJ,* 1968, Vol. 3, pp. 309–313.

9. David S. Paterson et. al., "Multiple Serotonergic Brainstem Abnormalities in Sudden Infant Death Syndrome," *Journal of American Medical Association,* Nov. 1, 2006, Vol. 296; pp. 2124–2132.

10. Vincent J. DiMaio and Dominick DiMaio, *Forensic Pathology* (Boca Raton, FL: CRC Press, 2001), pp. 330–331. The following are online resources for providing additional information on SIDS: First Candle, *www.firstcandle.org*; Interagency Panel on Sudden Infant Death Syndrome, "Guidelines for Death Scene Investigation of Sudden, Unexplained Infant Deaths," *www.cdc.gov/mmwr/preview/mmwrhtml/00042657.htm*; Office of Juvenile Justice and Delinquency Prevention "Recognizing When a Child's Injury or Illness is Caused by Abuse," *www.ncjrs.gov/pdffiles1/ojjdp/160938.pdf*; Canadian Association of Chiefs of Police "Code of Police Practice: A Guide for First-Line Officers," *www.rcmplearning.org/copp/encopp/d_infant.htm.*

11. Vincent J. DiMaio and Dominick DiMaio, *Forensic Pathology* (Boca Raton, FL: CRC Press, 2001), pp. 349–350.

12. David P. Southall, "Covert Video Recording of Life-Threatening Child Abuse: Lessons for Child Protection," *Pediatrics,* Nov. 1997, Vol. 100, No. 5, pp. 735–760; Sharon Begley, "The Nursery's Littlest Victim," *Newsweek,* September 22, 1997, p. 72.

13. Begley, "The Nursery's Littlest Victim," p. 67.

14. Randell Alexander and K. Kleinmann, *Diagnostic Imaging of Child Abuse* (Washington, D.C.: U.S. Department of Justice, 1996), pp. 6–9.

15. Bill Walsh. "Investigating Child Fatalities," Office of Justice Programs, Office of Juvenile Justice and Delinquency Prevention. August 2005, *www.ncjrs.gov/pdffiles1/ojjdp/209764.pdf.*

16. Rob Parrish, *Battered Child Syndrome: Investigating Physical Abuse* (Washington, D.C.: U.S. Department of Justice, 1996), pp. 9–10.

17. Stephen J. Boros and Larry C. Brubaker, "Munchausen Syndrome by Proxy: Case Accounts," *FBI Law Enforcement Bulletin*, 1992, Vol. 61, No. 6, pp. 16–20. These case reports were taken from this article.

18. James D. Regis, "The Battered Child," *Police Work*, April 1980, pp. 41–42.

19. Nicholas Kristof, "Seduction, Slavery and Sex," *The New York Times*, July 16, 2010.

20. Kenneth V. Lanning, *Child Molesters: A Behavioral Analysis for Law Enforcement Officers Investigating Cases of Child Sexual Exploitation*, 3rd ed. (Arlington, VA: National Center for Missing and Exploited Children, 1992), pp. 6–10. This entire discussion of child molesters has been reproduced (with minor changes) with permission. No part of this may be reproduced without the express written permission of the National Center for Missing and Exploited Children, 1-800-843-5678.

21. Ibid.

22. Debra Whitcomb, *When the Victim Is a Child* (Washington, D.C.: National Institute of Justice, 1992), pp. 15–20.

23. D. Floyd, testimony before President's Task Force on Victims of Crime, Final Report, December 1982, p. 51.

24. J. Waterman, "Development Considerations," in K. Mac-Farlane and J. Waterman, eds., *Sexual Abuse of Young Children* (New York: Guilford Press, 1986), pp. 15–29.

25. W. M. Friedrich, J. Fischer, D. Broughton, D. Houston, and C. R. Shafran, "Normative Sexual Behavior in Children: A Contemporary Sample," *Pediatrics*, Vol. 101, No. 4, April, p. 9.

26. A. Warren-Leubecker et al., "What Do Children Know about the Legal System and When Do They Know It? First Steps Down a Less-Traveled Path in Child Witness Research," S. J. Ceci, D. F. Ross, and M. P. Toglia, eds., *Perspectives on Children's Testimony* (New York: Springer Verlag, 1989), pp. 158–183.

27. M. A. Young, "Working with Victims Who Are Children or Adolescents: Using the Lessons of Child Development with Young Trauma Victims," *NOVA Newsletter*, 1989, Vol. 13.

28. Warren-Leubecker et al., "What Do Children Know about the Legal System"; K. J. Saywitz, "Children's Conceptions of the Legal System: 'Court Is a Place to Play Basketball,'" in Ceci et al., *Perspectives on Children's Testimony*, pp. 131–157. Also see S. P. Limber, G. B. Melton, and S. J. Rahe, "Legal Knowledge, Attitudes, and Reasoning Abilities of Witnesses," paper presented at AP-LS Division 41 Biennial Convention, Williamsburg, Virginia, March 1990.

29. R. Pynoos and S. Eth, "The Child Witness to Homicide," *Journal of Social Issues*, 1984, Vol. 40, p. 98.

30. K. J. Saywitz and C. Jaenicke, "Children's Understanding of Legal Terms: A Preliminary Report of Grade-Related Trends," paper presented at the Society for Research on Child Development Biennial Meeting, Baltimore, Maryland, April 1987.

31. Warren-Leubecker et al., "What Do Children Know about the Legal System?"

32. Whitcomb, *When the Victim Is a Child*, pp. 33–38. This discussion was adapted from this source.

33. Alabama, Connecticut, Michigan, New Jersey, New York, Pennsylvania, West Virginia, and Wyoming.

34. See, for example, *Cleveland v. State*, 490 N.R. 2nd 1140 (Ind. App. 1986); *People v. Garvie*, 148 Mich. App. 444, 384 N.W. 2d 796 (1986); *State v. Jenkins*, 326 N.W. 2d 67 (N.D. 1982).

35. E. Gray, "Children as Witnesses in Child Sexual Abuse Cases Study," Final Report submitted to the National Center on Child Abuse and Neglect under Grant No. 90-CA-1273, by the National Council of Jewish Women, New York, New York, 1990, p. 51. (Henceforth referred to as NCJW Study.)

36. K. R. Freemand and T. Estrada-Mullany, "Using Dolls to Interview Child Victims: Legal Concerns and Interview Procedures," *Research in Action*, National Institute of Justice, January/February 1988, p. 2.

37. White, pp. 472–473.

38. S. White and G. Santilli, "A Review of Clinical Practices and Research Data on Anatomical Dolls," *Journal of Interpersonal Violence*, Dec. 1988, Vol. 3, pp. 437–439.

39. L. Berliner, "Anatomical Dolls," *Journal of Interpersonal Violence*, Dec. 1988, Vol. 3, pp. 468–470; also see B. W. Boat and M. D. Everson, "Normative Data: How Non-Referred Young Children Interact with Anatomical Dolls," paper presented at the Symposium of Interviewing Children, cited in Berliner, "Anatomical Dolls," p. 469.

40. White and Santilli, "A Review of Clinical Practices," p. 431.

41. B. Boat and M. Everson, "Use of Anatomical Dolls among Professionals in Sexual Abuse Evaluations," *Child Abuse and Neglect*, 1988, Vol. 12, pp. 171–179.

42. K. MacFarlane and S. Krebs, "Techniques for Interviewing and Evidence Gathering," in MacFarlane and Waterman, *Sexual Abuse of Young Children*, pp. 74–75.

43. Ibid.

44. White and Santilli, "A Review of Clinical Practices," pp. 439–440.

45. MacFarlane and Krebs, "Techniques for Interviewing and Evidence Gathering," p. 87.

46. NCJW Study, pp. 439–440.

47. S. J. Ceci, D. Ross, and M. Toglia, "Age Differences in Suggestibility: Narrowing the Uncertainties," in S. J. Ceci, M. P. Toglia, and D. F. Ross, eds., *Children's Eyewitness Memory* (New York: Springer-Verlag, 1987), pp. 79–91.

48. H. Wakefield and R. Underwager, "Techniques for Interviewing Children in Sexual Abuse Cases," *VOCAL Perspective*, Summer 1989, pp. 7–15.

49. K. Saywitz et al., "Children's Memories of Genital Examinations: Implications for Cases of Child Sexual Assault," paper presented at the Society for Research in Child Development Meetings, Kansas City, Missouri, 1989.

50. J. R. Conte and J. R. Schuerman, "The Effects of Sexual Abuse on Children: A Multidimensional View," *Journal of Interpersonal Violence*, December 1987, Vol. 2, pp. 380–390.

51. W. N. Freidrich, R. L. Beilke, and A. J. Urquiza, "Children from Sexually Abusive Families: A Behavioral Comparison," *Journal of Interpersonal Violence*, Dec. 1987, Vol. 2, pp. 391–402.

52. J. Conte et al., "Evaluating Children's Report of Sexual Abuse: Results from a Survey of Professionals," unpublished manuscript, University of Chicago, undated, cited in J. E. B. Myers et al., "Expert Testimony in Child Sexual Abuse Litigation," *Nebraska Law Review,* 1989, Vol. 68, p. 75.

53. Whitcomb, *When the Victim Is a Child,* pp. 6–11.

54. D. Jones and J. McGraw, "Reliable and Fictitious Accounts of Sexual Abuse to Children," *Journal of Interpersonal Violence,* March 1987, Vol. 2, pp. 27–45.

55. Ibid.

56. J. Paradise, A. Rostain, and M. Nathanson, "Substantiation of Sexual Abuse Charges When Parents Dispute Custody or Visitation," *Pediatrics,* June 1988, Vol. 81, pp. 835–839.

57. See, for example, E. P. Benedek and D. H. Schetky, "Allegations of Sexual Abuse in Child Custody and Visitation Disputes," in D. H. Schetky and E. P. Benedek, eds., *Emerging Issues in Child Psychiatry and the Law* (New York: Brunner/Mazel, 1985), pp. 145–158; A. H. Green, "True and False Allegations of Sexual Abuse in Child Custody Disputes," *Journal of the American Academy of Child Psychiatry,* 1986, Vol. 25, pp. 449–456.

58. For an excellent summary of the drawbacks of such studies, see D. Corwin et al., "Child Sexual Abuse and Custody Disputes: No Easy Answers," *Journal of Interpersonal Violence,* March 1987, Vol. 2, pp. 91–105; also see L. Berliner, "Deciding Whether a Child Has Been Sexually Abused," in E. B. Nicholson, ed., *Sexual Abuse Allegations in Custody and Visitation Cases* (Washington, D.C.: American Bar Association, 1988), pp. 48–69.

59. N. Thoennes and J. Pearson, "Summary of Findings from the Sexual Abuse Allegations Project," in Nicholson, *Sexual Abuse Allegations,* pp. 1–21.

60. D. Finkelhor, L. M. Williams, and N. Burns, *Nursery Crimes: Sexual Abuse in Day Care* (Newbury Park, CA: Sage, 1988).

61. Kenneth V. Lanning, *Child Molesters: A Behavioral Analysis for Law Enforcement Officers Investigating Cases of Child Sexual Exploitation,* 3rd ed. (Arlington, VA: National Center for Missing and Exploited Children, 1992), pp. 24–31. This entire discussion of child pornography has been reproduced (with minor changes) with permission. No part of this may be reproduced without the express written permission of the National Center for Missing and Exploited Children, 1-800-843-5678.

62. R. W. Taylor, E. J. Fritsch, J. Liederbach, and T. J. Holt, *Digital Crime and Digital Terrorism,* Chapter 7: Sex Crimes, Victimization and Obscenity on the World Wide Web, 2nd ed. (Upper Saddle River, NJ: Prentice Hall, 2011), pp. 143, 183.

63. Defined as part of the United Nations General Assembly on the Promotion and Protection of the Rights of Children, September 20, 1995. Document available at *www.unhchr.ch/Huridocda/Huridoca.nsf/0/97dd6479be18883f80256719005e5661?Opendocument.*

64. "Review of the US Department of State Office to Monitor and Combat Trafficking in Persons TIP Report 2007." *The Protection Project* (Washington, D.C.: Johns Hopkins University, June 2007), p. 28, *www.theprotectionproject.org.*

65. E. Klain, "Prostitution of Children and Child-Sex Tourism: An Analysis of Domestic and International Responses" (Washington, D.C.: Office of Juvenile Justice and Delinquency Programs and National Center for Missing and Exploited Children, 1999) p. 37.

66. "State Seeks to Close Dutchess and Queens Based Travel Agency." Press release from the New York State Attorney General, August 20, 2003, *www.oag.state.ny.us/press/2003/aug/aug20a_03.html.*

67. "Child Sex Tourism," *Child Exploitation and Obscenity of the U.S. Department of Justice, www.justice.gov/criminal/ceos/sextour.html,* November 10, 2010.

68. E. Klain, "Prostitution of Children and Child-Sex Tourism: An Analysis of Domestic and International Responses" (Washington, D.C.: Office of Juvenile Justice and Delinquency Programs and National Center for Missing and Exploited Children, 1999) pp. 33–35.

69. F. Miko, "Trafficking in Persons: The U.S. and International Response," Congressional Research Service, Library of Congress (Washington D.C.: July 7, 2006).

70. E. Klain, "Prostitution of Children and Child-Sex Tourism: An Analysis of Domestic and International Responses" (Washington, D.C.: Office of Juvenile Justice and Delinquency Programs and National Center for Missing and Exploited Children, 1999) p. 33.

71. *The Paedo File,* End Child Prostitution, Child Pornography and Trafficking of Children for Sexual Purposes (EPCAT) Newsletter (EPCAT International: Bangkok, Thailand, April 1996), pp. 4–5.

72. E. Klain, "Prostitution of Children and Child-Sex Tourism: An Analysis of Domestic and International Responses" (Washington, D.C.: Office of Juvenile Justice and Delinquency Programs and National Center for Missing and Exploited Children, 1999) p. 37.

73. V. Silverman, "US Law Enforcement Targets Child Sex Tourism" (Washington D.C.: U.S. Department of State, December 17, 2003*). http://usinfo.state.gov/gi/Archive/2003/Dec/17-227348.html.*

74. "The Facts about Child Sex Tourism," Fact sheet from the U.S. Department of State Office to Monitor and Combat Trafficking in Persons, August 19, 2005, *www.state.gov/g/tip/rls/fs/2005/51351.htm.*

75. "Child Sex Tourism," Child Exploitation and Obscenity of the U.S. Department of Justice, *www.justice.gov/criminal/ceos/sextour.html.*

76. S. K. Andrews, U.S. Domestic Prosecution of the American International Sex Tourist: Efforts to Protect Children from Sexual Exploitation," *The Journal of Criminal Law and Criminology,* 2004, Vol. 94, 415–454.

77. The Child Pornography Prevention Act, U.S. Code Title 18, Section 2252: Certain Activities Relating to Material Involving the Sexual Exploitation of Minors.

78. U.S. Code, Title 18, Section 2251: Sexual Exploitation of Children.

79. In the Supreme Court of the United States, *John D. Ashcroft, Attorney General of the United States et al., Petitioners,* v. *The Free Speech Coalition et al., www.usdoj.gov/osg/briefs/2000/3mer/2mer/2000-0795.mer.aa.html.*

80. Supreme Court of the United States, *www.supremecourtus.gov/index.html.*

81. Donald M. Kerr, "Internet and Data Interception Capabilities Developed by the FBI," Statement for the Record,

U.S. House of Representatives, Committee on the Judiciary, Subcommittee on the Constitution, *www.cdt.org/security/carnivor/000724fbi.shtml*, July 24, 2000.

82. Kind Holger, "Combating Child Pornography on the Internet by the German Federal Criminal Police Office (BKA)."

83. "14 Nations Join to Bust Huge Internet Child Porn Ring," *www.cnn.com/WORLD/europe/9809/02/internet.porn.02/*.

84. J. Wolak et al., "Online Victimization of Youth: 5 Years Later" (Washington, D.C.: Office of Juvenile Justice and Delinquency Programs, Crimes Against Children Research Center, and National Center for Missing and Exploited Children, 2006) p. 17.

85. Ibid., p. 18.

86. V. Coleman-Wright, "For Detective, Kids' Safety Is First and Foremost." *American Police Beat*, May 2007, p. 70.

87. Information taken from Internet Crimes Against Children Task Force website, *www.icactraining.org/*, September 10, 2007.

88. J. Wolak, D. Finkelhor, and K. Mitchell, "Trends in Arrests of 'Online Predators,'" Crimes Against Children Research Center, 2009.

89. M. Huffman, "MySpace Deletes More Sex Offenders." ConsumerAffairs.com, July 25, 2007, *www.consumeraffairs.com/news04/2007/07/myspace_more.html*.

90. D. Goodin, "US States Press MySpace to Give Up Sex Offender Data." *The Register*, May 14, 2007, *www.theregister.co.uk/2007/05/14/myspace_offender_demand/*.

91. M. Huffman, "My Space Deletes More Sex Offenders."

92. V. Coleman-Wright, "For Detective, Kids' Safety Is First and Foremost."

93. National Conference of State Legislatures. School Bullying: Overview, *www.ncsl.org/Default.aspx?Tabld=12952*.

94. U.S. Department of Education, *Exploring the Nature and Prevention of Bullying*, *www2.ed.gov/admins/lead/safety/training/bullying/bullying_pg11.html*.

95. Raven Clabough, "Anti-Bullying Legislation in Massachusetts," *The New American*, May 4, 2010, *www.thenewamerican.com/index.php/culture/education/3468-anti-bullying-lesgislation-in-massachusetts*.

96. National Conference of State Legislatures.

97. D. Finkelhor, H. Hammer, and A. J. Sedlak, "Nonfamily Abducted Children: National Estimates and Characteristics," *National Incidence Study of Missing, Abducted, Runaway, and Thrownaway Children-2*, 2002, Washington, D.C.

98. J. O. Beasley, A. S. Hayne, K. Beyer, G. L. Cramer, S. B. Berson, Y. Muirhead, and J. I. Warren, "Patterns of Prior Offending by Child Abductors: A Comparison of Fatal and Non-Fatal Outcomes," *International Journal of Law and Psychiatry*, 2009, Vol. 32, pp. 273–280.

99. K. Hanfland, R. Keppel, and J. Weis, "Case Management for Missing Children: Homicide Investigation," Washington State Attorney General's Office, 1997.

100. Adapted from the FBI's *Child Abduction Response Plan*, Critical Incident Response Group, National Center for the Analysis of Violent Crime (Quantico, VA), pp. 15–16.

101. For more information, agencies can contact the NCAVC coordinator at their local FBI field office.

102. Interview with Supervisory Special Agent Mark Hilts, Federal Bureau of Investigation, NCAVC, Mar. 2, 1999.

103. L. G. Androm and C. J. Lent, "Cradle Robbers: A Study of the Infant Abductor," FBI Law Enforcement Bulletin, Sept. 1995, pp. 12–17.

104. W. D. Lord, M. C. Boudreaux, and K. V. Lanning, "Investigating Potential Child Abduction Cases: A Developmental Perspective," *FBI Law Enforcement Bulletin*, April 2001, Vol. 70, pp. 1–10.

105. These interviews were conducted with funds provided by Interagency Agreement #91-MC-004, issued through the cooperation of the Office of Juvenile Justice and Delinquency Prevention.

106. W. D. Lord, M. C. Boudreaux, and K. V. Lanning, "Investigating Potential Child Abduction Cases: A Developmental Perspective," FBI Law Enforcement Bulletin, April 2001, Vol. 70, pp. 1–10.

107. Ibid.

108. Ibid.

109. Ibid.

110. Ibid.

111. Ibid.

112. J. Robert Flores, *When Your Child Is Missing: A Family Guide to Survival*, Department of Justice, 2002, pp. 21–22.

113. For more information about the AMBER alert, visit *www.amberalert.gov*.

114. Federal Bureau of Investigation, *Child Abduction Response Plan*, p. 17.

115. 42 U.S.C. 14071; National Criminal Justice Association, *Sex Offender Community Notification Policy Report* (Washington, D.C.: Oct. 1997), p. 5.

116. The Edward Byrne Memorial State and Local Law Enforcement Assistance Program provides grants to states to "improve the functioning of the criminal justice system, with emphasis on violent crimes and serious offenders," *www.ojp.usdoj.gov/BJA/html/byrnef.htm*, accessed Feb. 22, 2000.

117. Scott Matson and Roxanne Lieb, *Sex Offender Registration: A Review of State Laws* (Olympia: Washington State Institute for Public Policy, July 1996), p. 5.

118. Edward Byrne Memorial, p. 1.

119. Ibid.

120. 104. P.L. 145, 100 Stat. 1345; Wetterling, "The Jacob Wetterling Story," p. 8.

121. C. L. Scott and J. B. Gerbasi, "Sex Offender Registration and Community Notification Challenges: The Supreme Court Continues," *The Journal of the American Academy of Psychiatry and the Law*, 2003, Vol. 31, 494–501.

122. 42 U.S.C 14072; Wetterling, ibid., pp. 8–9. Congress named the act after Lychner when she and her two daughters died in the TWA Flight 800 explosion off the coast of Long Island in July 1996.

123. The National Sex Offender Registry (NSOR), which became operational in 1997, initially served as a pointer system for a convicted sex offender's record in the Interstate Identification Index. The permanent registry—part of NCIC (National Crime Information Center) 2000—went online in 1999, replacing the earlier version. The NSOR flags sex offenders when agencies request authorized, fingerprint-based, criminal-history checks. Information provided by the Crimes

against Children Unit, Criminal Investigative Division, FBI Headquarters, Washington, D.C., Feb. 24, 2000.

124. The U.S. attorney general set October 2001 as the date by which all states should comply with DOJ standards relating to the Jacob Wetterling Act. To date, all states have developed sex-offender registries.

125. National Institute of Education, *Violent Schools—Safe Schools: The Safe School Study Report to the Congress*, Washington, D.C.: U.S. Department of Education, 1978.

126. National School Safety Center, "School Crime: Annual Statistical Snapshot," *School Safety* (Winter 1989).

127. J. Hall, "The Knife in the Book Bag," *Time* (May 22, 1993); T. Toch, T. Guest, and M. Guttman, "Violence in Schools: When Killers Come Home." *U.S. News and World Report* (Nov. 8, 1993).

128. "The School Shooter: A Threat Assessment Perspective." National Center for the Analysis of Violent Crime, FBI National Academy, Quantico, VA, 2000, pp. 2–9. (Much of this discussion on crime in school was adapted from this source.)

129. C. Malmquist, Homicidal Violence, malq001@atlas.socsci.umn.edu.

130. "The School Shooter: A Threat Assessment Perspective," pp. 16–21.

131. Glenn Stutzky, "How to Battle the School Bully," an interview with *ABC News, www.abcnews.go.com/sections/community/DailyNews/chat_bullying11298.html*, Nov. 29, 2001.

132. James Blair, "The Ethics of Using Juvenile Informants: Murder in California Prompts New Bill, Raises Questions about Whether Minors Should Be Operatives," *Christian Science Monitor, www.csmonitor.com/durable/1998/04/14/p3s1.htm*, Apr. 14, 1998.

133. "At Least 33 Dead in Virginia Rampage," *MSNBC and NBC News* April 17, 2007. See *www.msnbc.msn.com/id/18134671/*.

134. Commonwealth of Virginia, *Report of the Virginia Tech Review Panel.* PDF File, *www.governor.virginia.gov/TempContent/techPanelReport.cfm*, accessed August 31, 2007.

135. Michael Dorn, Senior Public Safety and Emergency Analyst—Janes Consultancy, "Home Searches: A Valuable Tool." *Campus Safety Journal*, Training Bulletins—Training Bulletin #8, 2003.

Chapter 12

1. *Assessment of United States in Trafficking in Persons Report 2010,* June 2010, (United States Department of State, 2010), p. 338.

2. U.S. Department of Justice, Office of Justice Programs, *Characteristics of Suspected Human Trafficking Incidents, 2007–2008* (Washington, D.C.: DOJ, January 2009).

3. *Assessment of United States in Trafficking in Persons Report 2010,* p. 339.

4. *The Crime of Human Trafficking: A Law Enforcement Guide to Identification and Investigation,* International Association of Chiefs of Police (2006), p. 3.

5. "Fact Sheet: Distinctions Between Human Smuggling and Human Trafficking," The Human Smuggling and Trafficking Center, January 2005, *www.justice.gov/crt/crim/smuggling_trafficking_facts.*

6. "Human Trafficking: Modern Enslavement of Immigrant Women in the United States," *American Civil Liberties Union* (May 31, 2007), *www.aclu.org/ womens-rights/human-trafficking-modern-enslavement-immigrant-women-united-states.*

7. 18 U.S.C. § 1589.

8. 18 U.S.C. § 1584.

9. 18 U.S.C. § 1581.

10. 22 U.S.C. § 7102 (4).

11. See, for example, Human Rights Center, University of California, Berkeley, and Free the Slaves, *Hidden Slaves: Forced Labor in the United States* (September 2004) [hereinafter *Hidden Slaves*], *www.hrcberkeley.org/download/hiddenslaves_report.*

12. International Labor Org., *A Global Alliance against Forced Labour,* 93rd Sess., Report I(B) at 10 (2005).

13. U.S. Department of State, *Trafficking in Persons Report, 2004* at 23 (2004).

14. *Hidden Slaves,* p. 1.

15. U.S. Department of State, *Trafficking in Persons Report, 2006* at 6 (2006) [hereinafter *2006 TIP Report*].

16. *Hidden Slaves,* p. 5.

17. Amy O'Neill Richard, Center for the Study of Intelligence, *International Trafficking in Women to the United States: A Contemporary Manifestation of Slavery and Organized Crime* (Nov. 1999) [hereinafter Richard, *International Trafficking in Women*], *www.cia.gov/csi/monograph/women/trafficking.*

18. Ibid., p. 3.

19. Steven Beardsley, "Brothers Receive 12-Year Prison Terms in Immokalee Human Slavery Case," *Naples Daily News,* 19 December 2008, *www.naplesnews.com/news/2008/dec/19/immokalee-brothers-get-prison-sentence-aliens-case/.*

20. "Victim of Slavery and Human Trafficking Is Awarded Large Sum by Jury," OC Immigration Attorney, *www.ocimmigrationattorney.com/blog/?p=773.*

21. J. Cwikel, B. Chudakov, M. Paikin, K. Agmon, and R. H. Belmaker, "Trafficked Female Sex Workers Awaiting Deportation: Comparison with Brothel Workers," *Archives of Women's Mental Health* 7(2004): 243–249. Early exposure to trauma also increases the chances that a woman will be recruited.

22. A. Aronowitz, *Coalitions against Trafficking in Human Beings in the Philippines: Research and Action. Final Report* (Geneva: United National Office on Drugs and Crime, Anti-Human Trafficking Unit, 2003). In one excellent study of women recruited in the Philippines, all women stated that they had willingly agreed to be transported to the country of destination; some even paid the travel costs up front. All those interviewed, however, subsequently fell into heavy debt and became enslaved in the sex trade.

23. Terry Coonan, "Human Trafficking: Victims' Voices in Florida," *Journal of Social Work Research and Evaluation* 5, No. 2 (2004): 207:216.

24. Ibid.

25. G. Caldwell, S. Galster, and N. Steinzor, *Crime and Servitude: An Expose of the Traffic in Women for Prostitution from the Newly Independent States* (Washington, D.C.: Global Survival Network, 1997). The United States is the number-one importer of mail-order brides and the number-one importer of Philippina women. One company charges men at modest sum for its catalog of Russian

women and holds a "mixer" in Russia to which U.S. men travel; the company charges the women a substantial amount, often their life savings, to travel to the mixer, the catch being that there are many more women at the mixer than there are men.

26. K. Lloyd, "Wives for Sale: The Modern International Mail-Order Bride Industry," *Northwestern Journal of International Law & Business* 20, No. 2 (2000): 341–368. Traffickers find marriage agencies and mail-order bride services attractive, because as legal businesses they can recruit women openly; they are also virtually unregulated. D. Hughes, (2004b). "The Role of 'Marriage Agencies' in the Sexual Exploitation and Trafficking of Women from the Former Soviet Union," *International Review of Victimology* 11, No. 1 (2004): 49–71. However, the overall extent to which traffickers use such businesses is unknown.

27. D. Hughes, *The Impact of the Use of New Communications and Information Technologies on Trafficking in Human Beings for Sexual Exploitation: A Study of the Users* (Strasbourg: Council of Europe, Committee for Equality between Women and Men, 2001).

28. E. Parrado, C. Flippen and C. McQuiston, "Use of Commercial Sex Workers among Hispanic Migrants in North Carolina: Implications for the Spread of HIV," *Perspectives on Sexual and Reproductive Health* 36 (2004): 150–156.

29. Janice G. Raymond and Donna M. Hughes, *Sex Trafficking of Women in the United States* (Coalition Against Trafficking Women, 2001), pp. 54–56, *www.uri.edu/artsci/wms/hughes/sex_traff_us.pdf.*

30. Graeme R. Newman, "The Exploitation of Trafficked Women" (U.S. Department of Justice: Office of Community Oriented Policing Services, February 2006), pp. 33–35.

31. D. Hughes, *Hiding in Plain Sight: A Practical Guide to Identifying Victims of Trafficking in the U.S. With Particular Emphasis on Victims of Sexual Trafficking as Defined by the Trafficking Victims Protection Act 2000* (Providence: University of Rhode Island, 2003), *www.uri.edu/artsci/wms/hughes/hiding_in_plain_sight.*

32. "Introduction to Human Trafficking," *Instructor's Manual* (St. Petersburg: Florida Regional Community Policing Institute, St. Petersburg College, 2006), pp. 26–29, 33–35, 44. (This discussion was adapted from this source.)

33. *Student Manual* (St. Petersburg College, Florida Regional Community Policing Institute, 2006), pp. 48–50.

34. Ibid., pp. 36–42.

35. Stacey Ivie and Natalie Nanasi, "The U-Visa: An Effective Resource for Law Enforcement," *FBI Law Enforcement Bulletin* (October 2009), *www.fbi.gov/publications/leb/2009/october2009/visa_feature.htm.*

36. New Classification for Victims of Criminal Activity; Eligibility for "U" Nonimmigrant Status, Background and Legislative Authority, *http://bibdaily.com/pdfs/E7-17807.pdf.* See also *www.ilrc.org/resources/U%20Visa/Frequently%20Asked%20Questions.html.*

37. *www.uscis.gov/files/pressrelease/U-visa_05Sept07.pdf.*

38. The U-visa is available to individuals with temporary immigration status (for example, student, employment-based, and tourist visas or Temporary Protected Status), as well as undocumented persons with no legal status.

39. Because of their experience and expertise, the authors use examples of domestic violence and other crimes against women throughout the article. However, the U-visa is available to both men and women and serves as a useful tool against a wide range of violent crimes.

40. 8 C.F.R. § 214.14(a)(2) (defining a "certifying agency" for U-visa purposes).

41. Pursuant to 8 U.S.C. 1184(p)(2), the maximum number of issued U-visas may not exceed 10,000 per fiscal year.

42. *Introduction to Human Trafficking, Student Manual,* St. Petersburg College, Florida Regional Community Policing Institute, 2006), pp. 26–29, 44.

Chapter 13

1. Federal Bureau of Investigation, *Crime in the United States—1999* (Washington, D.C.: Government Printing Office, 2000), p. 28.

2. Ibid.

3. Ibid., p. 29.

4. Bureau of Justice Statistics, *Criminal Victimization in the United States—1999* (Washington, D.C.: Bureau of Justice Statistics, 2000), p. 79, table 75.

5. Ibid., p. 80.

6. Ibid., p. 27, table 27.

7. Ibid., p. 39, table 37.

8. Bureau of Justice Statistics, *Criminal Victimization in the United States,* p. 32, table 32.

9. Bureau of Justice Statistics, *Criminal Victimization in the United States,* p. 41, table 43.

10. FBI, *Crime in the United States,* p. 29.

11. Matt Nelson, "Note, Tipster Help in Search for Bank Robber," *Duluth News-Tribune* (Minnesota), March 1, 2000.

12. "Two Plead Guilty in Robbery Try," *Las Vegas Review-Journal,* May 25, 2001.

13. "Deer River," *Duluth News-Tribune* (Minnesota), February 21, 2001.

14. See Werner J. Einstadter, "The Social Organization of Armed Robbery," *Social Problems,* 1969, Vol. 17, No. 1, p. 76. The broad categories are those identified by Einstadter; some of the content has been extended by the authors.

15. FBI, *Crime in the United States,* p. 28.

16. Bureau of Justice Statistics, *Criminal Victimization in the United States,* p. 38, table 36.

17. Ibid., p. 68, table 64.

18. Ibid., p. 69, table 65.

19. Ira Sommers and Deborah R. Baskin, "The Violent Context of Violent Female Offending," *Journal of Research in Crime and Delinquency,* May 1993, Vol. 30, No. 2, p. 147.

20. Bureau of Justice Statistics, *Criminal Victimization in the United States,* p. 39, table 37.

21. Michael J. Feeny, "Cameras Monitor Streets for Paterson Police," *Herald News* (Passaic, County, NJ, 31307), p. B-03.

22. Tod W. Burke and Charles O'Rear, "Armed Carjacking: A Violent Problem in Need of a Solution," *Police Chief,* January 1993, Vol. 60, No. 1, p. 18.

23. FBI, *An Analysis of Carjackings,* p. 3.

24. James T. Hurley, "Violent Crime Hits Home," *FBI Law Enforcement Bulletin,* June 1995, p. 10.

25. Howie Padilla, "Two Men Beat Up Couple in Their Home," *Star Tribune* (Minneapolis, MN), September 6, 2001.

26. Office of Banks and Real Estate, State of Illinois, "ATM Report," *www.obre.state.il.usa/agency/atmrpt.htm,* 1999, p. 1.

27. Ibid.

28. Ibid., pp. 4–5.

29. Ibid., p. 4.

30. Ibid.

31. Martha J. Smith, "Robbery of Taxi Drivers," U.S. Department of Justice, Office of Community Oriented Policing, 2005, pp 2, 5-36. (This discussion was adapted from this source.)

32. B. Schaller, "Causes and Solutions to Service Refusals," *GothamGazette.com* December 1999, *www.schallerconsultant.com/taxi/refusal.htm.*

33. Alicia Altizio and Diana York, "Robbery of Convenience Stores," *Problem-Oriented Guides for Police Problem-Specific Guides Series No. 49,* (Washington, D.C.: U.S. Department of Justice, Office of Community Oriented Policing Services, April 2007), pp. 6–32. (This discussion was adapted from this source.)

34. R. Hunter, "Convenience Store Robbery Revisited: A Review of Prevention Results," *Journal of Security Administration* 22, Nos. 1 & 2 (1999), pp. 1–13.

35. S. Lins and R. Erickson, "Stores Learn to Inconvenience Robbers," *Security Management* 42, No. 11 (1998): 49–53.

36. U.S. Department of Labor, OSHA, *Recommendations on Workplace Violence Prevention Programs in Late-Night Retail Establishments* OSHA 3153 (Washington, D.C.: Justice Research and Statistics Association, 1998).

37. F. Schreiber, "The Future of ATM Security," *Security Management* 38 (March Suppl., 1994): 18A–20A.

38. "Fighting Cargo Theft," *Transportation Topics, Trucking's Electronic Newsletter,* September 8, 1999: 4.

39. Ibid.

40. Deborah Lamm Weisel, U.S. Department of Justice, Office of Community Oriented Policing Services, March 2007, pp. 13–49. (This discussion of bank robbery was adapted from this source.)

41. M. Gill and R. Matthews. "Robbers on Robbery: Offenders Perspectives," in *Crime and Work: Studies in Security and Crime Prevention,* Vol. 1, M. Gill, ed. (Leicester: Perpetuity Press, 1994).

42. M. Gill and K. Pease, "Repeat Robbers: How are They Different?" in *Crime and Work: Increasing the Risk for Offenders,* Vol. II, M. Gill, ed. (Leicester: Perpetuity Press, 1998).

43. T. Gabor and A. Normandeau, "Preventing Armed Robbery through Opportunity Reduction: A Critical Analysis," *Journal of Security Administration* 12(1) (1989): 3–18.

44. H. Leineweber and H. Buchler. "Preventing Bank Robbery: The Offense from the Robber's Perspective," *Police Research in the Federal Republic of Germany,* E. Kube and H. Storzer, eds. (Berlin: Springer-Verlag, 1991).

45. J. Haran, "The Losers Game: A Sociological Profile of 500 Armed Robbers" (Ph.D. diss., Fordham University, 1982), University Microfilms.

46. T. Gabor and A. Normandeau, "Preventing Armed Robbery through Opportunity Reduction: A Critical Analysis," *Journal of Security Administration* 12(1) (1989): 3–18.

47. G. Camp, "Nothing to Lose: A Study of Bank Robbery in America" (Ph.D. diss., Yale University, 1968), Ann Arbor: Michigan University Microfilms.

48. D. Johnston, "Psychological Observations of Bank Robbery," *American Journal of Psychiatry* 135:11 (1978): 1377–1379.

49. M. Borzychki, "Bank Robbery in Australia," *Trends and Issues in Crime and Criminal Justice,* No. 253 (Canberra: Australian Institute of Criminology, 2003).

50. R. Matthews, *Armed Robbery: Police Responses.* Crime Detection and Prevention Series, Paper 78 (London: Home Office, Police Research Group, 1996).

51. J. Vardalis and T. Cox, "A Descriptive Analysis of Bank Robberies in Dade County, Florida, During 1994," *Journal of Security Administration* 21(2) (1998): 1–18.

52. Leineweber and Buchler, "Preventing Bank Robbery."

53. P. Van Koppen and R. Jansen, "The Time to Rob: Variations in Time and Number of Commercial Robberies," *Journal of Research in Crime and Delinquency* 36(1) (1999): 7–29.

54. P. Van Koppen and R. Jansen, "The Road to Robbery: Travel Patterns in Commercial Robberies," *British Journal of Criminology* 38(2) (1998): 230–247.

55. R. Erickson, *Armed Robbers and Their Crimes* (Seattle, WA: Athena Research Corporation, 1996).

56. F. Desroches, *Force and Fear: Robbery in Canada* (Toronto: Nelson Canada, 1995).

57. Johnston, "Psychological Observations of Bank Robbery."

58. Gabor et al., "Armed Robbery."

59. R. Erickson and A. Stenseth "Crimes of Convenience." *Security Management* 40(10) (1996).

60. Leineweber and Buchler, "Preventing Bank Robbery."

61. E. Kube, "Preventing Bank Robbery: Lessons from Interviewing Robbers," *Journal of Security Administration* 11(2) (1988): 78–83.

62. W. D. Nugent, P. Burns, and D. Cappell, *Risks and Rewards in Robbery Prevention and the Offender's Perspective* (Sydney, Australia: Australian Bankers Association, 1989).

63. W. Tiffany and J. Ketchel, "Psychological Deterrence in Robberies of Banks and Its Application to Other Institutions," *The Role of Behavioral Science in Physical Security,* NBS Special Publication 480-38 (Washington, D.C.: U.S. National Bureau of Standards, 1978).

64. Ibid.

65. S. Morrison and I. O'Donnell, *Armed Robbery: A Study in London* (Oxford, United Kingdom: Centre for Criminological Research, 1994).

66. S. Barancik, "FBI Data on Bank Robbery Contradict Movie Myths," *American Banker* 163(232) (1998): 2.

67. Tiffany and Ketchel, "Psychological Deterrence."

68. T. Hannan, "Bank Robberies and Bank Security Precautions," *Journal of Legal Studies* 11(1) (1982): 83–92.

69. Nugent et al., *Risks and Rewards in Robbery Prevention and the Offender's Perspective.*

70. Hannan, "Bank Robberies and Bank Security Precautions."

71. W. Saylor and M. Janus, *Bank Robberies: A Study of Bank Characteristics and Probabilities of Robbery.* Unpublished study, (Washington, D.C.: Office of Research, Federal Bureau of Prisons, 1981).

72. T. Baumer and M. Carrington, *The Robbery of Financial Institutions: Executive Summary* (Washington, D.C.: U.S. Department of Justice, National Institute of Justice, 1986).

73. Hannan, "Bank Robberies and Bank Security Precautions."

74. Nugent et al., *Risks and Rewards in Robbery Prevention and the Offender's Perspective.*

75. Kube, "Preventing Bank Robbery."

76. Gill and Pease, "Repeat Robbers: How are They Different?"

77. Vardalis and Cox, "A Descriptive Analysis."

78. J. Wise and B. Wise, *Bank Interiors and Bank Robberies: A Design Approach to Environment Security* (Rolling Meadows, IL: Bank Administration Institute, 1985).

79. Barancik, "FBI Data on Bank Robbery."

80. Ibid.

81. Gill and Matthews, "Robbers on Robbery."

82. J. Archea, "The Use of Architectural Props in the Conduct of Criminal Acts," *Journal of Architectural and Planning Research* 2(4) (1985): 245–259.

83. Charles Remsberg, *The Tactical Edge: Surviving High Patrol* (Northbrook, IL: Calibre Press, 1986), p. 251.

84. Ibid.

85. Ibid., p. 248.

86. Ibid., p. 253.

87. Ibid., p. 252.

88. Ibid.

89. The distinction between these types of stereotyping is taken from Jerry W. Baker and Carl P. Florez, "Robbery Response," *Police Chief*, October 1980, Vol. 47, No. 10, pp. 46–47.

90. Ibid., p. 47.

91. Ibid.

92. Coleman Cornelius, "Police Bag Bank Heist Suspect," *Denver Post*, December. 4, 1998.

93. Geoffrey P. Alpert, *Helicopters in Pursuit Operations* (Washington, D.C.: National Institute of Justice, 1998), p. 3, with some additions by the authors.

94. This information was obtained from the Miami-Dade (Florida) Police Department Robbery Bureau Standard Operating Procedure, pp. 7–10 through 7–14, April 4, 2004.

95. Kevin B. O'Leary, "Robbery 'Hoax': Shootings Real," *Boston Globe,* November 19, 1993, p. 1.

96. Richard Perez-Pena, "Teller Machine Robbery Was a Hoax, Police Say," *The New York Times,* February 19, 1994, p. A25.

97. For more information, see the website for Sirchie's CompphotoFitPlus Color, *http://sirchie.com/detail.asp?product _ID=CCID200.*

Chapter 14

1. Federal Bureau of Investigation (FBI), Crime Clock 2009, *www.FBI.gov/ucr/09cius/about/crime_clock.html,* December 2010.

2. FBI, Uniform Crime Reports, cius2009.

3. Ibid.

4. Ibid.

5. Rana Sampson, *False Burglar Alarms* (Washington, D.C.: U.S. Department of Justice, 2003), p. 1. Also see Rana Sampson, *False Burglar Alarms* (Washington, D.C.: Office of Community Oriented Policing Services, February 2007).

6. See Todd Keister, *Thefts of and from Cars on Residential Streets and Driveways* (Washington, D.C.: Office of Community Oriented Policing Services, February 2007).

7. C. Bennell and N. J. Jones, "Between a ROC and a Hard Place: A Method for Linking Serial Burglaries by Modus Operandi," *Journal of Investigative Psychology and Offender Profiling*, Vol. 2, No. 1, pp. 23–41, 2005.

8. Experienced investigators are familiar with these two possibilities. One limited study involving 221 total cases from San Diego and Dallas found only support for the replacement theory and even then it explained only a small number of repeat burglary victimizations. The study noted that the same items were taken in the first and second burglaries of the same residence more frequently than expected statistically, supporting the "replacement item" theory somewhat. See Ronald V. Clarke, Elizabeth Perkins, and Donald J. Smith, Jr., "Explaining Repeat Residential Burglaries: An Analysis of Property Stolen," in Graham Farrell and Ken Pease, *Editors Repeat Victimization,* Vol. 12 (Monsey, NY: Criminal Justice Press, 2001) pp. 119–132.

9. J. L. Schneider, "Prolific Burglars and the Role of Shoplifting," *Security Journal,* Vol. 16, No. 2, pp. 49–59, 2003.

10. Mildrade Cherfils, "Jury Convicts 'Spiderman,'" Associated Press, *www.canoe.ca/TopStories/Spiderman_dec8.html,* December 8, 1998.

11. Paulo Lima, staff writer, *The Bergen Record* Online, *www .bergen.com/bse/trainrob199811281.htm,* November 28, 1998.

12. Anderson County (Tennessee) Sheriff's Department, "Juvenile Burglary Ring Stopped," *News Release,* July 1, 2003.

13. Frank Main and Annie Sweeney, "Burglary Ring's Formula Worked for Decades," *Chicago Sun-Times,* January 2, 2005.

14. Bryan Joiner, "Codewise Crew Burglarized Queen's Homes for Millions," *Queen's Chronicle,* April 29, 2004.

15. See Richard A. Ballezza, "YACs Crime Groups," *FBI Law Enforcement Bulletin,* Vol. 67, No. 11, 1998, pp. 7–12.

16. Sandra Gonzales, "Ex-Cop Admits Burglary Charges," *San Jose Mercury News,* December 8, 1998.

17. Marvine Howe, "Anger Mixed with Sorrow for Organist Suspected in Church Burglaries," *The New York Times,* January 6, 1992, p. B4.

18. "FBI Recovers Norman Rockwell Paintings Stolen from Twin Cities Gallery," *Minneapolis Star Tribune,* December 13, 2001.

19. Marilyn Meyer, "Burglars Hit Titusville Bank," Florida Today.com, *www.flatoday/!newsroom/localstorya1264A.htm,* December 12, 2001, pp. 1–2.

20. Richard Perez-Pena, "3 Arrests Hit Burglary Ring in Manhattan," *The New York Times,* November 14, 1992, pp. 21–22.

21. "Loot Jams Va. Home of Alleged Superthief," *Atlanta Constitution,* December 16, 1980, p. 20D.

22. Ann All, "ATM Smash/Grabs Impact Industry," ATM Marketplace.com, March 18, 2004, p. 1.

23. Ibid.

24. For examples, see (no author) "Thieves Smash Store, Grab ATM," The BostonChannel.com, August 17, 2004, p. 1.

25. All, "ATM Smash/Grabs Impact Industry," p. 1.

26. Ibid., p. 2.

27. Ibid., p. 3.

28. See, for example, (no author) KATC3, Acadiana, Louisiana, "Man Arrested While Trying to Drive Off with ATM," December 10, 2004, and Ann All, "ATM News of the Weird," ATM Marketplace.com, January 21, 2005, p. 1.

29. (No author), "Ozark Man Charged in Attempted ATM Machine Break-ins," *Ozark Alabama News,* June 9, 2002, p. 2.

30. (No author) "ATM Burglary Tried with Shotgun," BillingsGazzette.com (Montana), June 18, 2000.

31. Bureau of Justice Statistics, *Criminal Victimization in the United States—2000* (Washington, D.C.: National Institute of Justice, 2002).

32. Ibid., Table 19, no page number in downloaded copy.

33. Wright and Decker, *Burglars on the Job*, p. 36.

34. Ibid., p. 37.

35. Ibid., p. 39.

36. Ibid., pp. 41–42.

37. Ibid., p. 43.

38. Ibid., p. 58.

39. Ibid., pp. 38, 58, with some restatement.

40. For example, see P. F. Cromwell, J. N. Olson, and D. W. Avary, "Who Buys Stolen Property? A New Look at Criminal Receiving," *Journal of Crime and Justice*, 1993, Vol. 16, No. 1, pp. 75–96.

41. Guy Trebay, "Shoplifting on a Grand Scale: Luxury Wear Stolen to Order," *The New York Times*, August 8, 2000, p. 8.

42. Federal Bureau of Investigation, "Operation American Dream," *www.fbi.gov/majcases/dream/dream.htm*, August 28, 2001, p. 2.

43. Richard Zitrin, "Two Accused of Fencing Loot Online," APB News.com, *www.apbnews.com/newscetern/breakingnews/2000/06/02/burglaries0602 _01.html*, June 2, 2000, p. 1.

44. Alexis Muellner, "Good Cop, Bad Cop Played in Miami Cargo Theft Sting," *www.southflorida.bcentral.com/southflorida/stores/1999/11/15/newscolumn3.html*, *South Florida Business Journal*, November 12, 1999, pp. 1–2.

45. Fort Lauderdale Police Department, "Investigative News," *www.ci.ftlaud.fl.us/police/cid1200.html*, December 2000, p. 8.

46. Ibid., p. 6.

47. Federal Bureau of Investigation, untitled news release, *www.geocities.com/pentagon/9719/129117.txt*, January 23, 1997, p. 2.

Chapter 15

1. This paragraph is restated with additions from John S. Baker, *The Sociological Origins of White Collar Crime* (Washington, D.C.: The Heritage Foundation, October 4, 2004), pp. 1–2.

2. David Young, "Pickpockets, Their Victims and Transit Police," *FBI Law Enforcement Bulletin*, 72 (12), December 2003, pp. 1–5; no author, ShanghaiDaily.com, "Pickpockets Attack Police," September 25, 2007; no author, "Pickpockets Target Oslo Police Chief," *Tech E-Newsletter*, May 25, 2007, with restatement and additions.

3. Crime Clock 2009, from Uniform Crime in the United States, 2009 (Washington, D.C.: Federal Bureau of Investigation, 2010), *www.fbi.gov/ucr/cius2009/about/crime_.clock.html*.

4. Uniform Crime in the United States, 2009 (Washington, D.C.: Federal Bureau of Investigation, 2010), *www.fbi.gov/ucr/cius2009/offenses/property-crime/larceny-theft.html*.

5. Uniform Crime in the United States, 2009 (Washington, D.C.: Federal Bureau of Investigation, 2010), *www.fbi.gov/ucr/cius2009/offenses/clearances/index.html*.

6. Uniform Crime in the United States, 2009 (Washington, D.C.: Federal Bureau of Investigation, 2010), *www.fbi.gov/ucr/cius2009/documents/index.html*.

7. Bureau of Justice Statistics, *Criminal Victimization in the United States* (Washington, D.C.: U.S. Department of Justice, December, 2006), Table 86. Printed from the Internet, no page number.

8. To learn more about theft by deception, see such sources as the New Jersey Statutes Annotated (N.J.S.A.) 2C:20-4.

9. Jack L. Hayes International, Inc., *22nd Annual Theft Survey* (Wesley Chapel, FL: Hayes International, 2010), *www.hayesinternational.com/thft_srvys.html*.

10. Michigan Retailers Association, "How Do I Spot Shoplifters?" February 16, 2005, p. 1, *www.retailers.com/eduandevents/ask/askshoplifters.html*.

11. Ibid.

12. Ibid.

13. No author, "Embezzlement/Employee Theft" (Fairmont, WV: National White Collar Crime Center), September 2002, p. 1.

14. Ibid., p. 2.

15. Uniform Crime in the United States, 2006 (Washington, D.C.: FBI, 2007), *www.fbi.gov/ucr.cius2006/Offenses/property _crime/burglary.html* and *www.fbi.gov/ucr.cius2006/Offenses/property_crime/motor_vehicle.html*.

16. Adopted from Rich Laufenbach, "Targeting Organized Retail Crime: Inside the Forensic Operations of One of the World's Largest Retailers," *The Police Chief*, Vol. LXXVI, No. 9, September 2009.

17. See Dean T. Olson, "Financing Terror, *FBI Law Enforcement Bulletin*, Vol. 76, No. 2, February 2007, pp. 1–5, and Mark Clayton, "Is Black-Market Baby Formula Financing Terrorism?" *The Christian Science Monitor*, June 29, 2005.

18. Federal Bureau of Investigation, "Copper Theft Threatens U.S. Critical Infrastructure," (Washington, D.C.: FBI, September 15, 2008), accessed March 17, 2011, *www.fbi.gov/news/stories/2008/december/copper-theft-intel-report-unclass*.

19. "Clark County Sheriff's Department Solves Major Copper Theft with Help from Statewide Online Tracking System and Metal Dealer." November 2, 2010, accessed March 17, 2011, *www.prweb.com/releases/prwebelecronic _reporting/metal_copper_theft/prweb4769064.htm*.

20. Adapted from Morris Greenberg, "Investigating property crimes: A checklist for success," PoliceOne.com, July 20, 2010, *www.policeone.com/police-products/investigation/articles/2142763-investigating-property-crimes-a-checklist-for-success*.

21. Sean B. Hoar, "Identity Theft: The Crime of the New Millennium," *United States Attorneys' USA Bulletin*, Vol. 49, No. 2, March 2001, p. 1.

22. Ibid., p. 1.

23. Lynn Langton and Katrina Baum, "Identity Theft Reported by Households, 2007-Statistical Tables," (Washington, D.C.: Bureau of Justice Statistics, June 2010); Federal Trade Commission, "Putting an End to Account-Hijacking Identity Theft," December 15, 2004, p.1.

24. United States General Accounting Office, *Identity Theft: Prevalence and Cost Appear to Be Growing* (Washington, D.C.: March 2002), p. 8.

25. Bill Husted, "Database Raid Fallout Escalates" *The Atlanta-Journal Constitution*, February 17, 2005.

26. Federal Trade Commission, *Identity Crime: When Bad Things Happen to Your Good Name* (Washington, D.C.:

September 2002), p. 3, with some restatement and additions.

27. See (no author) "Protect Your Identity," *PC World*, Vol. 22, No. 12, Dec. 2004, pp. 107–112.

28. Federal Trade Commission, *Identity Crime: When Bad Things Happen to Your Good Name*, pp. 2 and 9.

29. Richard Hamilton, *The Police Notebook* (Norman, OK: University of Oklahoma), January 7, 2005, pp. 14–17.

30. Ibid., pp. 13–14.

31. No author, "Stop Thieves from Stealing from You," *Consumer Reports*, October 3, 2003, p. 5.

32. Cindy Maggiulli, "Identity Theft Is a Risk on Campus," *The Ranger* (Amarillo College Newspaper), September 20, 2007.

33. Federal Trade Commission, *Identity Crime: When Bad Things Happen to Your Good Name*, p. 4.

34. Linda and Jay Foley, Executive Directors, Identity Theft Resource Center, "Identity Theft: The Aftermath 2003," Summer 2003, p. 5.

35. National Conference of State Legislatures, Identity Theft, 2007, *www.ncsl.org/programs/lis/privacy/idt-statures .htm*.

36. Linda and Jay Foley, "Identity Theft: The Aftermath 2003," p. 4.

37. Ibid., p. 8.

38. No author, "Credit Card Fraud" (Fairmont, WV: National White Collar Crime Center), Jan. 2003, p. 2.

39. Ibid., p. 1.

40. Ibid., pp. 1–2.

41. Laura Czekaj, "Card Scam Bust," *The Ottawa Sun*, July 23, 2004, p. 1.

42. No author, "Check Fraud" (Fairmont, WV: National White Collar Crime Center), September 2002, p. 1.

43. Barbara Hurst, Financial Institution Fraud Statistics," BankersOnLine.com, February 5, 2005, *http://Bankers-OnLine.com/security/gurus_sec090202c.html*.

44. Ian Dempsky, "Theft Operation 'Staggering,' Say Police," Tennessean.com, December 30, 2004, *www.Tennnessean .com/local/archives/04/12/63484418.shtml*.

45. Kara Platoni, "Trailers Are for Travelers," *East Bay Express* (Weekly Newspaper, Emeryville, CA), September 10, 2003, p. 2.

46. Ibid.

47. For information relating to the increase in fraud and con activity over the past three to five years, see the FBI website focused on fraud, *www.fbi.gov/scams-safety/fraud*.

48. No author, "Insurance Fraud," (Fairmont, WV: National White Collar Crime Center), September 2002, p. 1.

49. No author, "San Jose Father, Son Arrested on Auto Fraud Charges," *Insurance Journal*, Feb. 7, 2005, *www .insurancejournal.com/news/west/2005/02/07/50896.htm*.

50. No author, "Insurance Fraud: The Crime You Pay For," Coalition Against Insurance Fraud, February 9, 2005, p. 3.

51. No author, "Health Care Fraud" (Fairmont, WV: National White Collar Crime Center), September 2002, p. 2. For an overview of this subject, see Malcolm K. Sparrow, "Fraud Control in the Health Care Industry," (Washington, D.C.: National Institute of Justice), December 1998.

52. Ibid., p. 3.

53. Ibid., p. 1.

54. Ibid.

55. Ibid., pp. 1–2, and Oxford Health Plan, "Healthcare Fraud," 2005, p. 1, *www.oxhp.com/main/fraud/fraud.html*.

56. No author, "Insurance Fraud," (Fairmont, WV: National White Collar Crime Center), p. 3.

57. Ibid., p. 1.

58. Federal Bureau of Investigation, *2009 Financial Crimes Report, www.fbi.gov/stats-services/publications/financial -crimes-report-2009*.

59. No author, "Fraud and Organized Crime Intersect: Eurasian Enterprise Targeted" (Washington, D.C.: FBI), October 13, 2010, *www.fbi.gov/news/stories/2010/October/ medicare-fraud-organized-crime-bust/medicare-fraud-organized-crime-bust*.

60. Statement of John M. Taylor, Food and Drug Administration (no title), United States Senate's Special Committee on Aging, John B. Breaux, Chair, September 10, 2001, p. 1.

61. No author, "Big Apple Selects 10 'Rotten Apples'," *Insurance Journal*, April 5, 2004, p. 1, *http://insuranceJournal .com/magazines/east/2004/04/05/fraud*.

62. Federal Bureau of Investigation, *2009 Financial Crimes Report, www.fbi.gov/stats-services/publications/financial -crimes-report-2009*.

63. Ibid.

64. Ibid.

65. Ibid.

66. See Internet Crime Complaint Center, *www.ic3.gov/ default.aspx*.

67. Ibid.

68. Ibid.

69. Several Internet companies, such as eBay and PayPal, have extensive fraud alert and prevention programs aimed at educating would-be victims. For example, eBay has taken a proactive approach by sending their own email to customers, *http://reviews.ebay.com/ NEWEST-eBay-SCAM-ALERT-via-Email-see-detailed -pics-W0QQugidZ10000000003241637, accessed* December 18, 2010.

70. Modified from an actual report; however, the names and locations have been changed to protect the victim.

71. This information was provided by Bill Flowers, United States Secret Service, via e-mail on December 20, 2010. Agent Flowers correctly points out that most Nigerians are hard-working and honest and that these scams do not represent them as a whole.

72. There are a number of websites that discuss the bank-examiner and pigeon-drop schemes. For example, see this website, sponsored by the State of Missouri Attorney General's Office: *http://ago.mo.gov/publications/ bankexamine.htm*, accessed December 25, 2010.

73. There are a number of social science surveys that reflect conservative and patriotic values of senior citizens. See The Senior Citizen League for such surveys at *www.seniorleague.org*.

74. Federal Bureau of Investigation, Fraud Target: Senior Citizens, *www.fbi.gov/scams-safety/fraud/seniors*.

75. No author, "Money Laundering," (Montreal, Canada: Royal Canadian Mounted Police), January 26, 2005, p. 2.

76. Mark Motivans, Money Laundering Offenders, 1994–2001 (Washington, D.C.: Bureau of Justice Statistics), July 2003, p. 1.

77. No author, "Money Laundering," (Fairmont, WV: National White Collar Crime Center), August 2003, p. 1.

78. No author, "Economic Perspectives: The Fight against Money Laundering" (Washington, D.C.: U.S. Department of State), Vol. 6, No. 2, May 2001.

79. Ibid., p. 1.

80. No author, "Money Laundering," (Fairmont, WV: National White Collar Crime Center), Aug. 2003, p. 1.

81. Ibid., p. 2.

82. Bonni Tischler, Assistant Commissioner U.S. Customs Service, "The Columbian Black Market Peso Exchange," Statement before the Senate Caucus on International Drug Control, June 21, 1999, and no author, "Black Market Peso Exchange," *Dictionary of Financial Scam Terms*, January 26, 2005, p. 1.

83. Ibid., p. 1.

84. Ibid.

85. No author, "Money Laundering: Extent of Money Laundering through Credit Cards Is Unknown," Report to the Chairman, Permanent Subcommittee on Governmental Affairs, U.S. Senate (Washington, D.C.: United States General Accounting Office), July 2002, p. 3.

86. No author, "Securities/Investment Fraud" (Fairmont, WV: National White Collar Crime Center), June 2003, p. 1.

87. Ibid.

88. Ibid.

89. Federal Bureau of Investigation, *2009 Financial Crimes Report*, *www.fbi.gov/stats-services/publications/financial-crimes-report-2009*; Stephen Gandel, "Wall Street's Latest Downfall: Madoff Charged with Fraud," *Time Magazine*, December 12, 2008.

90. Federal Bureau of Investigation, *2007 Uniform Crime Report* (Washington, D.C.: USPO, 2008).

91. Ibid; and see Scott Burns, "Madoff's Case Topples Measures," *Dallas Morning News*, December 28, 2008, P. D-1.

92. Scott Burns, "Madoff's Case Topples Measures," *Dallas Morning News*, December 28, 2008, P. D-1.

93. Federal Bureau of Investigation, *2009 Financial Crimes Report*, *www.fbi.gov/stats-services/publications/financial-crimes-report-2009*; see also "Madoff Victims Win Biggest Settlement So Far," *Wall Street Journal*, December 17, 2010, p.1.

94. No author, "Pump and Dump Schemes," U.S. Securities and Exchange Commission, March 12, 2001, p. 1, *www.sec.gov/answers/pumpdump.htm*.

95. Ibid.

96. No author, "Microcap Stock: A Guide for Investors," U.S. Securities and Exchange Commission, Aug. 2004, pp. 1–2 is the source of information in this paragraph.

97. No author, "Securities/Investment Fraud" (Fairmont, WV: National White Collar Crime Center), June 2003, pp. 2–3.

98. No author, "Affinity Fraud: How to Avoid Scams That Target Groups," U.S. Securities and Exchange Commission, p. 2, *www.sec.gov/investor/pubs/affinity.htm*; also see *SEC v. A. B. Financing and Investments, Inc.*, and Anthony Blissett, Case No. 02-23487-CIV-Ungaro-Benages (South District, Florida, Dec. 6, 2002).

99. No author, "Securities/Investment Fraud" (Fairmont, WV: National White Collar Crime Center), June 2003, p. 3.

100. No author, "Insurance-Agent Scams," *Consumer Reports*, Aug. 2004, p. 5.

101. Ibid.

102. No author, "Pennsylvania Joins 25 States in Actions against Sellers of Payphone Schemes, Losses at Least $70 Million," news release, Pennsylvania Securities Commission, March 13, 2001, p. 1.

103. No author, "Certificates of Deposit: Tips for Savers," Federal Deposit Insurance Corporation, February 12, 2005, p. 1.

104. Ibid.

105. No author, "Broken Promises: Promissory Note Fraud," U.S. Securities and Exchange Commission, January 11, 2005, p. 1.

106. Ibid.

107. Ibid.

108. Ibid.

109. Ibid.

110. No author, "Common Fraud Schemes," Federal Bureau of Investigation, February 12, 2005, p. 7, *http://FBI.gov/majcases/fraud/fraudschemes.htm*.

111. No author, "Prime Investment Schemes," (Montreal, Canada: Royal Canadian Mounted Police), October 16, 2003, p. 1.

112. No author, "Insurance-Agent Scams," *Consumer Reports*, August 2004, p. 4.

113. Ibid.

114. Ibid.

115. No author, "FCC Consumer Advisory: 809 Phone Scam-Beware," (Washington, D.C.: Federal Trade Commission), Oct. 6, 2003, p. 1.

116. Family Safe Media, "Pornography Statistics 2008," *www.familysafemedia.com/pornography_statistics.html*, accessed December 22, 2010.

117. United States Postal Service, "Get Rich Quick? Don't Count on It!" Press Release, February 2, 2004, p. 1.

118. No author, "Consumer and Business Guide to Preventing Mail Fraud" (Washington, D.C.: U.S. Postal Service), 1999, p. 12.

119. Ibid., p. 20.

120. Ibid., p. 22.

121. Ibid., p. 16.

122. Ibid., p. 13.

Chapter 16

1. Federal Bureau of Investigation, *Crime in the United States, Uniform Crime Reports, 2009* available at *www.fbi.gov/ucr*.

2. Ibid.

3. Ibid.

4. Ibid.

5. Ibid.

6. Coyle, Tim, "Motorcycle Thefts," APB, the official publication of the International Association of Auto Theft Investigators, March, 2010, p. 15.

7. Joseph Weherle, Jr., CEO of National Insurance Crime Bureau (NICB), opening remarks to the 58th Annual Conference of the International Association of Auto Theft Investigators, August 22, 2010, Orlando, Florida.

8. Perry Stern, "MSN Autos," reprinted in the *Florida Auto Theft Intelligence Unit Newsletter*, Vol. 1, Issue 3, October 2008.

9. Citizens for Auto-Theft Responsibility, *CAR Newsletter*, Autumn 1992 (a quarterly publication of the not-for-profit public awareness and victim support organization, P.O. Box 3131, Palm Beach, FL 33480).

10. "NICB Goes Globe Trotting to Bring Back Stolen Cars," *APB* (official publication of the International Association of Auto Theft Investigators), November 1996, p. 63.

11. Speech by Lt. Greg Terp, Commander, Miami-Dade Police Department Auto Theft Task Force, Summit on Auto Theft in Florida 2002, Tampa, Florida, September 16, 2002.

12. NICB, "Doing a Double Take: Vehicle Clones Are a Street-Level Problem for Insurers," *Strategic Analysis Report*, Vol. 1, 2004, October 10, 2004.

13. Ibid.

14. Ibid.

15. National Auto Theft Bureau, 1990 Annual Report, p. 15.

16. National Insurance Crime Bureau, 2006, unpublished document.

17. Comments by David Shillingford, President, National Equipment Register, Summit on Auto Theft in Florida 2002, Tampa, Florida, September 16, 2002.

18. Gene Rutledge, "7 Character PIN for Off-Road Equipment Is Here," *APB*, July 1999, pp. 17–19.

19. "There's More than One Way to Stop a Thief," *APB*, March 2001, pp. 52, 58–59.

20. FIA International Research, "Contraband, Organized Crime, and the Threat to the Transportation and Supply Chain Function." Study conducted on behalf of the National Cargo Security Council, a coalition of public and private transportation organizations, September 2001, Executive Summary, p. 1.

21. Joseph Weherle, CEO, NICB, opening remarks, 58th Annual Conference, International Association of Auto Theft Investigators, Orlando, Florida. Mr. Wherele stated that there is no good data available on cargo theft losses and estimates range from $10 billion–$60 billion.

22. Remarks of Joseph Weherle, CEO, NICB.

23. Brian Shockley, "Automated License Plate Recognition," *APB*, the official publication of the International Association of Auto Theft Investigators, November 2008, p. 47. See also "Automated License Scan: The Ultimate 'Multi-Task' Tool for Patrol," *The Sheriff's Star*, official publication of the Florida Sheriff's Association, May/June 2009, p. 3, and Norman Gaumont, "The Role of Automatic License Plate Recognition Technology in Policing: Results from the Lower Mainland of British Columbia," *The Police Chief*, IACP, November 2008, pp. 50–59.

24. National Insurance Crime Bureau, *2010 Passenger Vehicle Identification Manual, 81st Edition* (Palos Hills, IL: NICB, 2010).

25. Ibid.

26. National Insurance Crime Bureau, *2010 Commercial Vehicle Identification Manual* (Palos Hills, IL: NICB, 2004).

27. National Automobile Theft Bureau, *2010 Heavy Equipment Identification Manual*, 1st ed. (Palos Hills, IL: NATB, 2010).

28. National Insurance Crime Bureau, *2010 Passenger Vehicle Identification Manual, 81st Edition*, front matter (Palos Hills, IL: NICB, 2010).

29. Federal Bureau of Investigation, "The New Generation of NCIC," *CJIS: A Newsletter for the Criminal Justice Community*, Vol. 3, No. 2, 1999, pp. 5–6.

30. Ibid.

31. Remarks of Joseph Weherle, CEO, NICB, 58th Annual Conference, International Association of Auto Theft Investigators, August 22, 2010, Orlando, Florida.

32. Ibid.

33. Information provided in a conversation with Sgt. Chris Bimonte, Miami-Dade Police Department, who represents the department on the North America Export Committee.

34. Comments by Senator Bill Nelson, Florida, Summit on Auto Theft in Florida 2002, Tampa, Florida, September 15, 2002.

35. Information provided by Sgt. Chris Bimonte.

36. Information provided by Sgt. Chris Bimonte.

37. Glenn Wheeler, "North American Export Committee Update," *APB*, March 2001, p. 11.

38. "NICB, ISO, and NER Form Industry Alliance to Combat Equipment Theft," Industry News section, *APB*, International Association of Auto Theft Investigators, July 2008, p. 13.

39. Ibid.

40. "Attorney General Issues Report on Component Part Markings," IAATI Legal News column, *APB*, November 2000, pp. 59, 61.

41. Ibid.

42. Ibid.

43. Ibid.

44. "Restoration of Altered or Obliterated Numbers," training bulletin, Alabama Department of Public Safety.

45. National Insurance Crime Bureau, *Fire Investigation Handbook* (Palos Hills, IL: NICB, 1995), pp. 31–67; National Fire Protection Association International, *NFPA 921 Guide for Fire and Explosion Investigations, 2001 Edition* (Quincy, MA: NFPA International, 2001), pp. 921–171 to 921–182.

46. This information was provided by the LoJack Corporation of Boston, Massachusetts.

47. "OnStar by GM," Industry News Section, *APB*, International Association of Auto Theft Investigators, November 2008, p. 67.

48. Much of the material on this topic is drawn from Phillip J. Crapeau, "Photo Inspection Helps Deter Auto Theft," *National Underwriter*, September 18, 1990.

49. Most of the material in this section is drawn from the Aviation Crime Prevention Institute, *Aviation Identification and Information Manual for Police Officers* (Frederick, MD: ACPI and the Aviation Insurance Industry, 1987) and from information supplied by Robert Collins, Aviation Crime Prevention Institute, Dec. 2001.

50. The address of the Aviation Crime Prevention Institute, Inc., is Post Office Box 30, Hagerstown, MD 21741-0030. Robert J. Collins, president of the institute, invites and welcomes inquiries and requests for assistance from law-enforcement agencies and officers. Telephone numbers for the institute are 800-969-5473 and 301-791-9791. The website is *www.acpi.org*.

51. Ibid.

52. Ibid.

Chapter 17

1. No author, Cyber Crime "More Profitable than Drugs," 9News, June 9, 2009, August 5, 2010, *http://news.ninemsn*

.com.au/technology/823443/cyber-crime-more-profitable-than-drugs. Attributed to speaker at Australian High Tech Crime Conference, Sydney.

2. Elinor Mills, "Study: CyberCrime Costs Firms $1 Trillion Globally," Security, January 28, 2009.

3. No author, Study: "One in Five On-Line Consumers Has Been Victim of CyberCrime," Consumer Reports Press Release, May 24, 2009.

4. Internet Crime Complaint Center, 2009 Internet Crime Report (Washington, D.C.: Bureau of Justice Assistance, 2010), p. 2.

5. No author, "A Cyber Crime Report," ParetoLogic, Inc, March 2008, p. 34, September 6, 2010, www.ParetoLogic.com.

6. Points 2, 5, and 8 are drawn from Olasanmi Omoneye Olufunke, "Computer Crimes and Counter Measures in the Nigerian Banking Sector, Journal of Internet Banking and Commerce, Vol. 15, No. 1 April 2010, p. 5.

7. Bill Chu, Thomas J. Holt, and Gail Joon Ahn, "Examining the Creation, Distribution, and Function of Malware Online," (Washington, D.C.: U.S. Department of Justice, March 2010), p. 5.

8. Ibid., pp. 41, 23.

9. Ibid., p. 42.

10. On this point see Mel Morris, "Intelligence, Knowledge and Organized Crime," Computer Fraud and Security, Issue 4, April 2010, pp. 13–15.

11. No author, "Top Cyber-Crime Threats for 2010," Sonic-WALL, August 20, 2010, www.SonicWALL.Com.

12. Rafael Etges and Emma Sutcliffe, "An Overview of Transnational Cyber Crime," Information Security Journal, Vol. 17, 2008, p. 91.

13. John Charlton, "Al Qaeda Buys Cyber Criminal Expertise," Computer Fraud and Security, Vol. 2005, Issue 3, March 2005, p. 2.

14. Ibid.

15. Clay Wilson, "Botnets, Cybercrime, and Cyberterrorism: Vulnerabilities and Policy Issues for Congress (Washington, D.C.: Congressional Research Service, January 2, 20008), p. CRS-11.

16. Mustaque Ahamad et al., "Emerging Cyber Threats for 2009," Georgia Institute of Technology, p. 2. Also see Reid Goldsborough, "Computer Zombies an Increasing Concern," Tech Directions, Vol. 69, Issue 8, March 2010, p. 15.

17. Rafael Etges and Emma Sutcliffe, "An Overview of Transnational Organized Cyber Crime," p. 92.

18. No author, "Hazards Lurk in Cameron Diaz Web Search Listings," USAToday, August 20, 2010.

19. Hassan Wahshat, Yasir Khalil, and Takialdin, "Computer Virus, Survey Study," International Journal of Computer Science and Network Security," Vol. 7, No. 4, April 2007, p. 308.

20. No author, "The 12 Costliest Computer Viruses Ever," Insure.com, August 3, 2010. http://insure.com/2010/08/03/The-12-Costliest-Computer-Viruses-Ever/.

21. Tom Zeller, Jr., "Protecting Yourself from Keylogging Thieves," The New York Times, February 27, 2006, p. 16.

22. Jean Thilmany, "Stealth Worms," Mechanical Engineering, Vol. 132, Issue 5, May 2010, p. 15 and Mark Bowden, "The Enemy Within," Atlantic Monthly, Vol. 305, Issue 5, June 2010, and Robert McMillan, "After One Year, 7 Million Conficker Infections," AllThingsDigital, Network-World.com, October 30, 2009, p. 1.

23. No author, "Defense Security Report, VeriSign, Distributed Denial of Service Attacks," July 11, 2008, p. 12.

24. Xin Luo and Qinyu Liao, "Awareness Education as the Key to Ransomware Prevention," Information Security Systems, Vol. 16, 2007, p. 195.

25. Ibid., p. 197.

26. No author, "A Cyber Crime Report, p. 6.

27. Jim Wingate, The Perfect Dead Drop, White Paper, BackBone Security, 2004.

28. Symantec, Trojan Horse, April 20, 2010, pp. 1–2. www.Symantec.com/security-response/writeup.jsp?docid=2004-021914-2822-99, August 16, 2010.

29. Ibid.

30. Arik Hesseldahl, "Spyware's Growing Arsenal," Business Week, online edition, August 16, 2006, p. 6.

31. Thorsten Holtz, Markus Engelberth, and Felix Freiling, "Learning More about the Underground Economy: A Case Study of Keyloggers and Dropzones," Laboratory for Dependable System, University of Mannheim, Germany, December 18, 2008, pp. 7–8.

32. Aaron Emigh, "The Crimeware Landscape: Malware, Phishing, Identity Theft, and Beyond," IronKey, Los Altos, California, September 19, 2006, p. 5.

33. See Michael Landi, "The Methods of Windows Rootkits," Journal of Applied Security Research, Vol. 4, Issue 2, 2009, pp. 389–426.

34. With restatement and additions, these points are drawn from Hollis Stambaugh et al., Electronic Crime Needs Assessment for State and Local Law Enforcement (Washington, D.C.: National Institute of Justice, 2001).

35. For a more extended view of this subject see Nathan Judish et al. (Washington, D.C.: U.S. Department of Justice, Computer Crime and Intellectual Property Section, 2009).

36. People v. Ledesma, 39 Cal 4th, 657, 703–704, 2006.

37. United States v. Bolin, 514 F.2d 554, 560–561, 1975, United States v. Ivy, 165 F.3rd, 397, 403, 1998 and United States v. Tibbs, 49 F.Supp.2d 47, 48–49, 53.

38. United States v. Sanchez, 32 F.3d 1330, 1994.

39. Jones v. State, 648 So.2d 669 (FL, 1994).

40. The impact of Georgia v. Randolph is discussed in greater detail in Renee E. Williams, "Third Party Consent Searches after Randolph: Dueling Approaches to Dueling Roommates," Boston Law Review, Vol. 87, No. 4, October 2007, pp. 937–968.

41. Georgia v. Randolph, 547 U.S. 103, 2006.

42. For a fuller treatment of this subject see Yule Kim, Protecting the U.S. Perimeter: Border Searches under the Fourth Amendment (Washington, D.C.: Congressional Research Service, June 29, 2009).

43. With changes and consolidation of points, the content in this and the remaining sections of this chapter are drawn from various portions of Katrina Rose, Electronic Crime Scene Investigation: An On-the-Scene Reference for First Responders (Washington, D.C.: National Institute of Justice, November 2009), most of it from pp. 6–22.

Chapter 18

1. Charles Swanson and Leonard Territo, "Agricultural Crime: Its Extent, Prevention and Control," FBI Law Enforcement Bulletin, 1980, Vol. 49, No. 5, p. 10. We originally estimated $3 billion annually. The figure in the

text is based on the assumption of less than a 3% annual increase in losses over the past 27 years.

2. For an extension of this and related propositions, see Charles Swanson, "Rural and Agricultural Crime," *Journal of Criminal Justice*, 1981, Vol. 9, No. 1, pp. 19–27.

3. Patricia Leigh Brown, "Someone Is Stealing Avocados," *The New York Times*, January 26, 2004.

4. E-mail, Laurie Hill to Charles Swanson, California Avocado Commission, October 2, 2007.

5. Jennifer Steinhauer, "Unusual Culprits Cripple Farms in California," *The New York Times*, July 31, 2007.

6. Ibid.

7. Christine Souza, "Vineyard Thieves Target Grapes, Harvest Supplies," California Farm Bureau Federation, September 19, 2007, p. 2.

8. Jesse McKinley, "Authorities Work to Crack Nut Crime Ring," *The New York Times*, October 2006.

9. Catherine E. Shoicet, "Thieves Strip Park's Palms," *St. Petersburg Times*, September 21, 2007.

10. Ibid.

11. FBI, Crime in the United States, 2006 (Washington, D.C.: FBI, 2009), Table 24. No page number in the Internet version of this document, *www.fbi.gov/ucr/cius2009/data.table_24.html.*

12. U.S. Department of Agriculture, Economic Research Service, U.S. Beef and Cattle Industry 2002–2005: Background Statistics and Information, p. 1, *www.ers.usda.gov/news/BSECoverage.htm.* For 2005 the National Agricultural Statistics Service (NASS) reported 190,000 cattle and calves lost to predation: 9.4% were attacks by mountain lions or bobcats, 12.9% involved dogs, 32.4% were killed by coyotes, and 45.3% "other or unknown predators." In contrast, that same year NASS accounted for only 21,000 head lost due to thefts, which seems very low; that same year Wyoming authorities reported 3,700 heads of cattle lost due to theft for just that state. That would mean Wyoming, one of the smaller cattle-producing states, had 17.6% of all cattle stolen, or nearly one in five.

13. Brian Brus, "Rustling Resurgence," *The Journal Record* (Oklahoma City), August 6, 2007.

14. Nelson Hernandez, "$75,000 in Bull Semen Stolen from Frederick Farm," *The Washington Post*, November 3, 2005.

15. Garance Burke and Olivia Munoz, "Hormone Theft Worries Rural Police, *Redding* (California) *Record*, February 23, 2007.

16. Mike Toner, "Brazen Fossil Hunters Are Cleaning Out U.S. Dinosaur Heritage," *Atlanta Journal Constitution*, August 23, 2001.

17. William L. Hamilton, "Jurassic Bark," *The New York Times*, December 1, 2005, and No author, "Petrified Wood Stolen on Federal Land," The Associated Press State and Local Wire, January 29, 2007.

18. Joe Corcoran, "High-Tech Measures Thwart Ginseng Poachers," *Voice of America News*, April 12, 2006, p. 1.

19. Ibid., p. 2, with additions.

20. Janet Heimlich, "Thorny Problem," *Texas Parks and Wildlife Magazine*, June 2003, p. 1.

21. No author, "Thieves Steal Hundreds of Millions of Dollars' Worth of Trees," *USA Today*, May 18, 2003.

22. Chuck Hayes, "Pennsylvania: Stop Theft! Timber Theft Growing Concern in Allegheny National Forest," *Times Observer* (Warren, Pennsylvania), July 14, 2006.

23. Warren Cornwall, "Maples Falling Victim to Backwoods Thieves," *The Seattle Times*, May 17, 2007.

24. No author, "Two Charged with Timber Theft from Medicine Bow National Forest," Associated Press, February 12, 2004.

25. David Windsor, "Timber Theft: A Solvable Crime," *Indiana Woodland Steward*, Spring 2001, Vol. 10, No. 1, pp. 1–3, *www.fnr.purdue.edu/inwood/past%20issues/timberth.htm.*

26. These points are drawn from Sgt. William Bacon, *Livestock Theft Investigation*, Los Angeles County Sheriff's Department, undated, p. 2, with modifications made by the authors.

27. Ibid., which is the source for the information in this paragraph.

28. Ibid.

29. Some of the information in this paragraph is drawn from ibid., pp. 5–6.

30. Ibid., p. 5.

31. Ibid.

32. E. N. Smith, "Modern Rustlers Steal Livestock via the Highway," *Seattle Times Com*, June 7, 1998, p. 1.

33. Ibid., p. 1.

34. Ibid., p. 12.

35. Ibid.

36. Bacon, *Livestock Theft Investigation*, p. 16, from which this paragraph was obtained with restatement.

37. Ibid., p. 24.

38. See *Utah Livestock Brand Book*, Utah Department of Agriculture, 2006.

39. These methods are identified in virtually all discussions of this topic. In preparing this edition we reviewed and drew a limited amount of restated content from Michael Neary, *Methods of Livestock Identification*, Purdue University Cooperative Extension, December 2002.

40. On this subject see No author, *A Sampling of Thoughts and Opinions on Electronic Identification*. The University of Tennessee, Center for Profitable Agriculture, 2004. In a small survey of farmers and ranchers it was found that among those who used a method of identification, 14.2% employed tattoos, 5.4% used brands, 77.4% used plastic ear tags, 1.8% relied on RFID devices, and 1.2% used other methods.

41. Several of these points were taken from Bacon, *Livestock Theft Investigation*, p. 17.

42. There are a number of articles on the use of DNA in wildlife investigations; as an illustration, see No author, "Wildlife Officers Use DNA Evidence to Solve Cold Case," *US States News*, August 21, 2006.

43. Randal C. Archibold, "Poachers in West Hunt Big Antlers to Feed Big Egos," *The New York Times*, December 9, 2006.

44. For example, see No author, "Thrill Killings Adding to Boost in Poaching of Nevada's Big Game," The Associated Press State and Local Wire, November 29, 2006.

45. Archibold, "Poachers in West Hunt Big Antlers to Feed Big Egos."

46. Ingrid Peritz, "Rich Hunters Used Copter to Stalk Terrified Moose," *The Globe and Mail*, Canada, December 7, 2006.

47. "Poachers Enlisted to Save Big Game," *The New York Times*, December 26, 1990, p. A28.

48. Press Release, New Mexico Department of Game and Fish, March 16, 2005.

49. Wency Leung, "Asia's Bile Trade Takes Its Toll of Canadian Bears," *South China Morning Post*, August 26, 2007.

50. Ibid.

51. Press release, The Humane Society of the United States, "Congress Aims to End the Black Market Trade in Bear Parts," July 18, 2007, *www.hsus.org/press_and _publications/press_releases*.

Chapter 19

1. National Fire Protection Association Fire Loss in the U.S. in 2008; U.S. Fire Administration, Intentionally Set Structure Fires; *www.usfa.dhs.gov/statistics/arson/*.

2. This information was obtained from "Stop Arson Now," a brochure published by the Florida Advisory Committee on Arson Prevention.

3. K. D. Moll, *Arson, Vandalism, and Violence: Law Enforcement Problems Affecting Fire Departments* (Washington, D.C.: Government Printing Office, 1977), pp. 20–21.

4. C. W. Stickney, "Recognizing Where Arson Exists," *Fireman Magazine*, September–December 1960, p. 3.

5. *Touched Off by Human Hands*, 1979. This booklet was originally published by the Illinois Advisory Committee on Arson Prevention in cooperation with the Illinois Chapter of the International Association of Arson Investigation and was reprinted for distribution by the State Farm Fire and Casualty Company, Bloomington, Illinois. Much of the information in this section was taken from this source, pp. 7–11.

6. Stickney, "Recognizing Where Arson Exists," p. 4.

7. Ibid., p. 8.

8. Ibid.

9. C. W. Stickney, "Recognizing Where Arson Exists," *Fire and Arson Investigator*, October–December 1970; W. A. Derr, "Wildland Fire Investigation: Information from Objects," paper presented at the 18th Annual Fire and Arson Investigators Seminar, Palm Springs, California, June 14–18, 1971.

10. National Fire Protection Association, *921 Guide for Fire and Explosives Investigation* (Quincy, MA: NFPA, 2008), pp. 921–940.

11. National Fire Protection Association, *921 Guide for Fire and Explosion Investigations* (Quincy, MA: NFPA, 2001), pp. 921–927, 921–928.

12. Ibid., p. 921–933.

13. Ibid., p. 921–933.

14. Ibid., p. 921–929.

15. *User's Manual for NFPA 921—Guide for Fire and Explosion Investigation* (2nd ed.) (Quincy, MA) National Fire Protection Association, Inc. 2005, p. 46.

16. Ibid., pp. 921–930.

17. B. P. Battle and P. B. Weston, *Arson: A Handbook of Detection and Investigation* (New York: Arco, 1972), pp. 19–28. Much of the information in this section was taken with permission from this source.

18. Joseph Toscano, *Motive, Means & Opportunity: A Guide to Fire Investigation*, American Re-Insurance Company, Princeton, NJ, 1996, pp. 87–88.

19. C. L. Karchmer, M. E. Walsh, and J. Greenfield, *Enforcement Manual: Approaches for Combating Arson for Profit Schemes* (Washington, D.C.: U.S. Department of Justice, 1981), pp. 15–31. This discussion was adapted from this source.

20. Joseph Toscano, *Motive, Means & Opportunity: A Guide to Arson Investigation*, American Re-Insurance Company, 1996, Princeton, NJ, pp. 10–23. Much of this discussion of other motives for arson was obtained with permission from this source.

21. Stickney, "Recognizing Where Arson Exists," 1960, pp. 11–12.

22. B. B. Caldwell, "The Examination of Exhibits in Suspected Arson Cases," *Royal Canadian Mounted Police Quarterly*, 1957, Vol. 22, pp. 103–108.

23. Stauffer, Eric and Doug Byron, "Alternative Fuels in Fire Debris Analysis: Biodiesel Basics," *Journal of Forensic Science* 52, No. 2 (March 2007): 371–379.

24. Ibid.

25. J. F. Bordeau, Q. Y. Kwan, W. E. Faragker, and G. C. Senault, *Arson and Arson Investigation* (Washington, D.C.: Government Printing Office, 1974), pp. 77–83. Much of the information in this section was taken from this source.

26. J. D. Nicol, "Recovery of Flammable Liquids from a Burned Structure," *Fire Engineering*, 1961, Vol. 114, p. 550.

27. D. Q. Burd, "Detection of Traces of Combustible Fluids in Arson Cases," *Journal of Criminal Law, Criminology, and Police Science*, 1960, Vol. 51, pp. 263–264; P. Rajeswaran and P. L. Kirk, "Identification of Gasoline, Waves, Greases, and Asphalts by Evaporation Chromatography," *Microchemical Journal*, 1962, Vol. 6, pp. 21–29.

28. R. Milliard and C. Thomas, "The Combustible Gas Detector (Souffer), an Evaluation," *Fire and Arson Investigator*, January–March 1976, pp. 48–50.

29. D. M. Lucas, "The Identification of Petroleum Products in Forensic Science by Gas Chromatography," *Journal of Forensic Sciences*, 1960, Vol. 5, No. 2, pp. 236–243.

30. P. L. Kirk, *Fire Investigation* (New York: Wiley, 1969), pp. 43–44; E. C. Crocker and L. B. Sjostrom, "Odor Detection and Thresholds," *Chemical Engineering News*, 1949, Vol. 27, pp. 1922–1931; and H. Zwaardemaber, "Camera Inorata," *Perfumery and Essential Oil Record*, 1921, Vol. 12, pp. 243–244.

31. P. L. Kirk, *Crime Investigation, Physical Evidence, and the Police Laboratory* (New York: Interscience, 1966), p. 717; H. P. Wonderling, "Arsonists—Their Methods and the Evidence," *International Association of Arson Investigators Newsletter*, October–December 1953, reprinted in *Selected Articles for Fire and Arson Investigators*, International Association of Arson Investigators, 1975; K. Ol'Khosvsbaya, "Colormetric Determination of Hydrocarbons, Gasoline, Kerosene and White Spent in the Air of Industrial Installations," *Gigiena Truda i Professional'nye Zabolevaniza*, 1971, Vol. 15, No. 11, pp. 57–58.

32. J. W. Girth, A. Jones, and T. A. Jones, "The Principle of Detection of Flammable Atmospheres by Catalytic Devices," *Combustion and Flame*, 1973, Vol. 21, pp. 303–312.

33. C. M. Lane, "Ultra-Violet Light . . . Gem or Junk," *Fire and Arson Investigator*, December 1975, Vol. 26, No. 2, pp. 40–42.

34. C. L. Karchmer, M. E. Walsh, and J. Greenfield, *Enforcement Manual: Approaches for Combating Arson for Profit Schemes* (Washington, D.C.: U.S. Department of Justice, 1981), pp. 249–252.

35. National Insurance Crime Bureau, *Fire Investigation Handbook* (Palos Hills, IL: NICB, 1995), pp. 24, 25.

36. The purpose of the National Insurance Crime Bureau is to investigate questionable insurance claims and cooperate with public law-enforcement agencies in securing the prosecution of insurance criminals.

37. National Insurance Crime Bureau, *Fire Investigation Handbook,* p. 26.

38. John Barracato, *Burning: A Guide to Fire Investigation* (Stamford, CT: Aetna Casualty and Surety, 1986), pp. 14–16.

39. National Fire Protection Association, *Guide for Fire and Explosion Investigations,* pp. 921–994.

40. Tim Dees, "Things That Go Boom in the Night," *Police* 34, No. 6 (2010): pp. 44, 46–47. (This discussion was adapted from this source.)

41. Smiths Detection is one of the largest manufacturers of IMS instruments for explosives detections, typically found at airport security checkpoints. In most cases an operator uses a glorified coffee filter to swab luggage or some other suspicious item and places it in a recess for analysis. More often than not a green light comes on and the traveler is free to go.

42. A Raman Laser, which works by measuring activity on the surface exposed or excited by the laser, produces a profile that is compared to that of the target substance. The effect is a detector that can be either fixed or handheld and costs a fraction of the IMS instrument. The microfluidic chips are consumed in the analysis process. The company plans to ship its first operational units this year.

43. George Buck, *Preparing for Terrorism* (Albany, NY: Delmar, 1998), pp. xi–xii.

44. James T. Thurman, *Practical Bomb Scene Investigation* (Boca Raton, FL: CRC Press, 2006): pp. 123–130. (This discussion of improvised explosive devices has been drawn directly from this source and modified with permission.)

45. Ian Sample, *The Guardian, Co, UK,* 27 December 2009, *www.guardian.co.uk/world/2009/dec/27/petn-pentaerythritol-trinitrate-explosive.*

46. National Fire Protection Association, *Guide for Fire and Explosion Investigations,* 1992, pp. 921-103–921-107.

47. James T. Thurman, *Practical Bomb Scene Investigation* (Boca Raton, FL) CRC 2006, pp. 251–259.

48. Detail packaging instructions for different types of evidence can be found in the FBI Laboratory Division Publication, *Handbook for Forensic Services,* as revised in 2003.

49. This checklist was provided by the U.S. Department of the Treasury, Bureau of Alcohol, Tobacco, and Firearms, 1999.

50. Ibid.

51. James T. Thurman, Practical Bomb Scene Investigation (Boca Raton, FL) CRC 2006, pp. 391–392. This information was obtained from this source with permission.

Chapter 20

1. The National Drug Intelligence Center (NDIC), established in 1993, is a component of the U.S. Department of Justice. The General Counterdrug Intelligence Plan, implemented in February 2000, designated NDIC as the nation's principal center for strategic domestic counterdrug intelligence. The NDIC produces national, regional, and state drug threat assessments, various drug information bulletins, and a series of pamphlets providing detailed information on specific drugs. The NDIC is a very valuable resource for local and state police officers engaged in drug enforcement in this country, and much of the description, usage, and abuse of drugs in this chapter is supported and grounded within the NDIC publications. See *www.usdoj.gov/ndic.*

2. Gregory Lee, *Global Drug Enforcement: Practical Investigative Techniques* (Boca Raton, FL: CRC Press, 2004), p. 19.

3. Several references and books have been developed to categorize individual drugs of abuse and articulate their specific effects on the physical body over the last 50 years. One of the first of these references was the landmark text by Samuel F. Levine, *Narcotics and Drug Abuse* (Cincinnati, OH: The W. H. Anderson Company, 1973). For additional references, see Erich Goode, *Drugs in American Society,* 5th ed. (New York: McGraw-Hill, 2000); James Inciardi and Karen McElrath's, *The American Drug Scene,* 4th ed. (Los Angeles, CA: Roxbury Press, 2004); and Carl Hart, Charles Ksir, and Oakley Ray, *Drugs, Society and Human Behavior,* 12th ed. (New York: McGraw-Hill, 2010).

4. David Holthouse, "The Chiva Game" (Denver, CO: Westworld, October 7, 2004).

5. Jane C. Maxwell, *Drug Abuse Trends* (Austin, TX: Texas Commission on Drug and Alcohol Abuse, June 1998).

6. Clyde B. McCoy and James A. Inciardi, *Sex, Drugs and the Continuing Spread of AIDS* (Los Angeles, CA: Roxbury Press, 1995).

7. David Holthouse, "The Chiva Game."

8. United Nations Office on Drugs and Crime, "The Global Heroin Market," *World Drug Report 2010, www.unodc.org/documents/wdr/WDR_2010/1.2_The_global_heroin_market.pdf.*

9. David Holthouse, "The Chiva Game."

10. Daniel Bates. "Police Warning over 'Cheese': Lethal Combination of Heroin and Cold Medicine behind 20 Deaths," *Daily Mail,* October 12, 2010, *www.dailymail.co.uk/news/article-1319865/Cheese-Heroin-cold-medicine-drug-20-school-childrens-deaths-NY.html.*

11. Donna Leinwand. "DEA Warns of Soft Drink-Cough Syrup Mix," *USA Today,* October 19, 2006, *www.usatoday.com/news/nation/2006-10-18-lean_x.htm?csp=34.*

12. "Prescription Cancer Drug Is a Narcotic of Choice," *Law Enforcement News,* February 14, 2001, p. 5.

13. Timothy Roche, "Potent Perils of a Miracle Drug," *Time,* Jan. 8, 2001.

14. Matthew Perrone, "FDA: Limited Benefit with Tamper-Proof OxyContin," *Associated Press,* September 22, 2009, *www.physorg.com/news172847086.html.*

15. "Heroin Use in Suburbs on the Rise," *ABCnews.com,* March 29, 2010, *http://abcnews.go.com/WN/heroin-suburbs-rise/story?id=10230269&page=1.*

16. U.S. Department of Health and Human Services, Substance Abuse and Mental Health Services Administration, *www.dasis.samhsa.gov/webtv/information.htm,* accessed December 16, 2010.

17. Todd F. Prough, "Investigating Opiate-Overdose Deaths," *FBI Law Enforcement Bulletin,* April 2009, pp. 27–31.

18. Ibid.

19. Carl Hart, Charles Ksir, and Oakley Ray, *Drugs, Society and Human Behavior.*

20. The controversy surrounding methadone treatment continues to be a hot topic in the drug research literature. See Charles E. Faupel, *Shooting Dope: Career Patterns in Hard-Core Heroin Users* (Gainesville, FL: University of Florida Press, 1991); James A. Inciardi, Frank M. Tims, and Bennet W. Fletcher, *Innovative Approaches in the Treatment of Drug Abuse: Program Models and Strategies* (Westport, CT: Greenwood Press, 1993); and *About Methadone,* 2nd ed. (Washington, D.C.: Drug Policy Alliance, 2004).

21. Carl Hart, Charles Ksir, and Oakley Ray, *Drugs, Society and Human Behavior.*

22. Robert C. Petersen, "Cocaine: An Overview," in *Drug Enforcement* (Washington, D.C.: Government Printing Office, 1977), pp. 9–12.

23. Carl Hart, Charles Ksir, and Oakley Ray, *Drugs, Society and Human Behavior.*

24. Ibid.

25. National Drug Intelligence Center, "Amphetamines—Fast Facts" (Washington, D.C.: U.S. Department of Justice, 2010). See *www.usdoj.gov/ndic.*

26. "Hawaii's Problems with 'Ice,'" *Police,* October 1989, p. 14.

27. See Combat Methamphetamine Epidemic Act 2005, Title VII of Public Law 109-177 (May 2006) at *www.deadiversion.usdoj.gov/meth/cma2005_general_info.pdf,* accessed December 18, 2010.

28. Patrik Jonsson, "Appalachia's New Cottage Industry: Meth," *Christian Science Monitor,* March 21, 2003.

29. Adapted and excerpted from "The Menace of Ice," *Time,* September 18, 1989, p. 28.

30. For a more detailed discussion of Strawberry Quick meth, see Donna Leiwand, *USA Today,* "DEA: Flavored Meth Use on the Rise," accessed at *http://usatoday.printthis.clickability.com/pt/cpt?action=cpt&title-DEQ%3A+Flavored+meth*; "Strawberry Meth: Email Fliers Warn of a New, Candy-Flavored Form of Methamphetamine Targeted at Young People Called Strawberry Meth or Strawberry Quick Meth," accessed at *http://urbanlegends.about.com/library/bl_strawberry_meth.htm*; "Candy-Flavored Meth Targets New Users," MY 2, 2007, accessed at *http://cbsnews.com/stories/2007/05/02/health/printable2752266.shtml.*

31. Donna Leinwand, "10 Held in Smuggling of 'Nazi Speed,'" *USA Today,* August 21, 2002, p. 1-A.

32. James McGiveny, "'Made in America': The New and Potent Methcathinone," *Police Chief,* April 1994, pp. 20–21 (this discussion was adapted with permission from this source). Methcathinone is also known as 2-methylamino-1-phenylpropan-1-one, n-methcathinone, monomethylproprion, and ephedrone; street names include *go, goob, sniff, crank, star, wonder star, bathtub speed, gaggers, wildcat,* and *cat.*

33. Todd Bensman, "Ancient Use, New Import," *Dallas Morning News,* June 27, 2002, p. A-21 and A-28. Also, see National Drug Intelligence Center, "Khat—Fast Facts" (Washington, D.C.: U.S. Department of Justice, 2004). See *www.usdoj.gov/ndic.*

34. Ibid.

35. National Drug Intelligence Center, "Barbiturates—Fast Facts" (Washington D.C.: U.S. Department of Justice, 2010). See *www.usdoj.gov/ndic.*

36. Robert C. Petersen and Richard C. Stillman, "Phencyclidine Abuse," in *Drug Enforcement* (Washington, D.C.: Government Printing Office, 1978), pp. 19–20. See National Drug Intelligence Center, "PCP—Fast Facts" (Washington, D.C.: U.S. Department of Justice, 2010). See *www.usdoj.gov/ndic.*

37. Raymond Hernandez, in "New Drug Battles, Use of Ecstasy among Young Soars," *The New York Times* on the Web, August 2, 2000.

38. "Way Found to Detect LSD in Humans," *Tampa Tribune,* September 8, 1972.

39. National Drug Intelligence Center, "LSD—Fast Facts" (Washington, D.C.: U.S. Department of Justice, 2010). See *www.usdoj.gov/ndic.*

40. National Drug Intelligence Center, "Foxy—Fast Facts" (Washington, D.C.: U.S. Department of Justice, 2010). See *www.usdoj.gov/ndic.*

41. National Drug Intelligence Center, "5-MeO-AMT—Fast Facts" (Washington, D.C.: U.S. Department of Justice, 2010). See *www.usdoj.gov/ndic.*

42. National Drug Intelligence Center, "Ketamine—Fast Facts" (Washington, D.C.: U.S. Department of Justice, 2010). See *www.usdoj.gov/ndic.*

43. Gregory Lee, *Global Drug Enforcement: Practical Investigative Techniques,* p. 43.

44. "Supreme Court Weighs Marijuana as Medicine," *CNN.com,* November 29, 2004, *www.cnn.com/2004/LAW/11/29/scotus.medical.marijuana.ap/index.html.*

45. Drug Policy Research Center, "Research Brief: Using Marijuana May Not Raise the Risk of Doing Harder Drugs" (Santa Monica, CA: RAND Corporation, 2002), *www.rand.org/publications/RB/RB6010/.*

46. "Marijuana Home Grow Operation," Crime Prevention and Information, Niagara Regional Police Service, *http://nrps.com/community/marijuana.asp.*

47. Ibid., pp. 2–3.

48. Wes Woods II, "Authorities Seize 14,000 Plants Worth $60 million to $80 million," *Inland Valley Daily Bulletin,* California, 2007.

49. Pierre Thomas and Lisa Jones. "Synthetic Marijuana: 'Legal' High a Dangerous Thrill for Young Americans," *ABC News,* November 22, 2010, *http://abcnews.go.com/US/synthetic-marijuana-legal-drug-scary-consequences/story?id=12211253&page=1.*

50. Ryan Grim. "K2 Crackdown: DEA Using Emergency Powers to Ban Fake Pot," *The Huffington Post,* November 24, 2010, *www.huffingtonpost.com/2010/11/24/dea-using-emergency-power_n_788149.html.*

51. See U.S. Code Title 21, Section 863.

52. National Drug Intelligence Center, "Drug Paraphernalia Prosecution: Stopping Criminal Facilitators of Drug Use," Information Brief (Washington, D.C.: U.S. Department of Justice, July 2003).

53. Gregory Lee, *Global Drug Enforcement: Practical Investigative Techniques,* p. 11.

54. National Drug Intelligence Center, "National Drug Threat Assessment 2010: Domestic Drug Flows" (Washington, D.C.: U.S. Department of Justice, May 2010).

55. Gregory Lee, *Global Drug Enforcement: Practical Investigative Techniques,* p. 12.

56. National Drug Intelligence Center, "National Drug Threat Assessment 2010: Domestic Drug Flows."

57. See Washington Post Online, *www.washingtonpost.com/wp-dyn/content/video/2010/11/05/VI201010110501962.html*, accessed December 18, 2010.

58. National Narcotics Intelligence Consumers Committee, "The NNICC Report 1995: The Supply of Illicit Drugs to the United States" (Washington, D.C.: U.S. Government Printing Office, 1996).

59. National Drug Intelligence Center, "National Drug Threat Assessment 2010: Domestic Drug Flows."

60. William Booth. "Mexico's Deadly Drug Violence Claims Hundreds of Lives in Past 5 Days," *Washington Post*, June 16, 2010, *www.washingtonpost.com/wp-dyn/content/article/2010/06/15/AR2010061503174.html*.

61. Randal C. Archibold. "Mexican Drug Cartel Spills Over, Alarming U.S." *The New York Times*, March 22, 2009, *www.nytimes.com/2009/03/23/us/23border.html*.

62. See Morgan Quitno, *America's Safest (and Most Dangerous) Cities* (Washington, D.C.: CQ Press, 2010); also, interview with Chief Gregory Allen by Dr. Robert W. Taylor on December 14, 2010. Dr. Taylor has been a consultant to the City of El Paso, Texas for the past 15 years.

63. Gregory Lee, *Global Drug Enforcement: Practical Investigative Techniques*, p. 7.

64. National Drug Intelligence Center, "National Drug Threat Assessment 2010: Domestic Drug Flows."

65. United Nations Office on Drugs and Crime, "The Global Heroin Market," *World Drug Report 2010*, *www.unodc.org/documents/wdr/WDR_2010/1.2_The_global_heroin_market.pdf*.

66. National Drug Intelligence Center, "National Drug Threat Assessment 2010: Domestic Drug Flows."

67. Ibid.

68. Jason Burke, "Europe Supplies World's Ecstasy," *The Observer*, September 1, 2002, *www.guardian.co.uk/drugs/Story/0%2C2763%2C784304%2C00.html*.

69. Paul Mahoney, *Narcotics Investigative Techniques* (Springfield, IL: Thomas Books, 1992), p. 5.

70. *New York* v. *Belton*, 452 US 454 (1981).

71. Gregory D. Lee, "Drug Informants, Motives, and Management," *FBI Law Enforcement Bulletin*, September 1993, pp. 10–15. This information was obtained with some modifications from this article.

72. Drug Enforcement Administration, *Agent's Manual*, Appendix B: "Domestic Operations Guideline, 2004."

73. Several police agencies have general orders, special guidelines, and/or policies relating to investigator-informant relationships. Such guidelines include specific direction on confidential informant management and control. Topics that should be addressed in these types of policies include (1) procedures to establish a person as a CI; (2) documenting contacts with the CI; (3) debriefing the CI; (4) restricting the use of the CI and protecting the identity of the CI; (5) designation of an informant control officer or supervisor; (6) documentation and registration of the CI; (7) documentation of payment to the CI and receipts; (8) developing control unit records on the CI; (9) using the CI in controlled purchases; and (10) using the CI in a search warrant affidavit. In addition, many departments require officers to attend special training on the management and control of confidential informants previous to their assignment in a narcotics or drug unit.

74. *DEA Integrity Assurance Notes*, 2004.

75. Paul Mahoney, *Narcotics Investigative Techniques*, p. 17.

76. Michael Lyman, *Practical Drug Enforcement*, pp. 10–13.

77. Gregory Lee, *Global Drug Enforcement: Practical Investigative Techniques*, pp. 92–93. Paul Mahoney, *Narcotics Investigative Techniques*, pp. 92–93.

78. Michael Lyman, *Practical Drug Enforcement*, pp. 6–7.

79. Ibid., p. 113.

80. Ibid., p. 127.

81. Gregory Lee, *Global Drug Enforcement: Practical Investigative Techniques*, p. 116.

82. Ibid., p. 123.

83. Michael Lyman, *Practical Drug Enforcement*, p. 31.

84. Ibid., p. 34.

85. Gregory Lee, *Global Drug Enforcement: Practical Investigative Techniques*, p. 147.

86. Paul Mahoney, *Narcotics Investigative Techniques*, pp. 309–310.

87. Ibid., p. 311.

88. Michael Lyman, *Practical Drug Enforcement*, pp. 156–159.

89. Paul Mahoney, *Narcotics Investigative Techniques*, pp. 312–314.

90. George Steffen and Samuel Candelaria, *Drug Interdiction: Partnerships, Legal Principles, and Investigative Methods for Law Enforcement* (Boca Raton, FL: CRC Press, 2003), pp. 73–84.

91. *B. C.* v. *Plumas Unified School District*, 192 F.3d 1260 (1999).

92. Gregory Lee, *Global Drug Enforcement: Practical Investigative Techniques*, pp. 164–165.

93. Drug Enforcement Administration, "Field Testing for Controlled Substances" (Washington, D.C.: National Training Institute, U.S. Department of Justice, 2000), pp. 1–6.

94. Office of National Drug Control Policy, "The High Intensity Drug Trafficking Area Program: An Overview," *www.whitehousedrugpolicy.gov/hidta/frames_overview.html*.

95. Washington/Baltimore HIDTA website, *www.hidta.org*.

96. Office of National Drug Control Policy, "North Texas HIDTA," *www.whitehousedrugpolicy.gov/hidta/frames_ntex.html*.

97. Charles Whitebread and Christopher Slobogin, *Criminal Procedure: An Analysis of Cases and Concepts* (New York: Foundation Press, 2000), p. 150.

98. *Illinois* v. *Gates*, 462 US 213 (1983).

99. Michael Lyman, *Practical Drug Enforcement*, p. 138.

100. Whitebread and Slobogin, *Criminal Procedure: An Analysis of Cases and Concepts*, p. 37.

101. *U.S.* v. *Leon*, 468 US 897 (1984).

102. *Nix* v. *Williams*, 467 US 431 (1984).

103. *Arizona* v. *Evans*, 514 US 1 (1995).

104. *California* v. *Acevado*, 500 US 565 (1991).

105. *Oliver* v. *U.S.*, 466 US 170 (1984).

106. Gregory Lee, *Global Drug Enforcement: Practical Investigative Techniques*, p. 148.

107. *Harris* v. *United States*, 390 US 234 (1968).

108. *Terry* v. *Ohio*, 392 US 1 (1968).

109. *Chimel* v. *California*, 395 US 752 (1969).

110. *New York* v. *Belton*, 452 US 454 (1981).

111. *Maryland* v. *Buie*, 494 US 395 (1990).

112. Paul Mahoney, *Narcotics Investigative Techniques*, p. 206.

113. Ibid., pp. 206–209.

114. There are a number of different techniques and methods for securing drug evidence. These two methods have been adapted from Gregory D. Lee, *Global Drug Enforcement: Practical Investigative Techniques,* p. 12.

115. Michael Lyman, *Practical Drug Enforcement,* p. 227.

116. Ibid.

117. Reprinted from Training Key 388, *Clandestine Laboratories* by L. Ray Brett. Copyright held by the International Association of Chiefs of Police, Inc., 1110 North Glebe Road. Suite 200, Arlington, VA 22201, U.S.A. Further reproduction without the express written permission from IACP is strictly prohibited.

118. Michael Cashman, "Meth Labs: Toxic Timebombs," *Police Chief,* February 1998, p. 44.

119. Ibid., pp. 44–45.

120. "New Meth Formula Avoids Anti-Drug Laws," *Associated Press,* August 24, 2009, *www.msnbc.msn.com/id/32542373/ns/us_news-crime_and_courts/.*

121. Michael Lyman, *Practical Drug Enforcement,* p. 45.

122. Ibid., pp. 45–46.

123. National Drug Intelligence Center, "Gangs and Drugs in the United States," *Drugs and Crime* (Washington, D.C.: U.S. Department of Justice, July 2003).

124. Ibid.

125. Presentation by Director R. Gil Kerlikowske at the Caruth Police Institute, Dallas Police Department, Lieutenant's Series II Final Training Session in Dallas, Texas on December 14, 2010.

Chapter 21

1. Office of the Historian, *Significant Terrorist Incidents, 1961–2001* (Washington, D.C.: U.S. Department of State, 2002), 10 pp. The information in this paragraph was extracted, with restatement, from this source.

2. National Counterterrorism Center, 2008 Report on Terrorism, 2009, Washington D.C.: Office of the Director of National Intelligence.

3. Phillip W. Thomas (Special Agent in Charge, Memphis Division, Federal Bureau of Investigation), "Statement for the Record before the House Committee on Government Reform, Subcommittee on Government Efficiency, Financial Management, and Intergovernmental Relations," March 1, 2002, p. 1.

4. The role of religion as a motivator or causation of terrorism has been argued by several scholars, with a recent focus on radical Islam and terrorism. See David C. Rapport, "Fear and Trembling: Terrorism in Three Religious Traditions," *American Political Science Review,* Vol. 78, No. 3 (September 1984); Walter Laqueur, *The Age of Terrorism* (Boston: Little, Brown, Inc., 1987); Mark Juergensmeyer, "Terror Mandated by God," *Terrorism and Political Violence,* Vol. 9, No. 2 (Summer 1997); Mark Juergensmeyer, *Terror in the Mind of God: The Global Rise of Religious Terrorism* (Berkeley and Los Angeles: University of California Press, 2000); Bruce Weitzman, *Religious Radicalism in the Greater Middle East.* Volume 4 (New York: Frank Cass Publications, 1997) p. 10; Jonathon R. White, "Political Eschatology: A Theology of Antigovernment Extremism," *American Behavioral Scientist,* 44, pp. 937–956 and *Terrorism: An Introduction,* 3rd ed. (Belmont, CA: Wadsworth Thomson Learning, 2003) pp. 46–61; Bruce Hoffman, "Holy Terror: The Implications of Terrorism Motivated by a Religious Imperative," *Studies in Conflict and Terrorism,* Vol. 18, pp. 271–284; John Murphy, *The Sword of Islam* (Amherst, MA: Prometheus Books, 2002); Lawrence Davidson, *Islamic Fundamentalism* (Westport, CT: Greenwood Press, 1998); and John Esposito, *Islam and the Straight Path* (New York: Oxford University Press, 1991); Bernard Lewis, *The Crisis of Islam: Holy War and Unholy Terrorism* (New York: Random House, 2004); Mark A. Gabriel, *Islam and Terror* (Lake Mary, FL: Frontline Books, 2002); Neil J. Kressel, *Bad Faith: The Days of Religious Extremism* (Amherst, NY: Prometheus Books, 2009); Eli Berman, *Radical, Religious and Violent: The New Economics of Terrorism* (Boston, MA: MIT Press, 2009); Moorthy S. Muthuswamy, *Defeating Political Islam: The New Cold War* (Amherst, NY: Prometheus Books, 2009); R. Joseph Hoffman (ed.), *The Just War and Jihad: Violence in Judaism, Christianity, and Islam* (Amherst, NY: Prometheus Books, 2010).

5. Lee Hancock, "Hasan's Hearing Resumes Monday as Focus Shifts to His Defense Team," *The Dallas Morning News,* November 14, 2010.

6. No author, "The Times Square Case," (Washington, D.C.: FBI), May 4, 2010, *www.fbi.gov/news/stories/2010/may/timessquare_050410/times-square-case;* no author, "Faisal Shahzad Sentenced in Manhattan Federal Court to Life in Prison for Attempted Car Bombing in Times Square," (Washington, D.C.: FBI), October 5, 2010, *http://newyork.fbi.gov/dojpressurel/pressrel10/nyfo100510.htm.*

7. Lansine Kaba, *The Wahhabiyya* (Evanston, IL: Northwestern University Press, 1974) and Lawrence Davidson, *Islamic Fundamentalism* (Westport, CT: Greenwood Press, 1998).

8. Henry Munson, *Islam and Revolution in the Middle East* (New Haven, CT: Yale University Press, 1989) and Ziyad Abu Amr, *Islamic Fundamentalism in the West Bank and Gaza* (Indianapolis, IN: Indiana University Press, 1994). In addition, Sayyid Qutb wrote over a hundred books mainly focusing on social justice and Islam. One of his central themes is the Islamic concept of *tawhid* (the singularity of God and, therefore, of the universe). See Sayyid Qutb, *Milestones* (Beirut, Lebanon: The Holy Quoran Publishing House, 1980).

9. Sun Tsu, *The Art of War,* translated by Lionel Gates (London: British Museum, 1910).

10. Malis Ruthven, *A Fury for God* (London: Hanover Books, 2002), pp. 170–171.

11. John Esposito, *Unholy War: Terror in the Name of Islam* (New York: Oxford University Press, 2002), pp. 9–11.

12. Ibid.

13. Congressional Research Service, "Terrorism: Near Eastern Groups and State Sponsors, 2002" (Washington, D.C.: Library of Congress, 2002), p. 16.

14. Esposito, pp. 13–14.

15. Ibid., pp. 18–21.

16. Dilip Hiro, *War Without End* (London: Routledge, 2002), pp. 267–274.

17. ABC News report, January 8, 2001, "Orders from Osama," *http://abcnews.go.com/sections/world/DailyNews/yemen010108.html.*

18. Zachary Abuza, *Militant Islam in Southeast Asia: A Crucible of Terror* (London: Rienner Publishers, 2003), pp. 127–128.

19. Tom Lasseter and Jonathan S. Landay, "Conditions Ripe for bin-Laden's Survival." *Dallas Morning News*, September 9, 2007.

20. "Al Qaeda in Yemen and Somalia: A Ticking Time Bomb," *United States Senate: Report to the Committee on Foreign Relations*, (Washington, D.C.: U.S. Government Printing Office, January 21, 2010).

21. Greg Miller, "US Charges 14 with Giving Support to Somali Insurgent Groups," *Washington Post*, August 6, 2010, *www.washingtonpost.com/wp-dyn/content/article/2010/08/05/AR2010080503683.html?sid=ST2010080504294.*

22. "Al Qaeda Supporter and Organizer of Jihad Training Camp in Oregon Sentenced in Manhattan Federal Court to Life in Prison" (Washington, D.C.: FBI), September 15, 2009, *http://newyork.fbi.gov/dojpressrel/pressrel09/nyfo091509.htm.*

23. Mike M. Ahlers and Brian Todd, "Al Qaeda Group Contemplated Poisoning Food in U.S., Officials Say," *CNN*, December 21, 2010, *http://edition.cnn.com/2010/US/12/21/al.qaeda.poison.plot/?htp=T2.*

24. Richard Esposito and Brian Ross, "Exclusive: Photos of the Northwest Airlines Flight 253 Bomb," *ABC News*, December 28, 2009, *http://abcnews.go.com/Blotter/northwest-airlines-flight-253-bomb-photos-exclusive/story?id=9436297.*

25. Craig Whitlock, "Al-Qaeda Is Rebuilt, Re-Stored and Renewed," *Washington Post*, September 10, 2007.

26. Ibid., pp. 128–132.

27. Ibid., pp. 133–136.

28. Ibid., pp. 153–166.

29. BBC News report, October, 9, 2003. "Timeline: Bali Bomb Trials," *http://news.bbc.co.uk/2/hi/asia-pacific/3126241.stm.*

30. Ibid., pp. 12–14.

31. Ibid., pp. 15.

32. Robin Wright, *Sacred Rage: The Wrath of Militant Islam* (New York: Simon and Schuster, 2001), p. 16.

33. Ibid., pp. 73–76.

34. Ibid., pp. 102–106.

35. Congressional Research Service, 2002, p. 6.

36. Council on Foreign Relations, "Terrorism Q and A: Hezbollah," *www.terrorismanswers.com/groups/hezbollah_print.html.*

37. BBC News report, February 16, 2001, "Israeli Killed in Hizbollah Attack," *http://news.bbc.co.uk/1/hi/world/middle_east/1173682.stm.*

38. Congressional Research Service, 2002, p. 7.

39. Associated Press report, Dec. 8, 2002, "Mombasa Bombing Reveals Possible al-Qaeda-Hizbollah Link," *www.lebanonwire.com/0212/02120805TGR.asp.*

40. Ibid.

41. Council on Foreign Relations, "Terrorism Q and A: Hezbollah."

42. International Policy Institute for Counter-Terrorism, "Terrorist Organizations: The Abu Nidal Organization," *www.ict.org.il/.*

43. BBC News, "Who are Hezbollah?" July 4, 2010, *http://news.bbc.co.uk/2/hi/middle_east/4314423.stm.*

44. Reuters, "US Wants to Build Up Hezbollah Moderates: Advisor," May 18, 2010, *www.reuters.com/article/idUSTRE64I0UM20100519.*

45. Ben Conery, "Hezbollah Uses Mexican Drug Routes into U.S.," *The WashingtonPost*, March 27, 2009, *www.washingtontimes.com/news/2009/mar/27/hezbollah-uses-mexican-drug-routes-into-us/?page=1.*

46. Joan Neuhaus Schaan, "Case Outlines Potential Terror Threat to U.S.," *Houston Chronicle*, September 19, 2009, *www.chron.com/disp/story.mpl/editorial/outlook/6627377.html* and John C. Thompson, "The New World Expansion of Hezbollah," *The Mackenzie Institute*, August 2010, *http://mackenzieinstitute.com/2010/hezbollah081810.htm.*

47. BBC Online, "Israel's History of Bomb Blasts."

48. United Press International, "Report: HAMAS Attacks Possible in the U.S.," March 16, 2003.

49. See Bruce Hoffman, "The Logic of Suicide Terrorism," *Atlantic Monthly*, June 2003, and The Palestinian Report, "An Interview with Eyad Sarraj," *Media Monitors Network*, 2001.

50. Dennis M. Lormel, (Chief, Financial Crimes Investigations, FBI), "Statement for the Record before the House Committee on Financial Services, Subcommittee on Oversight and Investigations," February 12, 2002, p. 9.

51. Justin Walker and Leila Golestrani, "Threat Analysis: Hamas and Hezbollah Sleeper Cells in the United States," *Urban Warfare Analysis Center*, March 18, 2009, *www.uwac-ok.com/research.html.*

52. Dale L. Watson (Executive Assistant Director, Counterterrorism and Counter Intelligence, FBI), "Statement for the Record on the Terrorist Threat Confronting the United States, before the Senate Select Committee on Intelligence," February 6, 2002, p. 3.

53. No author, "Al Qaeda Supporter Pleads Guilty to Supporting Terrorist Organization," (Washington, D.C.: FBI), May 19, 2010, *http://kansascity.fbi.gov/news/stories/2010/august/al-shabaab/al-shabaab.*

55. Michael Sheridan, "Attorney General Eric Holder Warns: The Real Threat to United States Is American-Born Terrorist," *New York Daily News*, December 21, 2010, *www.nydailynews.com/fdcp?1292951175623.*

56. BBC News, "Mexico's Drug War: Number of Dead Passes 30,000," December 16, 2010, *www.bbc.co.uk/news/world-latin-america-12012425.*

57. Jen Phillips, "Mexico's New Super-Cartel Ups Violence in Power Play," *Mother Jones*, April 13, 2010, *http://motherjones.com/mojo/2010/04/evolution-mexicos-cartel-war.*

58. Randal C. Archibold, "Mexican Drug Violence Spills Over, Alarming U.S.," *The New York Times*, March 23, 2009, *www.nytimes.com/2009/03/23/us/23border.html.*

59. Solomon Moore, "How US Became Stage for Mexican Drug Feud," *The New York Times*, December 9, 2009, *www.nytimes.com/2009/12/09/us/09border.html.*

60. Marc Lacey and Ginger Thompson, "Two Drug Slayings in Mexico Rock U.S. Consulate," *The New York Times*, March 14, 2010, *www.nytimes.com/2010/03/15/world/americas/15juarez.html.*

61. William Booth, "Mexican Pirates Attack Texas Fishermen on Falcon Lake, Which Straddles Border," *The Washington Post*, May 30, 2010, *www.washingtonpost.com/wp-dyn/content/article/2010/05/29/AR2010052903707.html.*

62. CNN, "Mexican Investigator in Falcon Lake Case Is Beheaded, Investigators Say," October 12, 2010, *http://*

articles.cnn.com/2010-10-12/justice/texas.falcon.lake. head_1_tamaulipas-state-mexican-investigator-search?_ s=PM:CRIME.

63. Ben Conery, "Hezbollah Uses Mexican Drug Routes into U.S.," *The Washington Post*, March 27, 2009, *www .washingtontimes.com/news/2009/mar/27/hezbollah-uses- mexican-drug-routes-into-us/?page=1*.

64. Ibid.

65. Brian Michael Jenkins, *Would-Be Warriors: Incidents of Jihadist Terrorist Radicalization in the United States Since September 11, 2001* (Arlington, VA: RAND Corporation 2010).

66. The George Washington University Homeland Security Policy Institute, "Out of the Shadows: Getting Ahead of Prisoner Radicalization," September 2006, *www .gwumc.edu/hspi/policy/PrisonerRadicalization.pdf*.

67. U.S. Department of Justice, "Pennsylvania Woman Indicted in Plot to Recruit Violent Jihadist Fighters and to Commit Murder Overseas" (Philadelphia Office Press Release: Federal Bureau of Investigation, March 9, 2010), see *http://philadelphia.fbi.gov/dojpressrel/pressrel10/ ph030910a.htm*.

68. S. Ackerman, "Pakistani Court Indicts 'Virginia Five,'" *The Washington Independent*, March 17, 2010, *http:// washingtonindependent.com/79446/pakistani-court-indicts -virginia-five*.

69. Andrea Elliot, "The Jihadist Next Door," *The New York Times*, January 27, 2010, *www.nytimes.com/2010/01/31/ magazine/31Jihadist-t.html?hp=&pagewanted=all*.

70. M. J. Stephey, "Daniel Boyd: A Homegrown Terrorist?" *Time Online*, July 30, 2009, *www.time.com/time/nationa/ article/0,8599,1913602,00.html*.

71. Rick "Ozzie" Nelson and Ben Bodurian, "A Growing Terrorist Threat? Assessing 'Homegrown Extremism' in the United States," *Center for International and Strategic Studies*, March 8, 2010, *www.csis.org/files/publication/ 100304_Nelson_GrowingTerroristThreat_Web.pdf*.

72. Associated Press, "Faisal Shahzad Kept Low Profile in U.S.," *CBS News*, May 4, 2010, *www.cbsnews.com/ stories/2010/05/04/national/main6459360.shtml*.

73. Bob Drogin and April Choi, "Teen Held in Alleged Portland Bomb Plot," *Los Angeles Times*, November 28, 2010, *http://articles.latimes.com/2010/nov/28/nation/la-na -portland-bomb-plot-20101128*.

74. Bob Drogin and Richard Serrano, "Baltimore Man Arrested in Foiled Terrorism Plot," *Los Angeles Times*, December 9, 2010, *http://articles.latimes.com/2010/dec/09/ nation/la-na-bomb-plot-arrest-20101209*.

75. Lolita C. Baldor, "Home-Grown Terror Threat Not Taken Seriously, Report Says," *The Washington Times*, September 15, 2010, *www.washingtontimes.com/news/2010/sep/15/ homegrown-terror-threat-not-taken-seriously/*.

76. Under current United States law, set forth in the USA PATRIOT ACT of 2005, acts of domestic terrorism are those which: "(A) involve acts dangerous to human life that are a violation of the criminal laws of the United States or of any State; (B) appear to be intended— (1) to intimidate or coerce a civilian population; (2) to influence the policy of a government by intimidation or coercion; or (3) to affect the conduct of a government by mass destruction, assassination, or kidnapping; and (C) occur primarily within the territorial jurisdiction of the United States." See also the FBI Terrorism Research and Analysis Center Memo, *Domestic Terrorism*, 1994.

77. Federal Bureau of Investigation, *Terrorism in the United States* (Washington, D.C.: FBI, 1996), p. 7.

78. Several important and relatively recent developments have helped to reduce the impact of right-wing, Christian Identity theology in the United States. First, the natural deaths of prominent leaders in the movement, including William Pierce, author of the *Turner Diaries* and a leader in the National Alliance and American Nazi Party, and the Reverend Richard Butler, pastor of the Church of Christ's Christians of Hayden Lake, Idaho, who died on September 8, 2004. In addition, several civil suits have been successfully litigated by Mr. Morris Dees and the Southern Poverty Law Center against the Christian Identity movement and the Ku Klux Klan.

79. Michael Barkum, *Religion and the Racist Right: The Origins of the Christian Identity Movement* (Chapel Hill, NC: The University of North Carolina Press, 1997).

80. Much of this discussion is informed by Anti-Defamation League, "Extremism in America," *www.adl.org/learn/ext _us/default.asp?LEARN_Cat=Extremism&LEARN_SubCat =Extremism_in_America&xpicked=1&item=0*.

81. See *United States v. Hutaree Members*, copy of federal indictment, *http://commons.wikimedia.org/wiki/File:Federal -hutaree-indictment-mar-2010.pdf*.

82. Much of this discussion is informed by the Southern Poverty Law Center, "Intelligence Project: Monitoring Hate and Extremist Activities," *www.splcenter.org/what -we-do/hate-and-extremism*.

83. J. J.McNabb, "Sovereign Citizen Kane," *Intelligence Report* (Birmingham, AL: Southern Poverty Law Center, Fall 2010), pp. 13–19.

84. Jerome Sherman, "Poplawski Called Unremorseful, *Pittsburgh Post Gazette*, April 8, 2009, *www.post-gazette .com/pg/09098/961304-53.stm*.

85. Heidi Beirich, "The Year in Nativism," *Intelligence Report* (Birmingham, AL: Southern Poverty Law Center, Spring 2010), *www.splcenter.org/get-informed/intelligence-report/ browse-all-issues/2010/spring/the-year-in-nativism*.

86. See Federal Bureau of Investigation, *Terrorism in the United States*, 1994.

87. Ibid.

88. James F. Jarboe (February 12, 2002) (Domestic Terrorism Section Chief, Federal Bureau of Investigation) "The Threat of Ecoterrorism," speech before the House of Resources Committee, Subcommittee on Forests and Forest Health.

89. Ibid.

90. Louis J. Freeh (Director, FBI) "Threat of Terrorism to the United States," speech before the U.S. Senate, Committees on Appropriations, Armed Services, and Select Committee on Intelligence (May 10, 2001).

91. Brent L. Smith, *Terrorism in America: Pipe Bombs and Pipe Dreams* (Albany, New York: State University of New York Press, 1994), p. 125.

92. Louis J. Freeh, *Threat of Terrorism to the United States*.

93. Brent L. Smith, *Terrorism in America: Pipe Bombs and Pipe Dreams*.

94. James F. Jarboe, "The Threat of Ecoterrorism."

95. Center for the Defense of Free Enterprise (CDFE), "Ecoterrorism," *www.cdfe.org/ecoterror.hml*.

96. See U.S. Department of Homeland Security, "Leftwing Extremists Likely to Increase Use of Cyber Attacks over the Coming Decade," *www.fas.org/irp/eprint/leftwing.pdf*.

97. Ibid.

98. James F. Jarboe, "The Threat of Ecoterrorism."

99. Off-Road.com, "A Short History of Ecoterrorism," *www.off-road.com/land/ecoterrorism_history.html*, viewed July 2003.

100. James F. Jarboe, "The Threat of Ecoterrorism."

101. Off-Road.com, "A Short History of Ecoterrorism."

102. Larry Copeland, "Domestic Terrorism: New Trouble at Home," p. 3.

103. See Blaine Harden, "11 Indicted in Eco-Terrorism Case," *Washington Post* (January 13, 2006) and U.S. Department of Homeland Security, Office of Intelligence and Analysis, *Domestic Extremism Digest*, March 2006.

104. Center for Arms Control and Non-Proliferation, "Financial Actions Against Terrorists," *www.armscontrolcenter.org/terrorism/issues/Financing.html*.

105. United States Mission to the United Nations, statement by James Shinn, Special Adviser to the U.S. Mission to the United States, on Agenda Item 160, Measures to Eliminate International Terrorism, in the Sixth Committee of the Fifty-Seventh Session of the United Nations General Assembly, October 2, 2002. USUN Press release #142-2 (02) October 3, 2002, *www.un.int/usa/02_142-2.htm*.

106. Financial Action Task Force on Money Laundering, "FATF Cracks Down on Terrorist Financing," October 31, 2001, *www1.oecd.org/fatf/pdf/PR-20011031_en.pdf*.

107. Canadian Foundation for Drug Policy, "The Scope of the Problem: The Value of Illegal Drugs for Terrorist and Criminal Organizations, 2001," *www.cfdp.ca/eoterror.htm*.

108. U.S. Drug Enforcement Administration, Drug Intelligence Brief, "Drugs and Terrorism; A New Perspective," p. 4.

109. Canadian Foundation for Drug Policy, "The Scope of the Problem: The Value of Illegal Drugs for Terrorist and Criminal Organizations."

110. U.S. Drug Enforcement Administration, Drug Intelligence Brief, "Drugs and Terrorism; A New Perspective," p. 5.

111. Ibid.

112. Ibid.

113. United Nations Office of Drugs and Crime, *The 2007 World Drug Report* (New York: UN Publications, 2007).

114. Jerry Seper, "Afghanistan Leads Again in Heroin Production," *The Washington Times*, August 12, 2003, *www.washingtontimes.com/functions/print.php?StoryID=20030811-100220-8928r*.

115. U.S. Drug Enforcement Administration, Drug Intelligence Brief, "Drugs and Terrorism; A New Perspective," p. 5.

116. Mark A. R. Kleiman, "Illicit Drugs and the Terrorist Threat: Causal Links and Implication for Domestic Drug Control Policy," *Congressional Research Service*, April 2004, pp. 1–2.

117. See "Thugs, Drugs and Coyotes on the U.S.-Mexican Border" (Austin, TX: Stratford Reports), March 14, 2010, and Sara A. Carter, "Terrorists Teaming with Drug Cartels," *Washington Times*, August 8, 2007.

118. International Policy Institute for Counter-Terrorism, "Peru Breaks Up FARC Arms Smuggling Ring," Press release, August 2000. *www.ict.org.il/spotlight/det.cfm?id=474*.

119. Eric Green, "U.S. Arrests Colombian for Trying to Buy Arms from Terrorist Groups," Embassy of the United States to Japan, *http://japan.usembassy.gov/e/p/tp-20040406-10.html*.

120. Terry Frieden, "Federal Agents Charge Four with Arms Smuggling," CNN.com, June 15, 2001, *http://archives.cnn.com/2001/LAW/06/15/arms.smuggling/*.

121. Jon Burstein, "Former Boca Jewelers Might Be Crucial to Arms Smuggling Case," *The South Florida Sun-Sentinel*, August 7, 2001, *http://billstclair.com/911timeline/2002/sunsentine1080701.html*.

122. Ibid.

123. From Internet discussion forum: Discussion42, "Terrorist Using ATMs and Fake Credit Cards for Financing," Dec. 11, 2004. *www.secularislam.org/discussion42/_disc42/000001fd.htm*.

124. "Fraud, ID Theft Finance Terror," *Chicago Tribune*, November 4, 2001, *www.chicagotribune.com/news/specials/chi-011104identity,0,5867496,print.story?*.

125. FBI Terror Task Force Probed Credit Card Fraud Case, *The Detroit News*, May 27, 2004, *www.detnews.com/2004/metro/0405/27/metro-165657.htm*.

126. William Billingslea, "Illicit Cigarette Trafficking and the Funding of Terrorism," *The Police Chief*, February 2004.

127. United States Action, remarks by President Bush in his announcements on the financial aspect of terrorism.

128. National Commission on Terrorist Attacks upon the United States, "Monograph on Terrorist Financing," pp. 87–113.

129. Ibid., pp. 114–130.

130. U.S. Immigration and Customs Enforcement—news release, "Holy Land Foundation, Leaders Accused of Providing Material Support to HAMAS Terrorist Organization," July 27, 2004, *www.ice.gov/graphics/news/newsreleases/articles/072704hamas.htm*.

131. U.S. Department of State, Office of International Information Programs, "U.S. Government Indicts 7 for Helping Finance Terrorist," December 19, 2002, *http://usinfo.org/wf-archive/2002/021219/epf405.htm*.

132. *The 9/11 Commission Report: Final Report of the National Commission on Terrorist Attacks Upon the United States* (New York: W.W. Norton & Company, 2004), p. 372.

133. Ibid., p. 172.

134. U.S. Department of State, Office of International Information Programs, Embassy of the United States of America, Jakarta, Indonesia. "Tracking Informal Terrorist Financing Next Task of U.S.-Led Coalition," speech by Kenneth W. Dam Deputy Secretary of the Treasury delivered to the Council on Foreign Relations New York, New York on June 8, 2002, June 11, 2002, p. 4, *www.usembassyjakarta.org/terrorism/coalition2.html*.

135. Kathleen Day, "Hawalah Cash Outlets Investigated as Source for Terror Funds," *Washington Post*, Nov. 7, 2001. Obtained through the Internet site for United States action, January 12, 2005, *www.unitedstatesaction.com/islam-money-changing.htm*.

136. Sina Lehmkuhler, "Countering Terrorist Financing: We Need a Long-Term Prioritizing Strategy," April 2003, p. 8, *www.homelandsecurity.org/journal/articles/Lehmkuhler.html*.

137. National Infrastructure Protection Center, *www.nipc.gov*, March 12, 2001, p. 1.

138. Watson, "Statement for the Record," pp. 7–8.

139. Donald M. Kerr (Assistant Director, Laboratory Division, Federal Bureau of Investigation), "Statement for the Record on Carnivore Diagnostic Tool" before the Senate Committee on the Judiciary, pp. 1–12, Sept. 6, 2000.

140. Ibid., p. 8.

141. United States Action, remarks by President Bush in his announcement on the financial aspect of terrorism.

142. Kathleen Millar, "Financing Terror: Profits from Counterfeit Goods Pay for Attacks," *U.S. Customs Today*, November 2002, *www.customs.ustreas.gov/xp/CustomsToday/2002/November/interpol.xml*.

143. Text of public testimony by Ronald K. Noble, Secretary General of Interpol on the links between intellectual property crime and terrorist financing, July 16, 2003, *www.interpol.com/Public/ICPO/speeches/SG20030716.asp?HM=1*.

144. United States Action, U.S. NEO-Nazi Group: National Alliance, January 12, 2005, *www.unitedstatesaction.com/national-alliance-nazi.htm*, p. 1.

145. Federal Bureau of Investigation, *Terrorism in the United States*, 1999, p. 44.

146. Watson, "Statement for the Record," p. 11.

147. International Association of Chiefs of Police, *Leading from the Front: Law Enforcement's Role in Combating Terrorism* (Alexandria, VA: IACP, 2001), p. 7.

148. For an important discussion of WMDs regarding the police, refer to Daniel R. Symonds, "A Guide to Selected Weapons of Mass Destruction," *Police Chief*, March 2003, pp. 19–29.

149. In January 2011, a series of incendiary letters were sent to government buildings in Washington, D.C., and Baltimore, Maryland. The letters were often addressed to high-level government officials, such as Janet Napolitano (Secretary of the Department of Homeland Security), but none of the packages exploded; rather they sparked and ignited causing significant disruption of services and chaos. Some postal workers reported minor burns to their fingers and hands, but no serious injuries resulted from these incidents, unlike the attacks sent to celebrities (for example, Tom Brokaw) after 9/11

in 2001, which resulted in several postal workers dying from handling letters filled with inhalation anthrax.

150. Christopher Rigopoulos, "The FBI Philadelphia Division's Hazardous Materials Response Team," *Police Chief*, March 2003, p. 20.

151. The singular of "bacteria."

152. *Thomas* v. *Inglesby et al.*, "Anthrax as a Biological Weapon," *Journal of the American Medical Association*, Vol. 281, 1999, p. 7.

153. U.S. Department of Defense, "Information Paper: Anthrax as a Biological Warfare Agent," *www.defenselink.mil/other_info/agent.html*, June 1998, p. 2.

154. Centers for Disease Control, "Use of Anthrax Vaccine in the United States," *Morbidity and Mortality Report*, December 15, 2000 (Vol. 49, No. RR-15), p. 3.

155. Centers for Disease Control, "Anthrax," *www.cdc.gov/ncidod/dbmd/diseaseinfo/anthrax_t.htm*, last reviewed January 10, 2011, p. 1.

156. Ibid.

157. National Domestic Preparedness Office, "On-Scene Commanders Guide for Responding to Biological and Chemical Threats" (Washington, D.C.: Nov. 1, 1999), p. 19.

158. Centers for Disease Control, "Interim Guidelines for Firefighters and Other First Responders for the Selection and Use of Protective Clothing and Respirators," *www.bt.cdc.gov/docuementsapp/anthrax/protective/10242001.asp*, January 10, 2011, p. 2.

159. Ibid.

160. Ibid., p. 3.

161. Ibid.

162. Ibid., p. 4.

163. National Domestic Preparedness Office, "On-Scene Commanders," p. 4, with minor additions by the authors.

164. Ibid., pp. 9–10.

165. Ibid., p. 10.

166. Steve Cain, *Agroterrorism: A Purdue Extension Backgrounder* (West Lafayette, IN: Purdue University 2001), p. 1.

167. Federal Bureau of Investigation, *Terrorism in the United States*, 1999, p. 240.

Chapter 22

1. 373 U.S. 83 (1963).

2. *Ohio v. Roberts*, 488 U.S. 56 (1982).

3. 124 S.Ct. 1354 (2004).

4. Crawford, 124 S.Ct. 1354, at 1374.